Aviation and the Law

Aviation and the Law

Fourth Edition

Laurence E. Gesell
Arizona State University

Paul Stephen Dempsey
McGill University

Coast Aire Publications

Library of Congress Catalog Card Number 2005901537

ISBN 978-1-890938-08-4

Printed in the United States of America

COAST AIRE PUBLICATIONS, LLC
2823 North Yucca Street
Chandler, Arizona 85224-1867
Office (480) 899-6151
Fax (480) 899-7918
E-mail coastaire@cox.net

ISBN 978-1-890938-08-6

9 781890 938086

iv

CONTENTS

CHAPTER 3
Constitutional Law and its Evolution

CHAPTER 4
United States Common Law

CHAPTER 5
Legal Research

CHAPTER 6
Aviation Security

CHAPTER 7
Ownership

CHAPTER 8
Airmen

CHAPTER 9
Consumerism

CHAPTER 14
Airports: and the Redistributive Function

CHAPTER 15
Airports: and the Protective Function

CHAPTER 16
Manufacturers' Liability

CHAPTER 17
Accident Investigation

CHAPTER 18
Insurance

CHAPTER 19
Private International Air law

CHAPTER 20
Public International Air Law

TABLES

FIGURES

CASE BRIEFS

Chapter 3—Constitutional Law and its Evolution

Chapter 4—United States Common Law

Chapter 5—Legal Research

Chapter 6—Aviation Security

Chapter 7—Ownership

Chapter 8—Airmen

Chapter 12—The Government as Landlord

Chapter 13—Airports: and the Proprietary Function

Chapter 14—Airports: and the Redistributive Function

Chapter 15—Airports: and the Protective Function

Chapter 16—Manufacturers' Liability

Chapter 17—Accident Investigation

Chapter 18—Insurance

Chapter 19—Private International Air law

PREFACE

The title, *Aviation and the Law*, is an intentional reflection upon the nature of law, for the study of aviation law must of necessity consider the field of aviation within the broader context of law as a whole. Aviation law is but an integral part of all law. It is, therefore, necessary to start from the beginning, to develop for the reader a basic understanding of the law, of its philosophy, and of its structure and due process, before addressing "aviation and the law" specifically. To this end, the book is assembled in six major sections, the first of which gives definition to law, touches upon notions of justice, fairness, the underlying theories of law, and upon morality—the latter being defined as it was by the ancient Greeks, as "social virtue."

Section One, comprised of Chapters 1 through 5, presents an historical perspective of the origins of Western law, and particularly of United States common law. Included are some thoughts of early philosophers such as Aristotle and Plato; the religious and natural doctrines of Saint Augustine and Saint Thomas Aquinas; the social contractarian theories of John Locke and especially of Jean Rousseau; the social utilitarian notions of John Stewart Mill; and the thoughts of more contemporary theorists including Donald Black, Milton Friedman, and John Rawls. The origins of U.S. law can be traced to the Code of Hammurabi, through Mosaic law, Roman law, Canon law, the Magna Carta, Napoleonic Code, and finally to the basic law of the land, the United States Constitution.

Section One expounds upon U.S. law by comparing criminal with civil law, by enumerating the basic rights of citizens and also by describing the various defenses which may be used against violations of those rights. These defenses give rise to the most common causes of litigation involving aviation. Finally, in the first section, aviation regulatory law is identified. The federal and state court systems are described. And, for the beginning researcher, there is a guide to legal research, with an orientation to the law library, including the

xxiii

procedure for tracing case law histories (or what is commonly referred to as "sheparding"). Integrated subsequently into Sections Two through Six are abstracts of actual court cases involving issues of related aviation concern.

Section Two, comprised of Chapter 6 alone, addresses criminal law as it relates to the air transportation system. Of primary concern are the issues of airport and airline security, air piracy, and other acts of criminal violence. Section Three, made up of Chapters 7 through 11, is an overview of civil (or tort) law in the field of aviation, focusing upon pertinent issues in their respective specialized areas, and supported by applicable case law. In this section the aviation industry is divided into the following representative areas: ownership, airmen, airlines, and fixed base operators. Section Four, Chapters 12 through 15, looks at airports and the role of government.

Section Five, Chapters 16 through 18, deals with manufacturers' liability, the transfer of liability through insurance, and liability for accidents, including an overview of the government's responsibility to investigate aircraft accidents and to promote aviation safety. Presented therein is a case study of an accident investigation conducted by the National Transportation Safety Board, and of how that given case was handled later in the civil court system. The case at hand is the infamous crash of Trans World Airlines Flight 514 near Dulles International Airport in 1976.

The final section of the book, made up of Chapters 19 and 20, is an introduction to international aviation law, including its historical development, the Warsaw System, bilateral governmental agreements in air transportation, competitive problems abroad, and exemplary court cases in this area.

As with previous editions, the purpose of this book is to provide students of aviation with a basic understanding of law, of the legal system, and of how the principles of law may be applied to the many aspects of air commerce and air transportation. Added to this latest edition are updates on the federal aviation security provisions since September 11, 2001, expansion in the area of international air law, as well as court cases of note decided since the last edition. For a more advanced treatment of the subject, read the companion to this text, *Air Commerce and the Law.*

2005   LEG/PSD

CHAPTER 1

PHILOSOPHY OF LAW

The law has different meanings, and almost everyone has different ideas of what law is or what it ought to be.

LAW'S COMPETING INTERESTS

Although the law ought to serve all citizens equally, it must do so in what has become a complex, pluralistic society. The law has different meanings, and almost everyone has different ideas of what law is or what it should be. By one definition, "law . . . is a body of rules of action or conduct prescribed by controlling authority, and having binding legal force."[1] "Justice," ideally, is synonymous with law, and refers to behavior in accord with both social ethics and with legal authority. Something *just* is in perfect and accurate balance. To *justify* something is to make it *equal* to something else. That is to say, in justice there is a balance between competing interests being served. These "competing" interests are enigmatic, but the law and its many aspects and interpretations can be represented by its dichotomies or, in other words, by its mutually exclusive yet coexisting orders.

Law is complex. And, one way to approach the study of any comprehensive subject is to break it down into its constituent parts or categories. Among the various ways to categorize law, it can be divided into its *substantive* and *procedural* forms. The former (substantive law) is concerned with the content, or substance, of the law. The latter (procedural law) governs the process of law.[2] Substantive law is theoretical. Procedural law is mechanical.

---

[1] *Black's Law Dictionary* (abridged 5th ed. 1983).
[2] James V. Calvi and Susan Colemen, *American Law and Legal Systems* (3rd ed. 1997).

Two dominant perspectives on scholarship in law and society are *instrumentalism,* and, by contrast, the *constitutive* view. Instrumentalism takes an external position and makes a sharp distinction between legal standards, on the one hand, and non-legal human activities, on the other. It conceives of law as a tool for sustaining or changing aspects of social life. The instrumentalists are interested in law's effectiveness. Law is designed to regulate activities, to declare what can or cannot be done. Law, to the instrumentalist, mirrors society.[3] That is to say, law follows morality, but is separate from it.

Explained as the antithesis of instrumentalism, in the constitutive perspective, law occasionally constructs new practices through meaning and interpretation. Law's meaning is internalized. It not only regulates what is in place, but it may bring into being new relations and meanings. Law's effects are seen in meanings and self-understandings rather than in the results of sanctions. As Sarat and Kearns submit,

> . . . *to acknowledge that law has meaning-making power is to acknowledge, contrary to the instrumentalist's general view, that some practices are not logically separable from, or intelligible apart from, the laws that shape them.*[4]

The constitutive perspective is looking for much deeper and more abstract meaning of law and its impact than "positive" instrumentalism. Its followers would suggest that instrumentalists are oversimplifying the effects of law by the importance they place in the advancement of the scientific, empirical, policy-focused aspect of legal realism. What constitutive theorists are interested in studying is the impact of the law where it is least recognizable and least problematic, where, to use Gramsci's phrase, law is "hegemonic."[5]

---

[3] Austin Sarat and Thomas R. Kearns, *Beyond the Great Divide: Forms of Legal Scholarship and Everyday Life,* in Austin Sarat and Thomas R. Kearns (eds.), Law in Everyday Life 21-61 (1993).

[4] *Id.*

[5] According to Gramsci, "hegemony" exists when the working class in advanced capitalistic societies believes that the ruling class interest is the same as interest of the larger society. *See* Antonio Gramsci, *Selections from Prison Notebooks* (1971).

Beyond instrumentalist and cognitive views, and in addition to substantive and procedural law, there are many other contrasting theories of law that can be demonstrated. Thomas Hobbes, for example, proclaimed two types of law. *Civil* is written, the other unwritten is *natural.* The law of nature and the civil law contain each other and are of equal extent. The laws of nature consist in equity, justice, gratitude, and other moral virtues. To obey the civil law, on the other hand, is to be "subdued by the sword."[6]

On the one hand, law is *positive*, or written. On the other, law is the normative moral fabric of society. *Natural law* theorists believe that laws of society, like the laws that govern the physical universe, are sown in nature. These laws, like God and nature, are eternal and immutable.[7] Conversely, some people believe law is constructed by associates, like a contract, and designed to protect and serve society.

Law can be utilitarian, serving the interests of the majority in a democratic way, while at the same time fulfilling the terms of the social contract, and thereby protecting the rights of the individual. In other words, law can look out for the interests of the whole of society, or of the individual part of society. One purpose of law in a civil society is to promote peaceful coexistence, yet law can be violent. Law can be lawful, and at the same time, it can be fair or equitable. It can be statutory, or it can be based on precedents and common law. It can be criminal or civil.

In the ancient Greek perspective, the universe can be described as part of the *physes* or of the *nomos*. It can be *sophic* or *mantic*. Another way of saying the same thing, but in the language of the Era of Enlightenment—and specifically in Immanuel Kant's words—is to say that laws are based either on *physics* or on *metaphysics*.[8]

What follows are some dichotomous ways of describing the law. Since law serves many purposes and means different things to a variety of people, there are many ways of describing what law is. To begin, most people view justice with a sense of fairness and equity.

---

[6] Thomas Hobbes, *Leviathan* (1651).

[7] James V. Calvi and Susan Coleman, *American Law and Legal Systems* 6 (3rd ed. 1997).

[8] *See* Immanuel Kant, *Fundamental Principles of the Metaphysic of Morals* (1785).

EQUITY AND FAIRNESS

In ancient Greek mythology, law is symbolized in the personage of Themis, who holds the scales of equity and fairness in the balance. As the famous 19th Century legal scholar, Henry Sumner Maine, points out, Homeric literature is far more trustworthy in presenting a picture of primitive, or basic law than are later writings and legal theories such as the "Law of Nature," or the "Social Compact" (i.e., the social contract).[9] In Maine's interpretation of Homer's *Iliad*, early societies "could only account for sustained or periodically recurring action by supposing a personal agent." Thus, a divine personage, *Aeolus*, represented the wind blowing; the sun rising and setting was a (divine) person, *Helios,* as was *Gaea*, the personification of Mother Earth yielding her increases. When a sovereign decided a dispute between subjects, or handed out a sentence, the judgment was assumed to be the result of direct inspiration from an incarnate being. For the ancient Greeks, the divine agent suggesting judicial awards to rulers and magistrates was *Themis*, the Goddess of Justice. *Themistes* were the actual awards or judgments.

It may be assumed that law's abiding theme, rooted in ancient Greek mythology, is comprised of philosophical notions of justice and fairness, as expounded upon by both Plato and then Aristotle. The modern philosopher John Rawls describes fairness, by rejecting utilitarianism, and viewing the social contract from a Kantian perspective.[10] The thrust of Rawls' theory of justice is conceptualized in what he terms "justice as fairness," fairness in this case meaning a balance of competing claims.[11]

Social utility (or utilitarianism) has for its guiding principle the securing of the most happiness possible for the greatest number of people (ergo, rule of the majority). The problem with serving a majority, of course, is that inevitably there results a non-served (even ill served) minority. In contrast, the social contract is a hypothetical agreement between a group of associates and the state, wherein the former relinquish some of their natural freedoms, and make promissory obliga-

---

[9] Henry Sumner Maine, *Ancient Law* (1861).
[10] John Rawls, *A Theory of Justice* (1971).
[11] *See* Ch. 2.

tions of responsibility, in exchange for the provision of certain protections and social welfare benefits from the latter, the state.[12]

Rawls envisions the construction of a social contract where the contracting associates, finding themselves in the "original position," devise two basic "principles of justice"—of equal liberties, and the fair distribution of inequalities among all associates.[13] Besides meting out fairness and equity, still another purpose for law is to resolve disputes. Law may not always resolve disputes "fairly," but hopefully it does resolve them. From a broad overview of rulings handed down, it would seem the courts are not looking to make any winners, but rather, to resolve issues in such a way that neither party comes out a total winner nor a total loser. In its abstractness, such a normative philosophy might be the most perfect justice possible in a world of imperfect people. Seemingly, no one person or group is either totally right or wrong, and by looking fairly at both sides of the story, there is, indeed, an attempt to balance the scales of justice.

THE NATURE OF LAW (OR OF HUMANITY)

Arguably, the nature of human beings is sociability and rationality.[14] To bring up the nature of law is to resume arguments posited by the ancient Greek philosophers Socrates and Plato, but especially Aristotle. The arguments are disputes about the nature of law and morality, and about the relationship of the two. *Morality* in this case meaning "virtue," with virtue generally being interpreted as "mastery." The opposite, *immoral*, does not necessarily mean sinful, as in the breaking of God's laws. But it does imply a violation of the norms of society.

The basic argument then, about what law is or is not, is between *morality* versus *law.* Morality is comprised of informally organized opinion, of deeply held convictions—ideals that are long-seated; in other words mastery, mastery of sociability and rationality. Law,

---

[12] Paul Stephen Dempsey and Laurence E. Gesell, *Air Commerce & the Law* 3 (2004).
[13] *See* Ch. 2.
[14] Thomas Hobbes, and others, have taken the position that in the "natural state," the human species are but savages. These theorists have used Darwinistic arguments to suggest that in anarchy (meaning here the absence of law) there would exist a perpetual war of each person against all others. Thomas Hobbes, *Leviathan* (1651). Conversely, Petr Kropotkin suggests that in anarchy the opposite of savagery would be the case; further suggesting that human beings (and, for that matter, all of the animal kingdom) survive through "mutual aid" rather than a war of survival. *See* Petr Kropotkin, *Mutual Aid* (1902).

strictly (or "positively") interpreted means rules (usually written) enacted and effected by a recognized social power (the government).[15]

Out of the above definitions come two schools of thought, the *positivists* and the *moralists*. The positivist asks, "What is the Law?" The moralist asks, "What is right and good?" Or alternatively, the moralist might ask, "What *ought* the law to be?" To demonstrate the thought and actions of moralists versus positivists by way of an aviation-related example, suppose a Federal Aviation Administration [FAA] safety inspector discovers an aviator who has been flying while not in possession of a pilot's license. Although the aviator is, in fact, a certificated airman, the aviator does not currently have personal possession of the pilot's certificate. Yet, the law (Federal Aviation Regulation Part 61.3a) states that,

> *No person may act as pilot in command or in any other capacity as a required pilot crewmember unless he has in his possession a current pilot certificate issued to him under this part.*

If the FAA inspector is a positivist, the inspector will cite the pilot for a clear violation of the regulations and, therefore, the commission of a grave offense worthy of sanction. If, on the other hand, the inspector is more of a moralist, the inspector may take into consideration the experience of the pilot with his or her many ratings and hours of flight time, the story that he or she simply forgot to bring the certificate, and the fact that no one was injured by the pilot's omission. As a moralist, the inspector may rationalize that it was not such a grave offense after all, and may therefore, send the pilot on his or her way with only a warning.

As one proceeds more deeply into the study of law, the pattern established by this basic argument—between morality (moralist) and law (positivist)—will be seen to repeat itself in comparison among various terms and notions. Although expressed in a variety of concepts, the law is seemingly under girded by these dichotomies. In other words, the law may be described by looking at its opposites. For instance, the competing legal theories identified by Henry Sumner

---

[15] In this sense, *positive law* may be interpreted as *instrumental*, and *moral law* as *constitutive*.

Maine (*supra*) as the "Law of Nature," and the "Social Compact," are but one example.

LAW AND JUSTICE

In a world of opposites, the ancient Greeks distinguished between *physes* (nature), and *nomos* (law). Greek writers speak of "two ways of viewing the world," which can be designated as *sophic* and *mantic*. The mantic (from *mantikos*) represents what is inspired, revealed, oracular, prophetic or divinatory. Sophic (from which came the term "sophisticated") signifies that which human kind have learned by their own wits. Philosophy thus had two beginnings; one represented by Anaximander and the other by Pythagoras. The latter held that only the gods knew what was what, and the philosopher was merely the messenger. Anaximander, on the other hand, sought to explain everything by investigation of the *physes*, the physical universe alone. The foundation of sophic thinking was "the elimination of the supernatural or superhuman from a description of the real world." In other words, anything that could not be weighed, measured, or sensed objectively was discounted.

Modern thought seemingly parallels the ancient Greek dichotomy of learning. As Hugh Nibley points out, "The *sophic* is simply the art of solving problems without the aid of any superhuman agency, which the *mantic*, on the other hand, is willing to solicit or accept."[16] For most of the 20th Century, discovering *truth* has been dominated by the *hypothetico-deductive* experimental (positivistic) approach— that is to say, by the *scientific* method. However, over the last 30 to 40 years there has evolved a popular movement away from the strictly "scientific" way of learning to a more normative mode, especially in the social sciences. *Evaluative* research, for example, is similar to traditional research in that it uses scientific (quantitative) methodologies and other empirical methods to produce information. But unlike experimental research, which declares itself to be "objective" and scientifically neutral, evaluation involves subjective (even mantic) input.

In his concept of "postpositivistic critical multiplism," Thomas Kuhn suggests that research *ought* to extend beyond the rigorous em-

---

[16] Hugh Nibley, *The Ancient State* (1991); *see also* Hugh Nibley, *Victoriosa Loquacitas: The Rise of Rhetoric and the Decline of Everything Else*, 20 Western Speech (1956); *see also*, Hugh Nibley, *Paths That Stray: Some Notes on Mantic and Sophic* (compiled around 1963).

pirical methods because "positivism" restricts the investigator's focus to non-subjective issues that can be arranged in factual law-like statements. In using the "multiplistic" approach, the attempt is to legitimate findings through "triangulation," or the use of multiple indicators to measure or test hypotheses.[17] Moreover, like law, evaluative research attempts to be fair. Scientific research is "conclusion oriented." Evaluation, on the other hand, is "decision oriented." As in a court of law, evaluation studies often represent an adversarial approach, which weighs the preponderance of evidence.

As with all learning, the ancient Greeks viewed law through dual perspectives. The tension between morality and positive law is one example. In the study of nature (*physes*), the sophic approach may have been preferred, as it has been in more recent times. With the law, however, the mantic philosophy was clearly dominant. As pointed out above, judgments came through "direct inspiration" from the gods. According to Nibley, *nomos* was "the moral order of society—itself."[18] To the Greeks, the essence of law was virtue and goodness—that a law-abiding person lived according to virtue.

Aristotle deserves especial attention in this area, for in his writings he distinguishes between, (1) justice as the *whole* (of society), and (2) justice as a *part* (the individual). As the "whole," the term justice is applied to being lawful; " . . . the just man is a moral man."[19] As a "part," justice is applied to being equal or fair. Aristotle focused on the latter, fairness and equity, and described three forms of justice:

- *Distributive* justice is the equality between equals. It is equal allocation, and things are meted out fairly to all;
- *Corrective* justice is equality between punishment and crime, that the punishment must not be less than, nor greater than the severity of the crime; and
- *Justice in Exchange* is equality between whatever goods are exchanged—that is to say, a "fair price."

To demonstrate how the above principles may be applied to aviation, look for example at the principle of distributive justice.

---

[17] Thomas Kuhn, *The Structure of Scientific Revolutions* (1962). *See also*, Thomas Kuhn, *Post-positivistic Critical Multiplism*, in R.L. Shotland and M.M. Mark, *Social Science and Social Policy* (1985).
[18] Hugh Nibley, *The Ancient State* (1991).
[19] Aristotle, *Nichomachean Ethics* (circa 336 B.C.).

Distributive justice is a foremost function of government, and most airports open to the public are owned and operated by a governmental agency, be it a city, county or special district (or authority). Follow, in the subsequent paragraphs, the economic philosophy of distributive justice as it is applied to airports and the manner in which airport authorities might charge for services and distribute wealth in a *utilitarian* fashion.

Distributive justice deals with the equitable treatment of all people individually and as a whole. Nicholas Rescher has described what he calls the "canons of distributive justice."[20] Rescher's canons specifically address economic justice:

- The *Canon of Equality* holds that all people must be treated equally, accepting the reality of differential claims and dessert —that is to say, treating all people impartially;
- The *Canon of Need* consists of treating people according to their requirements;
- The *Canon of Ability and/or Achievement* treats all according to their abilities or merit;
- The *Canon of Effort* treats all according to their sacrifice;
- The *Canon of Productivity* holds that people should be treated according to their productive contribution to the group;
- The *Canon of Supply and Demand* states that justice is the treatment of people according to the social value of their product, or on the basis of the relative scarcity of their service; and
- The *Canon of Social Utility* is justice, which advances the common good, or public interest, over the interests of the individual.

In the end, Rescher sums his canons into his *Canon of Claims*, wherein he states that distribution of justice is based upon a single, specific ground of claim which displaces all of the other canons. Distributive justice is according to legitimate claim. It is legitimate if it is defensible through the use of one or more of the supportive canons. Nevertheless, Rescher places emphasis on the canon of social utility. Likewise, John Stuart Mill stated that justice results from the

---

[20] Nicholas Rescher, *Distributive Justice* (1966).

maximization of social satisfaction (i.e., utility).[21] Thus, at least theoretically, it is justice if social utility is served—if it is *pragmatic* and makes most people happy!

R.M. Hare shares the same strong affinity for utilitarianism, but points out the antagonism between justice and utility.[22] Utility is expediency, not necessarily justice. John Rawls also recognized the inherent injustice of utilitarianism.[23]

Milton Friedman presents yet another utilitarian model[24] by looking at economic justice. Essentially adopting the canons of achievement, productivity, and maybe even supply and demand, he addresses distribution of income in an *allocative* way, "to each according to what he and the instruments he owns produces."[25] The justice of income is not primarily distributive, but rather is allocative.[26] "The essential function of payment in accordance with product in a market society is to enable resources to be allocated efficiently without compulsion, it is unlikely to be tolerated unless it is also regarded as yielding distributive justice." The major role of distribution in accordance with product is allocation without compulsion.

What is most applicable to airport economics is where Milton Friedman points out certain inequalities in the marketplace resulting from the differences in personal and property endowments. Because of these inequalities, and in the furtherance of social utility, governments (in this case, airport sponsors) find justice in the redistribution of private income for the good of all.

It has been postulated by economists (Milton Friedman, for example, and by Alfred Kahn, the former Civil Aeronautics Board Chairman and so-called "father of airline deregulation") that rate setting and cost recovery schemes should attempt to be "allocative" (i.e., to associate revenues with their cost-generating centers). But airports are

---

[21] John Stuart Mill, *Utilitarianism* (1863).

[22] R.M. Hare, *Justice and Equality*, in John Arthur and William Shaw (eds.), Justice and Economic Distribution (1978).

[23] John Rawls, *A Theory of Justice* (1971).

[24] Although Friedman might prefer to call it a "libertarian" model.

[25] *See* Milton Friedman, *The Social Responsibility of Business Is To Increase Its Profits*, New York Times Magazine (Sept. 1970); *see also Milton Friedman Responds*, Business and Society Review (spring 1972).

[26] Cost allocation, meaning the assignment of an item or group of items of investment, revenue, or cost to an object, activity, process or operation, in accordance with cost responsibilities, benefits received, or other measure of apportionment. *See* Paul Stephen Dempsey and Laurence E. Gesell, *Air Transportation: Foundations for the 21st Century* 512 (1997). *See generally*, 14 CFR 121, 135, 200-300, and SFAR 38-2 (Jan. 1, 1996).

not perfect markets. In fact, few airports are capable of economic independence.[27] Most airports cannot balance revenues with expenses, and therefore, cannot effectively allocate costs. Although cost allocation is stated as a desirable goal of airport management, true cost allocation is not attainable while at the same time providing well-rounded aviation services to the traveling public (i.e., the consumer).

Although it may appear unjust to cross-allocate resources from one cost center to another, a qualitative defense has shown income redistribution to be justifiable where it is necessary to satisfy social utility. Nevertheless, redistribution of wealth means "taking" from one to give to another.[28] In serving the interests of the majority, a minority may be disadvantaged. Hence, as John Rawls points out, utilitarianism "does not take seriously the distinction of persons."[29]

The result of all of this in actual application is that the government becomes a legitimized *Robin Hood*, whereby those who can afford it, pay more, and those who can least afford it, pay less. One tenant may be paying exorbitant rents, while a neighbor may be paying very low rent, or might even be subsidized. Take for example the airport-related costs to an automobile rental agency. Their rental contract normally calls for about 10% of their gross income to be paid to the airport for rental space and for the privilege of doing business on the airport. The net rent amounts to thousands of dollars per square foot of actually occupied terminal floor space. Compare this with rental of say only $20 or $30 dollars per square foot of floor space by the airlines.

Another example is the rate paid for parking automobiles versus the rate charged for temporary storage of an airplane. The fees, say $10 to $20 charged for overnight parking of an aircraft, may only marginally pay the costs of parking apron development, construction and maintenance. Conversely, one can pay as much or more to park a car for just two or three hours at some airports.

Automobile parking revenues and rents collected from auto rental agencies are major sources of income for an air carrier airport. Revenues from these two sources constitute the lion's share of surplus funds available to the airport sponsor, which can be used to make up for deficits in aviation-related land-use areas.

---

[27] Laurence E. Gesell, *The Administration of Public Airports* (3rd ed. 1992).

[28] Reference here is to the possible violation of the Fifth Amendment to the United States Constitution, and the "taking" of property without due process.

[29] John Rawls, *A Theory of Justice* (1971).

In cross allocating funds from one cost center to another, airports seemingly violate Aristotle's principle of distributive justice. And yet, it is legitimized by government in order to support the airport and to provide a facility for all. The practice is seemingly justified by the canon of social utility. But irrespective of the social advantages, the one paying the greater share of the burden may feel his or her individual rights are being violated, and the potential for a lawsuit is generated no matter how just the government's intentions. At any rate, from the above illustration it can be seen how the thoughts of Aristotle (and others) are not just the dusty rationale of some long since deceased philosopher. These ancient axioms have application today and can be found embodied in the daily practice of applied law.

NATURAL LAW

The application of law in ancient Egypt was far less complicated, and it was certainly less philosophical. So powerful was Pharaoh that he (and sometimes she) had only to say, "So let it be written, so let it be done."[30] Pharaoh was all-powerful because he was seen as a god incarnate. Moses, however, led the Israelites out of Egypt by following the dictates of a much higher authority. Later, the Romans, like Pharaoh, would rule with authority and the sovereignty of might. And the Roman Empire lasted for a thousand years. But then it too collapsed. Replacing it was the Holy Roman Empire, a combination of both church and state authority. Yet, the Holy Roman Empire was neither Roman nor an empire, nor did it turn out to be all that holy.

During the era of the Holy Roman Empire, sovereign power was again claimed to have originated in God. According to Roman Catholic theology, the Pope is chosen by God to be the "Vicar of Christ" on earth. Therefore, under the canon law of the Holy Roman Empire, the Pope was infallible. In a mixture of church and state, kings also claimed to have special dispensation. During the Age of Absolutism in Europe, the theory of the *divine right of kings* governed subjects' thinking about the source of the king's power.[31]

Just as the Pope was infallible in Church matters, the prevailing "hegemonic" belief was that the king (and a royal lineage) was, by his birthright, chosen by God. He was thereby granted the "divine right"

---

[30] Yul Brynner in *The Ten Commandments* (Cecil B. de Mille director, 1956).
[31] *See* James V. Calvi and Susan Coleman, *American Law and Legal Systems* 5-6 (3rd ed. 1997).

of exercising absolute rule over subjects in the realm. Emanating out of notions of absolute and infallible power came the expression "the king can do no wrong." Carried over from English common law, the concept of an infallible sovereign still holds true in America.

In the rationale of medieval thinkers, law came from God and was, therefore, eternal and immutable. However, during the Age of Enlightenment, theorists began to challenge the absolutism of popes and kings. Thomas More (1477-1535), for example, in *Utopia*, describes his form of socialism as an organization, which builds on the interests of the consumer.[32] In *Utopia*, More recounts a fictitious story about the travels of one Raphael Hythlodaye, who, in the course of a voyage to America, was left behind near Cape Frio. From there, he wanders about until, by chance, he comes upon the Island of Utopia. On Utopia, he finds an ideal constitution in operation, which provides for the welfare of all of its citizens.

Although the story is fiction, with a mythical geography, the names of real people, including More himself, participate in the dialogue with Hythlodaye. As a result, an air of reality pervades the whole of the story, leading many readers to believe the account to be real. The story, combined with other challenges presented by Thomas More against the king, clearly placed into question the power and authority of the King of England and eventually cost More his life by beheading in 1535.[33]

In feudal times, basing the economy of a society on the general welfare of the consumer (or individual) was a novel idea.[34] From the "seed" of individualism planted by More sprang up concepts of utilitarianism, the social contract, modern democracy and capitalism.

LAW AND SOCIETY

According to Calvi and Coleman, "The sociological theory of law holds that law represents a reflection of the values, mores, and culture of the society that produces it."[35] And, as the society changes, the law

---

[32] Thomas More, *Utopia* (1516).

[33] *See the Catholic Encyclopedia*, www.knight.org/advent (1997).

[34] Feudalism was the economic and social system in medieval Europe, in which land, worked by serfs, was held by vassals in exchange for military and other services to overlords. *Websters New World Dictionary* (1984).

[35] *I.e.*, that law follows morality.

will also change.[36] Viewed as a positive social force, law is a utilitarian mechanism that determines who is to receive certain benefits (e.g., social security, unemployment compensation, veteran's benefits, or distribution of welfare benefits). Ideally, law follows morality. Law, therefore, is symbolic as a reflection of society's values. By the law, new programs can be created, enhancing the economy and improving society. An example of the latter might be infrastructure construction including highways, waterways, airports and airways, and other forms of communication.

Law is *protective*. For example, it forbids behavior that causes harm—acts that are wrong in themselves (*malum in se*) such as murder, rape, arson, theft and so forth. It also forbids acts that are wrong merely because they have been prohibited by government (*malum prohibitum*), such as violation of traffic laws or a Federal Aviation Regulation [FAR].

Law also provides *predictability*. In Max Weber's perspective, it is "rational." It provides a measure of predictability so that individuals can conduct their affairs with some degree of certainty.[37]

Law was central to the 19th Century European founders of sociology. However, the sociology of law today is not a discipline with clear logical boundaries and a commonly agreed upon agenda. Nevertheless, over the past half century, the study of law and society began with the works of Karl Marx, Émile Durkheim, and Max Weber. Generally, they have been referred to as the trilogy of modern sociology. For Marx, Weber and Durkheim the relationship between law and society was a critical nexus for unraveling the general features of society and social change.[38] The common theme running through the works of all three theorists is the emphasis they each placed on the importance of the *division of labor* in society.

Because the division of labor is so central to scholarship of law and society, perhaps a fourth name, that of Adam Smith, should have been added to the list. Unfortunately, for reasons that are not altogether clear, the name of Adam Smith has been closely associated with the study of economics and American capitalism, and it has been glossed-over by modern sociologists. But it was Adam Smith who was concerned about the impact of division of labor upon society well

---

[36] James V. Calvi and Susan Coleman, *American Law and Legal Systems* 7 (3rd ed. 1997).
[37] *Id.* at 2-3.
[38] James M. Inverarity, Pat Lauderdale and Barry C. Feld, *Law and Society: Sociological Perspectives on Criminal Law* (1983).

before Marx, Weber and Durkheim. And, the works of all three of the latter-day social theorists reflect Adam Smith's assessment of the impact of the division of labor upon the *Wealth of Nations.*[39] Look for example at Durkheim's thesis for the doctorate, *The Division of Labor in Society.*[40] Section by section, it parallels Adam Smith's seminal contribution. Be that as it may, it is Marx, Weber and Durkheim who are generally recognized as the founders of modern sociology.[41]

THE CONTRIBUTION OF KARL MARX

Karl Marx (1818-1883) looked at social evolution as a function of the forces of production. By examining the transition from a feudal society to capitalism, Marx created a base-superstructure model to demonstrate the effect of the forces of production (tools, machines, work sites, raw materials, and labor power) in creating the relations of production (class structure, control of the forces of production, and consequent exploitation of workers by the owners of the means of production), which in turn create a superstructure (of legal and political institutions).[42]

Marx's basic argument was that capitalism is a transition to communism.[43] Central to understanding his argument, as Marx himself states, is to,

> . . . *grasp the essential connection between private property, avarice, and the separation of labour, capital and landed property; between exchange and competition, etc.; the*

---

[39] Adam Smith, *An Inquiry Into the Nature and Causes of the Wealth of Nations* (1776).

[40] Émile Durkheim, *De la division du travail social* (1893), English translation, The Division of Labour in Society (1933).

[41] *See generally* James M. Inverarity, Pat Lauderdale and Barry C. Feld, *Law and Society: Sociological Perspectives on Criminal Law* (1983), for the "contributions" of Marx, Weber, and Durkheim.

[42] *See* James M. Inverarity, Pat Lauderdale and Barry C. Feld, *Law and Society: Sociological Perspectives on Criminal Law* (1983).

[43] "Communism" was a term Karl Marx and Fredrich Engles chose to distinguish their brand from other forms of socialism, especially that of anarchists such as Pierre-Joseph Proudhon, of whom they were particularly scornful. *See* Gordon A. Craig, *Europe Since 1815* (alternate ed. 1974).

> *connection between this whole estrangement*
> *and the money system.*[44]

Additionally, it is essential to understand Marx's point that "it is men who change circumstances,"[45] and that "man's own deed (he is speaking here of the natural division of labor) becomes an alien power opposed to him, which enslaves him instead of being controlled by him."[46] Marx identifies an antagonism that exists within the framework of private property, and which expresses the subjection of the individual under the division of labor. The intent to abolish this conflict is one of the first concerns of communal life in an evolutionary process, Marx contends.

In the natural evolution of society as viewed by a Marxist, communal tribes (i.e., basic social groups) divide their labor. This division of labor becomes increasingly more specialized and evolves into capitalism and the ownership of private property. The antagonism between labor and capitalists intensifies as the owners of the forces of production increasingly exploit the work force. Capitalism is deconstructed by the process and becomes a new social (communal) form, re-emerging as Marx's ideal of *communism.*[47]

The re-introduction of capitalism into socialism, and its re-emergence as a new socialist form, one could interpret, is the "revolution" that Marx wrote about. It is not necessarily a military coup that Marx was referring to in his writings. Rather, "this evolution takes place naturally; in other words, is not subordinated to a general plan of freely combined individuals. . . ."[48]

Marx argues that this revolution must inevitably take place in order for most (the "proletariat") to achieve "self-activity." The "instruments of production . . .," he says, "must be made subject to each individual, and property to all. Modern universal intercourse can be controlled by individuals, therefore, only when controlled by all." It is

---

[44] Karl Marx, *Economic and Philosophic Manuscripts of 1844*, in Robert C. Tucker (ed.), The Marx-Engles Reader (2nd ed. 1978).

[45] Karl Marx, *Theses on Feuerbach*, in Robert C. Tucker (ed.), The Marx-Engles Reader (2nd ed. 1978).

[46] Karl Marx, *The German Ideology*, in Robert C. Tucker (ed.), The Marx-Engles Reader (2nd ed. 1978).

[47] *See* Laurence E. Gesell, *Airline Re-Regulation* (1990). Gesell refers to this evolutionary process as a "synergistic loop."

[48] Karl Marx, *The German Ideology*, in Robert C. Tucker (ed.), The Marx-Engles Reader (2nd ed. 1978).

here, however, where liberals and communists must part company. To coin Lowi, this would be "the end of liberalism."[49]

From a liberal perspective, Marx's concept of communism is unattainable. It is a conception of justice, and perfect justice is probably not possible in this life; or as Lawrence Friedman expresses it, "justice is never really total."[50] Marx's ideal of communism, if it could be totally achieved would, by definition, collapse upon itself, because "control by all" would signal a return to an original state of nature, elimination of the state and its laws, and, if Hobbes was right, result in a "war of all-against-all."[51] It would, therefore, proclaim the destruction of liberalism as a form of individualism—the very goal of Marx's concept of socialism.

Marx's brand of socialism is the antithesis of capitalism. In Marx's scheme of things, communism evolves from capitalism, and the two social forms are at odds. By extolling the virtues of capitalism, Adam Smith has been revered by business in America since the beginning of the Republic. Karl Marx holds the opposite distinction. The notoriety of Marx makes him the quintessential anti-capitalist. Where Smith viewed capitalism from its positive aspects, Marx saw only the dark side. Communism or what the Marxists believed was the second, or follow-on phase to socialism, was a radical political movement to overthrow the capitalist system. Adam Smith saw personal greed as a necessary factor in a healthy economy. To Marx, however, the "avarice of capitalism" stole from the workers what was rightfully theirs—their tools of production, and more importantly, "their labour power."[52] To understand the labor movement, it is useful, if not essential, to study Marxian theory. It is to Marxist doctrines that one must turn in the study of the history of labor law.[53]

It was Karl Marx who helped organize the International Workingmen's Association (the "First International") in 1864, and it was Marx who was active in affairs of the organization's General Council

---

[49] Theodore J. Lowi, *The End of Liberalism: The Second Republic of The United States* (2nd ed. 1979).

[50] Lawrence M. Friedman, *Total Justice* (1985).

[51] Thomas Hobbes, *Leviathan* (1651).

[52] Karl Marx, Wage Labour and Capital (1849) in Robert C. Tucker, The Marx-Engles Reader (2nd ed. 1978).

[53] Although Marx is generally recognized as the champion of the working class, he may not be the *best* representation of the persona of organized labor. Marx vies for the distinction along with his contemporary adversary, Pierre-Joseph Proudhon. Like Marx, Proudhon was a socialist, and also like Marx, he declared that "property is theft." *See* Paul Stephen Dempsey and Laurence E. Gesell, *Air Transportation: Foundations for the 21st Century* 353 (1997).

until 1871. Early labor organization in Europe was a socialist movement grounded in Marxist doctrine. The evolution of labor in America paralleled that of Europe, but *sans* socialism, at least until the 1930s.[54] After the Great Depression, organized labor in America turned increasingly to the State for its welfare and assistance.

THE CONTRIBUTION OF ÉMILE DURKHEIM

Émile Durkheim (1859-1917) also found error in Marx's assessment of the impact of the division of labor. In the preface of the second edition of his *Division of Labor*, Durkheim concludes that the evolution of the growing organization (of national corporations) which accompanies the division of labor has no connection with the communist ideal. In Durkheim's opinion, communism was not at all realistic. To him, it was no more than a psychological dream to revive a primitive social feeling.[55] In fact, Durkheim rejected all theoretical constructs of society that were formulated by what he considered to be purely "psychological" means.[56] Not only was he at odds with Marxism, he rejected theories of the social contract and of utilitarianism as well. Of the social contract, he said that Jean Jacques Rousseau[57] took a psychology, which contained no social elements for his starting point and constructed society as an artificial product which might coerce the individual by force, but which contained no moral obligation.[58]

Likewise, he argued that social order cannot be explained, as the Utilitarians sought to explain it, in terms of the enlightened self-interest (or happiness) of individuals.[59] To Durkheim, there had to be something other than individual tendencies, which bound society together. His was a concept of society as a moral construct, maintained through the development of a collective conscience. That "something" holding society together, he said, was *social solidarity.*[60]

---

[54] *Id.* at 353-357.

[55] *See* C.N. Starke, *Laws of Social Evolution and Social Ideals* 302 (1926).

[56] *Id.* at 314.

[57] Jean-Jacques Rousseau, *du contrat social* (The Social Contract) (1762).

[58] C.N. Starke, *Laws of Social Evolution and Social Ideals* 308 (1926).

[59] Thomas Raison (ed.) and Paul Barker (revised ed.), The Founding Fathers of Social Science 157-158 (1979).

[60] Note the parallel here between Durkheim's "social solidarity" and Adam Smith's "invisible hand." Both concepts are grounded in notions of a collective conscience.

Durkheim distinguished between two forms of social solidarity. *Mechanical solidarity*—characterized by consensus on values, collectively held sentiments and ideas, harmony of interests, and unity of purpose—was to be found in simple societies. *Organic solidarity*—arising from diversity of individual interests and characterized by interdependence and exchange—was to be found in advanced societies resting on the division of labor.[61]

In mechanical solidarity there are strong ties which bind members of society together. Conversely, organic solidarity has weak ties among members of a community. From mechanical solidarity comes repressive justice, which reaffirms common values through ritual forms of punishment. On the other hand, organic solidarity generates restitutive sanctions designed to restore disrupted relationships and return the offender to original status. Restitutive sanctions restore the offender by compensating the victim for loss or damage. Conversely, repressive sanctions are a "status degradation ceremony" that ostracizes the offender from the community.[62]

Currently, there is a trend toward restitutive sanctions as the resolution for violating society's norms.[63] Durkheim foresaw this trend, and he proposed that in developed societies civil law would increasingly replace criminal law. He also observed, " . . . that the degree to which a government possesses an absolutist character is not linked to any particular social type."[64] This led him to formulate the first of his *Two Laws of Penal Evolution*, which state that,

> *The intensity of punishment is the greater the more closely societies approximate to a less developed type—and the more the central power assumes an absolute character; and*

> *Deprivations of liberty, and of liberty alone, varying in time according to the seriousness of the crime, tend to become more the normal means of social control.*

---

[61] *See* James Inverarity, Pat Lauderdale and Barry Feld, *Law and Society: Sociological Perspectives on Criminal Law* 148-149 (1983); *See also* Thomas Raison (ed.) and Paul Barker (revised ed.), *The Founding Fathers of Social Science* 157-158 (1979).

[62] *Id.*

[63] *See* Donald Black, *The Behavior of Law* (1976).

[64] Émile Durkheim, *Two Laws of Penal Evolution* (1899).

Repressive and restitutive sanctions, like retribution and deterrence, are alternate forms of punishment, yet the focus of each is entirely different. Repressive sanctions are expiatory and designed around the offender by taking revenge—to retaliate and make the culprit atone. Conversely, restitutive sanctions involve reciprocity and a cooperative effort to restore conditions to an original state. Restitution includes the restoration of the deprived rights of the victims of rule-breaking, not just restitution of the offender by "paying him back." It might also include restitution of the offender to a state of compliance—with regulations for example.

Like other forms of regulation, certification of airmen through the Federal Aviation Regulations imposes limitations by threat of sanction.[65] With regard to sanctions, Durkheim predicted the current trend away from retribution and toward restitution as a way to resolve violation of society's norms. It follows that perhaps there ought to be a concurrent shift from retribution to restitution for the violators of government regulations as well. Unfortunately, centralized government enforcement still relies more heavily upon the retributive effects of punishment.

For example, the FAA developed a program to fulfill its statutory oversight obligations.[66] In the FAA's Compliance and Enforcement Program, formal enforcement action can take two forms. It can include administrative action such as warning letters, or it can take the form of legal action such as certificate suspension or revocation. Although it does have a restitutive component, fundamentally the FAA's program is retribution. Generally, it fails to recognize the necessity for, and the benefits of, more restitutive remedies.[67] Some critics see room for improvement in the current FAA enforcement program, which relies heavily upon retribution for corrective action.[68]

One might assume that airmen are honorable people, and that in general they are at all times attempting to comply with the FARs. One might, therefore, conclude that an airman's alleged non-compliance

---

[65] A. Stone, *Regulation and its Alternatives* (1982).

[66] Federal Aviation Administration, *Compliance and Enforcement Program*, Order 2150.3A (1988).

[67] Laurence E. Gesell and Robert Anderson, *Compliance and Enforcement: Aviation Safety In The Public Interest, Part II: Current Enforcement Program*, The J. of Aviation/Aerospace Education and Research (winter 1992).

[68] *See* Laurence E. Gesell and Robert Anderson, *Compliance and Enforcement: Aviation Safety in the Public Sector, Parts I, II, and III*, The J. of Aviation/Aerospace Education and Research (fall 1991, winter 1992, and spring 1992).

might be the result of lack of skills and/or knowledge. In the absence of any malice, the retributive effect of certificate suspension is arguably not the most appropriate way to handle airmen found in noncompliance with the rules.

Sanction taken only for its deterrent value is a unilateral form of redress that has a dubious chance of actually affecting offender rehabilitation in a remedial sense. Retribution fails to consider the benefits of positive interaction between the offender and the victim (in this case the state). In fact, it promotes the opposite effect by perpetuating any alienation between offender and victim. Restitution, on the other hand, provides a basis for restoring the breach of public trust precipitated by non-compliant action.[69] He may not have stated it the same way, but, essentially, that was Durkheim's point. In advanced societies, restitution is the preferred way of handling grievances.

THE CONTRIBUTION OF MAX WEBER

Like Émile Durkheim, Max Weber (1864-1920) was also a critic of Marx's communism. He was deeply concerned about the internal tensions of Western capitalist society, and from patriotic feelings, he sought to understand its institutional roots.[70] Weber is best known for his work in three areas: (1) the sociology of religion and its influence in the development of capitalism;[71] (2) political sociology and the analysis of politics and social stratification;[72] and (3) the development of systems of inquiry into the nature of social science.[73]

In Max Weber's methodology, there are two recurrent themes, the *ideal type* and *rationality*. His use of ideal types to describe his findings and observations was not an attempt to describe pure forms, but rather, it was an *observed* type against which other cases could be compared, and their deviation from the "ideal" measured. One of Weber's ideals was *capitalism*. Another was *bureaucracy*.

Key to understanding bureaucracy from Weber's perspective is to understand authority. Max Weber classified systems of authority into

---

[69] Laurence E. Gesell and Robert Anderson, *Compliance and Enforcement: Aviation Safety In The Public Sector, Part III: An Alternative Enforcement Program*, The J. of Aviation/Aerospace Education and Research (spring 1992).

[70] Timothy Raison (ed.) and Paul Barker (revised ed.), *The Founding Fathers of Social Science* (1979).

[71] *See* Max Weber, *The Protestant Ethic and the Spirit of Capitalism* (1904; Eng. trans. 1930).

[72] *See* Max Weber, *Wirtschaft und Gesellschaft* (Economy and Society) (Eng. trans. 1922).

[73] *See* Max Weber, *The Methodology of the Social Sciences* (1922; Eng. trans. 1949).

traditional authority, where the compulsion is to obey because leadership is formally identified; and *charismatic authority*, where the leader is followed because he or she possesses "unusual qualities." Bureaucracy is a system of rational-legal authority administered through bureaucrats, whose spheres of competence are precisely laid down.[74] It is a system for administering large organizations involving a (hierarchical) structure of authority, and a clearly defined set of rules and regulations to guide the decisions of bureaucrats who administer it. The characteristics of the ideal bureaucracy, said Weber, are *rationality* in decision making, *impersonality* in social relations, *routinized tasks*, and *centralized authority*.[75]

Bureaucracy has been criticized because of its impersonal relationships with clients, indecisiveness in dealing with unique circumstances, excessive paperwork and red tape, and for its unresponsiveness and delay. Because it is viewed by many analysts as an outmoded organizational structure, there has been an on-going search, at least since the 1980s, to find a viable replacement for Weberian bureaucracy. As Sadler points out, bureaucracy had its time and place, "ideally suited to the era of mass production," but now, "there is a growing international consensus that for the Western countries economic renaissance is dependent upon the cultural transformation of large-scale business, and in particular on the extent to which decaying bureaucracies can be replaced with dynamic organic cultures."[76]

Likewise, Deal and Kennedy "see a revolution on the horizon . . . a breakdown of the large, traditional hierarchical organizations that have dominated in the past."[77] What they envision is an "atomized" organization where there are no bosses. For their vision to work they suggest "strong cultural ties and a new kind of symbolic management will be required." Whether or not the bureaucratic, hierarchical form of business organization can really be replaced is still a matter of speculation, especially if one is contemplating cultural change within the corporation. Cultural change can be more readily accomplished (or controlled) through the centralization, not de-centralization of

---

[74] Timothy Raison (ed.) and Paul Barker (revised ed.), *The Founding Fathers of Social Science* 215-220 (1979).

[75] H.H. Gerth and C.W. Mills, from Max Weber: *Essays in Sociology* 196-198 (1948).

[76] P. Sadler, *Managerial Leadership in Post-Industrial Society* 124 (1988).

[77] T. Deal and A.A. Kennedy, *The Rites and Rituals of Corporate Life* (1982), in Stakeholders of the Organizational Mind 127 (Ian Mitroff, 1983).

management.[78] The bureaucratic form is still seen as necessary for the efficient operation of large organizations.

Nearly 100 years ago, Max Weber saw the ideal of bureaucracy as characteristic of the movement toward rational social organization in modern societies. Likewise, Émile Durkheim related the emergence of bureaucracy to the division of labor and the growing complexity of society. Max Weber's theory of bureaucracy remains today the most illuminating framework for analyzing large administrative systems. Certainly, federal, state and local governments are arranged in the bureaucratic form, including agencies like the FAA, state aeronautics authorities, and local airport sponsors—so are the major airlines and other large corporate structures.

From a Weberian point of view, the law is "rational." In Max Weber's perspective on capitalism (and the modern institutional order), the free market economy is dependent upon rational-legal authority, not only internal to the organization in its "bureaucracy," but also externally, upon the "rationality of economic action." As Anthony Giddens interprets Weber, "Modern rational capitalism has need, not only for the technical means of production, but of a calculable legal system and administration in terms of formal rules."[79] By "rational," Weber was referring to marketplace efficiency—the most rational means of orienting economic activity. As Inverarity, Lauderdale and Feld explain, rationality does not mean "reasonable" in the colloquial sense, but rather, is used in the technical sense to mean "rules and procedures."[80]

Of the three principal types of government regulation (i.e., economic, safety, and social regulation), the latter two (safety and social) can be expected to become increasingly more "rationalized" in the future. Safety is a universal need. On a continuum between what is unsafe and what is safe, an acceptable safety margin is never static. Rather, it is always being improved upon. A status quo in safety achievement, in effect, represents a *de facto* decline from where safety otherwise might have been. Therefore, safety programs and enhancements continuously strive for improvement.

---

[78] Paul Stephen Dempsey and Laurence E. Gesell, *Air Transportation: Foundations for the 21st Century* 100 (1997).

[79] Anthony Giddens, *Introduction*, in Max Weber (Talcott Parsons, trans.), The Protestant Ethic and The Spirit of Capitalism (1958/1976).

[80] *See* James Inverarity, Pat Lauderdale and Barry Feld, *Law and Society: Sociological Perspectives on Criminal Law* (1983).

Under the government's police powers there is a responsibility to protect the health, welfare and safety of society. Inasmuch as safety is not static, efforts must be continuously exerted by the government to improve upon it. As a result, one would expect that safety is an area wherein the government might be expected to be the most rational.

Safety and security are two sides of the same coin. Both have a common goal: to protect passengers, crew, cargo, and aircraft from harm. Their main difference, however, is that safety focuses on prevention from unintentional harm, while security focuses on intentional harm—parallel to the difference in the common law between negligence and intentional torts, respectively. Secure conditions demand rational rules to provide individuals assurance of their future safety and well being. For a degree of safety to be a rational or calculable expectation, it requires a network of supporting rules and regulations. It might be noted that the FAA's primary mission is aviation safety. The agency accomplishes its mission through certification and promulgation of regulations—the FARs. After September 11, 2001, security eclipsed other forms of safety with a watershed of Transportation Security Regulations [TSRs] emanating from the Transportation Security Agency [TSA].

Implicit in the government's continuing attempt to strive for ever-higher degrees of safety and security is that more regulations must be adopted to bring about increasingly more rational safety net. Therefore, one would assume that the future of safety and security regulation in air transportation portends the creation of more regulations yet to come. It is likewise the case with social regulation.

Social regulation has traditionally assumed different goals and objectives from its safety and economic counterparts. "Social regulation" (defined here as "environmental regulation") is much like safety regulation, in that social regulation monitors the environmental welfare of human beings. Like safety regulation, the social regulatory framework may be expected to expand. To curtail, if not control environmental pollution, it will require ever increasing regulatory controls to mitigate sources of pollution wherever practicable. Consequently, like safety and security regulation, the expectation is for government production of more environmental regulation in the future.[81]

---

[81] *See* Paul Stephen Dempsey and Laurence E. Gesell, *Air Transportation: Foundations for the 21st Century* 243-246 (1997).

LAW'S VIOLENCE

Simply stated, laws are rules, and control is brought about by enforcement of those rules. Regulation (a Federal Aviation Regulation, for example) may be defined as, " . . . a state-imposed limitation on the discretion that may be exercised by individuals or organizations, which is supported by the threat of sanction."[82] "Sanction" is another word for punishment. In his justification of the absolute power of the sovereign, Thomas Hobbes defined "punishment" as,

> . . . an evil inflicted by public authority on him that hath done or omitted that which is judged by the same authority to be a transgression of the law, to that end that the will of men may thereby the better be disposed to obedience.[83]

From his definition of punishment Hobbes was inferring, from the state's monopoly in the use of force, " . . . that neither private revenges nor injuries of private men can properly be styled punishment, because they proceed from public authority"—that is to say, there is a difference between revenge, which is private, and punishment, which is public.[84] The purpose of punishment is not retribution; rather, it is to restore law and order. Punishment is violence legitimized by the need for obedience to the law.[85] Punishment is designed to restore obedience—to control society, and thereby preclude a return to a natural state of anarchy.

In a less philosophical, and more pragmatic, even cynical viewpoint, the purpose for law in the contemporary sense, as well as during the days of Pharaoh, the Roman Empire, and all days in-between, at a minimum has been to maintain a civilized society. Absent the threat, prospect, or possibility of disorder and aggression, law would be unnecessary.[86] But in the world we all inhabit, there is *violence*. As Robert Cover suggests, We inhabit a *nomos*—a normative world. We

---

[82] Alan Stone, *Regulation and its Alternatives* 10 (1982).
[83] Thomas Hobbes, *Leviathan* (1651).
[84] *Id.*
[85] *Id.*
[86] *Id.*

constantly create and maintain a world of right and wrong, of lawful and unlawful, of valid and void.[87]

This image of nomos and law stands in stark contrast to a world of anarchy.[88] In such a world, law is always pulled in two directions, and as a result, there is "an essential tension in law."[89] "Justice," defined as meting out a balance, demands that violence be countered by a force equal to it—no different than confronting an invasion from without with an equal or superior counterattacking force from within. Few would enjoy the prospect of war, but personal harm and/or loss of freedom are unacceptable alternatives.

Paradoxically, though violence is the tool of the "unruly," it is violence itself that must be used to counter violence. Violence, thereby, becomes legitimated as the tool of law used by the state to control society. One might prefer denying the necessity of using violence in what one would like to believe is a "civilized" society, but as Sarat and Kearns state,

> *Violence stands before the law, unruly; it defies the law to protect us from its cruelest consequences. It demands that law respond in kind, and requires law to traffic in its own brand of force and coercion. It is thus that point of departure from which complete departure is impossible. It is the task of law and of much legal theory to insist, nonetheless, on the difference between the force that law uses and the unruly force beyond its borders. Legal theorists name the superiority of the former by calling it legitimate.*[90]

Defined as "punishment," violence may take any form along a continuum from sanction (for say a regulatory violation) to capital punishment (for murder). The most extreme violence the state can act out is that of the death penalty. Under any other circumstances than

---

[87] Robert Cover, *Nomos and Narrative*, 97 Harvard Law Review 4-5 (1983).

[88] Austin Sarat and Thomas R. Kearns, *Making Peace with Violence: Robert Cover on Law and Legal Theory*, in Austin Sarat and Thomas R. Kearns (eds.), Law's Violence 224 (1992).

[89] Martha Minow, Michael Ryan, and Austin Sarat (eds.) *Violence and the Law: Essays of Robert Cover* 1602 (1992).

[90] *Id.* at 211-251.

by lawfully prescribed means, an execution might also be described as murder. Note that the term, "execution," is legitimated by its own definition (e.g., "putting to death by a legal sentence") but which in and of itself may be insufficient justification for the act. Hence, how an act of murder (albeit by the state) can be legitimated has been a question of serious academic debate. As Robert Cover asks, how can law do homicidal deeds without itself being "jurispathic"?[91] In response to the question, in Cover one can find both a critic and an apologist for law's violence.

On the one hand, Cover insists that law is different from, and more than, violence. The purpose of law is the promotion of toleration, respect, and community. Conversely, unlawful violence is its own justification, against which the only viable alternative is force in kind. Law only reluctantly embraces legal force. The "unruly" are, by their nature, violent.[92] Cover thereby justifies law's violence by a difference principle. Yet, Cover himself is a self-proclaimed anarchist.[93] As such, he is a person one would hardly expect to condone state rule in any form. But Cover narrowly defines "anarchy" to mean " . . . the absence of rulers not the absence of law."[94] Accepting its necessity, law as applied in real life situations includes a certain kind of force.[95]

Karl Olivecrona approaches the legitimacy of law's violence more straightforward by making no apology for it. He argues that to create the belief that violence is alien to law, or of secondary importance, is a mistake. The fact that law uses violence is a reality that should not be masked. Apologists for law's violence create a "fatal illusion" and,

> . . . *law's real character is largely obscured and this is done by metaphysical ideas and expressions. It is not bluntly said, e.g., that the function of the courts is to determine the use of force. Instead their function is said to be the "administration of justice". . . .*[96]

---

[91] Robert Cover, *Nomos and Narrative*, 97 Harvard Law Review 4, 40 (1983).

[92] *See* Austin Sarat and Thomas R. Kearns, *Making Peace with Violence: Robert Cover on Law and Legal Theory*, in Austin Sarat and Thomas R. Kearns (eds.), Law's Violence 214 (1992).

[93] *Id.*

[94] Robert Cover, *Folktales of Justice: Tales of Jurisdiction*, 14 Capital University Law Review 179, 181 (1985).

[95] *See* Karl Olivecrona, *Law As Fact* 126, 134 (1939).

[96] *Id.* at 125.

Law's violence is what it is—violence. Execution is murder. And the force used by the state is legitimate, because that's what the state does (to "control" society). As stated by Jean Jacques Rousseau,

> *The death penalty inflicted upon criminals . . . is in order that we may not fall victims to an assassin that we consent to die if we ourselves turn assassins. In this treaty, so far from disposing of our own lives, we think only of securing them, and it is not to be assumed that any of the parties then expects to get hanged.*[97]

Within the social contract, or "treaty," envisioned by Rousseau, and implicit in the United States Constitution, the state has been empowered by the people to use such force in their defense. In "utilitarian" fashion, the majority can, if it so chooses, modify the limits of force employed by the state. At the extreme, if the majority is generally opposed to the very existence of the state, the only option is anarchy, and a return to a war of all-against-all.[98]

Majority rule is the essence of American democracy. Democracy in America is not perfect, but until a better system is devised, and subject to the will of the majority, it will have to suffice.

LEGISLATED JUSTICE

Law is supposed to follow morality. That is to say, the *morality* of a society, that precedes the law, should be reflected in *laws* that society later enacts. The hopeful outcome of legislation is that justice will become synonymous with the law. The term "just," therefore, denotes what is both lawful (positive) and fair (moral). Conversely, unlawful or unfair is unjust. Assuming the law to be just, the law-abiding person is just, the lawbreaker unjust.

It is the business of the legislative body to determine what is lawful. And, it is in legislature where morality and positive law theoretically come together. Unfortunately, not all law is moral. Because the two concepts theoretically intersect, the products of legislative bodies are deemed to be the *principles of justice*. The resultant law pre-

---

[97] Jean-Jacques Rousseau, *du contrat social* (The Social Contract) Book II (1762).
[98] *See* Thomas Hobbes, *Leviathan* (1651).

scribes certain conduct—examples being self-control, good temper, bravery and so forth. The Greeks would have considered these as attributes of virtue (i.e., mastery of sociability). It follows, then, that justice is perfect virtue, and a uniting of both positive and moral law. The system of law in America is the combination of common (moral) law and statutory (positive) law. Both will be addressed in more detail in subsequent chapters.

Where it is the job of the legislature to make (just) law, it is the responsibility of the judges (the judiciary) to try to equalize injustice which is found to consist of inequality under the law. As Aristotle pointed out, justice can only exist when people are (1) free and (2) have equality. Thus, a tyrant is considered by free persons to be unjust and tyranny to be illegal. In the social contract as it was envisioned by Rousseau, where the sovereign has abused its power, the people are justified in their disolvement of the (hypothetical) contract that has (in reality) been breached by the sovereign. This the American colonists did in 1776 with a formal Declaration of Independence.

Justice exists only when inter- (or mutual) relations are regulated by law. Aristotle suggested that justice can only exist between those where there is the possibility of injustice. Compare this with one of the first principles in the Declaration of Independence, "We hold these truths to be self evident, that all men are created equal. . . ." Said John Wise, "It follows as a common law of nature that every man esteem and treat another as one who is naturally his equal or who is a man as well as he."

The discussion of what was meant by "all men are created equal" involves a basic distinction pointed out by Alexis de Tocqueville that the *nature* of equality is separate from the *condition* of equality.[99] The authors of the Declaration of Independence presumably meant that all men are equal in their common nature of being endowed with the same basic rights to life, liberty and the pursuit of happiness. The condition of equality versus inequality is something else. All men are not born under equivalent economic and/or physical "conditions."

James Fennimore Cooper argued that nowhere in government is it laid down that equality is a governing principle. Cooper is referring to the condition of equality as opposed to its nature, by stating,

---

[99] Alex de Tocqueville, *Democracy in America* (1840).

> *Equality, in a social sense, may be divided into that of condition and that of rights. Equality of condition is incompatible with civilization and is found only to exist in those communities that are but slightly removed from the savage state. In practice, it can only mean a common misery.*[100]

As used in the Declaration of Independence, the term "equality" has nothing to do with inborn differences of physical stature, intelligence, or any other talents and capabilities; nor does it exclude inequalities which result from individual efforts and achievements. According to Cooper, and others, natural equality is the basis of social inequality, but which in turn is the basis of progress and civilization.

Democracy is not a perfect form of government, and Aristotle, on democracy and government, was highly skeptical of human motives. Rule by the elite seems a natural evolution, which leads to an imbalance of power. However, given a choice of political forms, democracy with its equality under law is the lesser of evils. Nevertheless, it warrants careful and continuous scrutiny. The founders of the Republic feared the abuse of power, and included in the American form of government are checks and balances to insure against abuses, and to provide justice by bringing the system back into equity.

In conclusion, to break the law, or to violate the rights of others, is an exercise of unrighteous dominion. As with abuse of power in government, the law is designed to equalize the violations of private citizens as well. How this is accomplished is subsequently described throughout this book by demonstrating how the law is structured and applied—in this case, its application to the field of aviation.

---

[100] *See* James Fennimore Cooper, *The American Democrat* (1838).

CHAPTER 2

ORIGIN OF LAW

*Out of the fear of a war of all-against-all, the rationality
of law has evolved over centuries of refinement.*

THE EVOLUTION OF WESTERN LAW [1]

Law has evolved through thousands of years of human experience.
The Greeks and Romans had systems of law, parts of which were
taken from the ancient Egyptians and Babylonians. And, Babylonian
laws were developed by people who lived even centuries before. Presented in this chapter is a chronological overview of the development
of Western law. Although simplified, if not in danger of being gro-
tesquely oversimplified, the overview does provide the reader with a
useful perspective on the evolution of modern law.

In describing modern law, U.S. Supreme Court Justice Oliver
Wendell Holmes, Jr. stated that U.S. common law, ". . . is the witness
and external deposit of our moral life. Its history is the history of the
moral development of the race." Holmes' philosophy was that, "The
life of the law has not been logic; it has been experience."[2] Law in the
United States developed as a response to a need to find solutions to
pressing issues of the times.[3] Although Holmes was specifically ad-

---

[1] The preponderance of information in this chapter is of historical nature. As such, it is common,
encyclopedic knowledge that has been summarized and condensed by the authors, who claim no
originality other than its reorganization. Where the works of individual authors have been used,
they have been appropriately cited. Rather than repeatedly citing the encyclopedic references
throughout the book, they are cited here just once. *Grolier Encyclopedia of Knowledge* (1991);
see also Encyclopædia Britannica (1969).

[2] Oliver Wendell Holmes, Jr., *The Common Law* (1881).

[3] James V. Calvi and Susan Coleman, *American Law and Legal Systems* 14 (3rd ed. 1997).

dressing the nature of U.S. common law, his philosophy is applicable across the ages as well.

Out of a fear of the "war of all-against-all" that Hobbes predicted, and of the dangers presented by the "unruly" in society, development of law has been a rational response to the constant threat of a breakdown by society. Society's existence hangs by a hair, and a modern community is at the mercy of a thousand dangers. Every day the community faces the possibility of such a breakdown—not from the forces of nature, but from sheer human unpredictability.[4] As Anthony Giddens interprets Max Weber, "Modern rational capitalism has need, not only of the technical means of production, but of a calculable legal system and administration in terms of formal rules."[5] The rationality of law minimizes the ever-present risks.

The rationality of law has evolved over centuries of refinement. One can see the beginnings of the development of law's rationalization in the earliest codification of society's rules.

CODE OF HAMMURABI

The first known legal system supported by a code of laws has as its origin the land of ancient Samaria, in the area commonly referred to as the "cradle of civilization" in modern day Iraq. The Acts of Babylonian kings can be traced as far back as 2370 BC, with the first known codification of their sovereign legislative acts occurring around 2130 BC. Then as now, legislative acts (or laws) tended to be formulated chronologically, and to have no other orderly form until otherwise arranged into a structured frame of reference. The process of organizing and arranging law by subject into a systematic form is by definition "codification." A code of laws provides society with easy reference to rules and standards by which it is expected to abide.

The entire body of law, however, is something more than a code of laws. Rather, it is the sum of all of the official and unofficial rules by which men and women live. But at a minimum, written codes can provide a legal framework upon which society can rely. Such was the case in ancient Babylon. Codification is fundamental to the structure of U.S. law as well. Examples are the *United States Code* and the

---

[4] Robert L. Heilbroner, *The Worldly Philosophers: The Lives, Times, and Ideas of the Great Social Thinkers* (2nd ed. 1972).

[5] Anthony Giddens, Introduction (1976), in Max Weber, The Protestant Ethic and the Spirit of Capitalism (Talcott Parsons trans. 1958).

Code of Federal Regulations, which are addressed, in subsequent chapters. The early Babylonian codes included legislative acts, other law including contract law, and a prescribed process for litigation.

Regarded as the most perfect legal monument of antiquity, and preserved by its carving in stone (literally, the law was "carved in stone"), is the Code of Hammurabi, King of Babylon in the 18th Century BC. In Hammurabi's Code were references to citizen's rights. It prescribed the social classes (according to station) to whom the law applied, defined social status, described property and ownership, the order of the family, and included a body of criminal law.

It is important to note from the above that the law may not apply to all people equally. To have laws to which one is subject is a personal right—even a cherished privilege. Without the law, one is denied access to justice and equality.[6] It was the privileged few to whom the Babylonian law applied. To have Roman citizenship was equally a privilege. The Romans extended the law liberally throughout the Empire, even to certain of the vanquished. Nevertheless, the law protected not everyone. Non-citizens, foreigners, and slaves were beyond the law's protection. Slavery was a commonly accepted practice amongst the Romans. Slavery, of course, is disenfranchisement to its extreme, and it was common throughout the world until the 19th Century. Unfortunately, it still exists today in remote, and in some not-so-remote conditions. Prostitution, for example, may entail compulsory servitude. Drug addiction, too, can take one into bondage.

Access to the law begins with a system of codification. As Henry Sumner Maine explains, "The most celebrated system of jurisprudence known to the world begins, as it ends, with a code." Maine went on to explain that, "From the commencement to the close of its history, the expositors of Roman Law consistently employed language which implied that the body of their system rested on the *Twelve Decemviral Tables*, and therefore on a basis of written law." More on Roman law, and the *Twelve Tables*, is presented below.

MOSAIC LAW

Not only are codes fundamental to law, legal forms the world over have roots in religious expression. The United States common law system, for example, is grounded in the Judeo-Christian experience.

---

[6] *See* Laura Nader (ed.), *No Access to Law: Alternatives to the American Judicial System* (1980).

Look, for example, at the laws of Moses. Mosaic Law prescribed the expected conduct for the twelve tribes of Israel. This ancient law is considered one of the earliest forms of *contract law*. Mosaic Law is the story of a partnership (or covenant) between man and God. The intent of the law was to develop the human race toward holiness and to help man become more godlike.

Inherent in Mosaic Law is an insistence on human rights—or said another way, for man to have free agency. Bear in mind that at the time of its origination, the tribes of Israel were in bondage under the Egyptians, and vividly recognized by the Israelites was the value of freedom—the keystone of any equitable system of law and justice.

The contract, or "covenant," states that in exchange for allegiance to God, man is to receive certain blessings, or benefits, from living the code. Note that by accepting Mosaic Law the Israelites were swearing their allegiance to their God, and no longer to any earthly ruler, or pseudo-god such as the pharaoh of Egypt. The only lawful authority for the Israelites was *natural law* that emanated from a more Supreme Being. It may follow that human beings are, therefore, ". . . endowed by their Creator with certain unalienable rights." Although the Israelites had a code of laws in the *Ten Commandments*, the adoption of "unalienable rights" suggests the supersedence of *natural* law over the *positive* law of the Egyptians.

Mosaic Law is more than just the *Ten Commandments* to which most people are familiar, but includes the five books of Moses—and *tradition.* The "codified" law starts in *Leviticus* with laws of cleanliness and sacrifice. Included also are laws of mercy and righteousness, of lawful marriage, and laws and ordinances concerning the Levitical priests, who were themselves the lawgivers and the interpreters of the law. It is in *Deuteronomy* where the Covenant is described, and where the familiar *Ten Commandments* can be found. It is here where Moses receives "The Law"—the law being the commandments, and judgments of God. Included are the laws of bearing false witness, slander, adultery, rape, divorce, usury, pledges (promises), war, and humanity. There also are the penalties assigned for disobedience of the aforementioned commandments. Along with laws against bearing false witness (perjury or lying) there is made a provision requiring two witnesses as documentary evidence. The laws of murder and manslaughter are found in the book of *Numbers*.

Something that serves as evidence or proof is a witness. When someone observes an event and then attests to that observation, his or her testimony gives witness of the validity of the event observed. There is a principle of law, as old as written history, which places reliance upon two or more witnesses to establish truth, and to serve as the burden of proof in establishing the facts. According to the laws of observance spoken of by Moses to the Israelites, a person thought guilty of a transgression was to be accused by one knowing or otherwise hearing of the wrongdoing. In *Deuteronomy*, it states:

> *At the mouth of two or three witnesses, shall he that is worthy of death be put to death but at the mouth of one witness he shall not be put to death.*[7]

Such reliance was placed upon the integrity of one's word that it was a transgression in its own right for someone to bear *false witness*. Compare the above excerpt with the following:

> *No Person shall be convicted of Treason unless on the Testimony of two Witnesses to the same overt Act, or on Confession in open Court.*[8]

So offended were American forebears over the unjust execution of Sir Walter Raleigh in 1618 for high treason, that the quotation above was included in the U.S. Constitution. It might be noted that Sir Walter Raleigh's conviction was obtained on the single deposition (i.e., written testimony) of one Lord Cobham, a prisoner, one who was not even examined in court, and who was known to have already retracted his accusation. Two witnesses to the same act are required by the U.S. Constitution, and the accused has the right to be confronted with the witnesses against him or her. The origin of this provision is, of course, thought to have come from Mosaic Law.

The fact that the Israelites placed sovereignty in God, and not in Pharaoh, is thought to have given rise to the foundations of *natural law* and of *democracy*. There was direct rule by God, but at the same

---

[7] *Deuteronomy* 17:26.
[8] U.S. Constitution, Article III.

time there was an insistence upon the independence (i.e., "free agency") of the (individual) person. The books of Moses are replete with examples of infractions of the law, which in and of themselves, demonstrate the acceptance of free agency by the Israelites. To violate the law individually or unilaterally one must have agency, or culpability, to do so.[9] However, in the case of the Israelites, it was up to God, not man, to punish, and the giver of the law in this case was an unseen ruler. Hence, at this point, the judges in God's behalf entered the picture. Although not the lawgiver *per se*, the High Priest, acting for God, became a governor of the laws.

Mosaic Law was based upon wisdom, understanding and righteousness. It entertained a far greater conception of equality and justice than say either Greek or, later, Roman law.

ROMAN LAW

The Romans craved color, texture, and decoration in their public and private spaces. Although the Romans produced beautiful and lasting works of art, they always felt inferior to the Greeks in art, literature, and science. But in government it was different. Governing was an art form mastered by the Romans. The following passage from Virgil's *Aeneid* makes the point:

> *The Greeks shape bronze statues so real they seem to breathe, and carve cold marble until it almost comes to life. The Greeks compose great orations, and measure the heavens so well they can predict the rising of the stars. But you, Romans, remember your great arts: to govern the people with authority, to establish peace under rule of law, to conquer the mighty, and show them mercy once they are conquered.*[10]

One of the most important legacies left behind by the Romans was their comprehensive body of statute and case law. The Greeks in-

---

[9] Culpability, or blameworthiness, requires a showing that a person acted purposely, knowingly, recklessly or negligently. *Black's Law Dictionary* (abridged 5th ed. 1983).

[10] Virgil, *Aenid VI*, 84753; *see also* T.R. Reid, *The Power and the Glory of the Roman Empire*, 192 National Geographic 26 (Jul. 1997).

vented the ideal of written law as a shield to protect individuals against one another and against the awesome power of the state, but it was the Romans who made it a rule of law. So fundamental is this rule of law to Western civilization that now it is commonly taken for granted. Yet, positive law is not a necessary aspect of the human condition. In East Asian nations, for example, the concept of written law and written contract is fairly weak. There, they may prefer to trust people, not laws, and to rely on innate human goodness (i.e., deontology) as the best guarantee of a civil society.[11]

As with the Greeks, Romans identified law with nature and with morality, but to the Romans the state of nature was synonymous with harmony. Citizens were regulated by reason. To live according to "reason" was to live "naturally." But the laws of nature and of reason took on new meaning with the Romans. The overriding principle became might; i.e., power over others. Dominant in the law was control through deterrence and retribution. Thus, one might ask, "reason" according to whom? The answer, of course, is reason according to who held the most power—an argument that "might is right."

During the early years of the Roman Republic, and in the ongoing struggle between ordinary people and the governing elite, the *plebeians* decided they would much rather rely on laws than on the whims of rulers. Under pressure from the *plebs*, the governing class was forced to issue written codes. The Romans thereafter gained a genuine respect for the rule of law. Even after the establishment of one-man rule, there was a tendency of the emperors to abide by legal dictates.[12]

The Romans synthesized what were considered to be "practical" rules and precepts into the *Twelve Tables*, which were published in the early period of the Republic, in about 450 BC. The *Twelve Tables* were a guiding set of moral principles and acceptable practices. Just over a thousand years later, during the Byzantine era, the Emperor, Justinian, re-codified Roman law again into the *Corpus Juris Civilis*—the Body of Civil Laws. By Justinian's time, Roman law had become complex and unmanageable. To set new order to the law, the laws were codified into fifty books known as *The Digest*. To keep the code up to date, periodically new laws were published as *The Novels*. Justinian's monumental compilation of the Digests, The Novels, and

---

[11] T.R. Reid, *The World According to Rome*, 192 National Geographic 64 (Aug. 1997).
[12] *Id.* at 64, 70.

the Revised Code, completed in AD 534, has served as the foundation of Western law ever since.[13]

The Roman legal process had profound influence on the American system. The U.S. system of common law, like the Roman system, is a combination of statutory and case law. During the era of the Roman Republic (549-509 BC), lawmaking was a bicameral activity. The American experiment used republican Rome as its model. Laws of the federal government must likewise go through two legislative bodies.[14]

It should be noted that law applied only to Roman citizens. Although the Romans were generous in extending citizenship, there was no established law for non-citizens. Without citizenship, a person had no civil rights. Citizenship was a prized possession, for it held the keys to the only personal, albeit limited, freedom available. Without the shield of citizenship a person was neither protected by a rational system of laws, nor free to interact in society. It is ironic that when one opposes, or otherwise runs contrary to the rule of the law, that same person often seeks protection from the same rule of law. When the Apostle Paul, for example, was threatened by the might of Rome, he sought refuge in the protection of his Roman citizenship.[15]

When brought before a Roman magistrate on charges something like inciting a riot, Paul was about to be beaten and jailed when he declared his citizenship. That changed everything. With citizens, it was not the Roman custom to hand over any man before he had faced his accusers and given an opportunity to defend himself against the charges.[16] Paul was permitted to remain free pending a trial. As a free man, Paul then asserted another prerogative of citizenship—to make an appeal directly to Rome. With the slowness of communication, probably coupled with a cumbersome bureaucratic process, Paul was left free for a matter of years. And since there is no record of the outcome, some scholars feel the charges were eventually dropped.[17] The earlier trial of Jesus was an altogether different matter.

When Jesus of Nazareth was brought before Pontius Pilate in AD 30, all the power lay on Pilate's side.[18] Apart from Jewish tradition,

---

[13] T.R. Reid, *The World According to Rome*, 192 National Geographic 68 (Aug. 1997).
[14] *Id.* at 62, 70.
[15] *Acts* 22.
[16] *Acts* 25.
[17] T.R. Reid, *The World According to Rome*, 192 National Geographic 70 (Aug. 1997).
[18] T.R. Reid, *The Power and the Glory of the Roman Empire*, 192 National Geographic 40 (Jul. 1997).

for which the Romans gave only tacit respect, Jesus was otherwise subject to relatively arbitrary treatment, even by a relatively minor procurator like Pontius Pilate.

Crucifixion, as was inflicted on Christ, was not a form of capital punishment imposed upon Roman citizens. Romans, sentenced to death, may have been given an opportunity to take hemlock, and thereby, to take their own lives in some dignity. But for foreigners and slaves, it was crucifixion.[19] If applied to freemen, the punishment was only used in the case of the vilest criminals, and degradation was a part of the infliction. Prior to the crucifixion, the victim was first scourged. In public, he was made to carry the crossbar to the execution site. The person was then stripped naked, stretched upon and either tied or, in the Roman custom, nailed to the cross. The cross was then set upright, and the person was left to await death.[20]

Death by crucifixion was the most lingering and painful of all forms of execution. The victim lived in ever-increasing torture for hours, sometimes days. Death came through the exhaustion caused by intense and unremitting pain, and congestion of organs incident to the strained and unnatural position of the body. In most cases, the body was left to rot, or to be devoured by birds and beasts.[21]

The floggings, physical abuse, and manner of death to which Jesus, as non-Roman, was subjected are well documented. But as Reid submits, Jesus had the power of an idea. Eventually, it was Christianity that would dominate the whole of the Roman Empire. Jesus' message, that every individual life was precious, addressed a human need that the Roman ethic did not consider.[22] The Christians gradually converted the entire Roman world, greatly assisted from within by the Emperor himself. Constantine, emperor from AD 306-337, had a vision of a cross with the words, *In hoc signo vinces* (In this sign you will conquer) engraved upon it. Although not yet converted to the religious practice, from that point Constantine took up the cause of Christianity and issued his famous edict of religious toleration.

---

[19] Although closely associated with Rome, crucifixion originated with the Phoenicians and Persians. It was practiced from about the 6th century BC until Constantine banned it in 337 AD

[20] *See* James E. Talmage, *Jesus the Christ* 65-67 (1916); *See also* John Wilkinson, *Jerusalem As Jesus Knew It* 151 (1978).

[21] *See Id.*

[22] *See* T.R. Reid, *The Power and the Glory of the Roman Empire*, 192 National Geographic (Jul. 1997).

CANON LAW

Although the Byzantine Empire continued for another thousand years, the final remnants of the old Roman Empire fell in AD 476. Constantine was the last emperor of the Roman Empire, and the first of the Byzantine Empire, the name given to the continuation of the former empire that had had its capital in Rome. Constantine moved the capital to Byzantium, from which the empire then took its name. The new capital was renamed Constantinople (what is now Istanbul).

The Early Byzantine period (AD 324-610) was highlighted by Constantine's deathbed conversion to Christianity, and by the founding of the city named after him. Another marked period was during the reign of the Emperor Justinian (AD 527-565), who tried to reunite the old Roman Empire. Under Justinian, the Byzantine Empire reached its greatest extent, after which time its influence over the West was no longer of any great significance. The near end of the Byzantine Era came as a result of its sacking by the Crusaders in the 13th Century. The era came to a final close when the Byzantines succumbed to the Ottoman Empire in 1453.

In the meantime, Constantine's conversion had made Christianity the most favored religion in the state, and after AD 380, it was the sole official religion. Subsequent to Constantine's rule, there occurred a gradual transition of power from the state to the Church. The Christian church and its bishop in Rome, the Pope, would come to dominate the Western World. With the fall of the Roman Empire, and the contraction of the Byzantine Empire to the area immediately around Constantinople, the one remaining stable institution within the geography of the old Roman Empire was the Roman Catholic Church. Unable to achieve national union, peoples who had been part of what had been the Roman Empire lived in a loose confederation known as the *Holy Roman Empire*. The beginnings of the Holy Roman Empire are associated with St. Augustine, who lived during the decaying years of Rome. In the 18th Century, Voltaire would proclaim it "neither holy, nor Roman, nor an empire." Because the Roman Catholic Church was the sole existing organized center of learning, the responsibility for propounding laws fell upon it.

Laws issued by the church during the Middle Ages were, by definition, canon. "Canon laws" are those governing a church, the regulations of a church, or the accepted doctrine of a church. Western law and philosophy, therefore, became steeped in the Christian tradition.

SAINT AUGUSTINE (AD 354-430)

To the Romans, Saint Augustine was a rebel who had fallen from a state of nature—meaning that he was not a "reasonable" person according to *their* terms. Saint Augustine, being an antagonist of Rome, was, by definition, "not reasonable." Accordingly, from the Roman perspective, Augustine was headed toward moral death, and his only salvation was to take refuge in Christian grace.

Saint Augustine, of course, took a very different view. For him, the Church was the exponent of the laws of God. The positive law of mortals could be disregarded if it happened to be in conflict with (natural) divine law. Even though positive law may have been intended as a remedy for the evils of sin, the laws of man were themselves, the product of sin. Therefore, according to Augustine, the Church had an obligation to rely upon natural law, and to intervene in positive law because of the contradiction. Thus, following the fall of Rome, and even though there was a recognized need for law and order, it would have been perceived as heathen (sinful) for the Church to have adhered to classical philosophy—the latter being grounded in the precepts of man.

Over the next 800 years, such strict doctrinal interpretation was subjected to societal pressures and changes. Consequently, the dogma had to be relaxed. By the 13th Century, the Holy Roman Empire was disintegrating, and in the interest of preserving church dominance, the doctrine was altered, *pragmatically*, to adapt to changing conditions. The reason for the change in attitude regarding the contradiction was rationalized away, and in a very mortal kind of way.[23]

SAINT THOMAS AQUINAS (1225-1274)

In his *Decretum Gratianum*, Saint Thomas Aquinas worked out a solution to the "contradiction" by identifying the laws of nature with the laws of man. His resolution lie in the fact that: (1) law is all em-

---

[23] To rationalize is to give reason or explanation that gives justification (or seems fair). It is to provide a natural explanation, and to make something, which is apparently irrational appear to be rational; in this case meaning "reasonable" and "acceptable."

bracing; and (2) law is ". . . nothing else than an ordinance of reason for the common good. . . ." In a very practical way, the Thomist system combined Greek philosophy, Roman Law, Christian teachings, and most of all pragmatism in an appeal to reason. The Law of God, according to the Thomists, was ". . . nothing else than the reason of divine wisdom. . . ."

With the Holy Roman Empire,[24] the Church was the first sovereign and authoritarian state in the Western Roman world. Focus on the church was to have an enduring effect. History reveals that when the Holy Roman Empire gradually broke up, it did so into smaller, separate states. Spiritual guidance emanated from the church through the historical Renaissance and Reformation periods. When the Holy Roman Empire came apart, there evolved the medieval notion of a United Christendom—that all of the states were related in the commonality of being Christian. Clearly, many of the teachings of Christ had fallen away, as evidenced by moral and ethical principles becoming subordinate to political expedience and even more rationalization. In short, reason fell away during the Dark Ages. The Dark Ages extended from the end of the fall of the Western Roman Empire until the revival of classical culture in the Renaissance. During that dark period, however, there was evidence of enlightenment. The first subject studied in the world's first university in 1088 was, of all things, law. It was the work of scholars at the University of Bologna that gathered abandoned shards of, and resurrected, Roman Law, making the growth of commercial activity again possible.

Important, though, is that there still existed through this period a perceived subordinate relationship between ruler and subjects, including the "divine right of kings." This was shortly to change.

MAGNA CARTA

In England in 1215, at Runnymeade, King John issued the first of a series of charters, which collectively are known as the *Magna Carta*—Great Charter. It was a major step toward establishing individual liberties and constitutional government. Even though the Magna Carta applied only to a small number of lords, barons, knights, and wealthy landowners, it was the beginning of guaranteed rights to all citizens.

---

[24] Which, it is said, "was neither Roman, nor holy, or was it an empire."

What the lords were demanding was "rationality" in the law.[25] The concessions the King was forced to sign were guarantees that he would henceforth conform to the law. Under duress and to appease the militant demands of these feudal barons, to avoid civil war, while at the same time to unify England against foreign invasion, the King made certain written concessions in this first issue known as the *Forest Charter*. So named, it is thought, because the contest supposedly arose out of the killing in the forest of one of the "king's deer" without his permission.

There were subsequent issues of revised charters in 1216 and in 1217. Bearing in mind that the original charter was signed unwillingly the versions of 1216 and 1217 contained some intentional omissions and alterations in the king's favor. This caused continued resentment amongst John's subjects.

King Henry III, as a child during the period following the *Forest Charter* and the Charters of 1216 and 1217, recognized the existence of certain basic (or natural) rights. When he became of age, and after sovereign power had descended to him, he issued a fourth charter known as the *Great Charter*. Together, all of the charters put in legal form a contract that led toward reforms in judicial and local administration. However, it was not yet a "constitution."

A constitution is a basic law in a politically organized body. The Magna Carta could not be considered by definition to be a constitution, but it did become a symbol of liberty against oppression. For whenever an individual considered himself to be wronged, he would thereafter refer to the Magna Carta in his defense against oppression.

After 1689, the English Bill of Rights supplanted the Magna Carta as the people's ensign of liberty. If it was commonly accepted that a certain act should not be committed, the Magna Carta, and later the Bill of Rights, became the cited authority. Although the Bill of Rights did, in fact, cite certain individual rights, albeit loosely, neither it nor the Magna Carta may have made any reference at all to certain cited offenses. It just became a matter of common acceptance that certain acts were illegal. Additionally, by that time the practice of making judicial rulings in England based upon the prior outcomes of other similar circumstances had already become common. Hence, one can see the emergence of what we know of today as common law.

---

[25] "Rationality" here meaning a consistent and calculable set of rules in the Weberian sense.

With the Magna Carta, the Bill of Rights, and the Era of Enlightenment, a new age of "natural law" theories emerged. As compared to Mosaic Law, there also evolved at this time a newer version of the social contract. Society sought to justify sovereign power (that subordinate relationship between ruler and subject), but at the same time to safeguard individuals from oppression. The histories of both England and France exemplify a struggle around this argument.

Perhaps attributed to the Magna Carta and to the English Bill of Rights, England is commonly thought of as having a "constitutional" government, though in fact, it has no written constitution. Nevertheless, it has been suggested that England does have an "implied" constitution based upon common law. Common law is also at the heart of U.S. law, and it was from England that the United States inherited it. How common law got to England, is somewhat of a mystery.

COMMON LAW

Up until the 5th Century, England was occupied by the Romans and, therefore, had no opportunity to develop a legal system of its own. Moreover, the Romans did not codify their law into the *Corpus Juris* until after their departure from England. Before then, Rome was still living by its *Twelve Tables*. Fundamentally, they were a set of moral principles and practices rather than a codified system of law. More importantly, whatever the form of Roman law, it applied only to Roman citizens, and not necessarily to the original inhabitants of the British Isles.

No one knows for sure of the true origin of common law, although seemingly it is traceable to the Norman invasions, and hence probably began with the Vikings. The Vikings were particularly active in plundering the coasts of Northern Europe between the 8th and 10th Centuries. It is plausible to assume that sometime after the Romans had departed, England sought to develop a system of law that was its own, and that from the Vikings the rudiments of common law were obtained. Thus, to some degree the English were practicing common law long before the Magna Carta. However, because the Magna Carta was seen to grant certain basic rights, it became a cornerstone for further enhancement of the common law practice. By mitigating the divine right of Kings, the English Bill of Rights prompted even greater reliance upon the commonly accepted practices of society.

In the United States, there are generally two basic forms of law: *case law* and *statutory law*. Although the U.S. common law system is made up of both forms, common law, *per se*, more specifically refers to the former. Statutory law is positive (i.e., written) and codified. Case law, on the other hand, is comprised of precedents (earlier decisions). Under the common law, precedents from earlier decisions are followed under the doctrine of *stare decisis*. Lower courts follow precedent established by higher courts. All courts tend to follow their own precedent. As a consequence, parties faced by similar factual circumstances are treated equally the same under the law. However, it is not a static system, for the common law evolves consistently with contemporary societal needs. Hence, where policy militates change, precedent can be abandoned. Unlike Hammurabi's Code, the common law is not chiseled into stone. It is a system of jurisprudence, which is based upon custom and tradition. Where stability and predictability is required—as in property and contracts—the law evolves little and *stare decisis* typically reigns. But in areas less dependent on commercial certainty—such as torts and Constitutional law—precedent is less strictly followed, and the law evolves at a more expeditious pace.

There is a parallel between what is moral and what is positive, compared to what is common law versus statutory law. Moral is nearly synonymous with the "commonly" accepted practices of society, whereas "statutes" are positive law.

The most important single root of the American legal system is common law, and it was imported directly from England. Between the time of the Magna Carta and when the Pilgrims arrived in America, England had 400 years to improve the common law system and for it to have become well established, or a "way of life," with those who settled the colonies. Amongst the settlers, there were few attorneys, or others knowledgeable of the law. The juridical process was, of necessity and by common acceptance, the resolution of differences according to traditions. Subsequently, law in the U.S. has become a combination of both statutory and common law.

NAPOLEONIC CODE

Not only is U.S. law rooted in English tradition, it is also of French origin, particularly in the heartland of America in what was once the Louisiana Territory. Much like the pleas for more justice which resulted in the Magna Carta, and later in the *Declaration of Independence* associated with the American Revolution, the battle cry of the French Revolution was *"Liberté, Égalité et Fraternité"* (liberty, equality and fraternity).

The French Revolution was conceived in oppression and in the violation of commonly accepted rights. So disregarding and uncaring were the aristocracy that Marie Antoinette, when told of the hunger of the peasants, is thought by tradition to have said with arrogant disregard, " . . . then let them eat cake." For this, and the mood of the revolution, she and many others were beheaded under the guillotine.

The French and the American revolutions occurred almost simultaneously in history. Also, they had common origins in oppression. Yet, it is interesting how the outcomes of each revolution were so different. Out of the violence of the French Revolution, and a cry for freedom, arose the reinstatement of a monarchy in the person of Napoleon Bonaparte. The conditions leading up to, and the aftermath following the French Revolution, were a period of anarchy. Absent law and order, it was a period of intense internal and external strife. It was a prolonged revolution, which included ten years of war. The disorder and confusion of the times presented the opportunity for a military rise to power by Napoleon, who eventually declared himself emperor. In America, when offered the like opportunity of becoming king, George Washington declined, preferring instead to retreat to private life at Mount Vernon. Upon his deathbed, Napoleon reportedly lamented that the French people wanted him to be another Washington, which he was not.

Although the results of the American and French revolutions were not the same, and the fact that the central figures were apparently driven by entirely different motives, the Napoleonic Era is important to U.S. law because of its influence in America through French colonization of the Louisiana Territory. Current laws, of the states that once made up the Louisiana Territory, reflect a tradition inherited from the Napoleonic Code. Hence, not only is Napoleon an important historical figure to the French, he is likewise important in American history.

Napoleon's father (Carlo Buonaparte) was a lawyer by practice and the family had its stock in ancient nobility. It is reasonable to assume that Napoleon must have been given some orientation towards law by his father. Napoleon began an academic education early in his life, but soon transferred to military training instead. Trained in the arts of war, Napoleon graduated from the French military academy at the age of sixteen. As a national hero in wars against the British, Napoleon rose to power.

Although the French had fashioned a constitution after the one in America, the French counterpart did not survive, and in fact, was followed by a series of non-enduring constitutions. Nearly ten years following the French Revolution, and after Napoleon had come to power, Napoleon's own Constitution of the Year VIII was adopted. By that time the French constitution had no mention of liberty, equality or fraternity—the very tenets of the French Revolution—nor did it guarantee any human rights. What it did accomplish was to give immense power(s) to the first counsel, namely to Napoleon and his ministers, generals and appointed civil servants.

Although not instituted by Napoleon himself, a codification of civil law was begun in 1790, shortly following the revolution. However, it was not promulgated until during Napoleon's reign in 1804. Hence, as a result of timing, it became known as the *Code Napoleon*.

The Napoleonic Code,

- gave form to administrative and organizational changes that occurred during the revolution;
- codified individual liberties, freedom of work and freedom of conscience;
- outlined the lay character of the state (i.e., officially, there were to be no nobility, but rather, only common citizens);
- gave equality before the law;
- protected property rights;
- gave greater liberty to employers (but showed little concern for employees); and
- addressed family issues such as marriage, divorce, and parental authority.

Although not uncommon for the times, only limited rights were granted to women.

Administrative reforms and reform of the judicial system embodied in the Napoleonic Code were more lasting than were any of the French constitutions. Conversely, the American Revolution gave rise to an enduring constitution. Yet, it is ironic that the revolutions of both countries sprang from the same notions of liberty and equality. Whereas in France the motto was "Liberty, Equality, Fraternity," in America the cry was, "Give me liberty or give me death"!

THE ECONOMIC REVOLUTION
(OR THE SECOND WAVE)

Probably the most important history leading to the development of modern law occurred over the past 400 years, during what Alvin Toffler refers to as the "Second Wave" (of social change).[26] The Second Wave is about the introduction of industrial mechanization and the mass movement from a predominantly agrarian economy to an economy based on mass-produced commodities.

Toffler uses the metaphor of ocean waves to describe three epoch changes in the social and economic evolution of humankind. His "wave front" analysis looks at history as a succession of rolling waves of change. But in "collision" of these waves, there are no clearly defined lines of demarcation. The simultaneous ebb and flow leaves one always begging the question of where the leading edge of one advancing wave begins and where the trailing edge of an ebbing tide leaves off. Like the metaphor, the incoming wave of social change overrides the retreating flow of outmoded customs and traditions.

The "First Wave" of change, Toffler suggests, was unleashed perhaps 10,000 years ago by the invention of agriculture.[27] The First Wave—the Agricultural Revolution—lasted thousands of years, but before it had played out, the "Second Wave" began rushing in. Toffler suggests the Second Wave of change was touched off by the Industrial Revolution, and it took only a few hundred years until now, when it, too, is about to ebb out. We are now at the dawning of the Third Wave—of what has been variously described as the computer age, communication age, technology age, and/or the electronics age.

Not being able to accurately predict the future, no one knows for sure where the Third Wave will take us. However, by looking at the historical example of the Second Wave's impact, what seems likely is that the Third Wave will be accompanied by catastrophic social change. As described by Toffler, he sees the Third Wave as a "powerful tide" that is,

---

[26] Alvin Toffler, *The Third Wave* (1980).

[27] *Id.* at 25-26.

> *. . . surging across much of the world today,*
> *creating a new, often bizarre, environment in*
> *which to work, play, marry, raise children, or*
> *retire.*[28]

The Second Wave introduced the same bewilderment to an agrarian society overtaken by industrialism. But, whereas Toffler suggests the Second Wave was "touched off by the industrial revolution," it really began well before that. The Industrial Revolution, *per se*, is generally recognized as a period lasting only about seventy years from 1760 to 1830. The Industrial Revolution represents only a small part of a much larger and longer-lasting event. Robert Heilbroner has described this larger event as the "Economic Revolution," and it began in the 15th Century, in the late Renaissance. He suggests the Economic Revolution began with the introduction of the market system and the concurrent need for economists.[29]

Heilbroner's "Economic Revolution" equates to Toffler's "Second Wave." It includes the transformation from feudalism to capitalism, the Era of Enlightenment, Industrial Revolution, the Progressive Era (and the shift from competitive capitalism to corporate capitalism),[30] and it overlaps the advent of the Third Wave.

Society, "being in constant danger of breaking down as a result of human unpredictability," has utilized three ways of guarding against such a calamity:

- the continuity of society can be ensured by organizing around *tradition*, by handing down the varied and necessary tasks from generation to generation according to custom and usage;

---

[28] *Id.* at 17.

[29] Robert Heilbroner, *The Worldly Philosophers: The Lives, Times and Ideas of the Great Economic Thinkers* 18 (4th ed. 1972).

[30] During the Progressive Era (from about 1890 until the beginning of World War I) "competitive capitalism," exemplified by many low technology enterprises, was transformed into "corporate capitalism," wherein the laissez-faire economic marketplace envisioned by Adam Smith in *The Wealth of Nations* (1776) was replaced by imperfect competition and the concentration of capital into fewer and fewer companies in any given market. Sociologically, the Progressive Era constitutes a "critical period" in the transformation of capitalism, akin to the major transformation from feudalism to capitalism. James Inverarity, Pat Lauderdale, and Barry Feld, *Law and Society: Sociological Perspectives on Criminal Law* (1983).

- it can use the whip of might and central *authoritarian rule*, thereby ensuring economic survival by the edict of authority and imposition of sanctions; or
- by using a *market system*, where the economic interplay of one person against another results in the necessary tasks of society getting done.

In the marketplace, each person does what is in his or her best monetary advantage. The lure of gain, not the pull of tradition or the whip of authority, is what steers people in the market. With the market system came economists and social philosophers who seemed to have awaited the invention of the marketplace. For, before there was a market, there was no need for either profession.[31]

The market system effectively began with the advent of the Economic Revolution. During the Middle Ages, there was no such thing as profit motive. There was no notion of monetary gain for gain's sake. There was no widespread and general struggle for wealth.

Although there have always been market places, as used above "the market" means a mechanism for sustaining and maintaining an entire society. There was no market system during the Middle Ages. The use of land, labor, and capital as agents of production could not yet be envisioned. There were lands of course, but they were not real estate to be bought and sold. Likewise, labor was not salable. Individuals could not sell their services to the highest bidder. Capital existed, in the sense of private wealth, but there was no impetus to risk one's capital possessions in new and aggressive ventures. Lacking land, labor, and capital, the Middle Ages lacked the concept of market. Lacking the market, society ran by custom and tradition.[32]

As Heilbroner explains,

> *The idea of "making a living" had not yet come into being. Economic life and social life were one and the same thing. Work was not yet a means to an end—the end being money and the things it buys. Work was an end in itself, encompassing, of course, money and com-*

---

[31] Robert Heilbroner, *The Worldly Philosophers: The Lives, Times and Ideas of the Great Economic Thinkers* 22-25 (4th ed. 1972).
[32] *Id.* at 25-27.

modities, but engaged in as part of a tradition, as a natural way of life. In a word, the great social invention of "the market" had not yet been made.[33]

The change from feudalism to capitalism was long and drawn out. It was not a peaceful evolution; it was an agonized convulsion of society, a revolution. Most heartfelt was the tragedy of the peasant. First to employ the land to their own advantage were lords who sought capital gain through the production of commodities. One of the first commodities was corn brought to Europe from the New World. Later it was wool.[34]

At the end of the 14th Century, the lack of labor, which was a consequence of the Black Death, had already induced landowners in England to retain land-workers in the villages. The lack of labor in the countryside, prompted landowners to try to dispense with labor altogether. By transforming the cornfields into pastures for sheep, relatively few shepherds were needed compared to those workers necessary to work the grain fields.[35] Common lands were confiscated and enclosed as grazing pastures. As a result, peasant farmers were excluded from a livelihood and forced to seek employment as farm workers, in a system that lacked enough jobs to fully employ them. Involuntarily placed in the most miserable of circumstances, and without the means of earning a living, they became beggars, and sometimes thieves, but usually paupers.

Society began pulling apart, and neither tradition nor threat of sanction could hold it together, although, the imposition of harsh punishment was tried. Alarmed at the increase in pauperism, migrant farm workers were prohibited from traveling beyond their local bounds and given only a pittance of relief to sustain them in their places of confinement. Wanderers were dealt with by whipping, branding, and mutilation. Ironically, by failing to understand the con-

---

[33] Robert Heilbroner, *The Worldly Philosophers: The Lives, Times and Ideas of the Great Economic Thinkers* 22-25 (4th ed. 1972).

[34] In British history, the Corn Laws were regulations restricting the import and export of grain, especially wheat. The general purpose of such laws, which dated from the 12th century, was to ensure a stable supply of domestic grain. Later, the laws were used to protect landowners (i.e., the producers) and to enrichen the state.

[35] *See* C.N. Starcke, *Laws of Social Evolution and Social Ideals* 12 (1926).

cept of a fluid, mobile work force, the ruling class prevented the only possible solution to the problem.[36]

With its essential components of land, labor, and capital, the market system was thus born in agony, an agony that began in the 14th Century, and lasted until well into the late 19th, even 20th Centuries. There is no single cause that one can point to, but the genesis of the market system may well have been the product of discrimination.

From the Judeo-Christian tradition, usury was a sin. In fact, the Church taught that "no Christian ought to be a merchant." But for the Jews, it was not so restrictive. Prohibited by European law from owning land and from entry into craft occupations, and like landworkers and other dispossessed serfs, Jews were confined to the villages. But fortunate for the Jews, the Church had placed severe restrictions on the taking of interest on loans (i.e., usury), and in profit taking in general by Christians. The limited competition in trade, commerce and banking provided opportunity for the Jewish community, and they became dependent upon this narrow range of economic activities for their livelihood. Marketing and banking provided an economic niche for the Jews, who thereby became the first capitalists in the medieval economy.[37] Thus, the early capitalists were not the pillars of society, but often its outcasts.[38]

The market system may also have begun with an attempt to return to Edward the Third's economic policy of the 14th Century. Its fundamental purpose had been to encourage foreign trade in order to promote consumers' interests in procuring more and cheaper goods (woolens, for example).

The policy of King Edward had been replaced by a policy to create a strong state that could use every possible means to enforce its will, in internal as well as external affairs. The consumers' interests became of less importance than the interests of producers did. The latter were to get the highest possible prices for their products in order to in turn enrich the state. The mercantilist policy[39] had its roots in the he-

---

[36] Robert Heilbroner, *The Worldly Philosophers: The Lives, Times and Ideas of the Great Economic Thinkers* 30 (4th ed. 1972); *see also* C.N. Starcke, *Laws of Social Evolution and Social Ideals* 7-11 (1926).

[37] James Inverarity, Pat Lauderdale, and Barry Feld, *Law and Society: Sociological Perspectives on Criminal Law* 72 (1983).

[38] *See e.g.* Max Weber, *The Protestant Ethic and the Spirit of Capitalism* (1904-1905).

[39] Mercantilism was an effort to build up the state's military and industrial strength. State intervention encouraged domestic industry, regulated production, controlled trading companies, placed restrictions such as tariffs and quotas on the importation of merchandise from other

gemony of the merchant elite thinking they could measure their own power, and that of the state, not by the well-being of the consumers, but by their own organs of power. It was against these conditions that Thomas More railed in his work, *Utopia.* It was a description of a well-regulated society where all consumers' interests were satisfied.[40]

Overwhelming poverty in the working class was everywhere. Workers were frustrated by their dual positions as both consumers and the material of production. The new "industrialists" were only interested in exploiting workers as much as possible, to reduce their wages as far as possible, and to extend their working hours as much as possible. The impossible social conditions called for a philosophy. Every age breeds its philosophers, apologists, critics, and reformers.[41] Answering the call were those who dreamed of preventing the violent increase of a landless town population, and others whose aim became the establishment of an organized set of associations, whose leaders would in a paternal way watch over the masses.[42]

The Renaissance and the Reformation had given way to the idealism in the Era of Enlightenment, and the emergence of what Heilbroner refers to as the "worldly philosophers."[43] These late 15th through 19th, even 20th Century scholars were, by-and-large, economic and social theorists who changed the way the world thinks. The delicate problem of society's survival was henceforth to be solved neither by custom nor by command, but by the free action of profit-seeking people brought together only by the market itself. The system was to be called "capitalism," and profit would soon be affirmed as an eternal and omnipresent attitude.[44]

From the "enlightened" scholars evolved each one's individual perception of social and economic justice—and in wide variance from socialism and communism, to liberal democracy and capitalism. What also came out of the Era of Enlightenment were the utilitarian and social contractarian philosophies. Social utility, together with the so-

---

countries, and sought out raw materials and markets through colonialism. The colonies were forced to sell their raw goods to the mother country, where they were turned into finished products, and then sold through compulsion back to the colonists. Mercantilists believed that a country's exports were one measure of its strength.

[40] C.N. Starcke, *Laws of Social Evolution and Social Ideals* 89 (1926).

[41] Robert Heilbroner, *The Worldly Philosophers: The Lives, Times and Ideas of the Great Economic Thinkers* 37 (4th ed. 1972).

[42] C.N. Starcke, *Laws of Social Evolution and Social Ideals* 10 (1926).

[43] Robert Heilbroner, *The Worldly Philosophers: The Lives, Times and Ideas of the Great Economic Thinkers* (4th ed. 1972).

[44] *Id.* at 37.

cial contract, form the moral foundation that law in the United States is built upon. Their proponents make up the genealogical tree forming the moral fabric of that foundation.

LAW AND ETHICS

Roscoe Pound argued that society's ethics, its moral ideas, give us the law.[45] Jean Jacques Rousseau stated,

> *What makes the constitution of a State really solid and lasting is the due observance of what is proper, so that the natural relations are always in agreement with the laws on every point, and law only serves, so to speak, to assure, accompany and rectify them.*[46]

Thus, stated as an axiom, "law follows morality." However, *morality* and *ethics* do not have the same meaning, and a distinction needs to be made. Although nearly synonymous, the terms have different origins and slightly different cultural connotations. "Ethics" stems from the Greek *ethos*, whereas "moral" is from the Latin (i.e., Roman) *mores*.

Ethics refers to personal character, or what it takes to be a good person. Ethics is also derived from the Greek *ta ethica*, meaning the nature of the virtuous life, or the right way to live.[47] In business or politics, for example, ethics has to do with proper decision-making. "Business ethics" seeks to understand business practice, institutions, and actions in light of human values.[48] In Pastin's conception, the ethics of a person or firm is simply, "the most fundamental ground rules by which the person or firm acts." "Good ethics," he says, is a matter of making "right decisions."[49]

---

[45] Roscoe Pound (1870-1964) was an American jurist, educator, and a leader in the reform of court administration in the United States.

[46] Jean Jacques Rousseau, *Du Compac Social, The Social Contract or Principles of Political Right* Book II (1762).

[47] David Theo Goldberg, *Ethical Theory and Social Issues* (2nd ed. 1995).

[48] Ethical Issues In Business 2 (T. Donaldson and P.H. Werhane eds., 1983).

[49] Mark Pastin, *The Hard Problems of Management: Gaining the Ethical Edge* xii, 24 (1986).

In the study of ethics, theorists have developed unique frameworks with which to understand ethics. Some of these *epistomologies* include:

- *Deontology* (*deontos*, Greek)—which is the study of rights and duty or obligations, with the belief that a person knows the difference between right and wrong; the moral rightness or wrongness of an act is to be defined in terms of its production of goodness or badness;
- *Descriptive Ethics*—describe how some people, members of cultures, or societies address moral issues;
- *Ethical Egoism*—approves of behavior motivated merely by an individual's desire for personal gain; it views behavior motivated by self-interest as ethical, and it looks at personal greed as collective altruism;
- *Metaethics*—is the analyzing of moral language; good and bad (or evil), right and wrong, propriety and impropriety, duties and rights, obligations and claims, or justice and injustice;
- *Natural Law Theories*—hold that moral principles or laws reflect the nature or rational order of things; that is to say, they exist in nature irrespective of human intervention;
- *Normative Ethics*—are an inquiry into the norms or principles of justifiable behavior and the values they embody; i.e., into what kinds of acts are right or permissible;
- *Right-based Theories*—take the basic concept of morality to be rights, freedoms and claims; assumed is an entitlement to act or have others act in a certain way; if one has a right to do something, then someone else has a correlative duty to act in a certain way;
- *Social Contract Theories*—take morality to consist of a set of rules establishing how members of society ought to treat each other—by hypothetical contract, which consists of giving up personal freedoms to a sovereign power in exchange for a set of rights, duties, and government protection;
- *Teleology* (*teleios*, Greek)—looks at the end consequences of a person's conduct; each class or kind of thing has an end (or *telos*) that will be good to the extent that it fulfills the natural functions of its kind;

- *Utilitarian Theories*—are based on the utility of what is useful is good; the moral worth of actions or rules is judged solely in terms of goodness or badness and the greatest utility (or happiness); that is to say, whatever promotes happiness for the most people is utility and therefore good; and
- *Virtue Theories*—where the study is of the moral character of the individual, rather than rightness or wrongness of actions.[50]

Ethics is the study of human behavior as related to right and wrong conduct.[51] It is the science that deals with conduct, in so far as it is considered as right or wrong, good or bad.[52] Ethics in ancient times signified *philosophia moralis* (moral philosophy), which was also called the *doctrine of duties*.[53] In the contemporary sense, "We might refer to someone's 'personal ethics' or character, while 'morality' is often used in discussions about social conventions and custom."[54]

Where the focus of ethics is on the individual, *morality* refers to the social rules that govern or limit one's conduct. Morality is about doing what is good or right. The Latin *mores* denotes *rectus*, meaning "straight" or "according to rule." "Good" is from the German *gut*, with the same root in Greek, meaning "valuable for some end."

Since ethics can be thought of as the study and science of morals,[55] in the contemporary sense, to be ethical is nearly synonymous with being moral. Ethics and morality, then, precedes the law and can include acts that are *malum in se* (wrong in and of themselves), because they are not right; as well as acts which society believes ought to be *malum prohibitum* (prohibited by government), because they are not good. Speeding, for example, is against the law. Yet, there is nothing inherently immoral about speed. But when it might endanger others, it becomes wrong. Likewise, there is nothing illegal about greed. But when the avarice of capitalism reaches beyond reasonable bounds it becomes immoral, sometimes resulting in what may be referred to as

---

[50] *See* David Theo Goldberg, *Ethical Theory and Social Issues* (2nd ed. 1995); *see also* Jacques P. Thiroux, *Ethics: Theory and Practice* (1977); *see also* William H. Shaw and Vincent Barry, *Moral Issues in Business* (5th ed. 1992).

[51] Herbert M. Bohlman and Mary Jane Dundas, *The Legal, Ethical and International Environment of Business* 34 (2nd ed. 1993).

[52] John Dewey and James H. Tufts, *Ethics* (revised ed. 1908/1932).

[53] Immanuel Kant, *Fundamental Principles of the Metaphysic of Morals* Introduction (1785).

[54] David Theo Goldberg, *Ethical Theory and Social Issues* 3 (2nd ed. 1995).

[55] Herbert M. Bohlman and Mary Jane Dundas, *The Legal, Ethical and International Environment of Business* 16, 29 (2nd ed. 1993).

"white collar crime."[56] Ivan Boesky and Michael Milken, for example, were not burglars, robbers, or common thieves, yet both went to prison for causing harm by what amounted to the same thing.[57] Stock manipulation is *malum prohibitum*, while theft is *malum in se*. In either case, there is an immoral gain at someone else's expense.

Law *malum prohibitum* is created by legislatures and, therefore, is subject to change. Conversely, acts *malum in se* are of eternal nature. In the latter case, one is motivated to do what is morally right out of either concern for others or just because it is right. Included in what is meant by morality are conventional norms against lying, cheating, stealing, or otherwise harming other people. Acts *malum in se*, and the prohibition against harming other human beings, are social conventions, which are fundamental to religious doctrines.

Most religions provide believers with an eternal or spiritual perspective. Additionally, they provide certain moral guidelines, values and commitments to adhere to as acceptable standards in this life. Much of law throughout the world is grounded in religious tenets, with Western law having its roots in the Judeo-Christian tradition. Its morality is likewise grounded in the utilitarian and social contractarian philosophies, each of which takes its inspiration from religious, although not necessarily Judeo-Christian, doctrine. One example of a religious tradition that runs parallel to the philosophies of utility and contract is the *Golden Rule*, which is to say, "do unto others what you would have them do unto you." The Golden Rule, or some derivation of it, seems to be a convention shared by the entire global population. Similar edicts can be found in all of the major world religions:[58]

- *Good people proceed while considering that what is best for others is best for themselves* (Hinduism).[59]
- *Thou shalt love thy neighbor as thyself* (Judaism).[60]
- *Therefore all things whatsoever you would that men should do unto you, do ye even so unto them* (Christianity).[61]

---

[56] *See* Ch. 9.

[57] In 1987, Ivan Boesky, a Wall Street speculator in corporate takeovers, plead guilty in federal court to a felony charge of stock manipulation. In 1990, Michael R. Milken, a junk bond financier at Drexel, Burnham and Lambert, plead guilty to six felonies, including conspiracy, securities fraud, mail fraud, and filing false tax forms. William H. Shaw and Vincent Barry, *Moral Issues in Business* (5th ed. 1992).

[58] William H. Shaw and Vincent Barry, Moral Issues in Business 9-10 (5th ed. 1992).

[59] *Hitopadesa*.

[60] *Leviticus* 19:18.

- *Hurt not others with that which pains yourself* (Buddhism).[62]
- *What you do not want done to yourself, do not to others* (Confucianism).[63]
- *No one of you is a believer until he loves for his brother what he loves for himself* (Islam).[64]
- *Treat the earth and all that dwell thereon with respect* (American Indian).[65]

In the Golden Rule, one can find the seeds of both the utilitarian and the social contractarian perspectives. Utilitarianism and the social contract are philosophical constructs that came out of the Era of Enlightenment, to be borrowed in the writing of the Declaration of Independence and the United States Constitution, and operationalized as fundamental principles in the basic law of the land. One can trace the historical development of each of the utilitarian and contractarian philosophies through a genealogy of its prophets.

UTILITARIANISM

Study of both the utilitarian as well as social contractarian perspectives begins best with Thomas More (1477-1535). More railed in his work, *Utopia*, at the idolization of money and at the idea that kings and merchants might consider themselves richer for having a well-filled exchequer, even though the citizens were destitute.[66] In criticizing the state, and policies that effectively made it impossible for commoners to be other than paupers and thieves, More was making (individual) human welfare the ultimate standard. Human welfare (or happiness) is the ultimate standard of right and wrong in utilitarianism. By his emphasis upon the consumer, More placed the individual before the state—a fundamental precept in the social contract.

Thomas More described his perfect commune in *Utopia*; a social organization built on the interests of the consumer. In the moral philosophy of the 18th Century this view found its philosophical formula

---

[61] *Matthew* 7:12.
[62] *Udanavarga* 5:18.
[63] *Analects* 15:23.
[64] *Traditions.*
[65] Anonymous, but most likely from the 19th century. Found on a poster by Paul H. Morgan (1994).
[66] C.N. Starcke, *Laws of Social Evolution and Social Ideas* 9, 12-13 (1926).

in the *doctrine of utility* and its principle: The greatest possible happiness of the greatest possible number. The "formula" for the principle of utility builds on the will of God. Based on the formula for utility, how one is to know the will of God is explained thusly:

> *The essence of God being love, only that which inspires benevolence towards one's fellowmen can be acknowledged as the will of God and, in this way, the welfare of humanity becomes the criterion of the Divine Law.*[67]

In this intricate train of thought, the criterion of virtue is the will of God. If society takes the place of God's will, it can only mean that universal welfare should be the leading principle of moral conduct.[68]

With the advent of the Industrial Revolution, but especially following to the American War of Independence, the colonies experienced a number of changing trade conditions. Demands for removal of obstacles to free trade gave credence to the thoughts of two contemporary writers in particular of the late 18th Century, Adam Smith and Jeremy Bentham.

ADAM SMITH (1723-1790)

Like Thomas More, Adam Smith also railed against the British Mercantile System. In 1759, he wrote his *Theory of Moral Sentiment*, which emphasized mutual sympathy and happiness as the decisive factor in social life. His seminal work, *An Inquiry into the Nature and Causes of the Wealth of Nations* (1776), was published in the same year as the Declaration of Independence. His latter work was timely in the transformation from a feudal society to capitalism and free trade. American capitalism was the ideal of that transformation.

Democratic capitalism is personified by Adam Smith, whose philosophical views epitomize the ideology of individualism and the free market under girding capitalism in America. In *Wealth of Nations*, Smith describes an economy where the market forces of capital, labor and the marketplace (or consumer) are perfectly balanced, and kept in balance by the "invisible hand" of competition. In his "per-

---

[67] *Id.* at 16-17.
[68] *Id.* at 16.

fectly" competitive system, the value of work resolves itself in fair wages for the worker, at the same time provides reasonable profits for the capitalist, and the consumer pays a "natural" (i.e., not inflated) price for commodities.

Smith best expressed the ideal of American capitalism in stating that, "By pursuing his own interest he (the individual) frequently promotes that of society more effectually than when he really intends to promote it." The invisible hand is more than an apology; it is the first discovery of a general sociological principle, that the collective result of individual behavior is not the same as the individual behavior. Effectively, personal greed can translate into collective altruism.[69]

By focusing on the (individual) consumer, Smith does not measure *The Wealth of Nations* by their passive riches, but by their active social processes, wherein the favorable condition of production lies in the consumer's interest and in a free and competitive market. His argument was that the division of labor and the specialization of production, the greatest possible market freedom, and the fewest possible artificial barriers to trade, are the conditions most favorable to the creation of wealth. Conversely, favoring the rich at the cost of the poor was a direct hindrance to the formation of wealth.[70] Smith conceptualizes a vision of perfect liberty, where an individual would be left "perfectly free to pursue his own interest his own way."[71] As disciples of Adam Smith, 20th Century neo-classical economists became the major proponents for airline deregulation in the 1970s.

JEREMY BENTHAM (1748-1832)

Adam Smith was a contemporary of Jeremy Bentham, and there was a close relationship between the two theorists.[72] Whereas Smith (an economist) had intended to prove that social welfare depends on harmony in the economic domain (where everybody could freely seek his own happiness), Bentham (a social engineer) was trying to prove that happiness depends on construction of the right social organization. He argued that the welfare of all depends on the welfare of each, and that social organization should aim at the construction of such

---

[69] *See* James Inverarity, Pat Lauderdale & Barry Feld, *Law and Society: Sociological Perspectives on Criminal Law* 96 (1983).

[70] *See* C.N. Starcke, *Laws of Social Evolution and Social Ideas* 9-10 (1926).

[71] Adam Smith, *An Inquiry Into the Nature and Causes of the Wealth of Nations* (1776).

[72] C.N. Starcke, *Laws of Social Evolution and Social Ideas* 19 (1926).

harmony.[73] Like Thomas More, what burned deepest in Bentham's soul was anger at the indifference of the state toward the victims of its (mercantilist) policy—the poor.

Although David Hume (1711-1776) and others had used the term "utility" in their moral writings, it was Jeremy Bentham who first formulated an explicitly utilitarian moral theory. Bentham's concept of social utility is a form of hedonism, and a belief that right conduct is determined by the balance of pleasure over pain that a given act can produce.[74]

An Introduction to the Principles of Morals and Legislation (1789) is probably Bentham's best known work. In it, he describes his doctrine of utility—that the aim of society ought to be achievement of the greatest happiness for the greatest number of people. Bentham's belief was that pain and pleasure could be measured quantitatively. If utility could be measured in quantitative terms, then it followed that ethical and social decision making might be reduced to a quasi-mathematical science. Bentham called his science "hedonistic" or "felicific calculus."

JOHN STUART MILL (1806-1873)

It was Jeremy Bentham who first formulated the theory of social utility, but it was seemingly his student, John Stuart Mill, who coined the term "utilitarianism." Mill was one of the Philosophical Radicals, or "Benthamites," who pursued various social and political reforms along the utilitarian lines laid down by Jeremy Bentham. However, in his most famous work, *Utilitarianism* (1863), Mill revised Bentham's version of utility. Where Bentham had suggested that all pleasures were of equal value, Mill differentiated the various pleasures, and argued for the superiority of the "higher pleasures of the mind."

Mill also gives some indication of an affinity for the social contract theory in his book, *On Liberty* (1859). In it, he suggests that only the principle of self-protection alone can justify either the state's tam-

---

[73] *Id.* at 18.

[74] There are two fundamental types of utilitarianism. In *Act Utilitarianism* there is one, and only one, moral obligation, the maximization of happiness, for which every action is to be judged according to how well it maximizes happiness. In *Rule Utilitarianism* utilitarian standards should be applied not to individual actions but to moral codes as a whole, suggesting that societies should adopt rules that maximize happiness. William H. Shaw and Vincent Barry, *Moral Issues in Business* 78 (5th ed. 1992).

pering with the liberty of the individual or any personal interference with another's freedom.

John Stuart Mill was not only a student of Jeremy Bentham, but he was also in the company of Claude Henri Comte de Saint Simon (1760-1825), August Comte (1798-1857), and the Utopian Socialists. Thus, Mill is included amongst the early sociologists who believed the means of production ought to be owned by those who use them.[75]

Saint Simon was revered by Émile Durkheim as the founder of sociology, but it was August Comte who coined the term *sociologie*.[76] Out of an industrial society, of mechanical, trivial and dull life, Mill (the sociologist) was interested in promoting the free and spontaneous growth of individuality.

In his theory of justice, Mill determined that justice involves a violation of the rights of the individual. And, if the individual has a right to something, then he has a valid claim on society to protect him in the possession of that thing (*à là* the social contract). What Mill's "utilitarianism" identifies as "rights" are certain moral rules, the observance of which is of utmost importance in maximization of happiness. The utilitarian theory of justice ties the question of economic distribution to the promotion of social well being, or happiness.[77]

Mill defended his brand of utility by conceiving the principle as Bentham had: happiness alone is desirable as an end, and it consists in pleasure and freedom from pain.[78] Mill defined utilitarianism as,

> . . . *[t]he creed which accepts as the foundation of morals, Utility, or the Greatest Happiness Principle, holds that actions are right in proportion as they tend to promote happiness, wrong as they tend to produce the reverse of happiness. By happiness is intended pleasure, and the absence of pain; by unhappiness, pain, and the privation of pleasure.*[79]

---

[75] The Industrial Revolution took the tools of production away from the workers and placed them in the hands of industrial capitalists, thus disenfranchising labor. *See* Paul Stephen Dempsey and Laurence E. Gesell, *Air Transportation: Foundations for the 21st Century* Chapter 6 (1997).

[76] Thomas Raison (ed.) and Paul Barker (revised ed.), *The Founding Fathers of Social Science* 33-63 (1963/1979).

[77] William H. Shaw and Vincent Barry, Moral Issues in Business 108-109 (5th ed. 1992).

[78] David Theo Goldberg, *Ethical Theory and Social Issues* 126 (2nd ed. 1995).

[79] John Stuart Mill, *Utilitarianism* Chapter II (1863).

Utilitarianism has popular appeal, because it is easy, said John Rawls.[80] Its appeal has been a function of its simplicity, egalitarianism, and comprehensiveness. According to Goldberg, utilitarianism,

> *. . . holds the promise of a single, simple and general quantitative calculus for ethics, government, economics, and the law . . . utilitarianism has continued to offer a method for determining efficient rules for law, politics, and economic distributions.*[81]

However, contemporary utilitarians no longer interpret "utility" simply as pleasure versus pain, but rather, refer to preferences, interests, benefits, welfare, or other technical references to distribution.[82] Utility interpreted this way is more in line with the philosophy of Henry Sidgwick.

Beyond utilitarianism, Mill's contribution also lay in his observance of the waste in duplication of parallel gas and water lines in London and the economies of scale inherent in natural monopolies.[83] It was this theory that lent support to the waves of economic regulation of the railroads in 1887, and the airlines, in 1935.

HENRY SIDGWICK (1838-1900)

Henry Sidgwick was an English philosopher best known for his ethical studies. His most prominent work was *Methods of Ethics* (1874). Although critical of the older utilitarians such as Jeremy Bentham and John Stuart Mill, Sidgwick formulated a utilitarian position that actions are right or wrong on the basis of their conformity with the general welfare. Sidgwick supported utilitarianism because he said it best described the morality of ordinary common sense.

VILFREDO PARETO (1848-1923)

Defined as the absence of pleasure or pain, utility is to be measured quantitatively in terms of its intensity, the span of time it lasts,

---

[80] John Rawls, *A Theory of Justice* (1971).
[81] David Theo Goldberg, *Ethical Theory and Social Issues* 128-129 (2nd ed. 1995).
[82] *Id.* at 129.
[83] John Stuart Mill, *Principles of Political Economy* 13 (1926).

its certainty of occurrence, and its immediacy or remoteness.[84] Perhaps no theorist has attempted to refine the calculus of measuring utility more than did Vilfredo Pareto. He was an economist turned socialist in his later life. Pareto was a rational economist who applied mathematical precision to sociology (and the social sciences) and the allocation of scarce resources.[85]

"Pareto optimality," for instance, is a utilitarian function used to satisfy a majority of the population. It differs from other utilitarian processes in that there are to be no losers when resources are distributed in a Pareto optimal fashion (i.e., anyone's gain cannot be to someone else's loss). When the distribution is "optimized," there is no way of making someone better off without making someone else worse off.[86]

To use an aviation-related example, when airlines market seats on a given flight, they attempt to perfectly satisfy all demands for seating categories. Pareto optimalization occurs when just the right numbers of seats are sold in accordance with the demand for each of the seating classes—first, business, and coach. As a result, a first-class or business-class passengers, willing to pay extra, receive superior service, but not at the expense of coach passengers who, for whatever reason, do not pay the premium. Equity and efficiency, or the relative values received are not at issue.[87]

CONTEMPORARY UTILITARIANS

As it has evolved, utilitarianism is a quantitative social science, which has, from its origination attracted economists to its ranks. To complete the genealogy of the utilitarians with modern counterparts to Adam Smith and Vilfredo Pareto, one of the economists might be John Maynard Keynes. And, if the *greatest liberty* amounts to the same thing as *greatest happiness*, then one might include Milton Friedman amongst the utilitarians.

---

[84] *Id.* at 117.
[85] Thomas Raison (ed.) and Paul Barker (revised ed.), *The Founding Fathers of Social Science* 126-35 (1963/1979).
[86] *See* Jeffrie Murphy and Jules Coleman, *The Philosophy of Law* 212-218 (1984).
[87] Paul Stephen Dempsey and Laurence E. Gesell, *Airline Management: Strategies for the 21st Century* Ch. 2 (1997).

John Maynard Keynes (1883-1946) was one of the most influential economists in the 20th Century.[88] Keynes' classic work, *The General Theory of Employment Interest and Money* (1936), was his response to the dilemma of the Great Depression. Millions of people were willing to work but could not find employment. Economic depression results when the total demand of consumers and investors is insufficient to purchase all the goods that society has produced. Industry cuts back on production, relies on its built-up inventories, and workers are laid off. Being simultaneously workers and consumers, without paychecks they cannot purchase the goods inventoried by the manufacturers, and the economy becomes a gridlock.

Keynes' answer to the dilemma was the "demand-side economics" adopted by Franklin D. Roosevelt.[89] It was Keynes' suggestion that during periods of high unemployment, the government needed to increase the money supply, to thus lower interest rates and stimulate business investment. Keynes also advocated a government fiscal policy of deficit spending on public works and other projects to increase the aggregate demand for goods and services.

Keynesian economics were a sharp departure from conventional economics, and his theory remains controversial today—as does the results of the New Deal of Roosevelt's administration. However, from a social utilitarian perspective, much pain and suffering was relieved as a result of the implementation of Keynes' ideas.

Milton Friedman (1912-), a leading exponent of free enterprise and the conservative point of view, offers a major alternative to Keynesian policy. Friedman argues that John Maynard Keynes incorrectly minimized the role of money and greatly exaggerated the effi-

---

[88] Reportedly, Keynes' work is derived from the economic philosophy of Silvio Gesell, who in turn studied the works of Pierre-Joseph Proudhon. Fundamentally, Gesell argued that the value of money is based upon the good faith and credit of the state, and not upon its backing by precious metal such as gold and/or silver. Pierre-Joseph Proudhon also noted the failure in reliance upon gold as a standard. *See* Silvio Gesell, *The Natural Economic Order*, Parts Three and Four (3rd ed. 1918). *See also* Pierre Joseph Proudhon, *What is Poverty?* Proudhon argued that economic "interest is not the product of material goods, but of an economic situation, a condition of the market." In *The Natural Economic Order*, Part One (3rd ed. 1918), Gesell's "conclusions are to the effect that capital must not be looked upon as a material commodity, but as a condition of the market, determined solely by demand and supply."

[89] Traditional economics had held that supply creates its own demand. Hence, the opposite of demand side economics is "supply side economics"—alternatively referred to as "trickledown economics." Trickledown economic theory was introduced in the United States by Andrew Mellon, Secretary of the Treasury for Presidents Coolidge, Harding, and Hoover. In the 1980s, President Reagan adopted a brand of trickledown economics that became known as "Reaganomics."

cacy of government taxing and spending policies.[90] Friedman suggests that the level of economic activity is largely determined by the quantity of money in the system.

Friedman also argues for a negative income tax, wherein payments to the poor would be made automatically when incomes fell below a certain level.[91] Thus, he is interested in rectifying an inequitable economic burden, thereby relieving pain and suffering, albeit indirectly.

Although their economic philosophies are from opposite poles, it might be noted that the social and economic problems that Keynes and Friedman attempted to solve are materially no different than those confronted by say Thomas More and Adam Smith respectively.

THE COMPACT OF LAW

Henry V. Poor, former associate dean of the Yale University Law School, succinctly describes law, as if it were a social contract. He states, "Law is the set of rules that we have established to make it easier for us to live with one another."[92] The rules of the game of law are conceived as granting the people rights and liberties, while at the same time subjecting them to duties and responsibilities. The social contract theory holds that a state is originally created through a voluntary agreement entered into by individuals living in a natural state of anarchy.

Although John Locke is generally thought of as the exponent of the social contract, the concept may be at least as old as the Romans. One can also find the theory in the writings of St. Thomas Aquinas.[93] In an argument suggesting that trust implies a contract, trust is the *mandatum* of Roman law, meaning a form of consensual contract. Whereas the Roman *mandatum* might imply something about the social contract, in the writings of St. Thomas Aquinas, the theory blossoms fully.

In the Thomist system, the teachings of the Bible, the doctrines of Roman law, and the principles of Aristotle's *Politics* are brought together. The Bible, for instance, teaches that law emanates from God.

---

[90] Milton Friedman and Anna J. Schwartz, *A Monetary History of the United States, 1867-1960* (1963).

[91] Milton Friedman, *Capitalism and Freedom* (1962).

[92] Readers Digest, *You and the Law* (Henry V. Poor, advisory ed. 1971).

[93] Sir Ernest Barker, *Introduction*, Social Contract: Essays by Locke, Hume, and Rousseau viii-x, xiii (1947).

But it also teaches that David made a covenant with his people. In the theory of Roman law, by *Lex Regia*, power conferred upon the emperor must proceed from the people. Finally, Aristotle seemed to favor a monarchy of the one best man. However, he also endorsed the right of the masses not only to elect the magistrate but also to call him to account. St. Thomas balances the three concepts of authority (the Bible, Roman law and Aristotle's politics) in the ideas of *principium*, *modus*, and *exercitium*.

As Sir Ernest Barker explains,

> *The principium, or essential substance of authority is ordained of God, . . . but its modus, or constitutional form (be it monarchy, aristocracy, democracy, or a mixed form), is determined by the people, . . . and its exercitum, or actual enjoyment is conferred—and as it is conferred may also be withdrawn—by the people.*[94]

Thus, in *De Regimine Principum*, St. Thomas states that government is instituted by the community, and may be revoked or limited by the community if the government is tyrannical. This was the general view through the Middle Ages. Feudalism, for example, was a system of contract, under which each man could say to his lord,

> *I will be to you faithful and true . . . on condition that you keep me as I am willing to deserve, and all that fulfil (sic) that our agreement was, when I to you submitted and chose your will.*[95]

From the Middle Ages, the enlightened philosophers eventually picked up on the concept of the social contract.

Whereas Thomas Hobbes used the concept of the social contract to justify the absolute power of the state,[96] with John Locke the social contract theory challenged the divine right of kings as the basis for a

---

[94] *Id.* at ix.
[95] From a Wessex document "Of Oaths" (circa AD 920), in Sir Ernest Barker, *Introduction*, Social Contract: Essays by Locke, Hume, and Rousseau ix (1947).
[96] Thomas Hobbes, *Leviathan* (1651).

state's legitimacy (see *infra*). In so doing, it laid the foundation for theories of constitutional government. Locke related law and government to the social contract, but did so from the perspective of individual rights, as did Jean Jacques Rousseau later. It was the political theory of Locke, which had a profound effect on England. It penetrated into France, and passed through Rousseau into the French Revolution. It was carried into the American colonies, and passed through Samuel Adams and Thomas Jefferson into the Declaration of Independence.[97]

To Locke and to Rousseau goes much of the credit for the principles and underlying philosophy of not only the American Declaration of Independence, but also of the United States Constitution. Both theorists are recognized for their conceptualizations of the social contract. Legal scholars in interpreting the Constitution often consult their writings. As will be seen later, Chapter 3 addresses the subject of Constitutional law, and relates to the U.S. Constitution as if it were a type of (written) social contract.

THOMAS HOBBES (1588-1679)

Thomas Hobbes, a 17th Century English philosopher, justified absolute government as the sole means of protecting society from the selfish nature of its individual members. His argument, based on the social contract, is presented in his most famous work, *Leviathan; or The Matter, Form, and Power of a Commonwealth, Ecclesiastical and Civil* (1651).

In *Leviathan*, Hobbes argues that the natural "condition of man" is constant "warre (sic) of every one against every one else." In making his argument, he uses the terms "warre" and "nature" interchangeably. The "right of nature," he says,

> . . . *is the liberty each man hath to use his own power as he will himself for the preservation of his own nature; that is to say, of his own life; and consequently, of doing anything which, in his own judgment and reason, he shall conceive to be the aptest means thereunto.*[98]

---

[97] Sir Ernest Barker, *Introduction*, Social Contract: Essays by Locke, Hume, and Rousseau xvi (1947).
[98] *Id.* at Ch. XIV.

So long as this natural right of every man to every thing exists, there can be no security for anyone. Seeking protection and self-preservation in the "war of all-against-all," civil society arises only by convention. From self-interest, people make peace and obtain security as a consequence of their delegation of total power to the state—which, in a state having absolute power, is a monarchy. Death, Hobbes says, is the worst of evils, and "The passions that incline men to peace are . . . fear of death. . . ."

Hobbes posits some fundamental laws of nature; the first of which he argues is to seek peace. The second law is derived from the first:

> . . . that a man be willing, when others are so too, as far as for peace and defence (sic) of himself he shall think it necessary, to lay down this right to all things; and be contented with so much liberty against himself.[99]

This mutual transferring of right is execution of the (social) contract, or what Hobbes calls the "mutual contract."[100] It need not require the swearing of an oath, "For a covenant, if lawful, binds in the sight of God, without the oath, as much as with it." One makes the covenant by conforming to the "laws of nature," which are "immutable and eternal." Once the contract has been made, in Hobbes' perspective, the subject is obligated irreversibly to obey its laws (which are the laws of nature), and of the commonwealth (e.g., the people of a state).

By civil laws, Hobbes understood to mean laws that men were bound to observe because they are members of a commonwealth. "Civil law is to every subject those rules which the Commonwealth hath commanded him. . . ."[101] Hobbes' mutual (or social) contract thereby grants absolute power to the sovereign. He concluded that rebellion against the state breaks society's basic contract and is punishable by whatever penalty the monarch may exact in order to protect all subjects from a return to the original state of nature.

---

[99] *Id.* Hobbes equates this law to the golden rule of the gospel: "Whatsoever you require that others should do to you, that do ye to them."

[100] *Id.* Ch. XV.

[101] Thomas Hobbes, *Leviathan* Ch. XXVI (1651).

JOHN LOCKE (1632-1704)

John Locke opposed Hobbes' view that people in the natural state are "nasty, brutish, and short." Instead, the natural state of man is one of happiness and tolerance. Men "are born free and rational." He also did not agree that individuals surrender their rights in exchange for an absolute sovereign who would be the source of all morality and law. Rather, the social contract preserves preexistent natural rights of the individual to life, liberty, property, and the pursuit of happiness.

Locke suggested there are two "foundations" (or human laws versus the law of God and the law of nature) that bear up societies. One is the natural inclination whereby all people desire sociable life and fellowship. The other an order (a social compact) expressly or secretly agreed upon. The latter is that which is called the law of a commonwealth.

Men being by nature free, equal, and independent, cannot be put out of their state of happiness and subjected to the political power of another without first giving their own consent. Such consent is freely given "by agreeing with other men, to join and unite into a community for their comfortable, safe, and peaceable living . . ." and ". . . a greater security against any that are not of it."[102] And, by consenting with others in a social compact to make one body politic under one government, each person puts himself "under an obligation to every one of that society to submit to the determination of the majority."

However, the agreement is not irreversible as it is in the case of Thomas Hobbes' contract. Locke was an advocate of civil and religious liberties. He denied the divine right of kings, arguing that government is based on the consent of the people. Locke set forth the view that the state exists to preserve the natural rights of its citizens. But when a government fails in that task, its citizens have the right—even the duty—to withdraw their support, and at times to rebel.

JEAN JACQUES ROUSSEAU (1712-1778)

In agreement with John Locke on the matter, Jean Jacques Rousseau stated,

---

[102] John Locke, *Concerning Civil Government* Ch. VIII (1690).

> *. . . there is in the State no fundamental law that cannot be revoked, not excluding the social compact itself; for if all citizens assembled of one accord to break the compact, it is impossible to doubt that it would be very legitimately broken.*[103]

However, Rousseau did not agree with Locke on the issue of the will of the majority. Rather, Rousseau maintained that the state was created to preserve freedom of the individual. The state is a unity, and as such expresses the general will for the common good of securing freedom, equality, and justice, regardless of the will of the majority. The majority may, in fact, wish for something contrary to the common good (e.g., slavery).

Another point of departure for Rousseau is in construction of the social contract. Locke, and others, had assumed the social contract to be an historical event. To Rousseau, the social contract was a theoretical construct, not a reality. In *The Social Contract*, he opens his dissertation by saying,

> *Man is born free; and everywhere he is in chains. One thinks himself the master of others, and still remains a greater slave than they.*[104]

He goes on to say that,

> *. . . since no man has a natural authority over his fellow, and force creates no right, we must conclude that conventions form the basis of all legitimate authority among men.*[105]

And in response to Hobbes, he states that,

> *. . . it is an empty and contradictory convention that sets up, on the one side, absolute author-*

---

[103] Jean Jacques Rousseau, *Du Compac Social, The Social Contract or Principles of Political Right* Book IV (1762).
[104] *Id.* at Book I § 1.
[105] *Id.* at Book I § 4.

ity, and, on the other, unlimited obedience. It is not clear that we can be under no obligation to a person from whom we have the right to exact everything.[106]

The "problem," he says,

. . . is to find a form of association which will defend and protect with the whole common force the person and goods of each associate, and in which each, while uniting himself with all, may still obey himself alone, and remain as free as before.[107]

This, he says, . . . "is the fundamental problem of which the Social Contract provides the solution."[108] And finally,

. . . each man, in giving himself to all, gives himself to nobody; and as there is no associate over whom he does not acquire the same right as he yields others over himself, he gains an equivalent for everything he loses, and an increase of force for the preservation of what he has.[109]

Within the social contract, as envisioned by Rousseau, there is found,

- an hypothetical association of individuals;
- who are willing to subordinate their freedoms to a government;
- that derives its authority from the people; and
- will use its sovereignty to defend and protect the person and goods of each of its associates.

---

[106] *Id.*
[107] *Id.* at Book I § 6.
[108] *Id.*
[109] *Id.*

Individual sovereignty is given up to the state in order to achieve freedom, equality, and justice. Jean Jacques Rousseau proclaimed that, "By social compact we have given the body politic existence and life; we have now by legislation to give it movement and will."[110] But when a state fails to act in a morally acceptable way, it ceases to exert genuine authority over the individual, who is then free to rebel.

IMMANUEL KANT (1724-1804)

A contemporary of Jean Jacques Rousseau's was Immanuel Kant, who formulated his own concept of the "original contract" theory.[111] To Kant there was a contractual basis for the just society that began from an original, or *a priori*, state of nature. "In all social contracts" Kant said, " . . . we find a union of many individuals for some common end which they all share." In the Kantian perspective, the social contract envisions an objective, hypothetical third person, in an "original position," contracting for conditions as yet unforeseen. Assumed is that the contracting person will not agree to conditions which might turn out to be adverse to that person's best interests, but rather, chooses to optimize conditions wherein he or she might later be situated.

JOHN RAWLS (1921-2002)

Recognizing the inherent injustices in not only the classical utilitarian, but the intuitionist's conceptions of justice as well, Rawls' guiding aim was to work out a theory of justice that would be a more viable alternative to those doctrines, which he says "have long dominated our philosophical tradition." His initial response was to strike a compromise between utility and the social contract.,[112] But his ultimate answer[113] was to return to the contractarian concept, to raise it to a higher level of abstraction, and to describe "justice as fairness" in the Kantian perspective—fairness in this case meaning a balance of competing claims.

---

[110] *Id.*

[111] *See* Immanuel Kant, *The Fundamental Principles of the Metaphysic of Morals* (1785).

[112] *See* John Rawls, *Outline of a Decision Procedure for Ethics*, The Philosophical Review 60 (1951); *see also* John Rawls, *Justice as Fairness*, The Philosophical Review 67 (1958); *see also* John Rawls, *The Sense of Justice*, The Philosophical Review 72 (1963).

[113] John Rawls, *A Theory of Justice* (1971).

Human rights are the outcome of Kant's "original contract."[114] Under girding Rawls' "original position" are his two basic *principles of justice*, which are:

> *The Liberty Principle—Each person is to have an equal right to the most extensive basic liberty compatible with a similar liberty for others;* and

> *The Difference Principle—Social and economic inequalities are to be arranged so that they are both: (a) reasonably expected to be to everyone's advantage, and (b) attached to positions and offices open to all.*[115]

CONCLUSION

Out of the Era of Enlightenment came the ethical foundations for the evolution of modern law. Utilitarians proclaim that universal welfare (or happiness) should be the leading principle in the conduct of life. The divine right of kings is thus supplanted as society takes the place of the will of God, which thereby describes what is called "natural law." As Calvi and Coleman explain, Thomas Jefferson incorporated the concept of natural law into the Declaration of Independence when he invoked the notion that men are endowed by their Creator with certain "inalienable rights." He also invoked the theory of the social contract, à là Locke and Rousseau,[116] when he emphatically stated that governments are instituted among men to protect those natural rights. And that when a sovereign abuses the power granted to it by its subjects, it is the right of the people to alter and abolish it. Jefferson then went on to list the abuses by George III.

The Declaration of Independence and its under girding philosophy, grounded in Locke and Rousseau, put a new twist on the relationship between the people and their government, by proclaiming that government derived its power from the consent of the governed,

---

[114] See *Immanuel Kant, Kant's Political Writings* (Hans Reiss, ed. and H.B. Nisbet, trans. 1970) in James Sterba, Justice: Alternative Political Perspectives (1980).

[115] John Rawls, *A Theory of Justice* (1971).

[116] Jean Jacques Rousseau, *Du Compac Social, The Social Contract or Principles of Political Right* Book (1762).

not by some accident of royal birth. Implicit in the concept of government by consent is the idea of majority rule.[117] American democracy is, by definition, utilitarian, because it attempts to provide the greatest happiness to the greatest number. It is, at the same time, grounded in the theory of the social contract, placing the individual before society and above the state. However, such a view is not without its critics.

David A.J. Richards, for example, demands that adherence to social utility, or to the social contract, ignores history by obfuscating "the interpretation of historical meaning of the American constitutional system." He argues that to understand the U.S. Constitution properly, one must "take seriously the multiple layers of interpretive history" the founders used in constructing the document. In short, interpreting the U.S. Constitution is no easy task that can be reduced to simple conventions like utilitarianism and the social contract. Rather, Richards is highly critical of both theoretical constructs, arguing on the one hand that John Locke was a much more "radical political thinker" than conventionalists have attributed to him, and that his "political theory has undergone and is still undergoing a sharp reassessment by critical historians."

On the other hand, Richards maintains that an "anti-utilitarian" theory of justice is superior to the utilitarian and a better reflection of moral reality (because it speaks to the rights of the individual). Interpretation of the First Amendment, and basic individual rights, Richards suggests, is articulated better by more contemporary theorists such as John Rawls, who argues for the priority of civil liberties over models of what Richards calls "religious toleration."[118]

However, the elusiveness of sorting out the "layers of interpretive history," that Richards finds necessary to understand constitutional construction, makes the ease of using conventional theories, such as utilitarianism and the social contract, appealing and instructive in understanding constitutional law. Hence, both the utilitarian and contractarian perspectives are instrumental in helping one to come to grips with the morality and substance of constitutional law. What follows in the next chapter, then, is an annotated rendition of the social contract known as *The Constitution of the United States.*

---

[117] *See* James V. Calvi and Susan Coleman, *American Law and Legal Systems* 56 (3rd 1997).
[118] David A.J. Richards, *Foundations of American Constitutionalism* 11-17 (1989).

Origin of Law

CHAPTER 3

CONSTITUTIONAL LAW
AND ITS EVOLUTION

*We the People of the United States, in Order to form a more perfect
Union, establish Justice, insure domestic Tranquillity, provide for
the common defence, promote the general Welfare, and secure the
Blessings of Liberty to our selves and our Posterity, do ordain and
establish this Constitution for the United States of America.*[1]

THE BIRTH OF REASON

After the Reformation and the Renaissance came the Enlightenment; and after the Age of Science came the Age of Reason.[2] Known
to the Germans as the *Aufklärung*, sometimes called the *Illumination*
by the English, the Age of Enlightenment is the historical period,
from about 1688 to 1776, during which time a new intellectual order
was established. Throughout the period, the older privileged class lost
ground to the Third Estate, or *bourgeoisie*. It was an intellectual
revolution, won by idealistic philosophers and romantic poets who
appealed to the masses to overthrow tradition and authority by the
exercise of the right of private judgment and an appeal to reason.

The cause of the triumph of reason over tradition during the Enlightenment can be found in a search for truth and the evolution of the

---

[1] The *Preamble to the United States Constitution. See e.g.*, Thomas James Norton, *The Constitution of the United States, Its Sources and Its Application* (1965); *see also* e.g., J. A. Richard
and James H. McCrocklin, *Our National Constitution: Origins, Development and Meaning*
(1957); *see also*, Edward C. Smith, *Introduction*, in The Constitution of the United States
(1969).
[2] Preserved Smith, *The Enlightenment* 1687-1776 (1934).

intellectual class to a dominant position in the state. Leaders of the Enlightenment found political leverage for subverting existing institutions and standards in the "laws of nature," beginning with the natural sciences. From natural science a new pattern was adopted in other fields of thought as well. As Preserved Smith explains,

> *Gradually, institutions, politics, religion, education, psychology, and esthetics, were subjected to the yoke of physics, were assumed to be amenable to natural law, and were investigated, criticized, explained, and reformed accordingly.*[3]

The first principle of Enlightenment was intellectualism. Secondly, the spirit of the era was practical and utilitarian. Third, the Enlightenment was optimistic of man's ability to win happiness. From reason sprang the recognition of social utility and the importance that individual happiness plays in the creation of justice.

The spirit of intellectualism grew out of an inquiry into the laws of physics and the development of that science as a mature academic discipline. Classical physics began in the field of mechanics, with the first laws of motion being codified by Sir Isaac Newton (1642-1727). The model for the physical, or natural sciences, was then adopted by the moral and social disciplines. The seminal works of Isaac Newton in the physical sciences and John Locke in the social sciences marked the beginning of the age.[4] But all subjects were thought to be amenable to natural law, and were investigated, criticized, explained, and reformed within the natural paradigm.[5]

In the limited sense, the natural sciences include descriptions of the earth and its productions such as zoology, botany, geology, mineralogy, and so forth. But in the broadest, most inclusive form, natural science may include anything that is natural in the universe. *Natural law* and *natural ethics* investigate the sense of right and wrong and of mutual obligation that is "natural" to mankind, as distinguished from the revealed law of God and/or the codified laws of man. *Natural religion* is a form that is distinguished from revealed religion, taking

---

[3] Preserved Smith, *The Enlightenment* 1687-1776 35 (1934).
[4] *Id.* at 21-40.
[5] *Id.* 32-35.

into consideration evidences of the existence and attributes of God as are afforded in nature and natural phenomenon. The idea of natural law, a natural ethics, and a natural religion became dominant in society and politics. Into art, into literature, and even into music, the thinkers of the 18th Century tried to introduce the principles of order and of natural law.[6]

The Enlightenment marks the beginning of a lost hegemony described as the "divine right of kings," the end of despotic rule in Europe, and the beginning of revolutions for liberty and freedom in the American colonies and in France. By the 17th Century, essentially all of the European states had become despotic. The nobles had actively seconded and the masses passively acquiesced in the claims of the state to unlimited control over its citizens.[7] However, by the late 17th Century, the ruling class had gone too far, the Age of Enlightenment dawned, and it was time for revolution.

In 1688, James II, King of England, fled to France. He had brought the English Revolution upon himself when he alienated virtually every politically and militarily significant segment of English society. In what is known as the "Glorious Revolution," the leaders of the major political factions in Parliament joined to drive James from the throne. By this bloodless revolution between 1688 and 1689, Parliament ended "divine right" in England and affirmed its supremacy over the monarch. In 1689, Parliament passed the English Bill of Rights limiting the powers of the monarchy over parliament.

Meanwhile, in France, the government became ever more despotic. During the last 30 years of his reign (1685-1715), Louis XIV strained the resources of that country to its limits in order to maintain the glory of his monarchy. Terrible wars, unwise government regulation of industry, trade and agriculture, and oppressive taxes took the country to near bankruptcy. The government reached deeper into the depths of despotism.

During the long reign of Louis XV (1715-1774) merchants and landowners began again to accumulate wealth, but peasants and the lower classes profited little. The final step in making the monarchy autocratic was taken by the suppression of the *Parlement de Paris* and of the local *parlements* by *coup d'état* in 1771.[8]

---

[6] *Id.* at 36-38.
[7] *Id.* at 28.
[8] Preserved Smith, *The Enlightenment* 1687-1776 29-30 (1934).

With the American Revolution having already taken place, by 1789 there was a revolution brewing in France as well. King Louis XVI, through inept management and his support of the colonists in the American War of Independence again took France to the brink of bankruptcy. The result was even harsher taxation on an already over-taxed population. Using the motto, *Liberté, Egalité, et Fraternité* (liberty, equality, and fraternity), the revolutionaries stormed the Bastille on July 14, 1789, and overthrew the monarchy.

THE DECLARATION OF INDEPENDENCE

It was only as a last resort that the American colonists declared their independence from Great Britain 23 years earlier. The colonists had sought to subordinate themselves to a sovereign ruler, and within the social contractarian perspective, to receive from that sovereign the blessings of security and a rational system of laws. Yet, they had been driven to the brink of anarchy, and were already beginning to experience political disorder, confusion, and violence—and the terror of the war of all-against-all—that absence of a rational order of government can bring. Prompting fear and disorder were "a train of abuses and usurpations" by the king of England.

Finding conditions intolerable, and to redress each of many oppressions they had been made to suffer, the colonists attempted on numerous occasions to petition King George III. For this purpose, Benjamin Franklin had been sent to England several times. But the colonist's pleas for relief were answered only by further injury.

In 1775, the year before formally declaring their independence, the colonists issued a lengthy *Declaration of the Causes and Necessity of Taking up Arms*, wherein they detailed their grievances. But showing their desire to remain subjects of the sovereign, they had explicitly denied any intention to separate from Great Britain, or to otherwise establish independent states.

Disregarding petitions to rectify their grievances, the King had re-fused to approve laws for the good of the colonies. In fact, he had shown himself to be a true despot, by placing the colonists outside of, and without law. Without equal access to the law, there could be nei-ther justice nor fairness. By way of abuse, oppression, and tyranny, King George had effectively breached the social contract and had opened the door to rebellion. As the colonists stated in the Declaration of Independence, ". . . . whenever any Form of Government be-comes destructive of these ends, it is the Right of the People to alter or to abolish it, and to institute new Government. . . ."

The "Laws of Nature and of Nature's God" were cited as the legal authority impelling the colonists to separate. "Throwing off" such a government was seen as not only the colonist's right, but their duty.

Many of the revolutionaries had already denounced the divine right of kings. And, they had adopted what by then had become popular philosophies including the utility and hedonism envisioned by Jeremy Bentham and Adam Smith, and the social contract as de-scribed by John Locke and by Jean Jacques Rousseau, as well as the writings of other "enlightened" theorists. The works of Charles De Montesquieu (1689-1755), for instance, are quoted oft by James Madison in the *Federalist*. As in England, so in America, the late 17th and 18th Centuries saw an emerging attraction to notions of Constitu-tional liberty. The colonists already believed that it was the people collectively who held the ultimate power to rule. Nevertheless, they were equally aware of the necessity of their consenting to a sovereign authority, and that such consent is a characteristic of even the most republican and democratic forms of government. They likewise un-derstood that they too must consent to sovereign rule—but it was with a caveat. The consent was to be granted only so long as the sovereign rule was lawful.

Under King George, sovereign rule had clearly despotic (i.e., not lawful). By 1776, the American colonists had found it necessary and unavoidable to separate themselves from Great Britain—but more specifically, that they remove themselves from the tyranny of King George. Marked by his actions as a tyrant, the colonists deemed George III unfit to rule them. Left with no other options, Thomas Jef-ferson was asked to draft a statement declaring the colonists' inde-pendence from England. The result was the *Declaration of Independ-ence*, which officially endorsed the ensuing Revolutionary War.

Cited in the main body of the Declaration of Independence are 26 indictments against the king for usurpations and tyrannical acts of oppression.[9] Among them were:

---

[9] *See* Appendix A.

- refusing to assent to laws for the public good;
- forbidding his governors to pass laws without his direct approval;
- extortion through refusal to pass other laws unless the people would relinquish their rights;
- distant (centralized) rule intended to make it fatiguing and frustrating to the colonists;
- reputed dissolvent of representative houses for opposing him;
- obstructing natural laws;
- obstructing the administration of justice;
- making judges dependent upon his will alone;
- creating a multitude of new administrative officers, harassing the people with their presence;
- keeping a standing army, subjecting the people to martial rather than civil law;
- failing to protect them and for waging war against them;
- plundering the coastal waters, burning towns and destroying lives; employing mercenaries to complete his works of death;
- exciting domestic insurrections and inciting the Indians against the people; and
- being a tyrant, thereby depriving the people of their basic liberties.

If justice exists only when people possess equality and freedom, then no level of justice is possible under tyranny. As the Israelites had done 4,000 years before, the colonists likewise made an appeal to natural law, and to a more supreme authority, by declaring certain "unalienable rights" endowed by their "Creator." Among these rights were life, liberty, and the pursuit of happiness—"That to secure these rights, Governments are instituted among Men, deriving their just powers from the consent of the governed." The colonists declared their independence, and began immediately to construct an altogether new social contract and the formation of a new government. Shortly following their separation from England, and in their desperate search for law and order, the revolutionaries sought to quickly replace their lost social compact and commonwealth. They nominated George Washington, amongst others, to be their king. Washington, of course, turned down the offer of the monarchy in favor of a democratic government yet to be designed.

PREAMBLE TO THE CONSTITUTION

Upon cessation of hostilities with the British in 1781, a new government was established within the framework of the newly formed *Articles of Confederation* (see Table 3.1, "Chronology of the U.S. Constitution"). Unfortunately, the Articles proved too easy for the separate and individual states to change, alter and/or amend. States also established barriers to trade. In order to assure a more lasting government, permanence would require a higher level of obligation to the maintenance of the federation, and all would have to agree. In 1787, a constitutional convention was assembled to rectify the weaknesses of the Articles of Confederation.

The *Preamble* of the U.S. Constitution reads as a resolution of that convention. It is the opening paragraph of the Constitution, and tells why the document was necessary. Looking at the constituent parts:

- *We the People of the United States*, implies a Republic, where the people form their own government, and it is with them that ultimate power rests.
- *In order to form a more perfect Union*, means a union of the states more perfect than it was under the Articles of Confederation. To be strong, the nation must be united, and not easily dissolved by the will of any one of its constituent parts.
- *In order to establish Justice*, in other words, means equality of all before the law. As in a social contract, all associates are subject to the law, entitled to its protection and responsible for obeying its provisions. The Constitution provides for police protection and for courts of justice and trial by a jury of peers.
- *In order to insure domestic Tranquility*, refers to the primary function within the social contract for the sovereign to protect each individual against a "war of all-against-all."
- *To provide for the common defense*, again refers to the obligation of the sovereign to protect its citizens. Provided under the Constitution is an army and navy, paid for out of a common (national) treasury, and for defense, not tyranny.

Table 3.1—CHRONOLOGY OF THE U.S. CONSTITUTION

1775

The American Revolution began. Hostilities did not end until 1781, when Lord Cornwallis surrendered at Yorktown, Virginia. A treaty was not secured until 1783.

1776

The Declaration of Independence was drafted stating why the colonists wanted to separate themselves from Great Britain.

1781

The Articles of Confederation were drawn up to give form to the new government. The Articles were loosely put together and proved too weak to adequately bind the colonies together.

1787

The U.S. Constitution is drafted as a foundation for government.

1788

The U.S. Constitution is adopted as the basic law of the land, effective in 1789, and ratified by all the states in 1790.

1791

The First Ten Amendments (The *Bill of Rights*) were added to the Constitution to delineate federal powers and guarantee the rights and liberties of the people.

- *To promote the general Welfare*, means both to safeguard and to improve upon the utility and well being of all the people and the promotion of the greatest happiness for the most people.
- *To secure the Blessings of Liberty to ourselves and our posterity*, suggests that in order to have justice, one must first have liberty, with long-term assurances of lasting freedom.
- *Do ordain and establish this Constitution for the United States of America*. With this, the framers of the Constitution gave form and solidarity to their new government through the creation of a basic law of the land.

Fundamentally, the U.S. Constitution is a document that prescribes the various political offices by which the government is organized. As Aristotle wrote, "A constitution is the organization of offices in a state, and determines what is to be the governing body and what is the end of each community." Each of the provisions in the Constitution has a separate history which when studied helps one to understand the document itself. The United States has an interesting system of "undoing power," and the Constitution was written with a fear of abuses by anybody. Wrote James Madison in 1788,

> *Wherever there is an interest and power to do wrong, wrong will generally be done, and not less readily by a powerful and interested party than by a powerful and interested prince.*[10]

In framing the governmental structure, and fearing the natural abuse of power, the founders built into the Constitution three separate powers. Immanuel Kant describes the three powers of the state as the Romans did, *potestas legislatoria, rectoria, et judiciaria*—the legislative power, the executive power, and the judiciary power:

- The *legislative* power of the sovereignty in the state is embodied in the person of the lawgiver;
- The *executive* power is embodied in the person of the ruler who administers the law; and

---

[10] In the *Federalist* (1787-1788).

- The *judiciary* power, embodied in the person of the judge, is the function of assigning every one what is his own, according to the law.[11]

It was Montesquieu, however, who first identified the executive, legislative, and judicial powers as they are classified in the Constitution. But John Locke distinguished the three powers a little differently.[12] Locke describes the three powers as legislative, executive, and *federative*. In explaining, he says there can be only one supreme power, the legislative, which is for the preservation of the commonwealth. The executive power is to execute the laws of the legislature. The federative power is for the execution of foreign policy. The executive and federative powers, although distinct, are both in the hands of the same person(s), who, in turn, is responsible to the people.[13]

Jean Jacques Rousseau identifies the powers of government similarly. "The legislative power belongs to the people, and can belong to it alone."[14] The "government, or supreme administration," he says, is the ". . . legitimate exercise of the executive power, and *prince* or *magistrate* the man or the body entrusted with that administration."[15]

The "government" in America is, as Rousseau described government, an intermediate body set up between the subjects (individually) and the sovereign (the subjects collectively), and consisting of three groups of "administrators"—the executive, the legislature, and the judiciary. The "executive" in America could have been a king. Instead, the chief executive is a president. With the President is an associate, the Vice President, and a Cabinet of the president's choosing (with the advice and consent of Congress).

The forum for Congress was borrowed from the Romans. During the era of the Roman Republic (509-549 BC), lawmaking was a bicameral activity. Legislation was passed by the *comitia*, an assembly of citizens. Representatives of the upper class, the senate, then approved it. And then it was issued in the name of the senate and the people of Rome. Laws in the United States, too, must go through two

---

[11] Immanuel Kant, *The Science of Right* §45 (1790).

[12] Sir Ernest Barker, *Introduction*, Social Contract: Essays by Locke, Hume, and Rousseau xxii (1947).

[13] John Locke, *Concerning Civil Government* Ch. XII (1690).

[14] Immanuel Kant, likewise, describes the legislative power as belonging only to ". . . the united will of the people." Immanuel Kant, *The Science of Right* §46 (1790).

[15] Jean Jacques Rousseau, *du compac social*, *The Social Contract or Principles of Political Right* Book III (1762).

legislative bodies. The House of Representatives represents the assembly of citizens, and, like its counterpart in ancient Rome, the U.S. Senate was originally designed as a chamber for the elite.[16] It was not until passage of the Seventeenth Amendment, in 1913, that ordinary people were allowed to vote for senators.[17]

Although the U.S. Constitution calls for the establishment of three separate powers as envisioned by Montesquieu, operationally, the separation of powers comes about as envisioned by Locke and Rousseau. As the "federative" power identified by John Locke emanates from the executive power, so too does the "judicial" power begin in the executive, and the legislative powers. A Supreme Court is mandated in Article III of the Constitution, but Supreme Court Justices are appointed by the President, with advice and consent of the Senate. And, "inferior courts," as necessary, are created by Congress. Both the executive and the legislature are directly responsible to the people.

Fighting to win support for ratification of the Constitution, Alexander Hamilton (1757-1804), James Madison (1751-1836), and John Jay (1745-1829) wrote a stream of articles between October 1787 and April 1788, which, when compiled in book form, became *The Federalist*. With regard to why three separate powers were necessary, James Madison explained,

> *The accumulation of all powers, legislative, executive, and judiciary, in the same hands, whether of one, a few, or many, and whether hereditary, self-appointed, or elective, may justly be pronounced the very definition of tyranny.*[18]

Beyond separation of powers, the concept of "checks and balances" ensured that each branch could circumscribe the powers of the other. For example, laws could not be passed without approval of both branches of the Congress, and usually, the President.[19] Such laws were subject to administration, enforcement and execution by the executive, and interpretation by the judiciary.

---

[16] T.R. Reid, *The World According To Rome*, 192 National Geographic 70 (Aug. 1997).
[17] *See* Appendix B.
[18] James Madison, The Federalist Number 47.
[19] With an overwhelming majority, the Congress could override a Presidential veto of a bill.

THE BASIC LAW OF THE LAND

The U.S. Constitution is the "basic law of the land." It is typical of most modern constitutions in that it was written by "constituent assemblies" of representatives of the people at large. The Constitution is grounded upon three principles:

- *separation of powers*;
- *citizens rights*; and
- *federalism.*

The Constitution did not provide for an entirely new government. Rather, the national government was to be a federation of 13 states that already existed prior to adoption of the Constitution. For the benefit of the whole, the national government was given supremacy— thus, the national motto, "Out of many, one." Federalism is formed by a compact between the separate states (being individual political units) which willingly subordinate their powers to the central or national government, while at the same time retaining other limited powers. It is a system unique to the United States.

The federal government represents the United States in foreign affairs and matters of national character. The National government is *supreme*, as in the highest authority or domain. Whereas, the State governments are *sovereign*, as in possessing independent authority.

ARTICLE ONE

The first article of the Constitution vests the legislative powers in a Congress comprised of two houses, a Senate with equal representation from each state, and a House of Representatives with representation by populace. The House of Representatives has a presiding officer, the *Speaker*, whom the members of the House elect. The Senate's *President* is a secondary role for the Vice President of the United States.

The duties and responsibilities of Congress, as outlined by Article One, are enumerated as follows:

- first and foremost is to make laws;

- to appropriate money by collecting taxes, duties, imports and excises; to pay debts or borrow money; to coin (make) money and regulate its value; and to provide the punishment for counterfeiting;

- to establish rules of naturalization of non-citizens; constitute inferior courts; promote the progress of science and useful arts, secure the exclusive rights for inventors, writers and discoverers; and

- to regulate commerce; fix the standards of weights and balances; create bankruptcy laws; establish post offices and postal (courier) roads; provide for common defense and general welfare; define and punish piracies and felonies on the high seas; to raise and support armies and navies; and declare war.

ARTICLE TWO

Executive power is *administrative*. The power of carrying out an organization's plans or purposes is "executive." It is the controlling and operational element of government.

Article Two vests with the President and a Vice President of the United States the executive power. It includes a responsibility to faithfully execute the laws. Demonstrative of the President's responsibilities is the oath of office repeated below:

> *I do solemnly swear (or affirm) that I will faithfully execute the Office of President of the United States, and will to the best of my ability, preserve, protect and defend the Constitution of the United States.*

The President commissions military officers, and is the Commander in Chief of the Army and Navy of the United States, and of state Militia when in service of the U.S.

Foreign policy is the exclusive domain of the President. It is the "federative" power identified by John Locke as the power ". . . of war and peace, leagues and alliances, and all the transactions with persons and communities without the commonwealth."[20] The President makes

---

[20] John Locke, *Concerning Civil Government* Ch. XII (1690).

treaties, with consent of Congress, receives ambassadors and otherwise makes and carries out the foreign policy of the United States.

The President appoints ambassadors, public ministers and counsels, Supreme Court justices and other officers. Included in the latter are members of the President's Cabinet; Secretary of State, Secretary of Defense, Secretary of Transportation, and so forth. The membership and organization of the Cabinet is subject to change with succeeding presidents.

Another power of the Presidency is that of reprieves and pardons for federal offenses, except impeachment.

ARTICLE THREE

Judicial power is vested in the U.S. Supreme Court, and in such other "inferior" courts (i.e., below the Supreme Court) which Congress may from, time to time, create. Federal judges are nominated by the President of the United States, and serve their term of office "during good behavior".

In order to preserve the system of checks and balances intended by the separation of powers, the writers of the Constitution protected the justices against intimidation from threats of removal or diminished salary, by giving to them their office for as long as they wanted and so long as their behavior remained such as is proper for a peaceable and law-abiding citizen.

The U.S. Supreme Court is comprised of the Chief Justice of the United States and such number of Associate Justices as may be fixed by Congress. Under current authority, established in 1948, there are nine Justices, eight Associate Justices, plus the Chief Justice.[21]

The Supreme Court hears cases:

- arising under the Constitution (the supreme law of the land). Essentially, national questions shall be tried in national courts;
- where the U.S. is a party;
- between two or more states;
- between a state and a citizen of another state; and
- between citizens of different states.

---

[21] 62 Stat. 869; 28 U.S.C. § 1.

The Constitution provides for trial by jury in all criminal cases save impeachment. The right to a trial by jury is mentioned in Article III, and in the Sixth Amendment. This right, however, may be waived by the accused. States have similar provisions, but the accused may not in all cases have the right to a jury trial in all state courts. Furthermore, Article III and Amendment VI apply to the *criminal* court system. The Seventh Amendment provides for jury trial in *civil* cases.

ARTICLE FOUR

Article Four contains certain states rights provisions, and guarantees to every state a republican form of government. In a Republic, such as the United States, its citizens hold the supreme or ultimate power. It is a "bottom-up" kind of government, rather than a "top-down" rule as in an absolute monarchy.

Many of the world's people still (willingly or unwillingly) view domination by a supreme power, and subjugation to the will of others as the expected norm. In some countries inequality may be sanctioned by law, custom, and/or tradition. The ideal in the American form of government, however, is quite the opposite. The expectation is that governmental officials are to respond to the will of the people.

Although at times appearing apathetic, Americans can become agitated when government is perceived as showing a deaf ear to the voice and will of the people. There was a social revolution in the 1960s, for example, which grew out of distrust for authority, and a subsequent reaction to what was perceived as an "Imperial" presidency. In the 1970s there was a return to "consumerism." But the 1980s mirrored a reflection upon the absolutism of 16th and 17th Century England, when the consumer was neglected in favor of a powerful and rich state. Ironically, the masses appeared to share in the hegemony that the "ruling class interest was the same as the interest of the larger of society."[22] What seemingly was of paramount importance was defeat of the "red threat," no matter the cost. At the expense of the "consumer," deficit spending on the military-industrial complex took the state to the brink of bankruptcy. In a minor social revolution, the political climate in early 1990's reflected widespread discontent with the federal bureaucracy and with politicians in general, and resulted in a popular movement to oust incumbents and to

---

[22] *See* Antonio Gramsci, *Selections from Prison Notebooks* (1971).

limit terms of office. The national elections of 2000 found the nation deeply divided. With the events of September 11, 2001, and the onset of the War on Terror, the national motto, "Out of many, one" took on renewed vigor. But by the elections of 2004 the nation appeared as divided as ever.

By occasionally flexing the power of the legislative branch, the voters send a message to the "executive" reminding them of the collective sovereignty of the people (in effect, "letting them know who is boss"). In a republican government the citizens of the various states hold the power of national government, executed through popularly elected officers and representatives. The Bill of Rights were adopted as the first ten amendments to the Constitution in order to assure that the legislative power, along with certain individual rights, remained with the people.

Out of the basic fear of abuse of power, and fearing that perhaps the Constitution transferred too much power from the states to the federal government, the Bill of Rights was drawn up within a year of the Constitution's ratification. The first ten amendments are supplementary to the concept of states rights found in Article IV.

ARTICLES FIVE, SIX, AND SEVEN

Article V makes provisions for adoption and ratification of constitutional amendments. Article VI declares the Constitution to be "the supreme law of the land." The second paragraph of Article VI is otherwise known as the *Supremacy Clause*. Article VII ratifies and establishes formal acceptance of the Constitution by those in attendance at the Convention in 1787.

THE BILL OF RIGHTS

Recall that the Declaration of Independence declared certain unalienable rights including life, liberty and the pursuit of happiness. The Constitution establishes the governmental institutions essential to protect those rights. To further insure the security of citizens' rights, the first ten amendments, popularly referred to as the *Bill of Rights*, came into being. One definition of democracy is that "people are free to live their lives as they wish, provided they obey the law which safeguards equal rights for all." This is the intent of the Constitution, as augmented and changed by its amendments.

The civil rights, or civil liberties, are the personal, natural rights guaranteed and protected specifically by the Constitution. The civil rights are enhanced by a number of Civil Rights Acts, which are federal statutes intended to supplement and give further force to basic personal rights guaranteed by the Constitution. For example, such acts prohibit discrimination based on race, color, age, sex, or religion.

The Bill of Rights can be conveniently divided into three areas:

- the so called *first claims*;
- the *restrictions* upon government; and
- other *unnamed rights*.

The first claims are freedoms of speech, of the press, of religion, and of peaceful assembly. A person has the right to say or to print what he or she wants, so long as what is said or printed does not harm others. A person may also worship as one chooses. There is the right to meet together and to petition the government. As noted above, King George III specifically denied the colonists this latter right.

The government restrictions prohibit it from interfering in the people's right to keep and bear arms. The government may not quarter soldiers in a person's home. It may not conduct searches except by warrant or probable cause, and it may not take a person's property without just compensation. The government cannot try a person twice on the same charges; an indictment for capital crime must be issued through a grand jury, a person cannot be forced to testify against oneself; and a person must be confronted by witnesses against him or her. A person may not be deprived of personal liberty unless it is according to law. If arrested, the accused must be informed of the charges. The government must provide a speedy trial, and in the district where the offense was committed. The government is forbidden to impose excessive bail, excessive fines or any cruel and unusual punishment.

To insure the states were not giving away any powers that did not immediately come to mind, the people were to retain all unnamed powers not specifically given to the federal government within the written body of the Constitution. However, the Bill of Rights became applicable to the states with the passage of the 14th Amendment, three years after the War Between the States concluded.

FIRST AMENDMENT

Guaranteed by the First Amendment are the *first claims*—freedom of religion, speech, press, and peaceable assembly. It seems ironic that those early colonists who had so recently emigrated from Europe because of religious persecution should be so intolerant of others in the practice of their religion. But such was the case, and it was imminently apparent that protection against religious intolerance needed to be embodied within the Constitution.

Freedom includes personal expression, both written and oral. Beginning in the 1960s, the U.S. Supreme Court expanded free speech guarantees, placing upon public officials and public figures the almost insurmountable barrier of proving that the alleged defamation was motivated by "actual malice" (knowledge of falsity or reckless disregard of the truth).[23]

The right to assemble peacefully was considered to exist even before the Constitution, and was incorporated in the Magna Carta. The Great Charter guaranteed certain rights (at least to a royal elite, and to churchmen). No one from within this select group was to be imprisoned or taken from his home except by legal, or due process. There was the right to appeal, to have a trial by jury, and the right not to be taxed without prior consent through representation.

The Great Charter was adopted in A.D. 1215. Four hundred years later, human rights again became an issue in England. In a redress of grievances, *The Petition of Rights*, another important document in the evolution of the U.S. Constitution, was submitted to the king in 1628. The Petition was rejected by King Charles I, who insisted upon his absolute sovereignty. Under strict or absolute sovereignty, "the king could do no wrong." He was, therefore, "above the law." By the time of the English *Bill of Rights* in 1689, it had been made clear that not even the king was above the law.

The English Bill of Rights was an "Act Declaring the Rights and Liberties of the Subject and Settling the Succession of the Crown." It declared:

> *That the pretended power of suspending the laws or the execution of laws by regal authority without consent of Parliament is illegal;*

---

[23] New York Times v. Sullivan, 376 U.S. 254 (1964).

That the pretended power of dispensing with laws or the execution of laws by regal authority, as it hath been assumed and exercised of late, is illegal;

That the commission for erecting the late Court of Commissioners for Ecclesiastical causes, and all other commissions and courts of like nature, are illegal and pernicious;

That levying money for or to the use of the Crown by pretence (sic) of prerogative, without grant of Parliament, for longer time, or in other manner than the same is or shall be granted, is illegal;

That the right of the subjects to petition the king, and all commitments and prosecutions for such petitioning are illegal;

That the raising or keeping a standing army within the kingdom in time of peace, unless it be with consent of Parliament, is against the law;

That the subjects which are Protestants may have arms for their defence (sic) suitable to their conditions and as allowed by law;

That election of members of Parliament ought to be free;

That the freedom of speech and debates or proceedings in Parliament ought not to be impeached or questioned in any court or place out of Parliament;

That excessive bail ought not to be required, nor excessive fines imposed, nor cruel and unusual punishments inflicted;

That jurors ought to be duly impanneled (sic) and returned, and jurors which pass upon men in trials for high treason ought to be freeholders;

That all grants and promises of fines and forfeitures of particular persons before conviction are illegal and void;

And that for redress of all grievances, and for the amending, strengthening and preserving of the laws, Parliaments ought to be held frequently.

In 1774, the colonists patterned a similar document, *The Declaration of Rights and Grievances*, after the English Bill of Rights. In addition, the English Bill of Rights was a point of departure for drafting the American Declaration of Independence. Furthermore, many of the passages in the English Bill of Rights are paralleled in the U.S. Constitution. Although it is not really a constitution, the English Bill of Rights has nevertheless been referred to as "England's Constitution."

Also guaranteed by the First Amendment are freedom of religion, and a prohibition against governmental establishment of religion. In the 1960s, this led the federal courts to prohibit prayer in the schools.

SECOND AMENDMENT

The Second Amendment guarantees the right to a well regulated militia. In addition, it also preserves the people's right to bear arms. This amendment is at the very core of contemporary gun control initiatives. Those who would have tighter control of personal weapons relate the right to bear arms only in association with organization of a "well regulated militia." Their interpretation grants the right to bear arms only to the military establishment, including the police, but not to private citizens. Interpreted by certain gun control advocates is that "militia" means the National Guard.

A more liberal interpretation by gun enthusiasts, on the other hand, argues it is the "people's" right, meaning each and every citizen's right, to have at least small arms, if not arms of unlimited scale. These people point out that "militia" is defined in the Militia Act of 1792, passed only five months after ratifying the Second Amendment. The Militia Act ordered every male citizen between the ages of 18 and 44 (i.e., the entire fighting-age population) to own the same type of rifle as used by the Continental Army during the Revolutionary War. This law required each "militiaman" to own the firearm most useful to the military of that time, which today might include automatic weapons. However, based on such an argument, it might also mean artillery, tanks, battleships and bombers; thereby begging the question of where the line might be drawn, if at all.

Gun control advocates would counter by arguing that the militia as the body of the people is an outdated concept, and that a citizen militia is no longer necessary. The argument remains unresolved.[24] Nevertheless, it could not have been the intent of the constitutional writers to authorize any *lawless* use of guns, nor to allow criminals to have guns. Thus, in the public interest, there does exist some right of government to restrict the bearing of arms under certain conditions—to carry them unrestricted aboard civil air transports for example.

THIRD AMENDMENT

The Third Amendment deals with the quartering of soldiers in private homes, and the right of the people to oppose it. Also implied in the Third Amendment is concern about the necessity of a standing army in time of peace.

Raising, and more specifically paying for the support of armies is expensive and extremely taxing upon governments, kings not excluded. Look, for instance, at the disproportionate share of the federal budget taken up by the Department of Defense. It was equally costly for the King of England to field an army, and especially expensive to support an army thousands of miles, and an ocean away. One way to help defray the cost was to house soldiers in private homes. It was

---

[24] *See* Scott Heller, *The Right to Bear Arms*, The Chronicle of Higher Education A8 (Jul. 21, 1995).

also a way to intimidate the colonists in who's homes the soldiers were quartered. As perceived by the colonists, if they were at peace with England, there was no apparent need for the army's presence among them, other than as an act of tyranny.

The government's cost for support of the army was shifted to private citizens, which became another form of "taxation without representation." Furthermore, the colonists were forced to house and support the very ones who were oppressing them. It is little wonder they were incensed about having the king's soldiers in their private homes.

FOURTH AMENDMENT

The right to be protected against *unreasonable* search and seizure is the essence of the Fourth Amendment. General search warrants were illegal in England, and were thought to be illegal in the Colonies as well. A general warrant supported by only vagueness was (and is) insufficient cause to search anyone's person or property. Yet, King George made it a common practice to imprison prominent people and to then search their houses without cause.

Note that the Fourth Amendment does not declare that one cannot be searched, only that one cannot be searched "unreasonably." As will be seen later when addressing the subject of aviation security, a search must be prompted by *probable cause*, which is something much more than mere suspicion. Otherwise, the motivation for a search must be listed as one of the authorized exceptions to the Fourth Amendment requirements.

The purpose of a legitimate search is to find incriminating evidence. It might also be noted that an (illegal) search can be used to destroy evidence as well—evidence which could be used in one's defense. Hence, to protect the rights of the innocent, it is necessary that proper procedures be established for the conduct of a search and, ostensibly, the seizure of evidence. Therefore, evidence that is improperly obtained is inadmissible in a court of law, no matter how incriminating it may be.

FIFTH AMENDMENT

The Fifth Amendment deals with answerability to the law, and it provides for rights relative to the *due process* of law. There are two due process clauses in the Constitution, one in the Fifth Amendment pertaining to the federal government, and another is in the Fourteenth Amendment, protecting persons against states actions. Due process is a term or phrase which encompasses certain fundamental rights or principles of justice which limit the government from depriving a person of life, liberty or property. Daniel Webster defined due process as ". . . law which hears before it condemns; which proceeds upon inquiry; and which renders judgment only after trial." The Supreme Court in 1855 decided due process was nearly synonymous with the law of the land. It is in the Constitutional guarantees—brought to this country as part of the laws of England and rooted in common law.

When one does not wish to be a witness against oneself, one may invoke the Fifth Amendment, which protects each citizen against self-incrimination. The individual is afforded protection against unjust interrogation and potentially forced confessions. It might be noted that compulsory self-incrimination existed in England as late as 400 years after Magna Carta.

The Fifth Amendment protects individuals against having life or limb placed in jeopardy more than once (i.e., *double jeopardy*); that is, a person may not be tried twice for the same offense. Otherwise, a person could be tried however many times it might take to result in a guilty verdict.

Invoking Fifth Amendment protection against self-incrimination is popularly understood, but a contemporary point at issue in many airport noise and environmental issues is another aspect of the Fifth Amendment, the unlawful "taking" of property. The Fifth Amendment also states that "no person shall . . . be deprived of life, liberty, or property, without due process of law; nor shall private property be taken for public use, without just compensation." The protection of property against government seizure can be traced to Roman Law. It is embodied in the Magna Carta. It can also be found in the Napoleonic Code.

SIXTH AMENDMENT

The Sixth Amendment states, "the accused shall enjoy the right to a speedy and public trial, by an impartial jury. . . ." The accused has the right to be informed of the accusations and to be confronted by the witnesses against him or her. Recall from Mosaic Law that two witnesses were required. This particular requirement also emanates from Roman Law where the accused had the right to be face-to-face with witnesses.

In a now famous case involving Clarence Earl Gideon, made popular in a movie starring the late Henry Fonda,[25] the Supreme Court interpreted that the Sixth Amendment also included the individual's right to be represented by counsel, even if he or she couldn't afford it.[26] The Court said that to be without counsel was tantamount to being deprived of due process, and was therefore in violation of the Constitution.

The *Gideon* trial was a State of Florida case, where the U.S. Supreme Court determined Mr. Gideon's U.S. Constitutional rights had been violated by the State in trying him undefended (i.e., not represented by legal counsel). In the *Gideon* case, however, Clarence Earl Gideon appealed to the U.S. Supreme Court to overturn a previous decision, which had upheld the state's right not to provide counsel.[27]

Furthermore, where provisions of the Constitution may or may not apply to states, the Fifth Amendment expressly exempts the military services from certain protections under the Constitution. In enumerating the responsibilities of Congress, Article I empowers the legislative body "to make Rules for the Government and Regulation of the land and naval Forces." Hence, for the military, there is a separate body of law known as the *Uniform Code of Military Justice* [UCMJ].

The Sixth Amendment provides in federal courts for speedy trials, meaning without unreasonable delay. Also included in the Sixth Amendment is the second mention in the Constitution of the right to trial by jury in federal criminal cases (also found in Article III). The intent is for the accused not to languish in jail, but rather, to have a reasonably speedy trial, by one's peers, and *where* the offense was committed; not in some far-removed distant and alien place.

SEVENTH AMENDMENT

Where Article III and the Sixth Amendment provide for jury trial in criminal cases, the Seventh Amendment protects the right to trial by jury in civil cases. However, in neither civil nor criminal cases

---

[25] Robert Collins (director), *Gideon's Trumpet* (1979).

[26] *See Gideon v. Wainright*, 372 U.S. 335 (1963).

[27] *Betts v. Brady*, 316 U.S. 455 (1942).

may the courts "re-examine the facts" found by the jury. That is to say, no judge may substitute his or her opinion for that of the jury. Higher courts to which the findings of a lower court are appealed do not normally review the findings of fact, but rather, examine only how the law was applied. There are occasions, however, when original and/or appellate courts may review the facts *de novo* (anew).

EIGHTH AMENDMENT

"Excessive bail shall not be required, nor excessive fines imposed, nor cruel and unusual punishments inflicted." At the time the Constitution was written, punishments, which today might be considered cruel or unusual, were then more commonplace. William Blackstone in 1758, for example, described "the punishment of high treason" as being "very solemn and terrible." The victim was hanged by the neck to near suffocation, then cut down to be castrated and have his severed genitals burned before his eyes. While still alive and conscious, he was disemboweled. The victim was then decapitated and the body quartered. Finally, the four parts of the corpus, plus the head, were put on display as an example for all to see, and left to rot or be eaten by the birds and wild animals. There seems to be no limit to man's inhumanity to man.

It is fortunate for people who live in civilized communities that such torture and mutilation would now be considered barbaric! Many people, in fact, view any form of capital punishment as inhumane and "uncivilized." It is ironic that today the tables are turned, and it is the English (although they are not alone in the civilized world), who find it barbaric that America still practices capital punishment. But for those opposed to the death penalty, they will have to console themselves with the fact that at least more "humane" forms of killing a person have been adopted. The preference for lethal injection, over say the gas chamber or the electric chair, is one example.

Irrespective of the merits of capital punishment, "cruel and unusual" punishment may be defined by contemporary societies in far more restrictive terms than it was in the 17th Century. Note, for example, in *Santa Monica Airport Assn. v. Santa Monica*, the courts found it "excessive" for the City to impose a fee of $5,000 to land a jet or $10,000 for it to take off during hours of prohibited operations.[28]

---

[28] *Santa Monica Airport Association v. City of Santa Monica*, 481 F.Supp. 927 (1979).

NINTH AMENDMENT

Although certain civil rights were listed in the first eight amendments, other unnamed rights were nevertheless retained by the people. These individual rights were not to be denied later simply for having not been specified in the Constitution. On the other hand, for the federal government, the powers enumerated in the Constitution were to be *all* it either possessed or could exercise, as expressed in the Tenth Amendment.

TENTH AMENDMENT

The Tenth Amendment is the *Reserved Powers Clause.* The powers not delegated to the federal government, nor expressly prevented to the states, are reserved to the states or to the people. There was widespread fear the national government might exercise powers not granted to it, or might otherwise abuse the powers it was given. Wrote Thomas Jefferson in 1823,

> *The States can best govern over home concerns and the General Government over foreign ones.*

Among the powers of the state not surrendered (i.e., those to remain with the states), wrote the Supreme Court in 1911, was the power "to guard the public morals, the public safety, and the public health, as well as to promote the public convenience and the common good." The foregoing is the definition of "police power." Application of police power will be demonstrated later on, especially in context with airport management-related issues.

OTHER AMENDMENTS

The original Bill of Rights is not all inclusive of the rights protected under the Constitution. Others expressly enumerate certain rights, namely:

- The *Eleventh Amendment* prohibits suits by individuals against states without their consent;
- The *Thirteenth Amendment* abolishes slavery;
- The *Fourteenth Amendment* protects the *privileges and immunities* of citizenship. A person born or naturalized is a citizen, and no state may treat an out-of-state citizen differently than it treats its own. The Fourteenth Amendment contains the second *due process* clause, protecting persons from deprivation of life, liberty or property without due process by state action. It also guarantees citizens *equal protection* under the law;
- The *Fifteenth Amendment* protects the right to vote, which cannot be denied because of race, color, or previous condition of servitude;
- The *Sixteenth Amendment* allows for (income) taxation;
- The *Nineteenth Amendment* provided women the right to vote;
- The *Twenty Fourth Amendment* bans the poll tax as an eligibility requirement to vote in Federal elections; and
- The *Twenty Sixth Amendment* guarantees the right to vote to anyone 18 years of age or older;

CONCLUSION

In 1987, the bicentennial year celebrating the birth of the U. S. Constitution, a bipartisan group, the Committee on the Constitutional System, was convened to study the effectiveness of the Constitution and its applicability to modern-day America. In its analyses, the committee reported that the separation of powers between the executive and legislative branches has guarded against tyranny as it was intended by the founding fathers, but that unfortunately, it has also produced government "deadlock," failed presidencies, and the chance for politicians to evade accountability. As examples, the system's inability to deal with arms control and with budget and trade deficits was cited. In the committee's opinion, the founders would be appalled by today's governmental stalemate and incoherence.[29]

In its report, a committee majority proposed changes in the Constitution, federal laws and party rules to improve collaboration be-

---

[29] Scripps Howard News Service, *Constitution Needs To Be Revised*, Tribune Newspapers (Jan. 20, 1987).

tween the White House and Congress, strengthen political parties, and take modest steps toward a parliamentary system, where the party in power is the same as the president.[30]

The committee's recommendations were not at all expected to be implemented any time in the near term, if ever. In fact, one member noted that some of the ideas were "way too far out." Nevertheless, the committee had hoped to stimulate debate. But perhaps the thought of revising the Constitution is too irreverent. Many Americans, including former President Ronald Reagan, and the epic novelist, James Michener, revere the United States Constitution as a sacred document. What this suggests, is that rather than changing the Constitution, maybe what is needed is to return conceptually and operationally to the basic document, as it was intended, and as it is written.

Upon the 200th anniversary of the U.S. Constitution, Ronald Reagan observed:

> *I can't help but marvel at the genius of our Founders. They believed first and foremost in freedom, which they approached abstractly and practically. They created with a sureness and originality so great and pure that I can't help but perceive the guiding hand of God, the first political system that insisted that power flows from the people to the state, not the other way around. They created a system in which We the People granted to the state certain rights. This revolutionary idea meant the state itself was not the giver of rights, but in fact, the recipient.[31]*

Said James A. Michener of the Constitution:

> *Fifty-five typical American citizens met and argued for 127 days during a ferociously hot Philadelphia summer and produced one of the magisterial documents of world history. Almost without being aware of their achieve-*

---

[30] *Id.*

[31] Ronald Reagan, *Why Its The Greatest*, Parade Magazine 4 (Sep. 15, 1985).

ment, they fashioned a nearly perfect instru-
ment of government . . . But I think they should
be praised mostly because they attended to
those profound principles by which free men
have through the centuries endeavored to gov-
ern themselves. The accumulated wisdom of
mankind speaks in this Constitution.[32]

Commonly referred to as "constitutional law," in this chapter a
fundamental description of the law of the land has been presented,
including the basic rights of every American citizen. What follows are
briefs for *Gideon v. Wainright*, and *Betts v. Brady*. As a matter of
format, case briefs cited in the body of the text are typically located at
the ends of chapters. If not at the end of the chapter, the brief may
appear elsewhere in the chapter, such as following a section.[33] Otherwise, the reader is referred to the law books.

In the following chapter, U.S. law will be described in general,
including definitions of commonly used terms and phrases, with particular attention given to terms used in cases cited in this book. Also
presented will be the first of many examples of how the law has been
applied in given (aviation-related) situations. Where this chapter has
outlined the individual rights of citizens, the subsequent chapter will
expound upon common causes for litigation, the available defenses,
and protection against wrongs when citizens' rights are violated.

We now examine the U.S. Supreme Court decision of *Betts v.
Brady*. Here, as throughout the book, we summarize the decision. The
reader is advised to consult the original decision for the language used
by the court.

BETTS v. BRADY
316 U.S. 456 (1942)

Are the Bill of Rights guarantees obligatory upon the states?

The petitioner, Betts, was indicted for robbery in the Circuit Court
of Carroll County, Maryland. Due to lack of funds, he was unable to
employ counsel, and so informed the judge at his arraignment. He

---

[32] James A. Michener, *The Secret of America*, Parade Magazine 6 (Sep. 15, 1985).
[33] *See* the "Table of Cases" in the *Contents*.

requested that counsel be appointed to him. The judge advised him that this would not be done, as it was not the practice of Carroll County to appoint counsel for indigent defendants, save in prosecutions for murder and rape.

Without waiving his asserted right to counsel, Mr. Betts pleaded not guilty and elected to be tried without a jury. At his request witnesses were summoned in his behalf. He cross-examined the State's witnesses and examined his own. The latter gave testimony tending to establish an alibi. Although afforded the opportunity, he did not take the witness stand. The judge found him guilty and imposed a sentence of eight years.

While serving his sentence, Betts filed with a judge of the Circuit Court for Washington County, Maryland, a petition for a writ of *habeas corpus* alleging that he had been deprived of the right to assistance of counsel guaranteed by the due process clause of the Fourteenth Amendment of the Constitution. The writ issued, the cause was heard, his contention was rejected, and he was remanded to the custody of the prison warden.

Some months later, a petition for a writ of *habeas corpus* was presented to the Chief Judge of the Court of Appeals of Maryland, setting up the same grounds as the former petition for the prisoner's release. The respondent was answered, a hearing was afforded, at which an agreed statement of facts was offered by counsel for the parties, the evidence taken at Betts' trial was incorporated in the record, and the cause was argued. The appeals court granted the writ, but denied the relief for which Betts had asked. He was remanded to the prison's custody.

Betts applied to the U.S. Supreme Court for, and was granted *certiorari*. In its review of the case, the Supreme Court looked at the historical record, and found that the constitutions of the 13 original states, as they were at the time of the federal union, exhibit great diversity in respect of the right to have counsel in criminal cases. In light of common law practice at the time the nation was formed, it is evident that the constitutional provisions, to the effect that a defendant should be "allowed" counsel or should have a right "to be heard by himself and his counsel," or that he might be heard by "either or both," at his election, were intended to do away with rules which *denied* representation by counsel in criminal prosecutions, but were not aimed to *compel* the State to provide counsel for a defendant. Hence, upon adoption of the Bill of Rights, the matter of appointment of counsel for defendants was dealt with by statute rather than by constitutional provision.

The constitutions of all the states, save one at the time of Betts' trial, contained provisions with respect to the assistance of counsel in criminal trials. Only nine state constitutions embodied a guarantee textually the same as that of the Sixth Amendment. In the fundamental law of most states, the language indicated only that a defendant was not to be denied the privilege of representation by counsel of his choice. This demonstrated to the Court that in the majority of the states, it had been the considered judgment of those states that appointment of counsel was not a fundamental right, essential to a fair trial. On the contrary, the matter had generally been deemed one of legislative policy.

The Court stated that (due process) of the Fourteenth Amendment prohibits the conviction and incarceration of one whose trial is offensive to the common and fundamental ideas of fairness and right. While want of counsel in a particular case may result in a conviction lacking in such fundamental fairness, the Court would not conclude that the (Fourteenth) Amendment embodies an inexorable command that no trial for any offense could be fairly conducted and justice accorded a defendant who is not represented by counsel.

The judgment of the lower courts was affirmed.

GIDEON v. WAINWRIGHT
372 U.S. 335 (1963)

Are the Bill of Rights guarantees obligatory on the States?

Clarence Earl Gideon was charged in a Florida state court with having broken into and entered a poolroom. Appearing in court without funds and without a lawyer, Gideon's plea was that "The United States Constitution says I am entitled to be represented by Counsel." He asked the court to appoint counsel for him, whereupon the judge said,

> *Mr. Gideon, I am sorry, but I cannot appoint Counsel to represent you in this case. Under the laws of the State of Florida, the only time*

> *the Court can appoint Counsel to represent a*
> *Defendant is when that person is charged with*
> *a capital offense. I am sorry, but I will have to*
> *deny your request to appoint Counsel to defend*
> *you in this case.*

Put to trial before a jury, Gideon conducted his defense about as well as could be expected from a layman. He made an opening statement to the jury, cross-examined the State's witnesses, presented witnesses in his own defense, declined to testify himself, and made a short argument "emphasizing his innocence to the charge contained in the information filed in this case." The jury returned a verdict of guilty, and Gideon was sentenced to serve five years in the state prison. Later, Gideon filed in the Florida Supreme Court a *habeas corpus* petition attacking his conviction and sentence on the ground the trial court's refusal to appoint counsel for him denied him rights "guaranteed by the Constitution and the Bill of Rights by the United States Government." The State Supreme Court, without an opinion, denied all relief.

Since 1942, when *Betts v. Brady*,[34] was decided by a divided U.S. Supreme Court, the problem of a defendant's "federal" constitutional right to counsel in a "state" court had been a continuing source of controversy and litigation in both state and federal courts. To give this problem another review, the Supreme Court here granted *certiorari*. The Court appointed counsel to represent him and requested both sides discuss in their briefs and oral arguments the following: "Should this Court's holding in *Betts v. Brady*, be reconsidered?"

Abe Fortas argued the cause for Gideon, and Bruce R. Jacob, Assistant Attorney General of Florida, argued the State's cause. The Assistant Attorney General of Alabama argued the cause of the State of Alabama, as *amicus curiae*, urging affirmance. The American Civil Liberties Union, as *amici curiae*, argued for reversal. Also as *amici curiae*, 22 state governments filed a brief urging reversal.

The facts upon which Betts claimed he had been unconstitutionally denied the right to have counsel appointed to assist him were strikingly like the facts upon which Gideon based his federal constitutional claim. Betts was indicted for robbery in a Maryland state court. On arraignment, he told the trial judge of his lack of funds to

---

[34] 316 U.S. 455.

hire a lawyer and asked the court to appoint one for him. Betts was advised it was not the practice in that county to appoint counsel for indigent defendants, except in murder and rape cases. He then pleaded not guilty, had witnesses summoned, cross-examined the State's witnesses, examined his own, and chose not to testify himself. He was found guilty by the judge, sitting without a jury, and sentenced to eight years in prison.

Like Gideon, Betts had sought release by *habeas corpus*, alleging he had been denied the right to assistance of counsel in violation of the Fourteenth Amendment. Betts was denied any relief, and on review the Supreme Court affirmed. It was held that a refusal to appoint counsel for an indigent defendant charged with a felony did not necessarily violate the Due Process Clause of the Fourteenth Amendment, which for reasons given the Court deemed to be the only applicable federal constitutional provision. The Court said:

> *Asserted denial (of due process) is to be tested by an appraisal of the totality of facts in a given case. That which may, in one setting, constitute a denial of fundamental fairness, shocking to the universal sense of justice, may, in other circumstances, and in the light of other considerations, fall short of such denial.*

The Sixth Amendment provides, "In all criminal prosecutions, Counsel for his defense." Until this case, the Supreme Court had construed this to mean that in "federal" courts counsel must be provided for defendants unable to employ counsel unless that right is waived.

The Court in *Betts* had ample precedent for acknowledging that those guarantees of the Bill of Rights, which are fundamental safeguards of liberty immune from federal abridgment, are equally protected against state invasion by the Due Process Clause. This same principle was recognized, explained, and applied in *Powell v. Alabama*.[35] The latter was a case upholding the right of counsel, where the Court held that the Fourteenth Amendment "embraced" those "fundamental principles of liberty and justice which lie at the base of all our civil and political institutions," even though they had been specifically dealt with in another part of the federal Constitution.

---

[35] 287 U.S. 45 (1932).

In many cases other than *Powell* and *Betts*, the Supreme Court has looked to the fundamental nature of original Bill of Rights guarantees to decide whether the Fourteenth Amendment makes them obligatory on the States. Explicitly recognized to be of this "fundamental nature," and therefore made immune from state invasion by the Fourteenth, or some part of it, are the First Amendment's freedoms of speech, press, religion, assembly, association, and petition for redress of grievances. For the same reason, though not always in precisely the same terminology, the Court has made obligatory on the States the Fifth Amendment's command that private property shall not be taken for public use without just compensation, the Fourth Amendment's prohibition of unreasonable searches and seizures, and the Eighth's ban on cruel and unusual punishment.

In the instant case, the Supreme Court said it accepted the court's assumption in *Betts v. Brady*, that a provision of the Bill of Rights which is "fundamental and essential to a fair trial" is made obligatory upon the States by the Fourteenth Amendment. This Supreme Court determined the Court in *Betts* was wrong, however, in concluding that the Sixth Amendment's guarantee of counsel is not one of these fundamental rights.

The Court in *Betts v. Brady* departed from the sound wisdom upon which the Court's holding in *Powell v. Alabama* rested. Florida, supported by two other States, had asked that *Betts v. Brady* be left intact. Twenty-two States, as friends of the Court, argued Betts was "an anachronism" when handed down, and that it should be overruled. The Court agreed.

The judgment was reversed and the cause remanded to the Supreme Court of Florida for further action consistent with this opinion.

CHAPTER 4

UNITED STATES COMMON LAW

*Law in the United States has statutes and codes, yet it is grounded
in common law. It has both civil and criminal elements.
And, it can be understood by both its substantive
theories and by its mechanical procedures.*

FRAMEWORK

Among its "competing interests," common law in the United States
meets the utilitarian interests of the majority, yet it also protects the
rights of the individuals within the social contract. The law promotes
peace, yet it is itself violent. It has its statutes and codes, yet it is derived from common law. It has both civil and criminal components.
And, the law may be understood by either its substantive theories, or
by its mechanical procedures. [1]

Substantive law is concerned with the content or substance of the
law. Legal definitions and legal theories are examples of substantive
law. Procedural law, on the other hand, is about the legal process. As
Calvi and Coleman suggest, procedural law consists of the "rules of
the game."[2]

The "rules" are written according to whether the substantive law is
civil or criminal. Civil matters and criminal matters are separate fields

---

[1] *See generally* James V. Calvi and Susan Coleman, *American Law and Legal Systems* (3rd ed.
1997); *see also* Donald L. Carper, Norbert J. Mietus, T.E. Shoemaker and Bill W. West, *Understanding The Law* (2nd ed. 1995); *see also* Readers Digest, *You and the Law* (Henry V. Poor,
advisory ed. 1971).
[2] James V. Calvi and Susan Coleman, *American Law and Legal Systems* 73 (3rd ed. 1997).

of law, yet together they are essential components of the U.S. common law system. Table 4.1, "Common Law System," illustrates the bifurcation of the law, delineates the areas of criminal law according to seriousness (and associated penalties), and subcategorizes civil law into its various areas around which attorneys tend to specialize.

One way of describing civil law is to define what it is not, which is criminal law. Criminal law proscribes specific rules which society has forbidden under threat of sanction. It involves the state's effort to prescribe individual conduct. In court, it manifests itself in an action brought by the state against a person (human or corporate). Civil law, on the other hand, focuses on relations and disputes between persons.[3] A civil action is brought to enforce, redress, or protect private rights. Conversely, it is the function of legislatures to decide what behavior will be made criminal and what penalties will be attached to violations of the law. In civil controversies, it is for individuals to work out their differences, albeit within a structured system of courts, case law, or by alternative forms of dispute resolution, and sometimes under the substantive commands of the legislature. For example, many states have promulgated the *Uniform Commercial Code*, governing traditionally common law aspects of contracts.

This chapter is focused on the domestic legal system. Note that "civil law" has quite a different meaning outside the United States. Civil law refers to the law prevailing in continental Europe and Latin America (and in Louisiana), based on legislatively codified Roman or French (Napoleonic Code) law. In contrast, the common law refers to Anglo-American court-made jurisprudence. Hence, the domestic criminal/civil law dichotomy in domestic U.S. law is quite different from, and should not be confused with, the common/civil law dichotomy that exists internationally.

There is a division within international law as well. Public international law refers to the law of nations, as expressed in international conventions, treaties, agreements, decisions of international tribunals, or customary law. Private international law refers to the law surrounding the rights and remedies of persons (individual and corporate) in commercial transactions, and in areas such as personal injury.

---

[3] The term *persons* includes natural persons, humans, and artificial persons, such as government bodies and different types of business entities, including corporations. Donald L. Carper, Norbert J. Mietus, T.E. Shoemaker and Bill W. West, *Understanding The Law* (2nd ed. 1995).

Table 4.1—COMMON LAW SYSTEM

Branches:	*Criminal*	*Civil*
Areas:	Felony Misdemeanor Infraction	Contract Real Property Probate Intellectual Property Corporate Family Creditors Rights Tort Administrative
Proof:	Beyond a Reasonable Doubt	Preponderance of the Evidence
Parties:	Public Grievance (State versus Individual)	Private Dispute (Individual versus Individual)
Sources of Law:	Constitution and Statutes	Judicial Precedent and Statutes
Purposes:	Punishment, Retribution	Restitution
Consequences:	Liberty at Issue	Money/Damages at Issue
Purpose:	Maintain Order	Resolve Disputes

CRIMINAL LAW

Criminal law is statutory. It is positive, written into penal codes. A crime is an act, or an omission, which has been defined and made punishable by law. Criminal behavior can be *malum in se*, "wrong in itself," or *malum prohibitum*, "prohibited by the state." Crimes that are *malum in se* have two characteristics: they involve highly moral overtones, and there is nearly universal consensus that the behavior is wrong. Murder and rape, for example, are types of behavior that are universally considered immoral.

Behavior that is *mallum prohibitum* is "criminal," merely because a legislative body has deemed it undesirable. Examples might be public safety and traffic control. But it might also include gambling or prostitution, both of which are forms of behavior, that some communities have embraced, while other communities have found offensive.[4]

In either case, *malum in se* or *malum prohibitum*, the purpose of substantive criminal law is to prevent harm to society. It declares what conduct is criminal, and it prescribes the punishment to be imposed for such conduct.

Criminal law is classified according to its severity and the penalties attached to it:

- A *felony* is a crime so serious it may be punishable by death or by imprisonment in a state or federal penitentiary. It is a crime referred to by the Constitution as "capital" or "infamous." Imprisonment is usually for more than one year.
- *Misdemeanors* are serious, but of less severity than felonies. They, accordingly, have associated with their commission less severe penalties. They are, nevertheless, still considered crime in its truest sense—a violation of statutory law punishable by fine and/or incarceration. The incarceration, typically in the county jail, is normally for a term less than one year.
- A *violation*, or in some states what may also be known as an *infraction*, is an offense, but is one normally considered something less than a crime. Although it involves violation of a stat-

---

[4] James V. Calvi and Susan Coleman, *American Law and Legal Systems* 161-162 (3rd ed. 1997).

ute, usually associated with it is a comparatively weaker ("civil") penalty—a fine for a traffic ticket for instance.

A *criminal action* is a determination of whether a defendant is guilty of an act committed against society and in violation of a penal statute. In finding a person guilty of a crime, there are common elements necessary in proving all crimes. These elements include *actus reus*, *mens rea*, *causation*, and *standard of proof.*

- *Actus reus* is a connection between an action and a crime. The person must have done a "guilty act."
- The second element, *mens rea*, has to do with the person's state of mind. To be guilty, the accused must have wrongful purpose in mind, a criminal intent, or a "guilty mind." Terms such as knowingly, willfully, intentionally, and purposely are used in demonstrating *mens rea*.
- The third element of a crime is *causation*. The "but for" test is used to determine causation. To be found guilty, the accused must have "caused" the act. Causation infers that "but for" the actions of the accused, the victim would not have been harmed.
- Finally, the *standard of proof* in a criminal action is "beyond reasonable doubt." Conversely, in a civil trial the standard is the "preponderance of the evidence."[5]

CIVIL LAW

Where criminal law is a violation against *society*, civil law involves injury to a *person*. Civil law is a broad category, including, for example, the law of property, contracts and torts. Torts involve the violation of an individual's right to freedom from bodily injury, property damage, injury to reputation, and/or a taking of individual rights without just cause. To constitute a tort, it must be clearly established that actual damage and/or injury did in fact occur. An act, even though malicious, which causes no damage, is insufficient cause for legal action. Furthermore, the accused must be directly or indirectly responsible for the damages caused either intentionally or by way of the person's neg-

---

[5] *Id.* at 163-168.

ligence. If the damages were unintentional, but nevertheless caused through accidental interference then the person at fault may have been "negligent," which is:

> . . . *the omission to do something which a reasonable man, guided by those ordinary considerations which ordinarily regulate human affairs, would do, or the doing of something which a reasonable and prudent man would not do.*[6]

It is conduct (or departure from the conduct expectable of a reasonably prudent person under like circumstances), which falls below the standard established by law for the protection of others.

The key element in negligence is the connection between the act and the injury resulting from it. Causation has two elements: *cause-in-fact*, and *proximate cause*. "Cause-in-fact" is the cause without which, the injury would not have occurred. "Proximate cause" (or, as it is sometimes called, "legal cause") is the foreseeable event to which an injury or loss can be attributed. As one court put it, "Proximate or legal causation is that combination of 'logic, common sense, justice, policy and precedent' that fixes a point in the chain of events, some foreseeable and some unforeseeable, beyond which the law will bar recovery."[7] A key element of proximate causation is "foreseeability"—whether defendant reasonably should have foreseen that his conduct might cause harm to plaintiff.[8]

Thus far, civil and criminal law have been described as separate and distinct categories of law which may be transgressed. It is possible, however, for a person to be guilty of trespassing the bounds of both civil and criminal law simultaneously. For example, a pilot may violate an FAR, thus violating a statutory code. While, or as a result of doing so, the pilot may injure a passenger, another pilot, or an innocent bystander, thereby causing a tort violation as well.

---

[6] *See Black's Law Dictionary* (abridged 5th ed. 1983).
[7] *People Express Airlines, Inc. v. Consolidated Rail Corp.*, 495 A.2d 107 (N.J. 1985).
[8] The seminal case is *Palsgraf v. Long Island R.R.*, 162 N.E. 99 (1928).

PROTECTION AGAINST WRONGS

Enumerated in the U.S. Constitution are basic civil rights. In this section those rights are reviewed in the context of practical application; that is to say, what are the available defenses against wrongs? Outlined below are the common causes for litigation when there has been some form of interference with personal rights.

- *Freedom of movement*—a person has the right to unrestricted freedom of movement. If a person has been illegally restrained, that person may file charges for *false arrest* or for *false imprisonment*.
- *Misuse of legal process*—on occasion public officials abuse their powers of office, willfully using them against individuals. A person has the right to be free from deliberate misuse of law and of the courts. Such violations give rise to charges of *malicious prosecution*.
- *Interference with person*—individuals have the right to be free from bodily injury, and not to be threatened. Charges of assault and battery may result; *assault* occurs where one, without consent, intentionally places another in apprehension of immediate physical harm, and *battery* if there has been unconsensual contact with another's person.
- *Peace of mind*—people have the right to freedom from unnecessary mental suffering. Malicious acts, which cause mental strain, are called *emotional anguish*.
- *Privacy*—individuals have the right to non-interference with their individual privacy. A person has the right to be left alone. There are several ways with which a person's privacy could have been tampered; for example, *illegal search* or *wiretapping*.
- *Interference with reputation*—the individual is expected to have freedom from unwarranted (and untruthful) attacks on his or her character. *Defamation* of character if written or printed is *libel*; if maliciously uttered it is *slander*.
- *Property rights*—a person has the right to unrestricted enjoyment and use of both real and personal property. If that right

117

has been violated, the person has been deprived of *quiet enjoyment*. If there has been undue annoyance, inconvenience, discomfort, or injury, which has caused the loss of quiet enjoyment, then there is *nuisance*. If there has been an unauthorized access onto land or into a building, then *trespass* has been committed. A person also has the right to unrestricted, uninterrupted enjoyment of one's personal property. If there has been interference with the right to personal property, the person doing it is said to be "converting" the property to his or her own (but unauthorized) use; the person is guilty of *conversion*. Contractual and business relationships are forms of property. If there has been an interference with contractual relationships, then there may have been *breach of contract*, or perhaps *breach of warranty*. Other interference with contractual relationships might involve *fraud*, *deceit* and/or *misrepresentation*. A person has the right to freedom from cheating and trickery.

COMMON TERMINOLOGY

In keeping with the theme of this chapter, to present a practical overview of U.S. law, this section is devoted to a glossary of commonly used terminology. It is by no means an exhaustive legal dictionary, but it does present for ready reference words and phrases used in this book, and terms which are considered pertinent to the case readings which subsequently follow. Additional terms, with their definitions, have been used in the body of the text.

- *Amicus curiae* is a Latin expression meaning "friend of the court." It is a bystander (usually an attorney) who volunteers information or states some matter of law for the assistance of the court. It may also be a person who is permitted to introduce evidence, or arguments, to protect his or her interests even though the person has no legal standing in the current case.
- *Appellant* is one who appeals the decision of a lower court to a higher court for review.
- *Appellee* is the other party in a litigation against whom an appeal is taken (also called the "respondent").

118

- *Affirm* is to confirm, ratify, or approve a judgment of a lower court.
- *Bailment* is the delivery of property by one (the *bailor*) to another (the *bailee*) in trust (or contract), and once the contract is fulfilled the property will be returned.
- *Caveat emptor* is a Latin phrase meaning, "let the buyer beware." According to this maxim a purchaser must examine, judge, and test before buying—and ultimately must be held responsible for his or her actions. It is a principle that has been generally outmoded by strict liability, warranty, and other consumer protection laws, which favor the consumer-buyer.
- *Condemnation* is the act of judicially converting private property to public use under *eminent domain*. Property is taken without consent of the owner, but with just compensation. *Inverse condemnation* occurs when a public entity takes or damages property without going through the legal procedure of condemnation, and does so without compensation to the owner. Conversely, *adverse possession* is a method of (private) acquisition of title to real property by possession for a statutory period under certain conditions.
- *Contract* is a legally enforceable agreement upon sufficient consideration. There is a subject or object over which there is an offer and acceptance agreed upon for some consideration (recompense). The essential elements of a contract are (1) competent parties, (2) the subject or object, (3) legal consideration, (4) mutuality of agreement (or assent), and (5) mutuality of obligation (i.e., both parties are bound by the terms).
- *Cross-claim* is a claim brought by a defendant in an action against the plaintiff.
- *Declaratory judgment* is one which declares the status, rights or duties of the parties involved but does not order any action to be taken.
- *Defendant* is the defender, the one against whom a claim or charge is brought. It is the one who denies a claim in a court action.
- *Demurrer* means that even if the facts stated by the other party are true, they do not constitute an enforceable claim.

- *De novo* means anew, afresh, a second time. In a *de novo* trial, the matter is tried anew; the same as if it had not been heard before and as if no decision had been previously rendered.
- *Deposition* is the testimony of a witness, conducted under oath outside of the courtroom.
- *Discovery* is the disclosure of facts, documents and evidence to the opposing party upon request.
- *Easement* is a liberty, privilege, or advantage that entitles its holder to some limited use or enjoyment in the land of another. The limited use might be the right to cross the land. An *avigation easement* provides the right to cross through or otherwise use the airspace overlying the property of another.
- *Eminent domain* is the inherent power of a sovereign government to take private property for public use.
- *Estoppel* is a condition that stops or prohibits action because of contradiction.
- *Freedom of Information Act* of 1966 provides entitlement to information from government files. Opposing it is the *Privacy Act* of 1980, which restricts acquisition of certain information.
- *Habeas corpus* in Latin means, "you have the body." In law it is the name given to a variety of writs, having for their objective to bring a party before a court or judge. When employed alone in common usage, and as the term has been used in this text, it is understood to mean *habeas corpus ad subjiciendum*, which is a writ directed to the person detaining another, and commanding that person to produce the "body" of the prisoner, or person detained.
- *Injunction* is a court order to stop.
- *Insurance* is a contract (policy) wherein payment of a premium (fee) is given in exchange for insurance (reimbursement) against loss incurred (at risk).
- *Insurance waiver* gives up the right to reimbursement under certain circumstances such as flying an airplane. An (aviation) *rider* may reinstate the coverage to include the category of activity otherwise excluded.
- *Interrogatories* are a series of questions.

- *Jurisdiction* is the power, authority, capacity, or right-to-act of a court within a given legal or geographic area.
- *Liability* is all manner of responsibilities, obligations, debts and assumptions of risk.
- *Litigation* is a legal contest, a lawsuit, or a contest by judicial process.
- *Negligence* is the omission of doing what a reasonable person would do, the failure to exercise "ordinary care," or to be "careless."
- *Plaintiff* is the one who begins a legal action. It may be the person who begins a personal action to recover damages for injury to his or her rights; i.e., the complaining party in a lawsuit. It may also be a defendant who is appealing the adverse decision of a lower court; that is to say, litigant roles may be reversed in an appeal.
- *Police power* is a governmental power to make and enforce reasonable laws and regulations in the interest of the general health, safety, welfare and morals of its citizens.
- *Preemption* is to usurp higher authority.
- *Proximate* is a complex term, perhaps best summarized in the phrase "legal cause"; it includes foreseeable harm to one to whom a duty is owed; it has also been described as the direct, immediate cause, without which an incident would not have happened. This latter concept is also a part of "but-for" causation.
- *Receiver* (or *trustee*) is appointed by the court to take into custody, management or control the property of another.
- *Remand* is to send back to the lower court.
- *Res ipsa loquitur* is a Latin term denoting that negligence is obvious. Literally it means, "the thing speaks for itself." Whenever the conditions surrounding an event are so extraordinary, it is presumed someone must be at fault; i.e., an accident in question could not have happened without negligence.
- *Reverse* is to annul, revoke, or to make void a legal decision. A higher court may "reverse" the decision of a lower court.
- *Trial* is the formal examination of the facts and evidence by a court of law. It is a judicial examination of the issues between

parties to a civil or criminal action in accordance with the law of the land.

- *Tort* is a civil wrong resulting in personal injury or property damage. It is separate, for example, from *contract* law, wherein there is breach of written or implied agreement. The three elements of every tort action are: (1) an *duty* to protect others against unreasonable risks; (2) a *failure to conform* to a reasonable standard; and (3) the conduct of the person supposedly at fault is so closely related to the incident as to have caused it—to have been the "but-for" and proximate *cause* resulting in *damages.*

- *Underwrite* is to assume risk by way of insurance.

- *Venue* is the place where injury happened, crime was committed, or where the accused is brought to trial.

- *Writ of certiorari* is an order in writing from a superior to an inferior court, directing the proceedings of a specified case be sent up for review. The U.S. Supreme Court customarily uses a *writ of certiorari* when it decides to review the decision of a lower court.

- *Writ of mandamus* literally interpreted means "we command." It is an order by the court to public officials, or to an inferior court, directing them to do or not to do something within the scope of their duties.

- *Zoning* partitions a local governmental jurisdiction by ordinance into authorized land use districts. It may also include regulations as to the structure and design of buildings within designated areas.

THE LEGAL SYSTEM

The sources of the law are found in constitutions, treaties, statutes, precedent, regulations, and court decisions. The legal system in the United States is commensurate with the rules of the game as defined by the U.S. Constitution. As with all social contracts, it is a system of *rights* and *duties.*

The U.S. common law system has as a framework the federal government alongside the governments of the different states. There are overlapping governmental systems, each with authority in some areas but not in others. There is the national system on one side, and the state and local governments on the other. Each system is comprised of executive, legislative, and judicial elements. Although similar in hierarchy, each of the judicial components (state versus federal) has its own individual structure.

Speaking of the balance of power among the executive, legislative and judicial branches, Alexander Hamilton said:

> *The executive not only dispenses the honors, but also holds the sword of the community. The legislative not only commands the purse, but also prescribes the rules by which the duties and rights of every citizen are to be regulated. The judiciary, on the contrary, has no influence of either the sword or the purse and can take no active resolution whatever. It may truly be said to have neither force nor will, but merely judgement. . . . The judiciary is beyond comparison the weakest of the three departments of power.*[9]

But, make no mistake. Irrespective of Hamilton's wisdom, the courts are pervasive, and they *do* have power.

FEDERAL COURTS

Recall from Chapter 3 that the Constitution provides in Article III for a Supreme Court, and that Article I empowers the legislative branch with the responsibility, "to constitute tribunals inferior to the Supreme Court." In other words, Congress may create additional courts, inferior to the Supreme Court, as it deems necessary. In practice, other courts have been formed as a result of overload upon the first and foremost Supreme Court.

---

[9] In the *Federalist* (a stream of articles, written between Oct. 1787 and Apr. 1788, by Alexander Hamilton, James Madison, and John Jay).

In the federal judicial system there is at least one *United States District Court* in each of the states, with more in heavily populated states. For example, there are two in California; a Northern U.S. District Court located in San Francisco, and a Southern U.S. District Court in Los Angeles.

Commonly referred to as "courts of original jurisdiction," the district courts have *general jurisdiction*, meaning they have the power to hear both civil and criminal cases. They are "original" in that trials start there. They are the *trial courts*.

In civil cases there are two restrictions on persons suing in the U.S. District Courts: (1) the plaintiff and defendant must be residents of different states, and (2) the amount of the lawsuit must be at least equal to an amount specified by law. There are also certain cases that belong exclusively in the U.S. District Courts, either because of constitutional reasons or because Congress has so dictated.

Alongside, and equal in stature with the U.S. District Courts, there are the courts of *limited jurisdiction*. They include: the *United States Court of Claims*, for lawsuits against the U.S.; the *United States Customs Court*, for tariff cases; the *U.S. Bankruptcy Court* to address debt reorganization and liquidation; and the *United States Tax Court*, handling cases under the Internal Revenue Code.

One of the attributes fundamentally inhering in a sovereign is that the sovereign cannot err (i.e., "the king can do no wrong"). Hence, an ancient principle of law states that a sovereign cannot be sued unless the sovereign consents to suit. Hence, absent consent, neither the federal government, nor the states, can be subject to suit by individuals.[10] In 1855, Congress created the Court of Claims to allow the U.S. government to be sued for damages under certain conditions. Said the Supreme Court in 1907, "Public policy forbids that the sovereign be sued without its consent, but that consent was given in some (but not all) cases by the creation of the Court of Claims."

Situated above the U.S. District Courts and the special courts are the *United States Courts of Appeal* (often called "circuit courts"), one in each of eleven United States circuits and one in the District of Columbia. The U.S. Courts of Appeal are concerned only with appeals,

---

[10] The sovereignty of states from suit was confirmed by the 11th Amendment to the Constitution.

or pleas for the reversal of decisions by lower courts or of federal administrative agencies.

The U.S. Court of Appeal was created in 1890, specifically to relieve the burden of the Supreme Court. Judges were at one time sent out on regular tours around an assigned territory, or district. Hence, they became known as "circuit court riders." Today, the circuit court judges sit within their defined districts. In 1909 Congress created the *United States Court of Customs Appeal* to review lower court decisions arising out of import duties.

The *United States Court of Military Appeals* is the court of last resort for appeals from court martial convictions (under the *Uniform Code of Military Justice*). The military appeals courts were formed through two delegated powers of Congress: (1) its power to create inferior courts, and (2) its power defined by Section 8, Article I, "to make rules for the government and regulation of the land and naval forces."

The highest court in the land, of course, is the *United States Supreme Court*, which entertains appeals from the federal appellate courts, sometimes directly from a U.S. District Court, and from the highest state courts on issues of interpretation of the U.S. Constitution. Review of lower court decisions is requested by filing a *writ of certiorari*. The Supreme Court then decides whether or not the legal questions of the case justify review by the Supreme Court.

STATE COURTS

The organization of state courts varies, but the general pattern of the various state judicial systems is similar to that of the federal judiciary. At the lowest level are the courts of limited jurisdiction, including *Small Claims Court*. Sometimes called the "people's court," "conciliation court," or "magistrate's court," small claims courts offer citizens the chance to resolve minor disputes without the need for lawyers. The maximum amount of damages recoverable ranges from $250 to $10,000, depending on the state. The most common maximum range is $1,500 to $2,500.[11]

---

[11] Donald L. Carper, Norbert J. Mietus, T.E. Shoemaker and Bill W. West, *Understanding the Law* 104 (2nd ed. 1995).

In most small claims courts, anyone with a grievance can bring suit for a nominal filing fee. However, one should file suit only after having exhausted other avenues for redress; for example, writing directly to the person or company involved in the complaint, or discussing the matter with an arbitrator. Other courts of limited jurisdiction include: *Traffic Court*, *Police Court*, and *Justice of the Peace*. Cases heard in these local courts frequently cannot be appealed.

States may also have within their system, special purpose courts along with the other local courts of limited jurisdiction. In some instances these special courts might also be "trial" courts. Examples of the special state courts are *Probate Court*, for settling wills and claims against estates; *Juvenile* or *Family Courts*, to settle domestic issues; and *Criminal Court* for trying criminal cases.

Above the special purpose local courts are the state courts of general jurisdiction—the trial courts. The courts of general jurisdiction handle both criminal as well as civil cases (which exceed a specified monetary amount). These state trial courts, usually known as *Superior Court*, have the responsibility of finding the facts of the case.

As in the federal system, the *state appellate courts* entertain only appeals from lower courts. Depending upon the size of a state, there may be more than one level of appellate courts. Since the trial courts find the facts in a particular case, the appellate court does not review the trial court's findings of fact, but rather decides whether the trial judge correctly applied the law.

The *State Supreme Court* hears appeals from all lower courts. It is the court of last resort, except for cases appealed on Constitutional grounds.

CIVIL PROCEDURE

The rules of procedure are similar for both the federal and state courts, as are the procedures for both civil and criminal trials. The discussion of the rules of procedure will begin with the process in the civil courts. Following that description, the principle differences between the civil and criminal procedures are reviewed. There are different types of civil actions, but by way of demonstration, a tort (or negligence) case is presented here as typical.[12]

Before any trial begins, be it civil or criminal, often there is an attempt to resolve the dispute outside of court through mediation, arbitration, or some other form of Alternative Dispute Resolution [ADR]. In some states, ADR is a mandatory part of the process that must be attempted in good faith before trial. As Justice Sandra Day O'Connor has stated,

> *The courts of this country should not be the places where the resolution of disputes begins. They should be the places where the disputes end—after alternative methods of resolving disputes have been considered and tried.[13]*

Following Abraham Lincoln's advice to law students,

> *Discourage litigation. Persuade your neighbors to compromise whenever you can. Point out to them how the nominal winner is often a real loser—in fees, expenses and waste of time.[14]*

Assuming ADR is unsuccessful, the trial procedure begins. Outlined below is the entire process in brief, from the *pretrial procedure* at the beginning, to the final *appeal* at the end.

PRETRIAL PROCESS

- Counsel for the plaintiff files a *complaint* with the court. In the complaint, the plaintiff describes the injury received, alleges negligence and liability by the defendant, and states the

---

[12] *See* James V. Calvi and Susan Coleman, *American Law and Legal Systems* 74-87 (3rd ed. 1997).

[13] Janice Roehl and Larry Ray, *Toward the Multi-Door Courthouse—Dispute Resolution Intake and Referral*, NIJ Reports 2-7 (Jul. 1987); *see also* James V. Calvi and Susan Coleman, *American Law and Legal Systems* 103 (3rd ed. 1997).

[14] Edward J. Kemp, *Abraham Lincoln's Philosophy of Common Sense* Vol. I 346 (1965); *see also* James V. Calvi and Susan Coleman, *American Law and Legal Systems* 102 (3rd ed. 1997).

remedy sought. The plaintiff may seek *general damages* to compensate for actual losses. The plaintiff may also seek *punitive damages*, to punish the defendant for the wrongdoing.

- After the complaint is filed, the defendant is formally *served* (i.e., notified that a legal action has been brought against him or her).

- Along with a copy of the complaint, the court issues a *summons* directing the defendant to submit an *answer* to the allegations made in the claim.

- Should the defendant fail to answer the summons, a default judgment is issued. Failure to respond is tantamount to an admission of guilt.

- Assuming the defendant does respond, the *discovery* process begins. During discovery, both sides obtain facts and information about the case from the other party in order to assist in preparation for trial. Discovery generally refers to disclosure by the defendant and/or plaintiff of facts, deeds, documents, or other things which are in the other party's exclusive knowledge or possession and which are necessary to the party seeking discovery. The tools of discovery include: depositions, written interrogatories, production of documents or things, permission to enter upon land or other property, physical and mental examinations, and requests for admission to files and otherwise confidential holdings.

- After discovery, either party may ask for *summary judgment* on a claim, counterclaim, or cross-claim, where there is no genuine issue of material fact, and where either party believes they are entitled to prevail as a matter of law.

THE TRIAL

- In the actual resolution of the conflict, the trial, the first order of business is to decide who will be the trier of fact. The parties may choose to have a *bench trial*, where the judge becomes the trier of fact. Or, they may choose a trial by *jury*, in which case prospective jurors (*venire*, or *venireman* in the singular) may be dismissed, with the final selection of jurors leading to an impaneled jury.

- After the jury is impaneled, each lawyer makes an *opening statement* to the jury, outlining the case, as it will be presented.

- The plaintiff's lawyer then begins by calling *witnesses*. The respective lawyers first subject the witnesses to direct examination (by the plaintiff's attorney), cross-examination (by the defendant's attorney), then redirect and re-cross-examine as necessary. During the oral examination of witnesses, the lawyers will submit physical *evidence* to substantiate their case.

- The process is then reversed with the defendant's attorney calling witnesses and submitting evidence.

- Following submission of all the oral and physical evidence, the two lawyers, beginning with the plaintiff's lawyer, address the jury for the final time with their closing statements, each summarizing their arguments.

PLEADINGS AND JURY DELIBERATION

- Once the evidentiary part of the trial is complete, either side may request a *directed verdict*. Where the party with the burden of proof has failed to present a *pima facie* case for jury consideration, the trial judge may order a verdict without allowing the jury to consider it. A *prima facie* case means there is sufficient evidence to render a reasonable conclusion in favor of the allegation asserted. Without *prima facie* evidence, as a matter of law, there can be only one verdict. Thus, the judge may direct the jury to find the only available verdict.

- Assuming formal pleadings have ceased, the judge *charges* the jury. In the judge's charge to the jury, the judge explains the applicable law, and describes what the jury must decide if they are to rule in favor of either party.

- After the jury has been charged, the case is formally submitted to them for deliberation.

- After the jury reaches a verdict, the foreman of the jury informs the bailiff, who in turn notifies the judge. Court is reconvened and the jury's verdict is formally read. This ends the trial stage. However, the person who loses has the right to ask the judge for a *judgment notwithstanding the verdict,* and to appeal to a higher court for review.

THE APPELLATE PROCESS

- Reasons for an appeal may vary, but they are usually of two categories: (1) the judge made an error regarding a question of law, or (2) there is a dispute over the amount of damages awarded.
- The first step in the appeal is for the appellant to file a *notice of appeal.* The appellant must *serve* (i.e., send) the appellee a copy of the statement of the issues to be appealed and a copy of the trial court's transcript.
- Counsel for both the appellant and the appellee must then file written briefs to the court. The *appellate brief* contains a summary of the facts of the case and presents written arguments on why the trial court acted correctly or incorrectly.
- The lawyers are then invited to present their *oral arguments* to the appellate court.
- The appellate court deliberates and then issues its decision. The minority of justices may wish to render a *dissenting opinion* as a matter of record, but the majority opinion is the final ruling.
- Not being satisfied with the appellate outcome, either party may then appeal to the state Supreme Court, or to the U.S. Supreme Court, as appropriate. Access to the Supreme Court is limited, and for most litigants the decision of the court of appeals stands. There are three ways in which a case may reach the Supreme Court: (1) as a matter of constitutional right, (2) where the Supreme Court itself decides it wishes to review a case, and (3) where the lower court seeks clarification on a question of law.

CRIMINAL PROCEDURE

The criminal process is similar to civil procedure, but with certain differences as noted in the following narrative.[15] In a civil trial the defendant may be found *responsible* (or *liable*). Conversely, in a criminal trial the defendant is either found *guilty* or *not guilty*. Note that there is no finding of *innocent*. In a criminal proceeding the person who is *factually guilty*—that is, one who really committed the crime—must be found *legally guilty* as well. Finding the person not guilty is not the same as finding the person innocent.

Whereas in a civil trial the weight of the evidence is sufficient to find the defendant liable, in a criminal trial the burden of proof weighs heavily on the state to demonstrate that the accused is guilty beyond a reasonable doubt. "Beyond a reasonable doubt" essentially means that all possible alternative explanations for what happened have been considered and rejected except one—the one concluding that the accused committed the crime.

PRETRIAL PROCEDURES

The criminal process begins with *arrest* of the defendant. The accused is taken into custody and brought before a magistrate for an *initial appearance*. The magistrate informs the accused of his or her right to a *preliminary hearing* and sets *bond*. Bond money is left, as security to ensure the accused does not flee. The accused may then be released on his or her own recognizance. Or, if no bond is set, or bond cannot otherwise be met, the accused may remain in jail awaiting trial.

The next step is the preliminary hearing to determine if there is *probable cause* to believe a crime has been committed, and whether there exists sufficient evidence to show that the accused committed the crime. Assuming the judge decides that sufficient probable cause exists, the accused is *bound over*, meaning the case is either turned over to a *grand jury*, or to a *prosecuting attorney*, to determine if the accused should be tried. A formal accusation by the grand jury or prosecutor is called an *indictment*. Following the indictment, the accused is

---

[15] James V. Calvi and Susan Coleman, *American Law and Legal Systems* 87-92 (3rd ed. 1997).

brought before a judge for *arraignment*, formally notifying the accused of the charges. The accused is then asked to enter a *plea* of guilty or not guilty. The accused may attempt a *plea bargain* at this point, pleading guilty in exchange for a lesser charge. Another option might be for the accused to plead *nolo contendre* (no contest), which is tantamount to a guilty plea, but a denial of any wrongdoing.

CRIMINAL TRIALS AND APPEALS

Whereas the outcome of a civil trial is merely an exchange of material things, a person's liberty, and sometimes one's life, is at risk in a criminal trial. Therefore, the burden of proof weighs heavy on the side of the accuser. The determination of legal guilt must be done with strict adherence to the rules of criminal procedure. The discovery process, for example, is very different in a criminal procedure, since the accused does not have to prove innocence. The state may be barred from discovery of evidence in the hands of the accused. Protected against *self-incrimination* by the Fifth Amendment, the accused cannot be forced to give a deposition, or to answer any interrogatories—nor can the accused be made to testify in court.

Another major difference between the civil and criminal procedures takes place in the trial phase. Once a jury is impaneled, the defendant is said to be in *jeopardy*. The Fifth Amendment protects the accused from being placed twice "in jeopardy of life and limb" (*double jeopardy*). If found guilty, the defendant may appeal the conviction based on errors made during the trial. However, once acquitted, the state cannot appeal the case, other than to seek clarification of a point of law for future reference.

ADMINISTRATIVE AGENCIES

Administrative law is derived from the rules, regulations, and procedures of governmental administrative agencies. The regulations of these agencies sometimes have the force and effect of law, and decisions are often rendered by these agencies in a way parallel to that of the courts. Examples of agencies, which embody administrative law at the federal level, are the Federal Aviation Administration and the National Transportation Safety Board. At the state level there are the State Aviation Commissions, or their counterparts.

For the courts to intervene in the affairs of government, evidence must convincingly show the actions taken by the government and its officials were either *arbitrary, capricious, an abuse of discretion,* or otherwise not in accordance with the law. Furthermore, before the courts may be expected to issue a *writ of mandamus* compelling administrative action, the injured party must have first exhausted all available remedies by appealing to and through the prescribed governmental process. If administrative law is to be tested in court, one or more of the following elements must be present, or the courts may refuse to hear the case on appeal:

- The actions taken by the government do not achieve the public purpose for which designed;
- What the government has done is vague and/or discriminatory;
- It is beyond the powers of the agency to do what it has done;
- The penalties imposed were administered without adequate notice;
- The agency has failed to provide due process; and/or
- Recognized legal rights have been violated.

COUNSEL

Addressed thus far in this chapter are the defenses normally employed at trial, and the structural foundation of the court system. Yet to be discussed are the people who provide the procedural expertise in the practice of law—the lawyers.[16]

A lawyer is chosen as one would choose a doctor, dentist, accountant or anyone who provides professional services. The first and obvious step, however, is to define the nature of the legal problem. One may start with a *general practitioner.* General practice lawyers handle a wide variety of legal problems. When problems are beyond their competence, they will refer clients to a *specialist* who has concentrated

---

[16] Information excerpted from, *How to Choose and Use a Lawyer,* published by the American Bar Association as a public service and distributed in cooperation with the U.S. Office of Consumer Affairs and the Consumer Information Center of the General Services Administration.

his or her practice in such areas as: litigation, criminal law, taxation, worker's compensation, labor relations, real property, probate and trust law, patents, and so forth (see Table 4.1, "Common Law System"). Obviously, the nature of the legal problem will help to define the type of lawyer needed.

Once the problem is defined, there are a number of ways to find a lawyer. Most people begin by asking for a referral from a personal acquaintance. Other common referral sources are employers, law school professors, administrators, consumer groups, and public interest organizations.

One can also find some answers in the public library in the *Martindale-Hubbell Law Directory*, which for more than one hundred years has published as complete a roster as possible of the members of the bar in the United States and Canada. The directory gives brief biographical sketches of many lawyers and describes the legal areas in which law firms practice.

In choosing a lawyer, the things to keep in mind are competence as well as accessibility and price. One way to judge competence is by the amount of time the lawyer has devoted to keeping up with changes in the law through continuing legal education. As to price, some lawyers make only a small charge, if any, for the first consultation. Thereafter, there are four principle methods for compensating a lawyer: (1) retainer, (2) contingent fee, (3) specific job, and (4) hourly rate.

When a lawyer is retained, a down payment is usually made toward the fee for specified legal services. In return for the retainer the attorney works for the client on an array of matters. Additional costs are added to the final bill for services involving extra time and effort.

Another fee arrangement used in certain non-criminal types of cases, especially in personal injury cases, is called a *contingent fee*. Such a fee is "contingent" upon the lawyer obtaining monetary recovery for the client. If no recovery is made, compensation may not be required. If an award is made, the fee will be a percentage of the recovery (commonly 30% to 40%). Court costs and out-of-pocket expenses are normally the responsibility of the client. Costs and expenses of litigation may be taken from the amount awarded or settled upon.

One of the most common methods employed by lawyers for charging fees is according to a prescribed fixed fee for the specific job (such as divorce proceedings, processing wills, purchase or sale of property, title examination, etc.). These are cases where the attorney can tell in advance approximately what the charges will be.

Sometimes the lawyer will base his or her charges on a fixed dollar amount for each hour spent on the client's behalf. The hourly rate may vary considerably from lawyer to lawyer.

PRECEDENT

Precedent is what common law is all about. It is the underlying principle of case law and of the American judicial system. A precedent is something said or done that may serve as an example or rule to authorize or justify a subsequent act of the same or analogous kind. It is synonymous with common law, or law based upon custom, tradition and what has been done before under similar circumstances.

Of importance is to be mindful of the precedents which each court and which each judicial system provides. Cases tried in state courts may or may not be acceptable as a precedent in another state. Federal court findings are valuable precedents in all states. The findings of a case tried in a lower court are normally not relied upon until the case has been appealed and heard by a higher court. Obviously, being the highest court in the land, U.S. Supreme Court rulings are the final word, and therefore provide the strongest precedents. Supreme Court rulings, however, are not cast in stone. The Supreme Court itself may overrule them in subsequent proceedings. In Chapter 3, the manner by which the Supreme Court may reverse prior rulings was demonstrated in the classic *Gideon* case. Since 1993, another benchmark case, *Roe v. Wade*, has come under scrutiny.[17]

In *Roe*, a majority of the nine Supreme Court justices ruled that a woman has a Constitutional right to privacy, which though nowhere explicitly stated in the Constitution, circumscribed the state's ability to deny her an abortion under certain circumstances. The ruling added fuel to the fire of an intense and lasting debate that seems to have no middle ground. For people who agree with the ruling, it was a triumph of women's rights and freedom of choice. For those who do not agree, the decision permitted murder of defenseless, unborn children.

---

[17] *Roe v. Wade*, 93 SCt 705 (1973).

To an objective outside observer, *Roe* is a study in the politics of overturning a Supreme Court precedent. The *Roe* decision was handed down by a primarily liberal Supreme Court. As conservatives, Ronald Reagan and George H.W. Bush both made commitments to appoint justices who would overturn *Roe*. In the years following the *Roe* decision, a more conservative Court reversed legislation imposing restrictions such as husband and parental vetoes, mandatory waiting periods and physician counseling.

By 1992, Harry Blackmun was the only member of the *Roe* majority still on the Court. Now he is gone. Gone also is Byron White, one of the original dissenters to *Roe*. The other remaining dissenter of the original *Roe* court is William Rehnquist, the current Chief Justice. The majority of the Court, including Rehnquist, are appointees of either Ronald Reagan or George H.W. Bush (Antonin Scalia, Anthony Kennedy, Sandra Day O'Connor, David Souter and Clarence Thomas). Gerald Ford also appointed John Paul Stevens, who incidentally is a strong supporter of a woman's right to choose. The remaining justices (Stephen G. Breyer and Ruth Bader Ginsburg) were appointed by Bill Clinton, the latter of which (Ginsburg) was instrumental in launching the Women's Rights Project of the American Civil Liberties Union in 1971. Conservative appointees of President George W. Bush may eventually overturn *Roe*. Hence, even the decisions of the highest court of appeal may not be permanent. The bottom line with respect to the subject of this chapter is to emphasize the importance of follow-up research to determine the most current precedents.

Legal research is the topic of the following chapter, but as an introduction, law cases are cited with the names of the parties to the case, and by reference to a nationally adopted system of filing and cataloging court proceedings. For example, in *United States v. Causby*, 382 U.S. 256-275 (1946), Thomas Lee Causby and his wife submitted a claim to the federal government for damages sustained as a result of operations at a nearby airfield operated by U.S. government military forces. The case citation (382 U.S. 256-275) refers to the 382nd volume of the *U.S. Supreme Court Reporter*, pages 256 to 275. At the end of the citation is the year of the trial (1946). Generally speaking, all cases are similarly identified.

An exception to naming the parties in a case is the use of *"in re"* in the case citation. This is the usual method of entitling a judicial proceeding in which there are no adversarial parties, but merely some subject concerning which judicial action is to be taken, such as an aircraft accident.

SAMPLE AVIATION CASE

The case which follows, *Newberger v. Pokrass*, is presented at this point as an introductory example of an aviation-related civil (tort) proceeding. Embodied in the case are the applications of many of the terms used in the preceding glossary such as plaintiff, defendant, negligence and *res ipsa loquitur*. Also demonstrated is the appeal process from a lower to a higher court. Interesting, is that not only was the pilot guilty of negligence, but his non-rated passenger was determined to share in the negligent operation of the aircraft as well. Here, as throughout this book, we summarize the case's salient conclusions. The reader is urged to consult the original decision (for which the citation follows the case name) for the language of court's actual decision.

NEWBERGER v. POKRASS
148 N.W.2d 80 (Wis. 1967)

Can a passenger share responsibility with the pilot in the negligent operation of an aircraft?

Melvin Newberger and Willard Pokrass were close personal friends and often made trips by airplane together. Pokrass owned his own twin-engine Apache airplane and often made trips to recreational areas. On December 28, 1962, Pokrass and Newberger planned a flight to Eagle River, Wisconsin, where the Pokrass family had a home with winter recreational facilities. Barbara Seely, also a friend, went along. They departed at 6:30 p.m. on a night flight into adverse weather conditions. When they reached the Wausau area, Pokrass received a report of unfavorable weather conditions at Rhinelander, so they landed at Oshkosh, had dinner, and waited for conditions at Rhinelander to clear.

They were on their way toward Rhinelander at about 10:30 p.m., but stopped in Wausau to refuel at about 12:15 a.m. Fifteen minutes later they were in the air again. Newberger told Pokrass he was sleepy and was going to sleep. Pokrass said he too was tired, and Newberger told Pokrass to wake him if he was needed. Newberger dozed off for a few minutes but woke up just before the plane struck the trees at 12:45 a.m. Newberger's testimony as contained in the Civil Aeronautics Board accident report, and which was submitted in evidence by all parties, was:

> *. . . I looked down, saw that we were going to hit the trees; and I yelled to Willard, "We are going to hit the trees." He said "I know," and he said nothing else. I believe that Willard answered in his sleep. I do not think he was aware of what was going on. I believe he must have dozed off and replied the way anybody would reply if a question was directed at someone who had dozed but wasn't sound asleep. . . .*

> *I find, after all of this time, that his answer was so foolish that I assume it must have been given in a dopey, sleepy condition. As I think back on it, the tone of his voice was such that he didn't sound as if he were aware of what was going on.*

When the plane crashed it became engulfed in flames, and the bodies of Pokrass and Seely were burned. Newberger survived the crash, but he spent the night in bitter cold at the site of the plane crash, awaiting rescue. He initially endured a 14-hour ordeal in a bitterly cold environment, followed by five weeks in the hospital, and was left with permanent injuries including the after-effects of having been burned and frostbitten.

Newberger brought suit against the estate of Willard Pokrass for the personal injuries he suffered. The jury found Pokrass 85% negligent, but also found Newberger 15% responsible for *contributory negligence*. In the jury's opinion Newberger could have possibly prevented the accident had he stayed awake. The jury awarded $55,000 for pain, suffering and disability, and $20,000 for loss of earnings. Judgment was entered on this verdict and the defendant (Pokrass estate) appealed. The appellants argued that: (1) there was no credible evidence to sustain negligence by the pilot (Pokrass), and (2) the trial court erred in determining *res ipsa loquitur* because it would require the testimony of an expert to prove anything the pilot did or failed to do was negligent. They also claimed the jury award for wage loss and for pain, suffering and disability was excessive.

The Wisconsin Supreme Court countered the appellant's arguments, stating Pokrass could have been found negligent in several respects: he set his course at a very low altitude in view of the very hilly terrain; his altimeter setting was faulty, resulting in his actually flying 170 feet lower than indicated; he ignored warnings to stay on the ground and of unfavorable weather reports; he flew at a very low altitude in view of the high winds and turbulent weather that existed; and he went to sleep while piloting the plane.

All mechanical failures were ruled out by the CAB accident investigation. Thus, a reasonable inference arises that the cause was human fault, and, therefore, *res ipsa loquitur* is proper. Negligence is presumed to be a factor.

The court also concluded the plaintiff's average income for the three years preceding the accident was $10,435.27, figures that alone support the award of $20,000 for lost wages. They also concluded the award of $55,000 for pain, suffering and disability was not excessive. There was the fourteen-hour overnight ordeal, the hospitalization, and further pain and suffering throughout the recuperation and which still occurred.

The court of appeals affirmed the lower court's judgment.

United States Common Law

CHAPTER 5

LEGAL RESEARCH

*Decisions handed down by the courts are written into books of law,
which when being researched requires a minimum of three steps.
The researcher who tries to short cut those three steps will often
take more time and be far less effective than the researcher
who methodically works through the steps in proper order.*

INTRODUCTION TO THE LAW LIBRARY

The purpose of this chapter is to introduce the reader to the law library, to describe the available publications, and to outline the process for conducting legal research. The focus is on the primary reference system, the *West National Reporter System*, but also included are introductions to the *Bancroft-Whitney* publications, topical references by the *Commerce Clearing House* [CCH], as well as statutory books, encyclopedias, and ancillary sources of case law materials. This is a "working" chapter to introduce the beginning researcher to resources particularly relevant to aviation law research.

Decisions handed down by the courts are published as legal digests. Law libraries are a repository for these books of law, and have as a primary source of law book materials the publications of a principal publisher, the West Publishing Company. Fundamental to conducting legal research is to focus upon the system of filing and cataloging court results developed by the West Company. West does not, however, publish everything found in the law library. Other companies publish works, which either augment the West system or provide information not otherwise readily available from West or from other sources.

The Bancroft-Whitney Company is a second prominent publisher of law books, in cooperation with The Lawyers Cooperative Publishing Company, who have jointly developed what they call the *Total Client-Service Library* [TCSL]. Although not as extensive as the West publications, the creators of the TCSL believe their system to be the first successful attempt in over 100 years (i.e.; since the West system originated in the late 19th Century) to develop a new system of legal research designed to meet the needs of the modern lawyer. Where West's *National Reporter System* concentrates on cataloging and cross referencing case law, the TCSL attempts to bring together resources which automatically guide and channel the researcher's efforts in a coordinated way.

In June of 1996, Bancroft-Whitney, Lawyers Cooperative Publishing, along with other companies belonging to the Thomson publishing conglomerate, merged with West Publishing to become the *West Group*.[1] The combination of the Thomson Corporation and West Publishing represented a $3.4 billion merger of two of the largest legal publishers in the United States.

Another major source of aviation law is published by the Commerce Clearing House, which is a publisher of topical reports. Aviation law is but one of the CCH specialty topics. The Commerce Clearing House brings together in one set of books, the aviation statutes, combined with aviation case law. In the CCH *Aviation Law Reporter* are four volumes:

- *Volume 1* contains federal statutes, a topical index, finding lists, and a table of cases;
- *Volume 1a* includes the Federal Aviation Regulations, and the Aviation Proceedings (otherwise referred to as "economic regulations") of the Department of Transportation;
- *Volume 2* has an annotated version of the Federal Aviation Act of 1958 (as amended), and a cumulative subject index; and
- *Volume 3* contains new court cases, current State laws, and an international law section.

---

[1] The West Group consists of Bancroft-Whitney, Clark Boardman Callaghan, Lawyers Cooperative Publishing, WESTLAW, and West Publishing.

In a continuing series, the CCH *Aviation Cases* is a full text reporter of decisions handed down by the federal and state courts on the subject of aviation law. Reporting the decisions of each case includes: the case name; the name of the court, docket number and decision date; case history with prior and subsequent decisions; head noting of main issues; and names of participating attorneys.

As with other libraries, law libraries have additional works including legal dictionaries (for example, *Blacks Law Dictionary*), encyclopedias (*Corpus Juris, Corpus Juris Secundum, American Jurisprudence*, etc.), and law periodicals. Importantly, there are papers, texts, and "hornbooks" (books explaining the rudiments or general principles of law) on given areas and topics of law. These various texts can often be used not only for their narrative information but also for their references and citations of significant law cases.

There is so much (for some perhaps even overwhelming) information housed in law libraries that it is easy to misperceive that all law has been cataloged, filed, and placed in the library. However, law libraries are not exhaustive. In fact, most law is not in the library at all. Remember that the common law system is based upon commonly accepted practices and habits of society, and upon precedent. In most cases court precedent has not been established until a higher court on appeal rules upon the issue. Not only that, most differences are settled long before they have a chance to make it to trial, let alone reach the appellate level.[2]

In saying that most law is to be found outside the law library, the point is this, law is a matter of sociability. It is what the Greeks referred to as "virtue." Recall from Chapter 1 that the essence of law to the ancient Greeks was virtue and goodness. People seem to get along by-and-large without the courts. Through a process of give-and-take, most people are generally able to resolve their disputes to some degree of mutual satisfaction, without reverting to arbitrators or to the formal legal process. Society's norms and how people work out their differences provide the bases for precedents upon which judges and juries

---

[2] To locate the results of cases not found in the law library, and cases that have not been appealed, it may be necessary to write directly to the clerk of the trial court which presided over the case in question, and to request a transcript of the proceedings. In some cases, where the issues were resolved at pre-trial settlements or otherwise settled out of court, if the parties are willing, and outside discussion is not otherwise prohibited by the terms of the settlement, one might obtain the results directly from those involved in the dispute.

find equity in the law. Precedents, although determined by the courts, are fundamentally a matter of what is acceptable to society.

Many lawyers today use the internet on-line subscription services of, primarily, Westlaw and Lexis/Nexis, to search their enormous databases within seconds. Whereas the law and related topics were once the exclusive domain of books and libraries, increasingly, these traditional sources are being replaced by on-line computer access. There are also significant "free" data bases of government agencies (such as the Department of Transportation [DOT] and Federal Aviation Administration [FAA]), which make available their governing statutes and regulations on their web sites, and the federal courts, which make available their decisions, and often, the briefs filed by lawyers in particular cases.

PRIMARY RESEARCH

Legal research entails common sense, coupled with some familiarity with the law library and perseverance in finding what one is looking for. This section is intended as a cursory guide to the law library, specifically oriented toward finding law as it relates to aviation. It might be noted that the West Publishing Company and Bancroft-Whitney/ Lawyers Cooperative Publishing Company each have published handbooks detailing how to conduct legal research when using their respective series of law books.[3]

In their text, *The Living Law: a guide to modern legal research*, Bancroft-Whitney suggests that every legal research project requires a minimum of three steps, and the researcher who tries to short cut those three steps will often take more time and be far less effective than the researcher who methodically works through the steps in proper order:

- *Step one* is to go to a *law finder* or "search book." A law finder directs the researcher where to go to find an answer. Included are: indexes, digests, tables, citators, and so forth. Keywords or numbers may be used for reference, or cases may be cited by name in alphabetic listings.

---

[3] West's Law Finder: *A Research Manual for Lawyers*; and *The Living Law: A Guide to Modern Legal Research*, by Bancroft-Whitney.

- *Step two* is to go to the law source that contains the statement of law. It may be a particular case, a statute, a regulation, or perhaps an administrative ruling. The statement of law describes what the law is on a given subject. Case law is restated in books called "reporters." Law may also be defined and explained in encyclopedias of law. Statutory law, on the other hand, may be found in tables of statutes, or may be arranged by code (i.e., "codified").

- *Step three* is to supplement the findings to insure that what has been found is the latest information available. For this purpose there are loose leaf releases, pocket publications, paperback volumes of the most current law, or one might check the *Shepard's* citation manual to trace a particular case to its conclusion.

LAW FINDERS

Since the legal system in the United States is one of common law and *precedent*, legal research must of necessity be oriented toward finding what the courts have decided in the past. As mentioned, there are various indexes, or law finders, available to help the researcher find what the courts have previously decided. These indexes to case law are commonly known as "digests."

In looking for cases in point, West suggests there are three methods of search: (1) by *descriptive words*, (2) by *topic*, and (3) by *table of cases*. Unless the researcher knows the case name, the descriptive word method is usually the most successful to use, and it is recommended that digests of descriptive words be consulted first before reverting to other means. Descriptive words describe the pertinent facts of the case or the legal question involved. There are thousands of words, arranged alphabetically in word digests, for cross referencing case law. Selecting descriptive words is critical, and as in using a thesaurus, synonyms, antonyms and closely related words should be used. Skill in choosing the most applicable words develops with practice, but West suggests that descriptive words naturally group themselves around five elements common to every case, the:

- parties;
- places and things;
- basis of action or issue;
- defense; and
- relief sought.

The easiest way to locate a case is to know the plaintiffs and/or defendant's names. If the researcher knows the name of the case, he or she can go directly to a digest, which contains a table of cases. Names of cases may be acquired from having heard of the case, from a hornbook, a casebook, or perhaps in a textbook on a particular topic of law. From the *Table of Cases* can be determined:

- the correct case title;
- parallel citations in more than one reporter;
- the case history; and
- other topics under which case law may have been classified.

The most difficult and least productive method of search for the novice is the *topic* method. Topic selection is similar to using descriptive words, but requires a more substantial educational foundation in law, and a thorough familiarity with topical classification. The average lawyer, for example, studies perhaps 30 or so legal subjects in law school, yet there are more than 400 topics in the West system. Despite the fact that commercial aviation is one of the nation's most important industries, and is an integral component of the tour and travel industry (arguably the world's largest industry), relatively few law schools teach courses in Aviation Law, and relatively few lawyers specialize in the practice of Aviation Law. There are only two graduate law programs in the world in this field—at McGill University, and at the University of Leiden.

Unless one is highly proficient in the practice of law, it is easy to end up researching the wrong topic. For this reason, the topic method of search is not ordinarily recommended for the beginning researcher.

The most ready access to aviation case law is to consult the Commerce Clearing House topical law reports. The CCH may have already done the work for the researcher. As stated earlier, Commerce

Clearing House brings together in one publication aviation statutes and aviation case law, to include new court cases. However, in researching CCH, it must be kept in mind that CCH law reports are "topical" and contain strictly aviation-related cases. As the title of this book implies, aviation law is but one aspect of the much larger picture of law. Cases in other topics may be relevant to the legal issue, but will be missed by a narrow focus on CCH ("aviation" only) publications.

Following a standardized pattern of indexing, the Commerce Clearing House indexing system includes a:

- *General Case Table*, which lists alphabetically the plaintiff/ defendant names;
- *Jurisdictional Case Table*, which lists cases by the jurisdiction within which they were decided; and a
- *Topical Index*, which is oriented toward aviation-related terms.

Because the CCH *Topical Index* is organized around aviation terminology, it may be more readily employed by the aviation researcher not trained in law than a more legalistic topical search in say West's system. The CCH *Topical Index* is the subject key to basic compilations, statutes, regulations and international documents in aviation.

REPORTER SYSTEMS

The system of reporting case law developed by Bancroft-Whitney and The Lawyers Cooperative Publishing Companies is the *American Law Reports* or *ALR* series. The ALR is to the Bancroft-Whitney system, what the *National Reporter System* is to the West system. It is a set of books which report all state appellate court decisions and decisions of the federal courts.

With the professed aim of providing "better service to the lawyer" (than they were then receiving), two young law book men in 1876 compiled a pamphlet known as *The Syllabi*. The purpose of *The Syllabi* was to furnish to the legal profession (specifically in Minnesota), a current compendium of recent adjudicated cases. From *The Syllabi*, the system grew to incorporate all of the states. *The Syllabi* was succeeded in 1879 by the *North Western Reporter*, and now includes the:

- *North Western Reporter;*
- *Pacific Reporter;*
- *North Eastern Reporter;*
- *Atlantic Reporter;*
- *South Western Reporter;*
- *Southern Reporter;* and the
- *South Eastern Reporter.*

Also included in the National Reporter System are the:

- *Supreme Court Reporter;*
- *Federal Reporter;*
- *Federal Supplement;*
- *Federal Rules Decisions;*
- *New York Supplement;* and the
- *California Reporter.*

The *Supreme Court Reporter* contains decisions of the U.S. Supreme Court. The *Federal Reporter* contains the opinions of the U.S. Court of Appeals, and of the U.S. Court of Customs and Patent Appeals. The *Federal Supplement* reports decisions of the U.S. Court of Claims, the U.S. District Courts and U.S. Customs Court.

The statements in the two preceding paragraphs referencing cases found in the *Federal Reporter* and *Federal Supplement* are perhaps an oversimplification, but one justified for purposes of aviation law research—recognizing that aviation is a comparatively recent topic in the body of law. The *Federal Reporter* and the *Federal Supplement* have both evolved concurrently with the creation of "inferior" federal courts. Decisions of the U.S. District Courts and U.S. Circuit Courts prior to 1880 are found in *Federal Cases,* a predecessor to the *Federal Reporter.* Likewise, U.S. District Court cases from 1880 to 1932 are in the *Federal Reporter,* rather than in the *Federal Supplement.* Decisions of now abolished courts like the U.S. Circuit Court and the U.S. Commerce Court, of the U.S. Court of Appeals (formerly the U.S. Circuit Court of Appeals), of the U.S. Court of Customs and Patent Appeals, and of the U.S. Emergency Court of Appeals may also be found in the *Federal Reporter.* Furthermore, U.S. District Court opinions not designated for publication in the *Federal Supplement* may be found in yet another publication, *Federal Rules Decisions*.

As can be seen, there is a proliferation of court decisions, which may be found in either the *Federal Reporter* or the *Federal Supplement*, the decisions of which may have little bearing on aviation law. Thus, for the sake of simplicity, and aviation law research specifically, if looking for decisions of the United States appellate court one should look in the *Federal Reporter*. For decisions of the U.S. District Courts and the Court of Claims one should refer to the *Federal Supplement*.

The *New York Supplement* and the *California Reporter* supplement the regional reporters. Due to more dense populations than found in other states, and the proportionally higher volume of court decisions coming from the states of New York and California, each of them has been assigned its own regional reporter. Notwithstanding, cases reported in the *California Reporter* will usually be found in the *Pacific Reporter* as well.

In Bancroft-Whitney's *Total Client-Service Library*, the principal reporters are the *ALR* series (1st, 2nd, 3rd, 4th, etc.), the *ALR Federal*, and the *United States Supreme Court Reports*. The *ALR* series primarily reports state cases of significance, with annotations and in-depth examinations. The *ALR Federal* reports federal matters with annotations. The *United States Supreme Court Reports*, as the name implies, contains annotated decisions of the U.S. Supreme Court.

Just as the U.S. Government has codified federal law, the states too have systems of codification. For many but not all of the states, West has published State annotated statutes and codes in a system patterned after the *United States Code Annotated*. Where there is no annotated state code available, the researcher may still go to a non-annotated compilation of state statutes, laws or codes to find aviation related state law. In some cases the states have excerpted from the state code the aviation related chapters and sections for compilation into one booklet. For example, the California Aeronautics Division has published *California Laws Relating to Aeronautics*.

AVIATION STATUTES

Congress has the power and responsibility to make laws. As one might recall from past civics classes, a member of Congress submits to the respective house of Congress a bill proposing a law be made. If the members of the respective house adopt the bill, it is then submitted to the other house for its approval. Assuming both houses of Congress adopt the bill, it then goes to the President, upon whose signature it becomes law. Such a law is known as an "Act of Congress" and will carry with it its popular name; for example, "The Federal Aviation Act of 1958."

The Act will also have associated with it a number of other titles and identifiers as well. It will have the number of the original bill submitted to either the House of Representatives (e.g., "H.R." number) or the Senate (e.g., "S." number). In the case of the 1958 Federal Aviation Act, it was Senate bill "S. 3880." The Act will also be known as a public law in accordance with its chronological adoption. For example, the Federal Aviation Act of 1958 was "Public Law 85-726," meaning that it was the 726th law of the 85th Congress. Additionally, the Act will have a numerical designator according to how it becomes codified. The Federal Aviation Act may be cited as "49 U.S.C. § 1301."

If the researcher knows the popular name of the act, the date it was adopted, and/or its Public Law (or "PL") number, the law can be found by looking in the publication, *United States Statutes at Large*, in the law library. Public Laws are chronologically filed in this publication of the U.S. Government Printing Office. For example, the Federal Aviation Act of 1958 is located in Volume 72, Part 1, page 731 of the aforementioned publication.

Since public laws are adopted chronologically, and are recorded in order, and because a researcher would otherwise have to sift through reams of pages looking for a specific law, another system of cross referencing and filing has been adopted. It is known as "codification." Recall that codification is nothing more than the process of collecting and arranging law systematically into a unified body called a "code." Codification of public law is entitled the *United States Code* [U.S.C.], and is published by the U.S. Government Printing Office. Subsequent to being organized as a codified body of law in the late 1800s, the United States Code has been periodically recompiled and updated. Beginning in 1926, it has been published every six years. In between editions, annual cumulative supplements are published in order to present the most current information. The most recent publication (as of this writing) is the 2000 edition, reflecting the general and permanent laws in effect as of January 2, 2001.

The United States Code is systematically organized under 50 Titles (see Table 5.1, "Titles of United States Code"); Title 49 establishes the DOT and FAA, and incorporates aviation with other forms of general transportation. Referring back to codification of the Federal Aviation Act of 1958, it is designated "49 U.S.C. § 1301 et seq." Within Title 49, "Transportation," there are five subdivisions of which Subtitle III is reserved for air transportation.

Congress enacted the first "Code of Laws of the United States" in 1926. Prior to that time, and as far back as 1874, Congress merely authorized the compilation and publication of general and permanent laws of the United States. The West Publishing Company was instrumental in preparing and submitting the first official United States Code, which Congress adopted in 1926. West helped prepare subsequent editions of the United States Code. And it continues to publish one of the available annotated versions of the United States Code. West's *United States Code Annotated* [U.S.C.A.] includes, with the text of the United States Code, practical editorial features to facilitate the researcher's understanding of the code, and which may save time. The U.S.C.A. is indexed much the same as other West publications, by incorporating three methods of search: (1) the fact method, (2) the topic method, and (3) the popular name method. Bancroft-Whitney provides a similar service with its publication, *United States Code Service*.

Because federal regulatory agencies derive their powers through Acts of Congress, the regulations that these agencies in turn promulgate have the force and effect of public law. The Federal Aviation Administration is such an agency, deriving its regulatory authority from the Federal Aviation Act of 1958. Its rules and regulations, the Federal Aviation Regulations [FARs], constitute positive law.

Codification of federal regulations appears in the U.S. Government Printing Office publication, *Code of Federal Regulations* [C.F.R.]. As the *United States Code* is organized by titles, the Code of Federal Regulations is likewise arranged. Titles 14 and 49 of the C.F.R. include regulations in the field of aeronautics and space. Chapter I of Title 14 contains the Federal Aviation Regulations.

Table 5.1—TITLES OF UNITED STATES CODE

1. General Provisions	28. Judiciary and Judicial Pro-
2. The Congress	cedure; and Appendix
3. The President	29. Labor
4. Flag and Seal, Seal of	30. Mineral Lands and Mining
Government, and the	31. Money and Finance
States	32. National Guard
5. Government Organization	33. Navigation and Navigable
and Employees; and Ap-	Waters
pendix	34. [Navy]
6. [Surety Bonds]	35. Patents
7. Agriculture	36. Patriotic Societies and Ob-
8. Aliens and Nationality	servances
9. Arbitration	37. Pay and Allowances of the
10. Armed Forces; and Ap-	Uniformed Services
pendix	38. Veterans Benefits
11. Bankruptcy; and Appendix	39. Postal Service
12. Banks and Banking	40. Public Buildings, Property
13. Census	and Works
14. Coast Guard	41. Public Contracts
15. Commerce and Trade	42. The Public Health and
16. Conservation	Welfare
17. Copyrights	43. Public Lands
18. Crimes and Criminal Pro-	44. Public Printing and Docu-
cedure; and Appendix	ments
19. Customs Duties	45. Railroads
20. Education	46. Shipping
21. Food and Drugs	47. Telegraphs, Telephones,
22. Foreign Relations and In-	and Radiotelegraphs
tercourse	48. Territories and Insular
23. Highways	Possessions
24. Hospitals and Asylums	49. Transportation
25. Indians	50. War and National Defense;
26. Internal Revenue Code	and Appendix
27. Intoxicating Liquors	

Table 5.2, "Federal Aviation Regulations," lists the Parts of Chapter I, Title 14 C.F.R. Note that the C.F.R. Parts coincide with the Federal Aviation Regulations. For example, C.F.R. Part 91 is the same as FAR Part 91, "General Operating and Flight Rules," and so forth.

Other guidance from the FAA is issued through *Advisory Circulars* [AC] and FAA *Orders*. FAA Orders are directives for *internal* use by FAA employees. While intended for internal use only, orders may affect those outside as well. Take for example FAA Order 7110.65, *Air Traffic Control*. It is the handbook that prescribes air traffic control procedures and phraseology for use by personnel providing air traffic control services. Under a different cover it is the same Air Traffic Control [ATC] handbook used by military and private contract civilian controllers as well. Furthermore, it is to the same procedures contained in Order 7110.65 to which all pilots are expected to adhere. Quoting from the FAA's explanation of the Advisory Circular system:

> *The FAA issues advisory circulars to inform the aviation public in a systematic way of non-regulatory material of interest. Unless incorporated into a regulation by reference, the contents of an advisory circular are not binding on the public. An AC is issued to provide guidance and information in its designated subject area or to show a method acceptable to the Administrator for complying with a related Federal Aviation Regulation.*

The implication is that FAA Orders and Advisory Circulars may not have the same force and effect as the FARs. But it should be recognized that the guidance found in ACs and in Orders originates from the same agency source. Therefore, in their practical application, and as interpreted by the FAA, ACs and Orders may take on the same importance as the FARs. In its management oversight of federally funded programs, for example, the FAA may insist upon conformance to standards specified in the Advisory Circulars. Similarly, the guidance for the managers of federally sponsored programs emanates from the Agency through its Orders.

Table 5.2—FEDERAL AVIATION REGULATIONS

SUB-CHAPTER A
DEFINITIONS

Part
1   Definitions and abbreviations

SUB-CHAPTER B
PROCEDURAL RULES

11   General rule-making procedures
13   Investigative and enforcement procedures
14   Rules implementing the Equal Access to Justice Act of 1980
15   Administrative claims under Federal Tort Claims Act
16   Rules of practice for Federally-assisted airport enforcement
        proceedings
17   Procedures for protests and contracts disputes

SUB-CHAPTER C
AIRCRAFT

21   Certification procedures for products and parts
23   Airworthiness standards: normal, utility, acrobatic, and
        commuter category airplanes
25   Airworthiness standards: transport category airplanes
27   Airworthiness standards: normal category rotorcraft
29   Airworthiness standards: transport category rotorcraft
31   Airworthiness standards: manned free balloons
33   Airworthiness standards: aircraft engines
34   Fuel venting and exhaust emission requirements for turbine
        engine powered airplanes
35   Airworthiness standards: propellers
36   Noise standards: aircraft type and airworthiness certification
39   Airworthiness directives
43   Maintenance, preventive maintenance, rebuilding, and
        alteration

SUB-CHAPTER G
AIR CARRIERS, AND OPERATORS FOR COMPENSATION OR HIRE: CERTIFICATION AND OPERATIONS

SUB-CHAPTER H
SCHOOLS AND OTHER CERTIFICATED AGENCIES

SUB-CHAPTER I
AIRPORTS

SUB-CHAPTER J
NAVIGATIONAL FACILITIES

SUB-CHAPTER K
ADMINISTRATIVE REGULATIONS

SUB-CHAPTERS L-M
[RESERVED]

SUB-CHAPTER N
WAR RISK INSURANCE

Source: Ch. I, Title 14 C.F.R. (as of Jan. 1, 2005).

In the *Advisory Circular Checklist*, the ACs are issued in a num-
bered-subject system, which in an orderly way corresponds to the subject areas of the Federal Aviation Regulations (and Title 14 C.F.R.,
Chapter I). In other words, the subject of FAR Part 61, "Certification:
Pilots, Flight Instructors, and Ground Instructors" is the same as Advisory Circular 61, "Certification: Pilots, Flight Instructors, and Ground
Instructors"; or FAR Part 91, "General Operating and Flight Rules,"
is the same as Advisory Circular 91; and so forth.

Whereas Chapter I, Title 14 of the Code of Federal Regulations is
reserved for the Federal Aviation Administration, Chapter II was
originally assigned to the Civil Aeronautics Board as "economic regulations." Subsequent to deregulation of the airlines, Chapter II has
been transferred to the Office of the Secretary, Department of Transportation. Chapter V is reserved for the National Aeronautics and
Space Administration. The economic regulations incorporated into Title 14, Chapter II, are shown on Table 5.3, "Aviation Proceedings."
New regulations, Title 14, Chapter III, applicable to private space
travel are shown on Table 5.4, "Commercial Space Transportation."

Regulations emanating from federal agencies like the FAA and the
National Transportation Safety Board [NTSB] fall within the realm of
administrative law. Another source of law may be the reports produced by the agency itself.

Until it was terminated in 1985, the CAB, through the U.S. Government Printing Office, published *Civil Aeronautics Board Reports*
annually, which reported its administrative law hearings. Those remaining administrative law functions, left by the CAB after deregulation, were transferred to the DOT, and the reports were discontinued.

SUPPLEMENTAL RESEARCH

Another work, not previously mentioned, yet salient to research in
aviation law, is published by Shepard's/McGraw Hill. *Shepard's Citations* are a compilation of citations to all cases reported in the
Reporters. The citations include affirmations, reversals and dismissals
by appellate courts, and by the U.S. Supreme Court. Through a procedure that has come to be known as "Shepardizing," case histories can
be traced in the Shepard's/McGraw Hill series.

Table 5.3—AVIATION PROCEEDINGS [4]

SUB-CHAPTER A
ECONOMIC REGULATIONS

Part

200 Definitions and instructions

201 Air carrier authority under Subtitle VII of Title 49 of the
United States Code [amended]

203 Waiver of Warsaw Convention liability limits and defenses

204 Data to support fitness determinations

205 Aircraft accident liability insurance

206 Certificates of public convenience and necessity:
Special authorizations and exemptions

207 Charter trips by U.S. scheduled air carriers

208 Charter trips by U.S. charter air carriers

211 Applications for permits to foreign air carriers

212 Charter trips by foreign air carriers

213 Terms, conditions and limitations of foreign air carrier
permits

214 Terms, conditions and limitations of foreign air carrier
permits authorizing charter transportation only

215 Use and change of names of air carriers, foreign air carriers
and commuter air carriers

216 Commingling of blind sector traffic by foreign air carriers

217 Reporting traffic statistics by foreign air carriers in civilian
scheduled, charter, and non-scheduled services

218 Lease by foreign air carriers or other foreign person of aircraft
with crew

221 Tariffs

222 Intermodal cargo services by foreign air carriers

223 Free and reduced-rate transportation

232 Transportation of mail, review of orders of Postmaster
General

234 Airline service quality performance reports

---

[4] Title 14, Chapter II was transferred from the Civil Aeronautics Board to the Department of
Transportation on Jan. 1, 1985. For a document giving the disposition of CAB regulations once the
Agency ceased to exist, *see* 50 FR 452, Jan. 4, 1985.

SUB-CHAPTER B
PROCEDURAL

Source: Title 14 C.F.R. Ch. II (as of Jan. 1, 2005).

Table 5.4—COMMERCIAL SPACE TRANSPORTATION

SUB-CHAPTER A
GENERAL

Part
400   Basis and scope
401   Organization and definitions

SUB-CHAPTER B
PROCEDURE

404   Regulations and Licensing requirements
405   Investigations and Enforcement
406   Investigations, enforcement, and administrative review

SUB-CHAPTER C
LICENSING

411   [Reserved]
412   License Application Procedures
415   Launch license
417-419   [Reserved]
420   License to operate a launch site
421-430   [Reserved]
431   Launch and reentry of a reusable launch vehicle (RLV)
432   [Reserved]
433   License to operate a reentry site
434   [Reserved]
435   Reentry of a reentry vehicle other than a reusable launch vehicle
      (RLV)
436-439   [Reserved]
440   Financial Responsibility
441-449   [Reserved]
450   Financial Responsibility
451-1199   [Reserved]

Source: Title 14 C.F.R. Ch. III (as of Jan. 1, 2005).

The Shepard's/McGraw Hill series includes reporter citations for each of the states (e.g., *Texas Citations, Arizona Citations*, etc.), as well as for the following regions:

- *Atlantic Citations*;
- *Northeastern Citations*;
- *Northwestern Citations*;
- *Pacific Citations*;
- *Southeastern Citations*;
- *Southwestern Citations*; and
- *New York Supplement.*

The Shepard's system is easy to use, and given at the beginning of each edition is a keynoted, illustrative case, with the citations to each cited case grouped in a standardized format. Included with the illustrative case citation are numbered blocks giving reference to case history and parallel citations, along with a table of abbreviations to decipher the encoded citations.

In supplementing case histories, one might also review the case findings in the CCH, West and other Reporters, which may include final disposition of the case at hand. For the most recent findings on the same or similar cases, all of the reporting publishers produce loose leaf or "pocket" issues of the most current court decisions.

With regard to currency of (federal) regulations, one may consult the *Federal Register* [FR]. The *Federal Register* supplements the Code of Federal Regulations. Mandated by federal law, certain documents must be published in the *Federal Register* as official, constructive notice to the world. In particular, it contains Notices of Proposed Rulemaking by federal agencies, inviting comments before Final Rules are adopted. To meet the requirements for giving public notice, the office of the Federal Register was established under the Federal Register Act. Documents, which must be filed and published, are:

- Presidential proclamations and Executive orders;
- each document or class of documents required to be published by act of Congress; and
- each document having general applicability and legal effect.

Because they are applicable generally and have legal force and effect, the Code of Federal Regulations (including FARs) are included in the public notification process. The *Federal Register* is published daily, Monday through Friday, and provides a uniform system for making available to the public regulations and legal notices issued by Federal agencies. An *Index* of entries appearing in the Federal Register is published periodically. A general index to the entire Code of Federal Regulations is found in the *CFR Index* and *Finding Aids*.

INTERNATIONAL AIR LAW

To this point, we have discussed research of domestic aviation law. Recognize also that there is a vast body of international aviation law as well. It is divided into two major areas—*Public International Air Law*, and *Private International Air Law*.

Public International Air Law can be found in a number of treaties and conventions between nations, the most important of which is the Chicago Convention of 1944. The Chicago Convention expresses certain requirements of nations in the area of aviation safety and navigation, and established the International Civil Aviation Organization [ICAO], headquartered in Montreal, and gave it jurisdiction over the many technical aspects of international civil aviation.[5] Most of ICAO's work has been focused on aviation safety, navigation, and security,[6] though it also has been the forum for updating liability and other pri-

---

[5] ICAO came into being on Apr. 4, 1944, when the Chicago Convention entered into force. It began operations in 1947 under the umbrella of the United Nations. Michael Milde, *The Chicago Convention—After Forty Years*, 9 Annals of Air & Space L. 119, 121 (1984). Gerald FitzGerald, *ICAO Now and in the Coming Decades*, in International Air Transport: Law Organization and Policies for the Future 47, 52 (N. Matte ed. 1976).

[6] Annex 17 of the Chicago Convention—Safeguarding International Civil Aviation Against Acts of Unlawful Interference—addresses aviation security. Annex 17 is supplemented by the *ICAO Security Manual for Safeguarding Civil Aviation Against Acts of Unlawful Interference* (Doc. 8973 – Restricted) (6th ed. 2002), first published in 1971, and its *Strategic Action Plan*. R.I.R. Abeyratne, *Some Recommendations for a New Legal and Regulatory Structure for the Management of the Offense of Unlawful Interference with Civil Aviation*, 25 Transp. L.J. 115, 121-130 (1998). For a review of the work ICAO has done in the area of security, *see* Paul Stephen Dempsey, *Aviation Security: The Role of Law in the War against Terrorism*, 41 Colum. J. Transnat'l L. 649 (2003), and Paul Stephen Dempsey, *Aerial Terrorism: Unilateral and Multilateral Responses to Aircraft Hijacking*, 2 Conn. J. Int'l L. 427 (1987).

vate law regimes in civil aviation.[7] Indeed, ICAO's principal objective is "ensuring the safety of international civil aviation worldwide. . . ."[8]

Article 12 of the Chicago Convention requires that every contracting State keep its regulations uniform, to the greatest extent possible, with those established under the Convention.[9]

Article 37 of the Convention attempts to achieve uniformity in air navigation, by requiring that every contracting State to cooperate in achieving the "highest practicable degree of uniformity in regulations, standards, procedures, and organization in relation to aircraft personnel, airways and auxiliary services in all matters in which uniformity will facilitate and improve air navigation."[10] The sentence that follows provides, "To this end [ICAO] shall adopt and amend from time to time . . . international standards and recommended practices and procedures" addressing various aspects of air navigation.[11] Hence, ICAO's 188 member States have an affirmative obligation to conform their domestic laws, rules and regulations to the international leveling standards adopted by ICAO.

The ICAO Council[12] is given the mandate to adopt international Standards and Recommended Practices [SARPs] on issues affecting the safety and efficiency of air navigation,[13] and for convenience, designate them as Annexes to the Chicago Convention. ICAO has issued SARPS, which effectively bind states to certain uniform standards, in the following fields:

---

[7] *See e.g.,* Paul Stephen Dempsey, *Pennies From Heaven: Breaking Through the Liability Limitations of Warsaw,* 22 Annals of Air & Space L. 267 (1997).

[8] ICAO Ass. Res. 32-11.

[9] "The elimination of the multitude of conflicting national aeronautical regulations, through the domestic implementation of the regulatory SARPs prescribed in the Annexes, would be an immense step toward facilitating international civil aviation." Thomas Buergenthal, *Law Making in the International Civil Aviation Organization* 102 (1969).

[10] Chicago Convention, Art. 37.

[11] *Id.*

[12] The ICAO Council, and not the Assembly, is the supreme body of the agency, for it holds the power to exercise both the quasi-legislative and quasi-judicial powers of the agency. *See* Peter Ateh-Afac Fossungu, *The ICAO Assembly: The Most Unsupreme of Supreme Organs in the United Nations System: A Critical Analysis of Assembly Sessions,* 26 Transp. L.J. 1 (1998).

[13] SARPs, designated for convenience as Annexes to the Convention, shall be effective in a period of time not less than three months after they are approved by a two-thirds vote of the ICAO Council, unless a majority of States register their disapproval within that period. Chicago Convention, Art. 37, 54(1), 90.

- Personnel Licensing;
- Rules of the Air;
- Meteorology;
- Aeronautical Charts;
- Units of Measurement to be Used in Air-Ground Communications;
- Operation of Aircraft, International Commercial Air Transport;
- Aircraft Nationality and Registration Marks;
- Airworthiness of Aircraft;
- Facilitation of International Air Transport;
- Aeronautical Telecommunication;
- Air Traffic Services;
- Search and Rescue;
- Aircraft Accident Inquiry;
- Aerodromes;
- Aeronautical Information Services;
- Environmental Protection;
- Security—Safeguarding International Civil Aviation against Acts of Unlawful Interference; and
- Annex 18: Safe Transport of Dangerous Goods by Air.

Although there is an obligation to attempt to achieve uniformity in law under Article 37, Article 38 of the Chicago Convention provides that any State finding it impracticable to comply with SARPs, or which has or adopts regulations different therefrom, "shall give immediate notification" to ICAO of the differences.[14] The Council is then obliged immediately to notify other States of such noncompliance.[15]

A number of other conventions govern other aviation issues, including security.[16] Moreover, traffic and other commercial aviation

---

[14] With respect to amendments to SARPs, under Article 38 of the Chicago Convention, any State that does not amend its own regulations to comply therewith, must notify ICAO within 60 days; and the ICAO Council shall, in turn, notify member States of the differences. Chicago Convention, Art. 38.

[15] Chicago Convention, Art. 38.

[16] Several multilateral conventions have been drafted under ICAO auspices addressing aviation security, including:
- *The Tokyo Convention of 1963* requires that a hijacked aircraft be restored to the aircraft commander and passengers be permitted to continue their journey. Convention on

rights between nations are distributed according to Bilateral Air Transport Agreements.

Private International Air Law consists of certain liability conventions (such as the Warsaw Convention of 1929, and the Montreal Convention of 1999), protocols thereto, inter-carrier agreements, and various court decisions.

These multilateral (and many bilateral) treaties and conventions are published in digests such as the CCH volumes, described above, and the United Nations Treaty Series. Once a decade, the principal International Air Law instruments are collected and published in McGill University's *Annals of Air & Space Law*. This information is also available on the Westlaw and Lexis/Nexis subscription services.

 Offenses and Certain Other Acts Committed on Board Aircraft, Sept. 14, 1963, 20 U.S.T. 2941, T.I.A.S. No. 6768, 704 U.N.T.S. 219, *reprinted in* 58 Am. J. Int'l L. 566 (1959), and 18 Annals of Air & Space L. 169 (1993), and Paul Stephen Dempsey, *Law & Foreign Policy in International Aviation* 433 (1987) [hereinafter Tokyo Convention].

- *The Hague Convention of 1970* declares hijacking to be an international "offense" and requires the state to which an aircraft is hijacked to extradite or exert jurisdiction over the hijacker and prosecute him, imposing "severe penalties" if he is found guilty. Convention for the Suppression of Unlawful Seizure of Aircraft, Dec. 16, 1970, 22 U.S.T. 1641, T.I.A.S. No. 7192, *reprinted in* 10 I.L.M. 133 (1971), 18 Annals of Air & Space L. 201 (1993), and Paul Stephen Dempsey, *Law & Foreign Policy in International Aviation* 441 (1987).

- *The Montreal Convention of 1971* not only expands the definition of "offense" to include communications of false information and unlawful acts against aircraft or air navigation facilities, but also requires prosecution thereof. Convention for the Suppression of Unlawful Acts Against the Safety of Civil Aviation, Sept. 23, 1971, 24 U.S.T. 567, 974 U.N.T.S. 177 (entered into force on Jan. 26, 1973, with 150 ratifications), reprinted in 18 Annals of Air & Space L. 224 (1993), and Paul Stephen Dempsey, *Law & Foreign Policy in International Aviation* 445 (1987). *See also* Paul Stephen Dempsey, William Thoms & Robert Hardaway, *Aviation Law & Regulation* § 9.13 (1993).

- *The Montreal Protocol of 1988*—the Protocol for the Suppression of Unlawful Acts of Violence at Airports Serving International Civil Aviation, Supplementary to the Convention for the Suppression of Unlawful Acts Against the Safety of Civil Aviation, added airport security to the international regime. ICAO Doc. 9518, reprinted in 18 Annals of Air & Space Law 253 (1993).

- *The Montreal Convention of 1991* prevents the manufacture, possession, and movement of unmarked explosives. Convention for the Suppression of Unlawful Acts Against the Safety of Civil Aviation, Sept. 23, 1971, 24 U.S.T. 564, T.I.A.S. No. 7570, *reprinted in* 10 I.L.M. 115, and 18 Annals of Air & Space L. 269 (1993).

CASE RESEARCH

In this section is presented a typical case citation, and how it can be traced through the system of law books. The case example is *Greater Westchester Home Owners Association v. City of Los Angeles*, which involved the Los Angeles International Airport and owners of homes immediately adjacent to the airport. It is a noise and land use issue.

Recall that the first step in legal research is to go to the digests. Looking at the "Defendant-Plaintiff Table A-L" in the *Ninth Decennial Digest* (of the American Digest System) 1976-1981, the case of *Greater Westchester Homeowners Association v. City of Los Angeles* will be found listed alphabetically under the defendant's (Los Angeles) name. It is cited as "603 P.2d 1329, 160 Cal. Rptr. 733 (Cal. S. Ct. 1979)." According to the digest entry, the case can be located in Volume 603 of the *Pacific Reporter*, on page 1329. It can also be found in Volume 160 of the *California Reporter*, on page 733, and so on. We also learn from the citation that the decision was handed down by the California Supreme Court in 1979.

The case can also be found in the *Ninth Decennial Digest*, "Table of Cases A-M" under a similar citation as that above. Included with the citation are some key "topical" terms including: "Eminent Domain" and "Municipal Corporation."

Suppose the researcher does not know the case name but is aware of the subject of the litigation. The researcher could look in the *Ninth Decennial Digest*, in the descriptive words section "Mines and Minerals-Negligence." In that volume, and under the term, "Municipal Corporation," the case of *Greater Westchester v. Los Angeles* is found, along with a brief description of the case and also its citing. The same would be true if looking under the descriptive words, "Eminent Domain." Using key words as clues, if one knew nothing more about the case than it involved the City of Los Angeles, looking under "Municipal Corporation," for example, could lead one to the case in point.

The index system thus leads the researcher ultimately to the *Pacific Reporter, second series*, where the case narrative in its entirety will be found. At this point, the first two steps of the research process are complete. Now suppose the researcher wants to know if the case was continued on appeal, and if so, what were the results? *Shepard's Citations* may now be consulted.

Recall the original case citation was "603 P.2d 1329." Looking for the Shepard's citation book corresponding to the case read in the *Pacific Reporter* leads the researcher to look at *Shepard's Pacific Reporter Citations* under Volume 603, page 1329. The case history there reported indicates the case was appealed to the U.S. Supreme Court but *certiorari* was denied, meaning the Supreme Court would not hear the case and it was thus terminated.

If the researcher wants to confirm the Shepard's citation he or she may then go to Volume 449 of *United States Reports* (for cases adjudged in the U.S. Supreme Court). There one would find that, indeed, the Supreme Court would not hear the case.

A short cut to the above process would be to first look in the CCH *Aviation Cases*. In the index of *Aviation Cases*, Volume 15, the case citations for *Greater Westchester v. Los Angeles* will also include the case history which indicates the case was ended by the Supreme Court's denial of *certiorari*. The complete text of the case can also be found in the CCH as well as West Publishing Co.'s *Pacific Reporter*, and *California Reporter* series.

CASE BRIEF

In this chapter, the beginning researcher has been guided through the process of legal research, including a description of how cases are cited. The final step in the process is to prepare a brief. A case brief is a synopsis of the findings. By definition, a "brief" is a detailed statement of a party's case. It is synonymous in law with "points and authorities." It is a condensed statement of the propositions of law which counsel desire to establish, indicating the reasons and authorities that sustain them. It is a vehicle of counsel to convey to an appellate court the essential facts of the client's case; a statement of the questions of law that counsel would have applied, and the application counsel desires made of it by the court. In other words, a case brief is a synopsis of a case.

In the research of case law books, a "brief" may also be an abstract of a given case. The hornbook reporting of especially long and complex cases are not uncommonly 20 to 30 pages in length. The purpose of a research brief, as is true in the normal use of the term is to condense the case for easy review of facts of the case and its outcome.

On Table 5.5, "Case Brief Outline," is one example of how to outline a case brief. Following the outline is an example of how *Greater Westchester v. City of Los Angeles* might be briefed.

The case of *Greater Westchester* was chosen for purposes of demonstrating the research process. The case is an interesting one, because the physical results of this issue can be seen around the perimeter of the airport today. If one were to visit Los Angeles International Airport, and to take a drive just north and east of the airport boundary, one would find acres of urban blight, where whole city blocks of residential housing have been raised. The people have been relocated, and left only are the vacant city blocks. The homes are gone, and all that remains are the city streets which sub-divide the area. It is a strange phenomenon to view what, until just a few years ago, were people's homes and neighborhood, but what is now laid waste in desolation. The area in effect has been made barren and lifeless as the result of the adverse environmental impact of the airport and its development. It is an excellent example to illustrate the extensive liability, which may be incurred in the operation of a public airport.

Table 5.5—CASE BRIEF OUTLINE

I   *CITATION*—the case name and official citation.
II   *PRINCIPLES*—the legal points made by the decision.
III   *FACTS OF THE CASE*
    A. *PLAINTIFF*—name and version of the facts.
    B. *CAUSE OF ACTION AND REMEDY SOUGHT*—the reason for or goal of the litigation.
    C. *DEFENDANT*—name and version of the facts if differing from Plaintiff's account.
    D. *DEFENSES*—to allegations of Plaintiff.
IV   *LOWER COURTS*—history of the litigation.
V   *ISSUES*—the legal questions.
VI   *HELD*—yes or no to the issues and the results.
VII   *RATIONALE*—reason for the decision.
VIII   *DISSENT*—basis for dissenting opinion.

GREATER WESTCHESTER HOMEOWNERS ASSOCIATION v. CITY OF LOS ANGELES
603 P.2d 1329 (Cal. S. Ct. 1979)

Is a municipality, which owns and operates an airport liable for personal injuries sustained by nearby residents, and caused by noise from aircraft using the facility?

Plaintiffs, as homeowners near the two north runways at Los Angeles International Airport, sued the City in *inverse condemnation* for property damage, and on a *nuisance* theory, for personal injuries caused from aircraft generated noise, smoke and vibrations.

In defense, the City argued that the nuisance claim was inappropriate for two reasons. First, the City argued that the noise emanated from aircraft in flight where the federal government exercises exclusive dominion. The airport operator was, therefore, federally preempted. Second, operation of aircraft is sanctioned by law and, therefore, the resulting aircraft noise emissions cannot constitute a nuisance. Civil Code 3482 provided: "Nothing which is done or maintained under the express authority of a statute can be deemed a nuisance." The California Supreme Court rejected both arguments.

Preemption as a defense normally infers sovereignty by the Federal government, which excludes local regulation of "aircraft in flight." In the FAA's view, federal law does not preempt the exercise of reasonable and nondiscriminatory proprietary control over land use planning, design and location of runways, aircraft noise limits, and curfews. Airport owners acting as proprietors can deny the use of their airports on the basis of noise considerations. Several courts have recognized the power of a proprietor to impose airport use restrictions that are reasonable and nondiscriminatory. Federal preemption *per se* is not a valid defense.

An *actionable nuisance* is defined as, "anything which is injurious to health, or is indecent or offensive to the senses, or an obstruction to the free use of property, so as to interfere with the comfortable enjoyment of life or property. . . ." It is recognized that a property owner has a constitutionally founded remedy of inverse condemnation for property damage or loss caused by noise. The Federal Aviation Act of 1958 provides that its terms shall not abridge "remedies now existing at common law or by statute. . . ." This clause preserves the validity of pre-existing nuisance causes of action. The City's reliance on immunity from nuisance liability was unpersuasive because "a statutory sanction cannot be pleaded in justification of acts which by general rules of law constitute a nuisance, unless the acts complained of are authorized by the express terms of the statute under which the justification is made. . . ." It must be "fairly stated that the legislature contemplated the doing of the very act which occasions the injury." Even if the activity causing the nuisance were authorized by statute, the manner in which the activity is performed may still constitute a nuisance. Governmental approval of aviation activity does not imply legislative approval of aircraft noise. The Court also found significant the City's involvement in the creation and maintenance of the nuisance in question was continuous. It was the City that decided to build and then expand the airport in the vicinity of a residential area. The Court held that the claims for personal injuries were founded upon nuisance that had not been federally preempted.

Plaintiffs were awarded damages for personal injuries sustained.

CHAPTER 6

AVIATION SECURITY

Where criminal activity has not been averted, there are established procedures used to identify and prosecute criminals guilty of carrying weapons and/or explosives aboard aircraft; assaulting, intimidating or threatening crew members, or otherwise attempting to engage in air piracy.

UNLAWFUL INTERFERENCE WITH AIRCRAFT AS A CRIME

Whereas the purpose for civil law is to protect the individual, criminal law is defined substantively as law, which has for its purpose the prevention of harm to society. Criminal law declares statutorily what conduct is criminal, and prescribes the punishment to be imposed for such conduct. In other words, it includes the definition of specific offenses and general principles of liability. Criminal laws are commonly codified into criminal, or penal, codes such as Title 18, "Crimes and Civil Procedure," of the United States Code, or in state penal codes such as California Penal Code.

Another example is Title IX, "Penalties," of the Federal Aviation Act of 1958, which prescribes the civil and criminal penalties for violating the provisions of the Act, or any rule, regulation, or order issued thereunder. Section 901 of Title IX prescribes Civil Penalties for the violation of safety and economic regulations. Any "person" who violates the safety and security rules and regulations is subject to a civil penalty (as prescribed in the Act) of $1,100 for each violation.[1]

---

[1] 49 U.S.C. 46301(a)(1). Per the Inflation Adjustment Act of 1990, as amended by the Debt Collection Improvement Act of 1996, federal agencies were to issue regulations adjusting their

Any person who operates aircraft "for the carriage of persons or property for compensation or hire," other than an "airman serving in the capacity of an airman," is subject to a civil penalty of not more than $11,000 for each violation.[2] A fine of $11,000 may also be the penalty for each violation related to the transportation of hazardous materials.[3]

Penalties assigned to those engaged in air commerce and air transportation[4] are intended for corporate entities such as the airlines, fixed base operators, and the airports that serve them. Furthermore, "each violation" has been defined by the courts to mean a violation for each "discrete" occurrence. For example, in *United States v. American Airlines*, a separate and individual violation occurred with each improper screening of a passenger's baggage.[5]

Whereas Section 901 of the Act prescribes the civil penalties attached to violations, or infractions of the rules and regulations, Section 902, *Criminal Penalties*, describes the crimes for which violators are guilty of misdemeanors and felonies. Section 902 lists the various types of crime which are of particular relevance to aviation by giving reference to Section 1472, Title 49, of the United States Code. The crimes identified in Section 902 include: air piracy, interference with crew members, carrying weapons and explosives aboard aircraft, forgery of certificates or aircraft markings, interference with air navigation, receiving illegal rebates, violations of the Hazardous Materials Transportation Act, falsifying records, and giving false information about the above crimes, such as falsely reporting a bomb.[6] Section 902 also gives reference to "certain crimes aboard aircraft," which in reality are nothing more than common street crime, made unique to aviation only because they may have been committed aboard an aircraft. Included are theft, assault, and so forth.

Although its scope has yet to be clearly defined, another area of criminal law that has received considerable attention over the past two or three decades is corporate crime. Albeit not included in the

---

covered civil monetary penalties for changes in the cost of living by Oct. 23, 1996, and then to make necessary adjustments at least once every four years thereafter. The penalties cited here and in footnotes 2 and 3 below represent adjustments as of Jan. 1, 2004.

[2] 49 U.S.C. 46301(a)(2).

[3] 49 U.S.C. 46301(a)(3)(A).

[4] *Air commerce* is generally defined as "the carriage by aircraft of persons or property for compensation or hire." When the carriage is by *common carrier*, it is defined as *air transportation*.

[5] *United States v. American Airlines*, 22 Avi. Rep. (CCH) ¶ 18,205 (1990).

[6] *See United States v. Feldman*, 10 Avi. Rep. (CCH) ¶ 18,351 (1969).

Federal Aviation Act as such, corporate deviance has been of particular concern in aviation since the advent of airline deregulation. "Deviance" is herein defined as "an act perceived by others as a departure from social norms." The most obvious corporate criminal activity (or deviance) allegedly occurring in aviation has been within the airline industry, and associated with anti-competitive activities of the airline companies subsequent to deregulation. Because it involves airlines specifically, it is appropriate to save the discussion about corporate deviance for the chapter on airlines. Hence, the discussion of corporate crime, or what has been otherwise described as "white collar crime," is deferred to Chapter 11. In this particular chapter, criminal law is addressed as it is generally manifest in the encompassing area of aviation security and as circumscribed by street crimes and acts of violence.

Title IX of the Federal Aviation Act specifies civil and criminal penalties, but it is generally fostered in the interest of aviation safety and security. Until recently it was the Federal Aviation Administration [FAA] Administrator who was required by Congress to provide persons traveling by air (transportation) protection from acts of criminal violence and air piracy. In carrying out its responsibilities, the FAA provided oversight and sponsored periodic courses in aviation security for the training of law enforcement officers, airline personnel, and others involved in security screening of passengers and development of airport and airline security programs. But the agency itself did not provide physical security. Subsequent to the events of September 11, 2001, and the creation of the Transportation Security Administration [TSA] within the Department of Homeland Security [DHS], the TSA has assumed the security responsibilities previously assigned to the FAA, including the screening process itself that had previously been performed by the airlines, the airports, or their contractors. Because of its sensitive nature and the fact that it might fall into the wrong hands, then as now certain information regarding security procedures is kept confidential.[7]

Since the 9/11 terrorist attacks against the World Trade Center and the Pentagon, terrorism has become the nightmare of the modern world. But the roots of terrorist acts against commercial aircraft go back as far as 1931 when Peruvian revolutionaries commandeered a

---

[7] *See Public Citizens, Inc., Aviation Consumer Action Project, and Families of Pan Am 103/Lockerbie v. Federal Aviation Administration*, CCH AVI 17,403 (1993).

non-commercial Ford Tri-Motor. The first hijacking of a U.S. commercial aircraft occurred in 1961.[8] On September 5 of that year Congress promptly amended Section 902 of the Federal Aviation Act to impose criminal penalties for hijacking.[9] Since then, the means by which terrorism has been manifest have been as brutal as they are imaginative, including hijacking aircraft, firing heat-seeking missiles at them, bombing aircraft and airport waiting lounges, gunning down passengers, and more recently, turning aircraft into guided missiles aimed at financial and governmental institutions.

During the infancy of civil aviation, a passenger's principal concerns were the skill of the pilot and the mechanical condition of the aircraft. Recent decades have added a third—aerial terrorism. Professor Paul Wilkinson points out that, "By the end of the 1980s aviation terrorism rivaled technical failure and pilot error as a cause of fatalities in civil aviation."[10] Hijackings account for the largest percentage of all attacks against civil aviation.[11] Other criminal acts involve: airport attacks;[12] bombings, attempted bombings, and shootings on civil aviation aircraft;[13] commandeering of aircraft;[14] general and charter

---

[8] *United States v. Davis*, 482 F.2d 893, 897-898 (9th Cir. 1973).

[9] Prior to 1961, hijacking an aircraft in the U.S. was usually held to be kidnapping or obstruction of commerce. *See Bearden v. United States*, 304 F.2d 532, 534-535 (5th Cir. 1962), *vacated on other grounds*, 372 U.S., 252 (1963), *obstructing commerce affd*, 320 F.2d 99, 104 (5th Cir. 1963), *cert. denied*, 376 U.S. 922 (1964). However, the Federal Aviation Act of 1958, Pub. L. No. 85-726, had authorized the FAA to issue such rules and regulations as necessary to provide for national security and safety in air transportation. It also prohibited the transportation of explosives or other dangerous articles in violation of FAA rules.
During the decade following the 1961 hijacking legislation, more than 120 attempts were made to hijack U.S. aircraft. *See* Paul Dempsey, William Thoms & Robert Hardaway, *Aviation Law & Regulation* Sec. 9.21 (1993).

[10] Paul Wilkinson, *Terrorism Versus Democracy—The Liberal State Response*, (2001).

[11] *U.S. Federal Aviation Administration, Criminal Acts Against Civil Aviation* 3 (2001).

[12] In the 1970s, airports in Tel Aviv and Athens were attacked; in the 1980s, airports in Rome, Munich and Vienna were attacked.

[13] The bombing of Air India flight 182 over the Irish Sea by Sikh separatists, killing all 329 aboard, and the bombing of Pan Am flight 103 over Lockerbie, Scotland, by operatives of the Libyan government, killing all 259 aboard, are notorious examples of explosions that destroyed commercial aircraft. North Korea is also widely believed responsible for a 1987 explosion of a Korean Airlines flight 858 over the Andaman Sea near Burma that killed all 115 passengers and crew aboard. In the late 1970s, surface-to-air missiles brought down Air Rhodesia aircraft. Mistaking it for a military aircraft, in 1988 the U.S.S. Vincennes fired missiles which brought down an Iran Air flight 655 A-300 commercial aircraft shortly after taking off from Bandar Abbas, killing all 290 people aboard. Earlier, in 1983, Soviet MIGs also brought down Korean Airlines flight 007, a Boeing 747 that had strayed over its territory, killing all 269 people aboard.

[14] Examples include the 1985 skyjackings of TWA flight 847 and Egypt Air flight 648. R.I.R. Abeyratne, *Legal and Regulatory Issues in International Aviation* 326 (1996).

aviation aircraft incidents;[15] off-airport facility attacks; and shootings at in-flight aircraft.[16]

ANTI-TERRORISM LAW AND POLICY[17]

The motives for aircraft hijacking are diverse, but international and domestic law have worked in a complimentary fashion to arrest aircraft hijacking, piracy, terrorism, and other forms of unlawful interference with commercial aviation as has United States' legislation addressing international and domestic problems related to aircraft hijacking and other forms of aerial terrorism. To better understand the historical response to aerial terrorism, a chronological understanding of the evolution of law and policy in aviation is essential, as the development of aviation policy has long been a reactive, rather than a proactive, process.[18] Presented below is an overview of international as well as domestic law and policy dealing with the threat of terrorism.

INTERNATIONAL AIR LAW

International law aimed at subduing threats and attacks on aviation and airport security is based upon several multilateral conventions drafted under the auspices of the United Nations and the International Civil Aviation Organization [ICAO],[19] including:

---

[15] In 2002, missiles were fired at an Israeli charter aircraft over Nigeria.

[16] These are the categories the FAA has used to report annual criminal incidents since 1986. *Id.*; *see also* , R.I.R. Abeyratne, *The Effects of Unlawful Interference with Civil Aviation on World Peace and Social Order,* 22 Transp. L.J. 449, 455, 461 (1995).

[17] This section was taken largely from Paul Stephen Dempsey and Laurence E. Gesell, *Air Commerce and the Law,* Ch. 15 (2004), and Laurence E. Gesell and Paul Stephen Dempsey, *Air Transportation: Foundations for the 21st Century* Ch. 11 (2005).

[18] For example, establishment of the FAA in 1958 followed three tragic crashes the preceding year, one that took the life of a U.S. Senator. Paul Stephen Dempsey and Laurence E. Gesell, *Air Transportation: Foundations for the 21st Century* 229-231 (1997).

[19] ICAO is composed of some 188 Contracting States and thereby encompasses virtually the entire civil aviation community. The basic aims and objectives of the ICAO are to ensure safe and orderly growth of international civil aviation throughout the world and to promote safety of flight in international air navigation. For discussion of the role of the ICAO, *see* Kotaite, *Security of International Civil Aviation-Role of ICAO,* 7 Annals Air & Space L. 95 (1982).

- *The Tokyo Convention of 1963*—the Convention on Offenses and Certain Other Acts Committed on Board Aircraft[20] requires that a hijacked aircraft be restored to the aircraft commander and passengers be permitted to continue their journey;
- *The Hague Convention of 1970*—the Convention for the Suppression of Unlawful Seizure of Aircraft[21] declares hijacking to be an international "offense" and requires that the State to which an aircraft is hijacked to extradite or exert jurisdiction over the hijacker and prosecute him, and impose "severe penalties" if he is found guilty;
- *The Montreal Convention of 1971*—the Convention for the Suppression of Unlawful Acts Against the Safety of Civil Aviation expands the definition of "offense" to include unlawful acts against aircraft or air navigation facilities, and the communication of false information, and requires prosecution thereof;
- *Annex 17*—in 1974, ICAO adopted Annex 17 to the Chicago Convention on Civil Aviation of 1944[22]; beyond incorporating several of the requirements of the Tokyo, Hague and Montreal Conventions, the Annex requires that member States establish a governmental institution to regulate security and a national civil aviation security program that prevents weapons, explosives or other dangerous devices aboard aircraft, the checking and screening of aircraft, passengers, baggage, cargo and mail, and requires security personnel be subjected to background checks, qualification requirements, and be adequately trained;
- *The Montreal Protocol of 1988*—the Protocol for the Suppression of Unlawful Acts of Violence at Airports Serving International Civil Aviation, Supplementary to the Convention for the Suppression of Unlawful Acts Against the Safety of Civil Aviation added airport security to the international regime; and

---

[20] Convention on Offenses and Certain Other Acts Committed on Board Aircraft, Sep. 14, 1963, 20 U.S.T. 2941, T.I.A.S. No. 6768, 704 U.N.T.S. 219, reprinted in 58 Am. J. Int'l L. 566 (1959) [hereinafter Tokyo Convention]. All subsequent citations are to the materials reprinted.
[21] Convention for the Suppression of Unlawful Seizure of Aircraft, Dec. 16, 1970, 22 U.S.T. 1641, T.I.A.S. No. 7192, reprinted in 10 I.L.M. 133 (1971) [hereinafter Hague Convention]. All subsequent cites are to the materials reprinted.
[22] Convention on International Civil Aviation, done Dec. 7, 1944, 61 Stat. 1180, T.I.A.S. No. 1591, 15 U.N.T.S. 295. *See* Dempsey, *The Role of the International Civil Aviation Organization on Deregulation, Discrimination, and Dispute Resolution,* 52 J. Air L. & Com. 529 (1987).

- *The Montreal Convention of 1991*—the Convention on the Marking of Plastic Explosives for the Purpose of Detection[23] prevented the manufacture, possession and movement of unmarked explosives.

In addition, several air security agreements have emerged entirely outside ICAO auspices, including the European Convention on the Suppression of Terrorism ("European Convention"),[24] and the Bonn Declaration on Hijacking ("Bonn Declaration").[25] The European Convention of 1977 provided that hijacking would not be deemed a political offense for purposes of extradition. The Bonn Declaration of 1978, an agreement of G-7 leaders, provided that all flights would be ceased immediately to or from any nation which refused to prosecute or extradite a hijacker, or return the hijacked aircraft.

Though constituting an important portion of the legal arsenal to curb acts of violence against civil aviation, the Conventions are limited in their application to contracting States.[26] Of the 188 ICAO member States, a number failed to ratify the Conventions, particularly the plastics explosive convention.[27] Nonetheless, ICAO members are obliged to comply with Annex 17 to the Chicago Convention, which incorporated several of the Conventions' requirements. The acceptance of the Conventions by a broad spectrum of the economic pow-

---

[23] Convention for the Suppression of Unlawful Acts Against the Safety of Civil Aviation, Sep. 23, 1971, 24 U.S.T. 564, T.I.A.S. No. 7570, reprinted in 10 I.L.M. 115 [hereinafter Montreal Convention].

[24] *European Convention on the Suppression of Terrorism*, opened for signature, Jan. 27, 1977, reprinted in 15 I.L.M. 1272 (1976).

[25] *Joint Statement on International Terrorism*, Pub. Papers 1308 (Jul. 17, 1978), reprinted in 17 I.L.M. 1285 (1978). The seven economic powers that participated in the drafting of the Bonn Declaration were Canada, France, West Germany, Italy, Japan, the United Kingdom and the United States.

[26] *The Convention for the Suppression of Unlawful Seizure of Aircraft*, Dec. 16, 1970, 22 U.S.T. 1643, 860 U.N.T.S. 105, entered into force Oct. 14, 1971, with 140 ratifications in 1994. *The Convention for the Suppression of Unlawful Acts Against the Safety of Civil Aviation*, Sep. 23, 1971, 24 U.S.T. 567, 974 U.N.T.S. 177, entered into force on Jan. 26, 1973, with 150 ratifications..

[27] Nicholas Matte, *Treatise on Air-Aeronautical Law* 372 (1981). As of 1981, 106 States had ratified the Tokyo Convention, and 109 had ratified the Montreal Convention. As of 2002, 173 States had ratified the Tokyo Convention, 175 had ratified Hague, and 176 had ratified Montreal. Of ICAO's 188 member States, 15 States had not ratified the Tokyo Convention of 1963, 13 had not ratified the Hague Convention of 1970, 12 had not ratified the Montreal Convention of 1971, and 108 had not ratified the Convention on the Marking of Plastic Explosives for the Purpose of Detection of 1991. *Status of Certain International Law Instruments*, 57 ICAO J. 35 (No. 6, 2002).

ers may lead to the development of customary international law[28] on the subject, in which case the provisions could be enforced against both signatories and non-signatories.

UNITED STATES DOMESTIC LAW

Along with its participation in multilateral conventions, resolutions, and declarations, since 1961 the United States government has attempted to combat aerial terrorism unilaterally through its own internal legislation. After defining hijacking as a federal crime in 1961, the United States discovered that the solution to this new type of terrorism was not to be realized by the imposition of penalties.[29] The problem was, and is, far more complex than traditional crimes. It follows then that unconventional measures may be necessary to rid the skies of would-be pirates.

The solution to this complex problem can only be realized by drafting legislation that improves airport security, destroys hijackers' incentives, and imposes sanctions not just on the hijacker himself, but on his support system and on any country willing to grant him a sanctuary. However, in the process of imposing extraordinary measures the possibility of trampling civil rights is proportionally increased. Moreover, freedom of movement is restricted, thereby becoming counterproductive to the very purpose of air transportation.

In the ensuing decades since 1961, the United States created a body of law designed to combat terrorism both domestically and abroad. Some of this legislation is intended to fulfill the nation's obligation as a party to the relevant international conventions or treaties, described above.[30] Still other laws have been enacted in response to the problem in United States domestic air travel caused by hijackings to Cuba.[31] Others still, were adopted to deal with particular catastro-

---

[28] Customary international law rule is common usage or state practice felt to be legally obligatory by those who follow it. Sasella, *The International Civil Aviation Organization: Its Contribution to International Law*. 8 Melb. U. L. Rev. 41 (1971).

[29] During the decade following the 1961 hijacking legislation, more than 120 attempts were made to hijack U.S. aircraft.

[30] *See* e.g., The Antihijacking Act of 1974, Pub. L. No. 93-366, § 101, 88 Stat. 409-410, 413 (1974) implements the Convention for the Suppression of Unlawful Acts Against the Safety of Civil Aviation (Hague Convention), 24 U.S.T. 564, T.I.A.S. No. 7570.

[31] As early as 1971, the FAA began to promulgate rules designed to increase security in and around the nation's airports, especially those airports located near large Cuban immigrant populations. For details about then current regulations, *see* 14 C.F.R. Part 107 (1986).

phes—Pan Am 103's explosion over Lockerbie, Scotland; TWA flight 800's explosion over Long Island, New York; and the World Trade Center/Pentagon attacks on September 11, 2001. Most of the statutes in force today can be divided into two broad categories: those designed to deter air piracy and those designed to punish the perpetrator. Succinctly summarized, the principal objectives of these laws were as follows:

- *The Antihijacking Act of 1974* implemented the Hague Convention of 1970; it imposed penalties for carrying weapons or explosives aboard aircraft, and a penalty of 20 years imprisonment or death if a passenger is killed during a hijacking; it authorized the President to suspend the landing rights of any nation that harbors hijackers.
- *The Air Transportation Security Act of 1974* authorized the screening of passengers and baggage for weapons.
- *The Aircraft Sabotage Act of 1984* implemented the Montreal Convention of 1971; it imposed penalties of up to $100,000 or 20 years imprisonment, or both, for hijacking, damage, destruction or disabling an aircraft or air navigation facility.
- *The International Security and Development Act of 1985* authorized expenditures for enhancing security at foreign airports.
- *The Foreign Security Airport Act of 1985* required the U.S. Department of Transportation Secretary to assess security at foreign airports, and notify the public or suspend service if a foreign airport fails to correct a security breach; it also required that foreign airlines serving the United States adopt and implement security procedures prescribed by the U.S. government.
- *The Aviation Security Improvement Act of 1990* mandated background checks for airline and airport employees, and imposed additional training, educational and employment standards upon them; it also required deployment of bomb-detection technology for baggage.
- *The Federal Aviation Administration Reauthorization Act of 1996* required passenger profiling, explosive detection technology, procedures for passenger/bag matching, and certification for screening companies.

- *The Omnibus Consolidated Appropriations Act of 1997* authorized the purchase of advanced screening equipment for baggage.
- *The Aviation Security Improvement Act of 2000* required fingerprinting and background checks of airport and airline security personnel at Category X airports.[32]
- *The Aviation and Transportation Security Act of 2001* federalized the airport screening function, establishing the new Transportation Security Administration under the Department of Transportation [DOT] to regulate security in all modes of transportation; it also enhanced baggage screening procedures, and imposed more stringent personnel qualifications on security employees.
- *The Homeland Security Act of 2002* consolidated 22 agencies, including the TSA, into a new cabinet-level Department of Homeland Security. The agency was given jurisdiction, *inter alia*, over transportation security, customs, immigration and agricultural inspections.

Under girding aviation regulation in the United States is the Federal Aviation Act, which assigns responsibility for safety and security and defines criminal activity while in flight and within the special aircraft jurisdiction of the United States. The aircraft is "in flight" from the moment when all external doors are closed following embarkation until the moment when one such door is opened for disembarkation. The "special aircraft jurisdiction" of the United States is: (1) any civil aircraft of U.S. registry, (2) aircraft of national defense forces of the U.S., (3) any other aircraft within the U.S., and (4) any aircraft outside the U.S. that has its next scheduled destination or last point of departure in the U.S. Listed in Section 902 of the Federal Aviation Act are a variety of crimes in aviation, but the crimes specifically related to aviation security are as follows:

- *Air Piracy*—is the seizure or exercise of control by force or violence or by any other form of intimidation and with wrongful intent of an aircraft while it is in flight, and within the special aircraft jurisdiction of the United States.

---

[32] 49 U.S.C. § 44903 (2002).

- *Attempt to Commit Air Piracy*—is committed when the aircraft is within the special aircraft jurisdiction of the U.S. even though the aircraft is not in flight at the time of attempted seizure or exercise of control, if the aircraft would have been in the special aircraft jurisdiction if the offense of air piracy had been completed.
- *Interference with Flight Crew Members or Flight Crew Attendants*—is a crime. Whoever, while aboard an aircraft within the special aircraft jurisdiction of the U.S., assaults, intimidates, or threatens any flight crew member or flight attendant of such aircraft,[33] so as to interfere with the performance by such member or attendant of his or her duties or to lessen the ability of such member or attendant to perform his or her duties is in violation of interference with flight crew members or flight crew attendants.[34]
- *Carrying Weapons or Explosives Aboard Aircraft*—is unauthorized except for law enforcement officers of any municipal or state government, or political subdivision thereof, or the federal government, who are otherwise authorized to carry arms. Whoever, not so authorized, while aboard an aircraft or who attempts to board an aircraft being operated by an air carrier in air transportation, has on or about his or her person a concealed deadly or dangerous weapon is in violation of federal law.[35]
- *False Information*—occurs whenever someone willfully and maliciously, or with reckless disregard for the safety of life, imparts or conveys or causes to be imparted or conveyed false

---

[33] Because their duties are passenger service-oriented, flight attendants are normally not considered as part of the crew. Rather, most airlines are organized with the flight attendants in their marketing departments. However, in the context of air piracy and crimes aboard aircraft, assault on a flight attendant is the same as an assault on one of the crew.

[34] *See Rombom v. United Airline,* Avi. Rep. (CCH) ¶ 18,300 (1994).

[35] It should be noted here that violation of many of the aviation security crimes might also be a violation of concurrent state law. Carriage of a concealed weapon, for example, may be in violation of State codes whether on an aircraft or not. Where an offense committed constitutes an offense against federal law only, criminal jurisdiction is vested exclusively in United States courts. Where offenses constitute violations of both federal and state law, there are two separate crimes committed, and two separate prosecutions may follow. Normally, prosecuting authorities (federal and state) decide under which law they wish to prosecute, and they will turn the suspect over to the selected authority. Otherwise, the first court exercising jurisdiction is entitled to carry its proceedings to a conclusion (including punishment), and the accused is then turned over to the other prosecuting authority for a second trial and additional punishment.

information, knowing the information to be false, concerning an attempt or alleged attempt being made or to be made. [36]

- *Other Crimes*—include "certain crimes" aboard aircraft as listed in Section 7, Title 18, U.S.C., including the following: assault, maiming, stealing personal property, murder, manslaughter (actual or attempted), rape, carnal knowledge, and taking of anything of value.

The Act makes these and all other aviation security crimes a federal offense, and vests with the Federal Bureau of Investigation [FBI] the exclusive jurisdiction of investigating these crimes.

AVIATION SECURITY PROCEDURES BEFORE 9/11 [37]

AIRPORT SECURITY

Before 9/11 and the subsequent reorganization of security agencies and regulations in the United States, the provisions of FAR Part 107, "Airport Security," and FAR Part 108, "Airplane Operator Security," formed the fundamental regulatory structure for the security of persons and property against acts of criminal violence and aircraft piracy. Part 107 provided for the control of access to air operations areas by unauthorized persons and ground vehicles. Further, no person was allowed entry to a "sterile" area without submitting to the screening of his or her person and property in accordance with the procedures being applied by the airport to control access to that area.

Part 108 was designed to prevent or deter the carriage aboard airplanes of any explosive, incendiary, or a deadly or dangerous weapon on or about each individual's person or accessible property, and the carriage of any explosive or incendiary in checked baggage. Under Part 108, the airlines were required to: prohibit unauthorized access to their airplanes; ensure that baggage carried aboard their aircraft was checked in by an identified agent; prohibit unauthorized access to

---

[36] Even making a joke containing false information is illegal. When someone makes a joke about the fact there may be a bomb in a suitcase, security personnel do not appreciate it. No matter how lightly intended, the person who passes on such false information is breaking the law, and may be prosecuted. There are those who have found out the hard way that jokes about bombs are no laughing matter. *See United States v. Feldman*, 10 Avi. Rep. (CCH) ¶ 18,351 (1969).

[37] This section is drawn heavily from Laurence E. Gesell, *The Administration of Public Airports* Ch. 12 (4th ed. 1999).

cargo and checked baggage; and conduct security inspections of their airplanes. A third regulation, FAR Part 109, "Indirect Air Carrier Security," provided additional protection against criminal activity. This part prescribed aviation security rules governing each air carrier (including air freight forwarders and cooperative shipping associations) engaged indirectly in air transportation of property. Each indirect air carrier was required to have a security program designed to prevent or deter the unauthorized introduction of explosives or incendiary devices into any package cargo intended for carriage by air.

These FARs were designed to ensure the security of airports serving scheduled air carriers and required them to have screening programs. Prior to the federalization of these functions, the air carriers have had the responsibility of preventing and deterring carriage of weapons and explosives aboard their aircraft by potential hijackers. Conversely, airports serving the applicable air carriers have been responsible for preventing and deterring unauthorized access to the air operations area, and for providing law enforcement support at passenger screening stations.

Since their inception in 1972, federal security regulations have been designed to meet hijacking and other criminal threats, as they were then perceived. Because of the historical decline in aircraft hijackings around the world, it was assumed that procedures had been adequate to protect the traveling public. The guard was let down. And as stated above, the tragic events of September 11, 2001 revealed the profound vulnerability of the U.S. transportation system.

For the most part these operations involved large transport type airplanes, generally conducted by air carriers with Certificates of Public Convenience and Necessity [PC&N] (originally issued by the Civil Aeronautics Board [CAB] and later by the DOT). Operating rules for these carriers were set out in FAR Part 121, and for this reason, FAA security regulations were initially placed in that part. After passage of the Airline Deregulation Act and the CAB's liberalized policies and broad authority granted to commuters to conduct scheduled operations with large aircraft, numerous commuter air carriers held authority to conduct operations similar to those previously conducted only by holders of CAB Certificates of PC&N. These airplanes operated over routes formerly served by PC&N certificate holders, and operations were conducted without being subject to full FAA security requirements.

To ensure consistent application of FAA's security rules and to achieve the necessary level of security, FAR 108, "Airplane and Airport Operator Security," evolved with security requirements based upon airplane complexity instead of CAB authorization. Note that the original Part 108 carried a different title than a later version, which applied to "airplane operators," but not airports. Airport responsibilities were then totally contained within Part 107, and Part 108 requirements, as pertaining to aircraft size, remained basically the same.

Part 108 categorized airplanes into three groups according to configured seating capacities: (1) over 60 seats; (2) 31 through 60 seats; and (3) less than 31 seats. The rationale used by the FAA assumed that the larger the aircraft, the more attractive it was for the potential hijacker. If an operator used aircraft with more than 60 seats the implementation of a full security program was required.

Part 108 required the adoption of a comprehensive security program for operations with 31 through 60-seat aircraft. The program had to be comparable to that required for operations with airplanes having more than 60 seats. But normally the operator would only have had to implement those portions of the program that called for having procedures for contacting a law enforcement agency and arranging for response to an incident when needed, and instructing crew members and other employees in the adopted procedures. However, each such operator was to be prepared to implement its full security program upon notification by the FAA that a threat existed.

For operators of small aircraft (1-30 seats) no security program was required unless passengers had uncontrolled access to a sterile area. In all cases where non-screened passengers were discharged into a sterile area provisions for security were required regardless of seating capacity. The carrier either had to screen the passengers properly, or otherwise control their access to the sterile area through surveillance and escort procedures or through the screening procedures of another carrier.

The Federal Aviation Act required the FAA Administrator to establish procedures for the inspection, detention and search of persons and property in air transportation and intrastate air transportation to assure their safety and to assure they would receive courteous and efficient treatment by local law enforcement personnel and the airlines. To this end, each certificate holder was required to conduct screening under a security program and to use the procedures included, and the facilities and equipment described, in its approved security program to prevent or deter the carriage aboard airplanes of any explosive, incendiary, or a deadly or dangerous weapon on or about each individual's person or accessible property, and the carriage of any explosive or incendiary in checked baggage.

SECURITY CHECKPOINT PROTOCOL

Airport security screening systems have varied principally only in where the screening takes place and have conformed to compliance with evolving legal precedence, unaltered since 9/11. At each screening point, appropriate signs advise the individual of the screening requirement and that the exercise of the individual's option to refuse to undergo the required screening process would result in denial of passage beyond the screening point. Additionally, wherever an X-ray baggage inspection system is used, appropriate signs must advise the individual of the X-ray inspection system.

The initial screening process is conducted using either a walk-through metal detector (or magnetometer) or a hand-held metal detector. If the person being screened does not alarm the detector, the person is cleared to proceed beyond the screening point. If the metal detector alarms, the person must be reprocessed to determine the cause of the alarm.

In reprocessing, the person causing the alarm divests his or her person of metal and is then reintroduced through the metal detector. If the walk-through metal detector continues to alarm during reprocessing, the person must undergo additional screening. The hand-held metal detector is then used to determine and isolate the area of the alarm. Once the area has been isolated, the cause of the alarm should be determined, with the passenger's assistance, through a consent frisk either by observation, physical inspection of outer garments, or by having the passenger present pocket contents for inspection. It was the law enforcement officer [LEO] who normally performed such frisks, if one was present. However, FAR Part 108 assumed that screeners might perform pat down or hand-held metal detector searches.[38] Having taken over this responsibility the Transportation Security Administration now performs this function. Under no circumstances is the passenger allowed beyond the screening point un-

---

[38] *See* 14 CFR Part 108, § 108.31 (2) (iv and v).

less screening personnel are first assured that the passenger is not carrying any dangerous objects.[39]

Property processing is conducted by using an X-ray device and/or by physical inspection of the item. If no weapon, explosive or incendiary device is discovered the carry-on article may be permitted beyond the screening point. Metal detectors are normally not used to screen carry-on articles. If during the screening process, a weapon, explosive, incendiary device, or other contraband were discovered, the LEO would take custody of the item and initiate appropriate law enforcement action.

Where security programs were required by FAR, both the airline(s) and the airport were required to have security programs in writing, signed by the operators, and approved by the FAA. The airport security program must include descriptions of:

- the *air operations area* (that portion of the airport designed and used for landing, take-off, or surface maneuvering of airplanes);
- areas on or adjacent to the airport which affect *security* of the air operations area;
- each *exclusive area* (an area where the air carrier exercises exclusive security responsibility);
- procedures, facilities, and equipment used to perform the *control functions* by the airport operator and by each air carrier;
- *notification procedures*;
- alternate security procedures for use in *emergencies* and other unusual conditions;
- the *system for maintaining records* of security related incidents; and
- the *law enforcement* support system and the peace officer training program.

The airport operator must provide law enforcement officers in the number and in a manner adequate to support the airport security program and each air carrier passenger screening system. Airport police

---

[39] It is of note that several of the 9/11 hijackers set off metal detectors at Washington's Dulles Airport. But surveillance camera tapes show that the screeners waved hand-held metal detectors around but never resolved what had set off the metal detectors. *See* Scott McCartney, *From X-rays to Cargo, Security Gaps Remain*, Wall St. J. (Wed., Jul. 28, 2004), at D2.

are full-fledged peace officers. They are uniformed, carry a badge, armed and authorized to use a firearm, and have authority to arrest (with or without a warrant) for felony crimes.

A recently added member to the airport law enforcement team, and one commonly accepted on many police departments, is the police dog. The canine program was launched in 1972 when a bomb-sniffing dog named Brandy found an explosives device on an airplane.[40] Many U.S. airports now have dogs trained to sniff and search baggage, aircraft and terminals for explosives. The FAA first employed bomb-detection dogs with the object of trying ". . . to have them [the dogs] located so that no airplane would ever be more than 30 minutes from an airport with dog teams." By 1986, there were between 60 and 70 dogs at airports across the country. Since then at least four agencies looking into airport security system deficiencies have called for the increased utilization of dogs. Following the attacks of 9/11 the federal Explosives Detection Canine Team Program has rapidly expanded to include more than 325 teams in 82 airports.[41]

In the past, the LEO had to be immediately available to the screening point. However, Part 107 then allowed for flexible response wherein the LEO could be summoned. The regulation stated, "each airport operator shall provide law enforcement officers in the number and in a manner adequate to support—its security program, and each passenger screening system. . . ." Much discretion was given to the FAA Administrator to determine the acceptability of each airport sponsor's law enforcement support system.[42]

---

[40] *TSA's Fine K-9s*, Airport Report Magazine (Jan./Feb. 2003), at 9, 11.

[41] *Id.*

[42] Subsequent to the TSA assuming responsibility for airport security, it has "looked at what is before it to be controlled," and has "rubricized" airport categories to its own liking. The TSA has been silent on what criteria it uses to categorize the airports. But generally they are categorized as Category I, II, II, etc., with the most prominent Category I airports being classified as Category X. With prior LEO response programs under Part 108, the response time varied depending upon the size of the airport. At Category I airports (screening over two million people annually) the response time could not exceed five minutes, and at selected Category IA airports could not exceed one minute. At Category II airports (screening 500,000 to two million) the response time was 10 minutes. At Category III (less than 500,000 to two million) the response time was 15 minutes. And, for Category IV airports (serving air carriers with less than 60 seats) the response time could be as much as 20 minutes. When previous flexible response programs were in effect, the air carrier had to have at the screening point a Checkpoint Security Supervisor [CSS] at Category I and II airports, or a Screener In Charge [SIC] at Category III and IV airports. The CSS was required to have training comparable to the LEO but did not have peace officer status.

Later procedures called for a Security Coordinator on the ground and in flight. For the latter, the pilot in command was designated as the "in-flight" security coordinator. No person could be used as a ground security coordinator unless, within the preceding 12 months, that person had satisfactorily completed security training. Likewise, a crewmember could not be used as an in-flight security coordinator unless that person had satisfactorily completed training (or recurrent training) within the preceding 12 months.

Security risks associated with airline employees became an issue with the crash of a Pacific Southwest Airlines [PSA] commuter jet near Paso Robles, California, in December 1987. The crash occurred after a former PSA employee, flying as a passenger, opened fire with a gun during the flight. The procedures to guard against air piracy that had been in place for nearly 20 years had served their purpose well, but there were loopholes. Moreover, with the introduction of "plastic" explosive materials, they were no longer as effective against the threat of concealed explosives. Emanating out of the PSA crash, the FAA in 1988 amended FAR Part 107 to require airport operators in their security programs to perform the following control functions:

- *controlling access* to each air operations area, including methods for preventing the entry of unauthorized persons and ground vehicles;
- *controlling movement* of persons and ground vehicles within each air operations area, including when appropriate, requirements for the display of identification; and
- promptly *detecting and taking action* to control each penetration, or attempted penetration, of an air operations area by a person whose entry was not authorized.

The airport operator was to ensure that access was denied immediately at the access point or points to individuals whose authority to have such access had changed. The system, method, or procedure had to be capable of limiting an individual's access by time and date. Effectively, this means the system was to be computer-controlled.

In March 1988, the FAA requested assistance from the National Research Council to initiate a study assisting the FAA Technical Center in evaluating methods for detecting concealed explosives, with the emphasis on highly energetic, plastic explosives in checked baggage. Soon afterward, the critical importance of explosive detection was highlighted by the destruction of Pan American World Airways flight 103 on December 21, 1988, by a terrorist bomb while in flight above Lockerbie, Scotland, killing all 270 persons aboard. Up to that time it was the worst aviation disaster of its kind in U.S. history.

The National Research Council's National Materials Advisory Board [NMAB] established a Committee on Commercial Aviation Security, composed of experts in areas of chemistry, physics, materials science, explosive materials, sophisticated analytical instrumentation, forensic science, and ordnance. The committee's primary conclusion was that "there does not appear to be any single detection technology that can provide levels of sensitivity and specificity that will have both a significant effect on reducing the threat and an acceptable impact on airport operations."[43]

The report by the Committee on Commercial Aviation Security to the FAA Technical Center analyzed a number of detection technologies and provided broad priorities for allocation of funding and research. The committee's recommendations were to:

- define a search strategy to optimize the mix of technologies available, with consideration of a *systems approach* employing layers of different devices with orthogonal detection capability;

- implement low-technology improvements including *bag-to-passenger matching* and *passenger profiling and/or interviewing*;

- define *performance criteria* for detection systems including as a guide for overall systems architecture, a minimum level of sensitivity and specificity, a minimum detectable amount of plastic explosives, vapor detection sensitivity range, and bag through-put rate;

- *reinforce baggage containers*, including improvements to the aircraft fuselage, as well as use of compressible padding to harden baggage containers against small explosive charges at altitude;

- establish standardized *operational tests* for all explosives detection systems to determine minimum detection capability, to

---

[43] Committee on Commercial Aviation Security, *Detection of Explosives for Commercial Aviation Security*, NMAB-471 (1993).

test the performance of the system, and to conduct field tests under airport operational conditions;

- develop standard positive controls for *solid and vapor detectors*;
- take advantage of *systems integration* opportunities for vapor detectors;
- explore the concept of *tagging* explosives and detonators to make them easily detectable by adding small quantities of materials during manufacturing that make them more observable by relatively inexpensive means; and to
- continue supporting the *exploration and development of new methods* that may be applicable to explosives detection.[44]

In response to the tragic loss of Pan Am 103, Presidential Executive Order 12686 established the President's Commission on Aviation Security and Terrorism. The Aviation Security Improvement Act of 1990 was enacted, in large part, to implement the recommendations of the President's Commission. The 1990 act amended the Federal Aviation Act of 1958 by adding a new sub-section, "Employment Standards," directing the FAA Administrator to prescribe minimum standards for the hiring and continued employment of air carrier and airport security personnel.

Subsequent to the 1988 bombing of Pan Am 103, FAR Part 107 was amended many times in piecemeal fashion and in response to individual aviation disasters. Reacting to the crash of TWA Flight 800 in 1996, the President's Commission alone made 57 recommendations for improving aviation safety. Between 1990 and 1999 both FAR Parts 107 and 108 had been in rewrite effectively for more than eight years. The final rewrite of 107 and 108 came just before the attacks in 2001. But much attention was being focused on requirements for security screening companies and personnel. A system called Threat Image Projection [TIP] was proposed for installation on then-existing baggage X-ray machines and designed to measure the performance of screeners by randomly placing realistic images of threatening objects onto the screen. The TIP system was one component of an overall computer-based Screener Proficiency Evaluation and Reporting System [SPEARS]. SPEARS was to be used to select, train,

---

[44] *Id.*

evaluate and monitor X-ray-screening employees.[45] Subsequent to 9/11 it was decided that the federal government would take over the screening function.

The Pan Am 103 accident highlighted not only the difficulty of detecting modern plastic explosives but also the growing capability of terrorist groups. The FAA effort to find a technical counter-terrorism solution accelerated in the aftermath of Flight 103. The FAA broadened its research in programs such as:

- working with aircraft manufacturers to develop techniques to *harden an aircraft* against the effects of a midair explosion;
- a major new initiative in the *human factors* of using technologies for screening;
- additional work in identifying suspects through the application of *profiles and questioning*; and
- special programs for *Thermal Neutron Analysis [TNA] enhancement*, the process of nuclear resonance absorption and vapor detection device.

When baggage is exposed to neutron radiation inside the TNA machine, the radiation activates elements in the bags, which then briefly emit gamma radiation measured by deflectors. The unique signature of gamma radiation can identify hidden objects. The FAA installed several TNA units at airports around the world, and although reportedly pleased with the results, remained officially undecided about proceeding with the TNA program.

Critics contend TNA is not cost-effective. Each machine costs about $1 million (U.S.), and it can have a high rate of false alarms, particularly when testing wool articles. Woolens contain high concentrations of nitrogen, and can be misidentified as explosives. In one test of the TNA, the machine processed 500 to 1,000 bags per day. When required to detect 2.5 pounds or more of explosives, the unit had a false alarm rate of about 5%. When set to detect less than one pound of explosives the rate went up to 15% and 20%.

Passage of the Aviation Security Improvement Act of 1990 temporarily blocked any further procurement of TNA devices pending more research. The act directed the FAA to "accelerate and expand the re-

---

[45] *See* Karl Bremer, *The Security Blues—Will Part 107 Rewrite Ever Surface?*, Airport Magazine (Mar./Apr. 1999), at 28-29.

search, development, and the implementation of technologies and procedures to counteract terrorist acts against civil aviation. The FAA requested that the Committee on Commercial Aviation Security be extended to provide advice regarding the implementation of the Aviation Security Improvement Act. The FAA asked for help in two key areas: systems analysis and architecture for explosive detection systems that could inspect passenger baggage and the development of test protocols and performance criteria for such systems.

In evaluating the "enemy" capabilities, against which counter-terrorist measure must be designed, the terrorist has literally dozens of choices of explosives. However, the explosive of choice seems to be the high energetic "plastics" that are widely available. Using plastic explosives, small, powerful bombs can be inexpensively constructed. These nitrogen-based (nitramine) explosives have three qualities that make them attractive to the terrorist:

- They have *high-energy yields* per unit weight;
- They have *small critical diameters* (i.e., the small diameter that can sustain detonation); and
- They require *little or no confinement* (i.e., heavy metal walls).

As a result, the focus in research and design of explosive detection devices is to search primarily for systems that can detect plastic explosives. Nevertheless, there are other types of explosives and devices that also pose significant threats. Thus, the Committee on Commercial Aviation Security found that "there does not appear to be any single detection technology" adequate to meet the threat. Therefore, the committee recommended a systems approach.

There are basically three general types of mechanical security detection techniques under consideration by the FAA: (1) *enhanced X-ray* machines; (2) *vapor detection* systems; and (3) *particle detection* equipment such as TNA. A fourth and far less sophisticated detection, yet highly efficient system involves the use of dogs to sniff out and detect explosives. Enhanced X-ray differentiates between organic and inorganic materials to aid in identifying explosives in luggage. Unlike X-ray machines, vapor detectors key on minute traces of explosive compounds captured in air samples.

Notwithstanding other technological advances in security technology, canine [K-9] units remain one of the most effective tools for combating crime and terrorism. For reasons that are not altogether understood, dogs are able to sense the volatility and possibly other characteristics of explosives. But more advanced, scientifically reliable technology is needed.

The terrorist bombing of Pan Am Flight 103 clearly demonstrated the need for new technology to detect explosives. The Aviation Security Improvement Act set a goal for the FAA to have new explosive detection equipment in place by November 1993. Questioning whether the goal had been met, members of Congress asked the Government Accounting Office [GAO] to examine the FAA's progress in developing new security technology and to specify actions the FAA could take to improve its security research program.

In May of 1994, the GAO reported that the FAA had made little progress toward meeting the goal for deploying new explosive detection systems. Although several devices had shown promise, technical problems had slowed the development and approval of the devices. The FAA's Aviation Security Research and Development Scientific Advisory Panel estimated it could take at least two to five more years before new devices could be approved for use by the airlines. Similarly, the FAA's efforts to enhance aircraft survivability following an internal explosion (by hardening baggage containers) were promising but were also several years from completion. Finally, the FAA lacked a strategy to guide its and the airlines' efforts to implement explosive detection equipment, nor had the FAA resolved such issues as cost, weight, and durability of hardened baggage containers.[46]

Unfortunately, within two years of the GAO report, on July 17, 1996, there was an explosion aboard Trans World Airlines Flight 800 just after takeoff. The explosion killed 230 people. No one knew for sure what caused the explosion. It could have been a mechanical malfunction, or there was a theory that because one of the fuel tanks was partially empty, the vapors in the tank may have exploded. But the possibility of a bomb having been placed aboard the aircraft or even a missile fired from the coast of Long Island Sound as the aircraft was climbing out was also suspected. Fearing sabotage, the White House Commission on Aviation Safety and Security was formed, chaired by Vice President Al Gore, to investigate what might be done to enhance aviation safety and security.

---

[46] Government Accounting Office, *Aviation Security: Development of New Security Technology Has Not Met Expectations*, GAO/RCED-94-142 (May 19, 1994).

On September 5, 1996, the Gore Commission announced its proposals to fight terrorism. Basically, the recommendations were a reiteration of what had already been presented:

- to install state-of-the-art *bomb-detecting equipment* in airports;
- to fund *research and development* necessary to make the technology more effective and readily available;
- increase the number of *bomb-sniffing dog teams*;
- mandatory *match between passengers and their luggage*; and
- better screening of passengers through computerized *profiles*.

The report itself highlights the fact that much of its work was based on addressing the public's emotional needs. As Robert Hahn laments, "the sad truth is that the threat of airline terrorism cannot be eliminated unless air travel is banned. . . ."[47] But as Al Gore resolved,

> *We may never see an end to terrorism, but we are sure going to do our level best to combat it and reduce to an absolute minimum level humanly possible the risk to American citizens traveling on airlines.*[48]

On October 9, 1996 President Clinton signed into law the Federal Aviation Administration Reauthorization Act, which included some wide-ranging security measures recommended by Al Gore's aviation security commission. The measure authorized the installation of new bomb-detection scanners to examine both carry-on and checked baggage at major airports, funding for new FBI agents to be assigned to airport security, increased inspection of mail on board flights, and increased the use of bomb-sniffing dogs.[49]

---

[47] *See* Karen Walker and Dave Knibb, *Blood, Sweat and Gore*, Airline Business (Apr. 1997).
[48] U.S. News Story Page, *Gore Announces Proposals to Fight Air Terrorism*, http://www.cnn.com/US/9609/05/airport.security/index.html (visited Feb. 18, 1999).
[49] U.S. News Story Page, *Clinton Signs Airport Security Measures Into Law*, http://www.cnn.com/US/9610/09/faa/index.html (visited Feb. 18, 1999).

AVIATION SECURITY PROCEDURES FOLLOWING 9/11[50]

Subsequent to the attacks of September 11, 2001, *U.S. News & World Report* reported "The terrorists flew on devil's wings in a horrifying moment, singular in history. They changed the course of a presidency, a nation, and, quite likely, the world." There was a strong suspicion that Osama bin Laden had choreographed the plan of terror and devastation that fundamentally changed the basic calculus for life for not only Americans but for millions of people around the world. But shortly following the attacks no one knew for sure who it was that had attacked the United States. Nevertheless, President George W. Bush immediately declared war. He just couldn't name the enemy.[51]

President Bush's formal response to the tragedy addresses two reasons why terrorism is—and will continue to be—a serious issue of concern for Americans: First, the characteristics of American society that its citizens cherish—freedom, openness, towering skyscrapers, and modern transportation systems—make the country vulnerable to terrorism of catastrophic proportions. America's vulnerability to terrorism will persist long after justice is brought to those responsible for the events of September 11. Second, the technological ability to launch destructive attacks against civilian populations and critical infrastructure spreads to more and more organizations and individuals with each passing year.[52] Another reason is that the very machine (the airplane) that helps to bring us all together by reducing both time and space, has made us all more vulnerable.[53]

Clearly, America's treasured personal freedoms coupled with its economic and political philosophies make the threat to the U.S. transportation system "a permanent condition," as bluntly noted by Bush in his address. In response, Congress and the Bush administration took many administrative and regulatory steps to stop the economic hemorrhage being experienced by the aviation industry. These re-

---

[50] This section draws heavily from Robin Sobotta and Laurence E. Gesell, *Airport and Aviation Security Addendum* (2003), to Laurence E. Gesell, The Administration of Public Airports (4th ed. 1999).

[51] Edward T. Pound, David E. Kaplan, Douglas Pasternak, Chitra Ragavan, Linda Robinson, Angie Cannon, Richard J. Newman, Mark Mazzetti, Bruce B. Auster, Kevin Whitlaw, Gloria Borger, Michael Tackett, Rochelle Sharpe, Ricardo Castillo, and Juli Hilliard, *Under Siege*, U.S. News & World Report (Sep. 24, 2001), at 10.

[52] George Bush, *Securing the Homeland Strengthening the Nation*, http://www.whitehouse.gov (visited 2003).

[53] *See* Editors, *The Security Puzzle*, Av. Wk. & Space Tech. (Aug. 23/30, 2004), at 56.

sulted in the passage of legislation and associated regulations that created a new cabinet-level office, new security regulations, and strengthened security procedures.

ORGANIZATIONAL CHANGES: FAA, TSA, AND THE DHS

With the November 2001 passage of the Aviation and Transportation Security Act [ATSA], several organizational and regulatory changes were prompted that, ultimately, have affected the aviation industry. The ATSA created the Transportation Security Administration and prompted several changes, including a mandate for 100% screening of all checked bags by air travelers and the requirement that all U.S. airport screening personnel be federally employed (with the exception of few select test programs for privatization). In addition, the ATSA mandated the fortification of commercial aircraft cockpit doors, additional federal air marshal presence on commercial aircraft, and hijack training for flight crews.

On March 1, 2003, the newly formed Department of Homeland Security [DHS] became responsible for oversight of the TSA.[54] "DHS is responsible for protecting the movement of international trade across U.S. borders, maximizing the security of the international supply chain, and for engaging foreign governments and trading partners in programs designed to identify and eliminate security threats before these arrive at U.S ports and borders."[55] Two weeks prior to its takeover by DHS, the TSA—which had already been granted the responsibility for security in all other modes of transportation—assumed all civil aviation security functions previously held by the FAA. In a *Federal Register* notice, TSA also announced the intended federalization of all airport security screeners and assumed responsibility "for the day-to-day security screening operations for passenger air transportation and intrastate air transportation under U.S.C. 44901 and 44935 . . . [including] hiring, training, testing, and deploying or arranging for Federal security screeners."

The TSA listed the major goals associated with its initial two-year plan (post 9/11) for major aviation security activities. Unfortunately, the TSA response to some deadlines was not timely or were met with

---

[54] Department of Homeland Security, *Travel and Transportation*, http://www.dhs.gov (visited 2003).
[55] *Id.*

questionable means (such as the 100% Explosive Detection Systems [EDS] checked bag deadline which was ultimately "achieved" a year late and with means other than EDS). Critics were concerned whether the Bush Administration was more concerned about pleasing politicians (to satisfy political agendas) and the public demand for improved customer service, than with achieving true security improvements. As of December 31, 2002, TSA claimed that "90% of bags can now be screened electronically [yet] several airports have received waivers that give them more time to install equipment."[56] Budgetary reasons have been repeatedly cited for the lack of timeliness or the "shortcuts" taken.

Airline executives, who are reluctant to appear publicly critical of the TSA, say that problems have cropped up for a variety of reasons, not all of them the agency's fault. In the rush to install baggage-screening systems by the deadline, the TSA resorted to screening many bags by having technicians wipe them with pads, and then analyze the pads for signs of explosives. The job could be automated by using scanning machines instead, but installing those giant machines, and the conveyor belts needed to make effective use of them, has lagged, partly for budgetary reasons. From the onset, airports have been asking for—and denied—the right to move ahead on putting security solutions into effect. "Until only recently, they were often met with hostility, then ignored, then informed that they would be told of the 'appropriate' solutions."[57]

REGULATORY CHANGES

Concomitantly with the organizational changes made at the federal level were several regulatory changes. The FARs previously forming the regulatory backbone of aviation security were replaced by Transportation Security Regulations [TSRs] (see Table 6.1, "Air Transportation Security Regulations Changes"). Although many of the changes are essentially a renumbering/relocation of FARs to TSRs there are a number of changes in the regulations of note, as discussed throughout this section. Nevertheless, the airport security architecture and protocol remains fundamentally the same, albeit

---

[56] Christopher Marquis, *Threats and Response: Airport Security: By Midnight, All Will be Set for Screening Checked Bags*, New York Times (Dec. 31, 2003), at A13.
[57] David Plavin, *Rushed Airport Security*, New York Times (Nov. 23, 2002), at A26.

beefed-up.[58] For example, the TSA has employed more frequent use of pat down searches,[59] to the dismay of civil liberties proponents.

Table 6.1—AIR TRANSPORTATION SECURITY REGULATION CHANGES

Regulatory Subject	New TSRs (49 CFR):	Largely Taken from old FARs (14 CFR):
Passenger Civil Aviation Security Service Fees	Part 1510	Part 129.3
Protection of Sensitive Security Information	Part 1520	Part 191
Civil Aviation Security (on-board security and other issues)	Part 1540	Portions of 107, 108 and 91.
Airport Security	Part 1542	Portions of 107, 108 and 91
Aircraft Operator Security: Air Carriers and Commercial Operators	Part 1544	Part 108
Foreign Air Carrier Security	Part 1546	Part 129
Indirect Air Carrier Security	Part 1548	Part 109
Aircraft Operator Security under General Operating and Flight Rules	Part 1550	SFAR 91

Source: Federal Register (Feb. 22, 2002), Vol. 67, No. 36, at 7939-8384.

---

[58] 49 CFR 1542 describes the airport security under the TSA.
[59] Transportation Security Administration Briefing Room, *Pat down, Other Screening Enhancements Must Be Carried Out Appropraitely*, http://www.tsa.gov (visited Dec. 31, 2004).

Passengers can thank Richard C. Reid, the infamous "shoe bomber,"[60] for having to take their shoes off at the check point, much to the discomfort of people with severe diabetes who are supposed to keep their feet covered at all times. Since the attacks of September 11, 2001, wherein hijackers took control of four airliners using box cutters, security procedures were modified to prohibit any sharp items being carried on board—even going to the extreme of prohibiting fingernail clippers.

A *New York Times* editorial warned that "airport operators and airlines should be concentrating on how to meet the requirements, not how to dodge them."[61] David Z. Plavin, President of the Airports Council International-North American said that, "No airports 'balked' at the baggage-screening deadline with which Congress encumbered the Transportation Security Administration. From the onset, airports have been asking for—and denied—the right to move ahead on putting security solutions into effect. Until only recently, they were often met with hostility, then ignored, then informed that they would be told of the 'appropriate' solutions."[62]

SECURITY PROCEDURES: NEEDED PROTECTION OR INVASION OF PRIVACY

While some analysts discuss the need to continue making meaningful improvements in aviation security, others feel the pendulum has swung too far in the opposite direction, particularly in the area of privacy concerns. American Civil Liberties Union [ACLU] legislative counselor Katie Corrigan suggested a "three-prong analysis" before Congress implements additional security measures.

First, any new security proposals must be genuinely effective rather than creating a false sense of security. Second, security measures should be implemented in a non-discriminatory manner. Individuals should not be subjected to intrusive searches or questioning based on their perceived or actual race, ethnic origin, or religion, or based on proxies for such characterizations. Finally, if a security measure is determined to be genuinely effective, the government should work to ensure that its implementation minimizes its costs to

---

[60] *See United States v. Richard Colvin Reid, a/k/a Abdul-Raheem, a/k/a Abdul Raheem, Abu Ibrahim*, Criminal No. 02-10013-WGY, U.S. Dist. Ct., Dist. of Mass. (2002).

[61] Editorial, *Airport Security*, New York Times (Sep. 20, 2002).

[62] Leo Plavin, *Rushed Airport Security*, New York Times (Nov. 23, 2002), at A26.

fundamental freedoms including the right to due process, privacy and equality.[63]

Of particular concern to the ACLU and others concerned about the strong potential for discrimination—particularly that based on gender, race or religion—is the possibility of compromised privacy when an airline collects and analyzes personal data in an effort to predetermine those who may be at higher risk of committing acts of air piracy. Using a FAA grant, Northwest Airlines developed the first profiling system, referred to as Computer-Assisted Passenger Prescreening System [CAPPS]. By analyzing more than 40 pieces of secret information collected by the airlines, the computer selects a number of individuals (referred to as "selectees"), as well as some randomly selected travelers, all of whom are subjected to heighten security procedures.[64] Currently, more advanced versions of CAPPS are being tested in the U.S., although for all intents and purposes CAPPS II is officially "dead." The government's controversial plan to screen passengers before they board the plane was officially terminated—but the TSA promised it would return in a new form with a new name. A DHS spokeswoman admitted that "The name CAPPS II may be dead, but the process of creating an automated passenger pre-screening system to replace [the then current] CAPPS will continue."[65]

CAPPS II was a limited, automated prescreening system authorized by Congress in the wake of 9/11. The intent is to modernize the prescreening process by authenticating travelers' identities and performing risk assessments to detect individuals who may pose a terrorist-related threat or who have outstanding federal or state warrants for crimes of violence. The TSA considers CAPPS II (or a derivative) to be a critical element in its "system of systems" approach to security including: thorough screening of baggage and passengers by highly trained federal employees, more impregnable aircraft through fortified cockpit doors and use of reinforced baggage containers, thousands of Federal Air Marshals aboard record numbers of flights, and armed and deputized Federal Flight Deck Officers.[66]

---

[63] Katie Corrigan, Testimony before the House Committee on Transportation and Infrastructure, Subcommittee on Aviation (Feb. 27, 2003).

[64] Id.

[65] Ryan Singel, *Life After Death for CAPPS?*, Wired News, http://www.wired.com (visited Sep. 13, 2004).

[66] U.S. Dept. of Homeland Security, *CAPPS II at a Glance*, a TSA Fact Sheet (Feb. 20, 2004).

Under CAPPS II, airlines were to ask passengers for expanded amounts of reservation information, including full name, date of birth, home address, and home-telephone number. With this expanded information, the system would quickly (i.e., within five seconds or so) verify the identity of the passenger and conduct a risk assessment utilizing commercially available data and current intelligence information. The risk assessment would result in a recommended screening level, categorized as: (1) no risk, (2) unknown or elevated risk, or (3) high risk. Once the system had computed a traveler's risk score it would send an encoded message to be printed on the boarding pass indicating the appropriate level of screening by screeners at security checkpoints.[67] On the positive side, this would work well for the *majority* of travelers, as most utilitarian proposals do. However, for the *minority*, including people misidentified by say having the same name as a suspected terrorist, it would deny them free access to travel. Thus, there is the potential for violating the basic rights of some people.

This is not the first time that profiling has been used in aviation security, or is it the first time that profiling has been challenged. ACLU's Corrigan claims, "Profiling is an ineffective security measure . . . not rooted in specific facts or evidence that an individual is a terrorist. Instead, [it] has been used pursuant to a cost-benefit analysis that certain security devices are too expensive to be used on each and every passenger."[68] Because the ACLU feels it is likely that terrorists will quickly learn the profile parameters, they will likely employ others who do not fit the profile to carry their bombs or hijack aircraft. Further, the ACLU is very concerned that privacy rights and illegal searches will result from "super profiles" that are reportedly being developed by the DOT, which is "funding private research on artificial intelligence techniques that would rate the risk of each passenger that boards a plane."[69]

Undaunted, the TSA announced in September 2004 that it would test a new pre-screening system for airline passengers known as "Secure Flight," which the TSA said will result in a more accurate, less intrusive screening process. Secure Flight replaced the controversial CAPPS II program. Under Secure Flight, the TSA would

---

[67] *Id.*
[68] Katie Corrigan, Testimony before the House Committee on Transportation and Infrastructure, Subcommittee on Aviation (Feb. 27, 2003).
[69] *Id.*

take over responsibility for checking airline passengers' names against watch lists—a function that under CAPPS was handled by the airlines.[70]

Predictably, the same groups who protested against CAPPS II asserted that the new program was little more than "a clone of the old one." The ACLU acknowledges that the job of government security officials is daunting. They endorse the goal of keeping terrorists off airplanes, but fear that a "capricious and unpredictable security bureaucracy" will trample on individual rights.[71]

In yet another "pre-screening program" the TSA is testing the viability of allowing frequent travelers to avoid random security checks at airports by providing personal information and biometrics data such as fingerprints or iris scans in advance. In 2004, five airports and four airlines were chosen and paired to work with the TSA on the Registered Traveler Pilot Program which was to last for 90 days to test the project.[72] In December of 2004 the government sought expansion of the Registered Traveler Program by adding more airports to the test program.[73]

AIRPORT SECURITY: CHANGES, TECHNOLOGY CONSIDERATIONS AND RISK ASSESSMENT

A variety of solutions to security concerns have been implemented at today's airports in the hopes of reducing the security risks. These include changes in personnel selection, training, and retention practices; increased use of canine security applications; new or increased perimeter and facility surveillance methods; and increased incorporation of new technologies. While many question the obvious (how would these actions have prevented 9/11?) others question the practicality or inconvenience to which they've been subjected since the 100% checked bag rule went into affect. Unfortunately, the federal government's security initiatives have been beset with negative externalities such as passenger delays, explosive

---

[70] The American Association of Airport Executives, *TSA Unveils New Screening System*, Airport Report (Sep. 1, 2004), at 1.

[71] David Hughes, *'Secure Flight' Draws Fire*, Av. Wk. & Space Tech. (Nov. 1, 2004), at 54. *See also* American Civil Liberties Union, *ACLU Calls New "Secure Flight" Passenger Profiling System Invasive, Inadequate and Ineffective*, ACLU News release (Oct. 26, 2004).

[72] Audrey Warren, *Frequent Flyers Line Up to Bypass Extra Searches*, Wall St. J. (Wed., Jul. 21, 2004), at D9.

[73] CNN.com, *TSA Seeks Registered Traveler Program Expansion* (Tues. Dec. 14, 2004).

detection systems false positives, and the challenges associated with the mandated installation of these very large, heavy and expensive pieces of equipment.

Perhaps the most visible of these security technology "solutions" are the explosive detection systems that travelers have seen introduced into airport lobbies, as required by the 100% checked bag screening initiative. Congress directed the federal government to screen all checked baggage for explosives by December 31, 2002. In response the TSA deployed 1,390 Explosive Detection Systems [EDS] and 7,601 Explosive Trace Detection Systems [ETD] at 441 commercial service airports. But critics contend that these machines have crowded airport lobbies and created safety and security concerns, decreased system efficiency, and unnecessarily increased TSA staffing requirements.[74]

Both types of devices the TSA uses to screen checked baggage for explosives (EDS and ETD) have limitations that impede operational efficiency and require additional backup screening methods. The ETD machines are roughly the same size as a common laser printer and cost only a few thousand dollars. They can detect minute traces of explosive residue, which may have been transferred to baggage surfaces through direct contact. The ETD machines have extremely high detection rates and very low false-positive rates. But, unfortunately, the process for collecting trace samples is slow, labor intensive, and highly susceptible to human error. They work best as a primary means of explosive detection at low-throughput airports. But to meet the baggage-screening deadline, TSA deployed ETD machines extensively.[75]

Conversely, EDS machines can be as large as a minivan, weigh up to 17,000 pounds and cost over $1 million each.[76] These machines can be highly automated and networked to scan bags by the hundreds each hour. They use Computer Tomography [CT] to scan objects and compare density to the density of known explosives. The problem is that these machines have high incidences of both false-positive and false-negative alarms. Many common objects

---

[74] U.S. House of Representatives, Subcommittee on Aviation, hearing on *In-Line Explosive Detection Systems: Financing and Development* (Jul. 14, 2004).

[75] *Id.*

[76] There are currently two manufacturers of EDS machines that have FAA and TSA approval. L-3 Communications Corporation produces the L-3 eXaminer EDX. InVision Technology, Inc. makes the InVision CTX. *Id.*

have densities similar to commercial and military grade explosives; thus there is a high number of false-positive indications. And since they require the presence of a sufficiently large mass of explosive to function properly, there is a high likelihood of a false-negative alarm if small amounts of explosive are present. One of the biggest problems is the size of the EDS machines. Most terminals require significant modification prior to installation.[77]

The aviation community has put pressure on the TSA to move the EDS machines out of terminal lobbies and to integrate them into the airport's automated baggage systems. They can be integrated "in-line" and configured to have higher explosive detection capabilities, on-screen alarm resolution, better false-positive rates, less staffing, lower maintenance, and less out-of-service time. Unfortunately, installation of an inline EDS would require extensive terminal modification at most airports.[78]

Introduction of federal TSA employees as screeners, installation of baggage screening equipment, and other modifications to the way passengers are screened have had a strong visual impact. One important change in airport security is the changing of the industry's perception of how to conduct a thorough risk assessment and, generally, the receptivity for application of new solutions to a variety of security-related concerns. "Effective risk management means moving from the concept of controlling crises to embracing the idea of making decisions proactively to forestall problems before they happen."[79] This more proactive approach includes consideration of both physical and financial risks.

Indeed, economic (including revenue considerations) and liability concerns have been elevated to an unprecedented status in risk planning. "Risk assessment entails estimating the magnitude of the identified risks in order to prioritize them on the basis of their po-

---

[77] Id.

[78] Necessary modifications include reinforced flooring, Information Technology [IT] networking, electrical upgrades, new conveyor systems, and sundry other new facilities. Airport officials have estimated the total cost for integration of EDS nationwide to be around $5 billion. As of Jul. 2004, eight airports had converted to full in-line operations, with an additional ninth airport in the process. An additional eight airports had signed letters of intent with the TSA. And 12 more had approved plans and were awaiting federal funding approval. Id.

[79] Gerald Fitzgerald, *Risk Assessment in a New Environment*, Airport Magazine (May/Jun. 2003), at 38.

tential ramifications. According to the level of risk, a notification plan is prepared to alert key decision-makers."[80]

SECURITY CHANGES: APPROACH, POLICY AND PERSONNEL

The impact on the aviation industry—and, in particular the airport industry—is only the beginning of a larger initiative to address the technological capabilities of those who wish to attack the "American Way of Life." These include changes in the cockpit and in the general perception of the "appropriate way" to handle hijackers or terrorists. Citizens once warned to act submissive are being raised to the status of heroes for their acts to thwart violence on board aircraft.

Likewise, there has been an about-face change in the federal government's policy on flight crew response to terrorists and/or hijackers on board aircraft. In keeping with this change was the push—and subsequent approval—to permit qualified airline pilots to carry weapons on-board aircraft. "Under Title XIV of the Homeland Security Act of 2002,[81] the Arming Pilots Against Terrorist Act established a program to deputize qualified volunteer commercial passenger airline pilots to serve as Federal Flight Deck Officers [FFDO], to defend the cockpit of an aircraft against acts of criminal violence or air piracy."[82]

While the FFDO program has already graduated and deployed a number of candidates, some concerns remain. For example, some perceive that the required psychological testing is "excessive and designed to fail a large number of candidates." In addition, the FFDOs are deputized for five years, so long as they re-qualify every six months. Some feel this amount of recurrent training is excessive. However, re-qualification with firearms every six months is not unusual for law enforcement officers. Also, at this time, the FFDOs are only permitted on domestic flights. As such, there is a concern about the fact that neither the TSA nor the State Department has engaged in discussions with foreign nations for recognition and acceptance of FFDOs internationally.[83]

---

[80] *Id.*

[81] P.L. 107-296.

[82] House of Representatives, Subcommittee on Aviation, Hearing on the status of the Flight Deck Officer Program (May 8, 2003).

[83] *Id.*

In addition to passenger and crew changes, the TSA initially rein-vigorated the Federal Air Marshal [FAM] program with increased personnel hires, modernized training facilities, increases in the num-ber of flight segments, and an increased budget. More recently, though, there have been budget reductions in this area. To make up for FAM shortages—particularly during heightened threat level con-ditions—the TSA has engaged in the cross training of some Customs agents as FAMs.

Federalizing more than 40,000 security screeners into TSA em-ployment was an additional signal in the federal government's overt assumption of the aviation security role at the nation's 400 plus com-mercial service airports. While some laud this as a necessary move to elevate security, others question whether the TSA's additional focus on customer service may compromise them from the original mission for which they were hired: deterring the carriage of weapons and acts of air piracy.[84]

FOURTH AMENDMENT CONSIDERATIONS

In the synopsis of the airport screening process (i.e., "security checkpoint protocol") presented above, it should be noted that there is an undertone of passive crime prevention. Whether it be law en-forcement officers or TSA agents, either is present at the security check point specifically to prevent hijacking. The officers are not there to search out broad criminal activity. Rather, they are there to observe the public generally, and the passengers or others being screened in particular, and to be on the alert for acts or potential acts of criminal violence aboard aircraft. However, if the screening proc-ess is not conducted strictly within the guidelines of the law, the screening process can readily become an illegal search.

These legal guidelines to which reference is given will be ex-pounded upon in subsequent paragraphs. Generally, however, recall that the Fourth Amendment of the U.S. Constitution protects people against illegal search and seizure:

> *The right of the people to be secure in their*
> *persons, houses, papers, and effects, against*

---

[84] Blake Morrison, *Feds Take Over Airport Screening: Better-trained Force Doesn't Shed Skep-tics*, USAToday (sometime in 2002), at A1.

*(unreasonable) searches and seizures, shall
not be violated, and no Warrants shall issue,
but upon (probable) cause, supported by Oath
or affirmation, and particularly describing the
place to be searched, and the persons or things
to be seized.*

The courts have determined that Fourth Amendment protection is not confined to the home. It extends to wherever the person may be, at the airport for instance. And, it is assumed every person may have secrets pertaining to his or her family, business or social relations. It is further assumed that a person's secrets may be no one else's business but their own. If one's personal affairs are disgraceful, they are nevertheless to be of no concern to others, and are not to be exposed without justifiable occasion. "Justifiable" is bounded by the terms of "probable cause." Search and seizure is not allowed unless the facts and circumstances would warrant a person of "reasonable" caution (certainty) to believe seizable property will be found on a particular person or in a particular place. It follows, then, that arrest should not take place unless the officer's information at the moment of arrest would warrant a person of reasonable caution in the belief that the suspect had committed or was committing an offense.

The situation of a passenger simply boarding an aircraft cannot in any way be construed to meet the above (probable cause) criteria for search and seizure. What, then, does constitute a legal search and seizure? The following are conditions under which a search may be authorized:

- upon a *warrant* (court order) based on probable cause;
- incident to *lawful arrest* based on probable cause;
- a *stop and frisk* search for dangerous weapons;
- a search of "mobile" premises;[85]
- *emergency administrative searches* (e.g., health and safety inspections); and/or
- upon *consent.*

---

[85] In other words, not attached to the ground, but movable such as a mobile home or trailer.

FOURTH AMENDMENT ENFORCEMENT

It is upon the latter two conditions stated above (emergency administrative searches and upon consent) that airport searches are authorized. If the passenger initially refuses to be searched, he or she must be allowed to freely depart. The judiciary has held that evidence obtained illegally cannot be used in court. The U.S. Supreme Court held in 1914, that evidence illegally obtained couldn't be used in federal prosecution for any purpose.[86] Conversely, in 1949, the U.S. Supreme Court held in *Wolf v. Colorado* that *state* courts were not constitutionally required to exclude illegally obtained evidence.[87] But in 1961, the U.S. Supreme Court reversed itself by overruling *Wolf*, and held that the Fourth Amendment *requires* the state courts to exclude evidence obtained through unlawful search and seizure.[88]

One search which may be conducted under conditions not requiring probable cause, is the stop and frisk, or so-called "pat down" search. This allowable exception was established in 1968 in *Terry v. Ohio*.[89] From the *Terry* case, the courts decided that an officer may, on *less* than probable cause, stop and frisk a suspect for weapons if the officer believes that criminal activity may occur, or that the person with whom the officer is dealing may be armed and dangerous.

The *Terry* precedent permits a law enforcement officer to stop and frisk a suspect based only on the officer's reasonable suspicion that a suspect probably has or will commit a crime. But keep in mind, suspicion means something more than a mere hunch, guesswork, gut feeling or intuition. It must be supported with facts, which the officer may later point to for the court, to justify his or her suspicion. Otherwise, the suspicion will not be considered by the courts to have been made by a reasonable person under similar circumstances.

A stop and frisk must be limited to a pat down search of a suspect for weapons that would be dangerous either to the officer or to others. Additionally, the crime, which is suspected, must be connected with a weapon. For example, one would not ordinarily associate a weapon with the violation of an infraction. Conversely, a potential hijacker would be expected to be armed and dangerous.

---

[86] *Weeks v. United States*, 232 U.S. 383 (1914).
[87] *Wolf v. Colorado*, 331 U.S. 25 (1949).
[88] *Mapp v. Ohio*, 367 U.S. 643 (1961).
[89] *Terry v. Ohio*, 392 U.S. 1 (1968).

In applying the *Terry* case to passenger screening situations, a prospective passenger may refuse to submit to a pat down search. In doing so the passenger forfeits the ability to board the aircraft. And even if the passenger were potentially armed, if the passenger leaves, the purpose of the FARs (now TSRs) for which the passenger screening procedures were designed to fulfill will have been served—not to catch criminals but to prevent hijackers from boarding aircraft.

In serving the intent of the law, a pat down search in a typical passenger-screening situation is to be used only as a last resort.[90] The passenger having failed to pass through a metal detector the first time, is then required to divest himself or herself of metal on his or her person and to resubmit to the metal detection screening device. The screening personnel may alternatively use a portable (hand held) detection device to determine the source location of the cause for alarm. What is of importance is the fact that a passenger alarming a metal detection device indicates only that the passenger has on his or her person unaccounted for metal. It does not provide reasonable grounds for suspicion that crime has, or is about to take place.

When a passenger has unaccounted for metal, which cannot be cleared by the screening personnel, the passenger is requested to consent to a pat down search. If the passenger declines the frisk and chooses instead to depart, the passenger ordinarily may do so. If on the other hand the passenger demands on entering, or attempts to enter the "sterile" area (meaning the area wherein all persons have been screened or otherwise cleared), or to board an aircraft, a pat down search is authorized. If a weapon or explosive device is found on that person, there is probable cause for arrest.

When a person consents to a frisk, the pat down search is limited to detection of weapons or explosives. If contraband is discovered, rather than weapons or explosives, it is admissible as evidence in court so long as it was found where a reasonable person might have searched specifically for weapons or explosives.

---

[90] The fact that the TSA has increased the use of pat down searches has generated some discussion and concern. Transportation Security Administration Briefing Room, *Pat down, Other Screening Enhancements Must Be Carried Out Appropraitely*, http://www.tsa.gov (visited Dec. 31, 2004).

CRIMINAL LAW

A person's right to privacy must be protected, and yet the government, for the health, safety and welfare of the traveling public requires that all passengers undergo metal detection device screening and search of carry-on items. Hence, in screening passengers there is a potential clash between individual rights and public safety. During the first decade following the implementation of airport security screening procedures there were 20 cases that reached the U.S. Court of Appeals for decision. None reached the Supreme Court.

Out of that body of 20 court cases, 16 involved contraband such as drugs, counterfeit money, and so forth. Four cases involved weapons. From these 20 cases have emanated certain established precedents:

- Passenger and baggage screening by means of a metal detection or other mechanical device *is a search* within the scope of the Fourth Amendment;
- Consent predicated on the denial of travel for refusal is *not a form of duress or coercion*; and
- Passenger screening searches fall within the *emergency administrative search doctrine exception* and are Constitutionally valid on the basis that the government has a compelling interest in air safety to require all persons desiring to fly on air carrier aircraft are required to undergo screening; moreover, the threat of air piracy is an emergency situation.

The case briefs that follow not only demonstrate the findings of the courts which support the above conclusions and points of law, they also provide a background to understand why and how the passenger screening procedures previously described evolved. There is such a fine line between lawful and unlawful screening of air passengers that it is extremely important for security screening personnel to adhere strictly to the established procedures. Upon assumption of the security screening responsibility, TSA was required to conform to the same legal guidelines and precedents as were imposed upon the FAA. Thus, when the TSA makes a unilateral decision to "enhance" the security procedures, it causes much discussion and concern amongst not only passengers but also watchdogs like the American Civil Liberties Union and others concerned with civil rights.

Follow, if you will, the chronological development of current air passenger screening procedures through evolving case law as presented in the following pages.

UNITED STATES v. BROWN
305 F. Supp. 415 (W.D. Tex. 1969)

At what point does the attempt to board an aircraft with a concealed weapon take place?

An unknown person advised the airline ticket agent he had seen the defendant drop an object that appeared to be either a weapon or a smoking pipe. An airport security guard was paged. The guard approached Benrus Eugene Brown and asked him if he had a weapon, to which the defendant, Brown, responded "yes." The guard did not give the defendant any of the constitutional warnings prescribed by the Supreme Court in *Miranda v. Arizona*.[91]

The government argued that when the defendant appeared at the customer service agent's desk, surrendered his ticket, and passed into the departure lounge, this constituted an "attempt to board an aircraft." At the time the defendant attempted to board, he was carrying a concealed deadly and dangerous weapon (a .22 caliber pistol).

The defendant, on the other hand, contended that such an attempt (i.e., to board) couldn't be consummated until the passenger actually "sets one foot on the aircraft itself."

The issues involved in this proceeding were:

- Did the acts of the defendant constitute an attempt to board an aircraft?
- Were statements made by the defendant at the time of his arrest admissible, in view of the fact that he was not given any warnings under the *Miranda* rule?
- Was the evidence which was seized from the defendant, that is, a .22 caliber pistol and an airplane ticket, illegally obtained from him as a result of an unlawful search and seizure?

The U.S. District Court answered the first question in the affirmative, and the second and third questions in the negative. If the defen-

---

[91] 384 U.S. 436 (1966).

dant's argument of "one foot on and one foot off" were allowed to prevail it would distort the meaning of the statute and frustrate the intent of Congress. *Black's Law Dictionary* defines "attempt" as "an effort or endeavor to accomplish a crime, amounting to more than mere preparation or planning it, which if not prevented, would have resulted in the full consummation of the act attempted, but which in fact, does not bring to pass the party's ultimate design."

At the time the security guard approached the defendant and began to question him, there was probable cause for the guard to believe an offense had been committed and that the defendant had, in fact, committed it. In addition, there is no doubt the security guard fully intended to take the defendant into custody if it became necessary for him to do so in order to determine whether or not the defendant had a weapon. Clearly, at that time, the accusatory stage of the proceedings had been reached, and the defendant was more than a mere suspect. He was, in fact, under arrest, and statements elicited from him by the security guard, absent the *Miranda* warnings, were inadmissible in evidence against him. However, the court was of the opinion the evidence that was admissible was sufficient to sustain a finding of guilty.

The Court found there was probable cause for the arrest, and the arrest was lawful. When a person is lawfully arrested, the officer has the right, without a search warrant, to make a contemporaneous search of the person of the accused for the fruits of, or the instrumentalities used to commit, the crime. The weapon as well as the ticket was, therefore, admissible in evidence.

UNITED STATES v. LOPEZ
328 F. Supp. 1077 (E.D.N.Y. 1971)

Is the use of a metal detector a reasonable search
allowable under the Fourth Amendment?

With his companion, Ernesto Perez Gonzalez, defendant, Frank Lorenzi Lopez, was apprehended on November 14, 1970, at John F. Kennedy International Airport, as he was about to board a Pan American flight bound for Puerto Rico. Two Deputy United States Marshals had been called to the Pan American premises where they were stationed in connection with the government's anti-hijacking program. An employee of Pan American had pointed out the two passengers as "selectees;" i.e., persons whose profile suggested a substantial likelihood they were potential hijackers. They had activated the magnetometer, and upon request, had failed to produce personal identifications.

The Marshals approached the two and asked if they would walk through the magnetometer again, first with, and then without, a small blue bag Gonzalez was carrying. Each of them did so, activating the device on both trips. The Marshals again requested identification, but none was produced. At this time, Gonzalez identified himself by his proper name, indicating the name Julio Lopez, which appeared on his ticket, was erroneous.

The two travelers were then asked to accompany the Marshals to a private area adjacent to the passenger-boarding ramp, where their outer clothing was patted down for weapons. A Marshal felt a hard object about four inches wide, six inches long, and three-quarters of an inch deep, under Lopez's clothing. A tinfoil covered plastic envelope, tightly packed with white powder, was discovered. Field-tested, the powder proved positive for heroin. Gonzalez and Lopez were then arrested.

For lack of evidence, Gonzalez was released. Lopez was tried in U.S. District Court, and charged with concealment and transportation of narcotics.

The Court discussed the physical search of the person under the concept in *Terry v. Ohio*,[92] and held that a search based on *Terry* is justified at the airport screening area. The criteria as set out by the Court in *Terry* must be met before a search can be made; to wit, ". . . the police must, whenever practicable, obtain advance judicial approval of searches and seizures through the warrant procedure. . . ."

No warrant was obtained for the search in this case, nor, as a practical matter could one have been expected. The anti-hijacking system depends upon being able to swiftly sift out potential hijackers for closer scrutiny while permitting all passengers including selectees to board unless weapons are discovered. Exigencies of time precluded the marshals from obtaining a warrant in this situation.

The government argued that continuing the boarding process after reading the posted and clearly observable signs that stated "Passengers and Baggage Subject to Search" amounted to implied consent to searches such as occurred in this case. But, the court found there was

---

[92] 392 U.S. 1 (1968).

no evidence of express consent. Therefore, the government failed to sustain its burden of establishing any sort of voluntary consent. Nevertheless, the court stated that the standard of probability which is required to justify intrusions at the frisk level have been variously stated. The *Terry* court concluded that,

> *[The] officer need not be absolutely certain that the individual is armed; the issue is whether a reasonably prudent man in the circumstances would be warranted in the belief that his safety or that of others was in danger.*

In this case, the location and size of the object, the fact that it was tightly packed and hard covered, and that it was large enough to be a container for a pistol or even explosive material, gave the Marshal ample cause to require removal from underneath defendant's clothing. Visual observation of the package covered with tinfoil would have increased the suspicion and apprehension of a reasonable officer. In fact, the court found the Marshal's conduct of this investigation was almost an exact model of the "frisk" approved in *Terry v. Ohio*.

The District Court concluded that contraband seized as a result of a properly circumscribed investigatory frisk predicated on information generated by a well administered federal anti-hijacking system is admissible in evidence. Such a seizure comports with established Fourth Amendment principles, and were it not for the special circumstances of this case, the court would not have hesitated to deny this motion to suppress.

While evidence discovered during a frisk pursuant to this anti-hijacking procedure would normally have been admissible, the special circumstances required suppression. The Pan American Passenger Service Manager issued a memorandum purporting to "update" the "profile" to be applied in the anti-hijacking screening procedure. This action was not authorized by Pan American Security Services, the United States Marshal Service, or the Federal Aviation Administration. It eliminated one criterion included in the official profile established by the FAA and added two additional categories.

Under the circumstances, the court assumed the "updated" profile was, in fact, employed in selecting the defendant Lopez. The procedure instituted by the FAA, the court said, was "abused."

The U.S. District Court concluded the anti-hijacking system could be a valuable and effective method of protecting millions of air travelers from the threat of violence and sudden death in the air. Properly supervised, it is also constitutional. Abuses such as the one, which occurred in this case, however, must be eliminated if evidence obtained in its operation is to be used in the courts. Defendant's motion to suppress the evidence was granted. Since without this evidence the government had no case, the indictment was dismissed.

UNITED STATES v. WARE
315 F. Supp. 1333 (W.D. Ok. 1970)

Is an unloaded gun considered a "dangerous" weapon?

A fellow passenger saw a pistol fall from the defendant, James Edward Ware's pocket, and it was reported to the airline. An officer approached the suspect, informed him of the information he had received, and conducted a pat down search. The officer removed a .25 caliber automatic pistol from the defendant's coat, and placed him under arrest for carrying a concealed weapon. The pistol was not loaded, and neither Mr. Ware nor his companion had ammunition.

The defendant was charged with attempting to board a commercial aircraft while carrying a concealed, dangerous weapon. He urged suppression of the pistol and all evidence resulting from its discovery and seizure, contending the search, seizure and arrest were unlawful and the unloaded pistol was not a dangerous weapon.

The U.S. District Court found that, under the circumstances disclosed by the evidence, the officer acted properly. The investigatory search and seizure were reasonable, the arrest was lawful, and the evidence procured thereby and resulting therefrom was admissible.

The purpose of Congress is to maintain public safety, and violation might be based on carrying or concealing an unloaded gun as well as a loaded gun. In interpreting the "dangerous weapon" provisions of various federal statutes, the courts have held that proper determination requires consideration of the entire context. It has been demonstrated many times that an airliner can be hijacked with an unloaded gun. The court concluded the unloaded .25 caliber automatic pistol in the defendant's pocket was a dangerous weapon, and overruled the defendant's motion to suppress the evidence.

HAVELOCK v. UNITED STATES
427 F.2d 987 (10th Cir. 1970)

*Is circumstantial evidence, largely based upon bizarre behavior,
sufficient to convict in an aircraft arson case?*

The evidence bore out that the appellant Lawrence B. Havelock used the aircraft lavatory facilities three times during a period of one hour and ten minutes, each time ostensibly for shaving. He was observed as nervous and almost overly polite. He was seen wearing yellow rubber gloves. He was seen stuffing a yellow object into his pocket or in-between the seats. He was the last person in the middle-aft restroom, a few minutes after which the door burst open and fire was discovered. He was observed near seat 14-C where yellow gloves containing matchbook covers were later found. He was also located near seat 11-C where other matching pieces of matchbook covers were found in an ashtray. The head of an arson squad testified that "undoubtedly a match has to be applied to something to leave this type of debris and damage to the floor itself." Additionally, from Havelock's hotel room was recovered a ticket bought for an earlier flight which was never taken, and he had taken out a $60,000 insurance policy naming his wife as beneficiary.

The inferences here pointed directly to Havelock as the guilty party, and he was tried and convicted by the lower court. Havelock appealed, arguing there was insufficient evidence to convict him, and the evidence taken from his hotel room was irrelevant and prejudicial.

The United States Court of Appeals found that even though the proof was not as weighty as direct evidence, it was not insufficient. As in most cases of willful burning of another person's property, because of the nature of the crime, direct evidence is seldom available to prove the accused participation. As to the allegedly prejudicial testimony and exhibits, the Court determined the evidence was not erroneously admitted. The sum of the hotel evidence, the court found illustrated sufficient fundamental features of a scheme that culminated in the fire aboard the aircraft in question. The judgment of the lower court was affirmed.

UNITED STATES v. LINDSEY
451 F. 2d 701 (3rd Cir. 1971)

May a suspect be frisked based upon observations
of suspicious appearance and behavior?

Marshal Brophy, an officer of the Anti-Hijacking Task Force, was monitoring passengers boarding Eastern Airlines Flight 427 bound for Atlanta, Georgia from Newark Airport. The Anti-Hijacking Task Force was an intergovernmental agency composed of the Justice Department, Federal Aviation Administration and airline industry personnel. About four minutes prior to the scheduled departure of Flight 427, Brophy observed defendant Bobby R. Lindsey rushing into the boarding lounge. Defendant handed a ticket to the ticket agent on duty and told him to "save a seat for Williams." The ticket agent noted it was in the name of "James Marshall," and made a gesture to Marshal Brophy, indicating the defendant should be watched. His suspicions aroused, the marshal continued to observe the defendant. Lindsey appeared nervous and was "looking about" and "perspiring."

When the moment of departure arrived, and the defendant moved towards the aircraft, Brophy approached the defendant, identified himself and asked for identification. Lindsey handed Brophy a Selective Service card bearing the name "Melvin Giles." The extreme anxiety noted before seemed to increase. By way of further identification, the defendant produced a Social Security card bearing his true name "Bobby R. Lindsey."

In the course of ascertaining the defendant's identity, Brophy noted two large bulges in Lindsey's coat pocket. Fearing the bulges might be weapons; the Marshal patted down the defendant to effect a weapons search. After feeling the bulges in the defendant's coat pocket, which he described as "very solid," Marshal Brophy extracted from the pocket two aluminum-wrapped packages, later found to contain heroin, which became the main prosecution evidence at trial. There was, of course, no search warrant.

Lindsey was tried and convicted in U.S. District Court and appealed. His contention was that the heroin was inadmissible evidence because it was obtained by an unlawful search and seizure. The government argued the heroin was lawfully seized under the circumstances, and relied upon *Terry v. Ohio.*[93]

In applying *Terry* to the case at hand, the U.S. Court of Appeals believed Marshal Brophy's reactions to the unusual behavior of the defendant were justified. In the context of a possible airplane hijacking with the enormous consequences which may flow therefrom, and in view of the limited time in which Brophy had to act, the level of suspicion required for a *Terry* investigative stop and protective search should be lowered. Therefore, despite the fact that it may be said the level of suspicion present in the instant case was lower than in *Terry*, it was sufficiently high to justify Marshal Brophy's actions. The judgment of the district court was affirmed.

UNITED STATES v. EPPERSON
454 F. 2d 769 (4th Cir. 1972)

What constitutes a legitimate search and seizure?

Cecil Epperson was arrested at Washington National Airport while boarding a flight to New York City. As Epperson passed through a magnetometer, the instrument disclosed an unusually high reading. The United States Marshal screening Epperson asked him if he was carrying a large amount of metal. Epperson produced several metal objects, but the device still gave a positive reading. Thereupon, the marshal searched the jacket Epperson was carrying and found a loaded .22 caliber pistol.

Defendant Epperson was convicted in the United States Magistrates Court, Alexandria, Virginia, of attempting to board an aircraft engaged in interstate commerce while carrying a concealed dangerous weapon. The decision of the Magistrates Court was sustained by the United States District Court, and Epperson appealed to the U.S. Court of Appeals. He claimed the pistol and ammunition should not have been introduced into evidence because they were the products of an illegal search. He argued that: (1) the use of the magnetometer was a "search," and (2) since there was no warrant and the circumstances did not fall within any of the recognized exceptions to the warrant requirement, the search was in violation of the Fourth Amendment.

---

[93] 392 U.S. 1 (1968).

The appellate court agreed that the use of the magnetometer in these circumstances was a "search" within the meaning of the Fourth Amendment. By this device a government officer, without permission, discerned metal on Epperson's person. That he did so electronically, rather than by patting down his outer clothing, may make the search more tolerable and less offensive—but it is still a search. Indeed, the very purpose and function of a magnetometer is to search for metal and disclose its presence in areas where there is a normal expectation of privacy.

The court also agreed the limited search by magnetometer did not fall within any of the recognized exceptions to the warrant requirement of the Fourth Amendment except that suggested by *Terry v. Ohio*,[94] wherein the limited scope and purpose of the search plus the element of danger and necessity for swift action excused getting a warrant. The Constitution does not forbid all searches and seizures; it forbids only those that are *unreasonable* The search for the sole purpose of discovering weapons and preventing air piracy fully justified the minimal invasion of personal privacy resulting from the use of a magnetometer. The use of the device cannot possibly be as annoying, frightening, and perhaps humiliating as being "frisked." The person scrutinized is not even aware of the examination. Thus, it is "reasonably related in scope to the circumstances which justified the interference in the first place."

Since the use of the magnetometer was justified, and hence the subsequent physical frisk was justified by the information developed by the magnetometer, and because the search was limited in scope to the circumstances which justified the interference in the first place, the search and seizure was not unreasonable. The U.S. Court of Appeals affirmed the conviction of the lower court.

UNITED STATES v. KROLL
481 F 2d 884 (8th Cir. 1973)

What constitutes unwarranted search and seizure?

The defendant, Gerald Frank Kroll, purchased a ticket for Trans World Airlines Flight 338 to Chicago, Illinois. The ticket seller determined the defendant was a possible hijacker and asked him to pro-

---

[94] 392 U.S. 1 (1968).

duce his driver's license for identification. The number of the driver's license was written on the defendant's tickets, which was notice to the passenger security detail at the boarding gate that the defendant fit the hijacker profile and should be searched.

The defendant passed through the magnetometer, which was activated by the metal hinges and lock on the attaché case he carried. The TWA security agent directed him to place the attaché case on a table and open it for inspection. A United States Marshal was working with the TWA agent and watched the search. The marshal became suspicious because the defendant did not open the file section in the upper part of the attaché case. The Marshal directed the defendant to open the file section. In the file section the Marshal could observe part of an ordinary white business envelope. It was light in weight, had a very small bulge, approximately one quarter inch thick and two inches across at one end of the envelope, and was otherwise limp and flat. The marshal felt the actions of the defendant were suspicious and, therefore, asked the defendant to empty the contents of the envelope into the case. The envelope contained a small plastic bag, within which was found an amphetamine and a partly consumed marijuana cigarette.

After an evidentiary hearing, the District Court granted defendant's pretrial motion to suppress the amphetamine, holding that while it was reasonable to inspect the defendant's attaché case, it was not reasonable to inspect the envelope contents. The government appealed, contending, first, the defendant consented to the search and, second, that it was a reasonable search for weapons or explosives.

The burden was upon the government to prove consent was, in fact, freely and voluntarily given. To sustain its burden, the government pointed out that warnings were posted at the airport advising passengers they were subject to being searched prior to boarding aircraft. It reasoned that, ". . . Where a person is clearly warned in advance that he will be searched and he still has time to withdraw as defendant did here, his conduct in seeking to board the plane must be inferred to include a free, voluntary and intelligent consent to be searched."

The District Court found this did not constitute consent to a search "in any meaningful sense," and the appellate court agreed. The Court said that compelling the defendant to choose between exercising Fourth Amendment rights and his right to travel constituted coercion;

the government could not be said to have established that the defendant freely and voluntarily consented to the search when to do otherwise would have meant foregoing the constitutional right to travel.

The district court also found no grounds had been established for believing the defendant was carrying explosives or weapons, but stated that the inspection of the attaché case was justified by the danger of air piracy. It held, however, that inspection of the envelope's contents exceeded the scope of the search permissible under the circumstances. The court defined "permissible search" as an inspection of that which may be "reasonably" deemed to conceal a weapon or explosives. Reasonableness in this context, the court said, was a matter of possibilities.

The District Court then held the probabilities of the situation were such that searching the envelope was unreasonable. It reasoned that given the size and condition of the envelope, and the small size of the bulge therein, the government had not established it was reasonable to believe it could contain a weapon or explosives—given the state of the art of miniaturization existing at the time of the search. Furthermore, in this case, nothing developed during the course of inspecting the attaché case to suggest it contained weapons or explosives.

The U.S. Court of Appeals affirmed the U.S. District Court's determination to allow suppression of the evidence.

UNITED STATES v. MORENO
475 F 2d 44 (5th Cir. 1973)

What constitutes a reasonable suspicion of a suspect's behavior?

Abraham Piña Moreno arrived in San Antonio International Airport aboard a Braniff Airlines flight from which he was observed deplaning by Deputy U.S. Marshal Granados. When Moreno came into the lounge area, he appeared to be looking for someone and was unusually wary of the airport security guards. He was visibly nervous as he proceeded into the main terminal area. This condition became more pronounced when he realized he was under surveillance. Shortly thereafter he entered a taxicab and left the airport.

About two hours later, Moreno returned and once again Granados began observing him. He went first to the Braniff ticket counter and got in line. Obviously very nervous, he switched from one line to another, several times before going to the Southwest Airlines counter where he finally bought a ticket. After purchasing the ticket he headed toward the gate of Southwest Airlines, looked straight at Officer Granados who was walking towards him, and he then went into a restroom located nearby. He seemed to be protecting or covering something, and there was a prominent bulge on the left side of Moreno's coat. This aroused the officer's suspicion that Moreno might be carrying some kind of weapon or explosive device, which could be used in an air piracy attempt.

Granados approached Moreno, identified himself and inquired whether anything was wrong. Moreno said he was a little nervous, adding he had just arrived in San Antonio the day before and taken a taxicab to the Baptist Memorial Hospital downtown. He was unhappy with the taxicab fare for the trip back to the airport. This account aroused Granados' suspicion still further, because he knew Moreno had arrived in San Antonio only a few hours earlier, and that he had gone to a bus station upon leaving the airport and not to the hospital as he claimed. After being asked twice to produce some identification, Moreno did so only after substantial hesitation. Finally, he removed a wallet from the inside left pocket of his coat and gave it to Granados, who by then was concerned Moreno might attempt to escape. Officer Granados stated that after he received the identification papers, Moreno "started to turn" and he thought Moreno was going to attempt to "run out of the restroom." Another officer was summoned and Moreno was escorted to the security office.

As they reached the security office a pat down search was conducted, after which Moreno was asked what he had in his inside coat pocket. He pulled out some papers, which obviously were not the cause of the bulge. He was then ordered to take his coat off and the ensuing search yielded three cellophane wrapped packages of heroin.

Prior to trial, Moreno filed a motion to suppress as evidence the heroin seized in the airport search. He contended that even if there were sufficient circumstances to justify a stop and frisk, the detention and subsequent search went far beyond the constitutionally permissible intrusion contemplated by *Terry v. Ohio*.[95] In denying the motion, the District Court recognized "the strong need for reasonable searches and seizures in furtherance of the public interest against air piracy." Accordingly, it concluded the arresting agents were reasonably

---

[95] 392 U.S. 1 (1968).

justified in believing Moreno might be armed and dangerous and in stopping and searching him pursuant to that belief.

Moreno was convicted in the United States District Court for unlawful possession of heroin in an attempt to distribute, and he appealed. The U.S. Court of Appeals held that in view of defendant's unusual nervousness, a condition which seemed to intensify after he realized he was being watched by an officer, the prominent bulge on the left side of the defendant's coat about which he seemed unusually apprehensive, the fact the defendant had just purchased an airline ticket and was headed in the direction of the airline gate, and in view of the fact that once confronted by police, the defendant appeared evasive and hesitant and lied about his previous destination, invasion of the defendant's personal sanctity entailed by his detention and warrantless airport search did not offend the Fourth Amendment .

The District Court's conviction was affirmed.

UNITED STATES v. ALBARADO
495 F 2d 799 (2nd Cir. 1974)

> *Does failure to clear the metal detector justify an*
> *immediate frisk?*

Ramon Albarado, an older man who spoke Spanish but not English, approached the boarding area of Pan American Flight 233 from New York's John F. Kennedy International Airport to Santo Domingo. Throughout the Pan Am terminal, and at the boarding gate, there were signs posted in both Spanish and English stating it is a federal crime to board an aircraft carrying a weapon and that passengers are subject to a search. In addition, there were announcements made at boarding time in both Spanish and English advising passengers that a search would be conducted.

Albarado's boarding line consisted of approximately 30 or 40 individuals ahead of him, five or six of who were stopped and patted down after they set off the magnetometer. Given his turn, Albarado placed his carry-on luggage on the table, and it was searched. He then passed through the magnetometer and activated it. The United States Customs Security Officer, Ronald Bliss, then motioned for Albarado to come over and open his coat, which he did. Bliss then patted him down and felt a bulge in his inside jacket pocket. At Bliss' request

Albarado removed the object. It was a package wrapped in aluminum foil, with a frontal size approximately that of United States currency and a thickness of about one-quarter inch. Bliss indicated to the defendant to open one end of the envelope. Albarado complied, without protest, and Bliss observed what he thought was a counterfeit $20 bill. The package was found to consist of 51 bogus $20 bills. Albarado claimed a stranger had approached him in front of his house and asked him to exchange the money in question. He explained the wrapping of the bogus bills was so they would not get wet. He also had approximately $2,360 in genuine currency on his person that was not wrapped in foil. Defendant was convicted in the U.S. District Court for possession of counterfeit currency and he appealed.

Each aspect of an airport search is a search within the meaning of the Fourth Amendment. In determining the reasonableness of a search, the need for the search must be balanced against the invasion of privacy involved. As concluded in *United States v. Bell*,[96] the use of a magnetometer is a reasonable search despite the small number of weapons detected in the course of a large number of searches. The absolutely minimal invasion of a passenger's privacy weighed against the great threat to hundreds of persons if a hijacker is able to proceed to the plane undetected provides justification for the search and makes it reasonable. While the magnetometer may be inefficient in that it searches every passenger, balanced against this is the absolutely minimal invasion of privacy involved. There is no detention at all, nor "probing into an individual's private life and thoughts. . . ." Passing through a magnetometer has none of the indignities involved in fingerprinting, paring of a person's fingernails, or a frisk. The use of the device does not excessively annoy, frighten or humiliate those who pass through it. A frisk, on the other hand, is considered a gross invasion of one's privacy.

The signs and highly visible magnetometers, coupled with the possibility of being frisked, serve as a deterrent. The hope is that any prospective hijacker will turn around and leave. Thus, while there is coercion to submit to the airport frisk, there is no compulsion. The legality of the search does not rest on a consent theory, but rather on the reasonableness of the total circumstances, that a passenger may withdraw at any time, plus the general knowledge that one is subject to a search if one flies, as weighed against the minimized invasion of

---

[96] 464 F.2d 667, *cert. denied* 409 U.S. 991 (1972)

the passengers' privacy. There is, of course, a compelling need for further investigation after an initial magnetometer reading indicates presence of metal. Without further investigation the magnetometer would not serve any valid purpose. It would be absurd to require airlines either to deny passage to everyone activating the magnetometer or to allow passage to anyone without discovering what activated it.

It should be noted that any further investigation after activation of the magnetometer is for the metal that did the activation; activating the magnetometer is not a general license to search for just anything. It is clear that, when compared with other methods, the frisk is "inefficient" in that a whole body may be frisked only to discover the keys in the passenger's pocket set the machine off. It would be easier and more effective merely to ask the passenger to remove all metal items and return through the magnetometer (a second time). This procedure is clearly preferred over the immediate frisk because, while still a search, it entails far less invasion of the privacy or dignity of a person than to have a stranger poke and pat one's body in various places.

The appellate court found the frisk to have been unlawful and reversed and remanded with directions that a motion to suppress the evidence be granted.

UNITED STATES v. BELL
464 F 2d 667 (2nd Cir. 1972)

*Does failure to clear the metal detector a second time
justify a frisk?*

Henry Bell entered LaGuardia Airport and purchased a ticket on Eastern Airlines Flight 101 to Atlanta, Georgia. Bell and the circumstances of his ticket purchase fell within the criteria of a "hijacker profile" developed by the Federal Aviation Administration in cooperation with the commercial airlines. He was therefore designated as a "selectee" by Ralph Whitfield, the ticket agent, and his ticket was given to him in an envelope that would identify him at the flight gate as a person who fell within the category of potential hijackers.

When Bell passed through the magnetometer, the device was activated indicating the presence of metal on his person. United States Deputy Marshal John Walsh requested that Bell pass through the magnetometer a second time. Bell complied and again the device registered. When asked for identification, Bell responded he had just been released from Tombs (jail) and that he was out on bail for attempted murder and narcotics charges. Walsh asked Bell if he minded being "patted down" and Bell responded, "Certainly not." Walsh proceeded behind the closed door of the jet way to pat down Bell from chest to hips and felt hard objects about four to five inches long in his raincoat pockets. Bell described the objects as "candy for his mother" and agreed to take one out of his pocket. It was a brown paper bag, which he again described as candy for his mother, but when opened at Walsh's request was seen to contain glassine envelopes, which Walsh believed to contain narcotics. Bell was then arrested and a search thereafter revealed the bulge in the other pocket was a similar bag. A field check at the airport revealed the 600 glassine envelopes in the bags contained heroin.

In U.S. District Court, Bell argued his Fifth and Sixth Amendment rights were infringed. Specifically, he said he was denied the right to confront witnesses against him, to the effective assistance of counsel, and to the right of a public trial. The government's justification for the barring of the public and the defendant, while permitting his counsel to participate, was based upon the compelling urgency of protecting the confidentiality of the "profile" which had been devised as a method to reduce the threat of hijacking. The courtroom was cleared of spectators and the defendant while the profile was disclosed. The court agreed it was not only desirable but also essential that if the profile system was to continue, it be kept confidential.

As to the denial of the Sixth Amendment right "to be confronted with the witnesses against him," Bell was present and represented by counsel who cross-examined the marshal and the ramp ticket agent who were present at the time of the stop and frisk. The court did not accept the argument that Bell's case was jeopardized by any lack of ability to confront the witnesses.

Bell also argued he was the victim of an unlawful search and seizure, to which the court did not agree. The marshal's request that he submit to a pat down search did constitute a "stop and frisk," under *Terry v. Ohio*,[97] but did not offend any Fourth Amendment rights of the defendant. The contention that the use of the magnetometer constituted an unreasonable search was, in the court's opinion, baseless.

---

[97] 392 U.S. 1 (1968).

The bodily pat down of Bell by Agent Walsh was a frisk fully consistent with the *Terry* test. In *Terry,* the Supreme Court rejected the concept that the police officer, conducting a stop and frisk, must have probable cause for making an arrest. There was no arrest here until after the contraband had been discovered. The Supreme Court in *Terry* required something less for the frisk, but still required that the police officer have a reasonable belief some criminal activity might take place and a reasonable belief the suspect may have a weapon which would present a danger to himself or others. Such were the circumstances in this case. The U.S. Court of Appeals affirmed the District Court conviction.

UNITED STATES v. BUSIC
592 F.2d 13 (2nd Cir. 1977)

> *Where should the trial take place of a case involving the*
> *hijacking of an aircraft en route?*

Trans World Airlines Flight 355 was scheduled to fly from LaGuardia Airport in New York to Chicago. Zvonko Busic, Julienne Busic, Petar Matanic, Frank Pesut and Mark Vlasic (the appellees) boarded the aircraft with a previously prepared typewritten hijack note. In addition, prior to boarding, the appellees had prepared several imitation dynamite sticks. Moments after takeoff, at an undetermined point beyond the boundaries of the Eastern District of New York, Zvonko Busic handed a note to a flight attendant for transmittal to the pilot. The note read in part, "This airplane is hijacked." Two to six minutes later, when the aircraft was in the vicinity of Buffalo, New York, the pilot received the message. Pursuant to the hijacker's orders, the pilot flew the airplane first to Montreal and then to Gander, Newfoundland, where 33 hostages were released prior to a transatlantic voyage. The hijackers eventually surrendered in Paris.

The grand jury charged the two Busics (Zvonko and Julienne), as well as Matanic, Pesut and Vlasic, with two counts of air piracy. The appellees moved to dismiss the substantive counts of the indictment because, they argued, venue was improper in the Eastern District. Judge Bartels of the Eastern District Court granted the motion, because ". . . they had not seized and exercised control over the aircraft before it had entered the airspace of the Western District of New York." The government appealed.

The Constitution, in Article III, Section 2, provides that trials,

> . . . *shall be held in the State where said Crimes shall have been committed; but when not committed within any State, the Trial shall be at such Place as the Congress may by Law have directed.*

The Sixth Amendment provides,

> *In all criminal prosecutions, the accused shall enjoy the right to a speedy and public trial, by an impartial jury of the State and district wherein the crime shall have been committed, which district shall have been previously ascertained by law. . . .*

In cases of air piracy, Congress by special statute[98] has determined that,

> . . . *whenever the offense is begun in one jurisdiction and completed in another, or committed in more than one jurisdiction, it may be dealt with, inquired of, tried, determined, and punished in any jurisdiction in which such offense was begun, continued, or completed, in the same manner as if the offense had been actually or wholly committed therein.*

The appellees contended that the essence of the crime of air piracy, according to the language of the Federal Aviation Act of 1958, is the intentional and forcible "seizure or exercise of control" of an aircraft. Thus, the offense charged here could not be committed until there was a transfer of control from the pilot to hijacker.

The United States Court of Appeals found the above to be a "tortured and hyperconstrictive" reading of the statute. Hijacking is by its

---

[98] 49 U.S.C. § 1473[a].

very nature a "continuous" crime. If the crime involves a continuous course of conduct, the offense may be tried wherever it was begun, continued or completed.

The Constitutional framer's mandate for a trial in the vicinity of the crime was meant to be a safeguard against injustice and hardship involved when the accused was prosecuted in a place remote from the accused's home and acquaintances. In the Air Piracy Act, Congress intended the government to enjoy the broadest possible choice of venue within constitutional bounds. To be tried in the Eastern District of New York would not result in any violations of the appellees' constitutional rights.

The Court decided that located within the Eastern District of New York is the airport where the hijackers boarded the plane, as is the metropolitan area where they resided and where they took significant steps toward commission of their crime. Accordingly, the Court of Appeals reversed the order of the District Court on the basis of improper venue, and remanded the case for trial.

UNITED STATES v. $124,570 [99]
873 F.2d 1240 (9th Cir. 1989)

May the airport security screening system be used to achieve ends unrelated to air safety?

On January 5, 1987, Wayne G. Campbell placed his locked briefcase on a conveyor belt leading to the X-ray scanner at the Seattle International Airport. Picking up a dark mass on the X-ray screen, the Flight Terminal Security (FTS) officer operating the scanner, Bonnie Boswell, asked Campbell to open the briefcase. With some reluctance, Campbell eventually agreed to do so privately. FTS officer Karen Kangas searched the case and found a very large quantity of currency. Kangas then questioned Campbell regarding his destination, returned his briefcase to him, and then released him.

Because large sums of cash are often associated with drug deals, FTS officers at the Seattle Airport had a policy of reporting any sum of U.S. currency over $10,000 to the United States Customs Service

---

[99] Material items used in connection with the drug trade are treated by the law as persons. Hence, the $124,570 is the defendant. Possession or use of property contrary to the law makes it subject to confiscation. Aircraft and money used in the trafficking of drugs are often seized and "named" as defendants, even though owners and/or operators may not be tried.

and Airport Police. Employees who reported such sums of money were paid $250 as a reward.

The information obtained by Karen Kangas was forwarded to Roger Guevarra, a Drug Enforcement Administration [DEA] agent in Los Angeles. Acting on this information, Guevarra and a second DEA agent, Christopher Amato, met Campbell's flight. They identified themselves to Campbell, and in response to their questioning, Campbell admitted he had $130,000 in his briefcase. He contended the money belonged to a friend of his in Encino, California, who had hired him to ransom a stolen painting.

Skeptical of his story, the agents took the briefcase to a nearby DEA office, and Campbell followed. Once there, Campbell opened the briefcase revealing bundles of currency, a substantial quantity of cigarette rolling papers and a receipt from a Seattle hotel indicating that Campbell had stayed there from January 3 to January 5, 1987.

The DEA agents photocopied the papers and returned to Campbell everything except the currency. On January 6, 1987, DEA agents used Smoky, a narcotics detecting dog, to test the currency for the odor of cocaine, heroin, marijuana and marijuana derivatives. Smoky's reactions indicated one or more of these substances had come in contact with the money.

The United States then filed a forfeiture action. Campbell filed a timely claim and answer, and moved to suppress the evidence uncovered by the search of his briefcase. The district court denied Campbell's motion to suppress and ruled that the currency was subject to forfeiture. Campbell appealed the district court's ruling.

The question before the court of appeals was whether the use of the airport security system to achieve ends unrelated to air safety violated the constitutional rights of commercial passengers. For precedent the court looked at *United States v. Davis*,[100] wherein it was decided a generalized law enforcement search of all passengers, as a condition for boarding a commercial aircraft, would plainly be unconstitutional. The appellate court also recognized the Supreme Court had repeatedly emphasized the importance of keeping criminal investigatory motives from "coloring" administrative searches.

The court determined the situation at the Seattle Airport plainly fell outside the administrative search rationale in *Davis*. The close working relationship between the FTS and law enforcement authori-

---

[100] 484 F. 2d 893, 910 (1973).

ties had a significant distorting effect on airport searches as approved in *Davis*. Having found no weapons or explosives in Campbell's briefcase, agent Kangas' legitimate interest in Campbell's identity and destination were at an end; there was no further safety-related justification for detaining Campbell and prying into his affairs.

The accommodation reached between law enforcement authorities and FTS officials made much sense from a law enforcement perspective. However, it effectively transformed a limited check for weapons and explosives into a general search for evidence of crime, substantially eroding the privacy rights of passengers. The order denying the motion to suppress was reversed. The order of forfeiture was vacated, and the case was remanded for further proceedings consistent with this opinion.

UNITED STATES v. $557,933.89
287 F.3d 66 (2nd Cir. 2002)

Under what circumstances may goods be seized as a result of a routine airport search and be subjected to civil forfeiture?

Ramon Mercado was passing through an American Airlines security checkpoint at New York LaGuardia Airport when the security officer asked if he could open Mercado's briefcase, and Mercado complied. It was full of money orders worth some half million dollars. The security guard detained the suitcase while contacting the Port Authority Police [PAP]. The PAP then brought in the Drug Enforcement Administration. Mercado was given a receipt for the money orders, and proceeded on the flight to Miami.

A "canine sniff" of the money orders subsequently revealed the presence of a narcotics residue. The DEA then instituted administrative forfeiture proceedings[101] on grounds of narcotics trafficking and money-laundering. Mercado argued the evidence should be suppressed because it was seized in violation of the Fourth Amendment. He subsequently pled guilty to one count of conspiracy to possess and distribute cocaine.

The Court held that a person possesses a privacy interest in the contents of personal luggage that enjoys Fourth Amendment protec-

---

[101] 19 U.S.C. § 1607.

tion. Moreover, consent to reasonable security searches at an airport does not constitute consent to unreasonable searches.

Conceding that airport personnel were permitted to search his briefcase for weapons, Mercado insisted that once they found none, they were obliged to close it up and send him on his way; they were not free to search for other illegal material unrelated to aviation security. The Court disagreed, citing the "plain view" doctrine, allowing law enforcement personnel to seize an item without a warrant so long as it is immediately apparent the object is connected with a criminal activity, and so long as they observe it from a lawful vantage point (that is, they have not violated the Fourth Amendment by being in a position to see the unlawful item). So long as the search of the passenger's carry-on bag was no more intrusive than necessary to accomplish its purpose of detecting weapons or explosives, such other criminal items in "plain view" may lawfully be seized. The Court found both the initial opening of the briefcase and seizure of the money orders and, based on probable cause, the K-9 bag sniff, were within the Fourth Amendment. Hence, administrative forfeiture of the money orders was proper.

PUBLIC CITIZEN v. FEDERAL AVIATION ADMINISTRATION
988 F.2d 186 (D.C. Cir. 1993)

To what extent may the FAA withhold security and staffing information from public disclosure?

In this case, the petitioners challenged the Federal Aviation Administration rules adopted pursuant to the Aviation Security Improvement Act of 1990 [ASIA], arguing that the rules were insufficiently detailed. The main thrust of their contention centered on the FAA's failure to publish the secret rules in the *Federal Register* and to allow public comment, in violation of the Freedom of Information Act of 1988, and the Administrative Procedure Act.

In 1988, terrorists succeeded in bombing Pan Am flight 103 over Lockerbie, Scotland, killing all passengers aboard. In response, the President of the United States created the Commission on Aviation Security and Terrorism, to conduct an appraisal of the practices and policy options available with respect to preventing terrorist acts involving aviation. The Commission's conclusion was that "the U.S.

civil aviation security system is seriously flawed . . . [and] needs major reform." According to the Commission, "the FAA [had] provided to the airlines and airports very little guidance and few standards for their use" in combating terrorism. Congress sought to remedy the problem by enacting the Aviation Security Improvement Act. Subsequently, the FAA adopted rules prescribing "minimum training requirements for new employees . . . and minimum staffing levels." But in its Notice of Proposed Rule Making [NPRM], the FAA chose not to disclose too much detail about the proposed security procedures. Its failure to disclose all of the details prompted the petitioners, who were not satisfied with the FAA's assurances, to bring suit.

Because Congress had committed the Aviation Security Improvement Act to the FAA's administration, the Court determined that *Chevron U.S.A. v. Natural Resources Defense Council* [102] provided the applicable standard. Summarizing the standard,

> *Under the Chevron analysis, judicial review of an agency's interpretation of a statute under its administration is limited to a two-step inquiry. At the first step, [the court] inquires into whether Congress has directly spoken to the precise question at issue. If [the court] can come to the unmistakable conclusion that Congress had an intention on the precise question at issue, [the] inquiry ends.*

> *However, if the statute before [the court] is silent or ambiguous with respect to the specific issue before [it], [the court] proceeds to the second step. At this stage, [the court] defers to the agency's interpretation of the statute if it is reasonable and consistent with the· statute's purpose; [the courts] are not free to impose [their] own construction on the statute, as would be necessary in the absence of an administrative interpretation.*

---

[102] 467 U.S. 837 (1984).

Deferring to the FAA's interpretation of the Aviation Security Improvement Act, the court upheld the rules as adopted, and concluded that Congress clearly intended for the FAA to retain the authority to promulgate security-sensitive rules in secret. The court further contended the FAA had rationally determined that to disclose the information the petitioners were seeking would have jeopardized passenger safety. Accordingly, the petitioners' motion to review the FAA's security-sensitive rules was denied.

ROMBOM v. UNITED AIRLINES
867 F. Supp. 214 (S.D.N.Y. 1994)

Under what conditions may a passenger be removed from a flight, and arrested for disruptive behavior?

On August 3, 1992, the plaintiff, Sarah Shepard Rombom, boarded a United Airlines flight in Chicago, destined for New York. However, Rombom and her traveling companion, Lani Adelamn, were removed from the plane before it departed, and were arrested by the Chicago Police. As the aircraft left the gate, a flight attendant had to stop reading the flight safety instructions to ask Rombom, Adelman, and three men with whom they were having conversation, to be quiet. The parties disagreed about what then ensued.

United claims that the group refused to comply with the flight attendant's requests to be quiet, and continued to act in a rambunctious manner during and after the safety instructions. The flight attendant sought assistance from the head flight attendant, Joyce Cunningham, who notified the pilot, K.S. Burbech, of the situation. Burbech instructed Cunningham to tell the offending passengers that they would be removed from the aircraft if they failed to behave properly. Cunningham relayed this message to Rombom and her associates, who allegedly reacted to this ultimatum by becoming even more ill mannered. Cunningham reported this response to Burbech, who decided to return to the gate. At the gate, members of the crew requested that the five offending passengers disembark. The group refused, and asserted that they would deplane only if escorted off by the police. The police were summoned, and at this point, the three men deplaned quietly and were not arrested. Rombom and Adelman, however, had a sharp exchange with the police officers, who arrested the women for disorderly conduct.

Rombom described quite a different scenario, and rejected United's characterization of her conduct as disruptive and a safety problem. She alleged that it was Cunningham who acted inappropriately and unprofessionally, in a rude and aggressive manner toward her and Adelman. Rombom claims that she and her friends became quiet when the flight attendant stopped the safety demonstration and asked the group to settle down. After the safety instructions, the group resumed its conversation. Cunningham then approached the group and repeatedly threatened to turn the plane around if they did not behave. One of the men replied that the group was doing nothing wrong, and challenged Cunningham to take whatever course of action she felt was appropriate. When Rombom asked what the problem was, Cunningham told her to mind her own business unless she wanted to be thrown off the plane. Subsequently, the pilot announced that he was turning back to the gate. Members of the flight crew then threatened to remove anybody who spoke out loud. As Rombom voluntarily exited the plane onto the gateway, a member of the crew said "[p]ut these two girls under arrest."

The charge against Rombom and Adelman was subsequently withdrawn, and it is unclear who pressed charges against them. Cunningham apparently signed the misdemeanor complaint, however, she denies that the signature on the complaint is hers. Nevertheless, the police handcuffed Rombom and charged her with disorderly conduct. As she was placed in the police car, Rombom said she saw "every passenger" staring at her. She sued United, Burbech, and Cunningham, claiming that as a result of the defendants' actions she suffered "great mental and physical distress . . . [and] was humiliated, made sick and injured her character and reputation. . . ."

Rombom's claims center around three distinct actions taken by the flight crew. First, she complains that the flight crew, especially Cunningham, acted in a "rude" and "unprofessional" manner. The second activity for which Rombom sought recovery was the pilot's decision to return to the gate. Finally, she alleged that the flight crew had her arrested out of spite.

United moved for summary judgment, alleging that Rombom's state tort claims were preempted by federal law. The Federal Aviation Regulations implicitly preempt Rombom's claims because these statutes and regulations mandated the actions taken by the flight crew. Under federal law, the pilot has discretion to refuse to transport a passenger who poses a threat to the safety of the flight.[103] And, even under the narrowest definition of services, a flight attendant who asks for quiet so that others may hear safety instructions is clearly performing a necessary service that cannot be construed as "rude." However, nothing in the statutes and regulations authorizes an air carrier to take any action, such as having a passenger arrested out of spite or maliciousness, where the arrest was not necessary to the provision of an airline service.

Thus, United's motion for summary judgment was partially granted with respect to any claims based on (1) the arguments the plaintiff had with the flight attendants, concerning her behavior, and (2) the pilot's decision to return to the gate. Summary judgment was denied with respect to any claims relating to United's role (if any) in having the plaintiff arrested.

UNITED STATES v. RICHARD COLVIN REID, A/K/A ABDUL-RAHEEM, A/K/A ABDUL RAHEEM, ABU IBRAHIM
Criminal No. 02-10013-WGY (D. Mass 2002) (unpublished)

Are avowed members of Al Qaeda, who have sworn allegiance to Osama Bin Laden, enemy combatants?

On a December 22, 2001 flight on American Airlines Flight 63 from Paris to Miami, British citizen Richard Reid attempted to light a fuse connected to plastic explosives in his shoe. He was subdued and restrained by passengers on that flight and taken into custody. The Grand Jury indicted Reid under nine counts and charged that at all times relevant to counts one and two, brought under 18 U.S.C. Chapter 113B, "Terrorism," Al Qaeda was a designated foreign terrorist organization under 8 U.S.C. Section 1189. And that at various times relevant to the counts Richard Reid received training from Al Qaeda in Afghanistan.

The nine counts brought against Richard Reid by the Grand Jury were:

---

[103] 49 U.S.C. §1511; 14 C.F.R. §§ 121.533 and 121.571.

- Count One—attempt to use a weapon of mass destruction (a destructive device consisting of an explosive bomb placed in each of his shoes) against nationals of the United States while such nationals were outside the United States, all in violation 18 U.S.C. Section 2332a (a) (1).

- Count Two—attempt to kill nationals of the United States while such nationals were outside the United States, in violation of 18 U.S.C. Section 2332 (b) (1).

- Count Three—placing on the aircraft explosive devices (contained in his footwear) in violation of 49 U.S.C. Sections 46505 (b) (3) and (c).

- Count Four—attempt to commit murder of more than one of the 183 passengers and 14 crewmembers aboard the aircraft in violation of 49 U.S.C. Section 46506 (1) and 18 U.S.C. Section 1113.

- Count Five—assaulting, intimidating, and interfering with the duties of Hermis Moutardier, a flight attendant on the aircraft in violation of 49 U.S.C. Section 46504.

- Count Six—assaulting, intimidating, and interfering with the duties of Cristina Jones, a flight attendant on the aircraft in violation of 49 U.S.C. Section 46504.

- Count Seven—attempt to set fire to, damage, destroy, disable, and wreck the American Airlines Flight 63 aircraft in violation of 18, U.S.C. Sections 32 (a) (1) and (7).

- Count Eight—carrying a firearm (the two destructive devices) during the commission of the above listed crimes in violation of 18 U.S.C. Section 924 (c).

- Count Nine—attempt to wreck, set fire to, and disable a mass transportation vehicle affecting interstate and foreign commerce in violation of 18 U.S.C. Section 1993 (a) (1) and (8).

Faced with the above nine counts, Reid surprised federal prosecutors by pleading guilty to all charges. He was found guilty of all charges, and during his sentencing hearing on January 30, 2003, Reid claimed to be a member of the Al Qaeda terrorist network, admitted allegiance to Osama Bin Laden, Islam and Allah, and declared himself an enemy of the United States.

The following is a partial transcript of the sentence hearing in which Reid was sentenced to life in prison for his confessed plan to try plan to try and blow up a jetliner with explosives he had hidden in his shoes. Given an opportunity to address the court, Richard Reid said the following:

> *I start by praising Allah because life today is no good. I bear witness to this and he alone is right to be worshiped. And I bear witness that Muhammad Sa'laat Alayhi as-Salaam is his last prophet and messenger who is sent to all of mankind for guidance, with the sound guidance for everyone.*
>
> *Concerning what the Court said? I admit, I admit my actions and I further, I further state that I done them. I further admit my allegiance to Osama bin Laden, to Islam, and to the religion of Allah. With regards to what you said about killing innocent people, I will say one thing. Your government has killed 2 million children in Iraq. If you want to think about something, against 2 million, I don't see no comparison. Your government has sponsored the rape and torture of Muslims in the prisons of Egypt and Turkey and Syria and Jordan with their money and with their weapons. I don't know, see what I done as being equal to rape and to torture, or to the deaths of the two million children in Iraq.*
>
> *So, for this reason, I think I ought not apologize for my actions. I am at war with your country. I'm at war with them not for personal reasons but because they have murdered more than, so many children and they have oppressed my religion and they have oppressed people for no reason except that they say we believe in Allah. This is the only reason that America sponsors Egypt. It's the only reason they sponsor Turkey. It's the only reason they back Israel.*

As far as the sentence is concerned, it's in your hand. Only really it is not even in your hand. It's in Allah's hand. I put my trust in Allah totally and I know that he will give victory to his religion. And he will give victory to those who believe and he will destroy those who wish to oppress the people because they believe in Allah. So you can judge and I leave you to judge. And I don't mind.

This is all I have to say. And I bear witness to Muhammad this is Allah's message.

Judge William Young sentenced Reid and made the following impassioned closing comments:

Mr. Richard C. Reid, hearken now to the sentence the Court imposes upon you . . . .we all know that the way we treat you, Mr. Reid, is the measure of our own liberties. On counts 1, 5 and 6 the Court sentences you to life in prison in the custody of the United States Attorney General. On counts 2, 3, 4 and 7, the Court sentences you to 20 years in prison on each count, the sentence on each count to run consecutive one with the other. That's 80 years. On Count 8 the Court sentences you to the mandatory 30 years consecutive to the 80 years just imposed. The Court imposes upon you on each of the eight counts a fine of $250,000 for the aggregate fine of $2 million. The Court accepts the government's recommendation with respect to restitution and orders restitution in the amount of $298.17 to Andre Bousquet and $5,784 to American Airlines. The Court imposes upon you the $800 special assessment.

The Court imposes upon you five years supervised release simply because the law requires it. But the life sentences are real life sentences so I need not go any further. This is the sentence that is provided for by our statutes. It is a fair and a just sentence. It is a righteous sentence.

Let me explain this to you. We are not afraid of any of your terrorist co-conspirators, Mr. Reid. We are Americans. We have been through the fire before. There is all too much war talk here. And I say that to everyone with the utmost respect. Here in this court where we deal with individuals as individuals, and care for individuals as individuals, as human beings we reach out for justice.

You are not an enemy combatant. You are a terrorist. You are not a soldier in any war. You are a terrorist. To give you that reference, to call you a soldier gives you far too much stature. Whether it is the officers of government who do it or your attorney who does it, or that happens to be your view, you are a terrorist. And we do not negotiate with terrorists. . . . We hunt them down one by one and bring them to justice. So war talk is way out of line in this court. . . . You're no warrior. I know warriors. You are a terrorist. A species of criminal guilty of multiple attempted murders.

In a very real sense Trooper Santiago had it right when first you were taken off that plane and into custody and you wondered where the press and where the TV crews were and you said you're no big deal. You're no big deal.

What your counsel, what your able counsel and what the equally able United States attorneys have grappled with and what I have as honestly as I know how tried to grapple with, is why you did something so horrific. What was it that led you here to this courtroom today? I have listened respectfully to what you have to say. And I ask you to search your heart and ask yourself what sort of unfathomable hate led you to do what you are guilty and admit you are guilty of doing.

And I have an answer for you. It may not satisfy you. But as I search this entire record it comes as close to understanding as I know. It seems to me you hate the one thing that to us is most precious. You hate our freedom. Our individual freedom. Our individual freedom to live as we choose, to come and go as we choose, to believe or not believe as we individually choose.

Here, in this society, the very winds carry freedom. They carry it everywhere from sea to shining sea. It is because we prize individual freedom so much that you are here in this beautiful courtroom. So that everyone can see, truly see that justice is administered fairly, individually, and discretely.

It is for freedom's sake that your lawyers are striving so vigorously on your behalf and have filed appeals, will go on in their, their representation of you before other judges. We care about it. Because we all know that the way we treat you, Mr. Reid, is the measure of our own liberties.

Make no mistake though. It is yet true that we will bear any burden; pay any price, to preserve our freedoms. Look around this courtroom. Mark it well. The world is not going to long remember what you or I say here. Day after tomorrow it will be forgotten. But this, however, will long endure. Here, in this courtroom, and courtrooms all across America, the American people will gather to see that justice, individual justice, justice, not war, individual justice is in fact being done.

The very President of the United States through his officers will have to come into courtrooms and lay out evidence on which specific matters can be judged, and juries of citizens will gather to sit and judge that evidence democratically, to mold and shape and refine our sense of justice.

See that flag, Mr. Reid? That's the flag of the United States of America. That flag will fly there long after this is all forgotten. That flag still stands for freedom. You know it always will. Custody, Mr. Officer. Stand him down.

Reid had one final retort:

That flag will be brought down on the Day of Judgment and you will see in front of your Lord and my Lord and then we will know.

Whereupon the defendant was removed from the courtroom.

CHAPTER 7

OWNERSHIP

Bankruptcy law gives the honest but unfortunate debtor a new opportunity in life and a clear field for future effort, unhampered by the pressure and discouragement of preexisting debt.

CIVIL LAW IN AVIATION

Whereas the previous chapter dealt with the criminal, or "positive," aspect of aviation law, this and succeeding chapters are about civil, or "moral" law within the field of aviation. In each chapter of this section there is a focus upon a principal topic within the field of aviation. These topics include ownership of aircraft and other aviation assets, airman rights and responsibilities, government regulatory responsibilities, airline-related issues including labor relations and passenger rights, and legal issues associated with management of public airports.

Where each of these chapters contains a focal topic, each chapter also incorporates salient sub-topics, which are closely associated to the principal subject. Bankruptcy, insurance, antitrust, torts, and environmental concerns are examples found among the variety of sub-topics. This chapter, dealing with the application of civil law in aviation, begins with the subject of *ownership*.

AIRCRAFT OWNERSHIP

In general, the owner of an aircraft is bound to use reasonable care to prevent injury to others. What is considered "reasonable" may vary from state to state, and may be determined only after careful consideration of each individual situation. Even so, federal law makes it clear that the aircraft owner as well as the aircraft operator may be held liable for its operation.[1] But under the common law rules of negligence, it is ordinarily the *operator*, and not the owner, who is at fault in incidences involving aircraft mishaps. Airman (or "operator") responsibilities are the subject of the subsequent chapter. The focus of this chapter is upon the owner, *title* (i.e., a claim or right to ownership), the means of *conveying* (i.e., transferring) ownership, and *title assurance*.

The first responsibility of the owner of an aircraft is to insure that the aircraft is properly registered with the Federal Aviation Administration [FAA].[2] Article 20 of the Chicago Convention requires that all aircraft display the nationality and registration marks of the state of registry. Article 33 of the Convention provides that Certificates of Airworthiness issued by a nation in conformity with the Chicago Convention shall be recognized as valid by other states.[3]

Title V of the Federal Aviation Act of 1958 Act provides that it is unlawful to operate an aircraft in the United States if it is not registered by its owner whenever the aircraft is owned by a U.S. citizen, by a foreign country granted permanent residence in the U.S., or by corporations doing business under laws of the United States.

The owner of an aircraft registered by the FAA Administrator is issued a certificate of registration, but not title. It is important to note that registration is not evidence of ownership; it is merely notification that the aircraft is duly registered with the FAA. The FAA is not a title-issuing agency, nor is it liable for title rights.[4] Unlike the combined registration and title issuance carried out by the various states with regard to automobiles, title to aircraft is by a separate legal form of conveyance or deed of title. In most states, the state not only licenses automobiles, but also receives proof of ownership and in exchange

---

[1] Federal Aviation Act of 1958, § 901.

[2] *See Dowell v. Beech*, CCH 11 AVI 17,831 (1970).

[3] U.S. courts have recognized the duty of the FAA to abide by its Article 33 Chicago Convention obligation to recognize as valid licenses issued by another signatory State, provided that the requirements underlying such licenses are equal or superior to those required under the Annexes. *Professional Pilots v. FAA*, 118 F.3d 758, 768 (D.C. Cir. 1997); *British Caledonian Airways v. Bond*, 665 F.2d 1153, 1162 (D.C. Cir. 1981). *See also, In the Matter of Evergreen Helicopters*, 2000 FAA Lexis 247 (2000).

[4] *See Koppie v. United States*, CCH AVI ¶ 17,680 (1993).

issues a certificate of title. However, with other vehicles such as boats, airplanes, trailers, and so forth, the state (like the FAA) may register only, without becoming involved in title issuance. Such is the case with the federal government and the national registration of aircraft. The FAA provides a centralized preemptive system of recording aircraft ownership which substitutes the multiplicity of state registration systems, but it does not "title" aircraft.

The FAA Administrator is charged with maintaining a system of recording any conveyance which affects title or interest in an aircraft (and engines over 750 hp), including any leases or mortgages which affect title. With reference to owner's liability, the federal law stipulates a person may not be held responsible for injury or death caused by aircraft unless the aircraft is in the person's "actual possession or control" at the time of the incident. Thus, the time of recording any changes in interest with the FAA can be of significance in liability litigation. Recordation with the FAA may also affect title. Recording interest in aircraft or engines with the FAA does not guarantee title, but it may provide priority in determining subsequent conflicting interests over title.[5]

In the purchase of an aircraft, the potential buyer is advised to follow five basic steps in the acquisition of a new airplane:

- First, a *title search* should be conducted to determine in a preliminary investigation if the person selling the aircraft has the right to do so.
- Second, the potential buyer(s) should attempt to determine if there are any liens or mortgages *encumbering* the sale. The seller may have the right to sell the aircraft, but might be transferring to the buyer not only the aircraft itself, but some liabilities as well. A title search may reveal faults in the title, and there are companies, which can be engaged to conduct title searches for potential buyers.[6]
- The third step is to obtain a formal (i.e., notarized) *bill of sale*.

---

[5] *See Atlas v. Twentieth Century*, CCH 10 AVI 17,502 (1967).
[6] For example, the Aircraft Owners and Pilots Association [AOPA] provides such a title search service; or one may otherwise employ an independent title company to perform this service.

- Fourth, all changes in interest (title, mortgages, etc.) should be *recorded* with the FAA.
- The fifth and final step is to obtain *title insurance*, just in case the title transferred turns out to be faulty. Even though the buyer may have taken reasonable precautions and conducted as thorough a title search as possible, something affecting the title may have been hidden or missing.

FORMS OF OWNERSHIP

The forms of aircraft ownership are generally three:

- *single ownership*;
- *partnership*; and
- *incorporation* (or some other form of limited liability).

In single ownership there is only one owner. Obviously, the advantage of single ownership is to have complete and sole control of the disposition of an aircraft. The disadvantage is that one person alone is responsible financially and for the liability of owning the aircraft.

A partnership includes more than one person having title to an aircraft. This is a common form of ownership, because it allows at least partial ownership where, otherwise, owning an airplane might be cost prohibitive. With shared ownership there may be limited access to the use of the aircraft. Additionally, not only is there responsibility for one's individual actions but there is joint liability for the actions of all partners as well.

The distinct status of a corporation sets its existence apart from the status of its individual shareholders. A "corporation" is "an artificial person or legal entity created by the state or the federal government." The business is treated by the law as a separate and distinct entity. As a legal "person," the business owns the aircraft, along with its other assets. Individual shareholders are generally free of the liabilities of the corporation. Moreover, their ownership is limited to shares in the company and not to any of the company's tangible assets and liability is ordinarily limited to their investment in their corporation. Similar to a corporation in terms of liability is a Limited Liability Company [LLC].

In many states, small, jointly owned companies may be granted the same limits to liability found with the corporation.

Sometimes, a partnership or corporation is formed whereby individuals enjoy fractional ownership in an aircraft. Like owners of a condominium, each has a right to use the common asset on a pre-defined basis.

A flying club, like a partnership, is a way to lower the individual cost of aircraft ownership and operation. However, a flying club may take more than one form of ownership. The preferred ownership in a flying club is to title the aircraft to the club as a *non-profit* corporation. Joint ownership (or partnership) is to be avoided, since it carries with it the same liabilities as a partnership—only magnified by the normally greater membership in a club versus a customary partnership of limited size. The specific interest of a corporate member is intangible. The ownership interest is controlled by the charter or agreement under which the club is formed. Usually there is no interest in any specific aircraft such as one might have in co-ownership of an airplane. Rather, members have joint ownership of the club as a whole.

AIRCRAFT MAINTENANCE

Although ownership brings with it certain privileges, the owner of an aircraft is restricted in the extent to which the aircraft may be personally maintained. Unless an aircraft owner is a certified aircraft mechanic, the owner may not personally perform other than preventive maintenance on the aircraft. Unlike an automobile, which can be maintained, overhauled, or re-built without a license to do so, an aircraft repair usually requires the services of a certified Aircraft and Powerplant [A&P] mechanic. Federal Aviation Regulation Part 43, "Maintenance, Preventive Maintenance, Rebuilding, and Alteration," provides that the holder of a pilot certificate may perform *preventive maintenance* only on an aircraft owned and operated by that pilot, so long as the aircraft is not used in commercial air carrier operations. Generally speaking, "preventive maintenance" is limited to work which does not involve "complex assembly operations."

Although not inclusive of all possible activities, the following is a general list of authorized preventive maintenance activities, including:

- changing and repair of landing gear tires and replacing wheels or skis;
- ground servicing (air, oil, fuel, grease, hydraulic fluids, and lubrication not requiring disassembly);
- cleaning and replacing fuel and oil strainers or filter elements;
- replacement of defective safety wiring and/or cotter keys;
- replacing or cleaning spark plugs and setting of spark plug gap clearance;
- replacing and servicing batteries;
- trouble shooting and repairing broken circuits in landing light wiring circuits, replacing bulbs, reflectors and lenses of position and landing lights, and removing, checking, and replacing magnetic chip detectors;
- replacing any hose connection except hydraulic connections, and replacing prefabricated fuel lines;
- refinishing exterior decorative coatings, and applying preservative or protective coatings;
- repairing upholstery and interior furnishings, replacing seats, seat parts, and safety belts, and replacing side windows where it does not interfere with the aircraft structure or operations; and
- replacing cowlings, and making small simple repairs to fairings, nonstructural cover plates, cowlings and small patches and reinforcements that do not change the contour of the surface.

Transgressing the provisions of FAR Part 43 can have serious ramifications. First of all, it is a violation of an FAR subject to fines, penalties and/or suspension of certification privileges. Second, the action may void any insurance coverage. Third, it may affect warranty and/or product liability protection. And finally, it could result in physical injury or death and a subsequent bar against recovery for damages, either personally or by one's survivors.

In 1983, for example, a home built aircraft crashed on the Central Coast of California, killing its two occupants. The aircraft purportedly crashed because of a simple, but unauthorized modification to a control trim tab on the canard. Even though the work on the trim tab was done by a fully certified A&P mechanic, it was nevertheless a modification not authorized by the factory. As both occupants—the owner and his mechanic-passenger—were directly responsible for the trim tab modification, not only are they dead, but their families were left financially unprotected. They had no insurance to cover the accident, nor were they able to otherwise recover for damages resulting from product liability.

OWNERSHIP AND THE TAX LAWS

One of the liabilities of aircraft ownership is taxation. Tax liability has two perspectives: taxes that must be paid and allowable tax deductions. Aircraft owners are customarily assessed an *ad valorem* tax[7] on their aircraft as personal, or chattel, property. Personal property taxes are collected by the governmental jurisdiction where the aircraft is permanently stored (often determined by where the airplane is physically located on "tax day," or the day chosen by the tax collector to inventory the taxable properties within the tax collector's jurisdiction). *Situs* (or location) of property, for tax purposes, is determined by whether the taxing authority has sufficient contact with the personal property sought to be taxed to justify in fairness the particular tax.[8]

Airlines may be liable for the taxes at the address used for registration purposes, but also by the states wherein the aircraft has operated, landed, or flown over.[9] Another tax, for which aircraft owners may be liable, is "possessory interest tax"—a property tax attached to the use of public properties by private citizens.[10] For example, an owner may be required to pay possessory interest taxes—over and above the rental fee—for use of an aircraft tie-down space on a public airport.

In addition to taxable areas, a question often raised by aircraft owners is to what extent they are allowed by the Internal Revenue Service [IRS] to deduct expenses connected with the use of their pri-

---

[7] *Ad valorem* is a tax imposed on the value of property; *see Black's Law Dictionary* (abridged 5th ed. 1983).
[8] *See Black's Law Dictionary* (abridged 5th ed. 1983).
[9] *See Northwest v. Minnesota*, 322 U.S. 292 (1944); *see also Northwest Airlines, and Republic Airlines v. State of Illinois*, CCH AVI 18,352 (1994).
[10] When real property is owned by the state for public use it is normally not subject to taxation. However, where the property is controlled by a private entity, such as through lease agreement, the subject property may be subject to taxation.

vately owned airplanes. The IRS has been critical of the business use of aircraft, and has, at times, employed what are seemingly arbitrary and discriminatory limitations on the use of especially personally owned (as opposed to corporate–owned) airplanes. It is not uncommon for a personal accountant to advise against claiming deductions for the business use of a personally owned aircraft—irrespective of the legitimacy—just to avoid a potential confrontation with the IRS.

There is no reference specifically to aviation-related expenses in the Internal Revenue Code; however, the Tax Reform Act of 1984 imposed strict rules on the personal use of aircraft. Effectively, the law defines "business use" of airplanes and restricts the deductions allowed if personal use of the airplane exceeds 49%.

Travel expense deductions ordinarily claimed in connection with the use of privately owned airplanes are normally claimed on the basis of deductions allowed under Sections 162 and 212 of the Internal Revenue Code. Expense related to a trade or business is allowed under Section 162. Deductions permitted under Section 212 relate to the management or maintenance of income-producing real property. In either case, only those business expenses that are ordinary, necessary and reasonable are deductible. "Ordinary expenses" are those which are common and accepted in the general industry or type of activity in which the taxpayer is engaged. "Necessary expense" has been interpreted to mean appropriate and helpful in the development of the taxpayer's business.[11] "Reasonable expenses" must be reasonable in *amount*, and must bear a ". . . reasonable and proximate relation to the production or collection of taxable income, or to the management, conservation, or maintenance of property held for the production of income.[12] Reasonableness is a question of fact to be determined in each individual case.

For example, in *Sartor v. the Internal Revenue Service*, the Tax Court determined that "by using the airplane, petitioner (Steven Sartor) was able to arrange a more flexible schedule which enabled him to maximize his sales opportunities."[13] Thus, the Court concluded ". . . that the travel expenses were necessary within the meaning of Section 162." In another instance (*Ballard v. the Internal Revenue Service*),

---

[11] *See Sartor v. the Internal Revenue Service*, 84,273 P-H Memo TC (1984).

[12] *See Ballard v. the Internal Revenue Service*, 84,662 P-H Memo TC (1984).

[13] *Sartor v. the Internal Revenue Service*, 84,273 P-H Memo TC (1984).

deductions were allowed in part for expenses of owning, operating and maintaining a Cessna 310 used for trips to income-producing property owned and managed by the petitioners (John and Patricia Ballard).[14] The plane was used only for brief, unaccompanied trips when needs of the rental property required the Ballard's presence. Periodic visits were required to supervise repairs and maintenance and to meet with legal counsel and local government officials. The deductions were reduced by the court, however, since they were found to be excessive in relation to costs of alternative means of transportation.

BANKRUPTCY

Article 1, Section 8 of the U.S. Constitution confers upon the Congress the power to enact "uniform Laws on the subject of Bankruptcies." Congress enacted the first Bankruptcy Code in 1978. Now codified in Title 11 of the United States Code, it has been amended many times. "Bankruptcy" is a state of judicially being declared insolvent. That is to say, it is a legal declaration to the effect that the fair value of the property and assets of an individual or of a corporation, or the flow of income being received by that "person" is insufficient to cover the person's debts. The property of one who has been declared bankrupt is subject to seizure and distribution among creditors. Bankruptcy proceedings may be classified as either voluntary or involuntary. A "voluntary bankruptcy" is filed by the *debtor*, whereas an "involuntary bankruptcy" is filed by the *creditors*.

The purpose of bankruptcy law is to give debtors a "fresh start" from burdensome debt. As the U.S. Supreme Court observed in *Local Loan v. Hunt*,[15] bankruptcy law "gives the honest but unfortunate debtor . . . a new opportunity in life and a clear field for future effort, unhampered by the pressure and discouragement of preexisting debt."[16]

Bankruptcies may also be categorized according to the Chapter (of the Federal Bankruptcy Code) under which they are filed. One often hears some company going bankrupt, and of the bankruptcy being referred to as either a "Chapter 7" or a "Chapter 11" bankruptcy. In the 1980's and 1990's, for example, several prominent airlines, including

---

[14] *Ballard v. the Internal Revenue Service*, 84,662 P-H Memo TC (1984).
[15] 292 U.S. 294 (1934).
[16] *Id.* at 244.

Braniff, Pan Am, TWA, Continental, Eastern and America West, continued to operate while under protection from a Chapter 11 bankruptcy. By 2004, Aloha Airlines, Hawaiian Airlines, American Trans Air, United Airlines and US Airways were in Chapter 11 bankruptcy. Unable to emerge successfully from bankruptcy, some carriers (e.g., Braniff, Pan Am, Eastern, et al.) ended their operations in spite of the protection from creditors afforded them. Other carriers, such as Swift Aire Lines (*infra*), terminated business outright under Chapter 7.

The references (i.e., Chapter 7, Chapter 11, et al.) are to procedures outlined by Chapter in the National Bankruptcy Act (Title II U.S.C.). The following is an overview of the contents of National Bankruptcy Act:

- *Chapter 7* is a liquidation. It is a complete termination of the business, and according to the Act is intended to ". . . close up the estate as expeditiously as possible. . . ." The trustee collects the debtor's assets, reduces them to cash, and distributes the proceeds to creditors on a pro-rate basis, though secured creditors may receive preferential treatment vis-à-vis unsecured creditors and stockholders.
- *Chapter 9* contains the procedures by which the debts of a municipality may be adjusted. Orange County, California, for instance, filed for bankruptcy under this Chapter on December 6, 1994, as a result of the county treasurer having lost $1.7 billion of taxpayers' money through investments in risky Wall Street securities.[17]
- *Chapter 11* is a reorganization, which leaves the "debtor in possession" [DIP].[18] For the first 120 days after the order for relief is filed, the DIP has the exclusive right to file a plan for reorganization to eventually make the company solvent, while in the meantime it remains in operation. A company that fails to reorganize successfully may find itself in Chapter 7 liquidation proceedings.

---

[17] *See* Public Policy Institute of California, *The Orange County Bankruptcy: Who's Next?*, in Research Brief (Apr. 1998), Issue No. 11.
[18] 11 U.S.C. § 1101.

- *Chapter 13* is an adjustment of the debts of an individual with a regular income. It is much like Chapter 11, but for the individual. In other words, a plan is formulated which may result ultimately in achieving solvency.

In bankruptcy proceedings a trustee (or receiver) is appointed by a Federal Bankruptcy Court. There are some 90 such courts, one in each U.S. judicial district. The trustee assumes responsibilities while the debtor is insolvent or unable to pay debts. The trustee's role is to take charge of the estate, investigate irregularities such as fraudulent transfer or preferential transfer, see that creditors are treated fairly, receive claims, liquidate property and/or distribute available funds. Under "avoiding powers," transfers of money or property concluded within the 90 days preceding bankruptcy can be avoided by the trustee and the assets forcibly returned to the bankrupt estate. Transactions by insiders may be avoided up to a year prior to filing.[19]

In an innovative approach, Continental Airlines, while under Frank Lorenzo's leadership, used the bankruptcy court in 1983 as a forum to impose new wage rates and working conditions upon the various employee groups.[20] Ironically, six years later, creditors used the bankruptcy court to remove Frank Lorenzo from his leadership at Eastern Airlines.[21] The Official Committee of Unsecured Creditors of Eastern requested the bankruptcy court appoint a Chapter 11 trustee to replace the debtor-in-possession (Lorenzo), in order "to enhance the value of the estate" and proceed toward a "viable reorganization."

More recently, when United's initial bid to receive a $1.8 billion federal loan guarantee was turned down by the Air Transportation Stabilization Board [ATSB] in December of 2002, the airline's CEO, Glenn Tilton then vowed to use the court process to craft a "transformational business model," which included draconian concessions on the part of labor. A week after being rejected by the ATSB, United filed for bankruptcy protection. Not surprisingly, labor responded with a "no confidence" vote in Tilton. United became the largest airline and sixth-largest U.S. company (by assets) in history to file under Chapter

---

[19] 11 U.S.C. §§ 101(31), 101(54), 547, and 548.
[20] *See* Ch. 9.
[21] *See In re Ionosphere Clubs, Inc. and Eastern Airlines, Inc., Debtors*, CCH 22 AVI 18,129 (1989).

11. In court documents, UAL listed assets of $22.7 billion and liabilities of $21.5 billion, and was facing $920 million of past due debt repayments looming within a week of the filing. Without the required loan guarantee, Tilton said the company had no choice.[22]

There were no indications of any wrongdoing at United, but where bankruptcy is involved irregularities such as fraudulent and/or preferential transfer are not uncommon. These irregularities result from attempts by debtors to retain assets at the expense of creditors. "Fraudulent transfer" is the transfer of money or property to "defraud" creditors. A common example of fraudulent transfer might be the transfer of company funds to immediate relatives just prior to filing for bankruptcy protection. Conversely, "preferential transfer" occurs when certain, "preferred" creditors are paid in full while leaving others partially or totally unpaid. It is an unfair distribution of limited assets. This could occur, for example, where a supplier is controlled by the same company as the insolvent company.

Common in bankruptcies are high levels of suspicion amongst creditors who feel (whether real or imaginary) a sense of being cheated when they become aware of the fact they may not receive what is due them because of business failure and subsequent bankruptcy proceedings. It is the responsibility of the trustee to protect the interests of creditors and to discern potential allegations of wrongdoing having a foundation, and to investigate those suspect irregularities.

In the case briefs which subsequently follow, the case of *Swift Aire Lines v. Crocker National Bank* is given as an example of an airline in bankruptcy, and more specifically is presented as an example of a trustee attempting to fulfill his responsibilities to see that all creditors were treated fairly, and to rectify any irregularities.[23] The allegations in *Swift* were twofold. First, Crocker Bank failed to live up it its obligation to honor an irrevocable letter of credit to Swift Aire for $775,000 based on a technicality. And second, Justin Colin, the principal stockholder in Swift, intentionally bankrupted the airline in a Chapter 7 filing in order to avoid personal responsibility for the aforementioned $775,000 letter of credit.

---

[22] Laurence E. Gesell and Paul Stephen Dempsey, *Air Transportation: Foundations for the 21ˢᵗ Century* 300 (2ⁿᵈ ed. 2005).

[23] *Swift Aire Lines, David Farmer as Trustee v. Crocker National Bank and Justin Colin*, 30 B.R. 490 (1983).

The trial court upheld the trustee's complaint against the bank for wrongful refusal to honor the letter of credit. As the lower court stated, Crocker's refusal to honor the letter of credit was an attempt to "elevate form over substance." In other words, Crocker relied upon the literal and "positive" terms of the contract, rather than any "moral" obligation it may have had to live up to the spirit of the agreement. It was also pointed out in the lower court proceedings that "The (Swift) Board of Directors, being controlled by Colin, might have been reluctant to draw on the letter of credit."

On appeal, however, the appellate court reversed the lower court's ruling sustaining Crocker's defense that there had not been "strict compliance" with the terms of the letter of credit agreement. Further, the Court found that by filing (Chapter 7) bankruptcy, Swift (controlled by Colin) had made it impossible for anyone to draw against the letter of credit. In short, the trial court determined Colin's actions to be a deceptive misrepresentation of his real intentions. The appellate court, on the other hand, found no (legal) irregularity in what Justin Colin had done in securing the credit agreement.

In yet another case, *Gary Aircraft v. General Dynamics*, questions of both security interests for buyers in the ordinary course of business, and of security interest in bankruptcy proceedings were at issue.[24] The effects of bankruptcy on creditors and others, however, are varied. Aircraft and other assets may be readily sold to liquidate debts, and to realize at least partial recovery by creditors. At a minimum, the assets will likely be tied up in the bankruptcy proceedings for months, and sometimes years, while claims are filed and the liquidation process takes place. Moreover, certain creditors have priority and will be paid before other general creditors. Taxes and administrative fees of the trustee (the appointed bankruptcy attorney) for instance are paid ahead of other creditors.

In aviation-related bankruptcies there are at least two mechanisms which avoid having property tied up in bankruptcy proceedings. Chapter 11 of the Bankruptcy Act provides that where there is a "purchase-money equipment security interest" (i.e., the right to demand and receive property), the creditor may have the right to take

---

[24] *Gary Aircraft Corporation v. General Dynamics*, 681 F.2d 365 (5th Cir. 1982), *cert. den.* 462 U.S. 1131 (1983).

possession of aircraft per the terms of a lease or conditional sales contract. Such a right connected with aircraft ownership is not affected by a court ruling to enjoin (i.e., prohibit) such a taking. Under Section 1110 of the Bankruptcy Act,[25] once an airline falls into bankruptcy, it enjoys an automatic stay from making lease payments on that asset for only 60 days after the filing of bankruptcy, after which the lessor is free to repossess the aircraft unless, within that period, it enters into an agreement to defer payments with the lessor.[26]

Another priority creditor may be the landlord in real property leasehold or rental agreements. The landlord is entitled to owed and on-going rents while the property is tied up in bankruptcy. In the case of an airport as the landlord, this creditor priority right may be of limited benefit. Airports are established to fulfill the transportation needs of the community, not to make money. Rental moneys (i.e., profits) are not the primary motivation for public airport sponsors. Rather, airports are a public service. Oftentimes, rental agreements with airlines and other commercial operators are established below cost in order to entice these various airport-related activities to conduct business at the sponsor's airport. Thus, with limited airport land and/or building assets tied up in bankruptcy, to the exclusion of other air carriers and airport operators, it may hold little consolation for the airport sponsor to receive the rental moneys in the interim, while public air transportation and commercial needs go unserved.

Referring to reorganization petitions of Braniff International and Continental Airlines, Paul B. Gaines, then Director of Aviation for Houston, Texas, said that, "During each of these painful proceedings, airport proprietors lost control over the use of aircraft gates and terminal space, and in some cases, these facilities sat idle when the bankrupt airline closed or reduced its operations." "This situation was compounded when other airlines were anxious to serve or expand their existing service, and the proprietor was precluded by law from making use of these scarce facilities." In other cases, the Chapter 11 carrier was able to lease out its protected gates reportedly at a profit, while paying the airport proprietor the below break-even cost of the lease.

---

[25] 11 U.S.C. § 1110.
[26] *Kimmelman v. Port Auth. of N.Y. & N.J.*, 344 F.3d 311, 320 (3rd Cir. 2003).

Although some large air carrier airports may have alternative terminal and airfield facilities available, the loss of any space at all at already-crowded airports is noticeably detrimental to airport operations. Imagine, then, the effect of bankruptcy on smaller airports where the loss of space used by even one carrier is proportionally magnified. Take the example of San Luis Obispo, on the Central Coast of California, where Swift Aire Lines was its primary carrier when the airline filed for bankruptcy under Chapter 7. Limited terminal space and an extensive corporate headquarters leasehold was tied up in court for nearly two years—ultimately to the inconvenience of nearly a quarter of a million enplaning passengers.

Fortunately, more recent amendments to the Bankruptcy Act now require an air carrier to relinquish unused terminal space. According to Paul Gaines, "The change in federal law will help assure that scarce airport gates and terminal space are made available to airlines willing and able to provide needed air service."

Through the decade of the 1980s, air carrier solvency was an issue of growing concern. Among others, Braniff was liquidated. Associated with a string of airline company bankruptcies was an undermining of consumer confidence in the airline industry. The high bankruptcy rate was followed by a period of consolidation among major carriers between about 1985 and 1987, coupled with a movement toward alignment of regional carriers under the umbrellas and colors of the larger, dominant airlines. At first, the prospect of consolidation offered a potential answer to industry wide insolvency. Unfortunately, the decade of the 1990s was entered under the threat of even more airline bankruptcies and the prospect of only three to six major carriers surviving in the United States. The losses were devastating. Between 1990 and 1994, the airline industry lost $12 billion, more than it had made in its entire history.[27] Pan Am and Eastern Airlines were liquidated, while TWA limped along until finally being acquired by American Airlines. And yet, the worst was yet to come.

By the mid-1990s, the crisis in the airline industry had subsided. Nevertheless, solvency of the major air carriers, Chapter 11 bankruptcies, and impending airline business closures under Chapter 7 contin-

---

[27] Paul Stephen Dempsey and Laurence E. Gesell, *Air Transportation: Foundations for the 21st Century* 221 (1997).

ued to be issues of concern.[28] During the first decade of the 21st Century, the air transportation industry was struggling to recover from by far the worst economic crisis in its history, the trauma of which was brought on by a series of setbacks that began with airline deregulation, followed by a rash of consumer complaints and safety concerns, constrained airport capacity resulting in inordinate traffic delays, economic recessions and spikes in oil prices, two wars in the Middle East, and topped off by acts of terrorism around the world and a system now constrained by heightened alert and enhanced security procedures.

In the process several traditional hub-and-spoke airlines have been brought to the very brink of extinction and bankruptcy.[29] Free market advocates cite a high cost structure as the cause of the most recent airline crisis and suggest that those costs can be lowered if not by negotiation then via the bankruptcy process.[30]

What follows are some examples of bankruptcy proceedings and other issues involving aviation-related property rights.

INTERNATIONAL ATLAS SERVICES v. TWENTIETH CENTURY AIRCRAFT
251 Cal. App. 2d 434 (Cal. App. 1967), *cert. den.* 398 U.S. 1038 (1968)

Does recordation of aircraft have priority over other
recordedtitle to its engines?

Twentieth Century Aircraft Company sold a Douglas DC-6B to President Airlines under a conditional sales contract. President Airlines employed International Atlas to service and maintain the aircraft. Atlas serviced the engines by substitution. An engine needing overhaul, or whose time had run out, was replaced by a newly overhauled engine with zero time on it. In turn, Atlas would take possession of an old engine and would overhaul and rebuild it. During a period (referred to as a "Quick Engine Change" [QEC]) when engines belonging to Atlas

---

[28] Editorial, *Courageous Steps Required to Reform Airlines*, Av. Wk & Space Tech. (Nov. 18, 2002), at 82.
[29] *See* Laurence E. Gesell and Paul Stephen Dempsey, *Air Transportation: Foundations for the 21st Century* 473 (2nd ed. 2005).
[30] *Id.*, at 444.

were installed on the aircraft, President Airlines defaulted on its conditional sales contract and Twentieth Century repossessed the aircraft. Atlas brought suit for possession of its engines.

Aircraft engines bear serial numbers for identification, and their ownership may be recorded with the FAA. However, Atlas relied upon the terms of its maintenance agreement with President Airlines to retain title to its engines, "Title to all spare QEC's and engines shall at all times remain in IAS (Atlas). . . . " Twentieth Century on the other hand, recorded its conditional sales contract with the FAA. The contract of sale required President Airlines to keep the aircraft in good order and repair, and to pay all expenses of maintenance and overhaul.

The trial court awarded judgment in favor of Twentieth Century, which had repossessed the aircraft as legal owner and conditional seller, even though California law in 1961[31] provided, "When things belonging to different owners have been united so as to form a single thing, and cannot be separated without injury, the whole belongs to the owner of the thing which forms the principal part; who must, however, reimburse the value of the residue to the other owner or surrender the whole to him." Atlas appealed.

During the trial appeal, Atlas' case was made even stronger under state law. Section 9314 of the California Commercial Code provided, ". . . a security interest in goods which attaches before they are installed in or affixed to other goods takes priority as to the goods installed or affixed (called in this section 'accessions') over the claims of all persons to the whole. . . . "

Under California law, Atlas should have recovered the engines. However, the California Court of Appeals determined that California law did not apply. The controversy was governed instead by federal law (Section 503 of the Federal Aviation Act of 1958, requiring recordation of aircraft/engine title with the FAA). Twentieth Century had to prevail since it had recorded its interest with the FAA, whereas Atlas had not. The Federal government may be said to have fully occupied the field of recordation of interests in aircraft and rights derived from recordation, and to have established paramount law in this area. This paramount interest under federal law effectively superseded any inconsistent state law.

---

[31] Cal. Civil Code § 1025.

The Appellate Court concluded that the failure of Atlas to record its interest in the engines installed on the aircraft to which Twentieth Century held title, which title the latter had properly recorded under federal law, subordinated its interest in the engines at the time of repossession to the interest of Twentieth Century in the aircraft as a whole. The California Court of Appeals affirmed the judgment of the lower court.

DOWELL v. BEECH ACCEPTANCE CORPORATION
476 P.2d 401 (Cal. 1970)

Does Federal recordation of aircraft interest supersede state law?

A Beechcraft Bonanza, single engine aircraft, was sold by Beechcraft Acceptance Corporation, the manufacturer, to one of its distributors, Nevadair. In turn, Nevadair made a conditional sale of the airplane to Tanger, a duly authorized Beechcraft dealer. Under the terms of the conditional sales contract, Tanger was not to sell the plane without Nevadair's consent. Tanger still owed Nevadair $20,000 on the plane. At the same time, Nevadair assigned its security interest to Beech. Beech knew that Tanger was an authorized Beechcraft dealer, and that the plane would be offered for sale. Beech recorded its assigned security interest in the airplane with the FAA.

Donald Dowell purchased the plane for $30,000 from Tanger, paying for it in full. Dowell had no knowledge or notice of Beech's security interest, nor did he complete a title search. He did not think it necessary since he was buying directly from the manufacturer's authorized dealer. Tanger promised Dowell they would register the sale with the FAA, but they failed to keep their promise. Beech removed the aircraft from Dowell without his knowledge or consent, and Dowell brought suit against Beech for return of the airplane or its value, for damages resulting from loss of use, and for punitive damages.

The trial court rendered judgment declaring Dowell to be the owner, and awarded him $175 compensatory damages for loss of use, and $1,000 punitive damages for oppressive conduct. The decision for the lower court was based in part on Section 9307 of the Uniform Commercial Code and upon California Code which both stated that a buyer in the ordinary course of business could take possession free of a security interest created by his seller, even though the security interest was perfected, and even though the buyer knew of its existence. Beechcraft, joined by Nevadair, appealed. The principal issue in the appeal was whether the federal system of recording aircraft interest affected priorities recognized by applicable state law. The California Court of Appeals reversed the lower court's imposition of $1,000 punitive damages, but in all other respects it affirmed the lower court's decision that Dowell be awarded ownership of the aircraft. The appellate court recognized the priority of federal recordation of aircraft interests, but determined from the history of the Federal Aviation Act of 1958 (and as far back as the McCarran Bill and the Civil Aeronautics Act of 1938) that it gave no support to the proposition that the recording provisions of the Act were designed to nullify state law. Beechcraft and Nevadair continued their appeal.

The California Supreme Court reversed the judgment granting possession of the disputed aircraft to Dowell, reversed the award of compensatory damages, and it followed, failed to sustain the award of punitive damages. For precedent, the Court looked to *International Atlas Services, Inc. v. Twentieth Century Aircraft Co.*[32]. To wit, the federal policy requiring recordation to protect previously acquired aircraft titles would be undermined if state law governed the rights of the parties irrespective of recordation. In the Court's words, "The federal policy to foster recordation is eviscerated by a rule which relies on state laws to protect the buyer in the ordinary course of business, even though he fails to undertake a simple title search which would have readily revealed all encumbrances." The case was reversed and remanded in favor of Beechcraft, the owner of recordation.

SHACKET v. PHILKO AVIATION
841 F.2d 166 (7th Cir. 1988)

Does actual notice of prior interest and purchaser's knowledge of the facts have a bearing on recordation of aircraft interest?

Philko Aviation, owned by Edward McArdle, became the lessor of facilities used by Roger Smith, an aircraft dealer. In November 1977, Smith agreed to sell Maurice and Sylvia Shacket a Piper airplane for

---

[32] 251 Cal. App. 2d 434 (Cal. App. 1967), *cert. den.* 398 U.S. 1038 (1968).

$290,000, payable by a trade-in of the Shackets' old plane plus $126,000 cash. The Shackets put down a $20,000 deposit. As Smith was not a piper dealer, he arranged to buy the plane from Clark Aviation for $239,000. On April 20, Clark delivered the plane together with a bill of sale to Smith, who in turn delivered it to the Shackets in exchange for the balance of the purchase price, the trade-in having already been delivered to Smith. Smith told the Shackets that, as was customary, he, as dealer, would take care of registering their title with the FAA.

The next day, Smith went to McArdle and showing him a phony purchase order, told him that he had contracted to sell a 1978 Piper Navajo (the plane he had just delivered to the Shackets) to a firm called Krueger Aviation for $290,000, and that he needed $152,000 to complete payment to Clark Aviation, from which he had bought the plane. McArdle agreed to have Philko advance the money. In exchange, Smith not only agreed to repay the money to Philko out of the sale proceeds, but in addition to those proceeds, would repay $60,000 that he owed one of McArdle's other companies. He also gave Philko a bill of sale for the aircraft. It was understood, however, that Philko would not take possession. Rather, the plane would be sold to Krueger, and Smith would pocket the difference between the purchase price and the $212,000 ($152,000 plus $60,000) destined for the McArdle companies. Smith, who still owed Clark $147,000 of the purchase price of the plane, now paid this off.

In May, Smith confessed to McArdle who in turn promptly filed with the FAA apparently in an attempt to secure his interest (over the Shacket's) in the aircraft. Following up on the progress of his own registration in early June, Shacket discovered Smith had disconnected his phone. Shacket, now fearful that Smith had not registered the aircraft as promised, immediately mailed to the FAA the temporary registration form that Smith had given him when he bought the plane, but it was too late. By then, the FAA records showed Philko as the owner. The FAA told Shacket he would need to have a bill of sale from Philko, which of course McArdle would not provide him.

The Shackets brought suit, asking for a declaratory judgment that they, not Philko, owned the plane. Philko counter-claimed, seeking damages for conversion, because the Shackets were in possession of what he considered was his plane. The case presented a classic dispute between two persons, each with defective title to the same property—the Shackets' title being defective because it was not recorded; Philko's being defective because he acquired a bill of sale from Smith who had no title.

The U.S. District Court held that the Shackets should prevail. The U.S. Court of Appeals affirmed, holding that the validity of the Shackets' title depended upon Illinois State law because they were bona fide purchasers who had taken possession of the aircraft. Philko they determined was not a bona fide purchaser under state law because it had not taken possession.

The Supreme Court disagreed because,

> . . . *if Philko had actual notice of the transfer to the Shackets or if, under state law, Philko failed to acquire or perfect the interest that it purports to assert for reasons wholly unrelated to the sale to the Shackets, Philko would not have an enforceable interest, and the Shackets would be entitled to retain possession of the aircraft[33].*

To the Supreme Court, the principal issue was whether Philko had *actual notice* of the sale to the Shackets when it obtained its own bill of sale. Although under the Federal Aviation Act, as interpreted by the Supreme Court, an unrecorded conveyance of an airplane, such as a sale by Smith to the Shackets, *normally* is trumped by a recorded interest, there is an exception for the case where the holder of that interest had "actual notice" of the prior unrecorded conveyance. Obviously, Philko had such notice at the time it mailed its bill of sale to the FAA.

The issue of notice must be distinguished from that of possession, which figured in the trial court's opinion affirmed at the appellate level. While holding that the federal recording system is preemptive, the Supreme Court disclaimed the ridiculous proposition that whoever files a bill of sale first is the true owner unless he or she has actual notice of prior sale. The filer must have a property interest, whether an ownership or a security interest to be filed. If Philko had actual notice

---

[33] 462 U.S. 406, 414 (1983).

of a prior sale, it was irrelevant whether they acted with reasonable diligence in attempting to record their title. The case was remanded to the appellate court to rule accordingly.

GARY AIRCRAFT v. GENERAL DYNAMICS
681 F.2d 365 (5th Cir. 1982), *cert. den.* 462 U.S. 1131 (1983)

Does federal recordation of aircraft interest displace state law assignment of priorities to interests in aircraft?

In December 1971, Gary Aircraft Corporation entered into a written letter of understanding with Frederick B. Ayer and Associates, Inc., expressing its intention to purchase four airplanes from Ayer, a dealer in aircraft. Interest in two of those aircraft became the issue in this case. Gary did not complete the transaction, but Arthur Stewart, its president, acting as an individual did carry out the transaction. At the time of sale, General Dynamics Corporation held interest, which had been recorded with the FAA, in the two aircraft under a security agreement executed by Ayer in 1962. Under that agreement, if Ayer was in default on its obligations to General Dynamics, Ayer was not authorized to sell the aircraft without the consent of General Dynamics. On the date of sale from Ayer to Stewart, Ayer was in fact in default to General Dynamics.

On January 4, 1972, only days after the sale, Gary initiated an aircraft title search through the Aircraft Owners and Pilots Association [AOPA], who reported the results one day later on January 5. Seven months later (in August), Stewart recorded his bill of sale with the FAA. Repeatedly, over the succeeding four years, Gary requested that Ayer secure release of the security interest held by General Dynamics. Without success in obtaining a release from General Dynamics, Stewart transferred the two planes, without consideration, to Gary in 1975. Gary in turn mortgaged the aircraft with the Victoria Bank and Trust Company, and Victoria Bank recorded its interest with the FAA.

General Dynamics hearing of the transfer of aircraft, unauthorized by the terms of their contract, made claim to their security interest in the airplanes. Subsequently, Gary filed Chapter 11 bankruptcy and the aircraft were then tied up in the bankruptcy proceedings. Through the bankruptcy court, Gary sought permission to sell one of the aircraft free and clear of liens. The court permitted the sale, and the proceeds were deposited with the court. The second airplane remained in Gary's possession. General Dynamics filed suit, arguing that:

- The Federal Aviation Act of 1958 granted General Dynamics priority, because it had recorded its security interest before Stewart purchased the aircraft;
- Even if the priority question did not govern, then Stewart could not qualify as a buyer in the ordinary course of business; and finally,
- Even if Stewart qualified as a buyer in the ordinary course of business, then Gary could not so qualify.

The Bankruptcy Court, affirmed by the District Court, held that Gary was entitled to the proceeds of the aircraft sold, and to possession of the second aircraft already in their hands—free and clear of any interest asserted by General Dynamics. The courts countered all three arguments presented by General Dynamics and concluded that the FAA does not govern priorities in interests in aircraft; that Stewart, as a buyer in the ordinary course of business, took free of General Dynamic's interest, and that Gary took the title of its transferor (Stewart). General Dynamics appealed to the U.S. Court of Appeals.

The appellate court concluded that, without question, section 506 of the Federal Aviation Act reserves some areas of regulation for the states by assigning questions of "validity" to state law. Whether Congress intended to preempt state law by federalizing "priorities" is not clear. The Supremacy Clause of the U.S. Constitution requires the courts to invalidate state law only if it conflicts with a federal statute. Thus, Texas law was preeminent in this case.

Under the Uniform Commercial Code, adopted by Texas and enacted as the Texas Business and Commerce Code, a buyer in the ordinary course of business is one who, in good faith and without knowledge that the sale to him is in violation of the ownership rights or security interests of a third party, buys from a person in the business of selling goods of that kind. Such a buyer takes free of a security interest created by his seller, even if that interest is perfected, and even if the buyer knows of its existence. The appellate court concluded that the law is designed to protect the innocent buyer against prior security interests in retail goods because he cannot be expected to discover those interests. Both Stewart and Gary were determined by the court to be such buyers in the ordinary course of business.

The ruling of the bankruptcy court, affirmed by the District Court, was affirmed by the Court of Appeals General Dynamics appealed to the U.S. Supreme Court but *certiorari* was denied in 1983.

KOPPIE v. UNITED STATES
1 F.3d 651 (7th Cir. 1993)

Is the Federal government liable for title assurance?

The plaintiff, Chad M. Koppie, sued Ligon "Air" and the FAA over the ownership of a Convair 880 airplane. Koppie claimed that Ligon "Air" was in control of the plane, which he rightly owned, and the FAA took the wrong side in the dispute by issuing a Certificate of Aircraft Registration to Ligon "Air" rather than to him.

Koppie purchased, or thought he had purchased, the Convair from Hudson General Corporation in 1987 for a mere $5,000, a strikingly good deal for an aircraft that originally cost $10 million. Hudson had obtained title through satisfaction of a garnishment lien against Ligon "Air," which owed it money for storing and maintaining the plane. But unbeknownst to Koppie, the aircraft had made its way back into the hands of Ligon "Air" through a circuitous route. Koppie took ownership subject to the recorded interest of Cromwell State Bank, the original lien holder, and Cromwell assigned its interest to something called the "880 Partnership," which then resold the plane to Ligon "Air." Both the "880 Partnership" and Ligon "Air" were owned by the same two people, Susan and Cliff Pettit. Koppie knew something was amiss when in June or July of 1987 he went to the airport to look after his plane and discovered Michael Potter, whom he thought was an agent of Ligon "Air," working on the aircraft.

In the meantime, Koppie had applied for a Certificate of Aircraft registration from the FAA. On June 23, 1987, he received a letter denying his request because of the conflicting claims over ownership. Having learned that his ownership of the plane was in serious dispute, Koppie signed two documents releasing whatever interests he might have had in the Convair in return for consideration of $36,000 from

Michael Potter. Koppie eventually received and accepted the money, and the plane was flown to South Africa where it remained.

Koppie then claimed that the release of his interests in the Convair was nullified by a subsequent document between him and Michael Potter and Western Continental Holdings, Ltd. But in the document, Potter and Western Continental Holdings acknowledged that they had no interest of any kind in the airplane. Clearly, it is impossible for a person who owns no interest in a piece of property to execute an agreement for consideration transferring ownership of the property to another. This would be akin to the proverbial "selling the Brooklyn Bridge." The document was meaningless. Thus, Koppie's earlier decision to accept $36,000 for the relinquishment of all claims to the Convair prevented him from complaining that he, not Ligon "Air," owned the aircraft. Irrespective, the FAA could not determine the ownership of the aircraft, and, therefore, could not issue a registration certificate.

More fundamentally, Koppie had alleged that under the Federal Tort Claims Act the FAA had wrongfully denied him a Certificate of Aircraft Registration, and had tortiously converted his property. The major flaw in his argument was that registering an aircraft with the FAA does not determine ownership and has no legal effect. The purpose of registering a plane is to define its nationality. Registration is not evidence of ownership of aircraft in any (court) proceeding in which ownership by a particular person is, or may be an issue. The statute[34] expressly forbids the kind of ownership claim made by Koppie based on certification. In essence, a Certificate of Aircraft Registration is worthless as for proving ownership. The judgments for both defendants (the United States and Ligon "Air") were affirmed.

SARTOR v. COMMISSIONER
T.C. Memo 1984-274 (May 22, 1984)

May a salesperson deduct for travel expenses incurred in business use of a personal airplane?

Steven F. Sartor and his wife Gwenn Sartor resided in Kaysville, Utah. Mr. Sartor was employed by Dixico, Inc. as an outside sales-

---

[34] 49 U.S.C. § 1401(f).

man. In 1978, he was assigned the sales territory of Utah, Idaho and Colorado. In 1980, his sales territory was expanded to include Washington, Oregon, Montana and Vancouver, Canada. Having obtained a commercial pilot's license in 1965, Sartor began using his personal Cessna 182 airplane for business in 1979. In 1980, he purchased 50% interest in a newer and larger Cessna T-206 airplane, because it was capable of safe flights in instrument flight conditions. At the same time, he began aircraft qualification and instrument flight training in the Cessna T-206.

Because there were less frequent commercial flights available, supposedly as a result of airline deregulation, it was necessary for him to use his own airplane. During 1980, Sartor used his airplane almost exclusively for business purposes, flying to see customers throughout his sales territory. Between 1980 and 1982, his sales bonus increased each year. In his 1980 income tax return, Sartor claimed three types of expenses in connection with the use of his airplane:

- travel expenses to visit clients;
- travel expenses to entertain his clients with scenic flights and fishing trips; and
- expenses for aircraft qualification.

The Internal Revenue Service [IRS] determined the Sartors were not entitled to the expense deductions because: (1) the airplane expenses were not "ordinary, necessary nor reasonable business expenses" under Section 162 of the Internal Revenue Code (in effect during the year in question), and (2) the entertainment expenses, because the Sartors had failed to satisfy the substantiation requirements under Section 274. In other words, the Sartors failed to adequately demonstrate the expenditures were "ordinary, necessary and reasonable" to the success of their business. The Sartors countered by arguing the travel and entertainment expenses were both necessary and reasonable because they allowed Mr. Sartor to be more successful.

Under Section 162, the term "necessary" has been interpreted to mean appropriate and helpful in the development of the taxpayer's business. The Tax Court found that Sartor's travel expenses, including the aircraft qualification expenses, were very helpful to him in his business. By using the airplane, Sartor was able to arrange a more flexible schedule, which enabled him to maximize his sales opportunities. Thus, the Court concluded the travel expenses were necessary within the meaning of Section 162. Additionally, the travel expenses were reasonable as well, the court concluded, because not only did Sartor have a "reasonable" expectation his bonuses would increase as a result of using the airplane, his bonus each year actually did increase. Additionally, the expenses were reasonable because the increased productivity helped to assure him of continued employment.

As for the other deductions, the Court agreed with the IRS that Sartor had failed to substantiate the entertainment expenses. Section 274 required an income earner to show that the predominant purpose of the entertainment expense was to further business, and that the mere generating of "goodwill" was not enough. Sartor could only show names of clients who accompanied him on trips. There were no statements concerning a business purpose.

The airplane-related travel expenses were allowed as deductions. The entertainment expenses were not allowed.

BALLARD v. COMMISSIONER
T.C. Memo 1984-662 (Dec. 20, 1984)

May an owner deduct travel expenses in connection with the use
of a personally-owned airplane and the maintenance
of income-producing property?

John and Patricia Ballard resided in Florissant, a suburb of St. Louis, Missouri, but owned and managed several apartment buildings in both St. Louis and Marathon, Florida. John Ballard traveled regularly from his home in St. Louis to Marathon and back. Patricia Ballard did not accompany her husband, but stayed behind to manage their properties in the St. Louis area.

Ballard was a command pilot with Ozark Air Lines, and had access to reduced air fares offered through interline agreements with Trans World Airlines and Eastern Airlines. He could have flown *standby* to his destination(s) on any one of the three carriers (i.e., Ozark, TWA or Eastern), and in fact did so on several occasions. He also traveled between St. Louis and Marathon in a 20-year old (1956) Cessna 310, a small twin-engine airplane. He used the plane exclusively for these trips, and did not fly it for pleasure. One hundred percent of the costs of owning, operating and maintaining the airplane were claimed as deductions under Section 212 of the Internal Revenue Code. The IRS Commissioner disallowed all of the airplane expenses and depreciation, determining that the expenses of owning, operating and maintaining an airplane were not deductible as "ordinary, necessary, and reasonable" business expenses under Section 212.

The IRS contended that the airplane expenses and depreciation substantially exceeded the gross rental income, before even considering any other expenses associated with the property. Furthermore, the IRS argued, a comparison of the income and expenses clearly demonstrated that the plane had no reasonable and proximate relationship to the production of income as required under Section 212. Finally, the expenses far exceeded the cost of available commercial flights.

The Ballards contended that the expenses were "ordinary, necessary, and reasonable" within the meaning of Section 212, because the expenses were within the scope of their overall business plan and within the framework of their other income-generating business activities, and reasonable in comparison with alternative means available to accomplish their business plan. At issue were:

- whether the Ballards had a dominant personal motive for these trips;
- whether the costs were ordinary and necessary expenses paid for the purposes provided in Section 212;
- whether the trips bore a reasonable or proximate relation to the production of income or management of income-producing property; and
- whether the costs themselves were reasonable.

The Court found that the IRS offered merely speculation as to the Ballard's personal reasons for the trips. The Ballards, on the other hand, demonstrated the appropriate purpose under Section 212 by detailing reasons why managing the Marathon property (a duplex) required periodic visits. The final factor, however, was whether the costs were reasonable. The costs were clearly greater than the cost of flying by commercial air. The Ballards failed to present any evidence as to why Mr. Ballard could not have flown as a standby passenger instead of using his personal airplane. The expenses of owning, operating, and maintaining the airplane were, therefore, excessive in relation to the costs of alternative means of transportation. The Court allowed deduction of an equivalent to the costs for trips by commercial airline.

NORTHWEST AIRLINES v. MINNESOTA
322 U.S. 292 (1944)

In which state does an interstate air carrier pay taxes?

The instant case arose because the state of Minnesota imposed a personal property assessment against the whole fleet of aircraft owned and operated by Northwest Airlines, an interstate air carrier. There was a question as to the state's authority to do so since only a part of the fleet was in the state on the "tax day" (the day when all taxable property within the state's jurisdiction was counted).

The case originated in the District Court for Ramsey County, and was appealed to the Supreme Court of the State of Minnesota, which ruled in favor of the State. Northwest petitioned the U.S. Supreme Court, on constitutional grounds, to review the case. On writ of *certiorari*, the U.S. Supreme Court reviewed the judgment of the state courts that had been in favor of the State of Minnesota.

Northwest Airlines maintained the tax violated both the Commerce Clause and De Process Clause of the U.S. Constitution. The Due Process Clause of the Fourteenth Amendment states, in part, "No State shall make or enforce any law which shall abridge the privileges or immunities of citizens of the United States; nor (under the Fifth Amendment) shall any State deprive any person of life, liberty, or property, without due process of law. . . ." The Commerce Clause is embodied in the duties and responsibilities of Congress as listed in Article I Section 8 of the U.S. Constitution, to wit, "The Congress shall have power . . . to regulate commerce with foreign Nations, and among the several states, and with Indian tribes."

In further argument, Northwest contended that even though the airline was chartered by Minnesota, that was not a controlling fact as to tangible property having a tax "situs" (the taxing jurisdiction of the state over property located in the domicile of the owner) elsewhere.

Many of the airline's aircraft were in other states on tax day and other jurisdictions could conceivably impose a personal property tax on the same aircraft. In prior cases, dealing not with aircraft, but with a company's rolling stock, it was determined that taxing would be proportionate among the taxing jurisdictions. Northwest contended that the location in Minnesota of the airline's main business office and maintenance hangar was not of controlling significance.

The State of Minnesota responded by stating that the tax did not violate the due process clause of the Constitution, because the planes *were* in Minnesota as much if not more than in other states. The airline was organized under the laws of Minnesota, and therefore, received the benefits of, and protection from the laws of that state. Most importantly, Northwest had failed to prove that any other state had jurisdiction to tax any of aircraft involved. They had not paid taxes to other states, they merely assumed that the precedents of prior rolling stock cases supported proportionate taxation, and that was an erroneous assumption. The tax did not violate the Commerce Clause, and it was argued by the state that it was in the best interests of the aviation industry that such taxes be sustained.

The question before the court, then, was whether the Commerce Clause or the Due Process Clause of the Fourteenth Amendment barred the State of Minnesota from enforcing the personal property tax it had laid on the entire fleet of airplanes owned by Northwest. For all the planes, St. Paul was the homeport registered with the Civil Aeronautics Authority, under whose Certificate of Public Convenience and Necessity [PC&N] Northwest operated. Northwest operated other maintenance bases, but the work of rebuilding and overhauling the planes was done in St. Paul. Details as to stopovers, other runs, the location of flying crew bases and of the usual facilities for aircraft, had no bearing on this case.

The tax in controversy was for the year 1939. All of Northwest's planes were in Minnesota from time to time during that year. The tax assessed by Minnesota was a tax assessed upon "all personal property of persons residing therein, including the property of corporations . . ." On May 1, 1939, the time fixed by Minnesota for assessing personal property subject to its tax, Northwest's Minnesota operations were 14% of its system wide mileage, and 16% of its scheduled plane mileage. Northwest based its personal property tax return for 1939 on the number of planes in Minnesota on May 1, 1939. Minnesota assessed a tax against Northwest on the basis of the entire fleet coming into Minnesota. The Supreme Court of Minnesota, with three judges dissenting, affirmed the judgment of a lower court in favor of the state.

In its findings the Supreme Court placed great reliance upon the early 20th Century decision of *New York C & H Railroad Co. v. Miller*.[35] In the *Miller* case, the New York Central Railroad introduced evidence that during the taxable years in question, a proportion of its cars, ranging from about 12% to 64%, was used outside of New York. This figure was arrived at by using the ratio between Central's mileage outside of New York and its total mileage. The state comptroller nevertheless ruled that all of Central's cars were taxable in New York, the state of domicile. The New York Court of Appeals remitted the proceedings to the comptroller to determine whether any of the rolling stock was used exclusively out of the state. No such evidence was introduced for any tax year. The comptroller made no reduction in the tax, and this action was affirmed by the Appellate Division, the Court of Appeals, and upon review in the instant case.

In announcing the conclusion and judgment of the Supreme Court in *Miller*, Justice Holmes observed that Minnesota was here taxing a corporation for all its property within the state during the tax year, no part of which received permanent protection from any other state. No other state could claim to tax as the state of the legal domicile as well as the home state of the fleet. No other state was the state, which gave Northwest the power to be, as well as the power to function. No other state could impose a tax that derived from the significant legal relation of creator and creature. Minnesota continued to safeguard Northwest and Minnesota alone could tax the personal property, which was attributable to Minnesota and to no other state.

It was not shown in the *Miller* case, and it was not shown in this case, that a part of the company had acquired residency elsewhere (i.e., taxing situs). That was the decisive feature of the *Miller* case, and was decisive in this case. The doctrine in the *Miller* Case, which was applied here, did not subject property permanently located outside of the domiciliary state to double taxation. But not to subject property that

---

[35] 202 U.S. 584 (1906).

had no locality other than the state of its owner's domicile to taxation would free such floating property from taxation everywhere.

The decision of the Supreme Court of Minnesota was affirmed, but not unanimously. Mr. Justice Stone dissented stating that in his opinion Minnesota did impose an unconstitutional tax on Northwest in violation of the Commerce Clause, and for that reason believed the judgment should have been reversed.

There were two justices who felt compelled to issue concurring statements. Mr. Justice Black concurred but did not want this case to "foreclose" consideration of the taxing rights of states other than Minnesota. Mr. Justice Jackson concurred, but made note that this was the first Supreme Court consideration of constitutional limitations upon state power to tax airplanes. Flight over a state confers no jurisdiction to tax. Landing, however, might confer jurisdiction to tax. Like any other article of personal property, a plane could land or remain within a state in such a way as to become a part of the property within the state. Mr. Justice Jackson said he concurred with the judgment, but only because the record seemed to establish Minnesota as a "home port" within the meaning of the case authority cited.

NORTHWEST AIRLINES v. THE DEPARTMENT OF REVENUE OF THE STATE OF ILLINOIS
692 N.E.2d 1264 (Ill. App. 1998)

May a state assess taxes for air carrier overflights of their state, even though the flights neither land in nor take off from airports in the state?

This case was an appeal from the decision of an Administrative Law Judge [ALJ). The ALJ affirmed the Department of Revenue's inclusion of Northwest Airlines and Republic Airlines[36] overflight miles in the Illinois income tax apportionment formula. The airlines did not dispute the requirement to apportion their business income derived from those services performed in Illinois. They did contend that overflights, which neither take off nor land in the state, are not "revenue

---

[36] On Aug. 12, 1986, NWA, Inc., the parent company of Northwest Airlines, acquired Republic Airlines as a wholly owned subsidiary of NWA, Inc. Republic merged into Northwest effective Nov. 19, 1986.

miles" (i.e. income) derived from doing business in the state, and therefore should not be taxed. The ALJ disagreed and issued a recommendation upholding the Department of Revenue. The airlines appealed.

The Department of Revenue's rationale for including overflights was based on the substantial number of airline revenue miles that were not apportioned to any state, which in the Department's view should be apportioned. The Department felt that because of the taxpayers' (the airlines) link to Illinois and the fact the miles were flown *over* the state, there was a sufficient nexus to connect to income. The airlines argued that the rules of statutory construction did not permit the expansion of the words "in this State," because the plain meaning of "in" does not include "over." The Department responded by stating "the legislature did not intend to exclude fly-over miles from the apportionment formula." The Department further contended that if overflight miles were not included in the tax apportionment formula, then they would not be taxable by any state and would be "nowhere miles," resulting in less than 100% apportionment. Agreeing, the ALJ's rationale, in part, was:

> *Activities in Illinois airspace are in Illinois. There is nothing in the statute to support the taxpayer's view that only the Illinois flyover miles of originating and departing flights should be included. . . . By considering those miles as being in Illinois while considering flyover miles as being over Illinois is making a distinction not contemplated by the statute.*

The ALJ also rejected the taxpayers' argument that overflights are in federal territory because "no miles would ever be attributed to any state. . . ." He argued that the airlines conduct regular activities in Illinois and get benefits from it. The right to fly over Illinois is a privilege and the airlines must share in the maintenance and cost of services available from the state. According to the ALJ, "Any contact with Illinois, no matter how minimal, is sufficient to subject all of an airline's Illinois flyover miles to taxation."

The U.S. Court of Appeals took exception, concluding that neither the language of the (Illinois tax) statute nor the legislative intent indicated that overflights were included in the language. Therefore, the

ALJ's decision, without any legal analysis, that overflights were included in the tax law was contrary to law. Courts "cannot read words into a statute unless those words are needed to give effect to the legislature's intent."[37] The court must apply the statute as written. Nevertheless, the court suggested that the Department of Revenue "may" possess the means to include overflight miles in the tax formula if certain requirements were met. The Department must first demonstrate there is sufficient nexus to support including other items in the tax formula. And second, it must demonstrate that the airline revenue miles are not taxed by any other state.

The decision of the ALJ was reversed as contrary to law, but the case was remanded in light of the above instructions for the Department to make specific findings as to the basis for taxation of overflights.

IN RE SWIFT AIRE LINES
30 B.R. 490 (9th Cir. 1983)

May a bank refuse to honor a letter of credit pursuant to the principle of strict compliance?

Swift Aire Lines was a commercial airline service financed primarily through Wells Fargo Bank. In 1980, Justin Colin purchased 80% stock ownership in the airline for $1,775,000. He agreed to contribute an additional $775,000 to Swift in the event that either Wells Fargo Bank or the Board of Directors of Swift determined in good faith that such funds were required by Swift for the continuing operation of its business. Colin was to deliver to Swift a bank letter of credit in the amount of $775,000 in the event such payment was required. Crocker National Bank issued an irrevocable letter of credit for $775,000 with Swift as beneficiary. The Board of Directors of Swift and Wells Fargo were each given the power to draw on the letter of credit. Note that Colin controlled the Swift Board of Directors and might have been reluctant to draw on the letter of credit if the business were faltering. But Colin agreed that the debtor could draw on the Crocker letter of credit even if Swift filed a petition under *any* chapter of bankruptcy.

---

[37] *Northern Trust Co. v. Bernardi*, 504 N.E.2d 89 (Ill.1987).

As a condition of the letter of credit, Crocker required a statement that Wells Fargo or Swift had demanded payment (from Colin) of the additional contribution, and that the amount remained unpaid for a period of five days. On September 15, 1981, Wells Fargo made formal demand on Colin for payment. On September 18, 1981, Swift (controlled by Colin) filed a Chapter 7 bankruptcy. Subsequently the trustee David Farmer was appointed, and on October 6, 1981, he presented documents to Crocker in attempt to draw against the letter of credit. On October 7, 1981, Crocker refused to honor the letter of credit because: the draft was not drawn by the beneficiary (Swift), who was now out of business; and the letter of credit required a statement from Wells Fargo which "must be manually signed" by the beneficiary and followed by the designation "Corporate Secretary, Swift Aire Lines, Inc." This requirement was not met since Swift was out of business and no longer had a corporate secretary.

The letter of credit required a statement from Wells Fargo that the "funds are required by Swift Aire Lines, Inc. for the continued operation of its business. . . ." Crocker contended this was a false statement, and therefore defective, because at the time it was presented (by Farmer as trustee) Swift was out of business and no longer needed the funds "for continued operation." Thus, Crocker maintained the trustee did not have the power to draw under the letter of credit agreement.

The trial court decided on March 25, 1982, that the trustee had filed the necessary documents to draw against the letter of credit, and the court entered a money judgment against Crocker in favor of the trustee for $775,000 principal plus interest and costs. It might be noted that Crocker had filed a third party complaint against Colin for indemnification in the event the trustee prevailed. The trial court struck the third party complaint, but Colin nevertheless subsequently filed for personal bankruptcy. Both Crocker and Colin appealed, contending that the trial court erred in concluding that the trustee *strictly* complied with the terms of the letter of credit.

The United States Bankruptcy Appellate Panels of the Ninth Circuit stated that there were only two alternative means of drawing on the letter of credit:

- The *first alternative* was that the Board of Directors of Swift had determined funds were needed for continued operation of the business; or
- The *second alternative* required a statement from Swift that Wells Fargo requested the additional contribution, signed by the corporate secretary of Swift, and that Wells Fargo had determined the funds to be necessary for continued operation of the business.

The appellate court determined that upon a filing of bankruptcy, Swift's officers and directors no longer had power or authority to deal with the estate. By filing bankruptcy, Swift (Colin) had made it impossible for Wells Fargo or Swift to draw against the letter of credit since there was no longer a corporate secretary able to act for the debtor.

The trial court had determined that the trustee was entitled to draw on the letter of credit because: bankruptcy law controls over conflicting state law; and Crocker was trying to "elevate form over substance." The appellate court disagreed stating the Bankruptcy Code did not give the trustee the power to automatically enforce payment if state law requiring strict compliance would dictate otherwise. The trial court's determination that Crocker's refusal to recognize the trustee, as beneficiary would only elevate form over substance was at odds with the doctrine of strict compliance. Pursuant to the principle of strict compliance, the trustee was precluded from requesting the letter of credit. The trial court's decision was reversed and the case remanded.

IN RE IONOSPHERE CLUBS
922 F.2d 984 (2nd Cir. 1990)

Under what conditions may a debtor-in-possession be removed?

On March 9, 1989, Eastern Air Lines and its affiliate Ionosphere Clubs, Inc., each filed a voluntary petition for relief under Chapter 11 of the Bankruptcy Code. Approximately 13 months after filing for bankruptcy, the Official Committee of Unsecured Creditors of Eastern (the "Committee") moved that the Court appoint a Chapter 11 trustee to replace the debtor-in-possession, Frank Lorenzo, "in order to enhance the value of the estate" and proceed toward a "viable reorganization." The Committee had lost all confidence in Eastern's management when Eastern announced to the Committee that it once again would have to renege on its previous agreement for debt repayment.

The Committee asserted that a court appointed trustee was warranted because:

- Eastern's devastating, constantly expanding and unending losses were extremely damaging to unsecured creditors, and, therefore, to the interests of the estate;
- Texas Air Corporation (the parent company) and Eastern had demonstrated their inability to project the results of proposed operations to the extent that the Committee had lost confidence in their stewardship of the business; and
- Eastern and Texas Air had repeatedly reneged on their plan of reorganization agreements with the Committee, such that the Committee had no confidence in the ability or willingness of the debtors and their common equity holder to adhere to basic understandings.

In a Chapter 11 bankruptcy, the debtor-in-possession has certain obligations:

- A debtor-in-possession must act as a "fiduciary of his creditors" to "protect and to conserve property in his possession for the benefit of creditors."[38]
- A debtor-in-possession has all the duties of a trustee in a Chapter 11 case, including the duty to protect and conserve property in its possession for the benefit of creditors.[39]
- A debtor-in-possession's fiduciary obligation to its creditors includes refraining from acting in a manner which could damage the estate, or hinder a successful reorganization of the business.[40]

---

[38] *In re Sharon Steel Corp.*, 871 F.2d 1217 (3rd Cir. 1989).
[39] *In re Devers*, 759 F. 2d 751, 754 (9th Cir. 1985).
[40] *In re Thurmond*, 41 Bankr. 464, 465 (Bkrtcy D. Or. 1983).

Throughout this case, Eastern had continually made operating projections, which it had failed to achieve, with resultant losses being borne by the unsecured creditors. The debtors were unable to make reliable operating estimates, even over short periods of time. Hence, the court found clear and convincing evidence, which mandated the appointment of a trustee.

The United States Trustee was directed to appoint an eminently qualified person, with the ability to continue to operate Eastern Air Lines as a going concern and to develop a viable business plan.

CHAPTER 8

AIRMEN

The FAA Administrator is to promote the safety of flight of civil aircraft in air commerce by prescribing rules, regulations, minimum standards, methods, and procedures. In doing so, the Administrator is given broad discretionary powers of authority and responsibility.

INTERNATIONAL AIR LAW

First adopted in 1948, Annex 1 to the Chicago Convention of 1944 addresses personnel licensing.[1] Under it, no one may act as a flight crewmember unless he holds a valid license in compliance with the Annex.[2] To secure a license or type rating,[3] the applicant must satisfy age,[4] knowledge,[5] experience,[6] flight instruction,[7] and skill[8] requirements.[9] The licensing process also must include a medical fitness

---

[1] ICAO, Annex 1 to the Convention on International Civil Aviation—Personnel Licensing (9th ed. Jul. 2001) [hereinafter Annex 1].

[2] Annex 1, § 1.2.1.

[3] Type ratings are established for aircraft, and for operating an aircraft under Instrument Flight Rules [IFR]. The second-in-command of an aircraft requiring more than a single pilot must also hold a type rating for that aircraft. Annex 1, § 2.1.7.

[4] The minimum age is 17 years. Annex 1 § 2.3.1.1. The minimum age for commercial pilots is 18 years. Annex 1 § 2.4.1.1. The minimum age for an airline transport pilot license is 21 years. Annex 1 § 2.5.1.1.

[5] Annex 1 §§ 2.3.1.2, 2.4.1.2, 2.5.1.2.

[6] The applicant may not have less than 40 hours of flight time. Annex 1 § 2.3.1.3. Applicants for a commercial pilots' license must have 200 hours of flight time, or 150 hours if completed during a course of approved training. Annex 1 § 2.4.1.3.1. Applicants for an airline transport pilot license must have 1,500 hours of flight time.

[7] Annex 1 §§ 2.3.1.4, 2.4.1.4, 2.5.1.4.

[8] Annex 1 §§ 2.3.1.5, 2.4.1.5, 2.5.1.5.

[9] Annex 1 §§ 2.1.1.3, 2.4.1.6, 2.5.1.6.

evaluation.[10] Similar requirements are established for flight navigators, flight engineers,[11] and aircraft maintenance personnel.[12]

Article 32 of the Chicago Convention requires that International Civil Aviation Organization [ICAO] member states shall issue certificates of competency and licenses to the pilot and operating crew of every aircraft registered in said state, and flown in international aviation.[13] With respect to flights above its territories, each state may refuse to recognize such certificates and licenses issued by another state to its own nationals.

Under Article 33 ICAO's 188 member states are obliged to recognize the validity of the certificates of airworthiness and personnel licenses issued by the nation in which the aircraft is registered, so long as the standards under which such certificates or licenses were rendered are at least as stringent as those established under the Chicago Convention.[14] Hence, a nation fails to comply with the Standing Rules of Procedure of the Assembly of the ICAO at its own peril, for there are implicit sanctions, and they are potentially severe. A state that fails to comply may find its airman, aircraft, air carrier, and/or airport certifications and licenses not recognized as valid by a foreign government, thereby terminating their operation to, from, or through its territories, isolating it from the global economy. Private sector insurance coverage for airlines and airports may be impossible to obtain. Moreover, the delinquent government would be responsible, and arguably liable, should an aircraft collision or other aviation tragedy occur whose proximate cause was the failure of the government to comply with relevant Standing Rules of Procedure.[15]

---

[10] Annex 1 § 1.2.4, and Ch. 6.

[11] Annex 1 Ch. 3.

[12] Annex 1 Ch. 4.

[13] Article 29 requires that flight crew members carry their licenses on board the aircraft they fly.

[14] A similar provision was included in Article 13 to the Paris Convention of 1919, the predecessor of the Chicago Convention. U.S. courts have recognized the duty of the FAA to abide by its Article 33 Chicago Convention obligation to recognize as valid licenses issued ay another Signatory State, provided that the requirements underlying such licenses are equal or superior to those required under the Annexes. *Professional Pilots v. FAA*, 118 F.3d 758, 768 (D.C. Cir. 1997); *British Caledonian Airways v. Bond*, 665 F.2d 1153, 1162 (D.C. Cir. 1981). *See also In the Matter of Evergreen Helicopters*, 2000 FAA Lexis 247 (2000).

[15] One might argue that the failure to notify ICAO of differences results in a presumption of full compliance with the standards at issue, and that such States should bear full legal liability for any harmful consequences of their non-compliance. *See* Michael Milde, The Chicago Convention—*Are Major Amendments Necessary or Desirable 50 Years Later?*, 19 Annals of Air & Space L. 401, 426 (1994).

FEDERAL JURISDICTION OVER AVIATION

In the United States, the Federal Aviation Administration holds plenary jurisdiction over aviation safety. The FAA licenses and regulates airline flight operations personnel (including flight crews, maintenance personnel and dispatchers),[16] and oversees airline safety, training and maintenance procedures,[17] technical flight standards,

---

[16] The FAA possesses wide discretion to revoke a pilot certificate under an emergency order pending expedited review (i.e., meaningful and timely review of certificate revocation–a post-deprivation hearing within a reasonable time, but with adequate time to prepare a defense, and with the right of the pilot to waive expedited proceedings in order to receive meaningful review of his claims). *Tur v. FAA*, 4 F.3d 766, 770 (9th Cir. 1993); *Grant v. NTSB*, 1483, 1485 (9th Cir. 1992); *Blackman v. Busey*, 938 F.2d 659, 664 (6th Cir. 1991); *Nevada Airlines, Inc. v. Bond*, 622 F.2d 1017 (9th Cir. 1980). As one court noted, "[T]he private interest at stake is [the pilot's] property interest in his airman's certificate. The governmental interest is the public safety and welfare. The importance of the latter justifies giving immediate effect to revocation orders 'where danger to the public is present.'" *Tur v. FAA*, 4 F.3d 766, 769 (9th Cir. 1993); *Morton v. Dow*, 525 F.2d 1302, 1305 (10th Cir. 1975).

Certain decisions of the FAA have been deemed not reviewable by the federal courts. For example, in *Adams v. Federal Aviation Administration*, 1 F.3d 955 (9th Cir. 1993), a pilot sought judicial review of the FAA's revocation of his pilot examiner designation. The court observed that the statute allowed the Secretary of Transportation (who delegated such authority to the FAA) to rescind any such delegation "for any reason which he deems appropriate." 49 U.S.C. § 1355(a) (2002). Thus, the statute provided no judicially manageable standard with which a court could review the exercise of such discretion, thereby leaving the FAA administrator's decision in such circumstances committed to agency discretion by law, and precluding judicial review thereof. 1 F.3d at 956. FAA regulations also allow suspension or revocation of a pilot's license based on a conviction for violating drug importation laws. 14 C.F.R. 61.15; *Pinney v. NTSB*, 993 F.2d 201 (10th Cir. 1993).

The NTSB holds broad jurisdiction over pilot certificates. It has held that "conduct on a single flight, generally in the form of recklessness or gross (or extreme) carelessness, is considered sufficiently egregious to demonstrate a lack of qualifications." *Administrator v. Wingo*, 4 N.T.S.B. 1304, 1305 (1984). The NTSB is not constrained to impose serious penalties only when a tragedy actually occurs. *Johnson v. NTSB*, 979 F.2d 618, 623 (7th Cir. 1992). The NTSB's mandate for protecting the public's safety requires that the Board be given wide discretion in imposing sanctions. *Hite v. NTSB*, 991 F.2d 17 (1st Cir. 1993). Even the failure of the NTSB to promulgate as a notice and comment rulemaking its standards for revocation of an airman's certificate has been deemed an exercise of reasonable discretion by the agency. *Hite v. NTSB*, 991 F.2d 17, 20-21 (1st Cir. 1993); *Rochna v. NTSB*, 929 F.2d 13 (1st Cir. 1991); *Tearney v. NTSB*, 868 F.2d 1451 (5th Cir. 1989), *cert. den.* 493 U.S. 937 (1989); *Komjathy v. NTSB*, 832 F.2d 1294 (D.C. Cir. 1987); *cert. den.* 486 U.S. 1057 (1988).

[17] An airline's flight personnel, flight and emergency procedure, aircraft and maintenance facilities are subject to periodic inspection and tests by the FAA. Common carriers and their crew must comply with the stringent requirements of Parts 121 and 135 of the FARs while private carriers must comply with the less stringent requirements of Part 91 of the FARs. 14 C.F.R. Parts 91, 121, 135 (2002). The policy behind this distinction is based on the right of the general public to be confident that the airlines that solicit their business operate under the highest standards of safety. *Woolsey v. NTSB*, 993 F.2d 516, 522 (5th Cir. 1993).

The FAA defines a "common carrier" as one that holds itself out to a definable segment of the public as willing to transport persons and property for compensation, indiscriminately. FAA Advisory Circular No. 120-112A (Apr. 24, 1986). The test is an objective one, relying on what

communications, aircraft certification,[18] and ground equipment. The FAA holds broad jurisdiction over navigation and air traffic control, including collision avoidance and wind shear detection. The primary mission of the FAA is safety. The U.S. General Accounting Office [GAO] summarized the FAA's comprehensive mission as:

> *Ensuring that all components of the air transportation system—including the airports, aircraft, and key personnel such as pilots—operate in a manner that maximizes aviation safety is a fundamental responsibility for FAA. FAA's aviation safety programs provide for the initial certification, periodic surveillance, and inspection of airlines, airports, repair stations, other aviation entities, pilots, and mechanics. These inspections are intended not only to detect actual violations but also to serve as part of an early warning system for identifying potential system wide weaknesses.*[19]

---

the carrier actually does rather than the label it embraces or the purposes that motivate such activity. *Woolsey v. NTSB*, 993 F.2d 516 (5th Cir. 1993); *Las Vegas Hacienda, Inc. v. CAB*, 298 F.2d 430 (9th Cir. 1962), *cert. den.* 369 U.S. 885 (1962). In the deregulated environment, the carrier need not maintain tariffs in order to be considered a common carrier; nor does the maintenance of separately negotiated contracts or occasional refusal to transport make it a private carrier. "What is crucial is that the common carrier defines itself through its own marketing efforts as being willing to carry any member of that segment of the public which it serves." *Woolsey v. NTSB*, 993 F.2d 516, 524 (5th Cir. 1993). *See generally* Paul Dempsey, Robert Hardaway & William Thoms, 2 *Aviation Law & Regulation* § 12 (1993).

[18] The FAA has implemented a number of requirements on aircraft manufacture and airline maintenance programs, including inspection and maintenance of aging aircraft (under the Aging Aircraft Safety Act of 1991), and corrosion control. The FAA has broad jurisdiction over aircraft certification and registration. Airlines must have and maintain FAA certificates of airworthiness for all of their aircraft.

Part of the government's comprehensive effort to promote aviation safety includes the promulgation of "Airworthiness Directives" [AD]. 14 C.F.R. §§ 39.1, 39.13 (2002). Design and construction standards for aircraft are included in the ADs. 14 C.F.R. §§ 23.601-23.1203 (2002). No person may lawfully operate an aircraft except in accordance with any applicable AD. 14 C.F.R. § 39.3 (2002). Under the Federal Aviation Act, "airworthiness" requires aircraft to be in conformance with the aircraft's type certificate, and be in condition for a safe flight. 49 U.S.C.App. § 1423 (2002). These requirements are not necessarily satisfied merely because the aircraft is flyable, or that it was flown without incident. *See Copsey v. NTSB*, 993 F.2d 736, 739 (10th Cir. 1993).

[19] U.S. General Accounting Office, *Federal Aviation Administration: Challenges in Modernizing the Agency* 9 (GAO/T-RCED/AIMD-00-87 Feb. 3, 2000).

The responsibilities for maintaining public safety in its use of the national airspace are extensive. The law provides; "The [Federal Aviation] Administrator shall prescribe air traffic regulations on the flight of aircraft (including regulations on safe altitudes) for—(A) navigating, protecting, and identifying aircraft; (B) protecting individuals and property on the ground; (C) using the navigable airspace efficiently; and (D) preventing collision between aircraft, between aircraft and land or water vehicles, and between aircraft and airborne objects."[20] Pursuant thereto, the FAA has created a National Air Traffic Control System [ATC].[21]

The U.S. aviation market is sufficiently large that it requires four agencies to administer its various aspects.. The National Transportation Safety Board[22] handles aircraft accident investigations mandated under Annex 6,[23] and appeals of decisions of the Administrator of the FAA.[24] Though it has no authority to issue regulations, the NTSB does have the responsibility to make regulatory recommendations to the FAA to avoid future accidents.[25] The Transportation Security Administration [TSA] of the U.S. Department of Homeland Security [DHS] regulates aviation security.[26] The Office of the Secretary of Transportation has jurisdiction over economic regulatory issues such as airline financial fitness, competition policy and consumer protec-

---

[20] 49 U.S.C. § 40103(b)(2) (2002).

[21] See Martin v. United States, 448 F. Supp. 855 (E.D. Ark. 1977).

[22] 49 U.S.C. § 1101, et seq. Annex VI. 49 CFR Parts 800, and 831.

[23] 49 U.S.C. §§ 1131-32 (2004). The NTSB describes its responsibilities as follows:
The [NTSB] is the agency charged with fulfilling the obligations of the United States under Annex 13 to the Chicago Convention on International Civil Aviation (8th ed., Jul. 1994), and does so consistent with State Department requirements and in coordination with that department. Annex 13 contains specific requirements for the notification, investigation, and reporting of certain incidents and accidents involving international civil aviation. In the case of an accident or incident in a foreign state involving civil aircraft of U.S. registry or manufacture, where the foreign state is a signatory to Annex 13 to the Chicago Convention of the International Civil Aviation Organization, the state of occurrence is responsible for the investigation. If the accident or incident occurs in a foreign state not bound by the provisions of Annex 13 to the Chicago Convention, or if the accident or incident involves a public aircraft (Annex 13 applies only to civil aircraft), the conduct of the investigation shall be in consonance with any agreement entered into between the U.S. and the foreign state.
Accident/Incident Investigation Procedures, 62 Fed. Reg. 3806 (Jan. 27, 1997).

[24] 49 U.S.C. § 1133 (2004).

[25] Paul Stephen Dempsey, William Thoms & Robert Hardaway, 2 Aviation Law & Regulation §§ 12.67–12.71 (1993).

[26] Paul Stephen Dempsey, Aviation Security: The Role of Law in the War against Terrorism, 41 Colum. J. Transnat'l L. 649, 717-719 (2003).

tion.[27] The DOT Secretary is statutorily commanded to assign and maintain safety as "the highest priority in air commerce."[28]

The Federal Aviation Administration (formerly Agency) was established by the Federal Aviation Act of 1958, and subsequently became a part of the U.S. Department of Transportation [DOT] upon the latter's creation in 1967.[29] The FAA is headed by an Administrator, appointed by the President with the advice and consent of the Senate for a term of five years. The Administrator is required to consider the maintenance and enhancement of safety and security as among the highest priorities in the public interest.[30] The FAA is charged with promoting aviation safety, ensuring the safe and efficient utilization of the national airspace,[31] and providing oversight of the U.S. airport system.[32] Though it does not own and operate airports (they are owned and operated by local, and usually local governmental, institutions),[33] the FAA issues airport operating certificates to air carrier airports, regulates them, and provides financial support to airports included in the National Plan of Integrated Airports [NPIAS].[34] The FAA handles all other aspect of airman, aircraft, airport, and airline safety, and provides air traffic control and navigation services.[35] Under U.S. law, actions of the Secretary of Transportation and of the

---

[27] For a review of the legislation passed by the U.S. to address aviation security, *see* Paul Stephen Dempsey, *Aviation Security: The Role of Law in the War against Terrorism*, 41 Colum. J. Transnat'l L. 649 (2003), and Paul Stephen Dempsey, *Aerial Terrorism: Unilateral and Multilateral Responses to Aircraft Hijacking*, 2 Conn. J. Int'l L. 427 (1987).

[28] 49 U.S.C. § 40101(a)(1) (2004).

[29] 49 U.S.C. subtitle I (2004). Following a series of accidents in the mid-1950s, the reaction of Congress was promulgation of the Federal Aviation Act of 1958, Pub. L. 85-726; 49 U.S.C. § 1300 *et sq.*, and creation of the Federal Aviation Agency (later to become the Federal Aviation Administration under the Department of Transportation Act of 1966). The accident investigation and recommendation responsibilities of the U.S. Civil Aeronautics Board (which had been created in 1938) were transferred to the FAA initially, and were re-delegated to the National Transportation Safety Board, made independent in 1974. Robert Hardaway, *Airport Regulation, Law and Public Policy* 19, 21 (1991). Paul Stephen Dempsey & Laurence E. Gesell, *Air Transportation: Foundations for the 21st Century* 229-231 (1997).

[30] 49 U.S.C. subtitle VII, 49 U.S.C. § 40101 *et seq* (2004).

[31] Navigation of U.S. airspace by foreign air carriers is governed by 40 U.S.S. § 41703 (2004).

[32] The FAA Administrator is charged with: promoting aviation safety; promoting aviation security; ensuring the safe and efficient utilization of the national airspace; overseeing of the US airport system; and supporting national defense requirements.

[33] Paul Stephen Dempsey, *Local Airport Regulation: The Constitutional Tension Between Police Power, Preemption & Takings*, 11 Penn St. Envt'l L. Rev. 1 (2002).

[34] 49 U.S.C. § 44706 (2004); 14 CFR Parts 71-109.

[35] Paul Stephen Dempsey, William Thoms & Robert Hardaway, 2 *Aviation Law & Regulation* § 12.48 – 12.54 (1993).

FAA Administrator must be consistent with the international obligations imposed by the Chicago Convention.[36]

The FAA has broad authority to conduct investigations.[37] The Administrator may delegate authority for issuance of pertinent orders, directives and instructions.[38] Given the size of commercial and general aviation in the U.S., many investigatory and oversight functions have been delegated, of necessity, to subordinate institutions,[39] and private persons.[40] The FAA Administrator holds broad rulemaking authority and discretionary powers.[41]

In the U.S., federal agencies are subject to the Constitutional requirement of providing due process of law prior to the deprivation of liberty and property.[42] The Administrative Procedure Act [43] requires notice and an opportunity to be heard (usually) before one is deprived of a governmental entitlement, such as an operating license. With some exceptions, federal agencies such as the FAA are also subject to certain transparency laws, including the Government in the Sunshine

---

[36] 49 U.S.C. § 40105(b) (2004).

[37] Paul Stephen Dempsey, William Thoms & Robert Hardaway, 2 *Aviation Law & Regulation* § 12.04 (1993).

[38] 49 U.S.C. § 106(f)(2)(c) (2004); 14 CFR Part 11-B Procedural Rules.

[39] Within the FAA, the safety oversight activities have been delegated to the Associate Administrator for Regulation and Certification [AVR]. Its principal organizational units are:

Flight Standard Services [AFS]—personnel licensing, certification and surveillance of operators and the airworthiness related to air carrier operations and aircraft maintenance;

Aircraft Certification Services [AIR]—airworthiness activities related to design and manufacturing;

Office of Aviation Medicine [AAM]—medical certification of aviation personnel, research, occupational health and substance abuse abatement.

The AFS oversees the region's airlines, establishes requirements for instrument procedures and flight inspection, coordinating these requirements with FAA headquarters in Washington, D.C.. The AFS secures compliance with FAA regulations, programs, standards and procedures governing the inspection, certification and surveillance of commercial and general aviation. It also examines, certifies and oversees flight and ground personnel, examiners and air agencies. Within each region, field activities are performed by the Flight Standard District Offices [FSDO], which are responsible for the day-to-day administration of the licensing process. See generally, Paul Stephen Dempsey, William Thoms & Robert Hardaway, 2 *Aviation Law & Regulation* § 12.04 (Butterworth 1993).

[40] The FAA delegates also certain certification and surveillance responsibilities to private persons under 14 C.F.R. Part 183. The FAA Administrator has broad authority to enter into contracts to fulfill its mandate. 49 U.S.C. § 106(1)(6) (2004).

[41] The FAA Administrator has discretion to issue such regulations, standards, and procedures as he deems appropriate. 49 U.S.C. § 40113(a) (2004). The Administrator is authorized to issue, rescind, and revise such regulations as may be necessary to carry out the FAA's mission. 49 U.S.C. § 106(f)(3) (2004).

[42] U.S. Const., 5th Amendment.

[43] 5 U.S.C. §§ 551-59, 701-06 (2004).

Act,[44] which ordinarily requires their meetings to be open to the public, as well as the Freedom of Information Act,[45] which ordinarily requires that agencies make available their internal documents available to the public upon demand. Exceptions exist for various reasons, including national security.

The FAA issues all licenses specified in Annex 1, promulgated by ICAO, and it validates foreign licenses.[46] After investigation, if found that the applicant is physically able[47] to perform the duties required for the airman certification, and possesses the appropriate qualifications, the Secretary will issue a certificate designating the capacity in which the applicant is authorized to operate, and the class, restrictions, and aircraft types for which certification is valid.[48] The certificate specifies its terms, conditions, and duration, physical fitness test, and any other qualifications deemed necessary in the interest of safety.[49] The FAA may prohibit a foreign national from receiving an airman certificate, or condition it upon reciprocal foreign treatment.[50]

The FAA also holds broad emergency powers to suspend or revoke various operating and airworthiness licenses and certificates. At various times, it has used such power to suspend operations of a certain aircraft type,[51] to suspend operations of an airline,[52] or to suspend

---

[44] 5 U.S.C. § 552b (2004).

[45] 5 U.S.C. § 552(b) (2004).

[46] In the U.S., certification of airmen is governed by 14 CFR Part 61 (Certification: Pilots, Flight Instructors, and Ground Instructors), Part 63 (Certification: Flight Crew members other than Pilots), Part 65 (Certification: Airmen Other Than Flight Crew members), Part 67 (Medical Standards and Certification), and 14 CFR 141 (Pilot Schools). These are complemented by FAA handbooks, such as FAA Order 8710.3C — *Pilot Examiner's Handbook*, FAA Order 1380.53.D — *Staffing Guide: Certification Engineers & Flight Test Pilots*; FAA Order 3000.22 — *Air Traffic Services Training*; FAA Order 3120.4J — *Air Traffic Technical Training*; FAA Order 3140.1 — *Flight Standards Service National Training Program*; FAA Order 3930.3 — *Air Traffic Control Specialist Health Program* FAA Order 7220.1A — *Certification and Rating Procedures* (ATC) FAA Order 8080.6B — *Conduct of Airmen Knowledge Tests*. FAA designated Aeronautical Medical Examiners [AME] conduct medical certification pursuant to 14 C.F.R § 97, and the FAA *Aeromedical Certification Manual*.

[47] The applicant must hold an FAA airman medical certificate. Paul Stephen Dempsey, William Thoms & Robert Hardaway, 2 *Aviation Law & Regulation* §§ 12.11-12.13 (1993).

[48] 49 U.S.C. § 44703 (2004). For example, mechanics and repairmen hold a different certification than do pilots. Paul Stephen Dempsey, William Thoms & Robert Hardaway, 2 *Aviation Law & Regulation* §§ 12.32-12.34 (1993).

[49] 49 U.S.C. § 44703 (2004). Paul Stephen Dempsey, William Thoms & Robert Hardaway, 2 *Aviation Law & Regulation* § 12.02 (1993).

[50] 49 U.S.C. § 44711 (2004).

[51] In 1979, after a crash in Chicago, the FAA grounded all DC-10 aircraft until it could determine the cause and prescribe a remedy.

[52] ValuJet began operations in Oct. 1993 with three aircraft. By 1996, it flew a fleet of 53 aircraft. On May 11, 1996, an oxygen canister exploded in the cargo hold in ValuJet Flight 592,

the operations of the entire airline industry.[53] In the United States, certain decisions rendered, or sanctions imposed, by the Administrator may be appealed to the NTSB.[54] For example, the FAA Administrator's decision to deny airman certification may be appealed to the NTSB.[55] Decisions of the NTSB may, in turn, be appealed to a U.S. Court of Appeals.[56] The FAA Administrator may promulgate regulations, and grant exemptions from them.[57]

AVIATION REGULATORY HISTORY

Like other forms of economic regulation in America, aviation regulation has its roots in the Progressive Era and the dramatic shift in the economic structure that took place during that period in history. The "Progressive Era" is described by historians as that period from just before the turn-of-the-century to about the end of World War I (1918). The Progressive Era is noted for its diverse reform movements, and it represents a critical period in the transformation of capitalism. Characterized by a large number of small competing firms using low technology, "competitive capitalism" was replaced by "corporate capitalism," represented by a small number of firms conducting large-scale production using high levels of technology.

In corporate capitalism, the state began to play more of a regulatory role in the economy. Unlike European nations, the U.S. avoided state ownership of the airlines. But recognizing the importance of air transport to the growth of the nation and its role in augmenting na-

---

causing it to crash in the Everglades, killing all 110 persons aboard. The FAA then accelerated and intensified its Special Emphasis Review of the carrier's operations which had begun the preceding Feb. In Jun. 1996, Valujet entered into a Consent Order with the FAA under which ValuJet agreed to suspend its operations and provide information demonstrating its qualifications to hold FAA operating authority. On Aug. 29, 1996, the FAA returned the carrier's FAA operating certificate to it. *See Application of Valujet Airlines*, DOT Order 96-9-36 (1996). *See* Paul Stephen Dempsey, *Predation, Competition & Antitrust Law: Turbulence in the Airline Industry*, 67 J. Air L. & Com. 685, 688 (2002).

[53] After four commercial aircraft were commandeered by Al-Qaeda operatives on the morning of Sep. 11, 2002—two flown into the New York World Trade Center and one into the Arlington, Va., Pentagon, the FAA issued an emergency order grounding all commercial aircraft from flying for three days. Paul Stephen Dempsey, *Aviation Security: The Role of Law in the War against Terrorism*, 41 Colum. J. Transnat'l L. 649, 712 (2003).

[54] 49 U.S.C. § 1133 (2004).

[55] 49 U.S.C. § 44703 (2004). Paul Stephen Dempsey, William Thoms & Robert Hardaway, 2 *Aviation Law & Regulation* §§ 12.02, 12/08 (1993).

[56] 49 U.S.C. § 1153 (2004). Paul Stephen Dempsey, William Thoms & Robert Hardaway, 2 *Aviation Law & Regulation* § 12.09 (1993).

[57] 49 U.S.C. § 44701(a)(2) (2004).

tional defense, the state took on a more active role in maintaining social and economic conditions to ensure the profitability of private enterprise. During the Progressive Era, the federal government increasingly began to regulate and control business organization and the consumption of commodities. It provided industry with "managed competition," a rational set of rules, and at times subsidies, to provide economic stability.

According to Max Weber, economic concentration evolved in the late 19th Century as a "rational" mechanism against excess competition in the marketplace. At its root was a desire to escape the rigors and uncertainties of competition and to rectify a market that business leaders could not otherwise control. Corporate growth was an attempt to stabilize and integrate the economy in such a way that would allow corporations to function in a predictable and secure economic environment wherein they would be assured of reasonable profits over the long run.[58]

As it turned out, the anti-competitive tactics of the giant national corporations, coupled with their sheer size, created as many political and legal problems as the economic uncertainties they resolved. The behavior of the railroad companies, especially, became a test of the *laissez-faire* marketplace and of the free enterprise system. Challenged directly was Adam Smith's "invisible hand" of competition. Lacking competition, the railroads set rates as they pleased, and in doing so, discriminated in particular against farmers as a group. Reaction to price discrimination practiced by the railroads became the basis for the consumer revolt by the agrarian society formed in 1867 known as the National Grange.[59]

The Granger movement is of significance in the evolution of government regulation (including the regulation of aviation), because it was the first time that American society regulated an industry by setting up a regulatory structure outside of the courts and the common law. Targeted specifically were the discriminatory rate practices of the railroads. The Granger movement of the 1870s was a demand for passage by individual states of measures to regulate the railroads, grain elevators and public warehouses. What eventually came out of the Granger movement in 1887 was the Act to Regulate Commerce,

---

[58] James Inverarity, Pat Lauderdale and Barry Feld, *Law and Society: Sociological Perspectives on Criminal Law* 223-225 (1983).

[59] *See* Laurence E. Gesell and Martin T. Farris, *Antitrust Irrelevance in Air Transportation and the Re-Defining of Price Discrimination* 57 J. of Air Law and Commerce (1991), at 173-197.

followed by a watershed of economic regulatory laws during the Progressive Era and beyond.

Aviation-related regulation in the United States can be traced to postal service programs linked with the promotion of air commerce. There had been experiments with the carriage of airmail as early as 1911, and by 1920, the Post Office Department had established four aeronautical stations, which maintained bonfires to assist aviators with aerial navigation at night. By the late 1920s, the bonfires had been replaced with beacon lights operated by the Department of Commerce Lighthouse Division. Navigation via electronic signals was introduced in the 1930s with the implementation of the Radio Range and its associated airway system.[60]

The bonfire attendants were replaced by lighthouse attendants, who themselves were replaced by radio range attendants, who in turn provided the additional service of radio relay for en route air traffic. The modern Flight Service Station [FSS] traces its origin to these early radio range attendants, and even earlier to bonfire attendants.

Air traffic control, *per se*, traces its beginnings to the Air Commerce Act of 1926, when the first aviation safety legislation was passed by the U.S. Congress. The purpose of the 1926 Act was to promote air commerce, and it charged the executive branch of the federal government with the operation and maintenance of an airway system, as well as with providing air navigation aids [NAVAIDS], and with the provision of safety in air commerce through a system of regulation. The Department of Commerce was tasked with monitoring air safety, and within it was created a Bureau of Air Commerce to promulgate air safety regulation. However, the actual function of controlling aircraft within the air traffic system was not assumed by the federal government for yet another decade.

In the early 1930s, the possibility of two aircraft arriving simultaneously over the same point and at the same altitude seemed remote, and there was no single agency serving as a unified control for airborne traffic. Rather, en route locations of (airline) company planes were monitored by each of the individual air carriers, and over their own separate and distinct radio frequencies. In the mid-1930s, there were three such airline-operated centers, one in Newark, one in Cleveland, and one in Chicago. In 1936, these three centers, which

---

[60] *See* Laurence E. Gesell, *Air Traffic Control: An Invitation to a Career* (1989).

constituted the skeletal beginnings of an air traffic control system, were turned over to the Bureau of Air Commerce.

On July 6, 1986, the FAA celebrated the first 50 years of air traffic control, recognizing as its beginning the government's assumption of responsibility for the above mentioned airline operated en route centers. It was not until 1941, however, that the federal government through the Civil Aeronautics Administration began operating air traffic control towers at terminal locations. What evolved was a modern air traffic control service made up of three separate service areas: terminal, en route, and flight service.

Airport, or "terminal" air traffic control service, is based upon observed or known traffic and airport conditions. En route air traffic control facilities provide services to aircraft under instrument flight rules [IFR] between departure and destination terminals. Flight Service Stations [FSS] are air traffic facilities which provide assistance to pilots such as flight briefings, en route advisory service, search and rescue services, assisting in emergency situations, relaying air traffic control clearances, disseminating aviation weather information, and originating Notices to Airmen [NOTAMS].

ECONOMIC REGULATION

For 20 years, air traffic control (and aviation safety in general) was seemingly a secondary role of government regulation in air transportation. Far greater attention was given to economic regulation of the airlines than was given to air safety. In the late 1920s, the fledgling air transportation industry was lacking in capital, engaged in destructive competition, and highly dependent for its survival upon revenues generated from government (mail) contracts. The air carriers were characterized as unwilling, or financially unable, to invest in new facilities; of operating obsolete equipment; of potentially being unsafe due to cost cutting; and of only marginally being able to maintain their operations with little or no growth. There were approximately 40 operating air transport companies, most of which either weak financially or otherwise failing. Ostensibly, there were more companies in operation than the early air transport market could viably support.

In 1928, Herbert Hoover was elected President, and in the gathering of his administration, he appointed Walter Folger Brown as Postmaster General. Since the time of Second Assistant Postmaster

General Otto Praeger (1915-1921), the postal service had assumed responsibility for developing commercial aviation. Brown continued this tradition and accepted his charge with a determination to ensure success in the area of air transportation and air commerce. His zeal was such that critics described him as having a "ruthless" will to succeed. That he developed political enemies was a natural outcome.

The Air Mail Act of 1930 was initiated by Walter Brown and drawn up in his office. The plan, or so-called "scheme," was to give Brown power to eliminate competitive bidding for airmail contracts, to force smaller companies out of business, and to give financial support to stronger corporations (including both manufactures of aircraft as well as the carriers themselves). Thereby, the forerunners of the U.S. aerospace industry as well as the airlines could be consolidated into more viable industries. Through the development of newer and larger airplanes, the aircraft manufacturing industry would expand. And commercial aviation would be developed and expanded by strongly encouraging, if not mandating an emphasis on the carriage of air passengers. Brown was indeed a controversial figure of whom many were critical. Nevertheless, in retrospect some analysts have suggested that perhaps he was 50 years ahead of his time, for consolidation became the undeniable outcome of airline deregulation in the 1980s.[61]

Brown's plan, however, came apart when Senator (later to become Supreme Court Justice) Hugo Black seized upon the political opportunity to include the air transportation system in a senate investigation of maritime contracts. Brown's allegedly dictatorial manipulation of airline (mail) contracts became the focal point of Black's Senate investigative subcommittee.

Subsequent to Hoover taking office, and shortly after appointing Walter Brown as Postmaster General, the stock market crashed in 1929, and the shadow of the Great Depression fell over the world. The economics of the times, and Walter Brown's (Republican) political affiliation, had a lot to do with how he would reorganize the air mail contracts. Whether intentional or not, supply-side economic theory would become a factor. Herbert Hoover inherited the so-called "trickle down" economic theory that had been introduced by Andrew Mellon, Secretary of the Treasury for Presidents Harding, Coolidge

---

[61] *See* Paul Stephen Dempsey and Laurence E. Gesell, *Air Transportation: Foundations for the 21st Century* 213-222 (1997); *see also* Laurence E. Gesell, *Airline Re-Regulation* (1990).

and finally Hoover. The trickle down theory became the standard economic philosophy of the Republican Party. It is the same fundamental theory that would be resurrected in the 1980s by President Ronald Reagan, to be repackaged as "Reaganomics."[62]

In historical context, with the U.S. mired down in the Great Depression, Herbert Hoover was by then being blamed for it, or at least for not doing enough about it, and his administration became the focus of public discontent and unrest. Hoover, personally, became an easy target for political attack from the opposition party, of which Hugo Black was a member. Just as the general attack upon Hoover had been exaggerated by assigning to him all or most of the blame for the depression, Black's subsequent political attack on Brown could be characterized as equally distorted.

Be that as it may, Franklin Delano Roosevelt, a democrat, was elected President in 1932. The Roosevelt administration adopted an economic strategy just opposite to that of the republican Hoover administration by embracing economic theories of John Maynard Keynes and a "bottom up" response to the depressed economy. That is to say, by putting people back to work it was theorized the total demand of both consumers and investors would be increased, thereby releasing the economy from the gridlock of the Depression.

Walter Brown was replaced by Postmaster James Farley who began to dismantle Brown's previous efforts; first, by charging the airlines with collusion and canceling all domestic airmail contracts; and secondly, by assigning the carriage of air mail to the Army. The latter move, however, proved to be a disaster resulting in multiple aircraft

---

[62] Trickle down, or "top down" economics assumes that if money is injected at the top, say in corporations, it will then "trickle down" by way of spending and wages, to be made available for re-spending by all in the economic chain down to the individual wage earner. Conversely, "bottom up" economics postulates that if money is made available at the bottom, say to the worker, goods and services purchased through demand will provide the economy to refurbish business and complete the economic chain. Andrew Mellon best expressed the trickle down economic theory by saying that, "The property of the middle and lower classes depends upon the good fortunes and light taxes of the rich." Louis Koenig, *The Chief Executive* 266-269 (3rd ed. 1975). Modern economic theory would refer to top down as "supply-side" economics, as opposed to, say "demand-side," or Keynesian economics. Supply-side economics call for more tax cuts, use of the market mechanism, and less governmental manipulation of the economy. Conversely, the Keynesian emphasis is on aggregate demand (spending) and government intervention. *See* Martin T. Farris and Stephen K. Happel, *Modern Managerial Economics* (1987). It was the under girding fundamentals of John Maynard Keynes' economic theories that were used by the Roosevelt administration to guide the United States out of the Depression. Prior to Roosevelt, however, the dominant paradigm was the trickle down theory of Andrew Mellon. Walter Brown would adopt the theory in his reorganization of the air mail service.

crashes, damage to property, and a needless loss of lives. The public air transportation system had been assigned to an Army, whose pilots were both inexperienced and ill equipped to assume responsibility for the carriage of airmail.

After only six months in operation, President Roosevelt ordered the Army to cease its airmail activities, and Congress passed the Air Mail Act of 1934. The 1934 act was *remedial* in that it was intended to counteract the supposed collusion allegedly occurring during Postmaster Brown's administration. It was at the same time *proactive*, because it also created a Federal Aviation Commission to study U.S. aviation policy and to make recommendations leading to more permanent air transportation legislation.

By the late 1930s, public policy had been significantly altered, and the political climate was ripe for strong economic regulation of not only the air transport industry, but of all forms of intercity public transportation was well. The political constituency that had been so critical of Brown's abuse of power were just as intent themselves upon using their powers to achieve their own political ends. The Roosevelt years were marked by strong marketplace intervention. And the 1930s were an era of increasing economic regulation in all sectors of industry, including transportation.

From the time the Act to Regulate Commerce was passed in 1887, the Interstate Commerce Commission had been given increasing authority to regulate the railroads and other forms of transportation. After 1920, the expansion of government regulatory authority was accelerated. By 1940, all five modes of public transportation (rail, water, highway, pipeline and air) were under some form of governmental regulation. The 1938 Civil Aeronautics Act (as amended by government reorganization in 1940) created the Civil Aeronautics Board [CAB] to economically regulate air transportation, and it was passed during a period of strong governmental regulation in all modes of transportation.

In part, the National Transportation Policy of 1940 read,

> *It is hereby declared to be the national transportation policy of the Congress to provide for fair and impartial regulation of all modes of transportation . . . to promote safe, adequate, economical, and efficient service*

> *and foster sound economic conditions in*
> *transportation . . . to encourage the establish-*
> *ment and maintenance of reasonable charges*
> *for transportation services, without unjust*
> *discrimination, undue preferences and advan-*
> *tages, or unfair or destructive competitive*
> *practices. . . . All of the provisions of this Act*
> *shall be administered and enforced with a view*
> *to carrying out the . . . policy.*

The 1938 Civil Aeronautics Act presented an altogether new law in air transportation, and with its passage came the repeal of all previous economic air commerce-related legislation. Its purpose was to provide for government (economic) regulation of air commerce, and to develop and promote growth in a stagnant air transportation market. The government intervened in the marketplace, reportedly so it could economically stabilize the industry, and theoretically to protect the rights of the traveling consumer.

With its "grandfather" clause, the Act created the Civil Aeronautics Board, which granted Certificates of Public Convenience and Necessity [PC&N] to the 16 then existing carriers.[63] Between 1938 and 1975, the CAB certificated some 86 new airlines to compete with the 16 "grandfathered" carriers, and exempted hundreds more from the certification requirements.[64] The CAB was given such pervasive power that hardly any proprietary act of consequence could happen within the industry without the federal government either knowing about it, or otherwise having it reported to them as mandated in the Uniform System of Accounts and Reports [USAR]. Furthermore, it was given authority to grant to the air carrier industry immunity against antitrust law, and allowed the government, through the CAB, to collectively set the rates for air transportation. The CAB would later be referred to as a "cartel" by proponents of airline deregulation.

---

[63] American, Braniff, Chicago & Southern (subsequently merged with Delta), Colonial (subsequently merged with Eastern), Continental, Delta, Eastern, Inland (subsequently merged with Eastern), Mid-Continent (subsequently merged with Braniff), National, Northeast, Penn Central (name changed to Capitol; merged with United), Transcontinental and Western (name changed to Trans World Airlines), United, and Western.

[64] Paul Dempsey, Robert Hardaway & William Thoms, *Aviation Law & Regulation* § 1.04 (1992).

Economic regulation of the airlines was introduced during the post-depression Roosevelt years. Like other programs of the New Deal, the Civil Aeronautics Act of 1938 was to have a lasting impression. The economic regulatory framework established by the 1938 Act was in place for 40 years, and was essentially unaltered until adoption of the Airline Deregulation Act in 1978.

DEREGULATION

The Airline Deregulation Act of 1978 reduced economic regulation, terminated the Civil Aeronautics Board (on Dec. 31, 1984) and its authority over pricing and entry, and shifted antitrust responsibility to the Justice Department. The effects of deregulation are mixed and varied, but clearly, more open competition resulted in rapid, and some would argue, unstable growth. Economist Alfred Kahn (the one widely viewed as the "father of airline deregulation") stated that, " . . . instability is the price we pay for competition."[65] The normative policies of the Act (Section 102) were to:

- maintain "safety as the highest priority in air commerce. . . .";
- make available "a variety of adequate, efficient, and low-priced services by air carriers. . . .";
- place "maximum reliance on competition;"
- develop and maintain "a sound regulatory environment. . . .;"
- prevent "unfair, deceptive, predatory or anticompetitive practices in air transportation. . . .;"
- avoid "unreasonable industry concentration, excessive market domination, and monopoly power. . . .;"
- encourage "entry into air transportation markets by new carriers . . . and the strengthening of small carriers so as to assure a more effective, competitive airline industry;"
- maintain a "comprehensive and convenient system of continuous scheduled service for small communities;" and
- "encourage efficient and well-managed carriers to earn adequate profits and to attract capital."

---

[65] Alfred E. Kahn, *Flying Among the Merger Clouds*, Time (Sep. 1986).

Airline deregulation significantly reduced government intervention in the air transportation marketplace. However, economic regulation was not eliminated entirely, nor was airline deregulation intended to reduce safety regulation. As Alfred Kahn stated,

> *We never deregulated safety. And I never intended to eliminate the antitrust laws; never intended to eliminate the responsibility of the government to build additional air capacity; never eliminated the responsibility of government to tax travelers enough and use the proceeds to hire safety inspectors, and fine airlines for safety violations, and (hire more) air traffic controllers.*[66]

AIR SAFETY INTERVENTION

In the mid-1950's, a series of accidents brought to surface an underlying need for significant safety enhancement in aviation. In 1956, a Trans World Airlines Constellation collided with a United Airlines DC-7 over the Grand Canyon. In early 1957, a Douglas Aircraft company-owned DC-7 collided with an U.S. Air Force F-89 over Sunland, California. The DC-7 crashed into a junior high school, killing three and injuring 70 others. In 1958, a third significant accident involved the collision of a United Airlines DC-7 and an USAF F-100 near Las Vegas, Nevada. The reaction of Congress, principally attributed to these three accidents, gave rise to the Federal Aviation Act of 1958,[67] and creation of the Federal Aviation Agency (later to become the Federal Aviation Administration under the Department of Transportation Act of 1966).

The 1958 Act superseded the Civil Aeronautics Act of 1938 by incorporating essentially the same economic provisions of the 1938 Act, but greatly expanding federal power in the area of air safety. The FAA became an independent agency, answerable only to Congress and to the President. The earlier Civil Aeronautics Administration (the FAA's predecessor) had been an administrative division within

---

[66] Alfred E. Kahn, *Deregulation: Is this the Tragic Consequences of Low Fares, More Competition*, an interview in the Arizona Republic (Aug. 23, 1987).
[67] PL 85-726; 49 U.S.C. 1300 *et seq.*

the Department of Commerce. On the other hand, the Federal Aviation Agency was made independent and given broader authority to promulgate and enforce aviation safety regulations. The FAA's primary responsibility was, and is, to promote safety through regulation.

A secondary mission is to promote air commerce. Yet, in 1996, Secretary of Transportation, Frederico Peña, was asking Congress to take away the FAA's responsibilities in promoting air commerce, suggesting there was a conflict of interest between regulatory and promotional functions. Irrespective, the FAA still retains its share of the responsibility for promoting air commerce; even in light of adopted economic deregulatory policy, and the perceived potential for conflict of interest.

Between safety and economic regulation, no other industry in the United States has been regulated more than has transportation. Even after passage of the Airline Deregulation Act, the term "deregulation" has, in the opinion of some, been a misnomer. More appropriately, there has been "regulatory reform." Granted, economic regulation has been significantly reduced, but other than removing price setting and route determinations, most of the CAB's responsibilities, including its many rules and regulations, were not eliminated. They were transferred to the DOT for enforcement. Prior to implementation of the 1978 Act, the CAB's rules and regulations were codified in Titles 14 and 49 of the Code of Federal Regulations, Chapter II, "Civil Aeronautics Board." 14 C.F.R., after deregulation, had its title changed to "Office of the Secretary, Department of Transportation—Aviation Proceedings." It is essentially the same code of law, albeit modified by deregulatory policy and given a different cover.

SAFETY REGULATION

U.S. aviation statutes and regulations comprehensively address all aspects of aviation safety.[68] As stated above, the primary mission of the FAA is safety. To carry out its mandate, the FAA promulgates its own set of rules in Title 14 C.F.R. Chapter I, "Federal Aviation

---

[68] The principal aviation statutory provisions of the U.S. are found in 49 U.S.C., enacted on 5 Jul. 1994, known as the Federal Aviation Act of 1958. The relevant statutory provisions governing civil aviation are set forth in Subtitle I-Department of Transportation [DOT], Subtitle II-Other Government Agencies (Chapter 11-National Transportation Safety Board [NTSB]), Subtitle III-General and Intermodal Programs (Ch. 51-Transportation of Hazardous Material), and Subtitle VII-Aviation Programs (Part A - Air Commerce and Safety).

Regulations." The basis for safety rules is found in Titles V, VI and VII of the Federal Aviation Act of 1958. Title V provides for a common system of registering civil aircraft; Title VI establishes minimum standards for aviation safety rules and regulations; and Title VII is concerned with rules and regulations of accident investigation.

The Federal government regulates safety in several ways: through aircraft registration, air traffic control, aircraft certification, accident investigation, and by certification of airmen. The Federal Aviation Act defines an "airman" as,

> . . . an individual who engages, as the person in command and or as pilot, mechanic, or member of the crew, in the navigation of aircraft while under way; and (except to the extent the Administrator may otherwise provide with respect to individuals employed outside the United States) any individual who is directly in charge of the inspection, maintenance, overhauling, or repair of aircraft, aircraft engines, propellers, or appliances; and any individual who serves in the capacity of aircraft dispatcher or air traffic control tower operator.

In other words, the term "airmen" applies to more than just pilots. An airman is any member of the aircrew. Aircraft mechanics and dispatchers are airmen as well. So are air traffic controllers. And, because aircraft fly in airspace controlled by the FAA and specifically by air traffic controllers, civil litigation involving airmen will likely include the federal government, air traffic controllers and/or the air traffic control system.

The U.S. government is sovereign and cannot be sued without its consent. In dealing with the government legally, airmen are given two principal avenues of legal recourse. First, the government allows itself to be sued under certain circumstances provided for in the Federal Tort Claims Act. Second, relief may be sought administratively through the provisions of the Administrative Procedure Act [APA]. The latter gives rise to a whole body of law known as "administrative law." It is an administrative court system which exists outside of the customary federal or state courts, but from which, appeal may be made to certain appellate courts. However, before appealing to the courts the litigant must first exhaust all available administrative channels before seeking judicial review.

THE ADMINISTRATIVE PROCEDURE ACT

The Administrative Procedure Act [APA] was enacted June 11, 1946. Chapter 5, Subchapter II, of the foregoing (5 U.S.C.) is entitled, "Administrative Procedure." Specifically, in the exercise of rule making under Title 49 U.S.C., the FAA Administrator is governed by the Administrative Procedure Act, as is the National Transportation Safety Board. The principles embodied in the APA have been adopted at all levels of government, and have become part of the due process of law. The Administrative Procedure Act provides for adjudication procedures outside of the normal judicial process. Any person who suffers a legal wrong because of any governmental agency action is entitled to judicial review as prescribed by statute.

Generally speaking, a person with a grievance must first appeal through the prescribed administrative channels before the case may be taken to the customary courts for review.[69] The administrative appeal normally begins with the agency concerned. If not satisfied at the originating agency level, an appeal usually may be pursued either within the agency, or at another governmental agency appointed as a reviewing authority. Thus, for example, the NTSB hears appeals from the administrative decisions of the FAA. If the issue cannot be resolved at the administrative level, and all possible administrative appeals have been expended, appeal may then be made to a United States Court of Appeals.

The administrative procedure is not intended to diminish the constitutional rights of any person, or rights otherwise recognized by law. Rather, its purpose is to preclude unnecessary intervention by the courts into the routines of government business. All citizens still have the protection of the Constitution. If, after the administrative process has been expended, there still remains legal cause, the case may be taken to the courts for satisfaction. In short, a plaintiff must expend his or her available administrative remedies, or channels, before appealing to the courts. The courts in general have upheld this principle,

---

[69] *See Gaunce v. De Vincentis*, CCH 17 AVI ¶ 18,403 (1983).

and where final administrative determinations have not yet been issued, but an appeal has nevertheless been submitted to the courts, the courts have remanded those cases back to the agency concerned. It is a specified requirement in all cases where suit is brought against the United States under the Federal Tort Claims Act [FTCA].

To illustrate the administrative process we examine the revocation or suspension of an airman's certificate. The FAA Administrator is empowered to regulate air safety through the issuance of safety certificates, an airman certificate (along with current medical certification) being one way of regulating safety. The Administrator also has the authority when necessary and in the interest of public safety to revoke the certificate. Where an airman certificate is suspended, amended, modified, revoked or denied, it may likely provoke an appeal by its holder. Before appealing, however, the alleged violator must first respond to the FAA, the agency having original jurisdiction.[70] After having exhausted the initial administrative remedy (i.e., responding to the FAA) and receiving an adverse decision, an appeal then may be made to a National Transportation Safety Board Administrative Law Judge [ALJ].

Appeals within the administrative legal system are heard by an ALJ, who is appointed by the government, in accordance with Civil Service Commission regulations, to conduct administrative hearings. Administrative law judges are government employees. The term may also apply to other presiding officers assigned to hold hearings. An administrative law judge functions as a trial judge, issues subpoenas, administers oaths, holds pre-hearing conferences, rules on procedural requests, and receives evidence. An ALJ is a public official authorized to decide questions brought in this case not before a court, but rather to an administrative hearing. Appeals from the administrative channels to the courts are not uncommon, and some examples are presented as briefs (or case studies) at the end of this chapter.

THE FEDERAL AVIATION ACT

The Federal Aviation Administration was established "to promote safety and to provide for the safe use of airspace." The FAA Administrator shall promote the safety of flight of civil aircraft in air commerce by prescribing rules, regulations, minimum standards, methods,

---

[70] *See* "Administrative Procedure," *infra.*

and procedures.[71] Additionally, the Department of Transportation Act of 1966 provides that certain "functions, powers, and duties" of the Secretary, pertaining to aviation safety, be assumed by the FAA Administrator.[72] The Administrator is given broad discretionary powers of authority and responsibility. The Administrator acts on behalf of the Secretary of Transportation, and the Administrator's authority and responsibilities are outlined in the Federal Aviation Act of 1958, as amended. In fulfilling its mandates, the FAA has been delegated a wide range of authority and responsibility with respect to the regulation of aviation. In responding to its predominate dictum of air safety in the public interest, the FAA has created an oversight mechanism known as the "Compliance and Enforcement Program."[73]

Under the provisions of Section 306 of the Federal Aviation Act, the Administrator is to give consideration to the requirements of national defense. Section 307 authorizes the development of plans and policy with respect to navigable airspace; the promulgation of rules and regulations with respect to the use of the airspace; and it provides for limitations necessary in order to insure the safety of aircraft and efficient use of the airspace. The Administrator may modify or revoke any rule or regulation developed pursuant to Section 307 when required "in the public interest." Additionally, the Administrator is responsible for providing personnel and facilities for the regulation and protection of air traffic; for prescribing rules and regulations regarding the flight of aircraft, and protection of persons and property on the ground; and for prescribing rules and regulations for the prevention of collision between two aircraft or an aircraft and another object. Furthermore, the Federal Aviation Act requires that the provisions of the Administrative Procedure Act [74] be implemented during the exercise of rule making authority. During the conduct of investigations, the

---

[71] The Federal Aviation Act of 1958, Title VI § 601, as amended.

[72] The Department of Transportation Act of 1966 § 6(c)(1).

[73] The description of the FAA's Compliance and Enforcement Program was synopsized from three journal articles: *See* Laurence E. Gesell and Robert Anderson, *Compliance and Enforcement: Aviation Safety in The Public Interest; Part I: Statutory Authority and Enforcement Procedures*, J. of Aviation/Aerospace Ed. & Research 13-19 (fall 1991); *see also* Laurence E. Gesell and Robert Anderson, *Compliance and Enforcement: Aviation Safety in the Public Interest; Part II: Current Enforcement Program*, J. of Aviation/Aerospace Ed. & Research 7-13 (winter 1992); *see also* Laurence E. Gesell and Robert Anderson, *Compliance and Enforcement: Aviation Safety in the Public Interest; Part III: An Alternative Restitutive Enforcement Program*, J. of Aviation/Aerospace Ed. & Research 24-30 (spring 1992).

[74] 5 U.S.C. § 5.

Administrator is authorized to take evidence, issue subpoenas, take depositions, and compel testimony.

The Administrator is bound by findings of the NTSB, subsequent to an appeal being filed by an applicant in response to the FAA's denial of application for the issuance or renewal of a certificate. The Administrator may re-examine any civil airman, and based on that examination, amend, suspend or revoke any certificate held.[75] Before taking any such action the Administrator shall advise the certificate holder as to any charges relied upon for the proposed action. Except in an emergency, the certificate holder will be given the opportunity to be heard as to why his or her certificate should not be suspended, revoked, or amended. The certificate holder may appeal any order issued by the Administrator to the NTSB, in which case the subject order is stayed. Unlike regular courts of appeal, the NTSB is not bound by finding of fact made by the Administrator.

The Administrator may assess a civil penalty for a violation of the Aviation Act, or a regulation, rule or order issued thereunder.[76] This action may be taken subject to a finding of violation. Congress established the fundamental policies for aviation regulation in the U.S. through passage of the Federal Aviation Act. The Administrative Procedure Act, codified within Title 5 of the United States Code, is the procedural apparatus used for processing alleged violations.

In order to carry out the government's oversight functions, rules, regulations and orders procedures have been developed under the authority of the Aviation Act. These functional mandates have the effect of law in that they were formulated under laws enacted through the legislative authority of Congress. Many of these rules and regulations are codified in the Code of Federal Regulations. Authoritative internal (FAA) directives known as "Orders" are also important regulatory tools, and are issued by persons holding the appropriate level of authority.

The FAA's Compliance and Enforcement Program[77] contains the policies and procedures to be utilized by certain employees of the FAA while conducting investigations of alleged non-compliance of the FARs, or provisions of the Federal Aviation Act. Another internal document, "Certification of Pilots and Flight Instructors," contains,

---

[75] Federal Aviation Act of 1958, Title VI § 609.
[76] Federal Aviation Act of 1958, Title VI § 905.
[77] FAA Order 2150.3A.

among other things, guidance information for FAA Inspectors regarding the acceptance of custody of an airman certificate.[78] In Title 49 of the Code of Federal Regulations,[79] there are regulations, applicable to the National Transportation Safety Board, which define the scope of the NTSB's procedural responsibilities. The statutory authority enabling aviation oversight is complex and is generated not only through the enactment of laws, such as the Department of Transportation Act of 1966 or the Federal Aviation Act of 1958, but by virtue of the multitude of rules, regulations and procedures created to carry out the stipulations in the subject laws.

ENFORCEMENT

Any person may file with the Secretary of Transportation a complaint with respect to anything done or omitted by any person in contravention of any provision of the Federal Aviation Act. In addition, the Secretary of Transportation (and by delegation, the Administrator) is empowered at any time to institute an investigation. This authority has been further delegated to various offices and individuals. Specifically, the FAA Chief Counsel, Deputy Chief Counsel, Assistant Chief Counsel, and each Regional Counsel have authority to respond on behalf of the Administrator during enforcement investigations.

In conducting investigations of alleged violations by certificate holding airmen, the operational arm of the FAA Counselors are the Inspectors in the field offices. Field offices "investigate, coordinate, and report violations of all regulations which are discovered within their geographical area and for which they have enforcement responsibility."[80] Furthermore, the Compliance and Enforcement Program contains the procedures and methods by which inspectors will conduct the investigations and assemble the final field report.

One important aspect of the FAA's enforcement program deals with "administrative disposition of certain violations."[81] Specifically, the FAA field office is responsible for processing an investigation and determining if an alleged violation requires legal enforcement action. If this determination is made, the field office (Supervising Inspector) is given latitude to take "administrative action."

---

[78] FAA Order 8710.4.
[79] 49 C.F.R. §§ 800-99.
[80] FAA Order 2150.3A, Ch. 3.
[81] *See* 14 C.F.R. §13.11.

Administrative action does not constitute a formal adjudication of the matter, but may be taken by issuing a warning notice or letter of correction. Neither the warning notice nor letter of correction indicates the FAA has made a finding of violation. Rather, the intent of this type of action is to identify a situation in which there may have been a violation, or in which corrective action would rectify a minor infraction, and issue notice that these circumstances have been corrected or should not occur again.

The decision whether or not to take administrative action as opposed to "legal enforcement action" (e.g., certificate suspension, revocation, civil penalty, etc.) is based on the applicability of four specific conditions pertaining to the alleged violation:

- No significant unsafe condition existed;
- Lack of competency or qualification was not involved;
- The violation was not deliberate; and
- The alleged violator has a constructive attitude toward complying with the regulations, and has not been involved in previous similar violations.

Legal enforcement and administrative actions are the two vehicles utilized by the FAA to carry out its enforcement responsibilities. In fulfilling these responsibilities, delegation of authority is necessary and is carried out as specified in the Federal Aviation Act as well as within the various rules, regulations, and orders created pursuant to the Act. The various individuals involved in the enforcement process, from the Administrator, to FAA Counsel, to FAA Field Office Inspector, are charged with the responsibility of formulating their responses to alleged violations with due consideration of air safety and the public interest.

ADMINISTRATIVE PROCEDURE

In order to understand the FAA enforcement program, a clear understanding of the procedural aspects involved is important. When an alleged violation by a certificate holding airman is investigated and processed, the entire procedure is governed by laws, rules, and regulations. The laws, such as the Department of Transportation Act, the Federal Aviation Act, the Administrative Procedure Act, and the various rules and regulations instituted thereunder, provide a consistent line of inquisition which, by design, is supposed to promote fairness to both sides of the dispute. The alleged violator is afforded certain Constitutional protections during the process and ultimately can seek to have his or her case heard by federal courts.

An investigation of an alleged violation can come from a variety of sources. However, air traffic control facilities, accident investigations, and public complaints are the most common sources. When information is made available to an FAA field office regarding an alleged violation, a letter announcing the initiation of an investigation is sent to the individual believed responsible. This letter advises the individual that certain facts and circumstances indicate a violation may have occurred. In the letter, the involved individual is given the opportunity to respond to the allegations and advise the FAA field office. After the field office has completed its investigation, a report of the findings is forwarded to the appropriate Regional Counsel.

Counsel for the FAA have authority to act on behalf of the Administrator during the conduct of investigations of alleged violations.[82] As a result of any investigation, when it is determined that safety in air commerce or air transportation and the public interest requires, an order amending, modifying, suspending, or revoking any airman certificate may be issued. If, after review of the investigatory data, the FAA believes a violation has occurred, counsel will issue the appropriate order. If action against an airman's certificate is proposed (as opposed to other forms of enforcement) FAA Counsel issues a Notice of Proposed Certificate Action, which states the charges or other reasons upon which the Administrator has based the proposed action. It contains four options, which the alleged violator may choose from in answering the charges:

- admit the charges and surrender his or her certificate;
- answer the charges in writing;
- request that an order be issued in accordance with the notice of proposed certificate action so that the certificate holder may appeal to the National Transportation Safety Board; or
- request an opportunity to be heard in an informal conference with FAA Counsel.

---

[82] 14 C.F.R. §13.19; *see also* Federal Aviation Act of 1958 § 609, and 49 U.S.C. §1429.

If the airman elects the third option above, and appeals the case to the NTSB, then the Administrator's order amending, modifying, suspending, or revoking the affected certificate is stayed. This is true unless the FAA finds that an *emergency* requiring immediate action exists in respect to safety in air commerce. In this case, the order of the Administrator takes affect immediately, and any appeal to the NTSB by the affected airmen does not stay the action of the mandate.

Upon appeal to the National Transportation Safety Board, the NTSB " . . . reviews in quasi-judicial proceedings, . . . orders by the Administrator modifying, amending, suspending, or revoking certificates."[83] Such proceedings are conducted under the provisions of the Administrative Procedure Act.[84] The initial appeal hearings are conducted by an Administrative Law Judge. The ALJ renders an *initial decision* after hearing the case in which the Administrator's previous order is now a complaint against the alleged violator. In the conduct of the hearing, the Board is not bound by the findings of fact of the Administrator, and the burden of proof, which is established by a preponderance of evidence, is upon the FAA. Of note is that when answering the complaint of the Administrator, the certificate holding airman is obligated to *deny* the allegation or else it may be construed as an admission of guilt.[85] Simply desiring a day in court, without being prepared to show where the order of the Administrator is incorrect, could be tantamount to an admission of wrongdoing.

After the ALJ makes an initial decision, the airman (respondent) can appeal this decision to the full National Transportation Safety Board. On appeal, the full Board will only consider procedural issues, such as:

- Are the findings of fact (in the original decision) supported by a preponderance of evidence that is reliable, probative, and substantial?
- Are conclusions made in accordance with precedent and policy?
- Are the questions on appeal substantial?
- Have any prejudicial errors occurred? [86]

---

[83] 49 C.F.R. § 800.3 (b).
[84] 5 U.S.C. § 551 et seq.
[85] 49 C.F.R. § 821.31.
[86] 49 C.F.R. § 821.49.

The Board has authority to change the ALJ's initial decision. If after receiving the decision and finding of the full Board, the respondent still desires to appeal, the law, in part, stipulates that "any order, affirmative or negative, issued by the Board . . . shall be subject to review by the Courts of Appeal of the United States. . . ."[87] There is also a review process of the appellate court's judgment by the U.S. Supreme Court upon *certiorari*,[88] although relative to the large number of appeals, it is rarely granted. The administrative process, through which an airman's certificate action may proceed, is charted on Figure 8.1, "Certificate Action Review Process."

RESTITUTION VERSUS RETRIBUTION

Certificated airmen are regulated by threat of sanction. Yet, there is a current trend away from *retribution*, and toward *restitution* as the way to resolve violations of society's norms.[89] Sanction of errant airmen by the FAA, however, remains primarily retributive. Repressive and restitutive sanctions, like retribution and deterrence, are alternate forms of punishment, but the focus of each is entirely different. Retributive sanctions are expiatory and designed around the offender. Restitutive sanctions involve reciprocity and cooperative effort to restore conditions to an original state. Restitution includes the restoration of the deprived rights of the victims of rule-breaking, not just restitution of the offender by "paying him back."

On the one hand, retribution is arguably not the most appropriate way to deal with all airmen found in non-compliance with the rules. Certificate sanction taken only for deterrence value is a unilateral form of redress, with dubious chances of actually affecting offender rehabilitation in a remedial sense. The retributive sanction fails to consider the benefits of positive interaction between the offender and the victim. When appropriate, a restitutive approach to enforcement, giving due consideration to the advantages of deterrence, provides the preferred basis for restoring the breach of public interest precipitated by the non-compliant action (i.e., violation) by an airman.

---

[87] 49 U.S.C. § 1486.

[88] as provided for in 28 U.S.C. § 1254.

[89] *See* Donald Black, *The Behavior of Law* (1976); *see also* Donald Black, *The Elementary Forms of Conflict Management*, in Law and Social Control Ch. 3 (1987); *see also* Donald Black, *Compensation and the Social Structure of Misfortune*, 21 Law and Society Review (1987); *see also* Laurence E. Gesell, *Airline Re-Regulation* (1990).

Figure 8.1—CERTIFICATE ACTION REVIEW PROCESS

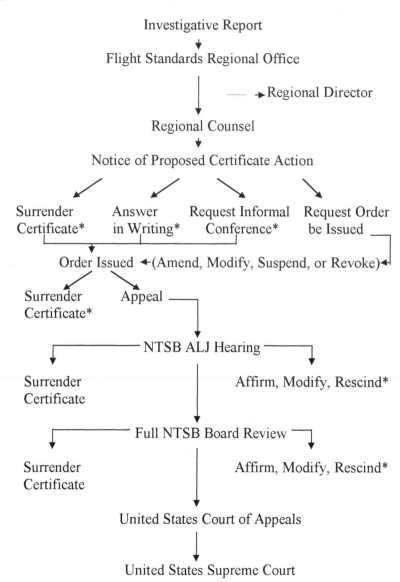

*Case may be resolved at any stage indicated by an asterisk.

On the other hand, the Compliance and Enforcement Program was developed by the FAA to fulfill its statutory oversight obligations. The FAA enforcement program resolves non-compliance by addressing both ends of the justice spectrum. From a restitutive perspective on one end, the administrative enforcement program allows the alleged offender to amend the wrong committed, theoretically restoring the system to its original state. On the other end lies the legal enforcement program and retribution. Deterrence is the objective of retributive sanctions. The system attempts to address both ends of the spectrum, but it is fundamentally retributive and fails to recognize the necessity for, and benefits of, more restitutive remedies.

Although allowing for restitutive remedies, the current administrative enforcement program is limited as to the type and nature of non-compliant activity that can be resolved through restitutive action. Without notable exception, most violations are handled within the legal enforcement program. Although the legal enforcement program has various elements, which on the surface purport flexibility, the effect of the underlying mechanism and basic process is predominantly retributive. Even so, the present limitations inherent in administrative action may not be totally inappropriate, in view of the fact that for many violations, mild restitution may not ensure future compliance.

Striking a balance between the mild restitutive notion of administrative action, and the retributive characteristics of legal enforcement, is the central focus of alternative programs studied by the FAA. Still, deterrence—the retributive goal of the FAA's certificate sanction program—is a valuable component of the enforcement process. Certificate sanctions (i.e., discipline) which deter future acts of non-compliance by the violator, as well as others who are similarly situated, on the surface seemingly serve a safety purpose and thereby enhance the public interest. The drawbacks of the purely retributive approach, however, are realized by envisioning the behavior that some violators are likely to display after receiving discipline.

For example, if an airman, in dealing with the vast complexities of today's airspace environment, inadvertently deviates from a procedural or communication requirement, then he or she is subject to a retributive sanction. This sanction might be a certificate suspension for say 60 days or more. Because of the deterrent effect of this sanction, this airman likely will not repeat the same violation. However, in avoiding the same circumstances that led to the prior violation, the airman may unknowingly create an even greater hazard to air safety than had originally occurred. For example, the airman may in the future, deviate around, over, or under a controlled airspace area in order to preclude the possibility of a procedural/communication mistake and additional confrontation with the FAA. This new routing followed by the airman may possibly deprive the air traffic control system of the advantages of knowing the whereabouts of the involved aircraft. The overall effect to the system may be a reduction in safety and, therefore, may be more detrimental to the public interest. Thus, retributive sanctions, alone, may fail to insure that the airman understands the entire scope of his or her non-compliant action.

Administering a disciplinary sanction, purely for deterrence purposes, attacks the *effect* of the non-compliant action, but fails to address the *cause*. Corrective justice demands equality between an infraction and its correlative punishment.[90] Selection of an appropriate sanction is aided by analyzing both cause and effect issues surrounding a non-compliant act.

ADMINISTRATIVE ACTION

As already stated, there are basically two sanctioning mechanisms within the FAA enforcement program; i.e., administrative action, consisting of warning letters and letters of correction; and legal enforcement action, consisting of emergency suspension, suspension, and/or deferred suspension. A "warning letter" (administrative action) is issued when more serious sanction is not necessary or desirable to deter repetition; and where, hypothetically, any average certificate holder might have done the same thing under similar circumstances. The warning letter is to bring to the attention of the violator the facts and circumstances of the occurrence. It is to advise, on the basis of available information, that such operations or practices are contrary to the regulations. Furthermore, it is to acknowledge the matter has been corrected and/or does not warrant legal enforcement action, and to request future compliance with the regulations. The letter is to be constructed so as to leave no doubt that a violation has occurred, but that the person involved is not charged with the violation.

A "letter of correction" (administrative action) is issued when the act is a type that can be corrected, and the alleged violator acknowl-

---

[90] *See* Aristotle, *Nichomachean Ethics* (circa 336 BC).

edges the violations (discrepancies, inadequacies, and areas of improvement). There is to be agreement that corrective action acceptable to the FAA is being taken, or will be taken within a reasonable time, or that satisfactory and prompt corrective action has been initiated. A letter of correction may also be used where the problem can be corrected by training, and its sole purpose is to correct *bona fide* non-compliance items. If corrective action is not completed as agreed, legal enforcement action may be taken.

Two programs have expanded the use of a letter of correction. One, entitled the "Air Carrier Internal Evaluation Program," was implemented in March of 1990. This program applies to operations conducted under FAR Part 121, "Operating requirements: Domestic, flag, and supplemental operations," and under Part 135, "Operating requirements: Commuter and on-demand operations and rules governing persons on board such aircraft." It provides for the issuance of a letter of correction in response to voluntary disclosure of infractions.

The other program, which also results in the issuance of a letter of correction, is entitled "Corrective Action through Remedial Training." This program was also implemented in March of 1990 and became a positive evolutionary step towards recognizing the value of restitution. There are several exclusionary elements of this program, however, which narrow the range and scope of those violations that may be included. An airman is ineligible for this program if:

- The offense severely compromised safety;
- The offense directly contributed to the cause of an accident; or
- The offense involved occurred when the certificate holder was operating for compensation or hire.[91]

In determining whether an act of non-compliance by an airman may be resolved with administrative action, certain conditions must be met:

- No significant unsafe condition can have existed;
- Lack of competency or qualification was not involved;
- The violation was not deliberate; and/or

---

[91] i.e., while operating under FAR Parts 121 or 135.

- The alleged violator has a constructive attitude toward compliance and does not have a history of similar violations.

With restitution as its underlying motive, with minor violations the element precipitating the allegation of non-compliance is normally addressed with an agreement for remedy reached between the FAA and the violator. This remedial-type approach effectively returns the system to its original state, which, of course, is the principal objective of restitution. The violator is not charged with non-compliance, nor is there a finding of violation. The FAA makes this concession in return for the promise and effect of some level of restitution. The downside of this type of action may be its lack of real deterrent value. At best, there is a mild retributive effect by way of the FAA's computer record keeping process known as the "Enforcement Information Subsystem" [EIS] tracking system, which enables the FAA to determine the exact violation/enforcement history of anyone who might have been involved in past non-compliant activity. Additionally, there still remains the possibility of this record being detrimental to future employment plans or aircraft insurance considerations, which, in effect, can be punitive.

The four elements (*supra*) that must be present before administrative action can be considered essentially define the concept of the program. With the exception of being able to objectively research the past record of the alleged violator, the remaining elements require a subjective assessment of the involved circumstances. There is, however, an Enforcement Sanction Guidance Table, which provides general guidelines for selecting an appropriate sanction for a given offense. Its purpose is to "assist, not replace, the exercise of prosecutorial judgment." This document also provides general guidance with respect to selecting specified ranges of appropriate sanctions. This general guidance requires a subjective analysis by those FAA individuals involved in the enforcement process.

The FAA has recognized that determination of the appropriate method for disposition of violation can best be accomplished in the field, rather than by Washington or Regional levels. In furthering the FAA decentralization program, and to provide greater discretion at the lowest operational level, authority is given to personnel at the field level to make final disposition by administrative action in place of legal enforcement action, whenever it is determined to be the most appropriate means of obtaining compliance with the Federal Aviation Regulations. The Administrator's policy with regard to this issue is clear, "the supervisor of the lowest operational field office of Flight Standards . . . will decide whether compliance may best be obtained through administrative action or through legal enforcement action."

It appears that the main limitations of the current FAA administrative enforcement program are:

- the limited number of violations which meet the stipulated criteria to be disposed of through administrative action;
- the stipulated conditions are too restrictive to accommodate all violations which do not warrant the legal enforcement process;
- the lack of real deterrent value; and
- the limited number of alternatives for the field office to select from in responding to the circumstances of the violation.

However, the following attributes appear to make the administrative enforcement program selectively effective:

- the expedient nature of resolution;
- the reduced expenditure of government resources;
- it is conceptually and practically restitutive, which promotes future informed compliance; and
- there is no finding of violation, thereby reducing potentially retributive undertones and subsequent adversarial relationship between the offender and the government.

LEGAL ENFORCEMENT ACTION

The other, and more predominant aspect of the FAA's enforcement program is legal enforcement action. The swiftest retribution is imposed through an "emergency suspension" (one form of legal enforcement action), which is imposed only when clearly needed in the public interest. It is not intended for punitive purposes, but rather is to be employed when there is evidence of lack of qualification, and/or when there is a probability that the holder of the certificate will probably continue to be in non-compliance.

Emergency suspension requires immediate coordination with the FAA Regional Flight Standards Division. The essence of this type of action most clearly personifies the literal reading of Section 609 of the Federal Aviation Act, "Amendment, Suspension, and Revocation of Certificates," regarding the justification which must be satisfied prior to the removal of an airman's privileges.[92] In a case of emergency suspension, the Administrator "determines that safety in air commerce or air transportation and the public interest requires. . . .," and as a result, the Administrator ". . . may issue an order amending, modifying, suspending, or revoking . . . and effective immediately." However, there are subsequent rights of appeal open to the affected airman to again recover his or her operating privileges.

The second form of legal enforcement action is punitive "suspension," which is used where it is necessary and imposed when:

- safety requires it;
- where technical proficiency and/or qualification mandates its use; and
- where a certificate holder does not satisfactorily accomplish the reexamination in an acceptable length of time.

Suspension of an airman's certificate is a frequently used legal sanction resulting from violations investigated by FAA Flight Standards District Offices [FSDOs]. The Compliance and Enforcement Program states, in part, that "if a certificate holder improperly exercises the privileges of that certificate, the natural consequence of that act is to lose the privileges for a period of time commensurate with the violation."[93]

This characterization of the certificate suspension sanction seems to justify the temporary removal of an airman's privileges solely for *punitive* purposes. Sanctions for punitive reasons, however, are clearly in contradiction with the foundation upon which the courts have determined certificate suspension for disciplinary purposes must be based; that is to say, as a *deterrence*. Look, for example, at *Pangburn v. CAB*.[94] The U.S. Court of Appeals supported the Civil Aeronautics Board right to impose a certificate suspension because of its "deterrence" value. The *Pangburn* case partially relied upon a review of *Wilson v. CAB*, wherein the *Wilson* Court recognized the "valuable

---

[92] *See Pastrana v. United States*, 746 F.2d 1447 (1984).

[93] FAA Order 2150.3A, § 206.

[94] *Pangburn v. Civil Aeronautics Board*, 311 F. 2d 349 (1st Cir. 1962).

deterrent effect" of certificate suspensions and an acceptance that suspensions could be imposed as a "deterrent sanction."[95]

One could argue there is more than a subtle difference between the imposition of a suspension (disciplinary action) solely for punitive purposes and the imposition of a suspension for deterrence value. Both of these philosophies embrace, albeit from a different perspective, a retributive notion. Judicial interpretation supports discipline to the extent that it acts as a deterrent to future violations. Conversely, discipline (solely punitive), as a natural consequence of the improper use of certificate privileges, is not similarly supported. This incongruity defines a fundamental difference in the administrative and judicial interpretations of Section 609 of the Aviation Act, and sets up certain suspensions for challenge in the courts.

A third form of legal enforcement action is "deferred suspension." It is imposed when corrective action by the violator would meet the objectives of the FAA enforcement program, and/or the case is too serious or does not meet the criteria for administrative action. This type of enforcement action is characteristically remedial in nature, and thus incorporates some restitutive qualities not present in other forms of suspension. Although the concept behind this type of action addresses violator rehabilitation, it does not appear to be a widely used tool. The Enforcement Sanction Guidance Table, which defines general guidelines for selecting appropriate sanctions, does not even provide for the application of a deferred suspension for airman operational types of violations. Moreover, there are certain inherent characteristics in the deferred suspension program, which would drastically reduce its effectiveness as an enforcement mechanism. For example, there may be an excessively long period of time between when the violation occurs and when the airman is advised of his or her capability to resolve the issue through corrective action.

During the normal investigation process the Inspector cannot be certain that his or her recommendations and analysis will be accepted, and, as such, discussing possible enforcement actions or sanctions with the violator is not permitted. As a result, the time period between when the violation is discovered and when the airman could be advised of any option to take corrective action, which is issued by FAA Regional Counsel through a Notice of Proposed Certificate Action, could be of considerable length.

---

[95] *Wilson v. Civil Aeronautics Board*, 244 F.2d 773 (1957).

Obviously, after a prolonged period of time it would be difficult to justify the need for, and rationalize the benefits of, operational remedial action. It would seem prudent that once identified, remedial action should be initiated immediately. Because of this aspect of the program, the deferred suspension option seems most appropriate for non-operational infractions, such as engineering and/or manufacturer-related violations. In another example, the effectiveness of a deferred suspension is reduced, because unlike administrative action, the FAA makes a *finding of violation*, thereby diluting the restitutive quality and enhancing the retributive aspect of this type of action. Unlike administrative action, an *order of suspension* is issued, although the actual time of suspension is waived.

Since the FAA makes a finding of violation, and actually issues an order of suspension (deferred), the overall punitive effect is similar to a normal suspension action. This effectively reduces the deferred suspension program's restitutive qualities in favor of a permanent retributive record of punishment. It appears that the initial assessment of the violation, which identified the need for remedial action as opposed to punishment, gets lost within a legal mechanism, which largely represses the potential effectiveness of the proposed solution.

In still another example, the mechanical elements of the deferred suspension action involve a significant expenditure of financial and human resources. In this regard, there is virtually no difference between deferred suspension and normal suspension. The investigating field office, various reviewing layers, and Regional Counsel, all become involved as in a standard certificate suspension action.

Conceptually, the availability of deferred suspension demonstrates a recognized need for remedial action for certain types of violations. Unfortunately, the process itself allows for only limited application. However, if the philosophy, embodied within the deferred suspension procedure, was infused into a process specifically tailored to address the proper balance between restitution and retribution, then ostensibly a significant enhancement to FAA's compliance and enforcement program could result. In summary, the FAA's aviation oversight responsibility, with its attendant enforcement program, is a complex issue. The enforcement tools available to address non-compliance are numerous and result in varying effects upon an airman's future propensity for informed compliance. A continued philosophical evolution, which recognizes the benefits of balancing retribution with the qualities of restitution, will unquestionably advance the goals of the FAA mission. Until then, the system of individual airman oversight will likely remain fundamentally retributive.

Examples of administrative law cases are presented at the end of the chapter. In the subsequent section, actions against the federal government for the failures of its individual employees to conform to reasonable standards are addressed. Where negligence is attributable to employees of the federal government, as opposed to the negligent acts of airmen, restitutive remedies are available.

FEDERAL TORT CLAIMS ACT

Under the English Common Law doctrine of sovereign immunity, "the king could do no wrong." Since the sovereign could do no wrong, it followed that neither the king nor his agents could be sued on any grounds unless *he* consented to it. The doctrine of sovereign immunity has been adopted in the U.S. and applies to federal and state governments, but neither of which is granted total immunity under the Constitution. The Fifth and Fourteenth Amendments, for example, prohibit the taking of property without just compensation. Furthermore, the federal government, initially by the Tucker Act and later through the Federal Tort Claims Act [FTCA], allows itself to be sued under circumstances where the tort actions of federal *employees* are involved. The Federal Torts Claims Act [96] provides, in part:

> *The United States shall be liable, respecting the provisions of this title relating to tort claims, in the same manner and to the same extent as a private individual under like circumstances, but shall not be liable for interest prior to judgment or for punitive damages.*[97]

The Federal Tort Claims Act grants the right to citizens to bring action against the federal government based upon *tort* for injury caused by an *employee* of a governmental agency.[98] A "tort" is a pri-

---

[96] 28 U.S.C.

[97] 28 U.S.C. § 2674.

[98] As the U.S. Supreme Court observed, "the test established by the Tort Claims Act for determining the United States' liability is whether a private person would be responsible for similar negligence under the laws of the State where the acts occurred." Hence, state tort law governs

vate wrong not based upon contract, which has been divided into two basic categories: *intentional* torts, or *unintentional* torts. Examples of intentional torts are libel, slander, assault, battery; i.e., damage intentionally inflicted upon another. An unintentional tort is *negligence*. The FTCA allows suit against the federal government for the unintentional tortious actions of its employees. Many states have comparable statutes allowing suit against them.

A "federal agency" includes the executive departments and corporations primarily acting as instrumentalities or agencies of the United States, but does not include any contractor with the United States. An "employee of the government" includes officers or employees of any federal agency, members of the military or naval forces of the United States, and persons acting on behalf of a federal agency in an official capacity, temporarily or permanently in the service of the United States, whether with or without compensation.

Contractors may also be categorized as employees.[99] Under the common law doctrine of *respondeat superior,* an employer can be held vicariously liable for the torts of its employees.[100] However, under the common law, if the tortfeasor was an independent contractor liability might flow to that independent contractor, rather than the person for whom the work is done.[101] Under the FTCA, liability extends to the United States for the "negligent or wrongful acts" of its employees, excluding vicarious liability for the acts of independent contractors.[102] The threshold question is whether the party committing the negligence is an independent contractor.

---

the circumstances, under which the U.S. is liable, though such liability is circumscribed by the explicit exemptions created in the legislation itself. *See* Paul Stephen Dempsey and Laurence E. Gesell, *Air Commerce and the Law* 732 (2004).

[99] *See Emelwon and McAlister v. United States,* CCH 10 AVI ¶ 17,718 (1968).

[100] Thus, the negligence of a driver or mechanic is imputed directly to the carrier for which they work, so long as they are acting within the "scope of employment," and not on a "frolic and detour." *The T.J. Hooper,* 60 F.2d 737 (2nd Cir. 1932); *Ira S. Bushey & Sons, Inc. v. United States,* 398 F.2d 167 (2nd Cir. 1968). A slight or minor deviation is not a "frolic and detour." *See Restatement (Second) of Agency* §§ 220, 229. The employer may, however, seek indemnification against the employee for any damages paid as a result of the employee's negligence.

[101] However, *see Restatement of Torts* § 427, which imposes liability upon the employer of an independent contractor where the work involves special dangers to others which is inherent in the nature of the work.

[102] *Aretz v. United States,* 604 F.2d 417, 426-427 (9th Cir. 1979); *Davis v. United States,* 2002 U.S. Dist. Lexis 25006 (E.D. La. 2003). The FTCA provides that the federal government is liable for manages "caused by the negligent or wrongful act or omission of any employee of the Government. . . ." 28 U.S.C. § 1346(b) (2002). An 'employee of the Government' is defined to include "officers or employees of any federal agency, members of the military or naval forces of the United States, and persons acting on behalf of a federal agency in an official capacity, tem-

Even where a court concludes that the independent contractor defense applies, the employer of the contractor may nevertheless be held liable: (1) for negligence in selecting, instructing or supervising the independent contractor; (2) where the duty is non-delegable (i.e., authority cannot be transferred); or (3) where the work to be performed is inherently dangerous.[103] The issue of whether a non-delegable duty exists as an exception to the independent contractor's defense in the context of FTCA litigation is one that has been addressed in more than 50 federal court decisions.[104] The circuits are clearly split on the issue, with the weight of authority having recognized the doctrine.[105]

As for "inherently dangerous, " the courts sometimes use the term to refer to both *ultrahazardous* activities, and to activities that are *dangerous under the particular circumstances* in which they are performed.[106] But these, in fact, are two entirely different concepts. The former ("ultrahazardous activities," a/k/a "abnormally dangerous" activities) are those for which, in many jurisdictions, strict liability is imposed under the common law. However, the imposition of strict liability is forbidden under the FTCA.[107] So if a court perceives the inherently dangerous concept to be synonymous with the strict liability concept of ultrahazardous activities, it will reject its application in the FTCA context.[108]

---

porarily or permanently . . . with or without compensation." 28 U.S.C. § 2671 (2002). The term 'federal agency' is defined to include "the executive departments, the military departments, independent establishments of the United States and corporations primarily acting as instrumentalities or agencies of the United States, but does not include any contractor with the United States." *Id. See Logue v. United States*, 412 U.S. 521 (1973), *see also United States v. Orleans*, 425 U.S. 807 (1976).

[103] James Henderson, Jr., Richard Pearson & John Siliciano, *The Torts Process* 155 (5th ed. 1999). *See also Merklin v. United States*, 788 F.2d 172, 175 (3rd Cir. 1986), which held that, under New Jersey law, "the employer may be liable for his contractor's negligence: (i) where the employer retains substantial control over the contractor's work; (ii) where the employer engages the contractor to perform 'inherently dangerous' work; and (iii) where the employer has negligently selected an incompetent contractor."

[104] Lexis search of Jan. 13, 2003.

[105] *See* Paul Stephen Dempsey and Laurence E. Gesell, *Air Commerce and the Law* 731-736 (2004).

[106] *Merklin v. United States*, 788 F.2d 172, 176 n. 4 (3rd Cir. 1986) (citing *Wilson v. Good Humor Corp.*, 757 F.2d 1293, 1295 (D.C. Cir. 1985), and *Toole v. United States*, 588 F.2d 403, 407 n.6 (3rd Cir. 1978)).

[107] *Dalehite v. United States*, 346 U.S. 15, 45 (1953) (Because the statute requires a negligent act, "liability does not arise by virtue either of United States ownership of an 'inherently dangerous commodity' or property, or of engaging in an 'extra-hazardous' activity.")

[108] However, not all courts have. The Eighth Circuit has held that when the government "hires an independent contractor to do extra-dangerous or ultrahazardous work [it] has a duty to exer-

However, the concept "inherently dangerous" is a term that also has a negligence dimension, and so long as it is the government's negligence—and not the vicarious liability of the subcontractor's—that is at issue, the FTCA affords a potential remedy. As one court put it, "When an activity is inherently dangerous, neither the owner, nor the contractor nor any agency with fiduciary duties concerning the activity may delegate the duty of safety to some other person or entity. The duty is nondelegable and that means that it stays where the law vests it, even if others in the chain of responsibility have a concomitant duty to ensure safety. . . ."[109]

The first section (1346) of the FTCA is the "Tucker Act" which deals with the United States as a defendant and with actions founded upon the U.S. Constitution and actions based upon contract. The main body (Sections 1402 through 2680) is the actual Federal Tort Claims Act, which was passed some time after the Tucker Act. Under the concept of sovereign immunity, the Government may not be sued unless it consents to suit. Under the Federal Tort Claims Act the federal government has set down the conditions under which it may be sued, namely upon employee negligence. The FTCA is excerpted and summarized in Table 8.1, "Federal Tort Claims Act."

Bearing in mind that not only are pilots "airmen," but that air traffic controllers, too, are airmen, interesting confrontations erupt within the legal system between these two types of "airmen." Air traffic controllers, by-and-large, are employees of the federal government and work directly for the FAA. Not uncommonly, an aircraft accident or incident involving a pilot or other crewmember will implicate, if not an air traffic controller *per se*, then at least the air traffic control system and in turn the federal government. When this happens the provisions of the Federal Tort Claims Act must allow for suits against the United States, before the FAA (as the Air Traffic Control employer) may be brought into court for damages.

---

cise reasonable care to see that the contractor takes proper precautions to protect those who might sustain injury from the work. This liability may be imposed on the United States as an employer, and it is not vicarious or strict liability, but rather a function of the employer's own negligence." *McMichael v. United States*, 751 F.2d 303, 310 (8th Cir. 1985).

[109] *Medicine v. United States*, 192 F. Supp. 2d 1052, 1066 (D. Mont. 2002) (concluding that felling trees in an area known for dangerous winds was an inherently dangerous activity imposing liability upon the federal government under the FTCA for injury to employees). *See* Paul Stephen Dempsey and Laurence E. Gesell, *Air Commerce and the Law* 737 (2004).

Table 8.1—FEDERAL TORT CLAIMS ACT

JURISDICTION

The district courts have original jurisdiction concurrent with the U.S. Court of Claims where the United States is the defendant, and where:

- civil action is taken against the United States for the recovery of any internal revenue tax; and
- where there is a claim, not above a specified amount, founded either upon the Constitution, any Act of Congress, any regulation of an executive department, or upon express or implied contracts with the United States. The district courts have exclusive jurisdiction over claims for injury or loss of property, or personal injury or death caused by the negligent or wrongful act or omission of any employee of the Government while acting within the scope (i.e., in line of duty) of the person's office or employment, under circumstances where a private person would be liable to the claimant in accordance with the law of the place where the act or omission occurred.

VENUE

Any civil action on a tort claim against the United States may be prosecuted only in the judicial district where the plaintiff resides or wherein the act or omission complained of occurred.

TIME LIMITATIONS

Appeals to the U.S. Court of Claims in tort claims cases shall be taken within 90 days after the entry of the final judgment of the district court. A tort claim against the United States shall be forever barred unless action is begun within *two years* after such claim accrues.

Table 8.1 (Cont'd)

U.S. LIABILITY

The United States shall be liable for tort claims in the same manner and to the same extent as a private individual under like circumstances. That is to say, for nominal and compensatory damages, but punitive damages are excluded.

PREREQUISITE AGENCY DISPOSITION

An action shall not be instituted upon a claim against the United States, which has been presented to a federal agency, unless such agency has made final disposition of the claim. In other words, *all administrative remedies and channels must be expended.*

FEDERAL EMPLOYEE PROTECTION

The *Attorney General shall defend* any civil action or proceeding brought in any court against an employee of the government who was acting in an official capacity at the time of the act or omission. A judgment under the Federal Tort Claims Act constitutes a complete bar to any action by the claimant, against the government employee whose act or omission gave rise to the claim.

EMPLOYEE DETERMINATION

Upon certification by the Attorney General that the defendant employee was acting within *the scope of the person's employment* at the time of the incident out of which the suit arose, any such civil action commenced in a state court shall be removed to the appropriate U.S. District Court. Should a district court determine that a case is not against the United States (such as against the employee for intentional tort), the case shall be remanded to the state courts.

Table 8.1 (Cont'd)

EXCEPTIONS

The provisions of the Federal Tort Claims Act do not apply to, among others, any claim based upon:

- an act or omission of a government employee *exercising due care* (i.e., not negligent) *in the execution of a statute or regulation*;
- the exercise or performance, or the failure to exercise or perform a *discretionary function*;
- the loss, miscarriage, or negligent transmission of letters or *postal matter*;
- assault, battery, false imprisonment, false arrest, malicious prosecution, abuse of process, libel, slander, misrepresentation, deceit, or interference with contract rights (i.e., *intentional torts*);
- combatant activities of the military or naval forces during time of war; and
- an incident *occurring in a foreign country.*

FEDERAL WAIVER OF SOVEREIGN IMMUNITY

English common law adopted the ancient Roman law maxim that "the King can do no wrong." Essentially, since the King, in effect, made and enforced the law, he could not be deemed subject to it, and was effectively incapable of doing wrong. American common law courts embraced the doctrine as well, and many states and some local governments codified it. But in recent decades, the doctrine has endured some constriction by both the common and statutory law.

Sometimes, the question arises whether an institution of the federal government (e.g., the DOT or one of its modal administrations, such as the FAA) is liable for injuries it may cause. After three decades of wrestling with the issue, dissatisfaction with the notoriously clumsy private bill device led Congress to codify the circumstances under which a federal agency will be liable for its torts in 1946.[110]

The FTCA provides, *inter alia*, that in tort actions, "The United States shall be liable . . . in the same manner and to the same extent as a private individual under like circumstances. . . ."[111] As the U.S. Supreme Court observed, "the test established by the Federal Tort Claims Act for determining the United States' liability is whether a private person would be responsible for similar negligence under the laws of the state where the acts occurred."[112] Hence, state tort law governs the circumstances, under which the U.S. is liable, though such liability is circumscribed by the explicit exemptions created in the legislation itself.[113] Under the FTCA, federal courts have exclusive jurisdiction over claims brought against the United States.[114]

Air traffic controllers, as individuals, may have their rights violated by the government as well. For example, in *DeHainaut v. Peña*, a group of air traffic controllers filed a class action suit against the government for its policy of indefinitely barring them from re-employment with the FAA.[115] Unfortunately, their claims for job reinstatement, for back pay, and for legal fees were denied.

What the air traffic controllers got caught up in was deregulation, including a social movement against organized labor that was much larger than anything they had expected. Airline deregulation, itself, was but part of a larger social revolution and demand for less government. The focus of the Airline Deregulation Act of 1978 was concern for the consumer. It was passed in response to Congressional and other investigations into airline regulation and on the heels of a regulatory reform movement in general. Deregulation was instituted because critics perceived economic regulation as inefficient, costly and ineffective. Even worse, the critics blamed industry for its mismanagement under the protective regulatory umbrella of the CAB. And, they accused government regulators of having been co-opted by the

---

[110] *Dahelite v. United States*, 346 U.S. 15, 24 (1953).
[111] 28 U.S.C. § 2674. The FTCA goes on to say that the federal government "shall not be liable for interest prior to judgment or for punitive damages." *Id.*
[112] *Rayonier, Inc. v. United States*, 352 U.S. 315, 319 (1957).
[113] *See* Scott Barash, *The Discretionary Function Exemption and Mandatory Regulations*, 54 U. Chi. L. Rev. 1300, 1302 (1995).
[114] 28 U.S.C. §§ 1346(b), 2674, 2680(a).
[115] *DeHainaut, v. Peña*, 32 F.3d 1066 (7th Cir. 1994).

very industries they were supposed to regulate. Industry and the government then tried to pass the buck by focusing the blame on labor.[116]

Collectively, government and (airline) industry leaders began systematically to dismantle organized labor. Some of the leaders were more aggressive than others were, and some were more direct with their intentions. Although their individual tactics varied, management in general spearheaded an attack against labor in an attempt to revolutionize the air transportation industry.

AIR TRAFFIC CONTROLLER RIGHTS

Although it did not involve airline workers, *per se*, the government's actions against air traffic controllers set the tone for the revolution. After a bitter fight between the Professional Air Traffic Controllers Association [PATCO] and the FAA over working conditions, a militant faction of controllers took charge of PATCO in early 1981.[117] PATCO leadership advocated a showdown with the FAA to finally force the issue. Despite being warned by the FAA, Congress, and the President, on August 3, 1981, members of PATCO struck in an attempt to secure for themselves higher and better wages, benefits and working conditions. It was declared an illegal strike by the Reagan administration, and thousands of air traffic controllers permanently lost their employment with the FAA.

The strike and resultant firings left the air traffic system seriously depleted of personnel. The remaining controller work force, reduced in numbers and experience by the firing of striking controllers, was expected to work continued overtime, to work long shifts, and to forego vacations. As late as 1984, six major control centers were operating with only 43% as many experienced controllers as before the strike, but still handling 95% of the pre-strike traffic volume.

More than 10,000 controllers participated in the illegal strike and were fired. The FAA claimed personnel requirements would be restored within two years; but nearly ten years passed before staffing levels were brought back up to normal. It was not until 1995, under the Clinton administration, and subsequent to the failed *DeHainaut v. Peña* class action suit, that any of the fired controllers were finally

---

[116] *See* Paul Stephen Dempsey and Laurence E. Gesell, *Air Transportation: Foundations for the 21st Century* Ch. 6 (1997).

[117] *See* Michael S. Nolan, *Fundamentals of Air Traffic Control* (1994); *see also* Laurence E. Gesell, *Air Traffic Control: An Invitation to a Career* (1987).

allowed to return to work. The fact that the administration carried a grudge for so many years could only have been out of spite. Nations, which have warred against the United States, have been forgiven in less time. The administration's failure to forgive the striking controllers, for so many years, was a clear indication of government's malice towards organized labor. It was indicative of the contempt for organized labor that under girded the government's post-deregulatory policies and actions.[118]

PILOT RIGHTS

Unfortunately, for pilots, the playing field is not even when it comes to challenging the federal government and/or individual air traffic controllers. By regulation, such cases begin with a presumption that the pilot (in command) is at fault.[119] In addition, this legal presumption has produced a mountain of statistics reflecting "pilot error" as the cause of most aircraft accidents. Likewise, there is a fundamental assumption that neither air traffic controllers nor the FAA have been found negligent in cases involving aircraft accidents, since it is already presumed that the pilot is the one most apt to be at fault. Thus, by virtue of the Federal Aviation Regulations, and the FAA's interpretation of those regulations, the burden of proof has been placed on the pilot. As a result, it is extremely difficult (although there have been exceptions) to demonstrate negligence on the part of air traffic control, or other FAA employees, and to in turn win a suit against the federal government on such grounds.

Demonstrating the philosophy that pilots have presumed responsibility in issues involving air traffic control, shown below is an excerpt from the *Basic Air Traffic Manual* [BATM], a reference training manual used during the 1980s by the FAA in instructing newly hired, prospective air traffic controllers:

> *A clearance issued by ATC is predicated on known traffic and physical airport conditions. An ATC clearance is an authorization by air traffic control, for the purpose of preventing*

---

[118] Paul Stephen Dempsey and Laurence E. Gesell, *Air Transportation: Foundations for the 21st Century* 369-370 (1997).
[119] 14 C.F.R. § 91.3.

> *collision between known aircraft, for an air-*
> *craft to proceed under specified conditions*
> *within controlled air space. It is not authori-*
> *zation for a pilot to deviate from any rule or*
> *regulation; neither is it permission to conduct*
> *unsafe aircraft operations. FAR 91.3(a) states:*
> *The pilot in command of an aircraft is directly*
> *responsible for, and is the final authority as to,*
> *the operation of that aircraft. If ATC issues a*
> *clearance that would cause a pilot to deviate*
> *from a rule or regulation, or in the pilot's*
> *opinion, would place the aircraft in jeopardy,*
> *it is the pilot's responsibility to request an*
> *amended clearance. Furthermore, if a pilot*
> *prefers to follow a different course of action,*
> *he is expected to inform ATC accordingly.*[120]

Implied in the BATM, and in the defense used by the FAA in most cases, is the premise by which counsel has sought in court to exonerate the FAA and to dismiss the agency from proximate responsibility for aircraft mishaps. The statement above, taken from the BATM, under girds the FAA's policy in this regard—a position which has been upheld in numerous court cases where ATC responsibility was in question. A classic example came as a result of the Trans World Airlines flight 514 crash near Dulles International Airport in 1974. The NTSB accident investigation report results demonstrated ATC error, but, nevertheless, blamed the pilots, because "they should have realized" the altitude published on an approach plate, from whence they were to commence an approach, might not be a safe altitude. In a subsequent lawsuit against the United States, the widows of the deceased pilots were unable to recover damages because the "primary negligence" was held by the pilots, who were not "helpless," and, therefore, held the "last clear chance" to avoid the accident.[121] Other similar cases follow in the briefs for this chapter.

---

[120] FAA Academy, *Basic Air Traffic Manual*, TM 12-0-3 (Sep. 1983).
[121] *Brock v. United States*, 14 Avi. Cas. (CCH) ¶ 19,246 (E.D. Va. 1977), *aff'd* 596 F.2d 92 (4th Cir. 1979).

GAUNCE v. DeVINCENTIS
708 F.2d 1290 (7th Cir. 1983)

*Must the administrative process be completed before the
judicial review process is commenced?*

The FAA sent notice to Martha Gaunce, informing her of the proposed revocation of her airman certificate for:

- operating an aircraft without having in her possession a current pilot or medical certificate;
- failing to have accomplished a current biennial flight review;
- violating air traffic control clearance;
- twice refusing to present her pilot logbook for inspection; and
- operating the aircraft carelessly, so as to endanger the life and property of another.

Gaunce was also informed of several options available to her. She chose to be heard in an informal conference.

Based on its finding that nothing occurred at the informal conference to alter the proposed revocation order, the FAA went ahead and issued its order of revocation. Gaunce was informed she could appeal to the National Transportation Safety Board. She did not appeal to the NTSB at that time (July 18, 1980), but did later appeal to the Board on November 30, 1980.

On December 3, 1980, only days after filing her appeal with the NTSB, she instituted suit against the FAA in the U.S. District Court. At issue was the claim that revocation of her airman certificate was a violation of the Fifth Amendment's due process requirements. Also at issue were claims for monetary damages against FAA employees. On the foregoing issues, the District Court summarily ruled in favor of the FAA on May 6, 1981. Gaunce filed her notice of appeal to the U.S. Court of Appeals on May 14, 1981. In the meantime, the NTSB affirmed the FAA revocation order, but modified it to suspension for 150 days and imposed a re-examination requirement.

The U.S. Court of Appeals determined the District Court erred in even hearing the complaint. The basic issue of whether the district court possessed subject matter jurisdiction had been completely ignored. Where Congress has provided a statutory procedure for review of an administrative order, such procedure is exclusive. An appellant may not dispense with the requirement of prior administrative review. It would have been improper for the U.S. Court of Appeals to decide on the issues raised in this case, because the appellant had not exhausted her administrative remedies. The statutes call for filing a petition in the court of appeals within 60 days of the conclusion of the administrative process. The time requirement had been totally ignored, and no reasonable grounds for ignoring it had been shown.

The Court of Appeals dismissed the appeal, vacated the District Court's judgment, and remanded the case to the district court with instructions to *dismiss* the complaint for lack of subject matter jurisdiction.

FERGUSON v. NATIONAL TRANSPORTATION SAFETY BOARD
678 F.2d 821 (9th Cir. 1982)

Is it reckless conduct for a pilot to land without
clearance at the wrong airport?

Lowell Ferguson was a pilot-in-command for Western Airlines, with over 12,000 hours of flying, and he had never been found in violation of any Federal Aviation Regulations. On a flight from Denver to Sheridan, Wyoming, Ferguson landed by mistake at the wrong airport. The flight was 35 minutes behind schedule. At night, but with unrestricted visibility, air traffic control offered a direct clearance to Sheridan along an airway, which passed directly over an airport in Buffalo, Wyoming. Ferguson accepted the new routing in order to save time and fuel. Neither Ferguson nor his co-pilot James Bastiani had flown into Sheridan before, but each thought the other had. At about 10:00 p.m., both pilots saw runway lights and commenced a visual approach to what they thought was Sheridan. It was not until the aircraft's nose wheel sank in the turnoff pad beyond the runway that Ferguson realized they had landed in Buffalo instead of Sheridan.

The FAA Administrator ordered suspension of Ferguson's Airline Transport Pilot certificate for 60 days, violating Ferguson with four sections of the Federal Aviation Regulations:

- deviating from an air traffic control clearance;
- landing at an airport not certified for air carrier operations;

- landing at an airport not listed in the Western Airlines Operations specifications; and
- operating an aircraft in a careless or reckless manner so as to endanger the life or property of another.

A hearing was held before an administrative law judge who affirmed the 60-day suspension. Ferguson filed an appeal, but the NTSB affirmed the suspension. The order of suspension was stayed, pending the disposition of the case by the U.S. Court of Appeals.

Ferguson felt he was qualified for a waiver of punishment under FAA Advisory Circular, AC 00-46B, because his actions in landing at the wrong airport were "inadvertent and not deliberate." The ALJ, affirmed by the NTSB, concluded that Ferguson's conduct was "reckless." Ferguson's argument in his appeal to the court was one of semantics. He contended that: (1) the NTSB improperly interpreted the phrase "inadvertent and not deliberate" and (2) the NTSB erred in affirming the conclusion that his action was "reckless."

The appellate court was limited in review of the NTSB decision by the standards of the Administrative Procedure Act. Unless the decision was "arbitrary, capricious, an abuse of discretion, or otherwise not in accordance with the law, or unsupported by substantial evidence," in an issue over semantics, the court was bound to give *deference to the administrative agency's interpretation of its own regulations*. The Administrator indicated that the FAA had established AC 00-46B in order to obtain information that would aid in discovering and preventing unsafe conditions. The first AC 00-46 included a waiver of certain disciplinary actions in return for a timely written report. The Advisory Circular expressly stated that the waiver applied "except with respect to reckless operations, criminal offenses, gross negligence, willful misconduct and accidents."

In the court's view the FAA did not intend to increase the number of circumstances in which waivers of punishment would apply. Thus, Ferguson's interpretation of the AC was erroneous and the FAA's was not. The court held that the NTSB did not abuse its discretion in interpreting AC 00-46B. Neither the historical background nor the language of the circular indicated that reckless conduct could be considered "inadvertent and not deliberate." It also concluded that the NTSB did not abuse its discretion in affirming the administrative law judge's conclusion that Ferguson's conduct was "reckless." Although he did not knowingly land his aircraft at the wrong airport, he should have known that his conduct demonstrated a gross disregard for safety and created an actual danger to life and property.

The court of appeals affirmed the decision of the NTSB.

SORENSON v. NATIONAL TRANSPORTATION SAFETY BOARD
684 F.2d 683 (10th Cir. 1982)

Is a pilot entitled to Miranda warnings before being cited for violation of Federal Aviation Regulations?

In September of 1979, Lee Sorenson, a commercial pilot, prepared to depart from the Fresno Air Terminal alone in his private airplane. On the way to his aircraft he was observed by witnesses who later testified he had trouble walking, his speech was slurred, he spilled coffee from his cup, he spilled a considerable amount of oil on his clothes, shoes and on the ground, and he smelled strongly of wine or alcohol. Airport security and members of the Air National Guard were called to investigate. Sorenson taxied his aircraft but was signaled to stop and deplane. A sobriety test was administered which required recital of the alphabet. Sorenson had trouble reciting past the letter "M." It was suggested that Sorenson wait a few hours before flying. There was neither arrest nor further incident. Sorenson walked away and did not return for several hours.

The Federal Aviation Administration ordered the revocation of Sorenson's pilot certificate based on the allegation that he was operating an aircraft while under the influence of alcohol. Sorenson appealed and at the hearing testified he was not intoxicated. He explained the smell of wine was from some wine spilled on his clothing the night before, and his bad back caused his unsteadiness and staggering. The ALJ found that Sorenson had violated the regulations as alleged; i.e., piloting an aircraft within eight hours of drinking alcoholic beverage or while under the influence of alcohol; and for reckless or careless operation of an aircraft. Sorenson appealed to the National Transportation Safety Board. The NTSB affirmed the Administrator's revocation of the pilot certificate.

Sorenson then appealed to the U.S. Court of Appeals claiming several evidentiary and constitutional errors, arguing:

- The Board's finding of intoxication was not supported by substantial evidence;
- His administrative hearing did not comply with the requirements of due process because the Administrator never presented empirical evidence of intoxication;
- The field sobriety test should have been excluded because he was not read his *Miranda* rights (i.e., the right to have an attorney present, the right to remain silent, etc.); and
- The Board's findings were not supported by sufficient evidence because the government's evidence constituted uncorroborated hearsay under the *Federal Rules of Evidence*.

To Sorenson's claims, the court determined:

- On review, the Board's findings of fact must be upheld if they are supported by substantial evidence in the record. The appellate court's function is not to weigh the evidence, or to evaluate the witnesses' credibility. The witnesses' observations were sufficient to establish that Sorenson was under the influence of alcohol;
- Circumstantial evidence may be used by the Administrator. The witnesses' observations provided substantial and direct evidence of his intoxication, and empirical evidence was not necessary to prove a violation of the regulations;
- The *Miranda* case concerned the admissibility of statements in a criminal proceeding obtained from a defendant questioned while in custody or otherwise significantly deprived of his freedom. Sorenson was allowed to leave, he was not detained nor questioned in a coercive way, he suffered no inconvenience, and his freedom was only briefly inhibited. It could not have been considered "custodial interrogation;" and
- Under the Administrative Procedure Act an agency need only exclude "irrelevant, immaterial or unduly repetitious evidence." Otherwise, any documentary or oral evidence may be received.

Finally, Sorenson contended that the regulations were unconstitutionally vague, because the phrase "under the influence of alcohol" is indefinite. In response, the Court said that the ordinary meaning of the words is clear. The regulations sufficiently informed (i.e., gave fair warning) to Sorenson, so his contention was without merit. The order of the Board was affirmed.

BOSSO v. WEITHONER
17 Av. Cas. (CCH) ¶ 17,708 (10th Cir. 1982)

Must the FAA Administrator grant an exception based upon a convincing showing that an applicant has fully recovered from disabilities?

In 1979, Armand Bosso applied to the Federal Aviation Administration for an airman's medical certificate. The certificate was first granted, but was then withdrawn because Mr. Bosso had a medical history of psychosis—a permanent disqualification. Bosso requested an extension of time within which he could seek review of the denial of his application. He then applied for an exemption from the limitations. To his petition for exemption, he attached extensive medical records and favorable reports of his present mental condition.

The petition for exemption was denied. The FAA neither refuted the favorable medical reports, nor did it provide explanation of the denial. Bosso sought a *writ of mandamus* to compel the FAA to grant the exemption or otherwise explain the denial.

The U.S. District Court dismissed the action for lack of jurisdiction. Bosso appealed the case, contending that both the Federal Aviation Act of 1958[122] and the principles of *due process* required the Administrator to make findings of fact explaining the denial. Bosso's interpretation of the Federal Aviation Act was that it meant the Administrator was required to state a factual analysis of determination of the evidence presented that Bosso had recovered from any illness and was entirely stable mentally.

The U.S. Court of Appeals stated that in making his argument, Bosso misunderstood the nature of the exemption process. The Administrator is permitted (i.e., at his *discretion*) to allow exemptions if such an exemption would be "in the public interest." The petitioner had to demonstrate a positive benefit to the public by an exemption, and not show simply that his flying would not be a public danger. The Administrator was not bound (again, it is "discretionary") to grant an

---

[122] 49 U.S.C. §§ 1301-1541.

exemption, even when the applicant could show he had fully recovered from his disability. The history of psychosis is a fact. The disqualifying regulation reflects an administrative determination that such a history presents enough danger to be sufficient for a permanent denial of a certificate. The Court expressed its sensitivity to the hardship and sense of unfairness felt by Bosso, but noted that Congress gave great discretionary power to the FAA. It should be noted the determination that psychosis is a permanent disqualification was not only an FAA administrative decision, it was also supported by a Flight Safety Foundation report as one of a set of disorders permitting permanent disqualification. The District Court's dismissal for lack of subject matter jurisdiction was affirmed.

PASTRANA v. UNITED STATES
746 F. 2d 1447 (11ᵗʰ Cir. 1984)

Is an airline pilot's certificate a Constitutionally protected
right under the Fifth Amendment?

On October 28, 1981, Raul Pastrana was the pilot-in-command of an Eastern Air Lines flight. During the landing rollout, the aircraft's left landing gear left the runway for a distance of about 200 feet. Mud covered the tires and dirt and grass had been ingested into an engine, resulting in cancellation of the subsequent flight with the aircraft. Bryant Chestnutt, in his capacity as an airline inspector for the FAA, requested a meeting with Pastrana and his crew, to which Pastrana refused to participate because he had not yet had an opportunity to meet with his union representative. Upon this refusal, Inspector Chestnutt served a letter to Pastrana ordering re-examination of his pilot qualifications. He also advised Eastern not to use Pastrana as pilot-in-command until satisfactory completion of the re-examination. On October 30, 1981, Eastern removed Pastrana from flight and pay status, predicated upon the FAA (Chestnutt's) directive. It was not until November 12, 1981, that the FAA Southern Region Counsel's office issued an Emergency Order of Suspension pursuant to statute (49 U.S.C. § 1429).

Captain Pastrana brought action against Chestnutt individually and in his official capacity as an employee of the FAA for suspending his pilot's certificate, and against Eastern Air Lines for the consequent suspension of his employment. He argued that:

- His pilot certificate was a prerequisite to his employment as a pilot with Eastern;
- Inspector Chestnutt acted under color of his authority to deprive him of his pilot certificate;
- Such action was beyond Chestnutt's statutory or regulatory authority; and
- Such illegal action deprived him of a constitutionally protected property interest without notice and hearing, and violated his right to due process under the Fifth Amendment.

The U.S. District Court dismissed Pastrana's various Constitutional tort claims against the United States and the FAA's employee Bryant Chestnutt, finding that a pre-suspension hearing was not required under 49 U.S.C. § 1429. In fact, the statute allowed appropriate FAA officials to suspend a pilot certificate in case of emergency. The doctrine of sovereign immunity bars suit against the U.S. where employees are exercising discretionary functions. The court also dismissed the claims against Eastern Air Lines. Pastrana appealed, not rebutting the doctrine of sovereign immunity, nor contesting the dismissal of his common law tort claims against Chestnutt, nor his claims against Eastern. Still at issue, however, was the potential civil liability of Inspector Chestnutt for allegedly acting beyond his authority in ordering Eastern not to use Pastrana as pilot-in-command.

The U.S. Court of Appeals reversed the finding of the District Court, and determined that Pastrana had asserted a Constitutionally protected right and an appropriate cause of action. Pastrana's pilot certificate, a predicate to his employment as a pilot, was determined to be a cognizable property interest protectable by the procedural due process requirement of the Fifth Amendment. 49 U.S.C. § 1429 granted the FAA Administrator the authority to re-examine any civilian pilot from time to time, and if the public interest in air safety required, the Administrator could amend, modify, suspend, or revoke a pilot's certificate as necessary. However, except in an emergency, no such order could take effect until the certificate holder had been given notice and an opportunity for a hearing. Investigators were not empowered to issue suspension orders, only a few high-ranking officials within the FAA were so empowered. Investigator Chestnutt (likely) exceeded his authority, but the appellate court stated it was up to a district court to find any potential liability. The dismissal by the District Court was vacated and the case remanded for further action.

EMELWON, INC. v. UNITED STATES
391 F.2d 9 (5th Cir. 1968)

Is a contractor an employee of the federal government?

The State of Florida, through its Game and Fresh Water Fish Commission, carried out an aerial spraying program for the United States Government. It was claimed that damage sustained by growing crops was the result of negligent spraying from an airplane of the herbicide *2,4-D* to eradicate water hyacinth and other noxious vegetation. Suit was brought against the United States under the Federal Tort Claims Act. The U.S. District Court directed a verdict for the United States on the ground that the State of Florida was neither an agent nor an employee of the United States, but was an independent contractor. Thus, the United States could not be liable under the Federal Tort Claims Act. The plaintiffs appealed.

The U.S. Court of Appeals held that in light of Florida law, the district court was in error, and failed to properly apply the law of Florida to the Federal Tort Claims Act. The FTCA imposes liability on the United States for acts of its employees. Florida law holds that the employer directly responsible for the legal duties its employees may have failed to discharge. Where an employer gains knowledge of a dangerous situation created by an independent contractor, it may incur liability through its failure to halt the operation or otherwise remove the danger. One who employs an independent contractor to engage in certain types of activity has a *non-delegable duty* to see to it that the independent contractor carries out its task in a non-negligent manner. Liability is imposed on the employer for its own failure to exercise reasonable care. The employer is liable for breach of its own non-delegable duty to take precautions against harm to third parties. It is enough that the employer has knowledge the independent contractor has created a situation, which poses the danger of injury to others.

Under the Federal Tort Claims Act the government is liable "in the same manner and to the same extent as a private individual under like circumstances. . . ." Under the extant circumstances, Florida law would permit the plaintiff to prove the employer of an independent contractor failed to exercise reasonable care. The plaintiff should have been allowed to have a jury decide whether employees of the United States negligently breached the duty imposed on an employer who discovers a dangerous situation created by its independent contractor, or to exercise reasonable care to prevent harm from an inherently dangerous activity carried out by an independent contractor.

The case was reversed and remanded.

WENZEL v. UNITED STATES
419 F.2d 260 (3rd Cir. 1969)

Is an air traffic controller negligent for information not considered the proximate cause of an accident?

Laurence Wenzel and his co-pilot took off from McChord Air Force Base in a commercial C-46 twin-engine cargo airplane. Six minutes after takeoff the plane's left engine developed a runaway propeller, and the crew requested permission to return to McChord. At that time the airplane was 13 miles northeast of McChord. The controller concluded that an emergency existed and he alerted the Radar Approach Control facility at McChord of the condition. As the plane was returning, the controller reported the position of the aircraft to the crew as being about nine miles northeast of McChord and "exactly five miles north of the runway at Thun Field." The crew otherwise had no knowledge of Thun Field, nor were they aware of its existence. Thus, the crew relied upon the controller for information regarding Thun Field. Upon learning of their proximity to Thun, the crew asked to have the field flash its landing lights and requested radar vector to Thun. The controller gave directional guidance and then volunteered "The length of the runway is 5300." As the plane approached for landing, it reported it was high and making a go-around. While over the runway, the plane turned left sharply, climbed over trees, and crashed a mile-and-a-half northeast of Thun. It was later determined by the court the actual length of the runway was 3,040 feet, but with a corrected length of only 2,667 feet.

Wenzel contended the defendant's negligence in reporting the correct runway length was the *proximate* cause of the accident. First, had the controller provided proper information, Wenzel would have probably proceeded back to McChord; and second, had the controller provided accurate information, a different approach and successful landing at Thun could have been accomplished.

The U.S. District Court found that Wenzel failed to sustain his burden of showing the defendant's negligence was a proximate cause of the accident. Wenzel appealed.

The U.S. Court of Appeals upheld the district court's findings that Wenzel did successfully execute a missed approach, and after that, crashed for some other unknown cause:

> *Whether the immediate cause of the crash was another runaway propeller or an explosion or too steep a banking turn too near the ground with wing tip contact with a ground obstruction is neither disclosed by nor to be inferred from the evidence in the case. . . . The controller did nothing to control or influence the handling of the aircraft which was in the exclusive control and the primary responsibility of the plaintiff as pilot. . . . In consequence of the long period of unconsciousness, which he suffered following the crash, the plaintiff was unable to recall any of the events immediately preceding the crash.*

The Court of Appeals determined the judgment of the District Court to be sound and right, and affirmed its decision.

SPURGIN-DIENST v. UNITED STATES
359 F.3d 451 (7th Cir. 2004)

> *Does the FAA have a duty to prohibit general aviation pilots from flying into bad weather?*

Piloting a small airplane with three passengers aboard, Daniel Sanders departed from Louisville, Kentucky, bound for Aurora, Illinois, when he encountered icing conditions, forcing an emergency landing at a small airport near New Lebanon, Indiana. Before departure and filing of a flight plan, he was given Airman's Meteorological Information [AIRMET] warning of "moderate rime or mixed icing along the entire route of the flight" to Aurora, and pilot reports of "light to moderate rime icing." While *en route*, he radioed the Evansville approach controller for icing reports in the area. The controller falsely reported there had been none for the last two hours, when in fact there had, though they referred to areas not in Sanders' flight path. As Sanders descended, he noted the ice building up on his wings causing his airplane to lose thrust and lift, and asked the controller to guide him to the closest airport. The controller informed Sanders that the closest airport was at New Lebanon, about 2.5 miles away, when in fact, it was five miles away. He crashed about five miles from the airport, killing all aboard.

The District Court Judge concluded that although Sanders had been misinformed and misdirected by ATC as he attempted to land, his decision to fly into icy conditions was the proximate cause of the crash. The Court of Appeals found that ATC was under no duty to prohibit a general aviation pilot from taking off in hazardous weather. It also agreed with the District Court's conclusion that the decedent knew he was flying into icing conditions, and that had the controllers provided more up-to-date information as requested, this information would not have led him to change course. Hence, the proximate cause of his death was his own decision to fly in poor weather conditions rather than the subsequent negligence of air traffic controllers.

THINGULDSTAD v. UNITED STATES
343 F. Supp. 51 (S.D. Ohio 1972)

> *Is detection of wake turbulence the responsibility*
> *of the pilot or of air traffic control?*

Arthur M. Thinguldstad was flying a Piper Cherokee on final approach to land at Port Columbus International Airport at Columbus, Ohio. His aircraft was overtaken by a Trans World Airlines Constellation and Thinguldstad crashed shortly thereafter. Ruth Thinguldstad alleged the United States, by and through its agents, employees of the FAA, was negligent in the manner in which they controlled and directed the aircraft flown by her husband and the TWA Constellation. She claimed that due to air traffic control negligence her husband's airplane encountered wake turbulence caused by the Constellation, and the turbulence caused the crash.

In 1966, when the crash occurred, the phenomenon of wake turbulence and wing tip vortices was well known and had been the subject of warnings to pilot's of small aircraft for a number of years. Ruth Thinguldstad alleged ATC was negligent for failing to give her husband timely and proper warning of wake turbulence, and in failing to maintain proper separation of the two aircraft. The Constellation overtook the Cherokee about seven miles from the runway end. ATC re-sequenced Thinguldstad's aircraft to land behind the TWA flight. Thinguldstad was asked by ATC if he wanted an alternate runway or if he preferred to follow the Constellation. He chose to land on the same runway. No warning of possible wake turbulence was given until about two minutes later, or about the time of the crash.

The United States argued that any encounter with wake turbulence would have taken place approximately 3.4 miles from the end of the runway. If wake turbulence were encountered 3.4 miles out, the evidence indicated Thinguldstad would have flown through it by the time he reached a spot over the impact point. Eyewitnesses testified the airplane nosed over and came straight down. Experts from both sides agreed that had Thinguldstad been caught in one of the vortex cores there would have been pitching or rolling of the aircraft.

The U.S. presented substantial evidence to indicate Mr. Thinguldstad crashed due to incapacitation from heart condition compounded by accumulation of carbon monoxide in the blood.

The Court determined the plaintiff had not met the burden of proof, and had not established, by a preponderance of the evidence, that any negligence on the part of the government employees was the proximate cause of the crash. The court further concluded there was a second and independent legal basis for denying any recovery by the plaintiff. The primary responsibility for the safe operation of an aircraft is upon the pilot. Moreover, the pilot must exercise ordinary care for personal safety. If Thinguldstad was indeed flying into wake turbulence, he was in the best position to realize it, and he took no evasive action. He even declined to accept the alternate runway for landing. Judgment was entered for the defendant.

FELDER v. UNITED STATES
543 F.2d 657 (9th Cir. 1976)

*Is air traffic control responsible for issuing warnings
of possible wake turbulence?*

A Lufthansa Airlines Boeing 707 was performing touch-and-go operations at Tucson International Airport, and had just taken off. Harry Felder was preparing to resume his flight to Phoenix, Arizona, in his Piper Comanche and was cleared for take-off. Felder was not given any cautionary warning of possible wake turbulence, and it was reasonable to infer from the evidence that Felder did not know the Boeing 707 had just departed. By the time he had reached the take-off point, the 707 was already airborne and was not readily visible to him. The Comanche climbed approximately 150 to 250 feet when Felder lost control. The plane flipped over abruptly, spiraled nose-down and crashed. Felder and two passengers were killed. The encounter with wake turbulence was determined to be the proximate cause of the crash.

The U.S. District Court determined that air traffic control was negligent when it failed to issue a wake turbulence warning to Felder when it cleared him for take-off, or when it failed to delay his departure until a possible wake turbulence encounter would have been avoided. The Court awarded monetary damages, but in making the award, the court deducted income taxes in computing future lost earnings. The U.S. appealed, objecting to the trial judge's calculations and attacking the total amount of the judgment as excessive and therefore punitive. Plaintiffs cross-appealed contending the District Judge erred as a matter of law in subtracting from their awards estimated income taxes that would have been paid on lost income.

Under the Federal Tort Claims Act the United States is liable for tort claims, in the same manner and to the same extent as a private individual under like circumstances, but shall not be liable for interest prior to judgment or for *punitive damages*. The purpose of the FTCA is compensation. It is intended to repay the amount of loss or injury sustained as a proximate result of government misconduct. Although the Act does not define "punitive damages," they may be thought of generally as damages intended to punish or deter. Failure to deduct income taxes would result in plaintiffs receiving greater financial support than they would have in the normal course of events. The Court determined the effect of such an award would be punitive and not permissible under the Federal Tort Claims Act.

The court also concluded it was necessary to reduce some of the awards and to increase one. However, rather than remand for recalculation, the appellate court calculated the awards itself. The U.S. Court of Appeals affirmed the District Court on the issue of damages, but remanded with directions to enter a modified judgment in the recalculated amount, incorporating deductions for income taxes.

MILLER v. UNITED STATES
587 F.2d 991 (9th Cir. 1978)

Must an air traffic controller issue a second
warning of wake turbulence?

Michael Lee Reilly was killed when the airplane in which he was riding as a passenger crashed at the Fairbanks International Airport. His mother, Helen E. Miller, brought suit against the United States under the Federal Tort Claims Act, claiming that the air traffic controller, an employee of the United States, had been negligent. The United States filed a third-party complaint against David A. Miller, the decedent's stepfather, who was pilot of the airplane. The District Court Judge, sitting without a jury, entered judgment in favor of Helen Miller, finding the United States and David Miller each 50% negligent in causing the death of Michael Reilly. Both the United States and Helen Miller appealed.

David Miller was performing touch-and-go landings in a two-seater Piper Colt airplane. Prior to the crash, Miller contacted the control tower and was advised by Audree Knutzen, the air traffic controller, that a Lockheed L-100 Hercules aircraft was departing the runway. Miller asked for authorization to execute a 360 degree turn to lose time. Knutzen was unable to approve the request because of following traffic, but told Miller he could extend his approach pattern for spacing. Miller agreed to the traffic pattern extension, and Knutzen advised him, "Caution, wake turbulence." Miller flew the extended approach and landed 4,000 to 5,000 feet down the runway approximately two minutes after the Hercules had departed. Miller rolled 300 to 400 feet down the runway before becoming airborne again. Shortly after becoming airborne, the Miller plane crashed.

The District Court Judge found that wake turbulence from the Hercules was the cause of the crash. Miller was found negligent in the manner he operated the airplane, and Knutzen was negligent in failing to conform to a reasonable standard to adequately warn Miller a second time. The Judge relied upon *United States v. Furumizo,*[123] wherein it was determined "the danger was extreme and the controllers knew it."

In the present case, however, there was no finding that the Miller aircraft faced an extreme danger or severe hazard (emergency situation). The appellate court determined Miller was advised of the departure of the Hercules, and as an experienced pilot this should have put him on notice about any possible wake turbulence. The controller then expressly warned Miller about wake turbulence. "This suggests that Miller may have had two warnings." Hence, the appellate court held that the trial judge erred in his determination of the controller's standard of conduct and the duty to give the additional warning. The judgment of the District Court against the United States was reversed.

IN RE AIR CRASH DISASTER AT NEW ORLEANS
544 F.2d 270 (6th Cir. 1976)

Is an air traffic control clearance for a low approach
the same as a "clearance to land?"

The pilot of a chartered DC-3 had been warned by air traffic control during a flight from Memphis to New Orleans that Moisant Field had visibility (600 feet) below the minimum requirement (2,400 feet) for landing. The pilot decided to continue to Moisant and asked for and received permission to come in for a low level approach and "look at it." Apparently relying upon the clearance to make a low level approach, but without ever asking for or receiving "clearance to land" the pilot made the approach, reported "the strobe lights in sight," and then descended below the decision height, at which point a missed approach should be commenced. The aircraft struck the runway at an angle, bounced but failed to gain altitude, then crashed in flames.

---

[123] 381 F.2d 965 (9th Cir. 1967)

Suit was filed claiming air traffic controller negligence. The plaintiffs argued the controller should have realized the crew would follow his advice, make an approach, descend to and, if practicable, continue below decision height and attempt to land. The plaintiffs contended the following transmission helped induce the pilot errors and the crash. Communications before commencing the approach were as follows:

- PILOT, "Ah roger, ah, will we be legal to make a pass and look at it?"
- CONTROLLER, "I can clear you for an approach, ah, yes, ah, you can make a low approach if you'd like."
- PILOT, "Ah, roger, well, if, ah, we can get contact with the ground will we be legal to land if that's six hundred feet?"
- CONTROLLER, "Four Two Delta, according to the approach plates if you get the runway or approach lights in sight, ah, correction on that, it says, ah, descent not authorized, well actually what it should say is that, ah, the approach plate is, ah, self explanatory. If you can see the runway or approach lights, affirmative, you can land."

Communications after commencing final approach were:

- PILOT, "Ah, roger, we're approaching the outer marker. We're going to make a low pass, see if we can pick up the lights."
- CONTROLLER, "Roger."
- PILOT, "Four Two Delta got the strobe lights in sight."
- CONTROLLER, "Roger."

The aircraft then descended and crashed. The plaintiffs argued that having placed the aircraft in a position of peril, the government was liable for the consequences that followed. The United States argued that the clearance to land is only given when it is asked for, and the pilot never asked for or received a clearance to land. The District Court Judge determined it was extremely unreasonable for the pilot to assume that he had a landing clearance, even if he had thought one had been implied earlier. He found that negligence of the pilot was "the sole proximate cause" of the crash. He also found negligence on the part of the controller, but that it was not the *proximate* cause. An air traffic controller is not expected to be able to quote verbatim regulations primarily designed for the pilot. The plaintiffs appealed.

The U.S. Court of Appeals looked for guidance in the Federal Aviation Regulations and in the *Airman's Information Manual.* FAR 91.115, "ATC clearance and flight plan required," read as follows:

> *No person may operate an aircraft in controlled airspace under IFR unless: (a) He has filed an IFR flight plan; and (b) He has received an appropriate ATC clearance.*

These same principles are spelled out even more clearly in the *Airman's Information Manual* with respect to the meaning of "Clearance":

> *A clearance issued by ATC is predicated on known traffic and known physical airport conditions. An ATC clearance means—an authorization by ATC, for the purpose of preventing collision between known aircraft, for an aircraft to proceed under specified conditions within controlled airspace. It is not authorized for a pilot to deviate from any rule or regulation nor to conduct unsafe operation of his aircraft. FAR 91.3(a) states:*

> *The pilot in command of an aircraft is directly responsible for, and is the final authority as to, the operation of that aircraft. If ATC issues a clearance that would cause a pilot to deviate from a rule or regulation, or in the pilot's opinion, would place the aircraft in jeopardy, it is the pilot's responsibility to request an amended clearance. Similarly, if a pilot prefers to follow a different course of action; e.g., land on a different runway, takeoff from the threshold instead of an intersection, etc., he is expected to inform ATC accordingly.*

> *When he requests a different course of action,*
> *however, the pilot is expected to cooperate so*
> *as to preclude disruption of traffic flow or*
> *creation of conflicting patterns.*

The appellate court determined that FAA regulations *require* a pilot to secure a clearance to land. They affirmed the judgment of the District Court. The District Judge's findings were not erroneous and he did not misapply the applicable FAA regulations.

DEHAINAUT v. PEÑA
32 F.3d 1066 (7th Cir. 1994)

> *Did the government's policy, of indefinitely barring from*
> *employment a group of former air traffic controllers,*
> *violate their constitutional rights?*

A group of former air traffic controllers, who had been fired for their participation in a 1981 strike against the federal government, filed a class action suit against the DOT, the FAA, and the Office of Personnel Management [OPM], seeking mandamus and injunctive relief and a declaratory judgment that OPM's policy of indefinitely barring them from employment with the FAA and related agencies was unconstitutional. Plaintiffs alleged that the policy violated the Constitution as a *bill of attainder*; an *ex post facto* law; a denial of *due process*; and a denial of *equal protection.*

The district court granted the defendant's motion to dismiss, and the plaintiffs appealed.

A federal statute provides that "[a]n individual may not accept or hold a position in the Government of the United States" if he "participates in a strike against the Government of the United States."[124] When a person is disqualified from continued employment, OPM, in its discretion, can debar that person from employment for three years, and the person may not be appointed to any position in the competitive service until his or her fitness for appointment has been re-determined.

On the first day of the strike in 1981, Ronald Reagan issued an ultimatum to the striking controllers to either return to work within 48

---

[124] 5 U.S.C. § 7311.

hours, or forfeit their jobs. Shortly thereafter, OPM announced that it intended to apply the maximum three-year debarment allowed by law. President Reagan, however, issued a directive modifying the debarment policy, concluding that the controllers, despite their strike participation, should be permitted to apply for federal employment outside the scope of the FAA and air traffic control. He further determined that it would be detrimental to the efficiency of operations at the FAA, and the safety of the air traffic control system, to permit the discharged controllers to return to the FAA. The Office of Personnel Management subsequently issued Federal Personnel Bulletin 731-6, announcing that:

> *All persons whose employment was terminated on account of the strike by air traffic controllers, which began on or about August 3, 1981, shall be determined not to be suitable for reinstatement or appointment in any position in the FAA, because it would be detrimental to the efficiency of that agency by interfacing with or preventing its effective performance of its duties and responsibilities.*

In response to the plaintiffs' allegations, the court first pointed out that a "bill of attainder" is a law that legislatively determines guilt and inflicts punishment upon an identifiable individual without provision of the protections of a judicial trial. In this case, however, the court could find neither a reasonable inference, nor "unmistakable evidence" of any punitive intent.

Second, the *ex post facto* provision of the U.S. Constitution[125] forbids Congress to enact any law "which imposes a punishment for an act which was not punishable at the time it was committed, or imposes additional punishment to that then prescribed." But the sanction levied here—ineligibility for certain federal jobs—is *civil*, not *criminal*, and from "earliest times," the Supreme Court has construed the *ex post facto* provision to apply only to criminal laws.

Third, the court did not find any violation of "due process." The disbarment from employment against striking employees[126] contem-

---

[125] U.S. Constitution Art. I, § 9.
[126] 5 U.S.C. § 7311.

plates the possibility of an indefinite ban. Moreover, Congress has delegated broad authority to the President to establish the qualifications and conditions of employment for civil servants. Additionally, the Director of OPM has broad discretion in interpreting a presidential directive relating to federal personnel matters. In the court's view, OPM had reasonably interpreted the language of the presidential ban upon the employment of controllers removed for striking.

Finally, as to the claim of "denied equal protection" under OPM's indefinite disbarment policy, the court stated that OPM's policy need only "withstand rational basis review." In the court's opinion, the explanations offered in the presidential directive rationally advanced the legitimate governmental objectives of safety and efficiency in the administration of the nation's air traffic system.

The U.S. Court of Appeals affirmed the district court's findings that: the Office of Personnel Management reasonably interpreted President Reagan's order regarding air traffic controllers who violated federal law by striking against the United States; OPM's policies implementing the presidential directive did not violate either the Bill of Attainder Clause or the *Ex Post Facto* Clause, and also did not deny the plaintiffs due process or equal protection of the law.

JIFRY v. FEDERAL AVIATION ADMINISTRATION
370 F.3d 1174 (D.C. Cir. 2004)

May the FAA abort the traditional "notice and comment"
rulemaking process in emergencies, and revoke airman
certificates of non-resident aliens on security grounds
without running afoul of the Fifth Amendment?

After the terrorist events of September 1, 2001, the nascent Transportation Security Administration promulgated regulations without notice having been published in the *Federal Register* and comment invited. Two pilots, who were non-residents and citizens of Saudi Arabia, appealed revocation of their airman certificates. They also objected to the regulations under which their certificates were revoked on grounds that they were improperly promulgated and denied them Fifth Amendment due process.

The U.S. Court of Appeals for the District of Columbia Circuit noted that Congress had given the FAA broad discretion to promulgate regulations prescribing safety and security in aviation.[127] The FAA may also "at any time" suspend or revoke an airman certificate if it determines that such action is necessary to advance "safety in air commerce" and "the public interest."[128] Particularly broad discretion is conferred regarding alien pilots.[129]

The FAA sent a letter to the pilots informing them that "based upon information available to us," they posed "a security risk to aviation or national security." The FAA revoked their certificates, and the two pilots appealed to the NTSB. Meanwhile, without notice and comment, the FAA and the TSA promulgated regulations providing for automatic suspension of airman certificates upon notification from TSA that the pilot poses a security threat.[130] Using these regulations, the FAA revoked the airman certificates of the two Saudi pilots. On appeal, the NTSB affirmed the revocations.

The Court noted that the Administrative Procedure Act includes a "good cause" exception, allowing rules to be promulgated without the traditional notice and comment requirements where "the agency for good cause finds . . . that notice and public procedure thereon are impracticable, unnecessary, or contrary to the public interest."[131] The Court observed that this exception bends the normal "notice and comment" procedural requirements in emergency situations where delay could result in serious harm. TSA argued that the regulations needed to be promulgated expeditiously "to prevent imminent hazard to aircraft, persons, and property within the United States." The Court upheld the regulations and the procedures under which they were adopted as necessary under the circumstances, and rationally related to the governmental need to protect the public.

An *ex parte* in camera review by the Court of the intelligence reports on the two Saudi pilots led it to conclude that substantial evidence also existed to support TSA's conclusion that the pilots were security risks. The Court also held that non-resident aliens without sufficient contacts with the United States are not entitled to Fifth Amendment protection.

---

[127] 49 U.S.C. § 44701(a)(5).
[128] 49 U.S.C. § 44709(a), (b).
[129] 49 U.S.C. § 44703(e).
[130] 14 CFR § 61.18; 49 CFR § 1540.117.
[131] 5 U.S.C. § 553(b)(3)(B).

Airmen

CHAPTER 9

CONSUMERISM

*Major airline corporations have enormous power. Such power
can result in tension between management and workers, between the
airlines and their customers, and among the airlines themselves.*

PREDOMINANT ISSUES

During the Progressive Era, *competitive capitalism*, exemplified by
many companies competing for a common share of the marketplace,
was transformed into *corporate capitalism.* It was a period from
around the turn-of-the-century to the advent of World War I, when the
laissez-faire competition envisioned by Adam Smith was replaced by
imperfect competition and concentration of capital.[1] With fewer and
much larger corporations, it was feared monopolies would have power
to distort the market, and would thereby disrupt the natural balance
between the marketplace forces of capital, labor and the consumer.

Today, airline companies are corporations with enormous power.
Hence, this chapter and the following two chapters address the tensions
among corporations, workers, and consumers. Legal issues in the airline industry seem to focus on three prevalent topics: consumer protection, labor relations, and corporate deviance (especially by way of
antitrust violations).

A "common carrier," is a company "engaged in the business of
transportation of persons or property from place to place for compensation, and which offers service to the public generally" (as opposed to

---

[1] *See* Adam Smith, *An Inquiry Into the Nature and Causes of the Wealth of Nations* (1776).

a "contract" or "private" carrier). The airlines are, by definition, common carriers. Because they are dealing directly with the public, it is natural that consumer relations would be a major function of an air carrier operation, and that likely there would be situations where differences between the consumer and the carrier could be settled only in court. Thus, consumer protection is at the forefront of air carrier-related legal concerns.

Additionally, in serving the general public, airlines employ large numbers of workers, many of whom are organized in unions. Labor relations, negotiations and litigation are of primary concern to airline management. This emphasis is reinforced by the provisions of the Railway Labor Act, the Airline Deregulation Act, and other federal rules and regulations protective of labor organizations.

In addition to being common carriers and employers, airlines are big business. And whenever big business is in competition, there are concerns of possible monopolistic abuse, unfair commercial practice, and consumer discrimination resulting in unfair rates and charges. Common between competing airlines is a variety of pricing strategies, which attempt to gain market leverage over other companies. When stretched beyond legal limits and the bounds of fair practice, such activities may be in violation of antitrust law.

In all three areas of legal concern, consumer protection, labor relations and antitrust law, the effects of deregulation are intertwined. The Airline Deregulation Act of 1978 reduced economic regulation of the airlines, terminated the Civil Aeronautics Board and its authority over fares, provided for free market entry and/or exit, and shifted antitrust responsibility (in part) from the government back to the airlines. The effects of deregulation are mixed and varied, but clearly, more open competition initially resulted in rapid, and as some analysts maintain, "unstable" growth.

Unstable growth had an effect upon consumers through crowding of airports, delays en route, and potentially lowered service levels. To the unions, deregulation was a disaster. Wages and benefits were significantly decreased, and it became increasingly more difficult for union representatives to negotiate with airline managers faced with stiff competition and reduced earnings. Moreover, fierce competition, combined with regulatory freedom, produced an environment conducive to antitrust abuses at the outset of deregulation.

The Airline Deregulation Act mandated regulatory reform, and as part of the regulatory reform process, provided for "sunset" of the Civil Aeronautics Board [CAB] and the transfer to other agencies of those CAB functions that were to continue. As amended by the Civil Aeronautics Board Sunset Act of 1984, the Airline Deregulation Act provided for transfer of certain functions to the Postal Service and the Justice Department. Most of the CAB functions remaining were transferred to the Department of Transportation [DOT], including:

- *Employee Protection*—providing for the determination of whether the termination of airline employees is due primarily to deregulation, thereby making them eligible for certain benefits;
- *Consumer Protection and Air Carrier Fitness*—programs affecting both foreign and domestic air transportation; and
- *Antitrust Authority*—providing for approval and antitrust immunity for mergers, interlocking relationships, and intercarrier agreements. Other than as it relates to agreements in foreign air transportation, this authority expired on January 1, 1989.

This and the two subsequent chapters address the central topics identified above.

CONSUMER PROTECTION

In Max Weber's perspective, economic concentration evolved in the late 19th Century as a "rational mechanism" against excess competition in the marketplace.[2] At its root was a desire to escape the rigors and uncertainties of competition and to rectify a market business leaders could not otherwise control. Corporate growth was an attempt to stabilize and integrate the economy in such a way that would allow corporations "to function in a predictable and secure environment that would permit reasonable profits over the long run."

The anticompetitive tactics of the emerging giant national corporations, coupled with their sheer size, enabled discriminatory practices against select consumers. For example, the railroads set rates as they

---

[2] *See* Max Weber, *The Theory of Social and Economic Organizations*, A.M. Henderson and Talcott Parsons (translators, 1947).

pleased, and in so doing discriminated in particular against farmers as a group. Reaction to price discrimination practiced by the railroads became the basis for the consumer revolt by the National Grange. What eventually emerged from the Granger movement of the 1870s was the Act to Regulate Commerce of 1887, followed by a subsequent string of economic regulatory laws (including the "antitrust laws") during the Progressive Era and well into the 1930s. Targeted specifically were the discriminatory rate practices of the railroads.

Early in the evolution of regulatory law, the focus shifted from *behavior* of the industry, manifested as discriminatory pricing and other abuses, to concerns about size and corporate (monopolistic) *structure*. Congress assumed the existence of a direct causal link between monopoly and consumer abuse. By 1872, monopolistic abuses were a nationwide problem, and a special committee was established in the U.S. Senate to study the issue. From that Senate committee came the *Windom Report* which concluded the railroads were, indeed, imposing unfair discrimination and extracting extortionate charges. It is of note that the focus of the Windom report was upon the *effects* of consumer abuse rather than its supposed *structural* causes. Still, the Windom Committee did recognize that although Adam Smith's "invisible hand" of competition might well be the ideal regulator, private competition, it said, "invariably ends in combination."[3]

To address widespread price discrimination, and partially as a consequence of the Windom report, the Senate and the House of Representatives separately drew up versions of regulatory bills. Unfortunately, the two houses became deadlocked over their different approaches to the matter, and to break the impasse, another special committee, the Cullom Committee, was appointed to investigate the railroad problem. In 1886, the Cullom Committee reported the existence of discriminatory abuses by the railroads, but in so doing, placed its emphasis not on consumer rights and the effects of the abuses, but on the assumption that the abuses resulted directly from monopoly power. Seemingly, the report altered the course of regulatory social control at this point by shifting the emphasis from the individual victim of discrimination and other consumer abuses to concerns about con-

---

[3] *See* Laurence E. Gesell and Martin T. Farris, *Antitrust Irrelevance in Air Transportation and the Re-Defining of Price Discrimination*, 57 The J. of Air Law and Commerce (1991).

trolling what the committee viewed as the fundamental structural cause of the abuse—monopolistic concentration.

Yet, consumer-oriented regulation was the idealism of legislation adopted during the Progressive Era, and it was during this time that the government, through its administrative powers, began increasingly to regulate and control business organization and the consumption of commodities. But rather than attempting to protect the consumer at the individual level, it was hoped government intervention at the corporate level would aid the individual by stabilizing the economy (and business) against "cutthroat" competition and the "evils" of monopoly. The shift from behavioral to structural control seemingly masked the fundamental ideology of consumer protection.

If it could be compared metaphorically with economic theory, social control at the organizational level would equate to "supply side" economics. Supply side or "trickle-down" economics attempts to encourage capital investment (traditionally through tax incentives), with the expectation that in turn jobs might be created and individual spending might expand the economy. The objective of antitrust law is to assure a competitive economy, based upon a belief that through competition at the corporate level, individual consumer wants will be satisfied at the lowest (i.e., economically efficient) price.

Unfortunately, antitrust law, transformed into administrative law by the Federal Aviation Act of 1958, and as interpreted by the courts, is designed to protect the airlines and not the consumer. As Ralph Nader contends consumers have been denied standing to file complaints or to participate in enforcement proceedings. As the Nader group has argued government regulation has advanced the interest of big business. The Civil Aeronautics Board, for example, may have been created for this very reason, at the urging of the airlines and because of a destructively competitive market.[4] The CAB became endowed with enormous powers to shape the destiny of air transportation, supposedly to protect the public's right to travel, but seemingly with an ulterior agenda of rationalizing the marketplace for industry.

By the 1970s, deregulatory proponents perceived that, rather than protecting the consumer, what had actually happened was the creation

---

[4] *See* M.J. Green (ed.), *The Monopoly Makers*: Ralph Nader's Study Group Report on Regulation and Competition (1973).

of an "imperfect cartel" bent upon satisfying air carriers, even to the detriment of the traveling public. They contended that what has happened in America as a result of government regulation in general, not just of the airlines, is a "collusion" of the two great forces in American society: government and industry.[5]

Perhaps the foremost leader in America on consumer advocacy rights has been Ralph Nader. He has been unique in his attempt to use political trials and to extend the meaning of political trials to include the civil courts as a means of political dissent. A "political trial," as defined by Michael Belknap, is:

> . . . *any trial or impeachment that immediately affects or is intended to affect the structure, personnel, or policies of government, that is the product or has its outcome determined by political controversy, or that results from the efforts of a group within society having control of the machinery of government to use the courts to disadvantage its rivals in a power struggle which is not itself immediately political or to preserve its own economic or social position.*[6]

POLITICAL COUNTER-DENUNCIATIONS

In whichever legal forum, civil or criminal, the legal strategy of the actors in a political trial will likely attempt to change the definition of the behavior of their opponents. Prosecution and/or the plaintiff will likely redefine the behavior of the defendant as criminal and/or a violation of civil rights. Pat Lauderdale suggests that the definition of behavior as political deviance is a product of counter-denunciations in the courtroom, and that the locus of political deviance is to be found in the interaction associated with (these) counter-denunciations, which shift the focus of attention from the deviant acts of one actor to the motives and behavior of the opposing party. Although the conditions of

---

[5] *See* Laurence E. Gesell, *Airline Re-Regulation* (1990).
[6] Michael Belknap (ed.), *American Political Trials* (1981).

political counter-denunciation are customarily circumscribed in terms of *criminal* proceedings, Lauderdale's descriptive outline (*infra*) has been modified herein to reflect more universal adaptation to other forms of litigation—civil and administrative, as well as criminal.[7]

Political trials are recognized as one means of mobilizing resources of a social movement by taking advantage of the courts to rally support for their cause, to enlarge membership, and to otherwise gain notoriety. The court proceedings can be used to redefine what society (in the norm) has labeled as criminal, or socially deviant activity, into issues of higher moral good. This redefinition may be used to differentiate between what is an ordinary criminal (or civil) trial, from one which can be categorized as "political."

The overall process of counter-denunciation is an attempt to re-define the actions of the prosecution to be perceived as less than legitimate, and the behavior of the defendants to be other than criminal, but rather, more legitimate than that of their accusers. This outline of political counter-denunciation may be seen not only as a means of describing a political trial, but also as a strategy for political deviance. Political counter-denunciations take one of six forms, any or all of which may be found in what may be defined as a "political trial":

- There may be an attempt to *remove* the alleged deviant behavior and/or the trial from its *everyday setting*;
- Defense may attempt to show that the actions of the opposing party (usually the prosecutor and/or plaintiff) are *motivated by private, or personal, cause*;
- In demonstrating the opposing party's private motivation, defense may *degrade* the *authority* of the prosecution;
- In the degradation of the prosecution, its *legitimacy* (and credibility) are thereby *undermined*;
- Defense may attempt to demonstrate *supra-personal motives* of the accused, to show that their behavior was not the result of selfish motivation; and
- If what the accused did was unselfish, it must therefore have been for some *higher moral reason*, and hence legitimated.[8]

---

[7] *See* Pat Lauderdale (ed.), *A Political Analysis of Deviance* (1980).
[8] *Id.*

One model for organizing a strategy for political dissent around the use of the civil courts is the Ralph Nader organization and the diversified action groups, which he formed in support of his consumer advocacy operations in the mid-1960s and early 1970s. The following section focuses upon the aviation consumer-related activities of both Nader personally, and of the Aviation Consumer Action Project [ACAP]. Below, we review the suits brought by the Nader organization variously against federal agencies and airline companies. The Nader movement is looked upon in retrospect, at its use of the civil courts in attempt to achieve its political ends and at the consequences of its actions. Although Ralph Nader has since denounced the deregulatory outcome, ostensibly, airline deregulation was, in part, a result of the Nader movement.

CONSUMER ADVOCACY

Stated literally, *caveat emptor* means, "let the buyer beware," which was once a commonly accepted legal principle in America. Under this concept the buyer was individually responsible for his or her own purchase decisions. If the consumer was dissatisfied with the purchase, for whatever reason—faulty, inferior or just ill suited to intended needs—the consumer was to blame for the faulty decision. Under this concept, the manufacturer or seller was responsible for the time and expense of producing the product and of making it available to the consumer. But once the product or service had been transferred, the producer carried no burden of responsibility beyond any expressed warranty conditions. In early common law, the consumer could deal directly with the manufacturer in hands-length bargaining, examine the goods before purchase, and protect himself thereafter, if necessary, with a contractual warranty. Until the mid-20th Century, this was the prevailing common law approach to products liability.

In the evolution of law society has found that because of their size and overwhelming power organizations have a disproportionate advantage over individuals, and in some cases enjoy a certain immunity from the law. In short, individuals have less access to the legal system, and less protection from it, than do organizations. This overwhelming advantage has given rise to a current trend toward increased liability for individual misfortune, and for the decisions of individuals as consumers. Starting in the late 1960s the courts began to recognize that in a complex and technical market economy the consumer cannot be expected to have sufficient knowledge and experience with the myriad of products available to adequately protect him or her in the common marketplace.

Since the 1970s, there has been a positive shift away from *caveat emptor*. Policy has gone from "let the buyer beware" to "let the producer beware." The burden of responsibility has shifted from the (individual) consumer to the (organized) producer. In the process of insuring against risk, there is a transfer of liability, or responsibility. In similar fashion, consumer protection attempts to shift responsibility from the consumer to the producer, the seller, or to the one responsible for placing the goods or services into the stream of commerce.

In the mid-1960s, while the courts were granting increasingly more protection to the unwary or otherwise victimized consumer (replacing traditional notions of *caveat emptor* with strict products liability) prompted by the consumer advocacy movement and the courts, Congress began passing legislation to protect the consumer. There was a wave of consumer-related legislation passed by Congress over the ensuing two decades. The era gave rise to contemporary notions of consumerism, a term which has taken on both positive and negative connotations. In the positive aspect, "consumerism" stands for the promotion of consumer interests.

Consumerism in the positive sense is a challenge to business to provide what is promised, to be honest, to inform the consuming public, to provide safe products with quality assurance, and to respond fairly to legitimate complaints. Consumerism is nothing more than a statement to industry that it should stand with integrity behind its products. Peter Drucker called consumerism "the shame of marketing," stating that if those in marketing were to look at business from the buyer's perspective rather than with the seller's viewpoint, there would have been no need for a consumer movement.

On the negative side, it is fair to say that some supposed consumer advocates may have been opportunists who seized upon popular issues only in support of their own self-motivated interests. Others, although well meaning, may have been overly zealous. Such extremism has led some critics in industry to view consumerism as an attack on the free enterprise system which, when carried to extremes, could only cripple industry. And in some cases, the activities of consumer advocates may have caused more harm than good, not only to industry but to the consumer as well. Nevertheless, most people would probably agree that the consumer advocacy initiative, which began in the 1960s, was a benefit to society overall. Moreover, it was a popular movement within American society and among political leaders.

In 1962, President John F. Kennedy presented a consumer message to Congress wherein he proclaimed his "four rights of consumers" and announced his commitment to consumer protection. Although consumer protection had been an intermittent public concern since the beginning of the Republic, the American public was ripe for a new consumer revolt. That revolt was led by Ralph Nader, and it began with the publication in 1965 of his book, *Unsafe at Any Speed.* The intent of this one actor, above all others, underscores the political tone of the most recent consumer crisis of note, and of the political trials associated with this movement. Nader's motivation, however, was not the result of any governmentally proclaimed commitment to protect the consuming public. Nader may have had an early faith in the efficacy of government, but he came to believe "that the impersonal forces of government cannot improve, and that in most cases they even compound, the impersonal activities of the corporations . . . ," which he has believed "ravage modern life." "Corporations should be driven out of business if they cannot provide decent environmental conditions," said Nader.[9] Ralph Nader's activities have been a personal and popular movement to change consumer and environmental policy. His cause has been a (political) crusade.

There are two points that made the activists' movement of the 1960s different from previous consumer crises. First of all, consumer protection policy had always been a government responsibility. Additionally, there have been two types of consumer advocacy groups, *private-interest groups*, and *public-interest groups*. The Granger movement was typical of the former, and exemplified by reactionary government policy in response to the demands of this special interest group. The movement of the 1960s, however, was characterized more by a concern for broad-based public welfare. Hence, it was a crusade and an appeal to a "higher moral good."

---

[9] *See* Ralph Nader, *The Consumer and Corporate Accountability* (1973).

Secondly, as a public-interest issue, the new consumer advocacy movement gained broad media coverage and experienced increasingly widespread popularity. Although he may have been seen initially by industry as a deviant, and hence as a threat. Rather, many consumer advocates have looked upon him as a saint. However, there should be no misgivings. Ralph Nader is a political revolutionary. "He is a revolutionary," says Charles McCarry, "in despair over what he regards as a society on the brink of shipwreck."[10] He is different from other revolutionaries only in his strategy. Rather than using the crime-related tactics of other more infamous political activists, Nader has employed, if not more peaceful, then at least more sophisticated means, through use of the civil rather than criminal courts. But he has not been beyond mobilization—and mass protest. In 1971, Nader gave a speech to a community college in Cleveland wherein his plea to the audience, "and to his larger audience, the whole American people," was for what he called "*ad hoc* power," or "non-institutional sources of power." What Nader was calling for was a citizen uprising, and "not necessarily one that works within the system."

Nader has had a three-phase battle plan in mind which "envisages an army of citizens equipped with information and resolve, marching on the capitals of their exploitation." Nader has said that he "want(s) to get people thinking that (traditional political activity) isn't enough and they're just fooling themselves unless they're part of it." Nader has been emphatic about his cause, and has indicated that "this country is in a battle between justice and suicide." Nader has been at war, and his three-phase battle strategy is comprised of: *Stage One*, where Nader, alone, was against the system; *Stage Two* was Nader and his "Raiders;" and *Stage Three* envisions development of models of social and political action.[11]

Stage One opened with the publication of *Unsafe at any Speed,* and Nader's ensuing battle with automotive manufactures. Stage Two followed the establishment, in 1968, of the Center for Study of Responsive Law, and his organization of other operations including the Aviation Consumer Action Project in the early 1970s. It was during the era of the mid-1970s that the preponderance of aviation-related

---

[10] Charles McCarry, *Citizen Nader* (1972).
[11] *See id.*

cases were brought by Nader and ACAP against certain aviation companies and the federal agencies in charge of regulating the air transportation industry.

CIVIL POLITICAL TRIALS

Incorporated into the law books are six cases, between 1972 and 1976, brought by ACAP variously against the CAB, FAA and DOT:

- In *Aviation Consumer Action Project v. Civil Aeronautics Board* (1972), ACAP attempted to challenge the statutory validity and Constitutionality of a CAB tariff ruling. The court dismissed the case because ACAP failed to pursue and exhaust its available administrative remedies.[12]
- *Aviation Consumer Action Project v. Civil Aeronautics Board*, (1973) was a challenge of CAB's sanction of the International Air Transport Association [IATA] power to impose fines upon its members. The court found no connection between U.S. law and IATA fines.[13]
- *Pillai, Goldwyn, and Aviation Consumer Action Project v. Civil Aeronautics Board* was a petition for review of a CAB order approving certain IATA agreements for the North Atlantic. The courts ruled in favor of ACAP, et al., and vacated the CAB order.[14]
- *Aviation Consumer Action Project v. Schaffe* was a challenge of FAA improper Notice of Proposed Rulemaking regarding the loading of radioactive materials on passenger-carrying aircraft. The court stayed the FAA order for 30 days pending proper amendment of Federal Aviation Regulations, but later dismissed the case as moot.[15]
- In *Aviation Consumer Action Project. v. Coleman*, the DOT, under its discretionary authority, had declared exemption under

---

[12] *Aviation Consumer Action Project v. Civil Aeronautics Board*, 480 F2d 1895, CCH 12 AVI ¶ 18,035 (1972).

[13] *Aviation Consumer Action Project v. Civil Aeronautics Board*, CCH 12 AVI ¶ 17,754 (1973).

[14] *Pillai, Goldwyn, and Aviation Consumer Action Project v. Civil Aeronautics Board*, 485 F2d 1018, CCH 12 AVI ¶ 18,036 (1973).

[15] *Aviation Consumer Action Project, et al., v. John H. Schaffer, Administrator, Federal Aviation Administration*, CCH 12 AVI ¶ 18,006 (1973).

the Hazardous Materials Transportation Act [HMTA] and ACAP challenged their authority to do so. The court enjoined DOT from issuing or renewing any exemption until (or unless) it was in full compliance with HMTA. On appeal the case was remanded and ordered vacated as moot.[16]

- *Aviation Consumer Action Project v. Civil Aeronautics Board* (1976) was an action under the Freedom of Information Act, to order the CAB to produce its decision concerning the merger of two airlines. The court ordered the CAB not to withhold related information unless it could be validly presumed under statutory provisions that information could be withheld.[17]

The six cases cited above, after reviewing the merits and substance of each suit, are seemingly innocuous. Since negligence of federal employees was not at issue, the only reasonable outcome of any of these cases would have been to force administrative change (*mandamus*) through the powers of the courts. The underlying problem of such actions is that the judicial branch (the courts) is highly reluctant (for Constitutional reasons) to interfere in the government's (i.e., executive branch) affairs. The very basis of the Administrative Procedure Act was to preclude any undue interference between the judicial and executive branches. In this sense, there is an administrative law barrier that precludes using the courts in this manner to bring about political or social change—or perhaps to obtain justice at all. Furthermore, the formal and legal (administrative) system allows the government to legitimate its control, and to coerce those who challenge it.

In reading these cases one can perceive feelings of discouragement, frustration and futility among the Nader group. Futile, in the sense that this kind of politico-legal strategy adopted by the Nader camp, of "pecking" at the government's administrative structure in an attempt to re-direct the bureaucracy, would seem to be a battle which could not be won unless the Nader forces could have had sufficient backing and could have been tenacious enough to somehow outlast the government's resolve. This was highly unlikely considering the government's

---

[16] *Aviation Consumer Action Project, et al. v. William T. Coleman, Secretary, Department of Transportation*, CCH 13 AVI 17,814 (1975).

[17] *Aviation Consumer Action Project v. Civil Aeronautics Board*, 412 F SUPP 1028, CCH 14 AVI 17,110, 418 F SUPP 634, CCH 14 AVI 17,411 (1976).

nearly unlimited resources. The only way this kind of war could likely be won is through the kind of mass citizen action Nader envisioned in Stage Three of his battle strategy, which had not yet materialized. The Nader movement began loosing steam in the mid-1970s during Stage Two when most of the trials cited in this writing took place and Stage Three may never become a reality.

Early trials brought by Nader, acting on his own, were similar to the ACAP cases cited above, and with like results:

- On appeal of an earlier district court ruling, in *Nader v. Federal Aviation Administration* (1971), Nader (and intervenors) requested the FAA Administrator impose an emergency ban against smoking on commercial aircraft. When the Administrator refused, this suit was brought against the FAA. However, the District Court ruled that the FAA's actions were within discretionary administrative powers granted the Administrator and the appellate court affirmed.[18]

- In *Nader v. Federal Aviation Administration* (1974), Nader joined with ACAP to challenge the FAA's approval of a policy permitting the airlines to use X-ray devices in airport terminals for inspection of carry-on baggage. The Court ordered the FAA to prepare an environmental assessment prior to its adoption of rules permitting the use of X-ray devices.[19]

By 1974, there was a break in the Nader strategy, with the opening chapter of *Nader v. Allegheny*,[20] which involved a seemingly unpretentious issue over Nader's boarding denial after having been issued a confirmed seat on an Allegheny Airline's flight. This case was more than a request for an administrative ruling change; it was a tort recovery action and a demand for both compensatory and punitive damages. In *Nader v. Allegheny*, the legal strategy shifted from demands for administrative changes in government, to a suit against a private corporation for (tort) damages. Notice, however, that the underlying scheme was still an attempt to force the CAB, through the powers of the courts, to modify its administrative rulings.

---

[18] *Nader, et al. v. Federal Aviation Administration, et al.*, 440 F 2d 292 (1971).

[19] *Nader, et al. v. Federal Aviation Administration*, 373 F. Supp. 1175 (1974).

[20] *Nader v. Allegheny*, 626 F 2d 1031 (1980).

Using a similar strategy in 1977, and with the same alleged violation at issue (i.e., overbooking practice), in *Nader v. Air Transport Association of America*, Nader claimed *antitrust* violations on the part of the airlines.[21] He argued the airlines at a specified meeting had:

> . . . *agreed not to compete either by ceasing to engage in overbooking, by modifying their reservation systems so as to significantly reduce the number of passengers denied boarding, by engaging in advertising relating to the practice of overbooking or the competitive risk of being denied boarding on competing airlines, or by warning persons making reservations that such reservations may not be honored because of overbooking.*

In essence, the court ruled that the administrative remedies had not been expended, and the alleged agreement was "basic to (that) regulatory scheme" where the CAB has the statutory authority. Apparently thwarted in his attempts at tort recovery, Nader then reverted to the long-tried strategy of "pecking" at the administrative process. In *Nader and Aviation Consumer Action Project v. the Civil Aeronautics Board; Air Transport Association*, Ralph Nader and ACAP challenged certain CAB guidelines governing the suspension of newly filed airline fares, which Nader claimed violated the Airline Deregulation Act of 1978.[22] The appellate court found no merit in Nader's argument and affirmed the lower court's ruling against him.

CIVIL COUNTER-DENUNCIATIONS

With frustration which surely must have accompanied the court findings, mostly against Nader and ACAP, what was the purpose for repeated attacks against the government and airline corporations if not political and conducted as part of some overall moral strategy? Although none of the Nader aviation trials can demonstrate all of the

---

[21] *Nader, et al. v. Air Transport Association of America*, 426 F. Supp. 1035 (1977).

[22] *Nader and Aviation Consumer Action Project v. The Civil Aeronautics Board; Air Transport Association*, 657 F 2d 453 (1981).

points, in the aggregate and when considering the actors, their intent, and the consequences of their actions, all six forms of political counter-denunciation identified in the outline above were satisfied:

- Each of the trials had an alternate agenda, *removed from the everyday issues* brought before the courts. Nader's long-standing battle against government "collusion" with corporations (in this case the airlines) was the political basis, or cause, behind these trials, irrespective of the specific charges.
- In Nader's perspective, the *private cause* of the opposition in these trials was the co-conspiracy of the government with the airlines, and that the government had seized "the legal and administrative apparatus . . . , turning government agencies into licensers of private monopolies."
- In each of the trials, there is an appeal to the courts, and an attempt to outflank the administrative process, thereby undermining and *degrading the authority* of the government.
- The *legitimacy of the government* is eroded by charges of collusion with private enterprise, at the public's expense. According to Nader, government economic regulation is a form of "corporate socialism, a condition of federal statecraft wherein public agencies control much of the private economy on behalf of a designated corporate clientele," and that the "consumer ultimately pays for the increased prices, encouraged waste, and retarded technology economic regulation fosters."
- As McCarry states, "Nader is not called upon for explanation because it is accepted that he represents the public interest."[23] Nader has used the media masterfully, and the press has created his image as a supra-personal *consumer champion*; and,
- In Nader's view, "business and government are allied in a system of greed and deception that is ruining the nation's natural resources and perverting its social purposes." His intent is thus presented as an "altruistic" war against that alliance and is legitimated by *higher moral reasons*.

---

[23] Charles McCarry, *Citizen Nader* (1972).

DEREGULATION OF THE AIRLINES

The consequences of Nader's political crusade against government regulators and the airlines, although oftentimes frustrated, have had a marginal influence upon regulatory policy and its revision. For instance, one result of *Nader v. Allegheny* was to prompt changes in the airlines' notification of passengers of their overbooking practice.

Six years after the Nader overbooking incident with Allegheny Airlines, and even before the case had reached its final conclusion, the CAB confirmed the court's opinion that the practice of overbooking is a material fact which should be brought to the attention of those purchasing tickets. This, the Board did by promulgating 14 C.F.R. 250, "Oversales," Sub-Section 250.11. This regulation requires carriers to post in their ticket offices and include with each ticket sold notice that,

> *Airline flights may be overbooked, and there is a slight chance that a seat will not be available on a flight for which a person has a confirmed reservation.*

In the broader picture, the Nader operations were at least partially instrumental in promoting passage of the Airline Deregulation Act of 1978. The movement to deregulate the airlines grew out of seemingly bipartisan reaction to expressed public concerns of excess governmental control from the lowest levels of municipal and county government to the federal level. At the latter level, and as early as 1974, attention was drawn to the alleged over-regulation of the airline industry when the Senate Administrative Practice and Procedure Subcommittee, chaired by Sen. Ted Kennedy (D-Mass.) examined the fairness of CAB policies. What emerged from the committee's hearings was an indictment of the Board's practices which were allegedly overprotective of the airlines, and that were generally anti-competitive. A report by the General Accounting Office indicated that with more competition based on price, airfares might have been as much as 25% cheaper.

The overall objective of airline deregulation was to return the industry to competitive capitalism, with many competing airlines, where none could control the market, and where all would have to actively participate in price competition. The scheme was to create a more perfect economic model of competition wherein prices would be driven down and the consumer would be the ultimate benefactor. The policy objectives of airline deregulation are prescribed in Section 102(a) of the Federal Aviation Act of 1958, as amended by the Airline Deregulation Act of 1978.[24] Although few people would like to return to the form of regulation practiced before airline deregulation, as measured against the *expressed* goals of the Airline Deregulation Act, deregulatory policy has clearly been a failure.[25] The government failed to sustain even one of the specified goals. More importantly, as measured against the stated objectives, deregulation failed to measure up to its obligations to the consumer.

After deregulation, Ralph Nader began to voice his concerns about the problems that deregulation had created. Nader's book, *Collision Course: The Truth about Airline Safety*,[26] is a chronicle of the problems he saw with deregulation. He concluded the airlines "wrecked themselves financially with these mergers, acquisitions, corporate raiders, and financial shenanigans. . . .The financial problems of deregulation are related to the safety problems."[27]

What is today commonly assigned as the purportedly positive results of airline deregulation have little association with the actual objectives set forth in the Deregulation Act's Statement of Policy. The fundamental and under girding objective of airline deregulation was to avoid industry concentration and return to a market of competitive capitalism, where there would be many competing companies earning sufficient profits to sustain a healthy economy that would attract capital investment. If one measures the success of airline deregulation in achievement of the expressed goals of the Airline Deregulation Act, deregulatory policy clearly failed to live up to its expectations.[28]

Per the explicit terms of the Airline Deregulation Act of 1978, the government was first to maintain "safety as the highest priority in air

---

[24] 49 U.S.C. § 1302 (a).

[25] *See* Laurence E. Gesell, *Airline Re-Regulation* (1990); *see also* Paul Stephen Dempsey, *Flying Blind: The Failure of Deregulation* (1990); *see also* Paul Stephen Dempsey and Andrew Goetz, *Airline Deregulation & Laissez-Faire Mythology* (1992).

[26] Ralph Nader & Wesley Smith, *Collision Course: The Truth about Airline Deregulation* (1993).

[27] CNN Transcripts, *Larry King Live* (Sep. 14, 1993).

[28] *See* Laurence E. Gesell and Paul Stephen Dempsey, Air Transportation: Foundations for the 21st Century 408-412 (2nd ed. 2005). *See also* Laurence E. Gesell and Martin T. Farris, *Airline Deregulation: An Evaluation of Goals and Objectives*, 21 Trans. L. J. (1992).

commerce." Air transportation remains the safest mode of travel, but the highest priority of deregulation was clearly not safety, it was marketplace efficiency. Even Alfred Kahn concedes the margin of safety may have eroded during the deregulatory peak and the scramble for higher load factors and marketplace shares.[29] Certainly, the significant aging of the U.S. fleet over the two decades following deregulation did not make commercial aviation safer. The second goal was to prevent any deterioration in safety.

Third, the government was to make available "a variety of adequate, efficient, and low-priced services by air carriers." Initially, there were a variety of airlines from which to choose, each offering competitive prices. Unfortunately, the quality of service declined as managers continued to utilize low fares as their principal competitive tool.

Fourth, the government was to place "maximum reliance on competitive market forces and on actual and potential competition." Intense competition led to either company failures or mergers, and the government relied almost exclusively upon the contestable market theory, which in the end proved to be invalid.

Fifth, the government was to develop and maintain "a sound regulatory environment." Open competition among airlines, however, leads to instability, and a non-rational marketplace. The deregulated market has been anything but "sound."

Sixth, the government was to prevent "unfair, predatory or anticompetitive practices in air transportation." The industry responded by inventing new ways to control the marketplace, such as the hub-and-spoke network, predatory pricing, and capacity dumping, while simultaneously the government turned its back on antitrust enforcement.

Seventh, the government was to avoid "unreasonable industry concentration, excessive market domination, and monopoly power." As the airlines became increasingly threatened financially by intense competition and the affects of economic recession, the government authorized the wholesale consolidation of the industry to levels unprecedented, and eventually gave the major airlines antitrust immunity to establish a three-member global cartel. In aviation policy, "globalization" is a euphemism for cartelization.

---

[29] Alfred Kahn, *Airline Deregulation—A Mixed Bag*, 16 Trans. L. J. 229, 251 (1988); Alfred Kahn, *Transportation Deregulation*, Econ. Development Q. 98 (1987); *Interview with Alfred Kahn*, USA Today, Oct. 5, 1988, at 13A.

Eighth, the government was to encourage "entry into air transportation markets by new carriers . . . and strengthen small carriers so as to assure a more effective, competitive airline industry." Instead, the DOT approved major mergers, while weaker commuters either ceased operating or were acquired by their dominant regional competitors or otherwise contractually aligned with them.

Ninth, the government was to maintain a "comprehensive and convenient system of continuous scheduled service for small communities." The promise of greater frequency of service to small communities brought with it so many disruptions in service and such higher prices that it has been neither "continuous" nor "convenient" for small communities across the nation.

Tenth, the government was to "encourage efficient and well-managed carriers to earn adequate profits and to attract capital." In the three decades since deregulation the air transportation landscape has been littered with airline failures and bankruptcies, and the industry twice lost all the money it had ever earned.

On the one hand, if one measures the success of airline deregulation by the stated objectives of the Airline Deregulation Act, it was a complete failure. On the other hand, if the industry and the traveling public are generally more satisfied with the current state of the airline industry than before 1978 then one must declare the airline deregulation experiment a success for consumerism. It is difficult, however, to understand why any stakeholder (investor, worker or consumer) in the air transportation marketplace would be so satisfied.

For the *owners* of the airlines, the first half of the 1990s was a financial disaster. A $12 billion loss in just four years (between 1990 and 1994) speaks for itself. But the worst was yet to come. The first three years of the 21st Century brought the industry to the brink of financial collapse, begging the government for financial assistance. Between 2001 and 2003 the airlines produced a cumulative loss of between $20 and $30 billion. With $100 billion accumulated debt, nearly $20 billion in under funded pension liability, and only about $2 billion in equity, not only is the airline industry without capital, its access to private capital markets is virtually nonexistent.[30]

---

[30] Paul Stephen Dempsey and Laurence E. Gesell, *Air Commerce and the Law* Preface (2004).

As for *organized labor*, workers were dealt a devastating blow, not only by a deregulatory policy that undermined industry viability, job stability, and resulted in the loss of an estimated 60,000 (and growing) career jobs, but by a government that failed to live up to its stated commitment to labor. Under the Airline Deregulation Act of 1978, workers were to be insulated from the instability anticipated with the introduction of a deregulated environment. Yet, displaced workers were systematically denied their Labor Protective Provisions [LPP] guaranteed under the Act itself.[31] And, government and management launched a two-pronged pincher attack against organized labor.

For the consuming public, there is a prevailing perception that the cost of travel by air is significantly lower since deregulation. And for the occasional leisure traveler this might be the case. However, as pointed out by the editors of *Aviation Week & Space Technology*, "many of the industry's best customers feel like they are being cheated and exploited. Business fares are near historical highs—on average 4-5 times more than the lowest leisure fares."[32] The reality is that the market is replete with price discrimination, the deception of code sharing, the inconvenience of the hub-and-spoke routing system that evolved since deregulation, and by other corporate strategies intended to circumvent the antitrust laws.[33] Moreover, real fares fell less in the decades subsequent to deregulation than in the decades preceding it.

The Airline Deregulation Act also preempted the states' ability to enforce their consumer protection laws on behalf of passengers, leaving that responsibility to a largely disinterested DOT. Thus, unique among nearly all U.S. industries, airlines may ignore state consumer protection laws. They may engage in "bait and switch" advertising practices (advertising, for example, a $79 fare for only 10% of inventory, which is quickly sold out), advertise a one-way fare when the price is only available on a round-trip purchase, offer a "confirmed reservation" on a flight that is overbooked, confiscate the nonrefundable ticket price from passengers who cannot make the flight, and prohibit them from giving the flight coupon to another traveler.

For the owners of the airlines, deregulation has been a financial disaster. Organized labor has been under assault since the inception of

---

[31] *Id.*
[32] *Courageous Steps Required to Reform Airlines*, Av. Wk. & Space Tech. (Nov. 18, 2002).
[33] *Id.*

airline deregulation. And, for the consuming public, it has been a mixed bag at best. In 1978, public opinion polls ranked airlines among the top industries in terms of customer satisfaction and confidence.[34] If a poll were taken today, would the American public see it the same way?[35]

THE AIRLINE DEREGULATION ACT'S PREEMPTION OF STATE CONSUMER PROTECTION

Two provisions of federal law have led to serious conflict regarding the dividing lines between state and federal jurisdiction over aviation. Congress added a savings clause to the Civil Aeronautics Act of 1938, which provided that nothing in the Act should be construed to "abridge or alter the remedies now existing at common law or by statute but that the provisions of this Act would be in addition to such remedies."[36] Subsequent recodifications of this act preserved this savings clause, giving the states jurisdiction over intrastate economic regulatory issues, as well as common law negligence and contract claims.

But with the promulgation of the Airline Deregulation Act of 1978, Congress was concerned that the states might attempt to exert economic regulation over the airline industry at a time when Congress had determined that entry and pricing regulation should be terminated. As a consequence, Congress added a provision which stated, "[A] state . . . may not enact or enforce a law, regulation, or other provision having the force and effect of law related to a price, route, or service of an air carrier. . . ."[37]

Under deregulation, some carriers began to engage in various methods of arguably false and misleading advertising that likely would not be tolerated in other industries. This led the National Association of Attorneys General [NAAG] to adopt detailed comprehensive guidelines for advertising and marketing practices in the airline industry. For example, they required that restrictions on promotional fares be in legible

---

[34] James W. Callison, *Airline Deregulation—Only Partially a Hoax: The Current Status of the Airline Deregulation Movement*, 45 J. of Air Law & Commerce (1980); *see also* Paul Dempsey, Robert Hardaway & William Thoms, *Aviation Law & Regulation* (1992).
[35] Paul Stephen Dempsey, *Erosion of the Regulatory Process in Transportation—The Winds of Change*, 41 ICC Practitioner's J. (Mar./Apr. 1980).
[36] 49 U.S.C. § 40120.
[37] 49 U.S.C. § 41713(b).

type, that round-trip purchase requirements be "clear and conspicuous" and include the round-trip price, that any "sale" or "discount" fares actually represent "a true savings over regularly available air fares," that any advertised fare "be available in sufficient quantity so as to meet reasonably foreseeable demand," so as to curtail the widespread airline industry practice of "bait and switch," and that restrictive changes in the frequent flyer programs be adopted prospectively only.[38] While the guidelines did not have the force and effect of law, they set a uniform national standard by which to measure airline practices. Several attorneys general warned airlines that they were violating the guidelines, implicitly threatening judicial action under their state consumer protection laws, while one explicitly threatened suit. The airlines retaliated with a suit of their own seeking a preliminary injunction, arguing that such state regulation of airlines was explicitly preempted by the above provision, and that being subjected to 51 different jurisdictions' view of appropriate advertising would unduly burden interstate commerce.

The U.S. Supreme Court in *Morales v. Trans World Airlines* [39] held that the airline fare advertising provisions of the NAAG guidelines were preempted by the Airline Deregulation Act, holding that the phrase "related to a price, route or service," is to be given broad construction, as if it read "if it has a connection with or reference to." The court found that the NAAG guideline requiring that advertised fares be available to meet reasonably foreseeable demand "would have a significant impact upon the airlines' ability to market their product, and hence a significant impact on the fares they charge."[40] The court then limited its holding, proclaiming that it does not "address whether state regulation of the nonprice aspects of fare advertising (for example, state laws preventing obscene depictions) would similarly 'relat[e] to' rates."[41] It also insisted that its decision would not give the airlines "carte blanche to lie and deceive consumers; the DOT retains the power to prohibit advertisements which in its opinion do not further competitive pricing."[42]

---

[38] 504 U.S. 374, 391 Appendix.
[39] 504 U.S. 374 (1992).
[40] 504 U.S. at 390.
[41] *Id.*
[42] *Id.*

After *Morales*, airlines began raising the preemption defense liberally in a multitude of state law actions, including state common law tort and contract actions. Some courts held that state tort law claims were preempted by the Airline Deregulation Act.[43] Others held that common law breach of contract and intentional infliction of emotional distress claims were preempted.[44] State law claims against anticompetitive practices surrounding Computer Reservation Systems [CRS] were preempted, with federal antitrust law deemed the exclusive means of private enforcement.[45] One court held that state contract and tort claims for denied boarding compensation were not preempted, although punitive damages for such injuries were preempted.[46]

These issues came to a head again before the U.S. Supreme Court in *American Airlines v. Wolens*,[47] a class action suit against American Airlines under both an Illinois consumer fraud statute and a common law breach of contract claim on grounds that American unilaterally and retroactively imposed restrictions on redemption of frequent flyer mileage award travel (specifically, capacity controls and blackout dates). The court found the statutory claim to be preempted by the Airline Deregulation Act, but did not read the preemption clause "to shelter airlines from suits alleging no violations of state-imposed obligations, but seeking recovery for the airline's alleged breach of its own, self-imposed undertakings."[48] It found that "[m]arket efficiency requires effective means to enforce private agreements." Thus, a state consumer protection or anti-fraud statute or regulation is preempted by the federal Airline Deregulation Act; a state common law cause of action apparently is not.

SAFETY PROTECTION

Measures to protect the traveling public have been a long-standing policy in an industry dominated by federal regulation. Notwithstanding

---

[43] *See e.g., Hodges v. Delta Airlines*, 4 F.3d 350 (5th Cir. 1993).

[44] *See e.g., Cannava v. USAir*, 1993 WL 565341 (D. Mass. 1993).

[45] *Frontier Airlines v. United Air Lines*, 758 F. Supp. 1399 (D. Colo. 1989).

[46] *West v. Northwest Airlines*, 995 F.2d 148 (9th Cir. 1993).

[47] 115 S.Ct. 817 (1995).

[48] *Id.* at 824. For a review of both the *Morales* and *Wolens* cases, *see* Jonathan Blacker, *"Fly To London for $298": The Battle Between Federal and State Regulation of Airfare Advertising Heats Up*, 61 J. Air L. & Com. 205 (1995).

the results of deregulatory policy, as well as the opinions of the Nader group and other critics of the governmental process, it may be stated that consumer advocacy in aviation began long before the era of consumerism, not only prompting public safety but to provide economic guarantees and consumer protection as well.

Following the sunset of the Civil Aeronautics Board on January 1, 1985, the responsibility for airline consumer protection matters, including consumer assistance and consumer protection regulation was assigned to a newly created Office of Community and Consumer Affairs, within the Department of Transportation's Office of Governmental Affairs. Consumerism is fundamentally an economic movement. To this end, economic regulations of the DOT include provisions designed to protect the air transportation consumer.

Section 601 of the Federal Aviation Act of 1958 empowers the FAA Administrator with the duty to promote safety of flight of civil aircraft in air commerce by prescribing and revising from time to time:

- minimum standards governing the design, materials, workmanship, construction, and performance of aircraft, aircraft engines, and propellers;
- reasonable rules and regulations and minimum standards governing the inspection, servicing, and overhaul of aircraft; aircraft engines, propellers and appliances; and the periods for, and manner in which inspections, servicing, and overhaul shall be made;
- reasonable rules and regulations governing the reserve supply of aircraft, aircraft engines, propellers, appliances, and aircraft fuel and oil;
- reasonable rules and regulations governing the maximum hours or periods of service airmen and other air carrier employees; and
- such other rules and regulations, or minimum standards, governing other practices, methods, and procedures, that the Administrator finds necessary to provide adequately for safety in commerce.

The Administrator promulgates and enforces rules and regulations designed to promote air commerce and safety. Air safety is regulated through issuance and/or revocation of certificates of airmen, aircraft, air carriers, air navigation facilities, air agencies, and air carrier airports. The Administrator may, from time to time, re-inspect any civil aircraft, aircraft engine, propeller, appliance, air navigation facility, or air agency, or may reexamine any civil airman. If, as a result of any such re-inspection or reexamination, or if, as a result of any other investigation made by the Administrator, a determination is made that safety in air commerce or air transportation and the public interest requires, the Administrator may issue an order amending, modifying, suspending, or revoking, in whole or in part, any type certificate, production certificate, airworthiness certificate, airman certificate, air carrier operating certificate, air navigation facility certificate, airport operating certificate, or air agency certificate.

Air carriers are required to refuse to transport any person who does not consent to a security search prior to boarding, or any property of any person who does not consent to a search or inspection of such property. Air carriers may also refuse transportation of a passenger or property when, in the opinion of the carrier, such transportation would or might be adverse to safety of flight.[49]

CONSUMER PROTECTION

Of the estimated 209 CAB functions transferred to DOT, seven were directly concerned with consumer protection, including 14 C.F.R. Parts: 250, "Oversales;" 252, "Smoking aboard aircraft;" 253, "Notice of terms of contract of carriage;" 374, "Implementation of the Consumer Credit Protection Act with respect to air carriers and foreign air carriers;" 379, "Nondiscrimination in federally assisted programs of the Board—Effectuation of Title VI of the Civil Rights Act of 1964;" and 382, "Nondiscrimination on the basis of handicap" (title since deleted). Title 14 C.F.R. Chapter II also provides consumer protection by requiring air carriers to be insured against liability for lost or damaged baggage, 14 C.F.R. Part 254, "Domestic baggage liabil-

---

[49] *See Robert F. Williams v. Trans World Airlines*, CCH 13 AVI ¶ 17,482 (1975).

ity;" and for aircraft accidents, 14 C.F.R. Part 205, "Aircraft Accident Liability Insurance."

In 1984, the final year of the CAB's operation, the number of consumer complaints against airlines filed with the CAB totaled 10,332. The largest category of complaints for U.S. carriers involved flight problems (28.1%), baggage related complaints (17.6%), and re-fund complaints (16.8%). The total complaints rose 14%, representing a significant increase over the previous year. The reported situation gave rise to real concerns of consumer protection in ensuing years, prompting the DOT to implement a consumer hot line and a method for reporting consumer complaints and on-time performance by the various airlines.

A common complaint against the airlines, exacerbated after de-regulation, is overbooking. It has been stated that "a reservation is a reservation, but not always a seat on a plane." To one degree or an-other most airlines practice overbooking, and it may be more common where break even load factors are most critical, such as where the lost revenue of just one empty seat can make the difference between profit or loss.

With a fully refundable ticket, it is relatively easy for a passenger to make a reservation and then not show. Before the advent of re-stricted ticketing, an estimated 20% of the passengers who made reser-vations did not meet their flights. Yet, an airline seat is a perishable commodity, and it is not so easy for the airline to make up for lost in-come. The value of the seat is lost forever. Hence, the airlines "over-book"; that is to say, they reserve or sell more tickets than there are seats available on the airplane.[50]

With larger, certificated carriers (i.e., with Certificates of Public Convenience and Necessity issued under Section 401 of the Aviation Act), there are provisions for compensating passengers who are denied boarding. However, established Denied Boarding Compensation [DBC] has its statutory limitations. The allowable monetary amounts may not fully compensate the passenger for losses when the passenger has been involuntarily bumped and may have had a potential loss of business due to a late or canceled arrival. Moreover, since deregula-tion, most tickets are nonrefundable and nontransferable. Hence, there

---

[50] *See Ralph Nader v. Allegheny Airlines*, 626 F.2d 1031 (1980).

is arguable inequity between allowing a carrier to keep the revenue derived from "no shows" as liquidated damages, yet allow carriers to overbook in order to sell more seats than are scheduled.

Another frequent complaint against airlines is that of lost or damaged baggage. Airline companies have taken into consideration the potentiality that luggage may be lost or damaged, and most airlines have established baggage rules as part of their adopted tariffs. The extent of airline liability is for reimbursement on the depreciated value of the baggage and its contents, as determined by the airline. Airlines will also pay for repairs to damaged luggage, and if damaged beyond repair will pay for the depreciated value of the luggage. If luggage is delayed, the airline may reimburse the passenger for rental or purchase of new clothing or equipment. However, if and when lost luggage is found and returned the passenger may be obliged to return the new, replacement items to the airline.

In international aviation, under the Warsaw Convention of 1929, carrier liability for air cargo or checked baggage is limited to 250 francs per kilogram (U.S. $9.07 per pound, or U.S. $20 per kilogram)[51] unless the shipper has declared a higher value and paid, if necessary, a supplementary fee, and the damages sustained meet or exceed such declared value.[52] Montreal Protocol No. 4 and the Montreal Con-

---

[51] *Hague Protocol*, 478 U.N.T.S. at 381. (amending *Warsaw Convention* art. 22). In most courts, prejudgment interest is also recoverable, the theory being that otherwise the plaintiff is not made whole. William J. Augello & George Carl Pezold, *Freight Claims in Plain English* (3rd ed. 1995) at § 16.4.4.

[52] Article 22(2) of the *Warsaw Convention* provides:

In the transportation of checked baggage and of goods, the liability of the carrier shall be limited to a sum of 250 francs per kilogram, unless the consignor has made, at the time when the package was handed over to the carrier, a special declaration of the value at delivery and has paid a supplementary sum if the case so requires. In that case the carrier will be liable to pay a sum not exceeding the declared sum, unless he proves that the sum is greater than the actual value to the consignor at delivery.

Warsaw Convention, supra note, art. 22(2). The *Hague Protocol* left liability at 250 francs per kilogram. One court noted that:

[T]he shipper who declares a separate value is no longer limited to a recovery based proportionately on the weight of the lost or damaged portion of the shipment. . . . [T]he special declaration provision of the *Warsaw Convention* is a simple bright-line liability rule for lost international shipments: if the shipper declares an additional value for a shipment, and pays an additional shipping charge, the carrier is liable for that value if the shipment is lost.

Williams Dental Co. v. Air Express Int'l, 824 F. Supp. 435 at 443 (S.D.N.Y. 1993), *aff'd* 17 F.3d 392 (2d Cir. 1993) (unpublished table decision).

Under the *Montreal Convention* of 1999, the liability of the carrier for damage to checked and unchecked baggage is limited to SDR 1000. *Montreal Convention*, art. 22(2); see also *id..*, Art. 17(4) (defining "baggage" as both checked and unchecked baggage). This limit, however, is not

vention of 1999 raised liability for cargo and checked baggage to 17 Special Drawing Rights [SDRs] per kilogram (about $25 per kilogram, or $11 per pound),[53] unless the shipper has made a special declaration of higher liability and paid a supplementary sum when required.[54] All three of these international agreements have been ratified by the U.S. Determining which is applicable to a given passenger depends upon which treaty is common to both the origination and destination nation (a ticketed round-trip itinerary considered as having the same origin and destination).

In the post-deregulation era, a growing proportion of the airline business has shifted to commuter airlines, many of which operate smaller, 15 to 20-passenger turboprop aircraft, or 50-75 seat regional jets. In many operational situations, to load these smaller aircraft with a full complement of passengers disallows the attendant carriage of the passengers' entire luggage, without exceeding the aircraft's allowable maximum gross weight. The result is delayed transport of the luggage on subsequent flights, and an inconvenience to the affected passengers. The practice of filling the aircraft to capacity, and intentionally leaving luggage behind without first notifying passengers, sets up a potential litigation to recover damages.[55]

The fear of loosing baggage en route has prompted many passengers to carry on board the aircraft as much luggage as possible. Excess baggage in the passenger compartment has become such a problem that some U.S. airlines may now restrict the passenger to one carry-on item, as is the practice in Europe already. In *Andrews v. United Airlines*, a passenger complained of being struck by baggage falling from an overhead bin.[56]

---

applicable if the passenger made a special declaration of interest in its delivery according to which the carrier would accept a higher limit of liability against supplementary payment. Because this declaration must be made at the time when the checked baggage was handed over to the carrier, it is unclear how to make such declaration for unchecked baggage.

[53] The Special Drawing Right [SDR] is a unit of currency used by the International Monetary Fund, comprised of an average value of a basket of currencies including the U.S. Dollar, British Pound, Japanese Yen, and EU Euro, and is published regularly in major newspapers. Warren Dean, Jr., *Aviation Liability Regimes in the New Millennium; Beyond the Wild Blue Yonder*, 28 Transp. L. J. 239, 245 (2001).

[54] *Montreal Protocol No. 4*, art. VII (amending *Warsaw Convention* art. 22).

[55] *See Daun v. Sun Aire*, CCH 17 ¶ AVI 17,536 (1982).

[56] *Andrews v. United Airlines*, CCH 24 AVI ¶ 18,072 (1994).

Another "baggage-related" issue relates to the carriage of animals aboard aircraft. Animals may be categorized in generally three ways: as *pets* accompanying passengers, as *service animals* for handicapped passengers, and as *cargo* being shipped. Although carriers have an obligation to treat all animals humanely, the rules applying to each category vary, as do the rules unilaterally self-imposed by the various airlines in their tariffs. Under regulation, these tariffs were subject to approval by the CAB, which reviewed them to determine whether their provisions were "just and reasonable." Post-deregulation, there is no government review of domestic tariffs. Therefore, these unilateral contract provisions should be viewed by courts as "contracts of adhesion" and held applicable only if not "unconscionable."

The discussion on service animals is deferred to the topic of passengers with disabilities below. However, with regard to the first category (pets), historically more than a half-million pets have taken to the skies in the U.S. each year, stowed in cargo or underneath passenger seats in the main cabin. But in recent years, airlines have steadily raised fees for transporting pets on domestic flights. In some instances it may cost more to transport an accompanying pet in the cargo hold than the price of its master's ticket in the main cabin. Most airlines will transport pets in the main cabin but charge a variety of prices for the service. The same is true of shipment in the hold. Some airlines allow pets to be checked as baggage. Others have created special pet programs. And certain airlines refuse to transport pets all together.[57]

Shipping animals can require special handling that some airlines consider more trouble than profitable. As a result, certain airlines have pulled out of what they consider to be the "treacherous" business of shipping pets and zoo animals. It can be treacherous for animal owners and their pets as well. There are instances where animals have either starved or froze to death because they were lost in shipment or otherwise died from exposure to the elements while left on tarmacs or in warehouses. A 1976 amendment to the Animal Welfare Act allows the Animal and Plant Health Inspection Service [APHIS] to penalize airlines for inhumane treatment of animals, but only after complaint. Under that law, US Airways was fined $50,000 after 46 forgotten ferrets

---

[57] Jane Costello, *High Air-Cargo Costs Are Pet Peeve*, Wall St. J. (Thurs., Apr. 11, 2002).

starved in an Evansville, Indiana warehouse, and two other incidences where 11 rodents were overheated.[58]

No one knows for sure the incidence rate of injuries to animals. Airlines have not been required to keep records on animals injured or killed during flight. And, it is difficult to estimate because airlines were either reluctant or would not even disclose how many animals fly each year. Thus, the number is highly disputed. Animal rights groups claim that thousands die in flight each year. The airlines say there are only a handful.[59] But even one death can be devastating to owners who consider their pets as part of the family. Unfortunately, damages for the loss of a pet on an airline can be reduced to so many pounds of cargo.

Concern for in-flight animal safety dates back at least to 1956 when the American Society for the Prevention of Cruelty to Animals [ASPCA] opened Animal Port, a holding area for animals in transit, and oversaw the handling of live cargo.[60] The dangers of shipping animals are well recognized, and in 2002 the FAA proposed stricter rules for the airlines to follow. But the proposed rules were met by stiff opposition from animal breeders and other commercial shippers of animals, fearing that new rules might do more harm than good to the commercial market. Animal rights activists would have preferred for carriers to monitor the condition of animals they transport as well as reporting any injuries or deaths to the FAA. But to their disappointment, the final rules included only a requirement that air carriers submit, to the DOT through the APHIS, a report on any incidents involving loss, injury or death of an animal during air transit by the carrier.[61]

CONTRACT OF CARRIAGE

An air carrier operating "large" aircraft must give notice of its terms of contract of carriage.[62] The ticket or other written instrument

---

[58] Ryan Dezember, *When Pigs Fly . . . FAA Rule Pits Breeders vs. Rights Activists*, Wall St. J. (Fri., Dec. 20, 2002), at B1.

[59] *Id.*

[60] *Id.*

[61] *See Rules and Regulations*, Federal Register (Aug. 11, 2003), Vol. 68, No. 154, at 47797-47800.

[62] As used here, "large aircraft" means any aircraft designed to have a maximum passenger capacity of more than 60 seats or a maximum payload capacity of more than 18,000 lbs. For application of certification under safety regulations, "large" may mean greater than 30 seats. For pilot type rating certification, it means aircraft of more than 12,500 lbs. maximum certificated takeoff weight.

which embodies the contract of carriage may incorporate the contract terms by reference (i.e., without stating full text), but upon request, each air carrier must provide free of charge by mail or other delivery service to passengers, a copy of the full text of its terms. Additionally, each air carrier must keep available at all times, free of charge, at all locations where tickets are sold within the United States, information sufficient to enable passengers to order the full text of such terms.

The terms of the contract of carriage may include:

- limits on the air carrier's liability for personal injury or death of passengers, and of loss damage, or delay of goods and baggage, including animals;[63]
- claim restrictions, including time periods within which passengers must file a claim or bring action against the carrier;
- rights of the carrier to change the terms of the contract;
- rules about reconfirmation of reservations, check-in times, and refusal to carry;[64] and
- rights of the carrier and limitations concerning delay or failure to perform service, including schedule changes, substitution of alternate air carrier or aircraft, and rerouting.[65]

Air carrier operators, flying aircraft with 60 seats or less, are exempt from requirements to file with the federal government, to print, or to keep open to public inspection, their tariffs showing all rates, fares and charges for air transportation between points served by it.[66] They are exempt except for tariffs for through-rates, fares and charges filed jointly with air carriers subject to the tariff rules. By definition a "commuter" air carrier is a scheduled air taxi, and may not be subject to the same rules as other air carriers (certificated under Section 401 of the Federal Aviation Act).

---

[63] *See Stevenson v. American Airlines*, CCH 24 AVI 17,341 (1992); *see also Gluckman v. American Airlines*, CCH 24 AVI ¶ 17,947 (1994).
[64] *See Goodman v. National Airlines*, CCH 8 AVI ¶ 18,406 (1964).
[65] *See Schaefer v. National Airlines* CCH 16 AVI ¶ 17,354 (1980).
[66] Federal Aviation Act of 1958, § 403.

OVERSALES

Stemming from the fact that often there are substantial changes in flight reservations before flights depart, and as a result of changes in passengers' plans and/or cancellation of their reservations, the airlines are authorized to "overbook." This practice was determined by the Civil Aeronautics Board, and later by the courts, to be in the public interest.[67] Because of multiple reservations made by a segment of the traveling public, and for "no-shows" who neglect to cancel reservations, in many cases, aircraft are not booked beyond capacity. To allow for the practice of overbooking, air carriers with respect to flight segments with large aircraft must compensate passengers whom the carrier has denied boarding because of overbooking.

In the event of an oversold flight, every carrier is to first request volunteers for denied boarding, before using any other boarding priority. A "volunteer" is a person who responds to the carrier's request for volunteers and who willingly accepts the carrier's offer of compensation, *in any amount*, in exchange for relinquishing the confirmed reserved space. If an insufficient number of volunteers come forward, the carrier may deny boarding to other passengers in accordance with its boarding priority rules. Every carrier must establish priority rules and criteria for determining which passengers holding confirmed reserved space shall be denied boarding on an oversold flight in the event that an insufficient number of volunteers come forward.

Subject to the exceptions providing for volunteers, air carriers are obligated to pay compensation to passengers denied boarding involuntarily from an oversold flight at the rate of 200% of the sum of the values of the passenger's remaining flight coupons up to the passenger's next stopover, or if none, to the passenger's final destination, with a maximum of $400. However, the compensation shall be one half the amount described above, with a $200 maximum, if the carrier arranges for comparable air transportation, or other transportation used by the passenger that, at the time either such arrangement is made, is planned to arrive at the airport of the passenger's next stopover or if none, at the airport of the passenger's destination, not later than two hours after the time the direct or connecting flight on which

---

[67] *See Ralph Nader v. Allegheny Airlines*, 626 F. 2d 1031 (1980).

confirmed space is held is planned to arrive in the case of interstate and overseas air transportation, or four hours after such time in the case of foreign air transportation.[68]

Carriers may offer free or reduced rate air transportation in lieu of the cash due; if (1) the value of the transportation benefit offered is equal to or greater than the cash payment otherwise required; and (2) the carrier informs the passenger of the amount of cash compensation which would otherwise be due and that the passenger may decline the transportation benefit and receive the cash payment. A passenger denied boarding involuntarily from an oversold flight is not eligible for denied boarding compensation if:

- the passenger does not comply fully with the carrier's contract of carriage or tariff provisions regarding ticketing, reconfirmation, check-in, and acceptability for transportation;[69]
- the flight for which the passenger holds confirmed reserved space is unable to accommodate that passenger because of substitution of equipment of lesser capacity when required by operational or safety reasons;
- the passenger is offered accommodations or is seated in a section of the aircraft other than that specified on the ticket at no extra charge, except that a passenger seated in a section for which a lower fare is charged shall be entitled to an appropriate refund; or
- the carrier arranges comparable air transportation, or other transportation used by the passenger at no extra cost to the passenger, that at the time such arrangements are made is planned to arrive at the airport of the passenger's next stopover or, if none, at the airport of the final destination, not later than one hour after the planned arrival time of the passenger's original flight or flights.

Passengers denied boarding involuntarily are to be furnished a written statement explaining the terms, conditions and limitations of denied boarding compensation, and describing the carrier's boarding

---

[68] See *Rousseff v. Western Airlines*, CCH 13 AVI ¶ 18,391 (1976).
[69] See *Goodman v. National Airlines* CCH 8 AVI ¶ 18,406 (1964).

priority rules and criteria. Furthermore, every carrier is required by regulations to display where tickets are sold and in a conspicuous public place a sign that is clearly visible and readable to the traveling public, which shall have printed thereon the following statement:

> *Airline flights may be overbooked, and there is a slight chance that a seat will not be available on a flight for which a person has a confirmed reservation. If the flight is overbooked, no one will be denied a seat until airline personnel first ask for volunteers willing to give up their reservation in exchange for a payment of the airline's choosing. If there are not enough volunteers the airline will deny boarding to other persons in accordance with its particular boarding priority. With few exceptions persons denied boarding involuntarily are entitled to compensation. The complete rules for the payment of compensation and each airline's boarding priorities are available at all airport ticket counters and boarding locations. Some airlines do not apply these consumer protections to travel from some foreign countries, although other consumer protections may be available. Check with your airline or your travel agent.*

SMOKING ABOARD AIRCRAFT

Between points within the United States and its territories, air carriers must prohibit all smoking on aircraft.[70] A $2,000 penalty may be imposed for tampering with a lavatory smoke alarm.

---

[70] 49 U.S.C. § 41706.

CONSUMER CREDIT PROTECTION

As already stated, there was a wave of consumer related federal legislation passed in the decades of the 1960s and 1970s. By the early 1980s, more than 50 consumer laws had been adopted. Included were laws related to consumer credit. As a result, all air carriers engaging in consumer credit transactions must comply with the consumer credit laws. Any violation of the following Acts of Congress is considered a violation of the 1958 Federal Aviation Act:

- *Consumer Credit Protection Act*, incorporating the following legislation:
- *Truth in Lending Act*, wherein exact finance charges must be divulged;
- *Fair Credit Reporting Act*, establishing procedures for correcting and explaining billing errors;
- *Equal Credit Opportunity Act*, making discrimination illegal;
- *Fair Debt Collection Practices Act*, which limit third party collector abuses; and
- *Electronic Fund Transfer Act*, which places controls on the electronic transfer of funds.

NONDISCRIMINATION

Air carriers under any federal program, or carriers receiving financial assistance from the federal government, may not discriminate in air transportation on grounds of race, color, or natural origin.[71] Subsequent to the terrorist attacks of September 11, 2001, the DOT began hearing reports of airlines unlawfully removing passengers of Middle Eastern or South Asian descent from flights and/or denying them permission to board. Responding to the reports of discrimination against passengers, the DOT brought its first complaint against American Airlines in April of 2003. The DOT's Aviation Enforcement Office alleged that the airline had "unlawfully" removed passengers from flights and denied boarding to passengers "because, or primarily be-

---

[71] *See Harris v. American Airlines*, CCH 24 AVI ¶ 17,156 (1992).

cause, the passengers were, or were perceived to be, of Arab, Middle Eastern, South Asian descent and/or Muslim."

Attempts to settle the issue through negotiations "proved unsuccessful." In a written statement, American said it "vehemently" denied the government allegations. Moreover, its employees "were following the directives of the President and the Attorney General to be vigilant in the face of terrorist threats" in the immediate aftermath of the attacks (which, incidentally, involved two of American's aircraft). It also pointed out immediately after the 9/11 attacks American's Chief Executive Officer [CEO] Donald Carty had urged the carrier's employees to treat all passengers, "particularly those of Arab, Muslim, or Middle Eastern backgrounds," with "tolerance and dignity." Irrespective, DOT sought to fine the carrier at least $65,000 for incidents involving at least 10 passengers.[72]

The DOT similarly brought charges against United Airlines in November 2003 that United had removed or denied boarding passengers in the weeks following September 11, 2001, based on perceptions that they were Arab, Muslim or Middle Eastern. Like American Airlines, the 9/11 attacks involved United aircraft as well. United denied the charges but entered into a consent decree whereby, though not required to pay a financial penalty, it agreed to improve civil rights training for pilots, flight attendants and customer service representatives.[73]

On March 2, 2004, the DOT reached a settlement with American Airlines over its charges that American had discriminated against passengers perceived to be Middle Eastern or South Asian descent. The settlement order found that "American acted in a manner inconsistent with federal laws that prohibit discrimination." It required American, without admitting to wrong doing, to provide civil rights training to its employees over a three-year period, and at an estimated cost of $1.5 million in order to resolve the allegations and avoid litigation.[74]

Not only are carriers prohibited from discriminating against passengers, but they may not recruit, advertise, hire, fire, upgrade, promote, demote, transfer, lay-off, terminate employees, nor establish rates of pay or other forms of compensation or benefits, select for

---

[72] Stephen Power, *American Air Hit by Federal Claim of Discrimination*, Wall St. J. (Mon., Apr. 28, 2003).

[73] *See World News Roundup*, Av. Wk. & Space Tech. (Nov. 24, 2003), at 16.

[74] *American Airlines Settles Discrimination Suit*, Airwise News (Mon., Jan. 10, 2005).

training or apprenticeship, use facilities, or otherwise treat employees discriminatorily.

To insure that handicapped persons receive adequate air transportation without unjust discrimination, the Rehabilitation Act of 1973 was passed to eliminate discrimination on the basis of handicap in any program or activity receiving federal financial assistance. In air transportation a "qualified handicapped person" is one who has a physical or mental impairment, but one whose carriage will not in the "reasonable expectation of air carrier personnel" jeopardize the safety of a flight or the health or safety of other persons.[75]

Under the Air Carrier Access Act of 1986,[76] carriers may not refuse transportation to people on the basis of handicap.[77] What is generally prohibited under the 1986 law is that carriers may not refuse transportation to people on the basis of handicap alone. Although carriers may still exclude persons with disabilities on safety grounds, they must provide written explanation of the decision. Moreover, carriers may require up to 48 hours advance notice for certain accommodations requiring preparation time such as respirator hook-up or transportation of a battery-powered wheelchair on a small aircraft. Nevertheless, carriers must accept battery-powered wheelchairs, including the batteries, and package the batteries as hazardous materials when necessary. But generally, carriers may not refuse transportation to people merely because they are disabled. Airlines are required to provide assistance boarding and within the cabin as well. Additionally, wheelchairs and other assistive devices have priority over other items for storage in the baggage compartment, and have priority for in-cabin storage over other passengers' items brought on board at the same time.

The Air Carrier Access Act became effective April 5, 1990. Since then several airlines have been charged with violation of the act, specifically with regards to accommodating wheelchair stowage. In a settlement approved in March of 2002, Northwest Airlines was ordered to pay $700,000 civil penalty and desist from future violations of rules prohibiting discrimination against passengers with disabilities. How-

---

[75] *See Adamsons v. American Airlines* CCH 17 AVI ¶ 17,781 (1982); *see also Walt Shinault v. American Airlines* CCH 22 AVI ¶ 18,420 (1990).

[76] 49 U.S.C. § 41705.

[77] As defined by the Air Carrier Access Act of 1986, a "qualified handicapped individual" is a handicapped person who validly obtains a ticket, comes to the airport for the flight, and meets non-discriminatory contract of carriage requirements that apply to everyone.

ever, Northwest could use the bulk of the fine to improve its services to the disabled.[78]

In September of 2003, three low-cost carriers (America West, Southwest Airlines and JetBlue) agreed to civil penalties totaling $750,000 to settle charges that they violated disabled-passenger laws and regulations by failing to provide stowage space for standard-size folding wheelchairs inside aircraft cabins. Each airline was to receive a credit for 90% of its share of the penalty for improving service to disabled passengers beyond federal requirements.[79]

All told, several carriers amassed more than $3 million in penalties in 2003. AirTran Airways was charged $125,000 for not providing appropriate room for stowage of wheelchairs on board. As a result the carrier set aside two seats in the rear of all aircraft for wheelchair storage. US Airways was fined in March 2003 for not providing adequate boarding and deplaning equipment for passengers using wheelchairs. Ryan International Airlines, a charter carrier, was fined $400,000 in September for similar violations.[80] For failing to provide mandatory accommodations for handicapped passengers, Frontier Airlines agreed in a consent order to stow a folded wheelchair on top of the last row of passenger seats on the right side of its Airbus A319 and its Boeing 737 aircraft.[81]

Pursuant to the Air Carrier Access Act, and in addition to wheelchairs and other assistive devices, "carriers shall permit dogs and other service animals used by persons with a disability to accompany the person on a flight." Moreover, "carriers shall permit a service animal to accompany a qualified individual with a disability in any seat in which the person sits, unless the animal obstructs an aisle or other area that must remain unobstructed in order to facilitate an emergency evacuation."[82]

Since the initial service animal guidance was published in 1996, a wider variety of animals have been trained to assist individuals with disabilities. Whereas in the past most service animals were guide dogs, today persons with disabilities use other animals such as cats and

---

[78] Staff Reporter, *Northwest to Pay Fine to Settle Complaint of Disabled Travelers*, Wall St. J. (Fri., Mar. 15, 2002), at B7.

[79] *World News Roundup*, Av. Wk. & Space Tech. (Sep. 1, 2003), at 18.

[80] Audrey Warren, *Airlines Incur Wheelchair Fines*, Wall St. J. (Wed., Oct. 15, 2003).

[81] *World News Roundup*, Av. Wk. & Space Tech. (Nov. 24, 2003), at 16.

[82] 14 C.F.R. § 382.55 (a) (1) and (2) (Jul. 2003).

monkeys not only to assist them with physical disabilities but to provide emotional support as well.[83] In 2003, the DOT clarified rules on service animals to include all manner of beasts if mental-health professionals declare that they are necessary for relieving stress and flying anxiety. On at least one occasion, Dan Shaw, who is legally blind, traveled on American Airlines with his guide horse Cuddles to make an appearance on the *Oprah Winfrey Show.*[84]

ESSENTIAL AIR SERVICE

Leading up to deregulation of the airline industry, legislators were concerned that, if given the opportunity, air carriers would exit unprofitable markets, leaving small communities without airport access. The Airline Deregulation Act of 1978 amended the Federal Aviation Act of 1958 to provide, for ten years after enactment, guaranteed essential air transportation to "eligible points"; that is, to communities that had therefore been provided certificated air carrier service. The Civil Aeronautics Board, and later the Department of Transportation, was delegated the responsibility periodically to review the determination of what was essential air transportation to each eligible point, and based upon such review and consultations with any interested community and with its state agency, make appropriate adjustments as to what constituted essential air transportation to that point.

In accordance with the guidelines promulgated under the Airline Deregulation Act of 1978, the CAB established procedures to be followed in designating eligible points and in determining essential air transportation levels for eligible points, and in the appeals and periodic reviews of these determinations.[85] The original authority for EAS expired in 1988. However, the program has been extended despite repeated attempts to eliminate it. Generally, Essential Air Service [EAS] determinations provided for:

---

[83] DOT Office of Public Affairs, *DOT Issues Guidance on Service Animals Based on Airline Industry/Disability Community Proposal* (Fri., May 9, 2003).

[84] *See* Scott McCartney, *The Stewardess Says, 'Why the Long Face?' A Horse in First Class*, Wall St. J. (Wed., May 21, 2003), at A1.

[85] *See Coastal Airlines v. Civil Aeronautics Board* CCH 17 AVI ¶ 18,444 (1983).

- service from the eligible point for up to two air transportation hubs;
- two round trips each weekday and two round trips over the weekend; and
- up to 160 available seats servicing 80 passengers per day with 40 seats each way.

NADER v. ALLEGHENY AIRLINES
626 F.2d 1031 (D.C. Cir. 1980)

May an airline overbook its flight by accepting more reservations than it can accommodate?

Ralph Nader was scheduled to address a rally in Hartford, Connecticut at noon on April 28, 1972. On April 25, 1972 he reserved a seat on Allegheny Airlines Flight 864, scheduled to depart from Washington, D.C., for Hartford at 10:15 a.m. on April 28. He held a *confirmed reservation* and arrived at the boarding and check-in area approximately five minutes before the scheduled departure time, but was told by Allegheny's agent that he could not be accommodated on Flight 864 because all the seats were occupied. He was offered an alternative air taxi flight by way of Philadelphia, but he decided not to accept it because of uncertainty as to whether he would arrive in Hartford in time for the noon rally. As a result, he was prevented from attending the rally.

Pursuant to CAB regulations, Allegheny mailed to Nader a check in the amount of $32.41 as denied boarding compensation. Nader's attorney returned the check to Allegheny, together with a letter characterizing the denied boarding compensation as a "wholly inadequate offer of settlement."

On July 7, 1972, Nader filed suit in the U.S. District Court, asserting Allegheny's liability on two theories: (1) a common law action based on fraudulent misrepresentation in that Allegheny failed to inform Nader of its booking practices; and (2) a statutory action under section 404(b) of the Federal Aviation Act of 1958, arising from Allegheny's alleged failure to afford Nader the boarding priority specified in its rules, filed with the Civil Aeronautics Board.

The federal District Court, sitting without a jury, entered a judgment for Nader on both claims, and awarded him a total of $10 in compensatory damages and $25,000 in punitive damages. On appeal, the U.S. Court of Appeals reversed the judgment based on Allegheny's alleged violation of Section 404(b), and the district court was instructed to make new findings of fact and conclusions of law. The award of punitive damages on the common law claim was reversed.

The appellate court pointed out that since punitive damages require a finding of malice or reckless disregard for the rights of others, the defendant's motivations are crucial; but "the trial judge never considered whether Allegheny reasonably believed that its policies were completely lawful, and in fact carried the approval of the Board." The U.S. Court of Appeals directed the district court to award punitive damages "only on the terms set forth in this opinion." The award of punitive damages on the statutory claim was reversed on the ground that Allegheny's conduct in applying its boarding priority rules contained no elements of intentional wrongdoing or conscious disregard for Nader's rights. Finally, the appellate court held that under the doctrine of primary jurisdiction the CAB must be allowed to determine whether failure to disclose the practice of overbooking was deceptive within the meaning of Section 411 of the Federal Aviation Act of 1958. The district court was instructed to stay further action on this issue pending reference to the CAB.

The decision was appealed, and the U.S. Supreme Court reversed the order of the appellate court, which had granted a stay to give the CAB an opportunity to act. The Supreme Court concluded that the common law action could be heard by the trial court without prior reference to the CAB. Accordingly, the appellate court entered an amended judgment and the case was remanded to the district court.

On remand, the district court found that Allegheny violated Section 404(b) of the Act, by its failure to board Nader in accordance with its own priority boarding rules. For this, the court awarded him $10 in compensatory damages. The court also found that Allegheny's failure to notify Nader of the chance that he would not be seated constituted fraudulent misrepresentation, and that "defendant Allegheny wantonly implemented its policy of nondisclosure and misrepresentation in conscious, deliberate, and callous disregard of the effect of its policy on its passengers, including plaintiff Nader." The court awarded Nader

$15,000 in punitive damages "to punish defendant Allegheny for its willful and wanton policy of nondisclosure and misrepresentation and . . . to deter defendant from engaging in such practices in the future."

Allegheny Airlines again appealed the judgment of the district court. On this final appeal Allegheny challenged only the award of compensatory and punitive damages on the claim based upon fraudulent misrepresentation.

Nader's reservation was not honored because Allegheny had accepted more reservations for flight 864 than it could accommodate. That is to say, the flight had been "overbooked." Overbooking is a common industry practice, designed to ensure each flight leaves with as few empty seats as possible despite the large number of "no-shows" (i.e., reservation-holding passengers who do not appear at flight time). The airlines try to predict the appropriate number of reservations necessary to fill each flight. In this way, they attempt to ensure the most efficient use of aircraft while preserving a flexible booking system that permits passengers to cancel and change reservations without notice or penalty. At times, the practice of overbooking results in oversales, which occur when more reservation-holding passengers than can be accommodated actually appear to board the flight. When this occurs, some passengers must be denied boarding (i.e., "bumped").

For all domestic airlines, oversales resulted in bumping an average of 5.4 passengers per 10,000 enplanements in 1972. Based on the 1972 experience of all domestic airlines, there was only slightly more than one chance in 2,000 that any particular passenger would be bumped on a given flight. The issues presented in this case were considered in context with the extended consideration the Civil Aeronautics Board had given to the practice of overbooking.

In 1967, the CAB rejected a proposal to include in its rules provisions requiring notice to passengers of an overbooked condition. Instead, the Board concluded the practice was in the public interest, because of substantial reservations turnover before flight departure time occasioned by changes in passengers' plans and cancellation of their reservations. In addition, the practice is used to allow for multiple reservations made by some passengers and for no-shows. Were the carrier prevented from overbooking, large numbers of passengers would be denied reservations on flights which, because of reservations turnover and no-shows, would depart with empty seats.

The court concluded that while it results in oversales, overbooking also contributes to flexibility and freedom in securing, changing, and canceling reservations. Controls on overbooking would reduce load factors, and the additional cost would ultimately be borne by the traveling public. In at least one level of analysis, the air carrier reservations systems in general benefit the traveling public.

This case presents two questions. First, was Allegheny liable to Nader in tort for fraudulent misrepresentations? And second, assuming such liability, was the award of punitive damages proper? As to the second question, the CAB expressed its approval of the practice of overbooking, concluding that "any rigid controls over overbooking, as now practiced, would inevitably lead to restriction on privileges, which contribute greatly to the convenience of air transportation. . . ." Thus, the award of punitive damages was determined to be in error.

As to the first question above, the elements in tort of fraudulent misrepresentation are:

- a false representation;
- in reference to a material fact;
- made with knowledge of its falsity;
- and with intent to deceive; and
- with action taken in reliance upon the representation.

The chance that a holder of a confirmed reservation would be boarded was approximately 99.95 out of 100. In light of this and other facts, the appellate court did not accept the district court's conclusion that Allegheny's failure to notify Nader of its overbooking practice was motivated by deceit and the desire to deprive him of information. The practice of overbooking was no secret, no covert operation, but was openly carried on, and Allegheny was entitled to believe any knowledgeable passenger knew of the practice. The lower court's finding that Allegheny harbored intent to deceive was contrary to the evidence. An airline, which intends to deceive by concealing facts, does not advertise the facts in public proceedings.

Only two days before he made his reservation on Allegheny flight 864, Nader was bumped from an American Airlines flight. Six months earlier he had been bumped by Eastern Air Lines. On both occasions he held a confirmed reservation. Nader "knew the facts" that a confirmed reservation did not exclude the possibility he might not be boarded. "One who has special knowledge, experience and competence may not be permitted to rely on statements for which the ordinary man might recover." It cannot be said that Nader relied on his confirmed reservation with Allegheny as a guarantee of passage. Hence, the court found there was no fraudulent misrepresentation, at least to a consumer as well informed as Ralph Nader. The U.S. Court of Appeals reversed the U.S. District Court's judgment for both compensatory and punitive damages and the case ended on this note.

LECKBEE v. CONTINENTAL AIRLINES
410 F.2d 1191 (5th Cir. 1969)

> *Is an airline liable for damages sustained as a result of exercising prudent judgment in an emergency situation?*

A Continental Airlines' four-engine turboprop began its take-off roll from the Greater Southwest Airport in Fort Worth, Texas. The aircraft was approaching lift-off speed when the captain's adjustable seat unexpectedly slid backwards away from the instrument panel and the controls. The Captain immediately aborted the take-off by retarding the throttles, and the aircraft was brought to a stop. Charles Leckbee, who was a passenger on the flight, about two months prior had undergone a surgical operation for the removal of a herniated disc in the lower region of his back. He alleged that the deceleration from the aborted take-off was so abrupt it threw him across his seat belt, causing injury to the bones, nerves, and soft tissues of his back.

The U.S. District Court concluded the evidence was insufficient to establish the malfunction as the proximate cause of Leckbee's injuries. The case was heard by a jury, but before the jury had a chance to deliberate the issues, the court directed a verdict in favor of Continental, stating there was no evidence from which the jury could find that Leckbee suffered an injury proximately caused by Continental's negligence. Leckbee appealed.

The U.S. Court of Appeals disagreed with the federal District Court. Proximate cause in Texas has two basic elements: (1) *cause in fact*, where but for the negligent act no harm would have been incurred; and (2) *foreseeability*, where a person of ordinary intelligence and prudence could anticipate the danger to others created by his or her negligent act. There was no negligence in the captain's actions to abort the take-off. Common sense suggests he exercised good judgment. However, the Appellate Court concluded a jury might justifiably find from the evidence that Continental's employees should have reasonably foreseen the danger to passengers created by a failure adequately to adjust the captain's seat. Because the seat came loose, it could be determined that that was the *cause in fact* of Leckbee's injuries. The judgment directed by the District Court was reversed and the case was remanded for a new trial.

ADAMSONS v. AMERICAN AIRLINES
444 N.E.2d 21 (N.Y. Ct. App. 1982)

> *Can a disabled person recover damages for the carrier's refusal to transport?*

While residing in Haiti, Hannelore Adamsons was stricken with an undiagnosed illness. Arrangements were made for her transportation to New York on defendant American Airlines. Initially it was explained to American's agents that although the plaintiff was paralyzed and in need of a wheelchair, she could sit up and her condition was not contagious. Upon these explained conditions American issued a first-class ticket. However, when the plaintiff arrived at the Port-au-Prince Airport she was crying out in pain and was obviously experiencing extreme discomfort. Further, it was noticed by American's employees that she had a catheter and disposal bag attached to her body. It was decided by the airline personnel that the plaintiff's health and the safety of the other passengers would be jeopardized if plaintiff were to be allowed to travel on the flight.

Two days later Adamsons flew to New York on Pan American World Airlines. Her illness was subsequently diagnosed as intermedulla hematoma on her spinal chord. Surgery was performed but was unsuccessful. The plaintiff remained paralyzed from the waist down. She filed suit for monetary damages against American claiming that its negligence in refusing to transport her, and the two-day delay in transportation, proximately caused her permanent paralysis. The action was submitted by the trial court to a jury to decide whether the defendant was negligent in refusing plaintiff passage. The jury returned a verdict of $525,000 for plaintiff. The (intermediate) Appellate Division affirmed the decision with one justice dissenting. The case was appealed.

The question before the New York Court of Appeals was whether the airline, in refusing passage to the plaintiff, properly exercised its authority under the Federal Aviation Act of 1958. The court held that it did. The Federal Aviation Act authorizes an air carrier to deny passage to any person "when in the opinion of the carrier, such transportation would or might be inimical (i.e., harmful) to safety of flight" (parenthetical added). It is abundantly clear that the decision to accept or refuse a passenger for air carriage lies exclusively with the airline. The court stated it did not believe "that Congress, in enacting the Federal Aviation Act, intended to test the airline's judgment to deny passage to certain persons by standards of negligence." Airline safety is too important. The law, therefore, endows the airline with discretion.

The Court of Appeals held that the trial court erred in submitting to the jury the question of whether the airline acted negligently. The standard, which should have been applied, was whether the decision was arbitrary, capricious or irrational, and thus constituting an abuse of discretion. As a matter of law, the defendant did not abuse its discretion in refusing to transport the plaintiff to New York. The airline could see how ill the passenger was. The illness was undiagnosed; the possibility of infectious origin had not been ruled out; her legs were paralyzed; and she had attached to her a Foley catheter. No special preparations had been made or requested to accommodate her.

There was no showing of arbitrariness. Accordingly, the order of the appellate division was reversed and the complaint dismissed.

ALAN SPORN v. METRO INTERNATIONAL AIRWAYS
17 Avi. (CCH) ¶ 18,207 (N.Y. S.Ct. 1983)

Is an airline liable for not meeting its published timetable?

Alan Sporn purchased a round trip ticket from Metro International Airways for passage from New York to Brussels and back. Take-off from Brussels was delayed three hours to permit the filming of the defendant's aircraft for a movie production. On behalf of himself and all others on the flight, Sporn filed suit for money damages on claims of fraudulent misrepresentation, breach of contract, rescission (i.e., annulling or unmaking of a contract) based on fraud, and a violation of General Business Law (e.g., false advertising).

The New York Supreme Court (which in New York is the trial court, rather than the supreme appellate court as in the other states) denied motion on breach of contract grounds. Neither timetable nor advertisement is a warranty of punctuality. In this case, a provision of the ticket stated that "times shown in timetable or elsewhere are not guaranteed and form no part of this contract." However, the publication of a timetable does impose an obligation to exercise all reasonable care to meet the timetable, and a carrier is liable when it negligently fails to keep the time published.

Motion was granted insofar as it sought "class action certification" (for a single alleged tortious act having harmed a large number of people and damages sustained by each almost certainly being insufficient to justify the expense inherent in any individual action). The court ordered defendant to furnish the plaintiff with the names and addresses of all persons on the flight, for purposes of consolidating the claims.

SCHAEFER v. NATIONAL AIRLINES
499 F. Supp. 920 (D. Md. 1980)

*What are passengers' rights in the event of an
airline flight cancellation?*

On March 25, 1979, plaintiff William Schaefer and his party (consisting of his wife, three family members and a business associate), had confirmed reservations on National Airlines Flight 106 from Miami, Florida to Washington, D.C. Schaefer and his family lived in Maryland and were attempting to return home from a week's vacation in Florida. Upon arrival at the airport in Miami, the plaintiff was informed that Flight 106 had been canceled, although no explanation was tendered.

Schaefer inquired about alternative transportation with Eastern Air Lines, only to be informed Eastern could not accommodate them. The plaintiff then discussed his problem with one of the defendant's agents. He was informed that defendant National Airlines could not offer them a flight home for two days. Schaefer expressed concern in that he had business meetings scheduled for the next day, which required his presence, his children had to return to school, and his business associate also needed to return to Maryland. Defendant National Airlines refunded the purchase price of the six return tickets and gave plaintiff $250 to help defray expenses. Plaintiff charted a private jet for $3,100 and returned home on that same day.

The reason for the cancellation of Flight 106 was that the aircraft scheduled to fly from Tampa, Florida, to Los Angeles, California, broke down in New York and the aircraft which was scheduled to fly Flight 106 was substituted for the Tampa-Los Angeles flight.

Schaefer brought this action against National alleging it breached its common law duty to him as a common carrier. He claimed as damages the expenses incurred as well as inconvenience, lost time, embarrassment, indignity, and wounded feelings. The plaintiff asked for $25,000 in actual damages and $200,000 in punitive damages.

National moved for summary judgment on the ground the tariff it was required to file with the CAB limited plaintiff's remedies to a refund of the purchase price of the ticket along with payment for certain incidental expenses, such as lodging and meals. In response, plaintiff argued that the portion of the tariff on which National relied was invalid and illegal and, thus, could not be raised as a defense.

National had complied with CAB rules in the event of a cancellation, and with the provisions of its filed tariffs. The U.S. District Court said it was well settled that a tariff, properly filed with the CAB, governs the rights and liabilities between a passenger and an airline. Limitations on liability contained within tariffs are binding on the parties even if the limitations are not embodied within the contract.

The plaintiff, however, posed an issue of invalidity of a CAB rule because it had subsequently been canceled for being "unjust, unreasonable, and unlawful." The court responded by stating the rule was effective at the time of the incident in question and, therefore, was valid. Summary judgment was granted in favor of the defendant National Airlines.

WILLIAMS v. TRANS WORLD AIRLINES
509 F.2d 942 (2nd Cir. 1975)

May an airline refuse to transport a passenger?

Robert F. Williams, a black, native-born American citizen, had lived in Monroe, North Carolina until he left his home August 27, 1961, for New York. He learned by radio on the afternoon of the following day that he had been indicted for an alleged kidnapping in North Carolina and a warrant had been issued to the Federal Bureau of Investigation for his arrest. To avoid prosecution he fled to Canada early in September 1961, and after approximately six weeks, he left for Cuba. He remained in Cuba until 1966, when he moved to the Peoples' Republic of China, where he and his family lived for approximately two years. In 1969, he decided to return to the United States and surrender to the authorities. He made a trip to Dar es Salaam, Tanzania, where he obtained from the U.S. Embassy a travel document or limited passport good only for a return to the United States. He and his family left China in August 1969, for Tanzania, and flew from there to Detroit, Michigan, later that month. Their arrival in Detroit was accompanied by a large demonstration at the airport.

On or about September 4, 1969, Williams purchased a ticket for air passage from Dar es Salaam to London, England, via United Arab Airlines, and thereafter from London by direct flight to Detroit, Michigan, on TWA. The ticket was issued in the name of "R. Franklin."

Meanwhile, on August 28, 1969, Joseph E. Flaherty, Security Representative for Trans World Airlines, received a telephone call from Special Agent John Sullivan of the Federal Bureau of Investigation [FBI] in New York who told Flaherty that Williams would be arriving at the Detroit airport on a TWA flight from London. He stated there was a warrant outstanding for Williams' arrest, that he was a fugitive, and there was a possibility of a demonstration when Williams arrived. The FBI, therefore, asked to have the aircraft parked somewhere other than at the passenger terminal or that it be rerouted to another airport.

After receiving the call, Flaherty contacted Richard Newman, TWA Staff Vice-President, Audit and Security, and advised him of the FBI's request. Newman in turn gave to the President of TWA, Forward Wiser, Jr., all of the information about Williams that had been received from Flaherty. TWA Vice-President and General Counsel, Raymond Fletcher, later advised Newman and another TWA Vice-President, that under the Federal Aviation Act the airline could refuse passage to Williams if he "would or might be inimical to safety of flight."

The ultimate decision to refuse Williams' passage was made by Wiser on September 4, 1969. At this point Williams was told that TWA had refused him passage to Detroit, although it offered to have him flown back to Cairo on United Arab Airlines, which Williams refused. Because he had neither a United States passport which allowed him general foreign travel nor a British visa, he was taken to Pentonville prison as an illegal immigrant, where he remained until September 12, 1969. TWA tried to make Williams an offer to transport him to Detroit if he would consent to be accompanied by a legal attaché of the United States Embassy in London, but the proposal failed to reach Williams in time. Williams never gave consent to an alternative offer by TWA to fly him from London to New York on the 5th.

On September 11, 1969, TWA completed arrangements with Williams' attorney in Detroit, pursuant to which the attorney was flown to London; and on September 12, he and Williams were taken by TWA on a special unscheduled non-stop flight to Detroit. Upon arrival at the airport there, two FBI agents took Williams into custody.

Williams instituted suit on January 26, 1970, against TWA alleging he was unjustly and unreasonably discriminated against in violation of the Federal Aviation Act, false imprisonment and breach of contract. The other allegations of his complaint were withdrawn either prior to or during the trial. The three remaining counts could only succeed in the event TWA was not authorized under the Aviation Act to refuse to carry Williams on September 6, 1969, in accordance with the terms of his ticket.

The central issue in this case, therefore, was whether, as a matter of law, it was reasonable under the circumstances for TWA to refuse to transport Williams, who was the holder of a valid and confirmed ticket, on the flight in question. The U.S. District Court ruled that the refusal was reasonable. Williams appealed.

The U.S. Court of Appeals pointed to the fact that one of the greatest hazards besetting the commercial transportation of passengers by air has been the hijacking of passenger planes. In order to meet this serious problem, Congress enacted appropriate legislation under the

Federal Aviation Act of 1958 authorizing an air carrier to refuse transportation to a passenger "when in the opinion of the air carrier, transportation would or might be inimical to the safety of flight."

However, the plaintiff brought this action on the theory that TWA's authority was severely limited because the Federal Aviation Act also forbids an airline to subject a person to "unjust discrimination or any undue or unreasonable prejudice or disadvantage in any respect whatever." The main thrust of Williams' case was that TWA had no right to rely upon the written and oral statements by the FBI, and that it was required to investigate the matters of which he was accused by the FBI and to make a thorough inquiry into his personal history as well.

In its decision the trial court found, in effect, there was no evidence to show that TWA, in refusing Williams passage on September 6th, took such action or was motivated in the slightest degree to do so, because of race, prejudice or discrimination. It further held that TWA's action was neither arbitrary nor unreasonable.

The U.S. Court of Appeals was of the opinion the findings and conclusions of the trial court were fully supported by the evidence before it, and that TWA's refusal to carry Williams on the flight for which he had a ticket was neither arbitrary nor in any way motivated by racial or political prejudice, but was, under the circumstances, reasonable and fully authorized.

The Federal Aviation Act expressly leaves the ascertainment of the necessity for denying passage to one seeking it, to the "opinion of the air carrier." The test of whether or not the airline properly exercised its power to refuse passage to an applicant or ticket-holder rests upon the facts and circumstances of the case as known to the airline at the time it formed its opinion and made its decision, and whether or not the opinion and decision were rational and reasonable and not capricious or arbitrary in light of those facts and circumstances. They are not to be tested by other facts later disclosed by hindsight.

The U.S. Court of Appeals held that the district court acted properly and reasonably, and its judgment was affirmed.

ROUSSEFF v. WESTERN AIRLINES
409 F. Supp. 1262 (C.D. Calif. 1976)

What recourse is available to a passenger re-routed
on an alternative, and inconvenient, flight?

On October 26, 1973, plaintiff Christ Rousseff boarded Western Airlines Flight 216 at Los Angeles. The flight was scheduled to arrive in Phoenix at 4:59 p.m., with an intermediate stop at San Diego. When Flight 216 arrived in San Diego, Rousseff was requested to disembark and was treated as a stand-by passenger on the flight from San Diego to Phoenix. He was not given a confirmed seat for the San Diego to Phoenix flight. Defendant Western Airlines re-routed the plaintiff from San Diego back to Los Angeles on Delta Airlines Flight 864, and from Los Angeles to Phoenix on Western Airlines Flight 724. Western Flight 724 was scheduled to arrive in Phoenix at 6:40 p.m., less than two hours from the scheduled arrival time of Flight 216. Plaintiff accepted and used the rerouted ticket provided by Western.

Plaintiff Rousseff brought suit in the U.S. District Court claiming unjust discrimination, unreasonable prejudice, disadvantage, and emotional harm. The district court judged the plaintiff had no remedy at law, because he was provided with alternative transportation, which would have gotten him to his destination within less than two hours from his originally scheduled time of arrival.

Under CAB regulation 14 C.F.R. Part 250, plaintiff's acceptance and use of the rerouted tickets provided by Western constituted liquidated damages for all damages suffered. Plaintiff was therefore barred from this action. Rousseff could not otherwise present substantial evidence to show he was entitled to any relief for either negligent or intentional infliction of emotional harm under California State law, nor could he present facts to support a claim for any unjust discrimination under the Federal Aviation Act of 1958.

COASTAL AIRLINES v. CIVIL AERONAUTICS BOARD
709 F.2d 119 (1st Cir. 1983)

*Could a party dissatisfied with essential air service
determinations, challenge the federal agency's
decision in court?*

Coastal Airlines, a losing applicant for one of the CAB's
subsidized routes, challenged a Board decision awarding Air Vermont
a one-year, $360,000 subsidy to provide six-day per week service to
Berlin, New Hampshire, and Newport, Vermont, from Burlington,
Vermont, and Boston. Generally, Coastal challenged the Board's procedures and sought to have the court determine essential service requirements—a duty and responsibility reserved to the CAB by Congress. Coastal claimed the CAB should not have included Newport in
its route selection, because Newport did not generate enough traffic to
satisfy the Board's general criteria as an eligible point.

The record suggests it was difficult for the Board to determine the
amount of the subsidy, the route configuration, and the carrier. The
CAB, its staff, the two towns, and the carriers disagreed with each
other, and the selection process involved repeated proceedings and reconsideration before a final decision was reached. But it is precisely
this kind of difficult decision that Congress entrusted to the CAB
rather than to the court.

Coastal sought to reargue the merits of the CAB's carrier selection
by disputing various Board findings about its own experience, Air
Vermont's preparedness, community support, and relative cost.
Coastal also challenged the Board's rejection of a certain type of aircraft (a Seneca II) that it proposed to put into service on the routes in
question.

Coastal filed objections to the procedures used by the CAB in its
contacts with the FAA about Logan landing rights. The U.S. Court of
Appeals, however, found Coastal's procedural objections totally without merit. The agency followed its own rules, the governing statutes,
and the Administrative Procedure Act [APA]. The court said that neither the Constitution, the APA, nor the agency's regulations required
the CAB to engage in a formal adjudicatory proceeding or to create
formal record to award a subsidy or grant.

The decision of the Board was affirmed. [Note: The responsibility for administering the EAS program was transferred from the CAB to the DOT in 1985].

STEVENSON v. AMERICAN AIRLINES
1992 U.S. Dist. Lexis 20195 (E.D. Pa. 1992)

Is there a limit placed on the value of an animal shipped as air cargo?

Edward and Cheryl Stevenson and their prize-winning dog were transported by American Airlines from Philadelphia to Chicago. The dog suffered heat exhaustion and died, as a result of the flight. The plaintiffs, the Stevensons, sued American Airlines for the loss of the dog. Defendant American Airlines filed a motion for pretrial summary judgment, on the theory that its liability for the loss is limited by the terms of the contract of carriage to the sum of $1250. The Stevensons argued they were not bound by the limitation (i.e., $1250), and they filed a cross-motion for summary judgment on all liability issues.

The applicable law in this case is reasonably clear. Federal law governs. For travel wholly between U.S. points, federal rules require any limit on an airline's baggage liability be at least $1250 per passenger. But excess valuation may be declared on certain types of articles. The decisive question here is whether the plaintiffs were afforded a fair opportunity to learn that the $1250 limitation would apply unless they sought, and paid for, additional coverage. In determining whether the passenger-shipper had reasonable notice of the limitation-of-liability provisions the test of reasonable *communicativeness* applies; the standard of which is normally decided by a judge rather than a jury.

The plaintiffs contended they never saw any of the conditions printed upon the ticket itself, and they were totally unaware of the $1250 limitation. However, the information was printed on their ticket(s). The Stevensons just failed to read it. The court said it was indeed unfortunate that the plaintiffs were not actually aware of the limitation provision, but as the defendant correctly pointed out, their ignorance was to no avail if they were afforded a reasonable opportunity to learn the limitation. In the judge's view, the information supplied on the ticket would have alerted a reasonable passenger to the fact that the contract of carriage contained some limitation on the carrier's liability for lost luggage—indeed, a reasonable passenger would not likely assume that the limitation did exceed $1250 per passenger.

The judge did note, however, that the limitation is $1250 per passenger, and therefor ruled that the passenger(s) could not recover more than $2500 for loss of jointly owned baggage (or the actual value of the dog at the time of the loss, whichever was less).

GLUCKMAN v. AMERICAN AIRLINES
1994 U.S. Dist. Lexis 17967 (S.D.N.Y. 1994)

What is the value of an animal shipped as "excess baggage"?

This action was for a breach of contract and various tort claims relating to American Airlines' failure to safely transport Andrew Gluckman's pet dog, Floyd. Before the court was the defendant's, American Airlines, motion to dismiss the complaint. American Airlines asked that, as a matter of law, the court enter judgment in Gluckman's favor in the amount of $1250 for the breach of obligation claim, and find in favor of American for the remaining tort claims.

Upon graduation from high school in the spring of 1988, Gluckman went camping out west with two high school friends. His parents purchased his round trip ticket from New York to Phoenix, as a gift. A golden retriever wandered into Gluckman's campsite, and the boys took him in and gave him food and water. Gluckman became attached to the dog, naming him Floyd.

On June 22, 1988 (well into the hot season in Arizona), Gluckman, who had never before bought an airline ticket for himself, telephoned American asking if there was a way to bring Floyd, a perfectly healthy, two-and-one-half-year-old golden retriever, in the passenger cabin of the airplane on the flight home. The agent told Gluckman that, in order to bring Floyd home Gluckman would have to put the dog in the baggage compartment. Gluckman could buy a special crate (for $80.85) for Floyd to ride in, and pay an additional $30 for Floyd's transport as excess baggage.

According to Gluckman, the ticket agent never disclosed that Floyd would be in any danger during the flight by virtue of the fact that he was traveling in the luggage compartment. Specifically, Gluckman claimed the agent did not warn him that:

- The cargo hold was not air-conditioned while the plane was on the ground;
- American could not monitor conditions in the cargo hold from the cockpit of the plane;
- The crew could not control the cargo area temperature; or
- The outdoor temperatures could not exceed safety limits set by defendant's own policies; placing a pet in the baggage compartment of an airplane in any temperature above 85 degrees or below 45 degrees Fahrenheit, if ground time was expected to exceed 45 minutes, was strictly forbidden by American;
- Nor did the ticket agent reveal to Gluckman that Floyd was, in the eyes of American, merely *baggage*, that the airline's liability for his injury or death was limited, or that Gluckman could insure the dog for more than the standard, limited amount if he desired.

The plane taxied away from the gate, but because of mechanical difficulties, the plane was forced to return to the gate, where it remained for over an hour. In Arizona, on that June day, the temperature climbed to 115 degrees Fahrenheit. The temperature in the unventilated baggage compartment, where Floyd was stowed, reached 140 degrees Fahrenheit. Gluckman disembarked the plane to make other travel arrangements, and he requested the dog be brought to him. When American's agents brought Floyd, Gluckman was devastated to find that Floyd had collapsed from the heat. Floyd was lying on his side panting; his face and paws were bloody; there was blood all over the crate; and the condition of the cage evidenced a panicked effort to escape.

After an unexplained delay of an additional 45 minutes American arranged to bring Floyd to a veterinarian. The veterinarian advised Gluckman that Floyd had suffered heat stroke and brain damage. Although Gluckman stayed with Floyd all night in intensive care, Floyd had to be put to sleep the next morning. In this action, Gluckman alleged that American's grossly negligent and reckless conduct resulted

411

in Floyd's destruction. Thus, he sought compensatory damages as a result of Floyd's death and his own emotional distress.

Although American conceded that its behavior was negligent and caused Floyd's death, it argued that its tariff legally precluded Gluckman from filing this suit more than one year after the incident in question. In the alternative, American requested that judgment be entered in Gluckman's favor in the amount of $1250, which represented the contractual limitation of liability set forth in the ticket. On the day of his return flight, Gluckman purchased an "Excess Baggage Ticket" (i.e., Floyd's ticket). On the face of Floyd's ticket, in writing less than one-sixteenth of an inch high, appeared the following: "Subject to tariff regulations. For conditions of contract see passenger ticket & baggage check." The Court found that the language contained in either "Floyd's ticket," or in Gluckman's ticket, was sufficient to constitute clear notice of the tariff.

As to the tort claims, in *Corso v. Crawford Dog and Cat Hospital, Inc.*,[86] the court ruled that "a pet occupies a special place somewhere in between a person and a piece of property." Gluckman thus contended that the courts of the State of New York having recognized a cause of action for loss of the companionship of a pet, sought a recovery in tort in this case. Unfortunately, the U.S. District Court of New York disagreed, finding that, ". . . *Corso*, and a few cases that follow it, (were) aberrations flying in the face of overwhelming authority to the contrary."

Accordingly, the District Court found that there is no independent cause of action for loss of the companionship of a pet. American may have failed to give the passenger reasonable notice as to the danger of placing an animal in the baggage compartment, but Gluckman's other claims for various torts, including negligent and intentional infliction of emotional distress, loss of companionship, and the dog's pain and suffering, were dismissed for failure to state a claim upon which relief could be granted. American's motion was granted in part and denied in part.

---

[86] 97 Misc.2d 530, 415 N.Y.S.2d 182 (1979).

LAMKIN v. BRANIFF AIRLINES
853 F. Supp. 20 (D. Mass. 1994)

Is an airline liable for burns sustained by a passenger
as the result of spilled coffee?

On March 15, 1985, Helen and George Lamkin were passengers on Braniff flight 500 from Miami to Boston. Shortly after take-off, a Braniff flight attendant served hot coffee to Helen Lamkin in a Styrofoam coffee cup with a narrow base. Mrs. Lamkin put the coffee on a folding shelf attached to the seat in front of her. The passenger seated in front of her moved the seat backwards, which caused the coffee cup on the folding shelf to spill its contents onto Mrs. Lamkin's lap. She sustained what was later diagnosed as second and third degree burns from the coffee. Mrs. Lamkin applied ice, apparently from the aircraft's galley, to the burned area.

On the day following the incident, a defective coffee maker was removed from the plane on which Mrs. Lamkin was injured. The evidence does not reveal the precise defect in the coffee maker, except that a note on a Braniff services form states that "there was no power to brew."

Mrs. Lamkin filed suit against Braniff, claiming negligence in hiring, instructing and training of its flight personnel in serving hot coffee and providing first aid, and in Braniff's use of an allegedly defective coffeemaker, seats, cup, and folding shelves. She also claimed that Braniff was negligent in failing to warn her about the excessively high temperature of the coffee, and in failing to warn the passengers about the hazards of moving the seat back.

As a common carrier, Braniff was subject to a high standard for care, and, according to the Supreme Judicial Court of Massachusetts, "the standard to which common carriers are held is the very highest, approaching that of an insurer." But while the standard may "approach" that of an insurer, the courts have not gone so far as to rule that a common carrier is in fact strictly liable for accidents which befall its passengers. Rather, "the carrier is not an insurer of the safety of its passengers, nor is it obliged by law to foresee and to guard against unlikely dangers and improbable harms."

In reviewing the facts of the case, and in light of a motion for summary dismissal, the U.S. District Court, as the trier of fact, determined that as a matter of law, all of the points necessary to demonstrate negligence were not presented. The plaintiffs (the Lamkins) had shown that: (1) Mrs. Lamkin was burned by hot coffee served by Braniff, and (2) a defective machine was removed the next day. The question thus raised was whether the plaintiffs had shown enough to support a finding by a factfinder that Braniff was negligent. The Court concluded they had not.

The plaintiffs failed to offer any evidence that Braniff knew or should have known that there was a defect in the coffee maker, which would cause it to brew extremely hot coffee. In fact, the plaintiffs had not even shown that there was a defect in the coffee maker that caused it to brew extremely hot coffee. They had not offered any evidence to show that Braniff or any of its employees knew or should have known that the coffee, which was actually served to Mrs. Lamkin, was extremely hot. In short, the plaintiffs simply failed to offer any evidence that would support a finding of negligence. The plaintiffs also failed to show how any behavior of the flight attendants after the coffee spilled exacerbated Mrs. Lamkin's injury. Nor did they offer any evidence as to how the seats, seat trays, or cups were defective. It could not even be demonstrated that the coffee was, indeed, too hot.

With regard to whether or not the coffee may have been over heated, the Court found instructive a New York coffee-spillage case with similar facts. In *Huppe v. Twenty-First Century Restaurants of America*,[87] the court stated:

> *Since plaintiffs clearly intended to purchase hot coffee and since coffee is customarily served and intended to be consumed as a hot beverage, plaintiffs must present evidentiary facts establishing that the coffee served by defendant was defective or unreasonably dangerous by virtue of being hotter than it should have been.*

---

[87] 497 N.Y.S.2d 306 (1985).

The District Court ruled that neither the plaintiff's expert nor common knowledge supported a finding that the mere occurrence of this accident showed *negligence*. Because the plaintiffs had failed to submit sufficient evidence to allow a jury to conclude that Braniff had acted negligently, the defendant's motion for summary judgment was granted.

ANDREWS v. UNITED AIRLINES
24 F.3d 39 (9th Cir. 1994)

*Is an air carrier responsible for damage caused by
a passenger's carry-on luggage?*

During the mad scramble that usually follows shortly after an airplane's arrival at the gate, a briefcase fell from an overhead compartment of a United Airlines aircraft and seriously injured the plaintiff, Billie Jean Andrews. No one knows who opened the compartment or what caused the briefcase to fall, and Andrew's didn't claim that airline personnel were involved in stowing the object or opening the bin. Her claim, rather, was that the injury was foreseeable and the airline didn't prevent it. The U.S. District Court dismissed the suit on summary judgment, and the U.S. Court of Appeals reviewed the case *de novo* (meaning "anew, afresh, or a second time").

Though United Airlines was "responsible for any, even the slightest, negligence and [was] required to do all that human care, vigilance, and foresight reasonable can do under all circumstances"[88] "[T]he degree of care and diligence which [it] must exercise is only such as can reasonably be exercised consistent with the character and mode of conveyance adopted and the practical operation of [its] business. . . ."

To show that United had not satisfied its duty of care toward its passengers, Mrs. Andrews presented the testimony of two witnesses, Janice Northcott, United's Manager of Inflight Safety, and Dr. David Thompson, a human factors expert. Northcott testified that in 1987, the airline had received 135 reports of items falling from overhead bins. As a result of these incidents, Northcott testified that United de-

---

[88] *See Acosta v. Southern California Rapid Transit District*, 2 Cal. 3d 19, 27 (1970), "it is not an insurer of its passengers"; *see Lopez v. Southern California Rapid Transit District*, 40 Cal. 3d 780, 785 (1985).

cided to add a warning to its arrival announcements, to wit, those items stored overhead might have shifted during flight and passengers should use caution in opening the bins. This announcement later became the industry standard. Nevertheless, United maintained that 135 reported incidents was trivial when spread over the millions of passengers traveling on its 175,000 flights every year.

Dr. Thompson testified that United's announcement was ineffective because passengers opening overhead bins couldn't see objects poised to fall until the bins were opened, by which time it was too late. He also testified that United could have taken additional steps to prevent the hazard, such as retrofitting its overhead bins with baggage nets, as some airlines had already done (e.g., British Airways and Virgin Atlantic).

The Court of Appeals concluded that the plaintiff had made a sufficient case to overcome summary judgment. United would be hard pressed to dispute that its passengers are subject to a hazard from objects falling out of overhead bins, considering the warning its flight crews give hundreds of times each day. Thus, a jury could have found United had failed to do "all that human care, vigilance, and foresight reasonably can do under all circumstances." A reasonable jury might conclude United should have done more; it might also find that United did enough. Either decision would be rational on the record presented to the district court, which means summary judgment was not appropriate. The case was reversed and remanded.

CHAPTER 10

LABOR RELATIONS

Organized labor bargains with many of the most influential
management in the country, including those in the public
sector. The business of unions is basically twofold;
collective bargaining and arbitration.

LABOR RELATIONS HISTORY

The tension and conflict between labor and management is as old as capitalism itself and the "division of labor" in society. Adam Smith was one of (if not) the first theorists to write about the division of labor. In his book, *An Inquiry Into the Nature and Causes of the Wealth of Nations*, written in 1776, Adam Smith described a vision of "perfect liberty" where an individual would be " . . . left perfectly free to pursue his own interest his own way . . . ," amidst an economic balance of the market forces of "capital, labor and the marketplace." In his ideal, the "invisible hand" of competition would maintain a *balance* within the marketplace, wherein the consumer would remain sovereign.

Unfortunately, the competitive capitalism of Adam Smith remains an illusive ideal, particularly in a modern world of corporate (even oligopolistic) capitalism. One can certainly question whether the consumer is, indeed, sovereign as envisioned in Adam Smith's laissez-faire marketplace. Moreover, the enmity between management and labor remains a contemporary reality. Considerably more enlightened management policies toward organized labor are in effect today than was the case several decades ago. However, the fact remains that unions are still far from welcome in the eyes of management.

Nevertheless, the pendulum in labor relations has made full swings. Judicial reaction to early attempts by labor to organize in order to improve working conditions was highly unfavorable. Applying doctrine established in early 18th Century England, U.S. courts initially condemned the concerted activities of worker's associations as "criminal conspiracies." They were deemed criminal because workers conspired to interrupt commerce to achieve their ends, and thus expose the overall public welfare to potential injury. As stated by the Philadelphia Mayor's Court in a case tried in 1806,

> *If this conspiracy was to be confined to the persons themselves, it would not be an offense against the law, but they go further . . . endeavoring to prevent, by threats, menaces, and other unlawful means, other journeymen from working at the usual prices, and that they compelled others to join them.*

By 1842, however, there was a break in the doctrine of criminal conspiracy, thus enabling labor to shift its emphasis from political action towards business unionism. Early unions began to flourish and some like the Knights of Labor survived the economic depressions of the late 19th Century.

Today, union strength is highly concentrated in blue-collar industrial areas that are strategic to U.S. economy. Even so, organized labor has thus far been notably unsuccessful in its attempt to organize such white collar (and fast-growing) sectors as trade, services, and finance. The net result over the past 30 years has been a slippage in union membership in the private sector, stimulated by the decline in industrialization of the U.S. caused by free trade. Early in the 21st Century, only about 15% of the U.S. labor force were still unionized and about a third of that was government employees. Still, organized labor bargains with many of the most influential management in the country, including those in the public sector.

The "business" of unions is basically twofold: *collective bargaining* and *arbitration*. *Black's Law Dictionary* defines "arbitration" as,

> *. . . an arrangement for taking and abiding by the judgment of selected persons in some disputed matter, instead of carrying it to established tribunals of justice, and is intended to avoid the formalities, the delay, the expense and vexation of ordinary litigation.*

"Compulsory arbitration" is that which occurs when the consent of one of the parties is enforced by statutory provisions. Examples are state statutes requiring compulsory arbitration of labor disputes involving public employees. Conversely, "voluntary" arbitration "is by mutual and free consent of the parties." On the other hand, arbitration is "binding" when the labor agreement is enforceable.

Collective bargaining is simply negotiations between an employer and union representatives of a collective body of workers over wages and working conditions. The central purposes of collective bargaining are rule making, compensation, and dispute resolution. Samuel Gompers of the American Federation of Labor [AFL] said, "The secret of this continuous progress (of the AFL) has been understanding the nature and possibilities of economic power and concentration on mobilization of that power."

What follows is a synopsis of early milestones in labor legislation:

- In 1890, the *Sherman Act* was enacted as a measure to discourage the concentration of smaller businesses into monopolies. It declared illegal "every contract, combination in the form of trust, or otherwise, or conspiracy in restraint of trade among the several states." It prescribed punishment by fine or imprisonment or both for "every person who shall monopolize, or attempt to monopolize, or combine or conspire . . . to monopolize any part of the trade or commerce among the several states." Under the provisions of this act, decisions handed down in 1911 by the Supreme Court ordered the dissolution of both Standard Oil Company and the American Tobacco Company. The Sherman Act was first considered exclusively a trade law, but in 1908 a court ruling held a labor union liable for damages for organizing a boycott. This provoked labor leaders whose determinations led to the Clayton Act of 1914.

- *The Clayton Act* of 1914 was intended to remove ambiguities in the Sherman Act by making certain specific practices illegal. Price discrimination among buyers was forbidden, along with exclusive selling and tying contracts, if their effect was to lessen competition. The Clayton Act explicitly clarified that nothing in the antitrust laws forbade formation of labor unions.
- *The Railway Labor Act* of 1926 [RLA][1] was the first comprehensive body of labor law promulgated by Congress. The RLA encompasses many of the foundational concepts of collective bargaining and dispute resolution in the labor/management context. The RLA was promulgated to ensure that labor disputes did not disrupt the railroad industry, which was essential for commerce. It was extended to airlines in 1936.
- *The Norris-LaGuardia Act* of 1932 was a great step toward removing the barriers to free organization. The Act had the effect of eliminating the worst abuses of the labor injunction. Unions were freed to engage in organizational activity, including boycotting and picketing by other than employees. This was the first significant pro-union act of Congress. Considerations of the unions are now commonplace, and provisions favorable to unions are often embodied in what would otherwise be non-labor related legislation. For instance, the Airline Deregulation Act of 1978 provides for the compensation of eligible airline employees who experience loss of employment as a result of the 1978 Act's implementation, even though the main purpose of the Act was to encourage free trade and the fundamental intent of the Act is totally unrelated to labor relations.
- The first positive assertion of the right of labor to bargain collectively was contained in S*ection 7a of The National Industrial Recovery Act* of 1933. Unfortunate for organized labor, there was no way to legally enforce the Act's stated principle. Two years later the NIRA was declared unconstitutional on grounds that had nothing to do with the labor section. Congress replaced Section 7a with a more elaborate law of labor relations. This was the *National Labor Relations Act*, more commonly known as the *Wagner Act* of 1935. The Wagner Act es-

---

[1] 44 Stat. 577 (1926).

tablished the principle of collective bargaining as the basis for industrial relations. Management was given the obligation of recognizing and dealing with labor organizations. The Act guaranteed workers the right to form and join labor organizations, and to engage in collective bargaining. The Act restricts employers from: restraining employees from organizing, interfering with the formation of a union, discriminating because of union membership, discharging an employee as a result of charges filed with a union, and refusing to bargain collectively.

- The *Taft-Hartley Act* of 1947, less commonly known as the *Labor-Management Relations Act*, was an amendment to the Wagner Act. The Taft-Hartley Act contained the opposing view that not only should a worker be protected by public policy to engage in union activities, but the worker also had the right *not* to join a union. The "closed-shop," where an employer hired only union workers, was outlawed. The Act also assumed that the interests of the union and of its members are not necessarily the same. The most important feature of the Taft-Hartley Act was its intent to regulate the unions in the public's interest. The Act prohibited unions from coercing employees into joining a union, causing an employer to discriminate against a non-union employee, charging excessive initiation fees, refusing to bargain collectively, causing an employer to pay for employment services not rendered (commonly referred to as "featherbedding"), or using the strike to force an employer to cease doing business (known as a "secondary boycott").

- The *Landrum-Griffin Act* of 1959, also known as the *Labor-Management Reporting and Disclosure Act*, was aimed at union leaders. It tightened restrictions on secondary boycotting and organized picketing, required detailed reporting of all financial transactions between unions and their officers and employees, and required the use of secret ballots in union elections. This Act developed a comprehensive program dealing with the rights of union members, the responsibilities of union leaders, and the use of union funds.

The Progressive Era was marked in particular by the passage of antitrust legislation. And before 1920, the chief emphasis in governmental regulation of transportation was to encourage competition and to protect the public from discriminatory rate practices, specifically by the railroads. However, after 1920 the railroad industry, which had become the primary mode of transportation over the previous six decades, was itself threatened by other evolving modes of transportation and increasing financial problems. Following the Transportation Act of 1920 there evolved a significant shift in U.S. policy which philosophically assumed governmental control would lead to increased efficiency of the transportation system and its facilities. It was believed that enforced competition had provided protection to the public through reduced rates, but that the net reduced income to the railroads resulted in insufficient revenue to meet expenses, and had not provided a fair rate of return on capital investment.

Title III of the Transportation Act of 1920 created a new agency, the U.S. Railroad Labor Board, which attempted to avoid interruptions to commerce by negotiating disputes. Title III was designed to deal with the sometimes-violent confrontations between labor and management in the railroad industry (including the major strikes of 1877, 1886, 1888, and 1894 and the 105 railroad strikes that broke out between 1899 and 1904).[2]

---

[2] In the 19th Century, the monopoly power wielded by Rockefeller's Standard Oil led to such deep rebates as to result in massive revenue losses by railroads. In 1877, Rockefeller insisted that the Pennsylvania Railroad cease oil refining or he would divert traffic to other roads. In the wake of Rockefeller's onslaught, the Pennsylvania fired hundreds of workers, slashed wages 20%, and doubled the length of trains without expanding crews. Also that year, the four major eastern railroads – the Pennsylvania, New York Central, Erie and Baltimore & Ohio [B&O]—set up a rate control pool, and cut wages by 10%. After the B&O announced wage cuts, a general railroad strike ensued. Wages had been reduced the prior year, yet dividends to stockholders were still being paid. It was one of the bloodiest battles in American labor history, resulting in dozens of fatalities. Trainmen at Martinsburg, W. Va., refused to handle freight trains; trains stopped at Grafton; fights broke out at Wheeling. To quell the uprising, state governors ordered out their militias, which Pres. Rutherford B. Hayes supplemented with federal troops. For a week, nearly the entire railroad system ground to a halt. Violence broke out in Baltimore, Chicago, St. Louis, St. Paul, Omaha and San Francisco. In Pittsburgh, a group of 20,000 strikers and supporters confronted 10,000 militiamen and police; 500 tank cars, 120 locomotives and 27 buildings were torched by trade unionists; 24 people died. William Withuhn, *Rails Across America: A History of Railroads in North America* 49 (1993). After burning more than 2,000 freight cars, the revolt subsided. Nonetheless, it inaugurated a new era of labor militancy in American industry. John Chernow, *Titan: The Life of John D. Rockefeller, Sr.* 201-202 (1998). It was the first great American industrial strike. William Withuhn, *Rails Across America: A History of Railroads in North America* 106 (1993). Working conditions on the railroads were difficult. Workers complained of long hours, no overtime pay, the lack of job security, and dangerous workplace conditions. In 1886, a bloody strike erupted on the Chicago, Burlington & Quincy Railroad. William Mahoney, *The Interstate Commerce Commission/Surface Transportation Board as Regulator of Labor's Rights and Deregulator of Rail-*

The 1920 Transportation Act increased the authority of the Interstate Commerce Commission by expanding its economic regulatory powers with regard to railroad management. With that extended economic authority also came the responsibility to settle railroad labor disputes. A national strike in 1922 revealed that the 1920 Act still was not the solution. So in 1926 Congress promulgated the Railway Labor Act,[3] the first legislation to force management to recognize and bargain with employee representatives.[4]

The Railway Labor Act enabled the establishment of two boards to mediate or facilitate labor disputes. Initially the National Railroad Adjustment Board was created to handle minor grievances. In 1934, the National Mediation Board came into being to help mediate major disputes. "Major" disputes involve contractual issues such as pay and working conditions; i.e., the substance of labor negotiations. "Minor" grievances arise from interpretations of contractual provisions.[5] With two national labor boards in place by 1934, there still was little by way of labor protection for airline personnel in the 1930s.[6] In 1936, the Railway Labor Act was amended to include airline workers. Specifically, the Act was extended to,

---

road's Obligations: The Contrived Collision of the Interstate Commerce Act with the Railway Labor Act, 24 Transp. L. J. 241, 245 (1997). In 1888 alone, 2,070 railway workers were killed, and another 20,148 were injured. In 1894, Eugene V. Debs and the American Railway Union staged a bitter, but unsuccessful, strike against wage reductions. *Russell Bourne, Americans on the Move: A History of Waterways, Railways and Highways* 100, 109 (1995). The Brotherhoods began to amalgamate to form unions. Promulgation of the Act to Regulate Commerce of 1887 and its creation of the Interstate Commerce Commission demonstrated the country's acknowledgment that railroads needed to be regulated. William Withuhn, *Rails Across America: A History of Railroads in North America* 106 (1993). The railroad industry pressed for establishment of Army bases in major cities, whose soldiers could be called out to quell strikes with force.
[3] 44 Stat. 577 (1926).
[4] For an excellent review of this history, *see* William Mahoney, *The Interstate Commerce Commission/Surface Transportation Board as Regulator of Labor's Rights and Deregulator of Railroad's Obligations: The Contrived Collision of the Interstate Commerce Act with the Railway Labor Act*, 24 Transp. L.J. 241 245-251 (1997).
[5] Where arbitration is refused there are provisions for the President of the United States to convene an Emergency Board to make recommendations. Effectively, emergency board proceedings allow for a 60 day cooling off period during which labor and management have an opportunity to reconcile differences. In 1997 an Emergency Board was convened by President Clinton to allow a cooling off period for labor and management at American Airlines. Fortunately, American Airlines and its pilots were able to work out their differences during the cooling off period, with no disruptions in service; *see* Paul Stephen Dempsey, Robert M. Hardaway and William E. Thoms, *Aviation Law and Regulation* (1992); *see also* Paul Stephen Dempsey and Laurence E. Gesell, *Air Transportation: Foundations for the 21st Century* (1997).
[6] *See Northwest Airlines v. Hoover*, 93 P.2d 346 (Wash. 1939).

> *. . . cover every common carrier by air engaged in interstate or foreign commerce, and every carrier by air transporting mail for or under contract with the United States Government, and every air pilot or other person who performs any work as an employee or subordinate official of such carrier or carriers. . . .*

CONTEMPORARY ISSUES

Labor protection has been an interwoven thread in transportation legislation since 1920. Labor provisions were also included in the Airline Deregulation Act of 1978 under Section 43. Employees of carriers whose work force was reduced by 7.5% or more as a direct consequence of deregulation are entitled to compensation. Section 43 was adopted as a labor protection device, but it is debatable whether the act has had any redeeming value at all for labor. Displaced employees have encountered great difficulty in recovering on claims filed under the provisions of Section 43.

From the outset, organized labor viewed the prospect of airline deregulation as potentially destructive of their cause, and only with reluctance did the unions accept its adoption—and then, only after Employee Protection Programs [EPP][7] had been incorporated. As it turned out, labor's apprehension was well grounded. The government later failed to live up to its obligations to provide the labor protective mechanisms incorporated into the deregulation act. Additionally, airline management generally took advantage of deregulatory policy and used it as a tool against organized labor. Statements from management that the Airline Deregulation Act " . . . was the greatest anti-labor act ever passed by an American Congress," or that "The government is forcing the airlines into a position in which national unionism cannot survive," give credence to union-related concerns and allegations.

Airline management brought into serious question whether under deregulation the provisions of the Railway Labor Act should not be drastically revised or that, in fact, there was even any similarity at all

---

[7] Sometimes referred to as *Labor Protective Provisions* [LPP].

between railroad and airline labor. In 1985, the U.S. Chamber of Commerce, acting on behalf of a number of airlines, petitioned the National Mediation Board to adopt guidelines for decertifying and eliminating union representation of airline employees under the Railway Labor Act. The Air Line Pilots Association's [ALPA] response to the petition was that the move, if successful, " . . . (would) reap bitter fruit in industrial strife over time."

It is possible, however, that the "move" (to decertify) was beyond labor politics. From an economic perspective, it may have transcended any one element as an issue larger than airline management, the unions, or both. For example, "the supporters of deregulation legislation did not accurately predict the dire consequences of their actions, or, if they suspected the fallout that would occur, chose to ignore the risks." Still, perceived by labor was a "strong anti-labor bias" on the part of management to decertify labor from the Railway Labor Act, and in other actions taken by the new "financial entrepreneurs" who had taken over management of the nation's airlines.

After passage of the Airline Deregulation Act, the CAB seemingly either avoided, or intentionally chose to ignore airline industry-related labor issues. In all claims placed before it, the Board failed to conclude that any of the airlines being evaluated incurred problems as a *direct* result of deregulation. Labor issues left unresolved at the termination of the CAB were handed over to the Department of Transportation in 1985. The DOT generally adopted a similar position that bankruptcies and other business disruptions were not caused by deregulation, but rather were the result of any one of numerous other factors not related to deregulatory policy. The predominant conclusion was that *mismanagement*, and not the effects of deregulation caused the failure of those affected airlines. Hence, the DOT, like the CAB before it, ruled that the employee protective provisions of the Airline Deregulation Act were not applicable, and claims under Section 43 (*de facto*) were unenforceable. But by the early 1990s, the legal process began working with limited success for pilots who had been previously unsuccessful with their claims under the employee protective provisions of the Airline Deregulation Act of 1978.[8]

---

[8] *See McDonald v. Piedmont Aviation*, CCH 24 AVI 17,190 (1992); *see also Air Line Pilots Association v. Federal Aviation Administration and Department of Transportation*, CCH 24

With the advent of deregulation, the industry suddenly found itself confronted with a labor crisis, when, for nearly four decades, labor relations had not been an issue. Deregulatory policy removed the mechanism (i.e., economic regulation) which enabled airlines to avoid cyclical bouts of destructive competition. After deregulation, and faced with intense competition from non-unionized new entrants, management of the established, but unionized, carriers suddenly needed to minimize operational costs and to maximize employee productivity and efficiency in order to compete—especially in markets where post-deregulation, non-union carriers had made significant in-roads.

The traditional airlines were (heavily) unionized and subject to collective bargaining agreements with relatively high wages and unproductive work rules. Carriers entering the market after deregulation were mostly non-union, with markedly lower labor costs. The difficulty of one carrier with high operational costs trying to compete with another carrier in the same market but with significantly lower costs is obvious. The competitive pressures on certain carriers increased dramatically, causing some to go bankrupt and forcing others to quickly find innovative ways to reduce their overhead. And the key to reducing overhead in any business is to cut the cost of labor.

The strains on labor relations had to come to a head. The competitive climate required established airlines to seek labor cost reductions and productivity enhancements. Concessions were made, but at some point the unions had to hold the line, and a labor-management front evolved, with both sides adopting rigid stances. Identified as the main issues between management and labor were: emergence of non-union airlines; restoration of lost wages from previous labor concessions; a share in the profits; growing Employee Stock Ownership Plans [ESOPs] for airlines; and "two-tier pay scales," under which newly hired personnel would be paid lower wage rates than other workers in similar jobs but having senior longevity.

In 1981, after a protracted dispute with the Federal Aviation Administration [FAA] over wages and working conditions, the Professional Air Traffic Controller Organization [PATCO] union declared a strike. Concluding that the strike was unlawful, and intent on sending a

---

AVI ¶ 17,693 (1993); *see also Ackerman, et al. v. Northwest Airlines*, CCH 24 AVI ¶ 18,115 (1994).

strong message that his government would not tolerate union disruptions, President Ronald Reagan responded by firing all 11,500 striking federal air traffic controllers and closing 80 towers.[9] The message was clear. The White House would stand behind management in confrontations with labor.

A key and prolonged battle in the deregulation-related labor confrontation occurred in the airline industry soon thereafter. Following a Leveraged Buy-Out [LBO] by Frank Lorenzo that saddled Continental Airlines with enormous debt, Lorenzo demanded significant wage reductions (to compensate for the LBO). Predictably, labor balked. Continental followed suit by filing for bankruptcy under Chapter 11 on September 24, 1983. Chapter 11 thereby became an innovative approach to resolving labor-related issues.

In effect, management closed down the "old" Continental, obtained protection through bankruptcy court, tore up the collective bargaining agreements, and started the "new" Continental by imposing new wage rates and working conditions The Air Line Pilots Association struck on October 1, 1983. The strike lasted nearly two years. And although ALPA contended it was not ". . . an end to the pilot strike at Continental," in September of 1985 ALPA authorized its striking members to submit bids on an estimated 450 job openings at Continental. By all traditional measures of labor negotiation, ALPA's acquiescence signaled the end of the strike. Union leaders were left with no other alternative. There was a breaking in ranks with some pilots threatening to disassociate themselves from ALPA, and secondly, court decisions had been unfavorable to the union. The federal bankruptcy judge had disallowed about $500 million in claims against Continental over management's rejection of union contracts.

Albeit much shorter lived than the Continental confrontation with labor, another critical battle occurred in the early 1980s between ALPA and United Airlines. The two-tier pay system became the pivotal issue. United had proclaimed its needs for a cost-effective labor contract in order to put itself on at least a near-equal footing with competition. ALPA feared the two-tier system would divide its ranks and reduce the effectiveness of the labor organization. Although

---

[9] L. Schoder, *Flying the Unfriendly Skies: The Effect of Airline Deregulation on Labor Relations*, 22 Transp. L. J. 105, 107 (1994).

United's management and union officials debated the two-tier issue for a year-and-a-half, negotiations did not come to a head until ALPA struck in May of 1985, accusing United of "union busting tactics." The strike lasted only 29 days and ended with a compromise two-tier pay system.[10]

By the failure of one specific objective of the Airline Deregulation Act, "to avoid industry concentration and return to a market of competitive capitalism," it can be argued that the so-called "deregulatory era" ended in the mid-1980s when the industry became even more concentrated than before the airlines were deregulated. Deregulatory policy, as Congress had intended, failed within ten years of its implementation. In the absence of sound regulatory policy the airlines have since floundered during what may be called the "post-deregulatory era." As of this writing, the airline industry is in dire straits and the prospectus can only be described as dour.[11]

"What has happened to the industry that emerged from a regulated environment to a feast-or-famine existence these last 25 years"? asks James Ott, reporter for *Aviation Week & Space Technology*.[12] Deregulatory opponents insist that the problems are proof that deregulation has failed and a return to regulation is the cure. And, arguably, the financial disintegration of the airline industry may well have been triggered by the Airline Deregulation Act in 1978. Yet, the industry has still managed to have its ups and downs. Thus, not all of the airlines' ills can be attributed to deregulatory failure or to lack of policy direction. There are other, intervening if not compounding variables. The current (economic) crisis is but the latest, and perhaps the worst, of *serial* setbacks, ranging from not just deregulation, but early safety concerns, consumer complaints, lack of air traffic and airport system capacity, terrorism, wars in the Middle East, economic recessions, and a couple of oil crises that have changed airlines worldwide.[13]

Whereas from the left there is growing demand for regulatory reform, on the right there is the call for just the opposite—more complete deregulation. Free market advocates cite high cost structure as the

---

[10] *See Air Line Pilots Association v. United Airlines*, CCH 19 AVI 17,613 (1985).
[11] Editorial, *Courageous Steps Required to Reform Airlines*, Av. Wk & Space Tech. (Nov. 18, 2002), at 82.
[12] James Ott, *Change, Or Else!*, Av. Wk. & Space Tech. (Jul. 21, 2003).
[13] *Id.*

cause of the airline crisis and suggest those costs can be lowered, if not by negotiation, then via the bankruptcy courts. That is to say, legitimizing use of the Bankruptcy Code to bust the unions, and thereby reduce labor costs. That is a lesson right out of the "Lorenzo School of Management," and it ignores history. Before the rise of unions life for the American worker was "nasty, brutish and short." It was out of desperation that workers united to gain collective power with which to improve their lot. And many of the living standards that most Americans now take for granted came from the efforts of labor unions.[14]

Rather than blaming labor for the ills of the industry, "Let failing airlines fail," shout the editors of *Aviation Week & Space Technology*. "Let there be no misunderstanding," they say, ". . . the management of these airlines have no one but themselves to blame for their predicament—their business model was broken long before terrorism changed the face of commercial air transportation."[15] Still, there is something different, something ominously terminal about the airlines now days.[16]

The result of the "deregulatory" experiment has been a disaster, leaving the industry on the brink of destruction. By the early 21st Century, with $100 billion accumulated debt, $18 billion in under-funded pension liability, and only $2 billion in equity, not only is the airline industry without capital, its access to private capital markets is virtually nonexistent. More than 150 airlines, both new entrants and incumbents, have fallen by the wayside.

It would seem the preponderance of airline labor complaints were rooted in the aftermath of deregulation, even though government denied it and apparently stonewalled attempts by affected workers to recover for damages. As John Peterpaul, Vice President, International Association of Machinists and Aerospace Workers, testified,

> *[We have] repeatedly come before Congress*
> *for a decade and a half sounding the alarm*
> *against the devastating impact of deregulation*
> *while we all watched in horror as the industry*

---

[14] James P. Hoffa, *Power of the People*, The American Legion Magazine (Sep. 2002), at 72. Mr. Hoffa is the general president of the International Brotherhood of Teamsters.

[15] Editorial, *Let Failing Airlines Fail*, Av. Wk. & Space Tech. (Mar. 8, 2004), at 70.

[16] Laurence E. Gesell and Paul Stephen Dempsey, *Air Transportation: Foundations for the 21st Century* 443-446 (2nd ed. 2005).

> *went into a tailspin. We take no pleasure in the*
> *fact that our prophecies have been fulfilled.*[17]

In the 10 years following airline deregulation, organized labor lost more than 60,000 *career* jobs. Irrespective, the air transportation industry has continued to expand according to pre-deregulation forecasts.[18] And even though the number of organized labor workers declined, overall employment increased, albeit largely with part-time help and less than career-type employment. By 1988 total airline employment topped 500,000 workers. And by 2000, employees numbered more than 700,000. The numbers dropped following the September 11, 2001, terrorist attacks and continued to fall as the Majors drastically restructured. Tragically, a work force that stood at 680,000 at the end of 2000 plummeted to an average of 601,000 in 2002, and to 561,000 in June 2003. Although career employment is down, total airline employment is still well above pre-deregulatory levels, and management continues to look for labor concessions, including reduced numbers.[19]

Ironically, management looks for more concessions from labor while, simultaneously, managers have practiced a dual standard and tried to insulate themselves with protected pensions, secure salaries, and bonuses.[20] Continued tension, with a lack of faith in management over time will yield only bitter fruit.

---

[17] Statement of John Peterpaul before the U.S. House of Representatives Subcommittee on Aviation, *Financial Condition of the Airline Industry*, 103rd Cong., 1st Sess. 498-499 (1993).

[18] Much of the growth experienced since 1978 apparently would have occurred irrespective of deregulation. *FAA Forecasts (1979-1990)*, which used pre-deregulation data in their formulation, projected growth from 197.3 million enplaning passengers in 1973, to 380.9 million passengers in 1988, and 453.9 million by 1990. As it happened, there were 419.2 million actual enplanements in 1988. This difference represents only 9% growth that at the outside could be attributed to the effects of deregulation. The actual growth trend subsequently drifted back toward the forecast projection trend, thus indicating no growth attributable to deregulation *per se*.

FAA Forecasts published in 1976 (i.e., well before deregulation) for fiscal years 1977-1988 held similar projections. The 1977-1988 forecasts predicted 393.2 million enplanements in 1988 or just 6% less than actual enplanements for that year. The projections in both 1976 and 1978, as well as the mean of the actual enplanement trend line, run generally parallel, which leads one to question whether deregulation had any effect at all upon increased travel by air. By stating that deregulation may have contributed even 6% or 9% of the growth is probably charitable, because actual enplanements regressed to the mean of all three projections. Laurence E. Gesell, *Airline Re-Regulation* 35 (1990).

[19] *See* Laurence E. Gesell and Paul Stephen Dempsey, *Air Transportation: Foundations for the 21st Century* 305-306 (2nd ed. 2005).

[20] *Id.* at 262-263.

EMPLOYMENT DISCRIMINATION

Unrelated to deregulation, but giving rise to another focal point in labor litigation have been changes in mandatory age-related retirement. A proliferation of age discrimination issues evolved subsequent to passage of the Age Discrimination in Employment Act of 1967. This act generally prohibits mandatory retirement before age 70 but allows for exceptions where age is "a *bona fide occupational qualification* reasonably necessary to normal business operations." Administrative or business convenience is not enough. To prove business necessity the employer must show two things. First, the business purpose is sufficiently compelling to override any discriminatory impact on the basis of age. And second any restrictions for it to actually and effectively carry out its business. The FAA's mandatory age-60 retirement for pilots has been upheld as lawful. In question, though, has been the necessity of flight engineers retiring at age 60. The FAA has a rule prohibiting airline pilots from flying past their 60th birthday, but the rule does not apply to flight engineers.

The FAA's mandatory age-60 retirement rule has been challenged many times, but as late as 2003 the Agency dismissed yet another challenge to its (now) 45 year old mandate requiring airline pilots to retire on their 60th birthday. In defense of its decision, the FAA rejected claims it has heard before, namely that the rule has always been about economic benefit to the airlines, not safety. However, it should be noted that ALPA has long supported the rule. [21]

The Age Discrimination in Employment Act applies to persons between the ages of 40 and 70. But age discrimination in employment in aviation is not necessarily restricted to those over 40 or those nearing retirement. Thirty years of age is oftentimes critical in hiring and otherwise beginning a career in aviation. For example, the FAA refuses to hire candidates for air traffic control positions who are over 30. Airlines in the past have had similar restrictions to employment.

It seems ironic that a person in his or her early 30s may be "too old." Certainly, there are active pilots who are over 30 flying for the airlines or air traffic controllers who are actively controlling traffic past the age of 30. But *working* pilots and controllers are just that.

---

[21] *Airline Outlook*, Av. Wk. & Space Tech. (Oct. 30, 2003), at 15.

They are already working and have established career status with their employers. Employers must sometimes make substantial investments in training their employees. Employers, likewise, are entitled to make reasonable determinations of career life expectancies of employees and to recover (or amortize) their investments. When it is tied to career life expectancy, age may be a *bona fide* occupational qualification.

Until the 1970s, many airlines imposed gender, height, weight, age, pregnancy and marital restrictions upon flight attendants. Airlines were interested in keeping their cabin crews female, young and attractive, as well as fresh, junior and inexpensive, with a rotation of mature flight attendants replaced by younger women. Hence, flight attendants were encouraged to leave after only a few years. In *Frank v. United Airlines*[22] the 9th Circuit U.S. Court of Appeals summarized the weight discrimination practice of major airlines:

> *During the 1960s and early 1970s, the standard practice among large commercial airlines was to hire only women as flight attendants. The airlines required their flight attendants to remain unmarried, to refrain from having children, to meet weight and appearance criteria, and to retire by the age of 35. Like other airlines, defendant United had a long-standing practice of requiring female flight attendants to maintain their weight below certain levels. After it began hiring male flight attendants in the wake of Diaz v. Pan Am World Airways, 442 F.2d 385 (5th Cir. 1971), United applied maximum weight requirements to both male and female flight attendants. Flight attendants—a group comprised of approximately 85% women during the time period relevant to this suit—are the only employees United has ever subjected to maximum weight requirements.*

---

[22] 216 F.3d 845 (9th Cir. 2000).

> *Between 1980 and 1994, United required fe-*
> *male flight attendants to weigh between 14 and*
> *25 pounds less than their male colleagues of*
> *the same height and age. For example, the*
> *maximum weight for a 5' 7'', 30-year-old*
> *woman was 142 pounds, while a man of the*
> *same height and age could weigh up to 161*
> *pounds. A 5' 11'', 50-year-old woman could*
> *weigh up to 162 pounds, while the limit for a*
> *man of the same height and age was 185*
> *pounds.*[23]

The court held that United was entitled to use facially discriminatory weight requirements only if it could demonstrated that the difference in treatment between men and women was reasonably necessary to the normal operation of the airline business and their job functions. Most of the restrictions imposed upon female flight attendants have been struck down over the years on grounds they fail to satisfy a *bona fide* work-related function. Attractiveness and youth have been deemed illegitimate conditions on employment.

Several federal laws have been enacted and programs created to prohibit various forms of discrimination.[24] These include:

- Title VI of the Civil Rights Act of 1964,[25] prohibits discrimination on the basis of race, color, or national origin;[26] Title VII prohibits such discrimination in the context of employment.[27]
- Title IX of the Education Amendments of 1972[28] prohibits discrimination on the basis of sex.

---

[23] 216 F.3d at 848 [citations and footnotes omitted].

[24] *See* Paul Stephen Dempsey and Laurence E. Gesell, *Air Commerce and the Law* 429-450 (2004).

[25] 42 U.S.C. § 2000d. This requirement is implemented by U.S. DOT Regulations, "Nondiscrimination in Federally-Assisted Programs of the Department of Transportation – Effectuation of Title VI of the Civil Rights Act," 49 C.F.R. Part 21.

[26] Requirements prohibiting discrimination on the basis of race, color, or national origin are set forth in Title VI of the Civil Rights Act of 1964, 42 U.S.C. § 2000d, and U.S. DOT regulations, "Nondiscrimination in Federally-Assisted Programs of the Department of Transportation—Effectuation of Title VI of the Civil Rights Act," 49 C.F.R. Part 21.

[27] 42 U.S.C. § 2000e.

[28] 20 U.S.C. §§ 1681, 1683, and 1685-1687.

- The Age Discrimination Act of 1975[29] prohibits age discrimination.

- Section 504 of the Rehabilitation Act of 1973[30] and the Americans with Disabilities Act of 1990[31] prohibit discrimination on the basis of handicaps.

- Title IX of the Education Amendments of 1972[32] and the Drug Abuse Office and Treatment Act of 1972[33] prohibit discrimination on the basis of drug abuse.

- The Comprehensive Alcohol Abuse and Alcoholism Prevention Act of 1970[34] prohibits discrimination on the basis of alcohol abuse or alcoholism.

- The Public Health Service Act of 1912[35], requires confidentiality of alcohol and drug abuse patient records.

- Section 1101(b) of the Transportation Equity Act for the 21st Century[36] provides for participation of disadvantaged business enterprises in Department of Transportation [DOT] programs.

- The Equal Pay Act of 1963[37] protects individuals who perform substantially equal work in the same company from sex-based wage discrimination.

---

[29] 42 U.S.C. §§ 6101 *et seq.*

[30] 29 U.S.C. § 794. U.S. DOT Regulations, *Nondiscrimination on the Basis of Handicap in Programs and Activities Receiving or Benefiting from Federal Financial Assistance*, 49 C.F.R. pt. 27 implementing 29 U.S.C. § 794 and 49 U.S.C. § 5301(d).

[31] 42 U.S.C. §§ 12101 et seq.; U.S. DOT regulations, *Transportation Services for Individuals with Disabilities (ADA)*, 49 C.F.R. Part 37. U.S. Equal Employment Opportunity Commission, *Regulations to Implement the Equal Employment Provisions of the Americans with Disabilities Act*, 29 C.F.R. Part 1630; Joint U.S. Architectural and Transportation Barriers Compliance Board/U.S. DOT regulations, *Americans With Disabilities (ADA) Accessibility Specifications for Transportation Vehicles*, 36 C.F.R. Part 1192 and 49 C.F.R. Part 38; U.S. DOJ regulations, *Nondiscrimination on the Basis of Disability in State and Local Government Services*, 28 C.F.R. Part 35; U.S. DOJ regulations, *Nondiscrimination on the Basis of Disability by Public Accommodations and in Commercial Facilities*, 28 C.F.R. Part 36; U.S. GSA regulations, *Accommodations for the Physically Handicapped*, 41 C.F.R. Subpart 101-119; U.S. DOT Regulations, *Transportation Services for Individuals with Disabilities (ADA)* 49 C.F.R. Part 37, Subpart H, *Over-the-Road Buses*, and joint U.S. Architectural and Transportation Barriers Compliance Board/U.S. DOT Regulations, *Americans With Disabilities (ADA) Accessibility Specifications for Transportation Vehicles*, 36 C.F.R. Part 1192 and 49 C.F.R. Part 38; FTA Regulations, *Transportation for Elderly and Handicapped Persons*, 49 C.F.R. Part 609, implementing 29 U.S.C. § 794 and 49 U.S.C. § 5301(d).

[32] 20 U.S.C. §§ 1681, 1683, 1685-1687.

[33] Pub. L. 92-255 (Mar. 21, 1972).

[34] Pub. L. 91-616 (Dec. 31, 1970).

[35] 42 U.S.C. §§ 290dd-3 and 290ee-3.

[36] 23 U.S.C. § 101 note.

- The Civil Rights Act of 1991[38] provides compensatory and punitive damages and attorneys' fees in cases of intentional employment discrimination.

Federal statutes prohibit discrimination in employment on the basis of sex, age, race, nationality or religion, but there are other forms of discrimination as well—height, for example.[39] And although the emphasis thus far has been on discrimination in employment, another issue is safety. Employers have a responsibility for providing workers with a safe work environment. The Occupational Safety and Health Administration established pursuant to the Occupational Safety and Health Act of 1970 [OSHA], develops and promulgates occupational safety and health standards. It develops and issues regulations; conducts investigations and inspections to determine the status of compliance with safety and health standards and regulations. And, the Administration issues citations and proposes penalties for noncompliance with safety and health standards and regulations. But irrespective of OSHA standards, they are not broad enough to cover all hazards in the work place. In 1994, a group of flight attendants employed by various airlines brought suit, on behalf of approximately 60,000 flight attendants, against the tobacco industry for injuries suffered from diseases and disorders caused by their exposure to secondhand cigarette smoke in airplane cabins.[40] It would appear that aviation employees have gone from an age of uncertain protection in the 1930s,[41] through what many considered years of overprotection between 1938 and 1978, and back to uncertainty in the post deregulatory era.

In reviewing cases of alleged discrimination in the workplace, courts use the burden-shifting framework for employment discrimination first articulated by the U.S. Supreme Court in *McDonnell Douglas Corp.v. Green.*[42] The framework for judicial assessment of a Title VII claim of discrimination under *McDonnell Douglas* involves a three-step process. First, the plaintiff must establish a *prima facie* case

---

[37] *Equal Pay Act of 1963*, Pub. L. No. 88-38, 29 U.S.C. § 206(d).

[38] Pub. L. 102-166 (Nov. 21, 1991); 42 U.S.C. § 1981.

[39] *See Novack, et al. v. Northwest Airlines*, CCH 24 AVI ¶ 18,346 (1995); *see also Sondel, et al. v. Northwest Airlines*, CCH 24 AVI ¶ 17,146 (1995).

[40] *See Broin v. Phillip Morris Companies, Inc.*, CCH 24 AVI ¶ 18,074 (1994).

[41] *See Northwest Airlines v. Hoover*, 93 P.2d 346 (Wash. 1939).

[42] 411 U.S. 792 (1973).

of discrimination.[43] If s/he succeeds, the burden shifts to the defendant to show a legitimate, non-discriminatory justification for the employment action.[44] If the defendant does so, the burden shifts again to the plaintiff to prove that the reasons advanced by the defendant were specious, and that its true motivation was discrimination.[45] The ultimate burden of proof, however, resides with the plaintiff.[46]

Case examples of discrimination in employment, as well as other airline-related labor disputes, are presented as follows:

NORTHWEST AIRLINES. v. HOOVER
93 P.2d 346 (Wash. 1939)

Were flight crews at one time discriminatorily excluded from workmen's compensation?

In the 1937 amendment of the Workmen's Compensation Act, pilots and instructors were omitted. Northwest Airlines, at that time an employer of 25 pilots and co-pilots and three stewardesses, appealed to the State of Washington Supreme Court to issue a *writ of mandamus* requiring the Washington State Department of Labor and Industries to recognize pilots, co-pilots and stewardesses within the provisions of the Act. Northwest had previously requested the Department of Labor and Industries take steps to bring the airline's employees under the Act, but the department had refused to do so.

---

[43] To prove a *prima facie* case of employment discrimination, a plaintiff must prove that (1) s/he is a member of a protected class, (2) who was qualified for the position, or was performing satisfactorily in it, (3) who suffered an adverse employment action (e.g., was not hired for, or was fired from the position), (4) under circumstances to give rise to an inference of discrimination based on his or her membership in the protected class.

[44] If plaintiff has established a *prima facie* case of discrimination, the burden shifts to the defendant to "articulate some legitimate, non-discriminatory reason" for the employment action. The employer must show that the employment practice is "job related for the position in question and consistent with business necessity. . . ."

[45] If the defendant provides a non-discriminatory reason for the employment action, the presumption of discrimination "simply drops out of the picture," and the governing standard is whether the evidence, taken as a whole, reasonably supports an inference of intentional discrimination. The ultimate burden of persuading the trier of fact that the defendant intentionally discriminated remains at all times with the plaintiff. Specifically, the plaintiff must prove that the legitimate reasons offered by the defendant were not its true reasons, but were instead a pretext for discrimination.

[46] *See* Paul Stephen Dempsey and Laurence E. Gesell, *Air Commerce and the Law* 434-439 (2004).

The Workmen's Compensation Act of 1911 established a new plan for the compensation of persons injured in hazardous industry. The Act was amended several times, and in 1923 it was amended bringing airplane pilots and instructors (Class 34-5) under the act. Between 1923 and 1937 the Act was amended several more times including changes to Class 34-5 rates of contribution. Listed among extra hazardous occupations were teaming, truck driving and motor delivery, including drivers and helpers, but the section contained no specific reference to persons engaged in air navigation. In 1937 the classifications were again amended and Class 35-4 was omitted, and for the first time there was included Class 34-3, "Airplane Manufacturing."

Northwest stated its airplanes were used in motor delivery, and its employees were engaged in driving the planes and in assisting in their operation while in the air. Northwest argued that as drivers, its employees were brought within the Act. It was argued that by dropping the classification "airplane pilots and instructors" and adding "motor delivery," the 1937 legislature intended to bring under the Act all workers engaged in the operation of an air transportation system, instead of including airplane pilots and instructors only.

The court rejected the argument, determining the intent of the legislature was to bring the business of airplane manufacturing under the Act, but not to include airplane pilots or instructors or other employees of air transportation companies engaged in "actual" flying. The court did not agree that "motor delivery" included airplanes. The court held that pilots, co-pilots, and stewardesses were not within the protection of the Workmen's Compensation Act.

MONROE v. UNITED AIRLINES
736 F.2d 394 (7th Cir. 1984)

Must all airline flight crewmembers retire at age 60?

Suit was filed against United Airlines for not permitting 112 flight deck crewmembers from serving as second officers (flight engineers) after the age of 60, allegedly in violation of the Age Discrimination in Employment Act of 1967. Plaintiffs were of two groups, the first consisting of pilots who were not permitted to transfer to second officer positions, and the second group made up of second officers who were not allowed to remain in their positions upon reaching the airline's long standing retirement age of 60. All plaintiffs asserted a claim to employment in the position of second officer after their 60th birthday.

The Age Discrimination in Employment Act [ADEA] makes it: (1) unlawful for an employer—with certain exceptions—to fail or refuse to hire or to discharge any individual or otherwise discriminate against any individual with respect to compensation, terms, conditions or employment because of that individual's age; and (2) to limit segregate or classify employees in any way that would deprive or tend to deprive any individual of employment opportunities or otherwise adversely affect his or her status as an employee because of the individual's age.

The exception to the above is that it is not unlawful for an employer to take any action which is otherwise prohibited where age is a Bona Fide Occupational Qualification [BFOQ]. A BFOQ is a consideration that is reasonably necessary to the normal operation of the particular business or where differentiation among employees is based on reasonable factors other than age. The purpose Congress intended in the ADEA is "to promote employment of older persons based on their ability rather than age;" and "to prohibit arbitrary age discrimination in employment." United Airlines admitted to having a general policy against employing any person as captain, first officer, or second officer after age 60. United contended its actions were justified because retirement after age 60 for all groups of airline pilots, including second officers, was a *bona fide* occupational qualification based on safety grounds. However, the FAA's age-60 rule for retirement did not apply to second officers, and in fact other airlines were at the time allowing flight engineers to work past 60.

United also asserted that because the group had not been serving as second officers, and were not qualified as second officers, they had no rights (under the collective bargaining agreement with ALPA) to transfer from captain and first officer to second officer—for which United would have to train and qualify them. Ironically, the Air Line Pilots Association sided with United rather than plaintiffs (members of ALPA), because it was ALPA which had signed the collective bargaining agreement, and it was they who were responsible for administering the contract and enforcing its terms.

The jury verdict held that United Airlines was in willful violation of the Age Discrimination in Employment Act. The U.S. District Court entered a preliminary injunction against United and ALPA to: (1) enjoin United from prohibiting (a) its second officers from working after age 60, or (b) its other flight personnel from transferring at age 60 to second officer; and (2) amend the collective bargaining agreement to conform to the foregoing provisions in number (1).

In response to the above court order, United and ALPA claimed to have met their re-negotiation obligations by assembling a Letter of Agreement [LOA] and submitting it to the court for approval. Under the LOA captains and first officers were made eligible to "bid down" to second officer vacancies, but any pilot who would not obtain a second officer ranking before age 60 would have to retire. If a crewmember were to: (1) bid for and receive a captain or first officer vacancy; and (2) were to thus become ineligible to bid down to second officer before reaching age 60 would have to retire at age 60. The result of such an agreement would permit pilots to retain (or obtain) captain or first officer only at the peril of losing any right to work past age 60. Captains and first officers would have to seize the first opportunity to bid down, long before they would reach age 60.

The court concluded the agreement was tantamount to punishing crewmembers who might exercise their rights under the Age Discrimination in Employment Act by electing to work past age 60. In the court's opinion, United and ALPA sought to win this lawsuit in long-range terms after having been unsuccessful in doing so before a jury in court. The court disapproved the agreement and reaffirmed the lower court's order to United and ALPA to bring themselves into compliance with the law.

SMITH v. PAN AMERICAN WORLD AIRWAYS
706 F.2d 771 (6th Cir. 1983)

> *Is an employer responsible for the discrimination based on*
> *sex, race and color of one employee against another?*

Sandra Richardson Smith was a black flight attendant for Pan American World Airways. In 1977, on a flight from London to Chicago, Guy Richard, a white male flight purser, allegedly referred to Smith in a racially derogatory manner and attempted to strike her.

Smith brought suit against her employer, Pan Am, because Richard had insulted her, the insult had racial overtones, Pan Am failed to discipline Richard or to take adequate precautions to insure persons with racist attitudes were not hired, and in so failing, Pan Am breached a duty of "ordinary care and caution it owed to her and deprived her of (equal) employment opportunity." In essence, Smith claimed Pan Am was guilty of racial discrimination in employment in violation of 42 U.S.C. § 1981 (i.e., equal rights under the law).

The airline made several unsuccessful attempts to arrange a hearing for Smith before company representatives, but Smith refused to attend because Richard would not be present. Furthermore, Pan Am was unaware, until the suit against them was filed, precisely what it was that Richard said, and for what exactly Smith would have them discipline him. Smith felt she had been "harassed" because of her race and her sex. As evidence, she alleged that "similar problems" had developed between Richard and other black female employees had "mailed letters" to Pan Am "and they (had) not disciplined Richard." She stated that an "investigation and a settlement conference" did take place, but "failed to resolve (her) grievance."

The U.S. District Court granted Pan Am's motion for summary judgment and dismissed the claims. Summary judgment was inappropriate for the racial discrimination claim for two reasons. First, the Equal Employment Opportunity Commission (per the Equal Employment Opportunity Act of 1972) had had no opportunity to mediate the claim as required. And second, Pan Am could not "be charged with having imposed any disparity of treatment . . . " in this case. The court found that Richard was Smith's "co-equal," with no authority to "hire, fire, promote or demote the plaintiff." Finally, the court found no evidence of "adverse employment action whatsoever" by Pan Am, no repetition, no prior history of similar events, and nothing to indicate the airline condoned Richard's remarks.

Smith appealed, but the U.S. Court of Appeals affirmed the district court's judgment, with the exception of reversing the district court's basing of its decision on Smith's failure to pursue EEOC remedies. There was no evidence of discriminatory purpose. As Pan Am said in its brief, this incident was quite obviously a "personality clash" between co-workers for which Section 1981, which prohibits racial discrimination in employment, provides no protection.

DEAN v. TRANS WORLD AIRLINES
708 F.2d 486 (9th Cir. 1983)

May a union pilot unilaterally decide to discontinue payment of dues?

John Dean, a Trans World Airlines pilot, was required by an agency shop agreement between TWA and the Air Line Pilots Association to pay an agency fee to ALPA. He protested the charge, characterizing it as an "unconstitutional tax," in numerous letters to ALPA. He accused ALPA, among other things, of using his fees for political expenditures in violation of the Supreme Court's holding in *International Association of Machinists v. Street*.[47] Unsatisfied with ALPA's response, Dean decided unilaterally to reduce his monthly payments to the union. He was sent several delinquency notices, including an itemized bill for all amounts owed. Finally, at ALPA's request and pursuant to the Agency shop agreement, TWA discharged Dean.

Dean sued for breach of contract and breach of duty of fair representation. The district court granted his motion for partial summary judgment ruling as a matter of law that Dean had raised a proper spending challenge under *Street*, and that his discharge was therefore unlawful. Trans World Airlines was ordered to reinstate Dean. TWA appealed the case. The U.S. Court of Appeals ruled that the district court erred when it granted summary judgment in Dean's favor.

International Association of Machinists v. Street prohibits unions from using the dues of a protesting employee to support political and ideological causes which the employee opposes. In *Street*, however, the Supreme Court held that protesting employees are not released from their dues-paying obligation simply because they believe a portion of their dues is being used for political expenditures—until final judgment in their favor is entered. To allow an injunction, restraining dues collections, could "interfere with the . . . unions' performance of those functions and duties which the Railway Labor Act places upon them to attain its goal of stability in the industry."

If courts cannot enjoin the collection of union dues, then an individual should not be permitted unilaterally to decide to reduce or

---

[47] 367 U.S. 740 (1961).

stop dues payment. The judgment of the district court was reversed and remanded.

AIR LINE PILOTS ASSOCIATION INTERNATIONAL v. UNITED AIRLINES
616 F. Supp. 849 (N.D. Ill. 1985)

Do the provisions of the Railway Labor Act apply to prospective employees of an airline?

The plaintiff, Air Line Pilots Association International, alleged that United Airlines violated several provisions of the Railway Labor Act.[48] The alleged acts were committed during a period of collective bargaining negotiations of a new agreement to replace the old. The allegations related to plans, which United had announced it intended to carry out if there was a strike by its pilots. On May 17, 1985, United's pilots did strike. On June 14, 1985, the pilots ratified a tentative agreement and thus ended the strike.

The back-to-work agreement provided that striking pilots would be returned to the same domicile, status and equipment to which they were assigned before the strike, with normal accrual of seniority. The parties agreed neither would "engage in nor condone any activities, which might constitute reprisals or recriminations as a result of the ALPA strike." United agreed ALPA would pursue its claims in federal court regarding: (1) the "Group of 500" pilots, (2) rebid of the airline, and (3) salaries for pilots hired as "fleet qualified." With the exception of the three outstanding issues enumerated, all other strike-related litigation and/or arbitration was dropped.

In the fall of 1984, United began to experience a shortage of pilots. Prior to this time United's practice was to *employ* student pilot applicants from the first day of training. Students were paid in accordance with United's agreement with ALPA and accrued pilot seniority from their first date of hire as student pilots. At this time, and because United was bargaining with ALPA, United chose to "pretrain" several hundred "applicants" who would be offered "formal employment once United had secured a cost competitive agreement with ALPA." United

---

[48] 45 U.S.C. § 151, *et seq.*

wanted the group, even though undergoing training, to be formally classified as "non-employees." This group of candidates became known as the "Group of 500," and the focal point of this litigation.

In April of 1985, those of the Group of 500 who had successfully completed initial training were offered employment effective May 17, 1985, whether or not there was a strike. In a letter from United's Director of Flight Standards, each student was informed a change to "permanent status will occur on May 17, 1985, or on the day you enter training whichever is later." The students were sent a letter by the Manager of Flight Employment confirming "employment" effective May 17, 1985. As the strike deadline of May 17 approached, United addressed a letter to the Group of 500 specifically requesting they report "at 0800 hours" to the Denver Flight Training Center on May 17.

When United first offered employment to the Group of 500, it did not hire them to serve as "crossovers" in a pilot strike. They were being hired to fill vacancies created by an expanding market. However, United did not want to put the new hires on the line until it "had a contract" with ALPA. As the May 17 strike deadline approached, United began to view the Group of 500 as a pool of trained replacements for striking pilots. United then told the Group if they did not cross the picket line and report to work on May 17, they would never work for United in the future. United issued seniority numbers, and placed on their payroll only those of the Group of 500 who reported to work on May 17.

When ALPA learned United intended to use the Group of 500 as replacements during a strike, it sent a letter to the Group encouraging them not to cross the picket line and few of the Group crossed ALPA's picket lines. Most of those who approached the picket lines refused to cross, but rather signed a report form provided by ALPA, which was subsequently supplied to United. Furthermore, many of those in the Group of 500, still undergoing initial training, departed the training facility when notified of the strike in progress.

Shortly after the strike commenced, United began implementing its flight operations strike plan, including a "rebid" of the airline, and the hiring of permanent replacements. "Bidding" is the pilot's seniority position defined as the combination of *status* (e.g., captain, first or second officer and type of aircraft flown) and *domicile* (from which pilot assignments originate and to which they return). United canceled all assignments of pilots, strikers and non-strikers to create vacancies in every position in the airline. United then allowed all non-striking pilots to bid for these jobs. Approximately 525 non-strikers participated in the bid, about half of them being management pilots.

Prior to the strike, United placed advertisements for what it called "fleet qualified permanent replacement pilots." These pilots, already flying for other airlines, were qualified to serve as captains or first officers. United offered to pay the fleet qualified candidates rates of $75,000 per year for captains and $50,000 per year for first officers. These rates were guaranteed minimums, so long as the pilots were employed by United. The rates were in excess of two tier wage scales to which both parties had recently agreed. In the 1985 agreement the maximum third year rate of pay for first officers was $41,125 per year; i.e., less than the $50,000 being paid to fleet qualified new hires.

The Air Line Pilots Association argued: (1) the Group of 500 were "employees" of United upon the first day of training. United stated that to allow the Group to return would "strategically hurt . . . in trying to operate through future strikes. . . .;" (2) United's re-bidding of the airline disadvantaged striking pilots by blocking them from new vacancies which would arise after the strike, and which otherwise would have been awarded to them. United intended to reward the loyalty of those pilots who had helped keep the airline running by giving them priority over former striking pilots with more seniority; and (3) the rates being paid to "fleet qualified" pilots were in excess of the new-hire rates under the 1985 agreement, and the "super-pay" had inherently destructive post-strike implications. United argued the lack of availability of qualified pilots at the time of the strike required the airline to offer pay sufficient to attract qualified replacements. This action was governed by the Railway Labor Act[RLA], which provides in part that, management and labor shall:

> . . . *exert every reasonable effort to make and maintain agreements concerning rates of pay, rules, and working conditions, and to settle all disputes . . . in order to avoid any interruption to commerce. . . .;*

employees shall have the right to organize and bargain collectively through representatives of their own choosing;

no carrier . . . shall deny or in any way question the right of its employees to join, organize, or assist in organizing the labor organization of their choice, and it shall be unlawful for any carrier to interfere in any way with the organization of its employees . . . , or to influence or coerce employees in an effort to induce them to join or remain or not to join or remain members of any labor organization;

no carrier . . . shall require any person seeking employment to sign a contract or agreement promising to join or not to join a labor organization; and

no carrier . . . shall change the rates of pay, rules, or working conditions of its employees, as a class, as embodied in agreements. . . .

In considering the permissible interpretation of the RLA, courts have turned to the National Labor Relations Act [NLRA],[49] as a back-up. In reaching its conclusions, the U.S. District Court relied upon the provisions of both the RLA and the NLRA as applied to the issues in this case.

The Court rejected ALPA's argument that the Group of 500 were employees of United upon their first day of training, because the training agreements expressly provided the student pilots were not employees during training. However, members of the Group of 500 had accepted United's offer of employment effective May 17, 1985. Furthermore, United declared their status to be "permanent" after May 17. United's belated attempt to require members of the Group to cross a lawful picket line as a condition of employment was unlawful under

---

[49] 29 U.S.C. § 152, *et seq.*

the RLA. United had denied employees the right to participate in a lawful strike on their first day of employment.

United also violated the RLA by unilaterally altering the "status quo" by instituting the "non-employee" training program. United could not have legally changed its historic practices and contractual commitments after it served notice of intended change in the earlier (1981) agreement with ALPA. After serving notice, "neither party may unilaterally alter the status quo." Moreover, United's treatment of the Group was unlawful even if they were not employees. The RLA provides that no carrier "shall require any person seeking employment to sign any contract or agreement promising to join or not to join a labor organization" (i.e., *any person*, not just *employees*). The NLRA reflects the same concern about pre-hire discrimination on the basis of union membership.

The Group of 500 were employees of United on May 17, 1985. United's condition that the student pilots cross a picket line on their first day of work was unlawful since the union remains the bargaining representative for "all employees in the designated craft, whether union members or not." United's contention that ALPA lacked standing on behalf of the Group was without merit.

As to United's re-bid of the airline at the conclusion of the strike, United agreed to return all pilots to their pre-strike assignments, thereby eliminating the vacancies posted for re-bid. Under the Railway Labor Act, an employer's right to hire replacements is based only on its needs to "continue in business." Its right to fill positions permanently is limited to those actually occupied and used to continue in business during a strike. In this case, however, no United pilot worked in a re-bid position during the strike. Rather, United planned to implement the re-bid awards to non-strikers only when new vacancies in those positions arose at some time after the strike had ended. United failed to justify the re-bid as reasonably necessary for its operations during the strike. Furthermore, there was evidence of United's intent of coercion and discrimination against union members by virtue of the re-bid procedure. United's stated policy was to "reward the loyalty of those pilots who help us keep this airline running." United's anti-union motivation in connection with the re-bidding of the airline invalidated the procedure notwithstanding other legitimate motives.

The third ALPA contention was of the salaries paid to the fleet-qualified pilots. They were in excess of the new hire rules under the 1985 agreement. The Air Line Pilots Association argued whatever business justifications may have existed during the strike for offering "super-pay" to incoming pilots, the inherently destructive post-strike implications outweighed the benefits. The Court disagreed. United had a reasonable requirement to offer pay sufficient to attract qualified applicants. Although super-pay might serve as a reminder of whom did and did not strike, it would not disadvantage striking pilots by changing their domiciles, lowering their salaries, or subjecting them to future layoffs. While a striking pilot might be unhappy having to serve with a less senior pilot earning a higher salary, United's business justification clearly outweighed the harm to striking pilots.

The Court concluded that United's policy of denying employment and accrued seniority to the Group of 500, and of conducting and attempting to implement the strike related re-bid of pilot positions violated the Railway Labor Act. The Court declared United's policy of paying super-pay to the fleet-qualified pilots did not violate the RLA. Therefore, judgment was entered in favor of the plaintiff on the claims regarding the Group of 500 and the re-bid of the airline. Judgment was entered in favor of the defendant regarding rates of pay for fleet qualified permanent replacements. United was directed and enjoined to restore the Group of 500 to status as employees. United was restricted and enjoined from implementing bid awards made to pilots during the strike, or from in any other way preferring non-strikers for any vacancies arisen since the strike or which would arise in the future.

PAN AMERICAN WORLD AIRWAYS v. CIVIL AERONAUTICS BOARD
683 F.2d 554 (D.C. Cir. 1982)

Is an airline management employee eligible for labor protection in a merger of companies?

Robert Wallace was an employee of National Airlines when it was acquired by Pan American World Airways in 1980. Wallace then accepted employment with Pan Am with whom he later had a dispute over his rights under the Employee Protection Program of the Airline

Deregulation Act of 1978, and the Civil Aeronautics Board's conditions in approving the merger of National and Pan Am. For many years, the Civil Aeronautics Board [CAB] had conditioned its approval of airline mergers upon acceptance of labor protective provisions "designed to protect the employees of the merged airlines from any adverse impact the merger may have on conditions of employment . . . and also to establish machinery for the peaceful settlement of any labor management disputes arising out of the merger."

Alleging violation of the EPP, Wallace filed a motion with the CAB asking it to compel arbitration over his dispute. He claimed lost entitlement to:

- "displacement allowance" because he had been "placed in a worse position with respect to compensation;" his "compensation" including bonuses, expense account remuneration, and lowered prospect of raises;
- entitlement to certain fringe benefits such as private office, secretary, credit cards, business travel, and job responsibility; and
- he had been changed from "middle-management" to "lower-level management," which constituted a denial of opportunities and continued employment in his former "class, craft, or field of endeavor." Wallace subsequently had to amend his original motion for arbitration because Pan Am gave him notice of employment termination. He thus sought to resolve the "cause, effect and remedy" of his dismissal.

Pan Am argued displacement allowance applied only to reduction in salary, contending that fringe benefits accrued only if the employee was entitled to a dismissal or displacement allowance. It also argued Wallace had not been required to change his field of endeavor. Wallace was still *management*, and they accordingly questioned whether he had any rights at all under EPP. Pan Am flatly denied Wallace had been fired in retaliation for filing a motion against them, but was fired along with 21 others, for economic reasons unrelated to merger.

In 1982, the CAB ordered arbitration of Wallace's claims, determining *compensation*, not simply *salary*. The Board also held that if indeed Wallace had been fired for retaliatory reasons it was "merger related." The allegation concerning discharge was subject to arbitration under EPP. Perquisites claimed by Wallace (i.e., private office, secretary, etc.) were at least arguable and should be resolved by arbitration. Upon appeal from Pan Am, the Board reconsidered and re-determined the perquisites were not part of Wallace's compensation, but were "simply aspects of (his) prior position with National which were necessary to carry out his employment responsibility." Finally, the Board held that Pan Am's assertion that management employees are excluded from EPP benefits was for an arbitrator to decide. In short, the CAB granted Wallace's motion to compel arbitration.

Pan Am appealed the case to the courts on grounds that the Board erred in three respects:

- Wallace's eligibility for employee protection;
- the claim for displacement benefits; and
- finding the dismissal claim arbitrable.

In reviewing the case the U.S. Court of Appeals found its scope of review narrow because under the Administrative Procedure Act the court could set aside the Board's action only if it was "arbitrary, capricious, an abuse of discretion, or otherwise not in accordance with law or . . . unsupported by substantial evidence. . . ." Each of the claims was reviewed within these limitations:

- *Wallace's eligibility for EPP benefits*—the Board left with the arbitrator whether the EPP coverage could be extended to management. The Board did not have the duty to resolve the question. By relegating the decision, the Board fulfilled its duty and acted within its discretion;
- *Wallace's displacement claim*—the Board quite properly did not in this case, and did not generally, address the merits of disputes. Arguments on merits are properly considered by an arbitrator; and
- *Wallace's dismissal claim*—the type of factual inquiry required to resolve the disagreement regarding the reason or reasons for Wallace's discharge was precisely the sort that lends itself to arbitration.

The appellate court held that the Board acted within the scope of its discretion in referring Wallace's claims to arbitration. The Board's order directing arbitration of Wallace's claims was affirmed.

BIGELOW v. HAWAIIAN AIRLINES
696 F. Supp. 1356 (D. Hawaii 1987)

What is the statute of limitations in claims for reemployment under the Employee Protective Provisions of the Airline Deregulation Act?

In this case, Hawaiian Airlines moved for partial summary judgment for the purpose of determining the proper statute of limitations applicable to plaintiffs David L. Bigelow's and Charles J. Edward's claims for reemployment under the Employee Protective Provisions of the Airline Deregulation Act of 1978. The EPP provides, in part, a duty to hire protected employees under the following conditions:

> *Each person who is a protected employee of an air carrier which is subject to regulation by the Civil Aeronautics Board who is furloughed or otherwise terminated by such an air carrier (other than for cause) prior to the last day of the ten-year period beginning on October 24, 1978 shall have first right of hire, regardless of age, in his occupational specialty, by any other air carrier hiring additional employees which held a certificate (of public convenience and necessity) prior to October 24, 1978. Each such carrier hiring additional employees shall have a duty to hire such person before they hire any other person, except that such air carrier may recall any of its own furloughed employees before hiring such a person.*

David Bigelow and Charles Edwards alleged they were furloughed by Continental Airlines, on or about September 24, 1983, when Continental ceased operations. Both alleged they unsuccessfully sought employment from Hawaiian Airlines. Bigelow tried twice in 1984, and once in 1986. Edwards alleged he unsuccessfully sought employment from Hawaiian once in 1984.

Employee Protective Provisions of the Airline Deregulation Act did not contain a limitations statute, nor did the (then) most recent EPP regulations promulgated by the Department of Labor. Since there was no statute of limitations applicable, the court had to "borrow the most suitable statute or other rule of timeliness from some other source."

Hawaiian Airlines proposed adoption of the six-month statute of limitations contained in the National Labor Relations Act of 1935. It argued that the plaintiffs' claims, which essentially were based upon unlawful refusals to hire, closely resembled an unfair labor practice covered under the NLRA. The court agreed the NLRA provision was the most appropriate and ruled accordingly. The defendant's motion for partial summary judgment declaring the six-month statute of limitations was granted.

McDONALD v. PIEDMONT AVIATION
930 F.2d 220 (2nd Cir. 1990)

What is the limitation on the duration of economic assistance payments under the Employee Protective Provisions of the Airline Deregulation Act?

Paul F. McDonald was an airline pilot, employed by Air New England until that carrier's demise in 1981. In late 1981, McDonald attempted to secure alternative employment with Piedmont Airlines, by exercising his statutory *first right of hire* under the Employee Protective Provisions of the Airline Deregulation Act of 1978, which generally granted certain employees of airlines adversely affected by deregulation a right to be hired first by surviving air carriers. The defendant Piedmont, however, refused to hire McDonald as a pilot, despite the fact that he met all relevant qualifications for that position.

Accordingly, McDonald filed suit against Piedmont in November of 1984, alleging the airline had violated the first-hire provisions of the Act. After ruling that the Act created an implied private right of action, and that McDonald's claim was timely brought, the U.S. District Court conducted a jury trial of the remaining issues in the case. The jury rejected Piedmont's excuses for refusing to hire McDonald, and awarded him compensatory damages in the amount of $2,226,920 for breach of statutory duty. This sum represented the difference between Mr. McDonald's projected lifetime earnings and benefits at Air Berlin, the non-certificated carrier which employed him after his rejection by Piedmont, and those he would have received had Piedmont complied with the law by offering him a job.[50]

Piedmont then appealed to the United State Court of Appeals.[51] The appellate court found that, while the airline violated its statutory duty, a 72-month limitation period on temporary economic assistance payments contained in the Act limited the damages that could be recovered for a violation of the statutory first right of hire. Despite persuasive arguments that the temporary economic assistance payments are unrelated to the length of an employee's first right of hire, the ruling of the appellate court limiting the pilot's damages to a 72-month period was followed. On remand, the district court adjusted the award to $474,722.78 (including interest) for projected earnings that McDonald would have earned between 1985 and 1987, had he been hired by Piedmont, and hypothetically fired by the airline six years later.

ACKERMAN v. NORTHWEST AIRLINES
54 F.3d 1389 (8th Cir. 1995)

When does the right of first hire benefit expire?

Plaintiffs in this case were 41 former Braniff Airways' pilots who alleged that Northwest Airlines violated their first hire rights under Section 43(d) of the Airline Deregulation Act of 1978. In May of 1982, Braniff abruptly ceased all operations. Twenty-nine of the 41 pilots alleged they applied for jobs with Northwest in 1982, shortly after Braniff ceased operations. In the meantime, Braniff Airways was reorganized as a subsidiary of the Dalport Corporation, and renamed Braniff, Inc. The "new" Braniff hired the plaintiff pilots in 1984, and continued to employ them until it ceased operations in 1989. Two of the 41 pilots applied for jobs with Northwest between 1984 and 1989.

---

[50] *See McDonald v. Piedmont Aviation*, 625 F. Supp. 762 (1986), and *McDonald v. Piedmont Aviation*, 695 F. Supp. 133 (1988).

[51] *See McDonald v. Piedmont Aviation*, 930 F.2d 220, *cert. den.* 112 S.Ct. 441 (1991).

All but three of the 41 pilots alleged they applied for jobs with North-west around October 1989, and 16 of the 41 pilots alleged they applied for jobs with Northwest in 1992.

Northwest moved for summary judgment, contending that:

- Plaintiffs could not state a claim for relief under Section 43(d) because Northwest's duty to hire expired on October 23, 1988;
- Plaintiffs could not state a claim for relief because their rights had been extinguished in 1984, when they were hired by Bra-niff, Inc.; and
- Most of the claims were time barred (by statute of limitations).

Northwest contended its duty to hire pilots under the Employee Protective Provisions of the Airline Deregulation Act expired on October 23, 1988, arguing that a U.S. District Court had held that a "covered carrier" (i.e., one holding a Certificate of Public Convenience and Necessity before the Airline Deregulation Act was passed in 1978) has no duty to give the right of first hire to protected employees after 1988, reasoning that "Congress limited the duration of Section 1552 to ten years, the period between 1978 and 1988".[52] However, this court respectfully disagreed with the *Crocker* court's construction of the duty to hire provision. The eligibility period does not purport to bar protected employees from exercising their rehire rights after 1988. "That statute defines 'protected employees' as those who are separated from employment between October 24, 1978 and October 24, 1988. . . . This time limit was chosen to define the group eligible for the benefits of the EPP, and is unrelated to the right of any one of them to bring a cause of action to enforce his rights, once established"[53]

Congress authorized the U.S. Department of Labor [DOL] to promulgate regulations that would implement the EPP. After a lengthy administrative process, the DOL released the regulations in 1985. The DOL determined that the right to first hire continues until a protected employee is hired by an air carrier that held a certificate before de-

---

[52] *See Crocker v. Piedmont Aviation*, 86-1673, *slip op.* (D.C. May 4, 1993). A slip opinion is an individual court decision published separately soon after it is rendered. Later, the decision is reported with others in bound volumes such as the *Reporter* series; *see Black's Law Dictionary*, abridged (5th ed. 1983).

[53] *See McDonald v. Piedmont Aviation*, 695 F. Supp. 133 (1988).

regulation, and that rehire rights are not lost upon employment by a non-certificated carrier.

As to the statute of limitation claim, which Northwest submitted barred the claims of the plaintiffs, because Congress did not provide a statute of limitations for Section 43(d), this court found it must borrow one from another source. It chose to borrow the one-year period applied to discrimination claims under the Minnesota Human Rights Act [MHRA], concluding, "a one year limitation period struck a proper balance between protecting valid claims and prohibiting the prosecution of stale ones."

The U.S. District Court concluded that the duty to hire under Section 43(d) remains in effect, and that Northwest, as a "covered carrier," must continue to hire protected employees. The court also held that the plaintiffs' employment with Braniff, Inc. did not extinguish their first hire rights under the EPP. Finally, the court held that the proper statute of limitations for the plaintiffs' claims under Section 43(d) is the one year period applied in the MHRA.

Northwest's motion to dismiss was denied. Its motion for summary judgment was granted insofar as the actions for certain plaintiffs are time barred; the motion for summary judgment was otherwise denied.

AIR LINE PILOTS ASSOCIATION v. DEPARTMENT OF TRANSPORTATION
3 F.3d 449 (D.C. Cir. 1993)

What are the qualifying conditions for unemployment compensation under the Employment Protective Program of the Airline Deregulation Act?

The Employment Protective Program of the Airline Deregulation Act [ADA] of 1978 authorizes the Secretary of Labor to provide limited unemployment compensation to certain airline industry employees who lose their jobs because of the deregulation provisions of the Act. In this appeal to the United States Court of Appeals, ALPA and the International Brotherhood of Teamsters challenged the conclusion of the DOT that certain airline workforce reductions were not *qualifying dislocations* making former employees eligible for the special unemployment benefits of the Act, which defines "qualifying dislocation" as,

> . . . a bankruptcy or major contraction of an
> air carrier . . ., occurring during the first 10
> complete calendar years occurring after Octo-
> ber 24, 1978, the major cause of which is the
> change in regulatory structure provided by
> [the Act], as determined by the Civil Aero-
> nautics Board.

The DOT's definition and application of the term "major cause" were the central issues in this case. The DOT had concluded that the ADA was not the major cause of the layoffs in question through an unconventional series of administrative proceedings. For the seven years prior to its sunset, the CAB was responsible for determining whether unemployed airline workers qualified for benefits under the EPP. The CAB began receiving applications from displaced airline workers in January of 1979. Although the CAB began to develop guidelines for processing EPP applications, it had neither rejected nor granted any applications before it ceased to exist at the end of 1984.[54] In a challenge brought by ALPA, the U.S. Court of Appeals held that the CAB had unreasonably delayed the processing of applications. The appellate court remanded for further proceedings, stating DOT would be subject to the Court's continuing jurisdiction.

After the Court's decision in *ALPA v. CAB*, the DOT adopted a "lead case" approach to processing EPP applications. DOT had received EPP applications from employees of 13 different airlines and chose lead cases involving five airlines to be litigated fully before Administrative Law Judges and then reviewed as a group by DOT. These lead cases involved employee dislocations at Braniff International Airways, Air New England, Mackey International Airlines, Pan American World Airways, and United Airlines. DOT stated that none of the lead cases would be reviewed until all had been decided by ALJs.

The Mackey International and Air New England cases were consolidated, and the then four ALJ decisions in the lead cases were issued between September of 1986 and February of 1990. The ALJ in *Braniff International Airways*,[55] concluded the major cause of Braniff's bank-

---

[54] *See Air Line Pilots Association v. Civil Aeronautics Board*, 750 F. 2d 81 (1984).
[55] DOT Docket No. 338978 (May 12, 1988),

ruptcy *was* the regulatory changes of the ADA. The ALJ in *United Air Lines*[56] held that the ADA *was* the major cause of one of the two workforce reductions at issue. The ALJs in the other lead cases, *Air New England* and *Pan Am*,[57] held that the major contractions at those airlines *were not* caused by the ADA.

The DOT reviewed all of the ALJ decisions and held, in its decision in "Employee Protective Program Investigations"[58] (i.e., the order under review in this case), that the ADA *was not* the major cause of *any* of the dislocations, essentially reversing the ALJ decisions in *Braniff* and *United*, and affirming them in *Air New England* and *Pan Am*. In *Braniff*, the DOT determined that the carrier's economic problems were "enabled" but not "caused" by the ADA. In its Order, the DOT defined "major cause" as follows:

> *If they [the airlines] failed because of other independent factors such as the PATCO [Professional Air Traffic Controllers] strike, the rise in jet fuel prices, or the recession, then no qualifying dislocation will be found. If they failed because of route or fare competition from carriers that entered [Braniff's] markets under ADA authority, or similar factors that are closely connected with the effects of ADA, then a qualifying dislocation may be found.*

The DOT applied its guidelines defining "caused by deregulation" to each of the five carriers involved in the lead cases and concluded that none of the workforce reductions were qualifying dislocations under the Act because they were all substantially caused by factors *unrelated* to the change in regulatory structure implemented in the ADA.

The portion of the DOT Order discussing the definition of "major cause" mentions only one of the four ALJ opinions, the decision in *Braniff*. Hence, the Court reviewed the facts surrounding the Braniff employee dislocation. The DOT Order involved a pure question of *statutory interpretation*—the definition of "major cause." The Court

---

[56] DOT Docket No. 38571 (Feb. 28, 1990),
[57] DOT Docket Nos. 40201 and 39783 (Sep. 22, 1986).
[58] DOT Order 91-9-20 (1991).

was obligated to uphold the administrative definition unless: (1) it constituted an unreasonable construction of the Act; or (2) the DOT's findings and constructions were "arbitrary, capricious, an abuse of discretion" or "unsupported by substantial evidence on the record."

The DOT's conclusions with respect to Braniff involved both standards of review, presented mixed questions of law and fact, and their conclusions failed under both standards. The DOT Order presented an interpretation of the EPP, which was internally inconsistent and therefore unreasonable and impermissible.[59] The DOT concluded on the one hand that Braniff management decisions that were "enabled" but not "compelled" by the Act were not caused by the changes in the airline regulatory structure. At the same time, the DOT considered competition from other carriers to have been caused by the Act despite the fact that competition was also "enabled" rather than "compelled."

The DOT's conclusion that the employee dislocation at Braniff International Airlines was not a "qualifying dislocation" under the ADA was internally inconsistent, and not supported by substantial evidence on the record, as was the DOT conclusion arbitrary and capricious that Braniff's expansion was not caused by the ADA. The U.S. Court of Appeals remanded to the Department of Transportation for proceedings consistent with this opinion, at which time the DOT could consider whether the basis of the remand could affect its determinations in other dislocations disposed of in the DOT Order.

SONDEL v. NORTHWEST AIRLINES
56 F.3d 934 (8th Cir. 1995)

Are minimum height requirements for hiring flight attendants discriminatory?

On June 8, 1992, Nimali Sondel filed a class action lawsuit in federal district court against Republic Airlines[60] and Northwest Airlines alleging disparate discrimination under Title VII of the Civil Rights Act of 1964 and the Minnesota Human Rights Act, a state law. The *gravamen* (i.e., the material part of the complaint) of both claims was

---

[59] *See Chevron v. Natural Resources Defense Council*, 467 U.S. 837 (1984).
[60] In 1986, Republic Airlines merged with Northwest Airlines and Northwest assumed all of Republic's liabilities.

that Republic and Northwest Airlines' 5'2" minimum height requirement for flight attendants. On July 27, 1992, eleven days after the state MHRA claim was dismissed from federal suit, Namili Sondel, Holly Novack, Kim Shaller, and Brenda Glapa filed for a class action suit in Minnesota State court on this MHRA claim. On September 30, 1993, the U.S. District Court certified the following class:

> . . . *all women who applied for employment with Northwest Airlines as flight attendants, who were under 5'2" (or were treated as if they were under 5'2") and who were rejected between October 10, 1991, and March 12, 1992.*

After being certified representatives in the federal suit, Novack, Shaller and Glapa attempted to certify a class action in the state court. However, the state court denied this motion for a variety of state rulings. The claims proceeded in a bench trial. On February 4, 1994, the state court issued a 31-page opinion in favor of Northwest, holding that: (1) Northwest's 5'2" height requirement did adversely impact upon women, but (2) the height requirement was manifestly related to the job by ensuring passenger safety, providing customer service, and reducing flight attendant injury. Northwest's ruling, therefore, did not violate state law. The plaintiffs appealed, and the Minnesota Court of Appeals affirmed.[61]

Following the decision of the state trial court, Northwest moved for summary judgment in the federal suit, asserting that the plaintiffs were barred by *res judicata* (i.e., the matter had already been settled in court) and *collateral estoppel* (meaning that the issue having been determined in court, cannot be used again between the same parties). The U.S. District Court granted summary judgment in favor of Northwest. The U.S. Court of Appeals reviewed the case *de novo* (i.e., anew), and affirmed the holding of the district court.

---

[61] *See Holly Novack, et al., appellants v. Northwest Airlines, Inc., respondents; Republic Airlines, defendant,* 525 N.W. 2d 592 (1995).

BROIN v. PHILIP MORRIS COMPANIES
641 So. 2d 888 (Fla. App. 1995)

*Is a class action certifiable by a group of nonsmokers claiming
to have been injured by secondhand cigarette smoke?*

Plaintiffs in this case were 30 nonsmokers who were flight attendants employed by various airlines based in the United States. They filed a *class action* against Phillip Morris Companies, Inc., and other companies that manufacture and sell tobacco. The suit was filed by the plaintiffs on their own behalf, and as class representatives on behalf of all similarly situated flight attendants. The class action suit was seeking damages under theories of strict liability, breach of implied warranty, negligence, fraud, misrepresentation, and conspiracy to commit fraud. The proposed class action consisted of approximately 60,000 flight attendants who were continuously forced to inhale smoke emitted from cigarettes passengers smoked in airplane cabins. The plaintiffs asserted they suffered from diseases and disorders caused by their exposure to secondhand cigarette smoke.

The defendants (Phillip Morris Companies, Inc., Philip Morris Incorporated, Philip Morris International, Inc., RJR Nabisco Holdings Corporation, RJR Nabisco Capital Corporation, RJR Nabisco, Inc., Loews Corporation, Lorillard, Inc., Lorillard Tobacco Company, Brooke Group LTD, American Brands, Inc., The American Tobacco Company, and Liggett Group, Inc.) filed motions to dismiss all class allegations in the complaint. The state of Florida trial court granted the motions, finding that the class was very large, the complaint presented issues of first impression, and the class representatives raised issues which might not be shared by the entire class. Furthermore, the trial court found that the representatives could not adequately safeguard the interests of the entire class. The plaintiffs (i.e., the 30 class representatives) instituted an appeal to the Florida District Court of Appeal, which disagreed with the lower court's conclusion that the complaint did not meet the requirements for certification as a class action.

There are four tests, which must be met to satisfy the requirements for class action certification: *numerosity, commonality, typicality*, and adequate *representation*.

The plaintiffs unquestionably met the first prong of the require-ment, "numerosity." More than 60,000 flight attendants were repre-sented. As to the second prong, the threshold of "commonality" is not high. A class suit is maintained where the subject of the action presents a question of common or general interest, and where all members of the class have a similar interest in obtaining the relief sought.[62] The alleged facts in this case demonstrated that the members of the class behaved in the same way, they were passive inhalers of secondhand smoke, and the defendants acted toward each member in a similar manner, by manufacturing the cigarettes that exuded the smoke. The class members all sought recovery under the same common interest, and shared a common interest in obtaining the relief sought.

Contrary to the defendant's assertion, the plaintiffs' legal claims need not be completely identical, only "typical." If class actions were dependent on class members presenting carbon copy claims, there would be few, if any, instances of class action litigation. The court in *Tenney v. City of Miami Beach*, held:

> *The very purpose of a class suit is to save a*
> *multiplicity of suits, to reduce the expense of*
> *litigation, to make legal processes more effec-*
> *tive and expeditious, and to make available a*
> *remedy that would not otherwise exist.*[63]

As to the fourth prong, the "adequacy of representation" require-ment is met if the named representatives have interests in common with the proposed class members and the representatives and their attorneys will properly prosecute the class action. For the reasons already stated, the representatives and the class members shared common interests. And finally, there was no reason to conclude that "representation" would not be "adequate."

The appellate court held that the complaint fulfilled the four re-quirements. It reversed the lower court's dismissal, and remanded the case.

---

[62] See *Imperial Towers Condominium, Inc. v. Brown*, 338 So. 2d 1081, 1084 (1976).
[63] 11 So. 2d 188, 189 (1942),

CHAPTER 11

ANTITRUST, PREDATION AND COMPETITION

Even today, crime in the streets generally receives more attention than does crime in the suites.

WHITE COLLAR CRIME

In the May 1907 issue of *The Atlantic Monthly*, Edward A. Ross described the criminaloid in American society. The "criminaloid" was a person protected from public condemnation because of his apparent respectability. He was "fortified by his connections with 'legitimate business'." What Ross called the criminaloid, today would be referred to as a "corporate criminal."

Over 30 years passed until Edwin H. Sutherland developed the concept of "white-collar crime" in 1940. In 1949 Sutherland carried out the first empirical study of illegal corporate behavior.[1] Irrespective of Sutherland's findings, throughout the decades of the 1940s, 1950s, and 1960s, crime in the United States continued to be defined solely in terms of traditional "street crimes." In the 1970s, Marshal Clinard,[2] working with others, including Richard Quinney[3] and Peter Yeager,[4] redefined "white-collar crime" and said it " . . . should have been entitled 'corporate crime'." Through the decade of the 1970s there was

---

[1] Edwin H. Sutherland, *A Theory of White-collar Crime* (1949).

[2] Marshal B. Clinard, *Corporate Ethics and Crime* (1983).

[3] *See* e.g., Marshal B. Clinard and Richard Quinney, *Criminal Behavior Systems: A Typology* (1973).

[4] *See* e.g., Marshal B. Clinard and Peter C. Yeager, *Corporate Crime* (1980).

increased recognition of corporate crime by criminologists like Clinard, Quinney and Yeager. But as they pointed out, even today "crime in the streets" generally receives more attention than does "crime in the suites." Moreover, ". . . as experienced investigators understand all too well, finding and punishing those responsible for your basic petty larceny is a whole lot easier than meting out justice for billions of dollars lost in deliberately opaque accounting schemes."[5]

Seemingly, corporate crime *does* pay. There is rarely any "corrective justice" in the prosecution of corporate crime.[6] Little equality exists between the punishment and the crime, with the punishment meted out being far less than the crime committed. It is not supposed to work that way. White-collar prison terms tend to be short when they are imposed at all. But when white-collar criminals are convicted, judges usually attach hefty fines to their sentences, as well as orders to pay restitution (i.e., compensation for victims' losses). The problem is that it is highly unlikely government will ever make the convicted felons fully pay. The amount of criminal debt owed but not collected in federal cases rose from $5.6 billion in 1995 to over $13 billion in 2002. Roane enumerates the reasons why more money is not retrieved:

- *In many restitution cases, investigators don't even look for forfeitable assets. In others, clearly unencumbered assets go untouched;*
- *When liens are filed, the Government Accounting Office [GAO] found, prosecutors typically wait from 400 to 600 days after the judgement date—a delay that significantly increases the risk that offenders will liquidate their assets and escape their obligations;* and
- *There is often little pattern to the way restitution is ordered or the manner in which it is collected, GAO reports show. Offenders with substantial assets may be asked to pay as little as $25 a month, while those with virtually no income may be assessed hundreds more.*[7]

---

[5] Marianne Lavelle, *Payback Time?*, U.S. News & Wld. Rpt. (Mar. 11, 2002), at 36.
[6] *See* Aristotle, *Nichomachean Ethics* (circa 336 BC).
[7] Kit R. Roane, *Getting Out of Jail Free*, U.S. News & Wld. Rpt. (Dec. 23, 2002), at 26.

After minimal punishment, convicted white-collar criminals often-times continue unabated with their lavish lifestyles.[8] The collapse of Enron and WorldCom led to billions of dollars in losses for investors and cost thousands of people their jobs. Adelphia's former Chief Executive Officer [CEO], John Rigas, and his son, Timothy Rigas, the Chief Financial Officer [CFO], were found guilty of fraud and conspiracy. They were convicted of hiding $2.3 billion in debt, deceiving investors, and lining their own pockets with company funds. All involved face the possibility of years in prison plus millions, if not billions of dollars in restitution. What price they will pay for their misdeeds and what lifestyles they might lead after the cases are settled

---

[8] Consider the following examples:

Michael Milken financed a frenzy of hostile takeovers with his junk bond underwriting, making billions of dollars for himself. Then, working with Ivan Boesky, traded on the takeover stocks, using insider information to ring up hundreds of millions in profits. Boesky paid a $100 million fine and served 22 months in jail. Left with an $800 million fortune, Milken lives in Encino, CA. In a divorce settlement from Seema Silberstein, heiress to the Beverly Hills Hotel fortune, Boesky got $20 million in cash and a $2.5 million house in La Jolla, CA.

Charles H. Keeting, Jr.'s Lincoln Savings & Loan empire collapsed in a heap of worthless junk bonds, wiping out the life savings of 23,000 senior citizens and costing taxpayers $3.4 billion. He served nearly five years in prison, the government seized the $300 million Phoenician Hotel, and investors got much of their money back by sueing Keeting's lawyers and accountants. In 2002, Keeting was back in Phoenix and working with an investment group based in the tax haven of Belize.

Convicted of fraud and tax evasion relating to the $70 million collapse of Sunbelt Savings, Edward McBirney was ordered to pay more than $7 million in restitution. He paid $32,910 and then nothing more for more than a year.

Larry Vineyard, former owner of Key Savings & Loan Assn., was convicted of conspiracy and bank fraud. The day he was indicted, he took out a $2.66 million advance on a loan, using the cash to buy a $963,000 house and to set up trusts for his sons and to pay expenses. He was sentenced to another three years for fraud related to the loan. Vineyard was to pay $5 million in restitution. The government managed to retrieve $1 million from Vineyard's family, but Vineyard himself paid nothing between 1996 and 2002, not even the mandatory $50 a month, even though at the time he was executive VP of a large real-estate firm in Dallas, and was also a top executive of other real estate concerns.

Jack L. Sternberg was sentenced to less than two years in prison for mail fraud related to a complex housing scheme. He was ordered to pay more than $1 million to scores of people he scammed out of homes. Records show that the U.S. Attorney's office released Sternberg from his debt after he paid less than $23,000.

Jack Dean Franks was convicted of fraud in connection with a failed Calif. Golf course and fraud related to the collapse of two savings and loans. The Federal Deposit Insurance Corporation [FDIC] says he has paid nothing of $1.2 million in restitution. In the meantime, he kept a home in the exclusive Balboa Bay Club Resort & Spa in Newport Beach, CA. He owned Equity funding Corp., a firm that bought the first 1,000 acres of a $30 million golf course development. And according to Federal Bureau of Investigation [FBI] affidavits, Franks owns more than $2.13 million in property in Mexico, other Calif. properties, a yacht, and two airplanes. *See* Kit R. Roane, *Getting Out of Jail Free*, U.S. News & Wld. Rpt. (Dec. 23, 2002), at 26. *See also* Marianne Lavelle, *Payback Time?*, U.S. News & Wld. Rpt. (Mar. 11, 2002), at 36.

remains uncertain. But in the end, these cases are "about cheating and lying" as well as pain and suffering endured by others as a result of it.[9] Unfairly or not, Martha Stewart's name is often lumped into the same news items with Enron's Kenneth Lay, Jeffrey Skilling, and Andrew Fastow, and with the Rigas officers of Adelphia, Bernie Ebbers of WorldCom, and Dennis Kozlowski of Tyco. Yet, Janet Tavakoli comes to Ms. Stewart's defense by arguing that Stewart's "behavior is nowhere near what they [Kenneth Lay, et al.] are alleged to have done in either psychology or consequences." Tavakoli would argue that what Martha Stewart did "is the closest thing to a victimless financial crime."[10] But such a position reflects the very nature of white-collar crime and the difficulty with defining it as "crime."

No doubt, Martha Stewart has paid more dearly than most convicted white-collar criminals. But the bottom line is that she did lie, and many (of her own employees and close friends) paid for it. The securities fraud charge against Ms. Stewart was thrown out, but she was found guilty of conspiracy, obstruction of justice, and two counts of making false statements to federal investigators about what led her to decide to sell 3,928 shares of her ImClone Systems stock.[11]

The high price Martha Stewart paid for her misdeed came not from the justice system but partially from legal defense costs and mostly from the court of public opinion. Where she paid the highest price was in devaluation of her stock ownership in Martha Stewart Living, dropping from nearly $20 per share (before her entanglements) to around $8.00 (during her trial). However, just after her sentencing the stock soared 37%, closing at nearly $12.[12]

From the courts, she received a lenient sentence within the federal guidelines: five months in prison, 5 months of home confinement, two years of supervised probation, and a $30,000 fine. She is still a very wealthy woman. Her fortune, once valued at more than $1 billion, re-

---

[9] The first criminal trial involving former Enron Corporation executives "is a case about cheating and lying" with Wall Street's help, said a prosecutor in the case. *See* Kristen Hays, *Enron Trial is About 'Cheating and Lying'*, Associated Press (Sep. 22, 2004).

[10] Janet Tavakoli, *Martha Stewart: The Irony Maiden Hates to Lose*, The Year Book, http://www.tavakolistructurefinance.com (visited Jan. 17, 2005).

[11] Ironically, on Dec. 27, 2001, while Martha Stewart was receiving the tip to sell that she would later be convicted of lying about, financier Carl Icahn began adding ImClone stock to his portfolio. Icahn made $250 million on ImClone shares he bought the fateful day Stewart sold hers. Leah Krauss, *Financier Icahn Makes Killing on ImClone*, United Press Int'l. (Apr. 29, 2004).

[12] Neil Irwin, *Stewart Stock Rallies After Sentencing*, Washington Post (Jul. 17, 2004), at E10.

mains in the range of $335 million.[13] But that is just for the time being. She is staging a comeback. As of this writing she was scheduled to revive her daily homemaking show in September of 2005. "Millions of people feel that Martha got a raw deal," said her producer Mark Burnett. "America loves comeback stories.[14]

Irrespective of Martha Stewart's status as an idol and her supposedly "victimless crime," corporate crime does more monetary damage in the United States than does ordinary crime.[15] Unfortunately, this fact is not generally recognized. Victims of corporate crimes are often unaware they have been taken.

The most troublesome issue with regard to public acknowledgment of corporate crime is definition. Even the question of whether there's even been a "crime" is often in question. As demonstrated by Marianne Lavelle, in order to send corporate criminals to jail:

- Prosecutors must show that wrongdoing was intentional, not just—as the accused will argue—the result of bad decision-making;
- Government investigators must cut through a thicket of business laws that shield corporate executives;
- They must rely on the most problematic of witnesses, colleagues who in many cases were accomplices; and
- Investigations and allegations take place in the public spotlight where the accused may be idolized by a following of fans.[16]

Corporate crime is not perceived with the same degree of threat as street crime. Even so, corporate violence does exist, and John Monahan, Raymond Novaco and Gilbert Geis have defined it as "behavior producing an unreasonable risk of physical harm to consumers,

---

[13] Dan Ackman, *Martha Stewart Found Guilty*, Forbes.com (Apr. 1, 2004).

[14] Carl Limbacher, *Martha Stewart to Get New TV Show*, NewsMax.com (Jan. 17, 2005).

[15] For example, investors' market losses in the Enron crash alone are estimated to be from $30 billion $60 billion. Compare that with the FBI's estimate of $15.9 billion worth of property reported stolen nationwide in 2000. Marianne Lavelle, *Payback Time?*, U.S. News & Wld. Rpt. (Mar. 11, 2002), at 36.

[16] *See id.*

employees, or other persons as a result of deliberate decision-making by corporate executives or culpable negligence on their part."[17]

Whether culpable or not, Phil Condit, the highly respected chairman and CEO of the Boeing Company, resigned just days after two other Boeing officials, Michael Sears and Darleen Druyan, were fired for an alleged breach of ethics. Sears was fired for unethical conduct in negotiating the hiring of Druyan, an Air Force missile defense expert, while she was still working for the Pentagon and was in a position to influence Boeing contracts.[18] The misdeeds, which Druyan only admitted late in the process (with a post-plea) and tried to hide by tampering with evidence, included favorable negotiations on the KC-767 tanker deal with the Air Force, a modernization contract for U.S. Air Force C-17 and North American Treaty Organization [NATO] E-3 Airborne Warning and Control System [AWACS] support.[19]

Boeing's Board of Directors accepted Condit's resignation after deciding "a new structure for the leadership of the company is needed." Chairman of the Board Lewis Platt praised Condit's "characteristic dignity and selflessness in recognizing that his resignation was for the good of the company."[20] Senator John McCain (R-Ariz.) called the incident "a national disgrace."[21] The bottom line is that the whole affair could be clearly described as a corporate crime, for which federal attorneys sought $170 million in civil penalties from Boeing.[22]

The concept of white-collar crime was developed to distinguish a body of criminal acts involving monetary offenses not ordinarily associated with criminality. Sutherland defined "white-collar crime" as "criminal acts committed by persons of the middle and upper socio-economic groups in connections with their occupations." Herbert Edelhertz, in 1970, defined white-collar crime as "an illegal act or series of illegal acts committed by nonphysical means and by

---

[17] John Monahan, Raymond Novaco and Gilbert Geis, *Corporate Violence: Research Strategies for Community Psychology*, in Daniel Adelson and Theodore Sarbin (eds.), Challenges for the Criminal Justice System (1979).

[18] Associated Press, *Boeing Chairman Phil Condit Resigns Amid Military Scandal*, News-Max.com Wires (Mon., Dec. 1, 2003).

[19] Robert Wall, *More Ill Wind*, Av. Wk. & Space Tech. (Oct. 11, 2004), at 45.

[20] Associated Press, *Boeing Chairman Phil Condit Resigns Amid Military Scandal*, News-Max.com Wires (Mon., Dec. 1, 2003).

[21] Robert Wall, *More Ill Wind*, Av. Wk. & Space Tech. (Oct. 11, 2004), at 45.

[22] Andy Pasztor and J. Lynn Lunsford, *U.S. to Seek Damages from Boeing*, Wall St. J. (Thurs., Dec. 18, 2003).

concealment or guile, to obtain money or property, to avoid payment or loss of money or property, or to obtain business or personal advantage."[23] Clinard and Yeager say that white-collar crime should be renamed because "corporate crime is *any* act committed by corporations that is punishable under administrative, civil, or criminal law."[24] This broadens the definition of crime beyond "occupation-related" crimes, and beyond criminal law.

THE DEREGULATORY MOVEMENT

Deregulation in 1978 reversed four decades of regulatory policy in air transportation.[25] Then it appeared as if deregulatory policy had made it easier for financial entrepreneurs to take advantage of the marketplace and to flourish unfairly in the airline industry. The editors of *Aviation Week and Space Technology*, for example, observed that airlines in the U.S. were traditionally managed by "airline people" committed to safety and service, but that they had been replaced by-and-large by "finance entrepreneurs," whose primary commitment is to the "bottom line."[26] This dramatic change in who ran the airlines, they argued, would seriously damage the air transportation system.[27]

Looking back upon the early railroad industry, when left to their own ends to compete, the inevitable result was collusion, merger, and monopoly. Regulation was imposed in 1887 was because of uncontrolled monopoly. Conversely, the beginning of motor transportation

---

[23] Herbert Edelhertz, *The Nature, Impact and Prosecution of White-collar Crime* (1970).

[24] Marshal B. Clinard and Peter C. Yeager, *Corporate Crime* (1980).

[25] *See generally*, Laurence E. Gesell, *Airline Re-Regulation* (1990).

[26] Editorial, *Keep the Sharks Out of Airline Waters*, Av. Wk. & Space Tech. (Aug. 14, 1989).

[27] Following up on the allegation made by the editors of *Aviation Week and Space Technology*, an empirical study was conducted to determine whether the finance-oriented management might have had a detrimental effect upon the industry and consumer welfare interests. In the final analysis, as suspected, in 1989 there was indeed an increase in the number of "finance-oriented" managers running the airline business. However, the effect upon the industry of the transition to more finance-oriented management is not altogether clear. On the one hand, an increase in finance-oriented managers should have been anticipated in a market expected to become intensely competitive. Hiring finance-oriented managers would seem to be an appropriate course to take if corporate culture is viewed as weak, and one is attempting to create a strong, profit-oriented, culture. On the other hand, with the sudden withdrawal of government economic oversight, and introduction of an openly competitive market economy, it should have likewise been anticipated that managers, using every tool at their disposal, would attempt to rationalize the marketplace to their advantage. *See* Laurence E. Gesell, *Airline Re-Regulation* (1990); *see also* Paul Stephen Dempsey and Laurence E. Gesell, *Air Transportation: Foundations for the 21st Century* (1997/2005).

brought with it ease of entry and minimum capital investment. But the result of rigorous competition was instability, and this, too, led ultimately to a clamor for regulation of motor carriers in 1935 and for air carriers in 1938.

Against this historical backdrop, regulation was instituted because the American public was unwilling to tolerate uncontrolled monopoly and equally reluctant to endure the vicissitudes of destructive competition. Yet, in the early 1960s there opened a deregulatory era, which began with a message from President Kennedy calling for more competition in transportation. The regulatory reform sentiment can be traced through the failure of Johnson's "Great Society" experiment, and the public perception of government as inefficient, costly and ineffective. The sentiment was personified in Ralph Nader's consumerism movement of the mid-1960s and early 1970s.

The deregulation movement can be summed up best by the allegation that regulation serves the private ends of those being regulated rather than the public welfare. Added to this were a series of studies which attempted to measure the social costs of (transportation) regulation: in motor transportation, railroads, and in the airlines. Finally, the railroad system was deteriorating in the populous Northeast, which led even further to questioning the efficacy of regulation. In sum, regulation was the focus of perceived consumer neglect, considerable social costs and misallocation of resources. The tone was being set for political reaction in the form of a series of deregulation acts which began initially with the Railroad Revitalization and Regulatory Reform Act (the so-called "4-R" Act) of 1976. The major thrust, however, of the deregulatory movement shifted to air transportation.

In response to congressional and other investigations into airline regulation, and on the heels of a deregulatory movement in general, President Carter's advisors urged him to declare his support for airline deregulation legislation. By supporting regulatory reform of the airlines, Carter endorsed a measure that was already well on its way toward enactment. The movement to deregulate the airline industry had begun during the previous administration, where Gerald Ford had placed deregulation as a key item on his agenda and had proposed an Aviation Act of 1975 to provide at least partial deregulation through more flexibility in setting rates and allowing for more freedom of entry by new carriers.

Ford's "Aviation Act" was never adopted, but the notion of deregulating the airline industry became one of the first items on Jimmy Carter's list of things to do. He appointed Alfred Kahn, an economics professor and a staunch advocate of deregulation, as chairman of the Civil Aeronautics Board. Kahn was not only in favor of deregulation, but he was thoroughly convinced deregulation could not work as a halfway measure, but rather, had to be complete.

With Carter's approval, the Civil Aeronautics Board [CAB] would experiment with less control over fares and routes. At about the same time, Carter made the decision to appoint only fervent deregulators to the Interstate Commerce Commission [ICC], and to reduce the Commission's size in order to provide a majority committed to deregulation. Thus, administrative deregulation began in earnest as the CAB's interpretation of economic regulation was modified 180 degrees by Kahn's concept of total deregulation. Kahn and the Carter administration proceeded overnight to reverse the provisions of the Federal Aviation Act and 40 years of regulatory precedent in aviation—and more than 90 years of economic regulatory policy if one traces the regulatory history back to the Act to Regulate Commerce of 1887.

Although Carter had scored major successes in the area of regulatory reform, and especially with the passage of the Airline Deregulation Act of 1978, Ronald Reagan, in what appeared to be a partisan display to outdo the Democrats, followed through with an even more intense commitment to providing greater regulatory relief for industry. Reagan issued Executive Order 12291, granting the Office of Management and Budget (OMB) super-agency status over regulations, and mandating economic analysis from executive branch agencies. It is of note that Reagan had called for reform proposals with titles such as: "Antitrust Remedies Improvements Act," the "Foreign Trade Antitrust Improvements Act," and the "Clayton Act Amendments." There can be little disagreement that Ronald Reagan favored the individual welfare interests of big business over both labor and the consumer. In theory, the wealth amassed by the rich would "trickle down" to the poor.

Within only two years of its adoption, the Airline Deregulation Act had been given an all new twist by the Reagan administration. Added to deregulatory policy was a White House pro-industry bias and a disdain for meaningful antitrust enforcement. Reagan became perhaps too enthusiastic about getting government altogether out of the regulation business. As deregulation zealot Michael Levine points out, "deregulation doesn't mean that government has *no* responsibilities." Nevertheless, Reagan was so intent on regulatory reform that the effect of his wholesale application of a cost-benefit analysis approach to regulatory policy led to the reordering of national priorities, not only in economic regulation, but away from safety and social regulation as well. The net effect of Reagan's withdrawal from government economic regulatory responsibility was to allow economic concentration within the airline industry, and thereby to significantly reduce free market competition.

By the mid 1980s, the Department of Transportation [DOT] began granting large-scale and wholesale mergers of airline companies, mergers that in the decade of the late 1960s and early 1970s (i.e., the consumer advocacy years), and perhaps even into the late 1970s (when the CAB was allegedly anti-competitive) would have been denied by the Board as destructive to competition.[28] The stage was being set for an organizational trend (back) toward oligopoly as it had been in the 1970s, in seeming contradiction to the adopted tenets of airline deregulation policy, and clearly not authorized under strict interpretation of the Federal Aviation Act of 1958 (Section 408), as amended by the Airline Deregulation Act of 1978.

Section 408 states (in part) that the government "shall not approve" an air carrier consolidation, merger, purchase, lease, operating contract, or acquisition of control, " . . . the effect of which in any region of the U.S. may be substantially to lessen competition, or to tend

---

[28] Domestic entry and ratemaking jurisdiction was phased out by the Airline Deregulation Act, but authority over mergers, consolidations, acquisitions, interlocking relationships and intercarrier agreements was transferred to the DOT on Jan. 1, 1985. The DOT's highly permissive policies with respect to mergers led to an explosion of such activity. The DOT approved each of the 21 mergers and acquisitions submitted to it, including the following: American-Air Cal; United-Pan Am (with various route systems); Delta-Western; Continental-People Express-Frontier-Eastern; Northwest-Republic; USAir-Piedmont; TWA-Ozark; and Southwest-Muse. Many of these mergers were approved under the then-prevailing neo-classical economics view that "contestability" of markets would arrest any anticompetitive conduct. The Northwest-Republic and TWA-Ozark mergers were vigorously opposed by the Department of Justice [DOJ] on grounds that they would create hub monopolies at Minneapolis and St. Louis, respectively. But at the time DOJ participated in an advisory capacity only, and again, DOT approved all mergers submitted to it (although a few were conditioned on a spin-off of certain routes and slots).

Finally, in 1989, Congress removed the DOT's merger jurisdiction and vested such review in the DOJ essentially to evaluate airline mergers, acquisitions, consolidations and interlocking relationships in the way it evaluates such transactions in any other U.S. industry. Since then, the pace of airline merger activity slowed significantly. Paul Stephen Dempsey and Laurence E. Gesell, *Air Commerce and the Law* 293 (2004).

to create a monopoly . . . " unless the effects of " . . . the proposed transaction are outweighed in the public interest. . . ." These are essentially the same criteria governing mergers in all U.S. industries, under section 7 of the Clayton Act. This caveat provided Reagan an opportunity to exercise the presidential prerogative, supposedly "in the public interest." Thus, the Reagan DOT successfully and unilaterally, through administrative regulation, redefined the terms and policy of the Deregulation Act, and there was "an almost total hands-off approach," where government went from total regulation to total deregulation.

Commenting on the failures of deregulation, Kahn states that "the principal failures, by far, have been on the part of government . . . to fulfill its responsibilities," and nowhere has there been more criticism—with the exception of safety—than about airline mergers. However, it is ironic that Kahn views the airline concentration issue as a reflection of what many advocates of deregulation would characterize as a "lamentable failure of the administration to enforce the policies of the antitrust laws." In his zeal to promote deregulation in the 1970s, Kahn remained silent on seemingly important aspects of government regulation which needed to be retained—on safety and antitrust enforcement, for example. It was Kahn himself, along with the Carter administration, who set the tone for the *total* deregulatory scenario that Reagan would later emulate, if not outdo. The Reagan administration could readily agree with Alfred Kahn that deregulation "must go all the way," and that Kahn's approach concurred with the Republican platform and party position. And from the perspective of *complete* deregulation advocated by Kahn, one might ask why antitrust enforcement should be excluded any less than other regulatory devices?

Carter's selection of Kahn to head the CAB posed an ominous threat to regulation. He had been waiting years to apply his economic theories, and he radically attacked the regulatory structure. It was Kahn's explicit desire to "so scramble the eggs that no one (would) ever be able to get them into their shells again." However, a total abdication from the regulatory mechanism was ill-advised. Those who would abolish regulation altogether ignore history as well as economic and political reality. History has demonstrated that regulation was instituted because competition without government controls had been tried and found wanting. The indictment is perhaps no less applicable to Kahn and the Carter administration, who remained silent on the merits of at least limited government intervention, than to Reagan. Nevertheless, it was an overly ambitious Reagan administration approach to deregulation, which led to an airline industry more concentrated than before deregulation, and with three times the debt as a result of overly leveraged buyouts.

THE ENVIRONMENT OF ANTITRUST

Thought of by many as the major problem area facing the air transportation industry in the post deregulation era was the potential for antitrust violation.[29] Airline deregulatory policy brought with it a proliferation of new entrants into the airline business, fierce competition between the airline companies, and a dynamic market force of rapidly changing technology. The increasing numbers of air carriers and the intense competition they practiced at the outset of the deregulatory era is reminiscent of the conditions which led up to adoption of the Civil Aeronautics Act in 1938 and an apparent need for economic and protective control of the air transportation industry in the first place. As new carriers entered the market, others left in revolving door fashion. It was an atmosphere conducive to antitrust violations. It is no wonder that some airline managers perceived a need to engage in aggressive (even potentially unfair) business practice as necessary to the survival of their airline—at a time when so many established companies succumbed to failure or bankruptcy following the onset of deregulation and coupled with a depressed airline economy in the early 1980s.

In the late 1930s the corrective action in response to destructive competition was thought to lie in increased governmental control and regulation. Fifty years later there was a completely different answer to a seemingly similar problem. This time the government was to allow the free market forces to correct the situation. And yet, the more things change the more they stay the same. History repeats itself in strange but interesting and mysterious ways. President Reagan adopted economic strategies in the 1980s that were much the same as those of President Hoover in the 1930s. The same "trickle down" economic theory adopted by Reagan in the 1980s, failed Hoover during the Great

---

[29] *See generally* Laurence E. Gesell and Martin T. Farris, *Antitrust Irrelevance in Air Transportation and the Re-Defining of Price Discrimination*, 57 J. of Air L. & Comm. (1991).

Depression and caused "the great humanitarian" to go down in infamy. Yet, the "trickle-down" theory was tried with a new twist on supply side economic policy.

It might be well to recall that the strategy developed by Herbert Hoover and Postmaster Walter Folger Brown in the early 1930s was ultimately designed to consolidate the industry into perhaps only three or four self-sufficient carriers. The Hoover administration was severely criticized for its fostering of the Air Mail Act of 1930, and the ensuing political reform by way of the (remedial) Air Mail Act of 1934, from which emanated the economic provisions later embodied in the Civil Aeronautics Act of 1938 which stayed in place for some 40 years (i.e., until deregulation in 1978). With the advent of deregulation it would seem that the independent market forces, reinforced by "Reagonomics" reoriented the industry in the same direction Postmaster Brown had originally planned 50 years before.

Evolving airline strategies after deregulation included movement toward consolidation of air carrier companies and aligning of smaller regional carriers under the umbrellas of major and national carriers into condensed hub-and-spoke networks. The road leading toward airline consolidation was bound to be full of antitrust "potholes."

Some 50 years before deregulation, Walter Brown had characterized the airlines as: unwilling or financially unable to invest in new equipment; using obsolete equipment; unsafe because of cost cutting; marginally able to maintain operations with no growth; and engaging in reckless competition. In the January 30, 1984, issue of *Newsweek*, the air transportation industry was described by that magazine's writers as an industry "recovering from devastating losses. . . .," "crippling fare wars. . . .," "in the new era of free wheeling competition. . . .," and "continuing pressure to cut costs. . . ." "Airlines old and new insisted they [were] not cutting corners on safety." However, one veteran airline captain and author John Nance reported, "You have to be naive to believe that airlines cut only frills, . . . carriers have always exceeded FAA regulation—but today I see an insidious trend."[30] Journalistic accounts of the U.S. airline industry's financial destruction published in the early 1990s and early 2000s looked remarkably familiar.

---

[30] John Nance to Leslie Stahl, in a CBS *Face the Nation* broadcast (day unknown, 1986).

The reporting by *Newsweek* in the 1980s was not much different than Walter Brown's perception in the 1930s. Certainly the airlines had matured as an industry, and the aircraft and airspace systems they were using were more technologically advanced. But when an airline company goes broke, it is still the same. Broke is broke! And airline managers may be expected to take whatever steps necessary to prevent failure. In a *laissez-faire* economy, it should be anticipated that managers will attempt to rationalize the marketplace to their own individual advantage—even if it means violation of antitrust laws. Robert Crandall,[31] then CEO of American Airlines, was thus caught-up in an attempt to so rationalize the industry to his airline's advantage.

1980 was a generally bad year for most airlines, and only one airline (Braniff) had greater losses than American. Yet Crandall is a hard driving, intensely competitive, and determined executive. He was intent on turning American around. As he says it, "I care a lot about whether we win or lose."[32] In 1980, his goal was not only to return American to profitability, but also to make the airline number one in the world. By 1989 it had become the number 1 in the U.S. and Crandall insisted, "We don't mind being the biggest airline, but that was never our objective. Our objective is to make American into the world's premier airline company." That means being tops in passenger service and employee relations and showing good profits in good times and bad.[33]

"Good profits," in bad times as well as good, seemingly eluded Crandall (and, for that matter, all of the CEOs of the large carriers). Nevertheless, American remained a dominant player because Crandall cut costs and continued to find ways to save on expenses, he generally kept peace with labor, built American's reputation for service, and therefore retained high-yield traffic. American was the laboratory for creating or perfecting several of the industry's most important innovations—computer reservations systems, frequent flyer programs, yield

---

[31] Robert Crandall was born in 1935, graduated from the U. of Rhode Island in 1957, and earned his M.B.A. from the Wharton School in 1960. After graduation from the U. of Rhode Island, he served in the U.S. Infantry in 1957, before returning to graduate school. Following graduate school, he went to work for the Eastman Kodak Co. until 1962, before moving to Hallmark Cards where he stayed until 1966. Before coming to American, Crandall had worked for TWA for seven years: from 1966 to 1970 he was assistant treasurer, from 1970 to 1971 he was VP for systems and data services, and from 1971 to 1972 he was VP and controller. He then moved to Bloomingdale Brothers in New York as Sr. VP and treasurer until Apr. of 1973, when he joined American.

[32] Doug Carroll, *American is Flying High*, USA Today (Wed., Jul. 19, 1989), at 1B.

[33] *Id.* at 2B.

management, and the hub-and-spoke system. Much of that is attributable to Crandall's determination to beat the competition, and his intellectual rigor and enjoyment of a good debate about a fresh idea. Henry Lefer, executive editor of *Air Transport World*, said that American had "the best management in the business . . . they've been very innovative and aggressive."[34]

At times, however, Crandall's aggressive action created legal difficulties. In early 1983, American and Crandall were charged with antitrust violations in a lawsuit filed by the Department of Justice after Braniff's Howard Putnam secretly taped a telephone call between the two men, wherein Crandall said, "Raise your . . . fares 20%; I'll raise mine the next morning." The charges were dropped by the trial court, reinstated by an appeals court, and ultimately settled in a Justice Department consent decree.

Ten years later, Mr. Crandall was in court again, this time charged with predatory behavior by two competitors. In 1992, he had guided the formulation of American's Value Pricing Plan, which was a bid to push the airline industry toward a simpler—and what Crandall contended would be a more profitable—fare structure. American took the lead in implementing a new structure, hoping others would follow.

Few analysts at the time disagreed with Crandall's notion that the industry had a real need to establish compensatory fares. There was plenty of business; but seemingly, the airlines were either not adequately managing yield or were otherwise simply not charging enough for services. Either way, they were loosing a lot of money and Crandall was trying to do something about it. Unfortunately for American, Continental and Northwest didn't appreciate the rationality in Crandall's actions, or at least did not see the rationalization as being favorable to other than American. Consequently, the two sued American for the losses they said were imposed on them by the Value Pricing Plan.

In trying to press its case, Joseph Jamail, the attorney for the plaintiff, asked Robert Crandall, "You really don't care about what happens to your competitors, do you?" In Crandall's response one can see the archetypal image of American Airlines. In true Milton Friedman fashion, he said, "I care about everybody, Mister Jamail, but I have a fiduciary responsibility to American Airline's stockholders and its employ-

---

[34] *Id.*

ees."[35] Crandall argued that he could not raise prices unless all other carriers raised theirs. In less than three hours of deliberation, the jury agreed, clearing both American and Crandall of the charges.[36]

While Crandall has often expressed the view that the predation claim by Northwest and Continental was completely unjustified, he has remorse that the earlier antitrust suit was such an embarrassment for himself and his colleagues. But sometimes there is a gray area between what is healthy competition and actually stepping over the line into antitrust violation.[37] How are managers to discern the difference between vigorous and predatory competition in order to "make right decisions"?[38] The whole issue of predation can cause much confusion amongst airline managers who may fail to understand fully what it is or how to counter it. With deregulation government wanted reduced prices and airlines were forced to compete in the marketplace. The competitive model relies on carriers vigorously challenging one another in an attempt to improve their position, yet antitrust law precludes airlines from doing their best to price competitors out of the market.[39]

ANTITRUST DEFINED

When predatory, "the predator deliberately incurs losses, in particular by setting prices below cost, in order to impose losses on the prey and force it to exit the market."[40] By definition a "trust" as used herein is a combination of business firms by agreement, and which reduces, or is intended to reduce, competition. Thus, "anti-trust" means to be against monopolistic agreements. Congress promulgated

---

[35] Friedman maintains that the corporate executive is an employee of the business, and therefore has a direct responsibility to conduct business in strict accordance with the employer's desires—to make a profit. The CEO has no social responsibilities, only to increase the profits of the business. *See* Milton Friedman, *The Social Responsibility of Business is to Increase its Profits*, in T. Donaldson and P. Werthane, Ethical Issues In Business: A Philosophical Approach (1983).

[36] James T. McKenna, *Crandall Fends off Lawyers at Trial*, Av. Wk. & Space Tech. (Aug. 2, 1993), at 40.

[37] For example, U.S. District Court Judge Robert M. Hill, in the original 1983 antitrust law suit, ruled that Crandall's "suggestion . . . was . . . not an attempt to fix prices." *See* Laurence E. Gesell and Martin T. Farris, *Antitrust Irrelevance In Air Transportation and the Redefining of Price Discrimination*, 57 J. of Air L. & Comm. (1991).

[38] *See* Mark Pastin, *The Hard Problems of Management: Gaining the Ethics Edge* xii, 24 (1986). "Good ethics . . . .," he says, "is a matter of making right decisions."

[39] John Dodgson and José Jorge, *Law of the Jungle*, Airline Business (May 1997), at 70.

[40] *Id.*

four separate competition laws to encourage competition and punish anti-competitive behavior: (1) the Sherman Act; (2) the Clayton Act; (3) the Robinson-Patman Act; and (4) the Federal Trade Commission Act. Each addresses a somewhat different problem with differing statutory thresholds, and the latter two do not apply to the airlines.[41]

In 1890, Congress enacted the Sherman Act to discourage the concentration of smaller businesses into monopolies. It declared illegal "every contract, combination in the form of trust, or otherwise, or conspiracy in restraint of trade. . . ." It prescribed punishment by fine or imprisonment or both for "every person who shall monopolize, or attempt to monopolize, or combine or conspire . . . to monopolize any part of the trade or commerce among the several states." Under the provisions of this act, decisions handed down in 1911 by the Supreme Court ordered the dissolution of the targeted Standard Oil Company and the American Tobacco Company. The act was to protect trade and commerce against unlawful restraints and monopolies.

The Clayton Act of 1914 was designed to supplement existing laws against unlawful restraints and monopolies and for other purposes. It was to remove ambiguities in the Sherman Act by making certain specific practices illegal. It forbid price discrimination among buyers, along with exclusive selling and tying contracts, if their effect was to lessen competition. The Clayton Act also made clear there was no provision in antitrust laws to forbid formation of labor unions.

Congress promulgated specific legislation to govern unfair and deceptive practices and unfair methods of competition in the airline industry. Moreover, the Airline Deregulation Act of 1978, which amended the Federal Aviation Act of 1958, explicitly provides that deregulation was not designed to condone unfair methods of competition, or deceptive, anti-competitive and monopolistic practices. Section 41712 (formerly section 411) of the Federal Aviation Act provides:

> *On the initiative of the Secretary of Transportation or the complaint of an air carrier . . . and if the Secretary considers it is in the public interest, the Secretary may investi-*

---

[41] Robinson-Patman applies to the sale of goods, not services, and the Federal Trade Commission Act explicitly excludes air carriers from its reach. *See* Paul Stephen Dempsey and Laurence E. Gesell, *Air Commerce and the Law* 275-280 (2004).

> *gate and decide whether an air carrier . . . has*
> *been or is engaged in an unfair or deceptive*
> *practice or an unfair method of competition in*
> *air transportation. . . . If the Secretary, after*
> *notice and an opportunity for a hearing, finds*
> *that an air carrier . . . is engaged in an unfair*
> *or deceptive practice or unfair method of*
> *competition, the Secretary shall order the air*
> *carrier . . . to stop the practice or method.*[42]

This statutory provision is modeled after, and indeed mirrors, Section 5 of the Federal Trade Commission Act.[43] According to Judge Posner, "Although the language of the corresponding section of the two acts is not identical, none of the differences seem deliberate, let alone material. . . . [S]ection 411 is essentially a copy of Section 5 of the Federal Trade Commission Act."[44]

In March of 1938, Congress empowered the FTC to prohibit "unfair or deceptive acts or practices in commerce," and "unfair methods of competition in commerce." Three months later, it promulgated the Civil Aeronautics Act of 1938 (which was later incorporated into the Federal Aviation Act of 1958), including Section 411 thereof, which gave the nascent CAB jurisdiction to prohibit unfair and deceptive practices and unfair methods of competition. Having given the CAB jurisdiction to enforce the unfair and deceptive practices/unfair methods of competition prohibition, Congress saw no need to have the FTC replicate the CAB's oversight. Thus, Section 5 of the Federal Trade Commission Act explicitly excludes "air carriers and foreign air carriers subject to the Federal Aviation Act" from its reach.[45]

---

[42] 49 U.S.C. § 41712 (2002).

[43] 15 U.S.C. § 45 (2002). *See United Air Lines v. Civil Aeronautics Bd.*, 766 F.2d 1107 (7th Cir. 1985).

[44] *United Air Lines*, 766 F.2d at 1112.

[45] The Federal Trade Commission Act provides, "The Commission is hereby empowered and directed to prevent persons, partnerships, or corporations, except . . . air carriers and foreign air carriers subject to the Federal Aviation Act of 1958 . . . from using unfair methods of competition in or affecting commerce and unfair or deceptive acts or practices in or affecting commerce." 15 U.S.C. § 45(a)(2) (2002).

With sunset of the CAB on January 1, 1985, jurisdiction under Section 411 was transferred from the CAB to the DOT. Noting that the CAB had issued rules under Section 411 since 1960, Judge Posner studied the legislative history of the Civil Aeronautics Board Sunset Act of 1984 and concluded, "Congress, looking forward to the period after abolition of the Board, was very concerned to preserve (in the Department of Transportation) authority to enforce Section 411. . . . And Congress was well aware that the Board had used rulemaking to enforce the section."[46] In that case, Posner, speaking for the Seventh Circuit, upheld the jurisdiction of the CAB to "make antitrust-like regulations by means of informal rulemaking."[47] The legislative history of the Civil Aeronautics Board Sunset Act emphasized the DOT's need to arrest anti-competitive practices:

> *There is also a strong need to preserve the Board's authority under Section 411 to ensure fair competition in air transportation. . . . Although the airline industry has been deregulated, this does not mean that there are no limits to competitive practices. As is the case with all industries, carriers must not engage in practices that would destroy the framework under which fair competition operates. Air carriers are prohibited, as are firms in other industries, from practices which are inconsistent with the antitrust laws or the somewhat broader prohibitions of Section 411 of the Federal Aviation Act (corresponding to Section 5 of the Federal Trade Commission Act) against unfair competitive practices.*[48]

Unless the DOT enforced the statutory prohibition against unfair and deceptive practices and unfair methods of competition, airlines would be in the unique position among U.S. industries of being abso-

---

[46] *United Air Lines*, 766 F.2d at 1112.

[47] *Id.* at 1120.

[48] H. R. Rep. No. 98-793, 98th Cong, 2nd Sess. 4-5 (1984).

lutely free to engage in such anti-competitive practices, contrary to the explicit wish of Congress in promulgating the Civil Aeronautics Act of 1938, the Federal Aviation Act of 1958, the Airline Deregulation Act of 1978, and the Civil Aeronautics Board Sunset Act of 1984. Every other industry in the U.S. economy is subject to the oversight of the FTC. Airlines are not. Nor are airlines subject to the deceptive practices regulation of the states, under the broad construction of the pre-emption provisions of the Airline Deregulation Act of 1978.[49]

Again, Section 5 of the Federal Trade Commission Act is essentially the equivalent of Section 411 [now Section 41712] of the Federal Aviation Act. The Supreme Court found that the "paramount aim" of Section 5 is to protect the public against evils likely to result from destruction of competition or restriction of it in substantial degree.[50] Section 5 is intended to combat, in their incipiency, trade practices that exhibit strong potential for stifling competition.[51] According to the Supreme Court, the fundamental question is whether the methods complained of are "unfair," and whether they produce substantial injury to the public by restricting competition in interstate trade and common liberty to engage therein.[52] Public policy is particularly concerned where unfair practices jeopardize or injure a present or potential competitor,[53] though an adverse effect on consumers may also trigger the prohibition.[54] The purpose of the legislation was to combat unfair practices, which if remained unchecked, probably would result in a violation of the antitrust laws (the Sherman and Clayton Acts).[55]

Both the FTC and DOT may forbid anti-competitive practices before they become sufficiently serious to violate the Sherman or Clayton Acts.[56] Indeed, the definition of "unfair methods of competition" is not

---

[49] *See Morales v. Trans World Airlines*, 504 U.S. 374 (1992).

[50] *FTC v. Raladam Co.*, 283 U.S. 643 (1931).

[51] *FTC v. Texaco*, 393 U.S. 223 (1968). It is not imperative, in order to bring into play the 'prophylactic' action of the FTC, to prove that a monopoly has been achieved, since one of the purposes of the Federal Trade Commission Act is to prevent potential injury by stopping unfair methods of competition in their incipiency." *Hastings Manufacturing Co. v. FTC*, 153 F.2d 253 (6th Cir. 1946).

[52] *Raladam*, 283 U.S. 643.

[53] *Id.*

[54] *FTC v. Sperry & Hutchinson Co.*, 405 U.S. 233 (1972).

[55] *Butterick Pub. Co. v. FTC*, 85 F.2d 522 (2nd Cir. 1936).

[56] *See Atlantic Refining Co. v. FTC*, 381 U.S. 367 (1965); *Pan American World Airways, Inc., v. United States*, 371 U.S. 296 (1963). If the purpose and practice of the anticompetitive activity runs

confined to those activities that were illegal under the common law, or condemned by the Sherman or Clayton Acts.[57] The DOT has acknowledged that its authority under this provision "allows us to define practices that do not violate the antitrust laws as unfair methods of competition, if they violate the spirit of the antitrust laws."[58] The U.S. Supreme Court has held: "Unfair or deceptive practices or unfair methods of competition," as used in Section 411 [now 41712], are broader concepts than the common-law ideas of unfair competition. The section is concerned not with punishment of wrongdoing or protection of injured competitors, but rather with protection of the public interest."[59]

Section 41712 provides that the Secretary shall take action against unfair and deceptive practices if he believes such action is in the "public interest." Congress explicitly defined the "public interest" in the Airline Deregulation Act to include the following:

> *[T]he Secretary of Transportation shall consider the following matters, among others, as being in the public interest. . . :*
>
> *(4) the availability of a variety of adequate, economic, efficient, and low-priced services without unreasonable discrimination or unfair or deceptive practices. . . .*
>
> *(9) preventing unfair, deceptive, predatory, or anti-competitive practices in air transportation.*
>
> *(10) avoiding unreasonable industry con-*

---

counter to the public policy declared in the Sherman and Clayton Acts, the FTC has jurisdiction to suppress it as an unfair method of competition. *Fashion Originators' Guild v. FTC*, 312 U.S. 457 (1941). The Federal Trade Commission Act was designed to bolster and supplement the Sherman and Clayton Acts as well as condemn as 'unfair methods of competition' existing violations of them. *FTC v. Motion Picture Adver. Co.*, 344 U.S. 392 (1953).

[57] *Motion Picture Adver. Co.*, 344 U.S. 392.

[58] 61 Fed. Reg. 42,208, 42,215. This interpretation is supported by *Sperry & Hutchinson Co. v. FTC*, 432 F.2d 146 (5th Cir. 1970), which held that under Sec. 5 of the Federal Trade Commission Act, the FTC could declare conduct "unfair" if it constituted either (1) a per se violation of antitrust policy, (2) a violation of the letter of the Sherman, Clayton or Robinson-Patman Acts, or (3) a violation of the spirit of these Acts. Similarly, the Third Circuit held that the Sherman Act acts as a guide or declaration of policy for the FTC in determining what constitutes an unfair method of competition. *New Jersey Wood Finishing Co. v. Minnesota Mining & Manuf. Co.*, 332 F.2d 346 (3rd Cir. 1964).

[59] *American Airlines v. North American Airlines*, 351 U.S. 79, 85 (1956) [citations omitted].

centration, excessive market domination, monopoly powers, and other conditions that would tend to allow at least one air carrier . . . unreasonably to increase prices, reduce service, or exclude competition in air transportation.

(11) maintaining a complete and convenient system of continuous scheduled interstate air transportation for small communities. . . .

(13) encouraging entry into air transportation markets by new and existing air carriers and the continued strengthening of small air carriers to ensure a more effective and competitive airline industry.[60]

Whereas the government is obligated to enforce the antitrust laws, it may on limited occasions provide immunity to antitrust enforcement if it is deemed to be in the public interest. Section 414 of the Aviation Act provided the Civil Aeronautics Board with authority to grant to air carriers limited immunity to the antitrust laws:

In any order made under Section 408, 409, or 412 of this Act, the Board may, as part of such order, exempt any person affected by such order from the operations of the "antitrust laws" set forth in Sub-Section (a) of the first section of the Clayton Act (15 U.S.C. 12) to the extent necessary to enable such person to proceed with the transaction specifically approved by the Board in such order and those transactions necessarily contemplated by such order, except that the Board may not exempt such person unless it determines that such exemption is required in the public interest. [Notwithstanding the preceding sentence, on the

---

[60] 49 U.S.C. § 40101 (2003). Restated, these are the goals and objectives of the Airline Deregulation Act of 1978.

> *basis of the findings required by Sub-Section (a)(2)(A)(i) of Section 412, the Board shall, as part of any order under such section which approves any contract, agreement, or request or any modification or cancellation thereof, exempt any person affected by such order from the operations of the "anti-trust laws" set forth in Sub-Section (a) of the first section of the Clayton Act (15 U.S.C. 12) to the extent necessary to enable such person to proceed with the transaction specifically approved by the Board in such order and with those trans-actions necessarily contemplated by such or-der.*] (Brackets added)

That portion within the [bracketed] area above was deleted by the Airline Deregulation Act of 1978. Sub-Section (a)(2)(A)(i), referred to within the brackets has to do with Board approval of mergers that re-duce or eliminate competition. Preceding the Airline Deregulation Act, anti-competitive agreements approved by the CAB were *entitled* to antitrust immunity, which the CAB had no discretion to deny. The De-regulation Act made two significant changes in this process. First, submission of joint operating agreements to the Board was made op-tional instead of mandatory. Second, the entitlement to antitrust immu-nity was limited; *mandatory immunity* was eliminated but the Board was granted the authority to confer *discretionary immunity*. The International Transportation Competition Act of 1979 amended the statute, reinstating the entitlement to mandatory immunity in limited circumstances.

The intent of Congress in passing the Airline Deregulation Act was to remove artificially imposed governmental constraints upon free trade in the air transportation industry. The overall scheme was to al-low the free enterprise system to function, and to ideally create a more perfect economic model of competition wherein prices would be driven down and the consumer would be the ultimate benefactor. In a perfect economy, there are many competitors, none of whom can control the market, and all whom must actively participate in price competition. The results, however, of artificially low air fares in the early 1980s were bankruptcies and air carrier failures. Given regulatory freedom, the economy rights itself by way of natural economic laws. Excess competition may be reduced or eliminated, if not by expansion and growth of surviving companies, then by merger. The mergers of the mid-1980s set the trend toward oligopoly. But that was not unique to the air transport industry. As Dreazen, Ip and Kulish point out, "Everywhere you look, powerful forces are driving American industries to consolidate into oligopolies—and the obstacles are getting less formidable."[61] Generally, there are tangible rewards for growing large, particularly in industries where fixed costs are especially high and the cost of serving each customer is low.

Even though large, consolidated companies have economies of scale and can theoretically offer lower unit costs. In practice, they typically do not. Oligopolistic prices tend to be higher, and oligopolies are highly reluctant to enter into price competition—conditions much the same as airline economics before deregulation, except for the allegations by some that air carrier management then had little incentive under government regulations to run the airlines efficiently. In the post-deregulatory era, airlines have moved toward consolidation; however, as Alfred Kahn has stated, the airline industry fails to behave like an "intelligent oligopoly."[62] Moreover, government intervention precludes airlines from economically rationalizing the marketplace. Look for example at the United Airlines' $4.3 billion proposal to buy US Airways in 2000. The government then assumed that because the two airlines were so strong, that by combining forces they would have acquired unlawful power to gouge consumers. Hence the antitrust authorities resolved to keep the two airlines safely apart. By 2005, both were in bankruptcy and it appeared that neither might survive.[63]

As of this writing, the cycle of airline concentration has been "fractionalized," and in its wake the legacy carriers are loosing their dominance in the industry, with several carriers threatened by insolvency and in bankruptcy. As the "airline crisis" slowly ebbs around the

---

[61] Yochi J. Dreazen, Greg Ip and Nicholas Kulish, *Why the Sudden Rise in the Urge to Form Oligopolies*, Wall St. J. (Mon. Feb. 25, 2002), at A1.

[62] Alfred Kahn, *Is it Time to Re-regulate the Airline Industry?*, The World Economy (Dec. 1982), Vol. 5, No. 4, at 343.

[63] Peter Huber, *Antitrust's Real Legacy*, Wall St. J. (Thurs., Dec. 26, 2002).

world, the profile of a revamped industry is taking shape.[64] A domestic airline industry is emerging that may be no longer dominated by the traditional hub-and-spoke system carriers. Based on the differential growth rates between the traditional and the low cost carriers, Edmund Greenslet, head of ESG Aviation Services, goes so far as to predict that the domestic share of the currently largest six U.S. carriers (American, Northwest, Delta, United, US Airways, and America West) plus Alaska Airlines, will shrink from 75% to 62% by 2010, drop another 12% by 2017, and settle in at around 45% by 2020.[65] However, assuming the major carriers restructure successfully, and further assuming they will diversify their services to match the competition, they may counter the advances made by the Low-Cost Carriers [LCCs]. Moreover, the proliferation of new-entrant, LCCs will present formidable competition amongst themselves.

Nevertheless, as Greenslet submits, "The domestic airline landscape is changing before our eyes, and the consequences for the traditional airlines are only beginning to be felt."[66] What is emerging is an air transportation system comprised of six principal market niches:

- long haul hub-and-spoke carriers,
- short haul point-to-point carriers,
- all cargo carriers,
- regional carriers,
- air charter carriers, and a
- small aircraft transportation system [SATs].

Accepting that the new and evolving air transport structure will be comprised of the above groupings, reasonable domestic market share assumptions for each of the passenger enplanement segments could conceivably be as follows: long haul hub-and-spoke carriers 45%;

---

[64] *See* Laurence E. Gesell and Paul Stephen Dempsey, *Air Transportation: Foundations for the 21st Century* 454-476 (2nd ed. 2005).
[65] Edmund S. Greenslet, quoted in Anthony Velocci, Jr., *Can Majors Shift Focus Fast Enough to Survive?*, Av. Wk. & Space Tech. (Nov. 18, 2002), at 52.
[66] *Id.*

short haul point-to-point carriers 25%; regional carriers 20%; with air charter networks and SATs sharing the remaining 10%.[67]

The consequences of this transformation of the industry leads one to conclude there may be less need for antitrust vigilance. As Roger Fones, transportation section chief in DOJ's Antitrust Division, suggests, "Antitrust laws aren't changing, but their application to aviation mergers might morph as market conditions deteriorate for the endangered network airlines." "As low-cost competitors expand their operations, the network carriers' market power wanes and they become less threatening to competition."[68]

But the problem with Mr. Fones' assessment is that herein lies the "tragedy of the commons."[69] The variety of options serving the various niches appears ideal—assuming capacity can and will be rationally matched against actual demand. But given the absence of sound aviation policy domestically, let alone internationally, the primordial instinct of the airlines will be to concentrate and produce excess capacity and to thereby destroy the marketplace commons. That is what airlines have always done absent government oversight. Unless there is government intervention to regulate the commons, it will inevitably be overgrazed to a tragic end. For another example of government intervention stifling oligopolistic concentration in the airline industry, look at the case of computer reservations systems.

COMPUTER RESERVATION SYSTEMS

The predominant antitrust issue left by the Civil Aeronautics Board upon its demise in 1985 involved airline Computer Reservations Systems [CRS]. In the days before CRS, airline reservations were made using the *Official Airline Guide* [OAG], by calling the airline reservations agents by telephone, or by referring to the electronic fare information published by the Airline Tariff Publishing Company. Today, the revolutionary shift toward automation and computerized systems has changed all that. Yet, at the outset, and well before the Internet

---

[67] Laurence E. Gesell and Paul Stephen Dempsey, *Air Transportation: Foundations for the 21st Century* 474 (2nd ed. 2005).

[68] Washington Outlook, *Antitrust Signals*, Av. Wk. & Space Tech. (Sep. 27, 2004), at 25.

[69] *See* Garrett Hardin, *The Tragedy of the Commons*, Science, Dec. 13, 1968, at 1243; *see also* Laurence E. Gesell, *Airline Re-Regulation* 126-127 (1990). *See also* Laurence E. Gesell and Paul Stephen Dempsey, *Air Transportation: Foundations for the 21st Century* 446-448 (2nd ed. 2005).

made such capabilities commonplace, there were only a handful of computerized reservations systems in the control of a select few carriers. The issue, then, became a matter of whether these select carriers were using their reservations systems to an *unfair* competitive advantage, and thus potentially in violation of antitrust law.

The predominant systems were American Airlines' *SABRE* and United Airlines' *APOLLO* systems, around which most of the controversy centered. Other leading systems are Trans World Airlines' *PARS II*, Eastern's *SYSTEM ONE* was another, and a late comer, Delta Airlines' *DATAS II*. In the late 1980s, of these systems, an estimated 70% of all reservations were made on either the *SABRE* or *APOLLO* systems. These were the primary distribution vehicles through which travel agents booked flights for passengers. Customer airlines of those systems accused the owners of the computer systems of taking unfair advantage of them, in some cases of raising charges from 300% to 500%, and of generally creating bias in the systems in favor of those major carriers who owned and operated them.

United and American countered by claiming that arrangement of computer displays to their advantage was only fair. It was they who took the chance and invested in the systems. The systems were designed to serve *their* companies, and they were entitled to return on their investment. Why shouldn't they (the owners and operators) gain advantage from their own systems? After all, they argued, they didn't invest millions of dollars in systems to serve their competition. Helping the competition would be a contradiction and contrary to what competition and the free enterprise system is all about.

The opposition, however, contended the investments were made and the systems were built before deregulation, when those carriers enjoyed the anti-competitive protection of the federal government. Under antitrust law's "essential facilities doctrine," the monopolist who controls access to the market must open it to competitors on fair and equal terms. If deregulation was to be successful, consumers needed free access to un-biased information on flights and fares. To have it any other way, the customers would be robbed of the opportunities that an open marketplace is intended to afford.

Either singly or collectively, a number of airlines filed suit on antitrust grounds against CRS system vendors.[70] The non-vendor airlines alleged that American and United, specifically, were restricting competition in four ways:

- displaying flight information in a biased manner;
- imposing discriminatory and extraordinarily high fees on competing carriers;
- using data to identify specific travel agents who could be induced or persuaded to divert their business; and
- by delaying entry of competing airlines' data into their systems.

Before its termination in 1985, the CAB established CRS rules and the DOT defended CAB's rules as a "rational program for preventing competitive harm and consumer injury." The Department of Justice was also asked to affirm those rules. The DOJ said its Antitrust Division would "continue to monitor the rules' ability to restore airline competition displaced by biased computer reservations systems." The Justice Department indicated it was too soon after the rules' implementation to determine their effectiveness, but stated the airline industry was "readily susceptible to monopolistic or joint monopolistic" behavior if entry barriers existed in markets. In a report issued in early 1986, the DOJ recommended against divestiture or further regulation of the computer reservations systems.

American, United, Eastern, TWA and Delta agreed to eliminate the use of secondary displays biased in favor of their own flights. In the meantime, action was taken independently by some domestic and foreign carriers to establish computer reservation systems of their own. People Express, for example, developed a system for travel agencies using TWA's PARS II. The International Air Transport Association [IATA] formed an "interest group" to investigate the establishment of a neutral industry booking system. The *Official Airline Guide* promised to offer reservations capability to its subscribers by the fall of 1985. A group of 24 U.S. and foreign carriers, which grew out of the IATA task force, offered to buy PARS from TWA. By 1986, a group

---

[70] *See In Re Passenger Computer Reservations Systems Antitrust Litigation*, CCH 21 AVI 17,732 (1988).

of 29 domestic and foreign carriers attempted to establish what it called the Neutral Industry Booking System, but the project was faced with significant monetary and operational barriers to entry. The computer reservation issue eventually subsided with the major operators agreeing not to bias the systems.

As early as 1984, the CAB promulgated rules attempting to eliminate CRS display bias by prohibiting CRSs from using carrier identity as a factor for editing and ranking airline services.[71] The rules also required each system to give participating airlines and subscribers a description of its display algorithms on request. Regulations promulgated by DOT in 1992 attempted to reduce architectural bias by eliminating features that favored the vendor airline (whose flights were previously accessed with fewer keystrokes), requiring equal functionality (to make all enhancements available to all airlines), and requiring each CRS owner to use identical procedures for loading fares and schedules (so that the vendor airline's fares and schedules were not loaded first).[72] After U.S. airlines divested themselves of CRSs, in 2004 the DOT repealed most of its CRS rules.[73]

In terms of oligopolistic efficiency, the industry's two largest players, American and United, lost control of a key asset that they had built themselves, and that were badly needed over the long-term to maintain stable profitability in a competitive environment.[74]

PREDATORY PRACTICES

Before deregulation, predation was scarcely an issue. Rates had to be filed in tariffs, and cost-justified as "just and reasonable" and "nondiscriminatory." New routes could be inaugurated only with regulatory approval. Hence, under regulation, there was little opportunity to bankrupt a competitor. But since deregulation, incumbent airlines have developed an arsenal of weapons to deter or punish smaller competitors, including:

---

[71] 49 Fed. Reg. 11,644 (Mar. 27, 1984). *See United Air Lines v. CAB*, 766 F.2d 1107 (7th Cir. 1985).

[72] Aviation Daily (Sep. 22, 1992), at 504.

[73] 69 Fed. Reg. 976 (Jan. 7, 2004).

[74] Peter Huber, *Antitrust's Real Legacy*, The Wall St. J. (Thurs., Dec. 26, 2002).

- dropping prices sharply;
- eliminating advance purchase and Saturday night stay-over restrictions;
- expanding the inventory of low-fare seats offered;
- increasing the number of flights and/or the size of aircraft;
- scheduling departures in close proximity to the new entrant's flights, sometimes boxing them in;
- offering passengers bonus frequent flyer miles;
- paying travel agent commission overrides to steer traffic toward the incumbent in the new entrant's markets;
- paying higher up front commission rates on routes where it competes with a new entrant;
- biasing their computer reservations systems against non-affiliated interline connections;
- refusing to enter into ticketing-and-baggage, joint-fare, and code-sharing relationships with the new entrant;
- refusing to lease gates, provide services, or sell parts to the new entrant;
- restricting airport operators with majority-in-interest clauses to prohibit the construction of gates and other infrastructure for new entrants; and
- prohibiting affiliated regional feeder airlines from entering into marketing agreements with the new entrant.

Although quieter than the antitrust issues surrounding the computer reservation systems, there was also some concern in the opening years of deregulation over predatory pricing and capacity dumping. "Predatory pricing" occurs when an airline establishes fares below the associated costs of producing service, specifically with the intent of driving competition out of business. It is a kind of "table-stakes poker" game where the one with the most chips or money, tries to out-last the other through a price war. "Capacity dumping" involves adding flight frequencies and seats to deny a competitor the ability to achieve break-even load factors. In the vernacular of the industry, an almost sure sign of potential predatory practices is the occurrence of "wingtipping" where one carrier will match another with a departing flight within five or ten minutes of the other, on the same route, and at a significantly reduced fare.

Like other forms of antitrust violation, predatory pricing is difficult to prove and therefore nearly impossible to enforce. In an intensely competitive environment, determining where fair market promotion leaves off, and where unfair pricing begins is problematic. A thin line is drawn between the violation of antitrust law and the conformance therewith. What must be determined is whether business is conducted fairly. But unfair business practice is a matter of perception. The Sherman and Clayton Acts have defined "unlawful" business practice with terms like "price discrimination," "monopoly," and "restraint of trade." Additionally, the Federal Aviation Act of 1958 describes fair competition in terms of whether it is "in the public interest." Section 41712 (formerly 411) of the Aviation Act grants the power to "investigate and determine whether any air carrier . . . has been or is engaged in unfair or deceptive practices or unfair methods of competition in air transportation . . . "

Thus, what is "unfair" is still a function of perception. It is a judgment call, a call between what is unfair competition on the one hand and free enterprise on the other. "Free enterprise," means having the freedom to take the business initiative. To quote a colloquial phrase, "Profit is not a dirty word," but in the pursuit of profit, the rights of competitors may sometimes be violated. As competition intensifies and a company's well-being appears threatened, managers of carriers under threat are quick to perceive the tactics of competitors as predatory. What follows is reflective of the intensely competitive environment that evolved subsequent to airline deregulation. The stories are typical of the predatory allegations that became rampant during the initial years of deregulation, and illustrate the competitive environment that erupted in the destabilized deregulatory marketplace.

One major problem of proof in a monopolization claim is that the allegedly predatory price is below cost. The difficulty lies in the fact that fixed costs bulk large in the airline industry as a percentage of fully allocated costs. Adding another passenger to a scheduled flight causes the airline to add little in terms of variable costs. Moreover, for a network airline, joint costs are spread over an array of flights, equipment and facilities, as well as different cabin classes, and therefore difficult to ascribe to any single flight. One promising approach might be to focus on the "opportunity costs" of the incumbent airline adding capacity to a market where a new entrant has emerged, rather than devoting that capacity to a market with higher margins.

In or about 1979, just after adoption of the Airline Deregulation Act, an individual or individuals from Golden Gate Airlines allegedly approached Swift Aire Lines' Chief Executive Officer and/or its corporate board members threatening to enter into intensive price war strategy if Swift did not agree to acquisition and merger with Golden Gate. During the 1979/1980 time frame, Golden Gate did, in fact, match Swift's flight schedule in many of its markets, and at deeply discounted rates of 50% or less than fares charged by Swift. Shortly thereafter, Swift was acquired by Golden Gate by purchase agreement. And not long afterward, both companies were put into Chapter 7 receivership, leaving California intrastate air transportation in shambles. Whether intentionally predatory or not, the business strategy on the part of Golden Gate's management was conclusively destructive.

Swift's primary replacement in the California Central Coast market was Wings West Airlines (now a part of the American Eagle system). Swift Airlines went bankrupt in September of 1981. Thereafter, Wings West rapidly expanded to serve the already developed market. Within a year, the airline was facing fierce and potentially unfair competition. In November of 1982, Wings West filed suit against Sun Aire Lines and its parent company, the DiGiorgio Corporation, charging that Sun Aire had engaged in below cost pricing practices designed to drive competitors from the Santa Maria, California, market.

In antitrust suits, the action may be civil, criminal, or both. Wings West sought civil compensation as well as an injunction against Sun Aire's allegedly anti-competitive pricing. Sun Aire had begun flying to Santa Maria in July of 1982. It had reduced its fares to a low of $19.50 to Los Angeles, compared to Wings West's $59 fare in the market prior to July. Cited as an example of Sun Aire's predatory strategy was the Yuma-Phoenix market once served by Cochise, where Sun Aire reduced its fares to $15 before Cochise abandoned the route. An agreement was reached and the Wings West case against Sun Aire was settled quietly out of court.

Perhaps the most intense competition for a domestic market in the deregulation era involved newly formed America West Airlines and Southwest Airlines (at the time, recently merged with Muse Air), both competing for the explosively growing Phoenix, Arizona, market. America West, with headquarters in Phoenix, was the largest carrier in terms of passenger boardings at Phoenix. Southwest, that reportedly tried to buy out America West in 1984, by 1985 was steadily building a secondary hub at Phoenix. Southwest's strategy was to establish dominance in the Phoenix marketplace. Southwest's officials said that in order to carry out their strategy, they had to be aggressive in terms of pricing—pricing not to be unprofitable but to be competitive. They publicly stated they would not do anything to justify charges of predatory pricing.

Accepting the operational deficit as advertising expense, Southwest had advertised an introductory fare of $9.00 one way Phoenix-Ontario, California, as a promotional fare. America West had been charging $45 one way to Ontario. It dropped its fare to $39 to match Southwest's regular fare of $39. Southwest subsequently dropped its one way Phoenix-Los Angeles fare to $29 and America West matched it.

The two carriers had been competing similarly between Phoenix and El Paso, Austin, Albuquerque, Los Angeles, San Diego and Las Vegas. But Southwest insisted that on a fully allocated cost basis, all Southwest fares were *remunerative*. If it can be demonstrated that at given load factors, the fare charged could recover costs and potentially produce profit, then by definition it is not predatory.

Reportedly, officials at America West alleged that, "Having moved to absorb Muse Air, Southwest, we believe, is now turning both barrels on us. . . ." A senior industry analyst told those same reporters,

> *It is pretty obvious that, having largely disposed of Muse Air, Southwest is going to make life even tougher for America West. Southwest had an easier time with Muse since it competed in every Muse market. Although it is head-to-head with America West in only selective markets, Southwest could do some damage here. Low fares will pressure America West and depress yields and could lead to difficulties for America West. . . .*

In April 1985, Muse Air had accepted a $60 million offer to be bought by rival Southwest. The latter immediately increased one-way fares on five routes where it had competed with Muse. The carrier admitted that it purposefully held down fares where it was in competition (with 40% of its assets) against Muse Air and America West. Southwest said its fare hikes were implemented because of increased operating costs.

In reviewing the takeover of Muse by Southwest, the DOJ's Antitrust Division said it approved the sale, but only because of the "failing company doctrine," under which an otherwise anti-competitive merger would not be challenged because one of the firms (Muse) was unlikely to meet its financial obligations or to successfully reorganize under bankruptcy, and probably could not find another qualified buyer.[75] In other words, Muse would have likely failed irrespective of its competition with Southwest. The Justice Department said it saw no significant antitrust issues in the deal. But America West was opposed to the sale, arguing that DOT's conclusions submitted to the DOJ for its consideration were seriously flawed.

It could be surmised that Southwest was engaged in conceivably unfair practice, but that was not demonstrated in court. Demonstrated only was an intense struggle to capture an increasingly lucrative market in a free enterprise system. Said Herb Kelleher, Chief Executive Officer of Southwest, "I like competition. . . . The airline business is the closest thing to war in peacetime."[76]

The carrier with the most carnivorous reputation for executing a "scorched earth" policy toward new entrants is Northwest Airlines, with a fortress hub in Minneapolis/St. Paul. Reno Air began operations out of Reno, Nevada, in July 1992. On February 10, 1993, Reno Air, then flying only seven jets, had the temerity to announce its intention to inaugurate thrice daily round-trip service between Reno and Minneapolis on April 1 at a fare of $95 one-way. Northwest had abandoned the route in 1991, because it was unprofitable. The day after Reno Air announced it would inaugurate Reno-Minneapolis service, Northwest retaliated by announcing it was beginning three round-trip daily flights

---

[75] It was under the failing company doctrine that American acquired TWA in 2001, an otherwise unacceptable merger under DOJ's anti-competitive guidelines. *See* Washington Outlook, *Antitrust Signals*, Av. Wk. & Space Tech. (Sep. 27, 2004).

[76] An interesting side note to the story involving Southwest is that Southwest had itself been the target of other airlines subsequently charged with antitrust violations; *See U.S. v. Braniff and Texas International Airlines*, CCH 15 AVI 17,388 (1978).

between Minneapolis and Reno on April 1.[77] The following day, Northwest announced it would begin new service to Reno, Nevada, from three of the West Coast cities served by Reno Air—Seattle, Los Angeles, and San Diego—on April 1, in effect, establishing a Northwest mini-hub at Reno, Nevada. These were routes not theretofore flown by Northwest. On May 1, 1993, Northwest announced it would begin a second daily flight from both Los Angles and Seattle to Reno. Northwest began offering bonus frequent flyer miles to passengers flying from Reno and commission overrides to travel agents booking passengers on Northwest.[78] Northwest also announced it would match Reno Air's fares, as low as $55 one-way over some segments.[79] Northwest offered the same fares on its *nonstop* flights from Minneapolis to Los Angeles, San Francisco, San Diego, Seattle, Ontario, and Portland as Reno Air offered to these cities in *connecting* service. By May 20th, the losses sustained caused Reno Air to reduce Minneapolis service to one flight per day.[80]

Senator Richard Bryan (D-Nev.) asked the Departments of Justice and Transportation to investigate whether Northwest was using "predatory pricing and scheduling practices" to run Reno Air out of business. According to Bryan, "The federal government should not let Northwest snuff out this airline just as it is getting its wings."[81] Transportation Secretary Federico Peña met with Northwest Airlines officials in March 1993, and gave them just two days to reconsider, or face the wrath of DOT. Northwest responded by abandoning its plans to start service to Reno from Seattle, Los Angeles, and San Diego, but continued its Minneapolis-Reno service.[82] Northwest retreated after Peña tacitly threatened regulatory or antitrust action.[83] But Reno Air was forced to abandon the Minneapolis-Reno market, ceasing service

---

[77] Earle Eldridge, *Bryan Calls for Probe of Reno Air's Competitors* (Mar. 3, 1993).

[78] Clinton Oster, Jr. & John Strong, *Predatory Practices in the U.S. Airline Industry* 8 (Jan. 15, 2001). The authors point out that commission overrides also played a role in the decision of Southwest Airlines to exit the Indianapolis-Detroit market, one of the few it has ever withdrawn from, and of Midwest Express to abandon the Milwaukee-Detroit market. *Id.* at 25.

[79] Frank Costello, *Is That a Predator Up There?*, J. of Comm. (May 11, 1993), at 8A.

[80] Clinton Oster, Jr. & John Strong, *Predatory Practices in the U.S. Airline Industry* 8 (Jan. 15, 2001).

[81] Earle Eldridge, *Bryan Calls for Probe of Reno Air's Competitors* (Mar. 3, 1993).

[82] *Northwest Forced to Drop Its Reno Plans*, Flight Int'l. (Apr. 7, 1993).

[83] Mark Clouatre, *The Legacy of Continental Airlines v. American Airlines: A Re-Evaluation of the Predatory Pricing Theory in the Airline Industry*, 60 J. Air L. & Com. 869, 914 (1995).

on June 1, 1993.[84] According to Professors Oster and Strong, "Following Reno's exit from the Reno to Minneapolis market, [Northwest's] fares increased quickly and steadily.[85] After Reno Air's withdrawal, Northwest's lowest fare increased 73% from $86 to $149, while its lowest refundable fare increased 320%, from $136 to $455. By the spring of 2000, Northwest's lowest seven-day advance purchase fare was $1,026.[86]

Decrying Northwest's "blatantly anticompetitive responses", Reno Air's General Counsel Bob Rowen alleged, "Northwest entered with excess capacity and reduced its fares. Industry experts agree that Northwest's purpose in doing so was to destroy the market, to push Reno Air out and deter other low fare airlines from entering Northwest's hubs."[87] In 1997, Reno Air filed an antitrust lawsuit against Northwest alleging unlawful monopolization. The suit contended that Northwest employed similar anticompetitive conduct against People Express, Icelandair, Midway Airlines and other new entrants at Minneapolis/St. Paul.[88] According to Rowen, Northwest "engaged in a variety of tactics, including below-cost pricing, to drive us from the market. These actions were predatory."[89] The case was dropped in April 1999, after American Airlines purchased Reno Air.[90]

Though the early 1990s brought about a proliferation of new entrant airlines, the late 1990s was an era of bankruptcies, liquidations and retrenchments for upstart airlines. Five new airlines per year emerged from 1990 to 1995. But from 1995 until early 1999, not a single new airline began service.[91] New entrants like Air South, Pan Am (which included Carnival Airlines), Western Pacific, Kiwi, and Sun Jet International fell into bankruptcy, while others were facing enormous financial difficulty. By 1999, new entrants accounted for

---

[84] Clinton Oster, Jr. & John Strong, *Predatory Practices in the U.S. Airline Industry* 8 (Jan. 15, 2001).

[85] *Id.*.

[86] Testimony of Bill LaMacchia, Jr., before the U.S. Senate Judiciary Comm., Subcomm. on Antitrust (May 2, 2000).

[87] Testimony of Bob Rowen before the U.S. Senate Commerce Comm. (Oct. 28, 1997).

[88] Tony Kennedy, *Reno Air Files Suit Against NWA*, Minneapolis Star Tribune (Apr. 17, 1997), at 1D.

[89] George Raine, *Battle On High*, San Francisco Examiner (May 22, 1998), at C-1.

[90] Katherine Yung, *Fair Fairs?*, Dallas Morning News (Mar. 1, 2000), at 1D.

[91] Address by DOT Deputy General Counsel Steven Okun before the Nova University Annual Conference on International Travel & Tourism (Ft. Lauderdale, FL, Apr. 13, 1999).

only 1.3% of the total market. From 1994 to 1999, while hub concentration was growing, competitive city-pair service declined 28%.[92]

Several new entrant airlines came together in 1996 to create the Air Carrier Association of America, which was initially formed to deal with the effort of the major airlines to shift the excise tax burden away from the largest airlines and onto the smaller, affordable airlines. But as they came together, the new entrants learned they had something else in common. The major airlines appeared to be on a homicidal mission to destroy the low-fare airlines.

The window of opportunity opened after the ValuJet catastrophe in the Everglades, in May of 1996. The DOT had been a champion of the competition brought to bear by the new entrant airlines, praising their annual $6 billion contribution to consumer savings as a clear success of deregulation.[93] But the Everglades crash occurred in an election year, and for political reasons, DOT soon found itself neutralized. The FAA grounded ValuJet's 53 aircraft. The question in the industry became, "Why did Delta allow ValuJet to grow so large? Why didn't Delta kill off ValuJet when it had the chance?"

According to the new entrants, that mind-set put a number of relatively smaller airlines in the cross hairs of the majors. For example, the world's largest airline, United, allegedly targeted Frontier and Western Pacific. American allegedly targeted Vanguard, Western Pacific, and Sun Jet International. Delta allegedly targeted ValuJet. Northwest allegedly targeted Spirit Airlines. Though the DOT had earlier been able to dissuade predation by "jaw-boning" the major airlines into engaging in responsible competitive behavior (by persuading Northwest and Delta to back off of their below-cost pricing and capacity dumping in markets entered by Reno and ValuJet, respectively), such moral persuasion no longer worked.

Low-fare new entrant airlines complained that the major airlines engage in below-cost pricing and capacity-dumping when a small affordable air carrier enters the markets they dominate, particularly when one dares to provide competition at their "Fortress Hubs." They allege that pricing and capacity are not the only predatory weapons in the

---

[92] Address by DOT Deputy General Counsel Steven Okun before the Nova University Annual Conference on International Travel & Tourism (Ft. Lauderdale, FL, Apr. 13, 1999).
[93] U.S. DOT, *The Low Cost Airline Service Revolution* (1996).

arsenal of the major airlines. Predatory behavior designed to suppress competition takes many forms.

According to the new entrants, capacity dumping and below-cost pricing were essential foundations of this campaign to eradicate competition. In each situation the tactics differed somewhat, but the alleged purpose was the same—destroy the low-cost airlines so as to raise consumer prices. Conversely, the major airlines claimed that the economic problems, which confronted the low-cost airlines, were because consumers shied away from them after the Everglades crash. But as the memory of the Everglades waned, new entrants alleged the major airlines engaged in the anticompetitive conduct.

After having received 32 complaints objecting to the predatory behavior of incumbent carriers (17 of which were filed by new entrant airlines), in April 1998, the DOT issued a proposed policy statement on unfair exclusionary conduct. The draft policy defined unfair exclusionary practices as a situation in which a major airline responds to new entry into its hub markets by cutting prices or increasing capacity in a way that either (1) causes it to forgo more revenue than all of the new entrant's capacity could have diverted from it, or (2) results in substantially lower operating profit—or greater operating losses—in the short run than would result from a reasonable alternative strategy for competing with the new entrant.[94]

Many such complaints were also lodged with the DOJ. In May 1999, the Justice Department filed the first antitrust lawsuit in its history alleging predatory conduct by a major airline in attempting to monopolize a market. The suit alleged that American Airlines lowered prices and changed capacity to force three new entrant airlines (i.e., Sun Jet International, Vanguard Airlines, and Western Pacific Airlines) to withdraw from the Dallas/Ft. Worth International Airport market, an airport in which American maintains a hub.[95] The Justice Department had earlier filed suit to block Northwest Airlines' acquisition of the controlling block of voting stock of Continental Airlines. The DOT later issued a milder policy, and the DOJ lost its antitrust

---

[94] U.S. General Accounting Office, *Aviation Competition: Information on the Department of Transportation's Proposed Policy* (Jul. 1999). DOT received more than 5,000 comments on the proposed policy. Testimony of Nancy McFadden before the Subcommittee on Aviation of the U.S. House Committee on Transportation and Infrastructure (Oct. 21, 1999). The final policy statement will not become effective until 12 months after it is received by Congress. Pub. L. 105-277.

[95] *U.S. v. AMR Corporation*, Civil Action No. 99-1180-JTM (D. Kan, filed May 13, 1999).

suit against American Airlines, but the new entrants were given a little breathing room to grow. Though SunJet International, Vanguard and Western Pacific were liquidated, Valujet (now AirTran) and Frontier grew at Atlanta and Denver, respectively.

MONOPOLIZATION UNDER THE ANTITRUST LAWS

As noted above, the unfair and deceptive practices/unfair methods of competition language of both Section 5 of the Federal Trade Commission Act and Section 41712 of the Federal Aviation Act have been interpreted to include such actions as assault the public interest, or the spirit of the antitrust laws. In this section, we examine predatory conduct in the airline industry that violates the spirit, if not the letter, of the Sherman and Clayton Acts.

Section 2 of the Sherman Act provides that "every person who shall monopolize, or attempt to monopolize . . . any part of the trade or commerce . . . is guilty of a felony."[96] A Section 2 claim can be brought against the use of monopoly power "to foreclose competition, to gain a competitive advantage, or to destroy a competitor."[97] Monopoly power is the power to control prices or exclude competition.[98] The creation or maintenance of a monopoly by illegitimate means is prohibited by section 2 of the Sherman Act. The offense of *attempting to create a monopoly* requires proof of (1) a specific intent to control prices or eliminate competition in a market (objective evidence of intent is sufficient); (2) predatory or anticompetitive conduct aimed at accomplishing this unlawful purpose; and (3) a dangerous probability of success (a realistic danger that if the defendant's conduct runs its course, it would create a monopoly).[99] Intention can be proven by establishing either intent to achieve monopoly power or an intent to drive

---

[96] Sec. 2 has two elements: (1) the possession of monopoly power in the relevant market, and (2) the willful acquisition or maintenance of that power, as distinguished from growth or development as a consequence of a superior product, business acumen, or historic accident.

[97] *United States v. Griffith*, 334 U.S. 100 (1948).

[98] *U.S. v. Grinell Corp.*, 384 U.S. 563, 571 (1966). Whether monopoly power exists or not depends on several factors, including the probable development of the industry, consumer demand, and defendant's market share. *Hayden Publishing Co. v. Cox Broadcasting Corp.*, 730 F.2d 64, 68 (2nd Cir. 1984).

[99] *Swift & Co. v. United States*, 196 U.S. 375 (1905); *Spectrum Sports, Inc. v. McQuillan*, 113 S.Ct. 884 (1993).

competitors from the market so that the dominant firm could later charge monopoly prices.

A claim of monopolization requires proof of (1) the possession of monopoly power in a relevant market and (2) the exercise of one or more impermissible exclusionary practices designed to strengthen or perpetuate its monopoly position (or put differently, conduct directed at "smothering competition").[100] Monopolization refers to activities that may be illegal if performed by the dominant firm in a relevant market.[101] Thus practices which do not in themselves constitute an antitrust violation may, in conjunction with overwhelming market power, violate Section 2.

Monopoly power is a large amount of market power, or the ability to reduce output and raise prices above marginal costs. Market share in a *relevant* market is generally accepted as an effective surrogate for direct measurement of market power. Generally speaking, the defendant must have 70% or more of the relevant geographic and product market. A "relevant geographic market" is an area where the dominant firm can increase its price without large numbers of consumers turning to alternative supply sources outside the area, or producers outside the area can quickly flood the area with substitute products.

The relevant geographic market in commercial aviation is certainly city-pairs; it may also include domination of a hub airport, where banks of flights from numerous cities enable an airline to dominate the city's local passenger market. In terms of the anticompetitive and monopolistic practices of a major hub airline directed at a new entrant, the relevant geographic market is the hub airport and its radiating city-pairs. Extensive studies of the consumer impact of hub monopolization conducted by the DOT and the General Accounting Office [GAO] conclude that a dominant airline charges prices between 19% and 27% higher for passengers beginning or ending their trips at a monopoly hub airport than prices for similar distances in competitive markets.

The *relevant product* requires an assessment of the products that are sufficiently close substitutes to compete effectively in each other's

---

[100] *U.S. v. Grinell Corp.*, 384 U.S. 563 (1966); *Berkey Photo v. Eastman Kodak*, 603 F.2d 263, 275 (2nd Cir. 1979).
[101] Herbert Hovencamp, *Economics and Federal Antitrust Law* 135 (1984); *Lorain Journal & Co. v. United States*, 342 U.S. 143 (1951).

markets.[102] Scheduled passenger air transportation is probably the relevant product market in commercial aviation (the competitive alternatives of rail, bus and automobile transport, or freight transportation, likely can be ignored).

One might argue that the relevant product markets in scheduled commercial aviation are non-stop passenger air transportation to and from a hub, and connecting service to and from other cities via the hub. One alternative product market to the non-stop market to and from a hub is connecting service via other hubs. However, connecting service is viewed by most consumers as an inferior product alternative to non-stop service, and has only a marginal competitive impact on non-stop service.

One who effectively controls a market may not lawfully use any exclusionary practice against a competitor, even though it is not technically a restraint of trade in violation of Section 1 of the Sherman Act.[103] A monopolist may not legitimately deter potential competitors from entering its market or existing rivals from increasing their output.[104] Under certain market conditions, the following constitute illegitimate exercises of monopoly power:

- Expansion of output or capacity.
- Predatory pricing.
- Pricing discrimination.
- Monopoly leveraging.
- Refusal to deal with a competitor.
- Refusal to share an essential facility.
- Raising rivals' costs.
- Exclusive dealing arrangements.

PREDATORY PRICING

The U.S. Supreme Court has never addressed the issue of predatory pricing and related anticompetitive practices in the context of a service

---

[102] Robert Pitofsky, *New Definitions of Relevant Market and the Assault of Antitrust*, 90 Colum. L. Rev. 1805 (1990).
[103] Herbert Hovencamp, *Economics and Federal Antitrust Law* 136-137 (1984).
[104] *Id.* at 138.

industry largely driven by network economies of scale and scope, such as commercial aviation.[105] The courts have made clear that key elements of antitrust analysis are to be tailored to fit the unique characteristics of the industry involved. The DOT has accurately summarized the economic characteristics of the airline industry which explain why predation sometimes is the *modus operandi* of a major carrier when faced with entry by a low-cost/low-fare airline.

Although the Supreme Court has said that predation rarely occurs and is even more rarely successful, our informal investigations suggest that the nature of the air transportation industry can at a minimum allow unfair exclusionary practices to succeed. Compared to firms in other industries, a major air carrier can price-discriminate to a much greater extent, adjust prices much faster, and shift resources between markets much more readily. Through booking and other data generated by computer reservations systems and other sources, air carriers have access to comprehensive, "real time" information on their competitors' activities and can thus respond to competitive initiatives more precisely and swiftly than firms in other industries. . . . These characteristics of the air transportation industry allow a major carrier to drive a new entrant from a local hub market. Having observed this behavior, other potential new entrants refrain from entering, leaving the major carrier free to reap greater profits indefinitely.[106]

The U.S. Supreme Court last addressed the issue of predatory pricing in a 1993 tobacco industry case of *Liggett & Myers v. Brown & Williamson Corp.*[107] The court re-emphasized that the antitrust laws

---

[105] Testimony of Mark Kahan before the Subcomm. on Aviation of the U.S. House of Representatives Committee on Trans. & Infrastructure (Apr. 23, 1998).

[106] U.S. DOT, Request for Comments in Docket OST-98-3717 (Apr. 6, 1998).

[107] 509 U.S. 209 (1993). In an earlier case, *Matsushita,* the Supreme Court observed:

> [T]he success of [predatory pricing] schemes is inherently uncertain: the short-run loss is definite, but the long-run gain depends on successfully neutralizing the competition. Moreover, it is not enough simply to achieve monopoly power, as monopoly pricing may breed quick entry by new competitors eager to share in the excess profits. The success of any predatory pricing scheme depends on maintaining monopoly power for long enough both to recoup the predator's losses and to harvest some additional gain. Absent some assurance that the hoped-for monopoly will materialize, and that it can be sustained for a significant period of time, '[the] predator must make a substantial investment with no assurance that it will pay off.'

were passed to protect competition, not competitors, and said that to sustain a *prima facie* case under Section 2 of the Sherman Act, a plaintiff had to prove the following:

- The prices complained of must be below an appropriate measure of its rival's costs.
- The below-cost pricing must be capable of producing the intended effects on the firm's rivals, such as driving them from the market. This requires an evaluation of the extent and duration of the alleged predation, the relative financial strength of the predator and its intended victim, and their respective incentives and will. The issue is whether, given the aggregate losses caused by the below-cost pricing, the intended target would likely succumb.
- The competitor must have a reasonable prospect (or a dangerous possibility) of recouping its short-term investment in below-cost prices by achieving longer-term monopoly profits. Once the rival is driven from the market, it must be likely that the predator will be able to raise prices above a competitive level adequate to recover the amounts expended on the predation, including the time value of the money invested in it. In other words, the predator must be able to obtain sufficient market power to set its prices above competitive levels for a sufficient period of time in order to earn excess profits beyond those lost during the period of below-cost pricing.[108]

In *Brown & Williamson*, the Supreme Court sustained dismissal of a $149 million jury award for Liggett, principally because it had failed to show how B&W, with only a 12% market share, could recover its investment in below-cost sales.

Matsushita Electric Industrial Co. v. Zenith Radio Corp., 475 U.S. 574, 589 (1995), citing Easterbrook, *Predatory Strategies and Counterstrategies*, 48 U. Chi. L. Rev. 263, 268 (1981).

The *Matsushita* decision involved an alleged conspiracy of Japanese television manufacturers. The court felt that a conspiracy among several firms to price below costs was unlikely both because predatory pricing is costly, and success is dependent on a host of uncertainties, making such schemes more likely to fail than succeed. *Id.* at 594. Single firm predation by a monopolist, however, may be more likely to be successful. Recall that antitrust law is to be applied on a case-by-case basis.

[108] *Brooke Group Ltd. v. Brown & Williamson Tobacco Co.*, 509 U.S. 209 (1993).

With respect to the first criterion, some courts have endorsed the "Areeda-Turner" test, which uses average variable costs as a proxy for marginal costs, although the U.S. Supreme Court has yet to prescribe which measure of cost should be used. In fact, the Court has held that "no consensus has yet been reached on the proper definition of predatory pricing" and left open the question of whether "above-cost pricing coupled with predatory intent is ever sufficient to state a claim of predation."[109] The Supreme Court has also emphasized that antitrust claims are to be resolved on a case-by-case basis, focusing on the particular facts before it.[110]

The difficulty of using variable costs as a proxy for an airline's marginal costs is that they are extremely small in the airline industry, and nowhere near what would be necessary to attain break-even. An additional passenger on a scheduled flight costs the airline "peanuts," literally and figuratively. If every airline priced every seat on the basis of average variable costs, all would be bankrupt within a year. Because commercial aviation is a capital intensive industry, with an extremely high ratio of fixed to variable costs, and some other measure (perhaps fully allocated costs or, as suggested above, incremental costs) is appropriate.

The Transportation Research Board [TRB] has recognized that, in attempting to determine whether behavior is predatory on the basis of pricing below costs, that an air carrier's marginal costs in a particular market—even short-run average variable costs—can be difficult to quantify retrospectively. However, the TRB concluded that opportunity cost—the value of the best alternative response that is foregone— is an appropriate method for assessing the costs of the alleged predatory conduct.[111]

Recognizing the difficulty of determining whether an airline's price cutting or capacity dumping constitutes an antitrust violation, because of the industry's obscure cost characteristics, the DOT has advocated a methodology focused on a firm's foregone revenue, rather than the relationship between price and cost.[112] The DOT has recognized that

---

[109] *Cargill, Inc. v. Monfort of Colorado*, 479 U.S. 104, 118 n. 12 (1986).

[110] *Eastman Kodak Company v. Image Technical Services, Inc.*, 504 U.S. 451 (1991).

[111] Transportation Research Board, *Entry and Competition in the U.S. Airline Industry: Issues and Opportunities*, E-7, E-8 (1999).

[112] U.S. General Accounting Office, *Aviation Competition: Information on the Department of Transportation's Proposed Policy* 12 (Jul. 1999).

the incremental cost of adding a passenger to a scheduled flight with empty seats is very low. The incremental cost of an additional passenger on a full flight is the foregone revenue lost from the passenger who cannot be accommodated. If an airline decides to add a flight or substitute a larger aircraft, the incremental cost would be additional costs incurred associated with those decisions.[113] Taking an aircraft from a more lucrative market to one less profitable involves incurring lost opportunity costs of the more productive and profitable use of that equipment.

In its antitrust suit against American Airlines, the Justice Department alleged that by increasing flight and seat capacity in city-pair markets entered by low cost carriers, American incurred increased costs in the form of the ownership and operating costs of additional aircraft allocated to those routes, as well as labor, fuel, food, sales and other costs which would not have been incurred absent the capacity increases. DOJ alleged that the additional revenues generated by the increased capacity were less than American's costs of allowing the flights as measured by (1) the flights' variable costs, (2) American's total costs of serving the routes, and (3) American's own measure of route profitability.[114] For its part, American insisted that its prices matched, but did not undercut, the new entrants' and covered American's variable costs.[115]

Fares designed to match a lower-cost competitor's fare are a competitive tool designed specifically to insure that market share is not lost through competitive air pricing. This is true whether or not airfare matching occurs at levels below either fully allocated cost or incremental cost. (Given a major carrier's scheduled departure frequency, market dominant frequent flyer plan and more expansive meal and customer amenities, one could also argue that a price match is, indeed, a price undercut. Moreover, mileage awards are a *de facto* form of price rebating, and therefore, price undercutting). Lowering prices below cost and below a competitor's prices may constitute anti-competitive or predatory behavior.

---

[113] *Id.* at 13.

[114] *U.S. v. AMR Corporation,* Civil Action No. 99-1180-JTM (D. Kan., filed May 13, 1999).

[115] American Airlines, *American Airlines' Response to Department of Justice's Allegations of Predatory Practices* (Press Release, May 13, 1999).

With respect to the *Brown & Williamson's* second criterion (the potential of below-cost pricing driving the rival from the market), an upstart airline's bookings plummet when a major carrier puts the new entrant in its cross-hairs. Because it earns supra-competitive profits in its monopoly markets, the incumbent airline can cross-subsidize below-cost pricing for an extended period of time in order to drive a smaller competitor out of business, unless of course, the major carrier is forced to abide by the antitrust and competition laws.

PRICE DISCRIMINATION

Another area of concern in antitrust law is "price discrimination," which Martin Farris and Stephen Happel define as a firm charging two or more different prices for essentially the same product "for reasons other than cost differences."[116] In order for price discrimination to occur and be successful, three conditions are essential:

- The firm must possess some degree of monopoly power;
- The firm must also be able to segregate or classify its customers into groups with different price elasticities; and
- It must be able to prevent resale from one segment of the market to another (i.e., arbitrage).

Price discrimination in American society is common, and from a purely economic standpoint may be neither good nor bad, but merely a description of a price action. From a legal perspective, however, "discrimination" is the act of treating one differently from another; that is, the act of unfairly, injuriously, and prejudicially distinguishing between persons or objects, where economically a sound and fair distinction does not exist. In "price discrimination," it means a higher rate, or a higher value, the resulting disadvantage involving a correlative discrimination. "Discrimination" means a distinction, as in treatment—especially an unfair or injurious distinction—specifically, an arbitrary imposition of unequal tariffs for substantially the same service. A carrier's failure to treat all alike under substantially similar conditions constitutes "unjust" discrimination.

---

[116] Martin T. Farris and Steven K. Happel, *Modern Managerial Economics* (1987).

Irrespective of precedents describing price discrimination as unfair or injurious, it may not be considered illegal under the antitrust laws unless there is an "attempt to monopolize." Furthermore, an attempted monopolization claim is encumbered by having to show:

- a specific intent to monopolize a *relevant market*;
- *predatory* or anti-competitive conduct; and
- a *dangerous probability of success*.

There have been major difficulties in interpreting just what constitutes price discrimination and whether competition was being lessened. Within the Clayton Act, price discrimination is not synonymous with "harmless differentiation," which is defined by Farris and Happel by its two defenses: (1) if it is due to allowances for *differences in cost*; and (2) if it is offered *in good faith*.[117]

The fact that price discrimination is against the law only if the effect of it may "substantially lessen competition or tend to create a monopoly" seems to be a fluke of legal evolution stemming from the interpretation of corporate abuse by the Cullom Committee.[118] The Cullom report, coupled with the results of *Wabash, St. Louis and Pacific Railway Co. v. Illinois*, wherein the Supreme Court decreed that the federal government alone had the power to regulate interstate commerce, led to passage of the Act to Regulate Commerce of 1887 (the Interstate Commerce Act) which was basically aimed at curbing monopoly, not rectifying consumer abuse *per se*.

Claims of unfair discrimination have long been unheeded by the courts because the plaintiff (usually a corporate entity) could not demonstrate (but on rare occasions) there had been an attempt to monopolize. Individual consumers are denied standing altogether.[119] The difficulty in interpreting antitrust violation, coupled with the historical masking of consumer rights would seem to indicate the need for revised antitrust legislation.[120]

---

[117] *Id.*

[118] *See* Ch. 9.

[119] *See Nader v. Allegheny Airlines, Inc.*, 626 F2d 1031 (1980).

[120] *See* Laurence E. Gesell and Martin T. Farris, *Antitrust Irrelevance in Air Transportation and the Re-Defining of Price Discrimination*, 57 J. of Air L. & Comm. (1991).

PAN AMERICAN WORLD AIRWAYS v. UNITED STATES
371 U.S. 296 (1963)

> *Did the CAB have jurisdiction over anti-competitive acts*
> *which occurred prior to the provisions for economic*
> *regulation in the 1938 Civil Aeronautics Act?*

This was a civil suit brought by the United States charging violations by Pan American World Airways, W. R. Grace & Co. (an American Flag Steamship line), and Pan American Grace Airways (Panagra), of the Sherman Act.[121] This suit, which the CAB requested the U.S. Attorney General to institute, charged two major restraints of trade. First, it was charged, Pan American and Grace, each of whom owned 50% of the Panagra stock, formed the latter company under an agreement that Panagra would have the exclusive right to traffic along the west coast of South America, free from Pan American competition, and that Pan American was to be free from competition of Panagra in other areas in South America and between the Canal zone and the United States. Second, Pan American and Grace conspired to monopolize and did monopolize air commerce between the eastern coastal areas of the United States and western coastal areas of South America and Buenos Aires. Pan American was also charged with using its 50% control over Panagra to prevent it from securing authority from the CAB to extend its route from the Canal Zone to the U.S.

In 1928, when Pan American and Grace entered into an agreement to form Panagra, air transportation was in its infancy. This was the first entry of an American air carrier on South America's west coast. Pan American in 1930 acquired the assets of an airline competing with it for air traffic from the U.S. to the north and east coasts of South America, and received a Post Office air mail subsidy contract.

The government's antitrust complaint alleged restraint of trade relating to a division of markets between the United States and South America, restraints imposed upon the jointly-owned air carrier by the two parent companies, and a conspiracy to monopolize transportation between the United States and South America.

---

[121] 15 U.S.C. §§ 1, 2, and 3.

The U.S. District Court found the joinder of the parent companies was not the result of a conspiracy, but was a lawful combination with legitimate ends. It was a pioneering venture in the days when air transportation was in its infancy, with its object being to promote United States business and trade in South America, and particularly the west coast of that continent. The understanding relating to the division of territories between the two airlines was not unreasonable under the circumstances and did not constitute a violation *per se* of the Sherman Act, and these two parties were not found guilty of any antitrust violations. However, the restraints which the parent air carrier exercised against the other carrier by its continued determination to suppress extension of such carrier to the United States, in itself constituted a monopolization of commerce in contravention of the provisions of the Sherman Act. Although the CAB approved through-flight agreements between the two carriers whereby equipment would be jointly used from the Canal Zone to the United States, such action did not relieve the offending carrier from the provisions of the Sherman Act under a claim that it was so relieved by operation of Section 414 of the Federal Aviation Act of 1958. Moreover, a contention that primary jurisdiction of the issues involved was in the CAB was rejected since many of the issues antedated the formation of the Civil Aeronautics Board and the passage of the Civil Aeronautics Act of 1938.

A decree was entered dismissing the complaint against the jointly-owned air carrier (Panagra) and the steamship line (W. R. Grace and Company). Pan American World Airways was ordered to divest itself of its stock in Panagra.

The case was appealed to the U. S. Supreme Court, which stated that when the transactions, challenged in this case as restraints of trade and monopoly, were first consummated, air carriers were not subject to pervasive regulation. However, in 1938 the Civil Aeronautics Act was passed which then regulated the industry under a regime designed to change the prior competitive system. The 1938 Act did not freeze the *status quo* nor attempt to legalize all existing practices. The CAB (under Section 411 of the Act) was given jurisdiction over "unfair practices" and "unfair methods of competition" even though they originated prior to 1938. The Board was given power to investigate and determine whether any air carrier, foreign air carrier, or ticket agent has been or is engaged in unfair or deceptive practices or unfair methods of competition in air transportation. The words "has been or is engaged in unfair . . . practices or unfair methods of competition" plainly include practices started before the 1938 Act and continued thereafter, as well as practices instituted after the effective date of the Act.

What was done in the pre-1938 days may be so disruptive of the regime visualized by the Act or so out of harmony with the statutory standards for competition set by the Act that it should be undone in proceedings under Section 411. The provisions for economic regulation in the Civil Aeronautics Act of 1938, which were reenacted without change in the Federal Aviation Act of 1958, displaced the Sherman Act insofar as all questions of injunctive relief against the division of territories or the allocation of routes or against combinations between common carriers and air carriers were concerned. Therefore, the questions presented in an antitrust complaint which charged that two parent carriers and their jointly-owned air carrier violated the Sherman Act by a division of markets between the United States and South America, restraints imposed upon the jointly-owned air carrier by the two parent air carriers, and a conspiracy to monopolize transportation between the United States and South America, had been entrusted to the CAB and the complaint should have been dismissed.

Accordingly, the Supreme Court reversed the judgment and remanded the case for proceedings in conformity with this opinion.

HUGHES TOOL CO. v. TRANS WORLD AIRLINES
409 U.S. 363 (1973)

Does the CAB (or any subsequent agency) have primary jurisdiction in airline antitrust cases, or may they be tried in court?

About five years after Trans World Airlines [TWA] was organized in 1934, Hughes Tool Company (Toolco) began to purchase common stock in the airline. Toolco was 100% owned and controlled by Howard Hughes. By 1944, it held 45% of the stock in TWA. By 1958, Toolco had increased to 78% its interest in TWA's common stock; from 1944 until December 1960, it nominated a majority of TWA's directors.

After 1955, the commercial air industry was largely converted to the use of jet aircraft. TWA's competitors began in that year to aid in the development of and to purchase jet planes. Prior to 1955, Toolco had entered into an arrangement with the General Dynamics Corporation (Convair) for the joint development of jet aircraft, but in that year the two companies terminated the arrangement. Toolco had also entered into a plan whereby it would develop and manufacture its own jet aircraft for sale or lease to TWA and its competitors. That plan was abandoned in 1956. During this period, Toolco arranged for the purchase on its own account of jet aircraft from Convair and the Boeing Company, these arrangements providing that Toolco could assign to TWA its rights to such aircraft.

Despite repeated requests by TWA, Toolco refused to assign any planes to TWA between 1956 and 1960. The only jet aircraft the defendants permitted TWA to use during this period were leased on a day-to-day basis by Toolco to TWA during 1959 and 1960 on condition that TWA would not purchase or lease aircraft from any other potential supplier. Some time prior to May 1960, Toolco and Atlas Corporation, which owned controlling stock interest in Northeast Airlines, entered upon a plan to have Northeast Airlines propose to TWA a merger of the two carriers. In November 1960, while the proposed merger plan was pending, Toolco diverted to Northeast six of the Convair jet aircraft, which by previous agreement it had assigned to TWA.

The defendants pursued a continuous policy of refusing to permit TWA to undertake equity financing except on the condition that Toolco increase its equity position in TWA; as a result, TWA was limited to obtaining funds through debt financing. When, in 1960, Toolco and Hughes finally agreed to outside financing for TWA, the cost of such financing had risen greatly and the financing could be arranged only on less favorable terms than had theretofore been available; terms which had already been secured by TWA's competitors. Under the 1960 financing arrangement, Toolco's stock in TWA was placed in a voting trust. The CAB approved this financing arrangement and the voting trust on December 29, 1960, finding these arrangements were in the public interest. Thereupon, the Metropolitan Life Insurance Company and the Equitable Life Assurance Society loaned TWA $92,800,000. And a group of banks, for which the Irving Trust Company acted as agent, loaned TWA $72,000,000. In March 1961

TWA's Board of Directors authorized the purchase of 26 Boeing jet aircraft. Thereafter, the defendants continued their attempts to have TWA purchase from Toolco jet aircraft, which Toolco had previously agreed to purchase from Convair. The defendants had also continued to press their demand for a merger of TWA and Northeast and had otherwise, despite the existence of the voting trust, attempted to prevent TWA from acquiring jet aircraft other than from Toolco.

TWA's complaint alleged the facts, heretofore stated, constituted violations of the Sherman and Clayton Antitrust Acts, insofar as the defendants had attempted to monopolize a substantial segment of interstate and foreign commerce and trade, had required that TWA boycott all suppliers of aircraft other than Toolco, and had agreed to provide financing and to sell aircraft to TWA on the condition that TWA not purchase or lease the goods of a competitor.

Relying upon the decision in *Pan American World Airways v. United States*[122] the defendant's asserted that the CAB possessed primary jurisdiction over these matters, and in the exercise of its powers, had approved all of the transactions alleged in the complaint and thereby immunized the defendants from the antitrust laws. The U.S. District Court held that nothing in the Federal Aviation Act precluded the court from asserting jurisdiction in this case, and the CAB's approval of various transactions between TWA and Toolco did not confer immunity upon the defendants from the operation of the antitrust laws. The U.S. Court of Appeals agreed. Nowhere in the Act is the CAB specifically charged with the duty of monitoring each transaction, which is ultimately effected between the carrier and its controller once an acquisition is approved. But the existence of this—which was employed in approving Toolco's acquisition of control over TWA—hardly supported the defendant's claim that Congress placed the regulation of everything which might flow from such transactions within the exclusive jurisdiction of the Civil Aeronautics Board. The complaint sufficiently stated a cause of action and established the district court's jurisdiction.

The history of this case was long and complex. It was originally instituted in 1961, and subsequently became the subject of many pretrial rulings, opinions and appeals. As stated above, the district court

---

[122] CCH 8 AVI 17,357 (1963).

ruled against the defendant's contention that the acts complained of were exempt from the antitrust laws by virtue of CAB orders.

In 1962, counsel for Toolco accepted a subpoena calling for Howard Hughes' personal appearance as a witness. After the court was informed the reclusive Hughes would refuse to appear for examination, it granted TWA's application for a default judgment. The Court of Appeals affirmed the ruling, but refused to pass upon the propriety of the entry of the default judgment. Rather, it referred to a special master the issue of damages on TWA's claim of $35 million, which the antitrust statute would *treble*.

In 1965, the U.S. Supreme Court dismissed *writs of certiorari*. The special master and the court then made preliminary rulings as to the effect of the default judgment. Some 11,000 pages of testimony were taken from experts in the fields of economics, engineering, finance and accounting. Over 800 exhibits containing 60,000 pages were admitted in evidence. The special master then rendered a 323 page report. Both parties objected to findings in the report, with the defendants generally arguing that conclusions of law were erroneous, and TWA claiming the award for damages was inadequate.

The U.S. Court of Appeals confirmed the report of the special master awarding damages in the sum of $137,611,435.95 (pursuant to 15 U.S.C.§ 15; i.e., treble damages). But on appeal, the U.S. Supreme Court held there was no antitrust violation because Toolco's *de facto* control of TWA had been approved by the Civil Aeronautics Board under section 408 of the Federal Aviation Act, which approval had thereby immunized the transactions from the application of the antitrust laws under section 414 of the Act.

ALOHA AIRLINES v. HAWAIIAN AIRLINES
489 F.2d 203 (9th Cir. 1973)

> *Does the Civil Aeronautics Board's authority to investigate*
> *unfair methods of competition withdraw from antitrust*
> *litigants the right to proceed for damages alleged to*
> *have occurred by reason of antitrust violations?*

Aloha Airlines alleged that Hawaiian Airlines, beginning as early as 1968 and continuing through 1970, engaged in an attempt to monopolize the Hawaiian inter-island air transportation system in violation of the Sherman Act. Plaintiff Aloha listed seven acts which defendant Hawaiian allegedly undertook "with the predatory intent and purpose of eliminating plaintiff as a viable competitor" and "with full knowledge of its impact on plaintiff and with the intent of injuring or destroying plaintiff." These were:

- excessive (*vis-à-vis* the needs of the public) flight schedules;
- excessive purchasing, ordering, leasing (or agreeing to lease) of aircraft;
- misrepresenting its schedules to the public;
- providing below cost servicing to interstate air carriers between stops;
- publicizing the fact that plaintiff and defendant should merge, while twice in bad faith renouncing merger agreements into which defendant had entered; and
- opposing before the CAB plaintiff's request for a subsidy.

As a result of these alleged practices, Aloha claimed it was damaged in the amount of $7,700,000. And it was asking for treble damages under Section 4 of the Clayton Act.

Hawaiian Airlines moved for an order to dismiss plaintiff's complaint on the grounds that (1) it failed to state a claim upon which relief could be granted, and/or (2) the trial court lacked jurisdiction over the subject matter and parties. Alternatively, on the same basis, defendant moved for an order to summary judgment as to all the claims alleged in the complaint.

Hawaiian Airlines' motions were based on four contentions. First, the CAB had exclusive jurisdiction over the subject matter of this action. Second, the CAB had primary jurisdiction and the Court should have waited for further proceedings by the Board. Third, plaintiff's complaint failed to allege the necessary elements for an attempt to monopolize which is prohibited by Section 2 of the Sherman Act. Fourth, *Eastern Railroad Conference v. Noerr Motor Freight* [123] forbids any antitrust claim based on defendant's opposition to Aloha's subsidy request before the CAB (for "Noerr-Pennington doctrine", see

---

[123] 365 U.S. 127 (1961).

U.S. v. Braniff. [124] The U.S. District Court found none of Hawaiian Airline's arguments convincing and denied the motion to dismiss. Subsequently, the Supreme Court decided *Trans World Airlines v. Howard Hughes, et al.,*[125] and Hawaiian Airlines renewed its motions, which were again denied.

Hawaiian Airlines appealed to the U.S. Court of Appeals. The appellate court affirmed the trial court's judgment. In response to Hawaiian's four contentions the court stated the following. First, the Federal Aviation Act of 1958 does not completely displace the antitrust laws, and, therefore, the CAB did not have exclusive jurisdiction where air carriers are concerned. The grant of authority to the Board by Section 411 did not withdraw the right to proceed for damages alleged to have occurred by reason of antitrust violation. It is significant that there was not then, nor had there ever been, any authority in the Board under Section 411 or elsewhere to make a factual determination as to the existence of all the ingredients of an antitrust suit under the Sherman Act. Second, the court pointed out the CAB had already dealt to the full extent of its ability with the matters at issue and there was nothing further to be remanded to it even if the "principle of primary jurisdiction" were to apply. It had already been determined that Aloha had been injured by "uneconomical overscheduling" (i.e., predatory pricing) by Hawaiian. As to the third and fourth contentions, the court held merely that the trial court had not erred in denying the motions. All other matters were still at an "interlocutory stage" (i.e., temporary or provisional), therefore there was no action for the appellate court to take.

The judgment was affirmed by the U.S. Court of Appeals. Hawaiian Airlines appealed to the U. S. Supreme Court but *certiorari* was denied.[126]

---

[124] CCH 15 AVI 17,388 (1978).
[125] 11 AVI 17,368 (1969).
[126] *Hawaiian Airlines v. Aloha Airlines*, 417 U.S. 913 (1974).

UNITED STATES v. BRANIFF AIRWAYS
453 F. Supp. 724 (W.D. Tex. 1978)

*Is the Civil Aeronautics Board vested with exclusive
or primary jurisdiction over criminal violations
of the antitrust laws?*

In 1977, a federal grand jury in and for the Western District of
Texas returned an indictment charging Braniff Airways, Inc., and
Texas International Airlines, Inc., in two counts with participation in a
combination and conspiracy in restraint of trade and commerce in violation of Section 1 of the Sherman Act, and with participation in
combination and conspiracy to monopolize trade and commerce in
violation of Section 2 of the Sherman Act.[127] Pursuant to an order of
the Court, the Government filed a detailed bill of particulars.

The defendants moved for an order dismissing the indictment. Four
principal grounds were presented:

- The Federal Aviation Act vests the Civil Aeronautics Board
  with exclusive jurisdiction over the criminal violations of the
  antitrust laws charged in the indictment;
- If the court rejected their claims of immunity, then, in the alternative, the court should apply the "doctrine of primary jurisdiction" and suspend this prosecution until certain Civil Aeronautics Board determinations were made; and
- Certain litigation, which was allegedly brought (as one of a series of overt acts) in furtherance of the conspiracy, was immunized from antitrust attack by the First Amendment and the
  Noerr-Pennington Doctrine. This doctrine refers to two
  Supreme Court decisions which have held that the First
  Amendment guarantees individuals the right to petition governmental bodies in an attempt to influence their decisions, even
  if the purpose and effect of such influence is anti-competitive.
  And fourth, Southwest Airlines' alleged unlicensed entry into
  the interstate market immunized defendants from this criminal
  prosecution.

---

[127] 15 U.S.C. §§ 1 and 2.

The indictment charged defendants with engaging in a classic antitrust conspiracy. It was narrowly drawn to cover restraints of trade and monopolization of the tri-city intrastate market in Texas. Defendants insisted that in the particular circumstances presented, the Federal Aviation Act displaced the Sherman Act, and that it was for the Civil Aeronautics Board alone to assess their conduct. The essence of their argument was that this case was governed by four decisions of the United States Supreme Court.[128] These decisions announce the rule that where market entry and industry practices are subject to the "pervasive supervisory authority" of a federal agency and there is such "plain repugnancy" between the antitrust laws and the agency's special public interest standards that, if the antitrust laws were applied to such practices "two regimes might collide," the agency's jurisdiction to regulate entry and competition in the industry "pre-empts the antitrust field" and bars the courts from imposing antitrust sanctions.

To the first argument, the District Court responded by restating that the Supreme Court had made it clear the Federal Aviation Act does not necessarily displace antitrust laws. As to the defendant's second argument, the clear intent of Congress is that an agreement to drive a competitor out of business is not in the public interest and thus not approvable by the CAB. Third, if litigation is used as an integral part of a scheme to destroy competition, that litigation can lose its First Amendment protection. The government was entitled to an opportunity to demonstrate at trial the precise nature of, and the extent to which the challenged conduct had exceeded lawful parameters. The resolution of this issue would have to abide the event of trial. Fourth, the Clayton Act provides that any person who shall be injured in his or her business or property by reason of anything forbidden in the antitrust laws may sue therefore.

The motions to dismiss were denied in all respects.

---

[128] *Pan American World Airways, Inc. v. United States*, CCH 8 AVI 17,357, 371 U.S. 296 (1963); *Hughes Tool Co. v. Trans World Airlines, Inc.*, CCH 12 AVI 17,694, 409 U.S. 363 (1973); *United States v. National Ass'n. of Securities Dealers, Inc.*, 422 U.S. 694 (1975); and *Gordon v. New York Stock Exchange, Inc.*, 422 U.S. 659 (1975).

INTERNATIONAL TRAVEL ARRANGERS v. WESTERN AIRLINES
623 F.2d 1255 (8th Cir. 1980)

In an antitrust dispute, does the CAB have primary jurisdiction where the dispute concerns allegedly unfair competitive practices?

International Travel Arrangers [ITA], a Minnesota Corporation, organized and arranged travel charter flights. The Minnesota State Automobile Association [MSAA] acted as a wholesaler and retailer for travel group charters organized and arranged by ITA.

Generally, ITA alleged at trial that Western Airlines, through a combination with its advertising agency, Batten, Barton, Durstine and Osborn [BBD&O], conducted a campaign aimed at preventing ITA's development of travel group charters [TGCs] from becoming a competitive threat to Western; that Western, by use of its monopoly power, further attempted to prevent ITA's program of TGCs from becoming a competitive threat; and that Western succeeded in its activities, thereby causing damage to ITA.

The U.S. District Court found that:

- Western's purpose in embarking on its anti-TGC campaign in the Twin Cities of Minneapolis and St. Paul, and other Minnesota cities, was to prevent the TGCs from becoming a competitive threat in this area;
- Its purpose was not to merely inform the public or to speak out on a political issue. If such had been the case, a substantially misleading or deceptive campaign would have been unnecessary;
- Western was aware that the natural and probable consequences of its veiled threats to MSAA to reduce preferred allocation space was to induce MSAA to cancel TGC plans it had with ITA; and
- Western's anti-TGC campaign was knowingly, intentionally, and purposefully designed to eliminate TGCs as a competitive force to Western's regularly scheduled air service, and Western was aware that such elimination of competition would be the natural and probable consequence of its conduct.

The Court concluded that BBD&O did in fact combine and conspire with Western in restraint of trade by knowingly and actively participating in anti-competitive conduct. Western entered into the combination with BBD&O with the specific intent to monopolize that portion of interstate commerce consisting of individually ticketed air transportation in the Twin Cities to Hawaii route.

The parties to this case stipulated a jury trial presided over by a United States Magistrate, and the district court ordered such. The trial proceeded on this basis. The jury returned a verdict in favor of ITA in the sum of $139,000. A new trial was granted by the district court on the basis that a jury trial presided over by a United States Magistrate was improper. The parties then stipulated to a retrial by the Magistrate acting as a Special Master. The stipulation and order thereon provided that the evidentiary proceedings and the jury trial would be deemed to be the proceedings before the Special Master. Adopting the conclusions and recommendations of the United States Magistrate acting as a Special Master, the district court found that Western violated Sections 1 and 2 of the Sherman Act and entered judgment of trebled damages of $361,596 ($120,537 x 3) against Western, and attorneys fees and costs, of $213,390.87 and $10,771.40, respectively, to ITA.

Western appealed to the U.S. Court of Appeals. Western challenged as clearly erroneous the Special Master's findings with respect to most of these factual allegations, and further specifically argued that the finding of a causal relationship between such alleged activities and ITA's alleged damages was clearly erroneous. Western also claimed the dispute should initially have been referred to the doctrine of primary jurisdiction inasmuch as the dispute concerned allegedly unfair competitive practices.

The court ruled that a determination by the CAB, as to whether or not the activities constituted unfair competition, would not necessarily have aided the court in arriving at an accommodation between the CAB regulations and the antitrust laws, for there would not necessarily exist a conflict even if the CAB decided one way and the court held the opposite. The district court properly had jurisdiction over this case.

The court of appeals affirmed the district court's conclusion that Western violated the Sherman Act. It also affirmed the damages awarded to International Travel Arrangers. It did not, however, affirm the calculated attorney's fees, concluding that the fee exceeded the outer limits of reasonableness. The attorney's fees were thus reduced to $161,003.75.

IN RE AIR PASSENGER COMPUTER RESERVATIONS SYSTEMS ANTITRUST LITIGATION
694 F. Supp. 1443 (C.D. Calif. 1988)

Does an airline's refusal to provide competitors reasonable access to its computerized reservations systems constitute an attempt to monopolize?

The plaintiffs, Continental Airlines and USAir, moved for a partial summary judgment that (1) the defendants American Airlines' and United Airlines' Computer Reservations Systems were "essential facilities"; and (2) defendants did not allow equal access to their essential facilities; and defendants had monopoly power.

The defendants made their own counter-motions under Section 2 of the Sherman Act.[129] Essential facilities doctrine imposes on a business that controls an essential facility, the obligation to provide its competitors reasonable access to that facility. An "essential facility" is one which cannot be reasonably duplicated and to which access is necessary if one wishes to compete. A facility is "essential" when competitors must have access to the facility to be able to compete meaningfully with the controlling firm. To be essential, "a facility need not be indispensable; it is sufficient if duplication of the facility would not be economically feasible and if denial of its use inflicts a severe handicap on potential market entrants," or the facility owner has the power to *monopolize* the market to which the facility is the "bottleneck."

"Monopoly power" focuses generally on a firm's ability to control prices or exclude competition. The Sherman Act does not prohibit monopoly itself, however, the elements of illegal monopolization under Section 2 of the Sherman Act are:

- possession of monopoly power in a relevant market;
- willful acquisition or maintenance (use) of that power; and
- causal antitrust injury.

---

[129] 15 U.S.C. § 2.

Monopolization is illegal if it is done to destroy competition. An attempted monopolization claim must show:

- specific intent to monopolize a relevant market;
- predatory or anti-competitive conduct; and
- a dangerous probability of success.

"Predatory pricing" refers to a firm's attempt to drive a competitor out of business, or to discourage a potential competitor from entering the market, by selling its output at an artificially low price. However, price reductions that constitute a legitimate competitive response to market conditions are competitive, not predatory. A determination of relevant market usually requires an inquiry into the nature of the product, and the geographical area of effective competition. A "relevant" service market is the smallest market for which, one, the elasticity of demand, and two, the elasticity of supply are sufficiently low that a firm with 100% of that market could profitably reduce output and increase price.

This case arose out of the defendants' ownership of Computerized Reservation Systems. A CRS is composed of computer terminals and printers in travel agents' offices that are telephonically linked to the vendor's computer. These CRSs were owned by various airlines and each system contained flight information for airlines other than the vendor airline. The vendor charged the travel agent for the use of its system, and travel agents charged other airlines fees for booking air transportation through the CRS. American Airlines owned the world's largest system, *SABRE*. United Airlines operated the second largest system, *APOLLO*. However, other systems also existed at the time of this trial, including: SystemsOne (or *SODA*) owned by Eastern Airlines; *PARS* run by TWA; and *DATAS II* owned by Delta Air Lines.

Although, in the 1970s and early 1980s, the vendors had allegedly "biased" their systems so as to display flight information favoring the vendor airline, in 1984 the CAB established rules requiring the vendors to make available an unbiased primary display. Nevertheless, display biasing is not necessarily an abuse of monopoly power since the activity does not depend upon the defendant's power to set prices or exclude competition. Display bias was an issue in this case, but the plaintiffs argued more forcefully that American held all other airlines captive by virtue of the essential need for access to the *SABRE* system; that both American and United were attempting monopolization of a relevant market and were exercising monopoly power; American was practicing predatory pricing, and both defendants were exercising price discrimination with an intent to monopolize.

The court granted summary judgments as follows:

- The defendants' motion on the plaintiff's claim based upon essential facilities doctrine was granted. The court concluded there were channels of distribution other than *SABRE*, because there were alternative CRS systems in competition with *SABRE*;

- The defendants' motion regarding monopolization and attempted monopolization was denied. The evidence indicated American was pricing *SABRE* below its marginal costs in order to gain a foothold (or "chokehold") in the market. Furthermore, a reasonable jury could infer that below cost pricing was taking place, and that it was undertaken for the purpose of later recouping lost profits through monopoly overcharges;

- Continental's motion regarding market power was denied. American, at that time, had never had more than fourteen percent of the air transportation market. A claim that a twelve to fourteen percent market share confers monopoly power was considered by the court to be absurd. The activity complained of must entail an abuse of monopoly power itself, as opposed to the mere use of competitive advantages which the defendant enjoys for some reasons distinct from its power to set prices or exclude competition;

- United's motion regarding monopolization of the national air transportation market, various local air transportation markets and both defendants' motions regarding certain local CRS markets were granted. The plaintiffs did not show that United possessed monopoly power in "a relevant market." They merely provided evidence indicating the defendants had a large market share in a "number of local markets." The plaintiffs provided no competent evidence supporting a claim that United monopolized the national air transportation market. Moreover, the plaintiff's could not show conclusively that United had "a dangerous probability of success." The plaintiffs' claimed that *SABRE* was its own relevant market, and American's contractual practices prevented travel agents from freely switching to competing CRSs. However, the court found that American's acquisition and maintenance of monopoly power was not an inevitable outcome;

- American's motion regarding attempted monopolization of specified markets (LaGuardia-Detroit, LaGuardia-Chicago, and Chicago-Los Angeles) was granted. Continental failed to present evidence supporting its contention that a city pair or hub constitutes a relevant market. A city pair cannot be a relevant market absent unusual conditions such as slot-constrained airports. A hub is merely a place to change planes during air travel between two other cities. Airlines do not sell air transportation to hubs; rather they sell air transportation between cities. A city is not a market because a "city is merely a collection of many city pairs that include that city." Therefore, plaintiffs had to show (1) specific intent to monopolize a hub or city pair, (2) predatory conduct or anti-competitive conduct directed to the accomplishment of that purpose, and (3) that defendants conduct was not ambiguous and was clearly predatory. The plaintiffs failed to do that;

- American's motion regarding attempted monopolization of the Dallas/Ft. Worth market was denied. The plaintiffs presented facts sufficient to support its contention that American attempted to monopolize the Dallas/Ft. Worth hub;

- United's motion regarding attempted monopolization of the national CRS market was denied. Specific intent can be inferred from the defendant's market power or predatory or anti-competitive conduct directed to accomplishing the unlawful purpose (of monopolization). There was competent evidence supporting the plaintiff's claim that the defendant engaged in predatory or anti-competitive conduct;

- United's motion regarding attempted monopolization of local CRS markets and local air transportation markets, and American's motion regarding local CRS markets was granted. The plaintiffs failed to produce evidence that United had monopolized various local air transportation markets;

- The defendants' motion on the plaintiff's monopoly leveraging theory was granted. The "monopoly leveraging theory" of liability holds that it is an act of monopolization for a firm having monopoly power in one market to exploit that power as a "lever" to secure competitive advantages in a second market. The use of monopoly power to gain advantage in another is a violation of Section 2 of the Sherman Act, even if there has not been an attempt to monopolize the second market. In this case, the court determined there was sufficient evidence to survive a motion for summary judgment. However, it did not appear that this particular monopoly leveraging theory was consistent with the requirements of Section 2. On that basis, the court would not grant the plaintiffs' motion; and finally,

- United's motion on Continental's claim for travel agent conspiracy was granted. Continental claimed that the same conduct, which they alleged to have constituted monopolization and attempted monopolization, also amounted to violations of the anti-conspiracy provisions of Section 1 of the Sherman Act. However, the plaintiffs failed to present any evidence that United's actions were anything but unilateral. A contract between United and *APOLLO* subscribers did not constitute a violation where the contract merely provided the terms upon which the parties would deal with one another during the course of the relationship.

REPUBLIC AIRLINES v. CIVIL AERONAUTICS BOARD
756 F.2d 1304 (8th Cir. 1985)

Is the Civil Aeronautics Board required
to grant antitrust immunity?

Before passage of the Airline Deregulation Act of 1978, the airlines were required to submit all joint operating agreements to the CAB for approval. If determined to be in the public's interest, the Board could approve anti-competitive agreements, and such agreements approved by the Board were entitled to antitrust immunity. The Airline Deregu-

lation Act made two significant changes. First, submission of joint operating agreements to the Board was made optional instead of mandatory. Second, entitlement to antitrust immunity was limited; mandatory
immunity was eliminated, but the Board was granted authority to confer discretionary immunity. With passage of the International Air
Transportation Competition Act of 1979, Congress amended the statutes reinstating the entitlement to mandatory immunity in limited circumstances. Limited mandatory immunity applied in situations where
the Board determined an agreement, though clearly anti-competitive,
should have been approved in the public interest. Antitrust immunity
for airline agreements was to be the exception, not the rule. Only those
agreements subject to serious risk of antitrust attack, yet providing
public benefits not reasonably obtainable by other means, were entitled
to mandatory antitrust immunity, and then only to the extent necessary.

This case was a petition for review of CAB Orders,[130] which approved after modification five agreements among domestic and international airlines regulating the marketing of air transportation. Appellants were contending that the Board decision to grant only temporary
immunity to the parties in these agreements, and the selective disapproval of certain provisions of the agreements, was contrary to the
Airline Deregulation Act. They maintained the agreements were entitled to mandatory immunity, and they would not enter the agreements
without indefinite antitrust immunity. The parties in this case were:

- Republic Airlines, Inc., an airline based in Minneapolis, Minnesota;
- the Air Transport Association of America [ATA], a trade association;
- the Air Traffic Conference of America [ATCA], the division of
  ATA which deals with the marketing of air transportation;
- the International Air Transport Association [IATA], a trade association representing foreign air carriers;
- the Association of Retail Travel Agents, Ltd. [ARTA], an association of retail travel agents; and
- the American Society of Travel Agents, Inc. [ASTA], another
  association of retail travel agents.

---

[130] 82-12-85, 99 CAB 1 (1982) and 83-3-127, 100 CAB 409 (1983).

Respondent was the CAB, supported by the DOJ. Intervenors were:

- Associated Travel Nationwide [ATN], an association of large volume travel agents;
- American Express Travel Related Services, Inc. (Amex), one of the largest travel agencies in the U.S.; and
- the National Passenger Traffic Association [NPTA] a trade association representing business travel departments [BTD] of major businesses and quasi-public agencies.

The proceeding, which culminated in this case, was an investigation by the CAB to determine how competition could best be introduced into the entire airline passenger and cargo marketing system. At the time, the marketing system was controlled by agreements entered into on behalf of the airlines by ATC and IATA with the advice and consultation of ASTA and ARTA. Five interrelated agreements provided a comprehensive travel agent system available to member airlines. So called "exclusivity" or "standards adherence" provisions of the agreements prohibited an airline from selling tickets except through agents who met the criteria established by the agreements for the granting of accredited agent status. The airlines by these agreements were forbidden from doing business with unaccredited agents.

The Board disapproved outright the exclusivity provisions, finding none of them necessary to meet transportation needs or for public benefit. It found that indefinite antitrust immunity was not required, rather, that only a temporary grant of antitrust immunity was needed in the transition period following passage of the Airline Deregulation Act. The petitioners sought to have the Board's actions declared unlawful and to have the orders remanded for further consideration by the Board. The Board argued that its orders should have been affirmed.

The petitioners charged that,

- The Board exceeded its authority without first balancing the anti-competitive effects;
- After engaging in a balancing-of-interests analysis, the Board would have required an indefinite grant of antitrust immunity;

- Even if not entitled to antitrust immunity, the public benefit of the agreements would compel a grant of antitrust immunity;
- The Board's failure to grant immunity was an abuse of discretion; and
- The Board's proceedings were irregular because the Board (1) conducted an illegal proceeding which made the administrative law judge's hearing meaningless, (2) the Board violated the Administrative Procedures Act by reaching a decision in secret, and (3) the Board prejudicially relied on extra-record evidence in reaching its decision.

The U.S. Court of Appeals responded by stating the Board was generally entitled to considerable deference in interpreting the statutes under which it operated. The court held that,

- The Board had power to excise anti-competitive provisions of agreements and grant approval to balance of the agreements, without making finding as to public benefits;
- Substantial evidence supported determination that exclusivity provisions of agreements raised serious antitrust concerns, and that these provisions were not needed to preserve benefits of the agreements;
- The Board correctly found that antitrust immunity was not required for approved agreements;
- Substantial evidence supported conclusions regarding exclusivity provisions of joint operating agreements, rules barring business travel departments from becoming accredited agents and opening of area settlement plan to agents selected outside common accreditation rules;
- The Board's forecasts of results of its decisions with respect to joint operating agreements were rational, based on consideration of all relevant factors and adequately explained;
- The Board's conclusions were rational and adequately supported by record; and
- Procedures followed by the Board were fair.

The court affirmed the CAB's orders with one dissenting vote. Circuit Judge Heaney disagreed, because, he said,

> *The record in this case reveals that the present system of airline ticket marketing and distribution has worked well for over 40 years. . . . The record also shows that the Board's decision will inevitably put thousands of small travel agents out of business . . . will allow certain entities to skim the cream from the top of the business . . . (and) . . . All of these harmful con-sequences to the existing air travel marketing and distribution system would have to be tolerated if the Board's manipulation of the system were consistent with the Federal Aviation Act and Airline Deregulation Act. In my view, however, the Board failed to engage in the public interest balancing analysis of the proposed agreements required by Section 412, and consequently failed to grant antitrust immunity to the agreements under Section 414. Thus, I would reverse the Board's order.*

CHAPTER 12

THE GOVERNMENT
AS LANDLORD

*Legal issues for fixed base operators center, on the one hand,
around rents, fees and charges imposed by the airport landlord,
and with fair and equitable treatment in leasehold agreements.
On the other hand, there are concerns about entrustment of
property to others, and the liabilities associated with bailment.*

THE GOVERNMENT LANDLORD

A Fixed Base Operator [FBO] is a private general aviation
commercial enterprise that offers flight training instruction, aircraft
maintenance and repair, aircraft refueling service, aircraft storage and
parking, and other ground support services to the general aviation
community. Fixed base operators provide these services from "fixed"
locations on airports.[1]

Because most public airports are owned and operated by state and
local governments, FBOs operating on those airports, of necessity,
become tenants of a government landlord. Airports are like public
utilities. They are characteristically monopolistic, having few if any
competitors. Airport tenants, including FBOs, have little or no choice
in shopping around for alternative airport facilities from which to

---

[1] Dempsey, Hardaway and Thoms suggest the term, "fixed base operator" originated during the
barnstorming era in America. The first airports were located on private property. Owners of such
property built what came to be known as "fixed bases," which served transient barnstormers as well
as other small aviation enterprises; *see* Paul Stephen Dempsey, Robert Hardaway, and William E.
Thoms, *Aviation Law and Regulation* 7-7 (1992).

"base" their operations. They become subject to a landlord unlike other landlords. In this case, the landlord is a governmental bureaucracy, with broad discretionary powers, and far reaching authority through its police powers. Additionally, the government landlord is partially insulated from responsibility for its actions through certain granted immunities from prosecution, which are afforded local governments. Airport tenants can find themselves in situations where it is difficult to negotiate for what they consider reasonable rental terms and conditions, or to receive equitable and non-discriminatory treatment. Therefore, rental agreements, and the right to conduct business are the foremost concerns of many FBOs. Hence, described herein are leasehold agreements and the conditions under which airport tenants are subjected.

Another prominent area of legal concern for fixed base operators is bailment, and the entrustment of property from one person to another. FBOs are primarily in the business of renting out their own property, and/or servicing the property of others. In either case, a bailment may occur, with its associated liabilities. Where the FBO has taken charge of the property of someone else, it must be properly secured. Conversely, when the FBO entrusts someone else with its property, it must be assured that such property will be used according to specified conditions, and in a manner which minimizes the FBO's liability exposure.

ECONOMIC PHILOSOPHY

At the heart of landlord/tenant agreements are leasehold rates. In the case of fixed base operator tenants, at issue is how much the airport is charging, and for what services and facilities the tenant has to pay. The answer to these questions depends upon where the airport lies within the scale of governmental functions. In utilitarian fashion, citizens generally pay taxes in exchange for the provision of services that will promote the most benefit to the most people. The question in many people's minds, however, is whether an airport ought to be one of the services freely provided to the general public. If it is, then the airport should be supported by general tax revenues, the way public parks or fire and police departments are. If, on the other hand, the airport serves only a select minority, then the elite group served by the airport should be the ones who bear the brunt, if not the entire costs of the government owning and operating the airport.

Proponents of the former philosophy will point out the economic benefits that an airport brings to the community. Airport advocates will hold to a position that these benefits accrue to the common welfare of the community, and that they far outweigh any deficit costs incurred in maintaining a public airport. Conversely, opponents will argue that airports are for the privileged few, and that governmental support of an airport constitutes a subsidy of special interests. Their opinion is moderated to some extent where common carriers and the notion of public transportation are interjected. Nevertheless, they will still maintain the airport *users* are the ones who should bear the costs for airport operation; "user charges" being defined as a payment over and above the user's obligations for support of the general government. Opponents to public airport subsidies argue that the individual beneficiaries can be identified, and, therefore, the proportional shares of the costs can be allocated to individuals on the basis of use. Under these conditions, the airport should operate as a commercial (enterprise) venture, and thereby pay its way, with little or no burden on taxpayers.

It may be safely assumed that airports probably lie somewhere in between the two foregoing positions. By statistical inference, airports are essential to modern transportation, and therefore, are necessary for a community's economic and social well-being. If an airport is essential to the welfare of the community, then there is an inherent obligation on the part of government to provide this service. That is, of course, if it is not otherwise provided by private interests. It is herein where lies the answer to ameliorating the two opposing arguments for and against public support of airports. Private enterprise, user charges, and the government, collectively support the operation of air transportation facilities. The degree to which the public sector must participate in subsidizing the airport is the political and legal issue. It should be noted that all but a select few airports are currently incapable of self support, and must rely on some form of subsidy for continued operation.[2] Moreover, the airport sponsor, when it is a city or a county, oftentimes has its own political/economic agenda, which may be contrary to the wishes and desires of the airport's tenants. In this competition

---

[2] *See* Laurence E. Gesell, *The Administration of Public Airports* (4th ed. 1999).

for limited general funds, an airport can come up short-changed and may do without the support necessary to sustain its full potential. To meet the difference in funding requirements, airport sponsors are turning to increased user charges in a cost-allocative fashion.

The establishment and collection of user charges and lease negotiations is a complex matter. It involves the underlying philosophy of airport management, the airport sponsor's adopted policy regarding rates and charges and the necessity for cost allocation, and the very concept of governmental (police) function to protect the health and welfare of all citizens. The functions of government can be classified into three general areas:

- *Protective services*—to defend the civil and property rights of individuals;
- *Redistributive activities*—to reallocate wealth for the economic welfare of society; and
- *Proprietary services*—to manage public properties and enterprise activities.

Airports are primarily a proprietary service, but to varying degrees are a function of all three forms of public service provision. In many cases, proprietary services provided by the government are in areas which otherwise would be performed by private, profit-making organizations. Generally, private enterprise has shown an interest in investing only in those sectors within the air transportation industry where there has been a reasonable expectation of profit—such as in the airlines, or, to a lesser extent, in ancillary services at airports.

Seemingly, if airports could have been viably developed and sustained within the private sector, they would have been. But low profits make airports, *per se*, unattractive as long-term business ventures. Historically, the private sector has shown little interest in airports as a business. As a result, airport ownership has been largely relegated to the governmental sector. Nevertheless, there are profit centers on airports wherein the private sector has been active. Examples include automobile rental, parking services, or restaurant and bar operations. Thus, amongst the airlines, airport concessionaires, and the government sponsor, airports have become joint public/private ventures. But the fundamental business relationship is underscored by a philosophy of public service that is paramount to the government sponsor.

The fact that airports are monopolistic is good reason for them to be operated by government. However, the (airport) monopoly presents inherent and potentially oppressive restrictions upon the operations of airport tenants—not the least of which may be a requirement to pay a full share of the airport facility and operations costs. Like public utilities such as municipal water, power or gas systems, the system users can be readily identified, and they can be expected to pay reasonable costs for the services they receive. The "free public use concept"— such as for use of parks, beaches, and so forth—is generally operable only where the individual beneficiaries cannot be readily identified, or where open use has been deemed to be in the public interest. Airports, however, are neither free to the public, nor are they a true "public utility," defined as:

- regulated within in its geographic area of operation;
- charges the public; and
- allows a percentage of return on investment (i.e., profit).

Aside from the fact that public utilities are usually *privately* owned, a public airport generally meets the three basic criteria, although philosophically they are neither to make a profit nor to lose money in the operation. Profit by the government is customarily considered an impingement upon the free enterprise system, since government represents unfair competition in what is otherwise expected to be a *laissez faire* economy.

Air transportation is a service industry, and from the government's perspective, the airport's product is the provision of a place for the service transaction to occur in the public interest. In making charges for airport facilities, the ideal of the government is to recover all or part of the cost of constructing, maintaining and operating the airport, but not to make a profit. Airport pricing schemes, therefore, are normally designed with the objective of breaking even, or at least reducing losses to a minimum. Revenue maximization is important in fulfilling the objective, but within reasonable expectations of not making a profit. As a result, entrepreneurship is not a typical skill found amongst airport managers. And until recently, there has been little incentive for airport sponsors to maximize revenues. Of more importance has been the politics of generating economic multiplier for the community, of which direct revenues in support of airport operations play a minor role. Where the airport sponsor has accepted federal funds for airport development, contractual assurances require that all moneys generated by the airport remain on the airport.

Airport charges can be categorized in two ways, as either *short-term* or *long-term*. Short-term arrangements are the most flexible and are generally based upon direct user fees. They are normally established in some form of rate structure or rental agreement. Direct user fees are comprised of those charges most directly associated with use of public areas such as landing fees, aircraft storage, transient tie-down fees and fuel flowage. Long-term agreements are leases (rather than rental) of land, terminal floor space, and other buildings.

Where the tenant is to develop capital improvements without governmental (or airport) assistance, it is often necessary to obtain long-term rights to property in order to secure favorable financing. Granting of long-term agreements, and the subsequent loss of flexibility, may be the price the airport must pay if it is unable or unwilling to finance capital improvements, but instead relegates that responsibility to the private sector. Nevertheless, the usual position taken by the airport sponsor is to attempt to minimize the length of long-term agreements. In deliberations over the terms and duration of a lease, there is the potential for confrontation. In the clash between public and private sectors, prospective tenants can become frustrated by the airport sponsor's concerns for what it believes are in the "public interest," pitted against their own overriding individual need to make a profit, and to locate on the airport under what they see as "reasonable" terms.

Assuming a long-term lease is negotiated to the tenant's satisfaction, the tenant acquires certain rights to the public property, but at the same time assumes a unique liability known as a "possessory interest tax." When real estate is transferred to the public sector, it is removed from the property tax rolls, and is no longer a source of revenue for the government. Conversely, if it is transferred to the private sector it is again taxable. If, however, title to property is retained by the government but turned over through rental or long-term lease to the private sector for private commercial purposes, this conversion of the land may again subject it to (possessory interest) taxation, the cost of which must be calculated into the tenant's financial prospectus.[3]

AIRPORT PRICING

With the advent of the "Proposition 13" movement in California in the 1970s, and the subsequent notion of decreased taxes and less government everywhere, over the past 30 years, there has been an attendant shift from general fund tax support for airport operations to a *user pays* philosophy. Airport users have always been expected to pay their fair share of costs, however, the notion of what is "reasonable and fair has been given broader meaning within improved concepts of government economic efficiency, and attempts to relate revenues to costs (i.e., cost allocation). With reduced general service tax bases, airport sponsors have become increasingly motivated to transfer more of the economic burden of operating the airport upon its users.

Inasmuch as airports are not supposed to make a profit, or at a minimum are to turn any profits back into the airport, the rates charged for providing specific services have been established to recover only the costs of providing those services. It is herein where the definition of "user pays" has taken on new meaning. True user pays philosophy demands that all costs of providing facilities be fully recovered. This includes administrative costs, operations and maintenance costs, capital recovery, and depreciation.

In the past, airport price structures have in most cases been established not so much as a function of cost allocation and the airport's need to recover costs, but more in accordance with what the market would bear, and comparative rates and charges of other nearby airports. In other words, there was a normative attempt to make charges "reasonable." This parity approach to rate setting in most cases kept user charges artificially low and did not provide for recovery of sufficient revenues to pay for the services rendered, let alone the needs for future capital investment.

Bringing rates more in line with actual fiscal requirements is a difficult and politically sensitive task, requiring extensive public relations

---

[3] *See Reading Municipal Airport Authority v. Schuylkill Valley School District*, CCH 12 AVI ¶ 17,307 (1972).

skills. Airport users are usually unreceptive to considering, as part of *their* obligation, the airport's need to recapture the fully allocated costs of providing airport facilities, such as land costs, initial construction costs, or the economic life and long-term amortization of facility improvements predicated upon future values of money. In short, they resist having to pay more for the same services they previously received at lower cost. They are quick to point out the lower charges (that serve their advantage) for similar services at nearby airports. They become unrealistic in their arguments to reduce the costs of providing services down to their simplest, yet unrealistic terms, amortized over a given period of time, at no interest, and not including sundry hidden costs associated with administering the services that they may feel ought to be a public obligation. Unfortunately, this is not much different than the approach taken in past years by airport management, although unknowingly, that set the rate structure at the airport sponsor's disadvantage to begin with.[4]

As rates are increased, the political backlash from airport users can sometimes be intolerable. Nobody likes to pay more, whether the increased charge is just or not. It can be extremely difficult for the airport sponsor to explain the reasons for increased prices to an irrational group of people who are concerned only with what they personally must pay, and not with the overall financial problems of the airport, nor of the public burden.

What constitutes a "reasonable" charge, then, remains subjective. It is a matter of personal perspective. In light of the fact that fewer than 70 airports in the United States are capable of fully paying their way, it is necessary for most airports to maximize their revenues.[5] However, revenue maximization should not occur at the price of injustice to airport tenants and other users. Each tenant must be able to generate sufficient revenues to recover its own costs, and to make a reasonable profit. If a tenant is unable to generate sufficient revenues, the laws of economics hypothesize the tenant will seek alternative opportunities elsewhere. Therein lies a dilemma. In a monopoly there are no alternative choices, the airport tenant must, voluntarily where possible, but

---

[4] *See* Laurence E. Gesell, *The Administration of Public Airports* (4th ed. 1999).
[5] *See id.*

involuntarily if necessary, obtain equitable lease arrangements. Sometimes it means taking the airport sponsor to court.

Rents and fees are perhaps the most common ground for disagreement between tenants and the airport sponsor, but this is by no means the only area where differences arise. Another prominent area of concern is in discrimination, or its opposite exclusive rights. Added to this is the possibility of antitrust violation. This issue is compounded by the fact that airports enjoy limited antitrust immunity, for which the airport sponsors may take advantage, and tenants may suffer.

Fixed base operators, especially when there is only one of them on an airport, often serve a dual role both as entrepreneurs and as managers of the airport for the airport sponsor. When FBOs develop a close (or at least closer than others) working relationship with the airport sponsor, they may receive preferential treatment over existing or potential competition. Outsiders wishing to provide competitive services on the airport may face discrimination. Conversely, should the FBO, already on the airport, fall out of favor with the airport sponsor, it may become the one discriminated against in favor of the new entrant.

Section 308 of the Federal Aviation Act[6] specifically prohibits exclusive rights by stating, "there shall be no exclusive right for the use of any landing area or air navigation facility upon which federal funds have been expended." Nevertheless, even though exclusivity is prohibited, the Federal Aviation Administration [FAA] has long supported a protectionist policy for airport operators—at times (unofficially) sanctioning the airport sponsor's decision to have only one FBO on its airport. In the philosophical dichotomy between providing open competition, while at the same time protecting certain businesses, airport managers find themselves squarely between competing interests and lawsuits erupt over charges of antitrust violation.

Under the terms of the Local Government Antitrust Act of 1984, Congress granted to local governments, including airport authorities, antitrust immunity limited to injunctive relief only. In other words, airports may still be sued for antitrust violations, but only to stop them from imposing, or otherwise allowing, unlawful anti-competitive conditions. The law removed the threat that localities and local officials could be liable for treble damages for antitrust violations.

---

[6] 49 U.S.C. § 1349(a).

Historically, airport operators, pressed by land restrictions and limited facilities, have oftentimes found it necessary to restrict the number of concessionaires and other tenants in order to maintain services at a level their limited facilities could handle. But, Supreme Court decisions in 1978 and 1982 stripped localities of assumed antitrust immunity as governmental agents of the state. Hundreds of antitrust suits against airports followed. The Local Government Antitrust Act of 1984 limits plaintiffs in antitrust suits against localities. In signing the bill (H.R. 6027) into law, President Reagan said that while antitrust laws "serve very important purposes, they were never intended to threaten public treasuries and the taxpayer's pocketbooks, or to disrupt good faith functioning of local units of government."

The case law examples at the end of the chapter specifically focusing on the antitrust issue as it applies to the airport landlord/tenant relationship. Demonstrated is the airport sponsor's responsibility in antitrust law as determined by contradicting court decisions. It was, by-and-large, a result of this vacillating judicial treatment, and the unacceptable liability being inflicted upon airport sponsors, that led to passage in late 1984 of the Local Government Antitrust Act which provided for antitrust immunity at public airports. The cases cited, follow chronologically the developing law in this area. In this vein, the reader is also referred to *Town of Hallie v. City of Eau Claire*,[7] a case involving neither airports nor FBOs, nor aviation at all, but is thought to be significant as the first municipal antitrust case to be heard by the Supreme Court since passage of the Local Government Antitrust Act the year before. This Wisconsin municipal antitrust case broadened the exemption from antitrust prosecution for localities, including airports.

ENTRUSTMENT TO OTHERS

Next to fiscal concerns associated with leasehold agreements, the second prominent area of concern with regard to fixed base operators in particular is the entrustment to them of their customers' property, namely their aircraft, and the entrustment of the FBO's aircraft to renters. A "bailment" occurs when personal property is handed over to another for a specific purpose, under either an express or implied

---

[7] 85 L. Ed 2d 24 (1985).

agreement. When the contract is completed or the purpose for which the property was delivered is fulfilled, it is understood that the property will be returned to its original owner.

Bailment occurs not only for commercial purposes such as rental, repair, cleaning, storage, and so forth, but lending property to a friend or neighbor creates a bailment as well. An aircraft delivered to a mechanic for repair creates a bailment. Allowing a friend to use an aircraft is also a bailment. The one (i.e., the owner) who delivers the aircraft to the mechanic is the "bailor." The one (e.g., the mechanic) to whom the property is delivered is the "bailee."

In a bailment the bailee has certain responsibilities. The bailee must reimburse the bailor for any loses or damages to the property while in the bailee's care.[8] The property must be returned in its original condition. Unless agreed upon beforehand, the bailee may not use the property for personal benefit. The bailor must assume certain responsibilities as well. If the bailor fails to retrieve the property within a reasonable period of time, the bailee may have the right to dispose of the property to satisfy the lien against it. If the bailee has taken reasonable precautions to protect the property, and yet the property is still damaged for reasons beyond the bailee's control, the bailor may be responsible for the property.[9] Should the bailor deliver the property to the bailee in faulty and dangerous condition, and not notify the bailee of the condition, the bailor may be responsible for damages or injury, which can be tied directly to the faulty condition.

Implied in a bailment are certain general rules covering the bailor's (i.e., the owner's) rights: The bailee,

- does not own the property, and possession reverts to the owner;
- may not dispose of the property (unless the bailor fails to fulfill the terms of the agreement);
- must be warned of hidden (dangerous) defects;
- must take reasonable care of the property;
- may be liable for loss or damage caused by the bailee's negligence;

---

[8] *See Quam v. Ryan*, 144 N.W. 2d 551 (1966).
[9] *See Clemson v. Butler*, 296 A. 2d 419 (1972).

- is generally not liable for loss or damage beyond the bailee's control;[10]
- must return the exact property received; and
- may not use the property without permission and if the bailee does, he or she is almost always liable for loss or damage. The wrongful use or wrongful taking of personal property is known as "conversion."

LIENS

A "lien" is a cloud on a title. Liens are sometimes referred to as "third party property rights." By definition, a lien is a legal claim on property as security (or interest) for a debt or charge—under which the property may be seized and sold to satisfy the debt. A lien can be in effect without actual possession of the property in question, such as an aircraft, or some other property.

Liens come in various forms, and lien holders are included in what are termed "favored creditors." That is, lienors (or lien holders) usually come ahead of others for what is owed them.[11] A seller, for example, may transfer title under a conditional bill of sale; the condition of the sale being that payment must be made in full before title is transferred. The seller holds a chattel mortgage. A "chattel" is (personal) property other than real property. The seller retains the right of repossession for non-payment.

Other common examples of liens include: lawyer's, mechanic's, storage, innkeeper's, garageman's, drycleaner's, and law violator's liens. For example, if a person stays in a motel, but fails to pay the bill, the innkeeper may retain the person's luggage as a lien. In the same way, ordinances have been written by local governments authorizing impound of aircraft for non-payment of tie-down or storage fees. Another example is a "mechanic's lien" (or "garageman's lien" in the case of an automobile repair). If an aircraft is left for repair, and the bill for the repairs is not met, the mechanic may refuse to surrender the aircraft until the bill is paid. Finally, a lien may be placed against

---

[10] *See Ebony and Ivory v. Hudson*, CCH 21 AVI 17,980 (1989).
[11] *See Southern Jersey Airways v. National Bank of Secaucus*, CCH 11 AVI 17,463 (1970).

property for non-payment of legal fees. This is called an "attorney's" or "lawyer's lien."

"Confiscation," or the act of seizing property by the government and converting it to public use, is a similar process. Whereas the lien is imposed as a civil penalty for failure to make good on a contract, the seizure of private property by the government, without compensation, is often done as a consequence of conviction for a crime, or because possession or use of the property was contrary to law. For example, property may be confiscated and secured against civil penalties for violations of Federal Aviation Regulations. Confiscation may occur in association with other federal violations as well; customs, drug enforcement, and postal violations are examples. Numerous aircraft have been seized for the illegal carriage of drugs, and some of these aircraft have not only been confiscated, but have been incorporated for use into customs and drug enforcement fleets.

Any property, including cash, may be confiscated, if it can be shown that the property is associated in any way with the trafficking of drugs.[12] Most property is ostensibly subject to lien action. Exceptions are real property, life insurance, clothing, and books and tools used for business. The following case briefs provide some examples of lien actions in the field of aviation, as well as antitrust and other airport-related issues.

WIGGINS AIRWAYS v. MASSACHUSETTS PORT AUTHORITY
362 F. 2d 52 (1st Cir. 1966)

*Under antitrust law, may an airport sponsor contract
exclusively with a sole fixed base operator?*

For many years prior to 1959, Wiggins Airways, Inc. and Van Dusen Aircraft Supplies conducted fixed base operations at Boston's Logan Airport. In 1959 the Massachusetts Port Authority took over operation of the airport and decided to have only one FBO on the airport. Wiggins' lease expired in 1959, and Van Dusen's lease was due to expire in 1961. The Authority invited expressions of interest from several fixed base operators, including Wiggins, Van Dusen, and

---

[12] *See United States v. $124,570*, CCH 21 AVI 18,378 (1989).

Butler Aviation, who was conducting similar operations throughout the country. All three expressed an interest to undertake the operation. It was Butler who was selected to be the single operator, and the plaintiff Wiggins was given notice to vacate its premises in not more than 90 days. Wiggins claimed it was forced to sell its business and equipment at Logan, and which Butler was able to buy at very low cost. A lease was executed between the Authority and Butler whereby the latter would take over Wiggins' hangar as of July 1, 1961, and the Van Dusen hangar as of January 1, 1962, following the expiration of the Van Dusen lease.

Wiggins filed a complaint with the FAA stating the decision to establish Butler as the sole and exclusive FBO violated the Federal Aviation Act of 1958 (49 U.S.C. Section 1349). The FAA Administrator intervened and instructed the Authority to grant Van Dusen an extension. The FAA also instructed the Authority to take steps to negotiate with all interested parties to correct the situation complained of. But it was too late for Wiggins who had sold everything and departed the airport. Van Dusen continued as an FBO on the airport.

Wiggins filed suit contending a member of the Port Authority had contacted Butler, and as a result of subsequent meetings the Authority and Butler entered into a conspiracy whereby the Authority would refuse to allow Wiggins to remain on the airport, and it would refuse to renew the Van Dusen lease, in violation of antitrust laws (15 U.S.C. Sections 15 and 26). Defendants responded, by stating that the Port Authority was acting as an agent of the Commonwealth of Massachusetts in the performance of a governmental function, and that a restraint or monopoly resulting from governmental action does not violate the Sherman Act. The United States District Court dismissed the suit on grounds that the complaint did not state a claim upon which relief could be granted, and Wiggins appealed.

The United States Court of Appeals agreed with the lower court's judgment stating, "We find nothing in the language of the Sherman Act or in its history which suggests its purpose was to restrain a state or its officers or agents from activities directed by its legislature. . . . The Sherman Act makes no mention of the state as such, and gives no hint that it was intended to restrain state action or official action directed by a state." The courts have repeatedly reaffirmed this principle.

As to the charges of conspiracy, the court could not find sufficient evidence—all the plaintiff alleged was that the Authority agreed with Butler to replace Wiggins and Van Dusen with Butler, and make Butler the sole and exclusive FBO at Logan. That was a simple agreement or arrangement. The fact that it was exclusive does not make it a conspiracy or illegal. The district court's decision was affirmed, and the U.S. Supreme Court denied *certiorari*.[13]

ALPHIN v. HENSON
392 F. Supp. 318 (D. Md. 1975)

May a sole fixed base operator, hired by the airport sponsor as its airport manager, exclude others wishing to provide competitive services from operating on an airport?

In 1930, and while working for Fairchild Industries, Richard Henson opened an airport on land owned by Fairchild. In 1934, the City of Hagerstown purchased the airport from Fairchild. Henson, while still employed by Fairchild, operated a fixed base operation part-time until he retired from Fairchild in 1964. After he retired, he was engaged full time at his FBO business. Henson had an involvement with the origination of the airport and its operation continuously from 1930 until this suit was filed in 1973; including the management of the airport for the city. In 1952 Henson was given the right to control all selling privileges and concession rights on the airport. The lease specifically provided that it should not be construed as granting Henson Aviation any exclusive right to conduct any activity at the airport contrary to the Civil Aeronautics Act of 1938; and that the lease "shall be subordinate to the provisions of any existing or future agreement between the city and the United States." A new lease with Henson was executed in 1972. The city was the recipient of financial assistance from the federal government for airport development and, therefore, was responsible for assurances to the federal government in its operation of the airport.

T. S. Alphin went to work for Fairchild in 1946, and shortly thereafter went to work for Henson as an aircraft mechanic until 1948 when

---

[13] 385 U. S. 947 (1966).

work dropped off. He then began doing aviation maintenance and repair work on his own. He would have liked to build a shop on the airport, but Henson told him there was no space available. He did part of his work in Henson's hangars (leased to Henson by the city) and took some of his work home. In 1966 Alphin purchased property adjacent to the airport and erected a building from which he conducted his maintenance and repair activities. With Henson's approval, he improved an airport service road so that he would have access to the airport.

The community of Hagerstown showed little interest in the airport until 1969, when it became apparent that a study was needed of the airport's operations and problems. The completed study recommended improvements to the airport and realignment of management practices. Pursuant to a resolution by the City Council, two contracts were negotiated with Henson Aviation. First, there was a lease as FBO, granting exclusive use of specific portions of the airport. Second, there was an agreement to provide airport management services.

Alphin subsequently asked Henson for a lease permitting him to do what he had already been doing for years without a lease. Henson sent Alphin a form of lease, to the provisions of which Alphin objected. Alphin then applied directly to the city for his lease. Henson recommended to the city that Alphin's proposal be rejected and Alphin filed suit. The U.S. District Court found that Henson's objection to Alphin's proposal was based in part upon Henson's reluctance to have competition.

The courts had held that: the antitrust laws were aimed at private action, not at governmental action; states, cities and governmental agencies could not be held liable for violations of the antitrust laws; and that restraints of trade which arose from valid governmental action could not give rise to private antitrust liability.

Insofar as any monopoly that Henson Aviation may have enjoyed as the result of the leases which the city entered into with Henson, it was not a monopoly that is unlawful under the antitrust laws. The city had the right to decide whether it was in the best interest of the public to enter into such a lease with one, or more, FBOs. Additionally, the city had the right to designate Henson as the airport manager. It was common practice in Maryland and elsewhere, for cities the size of Hagerstown to have the FBO act as its airport manager.

The FBO lease between the city and Henson did not grant Henson any exclusive right to furnish FBO services on the airport. Plaintiff Alphin failed to prove that the contract designating Henson as airport manager was intended by the city to authorize Henson to prevent other persons desiring to furnish FBO services on the airport from dealing directly with the city for such privileges. The relationship of Henson with the city did not violate the "non-exclusivity" provisions of the 1938 Act, and was under the approval of the FAA. It was not clear, however, that the FAA had approved the action of the Mayor in authorizing Henson to *negotiate* on behalf of the city with those persons wanting to conduct operations in competition with Henson.

Henson developed over the years a monopoly in the popular sense of the term, in some but not all commercial activities on the airport. When Henson, as airport manager, undertook to represent the city in negotiating a lease with Alphin and others who wished to provide FBO services in competition with Henson, and proposed to Alphin and others terms which would have protected Henson from competition, Henson went beyond the limits permitted by the antitrust laws. The U.S. District Court issued an injunction restraining Henson from attempting to monopolize any part of the business on the airport by negotiating on behalf of the city as airport manager. The court concluded that no broad injunction restraining the city in its operation of the airport should (or could) be granted, but did issue a narrow injunction restraining the city and its officials from permitting Henson to negotiate on behalf of the city with persons seeking permission to engage in activities on the airport which would compete with Henson.

NISWONGER v. AMERICAN AVIATION
411 F. Supp. 769 (E.D. Tenn. 1975).

Within the provisions of the Federal Aviation Act, may an airport sponsor contract exclusively with a sole fixed base operator?

Scott Niswonger, doing business as Greenville Air Service, applied to the Greeneville-Greene County, Tennessee Airport Authority to become an additional FBO at the airport. The Authority rejected the application, because, it said, all the ramp space then existing at the airport was leased to American Aviation, Inc. The Authority had leased

545

to American exclusively all the then available facilities suitable for aeronautical activities, and had thereby demonstrated its intention to exclude all other FBOs from doing business on the airport.

Niswonger sought a declaration from the court that the lease between American and the airport authority was void because it violated a federal statute, 49 U.S.C. Section 1349(a) (i.e., Section 308, the "non-exclusivity" provision of the 1958 Aviation Act). In its findings of fact, the trial court determined that the airport authority was a duly constituted public body, and an agent of the Town of Greeneville and Greene County, Tennessee. Greeneville and the County were municipal corporations, organized, existing and operating under the laws of the State of Tennessee.

It was also determined that there was available at the airport, space for an additional fixed base operator, and that American had been granted more area than it could actually use reasonably. The U.S. District Court concluded from 49 U.S.C. Section 1349(a) that ". . . there shall be no exclusive right for the use of any landing area or air navigation facility upon which federal funds have been expended. . . ." From FAA Advisory Circular 150/5190-2A of April 1972, the court determined the FAA's interpretation of "exclusive right" as denying,

> . . . *another from enjoying or exercising a like power, privilege or right. An exclusive right . . . conferred on one or more parties but excluding others from enjoying or exercising a similar right or rights . . . The leasing of all available airport land or facilities suitable for aeronautical activities to a single enterprise . . . (is) . . . evidence of an intent to exclude other . . . The amount of space leased to a single enterprise should be limited to that for which it can clearly demonstrate an actual need. . . .*

The court ruled the lease between American and the airport authority violated 49 U.S.C. Section 1349 to the extent that it granted to American exclusive use on the airport; and to such extent, it was void and inoperable. The U.S. Court of Appeals affirmed the lower court's decision.[14]

HERRICK'S AERO-AUTO-AQUA REPAIR SERVICE v. ALASKA
754 P.2d 1111 (Alaska 1988)

May itinerant mechanics compete on airports without meeting the same requirements as permanent tenants?

Herrick's Aero-Auto-Aqua Repair Service and other tenants on the Anchorage International Airport claimed it was unfair for them to meet certain insurance and airport permit requirements when itinerant mechanics at the airport were not subject to the same standards. Specifically, the lessees were required to provide insurance against public liability and to indemnify the airport for any damages caused. The lease agreements also restricted the types of business the lessees could pursue on their leaseholds.

Conversely, the mobile or itinerant mechanics provided services from their vehicles at their customers' tie-downs and slips, and had not obtained the statutorily required permits to conduct business on the airport. The airport sponsor knew of the itinerant operators, but took no action against them. The official airport tenants brought discriminatory enforcement charges against the Alaska Department of Transportation [ADOT], the airport operator, for not enforcing its rules with regard to the itinerant mechanics. This was a case of equal protection under the law. The lessees also alleged the airport breached its contract with them.

Both sides moved for summary judgment. The trial court granted summary judgment to the lessees and ordered ADOT to enforce its requirements, but only "to the extent that (ADOT was) fiscally capable . . . ." It did not order the regulations enforced against the itinerants. The summary judgment, however, dismissed the breach of contract claim. The lessees appealed the trial court's refusal to grant the relief requested.

---

[14] 529 F. 2d 526 (1976).

On appeal, ADOT presented three arguments. First, it argued that it would incur "significant financial impact" in enforcing its policy. In other words, ADOT claimed it was not economically feasible for it to enforce the rules with the itinerants. The court, however, stated that "savings will always be achieved by excluding a class of persons." Cost savings alone were not sufficient government objectives when equal protection was a consideration.

Second, ADOT argued the regulation was too cumbersome to enforce because itinerant mechanics were difficult to identify and with so many entrances to the airport, airport authorities could not possibly monitor the coming and goings of itinerant mechanics. The court responded by saying, "this argument simplifies to an admission that security at the airport [had] been poor." It would not allow the airport's "substandard performance to define constitutional requirements."

Finally, ADOT argued it was allowed to make exceptions to the regulations on a showing of "good cause." This was an argument that begs the question of what constitutes "good cause," which cannot be defined as a standard sufficient to derogate constitutional requirements.

The appellate court concluded that ADOT's enforcement policies violated the equal protection due to the lessees, but disagreed with the trial court's remedy. The case was remanded to the trial court for further proceedings consistent with this opinion.

GUTHRIE AIRCRAFT v. GENESEE COUNTY, N.Y.
494 F. Supp. 950 (W.D.N.Y. 1980)

Does an airport sponsor, as a governmental agency, have automatic exemption from antitrust laws?

The individual plaintiffs were Will S. Guthrie, Walter C. Guthrie and Walter C. Guthrie, Jr. Jointly the Guthries were the owners of the two corporate plaintiffs, Guthrie Aircraft and Batavia Aviation. The Guthries were conducting business as FBOs on the Genesee County Airport near Batavia, New York. The airport was owned and operated by Genesee County. In 1977, the county, through a series of actions, terminated Batavia Aviation as the fixed base operator of the airport. The plaintiffs alleged that,

- They were forced out of the airport terminal building and were not allowed to have any office space in their terminal;
- They were forced to remove their tools from the maintenance hangar even though other parties renting hangars at the airport were allowed to continue their use of the maintenance hangar;
- They were told that Prior Aviation would need *all* of the space at the airport for its operations which, they said, was untrue;
- Their hangar rent was raised 100%, and an additional 100% surcharge was imposed upon them alone;
- To avoid the higher rent they moved their operation to private property adjacent to the airport, but the county erected a snow fence to block their access to the airport; and
- The county refused to allow Exxon Company to deliver any aircraft fuel to them, or to allow them to deliver their own fuel.

Upon termination of activities at the airport by the plaintiffs, the county entered into an agreement with Prior Aviation Service, Inc., which then became the sole FBO at the airport. The plaintiffs brought suit alleging that the defendants contracted, combined and conspired to restrain trade in violation of the Sherman Antitrust Act (15 U.S.C. Sections 1 and 2), with the intent to eliminate them as competitors. They also claimed the county granted Prior an exclusive right to use the airport for air carrier activity, and otherwise discriminated against the plaintiffs, in violation of the Federal Aviation Act (49 U.S.C. Section 1301, *et seq.*, and 1349[a] in particular). The county had received federal funds to improve the airport, and the county agreed as part of the federal grant not to discriminate between air carriers using the facility. The plaintiffs alleged the county and Prior conspired to violate that agreement, and had, in fact, discriminated against Batavia Aviation with respect to rental and other rates. Plaintiffs alleged the County entered into an agreement with Prior, which granted exclusive rights in violation of the Federal Aviation Act.

The defendants moved to dismiss the claims on three grounds:

- *Standing of Individual Plaintiffs*—arguing the plaintiffs lacked standing because the complaint failed to allege any direct injury from the alleged antitrust violation;

- *Private Action under the Federal Aviation Act*—claiming the plaintiffs had no standing under the Act because no private right of action exists for the violation of the Act alleged in the complaint. (It should be noted that to maintain a private action it must appear that some personal right has been or is about to be invaded. Antitrust laws apply to business entities, not individuals. Additionally, the defendants asserted that plaintiffs' claim was subject of the primary jurisdiction of the Federal Aviation Administration, and the court should decline to exercise its jurisdiction pending a determination by the FAA).

- *State Action Exemption*—wherein it was contended the Sherman Antitrust Act does not apply to the conduct undertaken by a local government.

Referring to the language of the Clayton Antitrust Act, "any person who shall be injured in his business or property by reason of anything forbidden in the antitrust laws may sue therefore in any district court of the United States. . . ." In response to the motion regarding standing of the individual plaintiffs, the court determined that the pertinent language was "injured in his business or property." After review of the injuries itemized, the court could find that none alleged a *direct* injury to the individual plaintiffs as required by the antitrust laws.

As to whether there was private cause of action under the Federal Aviation Act of 1958, the court referred to *Touche Ross and Company v. Reddington*,[15] *Cannon v. University of Chicago*,[16] and *Cort v. Ash*,[17] wherein these decisions emphasized "the fact that a federal statute has been violated and some person harmed does not automatically give rise to a private cause of action in favor of that person." In the instant case, the court found no indication that the Federal Aviation Act was enacted for the benefit of a special class of which the plaintiffs were members—and this was the threshold question! The court said it had not been shown any legislative history evidencing any purpose to provide a private cause of action.

---

[15] 442 U.S. 560 (1979).
[16] 441 U. S. 677 (1979).
[17] 442 U.S. 66 (1975).

The plaintiffs relied heavily on *Niswonger v. American Aviation.*[18] However, this court pointed out that in Niswonger the district court did not find a private remedy under Section 1349(a). The relevant portion of that case pre-dated *Cort v. Ash, supra,* and the more recent Supreme Court decisions should be applied. The *Niswonger* decision was, therefore, discounted, and this court found that no private remedy exists under 49 U.S.C. § 1349(a) (the "non-exclusivity" clause).

In addressing the issue of governmental antitrust immunity, it was determined that a court must first examine state statutes to determine if there is any authorization for anti-competitive conduct. Furthermore, the terms of agreements on airports must provide for the operation of the airport as a *public* airport for the *general use* of the public. In the instant case, the court said it was not convinced that the legislature "contemplated" the action allegedly engaged in by the defendants, nor that the State of New York had manifested a policy to displace competition with regulation or monopoly in public service.

In this case, the defendants relied heavily on *E. W. Wiggins Airways, Inc. v. Massachusetts Port Authority,*[19] but *Wiggins* predated more recent Supreme Court decisions, especially in *City of Lafayette v. Louisiana Power and Light Company;*[20] and *Goldfarb v. Virginia State Bar,*[21] which had replaced the earlier decision of *Parker v. Brown,*[22] wherein the Supreme Court held that the antitrust laws were not intended to apply to state action. The decision in Wiggins was based on the theory that a blanket *Parker* antitrust immunity applied to *any* governmental action. That simply was no longer the law. The court resolved the motions to dismiss as follows:

- Defendant's motion to dismiss the plaintiff's claims insofar as they were brought by individual plaintiffs was granted;
- Defendant's motion to dismiss the plaintiff's claim under the Federal Aviation Act was granted; and
- Defendant's motion to dismiss the plaintiff's antitrust claims was denied.

---

[18] CCH 14 AVI ¶ 17,311 (1975).
[19] 362 F. 2d 52 (1966).
[20] 435 U.S. 389 (1978)
[21] 421 U.S. 773 (1975).
[22] 317 U.S. 341 (1943).

READING MUNICIPAL AIRPORT AUTHORITY v. SCHUYLKILL VALLEY SCHOOL DISTRICT
286 A.2d 5 (Pa. Commonwealth Ct. 1972)

*Are hangars, leased by an airport to a fixed base operator,
exempt from real property taxation?*

The Reading Municipal Airport Authority borrowed from a bank the money with which it purchased two steel buildings containing 16 T-hangars. It leased the T-hangar buildings to Reading Aviation Service, a fixed base operator. Reading Aviation in turn leased the 16 T-hangars to owners of private aircraft based at the airport. The issue in this case was whether the two buildings were entitled to exemption from local property taxation. The county tax assessor, as well as the Pennsylvania Court of Common Pleas, determined the buildings were not tax exempt. The airport authority appealed.

The Constitution of Pennsylvania provided, in part, "the General Assembly may by law exempt from taxation . . . that portion of public property that is actively and regularly used for public purposes." The appellate court noted further that the courts had embellished the constitutional and statutory authority with supplementary principles:

- A real property tax may be levied upon land owned by a public body not used for a public purpose but leased to a private individual for a commercial purpose (i.e., a "possessory interest);

- Public property used for a public purpose is entitled to be exempted although persons using the facility are required to pay reasonable charges for refreshment or special entertainment;

- The fact that properties of a public body are leased to private parties deriving profit therefrom, instead of being operated by the body, will not defeat the exemption if the properties are being used for the specifically authorized public purpose for which they were acquired;

- It is the use of the property, and not the use of the proceeds from the property, that determines whether tax exemption may constitutionally be granted;

- That property used commercially serves the convenience of public users will not justify an exemption, nor will the fact that the use is not indispensable or essential there to defeat exemption. The test is whether the property's use is reasonably necessary for the efficient operation of the facility; and
- It is a judicial question for ultimate determination of the courts as to whether use is public and, hence, entitled to exemption.

In the instant case, one scheduled airline operated out of Reading, producing 10% to 15% of the airport's operations. The balance of the activity or operation at the airport, was what is sometimes referred to as "general aviation," which used the facilities for landing and taking off, fueling, maintenance and hangarage of aircraft owned or operated by members of the public, individual and corporate.

Appellant Reading Municipal Airport Authority contended the 16 T-hangars were at least reasonably necessary to the operation of its airport. If they were not provided, the owners of the aircraft there housed might have moved from the airport, thus reducing the volume of business enjoyed by the FBO. Hence, the FBO's ability to meet the Authority's charge for its use of the airport would be diminished. As its brief stated, without the hangars it would "seriously (impair the Authority's) ability to obtain state and federal funds for continuing its ongoing program of maintenance and capital improvements."

The Authority had borrowed from a bank to acquire the hangars. The monthly payment necessary to service the loan was $788.08 over a period of 20 years. This was the exact amount of rent payable by Reading Aviation Service and the precise term of its occupancy. Furthermore, the lease imposed no obligation on Reading Aviation to sublet the T-hangars to users of the airport (i.e., the public), and did not require that the property be used for this purpose.

A copy of a typical T-hangar lease between Reading Aviation Service and a user was admitted into evidence. It contained the following significant provision:

> *The lessee shall have the right to use the facilities of the said airport for the purpose of flying the airplane stored in said hangar, but shall not engage in any commercial flying off*

*said field, nor conduct any business enterprise
at said airport.*

In previous cases, where property was held to be exempt from taxation, some measure of control was retained by the public body. Here, not only had the Authority relinquished all such control to a private enterprise, it had conditionally agreed the property might be used for a purpose other than that which it said justified the exemption.

The court recognized that T-hangars are an attractive feature of an airport devoted mainly to general aviation. If they are available for use by the general public, and, if under all the circumstances they are reasonably necessary to the functioning of the airport as a public instrumentality, their exemption is proper. However, where buildings are provided to a private business with no restriction as to use or charges for use, and available for rental by that private entity to persons of its unfettered choosing, there is not a public use.

The court believed not only did Reading Aviation Service give preference to users of its services, it exacted the condition that users not engage in competing business at the airport. Under these arrangements the property primarily served Reading Aviation Service and not the general public using the airport. It was, therefore, not entitled to the public subsidy of tax exemption. The Commonwealth Court of Pennsylvania affirmed the lower court's ruling.

QUAM v. NELSON RYAN FLIGHT SERVICE
144 N.W. 2d 551 (Minn. 1966)

*Who is responsible for severe storm damage to an aircraft
parked on the bailee's property?*

The plaintiff, Burton Quam, was assigned a parking place for his single engine airplane on the defendant's, Nelson-Ryan Flight Service, premises. While the plane was parked on the defendant's premises, one of the tie-down ropes broke during a severe storm. The airplane was thrown about in the storm resulting in damage to the plane. The trial court (Municipal Court, Hennepin County, Minnesota) indicated to the jury that,

- In order to recover on his claim, the plaintiff had to prove by the preponderance of the evidence that the rope furnished by the defendant was defective or insufficient for its use;
- The defendant's failure to furnish a rope sufficient for its intended use was a direct cause of the damage; and
- The plaintiff had to prove by a preponderance of the evidence the contributory negligence and assumption of risk of the defendant.

Jury in the trial court found there had been breach of duty on the part of Nelson-Ryan. As operator of a flight service that assigned to Burton Quam a place to keep his airplane, it failed to provide equipment which was safe for its intended use. Nelson-Ryan Flight Service appealed. On appeal, the Supreme Court of Minnesota ruled that one who furnishes equipment for compensation for a business use by another, under circumstances where the person retains the exclusive right to maintain the equipment, and it is foreseeable that damage might result from defects to it, owes a duty to use reasonable care to provide equipment which is safe for its intended use and free from defects of which the person has knowledge, or which could have been discovered by use of reasonable care.

On the basis of the record, there was a fact question as to whether or not the rope, which broke, was defective. The jury had the opportunity to examine the rope and could find fairly that there was, in fact, a breach of duty on the part of the defendant in failing to provide equipment that was "safe for its intended use."

The Supreme Court affirmed the finding of the lower court.

CLEMSON v. BUTLER AVIATION-FRIENDSHIP
296 A. 2d 419 (Md. 1972)

Is a bailee responsible for damages beyond the bailee's control?

John Clemson entrusted his airplane to Butler Aviation for repairs. While in Butler's care, the airplane was moved to a location 25 feet outside the door of Butler's hangar. It was a door regularly used by Butler employees, and where employees had to pass in the performance of their duties. Chocks were placed under the wheels, but the plane was not otherwise secured. On the afternoon of the fourth day after Clemson delivered the airplane for repairs, a Butler employee found a man sprawled across the front seats, the victim of suicide. The suicide victim was identified as the same person seen 20 minutes earlier trying to start the airplane. There was extensive damage done to the plane. The instrument panel had been smashed and apparently pieces of glass had been used in the suicide.

Clemson brought suit against Butler for loss of income because of damage to the airplane "while in the care and custody of Butler for repairs," and for the three-day delay in making the repairs. Butler counter-sued Clemson for the cost of the repairs. The Baltimore County Circuit Court entered judgment in each suit in favor of Butler. Clemson appealed, claiming:

- "The proximate cause of the damage to (his) aircraft" was "the act of (Butler) in taking possession of (Clemson's) aircraft, one, two or three days prior to the time when they would have an employee available to work on the requested repair";
- that "ordinary care and diligence would require (Butler) to permit the aircraft to remain in its place of safety on the north ramp . . . until (Butler) was ready to work on the repairs. . . .";
- that Butler's employees "could have reactivated the 'control lock' . . . which would have prevented the movement of the control surfaces"; and finally,
- the vandal should have been seen by Butler's employees.

The Court of Appeals of Maryland was of the opinion the bailee, Butler, had exercised ordinary care and diligence in safeguarding the airplane, and could not be held accountable for the activities of the suicide victim. No evidence was presented to indicate that Butler should have anticipated damage would take place. On the issue of timely repairs, there was no testimony that Butler failed to deliver the plane within a reasonable time.

The burden of proving negligence was Clemson's, and he failed to prove that Butler had not exercised ordinary care and diligence.

The trial court's conclusions were supported.

ANDERSON AVIATION SALES CO. v. PEREZ
508 P.2d 87 (Ariz. App. 1973)

*Is the renter of an airplane responsible for the certification
and currency of the pilot?*

Forrest Dockery, a pilot, was in the business of supplying used cars to Madison Chevrolet. Dockery arranged to fly five drivers to Blythe, California, to drive five used cars back to Phoenix, Arizona. Dockery arrived at Anderson Aviation's office at Sky Harbor Airport at about 6:30 p.m., and told Anderson's receptionist he was flying to Blythe and return. He then signed Anderson's lease agreement for a Piper Comanche. He appeared in a hurry, and stated he would file a flight plan in the air. On his preflight inspection, Dockery was observed for five or ten minutes by Anderson's chief pilot and managing agent. Dockery and his passengers took off at 7:01 p.m. for a night flight to Blythe. As the plane approached its destination the Flight Service Station [FSS] at Blythe reported the Blythe Airport had sustained a power failure and was without runway lights. Dockery first learned of the light outage when he called in over Quartzite for landing instructions. An automobile was placed at the end of the runway, with its lights on to help illuminate the runway. Expert testimony indicated that while attempting to land, Dockery became spatially disoriented and crashed. All in the plane perished.

The families of the deceased sued Dockery's estate, Anderson Aviation, and Madison Chevrolet. The latter settled out of court. The allegations were that Anderson leased the airplane to Dockery knowing he was not current to carry passengers at night.

Anderson argued that even if Dockery was not in compliance with Federal Aviation Regulations, it was not their responsibility to determine his qualifications. Per the general law in Arizona applicable to bailments, the liability of an aircraft owner is determined by the law applicable to torts on land. And, one who rents a car to an unlicensed driver is not liable under the "doctrine of negligent entrustment" since the lack of a license has no relevance to whether or not the bailee is competent to operate the vehicle.

The Superior Court of Maricopa County did not accept the defendant's argument, and stated " . . . an airplane and an automobile are different breeds of cat; what might not be negligence in the rental of a car could be gross negligence in the rental of a plane." In the end, the "reasonable man" text must govern. The jury verdict was against the defendant and Anderson appealed. But the Court of Appeals of Arizona sustained the Superior Court verdict, finding Anderson negligent for any one of several reasons:

- for allowing all arrangements to be handled by a receptionist when the chief pilot was available and under company policy should have handled the arrangements for the flight;
- for insufficient checking of the pilot's currency with Federal Aviation Regulations [FARs] and no check-out of the pilot for night flying;
- for allowing the pilot to take off without filing a flight plan; and
- for failing to notify the pilot of weather conditions over Blythe and that the lights were out on the landing strip.

The judgment of the trial court was affirmed.

SOUTHERN JERSEY AIRWAYS, INC. v. NATIONAL BANK OF SECAUCUS
261 A.2d 399 (N.J. App. 1970)

Does a mechanic's lien constitute a security interest which should be recorded?

The owner of an aircraft handed it over to Southern Jersey Airways for repair. Subsequently, the owner defaulted on his conditional sales agreement with the National Bank of Secaucus, and the latter appointed a bailiff to take possession of the airplane. The bailiff purported to take possession, and posted a notice of public sale. The bailiff sold the plane at public sale, and the bank purchased it as the highest bidder. However, throughout the entire process, the aircraft was physically in the hands of Southern Jersey Airways. They refused to surrender possession, relying upon their statutory mechanic's lien.

The Bank of Secaucus recorded its security agreement with the FAA. Southern Jersey Airways did not record its mechanic's lien until after the bank purported to seize and sell the aircraft (to itself) after default on the loan by the owner. The bank brought suit against Southern Jersey Airways for possession of the aircraft.

Under the Federal Aviation Act of 1958, the FAA maintains a system of both registration of aircraft ownership, and for recordation of conveyances of aircraft and of other security instruments. Recognizing the priority of recorded security interest in the federal system of aircraft registration,[23] and owing to the fact the bank recorded its interests prior to Jersey Airways filing of its mechanic's lien, the Atlantic County Court entered a judgment in favor of the bank.

In the appeal by Southern Jersey Airways, the New Jersey Superior Court, Appellate Division, did not place in question the priority of the federal recordation system. At issue, rather, was whether or not a mechanic's lien constitutes a recordable security interest. New Jersey law[24] granted a possessory lien for sums due for the storage, maintenance, keeping or repair of aircraft, and further stated, "The lien shall be superior to all other liens. . . ."[25] The Uniform Commercial Code, adopted in New Jersey reads, "When a person in the ordinary course of his business furnishes services or materials with respect to *goods subject to a security interest,* a lien upon goods in the possession of such person given by statute or rule of law for such materials or services *takes priority over a perfected security interest* unless the lien is statutory and the statute expressly provides otherwise."[26]

The appellate court was convinced that Congress, in passing the Federal Aviation Act, did not intend necessarily to displace and pre-empt all state law bearing upon priorities of lien and title interests in aircraft. Rather, it was the intent of Congress to substitute, for the multiplicity of state registration or recording systems, a single pre-emptive federal system. Most decisions involving the Federal Aviation Act have carefully delineated federal recording provisions as preemptive and exclusive only in respect of place, requirements of recording, and the effect of failing to record a federally recordable conveyance or instrument. It is erroneous to assume that Congress has preempted the entire field of conveyancing of interests in aircraft.

---

[23] *See* Ch. 7.
[24] N.J.S.A. § 2A:44-1.
[25] N.J.S.A. § 2A:44-2.
[26] N.J.S.A. § 12A:9-310 [emphasis supplied].

The statutory description of recordable rights makes it doubtful that Congress contemplated recordation of a mechanic's lien. A "conveyance" is defined in 49 U.S.C.A., as "a bill of sale, contract of conditional sale, mortgage, assignment of mortgage, or other instrument affecting title to or interest in, property." It is evident that the Federal Aviation Act contemplates a written instrument. Even if a lien were a recordable instrument, in the instant case, recording of the mechanic's lien would have afforded no constructive notice to the bank which had taken its interest previously. Additionally, a search of the record by the bank before its investment would not have discovered a mechanic's lien, even if it had been recorded.

The court concluded that,

- Failure to record the lien did not invalidate it;
- Federal recording of the bank's interest did not afford it priority over Southern Jersey Airway's recording (federal recordation is not a matter of a race to see who can record first); and
- The relative priorities in this case had to be determined according to state law, giving priority to a mechanic's lien.

The judgment was reversed and remanded.

STUBBS AVIATION SERVICE v. HOOK
467 N.E.2d 29 (Ind. App. 1984)

Is a fixed base operator responsible for an aircraft, stored on the FBO's property, when the aircraft owner retains keys to the aircraft?

Stubbs Aviation Service was a fixed base operator providing services from the Speedway Airport, part of the Indianapolis Airport Authority. Ralph Hook owned a Piper Cherokee airplane and had rented a tie-down space from Stubbs for storage of his aircraft. In December of 1979, Hook went to Stubb's office to pay his annual rental fee. He was there told that his airplane had been damaged two or three weeks earlier. In Hook's opinion, and in the opinion of a witness, the damage was caused by a ground vehicle.

The airplane was parked in a space designated by Stubbs, and Stubbs furnished the tie-down equipment. Stubbs possessed a set of keys for the airplane, and he moved it occasionally by using the key and/or by moving it manually. Hook and a friend retained keys to the airplane, and it was not necessary for pilots to check in with Stubb's office before using the airplane.

The trial court concluded Stubbs and Hook had made a bailment contract. Relying on this conclusion, and applying the doctrine of *res ipsa loquitur*, the trial court found Stubbs Aviation liable for the unexplained damage. Because the airport authority determined the location of the tie-down space, and the apportionment of rental fees, it too was held liable. Stubbs Aviation and the Airport Authority appealed arguing,

- *Res ipsa loquitur* was not applicable because the defendants did not control the airplane;
- The contract between Stubbs and Hook was not a bailment because the FBO did not have exclusive possession and control of the airplane;
- The Airport Authority should not have been liable because it did not manage the tie-down facilities; and
- The trial court erred by allowing the *speculative* cause of the damage.

Hook argued that the judgment could have been sustained on any one of three theories: bailment, *res ipsa loquitur*, or contract.

The Indiana Court of Appeals concluded that indeed Stubbs did not have exclusive possession and control, and therefore no bailment was created. In order for a bailment to exist, the bailed property must be delivered into the bailee's exclusive possession and accepted fully by the bailee. There must be such a full transfer, either actual or constructive, of the property to the bailee as to exclude the possession of the owner and all other persons and give to the bailee, for the time being, sole custody and control.

The doctrine of *res ipsa loquitur* is a mechanism for proving breach of a duty, once the duty has been established. Absent a bailment, Stubbs did not have a duty to provide safe storage. Hook did not introduce evidence that he had contracted for safe storage, he merely assumed it.

The judgment was reversed in favor of Stubbs Aviation and the Indianapolis Metropolitan Airport Authority.

CHAPTER 13

AIRPORTS: AND THE PROPRIETARY FUNCTION

Airport-related litigation typically involves one of three issues: land use control, property rights or the airport as a nuisance.

THE AIRPORT SPONSOR

Most airports in the United States are sponsored by governmental entities; that is to say, the traveling public is served through a system of government-owned and operated facilities. As described previously, the functions of government can be classified into three general areas: (1) proprietary services; (2) redistributive activities; and (3) protective services. Since most airports, open to the public, are owned and operated by governmental institutions, the previous chapter as well as this and the two subsequent chapters examine the liability associated with the three general areas of government service provision.

Because governmental services are socially pervasive, all three areas of service provision tend to overlap in related litigation. To give some semblance of order to the case law in this book, the cases have been generally arranged by service area (i.e., proprietary, redistributive, or protective). Cases presented in all three areas are interrelated, but an attempt was made to place them in the *most* related chapter. Nevertheless, and with some exceptions, what becomes clear from the subsequent readings is that the most notable areas for litigation involving airports are airport land use control, property rights, and cases emanating from airports as a nuisance, especially due to airport-related noise and other environmental concerns. The latter (the airport environment) is the overriding concern. Nevertheless, the imposition of airport rates and charges is another area giving rise to challenges from individual airport users and the public at large.

AIRPORT LITIGATION

Litigants have experimented with three principal causes in recovering damages: by claiming nuisance, charging trespass, and/or by inverse condemnation. The most successful method has been the latter, under which litigation is commenced on an allegation of an unconstitutional taking of property without just compensation.[1]

Land use regulatory controls are pursuant to police power—the power to protect the public health, safety, and welfare.[2] While the government may regulate the use of property, if regulation goes too far, it may becomes a "taking." The Fifth Amendment to the United States Constitution states in part, ". . . nor shall private property be taken for public use, without just compensation." Most state constitutions contain similar language.

When the state "takes" private property for public use, the owner must be justly compensated. In contrast, when there is only regulation of the uses of private property (police powers), compensation does not have to be paid, depending upon the intrusiveness of the regulation. Whether or not compensation is due, and how much, and whether there has been an invalid exercise of police power under the due process clause, are normally at the root of most land use cases.

Airport related noise, as a problem, is associated with people living in close proximity to airports. When citizens are subjected to noise in their habitats, they rebel and seek compensation for what they consider to be an intrusion on their peace and quiet. Although the federal government would seem to be the only entity clearly possessing sufficient authority to control airport noise, the liability for injury suffered by those living near airports has been clearly placed by the courts with the airport proprietor. Saddled by the courts with the responsibility for noise nuisance, yet lacking the authority to do much about it short of federal preemption, airports became increasingly more frustrated. With two cases ruled in favor of airport proprietors in 1985, airport sponsors were subsequently granted more authority to manage their noise control problems.

---

[1] *See Greater Westchester Homeowners v. City of Los Angeles,* 160 Cal. Rptr. 733 (1979).

[2] *See Harrell's Candy Kitchen v. Sarasota-Manatee Airport Authority,* 111 So. 2d 439 (1959).

In one case, the Port Authority of New York and New Jersey issued rules prohibiting aircraft, non-compliant with federal noise standards,[3] from using John F. Kennedy International Airport.[4] After receiving a federal exemption from the rules (in FAR Part 36), Arrow Air (an airline flying Douglas DC-8's from New York to Puerto Rico and other U.S. points) sought a temporary restraining order against enforcement of the local rule. The district court judge ruled in favor of the Port Authority on all three of Arrow's major arguments:

- that the carrier's exemption from FAR Part 36 should federally pre-empt locally adopted rules;
- that the Port Authority's rule placed undue burden on interstate commerce; and
- that the Port Authority acted discriminantly and arbitrarily in refusing to exempt Arrow from its rule.

According to the court in *Arrow*, airport proprietors now have significant leeway in formulating policies different from federal policies, provided they do not conflict. The airport's authority had been broadened subsequent to the Aviation Safety and Noise Abatement Act of 1979. In the court's opinion, "Congress has authorized airport proprietors to enact reasonable, non-discriminatory noise regulations. . . . The Port Authority's final rule fully meets these criteria, and any effect on commerce is both incidental and authorized by Congress."

Ecuatoriana Airlines challenged a similar noise rule at Los Angeles International Airport. The airline wanted to serve Los Angeles with a Boeing 707. The U.S. District Court denied Ecuatoriana's request for injunction against the Los Angeles Airport. Here again, the airline argued that the local rules were preempted by federal law. The court rejected the preemption argument, and also arguments that the rules violated treaty agreements and due process.

Even though the Federal Aviation Administration [FAA] had granted exemptions to the airlines, the federal courts in New York and Los Angeles ruled that since the airport is ultimately responsible for local noise suits, the airport must be given the authority to remedy the noise unacceptable to the community. Moreover, the courts ruled that because the federal government has chosen not to accept respon-

---

[3] 14 CFR Part 36, *Noise Standards: Aircraft Type and Airworthiness Certification.*
[4] *See Arrow Air v. Port Authority of New York and New Jersey,* 602 F. Supp. 314 (1985).

sibility for noise suits, and Congress (in the Aviation Safety and Noise Abatement Act of 1979) authorized airport proprietors to enact reasonable, non-discriminatory regulations, "local noise rules adopted by airports and meeting this criteria shall be upheld."

AIRPORT AUTHORITY

There are numerous privately owned airfields in the United States, some of which are open to the public while others are not, but few of these privately owned airports are of major importance in terms of the national air transportation system. Most of the airports in the National Plan of Integrated Airport Systems [NPIAS] are publicly owned and operated. Those privately owned airports that contribute significantly to the national air transportation system are rapidly disappearing.[5]

With few exceptions, public airport administration is structured within one of three standard forms of governmental organization. Most public airports are owned by a county, by a municipality, or by one of the sub-governmental entities known as "authorities" or "special districts." The exceptions to city, county, or special district ownership are the various state-owned airports, particularly in Alaska. At one time, Dulles International and Washington National Airports were also exceptions. They were owned and operated by the federal government, but in 1986, both airports were transferred to a newly organized airport authority for the greater Washington, D.C. metropolitan area.

The point isn't that there are no privately owned airports. In fact, there is a growing proliferation of private airfields. By 2004, there were more than 19,000 landing sites in the U.S. including airports, heliports, seaplane bases and airstrips. However, only about 5,314 of these airports were open to the public.[6] In most cases, privately owned airports are operated for the convenience of the owner, or for the use of a select few, and are not open for use by the general public. Less than 10% of airports open to the public are privately owned.

---

[5] *See* Laurence E. Gesell, *The Administration of Public Airports* (5th ed. 1999).

[6] Of the 19,000 plus facilities, 5,314 were open to the public. Of the airports open to the public, 3,489 are included in the 2001-2005 NPIAS and considered significant to national air transportation. And of the NPIAS airports, 546 are "commercial service airports," defined as "public airports receiving scheduled passenger service and having 2,500 or more enplaned passengers per year." FAA Report to Congress, *National Plan of Integrated Airport Systems 2001-2005*, (Aug. 28, 2002). *See also* Laurence E. Gesell and Paul Stephen Dempsey, *Air Transportation: Foundations for the 21st Century* (2nd ed. 2005).

Authority to operate airports has been deferred to states, and especially to local governments. Cities, counties and special districts derive their authority to operate airports from the state within which they are located. The source of authority given to states, and in turn to local governments to own and operate airports, is constitutionally grounded in the Tenth Amendment. The U.S. Constitution vests all government authority as specifically stated with the federal government. Otherwise, authority rests with the individual states, or with the people. In other words, state and local airports derive their powers through "enabling legislation" created by their individual state legislatures. In the case of state-owned airports, it is through legislation authorizing airport operation directly by the state. For county, city, and joint governmental operations (classified as airport authorities, port authorities, special districts, and so forth) the airport's "authority" is granted by the state through charters of incorporation or other organization of these sub-governmental entities.

PROPRIETARY NATURE OF AIRPORTS

The legal status of a public airport is different than that of a private airport. Privately owned airports are, by definition, private enterprises. Publicly owned airports are proprietary functions of the government. The courts have held that the acquisition, improvement, maintenance, and operation of a government-owned and -operated airport, for use by the general public and for the general benefit of the public, is within the scope of governmental services.[7] Nevertheless, public proprietary functions differ from private enterprise.

Unlike the private sector, public airport sponsors have the authority to acquire property for airport purposes through purchase, lease or through exercise of their power in eminent domain. They may also exercise their police powers to regulate operation of their airports. Promulgation of aviation related rules and regulations designed to protect the public safety, health and welfare have been upheld by the courts as a valid exercise of police power,[8] so long as the local regulations are reasonable and do not conflict with existing state or federal regulations.[9] Local governments may regulate their airports, but may

---

[7] See American Airlines, et al. v. Louisville and Jefferson County Air Board, CCH 6 AVI ¶ 17,587 (1959).

[8] See Stagg v. Municipal Court, 2 Cal App 3d 318 (1969).

[9] See American Airlines, Inc. v. Hempstead, 348 F.2d 369 (1968).

not regulate those aspects of aircraft operation which have been pre-empted by the federal government,[10] nor regulations which unduly burden interstate commerce.[11]

In dealing with a state government or with the federal government on tort issues, the private citizen may confront the doctrine of "sovereign immunity" when bringing suit against the government. In suits against the federal government, the action must be certified under the Federal Tort Claims Act. Such is not necessarily the case where the local government is the airport sponsor, but in the exercise of governmental functions, the airport sponsor may benefit from extension of the state's sovereign immunity. In some instances, the courts have held that the local government in its operation of the airport was acting in a purely "proprietary" capacity (in this instance meaning, "acting as a private enterprise"). In certain aspects of airport operation, the local government possesses all the necessary powers to operate an airport—to obtain or sell property, to regulate the airport, and to charge fees for its use. As proprietors, airports may charge fees to recoup the costs of operation, so long as the fees are reasonable.[12]

PASSENGER FACILITY CHARGES

Although prohibited for many years, the so called "head tax" is now accepted as a reasonable fee in the recovery of airport costs.[13] Until 1990, locally imposed per passenger charges were illegal in the United States, except for a brief period in 1972-1973, following a Supreme Court ruling that had legalized it.[14] In response to the court decision legalizing head taxes, certain airport sponsors rushed to impose related charges, with some collecting the taxes for off-airport, non-aviation related uses.

The Supreme Court ruling allowing the collection of per passenger taxes, with no restrictions placed on where the moneys might be applied, was in direct conflict with federal policy related to expenditures

---

[10] See Burbank v. Lockheed Air Terminal, Inc, 411 U.S. 624 (1973).

[11] See Santa Monica Airport Association v. City of Santa Monica, 481 F. Supp. 927 (1979).

[12] See American Airlines v. Massachusetts Port Authority, 560 F.2d 1036 (1979).

[13] See Laurence E. Gesell, The Administration of Public Airports 281-283 (3rd ed. 1992); See also Robert A. Bunnell, Passenger Facility Charges: Are We Finally Ready?, Airport (Jan./Feb. 1990).

[14] See Evansville-Vanderburgh Airport Authority District. v. Delta Airlines, 405 U.S. 707, 92 S.Ct. 1349, 31 L. Ed. 2d 620 (1972); see also Northeast Airlines, et al. v. New Hampshire Aeronautics Commission, et al., N.H. Supreme Court (Feb. 24, 1972).

from the Aviation Trust Fund. Moreover, federal agencies were strongly opposed to allowing airports to impose their own charges upon passengers who were already contributing to the Aviation Trust Fund by way of taxes collected by the airlines. To more fully understand the policy conflict, it should be realized that airport sponsors who receive Aviation Trust Fund assistance must give assurances to the federal government that all moneys generated at the airport will be returned to the airport, and will not be used for any other (i.e., non-airport) government activity.

The airlines, too, reacted to the court decision with understandable opposition, for fear that excessive taxes might drive consumer demand down. Hence, those opposing the imposition of local head taxes (i.e., federal agencies, the airlines, and consumer advocacy groups) successfully exhorted Congress subsequently into outlawing locally imposed charges.

In 1973, Richard Nixon signed into law the Anti-Head Tax Act, which prohibited the collection of taxes (by local authorities) based upon individual passenger enplanements. Following passage of the Act, President Nixon stated that he would have ". . . favored a moratorium rather than a prohibition on the taxes. . . .," so the issue could be studied more closely. He therefore directed the Secretary of Transportation to conduct a study of the prohibition. In 1974, the FAA completed its study and found that, while funds were needed for airport development, ". . . head taxes may or may not be the most effective way to increase financing." The issue was left open-ended, and consequently, the battle over head taxes continued, with local airports seeking alternative ways to finance airport development.

By 1988, airport proprietors collectively (principally through the then Airport Operators Council International, and the American Association of Airport Executives) declared that it was time once again to raise the issue of local funding. But, on this go-around, the head tax issue was combined with the overriding, critical and national issue of declining airport capacity and increasing delays being experienced in the air traffic and airspace system. Airport sponsors argued that a local funding mechanism was necessary to enhance capacity.

The airport owners' position was reinforced by Secretary of Transportation Samuel Skinner, who sought more local participation in funding the transportation system through user fees. Additionally, one of the central components of Mr. Skinner's national transportation policy for airport financing was a Passenger Facility Charge [PFC]. Sufficient congressional support was obtained, and by a vote of 405 to 15, the Aviation Safety and Capacity Expansion Act, which included PFCs, was passed in 1990. The Aviation Safety and Capacity Expansion Act is part of Title IX of the Omnibus Budget Reconciliation Act of 1990. Section 9110, entitled "Passenger Facility Charges," allows an airport to impose a fee of $1.00, $2.00, or $3.00 per enplaning passenger (at that airport) to help finance Department of Transportation [DOT] approved "airport-related projects." The fees collected (1) may not exceed amounts necessary to finance specified projects; and (2) must be used on eligible airport-related projects; i.e., the fees collected specifically *cannot* be applied to non-airport programs (though the DOT has approved the use of PFCs to build intermodal links to nearby rail and transit facilities). The PFC regulation was substantially amended on May 30, 2000, by the Aviation Investment and Reform Act for the 21st Century [AIR-21], authorizing the local imposition of a $1, $2, $3, $4, or $4.50 charge per enplaned passenger. The Act requires that air carriers collect the locally imposed fee as part of their ticketing of passengers. The airlines then transfer the funds to the airport sponsor. Although now legitimized, Passenger Facility Charges have not been imposed without challenge.[15]

FUNDING OF INTERMODAL PROJECTS[16]

Federal Aviation Regulations provide that airport access projects must preserve or enhance the capacity, safety or security of the national air transportation system, reduce noise, or provide an opportunity for enhanced competition between carriers.[17] Such projects must also be for exclusive use of the airport patrons and employees, be constructed on airport-owned land or rights of way, and be connected to the nearest public access of sufficient capacity.[18] The FAA insisted that AIP funds be limited to landside expenditures, "which encompasses the area from the airport boundary where the general public enters the airport property to the point where the public leaves the terminal building to board the aircraft. Typical eligible landside de-

---

[15] See *Northwest Airlines v. Federal Aviation Administration*, CCH 24 AVI 17,901 (1994).
[16] Portions of this section are derived from Paul Dempsey, *The Law of Intermodal Transportation: What It Was, What It Is, What It Should Be*, 27 Trans. L. J. 367 (2000).
[17] 14 C.F.R. Part 158.
[18] FAA Order 5100.3A, Para. 553(a), AIP Handbook (Oct. 24, 1989).

velopment items include such things as terminal buildings, entrance roadways and pedestrian walkways."[19] As we shall see, more recent interpretations by the FAA have liberalized this rather constricted view of the types of landside projects, which are appropriate for federal airport funding.

In 1996, the FAA approved the request of the Port Authority of New York and New Jersey to use PFC funds to extend Newark Airport's light-rail line 4,400 feet to an Amtrak/New Jersey Transit station off airport grounds.[20] Among the largest intermodal projects approved by the FAA for PFC funding was in 1998 for a $1.5 billion rail line linking New York's John F. Kennedy International Airport with the Long Island Rail Road and the E, J and Z subway lines to Manhattan at Jamaica Station, and to Howard Beach.[21] The FAA concluded PFC expenditures on the JFK rail link would satisfy the statutory and regulatory requirements by alleviating ground congestion on airport roadways and terminal frontages, by enhancing the efficient movement of airport employees, by freeing up capacity on the roadways for additional passengers, and by improving the airport's connection to the regional transportation network. It found, "Where ground access is shown to be a limiting factor to an airport's growth, a project to enhance ground access may qualify as preserving or enhancing capacity of the national air transportation system."[22] The FAA found the rail line would enable an additional 3.35 million passengers to use JFK annually by the year 2013, and "therefore must be construed to have a substantial capacity enhancement effect on JFK, as measured in air passengers accommodated by the airport."[23] The FAA concluded the rail link would "serve to preserve or enhance the capacity of JFK and the national air transportation system . . . ."[24] The $3 per ticket Passenger Facility Charge would generate about

---

[19] Quoted in U.S. DOT, *Intermodal Ground Access to Airports: A Planning Guide* 16, 202 (Dec. 1996).

[20] *Stalled Train to Kennedy Airport*, N.Y. Times, Jan. 30, 1998, at A20. Letter from FAA Associate Administrator Susan Kurland to Port Authority Ex. Dir. George Marlin (Nov. 6, 1996).

[21] The Port Authority of New York and New Jersey alleged that the line would create "a more efficient vehicular flow at the airport by removing buses, shuttle vans, and private autos currently used by air passengers, airport visitors, and airport employees at JFK . . . ", and that without the line, "ground access congestion would constrain projected O&D passenger growth at JFK and adversely affect the national air transportation system." Letter from FAA Associate Administrator Susan Kurland to Port Authority Ex. Dir. Robert Boyle of Feb. 9, 1998, at 20.

[22] *Id.* at 21.

[23] *Id.* at 24.

[24] *Id.*

$45-50 million a year, enabling the airport to pay off the cost of the line in 20 years.[25]

Rail lines at Atlanta, Chicago, Cleveland and Washington, D.C., have been financed by transit systems rather than airports. The Intermodal Surface Transportation Act [ISTEA] included a special appropriation for extension of the Bay Area Rapid Transit System [BART] to San Francisco International Airport [SFO]. The Federal Transit Administration committed $750 million, or about 64% to the $1.2 billion project. The remaining $417 will come from state and local funding sources.[26] The FAA approved airport funding for construction of a BART station at SFO.[27] The 8.7-mile extension, the largest since BART was built in the early 1970s, will have four stations. About 68,000 riders a day were expected to use the line when it opened in 2001.[28] The Federal Transit Administration has also committed to contributing 72% of the construction costs of the $399 million extension of the St. Louis Metrolink to Mid-America Airport in St. Clair County, Illinois. This light rail system already connects to St. Louis Lambert International Airport.[29]

REGULATORY FEES

Along with reasonable charges to recoup costs incurred in the operation of an airport, airport sponsors may also charge fees as a (governmental) regulatory function. Such charges might even include the imposition of fees intended to divert traffic to another airport.[30] Where proprietary regulations have been unreasonable or discriminatory, or especially where they have conflicted with (i.e., preempted) state or federal regulatory schemes, they have been held invalid. An example was the attempt in the mid-1980s to divert, or to otherwise discourage general aviation operations, including those by commuter

---

[25] Matthew Wald, *U.S. Approves Plan for Rail Link to Kennedy Airport*, N.Y. Times, Feb. 19, 1998.

[26] U.S. General Accounting Office, *Surface Infrastructure: Costs, Financing and Schedules for Large-Dollar Transportation Projects* 18 (Feb. 1998).

[27] Letter from FAA Associate Administrator Susan Kurland to SFO Airport Dir. John Martin (Oct. 18, 1996).

[28] Benjamin Pimentel, *BART's 4-Year Trip to SFO Starts Today*, San Francisco Examiner, Nov. 3, 1997, at 1.

[29] U.S. General Accounting Office, *Surface Infrastructure: Costs, Financing and Schedules for Large-Dollar Transportation Projects* 40 (Feb. 1998).

[30] *See Aircraft Owners and Pilots Association v. Port Authority of New York and New Jersey*, 305 F Supp. 93 (1969).

carriers, from using Boston Logan International Airport. Motivated by a desire to relieve congestion and improve efficiency at Logan, the Massachusetts Port Authority [MASSPORT] proposed implementation of its Program for Airport Capacity Efficiency [PACE] which would have dramatically increased landing fees. Three lawsuits, combined in a class action to challenge PACE, were brought by the National Business Aircraft Association [NBAA], the Aircraft Owners and Pilots Association [AOPA], and by the New England Legal Foundation with the Regional Airline Association. A federal district court judge upheld the fee increases as reasonable and non-discriminatory, and not preempted by federal law. Still, he questioned why the general aviation fee increase was so dramatic—between 250% to 300%.

Subsequent to the ruling in the District Court, a DOT Administrative Law Judge [ALJ] rendered his preliminary decision in the DOT's investigation of the MASSPORT fees. The ALJ's ruling stated the PACE proposal violated grant assurances pursuant to Section 511 of the Airport and Airway Improvement Act of 1982. The fees were not "fair and reasonable." The proposal was "discriminatory" under Section 511. It violated the Anti-Head Tax Act,[31] because it was not "reasonable." It "invaded" the authority of the DOT in violation of Section 307 of the Federal Aviation Act. The proposal was contrary to the prohibitions set forth in Section 105 of the Federal Aviation Act. It was preempted by federal law and thus unlawful. And, the fee structure violated the Commerce Clause of the U.S. Constitution.

The class action suit was finally settled in 1991, following a court decision in 1988, which ultimately found the higher fees to be unlawful. Under the settlement, those who paid excess fees were refunded the difference, plus one year's interest, minus fees and expenses. The settlement cost MASSPORT an estimated $2.68 million, plus interest.

In the majority view, courts have not regarded state laws as granting governmental immunity in the operation of public airports. Generally, airports are considered to be proprietary, with the same status as a similarly situated private enterprise. In these situations, the government sponsors have been held liable for torts as if they were private entities. An exception is where states have expressly granted tort immunity for local government operation of an airport.[32] In most in-

---

[31] 49 U.S.C. § 1513.
[32] *See Scotti v. Birmingham*, 337 So. 2d 350 (1967).

stances the local government's liability for torts arising from airport operation is the same as that of a private person. The general rule is that municipalities are immune from suit in the exercise of their governmental functions, but are not immune for their proprietary, or businesslike, activities.

LOCAL AIRPORT REGULATION[33]

Local governments, and airport proprietors, on occasion have attempted to regulate airport operations or airport development. These efforts have been inspired by local political opposition to airports, and in some instances by a desire to avoid nuisance and inverse condemnation litigation. They have been met with varying levels of success depending upon what is regulated, how it is regulated, and who is regulating it. A review of the cases reveals four major categories of activities for which local regulation has been attempted: (1) prohibition of new airline service; (2) regulation of air space; (3) noise regulation; and (4) land use restrictions.

PROHIBITION OF NEW AIRLINE SERVICE

When Dallas/Ft. Worth Airport [DFW] was contemplated in 1968, the cities of Dallas and Ft. Worth passed ordinances requiring a phase-out of the existing regional airports, including Love Field. Litigation seeking to extricate Southwest Airlines from Love and force it to fly out of DFW failed, with the court ruling that Southwest had "a federally declared right to the continued use of and access to Love Field, so long as Love Field remains open."[34]

In 1980, Congress passed the Wright Amendment,[35] restricting large jet service at Love to points in Texas and its adjacent states (New Mexico, Oklahoma, Arkansas and Louisiana). In 1997, Congress passed the Shelby Amendment,[36] which authorized large jet service from Love to three additional states (Kansas, Mississippi, and

---

[33] Portions of this section are derived from Paul Dempsey, *Local Airport Regulation: The Constitutional Tension Between Police Power, Preemption & Takings*, 11 Penn State Environmental L. Rev. 1 (2002).

[34] *Southwest Airlines Co. v. Texas Int'l Airlines, Inc.*, 546 F.2d 84, 103 (5tth Cir. 1977).

[35] Pub. L. 96-192, 29 Stat. 35 (1980).

[36] Pub. L. 105-66, 111 Stat. 1447 (1997).

Alabama), and authorized service to states beyond in aircraft having fewer than 57 seats.

In the late 1990s, the city of Ft. Worth brought suit to enforce the 1968 ordinance against Legend Airlines, a new entrant seeking to take advantage of the Shelby Amendment and inaugurate 56-seat jet service out of Love Field. The DOT issued a Declaratory Order holding that Ft. Worth could not enforce the ordinance, holding "the City of Ft. Worth may not enforce any commitment by the City of Dallas . . . to limit operations at Love Field, and the proprietary powers of the City of Dallas do not allow it to restrict services at Love Field authorized by federal law."[37]

Reviewing the DOT Order, in *American Airlines v. Department of Transportation,*[38] the Fifth Circuit U.S. Court of Appeals concluded that the Ordinance operated as limitations "relating to . . . routes" within the preemption provisions of the Airline Deregulation Act.[39] Nonetheless, since the city of Dallas owned and operated Love Field, the question was whether the Ordinance fell under the proprietary powers exception. The court noted that the scope of an owner's proprietary powers exemption had never been clearly articulated by the courts. It then set about to try to specify some perimeters for the exemption. The court noted that "local proprietors play an 'extremely limited role' in the regulation of aviation."[40] It noted that federal courts consistently have held "that an airport proprietor can use only 'reasonable, nonarbitrary, and nondiscriminatory rules that advance the local interest.'"[41] In each case where proprietary efforts to regulate such issues (such as noise or congestion) has been upheld, "the proposed restriction was targeted at alleviating an existing problem at the airport or in the surrounding neighborhood."[42]

Fort Worth argued that the prohibition on new service at Love Field was necessary in order to allocate traffic between that airport and DFW, so as to preserve the short haul nature of Love. The court

---

[37] Robert Gibreath and Paul Watler, *Perimeter Rules, Proprietary Powers, and the Airline Deregulation Act: A Tale of Two Cities,* 66 J. Air L. & Com. 223 (2000).

[38] 202 F.3d 788 (5th Cir. 2000).

[39] Robert Gibreath a Paul Watler, *Perimeter Rules, Proprietary Powers, and the Airline Deregulation Act: A Tale of Two Cities,* 66 J. Air L. & Com. 223 (2000).

[40] 202 F.3d at 806 (quoting *British Airways Bd. v. Port Authority,* 654 F.2d 1002, 1010 (2nd Cir. 1977).

[41] 202 F.3rd at 806 (quoting *National Helicopter Corp. v. City of New York,* 953 F. Supp. 1011 (D.N.Y. 1997)).

[42] 202 F.3d at 806.

observed that this was a novel rationale, one not theretofore embraced by any court as within the proprietary exemption. The court noted that it did "not limit the scope of proprietary rights to those which have been previously recognized," and that other non-discriminatory rules which advance a previously unrecognized local interest might qualify under the exemption.[43] But this one did not. The court concluded that Ft. Worth failed to offer "a viable alternative justification for the route limitations that might support extending the recognized scope of a proprietor's power" under the statutory exemption because it would extend that exemption beyond its "intended limited reach."[44] Not only was the Ordinance preempted, but contractual use agreements concluded by the cities and airlines that attempted to restrict service at Love were held preempted as well.[45]

Only in one case—and in a state court decision—was the right of the airport proprietor to prohibit commercial service at a regional airport upheld. In *Arapahoe County Airport v. Centennial Express Airlines*,[46] the Colorado Supreme Court upheld a municipal proprietor's ban on all commercial service at Centennial Airport, which theretofore had been used exclusively for private aircraft. The county proprietor proffered no rationale to support its restriction other than that failing to uphold its discretion would strip the Authority "of its ability and authority to manage the airport."[47] The Colorado court said, "the power to control an airport's size exists at the core of the proprietor's function and is especially strong where, as here, the prohibited use has never been allowed, or even contemplated."[48] The FAA responded by cutting all federal funds to Centennial Airport.[49]

The Fifth Circuit in *American Airlines* took a swing at the Colorado Supreme Court:

> *To the extent that Arapahoe holds that it is within an airport owner's proprietary powers to restrict service at a local airport without*

---

[43] 202 F.3d at 808.
[44] *Id.*
[45] 202 F.3d at 810-11.
[46] 959 P.2d 587 (Colo. 1998).
[47] 959 P.2d at 590.
[48] 956 P.2d at 595.
[49] "Airport proprietors who exceed their regulatory authority risk having federal funds withheld by the Federal Aviation Administration." *Alaska Airlines v. City of Long Beach*, 951 F.2d 977 (9th Cir. 1989).

articulating a viable purpose for the restriction, we view that case as deviating from the generally accepted rule that we adopt here. . . . We fear that under the rationale of Arapahoe, virtually any regional regulation enacted by a proprietor would fall within the proprietary powers exception. This would expand the regulatory role of municipal owners far beyond the 'extremely limited role' envisioned by the ADA.[50]

REGULATION OF AIRSPACE

In *United States v. City of New Haven*,[51] the Second Circuit U.S. Court of Appeals struck down the efforts of the town of East Haven to use the Connecticut courts to enjoin use by the city of New Haven to use a newly constructed runway at Tweed New Haven Airport whose flight approach was over East Haven. East Haven argued that the runway had been built in violation of state law. The court held that "state legislation purporting to deny access to navigable airspace would therefore constitute a forbidden exercise of the power which the federal government has asserted."[52] Also preempted were efforts by the Village of Cedarhurst to regulate flights at New York City's airports. Arguing that the aircraft constituted a public nuisance and were trespassing over public property, the Village attempted to prohibit flights at less than 1,000 feet in altitude. The court concluded that there was a "sufficient question of the validity of the Cedarhurst ordinance as against the supremacy of national power so that we are in no way justified in now declaring it valid."[53]

Similarly, efforts by the Town of Hempstead in its Unnecessary Noise Ordinance to regulate noise at New York John F. Kennedy International Airport were held preempted. The effect of the Ordinance was to prohibit aircraft from flying over the town and to significantly

---

[50] 202 F. 3d at 807.

[51] 496 F.2d 452 (2nd Cir. 1973).

[52] 496 F.2d at 454.

[53] *All American Airways v. Village of Cedarhurst*, 201 F.2d 273 (2nd Cir. 1953); *Allegheny Airlines v. Village of Cedarhurst*, 238 F.2d 812 (2nd Cir. 1956).

restrict their take-off and landing patterns.[54] It is now settled law that state and local governments are precluded from regulating aircraft in flight, as airspace allocation and use falls within the exclusive province of the federal government.[55]

NOISE REGULATION

To minimize legal liability and political discomfort, numerous local airports have taken action to reduce aircraft noise or mitigate its effects, including access or use regulations or restrictions.[56] However, local governments have been preempted from exercising their police powers to promulgate noise abatement requirements which affect aircraft flight patterns, or to impose curfews on unwilling airport proprietors.[57] Certain local governments and airport proprietors have imposed curfews on airport operations in attempt to eliminate aircraft noise during the night. Efforts by local governments that do not own and operate their airports to regulate noise have fared poorly.[58] The seminal case is *City of Burbank v. Lockheed Air Terminal.*[59]

In *Burbank,* the U.S. Supreme Court struck down a city ordinance placing an 11:00 p.m. to 7:00 a.m. curfew on flights from Hollywood-Burbank Airport as implicitly preempted by federal law. The City of Burbank did not own or operate the airport, but was merely a municipality imposing regulations. Writing for the court, Justice Douglas quoted from the legislative history of the Noise Control Act of 1972: "States and local governments are preempted from establishing or enforcing noise emission standards unless such standards are identical to standards prescribed in the bill."[60] Said Douglas, "If we were to uphold the Burbank ordinance and a significant number of munici-

---

[54] *American Airlines v. Town of Hempstead,* 272 F. Supp. 226 (E.D.N.Y. 1967), aff'd 398 F.2d 369 (2nd Cir. 1968), *cert. den.* 393 U.S. 1017 (1969).

[55] J. Scott Hamilton, *Allocation of Airspace ss a Scarce National Resource,* 22 Transp. L.J. 251, 261 (1994). Numerous courts have accepted the proposition that the federal government has preempted the area of flight control regulation to eliminate or reduce noise. *See San Diego Unified Port District v. Gianturco,* 651 F.2d 1306, 1315 n. 22 (9th Cir. 1981), and cases cited therein.

[56] James Gesualdi, *Gonna Fly Now: All the Noise About the Airport Access Problem,* 16 Hofstra L. Rev. 213, 221 (1987).

[57] *Id.*

[58] *See e.g., San Diego Unified Port District v. Gianturco,* 651 F.2d 1306 (9th Cir. 1981).

[59] 411 U.S. 624 (1973). *See* Mary Jo Soenksen, *Airports: Full of Sound and Fury and Conflicting Legal Views,* 12 Transp. L. J. 325 (1982).

[60] 411 U.S. at 634 (quoting from the Senate committee report).

palities followed suit, it is obvious that fractionalized control of the timing of takeoffs and landings would severely limit the flexibility of FAA in controlling air traffic flow. The difficulties in scheduling flights to avoid congestion and the concomitant decrease in safety would be compounded."[61] FAA's need to balance safety and efficiency in air transportation required a "uniform and exclusive" system of federal regulation.[62]

But in a footnote, Douglas drew a distinction between a city that owns an airport, vis-à-vis a city that does not, saying, "we are concerned here not with an ordinance imposed by the City of Burbank as 'proprietor' of the airport, but with the exercise of police power. . . . Thus authority that a municipality may have as a landlord is not necessarily congruent with its police power. We do not consider here what limits, if any, apply to a municipality as a proprietor."[63]

In dissent, Justice Rehnquist emphasized what the majority had not held:

> *A local governing body that owns and operates an airport is certainly not, by the Court's opinion, prohibited from closing down its facilities. A local governing body could likewise use its traditional police power to prevent the establishment of a new airport or the expansion of an existing one within its territorial jurisdiction by declining to grant the necessary zoning for such a facility.*[64]

---

[61] 411 U.S. at 639. However, *Burbank* was a 5-to-4 decision. Writing the dissent for four Justices, Justice Rehnquist quoted from the House committee report, which said, "The authority of State and local government to regulate use, operation, or movement of products is not affected at all by the bill." 411 U.S. at 641. According to Rehnquist, "Because noise regulation has traditionally been an area of local, not national, concern, in determining whether congressional legislation has, by implication, foreclosed remedial local enactments 'we start with the assumption that the historic police powers of the States were not to be superseded by the Federal Act unless that was the clear and manifest purpose of Congress.'" 411 U.S. at 643 (citing *Rice v. Santa Fe Elevator Corp.*, 331 U.S. 218, 230 (1947)). Rehnquist argued that because noise regulation traditionally has been a matter of local concern, federal statutes should not supersede the exercise of local police power unless Congress expressed a "clear and manifest" intent to do so. He noted that the "control of noise, sufficiently loud to be classified as a public nuisance at common law, would be a type of regulation well within the traditional scope of police power possessed by states and local governing bodies." 411 U.S. at 643.

[62] 411 U.S. at 638.

[63] 411 U.S. at 635 n.14.

[64] 411 U.S. at 653.

Because, under *Burbank*, airport proprietors or operators bear liability for excessive airport noise, they have been given special leeway in controlling the sources of airport noise. Before a municipality may abate airport noise, it must be exposed to potential or actual liability for excessive airport noise.[65] Numerous efforts of non-proprietor municipalities have been preempted, including:

- The City of Audubon Park attempted to regulate noise at Louisville's airport;[66]
- The Town of Gardiner sought to regulate parachute jumping, flight paths, and attendant aircraft noise;[67]
- The City of Blue Ash attempted to prescribe flight patterns;[68]
- The City of Clearwater tried to impose flight curfews;[69] and
- Tinicum Township sought to regulate noise at privately owned Van Zant Airport.[70]

Though airport proprietors may regulate use of the airports they control, efforts by local municipalities to regulate the flight of aircraft have been struck down as preempted by federal law. However, local governmental noise abatement plans that do not restrict operations have been upheld.[71] In *British Airways Board v. Port Authority of New York and New Jersey*,[72] the U.S. Court of Appeals for the Second Circuit, in concluding local restrictions on the flight of the supersonic Concorde aircraft were unlawful, summarized the dividing lines between federal and local jurisdiction in this area:

---

[65] *United States v. State of New York,* 552 F. Supp. 255, 263 (N.D.N.Y. 1982) ("The threat of commercial ruin from large, adverse monetary judgments [underlies] the 'fairness' rationale for the proprietor exemption. . . ." *Id.* at 264.)

[66] *American Airlines v. City of Audubon Park,* 297 F. Supp. 207 (W.D. Ky. 1968), aff'd 407 F.2d 1306 (6th Cir.), *cert. den.* 396 U.S. 845 (1969).

[67] *Blue Sky Entertainment v. Town of Gardiner,* 711 F. Supp. 678 (N.D.N.Y. 1989), *aff'd* 621 F.2d 277. However, the court found the following requirements of the town ordinance were not preempted: (1) a requirement that operators have a license; (2) the effort of the Town to hold the airport in violation of the ordinance if they fail to follow state or county law; (3) efforts to regulate land use; and (3) provisions of the ordinance seeking to impose penalties or revocation or suspension of the license if the law were violated.

[68] *United States v. City of Blue Ash,* 487 F. Supp. 135 (S.D. Ohio 1978).

[69] *Pirolo v. City of Clearwater,* 711 F.2d 1006 (11th Cir. 1983).

[70] *Country Aviation, Inc. v. Tinicum Township,* 1992 U.S. Dist. Lexis, 19803, 1992 WL 396782 (E.D. Pa. 1992), aff'd 9 F.3d 1539 (3rd Cir. 1993).

[71] *San Diego Unified Port Dist. v. Gianturco,* 651 F.2d 1306 (9th Cir. 1981); *City of Tipp City v. City of Dayton,* 204 F.R.D. 388, 2001 U.S. Dist. Lexis 23016 (S.D. Ohio 2001).

[72] 564 F.2d 1002 (2nd Cir. 1977).

Common sense . . . required that exclusive control of airspace allocation be concentrated at the national level, and communities were therefore preempted from attempting to regulate planes in flight. The task of protecting the local population from airport noise, however, has fallen to the agency, usually of local government, that owns and operates the airfield. It seemed fair to assume that the proprietor's intimate knowledge of local conditions, as well as his ability to acquire property and air easements and assure compatible land use, would result in a rational weighing of the costs and benefits of proposed service. Congress has consistently reaffirmed its commitment to this two-tiered scheme, and both the Supreme Court and the executive branch have recognized the important role of the airport proprietor in developing noise abatement programs consonant with local conditions.

The maintenance of a fair and efficient system of air commerce, of course, mandates that each airport operator be circumscribed to the issuance of reasonable, nonarbitrary and nondiscriminatory rules defining the permissible level of noise which can be created by aircraft using the airport. We must scrutinize all exercises of local power under this rubric to insure that impermissible parochial considerations do not unconstitutionally burden interstate commerce or inhibit the accomplishment of legitimate national goals. And, of course, our task [includes] monitoring the proprietor's observance of the strict statutory obligation to make his facility available for public use on fair and reasonable terms, and without unjust discrimination. . . .[73]

---

[73] 564 F.2d at 1010-1011 (citations and footnotes omitted). The court found that the Port Authority had failed to promulgate reasonable, nonarbitrary and nondiscriminatory noise regu-

Thus, though local governments have fared poorly in their attempts to regulate airport noise, airport proprietors have fared much better. The exposure of airport proprietors to trespass, nuisance and inverse condemnation legislation forces them to attempt to reduce negative environmental impacts. As a consequence, it is generally accepted that airport proprietors may exercise their proprietary powers to control noise by promulgating noise abatement and curfew regulations, provided that such regulations are fair, reasonable, and non-discriminatory, and do not unduly affect the free flow of interstate commerce.[74] For example, some airports impose flight curfews (prohibiting takeoffs and landings during certain late evening hours), prohibit the landing of Stage 2 aircraft, or establish perimeter rules prohibiting nonstop flights beyond a specified radius.[75]

For example, the City of Long Beach, which owned and operated Long Beach Municipal Airport, adopted a noise control ordinance that limited airlines to 15 flights per day and required the use of quieter equipment. In *Alaska Airlines v. City of Long* Beach,[76] the Ninth Circuit U.S. Court of Appeals held the ordinance was not preempted, and that the proprietor should be permitted "to enact noise ordinances under the municipal-proprietor exemption if it has a rational belief that the ordinance will reduce the possibility of liability or enhance the quality of a City's human environment."[77] The ordinance was also challenged on grounds that it impermissibly burdened interstate commerce. The court held that the ordinance could have been struck down on Commerce Clause grounds if its purpose was "to disfavor interstate commerce or its benefits were illusory or insignificant, but neither is the case."[78] Nor was the ordinance found to be arbitrary, capricious, or unrelated to a legitimate governmental purpose.[79] The

---

lations at Kennedy International Airport expeditiously. *See also United States v. State of New York,* 552 F. Supp. 255 (N.D.N.Y. 1982), which found a proprietor's curfew "overbroad, unreasonable, and arbitrary." *Id.* at 264.

[74] *City of Burbank v. Lockheed Air Terminal,* 411 U.S. 624 (1973). *See also National Aviation v. City of Hayward,* 418 F. Supp. 417 (N.D. Cal. 1976) (city airport proprietor prohibition of night operation of aircraft at noise above a specified level deemed only an incidental burden on interstate commerce); *Arrow Air, Inc. v. Port Authority,* 602 F. Supp. 314 (S.D.N.Y. 1985) (airport proprietors may establish "fair, even-handed and nondiscriminatory regulations" to limit noise).

[75] *See e.g., Western Air Lines v. Port Authority,* 817 F.2d 222 (2d Cir. 1987).

[76] 951 F.2d 977 (9th Cir. 1992).

[77] 951 F.2d at 982 (quoting *Santa Monica Airport Ass'n, v. City of Santa Monica,* 659 F.2d 100, 104 (9th Cir. 1981).

[78] 951 F.2d at 984.

[79] *Id.*

court found that "the goal of reducing airport noise to control liability and improve the aesthetics of the environment is a legitimate and permissible one."[80]

Similarly, in *Santa Monica Airport Association v. City of Santa Monica*,[81] the Ninth Circuit upheld several city ordinances imposed on a city-owned and -operated airport, including night curfews on takeoffs and landings, prohibitions on low aircraft approaches on weekends, prohibited helicopter flight training, and maximum noise levels of 100 dB; however, it struck down a prohibition against jets and a fine for jet operations on grounds that they would constitute an unreasonable burden on interstate commerce.[82] The court held that "the power of a municipal proprietor to regulate the use of its airport is not preempted by federal legislation. . . . Congress intended that municipal proprietors enact reasonable regulations to establish acceptable noise levels for airfields and their environs."[83]

Among the categories of restrictions designed to reduce noise by airport proprietors that have been upheld as not preempted under federal law are:

- Reasonable and nondiscriminatory noise control regulations;[84]
- Restrictions on the type of air service and type of aircraft serving the airport;[85]
- Limitations on the cumulative level of noise exposure at the airport;[86]
- Aircraft takeoff and landing fees as a means of controlling airport growth;[87] and
- Airport perimeter rules (restricting flights beyond a specified radius) designed to divert traffic to another regional airport, at least when imposed by a multi-airport authority.[88]

---

[80] *Id.*

[81] 659 F.2d 100 (9th Cir. 1981).

[82] 659 F.2d at 102. Donald Harper, *Regulation of Airport Noise at Major Airports: Past, Present & Future,* 17 Transp. L. J. 117, 135 (1988).

[83] "Congress intended to allow a municipality flexibility in fashioning its noise regulations." 659 F.2d at 104-05.

[84] *Santa Monica Airport Ass'n v. City of Santa Monica,* 481 F. Supp. 927 (C.D. Cal. 1979), aff'd 659 F.2d 100 (9th Cir. 1981).

[85] *Burbank Air Transport Ass'n v. Crotti,* 389 F. Supp. 58 (N.D. Cal. 1975).

[86] *Global Int'l Airways Corp. v. Port. Auth. of N.Y. & N.J.,* 727 F.2nd 246 (2d Cir. 1984).

[87] *Aircraft Owners & Pilot's Ass'n v. Port Auth of N.Y.,* 305 F. Supp. 93 (E.D.N.Y. 1969).

However, "overbroad, unreasonable and arbitrary" regulations may be struck down by the courts as imposing an unreasonable burden on interstate commerce.[88] The likelihood of running afoul of the Commerce Clause, as well as the Airline Deregulation Act's explicit preemption provision, is heightened when the airport restrictions fall upon commercial airlines, as opposed to general aviation aircraft.[90] Moreover, the courts have emphasized that noise restrictions must be fair, reasonable and nondiscriminatory, and intended to serve a legitimate public purpose.[91]

LAND USE REGULATION

Nearly every state has passed laws conferring authority to local governments to promulgate special airport zoning regulations and prohibit incompatible land uses.[92] Typically, zoning challenges fall into seven categories: (1) challenges by landowners of ordinances that designate "airport hazard areas" wherein development inconsistent

---

[88] Jonathan Cross, *Airport Perimeter Rules: An Exception to Federal Preemption,* 17 Trans. L. J. 101 (1988). However, perimeter rules imposed by a single airport not a part of a multi-airport system stand on shakier legal ground. *Id.* at 110.

"Proprietary restrictions which have been upheld by the courts include: a night curfew on all aircraft takeoffs and landings, a prohibition against low approaches and 'touch and go' landings on weekends, a prohibition against helicopter training flights, and the establishment and enforcement of maximum single event noise exposure levels against aircraft using the airport." J. Scott Hamilton, *Allocation of Airspace As a Scarce National Resource,* 22 Transp. L. J. 251, 265 (1994). Among the types of regulations imposed by airport proprietors, with some success, have been: "setting noise standards, both overall standards and those that apply to individual flight operations; banning or limiting flights at certain hours; regulating ground operations to reduce the amount of noise produced; banning or limiting training flights by aircraft operators; barring certain aircraft from using an airport; limiting growth in the total number of flights by a specific operator and/or requiring that an increase be accomplished only with a certain kind of aircraft; banning certain noisy aircraft entirely; requiring new airlines serving an airport to meet certain noise standards; and requiring gradual phase out of noise aircraft." Donald Harper, *Regulation of Airport Noise at Major Airports: Past, Present & Future,* 17 Transp. L. J. 117, 139 (1988).

[89] *See e.g., United States v. New York,* 552 F. Supp. 255 (N.D.N.Y. 1982), aff'd 708 F.2d 92 (2d Cir. 1983), *cert. denied* 466 U.S. 936 (1984) (curfew banning all flights from 11:00 p.m. to 7:00 a.m. held overbroad because it banned "all aircraft regardless of the degree of accompanying emitted noise"); *United States v. County of Westchester,* 571 F. Supp. 786 (S.D.N.Y. 1983) (similar curfew preempted as "unreasonable, arbitrary, discriminatory and overbroad").

[90] Donald Harper, *Regulation of Airport Noise at Major Airports: Past, Present & Future,* 17 Transp. L.J. 117, 135 (1988).

[91] James Gesualdi, *Gonna Fly Now: All the Noise about the Airport Access Problem,* 16 Hofstra L. Rev. 213, 256 (1987).

[92] Luis Zambrano, *Balancing the Rights of Landowners With the Needs of Airports: The Continuing Battle Over Noise,* 66 J. Air L. & Com. 445, 468 (2000).

with the hazard designation is prohibited; (2) allegations by landowners that the ordinances violate Equal Protection guaranteed by the U.S. and State Constitutions; (3) allegations that ordinances constitute a taking without just compensation and therefore violate the Due Process protections of the U.S. and State Constitutions; (4) challenges by landowners of ordinances that prohibit them from developing private airports or helipads; (5) allegations that non-conforming uses existing prior to the ordinance should be "grandfathered" in; (6) challenges by landowners that the zoning ordinances conflict with coordinated planning processes, such as the airport development plan or the state or metropolitan regional master plan; and (7) allegations that the ordinances are preempted by federal control of air transportation.[93]

Zoning is an area that appears relatively, though not totally, free from the federal preemption problems local governments face in other air transportation contexts. Though the federal government has preempted navigable airspace, state and local governments retain substantial control over land use.[94] The decision of where airports or aircraft operations will be located remains a particularly local decision.[95] Local governments retain significant authority over land use; the right not to have an airport in the first instance is a local decision.[96]

Generally speaking, local governments may regulate the land use around an airport so long as such zoning ordinance constitutes a reasonable and legitimate exercise of local police powers. The ordinance must (1) substantially relate to public health, safety, and general welfare; and (2) must be supported by a public interest sufficient for the

---

[93] Luis Zambrano, *Balancing the Rights of Landowners with the Needs of Airports: The Continuing Battle over Noise*, 66 J. Air L. & Com. 445, 470-471 (2000).

[94] *Wood v. City of Huntsville*, 384 So. 2d 1081 (Ala. 1980). "[T]here is a distinction between the regulation of the navigable airspace and the regulation of ground space to be used for aircraft landing sites. Although the regulation of the airspace of the United States has been preempted by Congress. . . ." the regulation of the location aircraft landing sites is not. *Gustafson v. City of Lake Angelus*, 76 F.3d 778 (6th cir. 1996). "Gustafson suggests that local governing bodies have exclusive control over air transportation up until the moment that the plane lifts off of the ground and enters airspace. . . . Gustafson seems to indicate that although local planning bodies can regulate every aspect of land development, the same governing bodies must stop regulating the moment a plane enters airspace, although the noise continues to impact the land." Luis Zambrano, *Balancing the Rights of Landowners With the Needs of Airports: The Continuing Battle Over Noise*, 66 J. Air L. & Com. 445, 464 (2000).

[95] *Bethman v. City of Ukian*, 216 Cal. App. 3d 1395 (1989).

[96] *Wright v. County of Winnebago*, 73 Ill. App. 3d at 344 (1979).

reasonable imposition of restrictions on surrounding land without having to compensate the property owner for loss of value.[97]

Local governments may exercise their police, land use and zoning powers to regulate the location, height and size of structures (for example, to prohibit the erection of a skyscraper at the end of a runway), so long as the regulation is imposed for a health or safety purpose unrelated to the regulation of noise or the use of navigable airspace.[98] Reasonable zoning ordinances that merely regulate or restrict airport location[99] or ground operations, or assure compatible land uses within the vicinity of the airport, have been deemed not federally preempted and within the police power of the government as appropriately related to health, safety or general welfare goals.[100] For example, owners of private landing strips seeking to create private airports have failed in their attempt to secure federal preemption of zoning prohibitions.[101] Paradoxically, without zoning, land around the airport perimeter may become high-density development because the land is not suitable from a market perspective for low-density use. For example, airport zoning may restrict land use so as to limit the height of structures in the aircraft approach paths to assured safety.[102]

---

[97] Luis Zambrano, *Balancing the Rights of Landowners With the Needs of Airports: The Continuing Battle Over Noise*, 66 J. Air L. & Com. 445, 469-470 (2000).

[98] Paul Stephen Dempsey, Robert Hardaway and William Thoms, *1 Aviation Law & Regulation* §§ 8.03-8.14 (1993). *See also*, Pamela Corrie, *An Assessment of the Role of Local Government in Environmental Regulation*, 5 UCLA J. Envtl. L. & Pol'y 145 (1986).

[99] *Gustafson v. City of Lake Angelus*, 76 F.3d 778 (6th Cir. 1996) (city ordinance prohibiting seaplanes landing on lakes not preempted); *Condor Corp. v. City of St. Paul*, 912 F.2d 215 (8th Cir. 1990) (city zoning ordinance prohibiting siting of heliport not preempted).

[100] Congress did not attempt to preempt the right of a local government to designate and regulate aircraft landing areas. "We find no purpose manifested in the Federal Aviation Act to preempt local law concerning the designation of landing sites for aircraft, including seaplanes. . . . The federal government, rather than 'preempting the field,' has not entered the field and exerts no control over the location of seaplane landing sites." *Gustafson v. City of Lake Angelus*, 76 F.3d 778, 787-788 (6th Cir. 1996)

[101] "These are all areas of valid local regulatory concern, none of which is federally preempted, and none of which inhibits in a proscribed fashion the free transit of navigable airspace. And just as certainly, no federal law gives a citizen the right to operate an airport free of local zoning control. *Faux-Burhans v. County Commissioners of Frederick County*, 674 F. Supp. 1172, 1174 (D. Md. 1987), *aff'd* 859 F.2d 149 (4th Cir. 1988), *cert. den.* 488 U.S. 1042 (1989). "As a policy matter, if federal preemption were found, . . . state and local governments, which are the only bodies that currently license privately operated helistops and heliports, would be shorn of this regulatory responsibility. Congress could not have intended to create a governmental vacuum with respect to privately operated helistops. *Garden State Farms, Inc. v. Bay*, 390 A.2d 1177 (N.J. 1978).

[102] Edward Ziegler, *Rathkopf's The Law of Zoning and Planning* § 60.01 (4th ed. 1999).

Other means of avoiding inverse condemnation litigation include land use planning and zoning around airport perimeters. Airport planners must project the "noise footprint" that will fall on surrounding land by virtue of aircraft operations, with an assumption that an impact above 65 Ldn is incompatible with the reasonably quiet use of residential real estate. Zoning such land for industrial or agricultural use, for example, can ameliorate legal and political problems. Zoning can be the most cost-effective means of avoiding inverse condemnation litigation.[103] An even more effective, albeit expensive, means of accomplishing the same goal is an outright purchase of all land which falls within the 65 Ldn noise footprint, using condemnation powers under eminent domain, if necessary, or purchasing "avigation easements" over surrounding land.[104] As one commentator noted, zoning is a "two-edged sword which local governments may use not only to protect airports from the encroachment of noise-sensitive residential developments, but also to protect residential communities from the encroachment of noise-generating airports.[105]

What follows are airport-related law cases associated with the proprietary function of government owned and operated airports, beginning with the landmark *United States v. Causby* case in 1946.[106] With respect to the environment, the responsibility for determining the permissible noise levels for aircraft using an airport remains with the airport proprietor. This precept originated from the *Causby* case, where the United States, as operator of a military field, was held responsible under the Fifth Amendment to the U.S. Constitution for rendering the Causby's property useless as a chicken farm because of low flying airplanes. The precedent set in the *Causby* case was extended to commercial airports in 1962, in *Griggs v. Allegheny Co.*, when it was held that the County, as the airport sponsor, was the entity that had decided to build an airport at a particular location, and that the County was therefore liable for the taking.[107]

---

[103] J. Scott Hamilton, *Allocation of Airspace as a Scarce National Resource*, 22 Trans. L. J. 251, 266 (1994).

[104] Scott Hamilton, *Planning for Noise Compatibility, in Airport Regulation*, Law & Public Policy 85-86 (R. Hardaway ed. 1991); Luis Zambrano, *Balancing the Rights of Landowners With the Needs of Airports: The Continuing Battle Over Noise*, 66 J. Air L. & Com. 445, 469 (2000).

[105] J. Scott Hamilton, *Allocation of Airspace as a Scarce National Resource*, 22 Trans. L. J. 251, 260 (1994).

[106] *United States v. Causby*, 328 U.S. 256 (1946).

[107] *Griggs v. Allegheny Co.*, 82 S.Ct. 531 (1962).

UNITED STATES v. CAUSBY
328 U.S. 256 (1946)

*Does the flight of aircraft over the property of another
constitute a taking?*

Thomas Lee Causby and his wife owned a 2.8 acre chicken farm underlying the approach path to a (leased) military airfield near Greensboro, North Carolina. The Causbys claimed that noise and glaring lights at night, of military planes landing or leaving the airport, interfered with the normal use of their property as a chicken farm and with the night's rest of their family. As a result, they had to give up their chicken business. As many as six to ten chickens were killed in one day when they became frightened and flew into walls. A total of 150 chickens were lost in this way. The Causbys submitted a claim to the federal government for the loss of their property. The claim ultimately reached the U.S. Supreme Court.

The federal government argued there was no taking since it had asserted control over the use of airspace. The flight of aircraft, here, was within the navigable airspace as defined in the 1926 Air Commerce Act and the Civil Aeronautics Act of 1938. Such flights were an exercise of the declared right of travel through the (public) airspace. Damages incidental to a lawful action are consequential and do not constitute a taking.

The Causbys argued that the use made of the property (the overlying airspace being a portion thereof) by the defendant amounted to a taking. Predicated upon an ancient maxim of real property, "He who owns the soil owns it to the heavens," the taking of airspace above plaintiff's property resulted in damage to the remainder of the property. Therefore, it was argued, the plaintiffs should recover both for the value of the part taken and for the damage done to the remainder.

This case reached the Supreme Court, whose opinion included an analysis of airspace, and whether or not the flights were within legally defined navigable airspace. The minimum navigable airspace defined by Congress was in terms of 300, 500 and 1,000 feet flight levels. Although the Civil Aeronautics Authority had been given jurisdiction to prescribe air traffic rules, the path of glide was not the minimum safe altitude of flight within the meaning of the statute. Congress had defined navigable airspace only in terms of the minimum safe altitudes of flight. The approach path was not considered to be the downward reach of the minimum prescribed altitudes.

The Supreme Court agreed with the lower U.S. Court of Claims that there had been a diminution of value in the property, and that the frequent and low-level flights (outside of the minimum prescribed altitudes) were the direct and immediate cause. Although ruling that compensation was due, the Supreme Court reversed the lower court's decision, because it had not found a precise description of the easement taken. It was not described in terms of frequency of flight, permissible altitude, or type of airplane. Nor was there a finding as to whether the easement taken was temporary or permanent. An accurate description of the property taken is essential. The case was remanded to the Court of Claims so that it could make the necessary findings in conformity with the higher court's opinion.

The use of land presupposes the use of some of the super-adjacent airspace. Invasion of the overlying airspace can affect the use of the land itself. The court's opinion seems to indicate mere flight over land does not constitute a taking, but rather must be attended by something else, such as noise and glare. The court found that flights over private land are not a taking unless flown so low and so frequently as to be a direct and immediate interference with enjoyment and use of the land.

In dissenting opinion, Justice Hugo Black said that the court's findings were "an opening wedge for an unwarranted judicial interference with the power of Congress to develop solutions for new and vital national problems." In his opinion, this case should have been "reversed on the grounds that there had been no 'taking' in the Constitutional sense." The Constitution entrusts Congress with full power to control all navigable airspace. Congress had already acted under that power. By statute, it had provided "the United States of America is . . . to possess and exercise complete and exclusive national sovereignty in the airspace above the United States." Congress had thus declared that the air is free, not subject to private ownership and not subject to delimitation by the courts. In Justice Black's opinion, the court elected to thwart the intent of Congress with its findings in this case.

BROWN v. CITY OF SIOUX CITY
49 N.W.2d 853 (Iowa 1951)

What is the airport's proprietary capacity as a landlord?

C.A. Brown sued the city of Sioux City, Iowa, alleging that in 1948, he rented certain property located at the municipal airport, for the purpose of maintaining and establishing colonies of bees thereon; that in August of that year the city was negligent in spraying the airport property with a poisonous substance called "chlordane," such that his bees were sprayed. The bees picked up the poisonous substance on their bodies and carried it back to the bee colonies, with the result that his bees died, his honey was permeated with the poisonous substance and rendered unfit, and the hives also were rendered unfit for further use. He alleged that the city operated the Sioux City Airport in its proprietary capacity. At the conclusion of the evidence, the trial court submitted to the jury the questions of defendant's negligence, plaintiff's freedom from contributory negligence, and whether the defendant was acting in a governmental or proprietary capacity. After a verdict for the plaintiff for $1,500, the trial court sustained the defendant's motion for judgment notwithstanding the verdict on the ground, "that the operation of the air base was a governmental function; that the farming operation in connection therewith was but an incident thereto." The plaintiff appealed.

In its review of the evidence, the Iowa Supreme Court concluded that the evidence was sufficient without testimony that the spray reached the grove rented by the plaintiff. The city rented the land to Brown for the express purpose of keeping bees. The city knew the bees would not be confined to this three-acre plot it rented to the plaintiff. The city knew, as do all persons that it would be impossible to confine bees without destroying their usefulness as honey producing insects. The city knew the bees would work out of the apiary and onto the adjoining fields. When the city, as plaintiff's landlord, sprayed a poison that would kill bees on the land adjoining the plot, without at least notice to plaintiff, it should have foreseen the ensuing damage. Unless the city is immunized against such an action based upon negligence, because its actions were in the performance of a governmental function, it should respond in damages.

The trial court held that "the operation of the air base was a governmental function." The Supreme Court concurred but stated that such a ruling did not demand setting aside the verdict. It is the established rule in Iowa, and in most jurisdictions, that a municipality, in the exercise of its purely governmental function, is not liable for negligence. But this rule of governmental immunity is to be strictly construed. The trial court held the city's "farming operation," in connection with the operation of the "air base" was "but an incident thereto." It makes little difference whether you call the city's farming operation incidental to the airport operation or not. The defendant chose to conduct its farming operations on the airport property by leasing to tenants. This it had a right to do in furtherance of an economical administration of the municipality.

The city could rent this land, derive revenue therefrom, and thereby cut the deficit for the operation of the airport, with a resulting lessening of the tax burden. But in renting for revenue, the city was functioning in its proprietary capacity. The city cannot accept and exercise the special privilege of leasing its property to tenants without assuming the responsibilities and liabilities flowing from that relationship. Surely the city in its capacity as landlord had the same duty all landlords assume, namely, to exercise ordinary care, so as not to injure a tenant in the occupancy of the leased premises. When renting the land, the city was acting in a proprietary capacity. The Iowa Supreme Court held that the city was engaged in its proprietary capacity when renting the airport property to Brown, and as such, it had the liability arising from the landlord and tenant relationship, including liability for negligent acts that damaged the plaintiff in his use of the leased acreage. The ruling of the trial court was reversed and the jury's verdict reinstated, and the cause was remanded for ruling on a motion for a new trial.

AMERICAN AIRLINES v. LOUISVILLE AND JEFFERSON COUNTY AIR BOARD
269 F.2d 811 (6th Cir. 1959)

Is an airport within the normal scope of governmental services?

In 1947, American Airlines, Trans World Airlines, and Eastern Air Lines entered into similar lease agreements with the Louisville and

Jefferson County Air Board for the use of facilities at Standiford Field (Louisville Airport), at certain agreed rentals for a period of ten years. The leases granted the airlines an option to renew for a like period. Article II of the leases provided that,

> . . . *Lessor hereby grants to Lessee an option to renew this lease for one . . . additional term of ten years . . . provided that Lessee shall notify Lessor in writing of Lessee's exercise of such option as to any such renewal term not less than six . . . months before the expiration of the original term hereof. . . .*

The airlines gave the Air Board timely notice of their renewal of their options and the renewals of the options were acknowledged by the Air Board. After the exercise of the options, certain negotiations took place between the parties in an attempt to agree upon the rentals for the renewal terms, but the parties were unable to reach an agreement. Article III (C) of the leases provided:

> . . . *In the event Lessee exercises its option to renew this Lease in accordance with the provisions hereof, the rentals, fees and charges for such renewal term shall be as mutually agreed upon between Lessor and Lessee prior to the end of the term. In the event that Lessor and Lessee do not mutually agree as to such rentals, fees and charges for any such renewal term, the same shall be determined by arbitration, as hereinafter provided, and pending such determination the rentals, fees and charges last in effect shall continue in full force and effect.*

Prior to the expiration of the original term of the leases, the Air Board and the airlines were unable to mutually agree upon rental terms for the renewal period. The original term of the leases expired on October 31, 1957. The airlines sought through the courts to enforce the arbitration provisions of the leases, which the Air Board refused to recognize as binding upon it.

The U.S. District Court declared in its memorandum opinion that the arbitration provisions of the leases were invalid and unenforceable, because "the Air Board was without authority to contract to delegate to arbitrators its public and discretionary duty to fix rentals for the use of the facilities of the airport." The memorandum opinion concluded that, "Having reached the conclusion the arbitration provisions of the leases are unenforceable and void and the Airlines are not entitled to specific performance of the void covenants of their leases, it is not necessary to consider the question of whether or not the establishment of renewal rentals is an arbitrable issue."

The leases were hence declared terminated as of the end of the original ten-year term on October 31, 1957, for lack of agreement by the parties as to an essential provision of the renewal term; namely, the rental fees and other charges to be paid by appellant airlines for facilities at Louisville airport during the forthcoming ten-year period. The airlines appealed the case. In its review, the U.S. Court of Appeals stated that the Air Board's attack, upon the validity of its covenant to submit the renewal rentals and fees to arbitration, rested upon a ground that goes to the very formation of the contract to arbitrate in the first place; in particular, the authority of the Air Board as a public body to make such a covenant. State law and not federal law governed. The District Court looked to the law of Kentucky in deciding whether the arbitration provisions of the leases here in question were invalid and unenforceable, because those provisions were beyond the authority of the Air Board. Its decision that they were invalid was predicated upon the conclusion that,

> . . . since the Air Board is a public body engaged in the performance of a public duty, it is subject to all general laws applicable to other political subdivision and without express statutory permission it is not permitted to delegate and surrender to others its official powers which are discretionary in character and require the exercise of judgment.

Having thus concluded the arbitration provisions in controversy were invalid, the District Court did not find it necessary to reach the issue as to whether the dispute was of such a character as to be arbitrable. If the appellate court were to assume, as did the District Court, that the arbitration provisions in the leases amounted to a delegation of municipal powers to private persons, authority for such delegation must be found, if at all, in the Kentucky statutes. Under Kentucky law, the Air Board was a municipal corporation, and as such was an instrumentality or agent of the State possessing, save as may otherwise be conferred by the Kentucky Constitution, only such power or authority as the Kentucky General Assembly by statute had expressly or impliedly granted. Kentucky's Revised Statutes provided that:

> *The purpose of the (Air) Board shall be to establish and maintain one or more airports and facilities to provide for transportation by air of passengers, property, express, and mail, and to provide one or more airports and facilities for the use of the Federal Government. The (Air) Board shall have such powers as may be necessary or desirable to promote aviation and the development of facilities for air travel and transportation.*
>
> *The (Air) Board shall employ necessary counsel, agents, and employees to carry out its work and functions and to prescribe such rules and regulations as it deems necessary.*

There being no express statutory grant of authority to the Air Board to delegate the power to fix rental fees and charges for the use of airport facilities, the specific question in this case was whether or not authority to delegate such power to others, such as arbitrators, was impliedly granted because "necessary or desirable" within the meaning of the Kentucky Revised Statutes as quoted above.

A review of the opinions of the Court of Appeals of Kentucky revealed that, in the absence of express statutory language so authorizing, a municipal corporation of Kentucky had no authority to delegate to others discretionary powers either expressly or impliedly conferred, unless the facts were such that delegation was necessary either to realization of objectives which the municipality was authorized or duty bound to accomplish, or to effective exercise of powers otherwise expressly or impliedly conferred.

The U.S. Court of Appeals had difficulty applying the rule stated above for two reasons. First, the Kentucky courts had never said *that* was the Kentucky rule, and second, there were no Kentucky cases, which expressly conferred upon a municipal corporation such as the Air Board not only those powers "necessary" but also those powers "desirable." As applied to the facts at bar, Kentucky law was uncertain. The appellate court determined it would be necessary for the district court to retain the cases, stay proceedings, and defer or abstain from future exercise of federal jurisdiction, pending determination by Kentucky courts of the questions of Kentucky law as discussed.

For the reasons stated, the summary judgments declaring that the airport leases terminated on October 31, 1957, and interlocutory orders of April 22, 1958, denying a prohibitory injunction staying the proceedings in the district court and refusing a mandatory injunction to compel arbitration, in each of the three cases, were set aside, and the cases remanded to the district court for further proceedings not inconsistent with this opinion.

GRIGGS v. ALLEGHENY COUNTY
369 U.S. 84 (1962)

Who is liable for a taking, which is the result of aircraft landing and taking off?

The Griggs owned a family residence that was 3,250 feet from the end of the northeast runway at the Greater Pittsburgh Airport. Due to sloping terrain, the petitioner's chimney was only 11 feet below the 40:1 glide angle to the runway. Regular and almost continuous flights over the house made it impossible for people to converse or talk on the telephone. The residents were unable to sleep, being frequently awakened by airplane noise. The windows would often rattle and at times plaster fell from the walls and ceilings. The house was rendered unusable as a family residence.

There was a taking of an air easement. But who was responsible for the unauthorized taking: the federal government, the aircraft owners, or the airport proprietor? A Board of Viewers appointed by the

Court of Common Pleas found that there had been a taking by the respondent, Allegheny County. On appeal the Supreme Court of Pennsylvania decided there was a taking, but that it was the federal government or the airlines, and not the respondent who was liable.

The case was appealed to the U.S. Supreme Court, which reversed the Pennsylvania Supreme Court's ruling, and found that it was the airport sponsor who was liable. Allegheny County was the promoter, owner, and lessor of the airport. It was the airport proprietor who took the air easement in the constitutional sense. The airport proprietor decided (subject to Civil Aeronautics Administration approval) where the airport would be built, what runways it would need, their direction and length, and what land and navigation easements would be needed. It is the local authority that decides to build an airport and where it is to be located—not the federal government. The conclusion of the U.S. Supreme Court was that the respondent in designing the airport had not acquired enough property.

The airlines were lessees of the airport proprietor, and their leases gave them the right to "land" and "takeoff." No flights were in violation of federal air regulations nor were they lower than necessary for safe landings and takeoffs. Thus, it must have been the airport proprietor that was responsible for the taking.

In dissenting opinion, Justices Black and Frankfurter agreed there had been a taking, but in their opinion, it was the federal government who was liable. The county designed the airport, but did so in compliance with federal requirements. Congress in 1938 declared that the United States has "complete and exclusive national sovereignty in the airspace above the United States." They stated, that "Having taken the airspace over Griggs' private property for public use, it was the United States which owed just compensation."

CITY OF BURBANK v. LOCKHEED AIR TERMINAL
411 U.S. 624 (1973)

*May a local government impose a curfew on jet operations
at a privately owned airport?*

In the early 1970s, the City of Burbank passed an ordinance prohibiting jet operations at the Hollywood-Burbank Airport between the hours of 11 p.m. and 7 a.m. Hollywood-Burbank Airport was then a privately owned facility, with scheduled operations by certificated air carriers. It is located within the Burbank City limits.

The critical issue in this case was an argument that the ordinance was invalid because Congress, by its enactment of the Federal Aviation Act of 1958 and the Noise Control Act of 1972, had preempted state and local control over aircraft noise. The Federal Aviation Act provides in part, "The United States of America is declared to possess and exercise complete and exclusive national sovereignty in the airspace of the United States. . . ." There is no express provision of preemption in the Noise Control Act, but the court concluded the scheme of federal regulation of aircraft noise is so pervasive that there is preemption. In conjunction with the Environmental Protection Agency [EPA], the FAA has full control over aircraft noise, preempting state and local oversight. Thus, state and local governments remain unable to use their police powers to control aircraft noise by regulating the flight of aircraft.

The U.S. Supreme Court held the Burbank ordinance invalid. The defendants submitted "that a municipality with jurisdiction over an airport has the power to impose a curfew on the airport, notwithstanding federal responsibility in the area." The court's response was that it was not concerned with an ordinance imposed by the city as proprietor of the airport, but rather with the exercise of police power. The court was not considering in this case what limits, if any apply to a municipality as a proprietor. There is a critical distinction between the local government as an airport proprietor and the local government as a regulatory agency.

Four justices dissented. In their opinion, it was an erroneous notion that legislation dealing with aircraft noise was so pervasive as to imply preemption. On the contrary, House and Senate committee reports explicitly stated that the 1972 Noise Control Act was not intended to alter the balance between state and federal regulation. The dissenting judges "start with the assumption that historic police powers of the states were not to be superseded by federal act unless that was the clear and manifest purpose of Congress."

The justices did concur in the following views:

- The federal government presently preempts the field of noise regulation insofar as it involves controlling the flight of aircraft;

- State and local governments will remain unable to use their police powers to control aircraft noise by regulating the flight of aircraft;
- The 1972 Noise Control Act does not affect the rights of a state or local agency, as the proprietor of an airport, from issuing regulations or establishing requirements as to the permissible level of noise which can be created by aircraft using the airport. Airport owners acting as proprietors may deny the use of their airports to aircraft on the basis of noise considerations so long as such exclusion is nondiscriminatory;
- Just as an airport owner is responsible for deciding how long the runways will be, so too is the owner responsible for obtaining noise easements necessary to permit the landing and takeoff of the airport. The federal government is in no position to require an airport to accept service by larger aircraft, and for that purpose to obtain longer runways; and,
- Likewise, the federal government is in no position to require an airport to accept service by noisier aircraft, and for that purpose to obtain additional noise easements. The issue is the service desired by the airport owner and the steps it is willing to take to obtain the service.

AIR TRANSPORT ASSOCIATION OF AMERICA v. CROTTI
389 F. Supp 58 (N.D. Cal. 1975)

May a state enforce noise regulations which provide that the violation thereof by any aircraft is deemed a misdemeanor?

The California Public Utilities Code required the California Department of Aeronautics to adopt noise regulations governing the operation of airports and of aircraft at all airports operating mandatorily under a permit issued by the state. Airports with a noise problem were responsible for establishing means of monitoring and measuring aircraft noise emissions and to meet California's airport noise standards. The Code recommended procedures that could be employed to help attain noise reductions, but no procedures were mandatory. Airport authorities could tailor their programs to their own peculiar needs.

The regulations and standards were in two categories. There was the Community Noise Equivalent Level [CNEL] to generally measure continued operation of airports and limit uses about the airport. There was also the Single Event Noise Exposure Level [SENEL] for prohibitions applied to the inseparable feature of noise generated by an (actual) aircraft directly engaged in flight. Violation of SENEL limits was punishable by a fine of $1,000 for each infraction.

The U.S. District Court heard the case. The plaintiff was the Air Transport Association of America [ATA], members of which included virtually all United States scheduled interstate air carriers. The defendants included the Director of Aeronautics for the State of California, J.R. Crotti, and several directors and managing officials of prominent airports in California.

The airlines contended California noise standards were invalid and unenforceable by virtue of the Supremacy and Commerce Clauses of the U.S. Constitution. The Noise Control Act of 1972, which amended the Federal Aviation Act of 1958, reaffirmed and reinforced the conclusion that the FAA, in conjunction with the Environmental Protection Agency [EPA], had full control over aircraft noise, thus preempting state and local control. The airlines' position was based upon the simple contention that any control and regulation of the levels of noise generated by aircraft in direct flight is preempted by the federal government, and they relied heavily upon the findings in *Burbank v. Lockheed Air Terminal*.[108] However, the court believed the airlines' total reliance upon *Burbank* to be misplaced since that case focused on a single police power ordinance of a municipality, not on an airport proprietor (as a private enterprise) intending to abate noise. "Authority that a municipality may have as a landlord is not necessarily congruent with its police power. We do not consider here what limits, if any, applied to a municipality as a proprietor."

The court held that, "It is now firmly established that the airport proprietor is responsible for the consequences which attend his operation of a public airport; his right to control the use of the airport is a necessary concomitant, whether it be directed by state police power or his own initiative." In California, there are imposed sanctions (namely suspension or revocation of licenses or permits to operate airports) against airport proprietors for failure to perform mandatory functions in control and regulation of aircraft operations.

The monitoring of airport noise is a passive function, which in no way intruded upon or affected flight operations or air commerce. The

---

[108] 411 U.S. 625 (1973).

court concluded that the CNEL provisions and regulations were not invalid, and that they did not delve into the regulation of aircraft operations in direct flight, a regulatory area that is preempted by the federal government under constitutional law.

Conversely, the court found the SENEL provisions and regulations of noise invalid because the measurements were taken when the aircraft was in direct flight, and because the levying of criminal fines for violation of the regulations was an unlawful exercise of police power in the federally exclusive domain of control over aircraft flights, airspace management, and in interstate and foreign commerce. The court concluded that airlines were entitled to a partial summary judgment declaring the SENEL regulations void and unenforceable, and in contravention of the Constitution and laws of the United States.

NATIONAL AVIATION v. CITY OF HAYWARD
418 F. Supp. 417 (N.D. Cal. 1976)

Can a municipality, as the airport proprietor, enforce an ordinance under its police powers which restricts aircraft operations and imposes a nighttime curfew?

The plaintiffs in this case were National Aviation, Paramount Air Services, and Career Aviation, commercial operators at the Hayward Air Terminal in California. Air Transport Association of America filed a brief as *amicus curiae* (i.e., interested third parties). The City of Hayward, as owner of the Hayward Air Terminal, passed an ordinance which prohibited all aircraft which exceeded a noise level of 75 dBA (decibels on the "A" scale, or that scale which equates most to human hearing) from landing or taking off from the Hayward Air Terminal between the hours of 11 p.m. and 7 a.m. The commercial airplane operators held contracts that required they operate between 11 p.m. and 7 a.m. Because of the ordinance, they had been required to shift their operations to other airports at allegedly large increases in the cost of their operations. They also claimed to have suffered other damages, including reductions to the net worth of their companies, loss of value of their leased properties and facilities at the Hayward Air Terminal, decreased and less flexible service capabilities, loss of goodwill, and the potential of criminal prosecution should their employees be unable to comply with the ordinance. They essentially argued that enactment of the ordinance increased their operating costs and reduced their corporate net worth.

Plaintiffs and *amicus* sought an injunction, arguing the ordinance was unconstitutional; first, because it invaded a field preempted by federal law; and second, because it imposed an unconstitutional burden on interstate commerce. Their contention was that the Noise Control Act of 1972, as it amends the Federal Aviation Act of 1958, preempts the area of noise regulation, therefore rendering the Hayward ordinance unconstitutional. Plaintiffs also claimed they were denied access to the Hayward air movement area, which was their contractual right. And, they claimed that Hayward by its ordinance was in breach of prior federal agreements.

In referring to the findings in *Burbank v. Lockheed Air Terminal*,[109] "State and local governments will remain unable to use their police powers to control aircraft noise regulating the flight of aircraft." "Airport owners acting as proprietors can presently deny the use of their airports to aircraft on the basis of noise considerations so long as such exclusion is nondiscriminatory." The *Burbank* court's finding of preemption was made only with regard to a non-proprietor municipality's attempt to regulate aircraft noise pursuant to its police power. It did not consider what limits, if any apply to a municipality as a proprietor.

The ordinance stated the City of Hayward, as the owner, operator, and proprietor of the airport, possessed authority to adopt reasonable rules regulating the use of the airport. The ordinance was passed pursuant to its police powers. The question here was whether the city's status as proprietor of the airport left it free to exercise its police powers without constraint by federal preemption. According to the *Burbank* findings, it could not.

In *Air Transport Association v. Crotti*,[110] the court rejected the argument that the federal government had preempted the entire field of airport noise regulation. The court wrote, "It is now firmly established that the airport proprietor is responsible for the consequences which attend his operation of a public airport; his right to control the use of the airport is a necessary concomitant, whether it be directed by state police power or his own initiative." The *Crotti* court stated that the right of airport proprietorship control is recognized and ex-

---

[109] 411 U.S. 624 (1973).
[110] 389 F. Supp. 58 (1975).

empted from preemption. Such interpretation overlooks the explicit statement of the *Burbank* findings, wherein the court was not considering "what limits, if any, apply to a municipality as a proprietor," and produce the result that a municipality owning an airport would be free to exercise police powers in the field of airport noise regulation.

The instant court found itself on the horns of a particularly sharp dilemma. It turned to the notion of legislative intent. "When Congress legislates in a field which the states have traditionally occupied, the power of the states are not to be superseded by the Federal Act unless that is the clear and manifest purpose of Congress." The court found the ordinance valid and not preempted. If there is a need for a uniform and exclusive system of federal regulation, Congress and the FAA can take appropriate steps to provide such a regulatory system. At the time, neither Congress nor the FAA appeared to have preempted the area. Therefore, the City of Hayward could not be enjoined from enforcing its ordinance on preemptive grounds. Nor could it be enjoined under the Commerce Clause of the U.S. Constitution. The Hayward ordinance was found to be a local concern with only incidental burden on interstate commerce. From the record, the plaintiffs had little problem in successfully shifting their operations to another airport.

As for breach of prior federal agreements, the court had difficulty with the plaintiff's standing as a third party beneficiary. Even if the plaintiffs had a right to raise these claims, the court was of the opinion that Hayward had made its airport available for public use on fair and reasonable terms, and had not breached agreements with the federal government to "prevent any land use either within or outside the boundaries of the airport which would limit its usefulness as an airport." Plaintiffs claimed the city would have had no need for the noise ordinance if it had complied with the federal agreements. Plaintiffs also claimed inverse condemnation because the ordinance had deprived them of access to the runways at Hayward Air Terminal, and thereby substantially decreased the value of their long-term leases. However, the court found that the plaintiffs had no absolute right to unrestricted use of the airport's runways at all hours of the day.

The plaintiffs motion for a preliminary injunction was denied. The defendant's motion for dismissal was denied. The defendant's motion to dismiss plaintiff's claims for damages was granted, as was the defendant motion to dismiss plaintiff's claim for inverse condemnation.

SANTA MONICA AIRPORT ASSOCIATION v. CITY OF SANTA MONICA
481 F. Supp. 927 (C.D. Cal. 1979)

Can an airport proprietor restrict aircraft operations for noise abatement; and specifically, can it impose a ban on jet operations?

In a move aimed at reducing aircraft noise, the City of Santa Monica imposed a series of ordinances restricting aircraft operations at the Santa Monica Municipal Airport. Included among these several prohibitive ordinances was:

- a total ban on *jet* aircraft either landing or taking off;
- a maximum single-event noise exposure level of 100 decibels [dB] on any operation;
- a night curfew of aircraft operations from 11 p.m. until 6 a.m.;
- no touch-and-go, stop-and-go and low approach operations on weekends and holidays; and,
- a prohibition against helicopter training operations.

The restrictive ordinances were challenged by the plaintiff, the Santa Monica Airport Association, a non-profit membership corporation consisting of pilots and owners of aircraft who use the airport. Plaintiff's intervenors (i.e., third parties to the case for protection of alleged interests) were the National Business Aircraft Association and the General Aviation Manufacturers Association. The FAA and the Aircraft Owners and Pilots Association entered as *amici curiae*.

The plaintiff's grounds of attack were on:

- violation of the Equal Protection Clause and the Commerce Clause of the United States Constitution;
- invalidity because of preemption arising from federal legislation and FAA regulations;
- breaches of the federal grant agreements between the FAA and the city; and,
- breaches of lease agreements between the city and airport tenants.

Plaintiffs contended the city's ordinances were preempted by the federal government; first, because Congress had legislated generally on the use of airspace and that the federal government thereby preempted that entire field; and second, because preemption exists by virtue of certain FAA regulations. Each of the five ordinances was challenged under the U.S. Constitution—on preemptive grounds, on equal protection grounds, and as an impermissible burden on interstate commerce.

At the outset, the U.S. District Court ruled out preemption on grounds that a municipal airport proprietor may exercise control over airport noise, providing such control is exercised reasonably, without discrimination, and without direct interference with commerce. In its tests in deciding constitutional validity regarding equal protection and the commerce clause, the court applied the same standard (as used by the U.S. Supreme Court) to each of the five ordinances. A general rule that emerged was the following:

> *Where the statute regulates evenhandedly to effectuate a legitimate local public interest, and its effects on interstate commerce are only incidental, it will be upheld unless the burden imposed on such commerce is clearly excessive in relation to the putative local benefits.*

To scrutinize each of the ordinances, and to insure that each did not represent an unconstitutional burden upon interstate commerce, or that neither inhibited the accomplishment of legitimate national goals the following steps were taken by the court:

- There was a determination as to whether there was an effect on interstate commerce;
- If there was any effect found, the next determination was whether the local body had acted within its province and whether the means of regulation chosen were reasonably adapted to the end sought; and,
- Whether there was a balancing of the burden imposed on interstate commerce against the local interests supporting the legislation.

As to all of the ordinances in question, except the jet ban, the court found them to be an indirect burden on interstate commerce. With the exception of the jet ban, all of the other ordinances were found valid in all respects. Claims of preemption of federal airspace jurisdiction were dismissed because the ordinances in question were regulations of noise made by airplanes landing and taking off from the defendant's airport, not regulations of airspace or flight.

The ordinance banning jets presented different legal questions. It was held unconstitutional on two alternative grounds—first, because it violated the Equal Protection Clause; and second, because it imposed an impermissible burden on interstate commerce. Business jets that could meet the single-event 100-dB level could not be validly excluded from the airport without being discriminated against unreasonably. The court also found the jet ban to be a direct burden on commerce, since it prohibited interstate travel of jets, even in those that could meet the local noise requirement.

As a subsidiary to the jet ban ordinance, the city had passed another ordinance imposing a fee of $5,000 for each landing of a jet and $10,000 for each jet take-off. The fee ordinances fell with the jet ban, which was held invalid. Even so, the court held such charges to be cruel and unusual punishment and unconstitutional as such.

Defendants had also offered evidence to the effect that aircraft noise is in some fashion directly related to incidences of disease and death among the surrounding residential population. The court found the evidence completely unconvincing. It found that no relationship had been shown between aircraft noise at its then present or alternative levels, and the incidence of death or disease among the Santa Monica population.

As to the intervenors' (NBAA and GAMA) claims of third party interests as beneficiaries of the federal grant agreements with the City, the court, supported by FAA opinion, dismissed the claims and found that none of the provisions relied on by the plaintiffs vested any private rights of action. The court also found that none of the conditions stipulated in individual leases with airport tenants had been violated by passage of the ordinances in question.

EVANSVILLE-VANDERBURGH AIRPORT AUTHORITY DISTRICT. v. DELTA AIR LINES
405 U.S. 707 (1972)

*Is a "head tax," imposed on individually enplaning passengers,
an unreasonable burden on interstate commerce?*

This case was heard upon *certiorari* from the United States Supreme Court to the Supreme Court of Indiana, but it also took into consideration a finding by the Supreme Court of New Hampshire on the same issue. The respondents, Delta Air Lines, challenged a "use and service charge" of $1.00 "for each passenger enplaning any commercial aircraft operated from the Dress Memorial Airport" in Evansville, Indiana. The funds were to be used for improvement and maintenance of the airport. The Indiana Supreme Court, upholding the lower court, held the charge to be an unreasonable burden on interstate commerce in violation of Article I, Section 8, of the U.S. Constitution.

Similarly, a New Hampshire statute levied a service charge of $1.00 for each passenger enplaning a scheduled commercial airliner weighing 12,500 pounds or more, and a 50¢ charge for each passenger enplaning a scheduled aircraft weighing less than 12,500 pounds. Fifty percent of the funds were allocated to the state's aeronautical fund, with the balance going to the municipalities or airport authorities owning the public landing areas. The New Hampshire Supreme Court sustained the constitutionality of the statute.

The Indiana and New Hampshire Supreme Courts differed in appraising their respective charges in terms of whether the charge was for the use of facilities in aid of travel provided by the public. The Indiana Supreme Court held that the Evansville charge "is not reasonably related to use of the facilities which benefit from the tax. . . ." On the other hand, the New Hampshire Supreme Court held that the New Hampshire charge was a "fee for the use of facilities furnished by the public" that did not "exceed reasonable compensation for the use provided."

The U.S. Supreme Court found their decisions concerning highway tolls to be instructive, establishing that the states are empowered to develop "uniform, fair and practical" standards for this type of fee. The court found that the Indiana and New Hampshire charges met those standards. First, neither fee discriminated against interstate commerce and travel. Second, the charges reflected a fair, if imperfect, approximation of the use of facilities for whose benefit they were imposed. Third, the airlines had not shown these fees to be excessive in relation to costs incurred by the taxing authorities.

The judgment of the Indiana Supreme Court was reversed. The judgment of the New Hampshire Supreme Court was affirmed. A charge designed only to make the user of state-provided facilities pay a reasonable fee to help defray the costs of their construction and maintenance constitutionally may be imposed on interstate and domestic users alike.

NORTHWEST AIRLINES v. FEDERAL AVIATION ADMINISTRATION
14 F.3d 64 (D.C. Cir. 1994)

Must an airport authority provide air carriers with written notice of individual projects being considered for funding through imposition of Passenger Facility Charges.

In 1990, Congress amended the Federal Aviation Act of 1958, to allow local public airport authorities to petition the FAA for permission to impose Passenger Facility Charges on passengers using the airport. The statute authorizes the FAA to "grant a public agency which controls a commercial service airport authority to impose a fee of $1.00, $2.00, or $3.00 for each paying passenger of an air carrier enplaned at such airport to finance eligible airport-related projects to be carried out in connection with such airport or any other airport which such agency controls." The FAA may only authorize an airport to collect PFCs in order to finance "specific . . . eligible airport-related project[s]. . . ." The statute further provides that "[b]efore submission of an application under [the PFC statute], a public agency shall provide reasonable notice to, and an opportunity for consultation with, air carriers operating at the airport." As part of the consultation process, the airport authority must provide air carriers with written notice of "individual projects being considered for funding through imposition" of PFCs.

On January 28, 1992, the Memphis-Shelby County Airport Authority requested permission to impose a $3.00 PFC on all passengers enplaned at Memphis International Airport. The application identified four primary projects to be financed with PFC revenue:

- the acquisition of land and the relocation of roadways and utilities to allow future airport development;
- construction of a new runway;
- reconstruction and extension of an existing runway; and,
- construction of a new taxiway.

Additionally, the application identified a backup project, should any one of the primary projects not be approved. This alternative proposal was to purchase homes in high noise corridors to reduce the impact of noise on communities surrounding the airport. Memphis failed to mention the alternative "noise compatibility project" when it consulted with Northwest and other airlines prior to submitting its PFC application.

The FAA authorized Memphis to impose a $3.00 PFC, and approved its runway and taxiway projects. However, Memphis had not yet secured the required environmental clearance to proceed with its runway and taxiway projects. Therefore, the FAA approved the noise compatibility project as an "alternative use" of the PFC revenues "in the event that one or more of the primary projects was not implemented." The FAA's decision authorized Memphis only to "impose" the PFC, but it did not yet grant approval to "use" the PFC revenue on any particular project.

Northwest Airlines petitioned the U.S. Court of Appeals for a review of the FAA's approval of the Memphis PFC. Northwest argued that FAA's failure to consider the economic and competitive effects of its decision rendered its ruling arbitrary and capricious. The airline also claimed that the FAA's approval of the PFC, based on the airport authority's proposed alternative project, violated the statutory requirement that PFC applications be tied to "specific projects," and that the airlines be consulted about each of these projects before the application is submitted. Finally, Northwest argued that the FAA violated the statute by allowing Memphis to impose PFCs on frequent flyer customers.

Each of Northwest's objections to the FAA's approval of the Memphis PFC ultimately attacked the FAA's interpretation of the PFC statute. Therefore, the court turned to precedent in *Chevron*

U.S.A. Inc. v. Natural Resources Defense Council, Inc,[111] which requires the court first to ask,

> . . . *whether Congress has directly spoken to the precise question at issue. If we can come to the unmistakable conclusion that Congress had an intention on the precise question at issue our inquiry ends there. . . . However, if the statute before us is silent or ambiguous with respect to the specific issue[s] before us, we proceed to the second step. At this stage, we defer to the agency's interpretation of the statute if it is reasonable and consistent with the statute's purpose.*

The appellate court did not reach Northwest's frequent flyer argument because the airline had failed to exhaust its administrative remedies as required. On the merits of Northwest's remaining challenges, the court deferred to the FAA's reasonable interpretation of the statute and rejected Northwest's petition. However, because the FAA did violate the consultation provisions of the statute with respect to the airport authority's proposed alternative project, the court concluded that Memphis could not expend its PFC funds to finance the alternative "noise compatibility project."

---

[111] 467 U.S. 837 (1984).

CHAPTER 14

AIRPORTS: AND THE
REDISTRIBUTIVE FUNCTION

*From a utilitarian perspective, the provision of balanced
airport services is necessary to serve the common
interests of most airport users.*

COST ALLOCATION

Professional accountants advocate the "allocation of costs" to specific user areas. The underlying philosophy suggests investment should be allocated according to relative economy and fitness. From the standpoint of sound economic principles, it is believed that user charges determine the appropriate amounts of investment. This economic principle calls for making user charges as direct as possible in attempt to relate cost to demand. Users of airport cost-centers must pay in proportion to their individual use, and the costs, which they themselves create. The more directly related the charges are to costs, the more ideal is the cost allocation process.

Although cost allocation is the ideal, it may not be a reasonable expectation.[1] From a practical standpoint, true cost allocation is not attainable on most airports, while simultaneously providing well-rounded aviation services to the public. The principle of cost allocation divides the airport into functional areas such as runways, ramps, hangars, and terminal buildings. Additionally, allocation may be determined by user category; e.g., air carrier, general aviation, concessionaire, and so forth. The expenses attributable to each area are es-

---

[1] *See Northwest Airlines v. County of Kent*, CCH 24 AVI ¶ 17,775 (1994).

tablished and charges made to recover each area's costs. It is a violation of the cost allocation principle to "cross allocate" (i.e., cross credit) revenues from one area to another, since this tends to break down the connection between cost and demand. An example would be to take air carrier terminal revenues to pay some of the costs associated with general aviation—to pay for a general aviation parking apron for instance; in other words, to cover costs for facilities not necessarily used by the one paying the charges.

Cost allocation is limited to the precept that price should be related to cost, but price discrimination (or the relative advantages and disadvantages of value-of-service pricing) inherently enter into airport rate setting schemes. The provision of balanced airport services makes cross-subsidization necessary from a utilitarian perspective; that is to say to serve the common interests of the *majority* of airport users.

Profit margins of all airport tenants are not equal. Often, non-aviation related entities generate more income than do those engaged directly in air commerce and air transportation. For example, a Fixed Base Operator [FBO] offering training and service has a much lower propensity for profit than an automobile rental agency.[2] It is not uncommon for concessionaires to contribute a proportionally larger share of revenue to the airport than many companies directly engaged in aviation activities *per se*. Hence, the airport becomes a legitimized Robin Hood by redistributing wealth amongst airport users. Although justified by utilitarian purposes, such price discrimination predisposes the potential for legal action to recover for perceived injustices suffered by the individual, or *minority* of airport users.

As previously discussed, at the heart of litigation associated with redistribution of wealth on an airport is the economic philosophy of the airport sponsor and rates it charges. Bringing rates in line with actual fiscal requirements is a difficult and politically sensitive task, requiring extensive public relations efforts. Airport users resist having to pay for the real costs of owning and operating an airport. As rates are increased to reflect actual costs, the backlash from airport users can escalate. Nobody likes to pay more, whether the increased charge is just or not. Neither does anyone like paying more than their fair share. More importantly, tenants totally reject paying for expenses

---

[2] *See Alamo Rent-A-Car v. Sarasota-Manatee*, CCH 20 AVI ¶ 18,175 (1987); *see also Airline Car Rental v. Shreveport*, CCH 21 AVI ¶ 17,201 (1987).

related to another airport user. Herein lies the root of most court cases involving the government redistribution service function.

REGULATION OF AIRPORT LANDING SLOTS [3]

Rationing scarce resources has never been an easy task. In a market system, resources are allocated to their highest valued use based upon the law of supply and demand—consumers bid for goods they want through the pricing system; producers promptly provide them to those bidding highest.[4] In contrast, public resources, particularly infrastructure built by government for public use, typically are rationed by government.[5] At many congested airports, where capacity arguably exceeds demand, governments have divided runway utilization into time-defined segments known as slots. A "slot" is the right to take off or land an aircraft—in effect, a "reservation."[6] By the end of the 1990s, more than 130 airports around the world were slot-controlled.[7] In the United States, four major U.S. airports are slot-constrained by federal decree—Chicago O'Hare, Washington National, and New York LaGuardia and Kennedy. A number of others (such as John Wayne Orange County Airport, California) are slot controlled by local airport proprietors, usually for purposes of reducing noise.

Landing slots are similar to gates in that both carry with them the economic equivalent of an operating certificate. Without a slot and a gate, an airline cannot operate. Where there is a finite number of such gates or slots, their value lies, in part, in their ability to create, on the one hand, or circumscribe, on the other, competition.[8] Therein lies the rub. Deregulation was supposed to eliminate operating certificates as barriers to entry.[9] Yet slots and gates are today's equivalent of op-

---

[3] Portions of this section are derived from Paul Dempsey, *Airport Landing Slots: Barriers to Entry and Impediments to Competition*, 16 Air & Space L. 20 (2001).

[4] Paul Dempsey, *Market Failure and Regulatory Failure as Catalysts for Political Change: The Choice Between Imperfect Competition and Imperfect Regulation*, 46 Washington & Lee L. Rev. 1 (1988).

[5] This section taken largely from Paul Stephen Dempsey and Laurence E. Gesell, *Air Commerce and the Law* 481-504 (2004).

[6] The European Union defines a slot as "the scheduled time of arrival or departure available or allocated to an aircraft movement on a specified date at an airport. . . ." EU Official Journal No. L014, 22/01/1993, at 1.

[7] Ruwantissa Abeyratne, *Management of Airport Congestion Through Slot Allocation*, 6 J. of Trans. Mgt. 29 (2000).

[8] Paul Dempsey, *Airport Planning & Development: A Global Survey* 441-487 (1999).

[9] Paul Dempsey, *The Rise & Fall of the Civil Aeronautics Board: Opening Wide the Floodgates of Entry*, 11 Transp. L. J. 91 (1979).

erating certificates. The ability to hoard landing slots and gates translates into the opportunity to erect barriers to entry and monopolize markets.[10] Market monopolization (and the consumer exploitation thereby enabled) has been the Achilles Heel of airline deregulation.[11]

Landing slot restrictions were originally imposed to reduce air traffic congestion and delays. Though technological and traffic management improvements over the ensuing decades have eliminated much of the original justification for such regulations at many airports, and despite the fact they effectively thwart efforts to achieve airline entry and pricing deregulation, they stubbornly linger on. Today, airports such as Newark, with far more significant congestion problems than those for which slots-constraints have been imposed, are slot-free.

New justifications have been advanced for their retention. Environmentalists fear elimination of slot restrictions will blast residents with noise.[12] Small communities fear slot elimination will cause them to lose access to congested airports. Incumbent airlines, which have spent millions of dollars hoarding slots, and lending institutions, which have used slots as collateral for airline loans, object to their removal on economic grounds. Though landing slots may well be a regulatory anachronism, they remain tenaciously embedded in aviation culture.

Several approaches have been attempted to ration slots, and each has produced its own set of problems:

- Governments or airports have distributed them to carriers via regulatory fiat.
- Governments have allowed airlines to divide them up by according antitrust immunity to scheduling committees.

---

[10] DOT Docket OST-97-2058-222 (May 21, 1998), citing Testimony of Donald J. Carty, p. 40, *AMR Corporation and American Airlines, Inc. v. UAL Corporation et al.*, USDC for the SDNY, 91 Civ 773-781 F. Supp. 292.

[11] "In most business contexts, competition provides healthy results. But in air travel, with a finite number of gates at publicly owned airports, the temptation exists for large air carriers to lock in access to gates with long-term contracts. Then they're free to charge a captive ridership whatever fares they choose. . . ." *Feds' Inquiry Ought to Wake Up Big Airlines*, Crain's Detroit Bus. (Mar. 16, 1998), at 8. *See also* Paul Dempsey and Andrew Goetz, *Airline Deregulation & Laissez Faire Mythology* 221-238 (1992).

[12] Paul Dempsey, *Airport Planning & Development: A Global Survey* 235-269 (1999).

- Governments have revoked slots from incumbents, or created a pool of new slots, for distribution to new entrant airlines, foreign carriers, or to provide service to small communities.
- Governments have allowed the bartering of slots; and
- Governments have transferred slots to airlines, and allowed them to buy, sell and trade slots in the market.

One promising rationing mechanism which has not been widely applied is "peak period" pricing, whereby carriers pay more for slots when demand is high, and less for slots when demand is low.

THE HIGH DENSITY SLOT RULE

Promulgated in 1968, the Department of Transportation [DOT] High Density Rule[13] designated several airports (i.e., Chicago O'Hare, New York's LaGuardia, Kennedy and Newark, and Ronald Reagan Washington National) as high density airports and regulated the number of permissible hourly Instrument Flight Rule [IFR] operations (takeoffs and landings).[14] The authority to take-off or land a single aircraft is referred to as a "slot." Thus, a round-trip flight to and from an airport requires two slots.

The 1968 High-Density Traffic Airport Rule originally addressed air traffic congestion on the East Coast. Although not part of the Rule, for a number of years the Federal Aviation Administration [FAA] controlled operations at several airports. Additional airports were added after the 1981 Professional Air Traffic Controllers Association [PATCO] strike, including Atlanta, Boston, Chicago O'Hare, Dallas/Ft. Worth, Denver, Newark and Philadelphia. In order to reduce administrative oversight, also beginning in 1968, the U.S. government[15] conferred antitrust immunity to scheduling committees, comprised of air carriers, to allocate slots among themselves. Because scheduling committees were heavily dominated by incumbent airlines, required unanimity, and there were no deadlock-breaking mechanisms, new entry was often stifled. Scheduling committees sometimes reached an impasse in order to resist efforts for new entry.

---

[13] 33 Fed. Reg. 17896 (1968).

[14] 14 CFR Part 39, Subparts K and S.

[15] Prior to its sunset on Dec. 31, 1984, the Civil Aeronautics Board performed this function; on Jan. 1, 1985, the DOT assumed that jurisdiction.

Occasionally, the FAA intervened, as it did in order to give the new-entrant airline New York Air (a non-union Texas Air subsidiary) slots to inaugurate an East Coast shuttle.[16]

Beyond the airline scheduling committees, the FAA experimented with other allocation methods. For a short while, the FAA permitted slot exchanges on a one-for-one basis. In 1982, the FAA experimented with a six-week experimental program permitting slot sales.[17] The High Density Rule has been amended several times since initially promulgated, to address issues such as the number of authorized operations,[18] specified controlled hours,[19] minimum percentage of slot use required to avoid forfeiture, and size of aircraft allowed at the airports.[20] Slot restrictions have the following characteristics:

- The number of slots varies from airport to airport;
- Slots are allocated among specified classes of users—air carriers, commuter carriers, and other operators; and
- Slots must be used 80% of the time over a two-month period or they will be considered dormant and withdrawn by the FAA.[21]

The DOT has less flexibility in changing slot restrictions at Washington National Airport, since they are now statutorily imposed.[22]

---

[16] Eileen Gleimer, *Slot Regulation At High Density Airports: How Did We Get Here and Where Are We Going?*, 61 J. Air L. & Com. 877, 885 (1996).

[17] 37 Fed. Reg. 25, 508 (1982). During this period, more than 300 slots were transferred, of which more than 190 were sold. Eileen Gleimer, *Slot Regulation At High Density Airports: How Did We Get Here and Where Are We Going?*, 61 J. Air L. & Com. 877, 884 n. 29 (1996).

[18] 45 Fed. Reg. 62,406 (1980).

[19] 49 Fed. Reg. 8237 (1984).

[20] 45 Fed. Reg. 62,406 (1980); 54 Fed. Reg. 38,843 (1989); 56 Fed. Reg. 41,200 (1991); 58 Fed. Reg. 39,610 (1993);

[21] Though special rules attempt to accommodate bankruptcy. *See* Eileen Gleimer, *Slot Regulation At High Density Airports: How Did We Get Here and Where Are We Going?*, 61 J. Air L. & Com. 877, 891-896 (1996).

[22] *The Metropolitan Washington Airport Act of 1986*, Pub. L. 99-591 prohibited any changes in the 37 hourly slots authorized for air carrier operations.

THE BUY-SELL SLOT RULE

In 1986, the rules were amended yet again to allow the purchase and sale of slots. The Buy-Sell Slot Rule was the brainchild of President Reagan's Office of Management and Budget [OMB] Director David Stockman. Promulgated in 1985, it permits airlines that hold slots to sell them at whatever the market will bear.[23]

The FAA "Buy-Sell" Rule became effective on April Fools' Day, 1986. It permits airlines to sell slots at the four High-Density airports (i.e., Kennedy, LaGuardia, O'Hare, and National), though the FAA insists the slots are not to be considered "proprietary rights."[24] The FAA reserved the right to revoke them at any time. Carriers holding slots on December 16, 1985, were "grandfathered" in—that is, they were effectively given the slots they held on that date. Slots not used regularly are deemed dormant and subject to recapture by the FAA,[25] and along with other newly available slots, can be distributed by lottery.[26] The FAA may also recapture slots for "operational reasons." International and general aviation slots are treated separately.[27] The Buy-Sell Rule also allows non-carriers to hold slots—something of significance for airlines wishing to use their slots as collateral for loans.[28] Moreover, in order to dodge the recapture of dormant slots, owners of slots were allowed to lease them to other carriers. Also, air carriers can allow commuter operators to utilize jet slots.

Four measures are used to determine the value of a slot:

- *The Economic Value of a Slot*—To the incumbent airline, the value of a slot is equivalent to the discounted present value of the net profit stream from the fare premium it is able to charge;

---

[23] *Stockman Urges Slot Auction at National*, Av. Week & Space Tech. (Jan. 17, 1983), at 34; Douglas Feaver, *Few FAA Proposals Depart from 'Open Skies' Air Traffic*, Washington Post, Feb. 4, 1984, at A1.

[24] 49 CFR § 93.233(a).

[25] Carriers with large numbers of slots can shift use between different slot numbers to cover non-use.

[26] Since 1986, the FAA has not held one additional lottery.

[27] 50 Fed. Reg. 52,180 (1985).

[28] Typically, the lender takes possession of the slot and leases it back to the carrier whose debt is secured by the collateral of the slot. Eileen Gleimer, *Slot Regulation At High Density Airports: How Did We Get Here and Where Are We Going?*, 61 J. Air L. & Com. 877, 902 (1996).

- *The Sales Value of a Slot*—To the prospective buyer, the value of a slot is the incremental earning power afforded by slot access; it will vary with the number of slots, the time period they represent, and the high density airport to which they provide access;

- *The Collateral Value of a Slot*—To the lender, their value will be discounted because of the risk associated with such collateral in terms of the possibility of recapture, or a change in governmental policy;

- *The Accounting Value of a Slot*—To the airline holding or seeking them, their value will vary depending upon the accounting treatment they are given, with some carriers bundling their value with gates, while others carrying them on their balance sheets at book value.[29]

PROBLEMS WITH THE BUY-SELL SLOT RULE

Parties opposed to the Buy-Sell rule objected on four grounds, saying it would: (1) give an undeserved "windfall" to incumbents; (2) increase air fares; (3) cause slots used for service to small communities to be outbid by carriers seeking to serve more lucrative routes; and (4) it would create anti-competitive incentives for large carriers to outbid smaller carriers for slots. Though history has since proven most of these objections correct, they fell upon deaf ears by a DOT determined to march forward.[30] As one source noted, "The DOT did not believe larger carriers would use their resources and the flexibility provided by the rule to dominate the markets and thereby create concentration at high density airports. . . . Reality has shown that the DOT's beliefs were quite naïve."[31]

Since promulgation of the Buy-Sell Slot Rule, by and large the major carriers have been the purchasers, and the early new entrant carriers the sellers, of slots. At the dawn of the 21st Century, the major U.S. airlines controlled 91% of all take-off and landing slots at National Airport, while their commuter affiliates controlled most of the

---

[29] Eileen Gleimer, *Slot Regulation At High Density Airports: How Did We Get Here and Where Are We Going?*, 61 J. Air L. & Com. 877, 900 (1996).
[30] Robert Hardaway, *The FAA "Buy-Sell" Rule: Airline Deregulation at the Crossroads*, 52 J. Air L. & Com. 1 (1986).
[31] Eileen Gleimer, *Slot Regulation At High Density Airports: How Did We Get Here and Where Are We Going?*, 61 J. Air L. & Com. 877, 896 n. 88 (1996).

rest (US Airways and its Shuttle affiliate alone controlled 39% of National's slots). In essence, the Buy/Sell Rule enabled the major carriers to generate significant monopoly power by virtue of the ability to hoard market share and effectively prohibit new entry made possible by slot ownership. As one source noted, "no meaningful access has been provided to new entrants since the buy-sell rule was enacted."[32]

The cost of purchasing slots at slot-constrained airports can be prohibitive for new entrants (though major carriers appear loathe selling them to new entrants at any price):[33]

- In 1996, it was reported that "new airlines have to pay as much as $2 million to buy a slot from one of the majors to fly into airports such as LaGuardia. . . ."[34]
- In 1993, slots at O'Hare traded at $2 million or more; United reported that each of its slots at O'Hare generates nearly $5 million on average in transportation revenue annually.[35]
- In 1992, USAir purchased 62 LaGuardia jet slots and 46 commuter slots, 6 national slots, a terminal under construction and flight kitchen for $61 million.[36]
- In 1991, USAir purchased 10 Washington National slots and 12 LaGuardia slots for $16.8 million (approximately $760,000 per slot).[37] USAir purchased 8 LaGuardia slots for $6 million (approximately $750,000 per slot).[38] American Airlines purchased 12 LaGuardia slots and 10 National slots for $21.4 million (approximately $970,000 per slot).[39] Continental purchased 35 LaGuardia slots by assuming $54 million in Eastern

---

[32] *Id.* at 877, 929.

[33] "[As a result of the Buy/Sell Rule] the carriers holding the slots have a grip on the traffic operating out of [Washington National, Chicago O'Hare, and New York Kennedy and LaGuardia Airports]. Slots at peak times are said to be worth several million dollars each, but new entrant carriers allege that slots cannot be purchased at any price." Sally Gethin, *Congress is Under Pressure To Limit the Influence of America's Powerful Hub and Spoke System*, Jane's Airport Rev. (Dec. 1, 1997), at 20.

[34] Ann Imse, *Federal Rules Hurt Discount Air Carriers*, Rocky Mountain News, Nov. 15, 1996), at 1B.

[35] Eileen Gleimer, *Slot Regulation At High Density Airports: How Did We Get Here and Where Are We Going?*, 61 J. Air L. & Com. 877, 900 (1996).

[36] Gary Rawlins and Larry Marshak, USA Today, Jan. 9, 1992, at 8B.

[37] Donna Rosato and Darren Summers, *Greenspan Raise*, USA Weekend (Nov. 23, 1991), at 10B.

[38] *Bankruptcy Court Begins Auction of Pan Am Assets*, Los Angeles Times, Dec. 10, 1991, at D3.

[39] *Stock Prices Fall*, Washington Post, Nov. 29, 1991.

Airlines debt (approximately $1.5 million per slot).[40] Delta purchased 5 LaGuardia slots for $3.5 million (approximately $700,000 per slot).[41]

- In 1990, American Airlines purchased 14 National and LaGuardia slots, and it was reported that "slots at National and LaGuardia typically sell for between $500,000 and $1 million each, depending on the time of day in which those landing and takeoff rights can be used."[42] American Airlines purchased 10 LaGuardia slots and two Canadian routes for $10 million.[43]

- A 1990 DOT study found that the value of all slots at the four high-density airports was approximately $3 billion, or $850,000 per slot. When accompanied by gates, the value of slots doubled.[44]

One source noted the reluctance of incumbent airlines to sell slots to new entrants, because, "carriers do not want slots to wind up in the hands of their competitors. In fact, the competitive considerations and reluctance to transfer slots may be greater when the potential buyer is a new entrant. . . ."[45] "Large carriers may also 'park' excess air carrier slots with their affiliated commuter airlines or code-sharing partners to keep them out of the hands of their competitors."[46]

As a consequence of these restrictions on new entry, average fares at LaGuardia were 35% higher than the average for 33 other airports.[47] Airline yields at Washington National Airport are among the highest in the nation as well. The FAA Buy-Sell Slot Rule has been widely criticized on grounds that it gave the incumbent airlines a windfall, and drove up the price of air transportation for consumers.[48] The Government Accounting Office [GAO] found that airports where

---

[40] *Auction Splits Up Eastern Airlines Assets*, Los Angeles Times, Feb. 5, 1991, at P3.

[41] *U.S. Airlines Bid for Eastern Remains*, USA Today, Feb. 6, 1991, at 8B.

[42] Stanley Ziemba, *Midway Sells 14 Slots in N.Y. and Washington*, Chicago Tribune, Oct. 13, 1990, at 1C.

[43] *Business Digest*, The Courier-Journal, Dec. 19, 1990, at 12B.

[44] Secretary's Task Force on Competition in the U.S. Domestic Airline Industry, *Airports, Air Traffic Control, and Related Concerns* (1990).

[45] Eileen Gleimer, *Slot Regulation At High Density Airports: How Did We Get Here and Where Are We Going?*, 61 J. Air L. & Com. 877, 907-908 (1996).

[46] *Id.* at 877, 910.

[47] U.S. General Accounting Office, *Airline Deregulation: Barriers to Entry Continue to Limit Competition in Several Key Domestic Markets* 21 (Oct. 1996).

[48] *See* Paul Dempsey, Robert Hardaway and William Thoms, 1 *Aviation Law & Regulation* § 7.25 (1993); Robert Hardaway, *Airport Regulation, Law and Public Policy* 197-205 (1991).

entry is limited by slot controls have about 7% higher air fares.[49] Airport access restrictions have been criticized on grounds they frustrate the open entry objectives and market force reliance fostered by the Airline Deregulation Act.[50] By 1997, DOT had concluded, "It would be far better for open competition if we did not have slot controlled airports."[51]

Pointing out that the oligopoly premium of a slot will vary with the extent of the incumbent firm's market share, Professor Robert Hardaway observed, "each slot held by an incumbent firm represents exactly one slot *not* held by a competitor. Each competitor eliminated from the market causes the demand curve facing the incumbent to become slightly steeper, thereby permitting the incumbent to reap, by degrees, a slightly higher oligopoly profit."[52] Shortly after the Buy-Sell Rule was promulgated, Hardaway accurately predicted, "because of the greater value of a slot to large firms, these firms may end up outbidding smaller firms. If this occurs, the following will result: (1) entry will be inhibited, thus permitting incumbent firms to face a steeply declining demand curve and enabling them to set prices at a profitable, but misallocative, level above marginal cost; and (2) combined with a "lose it or use it" provision, large outbidding firms may use slots for flights that do not cover variable costs in order to keep the slots and thus preserve an oligopoly profit on other flights."[53] Hardaway concluded that the Buy-Sell Rule "creates an economic incentive for large carriers to outbid small carriers for anti-competitive purposes."[54] He urged that a certain percentage of slots be recalled for redistribution, so as to flatten the slope of the demand curve for larger firms, reducing the anti-competitive incentive to hoard slots.

---

[49] Paul Dempsey, Robert Hardaway & William Thoms, 1 *Aviation Law & Regulation* § 5.05 (1993).

[50] *See* Robert Hardaway, *The FAA "Buy-Sell" Slot Rule: Airline Deregulation at the Crossroads*, 52 J. Air L. & Com. 1 (1986); James Gesualdi, *Gonna Fly Now: All the Noise About the Airport Access Problem*, 16 Hofstra L. Rev. 213 (1987); Eileen Gleimer, *Slot Regulation at High Density Airports: How Did We Get Here and Where Are We Going?*, 61 J. Air L. & Com. 877 (1996).

[51] DOT Response to Questions from Sen. Richard Shelby, Hearings on the Implications of Airport Deregulation (Oct. 21, 1997).

[52] Robert Hardaway, *The FAA "Buy-Sell" Rule: Airline Deregulation at the Crossroads*, 52 J. Air L. & Com. 1, 27 (1986).

[53] *Id.* at 1, 30.

[54] *Id.* at 1, 72.

THE FAA AUTHORIZATION ACT OF 1994

In 1993, the Baliles Commission urged the FAA to "review the rule that limits operations at 'high density' airports with the aim of either removing these artificial limits or raising them to the highest practicable level consistent with safety requirements."[55] The Federal Aviation Administration Authorization Act of 1994 authorized the Secretary of Transportation to grant exemptions from these requirements to enable new entrant air carriers[56] to provide air transportation at high density airports (other than Washington National Airport) if s/he finds both that the public interest so requires and that exceptional circumstances exist.[57] But until the late 1990s, several decisions of the DOT embraced a policy of not finding "exceptional circumstances" to exist where an incumbent already provided nonstop service in the market. In fact, DOT approved only two applications from new entrant airlines, and only in instances where the applicant's proposal would address a service void—markets which were large enough to support nonstop service but had none.[58]

This narrow interpretation[59] of the "exceptional circumstances" doctrine came under serious criticism by the GAO. In a 1996 report to Congress, the General Accounting Office found that "control of slots by a few airlines greatly deters entry at key airports in Chicago, New York and Washington."[60] The GAO recommended the Secretary of Transportation create a pool of available slots by withdrawing a reasonable number of slots from incumbent airlines, which received them through the grandfather process, and distribute them in a fashion that increases competition. Alternatively, GAO recommended that

---

[55] Nat'l Comm'n to Ensure a Strong Competitive Airline Industry Change, *Challenge and Competition: A Report to the President and Congress* (Aug. 1993).

[56] A "new entrant air carrier" is defined as an air carrier or commuter operator that holds or operates (or held and operated, since Dec. 16, 1985) fewer than 12 slots at the airport in question, not including international, Essential Air Services, or certain night time slots at Reagan or LaGuardia airports. 49 U.S.C. § 41714(h).

[57] 49 U.S.C. § 41714(c)(1).

[58] For example, in 1994 DOT granted Reno Air slot exemptions to serve O'Hare from Reno, Nevada, a market that then had no nonstop service. DOT Order 94-9-30 (1994).

[59] The DOT subsequently acknowledged that the standard had been applied narrowly. *See Application of Frontier Airlines*, DOT Order 97-10-17 (1997).

[60] Government Accounting Office report to Congress, report to Congress, *Airline Deregulation: Barriers to Entry Continue in Several Key Domestic Markets* (Oct. 1996).

Congress revise the legislative standard to "make the consideration of competitive benefits a key criterion. . . ."[61]

Responding to the GAO's study, DOT announced a new policy of viewing more favorably applications of new entrant airlines for waiver of the slot restrictions under the exceptional circumstances doctrine so as to improve competition in the market.[62] Adoption of the new policy made legislative amendment of the statutory criteria unnecessary. The DOT announced that henceforth it would find "exceptional circumstances" to exist warranting an exemption from the High Density Rule where: (1) applicants would fly jet aircraft that meet Stage 3 noise requirements in the market; (2) there is a reasonable expectation that the proposed service would be operationally and financially viable; and (3) the applicant either (a) will offer new non-stop service where none now exists, or (b) has a demonstrated potential to offer low-fare competition, there is single carrier service and the market could support competition, or the existing carriers do not provide meaningful competition.[63] Under these criteria, several new entrant airlines inaugurated new competitive service to a number of slot-constrained airports.[64]

Recognizing the High Density Rule as "a serious barrier to entry, which has had a dampening effect on domestic airline competition," DOT authorized 75 slot exemptions to a start-up airline, JetBlue, at New York Kennedy International Airport.[65] DOT also launched an experimental program of allocating slot exemptions to selected communities for the purpose of assisting them in securing service to slot-constrained airports.[66]

Major carriers alleged that the real reason for the new entrant's application for an exemption is that they want to avoid the expense of purchasing or leasing slots at a slot-constrained airport and thereby gain a competitive advantage by avoiding a normal cost of doing business. But one must realize that the major airlines received slots at National, LaGuardia, Kennedy and O'Hare Airports in the mid-1980s

---

[61] *Id.* at 23.

[62] DOT Response to the GAO Report (Jan. 6, 1997).

[63] *Id.*

[64] For example, the DOT awarded slot exemptions at New York LaGuardia Airport to Frontier Airlines, Spirit Airlines, Pro Air, AirTran, and American Trans Air.

[65] Application of New Air Corporation, DOT Order 99-9-11 (1999). New Air changed its name to JetBlue. JetBlue inaugurated service from New York Kennedy to Ft. Lauderdale, FL, on Feb. 11, 2000. It expects to serve 30 cities with 32 aircraft by 2002. *Business Wire* (Apr. 5, 2000).

[66] *Applications of the Communities of the Virginia Peninsula*, DOT Order 99-3-12 (1999).

without paying for or leasing them. Major airlines also lease the slots they received for free to other airlines. Yet, landing and takeoff slots are public resources. Rather than surrendering dormant slots to new entrant airlines, major airlines have turned these resources into private gain.[67] Moreover, the hypocrisy with which the major airlines make this argument is rather astounding. Paradoxically, the major carriers who protest so vehemently to domestic slot exemptions have been the most vociferous advocates in favor of slot exemptions for themselves at foreign airports such as London Heathrow and Tokyo Narita.

The 1994 Act also required DOT to conduct a study of the High Density Rule and report back to Congress, considering the following:

- whether improvements in technology and in the air traffic control system and the use of quieter aircraft would make it possible to eliminate the limitations on or increase the number of hourly aircraft operations;
- the effects of eliminating the High Density Rule, or increasing operations, on congestion, noise, competition, profitability, and safety;
- the impact on the Essential Air Services program, on the ability of new entrants to obtain reasonably timed slots, and the ability of foreign carriers to obtain slots; and
- the impact of the withdrawal of slots to support foreign air transportation.[68]

The DOT issued its report to Congress the following year. It noted that changing the High Density Rule would not adversely affect air safety since the rule plays only a secondary role to the FAA's air traffic management system. The study also found that O'Hare and National could support more growth. At Kennedy, DOT found that airfield capacity was well matched with the number of slots, while other infrastructure could accommodate additional traffic. At LaGuardia, the number of slots appeared slightly to exceed airfield capacity, though gate and landside capacity appeared sufficient to handle new growth. Using a cost/benefit analysis, discounting the additional revenue and passengers realized by slot rule elimination with the ad-

---

[67] For example, Midway Airlines owned 13 Washington National commuter slots that it leased to Air Canada for 10 years.

[68] 49 U.S.C. § 41714(e)(1).

ditional costs of delay, DOT found that O'Hare would enjoy a net benefit of $205 million per year, while at Kennedy the benefit would be only $7 million per year. At LaGuardia and National, however, the DOT found that elimination of the High Density Rule would result in net losses.[69]

THE PERIMETER RULES AND THE SHELBY AMENDMENT

In the late 1990s, Congress took additional action to reduce barriers to entry at airports. For example, the Wright Amendment of 1979 established a perimeter rule restricting air service at Dallas Love Field, limiting service to Texas and its adjacent states (i.e., New Mexico, Oklahoma, Arkansas and Louisiana). An exception to the rules allows service beyond if provided in aircraft with fewer than 56 seats.[70] In 1997, Congress passed the Shelby Amendment,[71] which allowed service from Love Field to additional states of Kansas, Mississippi and Alabama, and made it clear service beyond this area could be provided in aircraft having 56 seats even if such aircraft have been reconfigured to that size.[72] Despite the Congressional mandate, major airlines have devoted significant resources fighting new entry at Love Field.

Perimeter rules restrict competition not only at Dallas Love Field, but also at Washington National and at LaGuardia. Originally imposed by the CAB in the mid-1960s at 600 miles around National and expanded by the DOT to 1,000 miles in 1981, in the Washington Metropolitan Airport Act of 1986 Congress statutorily prescribed a perimeter of 1,250 miles. Under this statute, all aircraft taking off or landing from National must do so to or from an airport within a 1,250-mile radius from National. This restriction was criticized by the National Research Council's Transportation Research Board [TRB] in a 1999 study of competition in the U.S. airline industry, wherein the TRB stated: "These rules no longer serve their original purpose and have produced too many adverse side effects, including barriers to

---

[69] Eileen Gleimer, *Slot Regulation at High Density Airports: How Did We Get Here and Where Are We Going?*, 61 J. Air L. & Com. 877, 921-924 (1996).

[70] *International Air Transportation Competition Act of 1979* § 29, P.L. No. 96-192, 94 Stat. 35, 48-49 (1980). The amendment has never been codified. It was upheld as Constitutional in *State of Kansas v. United States*, 16 F.3d 436 (D.C. Cir. 1994).

[71] Department of Transportation and Related Agencies Appropriations Act § 337, P.L. No. 105-66, 111 Stat. 1425, 1447 (Oct. 27, 1997).

[72] *See Love Field Service Interpretation Proceeding*, DOT Order 98-12-27 (1998).

competition. These rules arbitrarily prevent some airlines from extending their networks to these airports; they discourage competition among airports in the region and among the airlines using these airports; and they are subject to chronic attempts by special interest groups to obtain exemptions."[73] Moreover, Washington National Airport's annual flight operations have declined since their high water mark in the early 1980s.[74]

CRITICISM OF GOVERNMENT RESTRICTIONS ON ENTRY

The Airline deregulation Act was supposed to eliminate restrictions on entry into the airline industry. Yet slot constraints and perimeter rules (as well as long-term gate leases and majority-in-interest clauses) continued to serve as serious impediments to entry decades after deregulation was adopted as national policy. Also in its 1999 report addressing competitive ramifications of slot controls, TRB stated that "increased opportunities for entry and competition in the domestic airline industry" are an important public interest goal. But there were obstacles to goal achievement, "including longstanding rules curbing access to some of the largest airports." The TRB also confirmed what other studies have found—that "high average fares in many of the city-pair markets involving the hub airports of major airlines have been a recurrent subject of public concern and policy debate during the past two decades" and that "slot-controlled airports consistently are among the highest-priced markets in the country." These criticisms of government constraints on entry at airports laid the foundation for legislation introduced by Senator John McCain (R-Ariz.) in 1999 to phase-out slot controls.

AVIATION INVESTMENT AND REFORM ACT

In February 2000, the DOT proposed elimination of many slot rules in order to increase new entry and promote competition.[75] On April 5, 2000, President Clinton signed into law, the Wendell H. Ford Aviation Investment and Reform Act for the 21st Century [AIR-21].[76]

---

[73] Transportation Research Board, *Special Report 255: Entry and Competition in the U.S. Airline Industry* (1999).
[74] *See* Paul Stephen Dempsey and Laurence E. Gesell, *Air Commerce and the Law* 501 (2004).
[75] Federal Document Clearing House (Apr. 14, 2000).
[76] PL 106-181.

Senator Wendell Ford observed, "this bill would loosen certain of the remaining federal regulatory restrictions to competition. These restrictions, like slot controls or the perimeter rule at National Airport, have limited the benefits of airline deregulation."[77]

AIR-21 began a phase-out of slot controls at LaGuardia, Kennedy and Chicago O'Hare. Slot restrictions were scheduled for elimination at O'Hare on July 1, 2002, as will the two New York airports by January 1, 2007. Airlines with limited operations could expand service at New York airports to 20 slots each, and at O'Hare to 30 slots each. There are no restrictions on adding regional jet flights, a change that is particularly beneficial for large airlines with regional aircraft. Almost immediately there were approximately 500 slot requests for regional jet operators. The real problem lay with capacity, gate and facility space for new entrants. As of May 1, 2000, slot exemptions for international service were no longer required at O'Hare.[78] But the congestion created by unlimited entry led DOT to encourage the carriers to enter into "voluntary" plans for capacity reduction, thereby peeling back the number of flight frequencies that slot elimination had generated.

AIR-21 also authorizes the DOT to grant up to 24 exemptions at National Airport, 12 within the 1,250-mile perimeter and 12 outside the perimeter. DOT may grant beyond-perimeter exemptions where the Secretary finds the exemptions will:

- provide domestic network benefits beyond the perimeter;
- increase competition by new entrant airlines or in multiple markets;
- not reduce travel options from small and medium hub airports within the perimeter; and
- not result in meaningfully increased travel delays.[79]

Additionally, in awarding slot exemptions, the Secretary may consider whether the carrier seeking a slot exemption provides maximum benefit to the U.S. economy, including U.S. jobs, while giving equal consideration to the consumer benefits associated with the award of

---

[77] Aviation Competition, Hearings before the Senate Comm. on Commerce, Science & Transportation (testimony of Sen. Wendell Ford) (Oct. 28, 1997).
[78] Id.
[79] 49 U.S.C. § 41718(a).

such exemptions.[80] These specific directives to issue slot exemptions where competition is increased by new entrants, and to consider the consumer benefits derived from slot exemptions, augment the existing statutory public interest considerations added to the Federal Aviation Act by the Airline Deregulation Act of 1978, to wit:

> *[T]he Secretary of Transportation shall consider the following matters, among others, as being in the public interest . . . :*
>
> *(4) the availability of a variety of adequate, economic, efficient, and low-priced services. . .*
>
> *(10) avoiding unreasonable industry concentration, excessive market domination, monopoly powers, and other conditions that would tend to allow at least one air carrier . . . unreasonably to increase prices, reduce service, or exclude competition in air transportation. . . .*
>
> *(13) encouraging entry into air transportation markets by new and existing air carriers and the continued strengthening of small air carriers to ensure a more effective and competitive airline industry.*[81]

Thus, enhancement of competition, reduction of barriers to entry, fostering of low-priced services, and continued strengthening of small carriers are primary policy imperatives of the Federal Aviation Act which govern its evaluation of applications for slot exemptions. As of the May 5th deadline for filing for slot exemptions at Washington National Airport, 19 applicants had requested permission to provide 104 new flights, 44 beyond the perimeter.[82] The DOT ultimately awarded six Washington National "beyond-perimeter" slots to America West Airlines (four from Phoenix, and two from Las Vega), two to Trans World Airlines (from Los Angeles), two to National Airlines (from Las Vegas), and two to Frontier Airlines (from Denver). Thus, new entrants received only four of the 12 slots allocated. Within the pe-

---

[80] 49 U.S.C. § 41715(c).

[81] 49 U.S.C. § 40101.

[82] Alan Sipress, *Airlines Battle to Land Slots at Reagan National*, Washington Post (May 15, 2000).

rimeter, the DOT awarded two slots to American Trans Air (from Chicago Midway), two to Midway Airlines (from Raleigh-Durham, N.C.), two to Midwest Express (from Des Moines), and four to Spirit Airlines (from points to be determined in South Carolina and Florida).[83]

Other new entrant airlines have been able to gain entry at LaGuardia, Kennedy and O'Hare. For example, Midway Airlines was able to secure nine slots at LaGuardia to replace slots that it had previously leased from an incumbent airline for $1.88 million per year.[84]

ANTITRUST IMMUNITY

Airports by their nature are monopolistic. There are few, if any, competitors. As previously pointed, the Airline Deregulation Act of 1978 discontinued antitrust immunity (in part) for the airlines. Subsequent to the Airline Deregulation Act, the courts and the Justice Department began to strictly enforce antitrust violations at the local government level. Supreme Court decisions in 1978 and 1982 virtually stripped local governments of any antitrust immunity that they may have assumed they shared with the states. Hundreds of antitrust suits against airports were subsequently filed. On the horns of a dilemma, airport operators needed to restrict the number of concessionaires such as restaurants, automobile parking lot companies, taxi operators, and others, in order to maintain services at levels the airport facilities were economically capable of accommodating.

In 1984, Congress passed the Local Government Antitrust Act to limit the liability of local governments, including airport authorities, to injunctive relief only. The law removed the threat of potential liability of treble (monetary) damages for antitrust violations. That is to say, a plaintiff could stop the local government from violating the antitrust laws, but was barred from seeking monetary compensation for damages. Historically, the courts have been reluctant to grant injunctions against public airports since such action could threaten the availability to the public of scheduled air transportation services.[85]

Although not related directly to aviation, but in fact dealing with monopoly over sewage treatment in the area of city services, in the

---

[83] *Slater Announces Slot Exemptions at Reagan National*, World Airport Wk., (Jul. 11, 2000).
[84] Testimony of Robert Ferguson before the Senate Judiciary Comm, FDHC Congressional Testimony (May 2, 2000).
[85] *See Loma Portal Civil Club v. American Airlines*, 394 P. 2d 548 (1964).

1985 Wisconsin municipal antitrust case of *Town of Hallie v. City of Eau Claire*, the U.S. Supreme Court broadened the exemption from antitrust prosecution for local governments including airports.[86]

TORT IMMUNITY

To varying degrees, public airports have historically been granted antitrust immunity, and in some instances tort immunity for their actions as governmental agencies. Airport sponsors generally have tort liability, particularly for proprietary operations. Most tort actions are the result of hazardous conditions, which contribute to accidents and personal injury or property loss. Liability for injury often results from lack of supervision or failure to exercise the due care of a reasonable person—in other words, to be "negligent." In most instances airport sponsors may be held liable for negligence on the part of the governmental agency or its employees, for failure to maintain the airport in a safe condition, failure to protect airport users and visitors (i.e., "business invitees") from reasonably foreseeable dangers,[87] or failure to discharge the duty of a bailee in caring for property of another. In tort liability, a *guest* in someone's home assumes some of the host's liability. A business invitee, on the other hand, is offered a higher degree of care than are non-commercial guests. The operator of a business, for example, must provide an invitee with ordinary care and warnings of known hazards. Airport management, as a proprietor, has a legal duty to prevent any conditions or actions, which in themselves create a dangerous or hazardous situation. The courts have held that airports must be kept safe for invitees and other users.[88]

The courts have not regarded state laws as broadly granting governmental immunity in the operation of public airports. Airports are generally viewed as proprietary in nature, and government sponsors are held liable for torts accordingly, except where states have expressly granted tort immunity for local government operation of an airport.[89] In most instances, the local government's liability, for torts arising from airport operation, is the same as that of a private person. The general rule is that municipalities enjoy sovereign immunity from

---

[86] *See Town of Hallie v. City of Eau Claire*, 85 L. Ed. 2d 24, (1985).
[87] *See Slapin v. Los Angeles International Airport*, 65 Cal. App. 3d 484 (1976).
[88] *See Brown v. Sioux City*, 49 NW 2d 853 (1951).
[89] *See Scotti v. Birmingham*, 337 SO 2d 350 (1967).

suit in the exercise of their governmental functions, but are not immune for their proprietary or businesslike activities.

For example, associated with its government police powers, an airport is responsible for preventing unauthorized access to air operations areas and for providing Law Enforcement Officers [LEOs]. The exercise of state police powers may afford certain immunities for the airport. However, in protecting the public against security risk, airport authorities must respect the civil rights of the traveling public. Airports are responsible for protecting the well-being of "invitees" (i.e., passengers and other airport customers) just as any other private enterprise. Precise contours of immunity differ under each state's common law.

AIRCRAFT OWNERS AND PILOTS ASSOCIATION v. PORT AUTHORITY OF NEW YORK
305 F. Supp. 93 (E.D.N.Y. 1969)

May an airport impose a fee in an attempt to divert traffic to another airport?

The Port Authority of New York and New Jersey was formed by interstate compact between the states of New York and New Jersey. The Authority operates John F. Kennedy International Airport, LaGuardia Airport and Newark Airport, and it also operates Teterboro Airport. Effective August 1, 1968, the Authority, for the professed purpose of relieving congestion and achieving maximum efficient operation of the three major airports, and with the professed intention of influencing general aviation operators to transfer their operations away from the runways and traffic control patterns at the three major airports during peak traffic periods, adopted a $25 minimum charge to be put into effect during defined peak operating periods, in lieu of the pre-existing $5.00 minimum fee. The peak hours were defined as from 8 a.m. until 10 a.m. on Monday through Friday, and from 3 p.m. until 8 p.m. on all seven days of the week. The fee applied in terms of $25 per takeoff, but it applied to any aircraft which either took off or landed during the peak hours, and which had a seating configuration of less than 25 passengers.

As originally adopted, there were two exceptions. First, all helicopters were excluded; and second, air taxis operating pursuant to

Authority permits issued to air taxi operators conducting regular service for airline connecting passengers at Kennedy, provided their aircraft operated at Kennedy from runways not used by the scheduled airlines. The $25 minimum fee openly and by design favored the large aircraft landings and takeoffs during peak hours, at the expense of small plane operations. And, in the small plane classification, it singled out for favored treatment air taxis, and particularly those conducting a connecting service to the airlines.

The FAA acknowledged the Authority's promulgation of the new regulations by issuing a statement to the effect that the regulations were intended to provide relief from excessive delays at certain major terminals and not to correct a safety problem. The regulations were intended to deal with the congestion problem and with the problem of air traffic controller workload. The prefatory statement of the FAA characterized the Authority's regulations as having been adopted for the express purpose of shifting general aviation traffic away from peak hours. Noted in the statement was that on September 11, 1968, the FAA itself had imposed an increased minimum charge for landing at Washington National Airport, put into effect to relieve congestion.

The plaintiff, Aircraft Owners and Pilots Association [AOPA], and 16 individual pilots and owners as plaintiffs and intervenors sued to enjoin the further enforcement by the defendant Port Authority of its "take-off" fee. The core of plaintiffs' attack was that the fee could neither relieve the landing and take-off congestion in terms of number of operations, nor contribute anything to safety. The argument, then, was that the fee was openly discriminatory. It was noted that nowhere does the law authorize discrimination in favor of air carriers. Explicitly and repeatedly, it was argued, the laws indicate the equality of right of access to air facilities—whether navigable air space or airports. The Aviation Act of 1958 provides that, "There shall be no exclusive right for the use of any landing area or air navigation facility upon which federal funds have been expended." Furthermore, the Port Authority had received over $48 million of federal grants. The Airport and Airway Development Act of 1970 provides for assurances from the airport sponsor in exchange for federal funds, to wit:

> *The airport to which the project relates will*
> *be available for public use on fair and reason-*
> *able terms and without unjust discrimination,*

*and The Sponsor will operate the Airport as
such for the use and benefit of the public. In
furtherance of this covenant (but without limiting its general applicability and effect), the
Sponsor specifically agrees that it will keep the
Airport open to all types, kinds, and classes of
aeronautical use without discrimination between such types, kinds, and classes: Provided,
That the Sponsor may establish such fair,
equal, and not unjustly discriminatory condition to be met by all users of the Airport as
may be necessary for the safe and efficient operation of the Airport; And Provided Further,
That the Sponsor may prohibit or limit any
given type, kind, or class of aeronautical use of
the Airport if such action is necessary for the
safe operation of the airport or necessary to
serve the civil aviation needs of the public.*

It was separately argued that the power of the FAA to regulate and
control air traffic, and the extent of its regulation of that traffic, particularly at the New York area, invalidated, on the "preemption doctrine," the attempt of the Authority further to regulate through charges
at the airport for the sole and only purpose of controlling traffic patterns. Defendant contended the new fee schedule was not in conflict
with any provision of federal law or any undertaking of the Authority
in connection with its receipt of federal grants of funds for airport
improvement, and that its fee schedule was reasonable and appropriate. The Port Authority argued there was no possibility of preemption,
and that there was at least qualified FAA approval of the fee schedule.

In deciding the discrimination issue, the U.S. District Court said
there was no basis for denying FAA and airport owners the power to
differentiate among kinds of flights. All persons have equal rights of
access to the navigable air space, but one aircraft approach may represent the right of over 150 passengers to have access to the navigable
airways and landing areas. The next plane may represent the right of
one or of two persons to have such access. To treat them alike in allocating scarce landing and take-off time and space is to ignore, and not
to recognize the basic right of equal access to airways and landing

areas. To treat the aircraft approach as the controlling consideration, which was the heart of the plaintiffs' contentions, would be to reduce everything to the safety considerations and to a blind application of the first-come, first-served principle. If "first-come, first-served" has validity as a principle, it would necessarily have to be limited by the inevitable qualification, "all other things being equal," which they rarely are. Considerations of safety and of efficient utilization of the air space are both valid grounds upon which to establish preferential assignments of landing and take-off times, and are perfectly compatible with the interest of every person in the protection of his or her freedom of access to navigable airways and related landing areas.

It cannot be said that the particular preferential system set up by the fee schedule was arbitrary, capricious, unreasonable or discriminatory. The test is not whether it was the wisest and best allocation of a scarce commodity that could have been made. In the context of the present case, it is fair to recognize that the willingness and ability to pay the increased charge may itself be an efficient means of locating an indefinable sub-classification of enhanced social utility in some kinds of general aviation that is not related to the passenger-carrying size of the aircraft.

Given the unquestioned fact of airport congestion at the three airports, the revised fee schedule drew a perfectly rational line in separating mass transportation and its ancillaries from other aviation. The efficient utilization of air space in the interest of the greatest number of users of the air space plainly justified the distinction between large and small aircraft. The district court granted the defendant's motion for summary judgment, and the action was dismissed.

TOWN OF NEW WINDSOR v. RONAN
329 F. Supp. 1286 (S.D.N.Y. 1971)

> *Can land be taken for airport development under*
> *eminent domain based upon probabilities, or*
> *must there be a clearly demonstrated need?*

This case centers on the fact that metropolitan areas are beset by problems of noise, congestion and danger with increasing jet air transportation and overtaxed airport facilities. There is a need for the development of airport facilities where congestion does not already exist. The area involved in the instant case is around Stewart Airport near Newburgh, New York.

The airport was purchased for operation by the Metropolitan Transportation Authority [MTA] in 1970. Subsequently, the New York Legislature passed an Act to authorize establishment of an airport at the Stewart site, for the accommodation of domestic and international air travel and freight transport. The Legislature appropriated $30 million for MTA to use for the costs of the enterprise. It was determined that the Stewart area should be taken and developed as one of the few available sites for probable expansion of the air transportation system. Immediate needs for the land were identified for explicit uses such as runways, facilities and a buffer zone. But beyond the defined development, it was intended that other development of the airport would only be in response to need. In other words, there was no clearly stipulated need for much of the land that was to be acquired through *eminent domain*.

Defendants were the MTA, its chairman (Ronan) and members, as well as various state and federal officials and agencies. Plaintiffs were three towns containing or adjoining the proposed development, and associations and corporations concerned with the land and environment. Plaintiffs sought a preliminary injunction against the MTA upon two propositions. First, enlargement of the Stewart Airport required approval by the Secretary of Transportation under the Airport and Airway Development Act; and second, the State could not seize title to the lands in question without such approval. Trial was held in the United States District Court.

The weakness of the plaintiffs' case on the merits defeated their motion. The court held that there was clear ground for a responsible judgment that the Stewart area was "one of the last viable" alternatives for the kind of jet airport facilities required in the near future. The state has the power to act rationally upon probabilities, if certainties are not available. The state may take more than it is positive it will need. According to the United States Constitution, and the Airport and Airway Development Act of 1970, it is permissible to take land projected as enlarged airport facilities where the projection includes a hope, or even a need, for federal approval and money. Under the provisions of the Airport and Airway Development Act, an agency must have title to the land, or an assured expectation of acquiring title as a condition precedent to federal approval. The court stated that it makes evident sense to take land and set it aside rather than to wait for a time when intervening development of homes and other buildings will have to be bought and razed.

SCOTTI v. CITY OF BIRMINGHAM
337 So. 2d 350 (Ala. 1976)

Is an airport immune from tort liability?

Joseph F. Scotti sued the City of Birmingham, Alabama, after sustaining injuries in a fall allegedly caused by a wet slippery mat at an entrance doorway of the Birmingham Municipal Airport. The defendant, City of Birmingham, filed a motion for summary judgment, contending it was immune from liability for its negligence at the airport. The motion was granted and the action dismissed. Scotti appealed from the judgment of dismissal. The Code section upon which the city primarily relied in its motion read:

> *Governmental function—the construction maintenance and operation of municipal airports is hereby declared a public governmental function, and no action or suit shall be brought or maintained against any municipality for or on account of the negligence of such municipality, or its officers, agents, servants or employees, in or about the construction, maintenance, operation superintendence or management of any municipal airport.* [90]

Scotti, however, maintained that as a consequence of the court's decision in *Jackson v. City of Florence*,[91] these statutes were inoperative and municipal immunity from tort liability was abolished, in whatever form and however it may have been established. The issue then was whether the decision in *Jackson* effectively removed immunity granted the city by the code sections mentioned above.

In *Jackson*, action was brought to recover from the City of Birmingham and several of its police officers for injuries which the offi-

---

[90] Code of Alabama, Title 4, Sec. 24.
[91] 294 Ala. 592, 320 So.2d 68 (1975).

cers, allegedly, negligently or willfully inflicted on the plaintiff during and following arrest. The circuit court sustained the city's *demurrer* and dismissed the complaint, and the plaintiff appealed. On appeal, the Alabama Supreme Court reversed judgment, and thereby abolished the "doctrine of municipal immunity," with the decision being applicable to the instant plaintiff and all others suffering injury thereafter.

The complaint claimed damages for personal injuries sustained by the plaintiff (Jackson) as a proximate result of the negligence and wantonness of a police officer acting in the line of duty. It was alleged the officer, while engaged as a police officer for the City of Florence, negligently assaulted and willfully or wantonly assaulted the plaintiff, an unarmed, 75 year old, 130 pound man by the use of excessive force, resulting in the plaintiff's loss of his right eye.

Appellant Jackson acknowledged that this was a "head-on" request for a re-examination and reconsideration of the broad question of whether Alabama municipal corporations should continue to enjoy immunity from liability for the wrongful acts of their agents acting within the line and scope of their employment. He further admitted that, for him to prevail, the Alabama Supreme Court had to overrule a long line of cases (i.e., reverse prior case-law precedent).

Alabama courts first considered the question of tort liability of municipalities in 1854. Four years later, the court declared cities to be immune to suit for torts committed by agents in the exercise of a governmental function. There followed a string of cases holding that municipalities were liable for torts committed in the exercise of their "proprietary" capacity (defined by this court as meaning "corporate"), but were immune from suit for the commission of torts in their "governmental" capacity (meaning governmental functions other than proprietary). In *Jackson*, the complaint was for damages sustained as a result of the city acting in a governmental capacity.

The court responded, by declaring the doctrine of governmental immunity has been universally condemned in an unending number of published statements by legal scholars and jurists. It is frequently stated that the doctrine cannot be defended on any logical basis. By the turn of the century, it was being criticized as unjust and irrational from many sources. However, there is no doubt that the doctrine was, by that time, firmly established in Alabama law by decisions of the Alabama Supreme Court; that is to say, the courts constructed the law, not the legislature. And yet, the concept of the "king can do no wrong" is the antithesis of the very concepts upon which the U.S. government was founded. Against this background the Alabama legislature, in 1907, enacted legislation in the area of tort immunity to municipalities. Although no mention was made in the statute of liability being restricted to corporate functions of the municipality, the Alabama Supreme Court in its determinations continued to distinguish between *governmental* function and *corporate* or *proprietary* functions.

It was apparent to the Supreme Court that the only force given to the enactment passed by the 1907 Legislature, in so far as changing the law of municipal immunity, was simply to perpetuate the law as it existed before the enactment. Since that time, the litigant suing a municipality in tort had to show that the function being performed, which resulted in his or her injury, was a corporate one. However, the only clue as to whether a particular function was governmental or corporate had to be found in cases expressly declaring that particular function to fall within one or the other category, and many incongruities resulted.

In its review in *Jackson*, the Alabama Supreme Court stated that as municipal immunity law had evolved, it was "judicial and not legislative in nature." The court thereby declared that it was not unreasonable to suspect the legislature in 1907 was reacting to a call for the abolition, and not perpetuation, of what was by that time recognized as an unjust rule of law. Perhaps the courts should have bowed to that legislative prerogative rather than take the course it did. The Supreme Court admitted to prior mistakes and suggested it should correct them. Thus, in the *Jackson* case, the Alabama Supreme Court, with a broad-brush determination, abolished municipal immunity for tort in that state. The decision, however, was not without dissent.

Taking into consideration the dissent in *Jackson*, and the extant Title 4 of the Alabama Code, the Alabama Supreme Court again reversed itself, and held in this case that the legislative language was unequivocal in granting immunity in connection with operation of airports. In a seeming contradiction, the court re-instituted the long established practice of granting immunity from tort wrongs.

The Alabama Supreme Court affirmed the circuit court judgment in favor of the city, finding it immune from suit for negligence.

SLAPIN v. LOS ANGELES INTERNATIONAL AIRPORT
135 Cal. Rptr. 296 (1976)

Is an airport liable for reasonably foreseeable dangers?

On January 22, 1974, plaintiff Herman Slapin was assaulted and severely injured by unknown persons while, as a paying patron, he was lawfully on Parking Lot Number Four near the American Airlines terminal at Los Angeles International Airport. He alleged that for some time prior to that date, the defendant airport knew the parking lot was dangerous and unsafe unless properly supervised, maintained, patrolled and protected. Additionally, the defendant knew the public relied upon such protection, maintenance and supervision. Nevertheless, the airport "carelessly, negligently, and improperly owned, operated, managed, maintained, supervised, controlled, lighted and secured said parking area in such a fashion and manner so as to maintain a dangerous condition of property." And, the airport "took inappropriate actions to either warn or protect the plaintiff. . . ." Plaintiff Madeline Slapin, Herman Slapin's wife, also sued for loss of conjugal society, comfort, affection and companionship.

The Superior Court of Los Angeles County sustained the city's *demurrer* to the complaint, that to the extent the plaintiffs' complaint sought recovery for failure of the city to provide sufficient patrolling or police protection at the parking lot, it failed to state a cause of action. A public entity is specifically *immunized* from liability for such failure by Section 835 of the Government Code.

Plaintiffs appealed, contending this immunity should not apply to a situation where the governmental entity is engaged in a proprietary function (i.e., operating a parking lot for paying patrons). This contention, the court said, was without merit because the former distinction between *proprietary* and *governmental* activities of a public entity was abolished by statutes enacted in 1963.

However, the main thrust of the plaintiffs' complaint was that the parking lot, particularly the insufficient lighting provided there, constituted a dangerous condition of property, rendering the governmental entity liable under Government Code Section 835, which stated:

Except as provided by statute, a public entity
is liable for injury caused by a dangerous con-

dition of its property if the plaintiff establishes that the property was in a dangerous condition at the time of the injury, that the injury was proximately caused by the dangerous condition, that the dangerous condition created a reasonably foreseeable risk of the kind of injury which was incurred, and that either;

(a) A negligent or wrongful act or omission of an employee of the public entity within the scope of his employment created the dangerous condition; or

(b) The public entity had actual or constructive notice of the dangerous condition under Section 835.2 and a sufficient time prior to the injury to have taken measures to protect against the dangerous condition.

Government Code Section 830 provided that "dangerous condition" means a condition of property that creates a substantial risk of injury when such property is used with due care in a manner in which it is reasonably foreseeable that it will be used. As to this aspect of the first amended complaint, the trial court erred in sustaining the *demurrer*—that a mugger thrives in dark public places is a matter of common knowledge. The California Court of Appeal held that plaintiffs were entitled to attempt to prove:

- The lighting of the parking lot created a substantial risk of a criminal assault and thus constituted a dangerous condition;
- The plaintiffs' injuries were proximately caused by the dangerous condition;
- The dangerous condition created a reasonably foreseeable risk of the kind of injury plaintiffs sustained; and,
- The defendant had actual or constructive notice of the dangerous condition in time to have taken measures to protect against it.

The court noted that a holding of liability based upon a failure to provide sufficient lighting at the parking lot would in no way interfere with the public entity's political discretion as to the amount of policing to provide at the parking lot. The judgment of the superior court was reversed and the cause remanded for further proceedings consistent with this opinion.

AMERICAN AIRLINES v. MASSACHUSETTS PORT AUTHORITY
560 F.2d 1036 (1st Cir. 1977)

May an airport charge for the utility of facilities not used?

Plaintiffs, 18 airlines, sought a declaratory judgment that the action of the Massachusetts Port Authority [MASSPORT], owner of Logan International Airport, in raising airlines' landing fees 52% in 1977, imposed an unconstitutional burden on interstate commerce. They announced they would pay only at the 1976 rate. MASSPORT counter-claimed for the unpaid difference between the 1976 and 1977 amounts. The U.S. District Court dismissed the complaint, and granted summary judgment for MASSPORT on its counterclaim. Plaintiffs appealed.

MASSPORT's action increased the landing fees paid by the airlines from $8.4 million to $12.6 million. Of the increase, $2.5 million was attributed to the cost of three projects totaling some $46 million. All projects were deemed by the airlines to be of little or no use to them. The first was a runway extension and construction project. Runway extensions had been planned and substantially built, as well as a Short Take Off and Landing [STOL] runway, but the work was brought to a halt because of state environmental law litigation. The runway extensions were converted into so called "extended runway safety areas" of dubious utility, according to the airlines. The STOL runway was obliterated. These projects had by this time run up a cost of from $4 million to $31 million. A second item accounting for the increased landing fee was the filling of a tidal area known as the Bird Island flats, a 280 acre plot of which 105 acres were vacant and held for future development. The cost of the flats was between $28 million and $41 million, the vacant part of which was alleged not to be of any use to the airlines. Finally, MASSPORT had included, in its landing fee charge, the cost of its commitment to pay the East Boston Neighborhood Health Center $100,000 a year for ten years for assistance in any airport disaster requiring emergency medical aid.

Plaintiffs and defendants each relied upon *Evansville-Vanderburgh Airport Authority District v. Delta Air Lines*,[92] wherein the court determined a tax may not be "excessive in comparison with the government benefit conferred." Standing on this language, the plaintiffs urged they were entitled to have *discovery* and to make the effort to prove the landing fee, particularly the dramatic 1977 increase, was not productive of any commensurate benefit to them. The district court seized on *Evansville's* formulation that a charge must not be "excessive in relation to costs incurred by the taxing authorities." MASSPORT relied on this language, as well, and alleged an impracticability of applying the airlines' formula of relation of tax to value received.

The U.S. Court of Appeals sided with MASSPORT, recognizing there was some language in *Evansville* that supported the plaintiff airlines, but that the overwhelming thrust of the language was toward a comparison of the tax with costs incurred in connection with construction of facilities. The appellate court stated it could not see how a federal system, recognizing state sovereignty, could work on a basis of customer judgments of benefits received. A state could supply facilities that would be of critical importance to some users, of moderate convenience to others, and of marginal use to the remainder. If taxes, such as landing fees, were to be subject to attack from each user, depending upon the particular utility, their imposition could be a matter of endless and shifting controversy. Such an approach would subject every taxing authority to judgments of courts as to the wisdom, foresight, and efficiency of its plans from the viewpoint of each affected customer.

This is not to say that states can run wild and tax users for all extravagances. The facilities must be relevant to the operation of the airport. And the revenue from the landing fee must be fairly consonant with the costs incurred. But within these broad parameters, users share both the benefits and the costs of an airport's decisions, including the imprudent ones. In this case, it was not disputed that the expenditures were actually incurred or that the fee was accurately calculated thereon. No contention of bad faith was advanced. All three of

---

[92] 405 U.S. 707, 92 S.Ct. 1349, 31 L. Ed. 2d 620 (1972).

the challenged expenditures were made for legitimate airport objectives. The appellate court affirmed the district court's summary judgment.

TOWN OF HALLIE v. CITY OF EAU CLAIRE
471 U.S. 34 (1985)

Are municipalities immune from U.S. antitrust laws?

A group of unincorporated Wisconsin townships filed suit against an adjacent city in the United States District Court for the Western District of Wisconsin, alleging the city had violated the Sherman Act by acquiring a monopoly over sewage treatment in the area, and providing service only to areas which were willing to be annexed by the city and to use its sewage collection services rather than those of the towns. The district court ruled in favor of the city, pointing to a Wisconsin law which authorized cities providing sewage services to limit the unincorporated areas covered by their service unless ordered by the state to service certain areas, and holding that the city's conduct fell within the "state action" exemption from the federal antitrust laws. The United States Court of Appeals for the Seventh Circuit affirmed.[93]

On *certiorari*, the United States Supreme Court affirmed. In an opinion by Chief Justice Powell, expressing the unanimous view of the court, it was held that anti-competitive conduct by a municipality is protected by the state action exemption to the federal antitrust laws where it is authorized by state law, even though the state does not compel or actively supervise the anti-competitive conduct or expressly assert that the law is intended to have an anti-competitive effect.

This case presents the question whether a municipality's anti-competitive activities are protected by the state action exemption to the federal antitrust laws established by *Parker v. Brown*,[94] when the activities are authorized, but not compelled, by the state, and the state does not actively supervise the anti-competitive conduct. The findings of the court were:

---

[93] *Town of Hallie. v. City of Eau Claire*, 700 F.2d 376.
[94] 317 U.S. 341, 87 L. Ed. 315, 63 S. Ct. 307 (1943).

- Municipalities are not beyond the reach of the federal antitrust laws by virtue of their status because they are not themselves sovereign; rather, in order to obtain the protection of the "state action" exemption, municipalities must demonstrate that their anti-competitive activities were authorized by the state pursuant to a clearly expressed state policy to displace competition with regulation or monopoly public service;
- A state legislature need not expressly state in a statute or its legislative history that it intends actions delegated to municipalities therein to have anti-competitive effects, in order for that statute to constitute a "clear articulation" of an anti-competitive policy and thus bring municipal actions based on that statute within the "state action" exemption from the federal antitrust laws;
- It is not necessary to show that a municipality's anti-competitive conduct was compelled by the state in order to find that the municipality acted pursuant to a clearly articulated state policy, and thus bring such conduct within the "state action" exemption from the federal antitrust laws; and,
- A municipality need not show that its anti-competitive conduct was actively supervised by the state in order to bring that conduct within the "state action" exemption from the federal antitrust laws.

Accordingly, the U.S. Supreme Court affirmed the judgement of the U.S. Court of Appeals.

ALAMO RENT-A-CAR v. SARASOTA-MANATEE AIRPORT AUTHORITY
825 F.2d 367 (11th Cir. 1987)

May an airport impose charges upon non-airport tenants who regularly use the airport for commercial purposes?

This case is one of a series of actions brought by off-airport automobile rental agencies in an attempt to avoid paying airport charges related to commercial automobile rental operations on certain airports, including the defendant in this case, the Sarasota-Manatee Airport Authority.[95]   In 1982, the Shreveport-Manatee Airport Authority began considering measures to alleviate ground traffic congestion, and to obtain revenue from operators of "courtesy vehicles" which transported customers to and from the main airport terminal and certain businesses on the airport. The Airport Authority was concerned with two categories of businesses: first, hotels and motels; and second, off-airport car rental companies. "Off-airport" car rental companies are car rental companies that do not rent facilities on airport property and thus must transport customers from the airport to their remote locations. In contrast, "on-airport" car rental companies lease counter space inside the airport terminal, as well as land adjacent to the terminal used for storing and maintaining cars.

On July 27, 1982, the Authority adopted two resolutions, one governing courtesy vehicles operated by hotels and motels, and one governing the off-airport car rental companies' courtesy vehicles. The resolution concerning hotels and motels established a monthly courtesy vehicle fee of $50 or $100, depending on the size of the vehicle, or an annual fee of $800 per vehicle. The resolution governing off-airport car rental companies, including Alamo, contained an extensive series of requirements for securing courtesy vehicle permits. For example, companies seeking a permit had to provide proof of financial responsibility, identify their managerial personnel, and pay a user fee. The user fee applicable to these car rental companies was "10% of all gross business receipts derived from the rental automobiles to passengers picked up at the airport."

For companies, including Alamo, conducting a substantial volume of business involving airport passengers, the 10% fee greatly exceeded the flat fee applicable to hotels and motels. On July 29, 1982, Alamo brought suit in the district court seeking to enjoin the Authority's imposition of the 10% user fee on it and other off-airport car rental companies. Alamo claimed the user fee violated the Equal Protection Clause of the United States Constitution, as well as other provisions of state and federal law. The U.S. District Court held that the user fee denied Alamo equal protection of the laws and permanently enjoined the enforcement of the user fee being charged off-airport companies.

---

[95] *See also Airline Car Rental, Inc. v. Shreveport Airport Authority,* CCH 21 AVI ¶17,201 (1987).

The U.S. Court of Appeals reversed the District Court's judgment on Alamo's equal protection challenge. Because the District Court did not reach several of Alamo's alternative grounds for relief, the appellate court remanded for consideration of those contentions. For example, the District Court did not reach Alamo's claims that the user fee: constituted an unreasonable burden on interstate commerce, denied it due process of law in violation of the Fourteenth Amendment and the Florida Constitution, and/or was enacted in violation of Florida's statutes.

AIRLINE CAR RENTAL v. SHREVEPORT AIRPORT AUTHORITY
667 F. Supp. 303 (W.D. La. 1987)

May an off-airport automobile rental company conduct business on an airport without an agreement with the airport?

In April of 1985 the Shreveport Airport Authority passed a resolution entitled "Resolution Establishing Regulations and Fees for Rental Car Businesses Operating at the Shreveport Regional Airport Without a Lease," whereby it stated that it was necessary to impose charges on entities which did not have contracts with the Airport Authority but nevertheless used airport facilities in the furtherance of their commercial enterprises. Specifically, the Authority intended to levy charges on non-tenant rental car businesses that picked up and supplied services to passengers from the airport.

The resolution required non-tenant rental car businesses to obtain from the Authority a Rental Car Non-Tenant Business Permit, which permit would be issued upon compliance with certain requirements, including an agreement "to pay for the duration of the permit to the Authority 7% of all gross business receipts derived from the rental of vehicles to passengers picked up at the Airport. . . . " In contrast, the on-airport tenants leased counter space within the airport terminal, and vehicle service and storage areas on airport grounds. In addition to rental fees, the on-airport tenants paid 10% of their gross receipts derived from car rental transactions consummated on the airport.

The plaintiff, Airline Car Rental, Inc., operated a car rental service located near the Shreveport Regional Airport at the time the resolution was passed and derived most of its revenue from customers who traveled through the airport, and who had already made reservations for the use of an Airline vehicle. In order to transport its customers from the airport to its facility, Airline operated a courtesy shuttle service from designated passenger loading zones at the airport to its premises. Prior to 1977, Airline leased one of three concession areas within the terminal facilities. In 1977, Airline lost its lease when three competing rental car businesses outbid it. Airline then moved to its location proximate to, but not on, the airport.

Airline brought action seeking declaratory, injunctive, and other relief from the resolution, on a variety of grounds including violation of: interstate commerce provisions, Sherman Antitrust Law, state antitrust laws, the Airport and Airway Development Act of 1970, the Airport Acceleration Act of 1973, the Civil Rights Act, Equal Protection under the U.S. Constitution, due process of law, the Louisiana Airport Authorities Law, and for *tortious* interference with Airline's business. The defendant Shreveport Airport filed a motion to dismiss claiming Airline had failed to state a claim upon which relief could be granted.

In a previous trial, the District Court, in *Airline Car Rental, Inc. v. Shreveport Airport Authority* [96] determined the plaintiff's motion for summary judgment should be denied and the defendant's motion granted in part and denied in part. In the instant case, the Airport Authority requested summary judgment dismissing each of Airline's remaining claims that the Authority adopted the resolution in violation of the Commerce Clause, and in violation of state and federal Equal Protection Clauses. Airline sought summary judgment only on the grounds that the resolution violated state and federal Equal Protection clauses and was adopted without lawful authority.

The U.S. District Court granted summary judgment in favor of the Airport Authority and against Airline Car Rental. The court found that the resolution was passed under lawful authority and it did not place an impermissible burden on interstate commerce. Because the resolution was solely an economic regulation, it had to be sustained if it furthered some appropriate state interest.[97] The court concluded that the resolution did further an appropriate state interest.

---

[96] CCH 21 AVI ¶ 17,192 (1986).
[97] *Sibley v. Board of Supervisors of Louisiana State University*, 477 So. 2d 1094, 1107-8 1985).

CONTINENTAL AIR LINES v. DEPARTMENT OF TRANSPORTATION
856 F.2d 209 (D.C. Cir. 1988)

May Dallas Love Field be served by all air carriers?

When the Dallas-Fort Worth Airport was built, Dallas Love Field was closed to interlining air carriers in order to ensure that operations would be transferred to the new Dallas-Fort Worth Airport [DFW]. The law closing Love Field to interlining traffic became known as the "Love Field Amendment" (to the Aviation Safety and Noise Abatement Act of 1979). Subsequent to the departure of all interlining air carriers from Love Field, and although challenged, Southwest Airlines continued its operations from there. It was able to do so because Southwest does not interline with other air carriers. Wishing to compete with Southwest Airlines at Love Field, Continental Airlines challenged the interpretation of the Love Field Amendment. In part, the Amendment read as follows:

> . . . *neither the Secretary of Transportation, the Civil Aeronautics Board, nor any other officer or employee of the United States shall issue, reissue, amend, revise or otherwise modify . . . any certificate or other authority to permit or otherwise authorize any person to provide the transportation of individuals, by air, as a common carrier for compensation or hire between Love Field, Texas, except (1) charter air transportation not to exceed ten flights per month, (2) air transportation provided by commuter airlines operating aircraft with a passenger capacity of 56 passengers or less. . .*

> *a common carrier between Love Field, Texas, except that a person providing service to a point outside of Texas from Love Field on November 1, 1979, may continue to provide service to such point.*

Additionally, and in part, Section 29(c)(1) of the Amendment read as follows:

> *(c) Sub-Sections (a) and (b) shall not apply with respect to . . . authorize transportation of individuals, by air, ON A FLIGHT between Love Field, Texas, and one or more points within the States of Louisiana, Arkansas, Oklahoma, New Mexico, and Texas by an air carrier, if (1) such carrier does not offer or provide any other through service or ticketing with another air carrier or foreign air carrier, and (2) such air carrier does not offer for sale transportation to or from, and the flight or air-craft does not serve, any point which is outside any such state.*

The fundamental question before this court was whether the Department of Transportation properly interpreted the Love Field Amendment so as to permit service at Love Field by Continental Air Lines, an "interlining" air carrier (that is, one with connecting flights with other airlines).

Faced with rather dreadfully framed language, the DOT nonetheless ruled that the statute, coupled with its legislative history, was "crystal clear." The DOT concluded that "the plain and literal meaning of Sub-Section (c) refers to a specific 'flight,' and Sub-clauses (1) and (2) which must logically be read together, describe restrictions applicable to the flight. As DOT summarized its view, "Congress intended to make Love Field a short-haul airport limited to turnaround intrastate service in five states . . . " and Sub-clauses (1) and (2) ". . . simply specify *interline* and on-line restrictions applicable to service at Love Field." It was this interpretation that came under challenge in this case.

In brief, the competing positions were as follows. Joined by Southwest Airlines, the DFW parties contended that the statute was plain and clear. In their view, Section 29(c)(1) "is a class restriction; the carrier cannot be of a class which provides through service or ticketing with another air carrier." The second clause, in turn, was seen as an" operational restriction." That is, "the air carrier cannot route its flight or sell transportation from Love Field to a point out-side of the five enumerated states."

For its part, DOT, joined on this issue by Continental Airlines, continued to maintain the statute was indeed plain and clear, but in quite the opposite way from that of the DFW/Southwest reading. DOT stressed that Congress' employment of the phrase, "on a flight," at the beginning of Sub-Section (c) most naturally should be inter-preted to mean that the restrictions found in (c)(1) and (c)(2) are ap-plicable solely to Love Field flights. The DOT reiterated the fact that Congress' intent in crafting the Love Field Amendment was solely to limit the airport to "short haul" service.

The two positions were at polar opposites. But according to the court neither interpretation was quite correct. Nevertheless, the DOT position was the closer of the two to congressional intent. The court's acceptance of DOT's interpretation allowed Continental to move into Love Field to inaugurate a Dallas to Houston service, notwithstanding the fact that the airline was an "interlining" carrier.

Although supporting DOT's interpretation of the entry provisions of the Love Field Amendment, Continental challenged a DOT ruling that passengers had to be "double-ticketed," which as described by DOT, "involves the purchase of two separate tickets: one for service from Love Field to a point within Texas or the four adjacent states (Love Field Service Area), and a separate, second ticket for service from that destination to a point beyond the authorized Love Service Area." Double-ticketed passengers are subject to certain inconven-iences, including separate fares and the need to reclaim any checked baggage at the connecting point and then recheck it on the next flight. Continental's challenge to the double-ticketing requirement was de-nied.

NORTHWEST AIRLINES v. COUNTY OF KENT
510 U.S. 355 (1994)

Is it an unlawful discrimination for airports to cross allocate costs and revenues amongst a variety of airport users?

Seven commercial airlines asserted that certain airport user fees charged them were unreasonable and discriminatory, in violation of the Anti-Head Tax Act [AHTA], and the Commerce Clause of the

U.S. Constitution. The user fees contested were charged by the Kent County International Airport in Grand Rapids, Michigan. The airport collected rent and fees from three groups of users: commercial airlines, general aviation, and non-aeronautical concessionaires.

Since 1968, the airport had allocated its costs and set charges to aircraft operators pursuant to a "cost of service" accounting system known as the "Buckley methodology."[98] The accounting system was designed to charge the airlines only for the cost of providing facilities and services they used. Under the system, the airport would first determine the costs of operating the airfield and the passenger terminal, and allocate these costs among the users of the facilities. Costs associated with airfield operations were allocated to the airlines and general aviation in proportion to their use of the airfield. No portion of the costs was allocated to the concessions. Costs associated with maintaining the airport terminal were allocated among the terminal tenants—the airlines and the concessions—in proportion to each tenant's square footage.

The airport would then establish fees and rates for each user group. It charged the airlines 100% of the costs allocated to them, in the form of aircraft landing and parking fees, and rent for terminal space occupied by the airlines. General aviation, however, was charged at a lower rate. The airport recovered from that user group a per gallon fuel flowage fee for local aircraft and a landing fee for aircraft based elsewhere. These fees accounted for only 20% of the airfield costs allocated to general aviation. In relation to costs, the airport thus "undercharged" general aviation. At the same time, measured by allocated costs, the airport vastly "overcharged" the concessions. The airlines paid a cost-based per square foot rate for their terminal space. The concessions, however, paid market rates for their space. The "market rates" (substantially meaning 10% of the concessionaire's gross receipts) exceeded the concession's allocated costs and yielded a sizable surplus. The surplus offset the general aviation shortfall of approximately $525,000 per year, and had swelled the airport's reserve fund by more than $1 million per year.

The airlines and the airport periodically negotiated and agreed upon fees, and following a new rate study made in 1986, the airport proposed increased fees. The airlines objected to the higher fees and failed to reach an agreement with the airport. Ultimately, the County

---

[98] *See* James C. Buckley, *Rental Fee Recommendations* (Feb. 1969).

Board of Aeronautics adopted an ordinance unilaterally increasing the fees. The airlines sued the airport, attacking:

- the airport's failure to allocate to the concessions a portion of the airfield costs;
- the surplus generated by the airport's fee structure; and,
- the airport's failure to charge general aviation 100% of its allocated airfield costs.

The airlines alleged the fees imposed on them were unreasonable, and thus unlawful, under the Anti-Head Tax Act of 1973, and the Airport and Airway Improvement Act of 1982 [AAIA]. They said the airport's treatment of general aviation discriminated against interstate commerce in favor of primarily local traffic, in violation of Article I, Section 8, Clause 3, of the U.S. Constitution, the "Commerce Clause."

The parties filed cross-motions for summary judgment. In the first of three opinions, the U.S. District Court denied motions, holding that the airport's cost methodology was not *per se* unreasonable. In its second opinion, the District Court held that the airlines had an implied right of action to challenge the fees under the AHTA, but not under the AAIA, and that the airlines had no cause of action under the Commerce Clause. Following a bench trial, the district court issued its third and final opinion, concluding that the challenged fees were not unreasonable under the ATHA.[99] The U.S. Court of Appeals affirmed the District Court's judgment in principal part.[100]

The U.S. Supreme Court granted *certiorari* to resolve a conflict between the instant case and another appellate court decision, which declared key parts of a similar fee structure unreasonable under the AHTA.[101] In *Evansville-Vanderburgh Airport Authority District v. Delta Air Lines*,[102] the Supreme Court held that the Commerce Clause does not prohibit states or municipalities from charging commercial airlines a "head tax" to defray the costs of airport construction and maintenance, so long as,

---

[99] *Northwest Airlines v. County of Kent*, 738 F. Supp. 1112 (1990).
[100] *Northwest Airlines v. County of Kent*, 955 F.2d 1054 (1992).
[101] *Indianapolis Airport Authority v. American Airlines, Inc.*, 733 F.2d 1262 (1984).
[102] 405 U.S. 707 (1972).

> *the toll is based on some fair approximation of*
> *use or privilege for use . . ., and is neither dis-*
> *criminatory against interstate commerce nor*
> *excessive in comparison with the governmental*
> *benefit conferred, it will pass constitutional*
> *muster, even though some other formula might*
> *reflect more exactly the relative use of the state*
> *facilities by individual users.*

Concerned that the court's decision in *Evansville* might prompt proliferation of local taxes burdensome to interstate air transportation, Congress enacted the Anti-Head Tax Act. The AHTA provides in part,

> *. . . nothing in this section shall prohibit a*
> *State (or political subdivision thereof . . .)*
> *owning or operating an airport from levying or*
> *collecting reasonable rental charges, landing*
> *fees, and other service charges from aircraft*
> *operators for the use of airport landing facili-*
> *ties.*

In the instant case, the fees were not found to be unreasonable under the Anti-Head Tax Act. However, the airlines asserted that, even if the airport's user fees were reasonable under the AHTA, they violated the Commerce Clause. The court responded by stating that it had already found the challenged fees reasonable under the AHTA, "through the lens" of *Evansville*—that is, under a reasonableness standard, that was taken from Commerce Clause jurisprudence. The U.S. Supreme Court affirmed the judgment of the Court of Appeals.

CHAPTER 15

AIRPORTS: AND THE
PROTECTIVE FUNCTION

*Police powers generally encompass two responsibilities, protection
and enforcement, which are sometimes seemingly at odds.*

FIRST CLAIMS

Protective services are subsumed within the "police powers" delegated by the states to the local governments, through which they adopt
such laws and regulations that tend to prevent the commission of fraud
and crime. Police powers are used to secure the comfort, safety, morals, health and prosperity of citizens, and to assure the protection of
individual civil liberties. Police powers generally encompass two responsibilities, *protection* and *enforcement*, which are sometimes
seemingly at odds. The primary concern in airport security procedures,
for example, is enforcement of the Fourth Amendment. Also of concern in airport liability, however, is protection of First Amendment (or
"first claims") rights. The first claims are freedom of speech, of the
press, of religion, and of peaceable assembly.

The airport has a responsibility to enforce First Amendment *violations* such as illegal communication of oral or written materials restricted by police power. A person is not free to overthrow civil order,
for instance. The limits of freedom of speech and of writing must be
considered in context with other clauses of the Constitution. Communications may not be indirect, or otherwise injurious to public morals,

private reputation or safety. A person may not, for example, give false information such as falsely reporting a bomb during airport screening.[1]

Conversely, the airport has an obligation to protect First Amendment *rights*.[2] However, balancing the rights of individuals against the rights of society is not always so discernible. For instance, religious or political activists have a right to practice free speech, particularly in a public place such as the airport. But many passengers may find the activists' practices to be a nuisance. In the public interest, the airport sponsor may regulate solicitation on the airport premises in a manner, which is reasonable or necessary.[3] However, because most airports are public property, ordinances that attempt to control the exercise of First Amendment rights must be limited and must legitimately serve the public interest.[4] The courts have overruled ordinances broadly disallowing First Amendment activities in airport terminals.

In *Jamison v. City of St. Louis*, evidence indicated the airport director's unvarying practice was to deny *all* requests for permission to protest or solicit except those accompanied by a court order.[5] Jesse Jamison, who believed he was discriminatorily discharged from his employment by an airline because of his mental illness, was denied permission by the airport director to peacefully protest his discharge, by standing silently in an unsecured spot on the terminal concourse with a sign stating the "Airline Discriminates Against the Handicapped." The U.S. Court of Appeals found the airport director's procedure for determining who could exercise First Amendment rights at the airport defective, because it gave the airport director complete and unguided discretion to rule on the exercise of First Amendment rights.

In another case, *Jews for Jesus*, the distribution of literature by a religious group was held to be protected speech, and the central terminal area of a major international airport was held to be a "public forum."[6] The airport board had adopted a resolution banning all First Amendment activity. Alan Howard Snyder, a minister of the Gospel for Jews for Jesus was threatened with arrest if he did not stop distributing literature on a pedestrian walkway in the Central Terminal Area.

---

[1] *See United States v. Feldman*, CCH AVI. ¶ 18,351 (1969).
[2] *See Multimedia Publishing v. Greenville-Spartanburg Airport*, CCH 24 AVI. ¶ 17,474 (1993).
[3] *State v. Daquino*, 361 U.S. 944 (1960).
[4] *International Society for Krishna Consciousness v. Englehardt*, 425 F. Supp. 176 (1976).
[5] 828 F 2d 1280 (1987).
[6] CCH 19 AVI. ¶ 18,401 (1986).

The U.S. Supreme Court ruled the airport board's desire to limit the uses of the airport complex to airport-related purposes did not justify the "total" denial of free speech exercise within the terminal. And in another similar case, *International Society for Krishna Consciousness v. Lee*, the courts did not enjoin the airport sponsor from enforcing its regulations with respect to the exercise of First Amendment rights in *non-public* areas of the airport.[7]

AVIATION ENVIRONMENT

Most airports that are open to the public are owned, operated, and regulated by governments, especially local governments. States and the federal government also have regulatory oversight responsibilities with regard to airports. Government regulation is in three basic forms. Two regulatory forms, economic and safety regulation, have been discussed elsewhere in this book. The first wave of government regulation was *economic*, in response to marketplace abuses during the Progressive Era and the inequities of an imperfect market. Economic regulation provides for the government marketplace control with respect to economic direction and performance of the regulated industry. Through economic regulation the government controls major economic decisions, including price, rate of return, as well as market entry and exit. Economic regulatory intervention was followed closely by *safety* regulation. This chapter introduces the third form of government control—*social regulation*.

Social regulation assumes different goals than either its economic or safety counterparts. Unlike the industry-specific orientation of both economic and safety regulation, social regulation is directed toward more global issues affecting society. Beginning in the mid-1960s, regulatory initiatives shifted increasingly to protection of the environment, the consumer and the worker. Assuming different goals and objectives than economic regulation, social regulation focuses upon specific attributes of production, such as product safety or pollution of the environment, without directly controlling economic decisions. Environmental law is the quintessential example of social regulation.

---

[7] *International Society for Krishna Consciousness v. Lee*, CCH AVI ¶ 17,270 1982).

Environmental management has come to the forefront as a principle function of airport management. Some described the 1990s as the "Decade of the Environment."[8] Among a flood of environmentally conscious initiatives were issues such as storm water runoff, underground storage tanks, noise and land-use compatibility. Protecting the environment is a continuing challenge that began in earnest in 1969. Recognizing the profound impact of human activity on the natural environment, and the critical importance of maintaining environmental quality, Congress enacted the National Environmental Policy Act of 1969 [NEPA]. This act has become the cornerstone of environmental legislation in the United States and is often referred to simply by its acronym, "NEPA," which is pronounced, "neepa." The main thrust of NEPA is to require an Environmental Impact Statement [EIS] whenever an environmental analysis shows that "major federal actions would significantly affect the quality of the human environment."

Responsible for formulating and recommending national policies to promote improvement of environmental quality in accordance with NEPA is the Council of Environmental Quality [CEQ].[9] Original guidelines for implementation of the National Environmental Policy Act were prepared by the CEQ in 1973. These rules were principally concerned with the preparation of an EIS and often resulted in reports which seemingly became their own end product and did little in the way of contributing to decisions which would further national environmental goals. In many cases the environmental review process became an obstacle to progress, without materially aiding in abating environmental concerns. The 1973 guidelines fostered inconsistent agency practices and interpretations of the laws, and resulted in excessive delays in processing environmental reports; with subsequent delays in proposed development.

In response to an executive order from President Jimmy Carter, the CEQ revised its guidelines in 1978, specifically to reduce paperwork and to make the statutorily required environmental analysis more use-

---

[8] The events of Sep. 11, 2001 would soon come to overshadow environmental issues as security became the primary concern, and if the 1990s were to be remembered as the "Decade of the Environment," the memory soon faded.

[9] The Council on Environmental Quality coordinates federal environmental efforts and works closely with agencies and other White House offices in the development of environmental policies and initiatives. The White House, Council on Environmental Quality, http://www.whitehouse.gov (visited Jan. 27, 2005).

ful. The new procedures were also intended to reduce delays in processing, and to promote better decisions. The most salient principle embodied within the revised guidelines is the use of an early "scoping" process to determine what the important issues are. The guidelines also emphasize real alternatives, reduce the length of environmental impact statements, require the use of plain language, and place time limitations in the NEPA process. Early decisions must be made as to whether or not an EIS is required.

Generally, the environment analysis entails two phases: the *assessment* phase and the *declaration* phase. The declaration phase results in the publication of one, or a combination, of four documents: (1) an Environmental Assessment, (2) Environmental Impact Statement, (3) a Finding of No Significant Impact, or (4) a Notice of Intent.

An Environmental Assessment [EA] serves several purposes: to provide evidence and analysis for determining whether to prepare an EIS or a finding of no significant impact, aid an agency's compliance with NEPA; facilitate preparation of an EIS, if necessary; and provide a discussion of the need for the proposal, impacts of the proposal, available alternatives, as well as a listing of those persons consulted in the process. For some time, the Federal Aviation Administration [FAA] had required preparation of an Environmental Impact Assessment Report [EIAR] prior to determining the necessity of an EIS. The EIAR was comparable to the EA as defined by the 1978 CEQ guidelines. Subsequently, the FAA adopted the term "environmental assessment" in place of the EIAR.

An Environmental Impact Statement is a detailed written statement of the environmental impact of the proposed action. Included are:

- any adverse environmental effects which cannot be avoided should the proposal be implemented;
- the relationship between local short-term uses of the human environment and the maintenance and enhancement of long-term productivity; and
- any irreversible and irretrievable commitments of resources which would be involved in the proposed action should it be implemented.

It should be noted that individual states might have enacted their own legislation similar to NEPA. For example, California has a State Environmental Quality Act. An Environmental Impact Report [EIR] is to California's State Environmental Quality Act, what, within the federal scheme, is an Environmental Impact Statement.

A Finding of No Significant Impact, or FONSI (pronounced, "fonzee"), presents the reasons why an action will not have a significant effect on the human environment, and why an EIS therefore will not be prepared. It includes the environmental assessment, or a summary review. A finding of no significant impact may also be known as a "Negative Declaration."

A Notice of Intent states that an EIS will be prepared and considered. It describes the proposed action and possible alternatives, describes the scoping process, and states the name and address of the person (or agency) responsible for issuing the EIS. Beyond the Environmental Policy Act of 1969, other legislation, which has significantly dealt with aviation and its relationship with the environment, are:

- the 1968 Amendment to the *Federal Aviation Act* of 1958 which added to the FAA's responsibility the control and abatement of aircraft noise and sonic boom;

- the *Airport and Airway Development Act* of 1970 which provided for development of airport and airway facilities adequate to meet future requirements of the air transportation system, and assured that airport development projects provided for the protection and enhancement of natural resources and quality of the environment;

- the *Clean Air Amendments* of 1970 which provided for promulgation of aircraft emission standards by the Environmental Protection Agency [EPA] with subsequent implementation and enforcement by the FAA; and most importantly,

- the *Noise Control Act* of 1972, which defined the responsibilities of FAA and EPA in the control of aircraft, noise. The 1972 Act also amended the Federal Aviation Act of 1958.

Add to these acts, the Clean Water Act of 1977, the Resource Conservation and Recovery Act of 1976, the Water Quality Act of 1987, and a host of other environmental policy acts which, either directly or indirectly, must be taken into consideration in conjunction with airports.

In 1979, the Aviation Safety and Noise Abatement Act became law. Prior legislation was concerned primarily with the negative impacts of aviation upon the community. In response to constraints being placed on airport operations, the Aviation and Noise Abatement Act assumes a reverse philosophy, by addressing the adverse impact of community encroachment upon the airport. It attempts to achieve the compatible coexistence of airports within the community. This philosophy, of sustained yet environmentally compatible growth, is sometimes referred to as "sustainable development."[10]

ENVIRONMENTAL POLICY
AND AIRPORT MASTER PLANNING

The passage of numerous environmental laws attest to the concern Congress has with regard to the environment and quality of human life. In airport planning and development, it is important to balance concerns for environmental feasibility with financial feasibility and/or engineering feasibility. "Environmental feasibility" means capable of being accomplished from an environmental standpoint. Environmental feasibility has several components, not the least of which is political acceptability. Another is compliance with regulatory and statutory requirements. Regulations for implementing the procedural provisions of the National Environmental Policy Act, issued by the President's Council on Environmental Quality, provide for three categories of environmental actions. Every proposed project will eventually be classified into one of these three categories: (1) actions normally requiring an EA; (2) actions normally requiring an EIS; and, (3) categorical exclusions.

For general guidelines as to which category a particular project may fall under see Table 15.1, "Environmental Action Choices."

---

[10] Sustainable development is "development that meets the needs of the present without compromising the ability of future generations to meet their own needs." Report of the World Commission on Environment and Development (1980). This was an early definition of sustainable development. *See* Organization for Economic Co-operation & Development [OECD], *Pollution Prevention & Control: Environmental Criteria for Sustainable Transport* 10 (1996); *see also* Laurence E. Gesell and Paul Stephen Dempsey, *Air Transportation: Foundations for the 21st Century*, Ch. 17 (2nd ed. 2005).

Table 15.1—ENVIRONMENTAL ACTION CHOICES

ACTIONS NORMALLY REQUIRING ENVIRONMENTAL IMPACT STATEMENT:

- First time airport layout plan [ALP] approval, or airport location approval for a commercial service airport located in a Standard Metropolitan Statistical Area [SMSA]; and/or,
- A new runway capable of handling air carrier aircraft at a commercial service airport in a SMSA.

ACTIONS NORMALLY REQUIRING ENVIRONMENTAL ASSESSMENT:

- New airport location;
- New runway;
- Major runway extension;
- Runway strengthening which would result in a noise increase over noise sensitive areas;
- Construction adversely affecting public roadway capacity;
- Relocation of residential units;
- Establishment/relocation of an Instrument Landing System [ILS]; or
- Approach Lighting System [ALS]; and/or
- Development affecting places of historical, architectural, archeological, or cultural significance; land acquisition for conversion of farmland; wetlands, coastal zones, or floodplains; endangered or threatened species.

CATEGORICAL EXCLUSIONS:

- Work on runways, taxiways, aprons, or loading ramps;
- Work on airfield lighting systems;
- Installation of airfield items such as segmented circles, wind indicators, or fencing;
- Construction of passenger handling facilities;
- Construction of entrance and service roadways;
- Grading or erosion control with no off-airport impacts;
- General landscaping;
- Noise compatibility projects;
- Land acquisition and relocation associated with any of the above projects;
- Federal releases of land; and/or
- Removal of displaced threshold.

Source: *Airport Environmental Handbook*, FAA Order 5050-4A (1985).

In general, actions "categorically excluded" are those that have been found, in normal circumstances, to have no potential for significant environmental impact. Actions normally requiring an EA sometimes have significant environmental impacts. Actions having significant impacts will require the preparation of an EIS. The purpose of an EA is to determine whether or not a proposed action will have, or is likely to have, one or more significant impacts. Based upon the findings reported in an EA, and other investigations deemed necessary, the FAA will prepare either a FONSI, or an EIS. It is often possible to adjust the plans so that potentially significant impacts can be alleviated, thus avoiding the necessity to prepare an EIS. Obviously, if there are two development choices available that will meet the need equally well, the one without significant impacts can be implemented more readily. Relatively few airport actions require an EIS, but if one is called for, preparation of the EIS in accordance with NEPA is the responsibility of the FAA.

The FAA does not approve a master plan *per se*. However, a major product of the master planning effort is the Airport Layout Plan [ALP], which the FAA must approve prior to an airport receiving federal funding for facility improvements. A sponsor seeking unconditional approval of a new or revised ALP must, if an environmental assessment is required, submit an EA with the ALP. The FAA will not approve a grant for airport development unless the airport sponsor has a current approved ALP. An ALP is approved unconditionally when all items on the ALP which are items normally requiring either an EA or an EIS have in fact received environmental approval.

Environmental work in connection with airport master planning must be undertaken by environmental professionals experienced with, and skilled in, the environmental disciplines—just as the skills of a professional soil or pavement engineer may be required. The purpose of an environmental assessment is to determine if the potential impacts are significant, explore alternatives and mitigation measures, and provide the information to determine whether or not an EIS is required.

The called "Environmental Assessment" document is simply a record of the preliminary investigations. After reviewing an EA, if the FAA determines there are no significant impacts or that with appropriate mitigation the impacts could be prevented or minimized to the point they are not significant, the FAA will issue a FONSI. On the other hand, if an EIS is required, it is the FAA's responsibility.

In considering potential impacts, procedural provisions of NEPA contain specific requirements on the subject of cumulative impact. NEPA provisions also introduce the concept of "tiering" of environmental actions. Although tiering and cumulative impact may, at first glance, appear to be contradictory, they are often mutually supportive terms. Cumulative impact stems from situations where individually minor, but collectively significant, actions take place over a period of time. The concept of tiering provides for making decisions when the time is ripe, but need not be made earlier. Even though environmental documentation and unconditional approval of the ALP may cover only the short term, the environmental documentation—whether it be a categorical exclusion, a FONSI, or an EIS—must consider the cumulative impacts of the short-term development over a longer period.

As part of the environmental impact assessment, there are statutory and/or regulatory requirements for public participation, and there are often political requirements as well. Environmental issues cannot be skirted, especially by the aviation community. When confronted by a concern about the environment, the airport manager must meet the issue head-on. Historical litigation has shown that if there is the slightest chance that a proposed action might be controversial on environmental grounds, it is far less trouble to confront the issue in a public information forum than to later resolve the issue in court. Citizen involvement, where appropriate, should be initiated at the earliest practical time and continued throughout the development of the proposed project in order to obtain meaningful input.

Each public participation program should be tailored to the situation. The more complex and far reaching the development proposed the more complex and far reaching should be the public involvement program. As a general guideline for public participation programs, the Council on Environmental Quality's regulatory requirements are to:

- make a diligent effort to involve the public in implementing NEPA procedures;
- provide public notice of NEPA related hearings, meetings, and the availability of environmental documentation;
- hold public hearings when appropriate;

- solicit information from the public; and to
- make findings of no significant impact and/or environmental impact statements and underlying documents available to the public.

Even if there appears to be neither public interest nor controversy, an opportunity for a public hearing is required by statute for: (1) a new airport; (2) a new runway; or (3) a major runway extension.

ENVIRONMENTAL IMPACT OF AVIATION

Aircraft noise is without question the severest environmental problem currently associated with airports. It can make an airport unpopular no matter how well the airport serves the transportation needs of the community, or how greatly it contributes to the community's economic well being. Aviation noise extends beyond the boundary of the airport, into areas over which the airport sponsor has no authority. However, the airport sponsor is considered responsible for noise resulting from aircraft operations. Due to the magnitude of the noise issue, particular attention is given to the environmental impact of noise in subsequent paragraphs devoted to the subject.

Besides noise, other environmental factors such as social impacts arise from the disruption of established communities, the necessity for relocation of people, altered transportation patterns, changes in employment, and so forth. Other than socioeconomic impacts, there are other potential impacts upon the man-made environment as well. Under various statutes, consideration must be given to the potential impacts of proposals upon public parks, recreation areas, wildlife or waterfowl refuges, historic sites, and historic and cultural properties, including archeological sites.

Though most of the problem of air pollution is caused by surface modes, particularly the automobile, increased concerns are being raised by air transportation, the fastest growing mode of transport and the only human enterprise to emit pollutants directly into the upper atmosphere.[11] Aircraft engines emit solid particulates, sulfur oxides, carbon monoxide, hydrocarbons and nitrogen oxides. The amounts of

---

[11] *See* Paul Stephen Dempsey and Laurence E. Gesell, *Air Commerce and the Law* Ch. 12 (2004).

each particular pollutant emitted are highly predicated not only upon the size of the aircraft, but also the type of engine used for propulsion; i.e., turbine versus reciprocating. As a rule, jets and other turbine-powered aircraft emit higher volumes of solid particulates and nitrogen oxides than do the piston aircraft. Conversely, piston powered aircraft discharge more carbon monoxide and hydrocarbons than do the jets.

Aside from aircraft as a point source, other sources of air pollution around airports might be from airport construction equipment, emissions from gasoline operated aircraft ground service equipment, automobile traffic entering and leaving the airport, exhaust from maintenance equipment, heating and air conditioning plants, and from fuel handling and storage systems. A major concern is with fuel vapor emissions. A prevailing environmental issue of the 1990s, focused on potential leakage from fuel storage facilities. The issue regarding underground storage systems is discussed below.

In 1973, the EPA established production standards to limit emissions of smoke, carbon monoxide, hydrocarbons, and nitrogen oxides. As originally drafted, the standards would have applied to all aircraft from the smallest single-engine plane to the largest commercial jetliner. However, in 1977, the EPA relaxed its standards applying to the general aviation fleet and made the standards applicable only to turbine airplanes having engines with at least 12,000 pounds of thrust.

With regard to airport master planning, there is wide evidence that aircraft engine emissions constitute only about one percent of the air pollutants in a typical metropolitan area. Although historically, airport and aircraft emissions were not considered significant contributors to the ambient air quality, they are becoming of increasing environmental concern. In airport planning and development, failure to obtain "Clean Air Certification" is a direct violation of airport sponsor assurances attached to federal funding.

Water quality is also a significant potential problem, depending upon current quality and quantity, and the location of proposed development with respect to sources. If the proposed development involves an airport location, runway location, or a major runway extension, then certification is required from the Governor of the State that there is reasonable assurance the project will be located, designed, constructed and operated in compliance with the applicable air and water quality standards. Impact upon water sources, especially from storm water discharge, will be subsequently covered in more detail.

Routine detailed inventory of biotic communities in environmental documents, as was common in the past, is no longer required. Consideration of biotic impact now emphasizes quality, not quantity. It is still necessary to be alert to potential impacts of significance on wildlife and waterfowl refuges and on water resources. Other areas requiring consideration are rare and endangered species, alteration of existing habitat, and wetlands. Special consideration has been extended to floodplains. If a proposal involves a 100-year floodplain, then mitigation measures may avoid significant impacts. Consistency of proposed development with approved coastal zone management programs is another requirement. If farmland is to be converted to other uses such as for an airport, it must be determined whether any of that land is prime or unique, or of state or local significance, which would be protected under the Farmland Protection Policy Act. Occasionally, wild and scenic rivers, light emissions, or solid waste disposal may be issues. For major developments in some areas, energy requirements, which are significant with respect to local supply, may be an issue. Finally, because of the surrounding habitat, drainage, water quality, human habitation or other situations particular to the development site, special mitigation measures must be taken during construction.

As can be seen, there is a myriad of environmental concerns when it comes to airport planning and development. Four of the most prominent operational concerns, are the ever-present issues of aircraft noise, but also wildlife impacts, storm water discharge, and concerns about potential leakage from underground fuel storage tanks. These environmental issues continue to prevail, but there are other concerns as well. In the 21st Century, three developments are likely to influence public policy in transportation:

- Concern exists about global warming and disintegration of the ozone level which shields the planet from ultraviolet radiation;
- Science will have a clearer understanding of the increasingly negative impact of transportation on the environment; and,
- Technological improvements in emission reductions from burning fossil fuels may be outpaced by growth in the transport

sector, making transportation a continuing concern as a pollution source.[12]

Airport planners and developers, of necessity, must concern themselves with environmental impact. Sustainable development has been embraced as a global mission.[13] "Sustainable transportation" has been defined as "transportation that does not endanger public health or ecosystems and meets mobility needs. . . ." Achieving a balance between societal needs and nature is indeed a difficult task, but not an impossible one. Sustainability does not insist that all transport should come to a halt. Rather, it attempts to promote a transportation system that is least offensive in terms of its consumption of the earth's resources and pollution of the earth's environment. What follows is a review of the four major areas of concern in airport development: underground tanks, storm water, wildlife, and noise.

UNDERGROUND STORAGE TANKS

Environmental concerns attached to potential leakage from underground storage tanks led to proposals in the mid-1980s for three-pronged legislation intended to prevent slow leak environmental contamination. First, *registration* of all tanks exceeding specified capacities would be required. Beginning in 1986, underground tanks of more than 1,100 gallons would have to be registered with appropriate state regulatory agencies. Second, recommended, but not required, would be regular tank inventory *control* programs including periodic environmental audits. Such audits would be systematic reviews and inspections of environmental records, files, facilities, operations and activities to assess whether the owner was in compliance with all applicable activities. Third, tank owners would assume *financial responsibility* for any fuel leak contamination, ostensibly through mandatory insurance coverage for those owners and operators who could not pay for damages out-of-pocket. Still under consideration in the preliminary plan-

---

[12] *See* Laurence E. Gesell and Paul Stephen Dempsey , *Air Transportation: Foundations for the 21st Century*, Ch. 17 (2nd ed 2005).
[13] The United Nations Conference on Environment and Development, known as the "Earth Summit," met in Rio de Janeiro in 1992. At Rio, 180 nations signed an agreement to roll back greenhouse gas emissions to 1990 levels by the year 2000.

ning was a "Superfund" via the creation of a leaking underground storage trust fund collected through additional taxation on fuels. Owners and operators of tanks would be required to show evidence of financial responsibility in the event of releases from their tanks. However, where financial resources of the owner/operator would not be available, such as insolvency or otherwise refusal to cooperate, the EPA could use the fund to pay for corrective action whenever necessary to protect human health and environment.

In 1984, Congress passed the Leaking Underground Storage Tank Liability and Standards Act, which mandated development of a federal regulatory program for underground tanks, and restricted the type of tanks which could be installed. In the meantime, the Environmental Protection Agency published interim rules stating that the only tanks that could be installed had to be designed, constructed and installed to prevent leaks due to corrosion or structural failure, and made of materials compatible with the substances stored. Cathodically protected steel tanks, and tanks constructed or clad with non-corrosive materials, were permitted if the cathodes would last the lifetime of the tank and if the non-corrosive materials were applied properly. Other than stipulating that tanks were to be installed correctly to prevent leaks, EPA gave little guidance on correct installation procedures.

In 1988, the EPA released its final rules covering the technical requirements for Underground Storage Tanks [UST]. These rules are published as the "Technical Standards and Corrective Action Requirements for Owners and Operators of Underground Storage Tanks."[14] Under these rules, owners of underground storage tanks are required to implement leak detection procedures and to upgrade or replace their tanks according to a time frame established by the EPA. Current law requires that fuel spills or leaks be reported to the EPA and, where there is any possibility of contamination reaching navigable waterways, the U.S. Coast Guard must also be notified.[15]

The EPA rules apply to "underground" storage tanks, which are defined as having "10% or more of their volume below ground." Excluded from the rules are farm and residential tanks containing less than 1,100 gallons and not used for commercial purposes; tanks used

---

[14] 40 C.F.R. § 280.
[15] 40 C.F.R. § 302.

for storing heating oil utilized on the premises where the tanks are located; tanks holding less than 110 gallons; and emergency spill and overfill tanks.

It should be understood that a few states (including California and Florida) had already established comprehensive programs covering UST systems prior to the adoption of federal guidelines in 1988. Moreover, each state has the option to implement the federal rules or develop its own set of guidelines, which are at least as stringent as those of the federal government. In other words, state regulations will likely be more comprehensive than the federal guidelines.

The Code of Federal Regulations address such areas as the design and installation of new tanks, required leak detection systems, piping, spill and overfill protection as well as record keeping and reporting.[16] The regulations allowed ten years (i.e., until 1998) for existent tanks and piping to be protected from corrosion and stated the methods that had been approved by the EPA. The regulations phased in leak detection over a five-year time frame, depending upon the age of the tanks. All tanks and piping had to have a leak detection system in place by the end of the five-year phase-in period (i.e., by December 1993).

Other areas included in the rules are corrective action and procedures for tank closures. If a UST system does not have corrosion protection and it remains closed "permanently" (defined as more than 12 months), three requirements must be met:

- The regulatory authority must be notified 30 days prior to closure;
- An environmental assessment must be completed by testing soils and/or groundwater samples to determine if the tank has caused a release which resulted in environmental damage; and
- Depending on local regulatory policies, an underground tank can be either removed or left in place, but in both cases the tank must be emptied and cleaned by removing all liquids, dangerous vapors and accumulated sludge.

In addition to the above rules, in 1986 Congress enacted the storage tank tax provision to the Superfund program that had been suggested

---

[16] 40 C.F.R. § 280.

earlier. A leaking underground storage tank trust fund, limited to $500 million, was financed by an additional 0.1 cent per gallon tax on motor fuels, including aviation fuels. The overall Superfund program is aimed at cleaning up abandoned hazardous waste sites, and was initially estimated to cost $8.5 billion, funded by a combination of taxes on the petroleum and chemical industries, general revenue taxes, and an environmental tax based on corporate incomes. With the passage of the Omnibus Budget Reconciliation Act of 1990,[17] Congress reimposed the Leaking Underground Storage Tank [LUST] Trust Fund Tax for five additional years, and at the same time removed the $500 million revenue ceiling. When the extension expired December 31, 1995, it was reinstated by the Taxpayer Relief Act of 1997 [18] for the period October 1997, through March 31, 2005.

Finally, "financial responsibility" was defined as the ability to finance at least one million dollars in cleanup costs per tank release. Financial responsibility can be demonstrated by several means: insurance, self insurance, establishment of an independent trust fund, the use of state funds dedicated for cleanup of leaking tanks, or a combination of these resources. The available option for most operators is insurance, and it should go without saying that most insurance underwriters will require proof that fuel storage systems aren't leaking before writing a pollution liability policy to cover them.

If any of the above rules are not met, the underground systems must be closed or replaced. Replacement presents two options: replace the old underground system with new tanks, or build aboveground. Aboveground storage is preferred for environmental reasons. The tanks are exposed for inspection, and there is less probability of undetected spills and leaks. The major concern about aboveground storage, however, involves safety. Historically, fire officials have felt that flammable liquids should be kept underground. Some communities may even have regulations prohibiting the installation of aboveground tanks. The advantages and disadvantages of each situation must be carefully evaluated to determine the most suitable solution to tank replacement.

---

[17] Pub. L. 101-508.
[18] Pub. L. 105-34.

STORM WATER DISCHARGE

Water pollution is perhaps the best understood of the environmental concerns, and therefore the easiest to rectify. Primary concerns associated with fuel tank leakage have to do with water contamination. Airport operations entail two kinds of water-related environmental impacts: (1) the effect upon *potable water intake*, and (2) *wastewater discharges*.

An airport is a point source for wastewater. If the airport chooses to treat its own wastewater, it must establish facilities, which meet federal standards in accordance with the Federal Water Pollution Control Act of 1972. If discharges of wastewater are into a municipal treatment system, the wastewater stream must be pretreated, if necessary, to make it compatible with the treatment system. By the same token, an airport may have its own well water, or may choose to tie into a local water system. If well water is used, it must be inspected and treated, as necessary, to insure potable quality.

The major source of water pollution is storm water run-off, which can remove contaminants from non-point sources that may not be easily identified. Storm water comes from all areas of the airport, and with it comes any spilled oil, fuel, loose debris, rubber tire deposits and a miscellaneous array of chemicals, paint strippers, cleaning solvents and deicing compounds. An adequate storm water drainage system is an operational necessity. A proper drainage system is a critical environmental consideration. The possibility that chemicals may be carried away by water run-off and subsequently cause ecological damage downstream is a deterrent to the use of specific types of weed killers on airports. Weed control is a major operational problem on an airport. Hence, great care must be exercised in the selection and application of chemicals to destroy them.

The Clean Water Act is intended to protect rivers and lakes from pollutants washing into these waters due to rainfall and snow melt. Section 402(p) of the Clean Water Act directs the EPA to establish storm water regulations. In 1990, the EPA published storm water discharge regulations for municipalities and certain industries including airports. Simply put, the regulations make airports responsible for storm water flows entering and leaving many sites on the airport. Furthermore, sheet flow coming onto airport grounds from a neighboring facility is also the airport's responsibility, unless it can be measured and sampled as it comes onsite.

Along with municipalities and other "industries," airports are required to obtain a National Pollutant Discharge Elimination System [NPDES] permit for discharge of storm water from areas directly related to manufacturing, processing, or raw materials storage to either surface waters (e.g., lakes, rivers, streams, creeks or ponds) or municipal storm sewers. Also targeted by the rules are airports with aircraft and runway de-icing operations, and facilities that use pesticides or herbicides to control weed growth, and facilities which use paints or solvents for their operations. The NPDES permits may be applied for either in an individual application or group application form. The method least preferred by owners and operators, because of cost, is to apply for an individual permit that requires the submission of sampling data for each out fall at each facility. The more preferred method allows industrial facilities, including airports, with similarly expected discharges to join together and submit a group application.

WILDLIFE CONTROL

Another ecological factor which can have a significant affect upon airport development and operation concerns wildlife, not only from the standpoint of the airport's impact upon the wildlife habitat, but of wildlife's effect upon airport operations as well.[19] The Federal Endangered Species Act protects species that are threatened or endangered. One of the most prominent examples of curtailed airport development caused by its potential impact upon wildlife occurred when Dade County, Florida, proposed an airport in the Florida Everglades as a replacement for Miami International. Through the decade of the 1970s the issue was contested on environmental grounds and the adverse impact the proposed airport would have on the Everglades.

Another outstanding example of stalled airport development occurred in the Antelope Valley near Palmdale, California, where the Los Angeles Airport Authority proposed a replacement airport for Los Angeles International Airport. The action was vehemently opposed by a

---

[19] *See Safeco v. Watertown*, CCH 16 AVI ¶ 18,201 (1981).

pro-environmental group. The Palmdale controversy also took place during the heavily pro-environmental era of the 1970s.

Noteworthy of the Florida Everglades and Antelope Valley issues, in both cases the proposed developments were to be in locations far removed from the urban settings of metropolitan Miami or Los Angeles, respectively. The remote locations were picked, at least in part, to avoid the significant impact that each proposed airport would have upon the human environment. Instead, each proposal met with strong opposition on behalf of the threatened wildlife habitats.

Not only can airports threaten wildlife, but wildlife can also be a serious threat to airports as well. Of principal concern are birds in the vicinity of the air movement area, which can be sucked into and destroy jet engines, but other forms of wildlife also may pose a problem, such as deer which run onto runways. In most cases proper fencing can keep large animals off the airport, and hunting teams can minimize on-airport control of mammals and reptiles. On the other hand, birds are much more difficult to control, and will often require the expertise of professionals experienced in bird control problems. Birds may also be protected, requiring permit application before eradication.

AIRCRAFT NOISE

Aircraft can pollute the environment in several ways, but based upon public reaction, apparently the worst pollutant of all is noise. Airplanes emit solid particulates, expel noxious gases, and theoretically can affect the ozone layer; but none of these possibilities has caused the turmoil that noise has. Across the nation, aircraft noise has sparked suits seeking relief from airport-related noise. Title 14 of the Code of Federal Regulations, Part 36, "Noise Standards: Aircraft Type and Airworthiness Certification," establishes acceptable approach, takeoff and sideline noise levels measured in decibels. Prior to implementation of 14 CFR Part 36, public opposition to airport noise was becoming increasingly vocal and sophisticated. In many instances, court actions were initiated to restrict or close airports. And yet, aircraft noise is not new; airplanes have always made noise. The original defense against aircraft noise was to remove airports as far from population centers as possible, so that noise would not be a problem. The theory that, "if there is no one to hear the noise there is no noise," worked fine in the beginning, but through the years the tendency of Americans has been to encroach upon airports by building homes and neighborhoods close to them, and then sue because airplane noise had supposedly brought the surrounding community to ruin.

Exemplary is the situation surrounding Dulles International Airport. Dulles was built on 10,000 acres in the Virginia countryside, specifically to remove airplane noise from the populated Washington, D.C. area. Construction began in 1958. By 1978, the new town of Reston had developed, nearby Herndon was growing rapidly, as were the other close-by communities of Manassas and Sterling Park. Several housing subdivisions had been built in and around each of these growing communities. The town of Centreville, which lies directly below a major approach and departure path, was planned by Fairfax County, from the outset, to be a major regional growth center. In just 20 years, land-use conflicts got out of hand. Yet, Dulles was to be the ideal airport design; planned, developed and operated under the expertise of the Federal Aviation Administration. Still, the planners did not effectively contemplate the ramifications of aircraft generated noise.

The primary concern with noise is the fact that it annoys people to the point where it constrains their activities. It interferes particularly with sleep and with communications. But what is "noise"? It is not just "sound." Noise, more specifically, is *unwanted* sound. It is a "nuisance," which is especially bothersome if it continues, as with the operation of an airport.[20]

Congress amended the Federal Aviation Act in 1968, to require the FAA to prescribe standards for noise measurement and abatement.[21] The FAA promulgated regulations thereunder for aircraft certification.[22] The Noise Control Act of 1972 gave the EPA a mandate to take an active role in the formulation and evaluation of noise standards, including aircraft noise, and in coordinating noise regulation with the FAA.[23] The EPA also regulates aircraft emissions.

The Aviation Safety and Noise Abatement Act of 1979 focused on reducing the impact of noise by establishing a system for airport noise

---

[20] *See Baker v. Burbank-Glendale-Pasadena Airport Authority*, 197 Cal. Rptr. 357 (1984).

[21] Pub. L. 90-411.

[22] 14 C.F.R. Parts 21 & 36.

[23] 49 U.S.C. § 4901-4918. *See City of Burbank v. Lockheed Air Terminal*, 411 U.S. 624 (1973).

compatibility land use planning.[24] That statute and the Clean Air Act of 1963, confer joint jurisdiction on the EPA and FAA to monitor and regulate aircraft engine noise and exhaust emissions. Airlines are required to comply with all applicable noise control regulations and exhaust emission standards. Noise abatement programs are generally aimed at reducing noise at the aircraft and/or airport source, but noise reduction strategies may be grouped into two major categories: (1) aircraft or engine modifications wherein the actual sound levels are reduced; and (2) flight, operational, and land use modifications which attempt to remove the sound from areas of adverse impact.

FEDERAL AVIATION REGULATION PART 36

By 1969, the FAA was already addressing aircraft noise through implementation of 14 CFR Part 36 (or "FAR Part 36."). Part 36 has been a progressive program, which initially set noise limitations on the manufacture of new aircraft. It has been extended to include the requirement for modification of noisy aircraft already existing. Since its issuance in 1969, FAR Part 36 has been amended many times to address noise at its (aircraft) source. FAR Part 36 does not address the removal of sound from areas of adverse impact.[25] With regard to aircraft noise, the removal of noise from areas of impact would come through subsequent legislation, ultimately leading to promulgation of FAR Part 150, "Airport Noise Compatibility Planning," and the establishment of Noise Exposure Maps [NEMs].

The Clean Air Act was amended by the Noise Pollution and Abatement Act of 1970, and the EPA Administrator was to establish an Office of Noise Abatement and Control. Congress subsequently declared that "inadequately controlled noise presented a growing danger to health and welfare of the Nation's populace." The Noise Pollution and Abatement Act was followed by the Noise Control Act of 1972. While the primary responsibility for control of noise rests with state and local governments, Congress felt that federal action was essential to deal with major noise sources (in commerce) requiring na-

---

[24] 49 U.S.C. § 2101-2124.
[25] Laurence E. Gesell, *The Administration of Public Airports* (4th ed. 1999).

tional uniformity treatment such as in transportation vehicles and equipment, machinery, appliances and other products in commerce.

Congress authorized and directed federal agencies, "within the fullest extent of their authority to carry out programs," to promote an environment free from noise that might jeopardize their health and welfare. The identification of major noise sources, noise criteria, and control technology was included. In aviation, the FAA Administrator was to conduct a study of:

- the adequacy of FAA flight and operational noise controls;
- the adequacy of noise emission standards on new and existing aircraft, together with recommendations on retrofitting and phase out of existing aircraft;
- the implications of identifying and achieving levels of cumulative noise exposure around airports; and,
- additional measures available to airports to control aircraft noise.

As a result of the FAA's study, subsequent changes were made to FAR Part 36. In aircraft design specification, Part 36 defines three stages of acceptable implementation. The acceptable decibel levels (or limits) for compliance with FAR Part 36 vary relative to aircraft weight, number of engines, and whether the engines are of high or low-bypass design. A 1977 amendment to FAR Part 36 established the noise designations for civil turbojet transport category aircraft as: "Stage 1," "Stage 2," and "Stage 3," (as the degree of control of noise emissions increased).

Stage 1 aircraft are those which, at the time of FAR Part 36 adoption in 1969, could not comply with the standards established by the regulation. Stage 2 were those aircraft that were in compliance with Part 36. The deadline for meeting Stage 2 requirements was January 1, 1985, after which all non-compliant, nonexempt aircraft were to be prohibited from operating at U.S. airports. In 1990, concern over aircraft noise led Congress to promulgate legislation banning most of the 2,300 Stage 2 aircraft in the U.S. fleet from U.S. airports by the end of

1999.[26] Waivers were granted until the end of 2003 if the airline had 85% of its fleet satisfying Stage 3 requirements by July 1, 1999.[27] On January 1, 2000, all aircraft over 75,000 pounds operating in the United States were required to meet the Stage 3 aircraft-noise certification standard.

FAR Part 36 prescribes noise standards for the issuance of type certificates (i.e. design certification) and for standard airworthiness certificates (i.e. operational certification under FAR Part 91). Federal Aviation Regulation Part 91 authorized exemption for carriers engaged in foreign air commerce. However, this latter exemption was modified by an international schedule for compliance with International Civil Aviation Organization [ICAO] Noise Standards which are substantially compatible with the standards set forth in FAR Parts 36 and 91, and by the Aviation Safety and Noise Abatement Act of 1979.

Through promulgation of FAR Part 36, the FAA effectively put a lid on aircraft noise escalation by establishing a ceiling on allowable noise produced by jet transport aircraft. Similar noise regulations may eventually involve all types of aircraft. Federal Aviation Regulation Part 36 has been a progressive program which initially set noise limitations on the manufacture of new aircraft. It was then extended to include the requirement for modification of already existent noisy aircraft. Due to the economics of retrofitting an already existing fleet, implementation of FAR Part 36 has been complex and controversial, but it can safely be stated that the trend of excessive aircraft noise is now downward. Eventually, all jet transports will meet FAR Part 36, Stage 3, requirements or better.

From initial adoption of FAR Part 36, the FAA had stated that compliance with FAR Part 36 could not be construed as a federal determination that aircraft were acceptable from a noise standpoint in *individual* airport environments. The responsibility for determining the permissible noise levels for aircraft using an airport remained with the airport proprietor.[28] However, the Airport Noise and Capacity Act of

---

[26] The terms, Stage 1, Stage 2 and Stage 3, are in reference to aircraft noise emission restrictions imposed by 14 C.F.R. Part 36.

[27] *Congress Mandates Phase out of Stage 2 Aircraft by End of Century*, Aviation Daily (Oct. 30, 1990), at 201.

[28] As already noted, this theory originated from the 1946 U.S. Supreme Court case of the *United States v. Causby*, 328 U.S. 256, where the U.S., as operator of a military field, was held responsible under the Fifth Amendment to the U.S. Constitution for rendering Causby's property useless as

1990 shifts authority away from airports to the FAA.[29] State nuisance and inverse condemnation law may nevertheless be used by individual citizens seeking to abate airport noise. A property owner still may allege that his or her property has been taken without just compensation in violation of the Fifth Amendment to the U.S. Constitution. The Noise Control Act of 1972 explicitly allows citizen suits against any person alleged to be in violation of any noise control requirement.[30]

In 2001, ICAO's Committee on Aviation Environmental Protection [CAEP] recommended adoption of new Chapter 4 noise standards that are 10 decibels lower, on a cumulative basis, than the Chapter 3 standards.[31] Because it is up to each ICAO member country to adopt noise standards, FAA has begun the rulemaking process to adopt the new standard. If adopted, the standards will apply to new designs submitted on or after January 1, 2006. On the basis of cost-benefit analysis, CAEP recommended there be no global phase out of aircraft meeting Chapter 3 noise standards.[32]

AVIATION SAFETY AND NOISE ABATEMENT ACT

Implementation of operational airport noise abatement strategies is the airport sponsor's responsibility. In this regard, the Department of Defense took an early lead in working toward airport compatibility when in 1973 it set forth DOD policy on achieving compatible use of public and private lands in the vicinity of military airfields. From the

---

a chicken farm because of low flying airplanes. The precedent set in the *Causby* case was extended to commercial airports in 1962 in *Griggs v. Allegheny Co.*, 82 S.Ct. 531, where it was held that the County (as the airport proprietor), and not the Federal government nor the airlines, was liable for the *taking* under the Fifth Amendment.

[29] John Jenkins, Jr., The Airport Noise and Capacity Act of 1990: Has Congress Finally Solved the Aircraft Noise Problem?, 59 J. Air L. & Com. 1023 (1994).

[30] *See* Laurence E. Gesell and Paul Stephen Dempsey , *Air Transportation: Foundations for the 21st Century* (2nd ed. 2005).

[31] ICAO noise "Chapters" are generally equivalent to U.S. "Stage 1, 2, and 3." The first generation of jet transports (e.g. Boeing 707 and Douglas DC-8) was not covered by ICAO Annex (16) and are therefore referred to as "non-noise certified" [NNC] airplanes. The initial standards for jet-powered aircraft designed before 1977 (e.g. Boeing 727 and Douglas DC-9) were included in Ch. 2. The Boeing 737-300/400, Boeing 767 and Airbus A319 are examples of "Chapter 3" aircraft types. *See* ICAO, *Aircraft Noise*, http://www.icao.int (visited Sep. 7, 2004).

[32] U.S. General Accounting Office, *Aviation and the Environment: Transition to Quieter Aircraft Occurred as Planned, but Concerns About Noise Persist* (Sep. 2001), at 8. *See* Laurennce E. Gesell and Paul Stephen Dempsey, *Air Transportation: Foundations for the 21st Century* 781 (2nd ed. 2005).

military's Air Installation Compatible Land Use Zones (AICUZ) program has evolved the federal government's Airport Noise Control and Land Use Compatibility Plans, or what have commonly become known as "FAR Part 150 Studies."

The purpose of the Aviation Safety and Noise Abatement Act of 1979 is to provide assistance to airport operators in preparing and carrying out noise compatibility programs, to provide assistance that assures continued safety in aviation, and for other purposes. The Act is a decisive one and has the express intent of standardizing noise measurement methodologies and land use compatibility programs in the U.S., and for the legal protection of threatened airports. By no later than one year after passage of the Noise Abatement Act, the Secretary of Transportation (in consultation with the Administrator of the Environmental Protection Agency and other appropriate agencies) was to:

- establish a single system of measuring noise;
- establish a single system for determining the exposure of individuals to aircraft noise; and
- identify land uses, which are normally compatible with various exposures of individuals to noise.

Advisory Circular AC 150/5050-6, "Airport-Land Use Compatibility Planning," contains recommended land use guidance charts which match acceptable noise limits with various land uses. A product of the FAR Part 150 Study is the Noise Exposure Map. The purpose of NEM is to depict the airport's present and future noise patterns, and the areas of present and future land use development which are not compatible with those noise patterns. The maps are prepared after consultation with the public, affected local governments, airport users, and the FAA. Utilizing local data and FAR Part 150 land use compatibility guidance, the sponsor determines and labels the non-compatible land uses, including noise sensitive uses such as residential areas, schools, hospitals, libraries, rest homes, and auditoriums. The maps and supporting data are submitted to the FAA for review and acceptance.

Upon acceptance of the NEM by FAA and publication by the sponsor, persons who subsequently acquire property in noise sensitive areas shall be presumed to have "constructive knowledge" of the existence of the NEM, and shall not be entitled to recover damages due to airport related noise. If a person by exercise of reasonable care would have known a fact, the person is deemed to have had constructive knowledge of such fact. Public recordation constitutes constructive knowledge.

The purpose of the airport's noise compatibility program is to formulate possible solutions to the noise problems identified by the noise exposure maps. This is a process in which a number of viable solutions are explored and the most workable of them are selected for full development. Total costs of each alternative are included in the considerations. The entire process is carried out in consultation with the affected local governments, the airport's users, those people impacted by the noise, and with the FAA. The program should include an implementation schedule, should identify who will be responsible for implementing the program, and should identify extent and source of the necessary funds. The total Noise Compatibility Program [NCP] is then submitted to FAA for approval.

After FAA acceptance of the NEM and publication of the availability of the NCP in the *Federal Register*, the agency has 180 days to complete its review and make a finding or it is approved by default except for any portion of a program relating to the use of flight procedures for noise control purposes. FAA approval of Part 150 Studies will be given only for those recommendations which,

- do not compromise safety;
- do not impose an undue burden on interstate or foreign commerce;
- do not discriminate for or against any group or class of users or operators;
- are meaningful and serve to provide real noise abatement;
- comply with federal airport grant agreements, which are funded by the flying public; and,
- do not conflict with or invade areas of responsibility vested in the federal government.

No part of the adopted noise map or related information, nor any part of the listed compatible land uses, can be admitted as evidence, or used for any other purpose in any suit or action seeking damages or other relief for the noise that results from the operation of an airport.

Further, no person acquiring property in an area surrounding an airport and included in the adopted noise map may recover damages for airport noise unless there has been a significant change in aircraft operations, change in airport layout, change in flight patterns, or increase in nighttime operations after the date of such property acquisition.

There is some concern that the provisions of this Act which prohibit recovery of damages resulting from aircraft noise may be unenforceable in court. The U.S. Constitution guarantees its citizens certain property rights, among which is the right to just compensation for property taken by a governmental entity. The right of a citizen to recover from inverse condemnation cannot be abrogated by Congress. However, the Act's provisions may prove more beneficial to airport sponsors in tort cases where nuisance is the issue rather than takings.

In a vein similar in philosophy to application of the Noise Exposure Map in FAR Part 150 Studies, when the cities of Burbank, Glendale and Pasadena, California, formed a Joint Powers Authority in order to purchase and operate the privately-owned Hollywood-Burbank Airport, they obtained funds for the acquisition from the federal government. In their contractual assurances, the cities were required by the FAA to comply with California Governmental Code Section 6546.1, which provided in part that "In operating the airport, the separate public entity (Joint Powers Authority) shall not permit or authorize any activity in conjunction with the airport which results in an increase in the size of the noise impact area."

In 1975, Lockheed Corporation (the previous airport owner) had applied for a variance from state noise standards. It was because of its inability to work a financially feasible solution to various problems created by aircraft noise, that Lockheed decided to divest itself of the Burbank Airport. Pursuant to the Airport and Airway Development Act of 1970, the FAA was required to assure that "all possible steps have been taken to minimize (any) adverse effect (upon the environment)." Thus, that responsibility was passed along to the new Joint Powers Authority among its newly adopted noise abatement rules. Air carriers were required to comply with FAR Part 36 and a resolution (Rule 7) which provided in part:

> . . . *any proposed increase in flight frequencies or such proposed implementation of serv-*

> *ice by a new carrier, shall be subject to the prior approval of the Commission, which approval shall not be granted except upon a determination by the Commission that such proposed increase in flight frequencies or such proposed implementation of service by a new carrier will be consistent with the provisions of the existing Grant Agreements between the Authority and the Federal Aviation Administration and any other applicable statutory or contractual restraints governing flight operations at the Airport. . . .*

Following adoption of Rule 7, and without Commission approval, Hughes Airwest increased its weekly schedule of flights at Burbank. The airport authority filed suit. The court ruled in favor of the airport, stating that its Rule 7 was a reasonable non-arbitrary and non-capricious regulation.[33]

On September 23, 1985, in *Baker et al. v. Burbank-Glendale-Pasadena Authority*, the California Supreme Court held that a public airport constitutes a "continuing nuisance." Under this ruling a plaintiff could bring successive actions against an airport, effectively providing that person with a perpetual annuity just for living near the airport. This, and other cases brought against the Burbank-Glendale-Pasadena Airport involved approximately 375 plaintiffs; with each plaintiff subsequent to the *Baker* decision filing new claims against the airport for $100,000 apiece for personal injuries and emotional distress, and $100,000 apiece for property damage—claims totaling approximately $75 million on a potentially recurring basis. The *Baker* decision was appealed to the U.S. Supreme Court for its consideration, but *certiorari* was denied. In light of decisions in *Baker* and in a companion case, *Blaine et al. v. Burbank-Glendale-Pasadena Airport Authority*, it is interesting to note that the airport not only had a Noise Exposure Map, but had repeatedly demonstrated its ability to reduce

---

[33] *See The Burbank-Glendale-Pasadena Airport Authority v. Hughes Air Corporation*, Superior Court of the State of California for the County of Los Angeles, Case No. 17926B (1980).

its impact upon the surrounding community by lowering its noise exposure (i.e., reducing the noise contours on the NEM).

FAR PART 36 EXEMPTIONS

In passing the Aviation Safety and Noise Abatement Act of 1979, Congress,

- preserved the regulatory requirement that certain aircraft (primarily B-707's and DC-9's) meet FAR Part 36 noise standards by January 1, 1985;
- specifically provided that the "Administrator of the Federal Aviation Administration shall . . . require all . . . foreign air carriers engaging in foreign air transportation to comply with the noise standards . . . at a phased rate of compliance similar to that in effect for aircraft registered in the United States"; and
- directed that administrative exemptions from FAR Part 36 compliance be granted only upon five conditions where: (1) a small carrier was involved, (2) upon a good faith compliance test consisting of making a deposit on noise attenuation equipment (e.g., "hush kits"), (3) needed technology to retrofit engines with noise attenuation devices was delayed or otherwise unavailable, (4) the carrier could suffer "financial havoc," and (5) the public would be deprived of valuable airline service.

Two airports especially affected by a mandate that all foreign air carriers come into compliance with FAR Part 36 were the international airports in Miami, Florida and Bangor, Maine, both of which petitioned the FAA for waivers from the noise rules. Bangor had 998 international operations annually, of which half were made by noncomplying aircraft, and involving eight European carriers. Miami International Airport is the second largest cargo airport in the U.S. As with Bangor, nearly 50% of its international cargo is handled by noncompliant aircraft, mostly from Latin America and the Caribbean.

The issue of noise compliance became political, and one of foreign policy pitting the FAA against the State Department. Miami International Airport sought intervention by the State Department on the grounds that strict enforcement would damage U.S. trade and foreign relations. Additionally, bilateral agreements with Latin American states would require revision to the detriment of the U.S. The Latin American carriers in particular, but other foreign carriers as well, claimed they were not financially able either to modify their aircraft, or to purchase new noise compliant airplanes. They claimed the noise rule was "provoking an economic crises for Latin American carriers."

The Department of State and the FAA were at loggerheads over the issue. The State Department was urging other nations to apply and/or reapply for exemptions to operate noise non-compliant transports in the U.S. The State Department even assisted some foreign carriers in drafting their applications for noise exemption for submittal to FAA. The FAA was caught in the middle by its congressional mandate, through the Aviation Safety and Noise Abatement Act, to strictly enforce FAR Parts 91 and 36. The FAA adopted the position that exemptions would be difficult to obtain. Those opposed to the granting of noise exemptions, however, were highly suspect of FAA's sincerity.

The House Foreign Affairs subcommittee on international operations held a hearing to discuss Miami International Airport's request for exemption. Both the House of Representatives and the Senate approved noise rule exemptions for Miami and Bangor. On October 16, 1984, President Reagan signed into law an amendment to FAR Part 36 that granted an extension to the January 1, 1985, deadline prohibiting any non-compliant aircraft from operating into the Miami and Bangor Airports. U.S. carriers who had spent millions of dollars to comply with the mandated noise regulations were highly disappointed by congressional actions. So were most U.S. airports and especially those looking for noise reduction at their locations. Certain airports had already adopted noise abatement rules requiring aircraft using their airports to comply with FAR Part 36 requirements. The American Association of Airport Executives [AAAE] approved a resolution opposing "any waiver exemptions or extensions" to FAA noise rules.

Following the victory in Congress on noise exemptions, certain foreign air carriers planned to file petitions to the FAA seeking suspension of the noise rule at other select airports. Targeted were Kennedy International and Los Angeles International Airports.

HARRELL'S CANDY KITCHEN v. SARASOTA-MANATEE AIRPORT AUTHORITY
111 So. 2d 439 (Fla. 1959)

Are airport height and hazard zoning regulations valid?

This case arose out of the imposition of vertical zoning regulations upon land belonging to appellant Harrell's Candy Kitchen. A complaint was filed by appellee, Sarasota-Manatee Airport Authority, to enjoin the erection of an ornamental superstructure atop a building under construction near the runway to a height in excess of that allowed by the regulations adopted by the Airport Zoning Board of Sarasota-Manatee Counties, Florida.

A temporary injunction was issued by the Circuit Court of Manatee County, and the property owners appealed by attacking the validity of the regulation because, they said, Chapter 333 of the zoning statute,

> *. . . constitutes a deprivation of the property of these defendants without due process of law; constitutes an unlawful taking of the property of these defendants without just compensation; constitutes an unlawful exercise of the police power of the State of Florida in that the subject matter of said Chapter bears no relationship to the public or general welfare as regards these defendants and their property; and constitutes a law too vague and uncertain to be enforceable.*

The trial court held that the airport regulations had been adopted pursuant to the provisions of Chapter 333 of the Florida Statutes; "that the declaration of the Legislature of the State of Florida in enacting the enabling act pursuant to which the airport zoning regulations in question were adopted is an entirely reasonable and correct statement of public policy"; that said regulations were valid, bore a substantial relation to the general welfare, and were duly and lawfully promulgated. The court issued an injunction requiring the defendants to reduce the height of their building.

The trial court noted defendants had failed to avail themselves of, much less exhaust, the administrative remedies that were prescribed for them by the airport zoning regulations. For this reason, the defendants had no standing in court to question the reasonableness of the height limits prescribed by the airport zoning regulations. Though the case was not decided on this point, the airport authority argued in the Florida Supreme Court that this alone required dismissal of the appeal.

The Supreme Court of Florida responded by saying the Airport Authority might well have proceeded in this litigation upon the theory that the appellants had not exhausted their administrative remedies in applying for a modification of the regulation as it related to this building and might have requested an order enjoining the construction of said building until the appellants had proceeded with and exhausted such remedies. However, the Airport Authority did not pursue this course, but chose instead to place squarely in issue the question of the validity and reasonableness of the regulations established by it. Having chosen this course, the authority could not then be permitted to pursue another course of action.

As to the validity of the zoning statute, the Florida Supreme Court said there is no longer any question concerning the power of the legislature to authorize agencies of the government to adopt and enforce zoning regulations. Such regulations not only promote the general welfare of the state and community served but also contribute to the proper and orderly development of land areas in the vicinity of airports. Zoning regulations duly enacted pursuant to lawful authority are *presumptively valid*, and the burden is upon he who attacks such regulation to carry the extraordinary burden of proving that it is unreasonable and bears no substantial relation to the public health, safety, morals and general welfare. The point of this case, then, was whether the regulation restricting the height of the building was reasonable.

The airport zoning regulations involved in this suit conformed in all details to the airport approach standards compiled by the Civil Aeronautics Administration [CAA]. These standards were the result of many years of experience by outstanding experts in the field of aviation, and compliance therewith was a precedent to federal aid in airport construction. Thus, the regulation was reasonably necessary to the safe operation of planes using the airport. Furthermore, the restriction in question as applied to the particular property could not be said to deprive the owner of the beneficial use of his land to such an extent that it violated constitutional rights or was otherwise unlawful.

The Supreme Court of Florida affirmed the judgment, and the decree of the Circuit Court of Manatee County.

SNEED v. COUNTY OF RIVERSIDE
32 Cal. Rptr. 318 (Cal. App. 1963)

May a local government pass an ordinance establishing airport operating areas and regulating height standards?

In the Fourth California District Court of Appeal, the plaintiff, Archie J. Sneed, claimed that, by ordinance, the County of Riverside took an air navigation easement over approximately 60 acres of his property. The easement ranged from four feet in height, at that part of the property closest to the airport, to 75 feet in height farthest away (the approach glide angle passed over a portion of plaintiff's property). The plaintiff owned 234.5 acres of improved property adjacent to an airport owned and operated by Riverside County. The property was used as a thoroughbred racehorse breeding and training farm and certain structures exceeded the height permitted by the ordinance.

The basic argument here, was whether a height limiting ordinance (i.e., "height and hazard zoning") was an authorized police power, or whether it was a taking of an air easement without payment of compensation as required under the Fifth Amendment to the U.S. Constitution, and under the provisions of the State Constitution. The California Constitution, Article I, Section 14 read in part, "Private property shall not be taken or damaged for public use without just compensation having first been made to, or paid unto court for, the owner. . . ."

California's enabling zoning law and zoning ordinance permitted elimination of airport hazards in approaches to airports through the exercise of police power "to the extent legally possible." And where "constitutional limitations" prevent such use of police power, the property (right) may be acquired by purchase, grant, or condemnation. Height restriction zoning had long been recognized as a valid exercise of police power, but not around airports. The old practice was to obtain air easements through purchase or grant.

Defendant County of Riverside contended the plaintiff failed to exhaust his administrative remedies, as required, before seeking judicial relief. The county's claim was that the plaintiff should have sought a permit from the Planning Commission with respect to non-conforming land uses or variances.

The court held that there is a distinction between commonly accepted and traditional height restriction zoning regulations of buildings and of airport approaches. In restricting building heights there is no invasion or trespass of the area above, whereas zoning of airport approaches contemplates actual use by airplanes of the airspace zoned. The court cited *Ackerman v. Port of Seattle*,[34] to wit:

> . . . *the authority of the government (always subject to constitutional safeguards) to regulate the use and utilization of private property for the promotion of the public welfare. . . . The difficulty arises in deciding whether a restriction is an exercise of the police power or an exercise of the eminent domain power. When private property rights are actually destroyed through the governmental action, then police power rules usually apply. But, when private property rights are taken from the individual and are conferred upon the public for public use, eminent domain principles are applicable.*

LOMA PORTAL CIVIC CLUB v. AMERICAN AIRLINES
394 P.2d 548 (Cal. 1964)

May airports and/or airlines be prohibited from creating noise, vibrations and other annoyances?

Plaintiffs were individuals who resided in the Loma Portal area of San Diego and a nonprofit corporation whose members were also residents of that area. Loma Portal lies to the west of Lindbergh Field, and

---

[34] 348 P.2d 664 (1960).

is in the flight path of the jet aircraft using that field's long runway. Defendants were commercial airlines, which flew passenger jets into and out of Lindbergh Field.

Lindbergh Field was owned and constructed by the City of San Diego. It had been in operation for over 35 years and has been used for regularly scheduled jet operations since 1960. The field is part of the national airport plan and is one of four major West Coast terminals. The master plan for its development had been approved by the Federal Aviation Agency. It had received grants of federal funds as a condition of which the city had agreed to the following: that it would "operate the airport for the public use and benefit; that it would operate in a suitable manner the airport and all facilities connected therewith which were necessary for airport purposes; that it would either by the adoption and enforcement of a zoning ordinance and regulations or by the acquisition of easements or other interests in lands or air space. . . ." And the city agreed it would prevent the use of land outside the airport's boundaries in any manner, which would create a hazard to the landing, taking off, or maneuvering of aircraft at the airport or otherwise limit the usefulness of the airport.

The airport operator, however, was not made a party to the suit. This is important, because in *Griggs v. County of Allegheny*,[35] it was held that the county, which owned and operated the airport, was obligated under the Fourteenth Amendment to compensate Griggs for the "taking" of his property. The fact that the glide paths there used were within the navigable airspace declared by Congress did not preclude the holding that there had been a taking of private property. The question of the rights of owners, *vis-à-vis* airlines, was not discussed by the court. The complaint in the instant case alleged that airline jets at San Diego flew,

> . . . *in great numbers at excessively low altitudes and within the air space immediately above or in close proximity to the homes of residents of the Loma Portal area . . . and below a safe altitude of flight; that in such flights such jet aircraft cause deafening, disturbing*

---

[35] 82 S.Ct. 531 (1962).

*and frightening noises and vibrations, disrupt
and interrupt sleep and repose and the use of
telephone, television and radio; disrupt, interrupt and prevent normal conversation and
communication; create fear, nervousness and
apprehension for personal safety; injuriously
affect the health, habits and material comforts
of plaintiffs, and prevent the normal use and
reasonable enjoyment of their homes.*

The plaintiffs sought from the court an injunction against the defendant airlines, prohibiting their operation of jet aircraft "at low altitudes in close proximity to such residences in such manner and at such
times as to interfere unreasonably with the normal use and enjoyment
by plaintiffs of their homes." There were no claims for damages, nor
did anything in the complaint indicate in monetary terms the amount of
damages sustained. This was important because it characterized the
case only as an action to *enjoin* a claimed nuisance, and not to recover
any damages for injury.

It is well established that public policy denies an injunction and
permits only the recovery of damages where private property has been
put to a public use by a public service corporation and the public interest has intervened. This principle is based upon a policy of protecting the public interest in the continuation of the use to which the property has been put. Under their leases with the city, the airlines had the
right to use the airport and all its appurtenances, including "the landing
field and any extensions thereof or additions thereto . . . and all other
conveniences for flying, landing and takeoffs. . . ."

Furthermore, the defendant airlines held FAA airworthiness certificates, commercial operator and air carrier operating certificates, and
certificates of public convenience and necessity, under which they were
obligated to provide "safe and adequate" service. An injunction will be
granted only when it is appropriate. In determining the availability of
injunctive relief, the court must consider the interests of third persons
and of the general public. In this case, the defendant's jet service was
in the public interest, and the public had come to rely on and have a
substantial stake in the continuation of that service.

It was also clear that it would have been contrary to the policy of the state to grant an injunction against flight operations in the vicinity of a public airport. The California Code of Civil Procedure provided:

> *Whenever any city, city and county, or county shall have established zones or districts under authority of law wherein certain manufacturing or commercial or airport uses are expressly permitted, except in an action to abate a public nuisance brought in the name of the people of the State of California, no person or persons, firm or corporation shall be enjoined or restrained by the injunctive process from the reasonable and necessary operation in any such industrial or commercial zone or airport of any use expressly permitted therein, nor shall such use be deemed a nuisance without evidence of the employment of unnecessary and injurious methods of operation. . . .*

The Supreme Court of California held that a request in Superior Court for an injunction to prohibit a nuisance was properly denied, as a matter of law, and under the circumstances of this case. There was an overriding public interest in the operation of aircraft with federal airworthiness certificates in federally certificated, scheduled passenger service, in a manner not creating imminent danger, and in accordance with applicable statutes and regulations. It was noted by the court that nothing in their findings were intended to be a determination of the rights of *landowners* who suffer from airplane annoyances to seek damages from the owners or operators of aircraft or to seek compensation from the owner or operator of an airport. Nor was any determination intended with respect to the rights of the parties when private airplanes and airports are involved. The court held here that under the facts of this case, (i.e., the operation of aircraft with federal airworthiness certificates in federally-certificated, scheduled passenger service, in conformity with federal safety regulations, in a manner not creating imminent danger, and in furtherance of the public interest in safe, regular air transportation of goods and passengers) an injunction is not available. The Superior Court judgment was affirmed.

AMERICAN AIRLINES v. TOWN OF HEMPSTEAD
398 F. 2d 369 (2nd Cir. 1968)

> *May local aviation rules and regulations conflict with existing state or federal regulations?*

The primarily residential Town of Hempstead, New York, lies to the east of John F. Kennedy International Airport [JFK]. The people of Hempstead were subjected to a noise problem so severe that the noise of aircraft over flight in Hempstead was frequently intense enough to interrupt sleep, conversation and the conduct of religious services. Additionally, it was sufficiently loud to submerge, for the duration of the maximum noise part of the over flight, the sound of radio, phonograph and television. The noise was frequently so intense as to interrupt classroom activities in schools, to be a source of discomfort to the ill, and a distraction to the well.

The case had nothing to do with questions of landowner's rights to compensation for over flights of their land, which might have amounted to a taking of their property. Nevertheless, there was inference that the airplane noise was a factor affecting decisions of people to acquire or dispose of interests in real property within the town. In an attempt to deal with the problem, the town added a new article to its "Unnecessary Noise Ordinance," forbidding anyone from operating a mechanism or device (including airplanes) which created a noise within the town exceeding either of two "limiting noise spectra."

The town argued that aircraft could fly over the Town of Hempstead in compliance both with the ordinance and with the FAA regulations governing landing and take-off patterns and procedures. There was no question, however, but that at the time the suit was brought, takeoffs and landings at JFK regularly produced noise exceeding the relevant limiting noise spectrum of the ordinance. Claiming the ordinance would prohibit airplanes using JFK from flying over the town, and thus would restrict the landing and take-off patterns and procedures normally adhered to by those airplanes, nine major U.S. flag air carriers, the Port of New York Authority, Charles H. Ruby, as president of the Air Line Pilots Association, three air line pilots, individually and as representatives of their class, and the Administrator of the Federal Aviation Administration (as *intervenor*), sued to enjoin the enforcement of the ordinance against them.

The U.S. District Court found that compliance with the ordinance would dictate the altitudes at which commercial aircraft could fly into and out of JFK, and that the flight requirements flowing from the ordinance would be, in large part, incompatible with existing traffic patterns and FAA procedures. Compliance would mean redesigning the flight patterns for JFK, together with a reintegration of the redesigned patterns with those for the other New York City airports. The safety margins of the existing procedures could not be preserved without restricting the traffic-handling capacity of JFK. And, there was no reliable evidence that a set of procedures could be devised for JFK in the then state of aviation development that would, assure compliance with the ordinance without substantial sacrifice of the interest in flight safety. The District Court therefore concluded that:

- The ordinance was an unconstitutional burden on interstate commerce;
- The area in which the ordinance operated had been preempted by federal legislation and regulation; and,
- The ordinance was in direct conflict with valid applicable federal regulation.

The Town of Hempstead appealed, still insisting that its alternate plan could steer most flights away from the town, thus assuring compliance with the ordinance. But the U.S. Court of Appeals concluded that any one of the district court's three conclusions was enough to make the ordinance invalid—that the ordinance was in conflict with applicable federal regulation was ample basis for affirmance. The FAA had promulgated extensive regulations, which unquestionably controlled the patterns and procedures of aircraft flying into and out of JFK. Compliance with the noise ordinance would have required alterations in the flight patterns and procedures established by federal regulations.

The U.S. District Court's order granting preliminary injunction was affirmed.

STAGG v. CITY OF SANTA MONICA
2 Cal. App. 3d 318 (1969)

Are aviation related rules and regulations designed to protect the public safety, health and welfare a valid exercise of police power?

On the night of January 2, 1968, R.E. Stagg piloted a jet aircraft which took off from Santa Monica Municipal Airport after 11 p.m. and before 7 a.m. the next morning. Santa Monica Municipal Code, Section 10105(a) provided:

> *No pure jet aircraft shall take off from the airport between the hours of 11:00 o'clock p.m. of one day and 7:00 a.m. the next day. The Airport Director or in his absence the watch commander of the Santa Monica Police Department may approve a take off during said hours, provided it appears to his satisfaction that an emergency involving life or death exists and approval is obtained before take off.*

On January 3, at the request of the airport director, a complaint was filed against Stagg by the City of Santa Monica in the local municipal court, charging him with violation of ordinance 10105(a). Following entry of a not guilty plea and setting of the matter for trial, Stagg made a motion to dismiss, which was denied. On May 10, Stagg filed a petition for a *writ of prohibition* in the superior court seeking to restrain the municipal court from proceeding with the trial. Stagg argued that the ordinance was an unconstitutional attempt to regulate a field preempted by both federal and state law.

On June 6, the superior court issued its memorandum and order granting the *writ of prohibition*. The court concluded the ordinance was invalid because its subject matter was preempted by state law. The court found it unnecessary to decide whether there was federal preemption. On June 13, the judgment granting the preemptory writ was entered. From this judgment the City of Santa Monica appealed.

As will be observed from the following discussion, the California Court of Appeal concluded that, as applied to the facts presented, the ordinance was valid. The appellate court found that the doctrine of federal preemption had no application here. In *Loma Portal Civic Club v. American Airlines,*[36] the court concluded that state action (and impliedly that of a political subdivision thereof) has not been precluded by any extensive pattern of federal regulation in the field of air transportation. The court stated:

> *A holding of federal preemption would have the effect of disabling the state from any action in the entire field, and placing in the federal government complete and sole responsibility for regulation of all aspects of that field. Such a holding by a single state court would have, of course, no effect on the conduct of other states with respect to regulation of that field, and unless Congress had in fact intended such preclusion of state regulation and were to carry out its responsibilities, there would result within that state a lacuna which the state would be powerless to fill. . . . To be sure, the supremacy case precludes the enforcement of state law which conflicts with federal law . . . and it is for this reason, not preemption, that a state may not prohibit that which federal authority directs.*

Concerning state regulations aimed at noise abatement, the court in *Loma Portal* observed:

> *Moreover, we note that noise abatement is a federal as well as a state aim, and when not inconsistent with safety . . . would not necessarily present a conflict with federal law but might well reinforce it.*

---

[36] 394 P.2d 548 (1964).

The appellate court disclosed no federal or California enactment, which directly conflicted with the ordinance in question. Both the federal government and the state of California had regulations governing the flight of aircraft. By virtue of its sovereignty over navigable airspace the United States has paramount power to regulate air traffic. The right of flight includes the right of safe access to public airports (i.e., the right of flight within the zone of approach and the right to land. Nothing is said about take off or departure from public airports).

The Superior Court determined the City of Santa Monica had no authority to pass the ordinance, because the state had reserved for itself the power to regulate all aspects of the air transportation field not reserved by the federal government. The appellate court disagreed. The airport was owned by the city, and a charter city has plenary (full) powers with respect to municipal affairs not expressly forbidden to it by the state. The operation of a municipally owned airport had been expressly committed by state statute to the local agency. The Government Code of California provided that a municipality may acquire property for use as an airport. The appellate court concluded that the city ordinance in question might also be upheld as a valid exercise of the municipality's police power. The California Constitution empowered cities and counties to make and enforce "such local, police, sanitary, and other regulations as are not in conflict with general laws."

The judgment was reversed.

VILLAGE OF WILLOUGHBY HILLS v. CORRIGAN
278 N.E.2d 658 (Ohio 1972)

Can airport zoning regulations designed to reduce airport hazards be adopted as an exercise of police powers?

Defendant was Cuyahoga County, owner and operator of the Cuyahoga County Airport, a portion of which extends into the village (now city) of Willoughby Hills in Lake County, Ohio. Plaintiffs were Willoughby Hills joined by petition filed by James and Bessie Chongris and Anton and Mildred Oblak, affected property owners.

The Boards of Commissioners of both Cuyahoga and Lake Counties, acting as the zoning board, adopted certain airport zoning regulations in the "airport hazard area." The plaintiffs filed suit alleging that the constitutional right of Willoughby Hills exclusively to enact and to enforce zoning regulations within its territorial limits had been infringed, and that property values had been depressed resulting in a taking of individual property rights and loss of tax revenues to the city. The defendant contended that the real property of the individual plaintiffs was subject to the jurisdiction and regulations of the Cuyahoga County Airport Zoning Board. The trial court entered judgment in favor of the defendant. The Court of Appeals reversed the lower court's judgment, and it was appealed to the Supreme Court of Ohio.

The trial court found there was no impairment of use, or diminution in value of the property in question. The Court of Appeals did not dispute actual findings of the trial court, but instead took the approach that the purpose sought by such airport zoning regulations could not be accomplished under police powers, but only through eminent domain. The Court of Appeals' conclusion was apparently based upon the rationale that all airport zoning regulations necessarily result in an unconstitutional taking of private property without compensation, irrespective of whether or not actual diminution of property has occurred.

The Ohio Supreme Court disagreed. It concluded that airport zoning regulations, at least those adopted in accordance with the provisions of the subject code and designed to reduce "airport hazards,"

> . . . may constitutionally be adopted as an exercise of the police powers of the State of Ohio, if such regulations are reasonably necessary to insure the safety of aircraft and of persons and property. However, if enforcement results in an unconstitutional taking, a court may enjoin the regulation or may direct the institution of eminent domain proceedings for the purpose of compensating the property owners.

In any zoning regulations restricting the use of land, there would appear to be a degree of taking, but the question of unconstitutional taking involves consideration of the extent the use of land is limited, and a judicial balancing of the loss against the benefits to society to be gained.

The court ruled that the subject zoning regulations were enacted as a proper exercise of the police power, and that they had a "substantial relation" to the "public safety" and "general welfare," though conceding that an airport may not in the guise of zoning, "convert" to the "public use" the "air rights" of property owners.

BRITISH AIRWAYS BOARD v. PORT AUTHORITY OF NEW YORK AND NEW JERSEY
564 F.2d 1002 (2nd Cir. 1977)

> *Can an authority restrict the use of its airport to*
> *specific aircraft pending the establishment of an*
> *applicable noise abatement regulation?*

At issue here was the supersonic jet airliner Concorde, its operators seeking use of the John F. Kennedy International Airport [JFK]. Plaintiffs-appellees were British Airways Board, and Compagnie Nationale Air France, both owners and operators of Concorde aircraft. Defendants-appellants were the Port Authority of New York and New Jersey and specified members and operators of JFK. *Amici curiae* were certain towns and villages, including the Town of Hempstead, and three persons with individual interests. This case went through several rounds of litigation, originally being tried in U.S. District Court, appealed to the U.S. Court of Appeals for the Second Circuit, back down to the District Court, and finally determined by the Second Circuit.

Surrounded by political implications, acceptance of the Concorde at airports in the United States became highly controversial. The President decided to permit supersonic transport aircraft service to 13 American cities under specified conditions. This decision came after 16 months of demonstration flights at Dulles International Airport. Similar tests were not conducted at Kennedy, because the plaintiffs refused to promulgate an acceptable noise rule for supersonic aircraft.

As early as 1958, the Port Authority had adopted 112 PNdB (perceived noise decibels) as the maximum permissible noise limit for all aircraft using Kennedy Airport. Until the instant case, no airplane meeting the 112 PNdB rule was denied access to the airport. The manufacturers of the Concorde proved, through testing at time of application to use Kennedy, and through follow up testing, that the Concorde could consistently meet a 109 PNdB standard. However, it was recognized by the U.S. Department of Transportation and by the Port Authority that there were unique low frequency vibrations produced by the Concorde which "were not necessarily reflected" in the current noise standard. In conjunction with the airlines' application to use U.S. airports, an Environmental Impact Statement was prepared by the FAA. The EIS concluded that,

> *This low frequency aspect will induce some perceptible vibration impact. However, while perceptible, the vibrational impact will not exceed any existing standards for structural damage. Since the low frequency content of Concorde's noise signature will produce some household rattle and interfere with communications, it will be annoying to residents in the immediate airport vicinity.*

The New York Legislature passed a bill banning all supersonic transports from Kennedy Airport (although this legislation was not binding on the Port Authority). The Port Authority banned the Concorde from Kennedy, initially for a period not to exceed six months, but then it was extended to a full year, and then to "a later date." The Port Authority's stated intention, for the time limits on the ban, was to give it the opportunity to project scientifically the community response to Concorde noise, and thereby to establish an appropriate noise regulation. During the course of events, the authority merely reiterated what had been known for years—that the Concorde had "unique characteristics including that on landing (it) has a high level of low frequency energy."

In the initial litigation, the District Court dissolved the Port Authority's ban, reasoning that the decision by the Secretary of Transportation (i.e., a federal decision to allow landing in the United States) preempted any contrary exercise of local authority. The Court of Appeals,

> *. . . held that federal law contemplated a limited role for airport proprietors. We decided that their task was to promulgate reasonable rules to abate noise in the airport and its environs. We also remanded for an evidentiary hearing to ascertain whether the Port Authority had exercised its responsibility in a "fair, reasonable and nondiscriminatory manner" or whether, as urged by the airlines and the United States, the thirteen month delay—as it was then—in promulgating a uniform noise standard for the Concorde was unreasonable, discriminatory and hence illegal.*

The District Court again struck down the Port Authority's ban on supersonic transport flights, concluding that for over a year the Authority had been "replowing old ground and doing re-reviews of scientific and theoretical data previously available." The Authority had no intention of setting either 112 PNdB or any other noise standard for the Concorde, thus creating an unreasonable, discriminatory and unfair impingement on commerce. The court enjoined the ban on the Concorde so long as it emitted no more noise than 112 PNdB.

On appeal, the Second Circuit said that,

> *The law simply will not tolerate the denial of rights by unwarranted official inaction. . . . There comes a time when relegating the solution of an issue to the indefinite future can so sap petitioners of hope and resources that a failure to resolve the issue within a reasonable period is tantamount to refusing to address it at all . . . The airlines should no longer be forced to suffer the consequences of such illegal delay.*

The court went on to state that its initial opinion in this case delineated the limited role Congress had reserved for airport proprietors in the U.S. system of aviation management. Exclusive control of airspace allocation is concentrated at the national level. Communities are pre-empted from regulating planes in flight, but the task of protecting the local population from airport noise belongs usually to the local government.

The important role of the airport proprietor in developing noise abatement programs consonant with local conditions was thus recognized. In its initial findings, the court found it fair to assume that the proprietor's intimate knowledge of local conditions would lead to the expeditious establishment of reasonable, non-arbitrary and nondiscriminatory noise regulations at Kennedy. The Port Authority did not do that, but rather, refused to allow the Concorde to land, when the airplane was capable of meeting the rule that was consistently applied to all other aircraft since 1958 (i.e., the 112 PNdB rule).

The appellate court affirmed the district court's order to dissolve the ban on the Concorde, but indicated its holding did not deny the Port Authority the power to adopt a new, uniform and reasonable noise standard in the future, assuming the Authority deemed the 112 PNdB rule to be inadequate.

BURBANK-GLENDALE-PASADENA AIRPORT AUTHORITY v. HUGHES AIR CORPORATION
Case No. NCC 17,926 B (Superior Court of the State of California for the County of Los Angeles 1980)

> *May an airport authority restrict the number of operations conducted by an airline?*

Plaintiffs in this case were the cities of Burbank, Glendale, and Pasadena, California (a.k.a. Joint Powers Authority). The defendant was the Hughes Air Corporation (d.b.a. Hughes Airwest). The City of Los Angeles appeared as *amicus curiae*. The case was heard by the Los Angeles Superior Court.

In 1977, the plaintiffs purchased the Hollywood-Burbank Airport, formerly owned and operated by Lockheed Corporation. In the early 1970s the State of California promulgated Noise Standards for California airports, and Lockheed was called upon to commence a noise-monitoring program. Since Lockheed had announced its intended sale of the airport, it applied for and was granted a variance from the

Noise Standards, subject to the condition, among others, that "During the term hereof (Lockheed) shall not permit or authorize any activity in connection with its airport, which results in an increase in the noise impact boundary. . . ."

Upon its acquisition of the airport, the Joint Powers Authority was compelled by the State Legislature to abide by terms stating, "In operating the airport, the separate public entity shall not permit or authorize any activity in conjunction with the airport which results in an increase in the size of the noise impact area. . . . " During that same period in time, the preparation of a combined Environmental Impact Report/Environmental Impact Statement was required to evaluate the environmental impact of the proposed sale of the Burbank Airport to a governmental entity. The FAA granted its approval of the EIR/EIS provided it "includes the condition that appropriate language will be included in a grant agreement for the proposed acquisition reflecting the commitments not to increase noise exposure. . . ."

The Authority entered into Airport Use Agreements with Continental Airlines, Pacific Southwest Airlines, and Hughes Airwest, subject to terms in each agreement that "This Agreement is subject and subordinate to the provisions of any agreements heretofore or hereafter made between the Authority and the United States," and that "Airline (Hughes) shall observe and obey all lawful and reasonable Rules and Regulations promulgated, from time to time by Authority. . . ." When the Authority began operation of the airport, several noise-related rules and regulations were initiated or continued in effect.

Hughes determined it would increase its flight schedules at the airport from a total of 134 operations per week to 196 per week, with a later reduction to 168 operations. The FAA advised the Authority that failure on the Authority's part to take action to prevent an increase in the airport's noise impact area could constitute an effective authorization of the increase, in violation of the Grant Agreement used in the Authority's acquisition of the airport.

The Authority adopted by emergency rule, and later by permanent rule adoption (of Noise Rule 7), that "no air carrier shall implement or continue in effect any increase in operations or weighted operations above the number of operations or weighted operations in effect for such air carrier during the week ending March 10, 1979, without the written approval of the commission. . . ." Hughes commenced increased operations without applying for permission to do so, and the Authority filed this action seeking a temporary restraining order, preliminary and permanent injunctive relief, and a declaratory judgment that Noise Rule 7 was valid and enforceable, and had been violated by Hughes.

In its conclusions of law, the court found the Noise Rule was reasonable, non-arbitrary, and non-capricious; did not impose unreasonable burden on interstate commerce; did not unjustly discriminate against or among airport users; did not unreasonably interfere with the objectives of the Airline Deregulation Act of 1978; did not create any exclusive use, as defined in the Federal Aviation Act of 1958; did not violate the due process or equal protection clauses of the United States or California Constitutions; and did not constitute an unlawful retroactive regulation. The court found the Noise Rule 7 of the Burbank-Glendale-Pasadena Airport Authority to be valid and enforceable, and permanently restrained Hughes Airwest from conducting additional operations.

SAFECO INSURANCE v. CITY OF WATERTOWN
529 F. Supp. 1220 (D.S.D. 1981)

*Is the airport sponsor responsible for warning air crews
of the possible presence of birds on the runway?*

Plaintiff, as *subrogee* of its insured, Kerr-McGee Corporation, brought these actions, (consolidated for trial) to recover for property damage to a twinjet Kerr-McGee aircraft which crashed on take-off from the Watertown Municipal Airport. The plaintiff brought action against the City of Watertown as operator of the Airport, and sued the United States under the Federal Tort Claims Act.

A Saberliner jet aircraft owned by the Kerr-McGee Corporation arrived at the airport in Watertown, South Dakota, at approximately 11:00 a.m. on Saturday, June 14, 1975. At approximately 4:30 p.m., the airplane began its departure. The crew was informed by employees of the Federal Aviation Administration in the Flight Service Station [FSS] at the airport that the visibility was about a mile and a quarter (the day was rainy), and that because of the prevailing wind, the favored runway was 17-35, running north-south.

The Saberliner taxied to the north end of Runway 17-35, turned, and started its take-off roll. About 3,000 to 3,500 feet down the 6,900 feet runway, the aircraft reached take-off speed and lifted off. Almost immediately, and while at an altitude of 25 to 100 feet, the plane encountered a flock of Franklin gulls. Some of the gulls were ingested into the airplane's two jet engines, all power was lost, and the pilot made an emergency landing in a field south of the airport. The pilot and co-pilot and one passenger received injuries; the Saberliner was a total loss. The parties stipulated the loss to be $1,787,872.

The plaintiff's first ground for recovery against the United States was that the FAA negligently certificated the Watertown Airport under 14 C.F.R. Part 139, "Certification and Operations: Land Airports Serving CAB Certificated Air Carriers," and, thereafter, was negligent in failing to enforce its regulations under that Part. Under the Part 139 certification process, an Airport Operations Manual must be submitted by the airport sponsor and approved by the FAA. Among many other requirements for the preparation of the airport operations manual, the applicant,

> . . . *must show that it has established instructions and procedures for the prevention or removal of factors on the airport that attract, or may attract, birds. However, the applicant need not show that it has established these instructions and procedures if the Administrator finds that a bird hazard does not exist and is not likely to exist.*

When Watertown submitted its airport operations manual in compliance with these regulations, it stated, under the category of "Birds," that there were "no problems at present time." The FAA accepted this statement and, without an independent inspection of the airport, approved the manual and issued a certificate to the airport in March, 1973. FAA thereafter conducted annual inspections. The Watertown airport's 1975 FAA inspection took place on June 4, ten days prior to the Saberliner accident. The report of this inspection, in a letter of June 6, 1975, from the Chief, Airport Certification Staff to the airport manager found "no discrepancies or violations to FAR Part 139." The plaintiff alleged the FAA knew or should have known that the Watertown Airport did in fact have a bird problem; that the FAA was negligent in allowing Watertown to have a valid certificate without requiring it to embark on a bird control program; and that the FAA was negligent in later failing to discover the bird problem, and in not thereafter requiring a bird control program.

To make out a cause of action under the Federal Tort Claims Act, the plaintiff had to overcome judicial precedent that the government does not incur liability for "discretionary" functions—that the mere provision for government safety inspections, or the ability to stop an activity for failure to comply with safety standards, does not impose liability on the government for failure to do so. A government safety program does not impose a special duty on the government. Thus, insofar as the complaint purported to state a cause of action against the United States for a negligent violation of 14 C.F.R. Part 139, either in issuing a certificate or the later failure to discover and correct the bird problem, had to be dismissed.

The basic elements of a negligence action are that there must be a duty owed by the defendant to the plaintiff, there was a breach of this duty, and the breach of the duty was the proximate cause of the plaintiff's injury. This court had no hesitation in finding that the operator of a public airport has a duty independent of federal statutes and regulations to the pilots using the airport to use reasonable care to keep the airport free from hazards—or at least to use reasonable care to warn of hazards not known to the pilots. However, the City of Watertown argued there had never been a problem with birds, specifically Franklin gulls, at the airport. In response to the city's contention, there seemed to have been almost a complete uniformity of opinion among the witnesses who were familiar with the Watertown Airport that gulls were there in substantial quantities from early Spring to late Fall for as long as any of the witnesses had been there.

Under the airport operations manual, which the airport was required to keep, the airport management was "responsible . . . for all General Supervision of the Watertown Municipal Airport." Further, federal regulations in 14 C.F.R. Part 139 (1975) indicated that it appeared to be the airport operator's duty to identify safety problems on the airport and to disseminate this information by Notices to Airmen [NOTAMs]. An FAA official testified that many of the airports in this

region had permanent NOTAMs, apparently printed in the *Airmens'
Information Manual*, and there was no indication why it would not
have been possible for one to be issued for the airport. The district
court found that the Watertown Airport, under the circumstances,
owed the pilots of the crashed Saberliner a duty to warn them of the
possible presence of gulls; that defendant City of Watertown breached
this duty by failing to so warn; and that the failure to warn was the
proximate cause of the crash.

The plaintiff also contended FAA employees at the Watertown Airport were negligent in failing to warn the Saberliner of gulls on the day
of the accident. These personnel were in the FSS located on the ground
floor of the airport terminal, and their duties involved the dissemination
of weather information and flight advisories. Flight Service Station
personnel may also relay air traffic clearances to pilots from an Air
Route Traffic Control Center, but they do not *control* air traffic. There
was no control tower at the airport. Rather, FSS personnel merely act
as a conduit of certain types of advisory information for pilots.

This advisory information includes hazards presented by birds, and
both of the FSS personnel on duty on June 14, 1975, acknowledged
they had issued bird warnings prior to the day of the accident. These
warnings, like the other information disseminated by FSS personnel,
were issued after the personnel had either made a direct observation of
a condition, or were informed of the existence of a condition by airport
management or pilot reports. On the day of the accident, however, FSS
personnel testified they neither saw gulls on the airport nor had they
received any reports of their presence.

The court determined that airport management could see the problems "close up," while the FSS personnel only appear to know of most
problems second-hand, and it would seem to cast an unreasonable burden on the FSS personnel to decide that some problem is of such magnitude it requires a permanent NOTAM without first receiving a decision to that effect from the management.

The "pilot in command of an aircraft is directly responsible for, and
is the final authority as to, the operation of that aircraft."[37] This includes a duty to see what can be seen, and to separate his or her aircraft from obstructions and hazards, including birds. Before the flight

---

[37] *See* FAR Part 91.3.

to Watertown, the pilot testified that he checked the NOTAMs for warnings on the Watertown Airport, and found nothing relating to birds. Before take-off, both the pilot and co-pilot looked down the runway, but saw no obstructions. When the Saberliner began to leave the ground, the co-pilot looked up, saw a flock of gulls around the Saberliner coming up from below, and told the pilot. Almost immediately thereafter, the aircraft lost power and crashed beyond the end of the runway.

Further, and of great importance in determining the crew's negligence, considered was the sheer difficulty of seeing the gulls. The gulls were apparently at a point about 3,500 feet from the north end where the Saberliner turned onto the runway. The court determined the crew had a "reasonable excuse for not seeing" the gulls on the runway in time to avoid the accident. Actions of the pilots were found not to be a proximate cause of the accident.

The U.S. District Court judgment was entered for the plaintiff against the defendant City of Watertown for the full stipulated value of the Saberliner.

CITY OF ATLANTA v. UNITED STATES
531 F. Supp. 506 (N.D. Ga. 1982)

*Is an Environmental Impact Statement required for projects planned
and adopted prior to the National Environmental Policy Act?*

In 1968, the City of Atlanta submitted an Airport Layout Plan [ALP] to the FAA. This Plan, which provided for a considerable upgrading of the facilities at Hartsfield International Airport, included four runways. The FAA approved the Plan on June 12, 1968. The National Environmental Policy Act became law on January 1, 1970.

Hartsfield had three runways. The city planned to construct a fourth runway to "increase the capacity of Hartsfield to handle flight operations and to aid the City in meeting anticipated demands for increased runway capacity." The FAA is responsible for maintaining air safety. To discharge this responsibility, it was required to construct navigational aids for the assistance of aircraft using the proposed runway, and to adopt takeoff and landing procedures for those aircraft and others "in the navigable airspace relating to the [proposed] fourth parallel runway." When completed, the runway could not be used until the FAA took these actions. These are the only actions the FAA, or any other agency of the federal government, would take with regard to the runway, which the city intended to construct with its own funds.

The question before the U.S. District Court was the applicability of the provisions of NEPA to these actions. The FAA contended that NEPA required it to prepare at least an Environmental Assessment before taking any action. The city disagreed and brought this action for a declaratory judgment that NEPA was inapplicable. The issue before the court was not the retroactive application of NEPA to federal actions taken before July 1, 1970; rather it was the application of NEPA to federal actions occurring after NEPA became effective in a project undertaken before NEPA's effective date.

According to the city, the FAA took its only "major federal action" with respect to the additional runway in 1968, when it approved the four-runway Plan. Later FAA involvement in placing the runway into operation was not sufficient to trigger NEPA, because all post NEPA environmental impacts were the necessary result of the pre-NEPA critical federal action. The FAA viewed its actions with respect to the runway in a different light. It argued that the installation of navigational aids and the development of flight paths and procedures were in themselves "major federal actions significantly affecting the quality of the human environment." Because they were post-NEPA major federal actions in a project that straddled NEPA's effective date, the FAA's contention was that NEPA applied.

In its determination, the district court turned to congressional intent, and upon regulations of the Council on Environmental Quality. While Congress did not specifically address the issue of applicability of NEPA to ongoing projects, it did direct that NEPA apply, "to the fullest extent possible." Regulations of the CEQ provided that, "NEPA shall continue to be applicable to actions begun before January 1, 1970, to the fullest extent possible." It was pointed out that many other courts in making their findings had relied upon this theme. Inasmuch as Congress intended NEPA to be applied "to the fullest extent possible," to its credit FAA was attempting to live up to this standard. The court held that FAA's approval of the four-runway plan in 1968 did not relieve it of its statutory duty to consider environmental factors in performing those post-NEPA actions necessary to make the runway operational. Defendant FAA's motion for summary judgment was granted. Plaintiff City of Atlanta's motion for summary judgment was denied.

ARROW AIR v. PORT AUTHORITY OF NEW YORK AND NEW JERSEY
602 F. Supp. 314 (D.N.Y. 1985)

May local airport sponsors enact reasonable, non-discriminatory
noise regulations formulated under policies differing
from federal policies?

Plaintiff, Arrow Air, Inc. (Arrow), a diversified passenger and cargo air carrier incorporated in 1981, sought to enjoin the Port Authority of New York and New Jersey (Port Authority), the owner and operator of John F. Kennedy International Airport [JFK], from enforcing its noise level restrictions. The restrictions became effective on January 1, 1985, and prevented Arrow from using Douglas DC-8, 60 series (DC-8-60) equipment, referred to as "Stage 1" aircraft, at JFK, since they did not comply with those noise restrictions.

Federal noise restrictions similarly prevented using such equipment, effective January 1, 1985. However, on an application filed by Arrow on August 2, 1984, the FAA granted Arrow, at the last minute, a limited exemption on December 28, 1984, until July 31, 1985, from the application of the federal restrictions. The Port Authority refused to grant a similar exemption from the noise requirement applicable at JFK to Arrow. Arrow sued for relief from the Port Authority's refusal to grant an exemption similar to the federal exemption.

Arrow intended to fly a DC-8-60, Stage 1, aircraft from JFK to Borinquen, Puerto Rico daily, and from JFK to Georgetown, Guyana, twice a week. The DC-8-60 aircraft did not comply with either Federal or Port Authority noise standards, both effective January 1, 1985, which required muted Stage 2 or 3 aircraft. Under the Federal Compliance Program promulgated by the FAA in December 1976, air carriers were required to phase-out and replace all their noisier and older aircraft by January 1, 1985. The FAA established a phased-in compliance schedule by grouping aircraft by noise characteristics; it termed these groupings "Stages." Stage 1 aircraft are the oldest and noisiest equipment such as the Boeing 707 and the DC-8-60. Stage 2 aircraft, which include the Boeing 747, are newer and somewhat quieter than the Stage 1 aircraft. Stage 3 aircraft are the most technically advanced and quietest aircraft, such as the Boeing 757, the Boeing 767, and the A-300. By January 1, 1985, all Stage 1 aircraft were to be replaced by Stage 2 or Stage 3 aircraft.

The Port Authority enacted a new Aircraft Noise Abatement Program on April 7, 1982. That program, like the FAA's, provided for phased-in compliance. The Port Authority's program consisted of an Interim Rule (520/0-00), a Nighttime Rule (530/0-00) (not questioned herein), and a Final Rule (540/0-00). The Interim Rule, which took effect on March 7, 1984, following a legal challenge, required air carriers to operate 75% of their four-engine aircraft movements with noise compliant equipment (i.e., with Stage 2 or Stage 3 equipment, or with any aircraft which is quieter than the noisiest Stage 2 aircraft operating at a particular Port Authority airport).

The Interim Rule also provided for a future owner's exemption (560/0-04) under which the Port Authority would treat a carrier's Stage 1 aircraft movements as Stage 2, where that carrier contracted with the Port Authority to utilize a Stage 3 aircraft at the Port Authority airports by January 1, 1985, and also had a lease or purchase agreement demonstrating that it would, in fact, have a Stage 3 aircraft by that date. The Port Authority's Final Rule, which took effect on January 1, 1985, provided that only noise compliant equipment could operate at the Port Authority's airports.

In applying for an injunction, Arrow's request was founded upon three arguments, that:

- The Port Authority's regulations were preempted by exemption from federal noise regulations;
- The Port Authority's rule placed undue burden on interstate commerce; and that,
- The Port Authority was discriminating against them.

As to preemption, the U.S. District Court stated that in numerous cases the federal courts have repeatedly affirmed the Port Authority's "power and . . . responsibility to establish fair, even-handed and non-discriminatory regulations designed to abate the effect of airplane noise on surrounding communities." The airport proprietor has authority to regulate aircraft noise. The Port Authority's Final Rule did not "stand as an obstacle to the accomplishment and execution of an established federal policy," nor did it impede FAA's purpose in granting Arrow an exemption, namely to permit Arrow to fly to San Juan. Moreover, the Final Rule reinforced the Aviation Safety and Noise Abatement Act of 1979 and Fleet Compliance Program's general policy of requiring air carriers to fly quiet, noise compliant aircraft by January 1, 1985, and thereafter.

The court responded to Arrow's urging that the Port Authority's regulation violated the Commerce Clause, because it imposed an undue burden on commerce, by stating that, "Evenhanded local regulation to effectuate a legitimate local public interest is valid unless preempted by federal action, . . . or unduly burdensome on maritime activities or interstate commerce." If a regulation is otherwise valid under the Commerce Clause, it is not rendered invalid simply because an operator has to change its market structure. Arrow claimed that it could not possibly compete on the Georgetown and Borinquen routes unless it could use the Port Authority's facilities in New York, and that it would be uneconomical to operate from JFK with the more expensive noise compliant equipment. However, Guyana Airways, Arrow's competitor on the Guyana route, operated its flights from JFK to Georgetown fully with noise compliant aircraft and charged the same price for its Georgetown service as Arrow. Finally, the court ruled the Port Authority had not discriminated against Arrow. Arrow had concentrated on leasing non-compliant aircraft.

Pursuant to a contractual agreement entered into by Arrow with the Port Authority on March 7, 1984, Arrow was granted a future owner's exemption from the Port Authority's Interim and Nighttime Rules, and permitted to conduct its operations at JFK and Newark International Airports with Stage 1 aircraft, and have those aircraft treated as Stage 2 aircraft, provided that it would lease, in December 1984, a DC-8-73 CF aircraft (a re-engined DC-8-60),, and a DC-10 aircraft, and immediately upon delivery place such aircraft in service at JFK and Newark Airports. In the future owner's exemption contract, Arrow also agreed to "comply with all other applicable provisions of the Port Authority's Interim, Nighttime, and Final Rules."

Arrow had not re-engined the specific DC-8 aircraft and the specified DC-10 aircraft was no longer in Arrow's fleet. Instead of having the DC-8 re-engined, Arrow scheduled this aircraft to be "hush kitted" by the Nacelle Corporation. Arrow planned to install so-called "hush kits" on its non-compliant Stage 1 aircraft to make them compliant by January 1, 1985. Arrow contracted, on October 15, 1984, with the Nacelle Corporation, a company 50% owned by George Batchelor, Chairman of Arrow's Board of Directors, for ten Hush Kits for its DC-8-60 aircraft. However, technology for the Hush Kits to quiet the noise from the DC-8-60 simply did not develop in time.

Since the Port Authority's Final Rule was not preempted, the Court had to determine whether it was being administered in a discriminatory manner. Arrow contended that the regulation was being administered in a discriminatory manner because the Port Authority permitted Icelandair to fly non-compliant DC-8-60 aircraft into JFK and allowed other air carriers to land non-compliant BAC 1-11s, Boeing 737s, and DC-9s into Port Authority airports. A qualified expert explained that the FAA Advisory Circular on aircraft noise shows that the BAC 1-11, Boeing 737, and DC-9 aircraft are quieter than the DC-8-60 aircraft on takeoffs and landings. The Port Authority's rule reasonably permitted certain two-engine aircraft to continue operating since they are quieter than the noisiest Stage 2 aircraft operating at JFK.

The Port Authority had authorized only one exemption to its Final Rule, and that was granted at the express request of the United States Department of State because of international policy considerations. Acting Secretary of State Van Dam requested that Icelandair be granted an exemption since it provided the only direct service between Iceland and the United States. Van Dam wrote, "This service is of significant strategic importance to the U.S. in light of the existence of military installations and equipment of the United States located in Iceland." The Port Authority authorized the Icelandair exemption because the Secretary of State said that it was necessary for national security. The Port Authority made a distinction based on a reasonable classification to give exemptions only when the air carrier could show that the exemption was in the national interest.

When local economic regulation is challenged as being discriminatory the court "presumes the constitutionality of the statutory discriminations and requires only that the classification challenged be rationally related to a legitimate state interest." The Port Authority had established reasonable procedures to make sure aircraft would conform to the noise requirements. In conclusion, the U.S. District Court stated, "It is manifest from our scheme of aviation management that Congress has consciously committed to airport owners the responsibility for determining the permissible levels of noise for the facility and its environs." Congress has authorized airport proprietors to enact reasonable, nondiscriminatory noise regulations. The complaint was dismissed.

C.A.R.E. NOW v. FEDERAL AVIATION ADMINISTRATION
854 F.2d 1326 (11th Cir. 1988)

May a reasonable decision by the FAA of a Finding of
No Significant Impact be successfully challenged?

Citizens Against Runway Extension Now (C.A.R.E. Now) petitioned the court to review the FAA's order approving a runway extension at DeKalb-Peachtree Airport, Georgia [PDK]. The purpose of the extension was to provide an increased margin of safety at the airport. C.A.R.E. Now was a non-profit civic organization consisting of homeowner associations and neighborhood groups in areas encircling PDK, contesting the runway extension.

In 1985, DeKalb County presented an Airport Layout Plan, which recommended the runway extension. The FAA approved the ALP. In order to comply with the National Environmental Policy Act of 1969, DeKalb County hired a private consulting firm to prepare an Environmental Assessment to ascertain the project's impact on the environment. The EA predicted noise exposure levels surrounding PDK would increase from 16,800 to 19,300 persons impacted because of the runway extension over the five-year period following completion of the extension. To mitigate the increased noise exposure, the EA proposed two measures. The first was a preferential runway use program designed to reduce the number of jets taking off in any one direction. The second mitigation measure was to have aircraft begin the takeoff roll 1,000 feet farther to the north on south departures.

The FAA issued its Finding of No Significant Impact. The FONSI noted that the EA had adequately discussed 11 development alternatives, including the alternatives of the use of another airport. The

FONSI also concluded that the EA complied with established FAA procedures in its methodology. Petitioners C.A.R.E. Now found the FONSI inadequate, and, therefore, filed this petition for review. Specifically, the petitioners asserted that the proposal created a reasonable possibility of a *significant impact* on the human environment, requiring the preparation of an Environmental Impact Statement under NEPA. The issues were:

- whether the impacts as presented by the FONSI were "significant" so as to require an EIS;
- whether the FONSI was deficient because the FAA failed to determine prudent alternatives to the project existed;
- whether the FONSI was deficient because the FAA failed to consider the cumulative impact of past, present, and reasonably foreseeable actions in finding that the project would not significantly impact the environment; and,
- whether the FAA erred in considering speculative mitigation measures in concluding that the project would have no significant impact on the environment.

The court found the utility of NEPA apparent in this case. Without NEPA, the FAA would not likely have imposed mitigation measures as conditions for the completion of the runway extension. With NEPA, however, the FAA was forced to consider the environmental consequences of its actions. As a result, PDK would experience enhanced safety with insignificant environmental consequences due to the implementation of effective mitigation measures.

The court's review was to determine if the record supported the critical findings and if the agency's decisions were reasonable. Because it found the FAA decision was reasonable, it denied the petition for review.

JEWS FOR JESUS v. BOARD OF AIRPORT COMMISSIONERS
785 F.2d 791 (9th Cir. 1986)

May religious materials be distributed in a public airport terminal?

Plaintiffs in this case were Jews for Jesus, Inc., a non-profit religious corporation, and Alan Howard Snyder, a minister of the Gospel for Jews for Jesus. The defendants were the City of Los Angeles and the Board of Airport Commissioners of the City of Los Angeles, collectively the operator of Los Angeles International Airport [LAX].

On July 13, 1983, the Airport Board adopted Resolution 13787, which stated in part:

> ... *the Central Terminal area at Los Angeles International Airport is not open for First Amendment activities by any individual and/or entity ... if any individual or entity engages in First Amendment activities within the Central Terminal Area at Los Angeles International Airport, the City Attorney of the City of Los Angeles is directed to institute appropriate litigation against such individual and/or entity to ensure compliance with this Policy statement of the Board of Airport Commissioners.*

On July 6, 1984, Alan Snyder was stopped by a Department of Airports peace officer while distributing free religious literature on a pedestrian walkway in the Central Terminal Area at LAX. The officer showed Snyder a copy of the resolution, explained that Snyder's activities violated the resolution, and requested Snyder leave LAX. The officer warned Snyder that the city would take legal action against him if he refused to leave as requested. Snyder stopped distributing leaflets and left the airport terminal.

Jews for Jesus and Snyder then filed suit against the airport, challenging the constitutionality of the resolution under both the California and Federal Constitutions. The district court held that the Central Terminal Area was a traditional public forum under federal law, and held that the resolution was facially unconstitutional under the United

States Constitution. On appeal, the U.S. Court of Appeals held that the distribution of literature by Jews for Jesus was protected speech and that the Central Terminal Area of the Los Angeles International Airport was a *public forum*. The governmental interests advanced by the Board were not sufficiently compelling to justify the total exclusion of those persons wishing to exercise free speech within the Central Terminal Area.

Los Angeles International Airport then appealed to the U.S. Supreme Court. The Supreme Court suggested that by prohibiting all protected expression, the Airport Board purported to create a virtual "First Amendment Free Zone." The Supreme Court could find no apparent saving construction of the resolution. The resolution expressly applied to all "First Amendment activities," and the words of the resolution left no room for a narrowing construction. A law that "confers on police a virtually unrestrained power to arrest and charge persons with a violation" of the resolution is unconstitutional because "the opportunity for abuse, especially where a statute has received a virtually open-ended interpretation, is self-evident."[38]

The Supreme Court concluded the resolution was substantially over broad, and was not fairly subject to a limiting construction. Accordingly it held that the resolution violated the First Amendment, and affirmed the judgment of the Court of Appeals.

INTERNATIONAL SOCIETY FOR KRISHNA CONSCIOUSNESS v. LEE
506 U.S. 805 (1992)

> *May religious organizations distribute materials*
> *in non-public areas of the airport?*

This action, alleging claims under the First and Fourteenth Amendments to the U.S. Constitution, began in 1975. Over the ensuing years it had been assigned to three successive federal district judges. A total of four complaints had been fashioned by the plaintiffs in an attempt to state actionable claims against the defendants. The plaintiffs sought a preliminary injunction against the enforcement by any of the

---

[38] *Lewis v. City of New Orleans,* 415 U.S. 130, 135-136 (1974).

defendants of certain of its regulations. The defendants collectively moved to dismiss the action for lack of jurisdiction.

Plaintiffs were the International Society for Krishna Consciousness, Incorporated [ISKCON], and Brian Rumbaugh, on behalf of all ISKCON members. Rumbaugh was a priest of ISKCON and President of the New York Temple of ISKCON. ISKCON is an international religious society, which espouses the religious and missionary views of Krishna Consciousness. It is a non-profit religious corporation. The defendants were the Port Authority of New York and New Jersey and its Superintendent of Police, Walter Lee, who by the time this action came to trial had died. The Port Authority is an entity created in 1921 by agreement between the states of New York and New Jersey. It operates the three airports involved in this action: LaGuardia, Kennedy and Newark International Airports.

The conflict in this case arose out of the desire of ISKCON members to conduct certain religious activities at the three airports. The plaintiffs described these activities as follows:

> *Hinduism as expressed by Krishna Consciousness imposes on its members the duty to perform a religious ritual in public places known as "Sankirtan," which consists of gratuitously disseminating religious tracts, sanctified flowers, or candy, and soliciting funds to support the Society. Sankirtan is directed to spreading religious truth as it is known to Krishna Consciousness, attracting new members, and supporting ISKCON's religious activities.*

In their complaint, the plaintiffs claimed they had attempted to perform Sankirtan at "those portions of Kennedy, LaGuardia and Newark International Airports open to the general public" according to agreement. The Port Authority had ". . . given to plaintiffs permission to distribute literature and solicit contributions only within certain limited public portions of certain of the terminals" at the airports. In all of the areas, pursuant to agreement, the plaintiffs had agreed to certain limitations on their performance of Sankirtan in that they had agreed to remain 25 feet from outer doors, security checkpoints, stairways, escalators, elevators, ticket counters, or anyone standing in line at any of the foregoing locations. ISKCON members did not enter private shops without permission, nor did they block entrances or exits of those shops. They did not chant or sing aloud or play musical instruments in the manner in which Sankirtan is frequently performed on the streets or in other open spaces.

The plaintiffs and the Port Authority had worked out an arrangement for the performance of the plaintiff's Sankirtan obligations in areas of the three airports not subject to airline lease agreements. The plaintiffs initially sought to reach similar agreements with the various airline tenants. Subsequently, they decided they no longer wished to deal with each of the airline tenants, but rather wished to enjoin the Port Authority from enforcing its regulations with respect to the exercise of First Amendment rights (within the leaseholds).

The plaintiff's request for injunctive relief was narrowly drawn. They requested only that the defendant be enjoined from enforcing the Port Authority's regulations at issue above. Since it was conceded that those regulations did not apply to non-commercial activity and were not being enforced by anyone in the leased areas, the plaintiff's motion was moot. The defendant's motion to dismiss for lack of jurisdiction was denied, but the plaintiff's motion for preliminary injunctive relief was likewise denied.

MULTIMEDIA PUBLISHING v. GREENVILLE-SPARTANBURG AIRPORT DISTRICT
991 F.2d 154 (4th Cir. 1993)

May an airport totally ban the placement of newsracks inside its airline passenger terminal?

Multimedia Publishing Company of South Carolina publishes the *Greenville News* and the *Greenville Piedmont*, both daily newspapers in South Carolina. The New York Times Company publishes the *Spartanburg Herald-Journal*, also a South Carolina daily. During the fall of 1988, before renovation of the Greenville-Spartanburg Airport terminal began, Multimedia contacted Dick Graham, then executive director of the airport, requesting permission to place newsracks in the passenger terminal building. Newspapers were then available only in the gift shop, and Multimedia had received complaints from business people in Greenville who weren't able to purchase them when arriving or departing outside the shop's hours of operation. Graham told Multimedia he didn't want to increase congestion in the small existing terminal by placing newsracks inside, but he promised to consult the renovation architects about providing newsrack space in the renovated facility, and he led companies to believe they could expect to place newsracks inside it.

Although Graham did ask the architect to consider newsrack placement, neither he nor his successor, Gary Jackson, pursued the matter further. When the architect contacted Jackson after renovation was under way, Jackson told him not to worry about newsracks because they wouldn't be permitted inside the new terminal. In November of 1989, when renovation was nearly complete, Multimedia asked Jackson when newsracks could be placed inside the new terminal. Citing aesthetic concerns, he flatly refused to permit newsracks in the terminal, although he later allowed the newspaper companies to place them in one of the airport's several parking areas.

In pressing for permission to place newsracks inside the terminal, Multimedia had offered to customize them, under the direction of the architect, to avoid detracting from the new terminal's aesthetics. Specifically, Multimedia had offered to paint them special colors, or place them inside wooden cabinets. Jackson never presented these offers to the Airport Commission, and indeed, consulted no one regarding the feasibility of customizing the newsracks to complement the terminal's decor.

Ultimately, the New York Times Company joined Multimedia's efforts, and together they brought suit against the airport. Jackson, acting alone, then prepared a list of justifications for banning newsracks. He claimed they:

- would mar the aesthetics of the terminal;
- cause gift-shop revenues to decrease;
- pose a pedestrian safety hazard;
- constitute a security risk because they might hold bombs; and,

- newsracks were unnecessary because adequate alternative means of distributing newspapers existed.

In a non-jury trial, the U.S. District Court found that the First Amendment protects distribution of newspapers through newsracks. It also determined that, for purposes of disseminating news, the Greenville-Spartanburg Airport is a public forum. Finally, the District Court concluded that it violated the newspaper companies' First Amendment rights. Accordingly, it enjoined the airport to permit the newspaper companies placing newsracks in eight locations inside the terminal building. The airport appealed.

The U.S. Court of Appeals determined the constitutionality of the airport's newsrack ban; first by deciding whether the distribution of newspapers through newsracks located on that property was entitled to First Amendment scrutiny. If it was, two further questions would be raised: (1) what type of forum for First Amendment purposes was this public property?; and (2) could the challenged ban survive the constitutional scrutiny appropriate to the regulation of expression in that type of forum?

The appellate court determined the airport's ban on newspaper vending machines violated the First Amendment of the United States Constitution, because it was not reasonably necessary to preserve the airport for its intended purpose of facilitating air travel and commercial activity. Although airport terminals are *not* a public forum, the government's power to regulate expressive activity on public property is still limited. In this case, the ban placed a substantial burden on the newspaper companies' expressive conduct within the terminal, since alternative for distributing newspapers—the airport gift shop and vending machines in a parking garage—were insufficient to provide easy access, unlimited availability, and visibility. The newspaper machines did not create major aesthetic problems; there was no evidence that the airport's concessionary revenue would be reduced by the presence of the machines; and the machines were inanimate objects that would create only a minimal amount of congestion. Concerns that a bomb might be placed in a newspaper machine were unfounded because the airport had never experienced a bomb threat, and, in fact, newspaper machines had never been used in any U.S. airport for the placement of a bomb.

Although during pendency of this appeal, it was established in International *Society for Krishna Consciousness, Inc. v. Lee,*[39] that airline terminals of the sort at issue in this case, are not public forums, this court concluded that the *total* ban here challenged was nevertheless unconstitutional. The appellate court therefore affirmed the district court's decision, declaring that the ban violated the First Amendment and had to be lifted.

---

[39] 112 S.Ct. 2701 (1992).

CHAPTER 16

MANUFACTURERS' LIABILITY

In manufacturing, there are three basic theories of liability:
negligence, express warranty in contract, and implied
warranty. Product liability is a fourth theory, although
it has its origins in both tort and contract law.

LIABILITY

"Liability" is a broad legal term including almost every character of hazard or responsibility. It may be defined as "an obligation one is bound in law or justice to do, pay, or make good something, which may be enforced by legal action." This and the subsequent two chapters are about liability. This chapter is about *contractual* obligations, as well as the duty aviation manufacturers have to consumers through *product liability*. The next chapter is about liability resulting from *negligence* and aircraft accidents. It is about liability when the type of accident is one that ordinarily does not happen in the absence of negligence (i.e., *res ipsa loquitur*). Then the subsequent chapter is about the transfer of liability by way of *insurance* contracts.

Product(s) liability is almost entirely a 20th Century development in law. It is concerned with injuries caused by products that are defectively manufactured, processed or distributed. The "products" area of law includes both tort and contract law, wherein legal actions are typically grounded in strict liability in tort or upon breach of any obligation or warranties associated with a contract. Product liability, as it relates to aviation, falls into a category of law, which may be referred to as "developed law." It is aviation law derived from other areas of the law and has undergone specific development in the context of aviation. Another example of developed law would be that of aviation insurance, which is the subject of Chapter 18.

Product liability stems from *strict liability* in tort. The development of product liability law is a reflection of the social evolution of law, whereby liability in the marketplace has shifted from "let the buyer beware" (*caveat emptor*), to "let the seller beware." The following paragraphs describe the evolution of (strict) liability as a sociological theory.

THE SOCIAL EVOLUTION OF LAW

Sociologists looking at economic life are interested in the changes industrialization causes in the occupational structure of a society. Strict liability is a story about the means of production in society, and the attendant shift in responsibility for individual actions from the small, family or clan grouping, to the individual personally, and then back to a larger, corporate group, as the "division of labor" becomes more specialized.[1] The principal means of production that a society uses—hunting and gathering, horticulture, pastoral life, agriculture, or industrialism—strongly influences the size and complexity of the society and the character of its cultural and social life.

Historically, there has been a general trend toward increased job specialization, a trend that has progressed most in modern industrial societies. Every human society, however large or small, establishes some division of labor. People are expected to specialize in their work because specialization promotes the welfare of society. Yet, in hunting and gathering societies, there is minimal division of labor. In more advanced horticultural and pastoral societies, and especially in agricultural societies, division of labor is greater. Still, in agricultural societies, and even in small-scale industrial societies of competitive capitalism, the individual typically produces the sum total of a given product.

But modern industrialism (i.e., corporate capitalism) breeds an entirely new form of division of labor in which each individual contributes only a minute part of the final product. The assembly line of the

---

[1] Or as Durkheim would argue, society is held together by "social solidarity," of which there are two general types. "Mechanical solidarity" is characterized by consensus on values, collectively held sentiments and ideas, harmony of interests, and unity of purpose, and is to be found in simple societies. "Organic solidarity," on the other hand, arises from diversity of individual interests and is characterized by interdependence and exchange. It is to be found in advanced societies and resting on the division of labor which is not just an expedient device for increasing human happiness, but a moral and social fact that holds society together. *See* Émile Durkheim, *The Division of Labor in Society* (1933).

modern automobile factory, where each worker's job is very narrowly described, has come to epitomize the division of labor in modern industry. The transition from competitive capitalism to corporate capitalism can be demonstrated by looking at the number of existing job specialties available at specific points in history. In 1850, for example, in the early stages of industrialism in the United States, the census recorded a total of 323 occupations. In contemporary America, according to the U.S. Department of Labor, there are more than 20,000 job specialties.

The writings of social theorists can also be used to describe the transition from competitive to corporate capitalism. In his 1776 treatise, *An Inquiry into the Nature and Causes of the Wealth of Nations,* Adam Smith described the tensions associated with the division of labor during a period of early competitive capitalism. In it, Adam Smith describes a vision of economic liberty, where an individual would be ". . . left perfectly free to pursue his own interest his own way. . . .," amidst an economic balance of the market forces of capital, labor and the marketplace (i.e., consumers).

Adam Smith wondered how it was possible that a community, where everyone was busily following each one's self-interest, did not come apart due to the pressures of competing interests. He questioned what it was that guided each individual's private business so that it conformed to the needs of the group. The controlling agent, he decided, was the " invisible hand" of competition, whereby "the private interests and passions of men" are led in the direction "which is most agreeable to the interest of the whole society." Self-interest acts as a driving power to guide individuals to whatever work society is willing to pay for. The avarice (or greed) of capitalism is regulated by competition. Each person, out to do the best for himself or herself, is faced with other similarly motivated individuals competing for the same market shares. The market thereby "self-regulates" both prices and quantities of goods according to the final arbiter of public demand. It also regulates the incomes of those who cooperate to produce those goods.

In Adam Smith's "perfectly balanced" economic system controlled by the invisible hand of competition, the value of work resolves itself in wages and profit, and the consumer pays a "natural" (i.e., not inflated) price for commodities. The problem, however, is that the real marketplace is imperfect, and inequities exist among market forces— most often to the greatest disadvantage of the consumer.

Today's market mechanism (what has been described as "corporate capitalism") is characterized by the huge size of its participants. The behavior of giant corporations, and equally giant unions, is totally different than the "competitive capitalism" of many small individual proprietors and workers. The sheer size of modern corporations enables them to withstand the pressures of competition, to disregard price fluctuations, and to consider what their self-interest shall be in the long run, rather than responding to the immediate day-to-day pressures of buying and selling.

In the 1930s, Émile Durkheim was apparently following the outline used by Adam Smith to describe the division of labor in *The Wealth of Nations*. In his seminal work, *The Division of Labor in Society* (1933), Durkheim tried to determine the social effects of the division of labor in modern societies. What Durkheim foresaw was a trend toward restitution as a resolution for violation of society's norms. His major theme was that a society is held together by its members' sharing of similar norms and values. Less developed societies are held together by what he called "mechanical solidarity." Because these societies are small, and because everyone is engaged in similar work, the members are all socialized in the same pattern share the same experiences, and hold common values.

Conversely, modern industrial societies are held together by what Durkheim called "organic solidarity" which is a much looser bond. Because these societies are large and the division of labor is highly diversified, its members hold different values and socialize in many varying patterns. Hence, the basis for social solidarity is no longer the similarity of the members, but rather, their differences. Because they are now interdependent, they must rely on one another (i.e., upon the group, rather than themselves) if their society is to function effectively.

Ironically, by emphasizing differences amongst people, it inevitably makes them more aware of themselves as individuals. In turn, these feelings of individualism undermine loyalty to the community and its shared values, sentiments and beliefs. The result is what Durkheim called "anomie," which is a state of "normlessness" in both the society and the individual. In Durkheim's view, the division of labor in modern society, and the resulting growth of individualism, would break down shared commitment to social norms. Having little commitment to shared norms people lack social guidelines for their personal conduct and are inclined to pursue their private desires without regard for the interests of society as a whole.

The increasing violation of society's norms necessitates reform in how society sanctions its deviates. In *The Division of Labor in Society*, Durkheim linked the evolution of sanction reform to transformations in social solidarity, described by him as either mechanical or organic. Durkheim asserted that repressive sanctions were the dominant form in "simple" societies typified by mechanical solidarity, and that restitutive sanctions were the predominant (more complex) form in societies having organic solidarity. Although there have been critics of Durkheim's assumptions, the trend in law is in fact moving from the repressive to the restitutive, at least in more developed societies typified by organic solidarity and decentralized authority.

Like Durkheim, the relationship between law and social structure is the subject of Donald Black's contemporary work.[2] Black looks upon law as a quantitative variable that increases or decreases from one setting to another. Law varies directly with organization. Organizations enjoy a disproportionate advantage over individuals, and in some cases increased organization may even provide immunity from the law. According to Black, "law is less likely to respond to organizational conduct as deviant, less likely to define it as criminal, and, even if so defining it, less likely to handle it as serious."

In short, and as Laura Nader and her colleagues have pointed out, individuals have less access to the legal system, and less protection from it, than do organizations.[3] In theory, this overwhelming legal advantage has given rise to a current trend toward increased organizational liability for individual misfortune. During the past century, compensation has become an increasingly common mode of conflict management and/or resolution. One of the elementary forms of social control is "conflict management"; that is to say the handling of grievances. Compensation is but a restitutive form of conflict management where the grievance is handled by a payment to the aggrieved. And, as Black has stated,

> *The classical point of departure in the theoretical discussion of compensation is Emile Durkheim's Division of Labor. He proposed that the compensatory style is directly related to the degree of interdependence in society. Since over time societies tend to exhibit an ever greater division of labor, which implies interdependence, compensation becomes increasingly prominent, progressively displacing the penal style of conflict management.*

---

[2] Donald Black, *The Behavior of Law* (1976); *see also* Donald Black, *Compensation and the Social Structure of Misfortune*, 21 Law and Society Review (1987); *see also* Donald Black, *The Elementary Forms of Conflict Management*, in School of Justice Studies, Arizona State University, New Directions in the Study of Justice, Ch. 3, Law and Social Control.

[3] Laura Nader (ed.), *No Access to Law: Alternatives to the American Judicial System* (1980).

Black's work incorporates Durkheim's theory of social solidarity, that restitutive sanctions would increasingly replace retributive (repressive) sanctions, and he notes that in the evolutionary perspective, the tendency to hold organizations strictly or even absolutely liable for the misfortunes of individuals is not altogether new.[4] In less developed societies, the practice is to hold the family or extended family (such as a clan) liable. However, one of the great historical transformations in many post-industrial societies has been the decline of the family. According to Black, individuals have become

> *. . . increasingly dependent upon organizations much as, in centuries past, they were dependent upon extended families. . . . The growing dependency of individuals upon organizations is reflected in an ever greater propensity to recruit organizations to compensate people for their misfortunes. . . . So returns a system of collective liability resembling practices long thought primitive. . . .*

Black states that "the evolution of compensation (thus) ultimately describes a circle, from one kind of collective liability to another." In other words, the current trend toward strict liability can be explained by looking at the past. But rather than describing a "circle," what surfaces is a synergistic, reiterative model which conceptually departs from one concept to another and then, in a reiterative process, is threaded back through the original concept to become yet another higher, more abstract form.

The model parallels the development of retributive to restitutive sanctions in social evolution of reform described by Durkheim. As Donald Black states, "The modern trend toward greater organizational liability appears to be a devolution toward a pattern of collective dependency characteristic of earlier societies before the decline of kinship." This model of human development may be referred to as a "synergistic loop,"[5] and expressed as follows:

---

[4] The doctrine of "strict liability" presumes the seller is liable for any and all defective or hazardous products, which unduly threaten a consumer's personal safety. In "absolute liability," the seller is responsible *without* fault or negligence; *see Black's Law Dictionary* (abridged 5th ed. 1983).

[5] *See* Laurence E. Gesell, *Airline Re-Regulation* (1990).

STRICT/ABSOLUTE LIABILITY
(CORPORATE RESPONSIBILITY)

TORT LIABILITY
(INDIVIDUAL NEGLIGENCE)

COLLECTIVE LIABILITY
(FAMILY/CLAN GROUP)

What is argued here is that Durkheim's central theorem remains today the dominant point of departure in explaining the modern trend toward strict or absolute liability and the increased liability of organizations for the welfare of individuals. Additionally, Durkheim's formulation applies convincingly to recent legal evolution. Post-industrial societies do appear to have more restitutive law relative to what Durkheim considered as ancient civilizations.

As Donald Black points out, organizations today are being held to an ever-broader standard of liability for the misfortunes of individuals. "An organization's mere association with an individual's misfortune increasingly leads to demands for compensation . . .," and "ultimately . . . a general theory of compensation will . . . address the conditions associated with voluntary compensation of all kinds." According to Black, liability can be collapsed into several categories:

- *Relative Liability*—arising from both injurious conduct and subjectivity of a particular kind;
- *Strict Liability*—arising from injurious conduct alone; and
- *Absolute Liability*—arising independently from injurious conduct and subjectivity.

Strict liability to a seller, manufacturer or supplier in products cases means that any one of them is liable only for injuries caused by a defect that existed in the product before it left their direct or indirect control. This differs from absolute liability where the supplier, seller, or manufacturer is considered an "insurer" of the product, and would therefore be held liable for any injury following from its use.

MANUFACTURERS' LIABILITY

For manufacturers of aviation products and for all products in general, there are three basic theories of liability:

- *Negligence*—based upon some failure to exercise reasonable care in the manner in which a product is made or assembled;
- *Contract*—including *express warranty,* where the manufacturer fails to live up to the specific terms of an agreement; and
- *Implied Warranty*—where, in recent decades, there has been a court trend toward placing greater responsibility on the manufacturer for defective products, and by imposing theories of strict liability on the manufacturer.

NEGLIGENCE

When negligence is obvious—that is, when the circumstances of a happening are so extraordinary that negligence is presumed—then the theory of *res ipsa loquitur* is usually invoked. As applied to the manufacture of aviation products, *res ipsa loquitur* would apply to situations where damage was caused directly by the obvious breakdown or failure of some product for which the manufacturer had responsibility in its production.

But all negligence is not that simple, nor so clearly circumscribed. It should be recalled that negligence exists when,

- There is a legal duty or *obligation to conform* to a reasonable standard to protect others;
- There is a *failure to conform* to that standard;
- The failure to conform was the *proximate cause* of the resulting injury; and
- Actual *damages* resulted.

The existence of a legal duty or obligation to protect others depends on the circumstances. Defenses available to the manufacturer against negligence liability are:

- *Assumption of Risk*—where the injured person was aware of the risk but ignored it;
- *Contributory Negligence*—where both parties are negligent and, therefore, the injured party's own lack of care might deprive him or her of the right to recover damages; and

- *Comparative Negligence*—which is similar to contributory negligence, but allows for an apportioning of the negligence responsibility according to relative degree (i.e., a percentage).

Negligence, then, is the essence of a "tort," which is defined as "a private or civil wrong by act or omission in doing what a reasonable person would do to protect others." It does not, however, include *breach of contract.*

CONTRACT LAW

A "contract" is a promise. To be enforceable, there must be an offer, acceptance, and consideration. It is an agreement between two people where each promises to do or not to do something. Contracts may be oral, or they may be written. They may be *expressed* and/or *implied.* The expressed provisions of a contract are the specific terms agreed upon. The "implied" provisions are those that in order to do justice the law imposes an agreement transcending the agreed upon terms of the contract.

When someone buys a product, that sale (or purchase) is a contract. Thus, sales are governed by the law of contracts. For a sale to be valid, it, like a contract, must meet certain criteria:

- There must be *mutual assent* (that is, an offer and acceptance), consisting of *mutuality of agreement* and *mutuality of obligation;*
- The parties must be legally *competent* (or capable) to make the transaction;
- There must be *consideration* (reason or compensation); and
- The subject matter of the sale must be *legal.*

Often, to give assurance to the buyer that a product is what it appears to be or is otherwise represented to be the seller will guarantee, usually in writing, the integrity of the product. Like other contracts, the warranty may be expressed or implied. In either case, the warranty becomes a part of the sales contract. The expressed warranty contains the specified terms of the guarantee.

Should there be an unjustified failure of the seller, or of the buyer, to perform the terms of the contract, when due, the provisions of the agreement will have been "breached"; that is to say, the contract is broken. If a contract is breached, then the law allows for the awarding of damages to return the injured party to the same position as if the contract had been performed. These are *nominal* awards where the damages are only slight. In extreme cases *punitive* or *exemplary* damages may be awarded as well, to punish the defaulting party, or otherwise to make an example of the person.[6]

A "defense" is that which is alleged by the defendant in a suit as a reason (in law or in fact) why the plaintiff should not recover what he or she seeks in the legal action. Common defenses to breach of warranty are:

- *Statute of Limitations*—which is the maximum time within which a legal action must be started;
- *Misleading Conduct*—where the actions of the other party may contribute to depriving the right to sue, often referred to as "estoppel";
- *Misunderstanding*—or a *mistake* made by both parties;
- *Fraud*—wherein a contract is the result of intentional deception, it is illegal, and therefore, unenforceable;
- *Duress*—where force or threats have been used;
- *Inability to Perform*—wherein it would be impossible to fulfill the terms of the contract;
- *Failure of Consideration*—which is a common breach where payment has not been made; and
- *Illegality of the Contract*—where the subject matter is not legal the contract is unenforceable.

IMPLIED WARRANTY

For decades, the old doctrine of *caveat emptor* was used in courts to deny legal satisfaction to anyone who had purchased faulty, or even harmful, merchandise. Under the doctrine of *caveat emptor*, translated from Latin and meaning "let the buyer beware," the consumer bought strictly at his or her own peril. More recently, however, the courts have come to realize that even if a buyer exercises ordinary care, he may be ill equipped to adequately protect himself against defective merchandise. The marketplace is simply too complex to protect the average buyer, who is normally not educated as to the myriad of diversified products. Thus, the courts have judicially transferred the greater share of liability to the manufacturer and to the vendor—those responsible for placing the product into the stream of commerce. And, in those cir-

---

[6] *See Miles v. Kavanaugh*, 350 So. 2d 1090 (1977).

cumstances where the dealer bought in good faith from the producer, the burden of liability may shift in total back to the manufacturer.

In either case the (corporate) manufacturer and/or seller is better situated economically to absorb catastrophic loss than is the (individual) consumer. With the advent of "consumerism" in the 1960s and 1970s, a proliferation of more than 50 laws were passed by Congress, with over 100 federal programs established to protect the consumer. Warranties beyond the terms of any specific agreement have been extended by these consumer protective laws and regulations. In the past, an express warranty had to be very explicit and describe exactly what was to be warranted. Today, greater reliance may be placed in what is (reasonably) implied by a contract.

Implied warranty is distinct from express warranty in that it is not dependent upon either the written or spoken words of the seller. Section 2-314 of the Uniform Commercial Code [UCC] provides that "a warranty that the goods shall be merchantable is implied in a contract for their sale if the seller is a merchant with respect to goods of that kind." Also stated in the UCC is the seller warrants the goods are fit for a particular purpose where the seller "at the time of contracting has reason to know any particular purpose for which the goods are required and that the buyer is relying on the seller's skill or judgment to select or furnish suitable goods." The buyer and seller, therefore, have a contractual relationship based upon such reliance.[7]

The implied warranty is a condition beyond the expressed terms of the contract, which the law suggests is a "reasonable expectation." In some cases, positive law dictates what is implied by way of statute. At other times, common law must be relied upon to determine what may be implied. Generally speaking, every sale implies the following warranties, that the

- seller has the legal right to sell the goods;
- goods are fit for the purposes intended;
- seller receives what was represented in the sale (i.e., not an unacceptable substitute); and
- the buyer will have exclusive possession of the goods.

PRODUCTS LIABILITY

Thus far, the discussion regarding manufacturer's liability, by-and-large, has been confined to responsibility for faulty goods. Liability for

---

[7] *See Pioneer Seed Co. v. Cessna Aircraft Co.*, CCH 16 AVI. ¶ 17,941 (1981).

goods that do not measure up to the consumer's expectations is one thing; liability for physical injury resulting from a defective product is a matter of an entirely different dimension. In cases where someone has been physically harmed, the most common ground for recovery is negligence. The early landmark decision, which set the stage for manufacturer negligence cases, was *MacPherson v. Buick Motor Co.*, where an automobile manufacturer was found liable to the consumer for a defective wooden spoke wheel.[8] Although a third party contractor produced the wheel, Buick held was responsible for the finished product.

An alternative approach to negligence is *breach of warranty.* In warranty cases the plaintiff has only to show that the product was not designed or constructed to fulfill its intended use. In warranty cases, however, early decisions required "privity of contract," which is a relationship of mutual interest existing only between the original parties to the contractual agreement. An implied warranty may extend to one not privy to the original contract between the manufacturer/seller and buyer. In 1960, the Supreme Court of New Jersey held in *Henningsen v. Bloomfield Motors* that the manufacturer and dealer of a defective automobile was liable for a breach of implied warranty, without any showing of negligence, and without privity.[9] Two years later, the Supreme Court of California developed the next evolutionary step of coupling tort with law of contracts in product liability cases. While the *Henningsen* decision was based upon a contractual theory of breach of implied warranty, the cause of action in *Greenman v. Yuba Power Products* was one of strict tort liability.[10]

A year later, in an aviation-related case, the New York Court of Appeals decided that regardless of privity of contract, an airplane manufacturer which puts a completed aircraft upon the market represents that it will safely do the job for which it is built.[11] The manufacturer is therefore liable for injuries if the product proves defective.

In the early 1960s, a new body of law emerged, known as "product liability." Having its origin in both tort and contract law, product liability includes assertions of both negligence and warranty. But a new basis of liability is involved—the principle of strict liability in tort. In strict liability, negligence on the part of the manufacturer need not be proven, only that the manufacturer breached a warranty, either expressed or implied, and that there is a causal relationship between the

---

[8] *MacPherson v. Buick Motor Co.*, 111 N.E. 1050 (1916).
[9] *Henningsen v. Bloomfield Motors, Inc.*, 161 A. 2d 69 (1960).
[10] *Greenman v. Yuba Power Products Inc.*, 377 P. 2d 897 (1962).
[11] *Goldberg v. Kollsman Instrument Corp.*, CCH 8 AVI. ¶ 17,629 (1963).

breach and the injury. In a way, it is the product itself that is liable—thus the term, "product liability." If the manufacturer designed and built the product, and the product caused injury because it was ill suited for its intended use, then the manufacturer is "strictly" liable. Even if the manufacturer has exercised all reasonable care, it is still responsible for the injury.

Every product liability case involves a definition of defect. In defining a "defect," it has been referred to as "an imperfection or condition not contemplated by the user or consumer." The *Restatement of Torts* (second), Section 402-A, considers "a defective condition unreason-ably dangerous to the user." The majority of courts have decided that "unreasonably dangerous" is inseparable from the definition of defect. There are three categories of defective products. Liability can be imposed for products that are defective because of: (1) the presence of a defect in the product at the time the defendant sold it (a manufacturing, production, or construction defect, sometimes termed the "lemon" product),[12] (2) a marketing defect—a failure of the defendant to warn the consumer of the risk (defective or nonexistent warning),[13] or (3) a design defect.[14] A defect must be proven. It must have existed at the time the product left the defendant's control, and it must have caused an injury.

EVOLUTION OF PRODUCTS LIABILITY

The development of the modern concept of products liability (or "enterprise" liability, as some refer to it) has proceeded through several stages. The steps in the metamorphosis were these:

- During the early Industrial Revolution, products liability was characterized by an emphasis on "privity" between buyer and seller,[15] with the remote manufacturer ordinarily being shielded from direct liability.[16]

---

[12] *See e.g., Pouncey v. Ford Motor Co.*, 464 F.2d 957 (5th Cir. 1972).

[13] *See e.g., Jackson v. Coast Paint & Lacquer Co.*, 499 F.2d 809 (9th Cir. 1974).

[14] *See e.g., Volkswagen of America, Inc. v. Young*, 272 Md. 201, 321 A.2d 737 (1974); *Barker v. Lull Engineering Co.*, 20 Cal. 3d 413; 573 P.2d 443; 143 Cal. Rptr. 225 (1978), 573 P.2d 443 (Cal. 1978).

[15] Early 19th Century common law in the United States followed that of England, which appeared to favor the position of defendants in personal injury cases on grounds of fostering the development of cottage industry. *See Priestly v. Fowler*, 3 Mees. & Wels 1, 150 Eng. Rep. 1030 (1837); *Albro v. The Agawam Canal* Co., 60 Mass. (6 Cushing) 75 (1850). One exception of this pro-defendant bias was the doctrine of *respondeat superior*, pursuant to which a master would be held liable for

- Exceptions to this strict rule gradually were carved out for (1) "an act of negligence of a manufacturer or vendor which is imminently dangerous to the life or health of mankind," (2) "an owner's act of negligence which causes injury to one who is invited by him to use his defective appliance upon the owner's premises," and (3) "one who sells or delivers an article which he knows to be imminently dangerous to life or limb to another without notice of its qualities is liable to any person who suffers an injury therefrom which might have been reasonably anticipated, whether there were any contractual relations between the parties or not."[17]

---

his servant's negligence causing injury to a stranger. *Farwell v. Boston & Worcester R. Corp.*, 45 Mass. (4 Met.) 49 (1842). Most courts during the early common law period denied recovery for personal injury where the plaintiff could show no privity of contract with the defendant. *Winterbottom v. Wright*, 152 Eng. Rep. 402 (Ex 1842); *Hasbrouck v. Armour & Co.*, 139 Wis. 357, 121 N.W. 357 (1909); *Lebourdais v. Vitrified Wheel Co.*, 194 Mass. 341, 80 N.E. 482 (1907). That is to say, no party could recover from another unless he had purchased the product directly from him. Even where privity existed, courts often denied recovery based upon the doctrine of *caveat emptor* ("let the buyer beware"). Thus, plaintiffs could not recover for contractual claims for latent defects unless they could prove a breach of express warranty, or the existence of fraud. *Seixas v. Woods*, 2 Caines 48 (S. Ct. N.Y. 1804). The buyer could protect himself contractually in arm's-length bargaining with the seller, or so it was assumed. In most cases, the buyer could examine the product before tendering the purchase price. If he hadn't the sense to insist upon the inclusion of a warranty in the contract of sale, and if the seller hadn't defrauded him, the buyer was simply stuck without a remedy, even where he was personally injured by the defective nature of the product.

[16] *Richard Epstein, Charles Gregory & Harry Kalven, Jr., Cases and Materials On Torts* 611 (5th ed. 1991). *See Winterbottom v. Wright*, 152 Eng. Rep. 402 (Ex. 1842), where a driver injured by a defective coach was barred from recovering because of the absence of privity of contract. Judge Abinger noted, "There is no privity of contract between these parties; and if the plaintiff can sue, every passenger, or even any person passing along the road, who was injured by the upsetting of the coach, might bring a similar action. Unless we confine the operation of such contracts as this to the parties who entered into them, the most absurd and outrageous consequences, to which I can see no limit, would ensue." *Id.* As one court noted, *Huset v. J.I. Case Threshing Machine Co.*, 120 F. 865, 871 (8th Cir. 1903), "The liability of the contractor or manufacturer for negligence in the construction or sale of the articles which he makes or vends is limited to the persons to whom he is liable under his contracts of construction or sale. . . . The general rule is that a contractor, manufacturer, or vendor is not liable to third parties who have no contractual relations with him for negligence. . . ." As the case law evolved, these rigid distinctions became blurred. For example, an exploding steam boiler causing only property damage was deemed not to be a dangerous instrument; no duty arising out of contract or law (tort) was deemed owed the plaintiff. *Losee v. Clute*, 51 N.Y. 494 (1873). But as courts became more sympathetic to the plight of plaintiffs suffering personal injury, they discovered means of sweeping aside traditional common law liability limitations based on the absence of privity of contractual relations between the parties.

[17] Liberalization of these strict rules began in cases where the defendant performed an act of negligence imminently dangerous to human life. *Thomas and Wife v. Winchester*, 6 N.Y. 397 (1852). Where the defendant's negligence put human life in imminent danger, he was held to have a duty of exercising caution beyond that arising out of the contract of sale. *Id.* Early distinctions were made between dangerous instruments, or products which in their nature were dangerous, and those which

- With Justice Cardozo's New York decision in *MacPherson v. Buick Motor Co.*,[18] courts began to jettison privity as a bar to recovery against remote manufacturers under negligence law.[19]

---

were not, the former requiring a higher degree of care, and therefore imposing upon their manufacturers (or sellers) a higher degree of potential liability. *Longemid v. Holliday*, 155 E.R. 752 (1852). On an *ad hoc* basis, courts during this period attempted to develop liability regimes based upon the nature of the commodity, which caused the injury. Thus, poison, gunpowder, spring guns, and torpedoes were deemed dangerous instruments; flywheels were not. *Loop v. Litchfield*, 42 N.Y. 351 (1870). Gradually, the courts began to focus on the issue of foreseeability of injury with respect to certain types of products as a basis for imposing a duty to exercise a higher standard of care. For example, in *Devlin v. Smith*, 89 N.Y. 470 (1882), a 19th Century New York decision, the court found the defendant liable for the death sustained by a carpenter who fell from a scaffold negligently built by it; there was no privity between the parties. The court found that a duty was nevertheless owed the carpenter because "misfortune to third persons not parties to the contract would be a natural and necessary consequence to the builder's negligence . . . such negligence would be an act imminently dangerous to human life." Although a scaffolding was arguably not a "dangerous instrument" *per se*, unless properly constructed it was a "most dangerous trap." Hence the act, not just the product, could be of such danger as to sweep aside the privity barrier. This was the beginning of the infamous assault on the citadel of privity. *Randy Knitwear, Inc. v. American Cyanamid Co.*, 11 N.Y.2d 5, 226 N.Y.S.2d 363, 181 N.E.2d 399 (1962). Other decisions broke through the traditional contract defenses such as *caveat emptor* by, for example, finding an implied warranty that the work was suitable and proper for the purposes for which the producer knew it was to be used. *Kellogg Bridge Co. v. Hamilton*, 110 U.S. 108 (1884); *Friend v. Childs Dining Hall Co.*, 231 Mass. 65, 120 N.E. 407 (1918). But other courts were still reluctant to go so far, limiting liability where there was no privity or fraud, or where the product was not imminently dangerous to human life or health. *Burkett v. Studebaker Bros. Mfg. Co.*, 126 Tenn. 467, 150 S.W. 421 (1912). One was quite prophetic in its rationale:

> *[I]f suits of the kind were sanctioned against manufacturers*
> *there would be no end to litigation, and practically no means, in*
> *the great majority of the cases, for the manufacturer to protect*
> *himself, and therefore that useful class of producers would be so*
> *loaded with litigation that their labor, skill, and enterprise would*
> *be greatly discouraged, if not destroyed, to the great detriment*
> *of the public welfare.*

Id. Nonetheless, two years later the same court allowed recovery for the ingestion of a cigar stub in a Coca-Cola bottle on grounds that "All medicines, foods, and beverages are articles of such kind as to be imminently dangerous to human life or health unless care is exercised in their preparation." *Boyd v. Coca-Cola Bottling Works,* 132 Tenn. 23, 177 S.W. 80 (1914).

[18] 111 N.E. 1050 (N.Y. 1916).

[19] A significant expansion in the law of products liability, and perhaps the beginning of the modern era of the law, was marked by Justice Benjamin Cardozo's powerful decision in *McPherson v. Buick Motor Co.*, 217 N.Y. 382, 111 N.E. 1050 (1916), involving a suit by the purchaser of a Buick against its manufacturer for a personal injury caused by a defective wheel made by a subcontractor. Cardozo rejected the traditional distinction between things "imminently dangerous to life" or "implements of destruction," such as poisons, explosives, and deadly weapons, and those not so dangerous. Instead, he emphasized the foreseeability of the injury if the product is negligently made, concluding that this foreseeability imposes upon the manufacturer a duty to exercise ordinary care. A neglect of such duty imposed liability for negligence. Sweeping aside the privity limitation, Cardozo held that such a duty was extended to all persons for whose use the thing is supplied before there was a reasonable opportunity to discover the defect. But Cardozo saw an important distinction in liability based on proximity or remoteness:

- Justice Traynor's concurring opinion provided the intellectual foundation for the movement toward strict liability in *Escola v. Coca-Cola Bottling Co.*,[20] in 1944. In addition to his focus on risk minimization (because the manufacturer is in a superior position to minimize the losses), and loss spreading (so that the cost of injury does not fall upon a single innocent consumer),[21] Traynor advanced several other rationales for strict products liability. He noted that although the doctrine of *res ipsa loquitur*, where applicable, offered an inference of defendant's negligence, nonetheless, that inference could be rebutted by an affirmative showing of proper care, often leaving the person injured by a defective product without an ability "to refute such evidence or identify the cause of the defect, for he can hardly be familiar with the manufacturing process as the manufacturer himself is."[22]

We are not required at this time to say that it is legitimate to go back to the manufacturer of the finished product and hold the manufacturers of the component part. To make their negligence a cause of imminent danger, an independent cause must often intervene; the manufacturer of the finished product must also fail in his duty of inspection. It may be that in those circumstances the negligence of the earlier members of the series is too remote to constitute, as to the ultimate user, an actionable wrong. We leave that question open.

Id. [citations omitted]. Thus, foreseeability of injury imposed a duty of ordinary care, the breach of which was actionable negligence, *see Ash v. Childs Dining Hall Co.*, 231 Mass. 86, 120 N.E. 396 (1918), unless there was no proximate cause. Cardozo would subsequently expand the notion of foreseeability, and the proximate cause limitation on duty and liability, in his seminal opinion in *Palsgraf v. Long Island R.R.*, 248 N.Y. 339, 162 N.E. 99 (1928): "[N]egligence in the air, so to speak, will not do. . . .[T]he orbit of the danger as disclosed to the eye of reasonable vigilance [is] the orbit of the duty. . . . The risk reasonably to be perceived defines the duty to be obeyed. . . ." *Id.* Nevertheless, some courts were reluctant to jump on board right away and sought to limit the expansion of liability to personal injury cases, holding that no such cause of action existed on such grounds where a loss to property (as opposed to personal injury) was suffered. *Windram Mfg. Co. v. Boston Blacking Co.*, 239 Mass. 123, 131 N.E. 454 (1921). Other courts got around this limitation by holding the breach of a duty imposed by a statute constituted negligence *per se*, as a matter of law, irrespective of whether recovery was sought for personal or property injury. *Pine Grove Poultry Farm, Inc. v. Newton By-Products Mfg. Co., Inc.*, 248 N.Y. 293, 162 N.E. 84 (1928).

[20] 150 P.2d 436 (Calif. 1944).

[21] As Judge Traynor was subsequently to observe, "The purpose of [strict products] liability is to insure that the costs of injuries resulting from defective products are borne by the manufacturers that put such products on the market rather than by the injured persons who are powerless to protect themselves." *Greenman v. Yuba Power Products*, 377 P.2d 897 (Cal. 1963).

[22] Traynor also noted that under already existing law, the retailer of a product was strictly liable to the consumer under an implied warranty of fitness for use and merchantable quality, which include a warranty of safety. The retailer forced to pay a judgment to an injured consumer could then bring

- Beginning with the New Jersey decision in *Henningsen v. Bloomfield Motors*,[23] in 1960, privity, as a bar to recovery against remote manufacturers, began to be swept aside in contracts actions, and implied warranties were extended to ultimate purchasers.[24] Standardized contractual disclaimers of liability were also swept aside in situations where the parties lacked equal bargaining power.[25]

- With the 1962 decision of *Greenman v. Yuba Power Products*,[26] strict liability began to be adopted to the exclusion of negligence principles, a trend solidified by the adoption of section 402A of the Restatement (Second) of Torts by the American Law Institute in 1965.[27]

- After the adoption of 402A, defective design and duty to warn cases were expanded under traditional negligence doctrine.

- Finally, heavily lobbied by insurance companies, beginning in the 1980s several state legislatures promulgated tort reform

---

suit against the manufacturer. This produced circuitous and wasteful litigation. Judicial efficiency could much be enhanced by allowing a direct suit by the consumer against the manufacturer based on its warranty. *Escola v. Coca-Cola Bottling Co. of Fresno*, 150 P.2d 436 (Cal. 1944). "As handicrafts have been replaced by mass production with its great markets and transportation facilities, the close relationship between the producer and consumer of a product has been altered. Manufacturing processes, frequently valuable secrets, are ordinarily either inaccessible to or beyond the ken of the general public. The consumer no longer has means or skill enough to investigate for himself the soundness of a product. . . ." *Id.*

[23] 161 A.2d 69 (N.J. 1960)

[24] Dean Prosser observed, "In the field of products liability, the date of the fall of the citadel of privity can be fixed with some certainty. It was May 9, 1960, when the Supreme Court of New Jersey announced the decision in *Henningsen v. Bloomfield Motors Inc.*" Prosser, *The Fall of the Citadel (Strict Liability to the Consumer)*, 50 Minn. L. Rev. 791 (1966).

[25] Still others held that actions brought for recovery under contractual warranties, express or implied, rather than tortuous negligence, continued to be limited by the requirement of privity of contract between the plaintiff and defendant. *Chysky v. Drake Bros. Co.*, 235 N.Y. 468, 139 N.E. 576 (1923). Nonetheless, some courts expanded the concept of privity to include family members of the individual who purchased the product. *Greenberg v. Lorenz*, 9 N.Y.2d 195, 213 N.Y.S.2d 39, 173 N.E.2d 773 (1961). Others allowed the introduction of the warranty as evidence in negligence cases. *Baxter v. Ford Motor Co.*, 168 Wash. 456, 12 P.2d 409 (1932).

[26] 377 P.2d 897 (Calif. 1963).

[27] Sec. 402A provides: One who sells any product in a defective condition unreasonable dangerous to the user or consumer or his property is subject to liability for physical harm thereby caused to the ultimate user or consumer, or to his property, if (a) the seller is engaged in the business of selling such a product, and (b) it is expected to and does reach the user or consumer without substantial change in the condition in which it is sold.

statutes limiting liability in various ways, including imposing limitations on damages and Statutes of Repose.[28]

ELEMENTS OF PRODUCTS LIABILITY ACTIONS

Product liability is regarded as a distinct area of law, although it has its origin in both tort and contract law. Hence, it shares basic characteristics with other lawsuits within the larger analogous classifications. If a products action is founded upon negligence, all of the elements of a negligence action must be present. Similarly, if the action is founded upon a failure to meet a warranty obligation, it must have the elements of any action grounded on breach of contract. That is to say, there must be a showing of the existence of a warranty, its breach, and of the injured party's right to recover. And finally, if the foundation of the action is strict liability in tort, the elements of that doctrine must be present. Table 16.1, "Elements of Products Actions," compares the necessary elements in each of the three principle foundations for manufacturer's liability actions.

DUTY TO WARN

The manufacturer is responsible for the goods it produces and, therefore, it has an inherent *duty to warn* consumers of its products, and of the dangers associated with their use. Liability for failure to warn may be predicated on negligence, breach of warranty, or strict liability in tort. Almost every product liability case includes a potential issue of failure to warn. There is a tendency to rely upon an alleged failure to warn in order to avoid having to demonstrate the existence of manufacturing or design defects. Thus, it may be said that the first line of defense in product liability issues is for the manufacturer to issue warnings.

Adequate warnings may insulate the manufacturer from liability caused by what otherwise may be a design defect. In court, the seriousness of the harm or injury that may result is the overriding concern in determining whether a duty to warn exists. Obviously, aviation-related products have the potential for disaster and extensive harm, and the duty to warn cannot be overly emphasized. Providing an adequate

---

[28] *See Richard Epstein, Charles Gregory & Harry Kalven, Jr., Cases and Materials on Torts* 611-12 (5th ed. 1991).

warning is, effectively, preventive maintenance. Conversely, there are after-the-fact defenses. Some of the common defenses used after an incident has occurred include warranty disclaimers, limitations of the warranty, contributory negligence, assumption of risk, and statute of limitations.

Table 16.1—ELEMENTS OF PRODUCTS ACTIONS

NEGLIGENCE	WARRANTY	PRODUCT LIABILITY
Reasonable duty exists to protect the safety of the injured party.	There is privity of contract in clearly expressed warranties.	Seller must be in the business of selling the product.
There has been a breach of that duty.	There is implied warranty of fitness, materials and workmanship.	Product had been placed in the stream of commerce by the seller.
An action, or failure to act, must be the proximate cause of the injury.	Notice of the breach must be presented to the merchant.	Product reached the consumer unchanged.
Actual damages must have been suffered.	Product must be damaged or defective.	Injury resulted from the Defective product

CONSEQUENCES

The *Henningson, Greenman*, and *Goldberg* cases cited previously were important building blocks in establishing this relatively new cause of action named "product liability." The plaintiff is no longer required to prove negligence on the manufacturer's part in producing the defective product. Rather, the focus shifted from the manufacturer to the performance of the product. Moreover, the cause of action has been simplified, and the plaintiff now has only to demonstrate who it was that placed the defective product into the "stream of commerce." Whoever places a defective product into the stream of commerce, be it the manufacturer, the wholesaler, or the retailer, if they are in the business of selling such products, may be held liable in product liability cases. And it matters not if the injured party obtained the product directly from the one who placed it in the stream of commerce.

The theory underlying product liability decisions is that society can more readily absorb catastrophic loss than can the individual. Those in the business of selling products are in the better position to absorb losses (and pass them on to other purchasers) than is the injured consumer. All of those who place the product in the stream of commerce have the ability to spread the risk amongst themselves. Hence, product liability law shifts the responsibility for liability from the individual to the corporate group.

The simplified cause of action has provided greater access to justice for the plaintiff in manufacturer's liability cases. However, most industry observers would agree that the evolution of product liability law has had a disastrous effect upon the general aviation aircraft manufacturing industry in the United States. During the same time when the consumer was being granted greater ease of recovery, the courts were adopting a philosophy that the merchant was in the better position to absorb losses for defective products. Simultaneously, the awards being granted by the courts went into a progressively upward spiral. The result was an increase, by order of magnitude, in the cost of product liability insurance premiums.

The decades of the 1960s and 1970s were marked by strong support from all three branches of government (executive, legislative and judicial) for the rights and protection of the consumer. Consumer advocates cried out a challenge to business and industry to stand behind their products. However, by the 1980s, the consumerism pendulum had swung so far that the situation was seemingly reversed and industry, not the consumer, became the victim.

The problem became so critical, particularly in the manufacture of general aviation aircraft, that the General Aviation Manufacturers Association [GAMA], terming product liability a top industry problem, issued what it considered industry's basic statement entitled "Product Liability Threatens U.S. General Aviation." Said Edward W. Stimpson, president of GAMA,

We, as manufacturers, accept responsibility for our products. . . . But even while general aviation safety has improved significantly, the cost of product liability has skyrocketed!

In 1985, it was reported that the cost of product liability insurance averaged $70,000 per aircraft, allocated among approximately 2,000 aircraft units delivered. In 1972, the cost was $2,111 per aircraft spread over 9,774 aircraft. And in 1962, the cost was just $51 in 6,778 deliveries. In less than five years between 1981 and 1985 the cost for product liability insurance rose over 500%, on average. In isolated cases, increases for specific companies were up to 3,000% in that same time frame. By 1986, the average cost of product liability insurance per airplane was about $80,000. The product liability price tag had risen higher than the cost of some single-engine airplanes. In May of 1986, Cessna announced it would no longer continue production of piston-powered aircraft, including their training airplanes. Piper Aircraft, another leading producer of low-cost trainers in the United States, subsequently went into bankruptcy, which stopped production of all of its line.

Who was to blame? The manufacturing industry accused the insurance industry of price gouging. Insurance companies said the problem stemmed from the high costs of liability judgments, which consequently forced them to increase their premium rates. Lawyers blamed the industry for what they perceived to be avoidable negligence on the part of manufacturers. Moreover, because airplane crashes often cause death or serious bodily injury, and because people who own their own airplanes tend to be higher-income, damage awards for such events tend to be large. Manufacturers brought the blame full-circle by saying it was the fault of overly generous juries, and self-perpetuation by the legal profession. Irrespective of whom was to blame, the effect of exorbitant costs for insurance, threatened the very survival of general aviation in the United States; at least as it had been previously known.

Beginning in 1986, there were several attempts by the federal government to resolve the issue legislatively. However, until 1994, none of the legislative proposals had been acceptable to all parties concerned. Seeking a fairer, more efficient way of protecting the consumer, while at the same time not victimizing the manufacturer, early legislative proposals from the aviation sector called for a uniform federal product liability law with an alternative *no-fault* claim system for expediting recovery of damages by those injured by defective products. Included was a procedure for filing claims for damages without alleging or proving fault. The injured party would be automatically compensated up to legally established limits. Alternatively, the injured party could still, at a later time, appeal to the courts for an increased judgment. Under such proposals it was suggested that most claims could be settled without costly and timely litigation.

Reportedly, the Association of Trial Lawyers of America opposed the proposals for no-fault insurance, and instead, advocated retention of the tort system to settle damage suits. Many attorneys maintained that no-fault proposals would punish consumers and would diminish their legal rights. In essence, attorneys argue that individual consumers are entitled to full recovery for damages, no matter what the impact upon the residual industry and the social costs resulting from the granting of high awards.

Irrespective of the trial lawyers' concerns, the critical nature of the situation was apparent to the aviation industry and to government, and something had to be done about it. The combination of an increasing number of product liability lawsuits, high jury settlement awards, and escalating insurance costs could not continue without imposing devastating effects upon the industry. And, absent the availability of aviation products at affordable costs, it would be the consumer who would become the ultimate victim.

On August 17, 1994, President Clinton signed into law product liability reform to reduce the liability faced by general aviation manufacturers. The General Aviation Revitalization Act of 1994 [GARA] placed an 18-year statute of repose (or limitation) on general aviation products. A "statute of limitations" prescribes limitations to the right of action on certain causes of action, triggered by the date the plaintiff knew, or should have known, he had a cause of action. In a product liability action, the defect in design or manufacture may not be known until years after the product was designed or manufactured. A "statute of repose" is triggered by the date the product is manufactured, irrespective of when the plaintiff knew or should have known of the defect. The GARA provides that after 18 years,

> *No civil action for damages for death or injury*
> *to persons or damage to property arising out*
> *of an accident involving a general aviation*
> *aircraft may be brought against the manufac-*
> *turer of the aircraft or the manufacturer of any*
> *new component, system, subassembly, or other*
> *part of the aircraft.*

The cost of liability insurance had substantially reduced the invest-ment into research and development by the general aviation manufac-turers, and it had slowed, in some cases stopped, production of certain general aviation aircraft. Following passage of GARA, manufacturers in the United States stepped up production of particularly small, sin-gle-engine airplanes.

What follows are cases which demonstrate the evolution of avia-tion-related product liability in the United States. Presented last, as an example of a product liability case, is *Brocklesby v. United States.*[29] In *Brocklesby*, the product at issue was an instrument approach chart published by Jeppesen and Company. In *Brocklesby*, survivors of the crew members of a World Airways aircraft that crashed near Cold Bay, Alaska in 1973 brought suit against the United States, because the U.S. Government had developed an allegedly defective instrument approach procedure used by the Jeppesen Company to publish the in-strument approach procedure in chart form. The Court of Appeals for the Ninth Circuit determined that an instrument approach chart is a product, and a defect in the Jeppesen chart properly resulted in a de-mand of strict product liability against Jeppesen, even though all the defects in the chart stemmed from the federal government's alleged failure to develop a safe instrument approach procedure. The court determined the chart manufacturer had to bear the costs of accidents proximately caused by the approach chart's defects.

In *Brocklesby*, the court determined the instrument approach chart manufactured by Jeppesen was the *proximate* cause of the accident. However, the National Transportation Safety Board [NTSB] found the *probable cause* of the accident was the captain's deviation from ap-proved procedures. Hence, *Brocklesby* is particularly interesting be-cause it not only provides an example of a product liability issue, but the results of this trial can be compared against findings by the NTSB looking at the same incident. As can be seen from this trial, and from the case study of the *TWA Flight 514* accident presented in Chapter

---

[29] *Brocklesby v. United States*, 767 F.2d 1288 (1985).

17, "Accident Investigation," the results of these two independent re-viewers are not always consistent.[30]

GOLDBERG v. KOLLSMAN INSTRUMENT CORP.
191 N.E.2d 81 (N.Y. 1963)

Who is strictly liable for a defective aircraft part, the manufacturer of the part, the manufacturer of the aircraft, or the airline that put the aircraft in service?

This was a suit by an administratrix for damages in the death of her daughter (Anneliese Goldberg) as the result of injuries suffered in a crash near LaGuardia Airport, New York City. The airplane, in which the daughter was a fare-paying passenger, was on a flight from Chicago to New York. American Airlines, Inc., owner and operator of the plane, was sued, along with Lockheed Aircraft Corporation and Kollsman Instrument Corporation, for negligence. The trial court dismissed the causes of action and the plaintiff appealed. Kollsman, manufacturer and supplier of the plane's altimeter, and Lockheed, maker of the plane itself, were charged with breaching their respective implied warranties of merchantability and fitness. Those breaches, it was alleged, caused the fatal crash. The New York Court of Appeals said that,

> *A breach of warranty, it is now clear, is not only a violation of the sales contract out of which the warranty arises but is a tortious wrong suable by a non-contracting party whose use of the warranted article is within the reasonable contemplation of the vendor or manufacturer.*

In *MacPherson v. Buick*[31] the court held the manufacturer was liable in negligence to the one who purchased a faulty Buick automobile from the dealer, thus developing the concept that to "things of danger" the manufacturer must answer to users for faulty design or manufacture. In *Greenman v. Yuba*,[32] a unanimous opinion imposed strict tort liability regardless of privity on a manufacturer in a case where a power tool threw a piece of wood at a user who was not the purchaser.

---

[30] *See Brock, et al. v. United States*, CCH 14 AVI. ¶ 18,246 (1977).
[31] 111 N.E. 1050 (1916).
[32] 377 P. 2d 897 (1962).

In *Greenman*, the California court said the purpose of such a holding was to see to it that the costs of injuries resulting from defective products are borne by the manufacturers who put the products on the market, rather than by injured persons who are powerless to protect themselves. Implicit in putting such articles on the market are representations that they will safely do the job for which they were built. However, in the instant case, the New York Court of Appeals did not think it necessary to extend this rule as to hold liable the manufacturer (defendant Kollsman) of a component part. Adequate protection was provided for the passengers by casting in liability the airplane manufacturer, which put into the market the completed aircraft.

The judgment appealed from was modified, without costs, so as to provide for the dismissal of the third (Kollsman) cause of action only. And, as so modified, the judgment was affirmed. But, two judges dissented stating the majority opinion was purely arbitrary, that the court's approach to the identification of an appropriate defendant did not answer the question: "Which enterprise should be selected if the selection is to be in accord with the rationale upon which the doctrine of strict products liability rests?"

If the carrier which immediately profited from plaintiff's custom is the proper party on which to fasten whatever enterprise liability the social conscience demands, enterprises that supply the devices with which the carrier conducts its business should not be subject to an action based on this theory. This seems most persuasive where the business that deals directly with the public is not merely a conduit for the distribution of the manufacturer's consumer goods, but assumes the responsibility of selecting and using those goods itself as a capital asset in the conduct of a service enterprise such as common carriage. In such a case, the relationship between the assembler of these goods and the air traveler is minimal as compared to that obtaining between the traveler and the carrier. In a theory of liability based, not on the regulation of conduct, but on economic considerations of distributing the risk of accidents that occur through no one's neglect, the enterprise most strategically placed to perform this function—the carrier, rather than the enterprise that supplies an assembled chattel thereto—is the logical subject of the liability, if liability there is to be. The two dissenting judges, therefore, were of the opinion that any claim in respect of an airplane accident that is grounded in strict enterprise liability should be fixed on the airline or none at all.

WILLIAMS v. CESSNA AIRCRAFT CORP.
376 F. Supp. 603 (N.D. Miss. 1974)

Is an aircraft manufacturer liable for secondary accidents ?

Plaintiffs were the wife and daughter of the decedent, Marion A. Williams, who was killed in an airplane crash. At the time of his death, Williams was the pilot of a Cessna 188 Agwagon, a fixed-wing aircraft utilized for agricultural purposes. The plaintiffs alleged the pilot's seat collapsed upon impact and the restraining or safety harness separated, allowing Williams to be thrown violently forward into the instrument panel. Plaintiffs did not specifically allege Williams could have survived the crash but for the failure of the seat and restraining harness. Rather, they alleged this was only one of a series of factors that proximately caused or contributed to his death.

Cessna did not deny that the seat collapsed and the harness separated. However, they contended as a matter of Mississippi law that it could not be held liable for the failure of the seat and harness—a so-called "second accident." The second accident doctrine apparently grew out of a series of suits involving automobile collisions. The plaintiff typically claimed his injuries were enhanced or aggravated by alleged defects inherent in the vehicle; that is, his injuries would have been less severe but for negligent design or construction.

In the instant case the initial accident was the crash of the aircraft rather than the failure of the seat and harness or the death of the pilot. Plaintiffs did not contend the failure of the seat and harness caused the aircraft to crash. On the contrary, the failure of these devices was attributed to the crash.

Mississippi law precluded imposition of liability on the basis of a second accident. The U.S. District Court concluded the failure of the seat and harness must be regarded as a separate or "second accident," and that the defendant, Cessna, was under no duty to design its seat and harness assembly, as a matter of ordinary intended usage, to withstand a high speed crash. Cessna's duty with respect to emergency landings or other situations was not before the court.

Even though a crash may have been a foreseeable result arising from the use of the aircraft, plaintiffs did not allege any set of facts that could demonstrate the seat and harness were flawed by hidden or latent defects which rendered the products unsafe for ordinary aircraft use. Plaintiffs, therefore, did not allege any facts that would justify the imposition of liability on Cessna as a result of the failure of the seat and harness. Judgment was rendered in favor of the defendant, Cessna.

BRUCE v. MARTIN-MARIETTA CORP.
544 F.2d 442 (10th Cir. 1976)

What constitutes a seller in the business of selling a product; and how long is a manufacturer/merchant liable for its products?

A Martin 404 was chartered to carry the Wichita State University team and some of its supporters to a football game in Logan, Utah. On October 2, 1970, the plane crashed into a mountain west of Silver Plume, Colorado. Seats in the passenger cabin broke loose from their floor attachments, were thrown forward against the bulkhead of the plane, and blocked exit. A fire then developed. Of the 40 persons on the plane, 32 died in the crash.

Martin manufactured the plane and sold it to Eastern Airlines in March 1952. Eastern used the plane for about ten years, and in 1962, sold it to Mohawk Airlines, which used it about three years and sold it to Ozark Airlines in 1965. In 1967, Ozark sold the plane to Fairchild-Hiller Corporation, a manufacturer of aircraft. The plane was in storage until sometime in 1970 when it was sold to Jack Richards Aircraft Company. Golden Eagle Aviation contracted with Wichita State University to provide transportation for its football games away from home. Golden Eagle supplied the crew and used the Richards aircraft.

Plaintiffs were persons injured, and representatives of persons killed, in the crash. The plaintiffs did not contend that any action of either defendant caused the plane to crash. Their claims were that the defendants' failures to design, manufacture, or maintain the plane in crashworthy condition caused the deaths, or enhanced the injuries, of the passengers. The alleged defects were the inadequacy of the seat fastenings and the lack of protection against fire. Plaintiffs sought recovery on theories of *negligence, implied warranty*, and *strict liability in tort*.

The classic statement of strict liability in tort is found in *Restatement of Torts* (second), Section 402A, which reads:

> *(1) One who sells any product in a defective condition unreasonably dangerous to the user or consumer or to his property is subject to liability for physical harm thereby caused to the ultimate user or consumer, or to his property, if*
>
> *(a) the seller is engaged in the business of selling such a product, and*

> *(b) it is expected to and does reach the user or consumer without substantial change in the condition in which it is sold.*
>
> *(2) The rule stated in Sub-Section (1) applies, although*
>
> *(a) the seller has exercised all possible care in the preparation and sale of his product, and*
>
> *(b) the user or consumer has not bought the product from or entered into any contractual relation with the seller.*

The plaintiffs' specific allegations related to the fire hazard and the adequacy of the seat fastenings. On the fire hazard, plaintiffs did not contest the Martin affidavit, which demonstrated not only compliance with air safety regulations, but also specific design features for protection against fire. The only fact shown by plaintiffs with regard to the seats that in 1970, 18 years after Martin made and sold the plane, airplane passenger seats, which would have withstood the crash, were in use. The record established that when the plane was made and first sold, its design was within the state of the art. The plaintiffs' affidavit, that 18 years after the manufacture and sale of the plane safer passenger seats were in use, was not relevant to the determination of whether Martin, by satisfying the 1952 state-of-art requirements, exercised reasonable care and, hence, was not negligent.

Plaintiffs contended state-of-art evidence is not material when the claim is based on strict liability. They argued that a showing of a design defective in 1970 established the plane was defective in 1952, the time of the original sale, absent a subsequent alteration of the plane.

To prove product liability (under Section 402A above), the plaintiff had to show that the product was dangerous beyond the expectation of the ordinary customer. State-of-art evidence helps to determine the expectation of the ordinary consumer. A consumer would not expect a Model T to have the safety features that are incorporated in automobiles made today. The same expectation applies to airplanes. Plaintiffs did not show that the ordinary consumer would expect a plane made in 1952 to have the safety features of one made in 1970.

In this action there was also question of concern similar to *second-collision* automobile cases,[33] because the plaintiffs' contention was that the plane was not "crashworthy." To this issue the court said that

---

[33] *See Williams v.Cessna*, CCH 13 AVI. ¶ 17,389 (1974).

proof of injuries in an airplane crash does not prove defective design and raises no presumption of defectiveness.

Along with Martin-Marietta, as the manufacturer of the airplane, Ozark Airlines was also named as a defendant because Ozark was an intermediate owner and seller of the plane. Plaintiffs said Ozark was engaged in the business of selling airplanes because it sold 40 planes to Fairchild. The court, however, stated that the number of planes sold is not determinative. Ozark was not a manufacturer, wholesaler, distributor or retailer. Ozark was a commercial air carrier, not a merchant or a person engaged in the business of selling airplanes.

The U.S. Court of Appeals affirmed the U.S. District Court's judgment in favor of Martin-Marietta and Ozark Airlines.

MILES v. KAVANAUGH
350 So.2d 1090 (Fla. 1977)

Is a non-commercial seller responsible for warranties?

In March 1973, the plaintiff, John Kavanaugh, answered a newspaper ad placed by the defendant, Richard Keenan, advertising the sale of a used 1956 Cessna 172 private airplane. Keenan stated the engine in the airplane had recently been completely overhauled, during which time a number of new mechanical parts had been placed in the engine. The defendant gave the plaintiff an engine and propeller logbook detailing the mechanical repair and flight history of the airplane, which the plaintiff carefully inspected.

The logbook reflected that on May 16, 1972, the engine had been given a major overhaul in which new mechanical parts were placed, all in conformity with the manufacturer's engine overhaul manual. The repair work had been done by the defendant, Kenneth L. "Dusty" Burrow, whose work was certified in the logbook by the defendant FAA inspector, Edward Miles. Kavanaugh specifically testified that he would not have purchased the airplane had he not been able to inspect and rely upon the information contained in the logbook.

Kavanaugh flew the airplane without incident for several months. Thereafter, he experienced an engine malfunction while the airplane was in flight. On December 5, 1973, just after takeoff, the engine began to lose power, shake violently and emit a loud clanking sound. Kavanaugh was barely able to land without crashing.

At considerable expense, Kavanaugh had to arrange for the airplane to be transported in parts to an aircraft repair shop where it was completely re-overhauled. It was there discovered that the prior overhaul had not included new parts as represented, and that the prior overhaul had been performed in a completely defective manner.

Kavanaugh sued the defendant Keenan, and the defendants Burrow and Miles, for breach of express warranty and misrepresentation. After a non-jury trial, the Circuit Court of Dade County awarded a judgment in favor of the plaintiff against all defendants in the amount of $5,800. Defendant Keenan appealed, questioning his liability on the sale of the airplane as well as the amount of damages awarded. Defendants Burrow and Miles appealed solely on the damages issue.

In the appeal to the District Court of Appeal of Florida, there were two issues: first, whether the seller expressly warranted the accuracy of the logbook; and second, whether the damages could include the expense of transporting the airplane for repairs, the expense of overhauling the airplane, and loss of use during repairs. Keenan argued that he never in so many words warranted the accuracy of the information contained in the logbook and was, in fact, ignorant of the admittedly false information contained therein. The court responded by stating that an express warranty need not be by words, but can be by conduct as well. Moreover, fraud is not an essential ingredient of an action for breach of express warranty. And, indeed, it is not even necessary that the seller have a specific intention to make an express warranty. It is sufficient that the warranty was made which formed part of the basis of the bargain. The court found such an express warranty in this case through Keenan's showing of the logbook to the plaintiff, without which this sale would never have been made. For breach of such warranty, Keenan was liable to Kavanaugh.

As to the measure of damages, the court held that such expenses and losses are recoverable when caused by the breach of warranty. Furthermore, the court was satisfied that the bill was reasonable. The lower court decision was affirmed.

PIONEER SEED CO. v. CESSNA AIRCRAFT CO.
16 Av. Cas. (CCH) ¶ 17,941 (E.D. Va. 1981)

What constitutes abnormal aircraft operation and therefore a waiver of warranty provisions?

The plaintiff was a South African Corporation which purchased a Cessna 441 turbo-propeller executive airplane from Commercial Air Services Limited, a duly authorized South African Cessna dealer. Prior to purchasing the subject aircraft, representatives from Pioneer went to Wichita, Kansas, to inspect a Cessna 441. They fully informed Cessna of the conditions under which the aircraft would operate, and the uses to which it would be put. Pioneer's regular pilot received training and instructions from Cessna in Wichita. Pioneer was engaged in agricultural activities and purchased the aircraft as a working piece of equipment for its business. Before a sale was consummated, Cessna represented to Pioneer that its aircraft had the capability to meet Pioneer's needs.

From the time Pioneer purchased the aircraft it was regularly serviced and well maintained. Pioneer did not make any alterations or modifications to the aircraft that would relieve Cessna from its warranty obligations. The aircraft had logged approximately 307 hours of flying time and was under the manufacturer's one-year warranty. The aircraft made a normal landing, reversed course, and taxied back on the runway. At the runway threshold, the aircraft started a left turn in the overrun area, headed for a parking place to the side of the threshold. During the course of the turn, the trunnion of the nose gear assembly suddenly failed, causing the nose gear to collapse. As a result of the collapse of the nose gear both propellers dug into the ground, both engines were badly shock-loaded, and major damage resulted. Pioneer filed suit against Cessna for breach of warranty.

Cessna and its South African agents and distributors advised Pioneer that the Cessna 441 could operate in South Africa, knowing that field conditions there imposed stress on nose wheel assemblies due to the nature of landing surfaces and other airport factors. Cessna knew at the time of the sale that the aircraft was to be operated from grass and sod airfields.

The U.S. District Court determined that Cessna should have known the 441 was not designed to operate from unimproved airports. The court determined Cessna was negligent in the manufacture of the aircraft in that it was foreseeable the trunnion had design defects for operation on non-improved surfaces. At the time of sale, the aircraft was defective and unreasonably dangerous for the use for which it was sold. Cessna breached its expressed and implied warranties that the 441 was fit for the operations conducted by Pioneer. The plaintiff was granted a judgment for $238,568, plus interest.

NEW YORK AIRWAYS, INC. v. UNITED TECHNOLOGIES CORPORATION
85 A.D. 2d. 936, 447 N.Y.S. 2d 84 (1981)[34]

*Does the product liability concept apply where both
the buyer and seller are sophisticated commercial
entities with equal bargaining strength ?*

In this action, New York Airways sought recovery of business losses and punitive damages resulting from the cessation of its operations in April 1979 following the crash at Newark International Airport of one of its Sikorsky S-61L helicopters. The accident was caused when one of the five tail rotor blades broke and separated from the tail rotor.

It is important to note that even though three passengers were killed, 12 passengers and three crew members were injured, this action did not involve a claim for personal injury, normally a part of a product liability action. The plaintiff's original complaint was in tort (negligence and strict product liability). The complaint was later amended to assert a warranty cause of action.

New York Airways contended that warranties on the tail rotor blade and on the aircraft itself covered defects in material and manufacture, and that these products were, in fact, defective. The defendant, United Technologies Corporation, moved for summary judgment asserting the plaintiff's claims were barred by disclaimers in the expressed warranties of the sellers contract which provided a warranty from defects in material manufacture, and further provided that the buyer's remedy be limited to repair or replacement at the seller's election provided that written notice of the defect be given within 90 days after first operation, but in no event later than one year after the date of delivery. The contract further provided:

*The foregoing warranties are exclusive and are
given and accepted in lieu of any and all other warranties, express or implied, including warranty of
merchantability. The remedies of the buyer for any
breach of warranty shall be limited to those provided herein to the exclusion of any and all other
remedies including, without limitation, incidental
or consequential damages*

---

[34] *See also* CCH 17 AVI ¶ 17,446 (1982).

The defendant contended the provisions above were controlling and should have barred the plaintiff's claim. Additionally, the defendant argued that, even if there was a breach of warranty, the statute of limitations of four years had expired.

The U.S. District Court held that the disclaimers were ineffective in this case. While this action did not involve a claim for personal injury, there was a crash that killed three and injured 15 others. If the underlying purpose of strict product liability was to protect consumers for products, which are unreasonably unsafe, not from those which are merely ineffective, a helicopter and its rotor blade are clearly such products.

Finally, the defendant wanted the court to superimpose upon the strict liability theory that this concept is viable only in transactions involving the consuming public and not in transactions with sophisticated commercial entities of "equal bargaining strength." The court did not agree. This strict tort liability cause of action was viable even though it was solely for recovery of economic loss and involved a transaction between commercial entities of equal bargaining strength. Accordingly, the U.S. District Court denied the defendant's motion.

McGEE v. CESSNA AIRCRAFT CO.
188 Cal. Rptr. 542 (Cal. App. 1983)

Does violation of a Federal Aviation Regulation constitute negligence in the manufacture of an airplane?

Helen McGee, a 53 year old mother of nine children, with approximately 125 hours of flying time, took off in a Cessna 177 Cardinal from Warner Hot Springs Airport. John H. Hedger owned the Cessna and he used it to teach flying, also having taught McGee how to fly. McGee and Hedger were good friends and flew many trips together. McGee would sit in the left-hand, pilot's, seat; Hedger would sit in the right-hand, instructor's, seat. Hedger did not charge McGee for all of their flying hours together, although McGee testified all of their flying hours were instructional, as she was a fledgling pilot.

On the day of the accident, Hedger was to observe McGee and a friend and to help them with cross-country flying and navigation. The crash occurred approximately a mile from the airport, about three minutes after they took off from Warner Hot Springs. When the aircraft crashed McGee and Hedger were rendered unconscious. The two passengers in the rear seats were thrown forward, but were not critically injured. All four occupants were wearing seat belts, but the aircraft was not equipped with shoulder harnesses. The two passengers in the rear were able to get out of the airplane through the right door. A fire began almost immediately. The passengers tried to get McGee out but they were not strong enough. They dragged Hedger from the aircraft and returned for McGee. McGee's legs were on fire. Other than some superficial facial injuries, McGee's injuries consisted of third and fourth degree burns, the severity of which resulted in amputation of both legs.

Both parties in this contest agreed McGee's severe and permanent injuries were caused by the post-crash fire. McGee maintained the fire was caused by Cessna's failure to design a sufficiently crashworthy aircraft. She asked "Why, in a clearly survivable crash, the aircraft did not protect her from enhanced injuries sustained by collision with the interior of the aircraft and exposure to the fire"? Cessna rebutted that the fire was a natural result of a violent crash, and the Cessna 177 Cardinal was sufficiently crashworthy.

McGee sued the manufacturer of the airplane, defendant Cessna Aircraft Company. A jury trial resulted in judgment for Cessna. The appellate court reversed, holding McGee should have been allowed to present her cause on a theory of strict liability, based on Cessna's failure to design a sufficiently crashworthy aircraft.

McGee presented her case to a second jury. The jury returned judgment for Cessna. McGee complained this judgment was the result of the trial court's failure to properly limit the evidence and correctly instruct the jury. On the instant appeal, two arguments were substantial. First, McGee asserted that the trial court failed to instruct the jury to shift the burden of proving proximate cause to Cessna because Cessna violated FAR Part 23.1191 concerning specifications for fire walls, and FAR Part 23.561, providing for protection of the occupants in emergency landing conditions. The failure of a person to exercise due care is presumed if:

- The person violated a statute, ordinance, or regulation;
- The violation was the proximate cause of the injury; and
- The injury resulted from violation of the regulation.

McGee cited these regulations to prove negligence *per se*, and as proof the aircraft was defectively designed because violation of an FAR is proof of a design defect. Under both a theory of negligence and strict liability for design defect, the burden of proof was on Cessna to prove the defect was not a proximate cause of the injury. Cessna's witness testified the aluminum firewall fittings of the Cardinal could not resist flame penetration for fifteen minutes as required by FAR.

Second, McGee argued the trial court erred in its instructions to the jury. The instruction given described "but for" causation and read:

> *A proximate cause of an injury is a cause which, in natural and continuous sequence, produces the injury, and without which the injury would not have occurred.*

McGee urged that the instruction should have described "substantial factor" causation, and should have been:

> *A legal cause of an injury is a cause that is a substantial factor in bringing about the injury.*

Where there are concurrent causes, California law provides that one cannot escape responsibility for his or her negligence on the ground that identical harm would have occurred without it. The appellate court found that the "substantial factor" instruction should have been given. The California Court of Appeals reversed the lower court judgment for the above two reasons.

BROCKLESBY v. UNITED STATES
767 F.2d 1288 (9ᵗʰ Cir. 1985)

Who is responsible for a defective instrument approach chart?

A World Airways aircraft crashed into a mountain near Cold Bay, Alaska, on September 8, 1973. All six crewmembers and occupants were killed. The aircraft (a Douglas DC-8-63F), and its contents were completely destroyed. Survivors of the crewmembers and World Airways brought an action against the U.S. government and Jeppesen and Company. The plaintiffs sought recovery for wrongful deaths and property damage caused by defects in an instrument approach procedure developed by the U.S. government and published by Jeppesen. Both actions were consolidated for trial in the U.S. District Court.

Standard Instrument Approach Procedures [SIAPs] are developed by the FAA. The SIAP is basically a collection of data and information about a particular airport in the form of a table. The procedure includes all appropriate aspects of the approach such as minimum altitudes, turns, headings, bearings, radio frequencies and procedures to follow if an approach is missed. Jeppesen then uses the FAA's data to produce the instrument approach procedure on a graphic approach chart used by pilots. World Airways pilots flying into the Cold Bay Alaska Airport were using a Jeppesen chart.

Since claims against the federal government are controlled by the Federal Tort Claims Act, the case in the district court was divided into two parts. A jury decided the claims against Jeppesen and the court decided the claims against the government. The case was submitted to the jury on three theories of liability: *strict liability, breach of warranty,* and *negligence.* The outcome was a verdict from the jury against Jeppesen. Had one of the three liability theories been inadequate or incomplete, the jury's verdict would have to have been reversed. The verdict against Jeppesen was in the amount of $11,630,000. The district court had awarded World Airways $6,155,580.81 in prejudgment interest for its claim of the market value of the aircraft. The court entered a final judgment for Jeppesen's liability in the amount of $12,785,580.81. The federal government settled with the plaintiffs for $5 million and was dismissed from the suit.

Of note is that prior to the trial in the district court, the federal government and Jeppesen had developed an "indemnity agreement," which is an agreement to repay for loss or damage. Once the government had settled with the plaintiffs and was dismissed from the suit, the court denied Jeppesen's motion to force by law the indemnity agreement. The indemnity agreement resolved claims between the government and Jeppesen, subject to various conditions not included in the trial record. The agreement was allowed into evidence in the trial over the objections of Jeppesen.

Jeppesen appealed to the U.S. Court of Appeals, based on two main issues: the indemnity agreement, and strict liability. However, the Court of Appeals denied Jeppesen's petition for reconsideration of the district court's decisions over Jeppesen's many arguments. Jeppesen argued that the indemnity agreement should have been inadmissible as evidence in determining liability according to *Federal Rule of Evidence* 408, "Compromise and Offers to Compromise." They felt the agreement was admitted only to prove liability. The appeals court disagreed; stating it was admitted to show the relationship between Jeppesen and the government and to attack the credibility of witnesses. Therefore, the district court was correct in allowing the indemnity agreement to be admitted as evidence. However, had Jeppesen objected to the admittance of the agreement on the basis of *unfair prejudice* under *Federal Rule of Evidence* 403, "Exclusion of Relevant Evidence on Grounds of Prejudice, Confusion, or Waste of Time," there would have been just cause for not allowing the indemnity agreement into evidence. In other words, Jeppesen had made an error by basing its objection on Rule 408.

Concerning liability, Jeppesen believed:

- The federal government's instrument procedure was not a "product" *per se*;
- Since the government's instrument approach procedure was defective, Jeppesen could not be held strictly liable; and
- There was not enough evidence to establish negligence.

The Court of Appeals pointed out that the issue was not whether the government's instrument approach procedure was a *product*, but whether Jeppesen's chart was a product. Since Jeppesen mass produces and markets the charts it was considered to be a defective product. The court cited Section 402-A of the *Restatement of Torts* (second):

> *The justification for strict liability is said to be that the seller, . . . has undertaken and assumed a special responsibility toward the consuming public who may be injured by it . . . public policy demands that the burden of accidental injuries caused by products . . . be placed upon those who market them.*

A second argument presented by Jeppesen was that it could not be strictly liable because the government's instrument approach procedure specifications were beyond its control. However, the court pointed to Jeppesen's production specifications manual, which required its employees to research any procedure thoroughly to "determine its validity and completeness" and to contact official sources to resolve any discrepancies. Jeppesen had the ability to detect an error and a way to correct it. The court felt Jeppesen had a "duty to test/duty to warn" the product that is marketed. Jeppesen failed to find a defect in the chart. Had it discovered the defect, it would have been required to warn the users of the chart. Jeppesen argued that to hold a manufacturer strictly liable for accurately republishing a government regulation was unfair. The court agreed, but found that the charts were more than a republication of the government procedures. Jeppesen turned them into a new form, a distinct product. Therefore, Jeppesen was responsible as manufacturer for insuring the charts were not unreasonably dangerous in their intended use.

The Court of Appeals concluded that the plaintiffs had introduced sufficient evidence to support a finding that the chart was defective. Jeppesen's argument against the allegations was that it had no power to change the government's approach procedure. Since the court had already found that this was not true, Jeppesen's defense in the appeal was invalid. The judgment of the district court was affirmed.

CHAPTER 17

ACCIDENT INVESTIGATION

Where negligence is obvious, res ipsa loquitur,
"the thing speaks for itself."

INTRODUCTION

The Civil Aeronautics Act of 1938 established an Air Safety Board, whose responsibilities included aircraft accident investigation. Under a 1940 reorganization plan, the Air Safety Board was eliminated, and the Civil Aeronautics Board [CAB] was created. The responsibility for accident investigation was transferred to the CAB, where it remained until 1966. The Department of Transportation Act of 1966 created the National Transportation Safety Board [NTSB], and placed it administratively under the Department of Transportation [DOT]. The Independent Safety Board Act of 1974 removed the NTSB from the DOT and made it an independent federal agency.

The primary mission of the independent NTSB is to investigate and determine the probable cause of accidents in all five modes of transportation (airway, railway, highway, waterway and pipeline). Then the job of the NTSB is to identify problems and propose changes so that the same type of accident does not happen again. It is not the purpose of the NTSB to either lay blame or to prosecute criminal behavior. In fact, "Criminal probes do not mix well with aviation accident inquiries."[1] "Not surprisingly," says Kenneth Quinn, former Federal Avia-

---

[1] For example, look at the parallel investigations conducted by the French and the British into the one and only crash of a Concorde aircraft in 2001. While the U.K.'s investigation team was al-

tion Administration [FAA] chief counsel, ". . . when individuals and company officials are aware of the possibility of criminal sanctions, they may refuse to cooperate with National Transportation Safety Board investigators by asserting their Fifth Amendment privilege against self-incrimination."[2] In accident investigation there needs to be a climate of cooperation and candor. Hence, blame is not the point.

In fulfillment of its mission, the NTSB makes rules and regulations governing the notification and reporting of aircraft accidents. All reports of investigations and findings are made public in the interest of public safety. The findings of the NTSB are often made available before damage suits associated with the accidents have begun.

One aspect of aircraft accident investigation concerns the availability of the information obtained by the NTSB for use as evidence in private litigation. Title 49 U.S.C., Section 1441(e) governs the use at trial of NTSB reports and provides:

> *No part of any report or reports of the National Transportation Safety Board relating to any accident or the investigation thereof, shall be admitted as evidence or used in any suit or action for damages growing out of any matter mentioned in such report or reports.*

The courts have held that this provision renders only the NTSB's *formal* reports as inadmissible, and does not require exclusion of testimony of investigators and others having firsthand factual knowledge concerning an accident. Federal cases which have looked at this provision have distinguished between the factual portion of the NTSB report and the portion which embraces a determination of probable cause, and have reached a consensus that Section 1441(e) only excludes that part

---

lowed to do its work unencumbered by prosecutors and courts, in France their investigation agency had to conduct its proceedings in parallel with the criminal inquiry. As a result, the French accident investigation moved very slowly and corrective action was delayed. Editorial, *Oil and Water, Cats and Dogs*, Av. Wk. & Space Tech. (Feb. 4, 2002), at 70.

[2] Kenneth P. Quinn, *Why Airline Crashes Aren't Criminal*, Air & Space (Dec. 2000/Jan. 2001), at 56.

of the report which expresses the agency view as to probable cause. The factual portions are admissible.[3]

The North Carolina Court of Appeals ruled that the factual portions of an aircraft accident report by the NTSB were admissible, for example, in an action seeking to recover for injuries suffered in the aircraft crash.[4] The Federal Aviation Act of 1958 required only the exclusion of that part of the report which expressed the agency view as to probable cause. Portions of the NTSB report that contained hearsay statements by pilots, witnesses and other non-officials who were not present to testify at trial were also properly excluded.

In another action, involving a wrongful death resulting from a helicopter crash that killed three men, it was determined by the appellate court that a trial court did not err in twice refusing to declare a mistrial after an expert witness repeated the NTSB's conclusions regarding the probable cause of the crash to the jury.[5] Prior to trial, a motion *in limine* was granted, excluding the NTSB report on the crash. However, testimony elicited at trial, mentioning the NTSB report, was not immediately objected to. A timely objection is necessary when an improper question has been asked in violation of a motion *in limine*.[6]

In the previous chapter, *Brocklesby v. United States* was presented as one example of an accident reviewed by both the courts and the NTSB. This chapter is devoted to looking at the relationship between the courts and the NTSB, and to looking extensively at another such comparative study involving the crash of Trans World Airlines Flight 514 at Berryville, Virginia, in 1974. The insuing legal action, *Brock v. United States*, is an example of how testimony and evidence taken from the same accident may be viewed, as it was in this instance, entirely differently by two independent reviewers.[7]

---

[3] *See Travelers Insurance Company v. Riggs*, 671 F. 2d 810, 816 (1982); *see also American Airlines v. United States*, 418 F. 2d 180, 196 (1969); *see also Berguido v. Eastern Airlines*, 317 F.2d 628, 631-32, *cert. den.*, 375 U.S. 895 (1963).

[4] *Bolick v. Sunbird Airlines, Inc.*, 386 SE 2d 76 (1989).

[5] *Davis v. Stallones, et al.*, CCH 21 AVI 17,361 (1987).

[6] A "motion *in limine*" is a written motion, which is usually made before or after the beginning of a jury trial for a protective order against prejudicial questions and statements. The purpose of such a motion is to avoid injection into trial, matters that are irrelevant, inadmissible and prejudicial.

[7] *Brock and Kresheck v. United States*, CCH 14 AV. ¶ 18,246 (1977).

NTSB CASE STUDY

The case study presented herein involved only one aircraft, Trans World Airlines Flight 514 [TWA 514], which crashed into a mountaintop near Berryville, Virginia on December 1, 1974, while on approach in rough weather into Dulles International Airport. TWA 514 was descending from its en route altitude for a non-precision instrument approach landing at Dulles International Airport during severe inclimate weather conditions. Forty-four miles from the airport, the aircraft was cleared by air traffic control [ATC] to begin its final approach. Upon receiving the approach clearance, the Captain, following the then generally accepted rules of procedure, began descent to the altitude published on his charts from which to commence the landing approach. The aircraft crashed into a mountainside, all aboard were killed and the wreckage strewn across the mountaintop.

The safety record in air transportation is remarkable, but demonstrated herein is the fact that the system is not infallible. The accident didn't just happen, it was caused either by the pilots, the air traffic controllers, or both; that is to say, *"res ipsa loquitur."* Where negligence is obvious, commonly invoked is the rule of evidence known as *res ipsa loquitur*, which, when translated, means, "the thing speaks for itself." In *res ipsa loquitur*, there is a presumption or inference that the defendant was negligent, which arises upon proof that the instrumentality causing injury (such as an aircraft) was in the defendant's exclusive control, and that the accident was one which ordinarily does not happen in the absence of negligence. Thus, the facts and circumstances "speak for themselves" that someone must be at fault. The negligence of the wrongdoer may be inferred from the mere fact that the accident that happened, with resulting injuries, would not have occurred were it not for negligence.[8]

Res ipsa loquitur is a legal rule allowing the plaintiff to shift the burden of proof on the negligence issue to the defendant.[9] The plaintiff must ordinarily prove three elements in order to shift the burden of proof to the defendant under *res ipsa loquitur*: (1) the accident is of a kind that ordinarily does not occur in the absence of someone's negli-

---

[8] *See Black's Law Dictionary* (abridged 5th ed. 1983).
[9] The English translation of the Latin phrase is "the thing speaks for itself."

gence; (2) it was caused by an agency or instrumentality within the exclusive control of the defendant; and (3) it must not have been due to any voluntary action or contribution on the part of the plaintiff.[10] If all three elements are satisfied, the jury may infer negligence on circumstantial evidence alone; even where there is no direct evidence of defendant's negligence.[11] Defendant has the burden of proving plaintiff assumed the risk of injury, or was contributorily negligent.

In this chapter, the findings of the NTSB investigation are compared against the results of a subsequent lawsuit and the court's analysis of the accident's probable cause. The stage is set first with an overview of the then-existing operating procedures, followed by the results of the investigation conducted by the NTSB, and finally, with how blame was ultimately resolved in the U.S. District Court.

Reference to aircraft accident investigation usually conjures up notions of the scene of the crash, the aircraft wreckage, and a team of specialists recording, analyzing and reporting the physical aspects of the accident scene. But to accident investigation there is a due process, legal aspect as well. In the Federal Aviation Act of 1958, Congress delegated to the NTSB the responsibility of investigating accidents, reporting the facts, conditions, and circumstances relating to each accident, and reporting the probable cause thereof in the interest of safety and of preventing possible recurrences. Along with the safety perspective, there is also the prospect of litigation subsequent to the aircraft accident investigation. Inevitably, where there has been an aircraft mishap, the principle of *res ipsa loquitur* will be invoked. That is to say, "the accident speaks for itself"—that someone must be at fault. Accidents don't just happen. They are caused. Presumed under the *res ipsa loquitur* doctrine is that the conditions which led to injury, would not have occurred had someone been more careful. If the responsible person was not exercising the caution of a reasonable person then, by definition, that person was "negligent."

NTSB accident investigation entails a search for the party or parties responsible for the accident, as well as conducting a physical in-

---

[10] *Ybarra v. Spangard*, 25 Cal. 2d 486, 154 P.2d 687 (1944); *Colmenares Vivas v. Sun Alliance Insurance Company*, 807 F.2d 1102 (1st Cir. 1986). Some states only require the first two prongs of the test. *See e.g., McGonigal v. Gearhart Industries, Inc.*, 788 F.2d 321 (5th Cir. 1986). *See also American Law Institute, Restatement (Second) of Torts* 328 (1966).
[11] *Colmenares Vivas v. Sun Alliance Insurance Company*, 807 F.2d 1102 (1st Cir. 1986).

vestigation of the wreckage itself. But the primary purpose for accident investigation is to promote safety awareness and accident prevention, not to find someone to blame. It is for the courts to determine negligence and who was at fault.[12]

This chapter deviates somewhat from the format otherwise used in this book. Presented herein is a case study, rather than a series of exemplary court decisions, of the accident which perhaps caused more controversy in the air transportation industry than any other accident since the collision of two air carriers over the Grand Canyon in 1956. That accident precipitated passage of what has been referred to as the "Constitution of Aviation," even the Federal Aviation Act of 1958.

An in-depth investigation of the nation's air traffic control system was subsequently conducted in conjunction with the NTSB hearings into the crash of the Trans World Airlines Boeing 727. The hearings began January 27, 1975, and lasted five days. An investigation of the air traffic control system concurrently resulted from a controversy that arose over the deficient procedures routinely used by air traffic control to direct aircraft into airports during instrument flight conditions using radar equipment. There appeared to be confusion between ATC and the pilot community over what exactly was meant by an "approach clearance." It became unclear as to what duties the air traffic controller had in issuing such a clearance, and what responsibilities the pilot accepted in adhering to the approach clearance. The controversy was over the issue of which minimum altitude descent was inherent in the clearance—the minimum for the aircraft's present position relative to the en route structure, or the lowest minimum for the approach procedure. What also came into question was an issue over the provision of radar services by ATC, and specifically, the meaning of the expression, "radar arrival."

---

[12] Similarly, a military accident board investigates a crash, comes up with the cause, and recommends corrective action to prevent a recurrence. In a separate action, the military judicial system follows up when blame is a factor, but it does not use information gathered by the accident board. *See* David M. North, Jr., *Let Judicial System Run its Course in Crash Cases*, Av. Wk. & Space Tech. (May 15, 2000), at 66.

OPERATIONAL PROCEDURES

What follows is just one opinion regarding the clarity of the then existing ATC procedures. But it should be observed that the commentary is thoroughly referenced, adequately supported by the testimony of expert witnesses at the NTSB hearings into this accident, and supported, in part, by (NTSB) dissenting opinion. The witnesses included experienced Department of Defense [DOD] air traffic control personnel, as well as seasoned civilian and military pilots with thousands of hours of experience flying in the air traffic and airspace system.

In compliance with the Federal Aviation Act, the FAA Administrator in the exercise and performance of his (or her) powers and duties, is to consider "the control of the use of the navigable airspace of the United States and the regulation of both civil and military operations in such airspace in the interest of the safety and efficiency of both." Likewise, the Administrator is responsible for "the development and operation of a *common* system of air traffic control and navigation for both military and civil aircraft." Augmented by DOD civilian employees, military controllers are trained, tested and facility-rated under the same rules employed by the FAA. They are, in fact, examined as to their proficiency by FAA examiners. It is by design a totally compatible system. However, DOD air traffic controllers are in separate agencies from the FAA; in the Army, Air Force, Navy and Marine Corps. They are, nevertheless, experts in the FAA's ATC system. Their professional opinion, unbiased through organizational separation from the FAA, makes them valuable expert witnesses in ATC related litigation.

By-and-large, the pilot witnesses, supported by DOD air traffic controllers, were of the opinion that given clearance for the approach, the TWA flight was cleared to the lowest minimum from which to commence an approach, in this case 1,800 feet mean sea level [MSL]. In testimony at the NTSB hearings, the FAA controllers disagreed. In their opinion, the Captain had sole responsibility for terrain clearance, and for maintaining altitude until such time as he was clear of all obstructions and could then safely descend to the appropriate minimum altitude from which to commence the final approach for landing.

In referring to the rules of procedure then in effect,[13] one would have thought there to be no confusion. However, confusion did arise in what were (typically) flexible radar procedures that had been developed by the local ATC facilities at most major airports handling high volumes of traffic. Although efficient, the ATC radar procedures often bore little relationship to any published material carried in the cockpit. Contributing to the problem was a waning familiarity with, and perhaps even deviation from, the basic controller handbooks[14] and a re-channeled focus upon the specific operational requirements of the individual facility where the controller was assigned, and upon the controllers own specific and specialized duties and responsibilities.

Controllers were of the opinion (an opinion that persists even today), that they are responsible for separation of aircraft flown under Instrument Flight Rules [IFR], from other IFR aircraft, but not for the separation of IFR aircraft from the ground. Operationally, however, altitude assignments by ATC were intended to accomplish both.[15] Controllers had the practical operational authority for altitude assignment, and to separate the legal responsibility from the authority to make such altitude assignments would seem unreasonable. But that is exactly what controllers and the system did.

So what did the rules say, and for what were the pilots and controllers individually responsible? In order to cover all aspects of an approach clearance from a radar vector, several possibilities are suggested (and it matters not whether they applied to the Dulles accident specifically). At the time of the accident (i.e., in the early 1970s), pilots were mandatorily required to adhere to ATC instructions when given altitude[16] or routing[17] assignments. They were also prohibited from operating an aircraft under IFR below applicable minimum altitudes.[18] In practical application, this meant below the published Minimum En route [MEA] and Minimum Obstruction [MOCA] Altitudes.[19]

---

[13] *Federal Aviation Regulations*, Part 91 (Aug. 23, 1974); *Terminal Air Traffic Control*, FAA Handbook 7110.8C (Oct. 1, 1974); United States Standard for *Terminal Instrument Procedures*, FAA Handbook 8260.3A (May 4, 1972); *Flight Procedures and Airspace*, FAA Handbook 8260.19 (Apr. 5, 1973).

[14] Handbook 7110-8C, and *Enroute Air Traffic Control*, FAA Handbook 7110.9C, Jul. 2, 1974.

[15] Handbook 7110-8C, § 791-92.

[16] 14 C.F.R. § 91.121 (Aug. 23,1974).

[17] 14 C.F.R. § 91.123 (Aug. 23,1974).

[18] 14 C.F.R. § 91.119 (Aug. 23, 1974).

[19] *Id.*

The pilot's responsibility, along with ultimate responsibility for the aircraft and its occupants, was, in simple form, to adhere to the ATC clearance. The application of that clearance is where the complication arose. Assignment of a proper clearance was the controller's job, and understanding that clearance was up to the pilot. On radar vectors, aircraft were not on published routes, and the pilot therefore had to rely upon the radar controller who was familiar with the Minimum Vectoring Altitudes [MVAs].[20] Charts depicting minimum vector routes or sectors are normally not available to the pilot in the cockpit.

In terminal areas, vectoring altitudes assigned could well have been below the published Minimum Sector Altitude [MSA] with which the pilot was aware. Many published transition legs were (and are) below the MSAs; and radar vectors were merely transition routes.[21] The published minimum sector altitude, if assigned by ATC to a lower level, may have alerted the pilot, but that did not necessarily mean that he could not be vectored at a lower altitude and still be clear of obstructions by the required distance.[22] The radar controller knew where those obstructions were and had them plotted on his screen.[23]

Now consider that the pilot had been given radar vectors taking him away from the published en route structure. The air traffic controller had to give him the reason for the vector.[24] That reason was important to him and had definite bearing on further clearances.

If the pilot was given vectors to a transition fix and subsequently given clearance for the approach, the clearance still required him to fly the transition route as published,[25] that being the last routing to which he had been assigned. If, on the other hand, he had been given vectors to a transition fix and subsequently issued instructions such as, "Upon intercepting the final approach course, you are cleared for the approach," then that would have been a new routing, and the last routing would no longer have been valid. If at the time there were no published minima applicable to the pilot's location, he should have had one assigned; otherwise, he was cleared to descend unrestricted to the lowest published altitude specified in the approach procedure prior to final

---

[20] Handbook 7110.8C, § 791 and 1333; Handbook 8260.19, Ch. 3, Sec. 9.
[21] Handbook 7110.8C, § 873.
[22] Handbook 8260.19, Ch. 3 § 9.
[23] Id.
[24] Handbook 7110.8C, § 1243.
[25] Handbook 7110.8C, § 1020; see also Airman's Information Manual 1-68 (Nov. 1974).

approach descent.[26] Upon issuing clearance for the approach, the controller was guaranteeing unrestricted descent to the lowest published altitude. If there were restrictions, then the controller had the responsibility and was supposed to either defer approach clearance until there were no restrictions or alternatively to issue an altitude restriction specifying at what point unrestricted descent could be made.[27]

Next, consider that the pilot had been taken off the en route structure for vectors to the final approach course. In this case, the radar vectors served as the transition legs[28] and the pilot should have been assigned an altitude. Vectors to final were normally expected to route the aircraft to the vicinity of the "approach gate."[29] The approach gate was that point on the final approach course which was one mile from the approach fix on the side away from the airport or five miles from the landing threshold, whichever was farther from the landing threshold.[30] At any rate, the controller was responsible for issuing the aircraft's position relative to the Final Approach Fix [FAF], or relative to the navigation aid that provided final approach guidance, or relative to the airport.[31]

In all cases, when the pilot was not on the published route structure, he was given azimuth and altitude instructions to return the aircraft to its route.[32] The controller was responsible for informing the pilot when the aircraft was observed in a position and on a track that would obviously cause the aircraft to deviate from its protected airspace.[33] When the aircraft was returned to the route structure and cleared for the approach, the pilot was expected to fly the approach as published.[34]

Apparently, the majority opinion of the NTSB did not share the same understanding of pilot/controller responsibilities just described. What follows are the results of the NTSB's investigation into the TWA 514 crash, the conclusions of which could not have been reached with the above understanding. The dissenting (minority) opinion, how-

---

[26] Handbook 7110-8C, § 1360.
[27] Id.
[28] Handbook 7110.8C, § 873.
[29] Handbook 7110.8C, § 1351 and 1352.
[30] Handbook 7110.8C, Definitions.
[31] Handbook 7110.8C, § 1360.
[32] Handbook 7110.8C, § 791, 1241 and 1242.
[33] Handbook 7110.8C, § 1244.
[34] 14. C.F.R. 91.116 (Aug. 23, 1974).

ever, was in harmony with the operating procedures as presented above.

NATIONAL TRANSPORTATION SAFETY BOARD
AIRCRAFT ACCIDENT REPORT [35]
No.: NTSB-AAR-75-16

SYNOPSIS

At 1110 eastern standard time, December 1, 1974, TWA Flight 514, a Boeing 727-231, N54328, crashed 25 nautical miles northwest of Dulles International Airport, Washington, DC. The accident occurred while the flight was descending for a VOR/DME approach[36] to Runway 12 at Dulles during instrument meteorological conditions. The 92 occupants—85 passengers and seven crewmembers—were killed and the aircraft was destroyed.

The NTSB determined that the probable cause of the accident was the crew's decision to descend to 1,800 feet before the aircraft had reached the approach segment where that minimum altitude applied. The crew's decision to descend was a result of inadequacies and lack of clarity in the air traffic control procedures which led to a misunderstanding on the part of the pilots and of the controllers regarding each other's responsibilities during operations in terminal areas under instrument meteorological conditions. Nevertheless, the examination of the plan view of the approach chart should have disclosed to the captain that a minimum altitude of 1,800 feet was not a safe altitude.

CONTRIBUTING FACTORS

The factors contributing to the accident were determined to be:

- The failure of the FAA to take timely action to resolve the confusion and misinterpretation of air traffic terminology although the Agency had been aware of the problem for several years;

---

[35] Trans World Airlines, Inc., Boeing 727-231, 54328, Berryville Virginia (DEC. 1, 1974).
[36] Very High Frequency Omni Directional Range, combined with Distance Measuring Equipment.

- The issuance of the approach clearance when the flight was 44 miles from the airport on an unpublished route without clearly defined minimum altitudes; and
- Inadequate depiction of altitude restrictions on the profile view of the approach chart for the VOR/DME approach to Runway 12 at Dulles International Airport.

HISTORY OF THE FLIGHT

Flight 514 was a regularly scheduled flight from Indianapolis, Indiana, to Washington, DC, with an intermediate stop at Columbus, Ohio (refer to Figure 17.1, "Descent Profile," for the flight sequence profile). There were 85 passengers and seven crewmembers aboard the aircraft when it departed Columbus. The flight departed Indianapolis at 0853 Eastern Standard Time, and arrived in Columbus at 0932.[37] The crew obtained weather and aircraft load information.

The flight departed Columbus at 1024, 11 minutes late. At 1036, the Cleveland Air Route Traffic Control Center [ARTCC] informed the crew of Flight 514 that no landings were being made at Washington National Airport because of high crosswinds, and that flights destined for that airport were either being held or being diverted to Dulles International Airport. At 1042, Cleveland ARTCC cleared Flight 514 to Dulles Airport via the Front Royal VOR (Very High Frequency Omnidirectional Range), and to maintain Flight Level [FL] 290.[38] At 1043, the controller cleared the flight to descent to FL 230 and to cross a point 40 miles west of Front Royal at that altitude. Control of the flight was then transferred to the Washington ARTCC and communications were established with that facility at 1048.

During the period between receipt of the amended flight release and the transfer of control to Washington ARTCC, the flight crew discussed the instrument approach to Runway 12, the navigational aids, and the runways at Dulles. When radio communications were reestablished with Washington ARTCC, the controller affirmed that he knew the flight was proceeding to Dulles.

---

[37] All times are eastern standard times expressed on 24 hour clock.
[38] "Flight level" is an altitude reference used above 18,000 feet mean sea level, using an altimeter setting of 29.92 inches of mercury.

Figure 17.1—DESCENT PROFILE

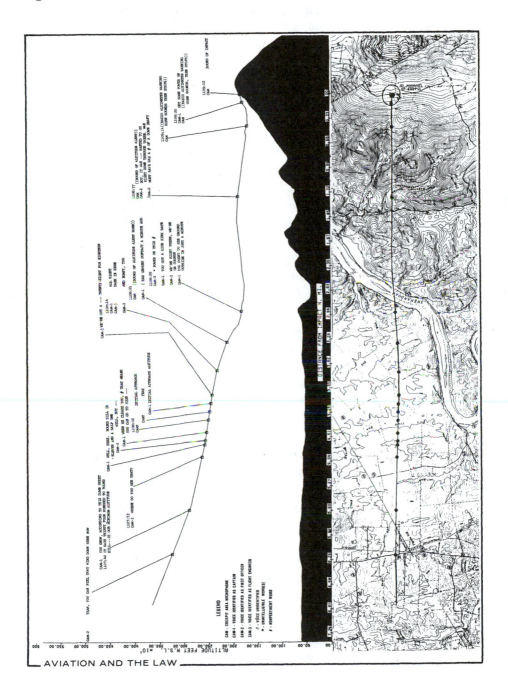

AVIATION AND THE LAW

773

Following contact with ARTCC, the Cockpit Voice Recorder [CVR] indicated that the crew discussed the various routings they might receive to conduct a VOR/DME approach to Runway 12 at Dulles. They considered the possibilities of proceeding via Front Royal VOR, via Martinsburg VOR, or proceeding on a straight-in clearance.

At 1051, the Washington ARTCC controller requested the flight's heading. After being told the flight was on a heading of 100 degrees, the controller cleared the crew to change to a heading of 090 degrees, to intercept the 300-degree radial of the Armel VOR, to cross a point 25 miles northwest of Armel to maintain 8,000 feet,[39] and ". . . the 300-degree radial will be for a VOR approach to Runway 12 at Dulles." The pilots again discussed the VOR/DME approach to Runway 12 at Dulles. At 1057, the crew again discussed items on the instrument approach chart including the Round Hill intersection, the final approach fix, the visual approach slope indicator and runway lights, and the airport diagram.

At 1059, the captain commented that the flight was descending from 11,000 feet to 8,000 feet. He then asked the controller if there were any weather obstructions between the flight and the airport. The controller replied that he did not see any significant weather along the route. At 1101, the controller cleared the flight to descend to and maintain 7,000 feet and to contact Dulles approach control. Twenty-six seconds later, the captain initiated a conversation with Dulles approach control and reported the aircraft was descending from 10,000 feet to maintain 7,000 feet. He also reported having received information "Charlie" transmitted on the Automatic Terminal Information Service [ATIS] broadcast. The controller replied with a clearance to proceed inbound to Armel and to expect a VOR/DME approach to Runway 12.

At 1104, the flight reported it was level at 7,000 feet. Five seconds after receiving that report, the controller said, "TWA 514, you're cleared for a VOR/DME approach to Runway 12." This clearance was acknowledged by the captain. The CVR recorded the sound of the landing gear warning horn followed by a comment from the captain that "Eighteen hundred is the bottom." The first officer then said,

---

[39] All altitudes and elevations are expressed in feet above mean sea level unless otherwise noted.

"Start down." The flight engineer said, "We're out here quite a ways. I better turn the heat down."

At 1105:06, the captain reviewed the field elevation, the minimum descent altitude, the final approach fix, and discussed the reason that no time to the missed approach was published. At 1106:15, the first officer commented that, "I hate the altitude jumping around." Then he commented that the instrument panel was bouncing around.

At 1106:42, the first officer said, "Gives you a headache after a while, watching this jumping around like that." At 1107:27, he said, ". . . you can feel that wind down here now." A few seconds later, the captain said, "You know, according to this dumb sheet it says thirty-four hundred to Round Hill . . . is our minimum altitude." The flight engineer then asked where the captain saw that and the captain replied, "Well, here. Round Hill is eleven and a half DME." The first officer said, "Well, but . . .," and the captain replied, "When he clears you, that means you can go to your. . . ." An unidentified voice said, "Initial approach," and another unidentified voice said, "Yeah!" Then the captain said "Initial approach altitude."

At 1108:14, the flight engineer said, "Dark in here," and the first officer stated, "And bumpy too." At 1108:25, the sound of an altitude alert horn was recorded. The captain said, "I had ground contact a minute ago," and the first officer replied, "Yeah, I did too." At 1108:29, the first officer said, "*power on this #."[40] The captain said, "Yeah . . . you got a high sink rate." The first officer replied, "Yeah." An unidentified voice said "We're going uphill," and the flight engineer replied, "We're right there, we're on course." Two voices responded, "Yeah!" The captain then said, "You ought to see ground outside in just a minute. . . . Hang in there boy." The flight engineer said, "We're getting seasick."

At 1108:57, the altitude alert sounded. Then the first officer said, "Boy, it was . . . wanted to go right down through there, man," to which an unidentified voice replied, "Yeah!" Then the first officer said, "Must have had a # of a down draft."

At 1109:14, the radio altimeter warning horn sounded and stopped. The first officer said, "Boy!" At 1109:20, the captain said, "Get some

---

[40] *Indicates unintelligible word(s); # indicates non-pertinent word(s).

power on." The radio altimeter warning horn sounded again and stopped. At 1109:22, the sound of impact was recorded.

At 1109:54, the approach controller called Flight 514 and said, "TWA 514, say your altitude." There was no response to this or subsequent calls. The controller subsequently testified he noticed on the radarscope that the flight's altitude was about 2,000 feet just before he called them. The Flight Data Recorder [FDR] readout indicated that after the aircraft left 7,000 feet, the descent was continuous with little rate variation until the indicated altitude was about 1,750 feet. The accident occurred on the west slope of Mount Weather, Virginia, about 25 nautical miles from Dulles, at an elevation of about 1,670 feet.

METEOROLOGICAL CONDITIONS

The weather in the area where the accident occurred was characterized by low clouds, rain mixed with occasional wet snow, and strong, gusty easterly winds. There were three SIGMETS in effect at the time of the accident.[41] They recommended caution due to ". . . moderate to severe mixed icing in clouds and precipitation above the freezing level" and embedded thunderstorms with tops near 40,000 feet. The cells were moving northeastward at 25 to 30 knots.

Ground witnesses in the accident area stated that, at about the time of the accident, the local weather was characterized by low ceilings, with visibilities ranging from 50 to 100 feet at the crash site. The wind was estimated at 40 miles per hour with stronger gusts. There was steady drizzle in the accident area.

Testimony at the public hearing indicated that an air traffic controller may vector flights to proceed to various points within the approach area to position the aircraft for execution of the approach. Aircraft are often vectored off published routes toward points on the approach path, and are often cleared to descend to altitudes below the published minimum altitude on the approach charts. Controllers and pilots have available to them the same information regarding Minimum Sector Altitudes [MSA] within 25 miles of airports, as well as minimum altitudes for various segments of an instrument approach. How-

---

[41] SIGMETS are advisory warnings of weather severe enough to be potentially hazardous to all aircraft. They are broadcast on navigation aid voice frequencies and by flight service stations. They are also transmitted on the Service A weather Teletype circuits.

ever, the controller also has available minimum vectoring altitudes, which the controller may use to clear aircraft to altitudes in certain areas, even when those altitudes are below the minimum altitudes depicted on the instrument approach charts in the pilot's possession. Pilots have no way of knowing the MVAs except through experience. Pilots testified that they had become accustomed to this sort of service and frequently did not know exactly where they were in relation to the terrain and obstacles depicted on their charts.

The testimony indicated pilots have become so accustomed to receiving assistance from the controllers that, unless advised by the controller, they do not know what type of services they are or are not receiving. Witnesses from FAA testified it is not necessary for pilots to know what services they are receiving, and that the pilot still has the ultimate responsibility for maintaining terrain clearance. In their testimony, the FAA referred to the pilot's responsibilities as outlined in 14 C.F.R. 91[42] and also found in 14 C.F.R. 121.[43]

INSTRUMENT APPROACH PROCEDURES

Instrument approach procedures are developed by the FAA according to prescribed, standardized methods contained in the *United States Standard for Terminal Instrument Procedures*, FAA Handbook 8260.3. The official document is FAA Form 8260.5, which contains all of the information required to depict and publish an instrument approach procedure. U.S. Government charts which depict the procedure are prepared and printed by the Department of Commerce, National Ocean Survey [NOS]. The charts prepared by NOS are used by air traffic controllers (and the military) while the Jeppesen charts are commonly used by air carrier flight crews.

---

[42] 14 C.F.R. 91.3(a), under "Responsibility and Authority of the Pilot in Command," stated, "The pilot in command of an aircraft is directly responsible for, and is the final authority as to, the operation of that aircraft."

[43] 14 C.F.R. 121.533 outlined the "Responsibility for Operational Control; Domestic Air Carriers." Paragraph (d) of 121.533 stated, "Each pilot in command of an aircraft is, during flight time, in command, of the aircraft and crew and is responsible for the safety of the passengers, crewmembers, cargo, and airplane."

The Jeppesen chart depicting the approach used by the crew of Flight 514 (see Figure 17.2, "Jeppesen Chart") was based on the data published by the FAA on Form 8260.5. However, there was no formal program of review or approval by the FAA in comparing the Jeppesen chart with the basic data on Form 8260.5. FAA requirements for instrument approach procedures[44] and Certificate Holders' Manual Requirements[45] are outlined in 14 CFR 121.

The Inter-Agency Air Cartographic Committee [IACC], composed of representatives from the Department of Defense, the Department of Commerce, and the FAA, has developed a manual containing U.S. specifications for use in the preparation of low-altitude instrument approach procedure charts. These specifications are used by cartographers in preparing NOS approach charts from the information on Form 8260.5. The third edition of the IACC manual, dated July 1971, states, in part, "These specifications shall be complied with without deviation until such time as they are amended by formal IACC action." Chapter III of the manual, Revision 9.c (35) and (36) dated January 1973, states under the heading "Profile" that, "A profile diagram of the instrument approach procedures shall be placed in the space provided below the plan view. All facilities, intersections, fixes, etc., used in, or pertinent to the approach procedure as portrayed in the plan view shall be shown."

The profile view of the VOR/DME approach to Runway 12 at Dulles Airport, as published by NOS (see Figure 17.3, "National Ocean Survey Chart"), depicted only the 6 DME fix and the final approach fix altitude of 1,800 feet. It did not depict the Round Hill intermediate approach fix altitude or the minimum altitudes associated with the routes inbound from the three initial approach fixes that were part of this procedure, although these data were displayed on the plan view. Form 8260.5 for this procedure did not list the requirement for the Round Hill intermediate fix to be included on the profile view.

---

[44] 14 C.F.R. 121.567, "Instrument Approach Procedures and IFR Landing Minimums," stated, "No person may make an instrument approach at an airport except in accordance with IFR weather minimums and instrument approach procedures set forth in the certificate holder's operations specifications."

[45] 14 C.F.R. 121.135, "Contents," stated, in part, that each manual required under C.F.R. 121.33 must include, "Appropriate information from the airport operations specifications, including for each airport...Instrument approach procedures...."

Figure 17.2—JEPPESEN CHART

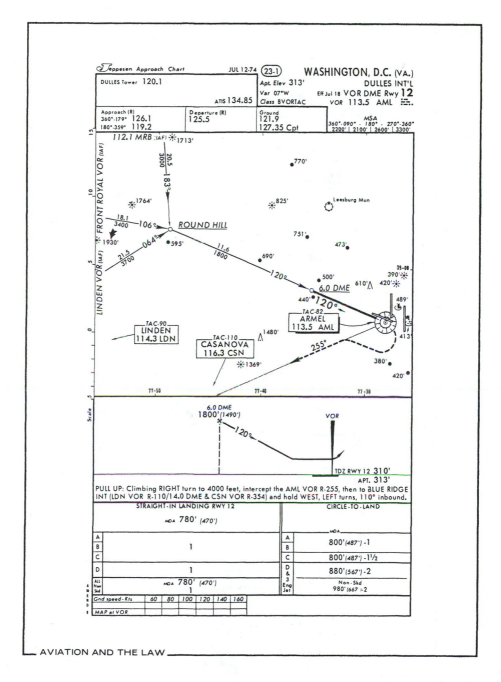

Figure 17.3—NATIONAL OCEAN SURVEY CHART

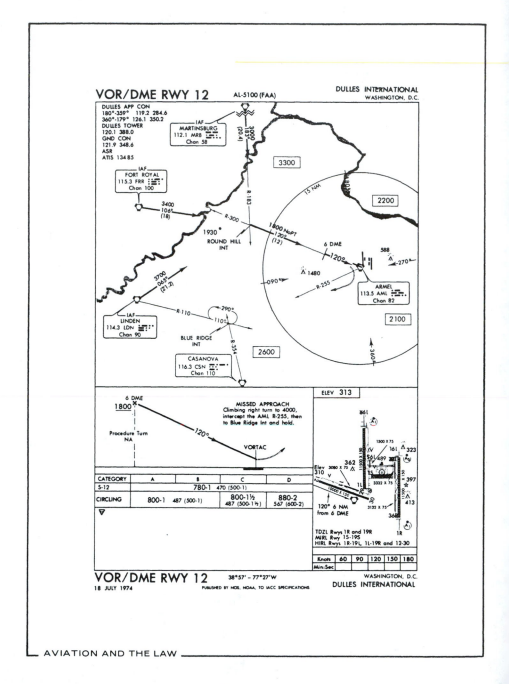

AIR TRAFFIC CONTROL MANUAL

The FAA Terminal *Air Traffic Control Manual*, Order 7110.8C, which was in effect on December 1, 1974, prescribed the air traffic control procedures and phraseology to be used by FAA personnel providing terminal air traffic control services. Controllers are required to be familiar with the provisions of this handbook, which pertain to their operational responsibility and to exercise their best judgments if they encounter situations not covered by the manual. The manual is offered for sale to the public,[46] but it is not routinely disseminated to flight crews.

Some portions of the *Air Traffic Control Manual* are used in air carrier training programs, and portions are used in some FAA publications to indoctrinate pilots regarding the air traffic control system. FAA witnesses testified that pilots do not need to know specifically the contents of the manual, including the application of radar services. Chapter 5 of the ATC manual deals with radar operations. Sections 2 through 6, as well as Section 9 of Chapter 5, define various aspects of radar operations including vectoring, radar handoffs, radar separation, radar arrivals, and radar identification. Section 9, "Radar Arrivals," Paragraph 1360, "Arrival Instructions," contains the following guides for controllers regarding an aircraft before it reaches the *approach gate*,[47] provided the aircraft was not conducting a radar approach:

> *Issue . . . approach clearance, except when conducting a radar approach. If terrain or traffic does not permit unrestricted descent to lowest published altitude specified in approach procedure prior to final approach descent, controllers shall: (1) Defer issuance of approach clearance until there are no restrictions or, (2) Issue altitude restrictions*

---

[46] The manual can be obtained from the Superintendent of Documents, Government Printing Office, Washington, D.C.

[47] The "approach gate" is a point on the final approach course which is one mile from the approach fix on the side away from the airport or five miles from the landing threshold, whichever is farther from the landing threshold.

with approach clearance specifying when or at
what point unrestricted descent can be made.

The FAA witnesses testified that Flight 514 was inbound to Armel by means of the pilot's own navigation, thereby relieving the controller of responsibility under Paragraph 1360 of the manual. The FAA witnesses also testified that IFR arrivals are routinely handled as "non-radar" arrivals in a radar environment, whenever the pilot is navigating without assistance from air traffic control. The witnesses testified that under these conditions, the pilot must provide his or her own terrain clearance. The air traffic control system provides only separation from other known IFR traffic. No official definitions were provided for the terms: "radar arrival" and "non-radar arrival."

The *Air Traffic Control Manual* stated the FAA provided three kinds of radar service:

- *radar separation*—when radar spacing of aircraft is accomplished in accordance with established FAA minima;
- *radar navigational guidance*—when vectoring aircraft to provide course guidance; and
- *radar monitoring*—defined as radar flight-following of an aircraft whose primary navigation is being performed by its pilot, to observe and note deviations from its authorized flight path, airway, or route.

As applied to the monitoring of instrument approaches from the final approach fix to the runway, radar monitoring also includes provisions for advice on aircraft position relative to approach fixes and advisories whenever the aircraft proceeds outside the prescribed safety zones. Discretionary instructions to controllers were that:

You have complete discretion for determining
if you are able to provide or continue to pro-
vide a service in a particular case.

Your decision not to provide or continue to
provide a service in a particular case is not

subject to question by the pilot and need not be made known to him.

Among the additional services that a controller could offer to a flight pursuant to Order 7110.8C were:

Issue an advisory to radar identified aircraft whenever radar observation reveals a situation which, in your judgment, is likely to affect the safety of the aircraft;[48] and

If you observe an automatic altitude report showing continuous deviation of 300 feet or more from the assigned altitude of an aircraft, issue altitude readout information to the pilot. Except during climb or descent, apply this procedure to aircraft whose automatic readout has been verified.[49]

The controller in this case stated that he saw the data block from Flight 514 show an indicated altitude of 2,000 feet, and he attempted to contact the flight at 1109:54. Prior to that time, the controller stated that the data was in a precipitation return and was "difficult to see."

HANDLING OF OTHER FLIGHTS

About one-half hour before the accident, an air carrier flight approached Dulles from the northwest and was cleared for a VOR/DME approach to Runway 12. The pilot of the flight said that because he was a considerable distance from the airport and was not given an altitude restriction to use before arriving on a published approach segment, he requested information regarding the minimum vectoring altitude at the flight's position. The controller gave the pilot the MVA and offered the flight a surveillance radar approach. The captain accepted the surveillance approach and landed without further incident.

---

[48] Paragraph 1545, "Safety Advisory."
[49] Paragraph 1546, "Altitude Deviation Information."

About six hours after the TWA 514 accident, a second air carrier aircraft approached Dulles from the southwest, and, at a point about 21 miles from Dulles, the captain asked the controller for the flight's position relative to the Round Hill intersection. The controller replied that he did not have Round Hill depicted on his radar. The captain later testified he was familiar with the terrain around Dulles and did not descend until after he was on the inbound heading to Runway 12 and inside 17.6 miles as indicated on his DME indicator.

REPORT OF UNSAFE CONDITIONS

In January of 1974, an air carrier in the United States initiated a Flight Safety Awareness Program. The purpose of the program was to encourage the carrier's pilots to report to the company any incident, or any suggestion, that could have safety implications, so that required remedial action could be taken. Under this program, an individual could make a report without identifying himself or his fellow crewmembers. The pilots were assured that the carrier would not take any punitive action as a result of information procured through this program. The carrier would not voluntarily divulge information secured in this program to any outside agency, which would permit identification of any individual involved. The carrier undertook to protect vigorously individual anonymity, unless the individual involved waived this protection.

In October of 1974, the carrier received a report under the above program. A crew reported they were approaching Dulles and after passing Front Royal at 6,500 feet, they were issued a clearance to descend to 4,000 feet and instructed to contact Dulles approach control. The crew anticipated an Instrument Landing System [ILS] approach to Runway 1R, but they were cleared for a VOR approach to Runway 12. After the captain reviewed the chart for the latter approach, he descended to 1,800 feet, intercepted the 300 degree radial (120 degrees inbound) to the Dulles VOR, and landed without incident.

After landing, the crew reviewed the approach and decided they had descended to 1,800 feet about 25 nautical miles from the VOR and were at that altitude before they reached the Round Hill intersection. The captain reported he believed at the time he made the approach a clearance for an approach authorized him to descend immediately to the final approach fix altitude. He had looked at the profile of the approach, saw the "1,800 feet" at the "six nautical mile DME fix," and overlooked the minimum altitude for the approach segment from the Front Royal VOR to Round Hill.

The carrier investigated this incident and contact was made with the FAA at the Dulles tower. The carrier's representative making this contact understood that in the future, a clearance for this approach would be issued when the flight was about 30 nautical miles from the airport. He also understood future flights would be radar monitored unless the controllers had other duties and activities that would preclude such action. The VOR/DME approach was reviewed with several company pilots and in each case, the chart was interpreted properly by the pilots. As a result of this investigation, the carrier believed it was not necessary to make any recommendations to the FAA or to change the carrier's procedures. However, they did publish a notice to all flight crews stating,

> *The extensive use of radar vectoring, in terminal areas, had led to some misunderstanding on the part of flight crews. Recent . . . events prompt these reminders:*
>
> 1. *The words "cleared for approach" generally put the flight crew on their own.*
> 2. *Don't start down to final approach fix altitude without reviewing other altitude minimums.*
> 3. *Inbound minimum altitudes to outer fixes are on the Jeppesen plates.*
> 4. *Flight crews should thoroughly familiarize themselves with the altitude information shown on approach and/or area charts for the terminals into which they are operating. This includes Minimum Sector Altitude [MSA] information.*

CONCLUSION

Considering the number of times the captain examined this chart after being informed that he was to divert to Dulles, the NTSB concluded he should have realized the minimum altitude of 1,800 feet might not be a safe altitude. The information available to the pilot, including the approach chart, should have alerted the crew that an unrestricted descent would be unsafe. Nevertheless, it appeared to the Board that there was a deficiency in the chart. This particular approach chart depicted the profile view from the final approach fix to the airport. It did not depict the intermediate fix, Round Hill, with its associated minimum altitudes. This information was available from the plan view of the chart, but it appears the crew gave their primary attention to the profile. If this was the case, it may have led the crew to discount the other information available on the chart and to continue their descent on the assumption it was permissible by reason of the clearance they had received.

A major question deserving consideration is the role of the ATC system in this accident. Specifically, why was TWA 514 not given an altitude restriction in its approach clearance? The testimony of all FAA witnesses, including the controller, was consistent in stating that,

- Flight 514 was not a "radar arrival";
- That because of this fact, the controller was not required to implement the provisions of Paragraph 1360 of the FAA Handbook 7110.8C; and that
- They considered TWA 514, after intercepting the 300 degree radial of Armel, as proceeding on its own navigation and as being responsible for its own obstacle clearance.

Federal Aviation Administration witnesses stated Flight 514 was not a radar arrival, because it had not been vectored to the final approach course. They did not consider the vector of Flight 514 by the Washington Center to intercept the 300-degree radial as being a vector to the final approach course, even though the VOR/DME approach procedure utilizes the 300-degree radial inbound from Round Hill. Particular emphasis was made by the FAA that the vector to the 300-degree radial occurred when the flight was approximately 80 miles from the airport and that it was vectored by the center on to an en route course. "Operational advantage" was indicated by the controllers as the reason for the vector to the 300-degree radial rather than to an initial approach fix on the approach procedure.

The counter position to FAA testimony is that Flight 514 *was* operating in a radar environment, was receiving at least one type of radar service, and was on a course which would lead directly to the Round Hill intermediate approach fix. Furthermore, the flight crew had been advised that the reason for the vector to the 300-degree radial was for a VOR/DME approach for Runway 12. Consequently, the aircraft should have received services, including altitude restrictions, as set forth in Paragraph 1360 of Order 7110.8C.

In evaluating these facts, the one issue present is whether the handling of Flight 514 required the provision of an altitude restriction. FAA witnesses agreed that, had Flight 514 been classified as a "radar arrival" within the meaning of the handbook, the flight would have been given an altitude restriction until it reached Round Hill. In resolving this issue, the Board had been troubled by the fact that ATC procedures are almost always dependent upon the usage of certain specified phrases and terms, many of which may have had no established definitions, and may have meant something different to controllers than to pilots. The term "radar control" is an example. The pilot witnesses believed that, when they were operating in a "radar environment," they were being "controlled" by radar procedures. The controller group was aware this was not always the case, but apparently the FAA did not perceive the difference of understanding between pilots and controllers. Efforts made by the FAA, to clarify when an aircraft was or was not radar controlled, did not eliminate the confusion.

The NTSB concluded that based on the criteria in Order 7110.8C, the system allowed for the classification and handling of Flight 514 as a "non-radar arrival." But the Board believed the flight should have been classified and handled as a "radar arrival." This, however, does not dispose of the issue of whether the ATC system should have provided for a redundancy that would have prevented, or consequently identified and corrected, a deviation by an aircraft from a clearance the controller expected it to follow. The system should clearly require controllers to give pilots specific information regarding their positions relative to the approach fix, and a minimum altitude to which the flight could descend before arriving at that fix. Pilots should not be faced with the necessity of choosing from among several courses of action to comply with a clearance.

The NTSB believed the clearance, under these circumstances, should have included an altitude restriction until the aircraft had reached a segment of the published approach procedure or the issuance of the approach clearance should have been deferred until the flight reached such segment. Therefore, the NTSB concluded the clearance was inadequate and its issuance and acceptance was the result of a "misunderstanding" between the pilot and the controller. The NTSB believed there was a lack of understanding between pilots and controllers generally in their interpretations of air traffic control procedures. There was also a lack of understanding about the meaning of some words and phrases used by both the controller and pilot in the handling of IFR traffic in the terminal area. In this case, there was no definition of the term "radar arrival" or "final approach course," nor, as indicated earlier, did there seem to be common understanding between pilots and controllers as to the meaning of "radar control."

The NTSB concluded it is essential that a lexicon of air traffic control words and phrases be developed and made available to all controllers and pilots who operate within the National Airspace System. Additionally, there should be one book of procedures for use by both pilots and controllers, so that each will understand what to expect of the other in all air traffic control situations. This manual must be used in the training of all pilots and controllers.

The need for such a lexicon and procedures manual is evident from the circumstances of this accident. Flight 514 was vectored to intercept the 300-degree radial of Armel, the reciprocal course of which coincides with the course for the intermediate and final approach segments of the published instrument approach procedure. The vector was given when the flight was more than 80 miles from the airport and at a point where the 300-degree radial of Armel was not a part of the instrument approach procedure. While proceeding inbound on the 300-degree radial of Armel, the flight would not have reached a segment of the published approach procedure until it arrived at Round Hill.

However, there was some testimony contending that Flight 514 was on its final approach course when the flight intercepted and was inbound on the 300-degree radial, and accordingly, that it was permissible for the pilot to descend to the minimum altitude of 1,800 feet prescribed for crossing the final approach fix of the VOR/DME instrument approach procedure. Irrespective, the Board concluded that qualified instrument pilots and air traffic controllers should know and understand beyond equivocation that the coincidence of the inbound course, being an extension of the final instrument approach course, does not permit descent to altitudes lower than those published for that air space segment, unless specifically authorized by ATC.

A clear, precise definition of "final approach course" and "final instrument approach course" should preclude future misunderstandings. Neither of these terms was defined in the *Airmans Information Manual* [AIM] at the time of this accident. However, the AIM glossary did contain a definition of "Final Approach-IFR" wherein the final instrument approach course is shown to be confined to the final approach segment of the instrument approach procedure and it begins at the final approach fix.

DISSENT

Two members of the Board dissented, and did not agree with the probable cause as stated by the majority. In their opinion, the probable cause was the failure of the controller to issue altitude restrictions in accordance with the *Terminal Air Traffic Control Handbook*, Order 7110.8C, Paragraph 1360(c), and also the failure of the pilot to adhere to the minimum sector altitude as depicted on the approach plate or to request clarification of the clearance. As a result, the pilot prematurely descended to 1,800 feet.

The flight was a "radar arrival" and, therefore, was entitled to altitude protection and terrain clearance. If the controller, as required by the then existing procedures for radar arrivals, had issued altitude restrictions with the approach clearance, or had deferred the clearance, the accident probably would not have occurred. On the other hand, if the pilot had either maintained the minimum sector altitude of 3,300 feet as depicted on the approach plate, or requested clarification of the clearance, there would not have been an accident. If the majority believed that under all the circumstances the flight should have been classified and handled as a radar arrival, then the flight was in fact a radar arrival, and the probable cause should so state. It would appear the majority believed the flight was a radar arrival but refused to make an unambiguous finding to that effect.

The Board majority attributed the failure of the controller to handle the flight as a radar arrival to be a "terminology difficulty" between pilots and controllers. However, it was not the pilots who were having any difficulty with terminology. They were following established procedures. The controllers may have had some difficulty with terminology, but the confusion was their own. The plain fact of the matter is that the controller simply did not treat the flight as a radar arrival as he should have. All the criteria of Paragraph 1360 for a radar arrival were present. Accordingly, the captain reasonably assumed he was a radar arrival, and that he would be given altitude restrictions if necessary. Not having received such restrictions, he initiated a descent to 1,800 feet.

The majority further stated "there is a general lack of understanding between pilots and controllers in their interpretations of air traffic control procedures." Yet, they found there was no misunderstanding in this instance on the part of the captain. As previously stated, he undoubtedly descended to 1,800 feet after receiving an approach clearance, because he was not issued an altitude restriction. If the controller was confused with regard to the application of Paragraph 1360, he should have asked for clarification from his supervisor. But there should have been no reason for confusion insofar as terminology is concerned. One of the most important functions of an air traffic controller is to possess the highest degree of knowledge in procedures and terminology, and to apply it with the greatest diligence and care.

In any event, the Board majority should have logically concluded that, in not handling the flight as a radar arrival, the Dulles controller did not properly apply the provisions of the controller's handbook. Furthermore, it appeared from the testimony of other controllers at the hearing that they would have handled the flight in a similar manner, which may in turn indicate a lack of understanding or comprehension by controllers, generally, regarding the application of Paragraph 1360.

The majority stated:

> . . . there was some testimony contending that
> Flight 514 was on its final approach course
> when the flight intercepted and was inbound

*on the 300-degree radial, and accordingly it
was permissible for the pilot to descend to the
minimum altitude of 1,800 feet prescribed for
crossing the final approach fix of the
VOR/DME instrument approach procedure.*

With all due respect, there was not merely "some testimony." Indeed, as hereinafter pointed out, there was *considerable* testimony and evidence from controllers, as well as pilots, to support the conclusion that the flight was on the final approach course and was a radar arrival. Nevertheless, despite their conclusion that the flight was a radar arrival, and, therefore, should have been provided altitude restrictions, the crew had at their disposal sufficient information, which should have prompted them either to refrain from descending below the minimum sector altitude or, at the very least, to have requested clarification of the clearance. Although the profile on the approach plate did not fully and accurately depict the various minimum altitudes associated with the entire approach, it appears there was adequate information on the plan view of the plate to alert a prudent pilot of the hazards of descending to an altitude of 1,800 feet prior to reaching the Round Hill intersection.

The existing air traffic control system and today's aircraft are highly complex and sophisticated. Neither can operate independent of each other—there must be a cooperative and coordinated effort on the part of both the pilots and the controllers if the system is to function efficiently and safely. The real issue in this accident was not one of inadequacy of terminology or lack of understanding between controllers and pilots. Rather, it was a failure on the part of both the controllers and pilots to utilize the ATC system properly and to its maximum capability.

BROCK v. UNITED STATES
CCH 14 Av. Cas. (CCH) ¶ 18,246 (E.D. Va. 1977)

*Was the crash of TWA Flight 514 the result of negligence on
the part of air traffic control, flight crew, and/or both?*

This was an action against the United States for the alleged wrong-ful death of the pilot and co-pilot of a Trans World Airline Boeing 727-231 aircraft, being operated as TWA Flight 514 (TWA 514) which crashed during an instrument approach to the Dulles International Airport (Dulles) on December 1, 1974. All aboard the aircraft were killed. The action was brought under the Federal Tort Claims Act.

The plaintiffs were widows of deceased crewmembers killed in the TWA 514 accident. It was their contention that the United States, through its air traffic controllers acting in the scope of their employment, was negligent in:

- failing to provide terrain clearance by failing to follow the provisions of the "Terminal Approach manual" of the FAA regarding "radar arrival" aircraft. The manual required the controller to defer issuance of an approach clearance if the terrain did not permit unrestricted descent to the lowest published altitude specified in approach procedure prior to final approach descent, or required the controller to issue altitude restrictions with the approach clearance specifying when or at what point unrestricted descent could be made;
- in failing to issue a safety advisory warning to TWA 514 that it had descended below the FAA's minimum safe vectoring altitude of 4,000 feet;
- by further failing to issue a safety advisory to TWA 514 when radar observations revealed it had further descended to the dangerous altitude of 2000 feet; and that
- the United States had the last clear chance to prevent the crash and deaths.

The government denied any negligence on the part of the FAA air traffic controllers and alleged the cause of the accident and the resulting deaths of plaintiffs' decedents was their own negligence. It also disputed the applicability of the last clear chance doctrine to this case.

On December 1, 1974, TWA 514 was operating as a scheduled passenger flight from Indianapolis, Indiana, to Washington National Airport, with an intermediate stop at Columbus, Ohio. Subsequent to takeoff from Columbus, the aircraft diverted to Dulles International Airport because of the weather conditions existing at Washington National Airport. TWA 514 on December 1, 1974, was the inaugural flight for TWA of its Indianapolis-Washington service.

At approximately 11:09:22 a.m., Eastern Standard Time, Flight 514 crashed into the west slope of Mount Weather, Clarke County, Virginia, at an elevation of 1,669 feet, approximately 20 nautical miles from Dulles. At the time of the crash, the aircraft had been cleared for a VOR/DME approach to Runway 12 at Dulles. A VOR/DME approach is a non-precision approach utilizing a Very High Frequency Omnidirectional Range [VOR] and Distance Measuring Equipment [DME]. By utilizing the VOR and DME equipment in conjunction with one another, a crew may execute a non-precision VOR/DME approach, which is an instrument approach by which the crew navigates its aircraft with reference to its airborne VOR and DME equipment. Such an approach may be conducted without any radar being present at all.

The VOR ground based station that TWA Flight 514 was utilizing on December 1, 1974, was the Armel VOR. In particular, the flight was utilizing the 300-degree radial of the VOR, and doing its own navigating along that radial by reference to its airborne VOR and DME equipment. By reference to the airborne equipment, not only could the crew determine its precise mileage from the Armel station, but it could also insure it maintained a course heading on the 300-degree radial by reference to the course deviation indicator.

In conjunction with using the airborne electronic equipment, the crew was also using an approved instrument approach procedure chart for the VOR/DME Runway 12 approach. The particular chart in this instance was published by the Jeppesen Company. It depicted frequency information, course information, altitude information and other information pertinent to the operation of TWA 514.

The flight crew of Flight 514 consisted of three individuals; Richard I. Brock was captain and pilot in command, Leonard W. Kresheck was co-pilot and first officer, and Thomas Safranek was flight engineer. The ground based air traffic control facility with which TWA Flight 514 was in radio contact at the time of the accident was the approach controller at the Dulles Terminal Radar Control room [TRACON], an FAA facility. On duty was FAA controller Dameron. The TRACON was equipped with aircraft surveillance radar with Automated Radar Terminal System [ARTS-III] capability. At the time of the accident, the radar and the ARTS-III equipment were operating.

In air traffic control service, two distinct radar services are offered: aircraft separation and terrain separation. No allegation was made of negligence in the performance of aircraft separation service. The pilot of an aircraft always exercises independent judgment in accepting a clearance from an FAA controller. By accepting any kind of clearance from an FAA controller, the pilot has implicitly exercised his or her independent judgment that the clearance will not jeopardize flight of the aircraft.

The second service FAA controllers can provide is terrain separation (i.e., providing clearances which ensure sufficient distance between the aircraft and the ground). Such a service is not automatic, however, but turns on when the aircraft in question is a radar arrival. As used in the industry, "radar arrival" includes an aircraft that specifically requests terrain separation assistance (e.g., a Ground Controlled Approach [GCA]), and an aircraft that is vectored by the controller to the final approach course of the airport. According to FAA testimony, simply being provided radar services such as aircraft separation does not make an aircraft a radar arrival. Nor does a good faith belief that one is a radar arrival, make the aircraft a radar arrival, if such belief is not reasonable under the circumstances. Stripped of jargon, what the Washington Center controller was saying to TWA 514 was this: Fly along a heading of 90 degrees until you intercept the Armel radio beacon at 300 degrees. Maintain eight thousand feet altitude. The Armel 300-degree radial will put you on course for a VOR approach to Runway 12 at Dulles.

The radar vector in the above exchange was the direction to fly a heading of 90 degrees. Until TWA 514 intercepted the Armel 300-degree radial, it was a radar arrival to Washington Center. It is only when an aircraft is following a heading given by an air traffic controller that the duty of terrain separation rests on the controller, since the aircraft may not know its position along that heading. Once an aircraft intercepts and turns onto a given radial of a VOR station, as TWA 514 did when it intercepted and turned onto the 300-degree radial of Armel, it can immediately determine how far away it is from the station and the airport through the use of its VOR/DME equipment.

While not wishing to belabor the point, the court thought it critical to understand the difference between being vectored to intercept a given radial of a VOR station, and being vectored to the final approach course. In both cases, the duty of the FAA air traffic controller is to provide both terrain and aircraft separation to the aircraft while it is on that vector. TWA 514 was not vectored to the final approach course. Rather, it was vectored to the 300-degree radial of Armel some 80 miles from the airport. At the point in space where it left the 90-degree heading and turned onto the 300-degree radial of Armel, TWA 514 was no longer on a radar vector supplied by an FAA controller. The plaintiffs' attempts to stretch the final approach course some 80 miles, and with it the duty to provide terrain separation, according to the court would have to fail.

If TWA 514 was not a radar arrival after it turned onto the Armel 300-degree radial, the question next presented was whether it again became a radar arrival pursuant to the clearance received from FAA controller Dameron at Dulles International Airport. "AR-1" is Dulles Approach Control, FAA Controller Dameron, and the pertinent exchanges were as follows:

Source	Content
TWA 514:	*Dulles Approach Control, TWA five fourteen, we're out of ten to maintain seven thousand, we have Charlie.*
AR-1:	*TWA five fourteen, Dulles, roger, proceed in-bound to Armel. Expect VOR/DME approach runway one two.*
TWA 514:	*Five fourteen, roger.*

(Minutes later)

TWA 514:	*TWA five fourteen level seven.*
AR-1:	*TWA five fourteen, roger.*
AR-1:	*TWA five fourteen, you're cleared for a VOR/DME to runway one two.*
TWA 514:	*Cleared for a DME, a VOR/DME approach runway one two, TWA five fourteen, roger.*

It is clear from the above exchange that FAA controller Dameron gave no vector to TWA 514, and that TWA 514 requested no radar assistance. There was substantial and credible evidence that the kind of clearance Dameron issued was one where only aircraft separation was provided. Dameron was undertaking to ensure that TWA 514 would not collide with other aircraft. The pilot retained the undertaking to ensure his aircraft would not collide with the ground. In summary, the Court found that TWA 514 was not a radar arrival within the meaning of Section 9 of the *Terminal Air Traffic Control Manual*, and thus, the provisions of Paragraph 1360 of that section did not apply.

Although the crew retained responsibility for terrain clearance, it may well be that TWA 514 thought Dameron was providing terrain separation, because the plaintiffs' next contention was that flight controller Dameron was negligent in failing to issue a safety advisory to TWA 514. The plaintiff contended FAA controller Dameron was negligent in failing to advise TWA 514 of its descent below 4,000 feet, the FAA's Minimum Vectoring Altitude [MVA] for the sector through which it was flying. The Court could not agree. Dameron testified he could not issue an aircraft an altitude below the MVA so long as it was on the radar vector. TWA 514, as discussed above, was not on a radar vector at any time after it intercepted the 300-degree radial of Armel. Additionally, Dameron did not issue TWA 514 any altitude clearances, much less one below the MVA for the sector in question. Dameron's testimony, which the court found credible, was that an aircraft on its own navigation would often descend to an altitude below the MVA altitude as shown on the chart. The pilot would be in possession of information, which the flight controller did not possess, and vice versa. Thus, a flight controller would not think it unusual to see such a descent and would not consider such a descent dangerous. The plaintiffs' attempt to impose a duty on Dameron in this regard had to fail, for the

Court was of the opinion that the duty would only arise had TWA 514 been on a radar vector (i.e., a "radar arrival"). Since the court had expressly found that TWA 514 was not on such a vector at the time, no duty arose.

Plaintiffs' next contended that FAA controller Dameron was negligent in failing to issue an advisory to TWA 514 when radar observation showed the aircraft to have descended below 2,000 feet some 58 seconds prior to impact. The Court did not decide in this case whether such a safety advisory was mandatory or simply a suggested procedure because Dameron testified that he should have given such an advisory had he had the time and ability to do so.

The Court resolved the conflict in favor of Dameron. He was a very credible witness. His testimony regarding his observation of the 2,000 feet altitude reading, an observation critical to the plaintiffs' case, is the only source of evidence that the 2,000 feet altitude reading ever appeared on the scope. He need have said nothing about this. Dameron did not impress the court as a self-serving witness.

With regard to contributory negligence, one need go no further than the transcript of the cockpit voice recorder prior to the impact. That transcript reads in part as follows:

Time	Source	Content
1107:48		
	CAM-1:	*You know, according to this dumb chit it says thirty-four hundred to Round Hill-is our minimum altitudes.*
1107:53		
	CAM-2:	*Where did you see that?*
	CAM-1:	*Well, here. Round Hill is eleven and a half DME.*
	CAM-2:	*Well, but. . .*
	CAM-1:	*When he clears you, goddamn it that means you can go to your. . .*
1108:02		
	CAM-?:	*Initial approach.*
	CAM-?:	*Yeah!*
	CAM-1:	*Initial approach altitude.*

	CAM-3:	*We're out a . . . twenty-eight for eighteen.*
	CAM-?:	*Right!*
	CAM-3:	*One to go.*
	CAM-2:	*Well, how come that son of a bitch didn't light up because we don't have the . . .*
1108:12		
	CAM-1:	*That's cause you got a thousand to go.*
	CAM-2:	*Well, we had the wrong numbers in it.*
1108:14		
	CAM-1:	*All right.*
	CAM-3:	*Dark in here.*
1108:20		
	CAM-2:	*And bumpy, too, ha ha ha ha.*
1108:25		
1108:27		
	CAM:	(Sound of altitude alert horn)
	CAM-1:	*I had ground contact a minute ago.*
	CAM-2:	*Yeah, I did, too!*
1108:29		
	CAM-?:	*. . . get some power on this son of a bitch!*
	CAM-1:	*Yeah!*
1108:33		
	CAM-1:	*You got a high sink rate.*
	CAM-2:	*Yeah!*
	CAM-?:	*We're going uphill.*
	CAM-?:	*We're right there, we're on course.*
	CAM-?:	(two voices simultaneously) *Yeah.*
1108:43		
	CAM-1:	*You ought to see ground outside in just a minute.*
	CAM-1:	*Hang in there, boy!*
1108:48		
	CAM-3:	*We're getting seasick!*
1108:57		
	CAM:	(Sound of altitude alert)
	CAM-2:	*Boy, it was . . . wanted to go right down through there, man.*
	CAM-?:	*Yeah!*

1109:01

    CAM-2:   *Must have had a hell of a down draft.*

1109:14

    CAM: (Radio altimeter warning horn sounds then
                stops)

1109:19

    CAM-2:   *Boy!*

1109:20

    CAM-1:   *Get some power on!*

1109:21

    CAM: (Radio altimeter warning horn sounds, then
                stops)

1109:22

    CAM: (Sound of impact)

The "chit" referred to above is the Jeppesen Approach Chart on which is shown the Minimum Sector Altitude [MSA] for the area in which the aircraft was traveling as being 3,300 feet, and 3,400 feet as the minimum altitude for this aircraft's heading toward Round Hill. Evident also from the transcript is the pilot's feeling that the clearance the controller previously had given them allowed them to descend to an altitude of 1,800 feet, when, as hereafter pointed out, in fact they were not allowed to descend to that altitude until after the aircraft had over-headed the facility, which in this case was Round Hill. The transcript further reveals that at 1108:21, a full minute prior to impact, the altitude alert horn sounded. This was an indication the aircraft was 500 feet above terrain. It sounded again at 1108:57 and 1109:14. Apparently, it was ignored by the entire crew. Nor did any member of the crew, as required by TWA training procedures, verbally notice the sounding. The court could not accept the plaintiffs' evidence that these horns are to be disregarded until on final approach. The argument that, because there was no evidence the crew was aware whether the alerts were true or spurious, they were relieved of the duty to heed them was incredulous.

Plaintiffs' position consistently was the advice given by the controller at 1104:16 that, "TWA 514, you're cleared for VOR/DME approach to runway one two," allowed them to descend to 1,800 feet. This, the court determined, was an incorrect interpretation of the clearance and those so interpreting it were negligent in doing so. The interpretation of "cleared for approach" as used in the *Airmen's Information Manual*, was the subject of correspondence between the FAA and TWA as early as 1970. The response of the FAA to the inquiry by TWA was as follows:

> *The phrase, "He should begin descent as soon as possible" was deleted, as it is not appropriate to the situation described. In other words, when the pilot is "cleared for an approach," it indicates that the type of approach to be executed is the pilot's choice, and such a clearance would include an altitude restriction if the controller deemed it necessary. It was felt that the deleted phrase could be misleading, particularly, to a pilot on a direct flight. It was felt that such pilot could forget his responsibility of obstruction clearance and descend to an initial approach altitude while still some distance from the airport, even if this altitude would be below obstruction clearance altitude in the area in which he is operating.*

Plaintiffs attempted to insulate the co-pilot, Kresheck, from the contributory negligence of the pilot, Brock. Clearly, of course, Brock could not abdicate his legal duties as the pilot in command by turning over the controls to Kresheck. Nevertheless, Kresheck had a duty as co-pilot to view the approach plate, to understand the clearance given, to be aware of the terrain, to be familiar with the FAA regulations, to bring to the attention of the captain any deviations from safe procedures, and when at the controls, to take such action as may be necessary and available to avoid the crash just as Brock would have, had he, Kresheck, been at the controls. In all of these duties, Kresheck failed.

The finding by the court that the United States was not guilty of primary negligence rendered it unnecessary to reach the issue whether the doctrine of last clear chance was applicable. Virginia divided its last clear chance plaintiffs into two categories: the *helpless* plaintiff and the *inattentive* plaintiff. Different duties were imposed on a defendant depending upon the category in which a particular plaintiff fell. A "helpless" plaintiff was one who would negligently place oneself in a situation of peril from which one physically would be unable to remove oneself. The "inattentive" plaintiff was one who would negligently placed oneself in a position of peril from which one physically would be unable to remove oneself, but would be unconscious of the personal peril.

Clearly the plaintiffs here were not helpless plaintiffs within the meaning of the above definition. The plaintiffs were the inattentive category. Even here, of course the availability of the doctrine to these plaintiffs presupposed the existence of sufficient time for effective action, a finding foreclosed by the court's contrary finding in its discussion of primary negligence. The doctrine of last clear chance has always been considered in reality a doctrine of proximate cause. This court found no lack of ordinary care or violation of any duty owed the aircraft on the part of the air traffic controller after he actually saw the peril of the aircraft. The last clear chance to avoid this accident was had by the crew, not the controller. If the crew had only heeded one of the many warnings available to them right up to the 1109:14 alert warning, the crash could have been avoided.

The U.S. District Court concluded the plaintiffs were not entitled to recover in this action.

LESSONS LEARNED

As tragic as certain events in life and death may be, still there is something to be gained from the experience. At a minimum, an aircraft accident ought to teach some lessons on how to avoid a reoccurrence. In addition to investigating accidents, the National Transportation Safety Board also has a duty to promote transportation safety by formulating safety improvement recommendations. It makes such recommendations to the Federal Aviation Administration. Out of the TWA 514 accident came at least four substantive changes; the first of which was a reconstruction of the VOR/DME Runway 12 instrument approach procedure into Dulles International Airport.

Second, the FAA developed a *Pilot/Controller Glossary*, which at a minimum is published in the *Airman's Information Manual* and in the *Air Traffic Control Handbook*. The glossary was compiled to promote a common understanding of the terms used in the air traffic control system. It includes those terms that are intended for pilot/controller communications. The terms are defined in an operational sense, which is applicable to both users and operators of the National Airspace System [NAS].

A third change involved the *Air Traffic Control Handbook* itself. Paragraph 1360, at the time of the TWA 514 accident read, in part, as follows:

> *Issue all of the following to an aircraft before it reaches the approach gate:*
>
> *c. Approach clearance, except when conducting a radar approach. If terrain or traffic does not permit unrestricted descent to lowest published altitude specified in approach procedure prior to final approach descent, controllers shall:*
>
> *(1) Defer issuance of approach clearance until there are no restrictions or,*
>
> *(2) Issue altitude restrictions with approach clearance specifying when or at what point unrestricted descent can be made.*

Subsequent to the TWA 514 accident, the *Air Traffic Control Handbook* was redesigned, and Paragraph 5-123 read, in part, as follows:

> *Issue all of the following to an aircraft before it reaches the approach gate:*
>
> *c. Approach clearance except when conducting a radar approach. Issue approach clearance only after the aircraft is:*

> *(1) Established on a segment of a published route or instrument approach procedure, or*
>
> *(2) Assigned an altitude to maintain until the aircraft is established on a segment of a published route or instrument approach procedure.*

A fourth change occurred in the standard procedures used by pilots. Operational instructions issued to pilots read, in part, as follows:

> *Operations on unpublished routes and use of radar in instrument approach procedures . . . When operating on an unpublished route or while operating on an unpublished route or while being radar vectored, the pilot, when an approach clearance is received, shall . . . maintain the last altitude assigned to that pilot until the aircraft is established on a segment of a published route or instrument approach procedure unless a different altitude is assigned by ATC.*

POSTSCRIPT

Irrespective of who might have been following proper procedure, and who might not have been, maybe the real (or "proximate") cause of the TWA 514 accident was inferred in the dissenting opinion of the NTSB aircraft accident report. It was the failure of both sides to communicate adequately. If there was an element of doubt, perhaps the controller should have been asked to repeat, or to otherwise clarify the clearance. Operation of the National Airspace System is clearly a team effort and communication amongst the team players is of paramount importance.

CHAPTER 18

INSURANCE

*Insurance is a rational attempt to escape the perils and uncertainties
of life through a mechanism of repayment for catastrophic losses,
either to oneself, or to another person negligently damaged.*

TORT LIABILITY

"Insurance" is a contract whereby one person undertakes to "indemnify" (or repay) another against loss, damage, or liability arising
from unknown and unexpected events. Liability for injury to others can
be costly, and often beyond the ability of the average person, or company, to bear alone. Insurance is one way by which the perils of life
and of business may be shared.

The principle of insurance is simple. Those exposed to similar hazards pay pre-established fees (called "premiums") into a central fund.
When a member of the group is exposed to one of the hazards for
which the member (or company) is insured, money is drawn from the
general fund to indemnify the insured person. In other words, the person is compensated for the loss incurred. Since many contribute to the
fund, and depending on the odds of occurrence, only a relatively few
suffer an actual loss, the cost of individual premiums is small relative
to the proportionally catastrophic effects of an accidental occurrence.

The field of insurance is particularly interrelated with two aspects
of law. First, because there is a contract (or policy) involved insurance
bears a direct relationship to the *law of contracts*. Second, liability
insurance is a matter of *tort law* because it provides protection when
someone brings a suit against the insured for loss or injury under circumstances where the court could find the person liable. A person is

"liable," that is, responsible or legally obligated, if he or she causes injury or loss to another person, either intentionally or negligently. The law views both types of actions as "torts."

Insurance has a long relationship with the aviation industry. The practice of insuring aviation interests began within eight years of the first successful controlled, powered flight by the Wright Brothers in 1903. At that time, a British insurance company, Lloyd's of London, developed an early policy to cover the legal liability of aircraft participating in an air meet. The first aircraft hull insurance was sold in 1917 by the Queen Insurance Company of America, and by 1920 the insurance market was expanded through such notable underwriters as the Home Insurance Company of America, the New York Fire Insurance Company, the Firemen's Fund Insurance Company, Globe and Rutgers Fire Insurance Company, and the National Liberty Insurance Company. Nevertheless, until World War II, aviation grew slowly, as did the aviation-related insurance industry. The field of aviation expanded rapidly following the war, and the demands for insurance coverage in the aviation field grew accordingly.

THE INSURANCE INDUSTRY

Those individuals who sell insurance are known as "agents" or "brokers." An insurance agent is employed by an insurance company to sell policies for it. That is, the person works for, and has the authority to act in behalf of, the insuring company. Conversely, an insurance "broker" is a middle person who represents the insured, and may obtain coverage for his or her client from any one of several insurance companies. A broker is an independent who is normally licensed to do business in one or more states.

The insurance "underwriter" is the company actually assuming the risk and the one responsible for paying the claims in the event of catastrophic loss. From the early days of aviation insurance, underwriters joined together to form aviation insurance groups. Through insurance groups, underwriters can spread the risks of a major, overwhelming occurrence. Prominent among these early aviation insurance groups was the United States Aircraft Insurance Group [USAIG], formed in 1928, and Associated Aviation Underwriters, formed a year later in 1929. Both of these two groups are active today. Other groups of underwriters in the domestic market have included: the Insurance Company of North America [INA], Aviation Office of America [AOA], South Eastern Aviation Underwriters [SEAU], Southern Marine Aviation [SMA], Avemco Insurance Company, and National Aviation.

There are also some foreign underwriters such as Lloyds of London, British Aviation Insurance Group and other European companies.

Traditional aviation coverage (see Table 18.1, "Aviation Insurance Terminology") comes in one of two forms, aircraft *hull* insurance and aviation *liability* insurance. Hull insurance covers physical damage to the aircraft itself such as crash, fire, theft or vandalism. Liability policies are written principally to cover the operation of aircraft and for operation of airports, including what is commonly referred to as "hangar keepers" insurance.[1] Reference is sometimes made to aviation "product liability" as a third category of aviation insurance. Product liability insurance is for coverage against claims caused by a defective product, or by improper service or repairs.

In most instances the hull damage provisions together with liability coverage are contained in comprehensive or combination aviation or aircraft policies, along with additional coverage such as medical payments, and passenger baggage and cargo liability. For example, airlines may have their aircraft liability insurance in "broad form," which covers most activities including denied boarding, baggage loss, intentional torts, and so forth.

Other forms of non-aviation insurance, *per se*, may be tied to aviation-related insurance, especially through policy exclusions such as an "aviation exclusion clause." An aviation exclusion invalidates policy coverage under circumstances specifically included in the exclusionary clause. For example, a normal life insurance policy may not cover the insured while that person is engaged in an aerial activity such as actually piloting an aircraft.[2]

Conversely, certain types of coverage may be included within the realm of aviation insurance. "Trip insurance," which an airline passenger may elect to purchase to cover lost expenses if a trip is cancelled or interrupted, is an example. Another form of travel insurance covers loss of life and limb. The latter form is really nothing more than short-term life insurance. The policy is in effect only for the duration of an air carrier flight.[3]

---

[1] *See Buffalo Air Park v. National General Insurance Co.*, CCH 15 AVI. ¶ 18,432 (1980).
[2] *See Hawkins v. State Life Insurance Co.*, CCH 13 AVI. ¶ 17,212 (1972).
[3] *See Lachs v. Fidelity and Casualty Co.*, 118 N.E. 2d 555 (1954).

ble 18.1—AVIATION INSURANCE TERMINOLOGY

AIRCRAFT INSURANCE
—in general, insures the owner for loss or damage
to the *aircraft*, and for *liability*.

Aircraft Hull Insurance—for physical loss or damage to the aircraft:

- *All Risk Basis-Not in Motion* is applicable to physical loss or damage while the aircraft is on the ground and not moving under its power or resulting momentum. This coverage includes a loss occurring while the aircraft is being pushed into the hangar or towed by a tractor, but does not insure against damage the aircraft may sustain while taxiing.
- *All Risk Basis* includes the conditions above, and adds physical loss or damage while the aircraft is taxiing and in flight.
- *Deductibles* are amounts, usually less than the total losses, for which the insured is responsible. Hull coverage can be written with or without deductibles. When coverage is written with deductibles, the amounts are stated in the declarations. Generally, a lesser amount will be applicable to *not-in-motion* losses, as contrasted to *in-motion* losses.
- *Aircraft Uses* may determine operational conditions under which the aircraft is insured.
- *In Motion* refers to while the aircraft is moving under its own power, or the momentum generated therefrom, or while it is in flight and, if the aircraft is a rotorcraft, any time the rotors are rotating.
- *Insured Value* is the amount, which is stated in the policy as the "Insured Value." Usually, this amount represents the purchase price of the aircraft, if new, or the current market value, if used.
- *Reinstatement* is a return to an original value. In the event of loss or damage, the insured value of an aircraft is reduced by the amount of such loss or damage. During repairs, the insured value is increased by the amount of repairs completed until the insured value of the aircraft as originally written is fully restored or "reinstated."

Aircraft Liability Insurance:

- *Bodily Injury, Excluding Passenger Liability* insures the liability for damages because of bodily injury, sickness, disease, mental anguish or death suffered by any person or persons other than passengers, resulting from an occurrence arising out of the ownership, maintenance or use of any insured aircraft.
- *Passenger Bodily Injury Liability* insures the liability for damages because of bodily injury, sickness, disease, mental anguish, or death suffered by any passenger or passengers due to any occurrences arising out of the ownership, maintenance or use of any insured aircraft.
- *Private Business and Pleasure* insurance is for individually owned aircraft used for the owner's personal purposes, and for which no charge is made or direct profit derived from use of the aircraft.
- *Industrial Aid (Business or Corporate Use)* insurance is for company-owned aircraft used for the transportation of executives, employees, and non-fare paying guests of the company in furtherance of the company's business interests.
- *Limited Commercial* insurance is for those aircraft used for profit making purposes such as instruction and rental to others, specifically excluding transportation of passengers or cargo for hire.
- *Commercial* insurance covers the same exposures as Limited Commercial insurance, but it includes passenger or cargo carrying for hire.
- *Special Purposes Uses* insurance includes such categories as crop dusting, spraying, hunting, seeding, banner towing or any use which by its nature requires more detailed evaluation and special rating.

Aircraft Hull Terms:

- *Aircraft* means the Aircraft described in the policy including the propulsion system and equipment usually installed in the Aircraft.
- *In Flight* means the time commencing with the actual take-off run of the aircraft and continuing thereafter until it has completed its landing roll. Or, if the aircraft is a rotorcraft, from

the time the rotors start to revolve under power for the purpose of flight until they subsequently cease to revolve.

- *Property Damage Liability* insures the liability for damages resulting from injury or destruction of property, including the loss of use thereof due to an occurrence arising out of the ownership, maintenance or use of any insured aircraft.
- *Single Limit Liability* the three classifications above may be written under a single limit and without a per person limitation.
- *Medical Expense* provides payment of medical, surgical, ambulance, hospital, professional nursing service and, in the event of death, reasonable funeral expenses.
- *Voluntary Settlement* provides that the underwriter will voluntarily pay an amount, not exceeding the voluntary settlement limits stated in the policy, in settlement of claims for dismemberment or death of passengers, regardless of the insured's liability.

Aircraft Liability Terms:

- *Aircraft*, with respect to liability coverage, is the aircraft described in the policy or any other aircraft being used as a temporary substitute.
- A *Passenger* is any person in or boarding the aircraft for the purpose of riding or flying therein.
- *Occurrence* means an accident, including continuous or repeated exposure to conditions, which results in bodily injury or property damage neither expected nor intended.
- *Airport and Fixed Base Operator's Liability* includes a wide range of policies designed for the particular needs of commercial aircraft and airport owners, operators and lessees.
- *Airport Premises and/or Operations* is coverage of ownership, maintenance or use of an airport. It is similar to owner's, landlord's and tenant's liability coverage against ordinary premises hazards, but includes aviation risks.
- *Contractual Liability* is coverage afforded the insured for the liability he or she assumes under the hold harmless provisions of a lease or contract agreement with others such as the airport owner and/or lessor, the gasoline or oil supplier, fuel equipment supplier and others.
- *Alterations and/or Construction* covers operations by independent contractors for the insured who may be covered for the

extension of runways, installation of new landing strips, demolition or alterations of existing structures, and the construction of hangars, administration buildings or repair shops.

- *Products and Completed Operations* is liability insurance for damages arising from products and completed operations hazards. It is for the supplier of aircraft products and for the airport owner and fixed base operator in relation to the manufacture, sale, and distribution of products, repairs and modifications to aircraft, and to the performance of services relating to aircraft products.
- *Hangarkeepers Liability* insures against liability for loss or damages to aircraft which are the property of others and in the custody of the Insured for safe keeping, storage or repairs and while in or on the described premises. Basic Hangarkeepers' coverage excludes aircraft while in flight. This insurance provides two limits of liability. The lower limit represents the insurer's maximum liability for any one aircraft, and the higher limit the maximum liability for any one loss.
- *Aircraft Manufacturers Products Liability* is insurance of the products liability exposures of manufacturers of aircraft, engines, and component parts. It provides coverage for damage arising out of the use of goods or products manufactured, sold, handled or distributed by the insured.
- *Workers Compensation and Employers Liability* insures employers engaged in aircraft operations.

Source: Associated Aviation Underwriters [AAU]. These are abbreviated definitions of terms used specifically by AAU, and are presented herein as exemplary only. Insurance terms may vary from one company to another, and may even vary from one policy form to another even within the same company. Specific policies must be consulted to determine precise meanings used therein.

Faced with vanishing commissions from airlines as well as other transportation providers, travel agents are finding new sources of revenue by selling trip insurance. These policies enable travel agents to collect up to 35% in sales commissions. In the last quarter of 2001, trip-insurance provider Travel Guard, alone, signed up 3,500 new travel agents to sell its product. However, consumers planning a trip are warned that although travel insurance can cover many unforeseen circumstances, there are plenty of exceptions, or exclusions for which they may not be aware.[4]

RISK SPREADING

In writing comprehensive policies, the inherent risks involved, and/or the extensive monetary costs, may be so great, that any one company, or even a group of insurance underwriters, may be unwilling to underwrite the total amount of a given policy by themselves. Spreading the risk does for underwriters what the insurance policy does for the individual.

To spread the risks, the policy may be covered to the full extent by several underwriters through either *horizontal* or *vertical* layering. For example, an insured may wish to have $100 million of insurance coverage. To meet this objective, Underwriter A may provide the first $10 million of coverage; Underwriter B covers the next $15 million; Underwriter C, the next $25 million; and Underwriter D, the upper $50 million limits. This would be an example of horizontal layering. In horizontal layering, if the damages were less than $25 million, only Underwriters A and B would be responsible for making payments to the insured.

Alternatively, suppose each underwriting company assumed a quota (or percentage) share of the total risk, with Underwriter A assuming say 10% of the risk; Underwriter B, 15%; Underwriter C, 25%; and Underwriter D, 50%. This would constitute vertical layering of the coverage limits. And where, say, the total coverage is the same $100 million, but where the total damages amount to only $25 million, under vertical layering, each of the underwriters would pay their portion of the insured's (actual) loss. Underwriter A would be responsible

---

[4] Brian J. O'Connor, *Travel Agents' Play: Trip Insurance*, Wall St. J. (Wed., Jul. 17, 2002), at D2.

for paying $2.5 million; Underwriter B would pay $3.75 million; Underwriter C, $6.25 million; and Underwriter D, $12.5 million.

RISK MANAGEMENT

The insurance industry has come to refer to its professional activity as "risk management," defined as, "the procedures and practices by which the industry recognizes and controls inherent and or environmental perils of a fortuitous nature, which by their occurrence would adversely affect either an individual or a business." Risk management is a formal management process that helps ensure financial stability and minimize losses. Through risk management, individuals, as well as corporate groups and public agencies, protect their assets and financial resources.

The elements of risk management may be described as:

- *analysis*, wherein there is recognition of risk exposure;
- *evaluation*, to measure potential or anticipated loses;
- *abatement*, to determine actions to be taken to reduce or eliminate risks such as loss control, safety programs and product integrity;
- *transfer* of the risk liability and reducing some of the known expense such as premiums or by contractual *hold harmless* provisions; and
- *risk accounting*, including an audit of the procedural aspects of risk management.

UNDERWRITER RESPONSIBILITIES

Insurance companies have two basic responsibilities to the insured, to *defend* and to *indemnify*. The first is the duty to defend the insured in court. This responsibility applies primarily to liability insurance. Inherent obligations in the duty to defend are to investigate claims, to retain attorneys, and pay associated costs including reasonable expenses of the insured, costs of experts, and costs of court exhibits and models. Appeals within the judicial system are also the responsibility of the insurer. The duty to defend is perhaps the most valuable provision of an aviation insurance policy. The cost of providing this service could well exceed the cost of paying damages.[5]

---

[5] *See Standard Oil Co. v. Hawaiian Insurance & Guarantee Co.*, CCH 17 AVI ¶18,410 (1982).

The second fundamental responsibility of the insurance provider is the duty to indemnify, or to pay damages according to the insurance agreement under terms such as "to pay on behalf of Insured all sums which the Insured shall become legally obligated to pay as damages" up to the policy limits less any deductible. A "deductible" is an amount of risk for which the insured is responsible, before the terms of an insurance policy become effective. For instance, say the policy is written with $10,000 limits and a $250 deductible; and say the actual damages incurred amount to $1,000. The insured is responsible in this case for paying the first $250 (the deductible) and the insurance company is responsible for the remaining $750 liability.

Rather than pay damages outright, the insurer may have the right to resolve the dispute through voluntary settlement. Normally, the insurance company also retains the right to subrogate. "Subrogation" is "the right of first party insurer to seek recovery from others who bear or share responsibility for loss or damage to the insured property." In other words, the insurance company pays the claims of the insured, but then assumes the right to make claims against any third parties who may have any responsibility in the losses suffered by the insured. Subrogation places the insurance company, which has paid out claims against the policy, in the same legal position as the insured was in originally, to make claims against third parties. If payment for damages is recovered by the insurance company, the insurer keeps the money. If damages are not recovered from the third party, the insurance company is nevertheless obligated to settle the claims for damages suffered by the insured.

Duties to defend and to indemnify have traditionally been the obligation of insurance companies over and above insurance policy limits, irrespective of the cost of providing these services. However, owing to the rapidly expanding costs of providing legal defense, the insurance industry could conceivably in the future take the position that costs of defense, including attorneys fees, are deductible from the total liability of the policy. For example, if the policy limits were $500,000 and it cost $100,000 to defend the case, there would be only $400,000 left to pay for damages. However, such an approach would significantly reduce insurers' incentives to hold down litigation costs and attorneys' fees, since they effectively could be passed on to the insured.

A problem plaguing aviation, as well as other industries has been not only the high cost of insurance premiums, but the very availability of insurance coverage as well. In the aerospace industry, it became a problem of epic proportions in the decade of the 1980s, particularly in the manufacture of light, general aviation airplanes. The costs for product liability insurance virtually brought to a halt the production of small, single-engine aircraft in the United States, until the government intervened by placing limitations on products liability claims.

Insurance coverage goes into effect according to contractual provisions. To be in effect, the policy need not necessarily be in writing,[6] nor if in writing, personally received by the insured. If the policy has been dropped in the mail, the courts normally consider that the policy has been *constructively delivered*. Many aviation policies are issued initially in a "binder," or by memorandum of a verbal contract given by the company or its agent to the insured. The binder and/or oral contract provides for temporary protection until a formal policy is issued. The binder sums up the coverage the insured agreed to purchase, even if the insured may not have as yet made a payment. However, if the insurance company does not issue a binder or an oral acceptance, the insurance coverage generally does not go into effect until the policy is delivered, albeit "constructively."

In filing claims with insurance companies, so long as the terms of the agreement have not been violated, the insurer will normally indemnify without complications, especially where claims are relatively simple and modest in cost. Where the case is more complicated, and where losses amount to large sums of money, it may take the insurance company or its adjuster more time to settle the account. The insurer will nevertheless, settle it. However, the insurance company may likely reject the claim if it thinks it has sufficient legal grounds for refusing to pay. Some insurance companies are infamous for being sticklers, but there is also the problem of the less than honest policyholder.

In obtaining insurance, there are two fundamental axioms. First, the insurance consumer owes "a duty to the underwriter to be honest." False statements made in acquiring insurance may later become grounds for breach of contract, thereby relieving the underwriter of its obligation. The second axiom admonishes the insurance consumer to "shop for a good company, not just cheap premiums." Under-priced premiums are normally associated with unreasonable exclusions in the policy, and a company with little intent of paying for losses.

What is considered sufficient grounds for non-payment may nevertheless be a matter of interpretation. An insurance policy is a contract like any other contract. If the insurer breaches the contract, the insured has the right to bring a legal action to compel the company to meet its obligations. This is the essence of the preponderance of litigation involving insurance claims, and of the exemplary cases that follow.

---

[6] *See GRP, Ltd. v. United States Aviation Underwriters*, CCH 14 AVI. ¶ 18,423 (1978).

WAR RISK INSURANCE

Before the tragic events of September 11, 2001, insurance carriers could calculate potential liability risk on the basis of the number of passengers a particular aircraft could seat or its cargo capacity, capped by the applicable liability regime and the value of the aircraft itself. But on September 11th, suicide hijackers turned commercial aircraft into guided missiles, aiming them at symbols of American economic and military prowess. After 9/11 the aviation insurance market could face the prospect of liability for damage to buildings and the high-salaried professionals working in them, and the potential proliferation of terrorist events, including the firing of heat-seeking missiles or other ground-based weapons at commercial aircraft. The United States was at war, and commercial aviation was among the most prominent of its casualties. Aircraft manufacturers were potentially at risk for their design of cockpit doors, and architects for their design of buildings unable to withstand the impact and combustion of penetrating commercial aircraft. The inability to predict frequency or degree of risk rendered the insurance carriers impotent to price it, thus creating market apoplexy.

Before the dawn of commercial aviation, insurance companies had placed war and terrorist risk insurance on a short leash in the maritime trade, insuring them separately, and allowing re-assessment and cancellation on short notice. In 1968, after the Israeli raid on Beirut International Airport, the London insurance market adopted the "War, Hi-Jacking and Other Perils Exclusion Clause" (AVN 48B), providing, *inter alia,* that policies did not cover acts of war, hostilities, sabotage, or hijacking.[7] But most coverage could be restored through a write back endorsement (AVN52C) inserted into the carrier's all-risk policy, or via a stand-alone war risks policy issued by war risk insurers, which gave insurers an option to cancel such coverage on seven days notice.[8]

On September 17, 2001, London aviation insurance underwriters announced they would cancel war risk coverage as of September 23rd.[9]

---

[7] *Int'l Air Transport Ass'n, The Liability Reporter* 53 (Feb. 2002).

[8] Richard Campbell, *Terrorism Insurance and War Risk Exclusions* (unpublished address before the ABA Tort Trial and Insurance Practice Section, Aviation and Space Law Committee, Washington, D.C., 2004).

[9] In 2004, aviation insurance underwriters announced they would exclude coverage for damages caused by dirty bombs, electromagnetic pulse devices, and biochemical materials.

They subsequently offered insurance at financially prohibitive levels (an average 91% increase in hull insurance premiums, and an 80% increase in liability insurance), capping liability at $50 million for third party liability war risk coverage.[10]

To ameliorate the devastating legal and financial impact of the events of September 11th on the U.S. airline industry, within three weeks the U.S. Congress passed the Air Transportation Safety and System Stabilization Act [ATSSSA],[11] which: (1) established federal war risk insurance for the industry;[12] (2) provided U.S. airlines with $15 billion in relief ($5 billion immediately, and up to $10 billion in guaranteed loans); (3) capped the liability of the two airlines involved—United Airlines and American Airlines—at their insurance limits, and eliminated punitive damages for September 11th claims;[13] and (4) established a no-fault September 11th Victims' Compensation Fund, directed by a Special Master who would determine compensation for damage to persons or property resulting from these terrorist events, as reduced by payments from collateral sources.[14] Liability for the events of September 11th eventually totaled nearly $40 billion.[15]

---

[10] Rod Margo, *War Risk Insurance in the Aftermath of September 11*, 18 ABA Air & Space Lawyer 16 (summer 2003).

[11] Pub. L. 107-42, 115 Stat. 230. *See* Kristin Buja Schroeder, *Failing to Prevent the Tragedy, but Facing the Trauma: The Aviation Disaster Family Assistance Act of 1996 and the Air Transportation Safety and System Stabilization Act of 2001*, 67 J. Air L. & Com. 189 (2002).

[12] ATSSSA reimbursed U.S. air carriers for the insurance premium increases to Oct. 1, 2002, and authorized the U.S. Department of Transportation [USDOT] to provide insurance and reinsurance for U.S. air carriers. DOT offered war risk coverage beyond the $50 million private market cap. ATSSSA also capped third party liability of U.S. airlines at $100 million, with the U.S. government assuming liability above that level. Rod Margo, *War Risk Insurance in the Aftermath of September 11*, 18 ABA Air & Space Lawyer 16, 19 (summer 2003). Fourteen months after the terrorist attacks on the World Trade Center and Pentagon, Congress passed the Homeland Security Act of 2002, which extended federal airline war risk insurance until Aug. 31, 2003 (and provided the Secretary with the discretionary authority to extend until the end of 2003). Pub. L. 107-296, 116 Stat. 2135 (Nov. 25, 2002). 49 U.SC. § 44302 (2004). This date was subsequently extended to Aug. 31, 2004, and then to Dec. 31, 2004, when the Secretary of Transportation concluded that war risk insurance was not commercially available on reasonable terms and conditions. 69 Fed. Reg. 5236 (Feb. 3, 2004).

[13] Subsequent legislation also capped liability for the aircraft manufacturers, the Port Authority of New York and New Jersey, the airports and the owners of the World Trade Center, to the limits of their insurance coverage. That amounted to about U.S. $1.5 billion per aircraft, and U.S. $650 million for the Port Authority. J. Grimaldi, *After a Respectful Pause, Lawyers Line Up to Sue*, Washington Post (Sep. 9, 2002), at E1.

[14] Responding to claims that the Special Master was imposing a *de facto* limit on liability, the court in *Colaio v. Feinberg*, 262 F. Supp. 2d 273 (S.D.N.Y. 2003), upheld the statute and the Special Master's schedule of liability. The Second Circuit affirmed the holding in *Schneider v. Feinberg*, 345 F.3d 135 (2nd Cir. 2003). Injured parties or estates that chose to forgo the Compensation Fund

Congress also promulgated the Terrorist Risk Insurance Act of 2002,[16] which filled the insurance void for a limited period of time, and the Aviation and Transportation Security Act [ATSA],[17] which federalized the airport security passenger and baggage screening function (which had theretofore been performed by U.S. airlines under Federal Aviation Regulations as an unfunded mandate), thereby indirectly and prospectively reducing carrier liability.[18]

---

could bring suit in the federal district court for the southern district of New York. If they decide to litigate they will have to establish traditional common law negligence and proximate cause, both of which may be formidable barriers to recovery. Thus, injured parties were given the alternative to file a claim for compensation from the Victims' Compensation Fund, directed by a Special Master, or file suit in the southern district of New York. *But see Burnett v. Al Baraka Investment and Development Corp.*, 274 F. Supp. 2d 86 (D.C. Cir. 2003) (ATSSSA's exclusive jurisdiction provision does not "encompass claims against Sep. 11 terrorists and their conspirators," and litigation may be pursued under the Anti-Terrorism Act, 18 U.S.C. § 2333, which allows any U.S. nationals injured by an act of international terrorism to file suit in any U.S. district court). Some 2,838 victims applied to the fund for compensation by the Dec. 22, 2003, deadline. *The Victims Compensation Fund: A Model for Future Mass Casualty Situations*, 29 Transp. L. J. 283, 297 (2002). Total payouts to victims exceeded $1.5 billion. *Id.* at 298. By Oct., 2004, the 9/11 Victims Compensation Fund had issued awards to 2,861 claimants, ranging to a low of $500 to a high of $8.6 million, after setoffs. http://www.usdoj.gov/victimcompensation/payments_injury.html (visited Oct. 12, 2004).

[15] It has been estimated that the total payout from government, insurers, and charities to 9/11 property damage and personal injury victims and their families exceeded $38 billion. Of that, insurers contributed more than $20 billion, while governmental institutions contributed $16 billion. Devlin Barrett, *Compensation for Sept. 11 Victims Tops $38 Billion*, Montreal Gazette (Nov. 9, 2004), at A23.

[16] Congress passed the *Terrorism Risk Insurance Act of 2002*, which created a three year federal Terrorism Insurance Program (until Dec. 31, 2005) administered by the Treasury Dept., to provide assistance to the insurance industry. Pub. L. No. 107-297 (Nov. 26, 2002). The U.S. established Equitime for U.S. carriers, while Europe established Eurotime. The International Civil Aviation Organization attempted to establish war risk insurance coverage under Globaltime as a non-profit entity backed by governmental guarantees which, as of this writing, has failed to achieve sufficient financial commitment to be implemented.

[17] Pub. L. 107-71, 15 Stat. 597.

[18] Actions for negligence for the negligence of screening functions performed by TSA employees will now have to be pursued under the Federal Tort Claims Act [FTCA], which provides:

> *The United States shall be liable, respecting the provisions of this title relating to tort claims, in the same manner and to the same extent as a private individual under like circumstances, but shall not be liable for interest prior to judgment or for punitive damages.*

28 U.S.C. § 2674. However, carriers may be liable for the security functions that remain with them, such as the negligence of ticketing agents in failing to designate the baggage of a suspicious passenger for enhanced screening, or the negligence of a pilot in leaving the cockpit door unlocked, for example. Often, the most significant exception to governmental liability under the FTCA is for a "discretionary function." Specifically, the Act's provisions do not apply, *inter alia*, to:

> *any claim based upon an act or omission of an employee of the Government, exercising due care, in the execution of a statute or regulation . . . or based on the exercise or perform-*

AIR CARRIER LIABILITY

Section 401 of the Federal Aviation Act of 1958 provides that, "No air carrier shall engage in any air transportation unless there is in force a certificate issued by the Board authorizing such carrier to engage in such transportation." Air carriers classified as "air taxi operators" are exempt from Section 401.[19] In order to protect travelers and shippers by aircraft operated by certificated air carriers, these air carriers must demonstrate their ability to compensate such travelers and shippers through adequate policies of insurance or plans for self-insurance in the amounts prescribed by the federal government for which the carrier(s) "may become liable for bodily injuries to or the death of any person, or for loss of or damage to property of others . . ." resulting from the operation or maintenance of (their) aircraft.

The economic regulations of the Department of Transportation require that certain air carriers waive the passenger liability limits[20] and certain defenses provided for in the Warsaw Convention. In so doing, the carriers subject themselves to liability for death or injury up to $75,000 per passenger. This requirement applies to all direct U.S. and

---

ance or the failure to exercise or perform a discretionary function or duty . . . whether or not the discretion be abused.

28 U.S.C. § 2680(a). *See* Paul Stephen Dempsey, *Privatization of the Air: Government Liability for Privatized Air Traffic Services*, 28 Annals of Air & Space L. 95, 109-111 (2003). The seminal federal case on the discretionary function exemption is *United States v. Varig*, 467 U.S. 797 (1984), a case involving the issue of whether the FAA should be liable for its alleged negligent failure to inspect a Boeing 707 aircraft that it had certified as airworthy but that crashed near Paris, France, when the lavatory caught fire. The U.S. Supreme Court held that it is "the nature of the conduct, rather than the status of the actor that governs whether the discretionary function applies . . . ." *Id.* at 813. The purpose of the exemption was to "prevent judicial 'second guessing' of legislative and administrative decisions [of federal agencies] grounded in social, economic, and political policy through the medium of an action in tort." *Id.* at 814. In *Varig*, the Supreme Court observed that Congress had given the FAA broad authority to establish and implement a comprehensive program of enforcement and compliance with aircraft safety standards, and held that the FAA's policy of "spot-checking" aircraft was acceptable based on the need of its employees "to make policy judgments regarding the degree of confidence that might reasonably be placed in a given manufacturer, the need to maximize compliance with FAA regulations, and the efficient allocation of agency resources." *Id.* at 820. Such discretionary acts were shielded from liability under the FTCA because they fell within the range of choices permitted by the Federal Aviation Act and were the results of policy determinations. Other U.S. Supreme Court decisions assessing the "discretionary function" exemption from liability have noted that conduct cannot be discretionary unless it involves an element of judgment or choice: "Where there is room for policy judgment and decision there is discretion." *Dalehite v. United States*, 346 U.S. 15, 34, 36 (1953): The exception protects "the discretion of the executive or the administrator to act according to one's judgment of the best course." The exemption applies "only to conduct that involves the permissible exercise of policy judgment." *Berkovitz by Berkovitz v. United States*, 486 U.S. 531 (1988).

[19] 14 C.F.R. Part 298.

[20] 14 C.F.R. Part 203 .

foreign direct air carriers except for air taxi operators (that are not commuter air carriers) as defined in Title 14 C.F.R. Part 298. In other words, all scheduled air carriers (both "Section 401" and "Part 298" carriers) must waive the Warsaw liability provisions. Moreover, the Montreal Convention of 1999 establishes strict liability up to 100,000 Special Drawing Rights [SDRs] (about $150,000), and presumptive liability beyond. The Montreal Convention applies to international round-trip flights from the U.S., and to international flights where the origin or destination is the U.S. and another nation, which has ratified the Montreal Convention. However, many nations still adhere to the Warsaw Convention, and certain passengers may be subjected to it, though if the flight is to or from the U.S., the Montreal Agreement lifts liability to $75,000 (and more, if "willful misconduct" on behalf of the carrier can be proven).

Though the Warsaw Convention was silent on the issue of whether insurance must be procured, Article 50 of the Montreal Convention of 1999 provides, "States Parties shall require their carriers to maintain adequate insurance covering their liability under this Convention. A carrier may be required by the State Party into which it operates to furnish evidence that it maintains adequate insurance covering its liability under this Convention."

U.S. and foreign direct air carriers must have in effect aircraft accident liability insurance coverage that satisfies federal requirements, and which are much higher than the Warsaw provisions. The minimum air carrier insurance requirements (except for air taxis) in the U.S. is $300,000 for bodily injury to or death of a person, or for damage to property of others, for any one person in any one occurrence, and a total of $20 million per involved aircraft for each occurrence, except that for aircraft of not more than sixty seats or 18,000 pounds maximum payload capacity, carriers need only maintain coverage of $2 million per involved aircraft for each occurrence.

Those air carriers classified as "air taxi operators" must have in effect liability insurance coverage for bodily injury to or death of aircraft passengers of at least $75,000 per person, and a limit for each occurrence in any one aircraft of at least an amount equal to the sum produced by multiplying $75,000 by 75% of the total number of passenger seats installed in the aircraft. Air taxis must also have liability coverage for bodily injury to or death of persons excluding passengers of $75,000 for any one person, and $300,000 for each occurrence; and must also have liability insurance for loss of or damage to property of $100,000 for each occurrence.

It should be kept in mind that these insurance requirements are for liability insurance, of sums that the carrier shall become legally obligated to pay as damages. However, air carriers are not insurers; i.e., they are not subject to absolute liability except under certain circumstances in foreign carriage, and *liability insurance* is not the same thing as *life insurance*.[21] For this reason, many travelers choose to purchase trip or travel insurance that is, in effect a short-term life insurance policy for the duration of the trip.[22]

BAGGAGE AND CARGO LIABILITY

Air carriers engaged in interstate and overseas transportation are required to maintain minimum levels of liability for loss, damage, or delay in the carriage of passenger baggage, and are required to provide certain types of notices to passengers. In any flight segment using an aircraft with more than 60 seats (i.e., "Section 401" carriers), an air carrier's minimum liability for provable direct or consequential damages resulting from the disappearance of, damage to or delay in delivery of a passenger's personal property, including baggage is not less than $1,250 for each passenger. An air carrier must provide to passengers, by conspicuous written material included on or with the passenger's ticket, either a notice of any monetary limitation on the carrier's baggage liability to passengers, or the following notice: "Federal rules require any limit on an airline's baggage liability to be at least $1,250 per passenger."

In international travel, baggage liability is set by the Warsaw Convention at 250 francs per kilogram unless special value was declared,[23] and 5,000 francs per passenger for unchecked baggage,[24] and at 1,000 SDRs (about $1,500) under the Montreal Convention of 1999.[25] Unless actual value is declared, air cargo is subject to the liability limitations shown in Table 18.2, "Limits of Liability for International Air Cargo." Following Table 18.2 are examples of aviation insurance related cases. Also see *Stevenson v. American Airlines*[26] and *Gluckman v. American Airlines*[27] in Chapter 9, "Consumerism."

---

[21] *Id.*

[22] *See Travelers Insurance Co. v. Morrow*, CCH 16 AVI. ¶ 17,605 (1981).

[23] Warsaw Convention, Art. 22(2).

[24] Warsaw Convention, Art. 22(3).

[25] Montreal Convention, Art. 22(2).

[26] *Edward Stevenson and Cheryl Stevenson v. American Airlines, Inc.*, CCH 24 AVI ¶ 17,341 (1992).

[27] *Andrew Gluckman (for himself and as representative of his dog, Floyd) v. American Airlines, Inc.*, CCH 24 AVI ¶ 17,947 (1994).

Table 18.2—LIMITS OF LIABILITY FOR
INTERNATIONAL AIR CARGO

Agreement	*Liability Limits*
The Warsaw Convention (1929)	250 "gold francs" per kg (US$20/kg; US$9.07/lb)
The Hague Protocol (1955)	Same, but explicitly based on total weight of package lost or damaged, or total weight of affected shipment
Montreal Protocol No. 4 (1975), and The Montreal Convention (1999)	17 SDRs per kg (US$25/kg; US$11/lb) Based on total weight of package lost or damaged, or total weight of affected shipment

BUFFALO AIR PARK. v. NATIONAL GENERAL INSURANCE CO.
15 Av. Cas. (CCH) ¶ 18,432 (N.Y.S.Ct. 1980)

Where more than one aircraft is damaged by the same event,
may the damage incurred by each aircraft be considered
a separate occurrence ?

This was an action brought by plaintiff airport operator, Buffalo Air Park, to determine the extent of its hangarkeeper's liability insurance coverage under the terms of a three-year liability insurance policy issued by defendant insurer, National General Insurance Company, on or about May 1, 1977. The dispute centered about the stated limits of the defendant's liability policy, insuring the plaintiff to the extent of $25,000 for any one aircraft and $25,000 for each occurrence. The issue arose as a result of the collapse of the snow-laden roof on the plaintiff's hangar. The accident damaged some 16 aircraft stored in the hangar. The claims of the various aircraft owners far exceeded the alleged policy limit of $25,000 for any one insured occurrence.

Plaintiff argued that the defendant's policy afforded insurance coverage up to a limit of $25,000 for each of the damaged aircraft. In other words, plaintiff contended that the collapse of the roof represented a separate and distinct occurrence as to each and every aircraft damaged thereby. The New York Supreme Court (which in New York, unlike the other 49 states, is the trial court) disagreed, stating that the pertinent policy provisions were made in plain, unambiguous and unequivocal language and was specifically limited to "$25,000 any one aircraft, $25,000 each occurrence, deductible $250."

The word "occurrence" was defined by the policy to mean,

> . . . an accident, or a continuous and repeated
> exposure to conditions, which results in injury
> during the policy period, provided the injury is
> accidentally caused. All damages arising out
> of such exposure to substantially the same
> conditions shall be considered as arising out
> of one occurrence.

As used in the policy, the phrase "one occurrence" clearly meant one accident; one single unexpected, unfortunate event; a single accidental happening or occurrence. While the collapse of plaintiff's roof may have entailed separate and distinct consequences to many aircraft, there was clearly only one single causative accident or event within the meaning of the policy. Under these circumstances the defendant's liability was limited to $25,000, less the deductible requirement of $250, and judgment was entered accordingly. Plaintiff's motion was denied.

HAWKINS v. STATE LIFE INSURANCE CO.
366 F. Supp. 1031 (E.D. Tenn. 1972)

Does an aviation exclusion in an insurance policy
include an aviator killed as a result of war?

This was an action, by the beneficiary of a life insurance policy, to recover the proceeds allegedly due and payable on the insured's death, which occurred June 11, 1968. The defendant, State Life Insurance Company, sought to defeat recovery on the ground that the circumstances of death precluded recovery under the aviation exclusion provision attached to the policy. The plaintiff, however, contended that the insured's death resulted from a *war risk* instead of an *aviation risk*.

When he applied to defendant for insurance, the insured represented that he would enter the United States Army as a pilot. In making the application, he signed a "Supplement to Application" concerning aviation, agreeing that the following would constitute a part of the policy.

> *This policy is issued subject to the express condition and agreement that the following risks are specifically excluded from the coverage afforded by this policy; notwithstanding anything contained in the policy to the contrary.*
>
> *Death of the Insured as a result of travel or flight in, or descent from or with any kind of aircraft, provided the Insured is a pilot, officer, or member of the crew of such aircraft, or is giving or receiving any kind of training or instruction or has any duties aboard such aircraft or requiring descent therefrom.*

The policy's "Premium Waiver Disability Provision" provided that no premiums would be waived if the disability of the insured resulted from "an act of war, declared or undeclared." The policy did not contain a war risk exclusion clause. This implied that war risks were contemplated as covered by the policy. Moreover, the defendant made no claim that war risks were excluded by this policy.

On the date of death the insured left his base in a light observation aircraft and did not return. His plane was found later that day. The Department of the Army's "Report of Casualty," which, by its own terms, was an official certificate of death, stated:

> *DIED 11 June 1968 in Vietnam from burns received while pilot aboard military aircraft which was hit by hostile fire, crashed and burned.*

In general, where an insurer seeks to avoid payment under an exclusion clause the insurer has the burden of showing the facts necessary to defeat recovery. Because the insurer chooses the language in its policies, its policies are construed against it and in favor of the insured.

The question presented in this case was whether the insured's death was within the scope of the aviation exclusion clause. Clearly the insured died while acting as pilot aboard an aircraft in flight, which descended and crashed at the time of his death. Thus, it might appear that recovery should have been barred under a literal interpretation of the aviation exclusion clause. On the other hand, the insured died from burns, which presumably resulted from a fire in his aircraft. The fire was caused either directly or indirectly by hostile action in a combat zone. Whether the hostile gunfire or the crash ignited the flames is immaterial. Either way the proximate cause of death was an act of war. These circumstances showed the insured's death to have been within both a war risk not excluded, and an aviation risk excluded by the policy. The problem was to which risk was his death to be attributed.

The U.S. District Court concluded that aviation was merely a "contributing cause" of death rather than a condition of Captain Hawkins' death but not its proximate cause. The proximate cause was the enemy fire. Facts of this case showed that the insured did not die as a result of aviation, but rather his death was a result of an act of war.

At the time the insurer entered into this contract with the insured, it knew that the insured was going to enter military service shortly thereafter as a pilot. It also knew that there was a military conflict in Southeast Asia where the insured might be assigned. Having accepted premium payments to the time of death, it could not then be permitted to deny liability for this combat death. Had it not been for an act of war his plane would not have crashed.

LACHS v. FIDELITY AND CASUALTY CO.
118 N.E. 2d 555 (N.Y. App. 1954)

*Must the language in an insurance policy be
clearly understood by the insured?*

The day before her death, the decedent made arrangements to fly on the following day. Upon arrival at the airline terminal the next day, the decedent purchased what was advertised as "Airline Trip Insurance" in the sum of $25,000 from an automatic insurance vending machine. She then went to the Consolidated Air Service Counter where she completed her flight arrangements and received from that agency a ticket on Miami Airline, Inc., a non-scheduled airline. In less than an hour she was dead as the result of a crash.

The defendant insurance company refused to honor the insurance policy stating that it intended only to insure passengers on a "scheduled" airline. The plaintiff (daughter and beneficiary of the decedent) claimed the vending machine was situated in front of the Consolidated Air Service counter at which decedent obtained her airline ticket, and that in letters ten times larger than any other words on the machine there appeared the words "Airline Trip Insurance." That is what the decedent believed she was buying.

The defendant insurer pointed to the fact that there was hanging on the wall where decedent picked up her ticket, a fairly large sign which bore the caption, "Non Scheduled Air Carriers Authorized to Conduct Business in This Terminal," and that there followed a list of ten carriers, among which was included "Miami Airline." The decedent should have realized she was flying on a non-scheduled airline. In part, the policy purchased by the decedent read, "This insurance shall apply only to such injuries sustained following the purchase by or for the Insured of a transportation ticket from . . . Scheduled Airline. . . ." The Court of Appeals of New York, however, recognized that "a contract of insurance, drawn by the insurer, must be read through the eyes of the average man on the street or the average housewife who purchases it. Neither of them is expected to carry a copy of the Civil Aeronautics Act of 1938, or Code of Federal Regulations, when taking a plane."

The defendant put one of its automatic vending machines in front of the ticket counter for the Consolidated Air Service, which was utilized by all non-scheduled airlines operating out of the airport as a processing point for their passengers. Before any passenger on a non-scheduled airline could receive a ticket, the passenger was required to present an "exchange order" at said counter. It could be found, the court said, that the insurer was inviting those passengers to insure themselves by its "Airline Trip Insurance."

The plaintiff defined "scheduled airline" by claiming that Miami Airline, Inc., maintained regular, published schedules of fares; schedules showing passenger mile rates; that it held itself out as maintaining regular schedules of flights; tickets were sold for stated hours of departure; and that it was licensed by the Civil Aeronautics Board to carry passengers and freight with large aircraft in interstate, overseas and foreign air transportation.

The definition suggested by the defendant in its brief seemed to the court to require more knowledge than the average layman has. According to the defendant a "Civilian Scheduled Airline" is an "air carrier which obtains a certificate of public convenience and necessity as provided in Section 401 of the Civil Aeronautics Act." It should be noted that the defense was not that a particular flight was not scheduled, but that the airline was not a "civilian" scheduled one. The attempt of defendant to establish that the term "Civilian Scheduled Airline" had a clear and definite meaning caused it to bring forward and present an enormous amount of proof extrinsic to the policy, including a statute, regulations, newspaper and magazine articles. By this mountain of work, it seemed to the court the defendant had established that "Civilian Scheduled Airline" was not at all free from ambiguity and vagueness—if it were not so, the contract of insurance itself would have disclosed the intent of the parties in entering into it.

The New York Court of Appeals (which in New York is the highest appellate court, although in every other state would be called the "Supreme Court") affirmed an order of the appellate division in favor of the plaintiff beneficiary. However, one judge dissented maintaining the policy clearly stated it was limited to flights by "Scheduled Airlines."

TRAVELERS INSURANCE CO. v. MORROW
645 F.2d 41 (10th Cir. 1981)

Does air trip insurance cover flights in private aircraft?

On January 4, 1979, Dale B. Morrow was contemplating a business trip to Honduras, Central America, with two business associates, one of whom was the pilot of a privately owned plane in which they were to make the trip. Morrow was desirous of obtaining insurance upon his life during the trip. He approached the counter in the airport at Tulsa, Oklahoma, where flight insurance was sold. He described the trip to the attendant, and advised her that it would be in a privately owned plane. The attendant selected Travelers Insurance Policy AT(5) from various policies available at the counter. At the Tulsa International Airport this policy was marketed through an independent company which had the insurance concession rights there. The local operation was through an arrangement with the independent company. Travelers had no control over the persons making sales from the booth. The printed AT(5) policy was complete, except for space to fill in the names and addresses of the insured and beneficiary, together with the amount of insurance, the name of the airline and flight number of the plane upon which the insured was to be a passenger. In the space where the flight number was to be recorded, the attendant wrote the words, "Private Air." Upon payment of $2.50, the policy was delivered to Morrow, who shortly thereafter gave it to his wife.

Policy AT(5) was the only Travelers insurance policy authorized for sale at the counter, and the attendant had authority to sell it to the public. The provisions of the policy limited coverage of an insured to injuries sustained while traveling on "Aircraft Operated by a Scheduled Air Carrier," as defined in Section 5 of the policy. Section 5 defined "a Scheduled Air Carrier" as one that held a Certificate of Public Convenience and Necessity issued by the United States Civil Aeronautics Board. The policy also provided that no agent had authority to change or waive any of its provisions. No claim was made that Policy AT(5) covered private plane flights. The evidence disclosed that Morrow was not advised of these provisions, and that he and the sales person assumed that the policy covered the Honduras trip.

Morrow was killed shortly after take-off from Oklahoma City, and subsequently Travelers Insurance Company brought this action seeking a judgment declaring non-liability on the $75,000 airplane flight life insurance policy issued to Morrow. Travelers argued that coverage in the policy was limited to passengers on regularly scheduled airline flights and did not provide coverage for passengers in private planes.

Norma Morrow, conceded that the AT(5) Travelers policy did not cover flights in private airplanes, and that the sales person at the Tulsa International Airport insurance booth did not have authority to change or modify the provisions of the policy. It was urged, however, that the representative at the Tulsa Airport had authority from Travelers Insurance Company to sell policies to passengers traveling on regularly scheduled flights, but that the attendant, by mistake sold such a policy to Morrow, representing that it was for a private flight, and that Travelers was *estopped* to deny liability. The trial court rejected this argument and found for the insurance company. Morrow appealed.

The U.S. Court of Appeals for the 10th Circuit stated that insurance policies are generally prepared by insurance companies, and ambiguities or uncertainties are strictly construed against the company. Generally, however, parties are bound by the policy provisions under the law of contracts. The failure of an insured to read the policy does not relieve him from its provisions. It is also fundamental that an insured is chargeable with knowledge of the terms of his insurance policy; has the duty to read and know the contents thereof; and is bound by the legal effect of its terms and provisions.

The law of Oklahoma is that, if its terms are free from doubt or ambiguity, an insurance policy must be permitted to speak for itself. Even in situations where obvious mistakes have been made, courts will not rewrite the contract between the parties, but will only enforce the legal obligations of the parties according to their original agreement. In Oklahoma, and elsewhere, the legal liability of an insurance company is generally limited to policy provisions. In the instant case the only actual authority of the agent for Travelers Insurance Company was to sell policies limited to regularly scheduled commercial flights.

To establish that an agent had apparent authority to bind its principal it must be shown that the principal knowingly permitted the agent to exercise the authority in question, or in some manner manifested its consent that such authority be exercised. The evidence in this case was without conflict that the only policy of Travelers Insurance Company which agents were authorized to sell was the AT(5) policy.

The insured's theory of "estoppel" would have permitted recovery for a risk that was not within the coverage of a policy, which had been sold by an agent who did not have authority to bind the insurance company for such risk. No authority was cited to support such a theory and the trial court's determination was affirmed.

STANDARD OIL CO. v. HAWAIIAN INSURANCE AND GUARANTY CO.
654 P.2d 1345 (Hawaii 1982)

Does the insurance company have a duty to defend even if the liability at issue is not one covered by the insurance policy?

The plaintiffs brought suit against defendant Hawaiian Insurance and Guaranty Company, Ltd. [HIG] to recover damages they allegedly sustained when HIG refused to defend actions brought against them by the heirs and executors of the pilot and the passengers of a plane which crashed on May 20, 1973. The airplane crash claimed the lives of the pilot, Dr. Robert C. H. Chung, and his passengers. The failure of the left engine to function had caused the aircraft to plummet to the ground. Investigation revealed that contaminants in the fuel strainer of the left engine might have been a cause of the engine failure. The tanks feeding the engine had been fueled from an aviation refueler truck covered by a liability insurance policy issued by HIG for the benefit of plaintiffs, Standard Oil Company of California [SOCAL], Air Service Corporation [ASC], and Universal Enterprises, d.b.a. Associated Aviation Activities [AAA].

Suits and cross-suits were filed by all parties, including: Dr. Chung's estate and the heirs of his passengers; the Chung estate against ASC and AAA, refuelers of the aircraft; and ASC and AAA against SOCAL as owner and renter of the fuel truck used to dispense aviation gasoline produced by SOCAL. Defendant SOCAL, through its attorneys, tendered to HIG the defense of its actions. Plaintiff HIG replied in writing that the issue was one of products liability, and that "[b]ased on the pleadings, our policy, which covers only comprehensive automobile liability, does not apply and therefore, we decline your tender to undertake the defense of Standard Oil under our policy."

Plaintiffs urged the circuit court to find as a matter of law that HIG had a duty to defend under the insurance policy. Defendant HIG answered the complaint by saying that it received late notice of the actions; that there had been a failure to give notice within a reasonable time as required by the insurance contract. The trial court concluded that HIG had waived notice. On appeal, the intermediate appellate court determined from the record that HIG had been given notice when SOCAL's attorneys contacted them.

The case was appealed to the Hawaii Supreme Court, which concluded that the intermediate appellate court had not erred. In the Supreme Court's view, HIG had received the required notice when even before SOCAL's attorneys notified them, they had received notice when Chung had filed complaints against ASC and AAA, operators of the truck insured by HIG. That should have alerted HIG to the possibility that the refueler truck *might* have been involved.

An insurer's duty to defend arises whenever there is a potential for indemnification liability of insurer to insured under the terms of the policy. The insured SOCAL had the right to expect its insurance company would make a determined effort to ascertain, not only from the pleadings, but also from the insurer's own independent investigation, whether the insured were entitled to defense representation under the policy.

> *An insurer must look beyond the effect of the pleadings and must consider any facts brought to its attention or any facts which it could reasonably discover in determining whether it has a duty to defend. . . . The duty to defend rests primarily on the possibility that coverage exists. This possibility may be remote, but if it exists the company owes the insured a defense. The possibility of coverage must be determined by a good-faith analysis of all information known to the insured or all information reasonably ascertainable by inquiry and investigation.*

The Hawaii Supreme Court affirmed the lower court decision in favor of Standard Oil.

GRP, LTD. v. UNITED STATES AVIATION UNDERWRITERS
261 N.W.2d 707 (Mich.1978)

*Does an oral agreement constitute a binding
contract of insurance coverage?*

In early 1974, Grand Rapids Label Company and Grand Rapids Forging and Steel Company decided to purchase an airplane for their joint use. A third equally owned corporation was to be formed and known as GRP, Ltd., for purposes of acquisition of the airplane. James Crosby, an independent insurance agent, was contacted for purposes of obtaining an insurance quotation for the as yet unpurchased airplane.

On April 25, 1974, Crosby attended a meeting with Paul Widener and Daniel Ek, who represented United States Aviation Underwriters [USAU]. Their discussions culminated in the composition of a "work sheet." The work sheet contained certain facts and figures dealing with the proposed operation of the airplane and the coverage desired. Later, the parties disagreed on whether the filling out of this "work sheet" was intended to be a firm quotation as to the conditions and cost of coverage. USAU contended that its intent was not to make the "work sheet" a quotation, because additional information was still needed. Daniel Ek admitted that he had checked a box on the work sheet entitled "quote" but contended that this had been inadvertent on his part. It was the position of GRP that as of April 25, 1974, they had a firm quotation for insurance coverage by USAU. Mr. Crosby testified that both Ek and Widener had indicated to him that the "work sheet" was indeed a quotation by USAU. Thereafter, Crosby sent a letter to GRP, which suggested that insurance coverage be secured from USAU. Ek took the position that he lacked authority to bind such coverage on his own. It is significant to note, however, that when Mr. Widener testified at trial, he indicated that Mr. Ek had told him that he (Ek) had declined to bind coverage because of pending questions with regard to pilot information, rather than because of any lack of authority to do so.

Shortly after May 3, 1974, GRP purchased the airplane, a Beechcraft Baron, a representative of GRP informed Mr. Crosby of the purchase and requested that he obtain the requisite insurance coverage. Mr. Crosby indicated the insurance was bound with USAU and would be effective on May 10, 1974. On May 14, 1974 the airplane crashed, killing the pilot and three passengers. Plaintiff, GRP Ltd., filed an action in circuit court seeking a declaration that at the time when the airplane crashed, there was a binding contract of insurance between it and defendant United States Aviation Underwriters, Inc. The trial court found that such a contract did, in fact, exist, and the Michigan Court of Appeals affirmed. The main thrust of USAU's argument was that there was "no meeting of the minds" as to the essential elements necessary to form a contract, and that the evidence was insufficient to support the trial court's finding that USAU had agreed to cover the risk.

On appeal to the Michigan Supreme Court, USAU argued the findings of the trial court should have been rejected, because they were based upon the preliminary finding that it is the custom in the aviation insurance industry to quote a risk only after a decision to bind has been made. USAU argued there was no support for that conclusion. However, even assuming USAU was correct in this regard, it was of no avail because the trial judge expressly found that on May 3, 1974, Crosby had been given authority to bind USAU with regard to both the quotation on voluntary settlement and with regard to the April 25, 1974 quotation.

USAU also contended that the decision of the trial court should have been set aside because there was no "meeting of the minds" with regard to the essential terms of the oral contract. In rejecting USAU's contentions on this point, the Court of Appeals indicated USAU's arguments were based upon a faulty premise, that there must be evidence in the record of express agreement on each and every essential term for a contract to be binding. Although it is regarded as essential that all elements of the contract should be agreed upon, it is not necessary this be done expressly. An oral contract of insurance will sustain an action, though no express agreement is made as to the amount of premium to be paid or the duration of the policy, if the intention of the parties to the contract in these particulars can be gathered from the circumstances of the case. The Court of Appeals, in applying this standard, found evidence in the record that would support a finding that every essential element of the contract had been agreed upon by the parties.

The Michigan Supreme Court reached the same conclusions as the Court of Appeals and affirmed. A valid oral contract of insurance existed between GRP and USAU when the airplane in question crashed.

POTTER v. RANGER INSURANCE CO.
732 F.2d 742 (9th Cir. 1984)

Must an aircraft's airworthiness certificate be in full force and effect for an insurance policy covering the aircraft to be in effect?

An insurance policy issued by the Ranger Insurance Company excluded coverage for an aircraft involved in a crash because the aircraft's airworthiness certificate was not in full force and effect at the time of the crash. The insured, Robert Potter, filed suit against the insurer, Ranger Insurance Company, for non-payment. The policy language read in part:

> *This policy does not apply: . . . 4. To Any Insured: . . . (b) who operates or permits the operation of the aircraft, while in flight, unless its airworthiness certificate is in full force and effect. . . .*

The U.S. District Court determined that exclusion 4(b) of the Ranger Insurance policy was ambiguous, and the defendant Ranger Insurance appealed. In its findings, the U.S. Court of Appeals for the 9th Circuit stated that when interpreting policy language, insurance policies are construed so as to provide coverage which a layman would have reasonably expected from the policy, and any ambiguity or uncertainty in an insurance clause is to be narrowly construed against the insurer. However, contracts are not rendered ambiguous by the mere fact that the parties do not agree on the meaning of a specific policy term. Ambiguity exists only when the policy terms at issue are subject to reasonably differing interpretations.

In interpreting exclusion 4(b), the U.S. District Court cited two aviation cases where the court found an insurance contract exclusion provision to be ambiguous and interpreted it as requiring knowledge and consent that the aircraft was operated in violation of certain regulations before coverage could be denied. In the instant case, both Potter and the District Court conceded that the exclusion language in the above two cited cases was less ambiguous than in the instant case; i.e., in the above two cases it was fairly clear that the exclusion only applied if the insured had knowledge of the violations. It was the opinion of this court the contract language in the instant case was readily distinguishable from the contract language in the above two cited cases.

In this case, exclusion 4(b) excluded from coverage any insured who "permits the operation of the aircraft while in flight unless its airworthiness certificate is in full force and effect." The placement of the word "unless directly preceding the language regarding the airworthiness certificate made it clear that the plane would not be covered unless there was a valid, effective airworthiness certificate. It was the appellate court's opinion that a lay person would reasonably expect after reading exclusion 4(b) that the insured would be denied coverage if the airworthiness certificate was not in effect, regardless of whether or not the insured had knowledge that it was not in effect. It was irrelevant that Potter did not have actual knowledge either that the certificate was ineffective or of the flight itself.

The district court decision was reversed and remanded.

BELLEFONTE UNDERWRITERS INSURANCE CO. v. ALFA AVIATION
312 S.E.2d 426 (N.C. 1984)

Must the pilot of an aircraft possess a current medical certificate for an insurance policy on the aircraft to be effective?

This action resulted from an airplane accident on June 20, 1978, in which the insured single-engine aircraft was destroyed, and the pilot, defendant William Axson Smith, Jr., and passengers Mary Jo Beck, William T. Taylor and Donna Stocks, were injured. Smith had rented the plane as the agent of his employer, defendant J.D. Dawson Company, from defendant Alfa Aviation, Inc., at Pitt-Greenville Airport in Greenville, North Carolina. Smith was attempting to land the plane at Riverside Campground in Belhaven when the crash occurred.

Two insurance policies in effect at the time of the accident had been issued to defendant Alfa Aviation by plaintiff Bellefonte Underwriters Insurance Company, Inc. One was an airport liability policy, required of Alfa Aviation under the terms of its lease from Pitt County-City of Greenville Airport Authority; the other was an aircraft policy covering the plane rented by Smith.

The plaintiff denied liability for all claims arising under both policies. Coverage under the airport liability policy was denied because of a specific exclusion stating, "This policy does not apply to any aircraft owned by, hired by, loaned to, or operated for the account of the Insured." Plaintiff maintained coverage under the aircraft policy was specifically excluded by a requirement that a lessee of an aircraft from Alfa Aviation have a current medical certificate meeting Federal Aviation Regulations. The aircraft policy specifically denied coverage "to any occurrence or to any loss or damage occurring while the aircraft is operated in flight by other than the pilot or pilots set forth under Item 7 of the Declaration." Item 7 provided that only pilots holding valid certificates would fly the aircraft and referred to Endorsement 15. Endorsement 15, the Pilot Clause Endorsement, also provided: "Only the following pilot(s) holding valid and effective pilot and medical certificates with ratings as required by the Federal Aviation Administration for the flight involved will operate the aircraft in flight."

During discovery, defendant Smith admitted the last medical certificate issued to him prior to the accident, pursuant to the FARs, was a third-class medical certificate issued October 16, 1975, two years and eight months before the crash. A third-class medical certificate expired 24 months after the date of examination.

When the injured defendants filed negligence suits against defendants Smith and Alfa Aviation, and they in turn sought coverage under the two policies underwritten by plaintiff, the plaintiff sought a declaratory judgment, contending that plaintiff had no duty under the policies to indemnify or defend Smith and Alfa Aviation. Defendants also joined in seeking relief by declaratory judgment. The trial court ruled as a matter of law that defendants were entitled to recovery under the terms of the insurance policies in question. Bellefonte Underwriters Insurance Company appealed.

Plaintiff insurance company contended the trial court erred in denying its motion for summary judgment, because express exclusions in both policies barred all coverage for defendants. The appellate court ruled that no causal connection was required between the breach of an exclusion limiting coverage to be denied under the medical certificate requirement. In other words, it was irrelevant that the accident was not caused by lack of a current medical certificate. The pilot could not lawfully act as pilot in command, since at the time of the crash he did not have the appropriate current medical certificate.

Plaintiff also argued that the airport liability policy issued to Alfa Aviation did not provide coverage for this accident, because the policy excluded "any aircraft owned by, hired by, loaned to or operated for the account of the Insured." The appellate court agreed with plaintiff, that since the aircraft in question was rented by Alfa Aviation to defendant Smith, it was excluded from coverage by the specific terms of the insurance contract. The North Carolina Court of Appeals reversed and remanded the cause of action.

EDMONDS v. UNITED STATES
642 F.2d 877 (1st Cir. 1981)

> *Must a pilot have a current biennial flight review for*
> *an insurance policy to be effective?*

On May 14, 1974, Dean Edmonds purchased a Beech Baron aircraft. Avemco Insurance Company subsequently issued an aircraft insurance policy to Edmonds effective May 15, 1974 for a period of one-year ("1974-1975 policy"). The 1974-1975 policy insured

Edmonds against personal injury and property damage while operating the aircraft. Item 7 of the "DECLARATIONS" section stated,

> *PILOTS: This policy applies when the aircraft is in flight, only while being operated by one of the following pilots, while such pilot is holding a valid and effective Pilot and Medical Certificate : (a) Dean S. Edmonds. . . .*

The 1974-1975 policy also contained a section entitled "EXCLUSIONS" and one entitled "CONDITIONS." Neither section set out a requirement that Edmonds undergo a periodic review of his piloting skills in order to qualify for coverage.

In 1974, the Federal Aviation Administration [FAA] amended Part 61 of the Federal Aviation Regulations by inserting therein Section 61.57, which provided in part:

> *(a) Flight Review. After November 1, 1974, no person may act as pilot in command of an aircraft unless, within the preceding 24 months, he has . . .*

> *(1) Accomplished a flight review given to him, in an aircraft for which he is rated, by an appropriately certified instructor or other person designated by the Administrator; and*

> *(2) Had his logbook endorsed by the person who gave him the review certifying that he has satisfactorily accomplished the flight review.*

Edmonds successfully completed a biennial flight review under the supervision of an FAA certified instructor on November 24, 1974. Prior to the expiration date of the 1974-1975 policy, Avemco sent Edmonds an "Aircraft Policy Renewal Information" form. The form included a questionnaire asking if the insured pilot(s) had a current biennial flight review. Edmonds checked the box indicating that he had a current biennial flight review and mailed the form to Avemco, which issued Edmonds a renewal policy ("1975-1976 policy"). Edmonds later received a new "DECLARATIONS" section. Item 7 of that section had been amended to read:

> *Item 7. PILOTS: This policy applies when the aircraft is in flight, only while being operated by one of the following pilots . . . who, (1) holds a valid and effective Pilot and Medical Certificate, (2) has a current biennial flight review. . . .*

In March of 1976, Avemco again sent Edmonds a policy renewal form. Edmonds replied that he had a current biennial flight review and mailed the form to Avemco, after which he received a renewal policy ("1976-1977 policy"). This renewal procedure was repeated again the following year. Edmonds indicated he had a current biennial flight review and mailed the form back to Avemco. Avemco subsequently issued a renewal policy ("1977-1978 policy"). As with the previous two policies, Item 7 of the "DECLARATIONS" section provided that the 1977-1978 policy "applied when the aircraft is in flight, only while being operated by one of the following pilots [Edmonds] . . . who . . . (2) has a current biennial flight review. . . ." The 1977-1978 policy also contained a new provision in the "EXCLUSIONS" section,

> *This policy does not apply:*
>
> *(g) Under Coverages A, B and C, to any aircraft while in flight . . .*
>
> *(3) being operated by a pilot not meeting the requirements set forth in item 7 of the declarations.*

When Edmonds returned the policy renewal form to Avemco to obtain the 1977-1978 policy, he did not have a current biennial flight review. His previous flight review took place on November 24, 1974, more than two years earlier. In 1977, Edmonds twice piloted an airplane accompanied by Gary Brigham, a demonstrator pilot employed by the Beech Air Company. Brigham later wrote to Avemco that Edmonds performed all of the maneuvers necessary to complete a biennial review during these flights. Brigham, however, was not an FAA certified instructor, did not have authority to conduct biennial flight reviews, and did not enter his finds in Edmonds' log book.

On January 14, 1978, Edmonds had an accident at Hanscom Field in Bedford, Massachusetts. As he brought his plane down for a landing on Runway 23, it hit a mound of snow and crashed. The aircraft was extensively damaged. Edmonds promptly filed a claim under the 1977-1978 policy. Avemco refused to honor his claim on the theory that by failing to maintain a current biennial flight review, Edmonds breached a condition precedent to Avemco's contractual duty. Edmonds then brought suit for damages against the United States, the Massachusetts Port Authority and Avemco. He alleged that Avemco breached its contract of insurance by refusing to cover the accident as required by the 1977-1978 policy. Massachusetts law governed this claim.

The U.S. District Court granted Avemco's motion for summary judgment, ruling that Edmonds was bound by Item 7 of the "DECLARATIONS," that Item 7 incorporated the federal regulatory standard for flight reviews, and that Edmonds did not comply with Item 7. The district court then turned to what it perceived as the more difficult question: whether Edmonds' failure to comply with Item 7 voided Avemco's obligations under the policy. The court noted that under Massachusetts law it was necessary to characterize Item 7 as either a "condition precedent," in which case, Avemco's obligation was terminated, or a "warranty or representation," in which case coverage could be voided only if the breach contributed to the accident or increased the insurer's risk.

In the district court's view, the standard for determining whether Item 7 was a condition precedent is set out in *Charles, Henry & Crowley Co. Inc. v. The Home Insurance Co.*:[28]

> *A statement made in an application for a policy of insurance may become a condition of the policy rather than remain a warranty or representation if: (1) the statement made by the insured relates essentially to the insurer's intelligent decision to issue the policy; and (2) the statement is made a condition precedent to recovery under the policy, either by using the precise words "condition precedent" or their equivalent.*

The U.S. District Court found that both branches of the standard were met in the instant case and ruled that Item 7 was a condition precedent. Accordingly, Edmonds' failure to comply with Item 7 prevented Avemco's duty of covering the accident from arising. Edmonds appealed. The U.S. Court of Appeals held that the district court prop-

---

[28] 349 Mass. 723, 726 (1965).

erly construed the term "current biennial flight review" as incorporating the federal regulatory standard, and that the District Court properly applied the *Charles* standard to the aircraft policy in this case. The U.S. District Court's decision was affirmed.

NATIONAL UNION FIRE INSURANCE v. ZUVER
750 P.2d 1274 (Wash. 1988)

> *Does a pilot's flight insurance coverage vary with the weather conditions during a flight?*

This case was a declaratory judgment action to determine insurance coverage under an aviation policy. The insured pilot, Phillip E. Strathy, took off at approximately 11:20 a.m. on June 19, 1983, in his Piper Cherokee airplane. His passengers included his three daughters and a friend, Thomas Zuver. Strathy departed from Martha Lake on a route to Eastern Washington that took him over the Cascade Mountains. Prior to takeoff, Strathy telephoned the Federal Aviation Administration Seattle Flight Service Station for a weather briefing. Other than a precaution for "mountains occasionally obscured," his flight plan was approved. Within one half-hour after departing, he crashed into Glacier Peak at the 10,000-foot level, killing all aboard.

Strathy was certified for visual flight rules [VFR] only. The crash occurred under weather conditions normally requiring an instrument flight rule [IFR] rating. Strathy's liability insurance carrier, the plaintiff in this case, National Union Fire Insurance Company, tendered a defense under a reservation of rights to disclaim coverage and filed this action for declaratory judgment. At issue was the interpretation of two related provisions in Strathy's insurance policy.

The first provision was an exclusionary clause, which provided,

> *This policy does not apply: . . . 2. To any insured while the aircraft is in flight . . . (b) if piloted by a pilot not properly certificated, qualified and rated under the current applicable Federal Air Regulations for the operation involved. . . .*

The second provision was a pilot warranty, which provided,

> *Insurance will be effective only when the operation of the insured aircraft . . . is by a pilot*

> *. . . who possesses a current and valid pilot certificate of the kind specified with appropriate ratings, . . . all as required by the Federal Aviation Administration for the flight involved. . . .*

In a split decision, the Court of Appeals in Washington State affirmed the trial court judgment that Strathy had violated Federal Aviation Regulations for visual flight and was thereby excluded from coverage under the policy. Representatives of the decedents' estates petitioned the Washington Supreme Court for review.

The term, "for the operation involved" was not defined in the policy, which created confusion with the pilot warranty endorsement phrase "for the flight involved." National contended the phrase "for the operation involved" was not ambiguous and required a different meaning than "for the flight involved," because the "operation" of the plane was not the same as the "flight" of the plane.

In the general rules for interpreting insurance contracts, if the policy language is clear and unambiguous, the court may not modify the contract or create ambiguity where none exists. However, it is a rule of insurance contract construction that an insurance policy must have meaning to lay persons, who, at their peril, may be legally bound or held to understand the nature and extent of its coverage. If any clause in the policy is ambiguous, a meaning and construction most favorable to the *insured* must be applied, even though the insurer may have intended another meaning.

National's insurance policy defined "in flight" as "the time commencing with the actual take-off run of the aircraft and continuing thereafter until it has completed its landing roll." Therefore, National argued, the phrase "for the operation involved" logically had a different meaning in the exclusion provision than "for the flight involved" had under the pilot warranty endorsement—the latter referring to the actual flight of the aircraft and the former designating who was qualified to operate the aircraft under the Federal Aviation Regulations.

The petitioners contended "operation involved" could just as reasonably mean the manner by which the entire flight was conducted. The court agreed the term "operation involved" was ambiguous, and thus construed it most favorably to the insured to mean the flight as a whole. However, a broader question affecting aviation insurance was whether a pilot's flight insurance coverage should vary with the weather conditions during the flight.

The petitioners argued that National's interpretation of paragraph 2(b) would force the courts to examine minutely every segment of a flight to determine when, in what manner, and for how long insurance coverage is in effect. If, as the petitioners urged, the flight is viewed as a whole, and the words "operation involved" meant conduct of the entire flight, then insureds will know with certainty whether insurance covers the operation of the aircraft for the flight involved. This latter interpretation and method was previously adopted by two courts (*National Insurance Underwriters v. King Craft Custom Products,*[29] and *Glover v. National Insurance Underwriters*[30]). These courts found insurance coverage should be determined at the inception of a flight. This approach is referred to as the "inception rule." According to *Glover,* "The weather conditions existing at the beginning of the flight should . . . be looked to in determining whether the flight is a VFR or an IFR flight."

In the instant case, the petitioners' argument was in line with the inception rule. In order to avoid any misunderstanding, the Washington Supreme Court emphasized it is the weather conditions at the time and place of departure, which are controlling. Therefore, Strathy was covered under the policy, and the Court of Appeals ruling was reversed.

TREMAROLI v. DELTA AIR LINES
458 N.Y.Supp.2d 159 (1983)

> *Can a passenger recover damages for hand held luggage lost in the airport security screening process ?*

Claimant Tremaroli submitted himself and his hand baggage to be searched as required under 14 C.F.R. 107 and 108, security screening required "to prevent or deter the carriage aboard airplanes of any explosive, incendiary device, or a deadly or dangerous weapon. . . ." The baggage was separated from Tremaroli when it was placed on a conveyor belt. As the baggage proceeded through the X-ray device, Tremaroli was himself going through a magnetometer (archway) security screening, and he was unable to observe his luggage. After he was screened he went to the conveyor belt and retrieved what he thought was his luggage. He later discovered he had picked up someone else's luggage that looked like his. He returned the mistaken luggage, but his was never returned to him. He instituted a small claims action in the

---

[29] 368 F. Supp. 476 (1973).
[30] 545 S.W. 2d 755 (1977).

Civil Court of the City of New York against Delta Air Lines and Ogden Security, Inc., to recover his losses.

Where control of lawful possession of personal property is transferred, as in the case of a security check, an implied *bailment* arises. The mere fact that the bailed item (the hand luggage) is lost does not make the bailee liable to the bailor. The bailee is not an insurer. However, the bailee can be liable for *negligence* or *conversion.* In such actions the bailor has the burden of establishing conversion or negligence. Upon proof of bailment, and failure to redeliver, a presumption arises that the bailee has converted the item bailed, or has negligently caused its loss. The burden of producing proof then shifts to the bailee. In this case the claimant established a *prima facie* case of negligence by showing that his baggage was in defendant's possession and had not been returned.

The court concluded the airlines have a duty to safeguard the passenger's hand baggage during their security procedures. Airlines encourage the passenger to carry valuables in carry-on luggage, not in hold luggage checked with the carrier and stored within the aircraft's freight compartment. Yet, the passenger is often separated from his or her hand luggage during the screening process, and thus is placed in a "Catch-22" situation. The security system should operate in such a manner that the airline is accountable to the public for the return of hand baggage. The public is under pressure to move as quickly as possible through the screening process. Hence, the duty of the airline is one of "reasonable conduct in light of the apparent risk." Delta breached its duty by not adequately foreseeing the claimant's dilemma and safeguarding his baggage.

The court awarded claimant's damages ($950) in the amount proven against the defendants. Since Delta had an agreement with Odgen Security wherein Ogden assumed liability for any actions, claims, losses, liabilities or expenses arising out of its services, Delta had an indemnification claim against Ogden for the $950. The court also found that liability limitations included in the carrier's tariff filed with the Civil Aeronautics Board was not applicable. A contract of carriage was not established, because the luggage was never placed on the airplane.

CHAPTER 19

PRIVATE INTERNATIONAL AIR LAW

*To facilitate international aviation, the world community has
concluded several treaties designed to provide certain uniform
rules of liability in international aviation.*

INTRODUCTION

Two international conventions stand out as paramount in international aviation rights and responsibilities. The first is the Warsaw Convention of 1929 (and its descendant, the Montreal Convention of 1999). The second is the Chicago Conference of 1944 (the subject of Chapter 20). These agreements laid the philosophical foundation for private and public international aviation law. This chapter as well as the final chapter address these two most important international legal regimes, and present an overview of international aviation law from a U.S. perspective.[1]

Every nation has complete and exclusive rights to its sovereign airspace. Therefore, in order to promote international air transportation, there must first exist favorable relationships between nations, supported by agreements allowing international air transportation to take place. The preponderance of these international air transport

---

[1]For a more detailed review on the Warsaw Convention and the subsequent development of the *Montreal Agreement* of 1966, *see* Andreas Lowenfeld and Allan Mendelsohn, *The United States and the Warsaw Convention* (1967) 80 Harvard L. Rev. For a European (especially British) view of international aviation law, *see* Carole Blackshaw, *Aviation Law & Regulation: A Framework for the Civil Aviation Industry* (1992). It was between the U.S. and Great Britain that the first international air transport agreement, the *Bermuda Agreement* of 1946, was written. *See also* Paul Stephen Dempsey and Laurence E. Gesell, *Air Commerce and the Law* Ch. 19 (2005).

agreements is in bilateral form; that is to say, the agreements are between two nations. But there are also a number of multinational agreements that many nations have ratified.

Control of international air transport may also arise from multinational political groupings such as the European Union [EU], or the long-standing International Civil Aviation Organization [ICAO]. Other international aviation organizations are formed at the industry level, such as the International Air Transport Association [IATA], or the Airports Council International [ACI].[2]

There have been a series of international conventions, which have formed the backbone of an international system of aviation law. The results of these conventions have contributed to international regulation of bilateral relations, air transport operations, security, and liability. First was the Chicago Conference of 1944, which established a basic framework of regulation essential to the development of international air transportation. More than 180 nations have ratified the Chicago Convention (and thereby become members of ICAO), which agreement is in three principal parts: Air Navigation, the International Civil Aviation Organization, and International Air Transport.

The Chicago Conference addressed such issues as sovereignty over airspace; traffic rights (commonly referred to as the "five freedoms"); aircraft nationality and registration; crew regulations; air navigation services; and the provision of airport facilities. Per Article 44 of the Chicago Convention, the purpose of ICAO was to "develop the principles and techniques of international air navigation and to foster the planning and development of international air transport." The other vital area of international aviation law originated with The *Convention for the Unification of Certain Rules Relating to International Transportation by Air*, otherwise known as the "Warsaw Convention."

THE WARSAW CONVENTION OF 1929

Recognized in the International Convention for Air Navigation of 1919 (commonly referred to as the "Paris Convention") was that each nation has complete and exclusive control of its territorial airspace, and thus may prevent the flight through its airspace of other nation's

---

[2] ACI was formerly known as the Airport Operators Council International [AOCI].

air carriers not having its permission. The Paris Convention established basic principles of air sovereignty, national registry of aircraft, and restrictions on the movement of military aircraft. It also established basic rules of aircraft airworthiness and competency of airmen.

The principal accomplishment of the Paris Convention was the establishment of airspace sovereignty theory, but the interim *Comite International Technique d'Experts Juridique Aériens* [CITEJA] was also created to begin work on a treaty for international air transportation relationships. The 1919 convention was followed by another convention in Paris in 1925, and later by the Warsaw Convention of 1929. The terms of the Warsaw Convention form a treaty, which has been ratified by more than 100 nations since 1929. The treaty was the end product of the work begun by the CITEJA.

The procedure for nations participating in the Warsaw Convention has been threefold. The first stage was for those attending the convention in 1929 to sign the treaty. The second stage was ratification, or formal adoption of the treaty. The final stage is completed when the terms of the Convention are actually put into force and effect by the respective nations—sometimes by incorporating the terms of the treaty into the laws and regulations of the individual nation. The Warsaw Convention was "adhered to," rather than "ratified" by the U.S.[3]

The purpose of the Warsaw Convention was twofold. First, with many different languages, customs, and legal systems in an evolving international air transportation marketplace, a certain degree of uniformity for tickets, waybills, claims arising out of international air transportation, and so forth, was desired. The second, and clearly the most important goal, was to limit the potential liability of the carrier in case of accidents where passengers might be killed or injured. The Convention shifted the burden of proof in accident liability cases to the carrier by making the carrier presumptively liable for damage sustained by a passenger in the course of an international flight. "International" was defined as air transportation between two contracting states or where the origin and destination are in the same contracting state, transportation with an agreed stopping place outside of the state.[4] All determinations regarding applicability of the Warsaw Con-

---

[3] See *Indemnity Insurance v. Pan American Airways*, CCH 1 AVI. ¶ 1247 (1944).
[4] Warsaw Convention, Art. 1.

vention are based on the origin and destination of the flight as specified on the ticket.[5] Where the passenger's ticket specified the origin in one nation, and the destination, we examine which treaty is common to them both. This might be the Warsaw Convention, Warsaw amended by one of its several Protocols (such as the Hague Protocol of 1955), or the Montreal Convention of 1999. Where the passenger's ticket specifies a round-trip international itinerary and origin and destination are the same, the most recent treaty ratified by it governs liability.

Article 28 of the Warsaw Convention provides four places of jurisdiction over airlines involved in accidents:

- where the carrier has its domicile;
- where the carrier has its principal place of business;
- where the carrier has a place of business through which the contract was made (i.e., where the ticket was purchased); and
- the place of destination.

While retaining the principle of liability on the basis of negligence, the Warsaw Convention shifted the burden of proof so that the carrier was *presumed* liable. In exchange for accepting the burden of proof in negligence cases, the Warsaw Convention limited the carrier's liability for each passenger's death or bodily injury resulting from an "accident"[6] (i.e., an unexpected or unusual event or happening external to the passenger) to 125,000 *Poincaré francs*,[7] or approximately $8,300 United States dollars. Hence, the essential bargain was a shift in the burden of proof, in return for a limit of liability exposure. Generally, signatory nations' airlines are liable for death, injury or damage to property that occurs during the "carriage by air" without proof of cause or liability. In this sense, the carriers were given strict liability as opposed to absolute liability.

Twelve, mostly European, countries had signed the Warsaw Convention in 1929. The United States did not participate in the work with CITEJA, and it was only an observer to the Warsaw Convention. Nevertheless, the U.S. is nearly a charter member. In 1933, the State De-

---

[5] *See Wyman and Bartlett v. Pan American World Airways, Inc.*, CCH 1 AVI. ¶ 1093 (1943).

[6] Warsaw Convention, Art. 17.

[7] The Warsaw Convention provides that the equivalent amount stipulated in *Poincaré* francs may be converted into any national currency in round figures.

partment transmitted its approval of the treaty to President Franklin Delano Roosevelt, who submitted the treaty to the Senate. On June 15, 1934, without debate, committee hearing, or report, the Senate gave its advice and consent by voice vote. The United States deposited its instrument of adherence with the Polish government on July 31, 1934, and President Roosevelt proclaimed the treaty 90 days later.

Debates concerning revision of the Warsaw Convention began almost immediately. Concerns centered on two issues. First, the liability limits were set far too low, particularly for U.S. citizens. The United States from the very outset has argued for increasing the liability limits. Subsequent amendments, such as the Hague Protocol in 1955, attempted to update and amend the Warsaw Convention, and double the liability limits (to approximately $16,600). The United States maintained all along that the liability limits were too low. But inasmuch as the U.S. was not able to obtain worldwide compliance to higher liability limits, it took unilateral steps to increase the limits for flights including stops in the United States.

The second concern centered on the meaning of "willful misconduct." Article 25 of the Warsaw Convention deprived the carrier of the benefits of the limits of liability if the damage was caused,

> . . . *by his willful misconduct or by such default on his part as, in accordance with the law of the court to which the case is submitted, is considered to be equivalent to willful misconduct.*

The meaning of willful misconduct has been criticized by legal scholars from the beginning as unclear. The language is obscure. It has led to differing interpretations in different countries and different courts.[8]

THE WARSAW SYSTEM

Since 1929, the Warsaw Convention has undergone several changes and amendments, not all of which have been ratified by the original

---

[8] *See In re Aircrash in Bali, Indonesia,* CCH 17 AVI. ¶ 17,416 (1982); *See also In re Korean Air Lines Disaster,* 704 F. Supp. 1135 (1988).

signatory nations. Conferences were held to discuss the Warsaw Convention in Cairo in 1946, Madrid in 1951, Paris in 1952, and Rio de Janeiro in 1953. Subsequent amendments and supplementary agreements have included the Hague Protocol of 1955, the Guadalajara Convention of 1961, the Guatemala Protocol of 1971, and the Montreal Protocols of 1975. Although not formally part of the Warsaw Convention updates, there was also the intercarrier Montreal Agreement of 1966. More recently, the International Air Transport Association unanimously endorsed the IATA Intercarrier Agreement (IIA) at the IATA Annual General Meeting in Kuala Lumpur on October 31, 1995—now referred to as the "Kuala Lumpur Accord."[9] Collectively, these international conferences, conventions and protocols make up the *Warsaw System.*

The Hague Protocol sought to increase carrier liability to 250,000 francs (about U.S. $16,600). Because the liability limits were still set too low, the United States was reluctant to ratify the Hague Protocol, and did not for more than half a century. One of the reasons for the delay was a concern about political reaction to the Protocol, stimulated in particular by a crash at Medicine Bow Peak, Wyoming, of a New York to San Francisco flight in October of 1955. Among those killed in the accident were five members of the Mormon Tabernacle Choir. Because tickets were purchased in Europe, they were covered by the Warsaw Convention. The accident caused discussions within the U.S. government of various proposals to exempt the domestic segments of a through journey from the effects of the Warsaw Convention. The United States did not ratify the Hague Protocol until 2003.

The Convention Supplementary to the Warsaw Convention, for the Unification of Certain Rules Relating to International Carriage by Air Performed by a Person Other Than the Contracting Carrier, more popularly known as the "Guadalajara Convention," was concluded in Guadalajara, Mexico, in 1961. The purpose of the Guadalajara Convention is expressed in its formal title. It dealt specifically with definition of the term "carrier." The U.S. did not ratify the Guadalajara Convention, but its essential terms have been incorporated into the Montreal Convention of 1999, extending liability to the underlying

---

[9] For a more detailed review of the Kuala Lumpur Accord of 1995, *see* Paul Stephen Dempsey, *Pennies from Heaven: Breaking Through the Liability Ceilings of Warsaw* (1997) XXII-I Annals of Air & Space Law.

carrier in a "wet lease" (lease of aircraft and crew), blocked space (sale of seats on a wholesale basis to another carrier), or code-share (use of another carrier's designator code for the flight number) basis.

Since Guadalajara there have been two major conventions: the Guatemala City Protocol of 1971 and the Montreal Protocols of 1975. The Guatemala City Protocol liberalized the circumstances under which recovery could be obtained, and set an absolute and unbreakable cap of 100,000 Special Drawing Rights [SDRs][10] on liability for passenger death or injury. Failing a sufficient number of ratifications, it never entered into force. The Montreal Protocols consisted of four separate protocols. Most of the changes found in the Guatemala and Montreal texts relate to liability limits, and the movement from gold francs to SDRs as the measure of the amount of liability. The United States ratified only Montreal Protocol No. 4, which principally affected air cargo liability. Many of its provisions also have been incorporated into the Montreal Convention of 1999.

One can become confused by the terminology, for much of it is named for Montreal, the home of both ICAO and IATA, and thus, the *de facto* capitol of international aviation, and the venue for many international conferences. One must try to keep in mind that the *Montreal Protocols* of 1975 sought to amend the Warsaw Convention. The *Montreal Agreement* of 1966 is not a treaty at all, but an international agreement that waives certain Warsaw defenses. The *Montreal Convention* of 1999 is a treaty that attempts to supplant the Warsaw system. Indeed, there is also a *Montreal Convention of 1971* that addresses unlawful interference with civil aviation.

THE MONTREAL AGREEMENT OF 1966

The Montreal *Protocols* of 1975 are not to be confused with the Montreal *Agreement* of 1966. The latter was an initiative of the International Air Transport Association. The Montreal Agreement was not an international treaty between nations, but rather was an agreement binding on contracting airlines. It was technically not a part of the Warsaw Convention.

---

[10] SDRs are a means of valuation established by the International Monetary Fund comprised of a "basket" of currencies of five industrialized nations.

The Montreal Agreement was a compromise establishing special limits of liability on air transportation affecting the United States. The Montreal Agreement provided that the signatory airlines accept *absolute liability* for injury to passengers up to a pre-described limit per passenger.[11] Under the Montreal Agreement: (1) the liability for each passenger for death or other bodily injury was calculated as the sum of either $75,000 inclusive of legal fees; or $58,000 exclusive of legal fees for a claim in a state where provision is made for separate award of legal fees and costs; and (2) the carrier was not to avail itself of Warsaw Convention defenses (including in particular, the "all necessary measures" defense). The plaintiff could still pierce the liability ceiling if it proved the carrier engaged in "willful misconduct."[12]

The Montreal Agreement had the status of a *special contract* under Article 22 of the Warsaw Convention. It applied to international transportation as defined in the Warsaw Convention, on airlines signatory to the agreement, provided that the intended journey included a point of departure or agreed stopping place in the United States.

The Montreal Agreement relating to liability limitations of the Warsaw Convention and the Hague Protocol was largely precipitated by an ultimatum from the United States. In November 1965, the U.S. denounced the Warsaw Convention, to become effective May 1966.[13] The United States offered to withdraw its denunciation before it became effective if, prior to May 1966, an international agreement could be reached that would substantially raise the limits of liability.

Because governments were unable to conclude a new multilateral agreement in such a short time, the international air carriers reached a private agreement in 1966, with participation of the Department of State, the Civil Aeronautics Board [CAB], and the International Air Transport Association. For passengers with a point of origin or destination in the United States the liability assumed by each signatory carrier was raised to $75,000 for each passenger meeting this special (U.S.) criterion. For all others not having a journey to or from the U.S. there was an individual per passenger liability of $8,290, or $16,580, as specified in the Warsaw Convention and Hague Protocol, respectively.

---

[11] *See In re Aircrash in Bali, Indonesia*, CCH 17 AVI. ¶ 17,416 (1982).

[12] Warsaw Convention, Art. 25.

[13] A six months' notice is required for withdrawal from the treaty.

The "Waiver of Warsaw Convention Liability Limits and Defenses," was adopted in conformance to the Montreal Agreement.[14] Under Part 203, participation in the Montreal Agreement was made mandatory. Part 203 requires that certain U.S. and foreign direct air carriers waive the passenger liability limits and certain carrier defenses in the Warsaw Convention in accordance with the provisions of CAB Agreement 18900, dated May 13, 1966. The participating carriers were required to give each of their passengers the notice required by the Montreal Agreement which was generally stated as follows:

> *Passengers on a journey involving an ultimate destination or a stop in a country other than the country of origin are advised that the provisions of the treaty known as the Warsaw Convention may be applicable to the entire journey, including any portion entirely within the country of origin or destination. For such passengers on a journey to, from, or with an agreed stopping place in the United States of America, the convention and special contracts of carriage embodied in applicable tariffs provide that the liability of [(name of carrier) and certain other carriers] parties to such contracts for death of or personal injury to passengers is limited in most cases to proven damages not to exceed U.S. $75,000 per passenger and that this liability up to such limit shall not depend on negligence on the part of the carrier. For such passengers traveling by a carrier not a party to such contracts or on a journey not to, from, or having an agreed stopping place in the United States of America, liability of the Carrier for personal injury to passengers is limited in most cases to approximately U.S. $10,000 or U.S. $20,000.*

---

[14] *See* 14 C.F.R. Part 203.

In 1974 a CAB Order made a provision for updated conversion of francs to dollars.[15] In the CAB conversion table, 125,000 francs converted to U.S. $10,000; 250,000 francs converted to U.S. $20,000.[16]

In accidents involving international flights, airline liability was limited by the Montreal Agreement to a maximum of $75,000 per passenger, absent proof of willful misconduct. The carriers agreed not to challenge claims on grounds that the airlines had undertaken all reasonable action to avoid the accident. Thus, plaintiffs could still break the $75,000 limit with proof of willful misconduct on the part of the carrier. "Willful misconduct" is conduct that is either intentional or committed under circumstances exhibiting a reckless disregard for the safety of others, knowing that danger exists. It is a conscious disregard for safety, and a gross deviation from standard conduct.[17] But it takes a lawsuit to demonstrate willful misconduct. Thus, in many cases, the only way that passengers or their decedents could secure realistic compensation was to sue airlines for (serious) negligence—a distressing, time-consuming, expensive and uncertain process, during which no compensation was payable. The Kuala Lumpur Accord has now changed all that, as did action taken unilaterally by the United States government for domestic air transportation liability limits.

Pursuant to recommendations of a study group, the Secretary of State recommended that the United States unilaterally enact legislation which would require CAB certificated carriers in international air transportation to provide automatic accident insurance for each of its passengers. In Section 401(q)(1), "Insurance and Liability," of the Federal Aviation Act of 1958 (49 U.S.C. 1371), U.S. law stipulates that: "No certificate shall be issued . . . unless . . . the air carrier . . . complies with regulations or orders issued by the Board governing the filing and approval of policies of insurance or plans for self insurance in the amount prescribed by the Board. . . ." This applies not only to U.S. airlines, but also to foreign air carriers operating to or from the United States. The intent of this law is to "protect travelers and ship-

---

[15] CAB Order 75-1-16 (1974).

[16] The calculations of the purchasing power of the dollar utilize a comparison of the Consumer Price Index for the years 1966 and 1993, based on U.S. Bureau of Labor Statistics. *See* Paul Stephen Dempsey, *Pennies from Heaven: Breaking Through the Liability Ceilings of Warsaw* (1997) XXII-I Annals of Air & Space Law, at 276.

[17] *See In re Korean Air Lines Disaster*, 704 F. Supp. 1135 (1988). *See also In re Aircrash in Bali, Indonesia*, CCH 17 AVI ¶ 17,416 (1982).

pers by aircraft operated by certificated air carriers" with "appropriate compensation." The requirements of the Federal Aviation Act with regard to insurance and liability are stipulated in 14 C.F.R. Part 205, "Aircraft Accident Liability Insurance." The minimum insurance requirement for air carriers per passenger is $300,000.

As for the limits of liability in international air transportation, an IATA working group, meeting in Washington, D.C., in August 1995, proposed no numerical limits on recoverable compensatory damages, with compensation to be calculated according to the law of the domicile of the passengers, but with preservation of the carrier defenses available under the Warsaw Convention and Hague Protocol (i.e., the "all necessary measures" clause). At a follow-up meeting, the IATA working group modified the carrier defenses in its "Agreement on Measures to Implement the IATA Intercarrier Agreement" [MIA], which provides for absolute carrier liability up to 100,000 SDRs, or the equivalent of about U.S. $150,000. However, the MIA also provides a fault-based system beyond 100,000 SDRs, with the burden of proving freedom from negligence on the carrier. For claims above 100,000 SDRs, the plaintiff (passengers or decedents) must prove only that there was an accident resulting in damages. But to avoid going over the 100,000 SDR limit, the defendant (airline) need only prove that it took "all necessary measures" to avoid the injury.[18]

On February 7, 1997, U.S carriers received approval from the U.S. Department of Transportation to modernize liability rules for passengers traveling on U.S. airlines. The Kuala Lumpur Accord is a vast improvement over the previous $75,000 ceiling limits of Warsaw/ Montreal, but it is still highly imperfect for U.S. citizens, where the average amount of damages for domestic aviation injury recovery ranges from $480,000 (for cases settled before trial) to $730,000 (for cases that go to trial). As Dempsey observes,

> . . . the merits of any solution to a problem depend on one's perspective. Depending upon how one views it, either the glass is half-empty, or it is half full. Compared with

---

[18] *See* Paul Stephen Dempsey, *Pennies from Heaven: Breaking Through the Liability Ceilings of Warsaw* (1997) XXII-I Annals of Air & Space Law, at 280.

> *$730,000, the Kuala Lumpur solution of*
> *$146,000 makes the glass appear half empty;*
> *compared with the Warsaw/Montreal status*
> *quo of $75,000, $146,000 makes the glass ap-*
> *pear half full* [19]

THE MONTREAL CONVENTION OF 1999

The Montreal Convention of 1999 [MC99] does not amend the Warsaw Convention, but instead is an entirely new treaty that seeks to replace the complex matrix of amending protocols and intercarrier agreements that evolved over the preceding 70 years with a unified, and more passenger-friendly, legal regime.[20] Among the most prominent features of MC99's liability regime are the following:

- Incorporating most of the liability provisions of the IATA Intercarrier Agreements, the Convention establishes a two-tier liability system, with strict liability up to 100,000 SDRs, and presumptive liability beyond;
- Unless special value is declared, loss and damage and delay of baggage results in maximum liability of 1,000 SDRs; destruction, loss, damage, or delay of cargo results in liability capped at 17 SDRs per kilogram;
- Carriers must maintain adequate insurance to cover their liability;
- The Convention's liability limits shall be reviewed every five years;
- The claimant may recover court costs and attorney's fees if the amount of damages awarded exceeds any written settlement offer made within six months of the accident but before suit is commenced (this is a "settlement inducement clause");
- The Convention introduces a "fifth jurisdiction" (of the passenger's domicile, if the carrier does business there) for personal injury or death (but not cargo and baggage) actions;

---

[19] *Id.*, at 281.
[20] *Ehrlich v. American Airlines*, 360 F.3d 366, 371 (2nd Cir. 2004).

- The Convention incorporates much of the liability regime of Montreal Protocol No. 4 relating to cargo;
- The formalities of the documents of carriage are not linked to the regime of liability and the carrier is not penalized for improper documentation.
- Arbitration clauses may be included in cargo air waybills;[21] and
- "Punitive, exemplary or other non-compensatory damages" are not recoverable.[22]

What follows are case examples emanating from the "Warsaw System."

INDEMNITY INSURANCE CO. v. PAN AMERICAN AIRWAYS 58 F. Supp. 338 (S.D.N.Y. 1944)

Are the limited liability provisions of the Warsaw Convention Constitutional?

The complaint in this case arose out of the crash of the Pan American Airways, *Yankee Clipper*, in the harbor of Lisbon, Portugal, on February 22, 1943. Recovery was sought of the damages suffered by the parents of Tamara Drasin Swan, who died in the crash. The action was brought by the compensation insurance carrier which, pursuant to its insurance contract with the decedent's employer, paid a compensation award to the parents of the deceased employee.

---

[21] The Montreal Convention allows the use of arbitration only with respect to carriage of cargo.

[22] *Compare* George Tompkins, Jr., *The Montreal Convention of 1999: This Is the Answer*, Aviation Q. 114-115 (Jul. 1999) (who views the new regime favorably), *with* Thomas Whalen, *The New Warsaw Convention: The Montreal Convention*, 25 Air & Space L. 12 (2000) (who does not). Reviews have been mixed. Other generally favorable treatments of the Warsaw Convention include Pablo De Leon and Werner Eyskens, *The Montreal Convention: Analysis of Some Aspects of the Attempted Modernization and Consolidation of the Warsaw System*, 66 J. Air L. & Com. 1155 (2001); Matthew R. Pickelman, Comment, *Draft Convention for the Unification of Certain Rules for International Carriage by Air: The Warsaw Convention Revisited for the Last Time?*, 64 J. Air L. & Com. 273 (1998); and Francis Lyall, *The Warsaw Convention—Cutting the Gordian Knot and the 1995 Intercarrier Agreement*, 22 Syracuse J. Int'l L. & Com. 67 (1996). For additional criticisms of the Montreal Convention, *see* Larry Moore, *The New Montreal Liability Convention, Major Changes in International Air Law: An End to the Warsaw Convention*, 9 Tul. J. Int'l & Comp. L. 223 (2001); Ludwig Weber, *ICAO's Initiative to Reform the Legal Framework for Air Carrier Liability*, 22 Annals Air & Space L. 59 (1997); and Sven Brise, *Economic Implications of Changing Passenger Limits in the Warsaw Liability System*, 22 Annals Air & Space L. 121 (1997).

Pan American Airways claimed the liability limitations under the Warsaw Convention of $8,291.87 (125,000 francs). The contract of transportation between the defendant Pan American Airways, and the deceased Tamara Swan, was expressly made subject to the limitation of the Warsaw Convention. Pan American also pled the failure of the plaintiff parents to file a claim in writing within thirty days after the event, as required by the contract of transportation.

The arguments relied on by the plaintiffs were four:

- The Warsaw Convention was unconstitutional because it encroached on the power of Congress to regulate commerce;
- The Warsaw Convention was inoperative because it was not self-executing and was never implemented by legislation;
- Being inoperative, it could not become effective as a contract between the carrier and the passenger; and
- The treaty was invalid in that its application would deprive the plaintiff of its property (under the Fifth Amendment) without due process of law.

According to the plaintiffs, the treaty professed to regulate foreign commerce—a power entrusted exclusively to Congress in Article I, Section 8 of the Constitution—without having received the approval of both houses of Congress. The U.S. declared its adoption of the Warsaw Convention by a *Declaration of Adherence*, advised by the Senate, and deposited on July 31, 1934. With "congressional" implementation by the Senate alone, it became effective for the U.S. on October 29, 1934.[23]

In response to plaintiff's first allegation of invalidation, the judge determined the treaty had been duly ratified in the manner prescribed by Congress. Treaties of commerce had been ratified in the manner challenged since the early days of the Republic. To the second charge, whether a treaty is self-executing, or requires implementation legislation, depends upon its terms, whether they call for further action or whether they are enforceable without legislation. The third point of contention was that the effectiveness of the contract of transportation

---

[23] See *Duff v. Varig Airlines, Inc.*, CCH 22 AVI. ¶ 17,367.

to limit the defendant's liability was predicated upon the "invalidity," or inoperativeness, of the treaty. As already stated, the treaty *was* valid, and since the premise failed, the argument had to fail. Finally, the argument, that the treaty was invalid because it deprived the plaintiff of property without "due-process," was rejected. The judge pointed out that, "statutes for the limitation of liability are no novelty."

The plaintiff's motion was denied.

CHUBB and SON v. ASIANA AIRLINES
214 F.3d 301, 304 (2nd Cir. 2000)

What liability rules apply if the origin nation has ratified the Hague Protocol (but not the Warsaw Convention), and the destination nation has ratified the Warsaw Convention (but not the Hague Protocol)?

In 1995, Asiana Airlines took delivery of 17 parcels containing computer chips from Samsung Electronics Co., agreeing to transport them from Seoul, South Korea, to San Francisco. Asiana instead flew them to Los Angeles and moved them to San Francisco via truck. Two of the 17 parcels, weighing a combined 35.3 kilograms and worth $583,000 were lost. The insurer, Chubb & Son, Inc., paid Samsung's claim and, thereby subrogated, brought suit against Asiana. Asiana invoked Article 22(2) of the Warsaw Convention which limits liability to $20 per kilogram of cargo lost, or in this case $706.00. Chubb argued that under Article 9 of that Convention, a carrier could not avail itself of the liability limitation of Article 22 if "the air waybill does not contain all the particulars set out in article 8(a) to (i) inclusive, and (q)[,]" and under article 8(c) the air waybill must specify the "agreed stopping places[.]"Accordingly, the insurer argued that because the aircraft stopped in Los Angeles, and Los Angeles was not listed in the air waybill as an agreed stopping place, the Article 22 liability limitation was inapplicable. The case became more complicated when Asiana filed a supplemental motion for summary judgment challenging the court's subject matter jurisdiction on grounds that the United States and South Korea were not in a treaty relationship with respect to the Warsaw Convention—the United States ratified the original Warsaw Convention while the Republic of Korea had ratified the

Hague Protocol, but did not separately adhere to the original Warsaw Convention.[24]

Applying the Vienna Convention on the Law of Treaties,[25] the U.S. Court of Appeals for the Second Circuit held that the ratification of two different liability regimes resulted in no common treaty in force between the United States and Korea.[26] Finding that "the parties to the Hague Protocol expressed an intention not to be bound by the original Warsaw Convention," the court held that at the time the cause of action arose, South Korea and the United States were signatories to two different treaties—the Hague Protocol and the Original Warsaw Convention, respectively.[27] Because the court found that these two nations were "not in treaty relations with regard to the international carriage of goods by air[,]" federal subject matter jurisdiction was deemed not to exist.[28] The court concluded that "no precedent in international law allows the creation of a separate treaty based on separate adherence by two states to different versions of a treaty, and it is not for the judiciary to alter, amend, or create an agreement between the United States and other states."[29]

---

[24] 214 F.3d 301, 304 (2nd Cir. 2000), *cert. den.* 533 U.S. 928 (2001) [hereinafter *Chubb*].

[25] *Vienna Convention on the Law of Treaties*, May 23, 1969, 1155 UNTS 331 (entered into force 27 Jan. 1980). Though the U.S. has never formally ratified the *Vienna Convention*, many courts have used it as a summary of customary principles of international law. Sean D. Murphy, *Contemporary Practice of the United States Relating to International Law*, 96 A.J.I.L. 706, 709 (2002).

[26] *Chubb*, 214 F.3d at 314. *See* Dana L. Christensen, *Comment: The Elusive Exercise of Jurisdiction over Air Transportation between the United States and South Korea*, 10 Pac. Rim L. & Pol'y J. 653, 688-689 (2001) (arguing that the *Chubb* decision was incorrectly decided).

[27] *Chubb*, 214 F.3d at 310 ("Those States that adhered to the *Hague Protocol* specifically adhered to the *Warsaw Convention* as amended at the Hague, not the Original *Warsaw Convention*. Thus, when South Korea adhered to the *Hague Protocol*, it indicated its intention not to be bound to the Original *Warsaw Convention*. Although it could have adhered separately to the Original *Warsaw Convention*, South Korea never exercised that option. South Korea is therefore not in a treaty relationship with the U.S. pursuant to the Original *Warsaw Convention*.") (internal citations omitted in parenthetical).

[28] *Id.* at 314. Federal subject matter jurisdiction exists for civil actions arising under, *inter alia*, treaties of the United States. 28 U.S.C. § 1331 (2003).

[29] *Chubb*, 214 F.3d at 314.

IN RE KOREAN AIR LINES DISASTER
704 F. Supp. 1135 (D.D.C. 1988)

*Under what conditions may the liability limits of the Warsaw
Convention be waived for willful misconduct?*

On September 1, 1983, 269 persons aboard Korean Air Lines
Flight 007 died while en route from New York to Seoul, South Korea.
The flight strayed off-course into Soviet airspace, and Soviet military
aircraft shot it down over the Sea of Japan. Many of the decedents'
representatives filed suit against several defendants, including Korean
Air Lines. Before the court in this trial was a motion brought by Korean Air Lines [KAL] for partial summary judgment dismissing the
plaintiff's complaints insofar as they sought damages against KAL in
excess of the Warsaw Convention limit for each passenger death.

The Warsaw Convention limits an air carrier's liability for each
passenger death unless the carrier is guilty of willful misconduct.
Thus, the issue in this trial was whether KAL had established that the
plaintiffs would not be able to adduce sufficient evidence to support a
finding that KAL was guilty of willful misconduct in the fateful flight.

The court defined "willful misconduct" as meaning,

> . . . *the intentional performance of an act (or
> failure to act) with knowledge that the act will
> probably result in injury or damage, or in
> some manner as to imply reckless disregard of
> the consequences of its performance, (or) a
> deliberate purpose not to discharge some duty
> necessary to safety.*

As plaintiffs would bear the burden of proving KAL's willful misconduct at trial, in order to recover damages greater than the Warsaw
limits, if the plaintiffs' proof on any element necessary to establish
willful misconduct was inadequate as a matter of law, then KAL was
entitled to summary judgment. However, giving plaintiffs the benefit of
all reasonable doubts, as the court had to do at this stage of the litigation, their evidence was capable of permissible inferences that would
establish each necessary element of willful misconduct. Plaintiffs ar-

gued that the crew of Flight 007 knew early on that, because of crew error prior to take-off, they were operating without a reliable Inertia Navigation System [INS], the primary means of navigating the flight. Instead of temporarily aborting the flight, to reprogram the INS, the crew decided to navigate the flight without the benefit of a reliable INS. This decision, in clear contravention of established procedures, was made to conceal their error that caused the INS to be either mis-programmed or misaligned. If they had aborted their flight to correct their error, they would have had to dump fuel; an action for which other KAL pilots had been disciplined in the past.

Korean Air Lines countered with an assertion there was no evidence as to the most probable cause of the accident. More particularly, KAL asserted the only inference that could be drawn from the "assumed deviation" was that the crew was negligent in failing to notice their deviation and to take corrective action. The court disagreed. The crew was repeatedly aware of their course deviation, but elected not to report it and take corrective action. The magnitude and duration of the deviation alleged here supported the inference that the crew realized its deviation some time prior to its last position report, but nevertheless continued the flight and continued to report being on course.

A claim of willful misconduct within the meaning of Article 25 of the Warsaw Convention has three essential elements:

- an *intentional act* or omission done with the conscious awareness that such an act or omission was wrongful;
- an *awareness* of the probable consequences of the act or omission; and
- a *causal relationship* between the act or omission and the injury sustained.

The crew's decision to conceal their error, rather than simply correct it, was an intentional act. Whether there was sufficient evidence for a conclusion the crew knew their INS system was unreliable was crucial to the awareness requirement. The court found there was sufficient evidence the crew knew that flying over the Soviet Union was prohibited, and that it was "dangerous." Finally, it was solely KAL's alleged misconduct that put the plane in the vulnerable position. And, it was solely KAL's failure to perceive the warnings, if given, that made the Soviet pilot's response possible. Korean Air Lines was in sole control of the airplane; only the crew had the ability to prevent the flight from entering Soviet airspace. It was found that warnings were given, and only the crew had the ability to heed the warnings. Therefore, there was evidence sufficient for a jury to conclude a causal connection between KAL's actions and the incident.

Korean Air Lines failed to carry its burden of persuading the court there were no disputed issues of fact that it was entitled to summary judgment as a matter of law. The motion was denied.

IN RE AIRCRASH IN BALI, INDONESIA
684 F.2d 1301 (9th Cir. 1982)

*Is state law preempted by the Warsaw Convention to the
extent that state law would prevent application of the
Convention's limitation on liability?*

A number of suits arose out of an air crash in Bali, Indonesia, on April 22, 1974, in which the plaintiffs' decedents and 104 other persons were killed. A jury found the defendant, Pan American World Airways (Pan Am), negligent, and awarded damages in excess of the Warsaw Convention liability limits. The U.S. District Court declined to reduce the verdicts to the Warsaw limits.

Pan Am appealed from the trial court's ruling that the Warsaw Convention was not applicable. The plaintiffs cross-appealed to attack evidentiary rulings made by the court in the course of the trial. The plaintiffs challenged the application, validity, and constitutionality of the Warsaw Convention, the Hague Protocol and the Montreal Agreement. They also attempted to avoid the liability limitations by showing willful misconduct on the part of Pan Am. The jury found no willful conduct. Plaintiffs, who would have been entitled to the benefit of the Montreal Agreement's provision of absolute liability up to a maximum of $75,000, chose instead to attack the Agreement and go to trial on *negligence* theories.

After the jury returned its verdict, the trial court ruled that, under California law, a decedent cannot by contract compromise a survivor's right to wrongful death recovery. Hence, they calculated, the contractual limitations imposed by the Warsaw Convention and subsequent agreements could have no operation. The court thus never reached the plaintiff's challenge to the constitutionality of the Warsaw Convention.

In refusing to apply the limitations on liability imposed by the War- saw Convention, the District Court relied on California law. It rea- soned that the Warsaw limitation is based on a contract between the passenger and the carrier. California does not permit a decedent to compromise by contract a survivor's right to wrongful death recovery. Any limitation based on a contract, therefore, can have no application against survivors under California law. The district court's decision presented two threshold questions. First, was the proper choice of law made? Second, does the Warsaw Convention preempt local law in re- spect to limitation of liability for wrongful death?

The Warsaw Convention requires recourse to local law to deter- mine certain issues. This was not disputed. However, Pan Am chal- lenged the court's choice of California law, although the jurisdiction of the federal district court in California was not challenged. Pan Am contended that either Virginia law, or the law of New South Wales, Australia, should have applied because descendent plaintiffs were resi- dents of these two locales. Apparently, either of these states' laws would have imposed a low dollar limit on wrongful death recovery, even in the absence of the Warsaw Convention. Irrespective, the court found Pan Am's argument unpersuasive since the plaintiffs' cases were filed in California.

The district court apparently did not consider whether the Warsaw Convention preempted the application of California's rule regarding the limitation by contract of wrongful death recoveries. It did not con- sider whether the application of California law would conflict with the Congressional scheme embodied in its adoption of the Warsaw Con- vention. The district court ruled that whatever its benefits were when it was ratified in 1934, the low limitation on liability could not be justified today by the conditions existing in 1934. However, the appel- late court knew of no doctrine that would allow it to examine congres- sional enactments to see if they still serve the purpose for which they were designed. Furthermore, Congress had ample opportunity to re- consider the wisdom of the Warsaw Convention, but it had yet to effect any changes.

Application of California law, as suggested in this case, necessarily conflicted with the congressional scheme. Accordingly, the Court of

Appeals held California law was preempted by the Warsaw Convention to the extent California law would prevent application of the Convention's limitation on liability. Plaintiffs then contended that if California law was preempted by the Warsaw Convention, the limitation on liability was unconstitutional. They made three constitutional challenges to the limitation, that the Warsaw Convention,

- is so arbitrary and unreasonable as to deprive them of substantive due process;
- deprived them of equal protection of the laws; and
- impermissibly burdened their constitutional right to travel.

The U.S. Court of Appeals for the 9th Circuit concluded that Article 22 of the Warsaw Convention is an economic regulation which would be Constitutional under the Commerce Clause—unless "arbitrary or unreasonable." The court found it to be neither arbitrary nor unreasonable, and therefore concluded it was not unconstitutional. The court also concluded the plaintiffs' third argument (of due process and right to travel) would fail if another remedy were available that would provide them with full compensation. The court found that such a remedy was available under the Tucker Act [30] if the liability limitation constituted a *taking* under the Fifth Amendment. However, no party to this litigation argued that the Warsaw Convention limitation constituted a *taking* entitling the plaintiffs to compensation by the United States under the just compensation clause of the Fifth Amendment.

Still unresolved in this case was the issue of willful misconduct. Records had been offered to the trial court showing the pilot in the fatal accident had made similar misstates in the past, of the kind causing this accident. Plaintiffs argued the pilot's mistakes in the past were evidence of habit and custom, that should have indicated to Pan Am he was likely to make the same mistake again. The records were offered to show that Pan Am had notice of the pilot's alleged incompetence, and Pan Am should not have allowed the pilot to fly.

Unfortunately, the trial court determined the records did not meet the standard for evidence of habit or custom. The appellate court disagreed. For the reasons stated, the judgment of the trial court was re-

---

[30] 28 U.S.C. § 1491.

versed, and the case was remanded for a new trial on the issue of willful misconduct.

EL AL ISRAEL AIRLINES v. TSENG
525 U.S. 155 (1999)

Does the Warsaw Convention provide the exclusive cause of action for international travel, or does the common law provide an alternative remedy?

This case involved an intrusive security search of Tsui Yuan Tseng at New York's John F. Kennedy International Airport during the process of embarking an El Al flight to Tel Aviv.[31] Pursuant to El Al's preboarding security procedures, a security guard questioned Ms. Tseng about her destination and travel plans, concluded her responses were illogical, and ranked her as a high risk passenger. She then was subjected to a 15-minute search of her baggage and person, during which she was required to remove her shoes, jacket and sweater, and to lower her blue jeans to midhip. A female security guard then examined her clothes by hand and by an electronic security wand.

Ms. Tseng testified that she was "really sick and very upset ... emotionally traumatized and disturbed" by the incident, causing her to undergo medical and psychiatric treatment upon her return from Israel. She filed an action in state court, asserting the torts of assault and false imprisonment. El Al had the case removed to federal district court, which held that the claim was governed by the Warsaw Convention; but the court concluded the claim was not cognizable under Article 17 because Ms. Tseng suffered no bodily injury (as explained above Warsaw does not permit "recovery for psychic or psychosomatic injury unaccompanied by bodily injury"), and her injury was not the result of an "accident."[32] On appeal, the Second Circuit agreed, but held that plaintiff's claims for assault and false imprisonment did not fall under Warsaw, and could be pursued under state tort law.

---

[31] *El Al Israel Airlines v. Tseng*, 525 U.S. 155 (1999). *See* Loryn Zerner, *Tseng v. El Al Israel Airlines and Article 25 of the Warsaw Convention: A Cloud Left Uncharted*, 14 Am. U. Int'l L. Rev. 1245 (1999); Jon Martin, *Tseng v. El Al Israel Airlines Ltd: The Second Circuit Further Weakens the Warsaw Convention*, 31 Conn. L. Rev. 297 (1998).

[32] 919 F. Supp. 155 (S.D.N.Y. 1996).

Article 24 of the Warsaw Convention provides that "cases covered by Article 17" may "only be brought subject to the conditions and limits set out in this convention."[33] The Supreme Court found that the "cardinal purpose" of Warsaw was to establish uniformity of law governing international aviation liability. It noted that the Second Circuit's construction "would encourage artful pleading by plaintiffs seeking to opt out of the Convention's liability scheme when local law promised recovery in excess of that prescribed by the treaty,"[34] thereby contravening Warsaw's overriding purpose of uniformity.

Examining the text of the Convention, its legislative history, its purpose, and the judicial precedent of other nations, the U.S. Supreme Court concluded that Warsaw "precludes a passenger from maintaining an action for personal injury damages under local law when her claim does not satisfy the conditions for liability under the Convention."[35] In other words, recovery for an injury caused by an accident occurring on an international itinerary, on board the aircraft or in the course of embarking or disembarking, "if not allowed under the [Warsaw] Convention, is not available at all."[36]

EASTERN AIRLINES v. FLOYD
499 U.S. 530 (1991)

May passengers recover for emotional injury
unaccompanied by physical injury?

Several passengers suffered mental distress when the Eastern Airlines Boeing 727, bound for the Bahamas, lost power in all three engines and began a sharp and terrifying descent. The flight crew informed the passengers it would be necessary to ditch the plane in the ocean. Miraculously, the pilots managed to restart the engines and land the jet safely at Miami International Airport. The passengers claimed to have suffered severe emotional (but not physical) injury nonetheless.

---

[33] Warsaw Convention, Art. 24.
[34] 525 U.S. at 170.
[35] *Id.* at 176.
[36] *Id.* at 161.

The U.S. Supreme Court held that Article 17 does not allow recovery for purely mental injuries.[37] This conclusion was based on the French translation (interpreting *"lesion corporelle"* to mean "bodily injury"),[38] and on the primary purpose of the Warsaw Convention—limiting liability in order to foster growth of the infant airline industry.[39] Writing for the majority, Justice Marshall concluded:

> *The narrower reading of 'lesion corporelle' also is consistent with the primary purpose of the contracting parties to the Convention: limiting the liability of air carriers in order to foster the growth of the fledgling commercial aviation industry. . . . Whatever may be the current view among Convention signatories, in 1929 the parties were more concerned with protecting air carriers and fostering a new industry than providing full recovery to injured passengers, and we read 'lesion corporelle' in a way that respects that legislative choice.*[40]

---

[37] 499 U.S. at 534. For a discussion of mental anguish claims under Article 17, *see* Louisa Collins, *Pre- and Post-Impact Pain and Suffering and Mental Anguish in Aviation Accidents*, 59 J. Air L. & Com. 402 (1994).

[38] 499 U.S. at 536, 542. For a discussion of *Floyd* and *"lesion corporelle" see* Dale Eaton, *Recovery for Purely Emotional Distress Under the Warsaw Convention: Narrow Constriction of Lesion Corporelle in Eastern Airlines, Inc. v. Floyd,* 1993 Wis. L. Rev. 563 (1993), and Gregory Sisk, *Recovery for Emotional Distress Under the Warsaw Convention: The Elusive Search for the French Legal Meaning of Lesion Corporelle,* 25 Tex. Int'l L.J. 127 (1990); *see also* Sheila Holmes, *Recovery For Purely Mental Injuries Under the Warsaw Convention,* 58 J. Air L. & Com. 1205 (1993).

[39] 499 U.S. at 546. *Adler v. Malev Hungarian Airlines,* 1992 WL 15144 (S.D.N.Y. 1992) ("Allowing state law causes of action alleging purely psychic injuries resulting from accidents occurring in international travel would frustrate the Convention's goals of uniformity and certainty in air carrier liability.")

[40] 499 U.S. 530, 546 (1991). This interpretation honors the compromise that was reached in Warsaw in 1929, and promotes uniformity, among its principal goals. In other words, the Court refused to read into the Convention the "modern reality" that was not foreseen in 1929 when the Convention was drafted.

AIR FRANCE v. SAKS
470 U.S. 392 (1985)

What kind of event constitutes an "accident" for which recovery may be had under the Warsaw Convention?

Saks involved a passenger who lost her hearing in one ear after a routine depressurization of an Air France aircraft landing normally at Los Angeles. In concluding that no Article 17 "accident" had occurred, Justice Sandra Day O'Connor, on behalf of the U.S. Supreme Court, emphasized several points:

- The definition of an accident under Article 17 should be flexibly applied after assessing all the circumstances surrounding the passenger's injuries;
- The "event or happening" that caused the passenger's injury must be abnormal, "unexpected or unusual";
- The event must be "external to the passenger," and not the passenger's own "internal reaction" to normal flight operations; and
- Where the evidence is contradictory, the trier of fact must determine whether an accident, so defined, has occurred.

Note that the term "accident" refers to the *cause* of the injury, rather than the injury itself.[41] In *Saks*, the court began by observing that Article 18 of the Warsaw Convention used the word "occurrence" in defining liability for lost or damaged baggage or cargo, and the word "accident" in Article 17, when addressing carrier liability for personal injury. Since the two terms are not synonymous, the drafters must have meant that they be given different meaning.

In *Saks*, the Supreme Court noted that the French legal definition of the term *"accident"* (relevant, of course, because French is the official language of the Warsaw Convention) when used to describe the cause of an injury, is a "fortuitous, unexpected, unusual, or unintended

---

[41] *Sakaria v. Trans World Airlines*, 8 F.3d 164, 170 (4th Cir. 1993), *cert. den.* 114 S.Ct. 1835 (1994).

event."[42] *Saks*, however, would reject the limitation that the event must be fortuitous or unintentional, wholly dropping these requirements from its reformulated definition of "accident." The Court found the text of the Convention to require that a "passenger's injury must be caused by an unexpected or unusual event."[43] Thus, the controlling French language of *"accident"* embraces the requirements that it be *fortuitous* and *unintended*.

In dictum, the Court in *Saks* found that even intentional torts caused by third persons could fall within the definition of an Article 17 accident, citing with approval several lower court decisions that found airline liability for damages caused by terrorist events, such as aircraft hijackings.[44] It must be emphasized that these are not cases in which intentional torts have been perpetuated by the defendant airline or its employees; these lower courts were, in effect, holding the carrier vicariously liable for the intentional torts of third persons.

According to Justice O'Connor, the *travaux préparatoires*[45] reveal that "Article 20(1) of the final draft contains the 'necessary measures' language which the Reporter believed would shield the carrier from liability for 'the accidents occur[r]ing to people by the fault of third parties' and for 'accidents occur[r]ing for any other cause.'"[46]

While observing that the definition of an accident should be flexibly applied, in *Saks*, the U.S. Supreme Court noted liability extends under Article 17 "only if a passenger's injury is caused by an unexpected or unusual event or happening that is *external to the passenger*. . .,"[47] concluding that a pre-existing condition or sensitivity of the passenger aggravated by "usual, normal, and expected" flight operations would not qualify as an accident.[48] The court did not address the question of

---

[42] 470 U.S. at 400, 105 S. Ct. at 1338.

[43] 470 U.S. at 400, 105 S. Ct. at 1343.

[44] The court cited *Evangelinos v. Trans World Airlines, Inc.*, 550 F.2d 152 (3rd Cir. 1977) (*en banc*) (carrier liable for passenger injuries suffered in terrorist attack in Athens, Greece, during embarkation); *Day v. Trans World Airlines*, 528 F.2d 31 (2nd Cir. 1975) (en banc), *cert. den.*, 429 U.S. 890 (1976) (carrier liable for injuries to passengers by terrorist attack suffered during flight embarkation at Athens, Greece, airport); and *Krystal v. British Overseas Airways Corp.*, 403 F. Supp. 1322 (C.D. Cal. 1975) (carrier liable for injuries suffered as a result of hijacking of an aircraft en route from Bombay to London).

[45] The *travaux préparatoires* are the minutes, or historical record, of the meetings resulting in adoption of international law.

[46] 470 U.S. at 402.

[47] 470 U.S. at 405, 105 S.Ct. at 1345.

[48] *Id.*

whether a pre-existing infirmity aggravated by unusual, abnormal and unexpected flight operations would constitute an Article 17 accident.

OLYMPIC AIRWAYS v. HUSAIN
124 S. Ct. 1221 (2003)

Does inaction constitute an "accident" for which recovery may be had under the Warsaw Convention?

Dr. Abib Hanson and his wife, Rubina Husain were flying aboard an Olympic Airways flight from Athens to San Francisco, seated in economy class, three rows from the smoking section. Hanson suffered from asthma. His wife asked a flight attendant several times to move him farther from the smoking section because he was "allergic to smoke." The flight attendant responded that there were no available seats, and that she was too busy to assist. In fact, there were available seats in economy class. Two hours into the flight, trying to get fresher air, Dr. Hanson walked forward in the cabin, and leaned against a seat near the galley. He felt ill. An allergist gave Dr. Hanson a shot of epinephrine, and administered cardiopulmonary resuscitation [CPR] and oxygen. Shortly thereafter, Dr. Hanson died. His heirs and estate filed a wrongful death action against Olympic Airways.

The principal issue was whether these circumstances constituted an "accident" under Article 17 of the Warsaw Convention. Like most of the critical terms in Article 17, precisely what kind of event constitutes an "accident" is nowhere defined in the Warsaw Convention.[49] Before *Husain,* the seminal case on the issue was *Air France v. Saks,*[50] handed down nearly two decades earlier.

The year before *Husain,* appellate court decisions in the United Kingdom and Australia had concluded that inaction could not constitute an Article 17 "accident." Both cases involved an allegation that passengers suffered Deep Vein Thrombosis [DVT] because of the failure of an airline to warn passengers that sitting for long periods of time

---

[49] *DeMarines v. KLM Royal Dutch Airlines,* 580 F.2d 1193, 1196 (3rd Cir. 1978).

[50] 470 U.S. 392, 105 S.Ct. 1338 (1985). More than 100 federal cases have addressed the question of what constitutes an aviation "accident" under Article 17 of the Warsaw Convention. *See also* Jeffrey Cahn, *Saks: A Clarification of the Warsaw Convention Passenger Liability Standards,* 16 U. Miami Int-Am. L. Rev. 539 (1985); *Lee Kreindler, Aviation Accident Law* § 11.04 (1994); *Stuart Speiser & Charles Krause, Aviation Tort Law* § 11.25 (1978).

may cause DVT. In *Deep Vein Thrombosis and Air Travel Group Litigation*,[51] the Master of Rolls of England's Court of Appeal concluded, "I cannot see, however, how inaction itself can ever properly be described as an accident. It is not an event; it is a non-event. Inaction is the antithesis of an accident."[52]

Six months later, in *Qantas Ltd. v.* Povey,[53] the appellate division of the Supreme Court of Victoria, Australia, concurred, concluding "a failure to do something . . . cannot be characterized as an event or happening. . . ."[54] The court went on to opine that a pilot's failure to drop the landing gear would not constitute an Article 17 accident, but the resulting crash of the aircraft would. Thus, although inaction could serve as the catalyst for an accident, and the accident could cause passenger injury or death, in and of itself, mere inaction does not meet the legal definition of an Article 17 "accident."[55]

In *Husain*, Olympic Airways argued that Article 17 requires an action on behalf of the carrier to satisfy the definition of an "accident," and that the flight attendant's refusal to move the decedent was mere inaction. The carrier emphasized the ambient smoke as the injury-producing event aggravating his pre-existing asthmatic condition leading to his death, not the flight attendant's failure to act or any violation of industry standards. In other words, the inaction of the flight attendant did not result in an "accident" causing the passenger's death; his own internal reaction to second-hand smoke did that, and second-hand smoke is not an unusual or unexpected event on an international flight.

But the federal courts considering Mr. Hanson's death focused on the flight attendant's failure to accede to his wife's requests. Finding for the plaintiff, the Federal District Court held that the flight attendant's actions were in "blatant disregard of industry standards and

---

[51] [2003] EWCA Civ. 1005, 2003 WL 21353471 (Jul. 3, 2003).

[52] [2003] EWCA Civ. 1005, p. 25, 2003 WL 21353471 (Lord Phillips, M.R.). He continued, "[T]he failure to warn of the risk of DVT, or to advise on precautions which would avoid or minimize that risk . . . cannot . . . be categorised [sic] as an accident. It was simply something that did not happen-a non-event. For this reason alone I would hold that the failure to warn of or to advise about the dangers of DVT is not capable of amounting to an accident under Article 17." *Id.* at 29

[53] [2003] VSCA 227 p. 17, 2003 WL 23000693 (Dec. 23, 2003).

[54] *Id.* (Ormiston, J.A.)

[55] Similarly, a lower federal court has held that failure to warn of the risk of DVT was not an Article 17 accident, thus precluding recovery by a passenger who suffered a stroke as a result of it. *Louis v. British Airways*, 2003 US Dist. Lexis 24750 (Nov. 17, 2003).

airline policies," and were therefore neither expected nor usual.[56] On appeal, the U.S. Court of Appeals for the Ninth Circuit affirmed, concluding that the flight attendant's refusal to reseat the decedent "was unexpected or unusual in light of industry standards, Olympic policy, and the simple nature of Dr. Hanson's requested accommodation."[57]

In an opinion written by Justice Clarence Thomas, the U.S. Supreme Court dismissed Olympic Airways' efforts to distinguish between the flight attendant's discourtesy, and the ambient smoke, as the injury producing event. The Court found that "Petitioner's statement that the flight attendant's failure to reseat Dr. Hanson was not the 'injury producing event' is nothing more than a bald assertion, unsupported by any law or argument."[58] The Court instead concluded there was more than a single injury-producing event, and that *both* the passenger's exposure to the second-hand smoke, and the refusal of the flight attendant to assist the passenger, contributed to his death.[59]

As to the distinction between action and inaction, the Court held that such a distinction might be relevant were this a common law torts case, but a negligence regime is not what is contemplated under the Warsaw Convention. Indeed, the Court cited *Saks* for the proposition that recovery may be had for intentional torts under Warsaw. What is contemplated under Article 17 is "an unexpected or unusual event or happening," and the refusal of a flight attendant to assist a passenger who requested assistance was such an event or happening.[60]

As to Olympic Airways' assertion that inaction cannot constitute an Article 17 accident, Justice Thomas posed an analogy. A Doctor informs the crew that a passenger aboard a flight will die unless he is moved to a hospital within one hour. Though it is industry policy to land at the nearest airport in such situations, Thomas posits, the crew chooses instead to disregard the request and does not land at an airport only 30 minutes away. Thomas cited a lower court decision for the proposition that "The notion that this is not an unusual event is staggering."[61] The Court also noted Article 25 provides that the liability

---

[56] 116 F. Supp. 2d 1121, 1134 (N.D. Cal. 2000).
[57] 316 F.2d 829, 837 (9th Cir. 2002).
[58] 124 S.Ct. at 1228.
[59] *Id.* at 1228.
[60] *Id.* at 1228-1229.
[61] *Id.* at 1229, citing *McCaskey v. Continental Airlines*, 159 F. Supp. 2d 562, 574 (S.D. Tex. 2001) (Warsaw claim existed where airline employees were rude prior to boarding, and subse-

caps of the Convention may be lifted for willful misconduct "or such default on [the carrier's] part as . . . is considered to be the equivalent to willful misconduct." Article 20(1) also provides that the "due care" defense is unavailable where the carrier fails to take "all necessary measures to avoid the damages." According to Thomas, "These provisions suggest that an air carrier's inaction can be the basis for liability."[62]

Justice Antonin Scalia wrote a dissent, the major portions of which were joined by Justice O'Connor. As the author of the Court's opinion in *Saks*, O'Connor's dissent lends credence to the notion that the Supreme Court in *Husain* strayed well beyond the bounds of *Saks*. Justice Scalia points out that the word "accident" could have two very different meanings: (1) something that is unintentional, or not "on purpose"; or (2) an unusual or unexpected event, intentional or not. According to Scalia, the Court in *Saks* adopted the latter view. This is a crucial distinction because, while inaction may be an accident in the former sense, whether it can be in the latter is questionable.[63] Scalia pointed to the above-described decisions rendered by courts in Australia and the United Kingdom, which held it cannot.

Recognizing uniformity of law was an important purpose of Warsaw,[64] Scalia observed that "Maintaining a coherent international body of treaty law requires us to give deference to the *legal rules* our treaty partners adopt."[65] He bluntly condemned the majority opinion, writing "Today's decision stands out for its failure to give any serious consideration to how the courts of our treaty partners have resolved the legal

---

quently failed to provide sufficient assistance to a passenger who suffered a stroke aboard a flight). But as Justice Scalia points out in dissent, the 11th Circuit denied recovery under Article 17 on facts similar to Thomas' hypothetical, in *Krys v. Lufthansa German Airlines*, 119 F.3d 1515 (11th Cir. 1997). The court there found that the failure of the crew to land the aircraft did not cause the passenger's heart attack. Because the heart attack was not caused by an "unexpected or unusual event external to the passenger" there was no Article 17 accident. Similarly, in *Walker v. Eastern Air Lines*, 775 F. Supp. 111 (S.D.N.Y. 1991), the court found that there was no Article 17 accident where it was alleged that inadequate care given by the cabin crew aggravated the passenger's preexisting asthma condition and contributed to his death.

[62] 124 S.Ct. at 1230.

[63] *Id.* at 1231.

[64] Wrote Scalia, "We can, and should, look to decisions of other signatories when we interpret treaty positions. Foreign constructions are evidence of the original shared understanding of the contracting parties. Moreover, it is reasonable to impute to the parties an intent that their respective courts strive to interpret the treaty consistently."

[65] 124 S.Ct. at 1233, footnote 2 [emphasis in original].

issues before us."[66] He used phrases like "sudden insularity" and "new abstemiousness with regard to foreign fare"[67] to express disappointment with the majority's failure to follow precedent in its sister common law jurisdictions in interpreting the Warsaw Convention. In a footnote to the majority opinion, Justice Thomas rejected this precedent, dismissing it as mere "opinions of intermediate appellate courts of our sister signatories," decided on different facts.[68]

Scalia retorted that the Supreme Court had on numerous occasions looked to appellate court decisions of other jurisdictions on matters of common treaty interpretation, and that the U.K. decision was authored by the Master of Rolls—"the chief judge of England's civil appellate court—a position thought by many to be even more influential than that of a Law Lord."[69] As to Thomas' view that the Australian and U.K. decisions were decided on different facts, Scalia rebutted, "*Deep Vein Thrombosis* and *Povey* hold in no uncertain terms that inaction cannot be an [Article 17] accident; not that inaction *consisting of a failure to warn of deep vein thrombosis cannot* be an accident."[70]

WALLACE v. KOREAN AIR LINES
214 F.3d 293 (2nd Cir. 2000)

Can the acts of a sexual predator be deemed an "accident" for which recovery from the airline may be had under Warsaw?

Three hours into a flight from Seoul to Los Angeles, Brandi Wallace "awoke in the darkened plane to find that Mr. Park [the male passenger seated next to her] had unbuckled her belt, unzipped and unbuttoned her jean shorts, and placed his hands into her underpants to fondle her." She awoke, turned away, and when he persisted, hit him hard, jumped over the two men seated next to her, and reported the incident to a flight attendant who reassigned her to another seat.

In *Wallace,* the U.S. Court of Appeals for the Second Circuit noted that courts wrestling with *Saks* had divided into two camps—those

---

[66] 124 S.Ct. at 1230.

[67] *Id.* at 1230-1231.

[68] *Id.* at 1229, footnote 9.

[69] *Id.* at at 1233.

[70] *Id.* at 1233, footnote 2 [emphasis in original].

holding an accident must arise from a risk that is characteristic of air travel, and those that have not. The court in *Wallace* avoided this "Talmudic debate" by embracing the flexibility articulated by *Saks* and finding the facts in the case satisfied either interpretation of "accident":

> *[I]t is plain that the characteristics of air travel increased Ms. Wallace's vulnerability to Mr. Park's assault. When Ms. Wallace took her seat in economy class on the KAL flight, she was cramped into a confined space beside two men she did not know, one of whom turned out to be a sexual predator. The lights were turned down and the sexual predator was left unsupervised in the dark. . . .*

> *[I]t is undisputed that for the entire duration of Mr. Park's attack not a single flight attendant noticed a problem. And it is not without significance that when Ms. Wallace woke up, she could not get away immediately, but had to endure another of Mr. Park's advances before clambering out to the aisle.*[71]

---

[71] 2 Avi. L. Rep. 17,869.

CHAPTER 20

PUBLIC INTERNATIONAL AIR LAW

Every nation enjoys complete and exclusive sovereignty over its airspace. Before there can be an exchange in international traffic rights, the nation over whose territory is to be flown must consent, usually in the form of a bilateral air transport agreement.

THE CHICAGO CONVENTION OF 1944

In 1944, the U.S. government invited allied world powers to Chicago with the objective of establishing an international aviation council, and to provide for worldwide airways.[1] The multilateral agreement that emerged was the Convention on International Civil Aviation, more popularly known simply as the "Chicago Convention," from which came certain principles and arrangements to facilitate international civil aviation. Among them were:

- a contractual format to be used as the basis for air transport agreements between nations;
- fundamental agreements to facilitate international air navigation; and
- the provisional development of the International Civil Aviation Organization [ICAO].

The Convention reaffirmed that every country has complete and exclusive sovereignty over airspace above its territory, and if the air-

---

[1] Paul Stephen Dempsey, *Law & Foreign Policy in International Aviation* 7 (Transnational 1987).

craft of one state were to transit the airspace of another, it must first obtain permission of the country whose airspace it will penetrate.

In Chicago, the United States promoted the position that airlines of all nations should have relatively unrestricted operating rights on international routes.[2] In the U.S. view, reliance on commercial air carriers to provide the quantity and quality of transport services demanded by consumers was preferable to economic regulation by government fiat.[3] In pursuit of this policy, American negotiators called for a multilateral granting of all of the so-called "five freedoms"[4] of the air and insisted that the determination of capacities,[5] frequencies,[6] and fares should be left to market forces rather than delegated to an international regulatory body.[7]

The "five freedoms" of the air for which the U.S. delegation called for multilateral recognition are as follows:

- *First freedom*—The civil aircraft of one country has the right to fly over the territory of another country without landing, provided the over flown country is notified in advance and approval is given.

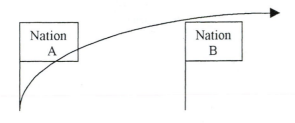

---

[2] *See* United Nations Information Organization [UNIO], *Report of the Chicago Convention on International Civil Aviation* 1, 4, 31 (1944). *But see* Anthony Sampson, *Empires of the Sky: The Politics, Contests and Cartels of World Airlines* 66-67 (1984).

[3] *See generally*, Anthony Sampson, *Empires of the Sky: The Politics, Contests and Cartels of World Airlines* 63-67 (1984); Nicholas Mateesco Matte, *Treatise on Air-Aeronautical Law* 128 (1981).

[4] Betsy Gidwitz, *The Politics of International Air Transport* 49-50 (1980); Ralph Azzie, *Specific Problems Solved by the Negotiation of Bilateral Air Agreements*, 13 McGill L. J. 303 (1967).

[5] Capacity refers to the available number of commercial seats on a specific aircraft-type multiplied by the flight frequency of that aircraft-type during a specific time period (usually one week) over a specific route.

[6] Frequency refers to the number of flights during a specific time period (usually one week) over a specific route.

[7] *See* Andreas Lowenfeld, *Aviation Law* § II-5 (1972).

- *Second freedom*—A civil aircraft of one country has the right to land in another country for technical reasons, such as refueling or maintenance, without offering any commercial service to or from that point.

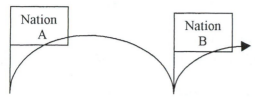

- *Third freedom*—An airline has the right to carry traffic from its country of registry to another country.

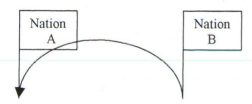

- *Fourth freedom*—An airline has the right to carry traffic from another country to its own country of registry.

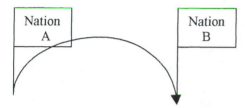

- *Fifth freedom*—An airline has the right to carry traffic between two countries outside its own country of registry so long as the flight originates or terminates in its own country of registry (subsequent practice has allowed "change of gauge" operations, whereby airlines transfer passengers between aircraft at a foreign point).

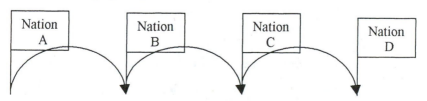

Some have argued that these were not really "freedoms" of the air at all, but restrictions. Actually, they were certainly freedoms if won in bilateral or multilateral negotiations, though usually exchanged on a *quid-pro-quo* basis. Otherwise, each state enjoyed complete and exclusive sovereignty above its territory to prohibit the exercise of such "freedoms."

In addition to the Chicago Convention, the Chicago conference also produced the *Transit Agreement*, which provided for the multilateral exchange of first and second freedoms.[8] More than 100 nations have since ratified the Transit Agreement. The Chicago conference also drafted the *Transport Agreement*, calling for the multilateral exchange of all five freedoms; but fewer than a dozen nations ratified it.[9] In the years since Chicago, several other freedoms of the air have been identified:

- *Sixth freedom—An* airline has the right to carry traffic between two foreign countries via its own country of registry. (Sixth freedom can also be viewed as a combination of third and fourth freedoms secured by the country of registry from two different countries).

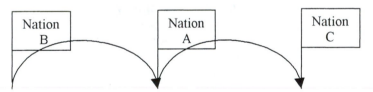

- *Seventh freedom—An* airline operating entirely outside one territory of its country of registry has the right to fly into another country and there discharge, or take on, traffic coming from, or destined to, a third country.

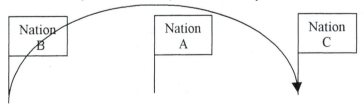

---

[8] International Air Services Transit Agreement, 59 Stat. 1693, T.I.A.S. No. 487, U.N.T.S. 389 (1951).
[9] International Air Transport Agreement, 59 Stat. 1701, T.I.A.S. No. 488, U.N.T.S. 387 (1953).

- *Eighth freedom—An* airline has the right to carry traffic from one point in the territory of a country to another point in the same country on a flight, which originates in the airline's home country. (This right is more commonly known as "consecutive cabotage," in which domestic traffic is reserved to domestic carriers).

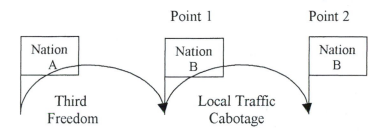

- *Ninth freedom—*An airline has the right to carry traffic from one point in the territory of a country to another point in the same country. (This right is "pure cabotage"). Article 7 of the Chicago Convention allows a nation to reserve cabotage to its own flag carriers; if it surrenders it to another state, it must do so on a nondiscriminatory basis.[10]

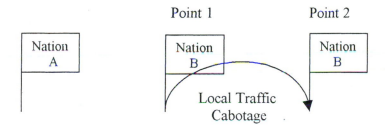

---

[10] Betsy Gidwitz, *The Politics of International Air Transport* 49-50 (1980). Bin Cheng, *The Law of International Air Transport* 13, 17 (1962). Professor Cheng has noted that "the more refined these distinctions become the more restrictive is the policy pursued; for every newborn 'freedom of the air' is in reality an additional shackle on the right to fly of foreign carriers, to be removed only at a price." *Id.* at 17. Paul Stephen Dempsey, *Law & Foreign Policy in International Aviation* 49-50 (Transnational 1987).

THE BERMUDA AGREEMENT

In 1946, representatives of the United States and the United Kingdom met at Bermuda to negotiate a bilateral agreement between the two countries outlining,

- the exchange of air rights;
- non-discriminatory practices;
- customs, duties and charges;
- airworthiness of aircraft and qualification of flight personnel;
- applicable laws and regulations;
- aircraft registration and ownership;
- rates and the procedures for ratemaking; and
- dispute resolution.[11]

The Bermuda bilateral air transport agreement between the U.S. and U.K. was the first of the so called major postwar "bilateral agreements," and it became the standard for U.S. bilateral agreements, from which was formed a United States Standard Form of Bilateral Agreements in 1953. The Bermuda style agreements became the standard for other bilateral agreements subsequently written. This form was used by the United States in negotiating bilateral agreements with several foreign countries, many of which remain in effect today. The form was meant only to be a guide, and all of its provisions are not necessarily contained in existing agreements. The form has been revised for use in more recent negotiations. The bilateral agreement with the United Kingdom has since been re-negotiated. The original agreement is now referred to as "Bermuda I," the subsequent agreement being "Bermuda II."

Actually, early U.S. drafts of the Chicago Convention included elaborate provisions for the limitation of carrier capacity. The United States also called for the strict recognition of cabotage in international aviation, thereby restricting foreign access to domestic traffic. Hence, the U.S. negotiating posture at Chicago was not as *laissez faire* as some historians have suggested.[12]

---

[11] Paul Stephen Dempsey, *Law & Foreign Policy in International Aviation* 53 (Transnational 1987).
[12] M. Willrich, *Energy and World Politics* 11-13 (1975).

THE INTERNATIONAL CIVIL AVIATION ORGANIZATION

Although the Chicago Conference failed in its attempt to formulate a comprehensive economic policy for international civil aviation or to effectuate an exchange of traffic rights, it laid the foundation for postwar establishment of the International Civil Aviation Organization.[13] The Provisional International Civil Aviation Organization [PICAO] functioned from June 6, 1945, until April 4, 1947. ICAO began operations April 4, 1947, and that same year was included under the umbrella of the United Nations' Economic and Social Council [ECOSOC]. ICAO was given responsibility for regulating the many technical aspects of international civil aviation.[14]

ICAO was vested with both quasi-legislative power (in its ability to adopt Standards and Recommended Practices [SARPs]), and quasi-judicial power (in its ability to settle disputes arising under the Chicago Convention).[15] It also holds quasi-judicial authority to resolve aviation disputes between nations. The nations attending the Chicago Conference conceded the need for uniform technical standards; consequently, the jurisdiction of the ICAO was extended to adopting SARPs (included as Annexes to the Chicago Convention for convenience) addressing such matters as aircraft licensing, airworthiness certification, registration of aircraft, international operating standards, and airways and communications controls.[16]

ICAO standards are binding, at least in the absence of a notification of the Council of a member state's inability to comply. The ICAO Council has adopted the following Annexes:

- *Annex 1: Personnel Licensing*[17]
- *Annex 2: Rules of the Air*[18]
- *Annex 3: Meteorology*
- *Annex 4: Aeronautical Charts*[19]

---

[13] *See* Andreas Lowenfeld, *Aviation Law* II-5 (1972).
[14] Michael Milde, *The Chicago Convention—After Forty Years*, 9 Annals of Air & Space L. 119, 121 (1984). FitzGerald, *ICAO Now and in the Coming Decades*, in International Air Transport: Law Organization and Policies For The Future 47, 52 (N. Matte ed. 1976).
[15] Michael Milde, *The Chicago Convention—After Forty Years*, 9 Annals of Air & Space L. 121, 123 (1984).
[16] R. Thornton, *International Airlines and Politics* 32, 34 (1970).
[17] Chicago Convention, Art 37(d).
[18] *Id.* Art. 37(c).
[19] *Id.* Art. 37(i).

- *Annex 5: Units of Measurement to be used in Air-Ground Communications*
- *Annex 6: Operation of Aircraft, International Commercial Air Transport*
- *Annex 7: Aircraft Nationality and Registration Marks*
- *Annex 8: Airworthiness of Aircraft*[20]
- *Annex 9: Facilitation of International Air Transport*[21]
- *Annex 10: Aeronautical Telecommunication*[22]
- *Annex 11: Air Traffic Services*[23]
- *Annex 12: Search and Rescue*[24]
- *Annex 13: Aircraft Accident Inquiry*[25]
- *Annex 14: Aerodromes*[26]
- *Annex 15: Aeronautical Information Services*
- *Annex 16: Environmental Protection*
- *Annex 17: Security—Safeguarding International Civil Aviation Against Acts of Unlawful Interference*
- *Annex 18: Safe Transport of Dangerous Goods by Air*[27]

The Chicago Convention gives ICAO responsibility beyond safety and navigation to accomplish such tasks as preventing ". . . economic waste caused by unreasonable competition . . ." and avoiding ". . . discrimination between contracting States. . . ."[28] However, as the above list reveals, ICAO has focused its energies primarily on issues surrounding air safety and navigation, leaving its jurisdiction over economic issues largely underutilized.[29] But with World Trade Organization in Geneva, and its General Agreement on Trade in Services [GATS] taking more of an interest in the economic affairs of airlines, many member states have urged ICAO to assert its dormant powers under the Chicago Convention in this arena. ICAO has issued

---

[20] *Id.* Art. 37(e).
[21] *Id.* Art. 37(j).
[22] *Id.* Art. 37(a).
[23] *Id.*
[24] *Id.* Art. 37(k).
[25] *Id.*
[26] *Id.* Art. 37(b).
[27] Paul Dempsey, *Law & Foreign Policy in International Aviation* 275 (1987).
[28] Chicago Convention, supra, Art 44(e), (g).
[29] Among the responsibilities given ICAO by the Chicago Convention are to meet the world's needs for ". . . safe, regular, efficient and economical air transport . . ." and to "[p]revent economic waste caused by unreasonable competition. . . ." Chicago Convention, Art. 44.

recommendations on a number of economic issues, including the extraterritorial application of competition laws, tariff setting, approval and enforcement, bias in computer reservations systems, and discrimination in airport, navigation and user fees.[30]

ICAO has been asked to exercise its formal dispute resolution functions on six occasions: *India v. Pakistan* (1952)—involving Pakistan's refusal to allow Indian commercial aircraft to fly over Pakistan; *United Kingdom v. Spain* (1969)—involving Spain's restriction of air space at Gibraltar; *Pakistan v. India* (1971)—involving India's refusal to allow Pakistani commercial aircraft to fly over India, and appealed to the International Court of Justice [ICJ]; *Cuba v. United States* (1998)—involving the U.S. refusal to allow Cuba's commercial aircraft to fly over the United States; and *United States v. Fifteen European States* (2003)—involving European Union [EU] noise emission regulations.[31] But as a political body, ICAO may be ill equipped to serve as a neutral adjudicator of disputes in the manner envisioned by its founders.[32]

ICAO also serves as the forum for the drafting of international conventions on aviation issues. For example, in the area of aviation security, ICAO served as the institution, which prepared, and facilitated the adoption and acceptance of the Tokyo Convention of 1963, the Hague Convention of 1970, and the Montreal Convention of 1971.[33] ICAO also has served as the forum for drafting the several conventions and protocols which have sought to update the Warsaw Convention on carrier liability. In addition to the role it has played in regulating the technical aspects of international civil aviation, ICAO has also succeeded in simplifying numerous economic aspects of the industry as well, such as facilitating customs procedures and visas. ICAO also assists the aviation industry by serving as a center for the collection and standardization of statistical data.[34] Today, ICAO is

---

[30] For a discussion of these activities, *see* Paul Dempsey, *Law & Foreign Policy in International Aviation* 276-293 (1987).

[31] *See* Paul Dempsey, *Law & Foreign Policy in International Aviation* 293-302 (1987); Paul Dempsey, *Flights of Fancy and Fights of Fury: Arbitration of Commercial and Political Disputes in International Aviation*, 32 Ga. J. Int'l & Comp. L. 231 (2004).

[32] Paul Dempsey, *Law & Foreign Policy in International Aviation* 300 (1987).

[33] *Id.* at 349-366, 443-449.

[34] R. Thornton, *International Airlines and Politics* 32 (1970). In addition to the role it has played in regulating the technical aspects of international civil aviation, the ICAO has also succeeded in simplifying numerous economic aspects of the industry as well, such as customs procedures and visas. *Id.* at 34. The ICAO also assists the aviation industry by serving as a center for the collection and standardization of statistical data. *Id.*

one of the largest and the most successful specialized U.N. agencies with more than 180 member nations.[35]

The International Civil Aviation Organization was created provisionally at the Chicago Conference, and now has its headquarters in Montreal, Canada. The ICAO has a General Assembly made up of representatives from member states, a governing Council elected by the members at large, a President who heads the Council, and a secretariat with five divisions:

- administration and services;
- legal;
- technical assistance;
- air transport; and
- air navigation to carry out the staff and administrative functions.

The aims and objectives of ICAO are to develop the principles and techniques of international air navigation and to foster the planning and development of international air transport so as to:

- insure the safe and orderly growth of international civil aviation throughout the world;
- encourage the arts of aircraft design and operation for peaceful purposes;
- encourage the development of airways, airports, and air navigation facilities for international civil aviation;
- meet the needs of the peoples of the world for safe, regular, efficient and economical air transport;
- prevent economic waste caused by unreasonable competition;
- insure that the rights of contracting states are fully respected and that every contracting state has a fair opportunity to operate international airlines;
- avoid discrimination between contracting states;
- promote safety of flight in international air navigation; and
- promote generally the development of all aspects of international civil aeronautics.

---

[35] Int'l Civil Aviation Org., Memorandum on ICAO, Addendum (1984).

THE EXTRATERRITORIAL REACH OF
U.S. ANTITRUST LAW

During World War II, the United States was the major producer of allied bombers and heavy air transports. This provided the U.S. with an aerospace manufacturing infrastructure unmatched anywhere in the world. With its dominance in the aerospace industry following WWII, the U.S. held a distinct competitive advantage over other countries competing for international air transportation markets.

The United States international air transport policy in 1946 encouraged expansion through continued progressive development of new aircraft by U.S. manufacturers, creating incentives that would in turn compel operational efficiency. The full economic potential would be recognized by widening the market. The expanding market would assure adequate cash flow for further capital improvement. And, U.S. carriers would carry a proportionally larger share of the world's travelers. It was a policy of free rein, and, in the air transportation vernacular, entailed no restrictions on "capacity."

Understandably, the British (and others), who did not have the same industrial advantages enjoyed by the United States, preferred capacity restrictions that would enable them to compete more equitably in international air transportation. Because the Chicago Convention failed to resolve international economic questions of commercial rights and rates, 31 countries met in Havana to establish an international association. The International Air Transport Association was formed out of its forerunner the International Air Traffic Association, which had been created in 1919 to standardize tickets and waybills. The primary purpose of IATA at its inception was the promotion of safe, regular, and economic air transportation, but the main function of IATA has been the (self) economic regulation of international air transportation. Major U.S. flag carriers subsequently joined IATA.

In negotiating the original Bermuda agreement, and considering U.S. international air transportation policy at the time, the United States made a major concession by concurring that international rates and fares would be subject to IATA agreement. The British, as well, gave concessions by accepting no predetermined limitations on capacity.

For nearly 20 years the bilateral agreement worked well, but by 1963, the concessions made earlier by each of the parties were becoming problematic to both sides. In 1963, IATA increased fares at a time when the Civil Aeronautics Board [CAB] decided fares should remain stable. The U.S. had agreed to abide by IATA established fares, and IATA prevailed in the dispute. But in order to maintain a U.S. dominance in international air transportation, the CAB granted to U.S. supplemental carriers permanent certificates of public convenience and necessity. With permanent authorization from the CAB, the supplementals were able to attract long-term financing for the purchase of new, or at least more, equipment. The supplementals flooded the international market with discounted charter flights, and millions of travelers were diverted to U.S. carriers, especially in the North Atlantic routes.

Several European countries wanted to limit charters, or in other words to reduce capacity, but supplemental carriers and charter airlines were not included or even considered in the bilateral documents. Many carriers tried to convince the CAB the proliferation of charter flights was destructive, that their impact was merely diversionary (i.e., did not create new and expanded market, but rather, took needed traffic from existing carriers leaving them with excess capacity).

As with deregulation in the U.S., price competition had been introduced to the international market. In the latter case not all were free to participate in IATA, including the U.S. carrier members and others. The free rein was enjoyed by charter, non-member carriers only so long as IATA chose to control the standard fares of all of its participants. By the early 1970s, only 20% of North Atlantic passengers were paying the full IATA fares, and IATA finally decided to invite the supplemental carriers to join. Ironically, many of the major carriers took up the charter business themselves. The North Atlantic market had excess capacity even before the supplementals joined IATA. When the majors took up chartering as well, the already highly competitive marketplace turned ruthless.

The Bermuda agreement had become ineffective, and the British announced their intention to terminate the agreement because of the destructively excess capacity offered by U.S. carriers in the North Atlantic market. A compromise was reached, and Bermuda II was signed in 1977, providing for more governmental involvement in approving routes. New carrier entrants would be pre-screened, and after review by IATA, proposed fares would be subject to governmental approval. The now defunct Laker Airways entered the United Kingdom-United States market under the provisions of Bermuda II.

The problem the U.S. had with Bermuda II, was that more governmental involvement meant government protection of the market. It was contrary to the principles embodied in the Airline Deregulation Act of 1978 and the popular movement in the U.S. toward less government in general. Additionally, it gave what President Carter considered to be an unfair advantage to the British. Keeping in mind that foreign policy is a Constitutionally granted responsibility assigned to the President, Jimmy Carter issued a new U.S. policy for international air transportation. The goals of the Carter policy were in line with deregulation, including:

- an innovative and competitive approach to pricing;
- liberalized charter operations;
- no limits on capacity; expansion of U.S. activity in the international market;
- more foreign gateways for U.S. carriers;
- integration of domestic and international air transportation service;
- development of international cargo service; and most importantly,
- elimination of discrimination and unfair competitive business practice.

It was a policy designed to encourage deregulation in the international scene, and to limit antitrust immunity, thereby subjecting international as well as U.S. carriers to Sherman and Clayton antitrust laws.[36] This policy gave rise to the International Air Transportation Competition Act of 1979,[37] which was to be the vehicle for implementing U.S. policy, and intended to increase international competition. It was Congress' international counterpart to the Airline Deregulation Act of 1978. By-and-large, it included the tenets of U.S. international air transport policy; to wit: open competition, consumer oriented fares, unrestricted charter operations, elimination of market

---

[36] *See Republic Airlines, Inc. v. Civil Aeronautics Board*, 756 F. 2d 1304 (1985).
[37] *See* Paul Stephen Dempsey, *Law & Foreign Policy in International Aviation* 45 (Transnational 1987).

restrictions, integrated domestic/international service, and fair non-discriminatory business practice. Furthermore, it included a unilateral agreement to provide more opportunity for foreign carriers to obtain access to the U.S. market in exchange for increased gateways overseas for U.S. carriers. The intent of the International Air Transportation Competition Act was to,

- promote competition;
- provide greater opportunities for U.S. carriers;
- establish new goals for international air transport negotiations; and
- generally extend the U.S. deregulation policy.

Foreign governments initially viewed deregulation with skepticism, and international opponents to deregulation argued:

- Deregulation, especially in the North Atlantic, would result in a loss of the regular high frequency service required by the business community, and would thus be detrimental to world commerce;
- Open competition results in overcapacity, and is inconsistent with a sound energy policy;
- The resultant overcapacity as evidenced in the North Atlantic market in the long run would result in financial disaster;
- Lower, yet stable, fares result only from careful governmental regulation of air transportation routes and fares; and
- It was foolish to talk about deregulation anyway, when there were so many other constraints indirectly regulating air transportation such as airport capacity, limited air traffic control capability, and so forth.

The arguments of the international community were not far removed from those of deregulatory opponents in the United States. The world seemed to be watching U.S. deregulation, while not necessarily going along with it. Many of the international carriers were either governmentally-owned, or their governments were otherwise highly involved in their operation for foreign policy and other political and economic reasons. Deregulation, and particularly U.S. antitrust laws, were not necessarily compatible with foreign airline operations or with their government's international air transportation policies. Some countries might never have been willing to conform to the principles of deregulation unless forced to by U.S. dominance. The British, for example, viewed antitrust as a key issue in air transport agreements with the U.S.

The British expressed their belief that the U.S. was systematically using its laws to extend deregulation internationally, and to use its laws to control international trade. Fearing the use of U.S. antitrust law as leverage against British carriers, the British Parliament felt compelled to pass their own trade protection law, and tried to invoke it when the liquidators for Laker Airways (an airline of British registry) brought suit against several airlines including British Airways in a U.S. court.[38]

In November 1982, a $1.05 billion civil antitrust suit was filed in the United States District Court in Washington, D.C., by the Laker Airways bankruptcy liquidator, against a number of transatlantic airlines including British Airways, and against the McDonnell-Douglas Corporation. The suit alleged there was a conspiracy among the defendants to drive Laker into bankruptcy through predatory pricing and to pressure lenders to deny financing to Laker. In May 1982, British Airways, on behalf of all 12 co-defendants in the civil action, made a formal offer of $65 million to settle the Laker antitrust suit. Provisions of the out-of-court settlement required Laker to give up all future claims, for their attorney to return or destroy all documents produced in the discovery proceedings, and not to use any of the information in any potential cases in the future.

Demonstrating the tight regulatory control that had evolved in the North Atlantic international market, Freddie Laker was quoted as saying that the 11 airline defendants wanted to "exclude (him) from re-entering into civil aviation," and the governments involved, "totally control international air transport in one form or another."

The Laker antitrust case was settled privately in July 1985. At the conclusion of the settlement, a British Airways spokesman commented,

> *As with our settlement with the liquidator, our agreement with Freddie Laker bears no admission of guilt on behalf of ourselves or the other*

---

[38] *See Laker v. Sabena, Belgian World Airlines,* 731 F.2d 909 (1984).

> *defendants to drive Laker out of business or to breach U.S. antitrust laws. The advantages to British Airways and the other defendants of ridding ourselves of all aspects of the Laker litigation for a very small fraction of the total amount claimed has encouraged all parties to reach a satisfactory out-of-court settlement.*

The Laker liquidator filed notice of settlement in U.S. District Court in Washington, September 30, 1985. Under the terms of the out-of-court settlement, $38 million went to institutional creditors; $22 million to former Laker employees and ticket holders; $8 million to Freddie Laker; and $12.5 million went to law firms representing the liquidator.

In 1984, the U.S. Department of Justice further aggravated international tension with a grand jury investigation into possible violations of U.S. antitrust laws by airlines operating between the U.S. and England. The grand jury was investigating charges of price-fixing and predatory practices by European and U.S. transatlantic carriers. Citing foreign policy concerns, President Reagan ordered the Justice Department to terminate its investigation. Political tension was already mounting from what the British protested as extraterritorial reach of U.S. antitrust laws, and concern over the viability of the Bermuda II agreement between the U.S. and Great Britain.

Back in 1978, the Civil Aeronautics Board had set out to withdraw antitrust immunity from ratemaking activities of the International Air Transport Association. The CAB had drawn the conclusion that IATA fare agreements substantially reduced competition, and it ordered IATA to *show cause* why U.S. airlines should not be withdrawn from, or prohibited from, participating in IATA's rate making conferences. The CAB's decision was later backed by the U.S. Court of Appeals.

Responsibility for final determination of the CAB's show cause order was transferred to the Department of Transportation upon termination of the CAB in January of 1985. In May 1985, the DOT ordered closed the nearly seven-year old show cause proceeding.[39] The same order authorized approval and continued antitrust immunity to IATA traffic conferences for five years. The DOT's conclusions were

---

[39] *See* Paul Dempsey, *Law & Foreign Policy in International Aviation* (1987).

that antitrust immunity of fare setting was required because of international comity and foreign policy considerations.

In *Laker Airways v. Sabena*, the court summarized the term "comity" as,

> *. . . the degree of deference that a domestic forum must pay to the act of a foreign government not otherwise binding on the forum . . . the central precept of comity teaches, that, when possible, the decisions of foreign tribunals should be given effect in domestic courts, since recognition fosters international cooperation and encourages reciprocity, thereby promoting . . . mutual expectations. The interests of both forums are advanced. . . . The rule of law is . . . encouraged, which benefits all nations.*[40]

The IATA show cause case, the Laker Airways suit, and other cases subsequently presented, illustrate examples of international related litigation in the air transport industry.

VIKING TRAVEL v. AIR FRANCE
1982 U.S. Dist. Lexis 18350 (E.D.N.Y. 1982)

What constitutes grounds for a class action suit?

This action was brought by Viking Travel against two U.S. air carriers and 15 foreign air carriers engaged in transatlantic air service. Viking alleged the airlines conspired with each other and with certain unnamed travel agents in the United States to engage in an unlawful rebate system in order to restrain competition in the sale of tickets for foreign air travel in violation of Sections 1 and 2 of the Sherman Antitrust Act of 1890. Viking sought treble damages pursuant to Section 4 of the Clayton Act of 1914, and injunctive relief pursuant to Section 16 of the Clayton Act. Viking sought class action certification of its suit under the Federal Rules of Civil Procedure (i.e., a *class action* suit). In order to certify a class under this rule, the plaintiff must meet

---

[40] *Laker Airways v. Sabena, Belgian World Airlines*, 731 F2d 909 (1984).

all four requirements set forth in Rule 23(a), and at least one of three requirements set forth in Rule 23(b):

- Rule 23(a)(1), *numerosity*, allows certification of a class only when the class is so numerous that "joinder of all members is impractical." Viking designated as a putative class all travel agents in the United States approved by the International Air Transport Association. Although this class was subject to diminution, as those agents who were allegedly co-conspirators would have to be weeded out, it would still have numbered in the thousands. This was more than sufficient to qualify for class action, but not so large as to make the suit unmanageable because of numbers alone. Thus, the require-ment of Rule 23(a)(1) was met.
- Rule 23(b)(1) is for *protection* of the defendant. Certification under Rule 23(b)(1) is appropriate when the prerequisites of Rule 23(a) are met and when bringing separate actions against the defendants by the individual class members would expose the defendants to the risk of being subject to incompatible standards of conduct. It is clear that in order for there to be in-compatible standards of conduct for the defendant to follow, other actions must be brought by individual members of the class. Since this action was commenced, no other actions had been brought. Because of the expense attached to such litiga-tion, it was highly unlikely that any would be. This made Rule 23(b)(1) certification inappropriate.
- Rule 23(b)(2), *injunction*, states that certification is appropri-ate only when the final relief sought relates predominantly to an injunction and not to damages. Plaintiff cited several cases, which purported to hold that Rule 23(b)(2) certification is ap-propriate where money damages are part of the relief sought. However, these cases either stated that while money may be granted under 23(b)(2), it cannot be the primary relief sought. In a treble damage antitrust case like the instant one, money damages are the primary relief sought. This principle has been recognized by courts across the nation. In light of the weight and pervasiveness of this authority, this court found Rule 23(b)(2) would be inappropriate.

- Rule 23(b)(3), *class predominance*, states that in order to obtain class certification under this rule, the plaintiff must meet all the prerequisites of Rule 23(a) and questions common to the class must predominate over individual questions and a class action must be the best method for fairly and efficiently resolving the controversy. As has been previously stated, the questions common to all members of the class in this case was the existence or non-existence of a conspiracy while the individual questions seem, at first glance, to concern damages only. The individual questions predominated over common ones. Moreover, a class action must be the most efficient method of resolving a controversy. Rule 23(b)(3) allows the court to consider the difficulties that would arise in management of a class action. In the instant case, the court determined that for all practical purposes, a class action would be unmanageable. Hundreds, perhaps thousands of mini-trials would be required to determine the question of impact. This alone seriously militated against the class action as an efficient tool. Thus, the plaintiff failed to satisfy any one of the Rule 23(b) requirements.

In conclusion, the plaintiff satisfied all four requirements of Rule 23(a), but could not satisfy any of the 23(b) requirements. Accordingly, the U.S. District Court dismissed the plaintiff's motion for class action certification.

LAKER AIRWAYS v. SABENA
731 F.2d 909 (D.C. Cir. 1984)

Are foreign air carriers subject to U.S. antitrust laws?

Laker Airways, Ltd., was founded as a charter airline in 1966. It began charter operations between the United States and the United Kingdom in 1970. As early as 1971, it sought to branch out into scheduled transatlantic air service. Laker hoped to gain a sizable share of the North Atlantic market by offering only basic air passage, with little or no in-flight amenities and non-essential services. Flying at a reduced cost would enable Laker to set rates much lower than those then charged by existing transatlantic air carriers.

Laker's potential competitors allegedly resisted the entry of this new carrier, delaying the commencement of Laker's novel economy service for several years. However, by 1977, Laker obtained the necessary authorizations from the United States and British governments, and inaugurated its low cost transatlantic airline service between London and New York.

The prices for scheduled transatlantic air service were substantially controlled by the International Air Transport Association, a trade organization of the world's largest air carriers. The IATA met annually to establish fixed fares for air carriage, which were implemented after authorization by national governments of the individual carriers. Laker's fares were approximately one-third of the competing fares offered by other transatlantic carriers, which were predominantly set under the auspices of IATA. The airline members of IATA allegedly perceived Laker's operations as a threat to their system of cartelized prices. The new competition not only jeopardized established markets of those carriers operating between the United Kingdom and the United States—such as British Airways and British Caledonian Airways—but also affected the demand for services provided by airlines flying direct routes between points in Continental Europe and the United States—such as Swiss Air Transport (Swissair), Lufthansa German Airlines (Lufthansa), KLM Royal Dutch Airlines, and Sabena Airlines—since some passengers allegedly found it cheaper to fly through London on Laker Airways, rather than direct on the other European transatlantic carriers. During meetings of IATA, in July and August 1977, the IATA airlines allegedly agreed to set rates at a predatory level to drive Laker out of business.

Notwithstanding this asserted predatory scheme, up until 1981, Laker managed to operate at a profit. At its zenith, Laker was carrying one out of every seven scheduled air passengers between the United States and England. However, during 1981, Laker's financial condition rapidly deteriorated. In mid-1981, the pound sterling declined precipitously. A large segment of Laker's revenue was in pounds, but most of its debts, such as those on its United States financed fleet of DC-10 aircraft, and expenses were in dollars. Already weakened by the asserted predatory pricing scheme, Laker ran into repayment difficulties. Fearing financial collapse, it sought to have its repayment obligations refinanced.

At this point, several airlines allegedly conspired to set even lower predatory prices. In October 1981, Pan American World Airways, Trans World Airlines, and British Airways dropped their fares for their full service flights equal to those charged by Laker for its no-frills service. They also allegedly paid high secret commissions to travel agents to divert potential customers from Laker. These activities further restricted Laker's income, exacerbating its perilous economic condition. At IATA meetings in December 1981, at Geneva, Switzerland, and in January 1982, at Hollywood, Florida, the IATA airlines allegedly laid plans to fix higher fares in the spring and summer of 1982 after Laker had been driven out of business. IATA members also interfered with Laker's attempt to reschedule its financial obligations. After Laker arranged a refinancing agreement, KLM, Sabena, and other IATA airlines allegedly pressured Laker's lenders to withhold the financing which had previously been promised. As a result of these alleged conspiracies, Laker was forced into liquidation under New Jersey law in early February 1982.

In the aftermath of these asserted conspiracies, Laker, through its liquidator, commenced an action in United States District Court for the District of Columbia to recover for the injuries sustained by the airline as a result of the alleged predatory pricing and unlawful interference with its refinancing arrangements. Laker's complaint filed on November 24, 1982 alleged two counts: (1) violation of United States antitrust laws, and (2) a common law intentional tort. Named as defendants were four American corporations, Pan American World Airways, Trans World Airlines, McDonnell Douglas Corp., and McDonnell Douglas Finance Corp., as well as four foreign airlines, British Airways, British Caledonian Airways, Lufthansa, and Swissair. Fearing that Laker would commence a second antitrust action against it Midland Bank, a British corporation involved in Laker's abortive refinancing attempt, filed a preemptive action in the United Kingdom's High Court of Justice on November 29, 1982, seeking to enjoin Laker from naming it as a defendant in any United States antitrust action. An injunction was issued the same day; this became a more permanent preliminary injunction on February 4, 1983.

Shortly thereafter, the four foreign defendants initiated a similar suit in the High Court of Justice. Their writs filed on January 21, 1983, sought: (1) a declaration that the four foreign defendants were not engaged in any unlawful combination or conspiracy; and (2) an injunction prohibiting Laker from taking any action in United States courts to redress an alleged violation by the defendants of United States antitrust laws. The writs specifically sought to compel Laker to dismiss its suit against the foreign defendants and to prohibit Laker from instituting any other proceedings in any non-English forum to redress any alleged violation of English or other laws prohibiting intentional or unlawful commercial injury. The substantive basis for the requested relief was the alleged inapplicability of United States antitrust laws under the Bermuda II Treaty, and the British Protection of Trading Interests Act. Shortly thereafter, Justice Parker issued an interlocutory injunction preventing Laker from taking any action in the United States courts or elsewhere to interfere with the proceedings the defendants were commencing in the High Court of Justice.

On January 24, 1983, to avoid being enjoined from continuing to sue the four United States defendants, Laker sought a temporary restraining order from the United States District Court, preventing the American defendants from instituting similar preemptive proceedings in England. The order was granted the same day, and later extended pending a hearing on Laker's motion for a preliminary injunction.

Approximately three weeks later, on February 15, 1983, Laker commenced in the district court a second antitrust suit. Appellants KLM and Sabena were named as defendants. A temporary restraining order was also entered against the appellants, preventing them from taking any action in a foreign court that would have impaired the district court's jurisdiction. This order was extended, pending a hearing on Laker's motion for a preliminary injunction.

On March 2, 1983, the British defendants successfully petitioned Justice Parker of the High Court of Justice to grant a second interim injunction against Laker preventing Laker from taking "any further steps" to prosecute its United States claim against the British airlines. Although the injunction was only designed to preserve the *status quo* pending a ruling by the High Court of Justice on the merits of the British airlines' suit seeking dismissal. The injunction prevented Laker from filing any discovery or other motions against British Airways and British Caledonian Airways.

At a hearing held five days later, Laker's motion for a preliminary injunction against the four American defendants, KLM, and Sabena was considered by the U.S. District Court. By order of March 7, 1983, and memorandum opinion dated March 9, 1983, the District Court granted a preliminary injunction. The terms of the injunction were designed only to "protect the jurisdiction of (the district court) over these proceedings" to the extent necessary to preserve "the rights of the plaintiff under the laws of the United States." The injunction prevented the defendants from taking any action before a foreign court or governmental authority that would interfere with the district court's jurisdiction over the matters alleged in the complaint. In its memorandum opinion, the court made it clear it would consider further narrowing the terms of the injunction at the request of any party as long as it would not leave the defendants "free to secure orders which would interfere with the litigation pending" before the district court. The court also consolidated Laker's two antitrust actions.

KLM Royal Dutch Airlines and Sabena Belgian World Airlines, joined by Swissair and Lufthansa, as *amici curiae*, appealed the March 7 order and the March 9 memorandum of the District Court, which enjoined KLM and Sabena from seeking an injunction against Laker's antitrust suit in the English courts. However, during the pendency of that appeal, the process of litigation and counter-litigation was continued in the United States and English courts. On March 29, 1983, Justice Parker vacated his March 2 injunction against Laker's prosecution of its antitrust suit against the foreign defendants. This interim injunction was then reinstated pending appeal.

In April and May 1983, Laker continued its efforts to proceed in its United States antitrust actions, while defending itself against the proceedings in the High Court of Justice which were designed to terminate its United States claims. On April 26, 1983, Laker issued a summons in the High Court of Justice seeking a dismissal or stay of the suits initiated by Lufthansa and Swissair. Laker also moved in the High Court of Justice for a discharge of the injunction granted on January 21, 1983. In a motion for partial summary judgment filed in the U.S. District Court, Laker affirmatively challenged the defendants' contentions that the action should be dismissed. By an opinion and order dated May 3, 1983, the District Court granted Laker's motion and held that jurisdiction did not have to be relinquished.

In a judgment read by Justice Parker on May 20, 1983, the High Court of Justice held that the injunctive relief requested by the British airlines was not justified, and it terminated claims for relief filed by British Caledonian Airways and British Airways. Justice Parker held that the application of U.S. antitrust laws to companies carrying on business in the United States was not contrary to British sovereignty, or the terms of the Bermuda II Treaty, at least while the dormant terms of the British Protection of Trading Interests Act had not been invoked. The judgment did recognize that a determination by the English Secretary of State that Britain's trading interests were negatively implicated by the United States antitrust action could change the result. However, at this point, before any intervention by the British Executive, the British court was willing to hold that Laker could not be prohibited from proceeding with its antitrust claims against British Airways and British Caledonian. The original interim injunctions were maintained, pending an appeal to the Court of Appeal by British Airways and British Caledonian.

The complexion of the controversy changed dramatically the next month, when the British Government invoked the provisions of the British Protection of Trading Interests Act. Upon a determination that measures taken to regulate international trade outside the United Kingdom "threaten to damage the trading interests of the United Kingdom," the Act authorized the English Secretary of State to require that any person conducting business in the United Kingdom disobey all foreign orders and cease all compliance with the foreign judicial or regulatory provisions designated by the Secretary of State. The Act authorized the Secretary of State to prevent United Kingdom courts from complying with requests for document production issued by foreign tribunals, and forbid enforcement of treble damage awards or antitrust judgments specified by the Secretary of State. On June 27, 1983, the Secretary of State for Trade and Industry cited his powers under the Act and issued an order and general directions prohibiting persons who conducted business in the United Kingdom, with the exception of American air carriers designated under the Bermuda II Treaty, from complying with "United States antitrust measures" in the district court arising out of any: (1) "agreement or arrangement (whether legally enforceable or not, to which a United Kingdom designated airline is a party"; or (2) "any act done by a U.K. designated airline" that relates to the provision of air carriage under the Bermuda II Treaty.

Laker applied for judicial review of the validity of the order and directions. The Court of Appeal considered this application with the appeals by British Airways and British Caledonian Airways of Justice

Parker's judgment of 20 May 1983. On July 26, 1983, the Court of Appeal announced its judgment that the order and directions were well within the power of the Secretary of State to issue, and hence valid. Because the order and directions of the British Executive prevented the British airline from complying with any requirements imposed by the U.S. District Court, and prohibited the airlines from relying on their own commercial documents located within the United Kingdom to defend themselves against Laker's charges, the Court of Appeal concluded the United States District Court action was "wholly untriable" and could only result in a "total denial of justice to" the British airlines. As a result, the Court of Appeal held that Laker must be permanently enjoined from proceeding with its United States antitrust claims against British Airways and British Caledonian.

After a hearing following judgment, the Court of Appeal granted an injunction: (1) restraining Laker from taking any steps against British Airways and British Caledonian in the United States action; and (2) directing Laker to use its best efforts to have British Airways and British Caledonian dismissed from the United States action. The second aspect of the injunction was stayed, pending appeal to the House of Lords. Subsequently, on October 21, 1983, Laker's summons to dismiss or stay the Lufthansa and Swissair action issued on April 26, 1983 was also adjourned, pending the outcome of Laker's appeal.

In summary, three months after Laker Airways filed an antitrust action in United States District Court for the District of Columbia against several defendants, including domestic British, and other foreign airlines, the foreign airlines filed suits in the High Court of Justice of the United Kingdom seeking an injunction forbidding Laker from prosecuting its U.S. antitrust action against the foreign defendants. After the High Court of Justice entered interim injunctions against Laker, the Court of Appeal issued a permanent injunction ordering Laker to take action to dismiss its suit against the British airlines. In the meantime, Laker responded by requesting injunctive relief in the United States District Court, arguing that a restraining order was necessary to prevent the remaining American defendants, and the additional foreign defendants Laker had named in a subsequent antitrust claim, from duplicating the foreign defendants' successful request for an English injunction compelling Laker to dismiss its suit against the defendants.

If the defendants had been permitted to file foreign injunctive actions, the U.S. District Court would have been effectively stripped of control over the claims—based on United States law—which it was in the process of adjudicating. Faced with no alternative but acquiescence in the termination of this jurisdiction by a foreign court's order, United States District Judge Harold H. Greene granted Laker's motion for a preliminary injunction restraining the remaining defendants from taking part in the foreign action designed to prevent the district court from hearing Laker's antitrust claims.

Supported by Swissair and Lufthansa, as *amici curiae*, KLM and Sabena challenged the United States District Court's preliminary injunction, on appeal in this case to the U.S. Court of Appeals for the District of Columbia Circuit. They claimed the injunction was unnecessary to protect the District Court's jurisdiction, and violated their right to take part in the "parallel" actions commenced in English courts. Denial of this opportunity, they asserted, flouted international principles of comity. Moreover, they charged that the district court ignored Britain's "paramount right" to apply British law to Laker, a British subject. Appellants and *amici* requested the appellate court overturn the district court's injunction as a clear abuse of discretion.

The U.S. Court of Appeals held that: (1) both the United States and Great Britain shared concurrent prescriptive jurisdiction over transactions giving rise to the plaintiff's antitrust claim; and (2) principles of comity and concurrent jurisdiction authorized defensive preliminary injunction designed to permit United States claim to go forward in the United States court free of foreign interference consisting of English proceedings designed solely to rob the United States court of its jurisdiction. KLM and Sabena, the court said, did not qualify under the general parallel rule because the foreign action they sought to join was interdictory and not parallel. It was instituted by the foreign defendants for the sole purpose of terminating the United States claim. The only conceivable benefit KLM and Sabena would reap, if the District Court's injunction were overturned, would be the right to attack the pending United States action in a foreign court. This would permit the appellants to avoid potential liability under the United States laws to which their business operations and treaty obligations have long subjected them. In these circumstances there was ample precedent justifying the defensive use of an antisuit injunction.

In its conclusion, the appellate court stated the conflict was precipitated by the attempts of another country to insulate its own business entities from the necessity of complying with legislation of our country designed to protect this country's domestic policies. At the root of the conflict were the fundamentally opposed policies of the United States and Great Britain regarding the desirability, scope, and implementation of legislation controlling anticompetitive and restrictive business practices.

No conceivable judicial disposition of this appeal could have removed the underlying conflict. Absent an explicit directive from Congress, this court had neither the authority nor the institutional resources to weigh the policy and political factors that had to be evaluated to resolve the competing claims of jurisdiction. The District Court's decision was affirmed and Laker's suit was allowed to proceed. Circuit Judge Starr dissented with deference to international comity, saying that, ". . . principles of comity among the courts of the international community counsel strongly against the injunction in the form issued here. The concept of comity of nations, a 'blend of courtesy and expedience,' was defined by the Supreme Court as the recognition which one nation allows within its territory to the legislative, executive or judicial acts of another nation, having due regard both to international duty and convenience, and to the rights of its own citizens or of other persons who are under the protection of its laws."

LAKER AIRWAYS v. PAN AMERICAN WORLD AIRWAYS
607 F. Supp. 324 (S.D.N.Y. 1985)

> *May the U.S. Courts be used to circumvent international*
> *air transportation agreements?*

In connection with the private civil action seeking treble damages for federal antitrust violations, alleged to have resulted in injury to Laker Airways Limited,[41] the Laker liquidator (residing in London and appointed in the United Kingdom) filed for *deposition subpoenas* upon the Midland Bank and Samuel Montagu & Co. Ltd. The subpoenas sought information and documents from Midland and Montagu who were non-party witnesses in the above antitrust suit. The movants Midland and Montagu requested the U.S. District Court

---

[41] *See Laker Airways v. Sabena, Belgian World Airlines*, 731 F. 2d 909 (1984).

quash the subpoenas. Midland and Montagu were not included in the antitrust suit. Implicit, however, was the suggestion that they were among the "lenders" believed by plaintiff to have colluded with Laker's competitors to deny financing to Laker.

Movants had not been sued because a court in the United Kingdom enjoined such action by the Laker liquidator. A motion was pending to vacate that injunction in light of a decision subsequently rendered by the House of Lords in a related case.[42] It was highly likely the injunction would be vacated in the due course of time, and, thereafter, movants would be named as additional parties. At the time the subpoenas were served, they were no more than non-party witnesses, entitled to have their pending motion adjudicated in accordance with the present state of the litigation. The subpoenas were extremely broad and burdensome as drafted. Although apparently intended only to elicit evidence for purposes of trial, to demonstrate such pressuring or collusion with regard to Midland and Montagu in their capacity as potential lenders to Laker, the demands extended as well to all papers relating to Sir Freddie Laker personally. Midland and Montagu denied they were pressured, and attributed the failure to make the loan to the continuous deterioration of the airline industry generally, and Laker in particular, in the latter part of 1981. All of Midland's activities, in connection with this matter, took place solely in the United Kingdom, and Midland's New York branch office had no involvement whatsoever with Laker. Similarly, Montagu had only a "representative office" which conducted no banking operations in New York. There were no files or documents in the New York Representative Office of Montagu concerning Laker, and no person at that office had any knowledge of the matters concerning Laker. The offices of both Midland and Montagu were not opened in New York until long after the events complained of by Laker in the antitrust action. Essentially, then, the deposition subpoenas sought to require Midland and Montagu, by officers having custody in the United Kingdom, to produce in New York for use in the antitrust litigation, documents and records regularly maintained at their home offices in London. This was inappropriate.

As a second reason to vacate, the court found the service of the subpoenas in New York was a transparent attempt to circumvent the Hague Convention on the Taking of Evidence Abroad in Civil or

---

[42] *British Airways v. Laker Airways,* 3 W.L.R. 416 (decided Jul. 19, 1984).

Commercial Matters,[43] which sets forth agreed international procedures for seeking evidence in this court from non-parties abroad. The
failure to use the Hague Convention was more than a mere technical-
ity. The extraterritorial jurisdiction asserted over foreign interests by
the American antitrust laws has long been a sore point with many foreign governments, including that of the United Kingdom.

The English Protection of Trading Interests Act of 1980 [PTIA]
authorizes and empowers the Secretary of State for Trade and Industry to interpose the official power of the British Government, so as to
prevent persons conducting business in the United Kingdom from
complying with foreign judicial or regulatory provisions designated
by the Secretary of State as intrusive upon that nation's sovereignty.
The attempt to effect the court subpoena was, in effect, an end run,
not only around the Hague Convention, but also around the PTIA.

In effect, this court was being asked to aid the plaintiff in the antitrust case in obtaining an order from the court which would cause the
Midland branch in New York and the Montagu agency to compel
their principals in London to violate British law by disgorging in
London and transferring to their New York offices, documents which
plaintiff would like to have seen, none of which were ever located in
New York. This was clearly an improper abuse of the subpoena
power of the court, and should not have been permitted. The U.S.
District Court granted the motions of Midland and Montagu to quash
the subpoenas.

BRITISH CALEDONIAN AIRWAYS v. BOND
665 F.2d 1153 (D.C. Cir. 1981)

*Must unilateral enforcement of international obligations of the
Chicago Convention follow the procedural requirements
embodied in those obligations?*

On May 25, 1979, an engine tore off the wing of American Airlines Flight 191, a DC-10, shortly after take-off from Chicago O'Hare
International Airport. All 271 passengers and crew on board the aircraft perished in the crash. Three days later, the FAA issued an Emergency Airworthiness Directive [EAD] requiring all U.S. operators of

---

[43] 28 U.S.C. § 1871.

DC-10s to inspect engine pylons. The following day, the FAA issued another EAD grounding all domestic DC-10s.

On June 5, 1979, the FAA Administrator issued an Emergency Order of Suspension (SFAR 40) for all airworthiness certificates for domestic DC-10 aircraft, and prohibited the operation in U.S. airspace of all foreign-registered DC-10 aircraft. While one can only speculate as to the motives, the suspension of foreign-flag aircraft arguably enhanced the safety of U.S. residents who might board them and also equalized the relative financial impact on U.S. carriers.

Several foreign-flag carriers objected. In *British Caledonian Airways*, the D.C. Circuit Court of Appeals found that the relevant airworthiness standards were properly promulgated by ICAO and set forth in Annex 8. The court also found that Article 33 of the Chicago Convention requires that "the judgment of the country of registry that an aircraft is airworthy must be respected, unless the country of registry is not observing the 'minimum standards' [of Annex 8]." It found that the requirements of Article 33 were self-executing, requiring no implementing legislation by the U.S. Congress.[44] But Congress had mandated, under former Section 1102 of the Federal Aviation Act of 1958, that the FAA Administrator must, in exercising and performing his powers and duties, "do so consistently with any obligation assumed by the United States in any treaty, convention, or agreement that may be in force between the United States and any foreign country or foreign countries."[45]

The court concluded that:

> . . . *because the Administrator at no time questioned whether the foreign governments met the minimum safety standards set by the ICAO, his issuance of SFAR 40 and his refusal to rescind the order after the foreign governments had revalidated the airworthi-*

---

[44] Occasionally, a national court has to intervene to force a governmental unit to abide by the nation's international obligations. Professor Kumm observes, "Whatever the reasons for widespread state compliance with international law, however, problems of noncompliance remain sufficiently widespread for national judicial actors to have a potentially significant role in the enforcement of international law." Mattias Kumm, *International Law in National Courts: The International Rule of Law and the Limits of the Internationalist Model*, 44 Va. J. Int'l L. 19, 23 (2003). U.S. courts have embraced various theories to enforce treaty obligations, including honor, natural law, contracts, and national interest. Detlev F. Vagts, *The United States and Its Treaties: Observance and Breach*, 95 Am. J. Int'l L. 313, 324-329 (2001).

[45] 49 U.S.C. § 1502 -1102, 49 U.S.C. § 40105(b).

*ness certificates for aircraft flying under their flags
would appear to have violated Article 33 and, therefore, section 1102.[46]*

There was but a single proper way for the FAA to restrict a foreign-flag carrier based upon the airworthiness of its aircraft: "If
doubts about airworthiness exist, one country may refuse to recognize
another country's certificate of airworthiness, but only if the certifi-
cating nation has not observed the minimum standards of airworthiness established in Annex 8 pursuant to Articles 33 and 27 of the Chicago Convention." The FAA Administrator had failed to do this. Ten
years later, the U.S. would launch a program to ferret out those nations not in compliance with Annex 8.[47]

GREATER TAMPA CHAMBER OF COMMERCE v.
GOLDSCHMIDT
627 F.2d 258 (D.C. Cir. 1980)

*What are the requirements of the Executive branch for
conclusion of a bilateral air transit agreement
exchanging traffic rights?*

Because every nation has exclusive sovereignty over the airspace
above its territory, international agreements are a prerequisite of
international air service. In the Bermuda Agreement of 1946 (now
referred to as "Bermuda I") the United States and the United Kingdom entered into such an agreement to govern air travel between the
two countries. The British eventually came to feel, however, that
Bermuda I permitted more flights on each route than were needed to

---

[46] The FAA also argued that Article 9 of the Chicago Convention gave it the authority to restrict
the flight of foreign aircraft into the United States. Article 9(b) authorizes a State "in exceptional circumstances or during a period of emergency, or in the interest of public safety, and
with immediate effect, temporarily to restrict or prohibit flying over the whole or any part of its
territory, on condition that such restriction or prohibition shall be applicable without distinction
of nationality. . . ." Chicago Convention, *supra* Note 11, Art. 9(b). The *British Caledonian* court
held that "Article 9 is aimed at restricting the territorial access of all aircraft, rather than restricting the movements of particular types of aircraft. . . . Article 9 permits a country to safeguard its airspace when entry by all aircraft would be dangerous or intrusive because of conditions on the ground. Article 9 does not allow one country to ban landing and take-off because of
doubts about the airworthiness of particular foreign aircraft, in derogation of Article 33." *British
Caledonian*, 655 F.2d at 1164.
[47] 49 U.S.C. § 44907(e).

meet the demand; planes flew with empty seats, and passengers had to be charged higher prices. On June 22, 1976, the United Kingdom notified the United States it intended to exercise its right to terminate that agreement.

When negotiations for a new agreement began, they were conducted by an American delegation chaired by Alan S. Boyd, whom President Carter had appointed special representative with the temporary personal rank of ambassador. The delegation included representatives of government agencies (among whom was the vice chairman of the Civil Aeronautics Board and advisors from the private sector). On July 23, 1977, Ambassador Boyd and Secretary of Transportation Brock Adams signed, on behalf of the United States, a second Bermuda Agreement (Bermuda II). Because Bermuda II is an "executive agreement," and not a "treaty," it was not submitted to the Senate for ratification.

Bermuda I imposed no bilateral restrictions on the number of airlines that could fly from a given gateway. Under Bermuda II, however, the United Kingdom could limit 13 gateways to non-stop service by only one American carrier, and could limit two gateways to non-stop service by two American carriers. On the recommendation of the CAB, the President awarded such "dual designation" to New York and Los Angeles.

Appellants were the Greater Tampa Chamber of Commerce; the Tampa Bay Area International Air Service Task Force; the Aviation Consumer Action Project; Hillsborough County, Florida; the City of Cleveland, Ohio; and 11 individuals. On March 23, 1978, they filed a complaint in the U.S. District Court, alleging that Bermuda II was an invalid agreement, and asked for declaratory and injunctive relief against the Secretary of Transportation, the Secretary of State, and the United States. Appellants identified as the injury which motivated the suit, the "anti-competitive" and therefore diminished quantity and quality of transatlantic air service available to them under Bermuda II. They alleged several "procedural" flaws in its execution:

First, Bermuda II is properly a treaty, and not an executive agreement, and therefore it should have been ratified by the Senate. Bermuda II must be a treaty because only treaties can override an act of Congress, and Bermuda II conflicts with the Federal Aviation Act of 1958. Specifically, the agreement conflicts with those portions of the Act which,

- mandate competition in air transportation "to the extent necessary to assure the sound development of an air transportation system;"
- provide that term, condition, or limitation of a certificate shall restrict the right of an air carrier to add to or change schedules, equipment, accommodations, and facilities for performing the authorized transportation and service as the development of the business and the demands of the public shall require. . . .; and
- require that, in approving rates, the CAB consider those factors specified by the Act.

Second, since 22 U.S.C. Section 901(c) permits the President to confer the personal rank of ambassador only "in connection with special missions for the President of an essentially limited and temporary nature of not exceeding six months," and since this was not such a mission, Mr. Boyd's appointment should have been submitted to the Senate for confirmation.

Third, appellees failed to carry out their duty to advise and consult with the CAB while Bermuda II was being negotiated. Nor did appellees consult with leaders of Congress to the extent prescribed by State Department Circular.

And Fourth, neither Mr. Boyd nor Secretary Adams was properly authorized to sign Bermuda II for the United States.

The U.S. District Court issued a memorandum opinion and an order. The opinion concluded that, despite appellees' arguments to the contrary, appellants had standing because they were injured by a diminution in air services appellants contended Bermuda II caused. The order granted appellees' request for summary judgment as to the questions of:

- whether Bermuda II and the Federal Aviation Act conflict;
- whether Ambassador Boyd and Secretary Adams were authorized to sign the agreement; and
- whether the President properly appointed Ambassador Boyd.

The order granted appellees' motion to dismiss as non-justifiable "political questions" the issues of: (1) whether Bermuda II should have been submitted to the Senate for ratification, and (2) whether appellees adequately consulted with the CAB during negotiations.

Appellants asked the U.S. Court of Appeals to reverse the U.S. District Court decision which would have declined to hold invalid the executive agreement then in effect between the United States and the United Kingdom, by which air travel between the two countries is regulated. Because the appellate court found appellants' complaint failed to allege facts showing a substantial likelihood that a grant of the relief sought would redress the appellants' asserted injuries, it held that appellants lacked standing to bring this action.

While the District Court may have been correct in concluding the appellants received less adequate air service than they might have received under Bermuda I, the U.S. Court of Appeals could not agree that that conclusion resolved the question of whether appellants had standing to have brought this suit. The district court did not evaluate appellants' standing in terms of the aspect of then current Supreme Court standing doctrine, which held that, absent a substantial likelihood that a federal court can redress the injury a plaintiff claims to have suffered, the plaintiff has no standing to invoke the court's power.

The U.S. Court of Appeals vacated the judgment of the District Court and remanded the case with instructions to dismiss the complaint.

APPENDIX A

THE DECLARATION OF INDEPENDENCE

July 4, 1776

WHEN, in the Course of human events, it becomes necessary for one people to dissolve the political bands which have connected them with another, and to assume among the powers of the earth, the separate and equal station to which the Laws of Nature and of Nature's God entitle them, a decent respect to the opinions of mankind requires that they should declare the causes which impel them to the separation.

We hold these truths to be self-evident, that all men are created equal, that they are endowed by their Creator with certain unalienable Rights, that among these are Life, Liberty and the pursuit of Happiness. That to secure these rights, Governments are instituted among Men, deriving their just powers from the consent of the governed. That whenever any Form of Government becomes destructive of these ends, it is the Right of the People to alter or to abolish it, and to institute new Government, laying its foundation on such principles and organizing its powers in such form, as to them shall seem most likely to effect their Safety and Happiness. Prudence, indeed, will dictate that Governments long established should not be changed for light and transient causes; and accordingly, all experience hath shewn, that mankind are more disposed to suffer, which evils are sufferable, than to right themselves by abolishing the forms to which they are accustomed. But when a long train of abuses and usurpations, pursuing invariably the same Object evinces a design to reduce them under absolute Despotism, it is their right, it is their duty, to throw off such Government, and to provide new Guards for their future security. Such has been the patient sufferance of these Colonies; and such is now the necessity which constrains them to alter their former Systems of Government. The history of the present King of Great Britain is a history of repeated injuries and usurpations, all having in direct object the establishment of an absolute Tyranny over these States. To prove this, let Facts be submitted to a candid world.

He has refused his Assent to Laws, the most wholesome and necessary for the public good.

He has forbidden his Governors to pass Laws of immediate and pressing importance, unless suspended in their operation till his Assent should be obtained, and when so suspended, he has utterly neglected to attend to them.

He has refused to pass other Laws for the accommodation of large districts of people, unless those people would relinquish the right of Representation in the Legislature, a right inestimable to them and formidable to tyrants only.

He has called together legislative bodies at places unusual, uncomfortable, and distant from the depository of their public Records, for the sole purpose of fatiguing them into compliance with his measures.

He has dissolved Representative Houses repeatedly, for opposing with manly firmness his invasions on the rights of the people.

He has refused for a long time, after such dissolutions, to cause others to be elected; whereby the Legislative powers, incapable of Annihilation, have returned to the People at large for their exercise; the State remaining in the meantime exposed to all the dangers of invasion from without, and convulsions within.

He has endeavoured to prevent the population of these States; for that purpose obstructing the Laws for Naturalization of Foreigners; refusing to pass others to encourage their migrations hither, and raising the conditions of new Appropriations of Lands.

He has obstructed the Administration of Justice, by refusing his Assent to Laws for establishing Judiciary powers.

He has made Judges dependent on his Will alone, for the tenure of their offices, and the amount and payment of their salaries.

He has erected a multitude of New Offices, and sent hither swarms of Officers to harass our people, and eat out their substance.

He has kept among us, in times of peace, Standing Armies, without the Consent of our legislatures.

He has affected to render the Military independent of and superior to the Civil power. He has combined with others to subject us to a jurisdiction foreign to our constitution and unacknowledged by our laws; giving his Assent to their Acts of pretended Legislation: For quartering large bodies of armed troops among us: For protecting them by a mock Trial from punishment for any Murders which they should commit on the Inhabitants of these States: For cutting off our Trade with all parts of the world: For imposing Taxes on us without our Consent: For depriving us in many cases of the benefits of Trial by Jury: For transporting us beyond Seas to be tried for pretended offences: For abolishing the free System of English Laws in a neigbouring Province, establishing therein an Arbitrary government, and enlarging its Boundaires so as to render it at once an example and fit instrument for introducing the same absolute rule into these Colonies: For taking away our Charters, abolishing our most valuable Laws and altering fundamentally the Forms of our Governments: For suspending our own Legislatures, and declaring themselves invested with power to legislate for us in all cases whatsoever.

He has abdicated Government here by declaring us out of his Protection and waging War against us.

He has plundered our seas, ravaged our Coasts, burnt our towns, and destroyed the lives of our people.

He is at this time transporting large Armies of foreign Mercenaries to complete the works of death, desolation and tyranny, already begun with circumstances of cruelty and perfidy scarcely paralleled in the most barbarous ages, and totally unworthy the Head of a civilized nation.

He has constrained our fellow Citizens taken Captive on the high Seas to bear Arms against their Country, to become the executioners of their friends and Brethren, or to fall themselves by their Hands.

He has excited domestic insurrections amongst us, and has endeavored to bring on the inhabitants of our frontiers, the merciless Indian Savages, whose known rule of warfare is an undistinguished destruction of all ages, sexes and conditions. In every stage of these Oppressions We have Petitioned for Redress in the most humble terms. Our repeated Petitions have been answered only by repeated injury. A

Prince, whose character is thus marked by every act which may define a Tyrant, is unfit to be the ruler of a free people. Nor have We been wanting in attentions to our British brethren. We have warned them from time to time of attempts by their legislature to extend an unwarrantable jurisdiction over us. We have reminded them of the circumstances of our emigration and settlement here. We have appealed to their native justice and magnanimity, and we have conjured them by the ties of our common kindred to disavow these usurpations, which would inevitably interrupt our connections and correspondence. They too have been deaf to the voice of justice and of consanguinity. We must, therefore, acquiesce in the necessity, which denounces our Separation, and hold them, as we hold the rest of mankind, Enemies in War, in Peace Friends.

WE THEREFORE, the REPRESENTATIVES OF THE UNITED STATES OF AMERICA, IN GENERAL CONGRESS, Assembled, appealing to the Supreme Judge of the world for the rectitude of our intentions, do, in the Name, and by authority of the good People of these Colonies, solemnly PUBLISH and DECLARE, That these United Colonies are, and of Right ought to be FREE AND INDEPENDENT STATES; that they are Absolved from all Allegiance to the British Crown, and that all political connection between them and the State of Great Britain is and ought to be totally dissolved; and that as FREE AND INDEPENDENT STATES may of right do. And for the support of this Declaration, with a firm reliance on the protection of Divine Providence, we mutually pledge to each other our Lives, our Fortunes, and our sacred Honor.

APPENDIX B

THE CONSTITUTION
OF THE
UNITED STATES OF AMERICA

Adopted July 2, 1788
Ratified May 29, 1790

Preamble

We the People of the United States, in Order to form a more perfect Union, establish Justice, insure domestic Tranquility, provide for the common defence, promote the general Welfare, and secure the Blessings of Liberty to our selves and our Posterity, do ordain and establish this Constitution for the United States of America.

ARTICLE I

Section 1. All legislative powers herein granted shall be vested in a Congress of the United States, which shall consist of a Senate and House of Representatives.

Section 2. The House of Representatives shall be composed of Members chosen every second Year by the People of the several States, and the Electors in each State shall have the Qualifications requisite for Electors of the most numerous Branch of the State Legislature.

No Person shall be a Representative who shall not have attained to the Age of twenty-five Years, and been seven Years a Citizen of the United States, and who shall not, when elected, be an Inhabitant of that State in which he shall be chosen.

Representatives and direct Taxes shall be apportioned among the several States which may be included within this Union; according to their respective Numbers, which shall be determined by adding to the whole Number of free Persons, including those bound to Service for a Term of Years, and excluding Indians not taxed, three fifths of all other Persons. The actual Enumeration shall be made within three Years after the first Meeting of the Congress of the United States, and within every subsequent Term of ten Years, in such Manner as they shall by Law direct. The Number of Representatives shall not exceed one for every thirty Thousand, but each State shall have at Least one Representative; and until such enumeration shall be made, the State of New Hampshire shall be entitled to chuse three, Massachusetts eight, Rhode-Island and Providence Plantations one, Connecticut five, New-York six, New Jersey four, Pennsylvania eight, Delaware one, Maryland six, Virginia ten, North Carolina five, South Carolina five, and Georgia three.

When vacancies happen in the Representation from any State, the Executive Authority thereof shall issue Writs of Election to fill such Vacancies.

The House of Representatives shall chuse their Speaker and other Officers; and shall have the sole Power of Impeachment.

Section 3. The Senate of the United States shall be composed of two Senators from each State, chosen by the Legislature thereof, for six Years; and each Senator shall have one Vote.

Immediately after they shall be assembled in Consequence of the first Election, they shall be divided as equally as may be into three Classes. The Seats of the Senators of the first Class shall be vacated at the Expiration of the second Year, of the second Class at the Expiration of the fourth Year, and of the third Class at the Expiration of the sixth Year, so that one-third may be chosen every second Year; and if Vacancies happen by Resignation, or otherwise, during the Recess of the Legislature of any State, the Executive thereof may make temporary Appointments until the next Meeting of the Legislature, which shall then fill such Vacancies.

No Person shall be a Senator who shall not have attained to the Age of thirty Years, and been nine Years a Citizen of the United States, and who shall not, when elected, be an Inhabitant of that State for which he shall be chosen.

The Vice President of the United States shall be President of the Senate, but shall have no Vote, unless they be equally divided.

The Senate shall chuse their other Officers, and also a President pro tempore, in the absence of the Vice President, or when he shall exercise the Office of President of the United States.

The Senate shall have the sole Power to try all Impeachments. When sitting for that Purpose, they shall be on Oath or Affirmation. When the President of the United States is tried, the Chief Justice shall preside: And no Person shall be convicted without the Concurrence of two thirds of the Members present.

Judgment in Cases of Impeachment shall not extend further than to removal from Office, and disqualification to hold and enjoy any Office of honor, Trust or Profit under the United States: but the Party convicted shall nevertheless be liable and subject to Indictment, Trial, Judgment and Punishment, according to Law.

Section 4. The Times, Places and Manner of holding Elections for Senators and Representatives, shall be prescribed in each State by the Legislature thereof; but the Congress may at any time by Law make or alter such Regulations, except as to the Place of Chusing Senators.

The Congress shall assemble at least once in every Year, and such Meeting shall be on the first Monday in December, unless they shall be Law appoint a different Day.

Section 5. Each House shall be the Judge of the Elections, Returns and Qualifications of its own Members, and a Majority of each shall constitute a Quorum to do Business; but a smaller number may adjourn from day to day, and may be authorized to compel the Attendance of absent Members, in such Manner, and under such Penalties as each House may provide.

Each House may determine the Rules of its Proceedings, punish its Members for disorderly Behavior, and, with the Concurrence of two thirds, expel a Member.

Each House shall keep a Journal of its Proceedings, and from time to time publish the same, excepting such Parts as may in their Judgment require Secrecy; and the Yeas and Nays of the Members of either House on any question shall, at the Desire of one fifth of those Present, be entered on the Journal.

Neither House, during the Session of Congress, shall, without the Consent of the other, adjourn for more than three days, nor to any other Place than that in which the two Houses shall be sitting.

Section 6. The Senators and Representatives shall receive a Compensation for their Services, to be ascertained by Law, and paid out of the Treasury of the United States. They shall in all Cases, except Treason, Felony and Breach of the Peace, be privileged from Arrest during their Attendance at the Session of their respective Houses, and in going to and returning from the same; and for any Speech or Debate in either House, they shall not be questioned in any other Place.

No Senator or Representative shall, during the Time for which he was elected, be appointed to any civil Office under the Authority of the United States, which shall have been created, or the Emoluments whereof shall have been encreased during such time; and no Person holding any Office under the United States, shall be a Member of either House during his Continuance in Office.

Section 7. All Bills for raising Revenue shall originate in the House of Representatives; but the Senate may propose or concur with Amendments as on other Bills.

Every Bill which shall have passed the House of Representatives and the Senate, shall, before it become a Law, be presented to the President of the United States; If he approve he shall sign it, but if not he shall return it, with his Objections to that House in which it shall have originated, who shall enter the Objections at large on their Journal, and proceed to reconsider it. If after such Reconsideration two thirds of that House shall agree to pass the Bill, it shall be sent, together with the Objections, to the other House, by which it shall likewise be reconsidered, and if approved by two thirds of that House, it shall become a Law. But in all such Cases the Votes of both Houses shall be determined by Yeas and Nays, and the Names of the Persons voting for and against the Bill shall be entered on the Journal of each House respectively. If any Bill shall not be returned by the President within ten Days (Sundays excepted) after it shall have been presented to him, the Same shall be a Law, in like Manner as if he had signed it, unless the Congress by their Adjournment prevent its Return, in which Case it shall not be a Law.

Every Order, Resolution, or Vote to which the Concurrence of the Senate and House of Representatives may be necessary (except on a question of Adjournment) shall be presented to the President of the United States; and before the Same shall take Effect, shall be approved by him, or being disapproved by him, shall be repassed by two thirds of the Senate and House of Representatives, according to the Rules and Limitations prescribed in the Case of a Bill.

Section 8. The Congress shall have Power To lay and collect Taxes, Duties, Imposts and Excises, to pay the Debts and provide for the common Defence and general Welfare of the United States; but all Duties, Imposes Excises shall be uniform throughout the United States;

To borrow money on the credit of the United States;

To regulate Commerce with foreign Nations, and among the several States, and with the Indian Tribes;

To establish an uniform Rule of Naturalization, and uniform Laws on the subject of Bankruptcies throughout the United States;

To coin Money, regulate the Value thereof, and of foreign Coin, and fix the Standard of Weights and Measures;

To provide for the Punishment of counterfeiting the Securities and current Coin of the United States;

To establish Post Offices and post Roads;

To promote the Progress of Science and useful Arts, by securing for limited Times to Authors and Inventors the exclusive Right to their respective Writings and Discoveries;

To constitute Tribunals inferior to the supreme Court;

To define and punish Piracies and Felonies committed on the high Seas, and Offenses against the Law of Nations;

To declare War, grant Letters of Marque and Reprisal, and make Rules concerning Captures on Land and Water;

To raise and support Armies, but no Appropriation of Money to that Use shall be for a longer Term than two Years;

To provide and maintain a Navy;

To make Rules for the Government and Regulation of the land and naval Forces;

To provide for calling forth the Militia to execute the Laws of the Union, suppress Insurrections and repel Invasions;

To provide for organizing, arming, and disciplining the Militia, and for governing such Part of them as may be employed in the Service of the United States, reserving to the States respectively, the Appointment of the Officers, and the Authority of training the Militia according to the discipline prescribed by Congress;

To exercise exclusive Legislation in all Cases whatsoever, over such District (not exceeding ten Miles square) as may, by Cession of particular States, and the acceptance of Congress, become the Seat of the Government of the United States, and to exercise like Authority over all Places purchased by the Consent of the Legislature of the State in which the Same shall be, for the Erection of Forts, Magazines, Arsenals, dock-Yards, and other needful Buildings;—And To make all Laws which shall be necessary and proper for carrying into Execution the foregoing Powers, and all other Powers vested by this Constitution in the Government of the United States, or in any Department or Officer thereof.

Section 9. The Migration or Importation of such Persons as any of the States now existing shall think proper to admit, shall not be prohibited by the Congress prior to the Year one thousand eight hundred and eight, but a tax or duty may be imposed on such Importation, not exceeding ten dollars for each Person.

The privilege of the Writ of Habeas Corpus shall not be suspended, unless when in Cases of Rebellion or Invasion the public Safety may require it.

No Bill of Attainder or ex post facto Law shall be passed.

No capitation, or other direct, Tax shall be laid, unless in Proportion to the Census of Enumeration herein before directed to be taken.

No tax or Duty shall be laid on Articles exported from any State.

No Preference shall be given by any Regulation of Commerce or Revenue to the Ports of one State over those of another; nor shall Vessels bound to, or from, one State, be obliged to enter, clear, or pay Duties in another.

No Money shall be drawn from the Treasury, but in Consequence of Appropriations made by Law; and a regular Statement and Account of the Receipts and Expenditures of all public Money shall be published from time to time.

No Title of Nobility shall be granted by the United States: And no Person holding any Office of Profit or Trust under them, shall, without the Consent of the Congress, accept of any present, Emolument, Office, or Title, of any kind whatever, from any King, Prince, or foreign State.

Section 10. No State shall enter into any Treaty, Alliance, or Confederation; grant Letters of Marque and Reprisal; coin Money, emit Bills of Credit; make any Thing but gold and silver Coin a Tender in Payment of Debts; pass any Bill of Attainder, ex post facto Law, or Law impairing the Obligation of Contracts, or grant any Title of Nobility.

No State shall, without the Consent of the Congress, lay any Imposts or Duties on Imports or Exports, except what may be absolutely necessary for executing its inspection Laws: and the net Produce of all Duties and Imposts, laid by any State on Imports or Exports, shall be for the Use of the Treasury of the United States; and all such Laws shall be subject to the Revision and Control of the Congress.

No State shall, without the Consent of Congress, lay any duty of Tonnage, keep Troops, or Ships of War in time of Peace, enter into any Agreement or Compact with another State, or with a foreign Power, or engage in War, unless actually invaded, or in such imminent Danger as will not admit of delay.

ARTICLE II

Section 1. The executive Power shall be vested in a President of the United States of America. He shall hold his Office during the Term of four Years, and, together with the Vice President, chosen for the same Term, be elected, as follows.

Each State shall appoint, in such Manner as the Legislature thereof may direct, a Number of Electors, equal to the whole Number of Senators and Representatives to which the State may be entitled in the Congress: but no Senator or Representative, or Person holding an Office of Trust or Profit under the United States, shall be appointed an Elector.

The Electors shall meet in their respective States, and vote by Ballot for two persons, of whom one at least shall not be an Inhabitant of the same State with themselves. And they shall make a List of all the Persons voted for, and of the Number of Votes for each; which List they shall sign and certify, and transmit sealed to the Seat of the Government of the United States, directed to the President of the Senate. The President of the Senate shall, in the Presence of the Senate and House of Representatives, open all the Certificates, and the Votes shall then be counted. The Person having the greatest Number of Votes, shall be the President, if such Number be a Majority of the whole Number of Electors appointed; and if there be more than one who have such Majority, and have an equal Number of Votes, then the House of Representatives shall immediately chuse by Ballot one of them for President; and if no Person have a Majority, then from the five highest on the List the said House shall in like Manner chuse the President. But in chusing the President, the Votes shall be taken by States, the Representation from each State having one Vote; a quorum for this Purpose shall consist of a Member or Members from two thirds of the States, and a Majority of all the States shall e necessary to a Choice. In every Case, after the Choice of the President, the Person having the greatest Number of Votes of the Electors shall be the Vice President. But if there should remain two or more who have equal Votes, the Senate shall chuse from them by Ballot the Vice President.

The Congress may determine the Time of chusing the Electors, and the Day on which they shall give their Votes; which Day shall be the same throughout the United States.

No person except a natural born Citizen, or a Citizen of the United States, at the time of the Adoption of this Constitution, shall be eligible to the Office of President; neither shall any Person be eligible to that Office who shall not have attained to the Age of thirty-five Years, and been fourteen Years a Resident within the United States.

[In Case of the Removal of the President from Office, or of his Death, Resignation, or Inability to discharge the Powers and Duties of the said Office, the same shall devolve on the Vice President, and the Congress may by Law, provide for the Case of Removal, Death, Resignation or Inability, both of the President and Vice President, declaring what Officer shall then act as President, and such Officer shall act accordingly, until the Disability be removed, or a President shall be elected.]

The President shall, at stated Times, receive for his Services, a Compensation, which shall neither be increased nor diminished during the Period for which he shall have been elected, and he shall not receive within that Period any other Emolument from the United States, or any of them.

Before he enter on the Execution of his Office, he shall take the following Oath or Affirmation: "I do solemnly swear (or affirm) that I will faithfully execute the Office of President of the United States, and will to the best of my Ability, preserve, protect and defend the Constitution of the United States."

Section 2. The President shall be Commander in Chief of the Army and Navy of the United States, and of the Militia of the several States, when called into the actual Service of the United States; he may require the Opinion in writing, of the principal Officer in each of the executive Departments, upon any subject relating to the Duties of their respective Offices, and he shall have Power to Grant Reprieves and Pardons for Offenses against the United States, except in Cases of Impeachment.

He shall have Power, by and with the Advise and Consent of the Senate, to make Treaties, provided two-thirds of the Senators present concur; and he shall nominate, and by and with the Advise and consent of the Senate, shall appoint Ambassadors, other public Ministers and Consuls, Judges of the supreme Court, and all other Officers of the United States, whose Appointments are not herein otherwise provided for, and which shall be established by Law; but the Congress may by Law vest the Appointment of such interior Officers, as they think proper, in the President alone, in the Courts of Law, or in the Heads of Departments.

The President shall have Power to fill up all Vacancies that may happen during the Recess of the Senate, by granting Commissions which shall expire at the End of their next Session.

Section 3. He shall from time to time give to the Congress Information of the State of the Union, and recommend to their Consideration such Measures as he shall judge necessary and expedient; he may, on extraordinary Occasions, convene both Houses, or either of them, and in Case of Disagreement between them, with Respect to the Time of Adjournment, he may adjourn them to such Time as he shall think proper; he shall receive Ambassadors and other public Ministers; he shall take Care that the Laws be faithfully executed, and shall Commission all the Officers of the United States.

Section 4. The President, Vice President and all civil Officers of the United States, shall be removed from Office in Impeachment for, and Conviction of, Treason, Bribery, or other high Crimes and Misdemeanors.

ARTICLE III

Section 1. The judicial Power of the United States, shall be vested in one supreme Court, and in such inferior Courts as the Congress may from time to time ordain and establish. The Judges, both of the supreme and inferior Courts, shall hold their Offices during good Beaviour, and shall, at stated Times, receive for their Services, a Compensation, which shall not be diminished during their Continuance in Office.

Section 2. The judicial Power shall extend to all Cases, in Law and Equity, arising under this Constitution, the Laws of the United States, and Treaties made, or which shall be made, under their Authority;—to all Cases affecting Ambassadors, other public Ministers and Consuls;—to all Cases of admiralty and maritime Jurisdiction;—to

Controversies to which the United States shall be a Party;—to Controversies between two or more States;—between a State and Citizens of another State;—between Citizens of different States;—between Citizens of the same State claiming Lands under Grants of different States, and between a State, or the Citizens thereof, and foreign States, Citizens or Subjects.

In all Cases affecting Ambassadors, other public Ministers and Consuls, and those in which a State shall be Party, the supreme Court shall have original Jurisdiction. In all the other Cases before mentioned, the supreme Court shall have appellate Jurisdiction, both as to Law and Fact, with such Exceptions, and under such Regulations as the Congress shall make.

The trial of all Crimes, except in Cases of Impeachment, shall be by Jury; and such Trial shall be held in the State where the said Crimes shall have been committed; but when not committed within any State, the Trial shall be at such Place or Places as the Congress may by Law have directed.

Section 3. Treason against the United States, shall consist only in levying War against them, or in adhering to their Enemies, giving them Aid and Comfort. No Person shall be convicted of Treason unless on the Testimony of two Witnesses to the same overt Act, or on Confession in open Court.

The Congress shall have Power to declare the Punishment of Treason, but no Attainder of Treason shall work Corruption of Blood, or Forfeiture except during the Life of the Person attainted.

ARTICLE IV

Section 1. Full Faith and Credit shall be given in each State to the public Acts, Records, and judicial Proceedings of every other State. And the Congress may by general Laws prescribe the Manner in which such Acts, Records and Proceedings shall be proved, and the Effect thereof.

Section 2. The Citizens of each State shall be entitled to all Privileges and Immunities of Citizens in the several States.

A Person charged in any State with Treason, Felony, or other Crime, who shall flee from Justice, and be found in another State, shall on demand of the executive Authority of the State from which he fled, be delivered up, to be removed to the State having Jurisdiction of the Crime.

No Person held to Service or Labour in one State, under the Laws thereof, escaping into another, shall, in Consequence of any Law or Regulation therein, be discharged from such Service or Labour, but shall be delivered up on Claim of the Party to whom such Service or Labour may be due.

Section 3. New States may be admitted by the Congress into this Union; but no new State shall be formed or erected within the Jurisdiction of any other State; nor any State be formed by the Junction of two or more States, or parts of States, without the Consent of the Legislatures of the States concerned as well as of the Congress.

The Congress shall have Power to dispose of and make all needful Rules and Regulations respecting the Territory or other Property belonging to the United States; and nothing in this Constitution shall be so construed as to Prejudice any Claims of the United States, or of any particular State.

Section 4. The United States shall guarantee to every State in this Union a Republican Form of Government, and shall protect each of them against Invasion; and on Application of the Legislature, or of the Executive (when the Legislature cannot be convened) against domestic Violence.

ARTICLE V

The Congress, whenever two-thirds of both Houses shall deem it necessary, shall propose Amendments to this Constitution, or, on the Application of the Legislatures of two-thirds of the several States, shall call a Convention for proposing Amendments, which, in either Case, shall be valid to all Intents and Purposes, as part of this Constitution, when ratified by the Legislatures of three-fourths of the several States, or by convention in three-fourths thereof, as the one or the other Mode of Ratification may be proposed by the Congress: Provided that no Amendment which may be made prior to the Year One thousand eight hundred and eight shall in any Manner affect the first and fourth Clauses in the Ninth Section of the first Article; and that no State, without its Consent, shall be deprived of its equal Suffrage in the Senate.

ARTICLE VI

All Debts contracted and Engagements entered into, before the Adoption of this Constitution, shall be as valid against the United States under this Constitution, as under the Confederation.

This Constitution, and the Laws of the United States which shall be made in Pursuance thereof; and all Treaties made, or which shall be made, under the Authority of the United States, shall be the supreme Law of the Land; and the Judges in every State shall be bound thereby, and Thing in the Constitution or Laws of any State to the Contrary notwithstanding.

The Senators and Representatives before mentioned, and the Members of the several State Legislatures, and all executive and judicial Officers, both of the United States and of the several States, shall be bound by Oath or Affirmation, to support this Constitution; but no religious Test shall ever be required as a Qualification to any Office or public Trust under the United States.

ARTICLE VII

The Ratification of the Conventions of nine States shall be sufficient for the Establishment of this Constitution between the States so ratifying the Same.

Done in Convention by the Unanimous Consent of the States present the Seventeenth Day of September in the Year of our Lord one thousand seven hundred and Eighty seven and of the Independence of the United States of America the Twelfth.

Witness whereof We have hereunto subscribed our Names.

THE FIRST TEN AMENDMENTS
known as
"THE BILL OF RIGHTS"

December 15, 1791

AMENDMENT I

Congress shall make no law respecting an establishment of religion, or prohibiting the free exercise thereof; or abridging the freedom of speech, or of the press; or the right of the people peaceably to assemble, and to petition the Government for a redress of grievances.

AMENDMENT II

A well regulated Militia, being necessary to the security of a free State, the right of the people to keep and bear Arms, shall not be infringed.

AMENDMENT III

No Soldier shall, in time of peace be quartered in any house, without the consent of the Owner, nor in time of war, but in a manner to be prescribed by law.

AMENDMENT IV

The right of the people to be secure in their persons, houses, papers, and effects, against unreasonable searches and seizures, shall not be violated, and no Warrants shall issue, but upon probable cause, supported by Oath or affirmation, and particularly describing the place to be searched, and the persons or things to be seized.

AMENDMENT V

No person shall be held to answer for a capital, or otherwise infamous crime, unless on a presentment or indictment of a Grand Jury, except in cases arising in the land or naval forces, or in the Militia, when in actual service in time of War or public danger; nor shall any person be subject for the same offence to be twice put in jeopardy of life or limb; nor shall be compelled in any criminal case to be a witness against himself, nor be deprived of life, liberty, or property, without due process of law; nor shall private property be taken for public use, without just compensation.

AMENDMENT VI

In all criminal prosecutions, the accused shall enjoy the right to a speedy and public trial, by an impartial jury of the State and district wherein the crime shall have been committed, which district shall have been previously ascertained by law, and to be informed of the nature and cause of the accusation; to be confronted with the witnesses against him; to have compulsory process for obtaining witnesses in his favor, and to have the Assistance of Counsel for his defence.

AMENDMENT VII

In suits at common law, where the value in controversy shall exceed twenty dollars, the right of trial by jury shall be preserved, and no fact tried by a jury, shall be otherwise reexamined in any Court of the United States, than according to the rules of the common law.

AMENDMENT VIII

Excessive bail shall not be required, nor excessive fines imposed, nor cruel and unusual punishments inflicted.

AMENDMENT IX

The enumeration in the Constitution, of certain rights, shall not be construed to deny or disparage others retained by the people.

AMENDMENT X

The powers not delegated to the United States by the Constitution, nor prohibited by it to the States, are reserved to the States respectively, or to the people.

AMENDMENT XI
(Ratified February 7, 1795)

The Judicial power of the United States shall not be construed to extend to any suit in law or equity, commenced or prosecuted against one of the United States by Citizens of another State, or by Citizens or Subjects of any Foreign State.

AMENDMENT XII
(Ratified July 27, 1804)

The Electors shall meet in their respective states and vote by ballot for President and Vice-President, one of whom, at least shall not be an inhabitant of the same state with themselves; they shall name in their ballots the person voted for as President, and in distinct ballots the person voted for as Vice-President;—and they shall make distinct lists of all persons voted for as President, and of all persons voted for as Vice-President, and of the number of votes for each, which lists they shall sign and certify, and transmit sealed to the seat of the government of the United States, directed to the President of the Senate;—The President of the Senate shall, in presence of the Senate and House of Representatives, open all the certificates and the votes shall then be counted;—The person having the greatest number of votes for President, shall be the President, if such number be a majority of the whole number of Electors appointed; and if no person have such majority, then from the persons having the highest numbers not exceeding three on the list of those voted for as President, the House of Representatives shall choose immediately, by ballot, the President. But in choosing the President, the votes shall be taken by states, the representation from each state having one vote; a quorum for this purpose shall consist of a member or members from two-thirds of the states, and a majority of all the states shall be necessary to a choice. And if the House of Representatives shall not choose a President whenever the right of choice shall devolve upon them, before the fourth day of March next following, then the Vice-President shall act as President, as in the case of the death or other constitutional disability of the President. The person having the greatest number of votes as Vice-President, shall be the Vice-President, if such number be a majority of the whole number of Electors appointed, and if no person have a majority, then from the two highest numbers on the list, the Senate shall choose the Vice-President; a quorum for the purpose shall consist of two-thirds of the whole number of Senators, and a majority of the whole number shall be necessary to a choice. But no person constitutionally ineligible to the office of President shall be eligible to that of Vice-President of the United States.

AMENDMENT XIII
(Ratified December 6, 1865)

Section 1. Neither slavery nor involuntary servitude, except as a punishment for crime whereof the party shall have been duly convicted, shall exist within the United States, or any place subject to their jurisdiction.

Section 2. Congress shall have power to enforce this article by appropriate legislation.

AMENDMENT XIV
(Ratified July 9, 1868)

Section 1. All persons born or naturalized in the United States, and subject to the jurisdiction thereof, are citizens of the United States and of the State wherein they reside. No State shall make or enforce any law which shall abridge the privileges or immunities of citizens of the United States; nor shall any State deprive any person of life, liberty, or property, without due process of law; nor deny to any person within its jurisdiction the equal protection of the laws.

Section 2. Representatives shall be apportioned among the several States according to their respective numbers, counting the whole number of persons in each State, excluding Indians not taxed. But when the right to vote at any election for the choice of electors for President and Vice-President of the United States, Representatives in Congress, the Executive and Judicial officers of a State, or the members of the Legislature thereof, is denied to any of the male inhabitants of such State, being twenty-one years of age, and citizens of the United States, or in any way abridged, except for participation in rebellion, or other crime, the basis of representation therein shall be reduced in the proportion which the number of such male citizens shall bear to the whole number of male citizens twenty-one years of age in such State.

Section 3. No person shall be a Senator or Representative in Congress, or elector of President and Vice-President, or hold any office, civil or military, under the United States, or under any State, who, having previously taken an oath, as a member of Congress, or as an officer of the United States, or as a member of any State legislature, or as an executive or judicial officer of any State, to support the Constitution of the United States, shall have engaged in insurrection or rebellion against the same, or given aid or comfort to the enemies thereof. But Congress may by a vote of two-thirds of each House, remove such disability.

Section 4. The validity of the public debt of the United States, authorized by law, including debts incurred for payment of pensions and bounties for services in suppressing insurrection or rebellion, shall not be questioned. But neither the United States nor any State shall assume or pay any debt or obligation incurred in aid of insurrection or rebellion against the United States, or any claim for the loss or emancipation of any slave; but all such debts, obligations and claims shall be held illegal and void.

Section 5. The Congress shall have power to enforce, by appropriate legislation, the provisions of this article.

AMENDMENT XV
(Ratified February 3, 1870)

Section 1. The right of citizens of the United States to vote shall not be denied or abridged by the United States or by any State on account of race, color, or previous condition of servitude.

Section 2. The Congress shall have power to enforce this article by appropriate legislation.

AMENDMENT XVI
(Ratified February 13, 1913)

The Congress shall have power to lay and collect taxes on incomes, from whatever source derived, without apportionment among the several States, and without regard to any census or enumeration.

AMENDMENT XVII
(Ratified April 8, 1913)

The Senate of the United States shall be composed of two Senators from each State, elected by the people thereof, for six years; and each Senator shall have one vote. The electors in each State shall have the qualifications requisite for electors of the most numerous branch of the State legislatures.

When vacancies happen in the representation of any State in the Senate, the executive authority of such State shall issue writs of election to fill such vacancies: Provided, That the legislature of any State may empower the executive thereof to make temporary appointments until the people fill the vacancies by election as the legislature may direct.

This amendment shall not be so construed as to affect the election or term of any Senator chosen before it becomes valid as part of the Constitution.

AMENDMENT XVIII
(Ratified January 16, 1919)

Section 1. After one year from the ratification of this article the manufacture, sale, or transportation of intoxicating liquors within, the importation thereof into, or the exportation thereof from the United States and all territory subject to the jurisdiction thereof for beverage purposes is hereby prohibited.

Section 2. The Congress and the several States shall have concurrent power to enforce this article by appropriate legislation.

Section 3. This article shall be inoperative unless it shall have been ratified as an amendment to the Constitution by the legislatures of the several States as provided in the Constitution, within seven years from the date of the submission hereof to the States by the Congress.

AMENDMENT XIX
(Ratified August 18, 1920)

The right of citizens of the United States to vote shall not be denied or abridged by the United States or by any State on account of sex.

Congress shall have power to enforce this article by appropriate legislation.

AMENDMENT XX
(Ratified January 23, 1933)

Section 1. The terms of the President and Vice President shall end at noon on the 20th day of January, and the terms of Senators and Representatives at noon on the 3rd day of January, of the years in which such terms would have ended if this article had not been ratified; and the terms of their successors shall then begin.

Section 2. The Congress shall assemble at least once in every year, and such meeting shall begin at noon on the 3rd day of January, unless they shall be law appoint a different day.

Section 3. If, at the time fixed for the beginning of the term of the President, the President elect shall have died, the Vice President elect shall become President. If a President shall not have been chosen before the time fixed for the beginning of his term, or if the President elect shall have failed to qualify, then the Vice elect shall act as President until a President shall have qualified; and the Congress may be law provide for the case wherein neither a President elect nor a Vice President elect shall have qualified, declaring who shall then act as President, or the manner in which one who is to act shall be selected, and such person shall act accordingly until a President or Vice President shall have qualified.

Section 4. The Congress may be law provide for the case of the death of any of the persons from whom the House of Representatives may choose a President whenever the right of choice shall have devolved upon them, and for the case of the death of any of the persons from whom the Senate may choose a Vice President whenever the right of choice shall have devolved upon them.

Section 5. Sections 1 and 2 shall take effect on the 15th day of October following the ratifications of this article.

Section 6. This article shall be inoperative unless it shall have been ratified as an amendment to the Constitution by the legislature of three-fourths of the several States within seven years from the date of its submission.

AMENDMENT XXI
(Ratified December 5, 1933)

Section 1. The eighteenth article of amendment to the Constitution of the United States is hereby repealed.

Section 2. The transportation or importation into any State, Territory, or possession of the United States for delivery or use therein of intoxicating liquors, in violation of the laws thereof, is hereby prohibited.

Section 3. This article shall be inoperative unless it shall have been ratified as an amendment to the Constitution by conventions in the several States, as provided in the Constitution, within seven years from the date of the submission hereof to the States by the Congress.

AMENDMENT XXII
(Ratified February 27, 1951)

Section 1. No person shall be elected to the office of the President more than twice, and no person who has held the office of President, or acted as President, for more than two years of a term to which some other person was elected President shall be elected to the office of the President more than once. But this Article shall not apply to any person holding the office President when this Article was proposed by the Congress, and shall not prevent any person who may be holding the office of President, or acting as President, during the term within which this Article becomes operative from holding the office of President or acting as President during the remainder of such term.

Section 2. This article shall be inoperative unless it shall have been ratified as an amendment to the Constitution by the legislatures of three-fourths of the several States within seven years from the date of its submission to the States by the Congress.

AMENDMENT XXIII
(Ratified March 29, 1961)

Section 1. The District constituting the seat of Government of the United States shall appoint in such manner as the Congress may direct:

A number of electors of President and Vice President equal to the whole number of Senators and Representatives in Congress to which the District would entitle if it were a State, but in no event more than the least populous State; they shall be in addition to those appointed by the States, but they shall be considered, for the purposes of the election of President and Vice President, to be electors appointed by a State; and they shall meet in the District and perform such duties as provided by the twelfth article of amendment.

Section 2. The Congress shall have power to enforce this article by appropriate legislation.

AMENDMENT XXIV
(Ratified January 23, 1964)

Section 1. The right of citizens of the United States to vote in any primary or other election for President or Vice President, for electors for President or Vice President, or for Senator or Representative in Congress, shall not be denied or abridged by the United States or any State by reason of failure to pay any poll tax or other tax.

Section 2. The Congress shall have power to enforce this article by appropriate legislation.

AMENDMENT XXV
(Ratified February 10, 1967)

Section 1. In case of the removal of the President from office or of his death or resignation, the Vice President shall become President.

Section 2. Whenever there is a vacancy in the office of the Vice President, the President shall nominate a Vice President who shall take office upon confirmation by a majority vote of both Houses of Congress.

Section 3. Whenever the President transmits to the President pro tempore of the Senate and the Speaker of the House of Representatives his written declaration that he is unable to discharge the powers and duties of his office, and until he transmits to them a written declaration to the contrary, such powers and duties shall be discharged by the Vice President as Acting President.

Section 4. Whenever the Vice President and a majority of either the principal officers of the executive departments or of such other body as Congress may by law provide, transmit to the President pro tempore of the Senate and the Speaker of the House of Representatives their written declaration that the President is unable to discharge the powers and duties of his office, the Vice President shall immediately assume the powers and duties of the office as Acting President.

Thereafter, when the President transmits to the President pro tempore of the Senate and the Speaker of the House of Representatives his written declaration that no inability exists, he shall resume the powers and duties of his office unless the Vice President and a majority of either the principal officers of the executive department or of such other body as Congress may be law provide, transmit within four days to the President pro tempore of the Senate and the Speaker of the House of Representatives their written declaration that the President is unable to discharge the powers and duties of his office. Thereupon Congress shall decide the issue, assembling within forty-eight hours for that purpose if not in session. If the Congress, within twenty-one days after receipt of the latter written declaration, or, if Congress is not in session, within twenty-one days after Congress is required to assemble, determines by two-thirds vote of both Houses that the President is unable to discharge the powers and duties of his office, the Vice President shall continue to discharge the same as Acting President; otherwise, the President shall resume the powers and duties of his office.

AMENDMENT XXVI
(Ratified July 1, 1971)

Section 1. The right of citizens of the United States, who are eighteen years of age or older, to vote shall not be denied or abridged by the United States or by any State on account of age.

Section 2. The Congress shall have power to enforce this article by appropriate legislation.

APPENDIX C

UNITED STATES STANDARD FORM OF BILATERAL AIR TRANSPORT AGREEMENT

(1953)

The Government of the United States of America and the Government of _____, Desiring to conclude an Agreement for the purpose of promoting air communications between their respective territories, Have accordingly appointed authorized representatives for this purpose, who have agreed as follows:

ARTICLE 1

For the purposes of the present Agreement:

(A) The term "aeronautical authorities" shall mean in the case of the United States of America, the Civil Aeronautics Board and any person or agency authorized to perform the functions exercised at the present time by the Civil Aeronautics Board and, in the case of _____, and _____ and any person or agency authorized to perform the functions exercised at present by the said _____.

(B) The term "designated airline" shall mean an airline that one contracting party has notified the other contracting party, in writing, to be the airline which will operate a specific route or routes listed in the Schedule of this Agreement.

(C) The term "territory" in relation to a State shall mean the land areas and territorial waters adjacent thereto under the sovereignty, suzerainty, protection, mandate or trusteeship of that State.

(D) The term "air service" shall mean any scheduled air service performed by aircraft for the public transport of passengers, mail or cargo.

(E) The term "international air service" shall mean an air service-which passes through the air space over the territory of more than one State.

(F) The term "stop for non-traffic purposes" shall mean a landing for any purpose other than taking on or discharging passengers, cargo or mail.

ARTICLE 2

Each contracting party grants to the other contracting party rights necessary for the conduct of air services by the designated airlines, as follows: the rights of transit, of stops for non-traffic purposes, and of commercial entry and departure for international traffic in passengers, cargo, and mail at the points in its territory named on each of the routes specified in the appropriate paragraph of the Schedule annexed to the present Agreement.

ARTICLE 3

Air service on a specified route may be inaugurated by an airline or airlines of one contracting party at any time after that contracting party has designated such airline or airlines for that route and the other contracting party has given the appropriate operating permission. Such other party shall, subject to Article 4, be bound to give this permission provided that the designated airline or airlines may be required to qualify before the competent aeronautical authorities of that party, under the laws and regulations normally applied by these authorities, before being permitted to engage in the operations contemplated by this Agreement.

ARTICLE 4

Each contracting party reserves the right to withhold or revoke the operating permission provided for in Article 3 of this Agreement from an airline designated by the other contracting party in the event that it is not satisfied that substantial ownership and effective control of such airline are vested in nationals of the other contracting party, or in case of failure by such airline to comply with the laws and regulations referred to in Article 5 hereof, or in case of the failure of the airline or the government designating it otherwise to perform its obligations hereunder, or to fulfill the conditions under which the rights are granted in accordance with this Agreement.

ARTICLE 5

(A) The laws and regulations of one contracting party relating to the admission to or departure from its territory of aircraft engaged in international air navigation, or to the operation and navigation of such aircraft while within its territory, shall be applied to the aircraft of the airline or airlines designated by the other contracting party, and shall be complied with by such aircraft upon entering or departing, from and while within the territory of the first contracting party.

(B) The laws and regulations of one contracting party relating to the admission to or departure from its territory of passengers, crew, or cargo of aircraft, such as regulations relating to entry, clearance, immigration, passports, customs, and quarantine shall be complied with by or on behalf of such passengers, crew or cargo of the other contracting party upon entrance into or departure from, and while within the territory of the first contracting party.

ARTICLE 6

Certificates of airworthiness, certificates of competency and licenses issued or rendered valid by one contracting party, and still in force, shall be recognized as valid by the other contracting party for the purpose of operating the routes and services provided for in this

Agreement, provided that the requirements under which such certificates or licenses were issued or rendered valid are equal to or above
the minimum standards which may be established pursuant to the Convention on International Civil Aviation. Each contracting party reserves the right, however, to refuse to recognize, for the purpose of
flight above its own territory, certificates of competency and licenses
granted to its own nationals by another State.

ARTICLE 7

In order to prevent discriminatory practices and to assure equality
of treatment, both contracting parties agree that:

(A) Each of the contracting parties may impose or permit   to be
imposed just and reasonable charges for the use of public airports and other facilities under its control. Each of the contracting parties agrees, however, that these charges shall not be
higher than would be paid for the use of such airports and facilities by its national aircraft engaged in similar international
services.

(B) Fuel, lubricating oils, consumable technical supplies, spare
parts, regular equipment, and stores introduced into the territory of one contracting party by the other contracting party or
its nationals, and intended solely for use by aircraft of such
contracting party shall be exempt on a basis of reciprocity from
customs duties, inspection fees and other national duties or
charged.

(C) Fuel, lubricating oils, other consumable technical supplies,
spare parts, regular equipment, and stores retained on board
aircraft of the airlines of one contracting party authorized to
operate the routes and services provided for in this Agreement
shall, upon arriving in or leaving the territory of the other contracting party, be exempt on a basis of reciprocity from customs duties, inspection fees and other national duties or
charges, even though such supplies be used or consumer by
such aircraft on flights in that territory.

(D) Fuel, lubricating oils, other consumable technical supplies,
spare parts, regular equipment, and stores taken on board air-

craft of the airlines of one contracting party in the territory of the other and used in international services shall be exempt on a basis of reciprocity from customs duties, exercise taxes, inspection fees and other national duties or charges.

ARTICLE 8

There shall be a fair and equal opportunity for the airlines of each contracting party to operate on any route covered by this Agreement.

ARTICLE 9

In the operation by the airlines of either contracting party of the trunk services described in this Agreement, the interest of the airlines of the other contracting party shall be taken into consideration so as not to affect unduly the services which the latter provides on all or part of the same routes.

ARTICLE 10

The air services made available to the public by the airlines operating under this Agreement shall bear a close relationship to the requirements of the public for such services.

It is the understanding of both contracting parties that services provided by a designated airline under the present Agreement shall retain as their primary objective the provision of capacity adequate to the traffic demands between the country of which such airline is a national and the countries of ultimate destination of the traffic. The right to embark or disembark on such services international traffic destined for and coming from third countries at a point or points on the routes specified in this Agreement shall be applied in accordance with the general principles of orderly development to which both contracting parties subscribe and shall be subject to the general principle that capacity should be related:

(A) to traffic requirements between the country of origin and the countries of ultimate destination of the traffic;

(B) to the requirements of through airline operation; and

(C) to the traffic requirements of the area through which the airline passes after taking account of local and regional services.

ARTICLE 11

Rates to be charged on the routes provided for in this Agreement shall be reasonable, due regard being paid to all relevant factors, such as cost of operation, reasonable profit, and the rates charged by any other carriers, as well as the characteristics of each service, and shall be determined in accordance with the following paragraphs:

(A) The rates to be charged by the airlines of either contracting party between points in the territory of the United States and points in the territory of _____ referred to in the annexed Schedule shall, consistent with the provisions of the present Agreement, be subject to the approval of the aeronautical authorities of the contracting parties, who shall act in accordance with their obligations under this Agreement, within the limits of their legal powers.

(B) Any rate proposed by an airline of either contracting party shall be filed with the aeronautical authorities of both contracting parties at least thirty (30) days before the proposed date of introduction; provided that this period of thirty (30) days may be reduced in particular cases if so agreed by the aeronautical authorities of each contracting party.

(C) During any period for which the Civil Aeronautics Board of the United States has approved the traffic conference procedures of the International Air Transport Association (hereinafter called IATA), any rate agreements concluded through these procedures and involving United States airlines will be subject to approval of the Board. Rate agreements concluded through this machinery may also be required to be subject to the approval of the aeronautical authorities of the _____ pursuant to the principles enunciated in paragraph (A) above.

(D) The contracting parties agree that the procedure described in paragraphs (E), (F), and (G) of this Article shall apply:

1. If, during the period of the approval by both contracting parties of the IATA traffic conference procedure, either, any specific rate agreement is not approved within a reasonable time by either contracting party, or, a conference of IATA is unable to agree on a rate, or
2. At any time no IATA procedure is applicable, or
3. If either contracting party at any time withdraws or fails to renew its approval of that part of the IATA traffic conference procedure relevant to this Article.

(E) In the event that power is conferred by law upon the aeronautical authorities of the United States to fix fair and economic rates for the transport of persons and property by air on international services and to suspend proposed rates in a manner comparable to that in which the Civil Aeronautics Board at present is empowered to act with respect to such rates for the transport of persons and property by air within the United States, each of the contracting parties shall thereafter exercise its authority in such manner as to prevent any rate or rates proposed by one of its airlines for services from the territory of one contracting party to a point or points in the territory of the other contracting party from becoming effective, if in the judgment of the aeronautical authorities of the contracting party whose airline or airlines is or are proposing such rate, that rate is unfair or uneconomic. If one of the contracting parties on receipt of the notification referred to in paragraph (B) above is dissatisfied with the rate proposed by the airline or airlines of the other contracting party, it shall so notify the other contracting party prior to the expiry of the first fifteen (15) of the thirty (30) days referred to, and the contracting parties shall endeavor to reach agreement on the appropriate rate.

In the event that such agreement is reached, each contracting party will exercise its best efforts to put such rate into effect as regards it airline or airlines.

If agreement has not been reached at the end of the thirty (30) day period referred to in paragraph (B) above, the proposed rate may, unless the aeronautical authorities of the country of the air carrier concerned see fit to suspend its application, go into effect provisionally pending the settlement of

any dispute in accordance with the procedure outlined in paragraph (G) below.

(F) Prior to the time when such power may be conferred upon the aeronautical authorities of the United States, if one of the contracting parties is dissatisfied with any rate proposed by the airline or airlines of either contracting party for services from the territory of one contracting party to a point or points in the territory of the other contracting party, it shall so notify the other prior to the expiry of the first fifteen (15) of the thirty (30) day period referred to in paragraph (B) above, and the contracting parties shall endeavor to reach agreement on the appropriate rate.

In the event that such agreement is reached, each contracting party will use its best efforts to cause such agreed rate to be put into effect by its airline or airlines.

It is recognized that if no such agreement can be reached prior to the expiry of such thirty (30) days, the contracting party raising the objection to the rate may take such steps as it may consider necessary to prevent the inauguration or continuation of the service in question at the rate complained of.

(G) When in any case under paragraphs (E) or (F) of this Article the aeronautical authorities of the two contracting parties cannot agree within a reasonable time upon the appropriate rate after consultation initiated by the complaint of one contracting party concerning the proposed rate or an existing rate of the airline or airlines of the other contracting party, upon the request of either, the terms of Article 13 of this Agreement shall apply.

ARTICLE 12

Consultation between the competent authorities of both contracting parties may be requested at any time by either contracting party for the purpose of discussing the interpretation, application, or amendment of the Agreement or Schedule. Such consultation shall begin within a period of sixty (60) days from the date of the receipt of the request by the Department of State of the United States of America or the _____ of _____ as the case may be. Should agreement be reached on

946

amendment of the Agreement or its route schedule, such amendment will come into effect upon confirmation by an exchange of diplomatic notes.

ARTICLE 13

Except as otherwise provided in this Agreement, any dispute between the contracting parties relative to the interpretation or application of this Agreement which cannot be settled through consultation shall be submitted for an advisory report to a tribunal of three arbitrators, one to be named by each contracting party, and the third to be agreed upon by the two arbitrators so chosen, provided that such third arbitrator shall not be a national of either contracting party. Each of the contracting parties shall designate an arbitrator within two months of the date of delivery by either party to the other party of a diplomatic note requesting arbitration of a dispute; and the third arbitrator shall be agreed upon within one month after such period of two months.

If either of the contracting parties fails to designate its own arbitrator within two months, or if the third arbitrator is not agreed upon within the time limit indicated, either party may request the President of the International Court of Justice to make the necessary appointment or appointments by choosing the arbitrator or arbitrators.

The contracting parties will use their best efforts under the powers available to them to put into effect the opinion expressed in any such advisory report. A moiety of the expenses of the arbitral tribunal shall be borne by each party.

ARTICLE 14

This Agreement, all amendments thereto, and contracts connected therewith shall be registered with the International Civil Aviation Organization.

ARTICLE 15

If a general multilateral air transport Convention accepted by both contracting parties enters into force, the present Agreement shall be amended so as to conform with the provision of such Convention.

ARTICLE 16

Either of the contracting parties may at any time notify the other of its intention to terminate the present Agreement. Such a notice shall be sent simultaneously to the International Civil Aviation Organization. In the event such communication is made, this Agreement shall terminate one year after the date of its receipt, unless by agreement between the contracting parties the notice of intention to terminate is withdrawn before the expiration of that time. If the other contracting party fails to acknowledge receipt, notice shall be deemed as having been received fourteen days after its receipt by the International Civil Aviation Organization.

ARTICLE 17

This Agreement will come into force on the day it is signed.

In witness whereof, the undersigned, being duly authorized by their respective Governments, have signed the present Agreement.

Done in duplicate at _____ this _____ day of _____ 195 ___.

For the Government of the United States of America:

For the Government of _____:

SCHEDULE

1. An airline or airlines designed by the Government of the United States shall be entitled to operate air services on each of the air routes specified via intermediate points, in both directions, and to make scheduled landings in _____ at the points specified in this paragraph:

2. An airline or airlines designed by the Government of _____ shall be entitled to operate air services on each of the air routes specified via intermediate points, in both directions and to make scheduled landings in the United States at the points specified in this paragraph:

3. Points on any of the specified routes may at the option of the designated airline be omitted on any or all flights.

To be inserted as Article 16 in agreements in which the intermediate points are specified in the route schedule.

Changes made by either contracting party in points on its routes described in the Schedule except changes in points in the territory of the other contracting party, shall not require amendment of the Schedule. The aeronautical authorities of either contracting party may therefore proceed unilaterally to make such changes, provided, however, that notice of any change is given without delay to the aeronautical authorities of the other contracting.

If such other aeronautical authorities find that, having regard to the principles set forth in Article 10 of the present Agreement, interests of their airline or airlines are prejudiced by the carriage by the airline or airlines of the first contracting party of traffic between the territory of the second contracting party and the new point in the territory of the third country, the authorities of the two contracting parties shall consult with a view to arriving at a satisfactory agreement.

Bilateral Air Transport Agreement

APPENDIX D

INDEX

WORDS AND PHRASES

Index

Index

gates, 613, 624, 626-627
gateways, 887, 906
General Accounting Office, 195, 371,
    498, 500, 504, 620, 622, 679
General Agreement on Trade in Services,
    882
General Aviation Manufacturers
    Association, 603, 605, 743
General Aviation Revitalization Act, 744
general aviation, 572, 584, 611, 617, 631-
    632, 634, 651-652, 742-745
general case able, 147
General Dynamics Corporation (Convair),
    257, 266-268, 511
General operating and flight rules, 153,
    155
Genesee County Airport, 548
give me liberty or give me death, 48
globalization, 373
Globe and Rutgers Fire Insurance Co.,
    806
Glorious Revolution; see English
    Revolution
Goddess of Justice, 4
Golden Eagle Aviation, 749
Golden Gate Airlines, 492
golden rule, 57-58
good faith, 278, 507, 538
Good Humor Corp., 323
goodwill, 271
Gore Commission, 196
Government Accounting Office, 195, 620
government intervention, 296-298, 300,
    303, 359, 486
government misconduct, 345
government protection, 887
government restrictions, 93
governmental functions/services, 532,
    567-568, 574, 590-591
Grand Rapids Forging and Steel Co., 831
Grand Rapids Label Company, 831
grandfather clause, 298, 585, 617, 622
Granger movement, 292, 358, 364
grants, federal, 603, 605, 632-633, 703
gravamen, 457
Great Charter, 43, 94
Great Depression, 18, 65, 295-296, 472
Great Society, 468
Greater Pittsburgh Airport, 595
Greater Southwest Airport, 399
Greater Westchester Home Owners
    Association, 168, 170-171, 564
greatest happiness principle, 62
greed; see avarice of capitalism

Greek mythology/philosophy, 4, 31, 36-
    37, 42, 143
Greeneville-Greene County, Tennessee
    Airport Authority, 545
Greenville Air Service, 545
Greenville-Spartanburg Airport, 656, 719,
    721
grievance, 440
group of 500, 442-445, 447, 500
Guadalajara Convention, 848
Guatemala City Protocol, 848-849
guilty, 115-116, 118, 131-132, 137
gulls, 705-708
gun control, 97
guns; see weapons
gut, 56
Guyana Airways, 712
habeas corpus, 106, 108-109, 120
habit and custom, 863
Hague Convention, 178-179, 181, 883,
    902-903
Hague Protocol, 846-848, 850, 853, 857-
    858, 861, 882
handicapped persons, 161, 380, 392, 656
hangars, 274, 544, 549, 552-554, 611,
    807, 811
Hanscom Field, 837
happiness, 4, 18, 29, 56, 58-62, 64, 70,
    74-75, 78, 81-82, 85, 92, 724
harassment, 440
harmless differentiation, 507
Harrell's Candy Kitchen, 564, 686
Hartsfield International Airport, 708
Hawaii Supreme Court, 830
Hawaiian Airlines, 254, 450-451, 513-515
Hawaiian Insurance and Guaranty Co.,
    Ltd., 813, 829
Hayward Air Terminal, 600, 602
hazardous industry, 437
Hazardous Materials Transportation Act,
    174, 367
hazardous materials, 174
hazards, 805, 810-811
head taxes, 568-569, 606
health, 344, 567, 655, 668-669, 676-677,
    687, 691, 695
hearings, 310, 334, 336, 339-440, 527,
    766, 896, 899
hearsay, 336, 763
hedonism, 61
hegemony, 2, 12, 79, 91
helicopters, 631
helios, 4
heliports, 566

Index

Index

National Labor Relations Act, 420, 445, 451
National Liberty Insurance Co., 806
National Materials Advisory Board of the National Research Council, 191
National Mediation Board, 423, 425
National Ocean Survey, 777
National Passenger Traffic Association, 526
National Plan of Integrated Airport Systems, 566
National Pollutant Discharge Elimination System permit, 673
National Railroad Adjustment Board, 423
National Reporter System, 142
National Research Council, 190-191
National Transportation Policy, 297
National Transportation Safety Board, 303-304, 306-307, 309-310, 331-335, 745, 761-763, 765, 767, 770-771, 788, 801, 803
National Union Fire Insurance Co., 839
natural consequence, 319
naturalization of citizens, 89
navigable airspace, 588, 767
navigation aids (NAVAIDS), 178, 293, 380, 537, 632, 708-709, 770, 772, 776, 793
navigation, 177-178, 181, 293, 302, 437, 546, 782, 786, 796, 844, 860, 875, 882, 884
negative declaration; *see* finding of no significant impact
negligence defined, 116
negligence, 116, 121, 127, 137-139, 246, 321-325, 327, 330-331, 334, 340-348, 367, 376, 399-402, 407, 411-415, 466, 539, 556, 558, 590-591, 630, 636-640, 705-707, 723, 728-731, 734, 736-743, 746, 749, 754-759, 761, 764-766, 792-794, 796-801, 806, 835, 842, 846, 851-853, 860-861, 871
negligence, comparative, 731
negligence, contributory, 138, 346, 555, 590, 730, 796-797, 800
negligent entrustment, 557
negotiations, 356, 419, 428, 442, 530, 545, 880, 885, 888, 907
Nelson-Ryan Flight Service, 554-555
Neutral Industry Booking System, 489
New Deal, 65, 299
new entrant airlines, 429, 615, 622-624, 627, 629

New Hampshire Aeronautics Commission, 568
New Jersey Superior Court, Appellate Division, 559
New York Air, 616
New York Airways, 754
New York C & H Railroad, 275
New York Court of Appeals, 401, 734, 746-747, 827
New York Fire Insurance Co., 806
New York Metropolitan Transportation Authority, 635
New York Stock Exchange, 517
New York Supplement, 148-149, 163
New York Supreme Court, 402, 823
Newark International Airport, 615, 631, 712, 718, 754
news media, 94, 110, 655
newsracks, 719-721
Noerr Motor Freight, 514
Noerr Pennington Doctrine, 514, 516
noise compatibility program, 681
Noise Control Act, 578, 597-599, 601, 660, 675-676, 679
noise exposure map, 676, 680-684
Noise Pollution and Abatement Act, 676
noise stage levels (I, II and III), 2, 582, 623, 677-679, 710-713
noise, 99, 171, 563-565, 570, 574-575, 577-589, 595, 597-605, 608-609, 613-614, 623-624, 634, 658, 660, 662, 665, 667-668, 674-682, 684-685, 689, 693-694, 696, 699-703, 710-714
nolo contendre, 132
nomos, 3, 7-8, 25-26
non-delegable duty, 323-324, 340
nondisclosure, 396
non-exclusivity, 545-546, 551
Norris LaGuardia Act, 420
North American Treaty Organization, 466
North Atlantic market, 886, 888-889, 893
North Carolina Court of Appeals, 763, 835
North Eastern Reporter, 148
North Western Reporter, 148
Northeast Airlines, 511-512, 568
Northeastern Citations, 163
Northwest Airlines, 202, 251, 273-274, 276, 378, 392, 423, 426, 435-437, 452-454, 457-458, 470, 475-476, 485, 494-498, 570, 608, 611, 652
Northwestern Reporter, 147
notary, 247
notice of proposed rule making, 235, 366

972

Index

radar environment, 223, 341, 766, 768-770, 781-783, 785-792, 794-797, 803
radio altimeter warning horn, 775
radio range, 293
radioactive materials, 366
Railroad Labor Board, 422
Railroad Revitalization and Regulatory Reform Act, 468
railroads, 292, 467-468
Railway Labor Act, 356, 420, 424-426, 441-442, 444-445, 447
Ranger Insurance Co. , 832
rape, 34, 184
rate setting, parity approach to, 535
rates and charges, 11, 298, 356-357, 386, 492, 506, 532-533, 535-536, 549, 552, 564, 612, 651, 880, 885, 890, 907; *see also* price competition
ratification, 84, 92, 442, 844-847, 849, 856-858, 862, 906, 908
rational, 23, 38, 41, 292, 357, 373, 406, 527, 805
rationality of economic action, 5-6, 21-23, 31-32, 41-43, 359, 467, 474, 486
Reading Aviation Service, 552-554
Reading Municipal Airport, 535, 552-553
Reaganomics, 65, 296, 473
reasonable doubt, 115, 131
reasonable man doctrine, 121, 210-211, 216, 558, 630, 765
reasonableness, 37, 41, 122, 209-211, 214, 216-217, 221-224, 226, 228-229, 234-235, 245, 248, 252, 266, 270-272, 292, 315, 324, 333, 340-341, 347-348, 357, 367, 379, 392, 396, 400, 402-403, 405-407, 409, 412, 415-416, 432, 438, 444, 447, 520, 522, 530, 532-536, 539, 546, 552, 555-556, 558, 567-568, 572-573, 575, 581, 583, 586, 601-602, 604, 606-607, 609, 611, 622-623, 630, 632-633, 653, 656, 666, 681, 683, 686-687, 691-692, 701-704, 706, 708, 710, 713-715, 730-731, 733, 735, 746, 750, 752, 768, 852, 859, 863, 882, 884
rebates, 174, 505, 891
receivership, 121, 255, 492
reciprocity, 311, 891
reckless disregard, 333, 396, 852, 859
recordable security interest, 559-560
recovery, 855, 859
rectoria, 85
rectus, 56
redistribution of wealth, 532, 563, 612
reform movements, 291

Reformation, 42, 53, 77
refundable ticket, 381
refusal to transport, 380, 384, 386, 400, 404-406
regional carriers, 485-486
Regional Counsel, Federal Aviation Administration, 307, 309, 319-320, 338
Regional Flight Standards Division, Federal Aviation Administration, 317
regional jets, 383, 627
regulation, 6, 25, 325, 327-328, 330-331, 349, 359, 428, 467-473, 488, 508-510, 512, 564, 567-568, 572, 594, 596-598, 600-605, 655, 657, 661, 664, 668-672, 675-676, 678, 684-687, 689-690, 692-699, 702-703, 705-706, 709-711, 714, 718-719, 747, 756, 759
regulation, administrative, 471
regulation, economic, 142, 158, 173, 294, 297-301, 328, 356, 358, 370, 379, 423, 469-470, 508, 510, 657, 713, 856, 863, 885; *see also* intervention, government
regulation, safety, 24, 173, 300-301, 304, 470, 657
regulation, social, 23-24, 470, 657
regulatory reform, 356-357, 428
Rehabilitation Act, 392, 434
rehabilitation, 319
relevant geographic market, 499-501, 507, 520-523
reliance on competitive market forces, 373
religion, 33, 39, 75, 94, 110, 655-656, 693, 716-718
remand, 121, 396, 416, 589, 591, 595
remedial, 319-320
remedy at law, 407
Renaissance, 42, 49, 53, 77
Reno Air, 494-496
rental agreements, 11, 253, 258, 272, 529-530, 534, 537, 549, 553-554, 557-558, 560-561
Rental Car Non-Tenant Business Permit, 646
reorganization, 254-255, 258, 281, 295-296, 494
reporters, 145, 158
repossession, 261-262
repressive sanctions, 20
reprisals or recriminations, 442
Republic Airlines, 457-458, 524-525, 887
reputation, 117
rerouted ticket, 407

Index

Index

LIST OF NAMES

Index

Index

Index

ABOUT THE AUTHORS

LAURENCE E. GESELL

Laurence E. Gesell is Professor of Air Transportation Management in the College of Technology and Applied Science at Arizona State University East and Professor of Transportation in the Interdisciplinary Studies in Transportation Systems Certificate Program in the Graduate College on the ASU Main Campus. Previous faculty appointments have included Adjunct Professor in the Extended Campus of Embry-Riddle Aeronautical University (1986-1989); Lecturer in the College of Business at California Polytechnic State University in San Luis Obispo (1983-1984); and Instructor in the Department of Aviation at Northern Virginia Community College (1976-1979).

Prior to accepting his appointment at Arizona State University in 1984, Laurence Gesell was the Airports Manager for the County of San Luis Obispo, California (1979-1984). He is an Accredited Airport Executive [A.A.E.] with the American Association of Airport Executives and Certified Airport Executive [C.A.E.] with the Southwest Chapter of the American Association of Airport Executives. From 1973-1979, he was an aviation consultant and airport planning project manager with Howard, Needles, Tammen and Bergendoff, a leading design firm of architects, engineers and planners. Dr. Gesell is a commercially rated pilot, retired Lieutenant Colonel and Master Army Aviator. He is a veteran of the Vietnam conflict, where he was awarded the Army Commendation Medal, two Bronze Stars, 39 Air Medals (including one for valor), and the Distinguished Flying Cross.

Laurence Gesell holds the following degrees: B.A. (in Public Administration), Upper Iowa University (1976); M.P.A., University of San Francisco (1982); and Ph.D. (in Justice Studies), Arizona State University (1990). He has authored 17 books, numerous professional papers, journal articles and final consultant reports. His principal areas of teaching and research interest are air transportation systems management and planning, public policy and regulation, as well as justice, law and society and ethical foundations of law.

PAUL STEPHEN DEMPSEY

Paul Stephen Dempsey is Tomlinson Professor of Global Governance in Air and Space Law and Director of the Institute of Air and Space Law at McGill University, in Montreal, Canada. From 1979-2002, he held the endowed chair as Professor of Transportation Law and Director of the Transportation Law Program at the University of Denver. He was also Director of the National Center for Intermodal Transportation. From 1975-1979, he served as an attorney with the Civil Aeronautics Board and the Interstate Commerce Commission in Washington, D.C., and in 1981 he was Legal Advisor to the Chairman of the I.C.C.

Dr. Dempsey is also Vice Chairman and Director of Frontier Airlines, Inc., and Director of the Jordan Center for Aviation Safety Security, in Amman, Jordan. He has served as a founder and first Chairman of the Board of Governors of the Certified Claims Professional Accreditation Council, Inc., and President and Director of the Genesee Foundation, Inc. He has also served as a consultant to U.S. and foreign airlines, railroads, motor carriers, transportation labor organizations, government agencies, and telecommunications companies.

Paul Dempsey holds the following degrees: A.B.J., University of Georgia (1972); J.D., University of Georgia (1975); LL.M., George Washington University (1978); and D.C.L., McGill University (1987). He has written more than 50 law review and professional journal articles, scores of newspaper and news magazine editorials and several books. His principal areas of teaching and research interest are transportation law, aviation law and regulation.